PRINCIPLES OF
ECONOMICS

PRINCIPLES OF
ECONOMICS

ROBERT H. FRANK
Cornell University

BEN S. BERNANKE
Princeton University

McGraw-Hill
Irwin

Boston   Burr Ridge, IL   Dubuque, IA   Madison, WI   New York   San Francisco   St. Louis
Bangkok   Bogotá   Caracas   Lisbon   London   Madrid
Mexico City   Milan   New Delhi   Seoul   Singapore   Sydney   Taipei   Toronto

McGraw-Hill Higher Education

A Division of The McGraw-Hill Companies

PRINCIPLES OF ECONOMICS

Published by McGraw-Hill/Irwin, an imprint of The McGraw-Hill Companies, Inc., 1221 Avenue of the Americas, New York, NY, 10020. Copyright © 2001, by The McGraw-Hill Companies, Inc. All rights reserved. No part of this publication may be reproduced or distributed in any form or by any means, or stored in a data base or retrieval system, without the prior written consent of The McGraw-Hill Companies, Inc., including, but not limited to, in any network or other electronic storage or transmission, or broadcast for distance learning. Some ancillaries, including electronic and print components, may not be available to customers outside the United States.

This book is printed on acid-free paper.

1 2 3 4 5 6 7 8 9 0 KPH/KPH 0 9 8 7 6 5 4 3 2 1 0

ISBN   0-07-228962-7

Cover: Leaded glass window designed by Frank Lloyd Wright for the Avery Coonley Playhouse, Riverside, Illinois, circa 1912, 61 cm x 97.5 cm

Photo: Christie's Images, New York

Design of book: The images in the design of this book are based on elements of the architecture of Frank Lloyd Wright (1867–1959), specifically from the leaded glass windows seen in many of his houses. Wright's design was rooted in nature and based on simplicity and harmony. His windows use elemental geometry to abstract natural forms, complementing and framing the natural world outside. This concept of seeing the world through an elegantly structured framework ties in nicely to the idea of framing one's view of the world through the window of economics.

The typeface used for some of the elements was taken from the Arts and Crafts movement. The typeface, as well as the color palette, bring in the feeling of that movement in a way that complements the geometric elements of Wright's windows. The Economic Naturalist icon is visually set apart from the more geometric elements but is a representation of the inspirational force behind all of Wright's work.

Publisher: *Gary Burke*
Executive editor: *Paul Shensa*
Development editor: *Tom Thompson*
Marketing manager: *Martin Quinn*
Senior project manager: *Jean Lou Hess*
Senior production supervisor: *Michael McCormick*
Designer: *Jill Kongabel/Matthew Baldwin*
Art editor: *Nora Agbayani*
Supplement coordinator: *Becky Szura*
New media: *Ann Rogula*
Illustrators: *Mick Stevens, Elliott Banfield, Brian Barneclo, and Gini Curl*
Compositor: *GTS Graphics, Inc.*
Typeface: *10/12 Sabon Roman*
Printer: *Quebecor World/Hawkins*

Library of Congress Cataloging-in-Publication Data

Frank, Robert H.
    Principles of economics / Robert H. Frank, Ben S. Bernanke
        p. cm.
    Includes index.
    ISBN 0-07-228962-7
    1. Economics. I. Bernanke, Ben. II. Title.

    HB171.5 .F734 2001
    330--dc21

                                                      00-061281

www.mhhe.com

DEDICATION

For Ellen

R. H. F.

For Anna

B. S. B.

ROBERT H. FRANK

Professor Frank received his B.S. from Georgia Tech in 1966, then taught math and science for two years as a Peace Corps volunteer in rural Nepal. He received his M.A. in statistics in 1971 and his Ph.D. in economics in 1972 from the University of California at Berkeley. He is the Goldwin Smith Professor of Economics at Cornell University, where he has taught since 1972, and where he currently holds a joint appointment in the Department of Economics and the Johnson Graduate School of Management. During a leave of absence from Cornell he served as chief economist for the Civil Aeronautics Board (1978–1980), a Fellow at the Center for Advanced Study in the Behavioral Sciences (1992–1993), and Professor of American Civilization at l'École des Hautes Études en Sciences Sociales in Paris (2000–2001).

Professor Frank is the author of a best-selling intermediate economics textbook—*Microeconomics and Behavior,* Fourth Edition (McGraw-Hill/Irwin, 2000). He has published on a variety of subjects, including price and wage discrimination, public utility pricing, the measurement of unemployment spell lengths, and the distributional consequences of direct foreign investment. His research has focused on rivalry and cooperation in economic and social behavior. His books on these themes include *Choosing the Right Pond: Human Behavior and the Quest for Status* (Oxford University Press, 1985) and *Passions Within Reason: The Strategic Role of the Emotions* (W.W. Norton, 1988). He and Philip Cook are coauthors of *The Winner-Take-All Society* (The Free Press, 1995), which received a Critic's Choice Award and appeared on both the *New York Times* Notable Books list and *Business Week* Ten Best list for 1995. His most recent general interest publication, *Luxury Fever* (The Free Press, 1999), was named to the *Knight-Ridder* Best Books list for 1999. He has been awarded an Andrew W. Mellon Professorship (1987–1990), a Kenan Enterprise Award (1993), and a Merrill Scholars Program Outstanding Educator Citation (1991). Professor Frank's introductory microeconomics course has graduated more than 5,000 enthusiastic economic naturalists over the years.

BEN S. BERNANKE

Professor Bernanke received his B.A. in economics from Harvard University in 1975 and his Ph.D. in economics from MIT in 1979. He taught at the Stanford Graduate School of Business from 1979 to 1985 and moved to Princeton University in 1985, where he is the Howard Harrison and Gabrielle Snyder Beck Professor of Economics and Public Affairs, and where he is currently Chairman of the Economics Department. He has consulted for the Board of Governors of the Federal Reserve, the European Central Bank, and other central banks, and he serves on a U.S. State Department committee that advises the Israeli government on economic policy. He is a Fellow of the Econometric Society, a Guggenheim Fellow, and a Research Associate of the National Bureau of Economic Research. He has been a visiting scholar at the Federal Reserve System in Boston, Philadelphia, and New York, and he is currently an advisor to the Federal Reserve Bank of New York.

Professor Bernanke's intermediate textbook, with Andrew Abel, *Macroeconomics,* Fourth Edition (Addison-Wesley, 2001), is a best seller in its field. He has authored more than 50 scholarly publications in macroeconomics, macroeconomic history, and finance. He has done significant research on the causes of the Great Depression, the role of financial markets and institutions in the business cycle, and measuring the effects of monetary policy on the economy. His two most recent books, both published by Princeton University Press, include *Inflation Targeting: Lessons from the International Experience* (with coauthors) and *Essays on the Great Depression.* He is a coeditor of the *NBER Macroeconomics Annual* and the *Journal of Business,* and he serves as associate editor for the *Journal of Financial Intermediation;* the *Journal of Money, Credit, and Banking;* and the *Review of Economics and Statistics.* He is also a member of the Editorial Board of the *Journal of Macroeconomics.* Professor Bernanke has taught principles of economics at both Stanford and Princeton.

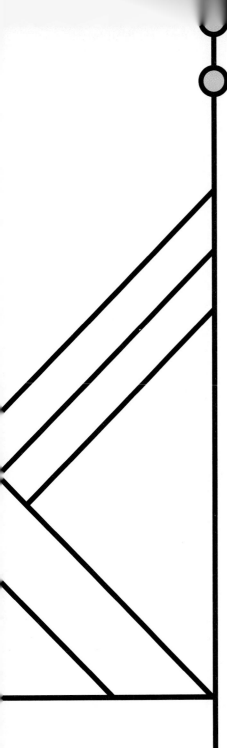

D ozens of principles of economics textbooks are available, and new entries into the market appear regularly. But with many copycats and few innovators, instructors' real choices are more limited than these numbers would suggest. We wrote this book from the conviction, born of long experience in the classroom, that there is a different, and better, way to introduce beginning students to economics. In bare bones, the philosophy of this text rests on two pillars: (1) the development and repeated application of a set of core economic principles, without the usual clutter, and (2) an active, student-centered approach to learning.

A SIMPLE AGENDA

The best way to teach introductory economics—or virtually any subject, for that matter—is to expose students to repeated applications of a short list of the core ideas of the discipline. But whose short list? If we asked a thousand economists to provide their own versions, we'd get a thousand different lists. Yet to dwell on their differences would be to miss their essential similarities. Indeed, we suspect that almost all the lists would contain variants of propositions like these:

The Scarcity Principle: Having more of one good thing usually means having less of another.

The Cost-Benefit Principle: Take no action unless its marginal benefit is at least as great as its marginal cost.

The Principle of Unequal Costs: Some costs (e.g., opportunity and marginal) matter in making decisions; other costs (e.g., sunk, average) don't.

The Principle of Comparative Advantage: Everyone does best when each concentrates on the activity for which he or she is relatively most productive.

The Principle of Increasing Opportunity Cost: Use the resources with the lowest opportunity cost before turning to those with higher opportunity costs.

The Equilibrium Principle: A market in equilibrium leaves no unexploited opportunities for individuals, but may not exploit all gains achievable through collective action.

The Efficiency Principle: Efficiency is an important social goal, because when the economic pie grows larger, everyone can have a larger slice.

Our point is not that this is the best short list, but that the introductory course will be taught most effectively if it begins with a well-articulated short list of some sort, and then doggedly hammers away at it, illustrating and applying each principle in context after context. It may be hackneyed to say, but it is nonetheless true that economics is a way of thinking, not a fixed body of facts to be memorized. Beginning students often find the economic way of thinking alien and difficult to master. Repetition and focus on a few core principles are the key to developing economic thinking skills, in the same way that they are the key to learning to play the saxophone or hit an overhead smash in tennis.

LESS IS MORE

Of course, many introductory economics textbooks pay lip service to the concepts of core ideas and thinking like an economist. And to be sure, versions of the core principles are found in many books—but often so is virtually every other economic principle that has surfaced over the past 200 years! The mind-boggling detail of these books—many of them thousand-plus-page encyclopedic reference tomes—could not have been purposely designed to camouflage more effectively the handful of principles that really matter.

All too often, students leave the introductory course never having fully grasped the essence of economic fundamentals. For example, the concept of opportunity cost—so utterly central to our understanding of what it means to think like an economist—is but one among hundreds of other concepts that go by in a blur. Opportunity cost is more important than, say, the idea that the short-run average cost curve is tangent to the long-run average cost curve at the optimal output level. But students would never realize that from the relative emphasis these topics receive in most of our introductory textbooks.

We consciously decided to write a textbook, not an encyclopedia. Our coverage includes what we believe to be the essential economic ideas and issues of the day. We have pruned much of the accumulated undergrowth, confident that students' shortest path to clear thinking about economic issues lies in becoming fluent in the basic tools of economic analysis—not in being inundated with more ideas, facts, and opinions than they can reasonably assimilate.

Repetition, however, consumes time and space. So notwithstanding our firm belief in the less-is-more approach, our book does not enter the market with the shortest page count. Instructors with Ph.D.s in economics may wonder whether so much repetition is really necessary, fearing that they will bore their students by exposing them to yet another application of the opportunity cost concept. To many, it will seem that the same time would be better spent discussing why the average fixed cost curve is asymptotic to the quantity axis.

At some point, it surely *is* better to move on to the technical properties of the average fixed cost curve. But in our view that point does not come during the principles course. For decades, each of us has had the privilege of teaching some of the best undergraduates in the world. This experience has persuaded us that when we attempt to teach less, we end up teaching more.

ECONOMIC NATURALISM

In our efforts to train students to think like economists, we aim not just for them to be *able* to apply core economic principles, but also to have an *inclination* to do so. The most effective strategy we have discovered for achieving that goal is to encourage students to become "economic naturalists." Studying biology enables people to observe and marvel at many details of the natural environment that would otherwise have escaped notice. For the naturalist, a walk in a quiet wood becomes an adventure. In much the same way, studying economics can enable students to see the everyday details of ordinary existence in a bright new light. Throughout the text, *Economic Naturalist* examples show students the relevance of economics to their world.

To illustrate, an economic naturalist is someone like Bill Tjoa, a recent student who asked, "Why do the keypad buttons on drive-up automatic teller machines have Braille dots?" A plausible answer, he reasoned, is that once the keypad molds have been manufactured, the cost of producing buttons with Braille dots is no higher than the cost of producing smooth ones. Making both types would require separate sets of molds and separate batches of inventory. If the patrons of drive-up machines found buttons with Braille dots harder to use, these extra costs might be worth incurring. But since the dots pose no difficulty for sighted users, the best and cheapest solution is to produce only keypads with dots.

In response to our challenge to employ economic principles to cast light on their own experiences, our students have tackled a host of other fascinating questions. Some recent examples from our classes:

- Why do brides spend so much money on wedding dresses, while grooms often rent cheap tuxedos, even though grooms could potentially wear their tuxedos on many other occasions and brides will never wear their dresses again? (Jennifer Dulski)

- Why, despite the proliferation of electrical appliances in the last century, do electrical outlets in newly built houses still have only two receptacles? (Beth Wollberg)

- Why do top female models earn so much more than top male models? (Fran Adams)

- Why are child safety seats required in cars but not in airplanes?" (Greg Balet)

Once students realize that they can pose and answer such questions on their own, they're hooked. A lifetime trajectory begins in which their mastery of economic principles not only doesn't decay with each year after completion of the course, but actually soars higher.

ACTIVE LEARNING

Our second guiding principle has been that active involvement by students—"student-centered" learning, in the jargon—is an essential part of an effective learning process. Merely understanding a concept—in the sense of being able to answer a test question about it the next day—is different from really *knowing* it. Even the brightest students never fully internalize a concept unless they use it repeatedly. So throughout the book, we use a number of devices to foster active learning.

- **Worked Examples.** New ideas and concepts are not simply asserted, as in most books. Instead, they are introduced by means of simple examples, usually numerical, which are worked through step-by-step in the text. These examples display the reasoning process used to reach the economic conclusion or insight, and they provide a model for the student to apply when working exercises and problems.

- **Exercises.** Following many examples, and indeed throughout each chapter, we pose in-text exercises that challenge the student to test and extend his or her understanding of the ideas being discussed. Worked-out answers to in-text exercises are provided at the end of the chapter, allowing immediate feedback.

- **Anecdotes and Illustrations.** Active learning is more likely to happen when students are engaged and motivated. We agree with Mary Poppins that a spoonful of sugar helps the medicine go down (even if the medicine is not so unpleasant). In that spirit, we have tried to make reading this text an enjoyable experience. We begin every chapter with an anecdote that motivates the discussion, and we illustrate the ideas with memorable cartoons, photographs, and original line drawings. Most important, we have striven to minimize jargon and keep the writing direct and student friendly.

- **Recap Boxes and Summaries.** To keep students focused on the forest as well as the trees, at strategic points in each chapter we have provided "recap boxes." Recaps put into a nutshell the main ideas of the previous section. The recap boxes are themselves recapitulated by bulleted end-of-chapter summaries, which are also designed to review the most important concepts presented in the chapter.

- **Core Principles Icon.** Throughout the book, whenever one of the core principles is discussed, a small icon will appear in the margin, thereby reinforcing the importance of those principles.

- **Review Questions and Problems.** Questions for review at the end of each chapter encourage the student to self-test understanding of the main ideas of the chapter. End-of-chapter problems are carefully crafted to help students internalize and extend core concepts.

THOROUGHLY MODERN MICRO

Although we believe pedagogy is extremely important, ours is not solely a book about pedagogy. Indeed, the decision about what to teach was at least as important to us as the decision of how to teach it. For example, because we believe that the most central concern of economics is efficiency, we have devoted extensive space to the concept of *economic surplus*. Introduced in Chapter 1 and applied repeatedly in Chapters 2–6, this concept is developed more fully in Chapter 7 than in any leading introductory text. Throughout the book, it underlies our ongoing argument in support of economic efficiency as an important social goal. Rather than speaking of tradeoffs between efficiency and other goals, we stress that maximizing economic surplus aids the achievement of all goals, both public and private.

A particularly distinctive feature of our book is its focus on the *normative implications of economic theory for decision making*. Basic economic reasoning tells us that rational individuals should ignore sunk costs when making choices, for example, yet many people are in fact strongly influenced by them. (Someone who has purchased a ticket for an NBA playoff game for $100 is, in practice, much more likely to drive through a snowstorm to get to the game than is an equally avid fan who won a ticket in a raffle.) Chapter 2 is devoted entirely to three pitfalls that are both widespread and important: the tendency to ignore opportunity costs, the tendency *not* to ignore sunk costs, and the tendency to confuse average and marginal costs and benefits. Throughout the book, we call students' attention to situations in which they themselves are likely to face similarly problematic choices.

Our goal of training economic naturalists has also helped dictate which topics to cover and which to leave out. Other things being equal, the more a topic enables us to make sense of our observations and experience, the stronger the case for including it. Thus, we are troubled that many people receive college degrees without ever having been exposed to ideas like the prisoner's dilemma or the tragedy of the commons. These and other *simple applications of game theory* are not only ideal vehicles for illustrating several of the core ideas of economics, but they also have enormous power to explain events in the world. In Chapter 10, we introduce students to the principles of games and strategic behavior in a highly intuitive way that does not rely on formal mathematics. We develop a limited number of simple principles that have proved entirely accessible to freshmen. In our experience, students are delighted to learn that these few principles can explain, among other things, why urban freeways are too crowded, why whales have been hunted to near extinction, why North Atlantic fisheries are near collapse, why the ozone layer is in danger, why many people fail to vote, and why the National Hockey League has a helmet rule.

MACRO AT THE FRONTIER

Our chapters on macroeconomics bring the best recent thinking in the field within the grasp of the beginning student. We avoid doctrinal disputes and lengthy detours into the history of thought. Instead, we treat the world economy as our laboratory, showing how basic economic ideas can help to explain important recent events (such as the Asian financial crisis) and longer-term trends (such as widening inequality in real wages).

In recent years, a changing set of real-world concerns and new developments in the discipline have reduced the field's traditional emphasis on cyclical fluctuations, in favor of *greater attention to long-run issues* such as economic growth, productivity, the evolution of real wages, and capital formation. Reflecting this shift in emphasis, we present a four-chapter, in-depth treatment of these long-run issues, prior to our analysis of short-run fluctuations. Chapter 20 provides an overview of the massive social transformation created by economic growth in the industrialized world, then analyzes the factors underlying this remarkable record. Subsequent chapters discuss how these trends have affected, and been affected by, developments in factor markets and financial markets.

Following our analysis of long-term trends, we present in Chapters 24–27 a *modernized treatment of short-term fluctuations and stabilization policy.* Throughout this section we emphasize the important distinction between the short-run and long-run behavior of the economy. In the short run, firms facing costs of changing prices will meet the demand forthcoming at their preset prices, creating a role for aggregate demand in the determination of output. In principle at least, sufficiently nimble monetary and fiscal policies can help to stabilize demand and output in the short run. In the long run, however, the economy tends toward full employment, and the effects of aggregate demand stimulus are felt primarily on the price level. Our model of short-run fluctuations includes two innovations that both simplify the analysis and make it more realistic. First, consistent with both media reporting and recent research on the central bank reaction function, we treat the interest rate rather than the money supply as the instrument of Fed policy. Second, our analysis of aggregate demand and aggregate supply relates output to inflation, rather than to the price level, sidestepping the necessity of a separate derivation of the link between the output gap and inflation.

A modern macro text must confront head on the *globalization of trading and financial relationships.* Our book places a heavy emphasis on globalization and its effects, starting with an analysis of the effects of globalization on real wage inequality (Chapter 21) and progressing to such issues as the benefits of trade, the causes and effects of protectionism, the role of capital flows in domestic capital formation, the link between exchange rates and monetary policy, and the sources of speculative attacks on currencies. We also use comparative examples throughout, drawing lessons from *differing national experiences* in terms of growth, wages, unemployment, saving, and stabilization policy. These comparisons invite the student to be an Economic Naturalist on a larger scale: to ask the question, Why do economic outcomes differ so much among countries?

ORGANIZATION OF MICROECONOMICS

The sixteen chapters of the microeconomics split are divided into four parts of four chapters each. Part 1, which is also included in the macroeconomics split, introduces students to the most basic ideas of economics, including all the core principles that will be used throughout the book. Chapter 1 focuses on the ideas of scarcity, tradeoffs, costs, and benefits, including the fundamental notion that the desirability of any action depends on its marginal costs and benefits. Following Chapter 1 is a brief appendix that reviews the basic mathematical tools—working with equations, graphs, and tables—that students will need for the course. As mentioned earlier, Chapter 2 extends the discussion of Chapter 1 by examining some common pitfalls for decision makers, such as the sunk cost fallacy. Chapter 3 introduces the ideas of specialization and gains from trade. Finally, Chapter 4 provides an introductory overview of the tools of supply-and-demand analysis.

Part 2 explores in greater detail the concepts of demand, supply, economic surplus, and efficiency in the context of pure competition. Building on the introduction to supply and demand in Chapter 4, Chapter 5 shows how demand curves are generated by the fact that people spend their limited income in rational ways. This chapter also discusses the concept of price elasticity and its uses. Chapter 6 turns to the sellers' side of the market, showing how upward-sloping supply curves follow from profit-maximizing decisions by producers. Chapter 7 develops the concept of economic surplus and explains Adam Smith's crucial insight—that when demand and supply curves fully reflect social benefits and costs, competitive markets maximize economic surplus. Finally, Chapter 8 examines the idea of economic profit and clarifies how the quest for profit drives competitive firms to provide a socially efficient allocation of resources.

In Part 3 we study deviations from the ideal of pure competition, emphasizing that outcomes in such situations need no longer be socially efficient. Chapter 9 examines one important type of deviation from competition, the existence of monopolistic and oligopolistic firms. When only a few producers exist in a market—and in many other noncompetitive situations—behavior often takes on a strategic component. Building on this observation, Chapter 10 introduces some elementary tools of game theory, demonstrating their applicability to a variety of economic situations. Chapter 11 considers the effects of externalities—situations in which supply and demand curves do not capture the full social costs and benefits of people's choices. We show that elementary game theory—including the ideas of the prisoner's dilemma, the arms race, and the tragedy of the commons—are quite useful for analyzing many situations with externalities. Chapter 12 examines yet another deviation from the competitive ideal, the case of incomplete or asymmetric information. Among many other examples, Chapter 12 includes a discussion of the "lemons" problem in the used-car market and an explanation of why clients prefer lawyers who wear expensive suits.

Finally, Part 4 uses the tools that have been developed to approach some issues of applied economics and economic policy. Chapter 13 tackles the question of why some people earn so much more than others, with attention to factors ranging from human capital investment to discrimination to "winner-take-all" markets. Chapter 14 shows how economic principles can be used to design economic policies that mitigate the effects of market imperfections, including anti-trust policies and policies about health care, the environment, and crime. Chapter 15 discusses public goods and taxation, as well as broader issues concerning the government's role in the economy. Completing the micro split, Chapter 16 extends the analysis of Chapter 15 by considering the benefits and pitfalls of government policies to redistribute income and reduce poverty.

ORGANIZATION OF MACROECONOMICS

The macroeconomics split begins with Part 1 (Chapters 1–4), which introduces basic economic concepts, including the core principles. Part 5 then brings the student into the realm of macroeconomics: Chapter 17 gives an overview of the issues that macroeconomists study, and of basic tools such as aggregation. Chapters 18 and 19 focus on issues of measurement: Chapter 18 looks at measures of real activity, such as GDP and the unemployment rate, and Chapter 19 considers measures of the price level and inflation. A theme of both of these chapters is that economic measurement is imperfect, and that intelligent consumers of economic statistics must be aware of their weaknesses as well as their strengths.

No topic in economics is more important to human well-being than the sources of long-term output and productivity growth. Reflecting that importance, the four chapters of Part 6 focus on long-run economic performance. Chapter 20 reviews the remarkable record of long-term economic growth and discusses the factors (such as the creation of human and physical capital, and improvements in technology) that have contributed to growth. Chapter 21 studies how economic growth, modernization, and globalization have affected workers' real wages and employment prospects. Turning from labor to capital, Chapter 22 analyzes the determinants of household saving and national saving, and shows how a nation's saving provides the funding needed for creating new capital. Saving and capital investment are mediated by financial markets, which are discussed in Chapter 23. This chapter also introduces the concept of money and discusses how the Federal Reserve controls the amount of money in circulation.

With the analysis of the long run as background, Part 7 studies the short-run behavior of the economy, including cyclical fluctuations and stabilization policy. Chapter 24 introduces short-term fluctuations in the economy and includes descriptions of business cycle dating, the U.S. experience with recessions and expansions, and the characteristic behavior of variables such as unemployment and inflation during cycles. In contrast to the situation in the long run, in which supply conditions are paramount in determining output, in the short run changes in aggregate spending can affect output. Chapter 25 looks at the relationship between aggregate demand in the very short run, when prices are fixed and firms simply meet the demand for their output. In this setting, government policies that affect aggregate demand, such as changes in government spending, can help to eliminate output gaps. Maintaining the short-run focus, Chapter 26 adds monetary policy and the Federal Reserve to the story. Chapter 27 moves from the short run to the long run by showing how adjustment in inflation eliminates output gaps over time. The chapter also considers other sources of inflation, notably aggregate supply shocks, and the policy dilemmas that these create.

Throughout the text we draw international comparisons, and allude to the effects of international factors on the economy (as when Chapter 21 analyzes the effects of trade on wage inequality). However, in Part 8 the focus is entirely on the international dimensions of the economy. Chapter 28 extends Chapter 3's analysis of comparative advantage to look at the case for and against free trade. This chapter also discusses how international capital flows augment the domestic pool of saving. Chapter 29 discusses the role of exchange rates in the economy and includes analyses of speculative attacks and the constraints that the exchange-rate regime places on domestic monetary policy.

THE CHALLENGE

The world is a more competitive place now than it was when we started teaching in the 1970s. In arena after arena, business as usual is no longer good enough. Baseball players used to drink beer and go fishing during the off-season, but they now lift weights and ride exercise bicycles. Assistant professors used to work on their houses on weekends, but the current crop can now be found most weekends at the office. The competition for student attention has grown similarly more intense. There are many tempting courses in the typical college curriculum, and even more tempting diversions outside the classroom. Students are freer than ever to pick and choose.

Yet many of us seem to operate under the illusion that most freshmen arrive with a burning desire to become economics majors. And many of us seem not yet to have recognized that students' cognitive abilities and powers of concentration are scarce resources. To hold our ground we must become not only more selective in what we teach, but also more effective as advocates for our discipline. We must persuade students that we offer something of value.

A well-conceived and well-executed introductory course in economics can teach our students more about society and human behavior in a single term than virtually any other course in the university. This course can and should be an intellectual adventure of the first order. Not all students who take the kind of course we envisioned when writing this book will go on to become economics majors, of course. But many will, and even those who do not will leave with a sense of admiration for the power of economic ideas.

A salesperson knows that he or she often gets only one chance to make a good first impression on a potential customer. Analogously, the principles course is often our only shot at helping students appreciate the value of economics. By trying to teach them everything we know—rather than teaching them the most important things we know—we too often squander this opportunity.

SUPPLEMENTS

We believe that an ancillary package is most useful if each element in it is part of a well-considered whole. In order to ensure that our package was as integrated as possible, two solid economists and excellent teachers—Jack Mogab and Bruce McClung at Southwest Texas State University—were charged with overseeing the program. They suggested candidates, gave us advice, and provided feedback for virtually all of the components. Additionally, Jack and Bruce wrote the Study Guide and Bruce wrote the micro test bank.

FOR THE INSTRUCTOR

- **Instructor's Manual.** Prepared by Margaret Ray at Mary Washington College, this manual will be extremely useful for all teachers, but especially for those new to the job. It offers suggestions for using the Study Guide, the test bank, the Economic Naturalists, and cartoons and music for teaching; it supplies sample syllabi with assignments, sample exams, and supplemental material; and it provides for each chapter an overview, an outline, teaching objectives, Economic Naturalist discussion questions, answers to textbook questions and problems, a homework assignment with answers, and a sample quiz with answers.

- **Test Banks.** Prepared by Bruce McClung at Southwest Texas State University (micro) and Nancy Jianakoplos at Colorado State University (macro), these manuals contain more than 5,000 multiple-choice questions categorized by Learning Objective (from the Study Guide); Learning Level (knowledge, comprehension, application, analysis); Type (graph, calculation, word problem); and Source (textbook, Study Guide, Web, unique).

- **Computerized Test Banks.** The print test banks (micro and macro) are also available in the latest Diploma test-generating software, ensuring maximum flexibility in test preparation, including the reconfiguring of graphing exercises. This Brownstone program is the gold standard of testing programs.

- **PowerPoints.** Prepared by Rebecca Campbell at Southwest Texas State University, these slides contain all of the illustrations in the textbook, along with a detailed, chapter-by-chapter review of the important ideas presented in the textbook. They are available in micro and macro packages.

- **Overhead Transparencies.** These more than 250, four-color acetates contain all the illustrations presented in the textbook. They are available in micro and macro packages.

- **Videos.** Produced by Paul Solman, business and economics correspondent for the Lehrer News Hour and WGBH Boston, these five 10-minute segments, available on CD or tape, cover five core concepts in economics.

- **Instructor's CD-ROM.** This remarkable Windows software program, which contains the Instructor's Manual, the Computerized Test Banks, and the PowerPoints, also allows the instructor to create presentations from any of the materials on the CD or from additional material that can be imported.

- **Web Site.** The development and design of the site was overseen by Scott Simkins at North Carolina A&T State University, and much of the content was provided either by Scott or by Jim Barbour at Elon College. Both of these experienced teachers are in the forefront of a movement to make teaching using the Web easier and more valuable. For teachers there are, among other things, an online newsletter called "Teaching Using the Web" (coordinated by Mark Maier at Glendale College); the Instructor's Manual; the PowerPoints; Economics on the Web, an annotated set of URLs/links to sites of interest to economists; along with a description of what's on the student site and some Optional Material from the book.

FOR THE STUDENT

- **Study Guide.** Written by Jack Mogab and Bruce McClung at Southwest Texas State University, these three books—for Economics, Microeconomics, and Macroeconomics—provide the following elements for each chapter: a Key Point Review; a Learning Objective Grid; and Self-Tests (Key Term Matching, Multiple Choice, Problems) with answers.

- **DiscoverEcon.** This menu-driven software was developed by Gerald Nelson at the University of Illinois. It provides students with a book-specific tutorial for either microeconomics or macroeconomics. Each chapter offers two essay questions and a multiple-choice test, and when appropriate, interactive graphing problems let students observe how the economic picture is altered as data is changed. There are also links to the textbook glossary.

- **Web Site.** Based on the idea that the single most important feature of any web site is quizzing and feedback, each chapter begins with an Electronic Learning Session (eLS). Each eLS opens with a brief recap of the chapter and is followed by a pretest with answers and analysis; the test is then followed by a set of study sessions based on Economic Naturalist Exercises, Graphing Exercises, PowerPoints, and Key Terms; and the study session is finally followed by a posttest, with answers and analysis. The site also contains such useful and exciting features as Interpreting the News—articles and summaries of relevant articles with analysis and discussion questions; Videos—10-minute segments on key concepts produced by Paul Solman of WGBH in Boston; e-mail Updates—periodic sending of information/study tips; the Glossary from the textbook; and Economics on the Web—annotated URLs useful for economics students.

ACKNOWLEDGMENTS

Our thanks first and foremost go to our publisher, Gary Burke, for his unwavering faith in our project over the past several years. In an industry known for sticking with proven formulas, he has been willing from the outset to gamble that the market will embrace our somewhat unorthodox vision. Without his support and encouragement, we never could have produced this book. Tom Thompson, our development editor, was enormously helpful as he guided us with intelligence, patience, and tact through three major revisions of the original manuscript. We also thank Paul Shensa, the Executive Editor, whose considerable experience, insightful suggestions, and extensive knowledge of the marketplace were of great help. We are especially grateful to Betty Morgan, our superb manuscript editor.

And we are also grateful to the production team, whose professionalism was outstanding: Jean Lou Hess, Senior Project Manager; Michael McCormick, Senior Production Supervisor; Jill Kongabel and Matthew Baldwin, Designers; Nora Agbayani, Art Editor; Becky Szura, Supplements Coordinator; and Ann Rogula, New Media Producer.

Finally, our sincere thanks to the following teachers and colleagues, whose thorough reviews and thoughtful suggestions led to innumerable substantive improvements:

Ercument Aksoy
Los Angeles Valley College

Richard Anderson
Texas A&M University

Daniel Berkowitz
University of Pittsburgh

Guatam Bhattacharya
University of Kansas

Scott Bierman
Carleton College

Kelly Blanchard
Purdue Universtiy

Bruce Blonigen
University of Oregon

Beth Bogan
Princeton University

George Borts
Brown University

Nancy Brooks
University of Vermont

Douglas Brown
Georgetown University

Marie Bussings-Burk
Southern Indiana University

David Carr
University of Colorado

Jack Chambless
Valencia Community College

James Cover
University of Alabama

Carl Davidson
Michigan State University

Paul DePippo
Glendale Community College

Lynn Pierson Doti
Chapman College

Donald Dutkowsky
Syracuse University

Nancy Fox
Saint Joseph's College

Geoffrey Gee
California State University–Fullerton

Jonah Gelbach
University of Maryland

Linda Ghent
East Carolina University

Kirk Gifford
Ricks College

Robert Gillette
University of Kentucky

Stephen Gohman
University of Louisville

Refet Gurkaynak
Princeton University

Mary Jean Horney
Furman University

Nancy Jianakoplos
Colorado State University

Robert Johnson
University of San Diego

William Kerby
California State University–Sacramento

Herbert Kiesling
Indiana University

Bruce Kingma
State University of New York–Albany

Hannes Kvaran
Glendale Community College

Leonard Lardaro
University of Rhode Island

Anthony Lima
California State University–Hayward

Tom Love
North Central University

Steven McCafferty
The Ohio State University

Edward McNertney
Texas Christian University

William Merrill
Iowa State University

Paul Nelson
Northeast Louisiana State
University

Neil Niman
University of New Hampshire

Norman Obst
Michigan State University

Charles Okeke
Community College of Southern
Nevada

Duane Oyen
University of Wisconsin–Eau
Claire

Theodore Palivos
Louisiana State University

Michael Potepan
San Francisco State University

Steve Robinson
University of North Carolina–
Wilmington

Christina Romer
University of California–Berkeley

David Romer
University of California–Berkeley

Greg Rose
Sacramento City College

Robert Rossana
Wayne State University

Richard Salvucci
Trinity University

Edward Scahill
University of Scranton

Pamela Schmitt
Indiana University

Dennis Starleaf
Iowa State University

Esther-Mirjam Sent
University of Notre Dame

John Solow
University of Iowa

Helen Tauchen
University of North
Carolina–Chapel Hill

Kay Unger
University of Montana

Stephan Weiler
Colorado State University

Jeffrey Weiss
City University of New
York–Baruch College

Richard Winkelman
Arizona State University

Mark Wohar
University of Nebraska–Omaha

Louise Wolitz
University of Texas–Austin

Darrel Young
University of Texas–Austin

Zenon Zygmont
Western Oregon University

PART 8 The International Economy

Chapter 28 International Trade and Capital Flows 765

Chapter 29 Exchange Rates and the Open Economy 801

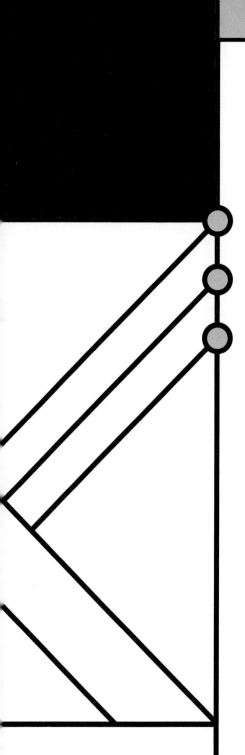

PART

1

INTRODUCTION

As you begin the study of economics, perhaps the most important thing to realize is that economics is *not* a collection of settled facts to be copied down and memorized. Mark Twain once said that nothing is older than yesterday's newspaper, and the same can be said of yesterday's economic statistics. Indeed, the only prediction about the economy that can be confidently made is that there will continue to be large, and largely unpredictable, changes.

If economics is not a set of durable facts, then what is it? Fundamentally, it is a *way of thinking* about the world. Over many years economists have developed some simple but widely applicable principles that are useful for understanding almost any economic situation, from the relatively simple economic decisions that individuals make every day to the workings of highly complex markets, such as international financial markets. The principal objective of this book, and of this course, is to help you learn these principles and how to apply them to a variety of economic questions and issues.

The four chapters of Part 1 lay out the basic economic principles that will be used throughout the book. Chapter 1 introduces the notion of scarcity—the unavoidable fact that, although our needs and wants are boundless, the resources available to satisfy them are limited. The chapter goes on to show that deciding whether to take an action by comparing the cost and benefit of the action provides a useful approach for dealing with the inevitable trade-offs that scarcity creates. Chapter 2 looks at some additional important principles for effective economic decision making, in the process identifying several pitfalls that plague many decision makers. Chapter 3 goes beyond individual decision making to consider trade among both individuals and countries. An important reason for trade is that it permits people (or countries) to specialize in the production of particular goods and services, which in turn enhances productivity and raises standards of living. Finally, Chapter 4 presents an overview of the concepts of supply and demand, perhaps the most basic and familiar tools of economists.

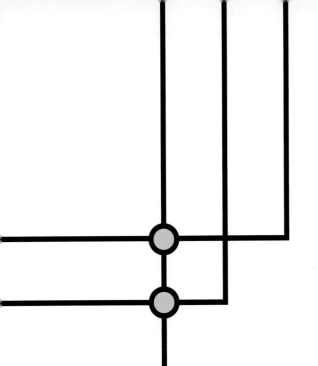

THINKING LIKE AN ECONOMIST

■

How many students are in your introductory economics class? Some classes have just 20 or so. Others average 35, 100, or 200 students. At some schools, introductory economics classes may have as many as 2,000 students. What size is best?

If cost were no object, the best size for an introductory economics course—or any other course, for that matter—might be only a single student. Think about it: the whole course, all term long, with just you and your professor! Everything could be custom-tailored to your own background and ability, allowing you to cover the material at just the right pace. The tutorial format would also promote close communication and personal trust between you and your professor. And your grade would depend more heavily on what you actually learned than on the vagaries of multiple-choice exams. We may even suppose, for the sake of discussion, that studies by educational psychologists prove definitively that students learn best in the tutorial format.

Why, then, do so many universities continue to schedule introductory classes with hundreds of students? The simple reason is that costs *do* matter. They matter not just to the university administrators who must build classrooms and pay faculty salaries but also to *you*. The direct cost of providing you with your own personal introductory economics course—most notably, the professor's salary and the expense of providing a classroom in which to meet—might easily top $20,000. *Someone* has to pay these costs. In private universities, a large share of the cost would be recovered directly from higher tuition payments; in state universities, the burden would be split between higher tuition payments and higher tax payments. But in either case, the course would be unaffordable for many, if not most, students.

With a larger class size, of course, the cost per student goes down. For example, in a class of 300 students, the cost of an introductory economics

Are small classes "better" than large ones?

course might come to as little as $100 per student. Needless to say, a class that large would compromise the quality of the learning environment. But compared to the custom tutorial format, it would be dramatically more affordable.

In choosing what size introductory economics course to offer, then, university administrators confront a classic economic trade-off. In making the class larger, they lower the quality of instruction—a bad thing; but at the same time, they reduce costs and hence the tuition students must pay—a good thing.

ECONOMICS: STUDYING CHOICE IN A WORLD OF SCARCITY

Even in rich societies like the United States, *scarcity* is a fundamental fact of life. There is never enough time, money, or energy to do everything we want to do or have everything we would like to have. **Economics** is the study of how people make choices under conditions of scarcity and of the results of those choices for society.

In the class-size example just discussed, a motivated economics student might definitely prefer to be in a class of 20 rather than a class of 100, everything else being equal. But other things, of course, are not equal. Students can enjoy the benefits of having smaller classes, but only at the price of having less money for other activities. The student's choice inevitably will come down to the relative importance of competing activities.

That such trade-offs are widespread and important is one of the core principles of economics. We call it the **scarcity principle**, because the simple fact of scarcity makes trade-offs necessary. Another name for the scarcity principle is the **no-free-lunch principle** (which comes from the observation that even a lunch that is given to you takes time to eat—time you could have spent doing other useful things).

The Scarcity Principle (or the No-Free-Lunch Principle):
Although we have boundless needs and wants, the resources available to us are limited. So having more of one good thing usually means having less of another.

economics the study of how people make choices under conditions of scarcity and of the results of those choices for society

Inherent in the idea of a trade-off is the fact that choice involves compromise between competing interests. Economists resolve such trade-offs by using **cost-benefit analysis**, which is based on the disarmingly simple principle that an action should be taken if, and only if, its benefits exceed its costs. We call this statement the **cost-benefit principle**, and it, too, is one of the core principles of economics:

The Cost-Benefit Principle: An individual (or a firm or a society) should take an action if, and only if, the extra benefits from taking the action are at least as great as the extra costs.

With the cost-benefit principle in mind, let's think about our class-size question again. Imagine that classrooms come in only two sizes—100-seat lecture halls and 20-seat classrooms—and that your university currently offers introductory economics courses to classes of 100 students. Question: Should administrators reduce the class size to 20 students? Answer: Reduce if, and only if, the value of the improvement in instruction outweighs its additional cost.

This rule sounds simple, but to apply it we need some way to measure the relevant costs and benefits—a task that is often difficult in practice. If we make a few simplifying assumptions, however, we can see how the analysis might work. On the cost side, suppose that the only relevant expenses are the professor's salary and the cost of a classroom big enough to hold the class. Imagine that the professor is paid $20,000 per course and that classroom space can be obtained at a cost of $30 per student per semester. Suppose further that the university charges tuition for the course equal to the direct costs of providing it. At the current class size of 100 students, the total cost is $23,000—$20,000 for the professor plus 100($30) = $3,000 for the classroom—which means that tuition is $230 per student. But if there were just 20 students in the class, the total cost would be $20,000 + 20($30) = $20,600—so tuition would be $1,030 per student.

The cost of reducing class size from 100 to 20 is simply the difference between the two tuition figures just calculated, namely, $1,030 − $230 = $800 per student. Should administrators switch to the smaller class size? If they apply the cost-benefit principle, they will realize that *the reduction in class size makes sense only if the value to students of attending the smaller class is at least $800 greater than the value of attending the larger class.*

Would you yourself (or your parents, if they are paying your tuition) be willing to part with an extra $800 for a smaller economics class? If not, and if other students feel the same way, then sticking with the larger class size makes sense. But if you and others would be willing to pay the extra tuition, then reducing the class size to 20 makes good economic sense.

Notice that the "best" class size, from an economic point of view, may not be the same as the "best" size from the point of view of an educational psychologist. The difference arises because the economic definition of "best" takes into account both the benefits *and* the costs of different class sizes. The psychologist ignores costs and looks only at the learning benefits of different class sizes.

In practice, of course, different people will feel differently about the value of smaller classes. People with high incomes, for example, tend to be willing to pay more for the advantage, which helps to explain why average class size is smaller, and tuition higher, at those private schools whose students come predominantly from high-income families.

The cost-benefit framework for thinking about the class-size problem also suggests a possible reason for the gradual increase in average class size that has been taking place in American colleges and universities. During the last 15 years, professors' salaries and the cost of classrooms have risen sharply, making smaller classes more costly. During the same period, median family income—and hence the willingness to pay for smaller classes—has remained roughly constant. When the cost of offering smaller classes goes up but willingness to pay for smaller classes does not, universities shift to larger class sizes.

Scarcity and the trade-offs that result also apply to resources other than money. Bill Gates is the richest man on earth. His wealth has been estimated at over $100 billion—more than the combined wealth of the poorest 40 percent of Americans. Gates has enough money to buy more houses, cars, vacations, and other consumer goods than he could possibly use. Yet Gates, like the rest of us, has only 24 hours each day and a limited amount of energy. So even he confronts trade-offs, in that any activity he pursues—whether it is building his business empire or planning the construction of his mansion—uses up time and energy that he could otherwise spend on other things. Indeed, someone once calculated that the value of Gates's time is so great that pausing to pick up a $100 bill from the sidewalk simply wouldn't be worth his while.

If Bill Gates saw a $100 bill lying on the sidewalk, would it be worth his time to pick it up?

APPLYING THE COST-BENEFIT PRINCIPLE

In studying choice under scarcity, we'll usually begin with the premise that people are **rational,** which means they have well-defined goals and try to fulfill them as best they can. The cost-benefit principle illustrated in the class-size example is a fundamental tool for the study of how rational people make choices.

rational person someone with well-defined goals who tries to fulfill those goals as best he or she can

As in the class-size example, often the only real difficulty in applying the cost-benefit rule is to come up with reasonable measures of the relevant benefits and costs. Only in rare instances will exact dollar measures be conveniently available. But the cost-benefit framework can lend structure to your thinking even when no relevant market data are available.

RESERVATION PRICES

To illustrate how we proceed in such cases, the following example asks you to decide whether to perform an action whose cost and benefits are described only in vague, qualitative terms.

EXAMPLE 1.1

Should you iron your shirt before going out?

You have a date for dinner in an hour, when suddenly you realize that your only clean shirt is not ironed. It doesn't look terrible, and you could certainly wear it if you had to. But you'd look and feel a little better if it were ironed, and you have the time to do it. On the other hand, you don't like to iron, and you will need 20 minutes to do the job—time that you could spend doing other things.

The cost-benefit principle says you should iron your shirt if the benefit of doing so exceeds the cost. The problem is that we don't have convenient ways to measure those benefits and costs. We can take a few simple steps, however, to generate useful estimates.

In dollar terms, the *benefit* of ironing your shirt may be defined as the largest amount of money you would be willing to pay to wear a pressed shirt to dinner rather than an unpressed shirt. How could you determine that amount? Here's a simple thought experiment that will give you an approximate estimate.

Imagine that a genie has offered to iron your shirt for a fee. If the fee were only a penny, would you accept? Assuming so, your benefit from having a pressed shirt must be at least 1 cent. If the genie's fee were $50, would you pay it? Probably not, in which case your benefit from having a pressed shirt must be less than $50. Somewhere between these two extremes lies the highest price you would be willing to pay to have your shirt ironed. To discover this price, imagine that the genie auctions off his services, starting with a price of 1 cent and raising it gradually until you refuse his last offer. For example, if you would accept the genie's offer to iron your shirt for $2.25 but would refuse the offer at $2.26, then the benefit to you of having a pressed shirt is $2.25. Another name for this benefit is your **reservation price** for having your shirt pressed—the highest price you would be willing to pay for that service.

A similar strategy can be used to estimate the cost of ironing your shirt. This time, we want to find out the most you'd be willing to pay to avoid ironing your shirt. This is what we mean by the cost of ironing your shirt. So imagine that someone offers to hire you to iron *his* shirt for a payment of, say, $50. Would you accept? If so, we know that your cost of ironing a shirt must be less than $50. Now imagine the offer being reduced in small increments until you finally refuse the last offer. For example, if you would iron someone's shirt for $2.00 but not for $1.99, then your cost of ironing a shirt is $2.00.

In this example, the benefit of ironing your shirt (your reservation price for *having* a pressed shirt) is $2.25, and your cost for a pressed shirt (your reservation price for *ironing* the shirt) is $2.00. Because your benefit exceeds your cost, your best course of action is to iron your shirt.

reservation price the highest price someone is willing to pay to obtain any good or service, or the lowest payment someone would accept for giving up a good or performing a service

ECONOMIC SURPLUS

economic surplus the economic surplus from taking any action is the benefit of taking the action minus its cost

In Example 1.1, ironing your shirt generated an **economic surplus** of $0.25, the difference between your benefit from ironing your shirt and your cost of ironing it. In general, your goal as an economic decision maker is to choose those actions that generate the largest possible economic surplus. This means taking all actions that yield a positive economic surplus, which is just another way of restating the cost-benefit principle.

OPPORTUNITY COST

Note that the fact that your best choice is to iron your shirt doesn't imply that you *enjoy* ironing it, any more than choosing a large class means that you prefer large classes to small ones. It simply means that ironing your shirt is less unpleasant than the prospect of showing up for dinner in a wrinkled shirt. Once again, you've faced a trade-off—in this case, the choice between a pressed shirt and the free time gained by going without one.

Needless to say, your mental auctions could have produced a different outcome. Suppose, for example, that the time you would need to iron your shirt is the only time you have left to study for a difficult test the next day. Or suppose you are watching one of your favorite movies on cable or that you are tired and would love a short nap. In such cases, we say that the **opportunity cost** of ironing your shirt—that is, the value of what you must sacrifice to iron your shirt—is high, and you are more likely to decide against ironing it.

In this example, if watching the last 20 minutes of the cable TV movie is the most valuable opportunity that conflicts with ironing, the opportunity cost of ironing your shirt is the dollar value you place on pursuing that opportunity—that is, the largest amount you'd be willing to pay to avoid missing the end of the movie. Note that the opportunity cost of ironing your shirt is *not* the combined value of *all* possible activities you could have pursued, but only the value of your *best* alternative—the one you would have chosen had you not ironed your shirt.

Throughout the text we will pose exercises like the one that follows. You'll find that pausing to answer them will help you to master key concepts in economics. Because doing these exercises isn't very costly (indeed, many students report that they are actually fun), the cost-benefit principle indicates that it's well worth your while to do them.

opportunity cost the opportunity cost of an activity is the value of the next-best alternative that must be forgone to undertake the activity

EXERCISE 1.1

If your reservation price for *having* an ironed shirt is $3 and your reservation price for *ironing* your shirt is $4, how much economic surplus would you receive from ironing your shirt? Should you iron it?

What is the opportunity cost of attending tonight's Eric Clapton concert?   **EXAMPLE 1.2**

It's rock 'n' roll hall of fame night. Eric Clapton is performing at 8 P.M. on the University of Minnesota campus, where your student ID card entitles you to free admission to all university events. Your only other alternative is to attend an 8 P.M. Bob Dylan concert at the Metrodome. Admission to the Dylan concert is $30, and you value the time and trouble involved in making the round-trip to the Metrodome at $10. If your reservation price for hearing Dylan is $50, what is your opportunity cost of attending the Clapton concert? What is your smallest reservation price for hearing Clapton that would make the Clapton concert your first choice?

By attending the Clapton concert, you give up the economic surplus you would have received by attending the Dylan concert, which is your reservation price for hearing Dylan minus the ticket price minus the cost of the trip to the Metrodome: $50 − $30 − $10 = $10. So $10 is your opportunity cost of hearing Clapton—the value of all you must sacrifice to hear him. You should attend the Clapton concert only if your reservation price for hearing Clapton is at least $10.

EXAMPLE 1.3   **Refer to Example 1.2. Suppose your reservation price for hearing Clapton is $8? What would be your opportunity cost of hearing the Dylan concert? Which concert should you attend?**

The question we must answer is "What is the value of everything you give up to attend the Dylan concert?" You give up the chance to hear Clapton, which is worth $8 to you; you give up $30 to buy the Dylan ticket; and you give up the chance to avoid the trip to the Metrodome, which is worth $10 to you. So the total value of what you give up is $8 + $30 + $10 = $48, and since this is less than your reservation price for hearing Dylan, you should attend the Dylan concert. (This is consistent with the conclusion from Example 1.2 that you should hear Dylan if your reservation price for hearing Clapton is less than $10.)

THE ROLE OF ECONOMIC MODELS

Economists use the cost-benefit principle as an abstract model of how an idealized rational individual would choose among competing alternatives. (By *abstract model* we mean a simplified description that captures the essential elements of a situation and allows us to analyze them in a logical way.) A computer model of a complex phenomenon like climate change, which must ignore many details and includes only the major forces at work, is an example of an abstract model.

Noneconomists are sometimes harshly critical of the economist's cost-benefit model on the grounds that people in the real world never conduct hypothetical mental auctions before deciding whether to iron their shirts. But this criticism betrays a fundamental misunderstanding of how abstract models can help to explain and predict human behavior. Economists know perfectly well that people don't conduct hypothetical mental auctions when they make simple decisions. All the cost-benefit principle really says is that a rational decision is one that is explicitly or implicitly based on a weighing of costs and benefits.

Most of us make sensible decisions most of the time, without being consciously aware that we are weighing costs and benefits, just as most people ride a bike without being consciously aware of what keeps them from falling. Through trial and error, we gradually learn what kinds of choices tend to work best in different contexts, just as bicycle riders internalize the relevant laws of physics, usually without being consciously aware of them.

Even so, learning the explicit principles of cost-benefit analysis can help us make better decisions, just as knowing about physics can help in learning to ride a bicycle. For instance, when a young economist was teaching his oldest son to ride a bike, he followed the time-honored tradition of running alongside the bike and holding onto his son, then giving him a push and hoping for the best. After several hours and many skinned elbows and knees, his son finally got it. A year later, someone pointed out that the trick to riding a bike is to turn slightly in whichever direction the bike is leaning. Of course! The economist passed that information along to his second son, who learned to ride almost instantly.

TO WHAT EXTENT SHOULD AN ACTIVITY BE PURSUED?

The pressed-shirt example involved the choice of whether or not to engage in an activity. But in many situations, as in the following example, the issue is not whether to pursue the activity at all but rather the *extent* to which it should be pursued.

How many pounds of compost should Heather use on her tomato patch?   **EXAMPLE 1.4**

To earn extra money over the summer, Heather grows tomatoes and sells them at the farmers' market for 20 cents per pound. By adding compost to her garden, she can increase her summer's yield, as shown in the table below. If compost costs 25 cents per pound and her goal is to make as much money as possible, how many pounds of compost should she add?

Pounds of compost	Pounds of tomatoes
0	100
1	120
2	125
3	128
4	130
5	131
6	131.5

To answer this question, note that questions of the form "Should Heather *pursue some activity*?" can be translated into the form "How many pounds of compost should Heather add?" by repeatedly posing the question "Should Heather *add an additional pound of compost*?" The answer, of course, is that Heather should add an additional pound of compost if its benefit is greater than or equal to its cost. The benefit of adding a pound of compost is the extra revenue she will get from the extra tomatoes that result; the cost of adding a pound of compost is 25 cents. If Heather starts out with no compost, she'll get 20 extra pounds of tomatoes—or 20($0.20) = $4 of extra revenue—by adding the first pound of compost. Clearly it pays to add the first pound of compost. Similar reasoning justifies adding the second, third, and fourth pounds of compost. (By adding the fourth pound of compost Heather will get 2 extra pounds of tomatoes, or 40 cents in extra revenue, which more than covers the 25-cent cost of the extra compost.) But note that if she were to add the fifth pound of compost, she'd get only one extra pound of tomatoes, whose 20-cent value is less than the cost of the compost. So Heather should add 4 pounds of compost and no more.

EXERCISE 1.2

In Example 1.4, if the cost of compost had been 50 cents/pound, not 25 cents, how many pounds of compost should Heather have added?

RATIONALITY AND IMPERFECT DECISION MAKERS

Imagine you are confronted with the question "Should I perform some action?" in which "perform some action" could mean anything from "eat another cookie" to "choose Wisconsin over Ohio State." The cost-benefit principle says that if the benefits of the action exceed its costs, then you should do it; but if the benefits fall short of the costs, then you should not do it. If its benefits and costs happen to be exactly equal, then it doesn't matter whether you perform the action or not.

Rational people will apply the cost-benefit principle most of the time, although probably in an intuitive and approximate way, rather than through explicit and precise calculation. To the extent that people are rational, their tendency to compare costs and benefits will help economists to predict their likely behavior. For example, we can predict that students from wealthy families are more likely than others to attend colleges that offer small classes.

As the next examples will make clear, however, the cost-benefit principle also proves helpful in another way. These examples demonstrate that people aren't born with an infallible instinct for weighing the relevant costs and benefits of daily decisions. Indeed, one of the rewards of teaching economics is to see how quickly it transforms students into better decision makers.

EXAMPLE 1.5

Should you drive downtown to save $10 on a $20 computer game? Should you drive downtown to save $10 on a $1,050 laptop computer?

Imagine you are about to buy a $20 computer game at the nearby campus store when a friend tells you that the same game is on sale at a downtown store for only $10. Would you drive downtown, or would you buy the game at the campus store?

Now imagine that you are about to buy a $1,050 laptop computer at the nearby campus store when a friend tells you that the store downtown has the same computer for only $1,040. Would you drive downtown this time?

In the first instance, the benefit of driving downtown is the $10 you will save on the game. To estimate the cost of driving downtown, simply ask yourself this question: "What is the minimum dollar amount that someone would have to pay me before I'd be willing to drive downtown and back?" Your answer to this question is your cost of driving downtown. If you'd be willing to do it for less than $10, then you should drive downtown. Otherwise, you should buy the game from the campus store. Since the cost of driving downtown is higher for some students than for others, different people will choose differently. But although there is no uniquely correct answer to this question, most students say they would shop downtown for the game.

So far, so good. But now let's consider whether to drive downtown for the laptop computer. Again, there is no uniquely correct answer, but most students now respond that they would shop at the campus store, saying "It's not worth it to drive downtown to save $10 on a laptop costing more than $1,000." But here we have a contradiction. The benefit of driving downtown to buy the laptop is $10—exactly the same as for the computer game. And the cost of driving downtown must also be the same in both cases, since whatever inconvenience and other expense the trip entails cannot logically depend on the trip's purpose. Finally, since the respective costs and benefits of the trips are identical, someone who finds it worthwhile to drive downtown in the first case should also find it worthwhile in the second. Yet as noted, most students respond differently in the two cases.

Many feel that a $10 savings on a laptop computer is insignificant because it is such a small *proportion* of the computer's price. Yet the proportion one saves on the purchase is simply not relevant to the decision. Regardless of how big that proportion is, you should take the trip if, and only if, the dollar amount you save is enough to compensate you for the trip's cost.

EXERCISE 1.3

Which is more valuable, saving $100 on a $2,000 plane ticket to Tokyo or saving $90 on a $200 plane ticket to Chicago?

EXERCISE 1.4

Ask your roommates or other friends outside class to consider the questions posed in Example 1.5 and Exercise 1.3. How do you expect they will answer? Do you think those who would choose differently in the two cases will accept your explanation for why such behavior cannot be rational?

Here is another example in which many people find it difficult to apply the cost-benefit principle correctly:

EXAMPLE 1.6

Would you buy a theater ticket after losing a $10 bill? Would you buy a second ticket after losing the first?

Imagine that you've just arrived at the theater to buy your ticket when you discover that you've lost a $10 bill from your wallet. Would you buy a ticket and see the play anyway? (You have enough money left to do that.)

Now suppose that you've just arrived at the theater when you discover that you've lost the $10 ticket you purchased earlier. Would you buy another ticket and see the play anyway?

As in Example 1.5, many people say they would choose differently in these two cases. Psychologists Daniel Kahneman and Amos Tversky found that most subjects would go ahead and see the play after losing a $10 bill but would not do so after losing a ticket they had already purchased.[1] According to the cost-benefit criterion, however, choosing differently in these cases is not rational. After all, the benefit of seeing the play is the same in both cases, and the cost of seeing the play—at the moment you must decide—is exactly $10 in both.

Many people seem to feel that in the case of the lost ticket, the cost of seeing the play is not $10 but $20, the price of two tickets. In terms of the financial consequences, however, the loss of a ticket is clearly no different from the loss of a $10 bill. In each case, you must decide whether seeing the play is worth spending $10. If it is, you should see it; otherwise not. Whichever your answer, it must be the same in both cases if you are rational.

Examples 1.5 and 1.6 make the point that people sometimes choose irrationally. Not only that, the errors they make tend to be systematic: People not only make inconsistent choices, but their inconsistencies also exhibit a strong pattern.

Some economists become defensive at the mere mention of the possibility that people sometimes choose irrationally, and most textbooks don't even call attention to this possibility. We find this a curious posture, for in our view, the fact that people do not always choose rationally makes the study of economics all the more useful. And as we'll see, learning how to identify situations in which we are least apt to weigh costs and benefits correctly promises to make all of us better decision makers.

That said, we must stress that our purpose in presenting Examples 1.5 and 1.6 was not to suggest that people *generally* make irrational choices. On the contrary, most people appear to choose sensibly most of the time, especially when their decisions are important or familiar ones. The economist's focus on rational choice thus offers not only useful advice about making better decisions but also a basis for predicting and explaining human behavior. We used the cost-benefit approach in this way when discussing how rising faculty salaries and building costs have led to larger class sizes. And as we will see, similar reasoning helps to explain human behavior in virtually every other domain.

WEIGHING BENEFITS AND COSTS GRAPHICALLY

Sometimes, as in the following example, a graph proves a convenient form in which to express the costs and benefits of various levels of an activity.

EXAMPLE 1.7

How much memory should your computer have?

Suppose you can add random-access memory (RAM) to your computer at a cost of $5 per megabyte. Suppose also that the value to you of an additional megabyte of memory, measured in terms of your willingness to pay for it, is as shown by curve *MB* in Figure 1.1. How many megabytes of memory should you purchase?

---

[1]Amos Tversky and Daniel Kahneman, "The Framing of Decisions and the Psychology of Choice," *Science*, **211**:453–458, 1981.

FIGURE 1.1
The Marginal Cost and Benefit of Additional RAM.
Curve *MB* plots the benefit of adding an additional megabyte of memory. Curve *MC* plots the cost of an additional megabyte of memory. It is rational to continue adding memory as long as the marginal benefit of memory (curve *MB*) lies above the marginal cost of memory (curve *MC*). The optimal amount of RAM is 30 megabytes, the amount for which the marginal benefit of memory is equal to its marginal cost.

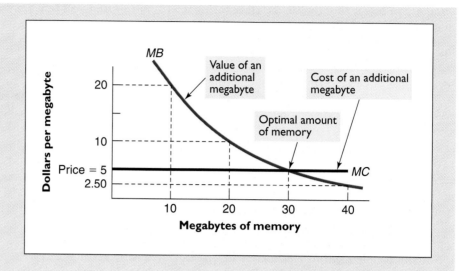

marginal benefit the marginal benefit of an activity is the increase in total benefit that results from carrying out one additional unit of the activity.

marginal cost the marginal cost of an activity is the increase in total cost that results from carrying out one additional unit of the activity.

Curve *MB* plots the value to you of an additional megabyte of memory (measured in dollars per megabyte, on the vertical axis) as a function of your computer's existing memory (measured in megabytes, on the horizontal axis). For example, the value of additional memory is $20 per megabyte if your computer has 10 megabytes of memory but only $10 if it has 20 megabytes. Curve *MB* is often called the **marginal benefit** curve, to emphasize that it shows not the *total* value of memory but the value of having *an additional unit* of memory. (*Marginal* means "extra" or "additional.")

Curve *MC* in Figure 1.1 shows the cost, in dollars, of adding an additional megabyte, assumed constant at $5. This curve is often called the **marginal cost** curve, to emphasize that it represents not the total cost of memory but the cost of adding an additional unit. The fact that curve *MC* is horizontal at $5 means that no matter how much memory your computer has, you can always add an extra megabyte at a cost of exactly $5. (Later on, we will consider examples in which the cost of adding additional units depends on the number of units you already have.)

Once we know the relevant marginal benefit and cost curves, finding the optimal quantity of memory is straightforward. Note in Figure 1.1 that if the quantity of memory your computer has is less than 30 megabytes, then the marginal benefit of adding memory (as measured by curve *MB*) is greater than its marginal cost (as measured by curve *MC*). So you should add memory if your computer currently has less than 30 megabytes.

Conversely, note that if your computer has more than 30 megabytes of memory, the marginal benefit of memory is less than its marginal cost, in which case you should have bought less memory. The optimal amount of memory is thus 30 megabytes, the amount at which the marginal benefit of memory exactly equals its marginal cost.

A common question prompted by Example 1.7 is "Why should I bother to add the thirtieth megabyte of memory if its marginal benefit is no greater than its marginal cost?" The answer is that at any amount less than 30 megabytes, the marginal benefit of memory exceeds its marginal cost. Suppose, for example, that your computer had only 29.9 megabytes of memory. The marginal benefit of additional memory would then be greater than its marginal cost (albeit by only a tiny margin), which means that you should expand. The same reasoning would apply if your computer had 29.99 megabytes, or even 29.99999. So you can always do better by expanding unless you've already got 30 megabytes.[2]

RECAP   COST-BENEFIT ANALYSIS

Scarcity is a basic fact of economic life. Because of it, having more of one good thing almost always means having less of another (the scarcity principle). Economics is devoted to studying how we can make intelligent choices in a world of scarcity.

The cost-benefit principle holds that an individual (or a firm or a society) should take an action if, and only if, the extra benefit from taking the action is at least as great as the extra cost. The benefit of taking any action minus the cost of taking the action is called the *economic surplus* from that action. Hence the cost-benefit principle suggests that we take only those actions with positive economic surplus.

Applying the cost-benefit principle requires measurement. The benefit of an action is your *reservation price* for having the action performed, the most you would be willing to pay someone to perform it. The cost of an action is the value of everything you must sacrifice to perform the action.

The cost-benefit principle applies not only to all-or-nothing decisions but also to decisions regarding the extent to which an activity should be pursued. The rule is to keep performing the action as long as the marginal benefit of the action exceeds its marginal cost.

ECONOMICS: MICRO AND MACRO

By convention, we use the term **microeconomics** to describe the study of individual choices and of group behavior in individual markets. **Macroeconomics,** by contrast, is the study of the performance of national economies and of the policies that governments use to try to affect that performance. Macroeconomics tries to understand the determinants of such things as the national unemployment rate, the overall price level, and the total value of national output. Chapter 17 contains a much more detailed introduction to the issues and methods of macroeconomics.

Our focus in this chapter and the next is on issues that confront the individual decision maker. Further on, we'll consider economic models of groups of individuals, such as all buyers or all sellers in a specific market. Later still we will turn to broader economic issues and measures.

No matter which of these levels is our focus, however, our thinking will be shaped by the fact that although economic needs and wants are effectively unlimited, the material and human resources that can be used to satisfy them are finite. Clear thinking about economic problems must therefore always take into account the idea of trade-offs—the idea that having more of one good thing usually means having less of another. Our economy and our society are shaped to a substantial degree by the choices people have made when faced with trade-offs.

microeconomics the study of individual choice under scarcity and its implications for the behavior of prices and quantities in individual markets

macroeconomics the study of the performance of national economies and the policies that governments use to try to improve that performance.

---

[2]Note that in this example we treated your computer's memory bank as a perfectly divisible quantity. In practice, however, computer memory can be increased only by adding chunks of discrete size. A more realistic account of your decision of how much memory to buy for your computer would advise you to add the next chunk of memory if its benefit exceeds its cost. The optimal quantity of memory could then be an amount for which the benefit of the last chunk was greater than its cost. In that case, the benefit of the next discrete chunk would be less than its cost.

THE PHILOSOPHY OF THIS TEXT

Choosing the number of students to register in each class is just one of many important decisions in planning an introductory economics course. Another decision, to which the scarcity principle applies just as strongly, concerns which of many different topics to include on the course syllabus. There is a virtually inexhaustible set of topics and issues that might be covered in an introductory course, but only limited time in which to cover them. There's no free lunch. Covering some topics inevitably means omitting others.

All textbook authors are necessarily forced to pick and choose. A textbook that covered *all* the issues ever written about in economics would take up more than a whole floor of your campus library. It is our firm view that most introductory textbooks try to cover far too much. One reason each of us was drawn to the study of economics was that a relatively short list of the discipline's core ideas can explain a great deal of the behavior and events we see in the world around us. So rather than cover a large number of ideas at a superficial level, our strategy is to focus on this short list of core ideas, returning to each entry again and again, in many different contexts. This strategy will enable you to internalize these ideas remarkably well in the brief span of a single course. And the benefit of learning a small number of important ideas well will far outweigh the cost of having to ignore a host of other, less important ideas.

So far, we've already encountered two core ideas: the scarcity principle and the cost-benefit principle. As these core ideas reemerge in the course of our discussions, we'll call your attention to them. And shortly after a new core idea appears, we'll highlight it by formally restating it.

A second important element in the philosophy of this text is our belief in the importance of active learning. In the same way that you can learn Spanish only by speaking and writing it, or tennis only by playing the game, you can learn economics only by *doing* economics. Because we want you to learn how to do economics, rather than just to read or listen passively as the authors or your instructor does economics, we will make every effort to encourage you to stay actively involved.

For example, instead of just telling you about an idea, we will usually first motivate the idea by showing you how it works in the context of a specific example. Often, these examples will be followed by exercises for you to try, as well as applications that show the relevance of the idea to real life. Try working the exercises *before* looking up the answers (which are in the back of the book).

Think critically about the applications: Do you see how they illustrate the point being made? Do they give you new insight into the issue? Work problems at the end of the chapter, and take extra care with those relating to points that you do not fully understand. Apply economic principles to the world around you. (We'll say more about this when we discuss Economic Naturalism below.) Finally, when you come across an idea or example that you find interesting, tell a friend about it. You'll be surprised to discover how much the mere act of explaining it helps you understand and remember the underlying principles. The more actively you can become engaged in the learning process, the more effective your learning will be.

ECONOMIC NATURALISM

With the rudiments of the cost-benefit framework under your belt, you are now in a position to become an "economic naturalist," someone who uses insights from economics to help make sense of observations from everyday life. People who have studied biology are able to observe and marvel at many details of nature that would otherwise have escaped their notice. For example, while the novice may see only trees on a walk in the woods in early April, the biology student notices many different species of trees and understands why some are already into leaf while others still lie dormant. Likewise, the novice may notice that in some animal species, males are much larger than females, but the biology student knows that that pattern occurs only in species in which males take several mates. Natural selection favors larger males because their greater size helps them to prevail in the often bloody contests among males for access to females. By contrast, males tend to be roughly the same size as females in monogamous species, in which there is much less fighting for mates.

In similar fashion, learning a few simple economic principles enables us to see the mundane details of ordinary human existence in a new light. Whereas the uninitiated often fail even to notice these details, the economic naturalist not only sees them but becomes actively engaged in the attempt to understand them. Let's consider a few examples of questions economic naturalists might pose for themselves.

Why do today's computers have so much more random-access memory (RAM) than the computers of just a few years ago?

Computers sold today typically come with at least 32 megabytes of RAM, often 64. Just a few short years ago, however, personal computers rarely had more than 2 megabytes of RAM. Why this dramatic increase?

To understand this change, the economic naturalist looks for changes in the underlying costs and benefits of RAM. Having more memory is obviously a benefit, since it enables the computer to carry out more complex tasks. But memory is also costly, and this limits the amount of memory we buy. Perhaps the most important reason for the greater amount of RAM in today's computers is the dramatic drop in cost made possible by new production methods. Whereas RAM once sold for several hundred dollars per megabyte, it now costs less than $10 per megabyte. As shown in Figure 1.2, for example, a fall in the marginal cost of RAM from $10 to $5 per megabyte increases the optimal amount of memory from 20 to 30 megabytes.

Important changes have occurred on the benefit side as well. For example, graphics software uses large amounts of memory, and the drop in RAM prices has encouraged developers to make much more intensive use of graphics. The new programs are more attractive than older programs, but a computer needs a lot of extra memory to run them. The availability of these programs has thus increased the benefit of adding extra memory and in so doing has helped to fuel the move toward greater amounts of RAM.

Graphically, we represent an increase in the value of additional memory as an upward movement of the marginal benefit curve. Figure 1.3, for example, portrays an upward shift in the marginal benefit curve from curve *MB* to curve *MB'*. Such a shift means that the consumer now finds extra memory more valuable than before, no matter how much memory his or her computer has. The upward shift in the marginal benefit curve in Figure 1.3 increases the optimal amount of RAM from 30 to 40 megabytes.

ECONOMIC NATURALIST 1.1

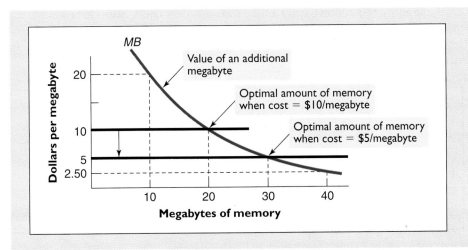

FIGURE 1.2
Falling RAM Prices Increase the Optimal Amount of Memory.
When the price of memory falls from $10 per megabyte to $5 per megabyte, the optimal amount of memory increases from 20 to 30 megabytes.

FIGURE 1.3
An Increase in the Marginal Benefit of RAM Increases the Optimal Amount of Memory.
When the marginal benefit of RAM increases (when curve *MB* shifts up to become curve *MB'*), the optimal amount of memory increases from 30 to 40 megabytes.

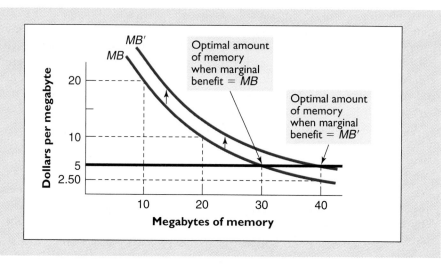

As long as we're on the subject, let's consider one more computer-related example.

Why do many hardware manufacturers include more than $1,000 worth of free software with a computer selling for only slightly more than that?

The software industry is different from many others in the sense that its customers care a great deal about product compatibility. When you and your classmates are working on a project together, for example, your task will be much simpler if you all use the same word-processing program. Likewise, an executive's life will be easier at tax time if her financial software is the same as her accountant's.

The implication is that the benefit of owning and using any given software program increases with the number of other people who use that same product. This unusual relationship gives the producers of the most popular programs an enormous advantage and often makes it hard for new programs to break into the market.

Recognizing this pattern, the Intuit Corporation offered computer makers free copies of *Quicken,* its personal financial-management software. Computer makers, for their part, were only too happy to include the program, since it made their new computers more attractive to buyers. *Quicken* soon became the standard for personal financial-management programs. By giving away free copies of the program, Intuit "primed the pump," creating an enormous demand for upgrades of *Quicken* and for more advanced versions of related software. Thus *TurboTax* and *Macintax,* Intuit's personal income tax software, have become the standards for tax-preparation programs.

Inspired by this success story, other software developers have jumped onto the bandwagon. Most hardware now comes bundled with a host of free software programs. Some software developers are even rumored to *pay* computer makers to include their programs!

The free-software example illustrates a case in which the *benefit* of a product depends on the number of other people who own that product. As the next example demonstrates, the *cost* of a product may also depend on the number of others who own it.

Why don't auto manufacturers make cars without heaters?

Virtually every new car sold in the United States today has a heater. But not every car has a CD player. Why this difference?

One might be tempted to answer that although everyone *needs* a heater, people can get along without CD players. Yet heaters are of little use in places like Hawaii and southern California. What is more, cars produced as recently as the 1950s did *not* all have heaters. (The classified ad that led one young economic naturalist to his first car, a 1955 Pontiac, boasted that the vehicle had a radio, heater, and whitewall tires.)

Although heaters cost extra money to manufacture and are not useful in all parts of the country, they do not cost *much* money and are useful on at least a few days each year in most parts of the country. As time passed and people's incomes grew, manufacturers found that people were ordering fewer and fewer cars without heaters. At some point it actually became cheaper to put heaters in *all* cars, rather than bear the administrative expense of making some cars with heaters and others without. No doubt a few buyers would still order a car without a heater if they could save some money in the process. But catering to these customers is just no longer worth it.

Similar reasoning explains why certain cars today cannot be purchased without a CD player. Buyers of the 2001 BMW 740iL, for example, got a CD player whether they wanted one or not. Most buyers of this car, which sells for approximately $70,000, have high incomes, so the overwhelming majority of them would have chosen to order a CD player had it been sold as an option. Because of the savings made possible when all cars are produced with the same equipment, it would have actually cost BMW more to supply cars for the few who would want them without CD players.

The insights afforded by the preceding example suggest an answer to the following strange question:

Why do the keypad buttons on drive-up automatic teller machines have Braille dots?

Braille dots on elevator buttons and on the keypads of walk-up automatic teller machines enable blind persons to participate more fully in the normal flow of daily activity. But even though blind people can do many remarkable things, they cannot drive automobiles on public roads. Why, then, do the manufacturers of automatic teller machines install Braille dots on the machines at drive-up locations?

The answer to this riddle is that once the keypad molds have been manufactured, the cost of producing buttons with Braille dots is no higher than the cost of producing smooth buttons. Making both would require separate sets of molds and two different types of inventory. If the patrons of drive-up machines found buttons with Braille dots harder to use, there might be a reason to incur these extra costs. But since the dots pose no difficulty for sighted users, the best and cheapest solution is to produce only keypads with dots.

The preceding example was suggested by Cornell student Bill Tjoa, in response to the following assignment:

EXERCISE 1.5

In 750 words or less, use cost-benefit analysis to explain some pattern of events or behavior you have observed in your own environment.

Why do the keypad buttons on drive-up automatic teller machines have Braille dots?

There is probably no more useful step you can take in your study of economics than to perform several iterations of the assignment in Exercise 1.5. Students who do so almost invariably become lifelong economic naturalists. Their mastery of economic concepts not only does not decay with the passage of time, it actually grows stronger. We urge you, in the strongest possible terms, to make this investment!

■ SUMMARY ■

• Economics is the study of how people make choices under conditions of scarcity and of the results of those choices for society. Economic analysis of human behavior begins with the assumption that people are rational—that they have well-defined goals and try to achieve them as best they can. In trying to achieve their goals, people normally face trade-offs: Because material and human resources are limited, having more of one good thing means making do with less of some other good thing.

• Our focus in this chapter was on how rational people make choices between alternative courses of action. Our basic tool for analyzing these decisions is cost-benefit analysis. The cost-benefit principle says that a person should take an action if, and only if, the benefit of that action is at least as great as its cost. The benefit of an action is measured as the

largest dollar amount the person would be willing to pay to take the action. The cost of an action is measured as the dollar value of everything the person must give up to take the action.

• Often the question is not whether to pursue an activity but rather how many units of it to pursue. In these cases, the rational actor pursues additional units as long as the marginal benefit of the activity (the benefit from pursuing an additional unit of it) exceeds its marginal cost (the cost of pursuing an additional unit of it).

• In using the cost-benefit framework, we need not presume that people choose rationally all the time. Indeed, we saw examples in which people's choices departed in systematic ways from what rational decision makers would have chosen.

■ CORE PRINCIPLES ■

The Scarcity Principle (or No-Free-Lunch Principle)
Although we have boundless needs and wants, the resources available to us are limited. So having more of one good thing usually means having less of another.

The Cost-Benefit Principle
An individual (or a firm or a society) should take an action if, and only if, the extra benefits from taking the action are at least as great as the extra costs.

■ KEY TERMS ■

economic surplus (6)   marginal benefit (12)   opportunity cost (7)
economics (4)   marginal cost (12)   rational person (5)
macroeconomics (13)   microeconomics (13)   reservation price (6)

■ REVIEW QUESTIONS ■

1. A friend of yours on the tennis team says, "Private tennis lessons are definitely better than group lessons." Explain what you think your friend means by this statement. Then use the cost-benefit principle to explain why private lessons are not necessarily the best choice for everyone.

2. Assuming that both care equally about improving their tennis games, who is likely to have a higher reservation price for private tennis lessons: a McDonald's clerk or a computer programmer?

3. One of the two bicycle shops near campus is having a sale on new mountain bikes. Sam nonetheless decides to buy his new bike from the other shop, paying $30 more in the process. Describe an example of conditions under which his decision might nonetheless be considered rational.

4. True or false: Your willingness to drive downtown to save $30 on a new appliance should depend on what fraction of the total selling price $30 is. Explain.

5. Both the economics and the sociology departments have scheduled their faculty meetings on the first Wednesday of each month at 4:00 P.M. The economics department has a policy of starting its meetings at 4 o'clock sharp. The sociology department's policy is to start once 80 percent of the faculty has arrived. Discuss the relative merits of these two policies.

■ PROBLEMS ■

---

1. Your reservation price for having a freshly washed car when you go out to dinner is $6. The smallest amount for which you would be willing to wash someone else's car is $3.50. You are going out to dinner this evening, and your car is dirty. How much economic surplus would you receive from washing it?

2. To earn extra money in the summer, you grow tomatoes and sell them at the farmers' market for 30 cents per pound. By adding compost to your garden, you can increase your yield as shown in the following table. If compost costs 50 cents per pound and your goal is to make as much money as possible, how many pounds of compost should you add?

Pounds of compost	Pounds of tomatoes
0	100
1	120
2	125
3	128
4	130
5	131
6	131.5

3. For each long distance call anywhere in the continental United States, a new phone service will charge users 30 cents per minute for the first 2 minutes and 2 cents per minute for additional minutes in each call. Tom's current phone service charges 10 cents per minute for all calls, and his calls are never shorter than 7 minutes. If Tom's dorm switches to the new phone service, what will happen to the average length of his calls?

4. The meal plan at university A lets students eat as much as they like for a fixed fee of $500 per semester. The average student there eats 250 pounds of food per semester. University B charges $500 for a book of meal tickets that entitles the student to eat 250 pounds of food per semester. If the student eats more than 250 pounds, he or she pays extra; if the student eats less, he or she gets a refund. If students are rational, at which university will average food consumption be higher? Explain briefly.

5. Suppose random-access memory can be added to your computer at a cost of $10 per megabyte. Suppose also that the value to you of an additional megabyte of memory, measured in terms of your willingness to pay, is as shown in the following diagram. How many megabytes of memory should you purchase? Explain briefly.

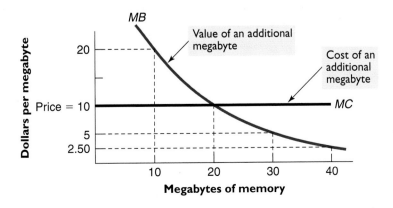

6. Residents of your city are charged a fixed weekly fee of $6 for garbage collection. They are allowed to put out as many cans as they wish. The average household disposes of three cans of garbage per week under this plan. Now suppose that your city changes to a "tag" system. Each can of refuse to be collected must have a tag affixed to it. The tags cost $2 each and are not reusable. What effect do you think the introduction of the tag system will have on the total quantity of garbage collected in your city? Explain briefly.

7. Once a week, Smith purchases a six-pack of cola and puts it in his refrigerator for his two children. He invariably discovers that all six cans are gone on the first day. Jones also purchases a six-pack of cola once a week for his two children, but unlike Smith, he tells them that each may drink no more than three cans. Explain briefly why the cola lasts much longer at Jones's house than at Smith's.

8. The Wallflowers will give a free concert on the Emory University campus the same night The Traveling Wilburys will perform at a club in Buckhead. The club charges a $3 fee at the door. You choose the Wallflowers concert, but your next best choice for the evening is to hear The Wilburys. Your opportunity cost of hearing the Wallflowers is:
   a. The dollar value to you of hearing The Traveling Wilburys minus the time and money cost of driving to Buckhead and paying the door fee
   b. The time and money cost of driving to Buckhead and paying the door fee
   c. The dollar value to you of hearing The Traveling Wilburys plus the time and money cost of driving to Buckhead and paying the door fee
   d. The study time lost for Econ 101 while you listen to the Wallflowers

9. Same as Problem 8 except that this time you prefer The Traveling Wilburys and The Wallflowers would be your second choice. Your opportunity cost of going to hear The Traveling Wilburys is:
   a. The club's door fee
   b. The dollar value to you of hearing The Wallflowers minus the time and money cost of driving to Buckhead and paying the door fee
   c. The dollar value to you of hearing The Traveling Wilburys minus the time and money cost of driving to Buckhead and paying the door fee
   d. The dollar value to you of hearing The Wallflowers plus the time and money cost of driving to Buckhead plus the $3 door fee
   e. The study time lost for Econ 101 while you drive and while you listen to The Traveling Wilburys

10. As in Problem 8, The Wallflowers will give a free concert on the Emory University campus the same night The Traveling Wilburys will perform at a club in Buckhead. The club charges a $3 fee at the door. Suppose the dollar value to you of hearing The Wallflowers is $6 and the cost of your round-trip drive to Buckhead is $5. If the dollar value to you of hearing The Traveling Wilburys is $15:
    a. Which choice should you make and how much economic surplus would you receive from your evening?
    b. How would your answers be different if the dollar value of hearing The Wallflowers were $8?

■ ANSWERS TO IN-CHAPTER EXERCISES ■

1.1 The economic surplus from ironing your shirt would be $3 − $4 = − $1. Because the surplus from ironing your shirt would be negative, you should not iron it.

1.2 Adding the third pound of compost makes sense, because it increases revenue by 60 cents and costs only 50 cents. But the fourth pound of compost does not make sense, because it adds only 40 cents to revenue.

1.3 Saving $100 is $10 more valuable than saving $90, even though the percentage savings is much greater in the case of the Chicago ticket.

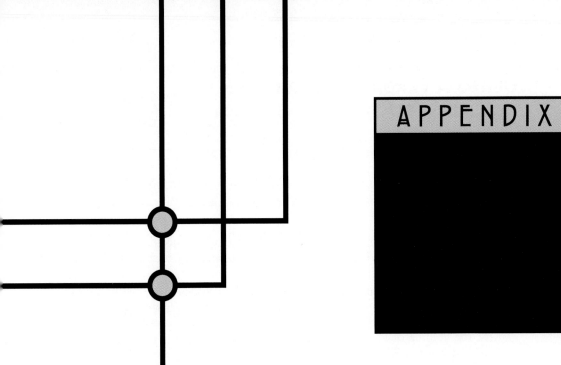

WORKING WITH EQUATIONS, GRAPHS, AND TABLES

■

Although many of the examples and most of the end-of-chapter problems in this book are quantitative, none require mathematical skills beyond rudimentary high school algebra and geometry. In this brief appendix we review some of the skills you'll need for dealing with these examples and problems.

One important skill is to be able to read simple verbal descriptions and translate the information they provide into the relevant equations or graphs. You'll also need to be able to translate information given in tabular form into an equation or graph, and sometimes you'll need to translate graphical information into a table or equation. The following examples illustrate all the tools you'll need.

USING A VERBAL DESCRIPTION TO CONSTRUCT AN EQUATION

We begin with an example that shows how to construct a long-distance telephone billing equation from a verbal description of the billing plan.

EXAMPLE A.1

equation a mathematical expression that describes the relationship between two or more variables

variable a quantity that is free to take a range of different values

dependent variable a variable in an equation whose value is determined by the value taken by another variable in the equation

independent variable a variable in an equation whose value determines the value taken by another variable in the equation

constant (or parameter) a quantity that is fixed in value

Your long-distance telephone plan charges you $5/month plus 10 cents/minute for long-distance calls. Write an equation that describes your monthly telephone bill.

An **equation** is a simple mathematical expression that describes the relationship between two or more **variables,** or quantities that are free to assume different values in some range. The most common type of equation we'll work with contains two types of variables: **dependent variable** and **independent variable.** In this example, the dependent variable is the dollar amount of your monthly telephone bill, and the independent variable is the variable on which your bill depends, namely, the volume of long-distance calls you make during the month. Your bill also depends on the $5 monthly fee and the 10 cents/minute charge. But in this example, those amounts are **constants,** not variables. A constant, also called a **parameter,** is a quantity in an equation that is fixed in value, not free to vary. As the terms suggest, the dependent variable describes an outcome that depends on the value taken by the independent variable.

Once you've identified the dependent variable and the independent variable, choose simple symbols to represent them. In algebra courses, X is typically used to represent the independent variable and Y the dependent variable. Many people find it easier to remember what the variables stand for, however, if they choose symbols that are linked in some straightforward way to the quantities that the variables represent. Thus, in this example, we might use B to represent your monthly *bill* in dollars and T to represent the total *time* in minutes you spent during the month on long-distance calls.

Having identified the relevant variables and chosen symbols to represent them, you are now in a position to write the equation that links them:

$$B = 5 + 0.10T, \tag{A.1}$$

where B is your monthly long-distance bill in dollars and T is your monthly total long-distance calling time in minutes. The fixed monthly fee (5) and the charge per minute (0.10) are parameters in this equation. Note the importance of being clear about the units of measure. Because B represents the monthly bill in dollars, we must also express the fixed monthly fee and the per-minute charge in dollars, which is why the latter number appears in equation A.1 as 0.10 rather than 10. Equation A.1 follows the normal convention in which the dependent variable appears by itself on the left-hand side while the dependent variable or variables and constants appear on the right-hand side.

Once we have the equation for the monthly bill, we can use it to calculate how much you'll owe as a function of your monthly volume of long-distance calls. For example, if you make 32 minutes of calls, you can calculate your monthly bill by simply substituting 32 minutes for T in equation A.1:

$$B = 5 + 0.10(32) = 8.20. \tag{A.2}$$

Your monthly bill when you make 32 minutes of calls is thus equal to $8.20.

EXERCISE A.1

Under the monthly billing plan described in Example A.1, how much would you owe for a month during which you made 45 minutes of long-distance calls?

GRAPHING THE EQUATION OF A STRAIGHT LINE

The next example shows how to portray the billing plan described in Example A.1 as a graph.

Construct a graph that portrays the monthly long-distance telephone billing plan described in Example A.1, putting your telephone charges, in dollars per month, on the vertical axis, and your total volume of calls, in minutes per month, on the horizontal axis.

EXAMPLE A.2

The first step in responding to this instruction is the one we just took, namely, to translate the verbal description of the billing plan into an equation. When graphing an equation, the normal convention is to use the vertical axis to represent the dependent variable and the horizontal axis to represent the independent variable. In Figure A.1, we therefore put B on the vertical axis and T on the horizontal axis. One way to construct the graph shown in the figure

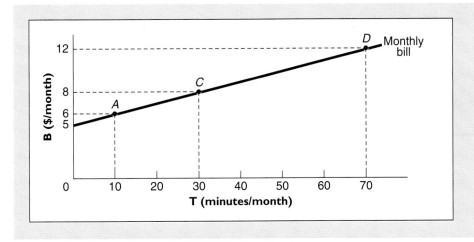

FIGURE A.1
The Monthly Telephone Bill in Example A.1.
The graph of the equation $B = 5 + 0.10T$ is the straight line shown. Its vertical intercept is 5, and its slope is 0.10.

is to begin by plotting the monthly bill values that correspond to several different total amounts of long-distance calls. For example, someone who makes 10 minutes of calls during the month would have a bill of $B = 5 + 0.10(10)$ = $6. Thus, in Figure A.1 the value of 10 minutes/month on the horizontal axis corresponds to a bill of $6/month on the vertical axis (point A). Someone who makes 30 minutes of long-distance calls during the month will have a monthly bill of $B = 5 + 0.10(30)$ = $8, so the value of 30 minutes/month on the horizontal axis corresponds to $8/month on the vertical axis (point C). Similarly, someone who makes 70 minutes of long-distance calls during the month will have a monthly bill of $B = 5 + 0.10(70)$ = $12, so the value of 70 minutes on the horizontal axis corresponds to $12 on the vertical axis (point D). The line joining these points is the graph of the monthly billing equation A.1.

As shown in Figure A.1, the graph of the equation $B = 5 + 0.10T$ is a straight line. The parameter 5 is the **vertical intercept** of the line—the value of B when $T = 0$, or the point at which the line intersects the vertical axis. The parameter

vertical intercept in a straight line, the value taken by the dependent variable when the independent variable equals zero

slope in a straight line, the ratio of the vertical distance the straight line travels between any two points *(rise)* to the corresponding horizontal distance *(run)*

0.10 is the **slope** of the line, which is the ratio of the **rise** of the line to the corresponding **run**. The ratio rise/run is simply the vertical distance between any two points on the line divided by the horizontal distance between those points. For example, if we choose points A and C in Figure A.1, the rise is $8 - 6 = 2$ and the corresponding run is $30 - 10 = 20$, so rise/run $= 2/20 = 0.10$. More generally, for the graph of any equation $Y = a + bX$, the parameter a is the vertical intercept and the parameter b is the slope.

DERIVING THE EQUATION OF A STRAIGHT LINE FROM ITS GRAPH

The next example shows how to derive the equation for a straight line from a graph of the line.

EXAMPLE A.3

Figure A.2 shows the graph of the monthly billing plan for a new long-distance plan. What is the equation for this graph? How much is the fixed monthly fee under this plan? How much is the charge per minute?

FIGURE A.2
Another Monthly Long-Distance Plan.
The vertical distance between points A and C is $12 - 8 = 4$ units, and the horizontal distance between points A and C is $40 - 20 = 20$, so the slope of the line is $4/20 = 1/5 = 0.20$. The vertical intercept (the value of B when $T = 0$) is 4. So the equation for the billing plan shown is $B = 4 + 0.20T$.

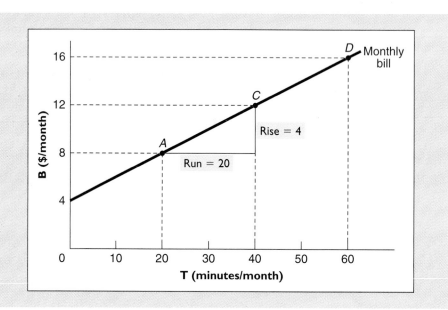

The slope of the line shown is the rise between any two points divided by the corresponding run. For points A and C, rise $= 12 - 8 = 4$, and run $= 40 - 20 = 20$, so the slope equals rise/run $= 4/20 = 1/5 = 0.20$. And since the horizontal intercept of the line is 4, its equation must be given by

$$B = 4 + 0.20T. \tag{A.3}$$

Under this plan, the fixed monthly fee is the value of the bill when $T = 0$, which is \$4. The charge per minute is the slope of the billing line, 0.20, or 20 cents/minute.

EXERCISE A.2

Write the equation for the billing plan shown in the accompanying graph. How much is its fixed monthly fee? Its charge per minute?

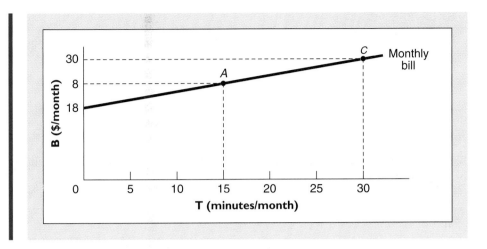

CHANGES IN THE VERTICAL INTERCEPT AND SLOPE

Examples A.4 and A.5 and Exercises A.3 and A.4 provide practice in seeing how a line shifts with a change in its vertical intercept or slope.

Show how the billing plan whose graph is in Figure A.2 would change if the monthly fixed fee were increased from $4 to $8.

An increase in the monthly fixed fee from $4 to $8 would increase the vertical intercept of the billing plan by $4 but would leave its slope unchanged. An increase in the fixed fee thus leads to a parallel upward shift in the billing plan by $4, as shown in Figure A.3. For any given number of minutes of long-distance calls, the monthly charge on the new bill will be $4 higher than on the old bill.

EXAMPLE A.4

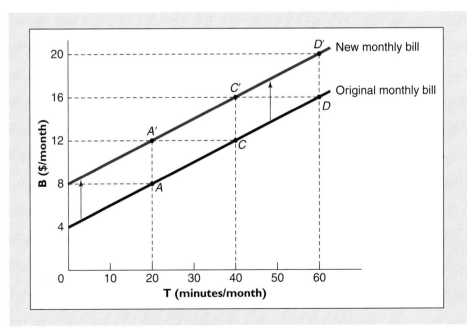

FIGURE A.3
The Effect of an Increase in the Vertical Intercept.
An increase in the vertical intercept of a straight line produces an upward parallel shift in the line.

Thus 20 minutes of calls per month costs $8 under the original plan (point *A*) but $12 under the new plan (point *A'*). And 40 minutes costs $12 under the original plan (point *C*), $16 under the new plan (point *C'*); and 60 minutes costs $16 under the original plan (point *D*), $20 under the new plan (point *D'*).

EXERCISE A.3

Show how the billing plan whose graph is in Figure A.2 would change if the monthly fixed fee were reduced from $4 to $2.

EXAMPLE A.5

Show how the billing plan whose graph is in Figure A.2 would change if the charge per minute were increased from 20 cents to 40 cents.

Because the monthly fixed fee is unchanged, the vertical intercept of the new billing plan continues to be 4. But the slope of the new plan, shown in Figure A.4, is 0.40, or twice the slope of the original plan. More generally, in the equation $Y = a + bX$, an increase in b makes the slope of the graph of the equation steeper.

FIGURE A.4

The Effect of an Increase in the Charge per Minute.
Because the fixed monthly fee continues to be $4, the vertical intercept of the new plan is the same as that of the original plan. With the new charge per minute of 40 cents, the slope of the billing plan rises from 0.20 to 0.40.

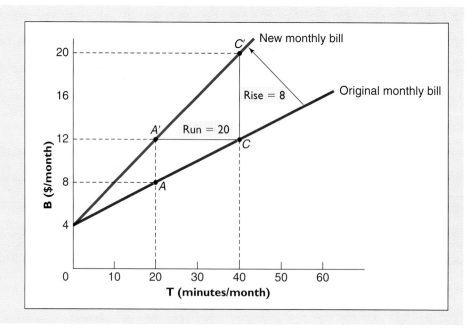

EXERCISE A.4

Show how the billing plan whose graph is in Figure A.2 would change if the charge per minute were reduced from 20 cents to 10 cents.

Exercise A.4 illustrates the general rule that in an equation $Y = a + bX$, a reduction in b makes the slope of the graph of the equation less steep.

CONSTRUCTING EQUATIONS AND GRAPHS FROM TABLES

Example A.6 and Exercise A.5 show how to transform tabular information into an equation or graph.

EXAMPLE A.6

Table A.1 shows four points from a monthly long-distance telephone billing equation. If all points on this billing equation lie on a straight line, find the vertical intercept of the equation and graph it. What is the monthly fixed fee? What is the charge per minute? Calculate the total bill for a month with 1 hour of long-distance calls.

TABLE A.1
Points on a Long-Distance Billing Plan

Long-distance bill ($/month)	Total long-distance calls (minutes/month)
10.50	10
11.00	20
11.50	30
12.00	40

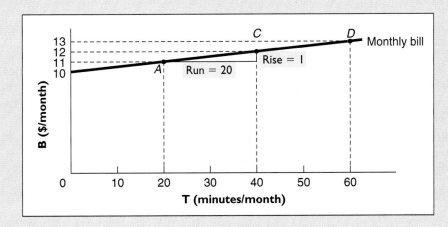

FIGURE A.5
Plotting the Monthly Billing Equation from a Sample of Points.
Point *A* is taken from row 2, Table A.1, and point *C* from row 4. The monthly billing plan is the straight line that passes through these points.

One approach to this problem is simply to plot any two points from the table on a graph. Since we are told that the billing equation is a straight line, that line must be the one that passes through any two of its points. Thus, in Figure A.5 we use *A* to denote the point from Table A.1 for which a monthly bill of $11 corresponds to 20 minutes/month of calls (second row) and *C* to denote the point for which a monthly bill of $12 corresponds to 40 minutes/month of calls (fourth row). The straight line passing through these points is the graph of the billing equation.

Unless you have a steady hand, however, or use extremely large graph paper, the method of extending a line between two points on the billing plan is unlikely to be very accurate. An alternative approach is to calculate the equation for the billing plan directly. Since the equation is a straight line, we know that it takes the general form $B = f + sT$, where f is the fixed monthly fee and s is the slope. Our goal is to calculate the vertical intercept f and the slope s. From the same two points we plotted earlier, *A* and *C*, we can calculate the slope of the billing plan as $s = \text{rise/run} = 1/20 = 0.05$.

So all that remains is to calculate f, the fixed monthly fee. At point *C* on the billing plan, the total monthly bill is $12 for 40 minutes, so we can substitute $B = 12$, $s = 0.05$, and $T = 40$ into the general equation $B = f + sT$ to obtain

$$12 = f + 0.05(40), \tag{A.4}$$

or

$$12 = f + 2, \tag{A.5}$$

which solves for $f = 10$. So the monthly billing equation must be

$$B = 10 + 0.05T. \tag{A.6}$$

For this billing equation, the fixed fee is $10/month, the calling charge is 5 cents/minute ($0.05/minute), and the total bill for a month with 1 hour of long-distance calls is $B = 10 + 0.05(60) = \$13$, just as shown in Figure A.5.

EXERCISE A.5

The following table shows four points from a monthly long-distance telephone billing plan.

Long-distance bill ($/month)	Total long-distance calls (minutes/month)
20.00	10
30.00	20
40.00	30
50.00	40

If all points on this billing plan lie on a straight line, find the vertical intercept of the corresponding equation without graphing it. What is the monthly fixed fee? What is the charge per minute? How much would the charges be for 1 hour of long-distance calls per month?

▪ KEY TERMS ▪

constant (22)
dependent variable (22)
equation (22)
independent variable (22)

parameter (22)
rise (24)
run (24)
slope (24)

variable (22)
vertical intercept (23)

▪ ANSWERS TO IN-APPENDIX EXERCISES ▪

A.1 To calculate your monthly bill for 45 minutes of calls, substitute 45 minutes for T in equation A.1 to get $B = 5 + 0.10(45) = \$9.50$.

A.2 Calculating the slope using points A and C, we have rise $= 30 - 24 = 6$ and run $= 30 - 15 = 15$, so rise/run $= 6/15 = 2/5 = 0.40$. And since the horizontal intercept of the line is 18, its equation is $B = 18 + 0.40T$. Under this plan, the fixed monthly fee is $18, and the charge per minute is the slope of the billing line, 0.40, or 40 cents/minute.

A.3 A $2 reduction in the monthly fixed fee would produce a downward parallel shift in the billing plan by $2.

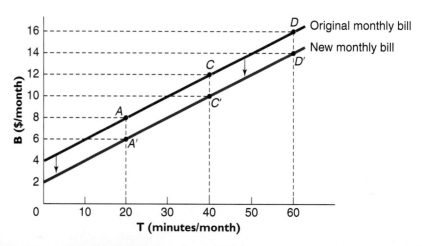

A.4 With an unchanged monthly fixed fee, the vertical intercept of the new billing plan continues to be 4. The slope of the new plan is 0.10, half the slope of the original plan.

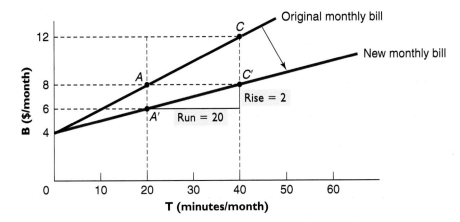

A.5 Let the billing equation be $B = f + sT$, where f is the fixed monthly fee and s is the slope. From the first two points in the table, calculate the slope s = rise/run = 10/10 = 1.0. To calculate f, we can use the information in row 1 of the table to write the billing equation as $20 = f + 1.0(10)$ and solve for $f = 10$. So the monthly billing equation must be $B = 10 + 1.0T$. For this billing equation, the fixed fee is \$10/month, the calling charge is \$1/minute, and the total bill for a month with 1 hour of long-distance calls is $B = 10 + 1.0(60) = \$70$.

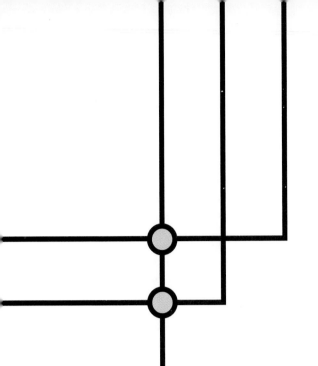

SOME COMMON PITFALLS
FOR DECISION MAKERS

T he protagonist of Roald Dahl's short story "Royal Jelly" is a bee-keeper whose infant daughter's physical development is seriously threatened by her inability to digest food. All medical interventions have failed. In desperation, the beekeeper decides to treat his daughter with massive doses of royal jelly, the substance that causes an ordinary bee to develop into a queen bee.

Only minute quantities of royal jelly are produced in any one bee colony. Because of its seemingly magical power to stimulate development, not just in bees but also in other creatures, the substance is astronomically expensive. The beekeeper's good fortune, as Dahl describes it, is that his occupation gives him access to large quantities of the precious stuff, which otherwise would have been far too expensive for a man of his modest means.

In any event, the new therapy seems to work—the baby immediately begins to gain weight when the royal jelly is mixed with her milk. Character-istically, Dahl ends his tale with a chilling twist. While changing their daughter's diaper one morning, the horrified parents notice that her torso has begun to take on the unmistakable contours of a queen bee's thorax.

Our interest in Dahl's fable lies not in its macabre ending but in its implicit claim that, to the beekeeper, royal jelly was essentially a free good. Of course, it was not a free good at all, for if the beekeeper had not fed the jelly to his daughter, he could have sold it in the marketplace. The amount for which he could have sold it was the opportunity cost of using the substance as he did. In this sense, then, the royal jelly was no less costly to the beekeeper than it would have been to an accountant or a school teacher. And he was therefore in no better position to provide it to his daughter than any other person of similar means. (Of course, in calculating how wealthy the beekeeper is, we have to take into account the value of his access to the royal jelly! Looking only at his earnings from the sale of honey would understate the total economic compensation he received from beekeeping.)

The fact that the beekeeper ignored the opportunity cost of the royal jelly when deciding whether to give it to his daughter does not mean that his decision was wrong. When a family member's health is threatened, most of us are willing to pay whatever we can afford in an effort to help. Thus, even though the opportunity cost of the royal jelly was high, its benefit might have been even higher, in which case the right decision would have been to administer it. But in that case, it would also have been the right decision for a schoolteacher or anyone else of similar means and circumstances. The important point is that using a good we already happen to own is not free.

As we noted in Chapter 1, the cost-benefit principle suggests that an introductory economics course should emphasize a short list of those principles with the greatest power to predict and explain behavior. But it also suggests that among those principles, we should focus especially on those that are most difficult to master. As we explore the cost-benefit approach in greater detail in this chapter, then, we will emphasize the errors people commonly make when trying to implement it. People often tend to ignore certain costs that they ought to take into account, for example, and sometimes they are influenced by costs that are irrelevant to the decision at hand. It is also common for people to base decisions on average costs and benefits instead of on the marginal costs and benefits called for by the cost-benefit principle.

PITFALL 1: IGNORING OPPORTUNITY COSTS

Sherlock Holmes, Arthur Conan Doyle's legendary detective, was successful because he saw details that most others overlooked. In *Silver Blaze,* Holmes is called on to investigate the theft of an expensive racehorse from its stable. A Scotland Yard inspector assigned to the case asks Holmes whether some particular aspect of the crime required further study. "Yes," Holmes replies, and describes "the curious incident of the dog in the nighttime." "The dog did nothing in the nighttime," responds the puzzled inspector. But as Holmes realized, that was precisely the problem. The watchdog's failure to bark when Silver Blaze was stolen meant that the watchdog knew the thief. This clue substantially reduced the number of suspects and eventually led to the thief's apprehension.

Opportunity costs are like dogs that fail to bark in the night.

Just as we often don't notice when a dog fails to bark, many of us tend to overlook the implicit value of activities that fail to happen. As we saw in Chapter 1, however, intelligent decisions require taking the value of forgone opportunities properly into account.

RECOGNIZING THE RELEVANT ALTERNATIVE

The opportunity cost of an activity, once again, is the value of the next-best alternative that must be forgone to engage in that activity. If ironing your shirt means not watching the last 20 minutes of a movie, then the value to you of watching the end of the movie is an opportunity cost of ironing your shirt. Many people make bad decisions because they tend to ignore the value of such forgone opportunities. To avoid overlooking opportunity costs, economists often translate questions such as "Should I iron my shirt?" into ones such as "Should I iron my shirt or watch the end of the movie?"

EXAMPLE 2.1

Should you use your frequent-flyer coupon to fly to Fort Lauderdale for spring break?

With spring break only a week away, you are still undecided about whether to go to Fort Lauderdale with a group of classmates at the University of Iowa. The round-trip airfare from Cedar Rapids is $500, but you have a frequent-flyer coupon you could use to pay for the trip. All other relevant costs for the vacation week at the beach total exactly $1,000. Your reservation price for the Fort Lauderdale vacation is $1,350. Your only alternative use for your frequent-flyer coupon is for your plane trip to Boston the weekend after spring break to attend your brother's wedding. (Your coupon expires shortly thereafter.) If the Cedar Rapids–Boston round-trip airfare is $400, should you use your frequent-flyer coupon to fly to Fort Lauderdale for spring break?

The cost-benefit criterion tells us that you should go to Fort Lauderdale if the benefits of the trip exceed its costs. If not for the complication of the frequent-flyer coupon, solving this problem would be a straightforward matter of comparing your reservation price for the week at the beach (your benefit from the trip) to the sum of all relevant costs. And since your airfare and other costs would sum to $1,500, or $150 more than your reservation price for the trip, you would not go to Fort Lauderdale.

But what about the possibility of using your frequent-flyer coupon to make the trip? Using it for that purpose might make the flight to Fort Lauderdale seem free, suggesting you would reap an economic surplus of $350 by making the trip. But doing so would also mean you would have to fork over $400 for your airfare to Boston. So the opportunity cost of using your coupon to go to Fort Lauderdale is really $400. If you use it for that purpose, the trip still ends up being a loser. In cases like these, you are much more likely to decide sensibly if you ask yourself, "Should I use my frequent-flyer coupon for this trip or save it for an upcoming trip?"

We cannot emphasize strongly enough that the key to using the concept of opportunity cost correctly lies in recognizing precisely what taking a given action prevents us from doing. To illustrate, suppose we modify Example 1.2 slightly, as follows:

EXAMPLE 2.2

Same as Example 2.1, except that now your frequent-flyer coupon expires in a week, so your only chance to use it will be for the Fort Lauderdale trip. Should you use your coupon?

Since you now have no alternative use for your coupon, the opportunity cost of using it to pay for the Fort Lauderdale trip is zero. That means your economic surplus from the trip will be $1,350 − $1,000 = $350 > 0, so you should use your coupon and go to Fort Lauderdale.

THE TIME VALUE OF MONEY

We saw that taking an action now often means being unable to take some other action in the future. To take the value of future opportunities properly into account, we need to be able to weigh future costs and benefits against those we incur or receive in the present. As the next example illustrates, having to pay someone a dollar 1 year from now is not the same as having to pay someone a dollar today.

EXAMPLE 2.3

Same as Example 2.1, except that now your best alternative use for your frequent-flyer coupon is for a flight you expect to take 1 year from now, for which the airfare is $363. If your savings account pays 10 percent interest per year, should you go to Fort Lauderdale?

Is your flight to Fort Lauderdale "free" if you travel on a frequent flyer coupon?

How does this new information alter the opportunity cost of using your coupon to travel to Fort Lauderdale? Using it now means having to pay $363 for your flight 1 year from now. The opportunity cost of using the coupon now might therefore seem to be exactly $363. But this way of thinking about the coupon misses an important aspect of opportunity cost.

The question you must ask yourself is "How much should I be willing to pay *today* to avoid making an airfare payment of $363 *one year from now?* To answer this question, you should simply ask, "How much would I have to put in my savings account today, at 10 percent annual interest, to have $363 one year from now?" The answer is $330, since that amount will earn $33 in interest (10 percent of $330) over the next year, for a total of $363.

Your economic surplus from the Fort Lauderdale trip is therefore $1,350 − $1,000 − $330 = $20, which means you should take the trip to the beach.

EXERCISE 2.1

Would your answer to Example 2.3 have been different if the annual interest rate had been 2 percent instead of 10 percent? (*Hint:* Would a deposit of $350 in your account today earn enough money to pay for your $363 air ticket 1 year from now?)

Example 2.3 and Exercise 2.1 drive home the point that the opportunity cost of a dollar spent today is not the same as the opportunity cost of a dollar spent 1 year from now. In general, the opportunity cost of resources that are expended in the future will be lower than the opportunity cost of resources that are expended in the present. The reason involves the **time value of money**—the fact that money deposited in an interest-bearing account today will grow in value over time. Indeed, the very fact that banks and other borrowers pay interest is a consequence of the opportunity cost concept.

time value of money the fact that a given dollar amount today is equivalent to a larger dollar amount in the future, because the money can be invested in an interest-bearing account in the meantime

Suppose, for example, that you owned a bank and someone deposited $1 million on January 1 without expecting to receive interest. You could then take the money and buy a productive asset, like a stock of mushrooms that would grow on an otherwise useless plot of land you own. Suppose mushrooms grow at the rate of 10 percent each year, and they sell for a constant price per pound. At the end of the year you could sell the mushrooms for $1.1 million and have $100,000 more than you started with.

But if that same option is available to the person who put his money in your bank, why should he give *you* the $100,000 he could have earned? Being a practical man, he will be willing to let you use his money only if you compensate him for the opportunity cost of not using it himself.

As the following example makes clear, paying interest on borrowed money is really no more than reimbursing the lender for the opportunity cost of not being able to use the money he has lent.

EXAMPLE 2.4

How much interest should Tom charge Dick?

Tom is a mushroom farmer. He invests all his spare cash in additional mushrooms, which require no labor and grow on otherwise useless land behind his barn. The mushrooms triple in weight during their first year, after which time they are harvested and sold at a constant price per pound. Tom's friend Dick asks Tom for a loan of $200, which he promises to repay after 1 year. How much interest must Dick pay Tom for Tom to be no worse off than if he had not made the loan?

If Tom kept the $200 and invested it in additional mushrooms, he would have 3($200) = $600 worth of mushrooms to sell after 1 year. Dick must therefore give Tom $600 − $200 = $400 in interest to prevent Tom from losing money on the loan.

Why do many people feel it is "unfair" to charge interest on a loan made to a friend or family member?

If a friend had asked you to pick up a concert ticket for her when you stopped at the Ticketmaster office, she would expect to reimburse you for the $50 you spent for it. Yet many people feel it would be unfair if you charged that same friend interest on money you loaned her. Why this difference?

Suppose you gave a friend a 1-year loan of $1,000, money that otherwise would have remained in your savings account earning interest at the annual rate of 5 percent. Had the money remained in your account, you would have earned $50 in interest. If your friend does not pay you interest on the loan, you will thus be $50 poorer at the end of the year than if you had not made her the loan. That is the opportunity cost of making her the loan. But because the $50 of forgone interest is not an explicit cost, many people tend to think of it as somehow different from other costs. To them, charging interest may seem as if you are profiting at your friend's expense. Yet it is no more unfair to ask a friend to reimburse you for interest forgone than to ask her to reimburse you for the cost of a concert ticket. If you want to make a gift of $50 to your friend—either by not accepting reimbursement for a concert ticket or by not charging interest on a loan—that is of course your privilege. But we generally do not describe people who fail to make gifts as being "unfair."

The preceding example illustrates the reciprocal relationship between costs and benefits. When taking an action results in your failing to receive a benefit that you otherwise would have received, that is a cost of taking the action. Loaning a friend money entails a cost because it results in your failure to receive the interest you would have earned had the money remained in your count. By the same token, failure to incur a cost amounts to the same thing as receiving a benefit.

As simple as the concept of opportunity cost is, it is one of the most important in economics. The art in applying the concept correctly lies in being able to recognize the most valuable alternative to a given activity.

"Just getting the hell out of here is worth the price of admission."

RECAP **THE PITFALL OF IGNORING OPPORTUNITY COSTS**

When performing a cost-benefit analysis of an action, it is important to account for all relevant *opportunity costs,* defined as the values of the most highly valued alternatives that must be forgone to carry out the action. A resource (such as a frequent-flyer coupon) may have a high opportunity cost, even if you originally got it "for free," if its best alternative use has high value. The identical resource may have a low opportunity cost, however, if it has no good alternative uses.

In calculating opportunity costs, it is important to take account of the time value of money. Because money can be invested in an interest-bearing account, a dollar paid or received in the future is worth less than a dollar paid or received today.

PITFALL 2: FAILURE TO IGNORE SUNK COSTS

The opportunity cost pitfall is one in which people ignore costs they ought to take into account. In another common pitfall, the reverse is true: People are influenced by costs they ought to ignore. *The only costs that should influence a decision about whether to take an action are those that we can avoid by not taking the action.* As a practical matter, however, many decision makers appear to be influenced by **sunk costs**—costs that are beyond recovery at the moment a decision is made. For example, money spent on a nontransferable, nonrefundable airline ticket is a sunk cost.

sunk cost a cost that is beyond recovery at the moment a decision must be made

Because sunk costs must be borne *whether or not an action is taken,* they are irrelevant to the decision of whether to take the action. The sunk cost pitfall (the mistake of being influenced by sunk costs) is illustrated clearly in the following examples.

EXAMPLE 2.5

Should you drive through a snowstorm to get to a basketball game?

You and your friend Joe have identical tastes. At 2 P.M. you go to the local Ticketmaster outlet and buy a $30 ticket to a basketball game to be played that night in Syracuse, 50 miles north of your home in Ithaca. Joe plans to attend the same game, but because he cannot get to the Ticketmaster outlet, he plans to buy his ticket at the game. Tickets sold at the game cost only $25, because they carry no Ticketmaster surcharge. (Many people nonetheless pay the higher price at Ticketmaster, to be sure of getting good seats.) At 4 P.M. an unexpected snowstorm begins, making the prospect of the drive to Syracuse much less attractive than before (but assuring the availability of good seats). If both you and Joe are rational, is one of you more likely to attend the game than the other?

Since you have already bought your ticket, the $30 you spent on it is a sunk cost. It is money you cannot recover, whether or not you go to the game. In deciding whether to see the game, then, you should compare the benefit of seeing the game (as measured by your reservation price, the largest dollar amount you would be willing to pay to see it) to only those *additional* costs you must incur to see the game (the opportunity cost of your time, whatever cost you assign to driving through the snowstorm, etc.). But you should not include the cost of your ticket. That is $30 you will never see again, whether you go to the game or not.

Joe, too, must weigh the opportunity cost of his time and the hassle of the drive in deciding whether to attend the game. But he must also weigh the $25 he will have to spend for his ticket. At the moment of deciding, therefore, the remaining costs Joe must incur to see the game are $25 higher than the remaining costs for you. And since you both have identical tastes—that is, since your respective benefits of attending the game are exactly the same—Joe should be less likely to make the trip. You might think the cost of seeing the game is higher for you, since your ticket cost $30, whereas Joe's will cost only $25. But at the moment of deciding whether to make the drive, the $25 is a relevant cost for Joe, whereas your $30 is a sunk cost, and hence an irrelevant one for you.

Now suppose we change the structure of Example 2.5 slightly.

Same as Example 2.5, except now a friend gives Joe a free ticket to the game at 2 P.M. Is one of you more likely to attend the game than the other?

EXAMPLE 2.6

This time neither of you faces any additional ticket expenses at the moment you must decide whether to drive through the snowstorm. Since your respective costs and benefits are the same, your decisions about whether to make the trip should also be the same.

According to the cost-benefit criterion, the decision to attend the game should not depend on whether someone bought a ticket or was given one. Yet people often seem to decide differently in the two cases. In particular, people who paid cash for a ticket often feel a need to use it, "to avoid wasting $30." People who get a free ticket seem to feel much more comfortable with the notion of staying home.

Such differences in judgment are almost surely the result of faulty reasoning. A rational decision maker weighs the benefit of seeing the game against only the *additional* costs he must incur to see it—in this example, the opportunity cost of time and the psychological cost and physical risk of driving through the snowstorm. How he came to possess a ticket in the first place has no bearing on either the relevant benefits or the relevant costs.

Here's another example in which many people seem to take sunk costs into account when they shouldn't.

How much should you eat at an all-you-can-eat restaurant?

EXAMPLE 2.7

Sangam, an Indian restaurant in Philadelphia, offers an all-you-can-eat lunch buffet for $5. Customers pay $5 at the door, and no matter how many times they refill their plates, there is no additional charge. One day, as a goodwill gesture, the owner of the restaurant tells 20 randomly selected guests that their lunch is on the house. The remaining guests pay the usual price. If all diners are rational, will there be any difference in the average quantity of food consumed by people in these two groups?

Having eaten their first helping, diners in each group confront the following question: "Should I go back for another helping?" If the benefit of so doing exceeds the cost, the answer is yes; otherwise it is no. Note that at the moment of decision about a second helping, the $5 charge for the lunch is a sunk cost. Those who paid it have no way to recover it. Thus, for both groups, the (extra) cost of another helping is exactly zero. And since the people who received the free lunch were chosen at random, there is no reason to suppose that their appetites are different from those of other diners. The benefit of another helping should be the same, on average, for people in both groups. And since their respective costs and benefits of an additional helping are the same, the two groups should eat the same number of helpings, on average.

Psychologists and economists have found experimental evidence, however, that people in such groups do not eat similar amounts.[1] In particular, those for whom the luncheon charge is waived tend to eat substantially less than those for whom the charge is not waived. People in the latter group seem somehow determined to "get their money's worth." Their implicit goal is apparently to minimize

---

[1]See, for example, Richard Thaler, "Toward a Positive Theory of Consumer Choice," *Journal of Economic Behavior and Organization,* 1(1), 1980.

the average cost per bite of the food they eat. Yet minimizing average cost is not a particularly sensible objective. It brings to mind the man who drove his car on the highway at night, even though he had nowhere to go, because he wanted to boost his average fuel economy. The irony is that diners who are determined to get their money's worth usually end up eating too much, as evidenced later by their regrets about having gone back for their last helpings.

The fact that the cost-benefit criterion may fail the test of prediction in examples like these does nothing to invalidate its advice about what people *should* do. If you are letting sunk costs influence your decisions, you can do better by changing your behavior.

One final sunk cost example:

EXAMPLE 2.8   **Should Jennifer go to the theater or have dinner with John?**

Jennifer has purchased a $50 theater ticket. On the day before the performance, John invites her to dinner the next evening. John is her chemistry lab partner, and Jennifer has been hoping he would ask her out. If she had known about John's invitation before buying the theater ticket, she would have accepted without hesitation. But it is too late to sell her theater ticket, and since John has no interest in the theater, she cannot attend both the play and the dinner. True or false: If Jennifer is rational, she will go to dinner anyway.

First a brief word about the criterion for deciding whether a statement is true or false. For a statement to be true, it must be true in *all* circumstances. If a statement can be shown to be false under *some* circumstances, it is false by definition. It need not always be untrue. So to rule on the statement posed in this example, we must ask whether it *might not* be true under some circumstances.

We'll use R^T to denote Jennifer's reservation price for going to the theater and R^D to denote her reservation price for going to dinner with John. Jennifer doesn't need to pay any money if she goes to the dinner, and since the opportunity cost of her time is the same for the two events, she can ignore that as a factor. So Jennifer's economic surplus from going to dinner with John will be R^D. Before she bought her theater ticket, the net surplus Jennifer expected to receive from going to the theater was $R^T - \$50$—the difference between her reservation price for the play and the price of a ticket.

Now, the fact that Jennifer would have chosen dinner over the theater if she had not yet bought a ticket tells us that $R^D > R^T - \$50$. *But since her theater ticket* is *already paid for, its $50 price is a sunk cost.* So Jennifer's economic surplus from going to the theater *at the moment she has to decide* will be R^T, not $R^T - \$50$. Thus she should go out to dinner with John only if $R^D > R^T$. From the information given, that may or may not be the case.

To illustrate, suppose $R^D = \$70$ and $R^T = \$80$. In that case, Jennifer would have chosen dinner over the theater before buying her ticket, because her surplus from attending the dinner ($R^D = \$70$) would have been greater than her net surplus from attending the theater ($R^T - \$50 = \$30$). But after she buys her ticket, the $50 becomes a sunk cost and thus is no longer relevant to her decision. Jennifer would gain an $80 benefit by going to the theater, and because that is more than the $70 benefit she would gain by going out to dinner with John, she would choose the theater. Because the true-false statement does not hold in this case, it is false.

EXERCISE 2.2

Refer to Example 2.8. Give examples of values of Jennifer's reservation prices for the dinner and the theater performance that are consistent with the description given in the example, but for which Jennifer's best bet *would* be to go to dinner with John.

> **RECAP** | **THE PITFALL OF NOT IGNORING SUNK COSTS**
>
> When deciding whether to perform an action, it is important to ignore sunk costs—those costs that cannot be avoided even if the action is not taken. Even though a ticket to a concert may have cost you $100, if you have already bought it and cannot sell it to anyone else, the $100 is a sunk cost and should not influence your decision about whether to go to the concert.

PITFALL 3: FAILURE TO UNDERSTAND THE AVERAGE-MARGINAL DISTINCTION

As we have seen, bad decisions often result from failure to take proper account of opportunity costs and from failure to ignore sunk costs. Another common source of difficulty is confusion involving the distinction between average and marginal costs and benefits.

THE RELEVANT COSTS AND BENEFITS ARE ALWAYS MARGINAL

The cost-benefit framework emphasizes that the only relevant costs and benefits in deciding whether to pursue an activity further are *marginal* costs and benefits—those costs and benefits that correspond to the *increment* of activity under consideration. In many contexts, however, people seem more inclined to compare **average costs** and **average benefits**—total cost or benefit per unit of activity.

As Example 2.9 makes clear, increasing the level of an activity may not be justified, even though its average benefit at the current level is significantly greater than its average cost.

average cost total cost of undertaking *n* units of an activity divided by *n*

average benefit total benefit of undertaking *n* units of an activity divided by *n*

Should NASA expand the space shuttle program from four launches per year to five?

EXAMPLE 2.9

Professor Kösten Banifoot, a prominent supporter of the NASA space shuttle program, has estimated that the gains from the program are currently $24 billion per year (an average of $6 billion per launch) and that its costs are currently $20 billion per year (an average of $5 billion per launch). True or false: If these estimates are correct, NASA should definitely expand the program.

To decide whether an additional launch makes sense, we need to compare the cost of adding that launch with the benefit of adding it. The *average* benefit and *average* cost per launch for all shuttles launched thus far simply are not useful in deciding whether to expand the program. Of course, the average cost of the launches undertaken so far *might* be the same as the cost of adding another launch. But it also might be either higher or lower than the marginal cost of a launch. The same statement holds true regarding average and marginal benefits.

Suppose, for example, that the benefit of an additional launch is in fact the same as the average benefit per launch thus far, namely, $6 billion. Should NASA add another launch? Not if the cost of adding the fifth launch would be more than $6 billion. Suppose the relationship between the number of shuttles launched and the total cost of the program is as described in Table 2.1.

At the current level of four launches per year, the average cost is $20 billion/4 = $5 billion per launch. But adding a fifth launch would raise costs from $20 billion to $30 billion, so the marginal cost of the fifth launch is $10 billion. If the benefit of an additional launch is constant at $6 billion, increasing the number of launches would make no sense. Indeed, the fourth launch itself would not be justified, since it cost $8 billion and produced only $6 billion in additional

TABLE 2.1
How Total Cost Varies with the Number of Launches

Number of launches per year	Total costs per year ($billions)
1	6
2	8
3	12
4	20
5	30

benefits. On the basis of the numbers shown in the table, which are completely consistent with Professor Banifoot's data on average costs and benefits, the optimal number of launches would be only three per year.

Here's an exercise that further illustrates the importance of the average-marginal distinction.

EXERCISE 2.3

Should a basketball team's best player take all the team's shots?

A professional basketball team has a new assistant coach. The assistant notices that one player scores on a higher percentage of his shots than other players. Based on this information, the assistant suggests to the head coach that the star player should take *all* the shots. That way, the assistant reasons, the team will score more points and win more games.

On hearing this suggestion, the head coach fires her assistant for incompetence. What was wrong with the assistant's idea?

One of the most important practical questions we confront in life is that of how to divide our time between competing activities. As the Example 2.10 illustrates, we won't answer this question intelligently unless we're careful to distinguish between average and marginal benefits.

EXAMPLE 2.10

How should members of a group allocate their effort in a foraging task?

Suppose you and three friends are shipwrecked on an island. Coconut trees, which grow in clusters on both the north and south ends of the island, are your only source of food. For the past year, you and one friend have been gathering coconuts from the north end of the island, and the other two have been gathering them from the south. You and your partner have been bringing back a total of 16 coconuts each day, while your other two friends have been bringing back only 12. These harvests appear to be sustainable indefinitely. True or false: If one of the others joins the two of you on the north end of the island, your total harvest of coconuts will rise.

This statement is false for the same reason that Professor Banifoot's statement was false in Example 2.9. All we know is that the average benefit per forager is 8 coconuts on the north end of the island and 6 coconuts on the south end. We should shift someone from the south end to the north end only if the increase in coconuts gathered at the north end is more than the corresponding reduction in coconuts gathered at the south end. But suppose the relationship between the number of foragers and the total harvest at each end of the island is as shown in Table 2.2.

As the numbers in the table indicate, the current allocation of two foragers at each end of the island yields a total of 28 coconuts a day. Shifting one forager from the south end to the north will increase the number of coconuts harvested from the north end by 3 per day but will reduce the harvest from the south end

TABLE 2.2
How Coconut Harvests Depend on the Number of Foragers

		North end	South end
	1	12 coconuts/day	6 coconuts/day
Number	2	16 coconuts/day	12 coconuts/day
of foragers	3	19 coconuts/day	18 coconuts/day
	4	21 coconuts/day	24 coconuts/day

by 6, for a net reduction of 3 coconuts per day. Even though the average harvest is greater on the north end of the island, the marginal benefit of an additional forager is greater on the south end. Thus, if either you or your partner were to join the other two at the south end, the daily harvest from the north end would go down by 4 coconuts, while the harvest from the south end would go up by 6—a net gain of 2 coconuts per day.

We must emphasize again that the fact that the statements in the preceding examples were false does not mean that they could not have been true under at least some circumstances. For instance, the relationship between foragers and harvests shown in Table 2.3 is also consistent with the information given in Example 2.10. Given this relationship, sending not just one but two extra persons to the north end of the island would make sense.

TABLE 2.3
Another Example of How Coconut Harvests Depend on the Number of Foragers

		North end	South end
	1	8 coconuts/day	6 coconuts/day
Number	2	16 coconuts/day	12 coconuts/day
of foragers	3	24 coconuts/day	18 coconuts/day
	4	32 coconuts/day	24 coconuts/day

In sum, the statements in Examples 2.9 and 2.10 were false because they were based on information about average benefits or costs rather than marginal benefits or costs. To be considered true, a statement must be true in *all* circumstances; it is false if it fails to hold in even a single case.

EXERCISE 2.4

Refer to Example 2.10. If there had been not four but five of you on the island and productivity was as described in Table 2.2, how many should have foraged at each end?

Example 2.10 and Exercise 2.4, in which the problem was to allocate labor between two coconut patches, illustrate the following simple but important rule:

The criterion for allocating a resource efficiently across different activities is to allocate each unit of the resource to the production activity in which its marginal benefit is highest.

This rule applies to cases in which the resources to be allocated are not finely divisible. For instance, we cannot have 2.62 foragers on one end of the island.

In other cases, the resource to be allocated may be perfectly divisible. For example, students taking an exam have an important resource—their time—to apportion among various questions in any way they choose. For a resource that is perfectly divisible, the rule becomes:

Allocate the resource so that its marginal benefit is the same in every activity.

Applied to the task of allocating one's time on an exam, this rule suggests that the optimal allocation is one in which the number of additional points earned from the last unit of time spent on a question must be the same for all questions. Suppose a student had not allocated her time according to this rule—for example, suppose she had earned 6 points from the last unit of time spent on one question and only 2 points from the last unit of time spent on another. If her last moments spent on the first question were more productive than her last moments spent on the second, she can boost her point total score by spending more time on the first question and less time on the second.

This idea *seems* easy enough. But just as an experiment, ask several friends to consider the following example.

EXAMPLE 2.11

How should you allocate your time on an exam?

Suppose that in the last minute you devoted to question 1 on your physics exam you earned 4 extra points, while in the last minute you devoted to question 2 you earned 10 extra points. The total number of points you earned on these two questions were 48 and 12, respectively, and the total time you spent on each was the same. If you could take the exam again, how—if at all—would you reallocate your time between these questions?

Even though you earned four times as many points from the first question than from the second, the last minute you spent on question 2 added 6 more points to your total score than the last minute you spent on question 1. That means you should have spent more time on question 2.

How did your friends do with this problem? As obvious as the answer might seem, many people—especially those who have not had a good course in economics—often do not grasp the underlying idea. They are distracted by the fact that the average point yield per unit of time spent on question 1 is so much higher than the average yield on question 2. But that comparison, by itself, tells us nothing about how to reallocate our time.

A similar misunderstanding of the average-marginal distinction recently led a dean at a large university to complain that the university's development office had grown too large. The number of employees in this office, which raises funds for the university, had more than doubled during the past decade. To back up his claim that this growth was a bad thing, the dean cited the fact that the amount of money raised per fund-raiser was only one-third as much as it had been 10 years before. But this observation tells us nothing about whether the dean's claim is true. From the university's point of view, the number of fund-raisers should be reduced by 1 only if so doing will reduce the total funds raised by less than the cost of that employee. The fact that the average amount of money raised per employee is much smaller than it once was simply does not tell us whether that is so.

fixed cost a cost that does not vary with the level of an activity

variable cost a cost that varies with the level of activity

FIXED AND VARIABLE COSTS

Sometimes the failure to distinguish between average and marginal costs arises from a failure to distinguish between **fixed costs**—costs that do not vary with the level of an activity—and **variable costs**—costs that do vary with the level of activity.

For example, the membership fee you pay to join most health clubs is the same whether you visit the club four times a week or only once a month. This fee is a fixed cost. Once you have paid it, it is *usually* also a sunk cost—but not always. Some health clubs offer an introductory period in which a membership may be canceled with a full refund. In such cases the membership fee is a fixed cost but not a sunk cost.

Many health clubs also have tennis or racquetball courts for which they charge hourly court fees. Because these charges depend on the number of hours you play, they are variable costs. If you've already become a member and are deciding how many times a week to play racquetball, you should ignore the membership fee but take into account the hourly court fee.

How is a fixed cost different from a sunk cost? Since a sunk cost is one that is irretrievably committed, it cannot vary with the level of an activity. All sunk costs are therefore also fixed costs. But not all fixed costs are sunk costs (as in the example of a refundable membership fee).

As the next example makes clear, the ability to distinguish between fixed and variable costs is important component to sound business decisions.

Should Commercial Airlines cancel its 10:00 A.M. flight?

In an effort to improve profitability, managers of a passenger airline have considered canceling flights on the least heavily traveled routes. The typical aircraft in the airline's fleet makes 1,000 flights a year and generates the following yearly costs:

EXAMPLE 2.12

Annual interest on money borrowed to buy plane	$ 400,000
Annual interest on money borrowed to buy other equipment	400,000
Fuel	400,000
Flight crew salaries	500,000
Maintenance labor	300,000
Total	$2,000,000

Flight crew salaries and maintenance labor are constant amounts for each flight. One flight that may be dropped currently uses an aircraft that makes 1,000 flights a year, at an average cost of $2,000 per flight. An average of 30 passengers travel on this flight at a ticket price of $60 each, for total ticket revenue of $1,800 per flight. Since this flight's revenue is less than its cost, the managers cancel the flight. Is their decision a good one?

The decision is faulty because the managers have failed to distinguish between fixed and variable costs. The labor and fuel expenses they have listed are variable, but interest expenses are fixed. Because labor and fuel expenses total only $1,200 per flight—much less than the flight's $1,800 ticket revenue—the flight should not be canceled.

Needless to say, Commercial Airlines could not hope to remain in business if the ticket revenue from *each* of its flights fell short of the average cost of operating that flight. But the criterion for deciding whether any *particular* flight makes sense is to compare its ticket revenues only to those extra costs generated by that flight.

Failure to appreciate the importance of the average-marginal distinction is an important source of error, not just within the world of business but in academia, government—indeed, virtually every sphere of professional and personal life. And a little bit of knowledge can sometimes be a dangerous thing. For example, tennis star Andre Agassi appears to know what a fixed cost is but seems confused about the extent to which such costs matter in deciding how to use his $12 million jet aircraft. "There are certain fixed costs when you own a plane," he explained during a break in the action at a recent tournament, "so the more you fly it the more economic sense it makes. . . ." Exactly right! But Agassi then went on to say, "The first flight after I bought it, I took some friends to Palm Springs for lunch." Taking the plane on such trips does indeed reduce the average fixed cost per flight. But to take frivolous trips solely for the *purpose* of reducing average cost per flight makes no more sense than driving aimlessly on the highway to improve your car's average fuel economy.

RECAP **THE PITFALL OF USING AVERAGE INSTEAD OF MARGINAL COSTS AND BENEFITS**

Decision makers often have ready information about the total cost and benefit of an activity, and from these it is simple to compute the activity's average cost and benefit. A common mistake is to conclude that an activity should be increased if its average benefit exceeds its average cost. The cost-benefit principle tells us that the level of an activity should be increased if, and only if, the *marginal* benefit of doing so exceeds the *marginal* cost.

The conclusion that some costs, especially marginal costs and opportunity costs, are important, while others, like sunk costs and average costs, are irrelevant to decision making is implicit in our original statement of the cost-benefit principle (an action should be taken if, and only if, the extra benefits of taking it exceed the extra costs). Yet so important are the pitfalls of ignoring opportunity costs and taking sunk costs into account, and of confusing average with marginal costs, we enumerate these pitfalls separately as one of the core ideas for repeated emphasis.

Not All Costs Matter Equally: Some costs (e.g., opportunity costs, marginal costs) matter in making decisions; other costs (e.g., sunk costs, average costs) don't.

■ SUMMARY ■

- Our focus in this chapter was on three common pitfalls that plague decision makers in all walks of life. The first involved the failure to consider opportunity costs. The opportunity cost of an activity is the value of the next-best alternative that must be forgone to engage in that activity. Many people make bad decisions because they tend to ignore the value of forgone opportunities. We are less likely to make this mistake if we translate questions such as "Should I iron my shirt?" into ones such as "Should I iron my shirt or study for my math test?" Posing the question in this way makes relevant opportunity costs difficult to ignore. Thus, if you ask yourself "Should I use my one frequent-flyer coupon on the next flight I take?" you are more likely to decide incorrectly than if you ask "Should I use my one frequent-flyer coupon on the next flight, or should I wait and use it on another flight?"

- The second pitfall involved the tendency not to ignore sunk costs. A sunk cost is a cost that is already irretrievably committed at the moment a decision must be made. In deciding whether to drive through a snowstorm to see a concert, the amount you have already paid for your ticket simply should not matter. In deciding whether to pursue an activity, the only costs and benefits that matter are the ones that will change with your pursuit of that activity. All other costs and benefits are irrelevant.

- The third and final pitfall was the tendency to confuse average and marginal costs and benefits. In deciding whether to increase the number of space shuttle flights, comparing the average cost of current shuttle flights with their average benefit is not instructive. Instead, we must compare the cost of an additional shuttle flight with the benefit of an additional shuttle flight. Such a comparison will often yield different results from a comparison of average costs and benefits.

▪ CORE PRINCIPLES ▪

Not All Costs Matter Equally
Some costs (e.g., opportunity costs, marginal costs) matter in making decisions; other costs (e.g., sunk costs, average costs) don't.

▪ KEY TERMS ▪

---

average benefit (39)
average cost (39)

fixed cost (42)
sunk cost (36)

time value of money (34)
variable cost (42)

▪ REVIEW QUESTIONS ▪

---

1. Why might someone who is trying to decide whether to see a movie be more likely to focus on the $9 ticket price than on the $20 she would fail to earn by not babysitting?

2. Many people think of their air travel as being free when they use frequent-flyer coupons. Explain why these people are likely to make wasteful travel decisions.

3. A friend has allowed you to use her off-campus parking space while she is away for her junior year abroad. If many other students are eager to rent parking spaces off-

campus, do you think your friend would be "unfair" to charge you for the use of her parking space?

4. Why is a lottery ticket that pays you $10 million now worth more than a lottery ticket that pays you $1 million each year for the next 10 years?

5. Is the nonrefundable tuition payment you made to your university this semester a sunk cost? Is it a fixed cost? How would your answers differ if your university were to offer a full tuition refund to any student who dropped out of school during the first 2 months of the semester?

▪ PROBLEMS ▪

---

1. Tom is a mushroom farmer. He invests all his spare cash in additional mushrooms, which grow on otherwise useless land behind his barn. The mushrooms double in weight during their first year, after which time they are harvested and sold at a constant price per pound. Tom's friend Dick asks Tom for a loan of $200, which he promises to repay after 1 year. How much interest will Dick have to pay Tom for Tom to be no worse off than if he had not made the loan? Explain briefly.

2. When John increased his computer's random-access memory by 10 megabytes, the total benefit he received from using the computer went up $55. John purchased the additional memory at a cost of $5 per megabyte, for a total cost of $50.
   a. How much economic surplus did John receive from the additional memory? Explain briefly.
   b. True or false: Because the total benefit of the additional memory was larger than its total cost, John should have added more than 10 megabytes of memory. Explain briefly.

3. A shirt company spends $1,000 per week on rent for its factory. Each shirt made at the factory requires $2 worth of cloth and $6 worth of labor and energy. If the factory produces 2,000 shirts per week:
   a. What is the average cost of a shirt?
   b. What is the marginal cost of a shirt?

   If the factory produces 3,000 shirts per week:
   c. What is the average cost of a shirt?
   d. What is the marginal cost of a shirt?

4. Fred owns four fishing boats on Seneca Lake. He knows from experience the following information about the catch per boat depending on the total number of boats he sends to either the north or south end of the lake. Based on the table below, what is the optimal allocation of Fred's boats?

Number of boats at north end	Catch per boat	Number of boats at south end	Catch per boat
1	100	1	75
2	80	2	75
3	60	3	75
4	40	4	75

5. You are shipwrecked on an island and must live only on coconuts and crabs. You divide your 8 hours of daylight between gathering coconuts and catching crabs. The following table shows how your daily crab and coconut harvests vary depending how you allocate your time.

Hours spent catching crabs	Total number of crabs caught	Hours spent gathering coconuts	Total number of gathered coconuts
1	8	1	6
2	17	2	11
3	23	3	16
4	28	4	20
5	31	5	23
6	34	6	24
7	37	7	24
8	39	8	24

   If your aim is to maximize the number of crabs plus coconuts you acquire daily, how much of your time should you spend gathering coconuts? How much time should you spend catching crabs? How many coconuts and crabs will you harvest each day? (*Hint*: Efficient allocation of your time requires you to allocate each hour to the activity that yields the higher marginal benefit.)

6. You have won a prize in a state lottery. In exchange for your lottery ticket, the state government will send you a check for $424 one year from now. If bank deposits pay interest at the rate of 6 percent a year, and you already have several thousand dollars in your account, what is the lowest price at which you would be willing to sell your lottery ticket today?

7. A group has chartered a bus trip to Niagara Falls. The driver's fee is $100, the bus rental $500, and the fuel charge $75. The driver's fee is nonrefundable, but the bus rental may be canceled a week in advance at a charge of $100. At $25 a ticket, how many people must buy tickets a week before so that canceling the trip definitely will not pay?

8. Sam bought a Trek bicycle for $800 instead of a Cannondale for $1,000. Now he finds out that another bike store in town is selling the Cannondale for $800. Mike, Sam's friend, offers him $600 for his Trek. If Sam is a rational consumer, should he sell Mike his Trek and buy the Cannondale?

9. Mary planned to travel to Chicago to see Cheryl Crow in a free Lincoln Park concert, and had already purchased her $50 round-trip bus ticket (nonrefundable, nontransferable) when she found out that Adam Sandler was giving a show on the University of Illinois campus that same night for $50. Had she known about the Adam Sandler show before she bought her bus ticket, she would have chosen to go to the Sandler show. If she is a rational person and her friend Sally offers to give her one of several extra tickets she has for the Sandler show, what should she do?

10. Mandy and Tom, who live in Eugene, Oregon, have identical tastes. They both plan to attend a Paula Cole concert at the State Theater. The tickets cost $20. Mandy has bought her ticket by phone using her credit card, but Tom, who doesn't have a credit card, plans to buy his ticket at the door. On the same evening the university announces a surprise free fireworks display on campus. If Mandy had known about the fireworks display in advance, she would not have bought the theater ticket. True or false: Assuming Mandy and Tom are rational and that Mandy cannot resell her ticket, it follows that Mandy will go to the concert, while Tom will go to the fireworks display. Explain briefly.

■ ANSWERS TO IN-CHAPTER EXERCISES ■

2.1 As before, using your frequent-flyer coupon means having to pay $363 for your airfare 1 year from now. How much would you be willing to spend today to avoid having to pay $363 one year from now? Suppose you deposit $350 in your account today at 2 percent interest. By the end of one year your account would be worth $357 (the original $350 plus $7 in interest). Because that amount is not enough to pay for your $363 air ticket, the opportunity cost of using the frequent-flyer coupon now must be *more* than $350. And that means that the cost of the trip to Fort Lauderdale is greater than its $1,350 benefit, so you shouldn't go to Fort Lauderdale.

2.2 Suppose Jennifer's reservation price for attending the dinner with John is $80 and her reservation price for attending the theater is $70. With these reservation prices, she would have chosen the dinner with John had she known about it in advance. And she should also have dinner with John even if she bought a theater ticket before learning of that opportunity.

2.3 If the star player takes one more shot, some other player must take one less. The fact that the star player's *average* success rate is higher than the other player's does not mean that the probability of making his *next* shot (the marginal benefit of having him shoot once more) is higher than the probability of another player making his next shot. Indeed, if the best player took all his team's shots, the other team would focus its defensive effort entirely on him, in which case letting others shoot would definitely pay.

2.4 With 4 of you, the optimal allocation was to send 3 to the south end and 1 to the north end. Starting with that allocation, you should send the fifth person to whichever end would result in the higher marginal gain. Sending the fifth person to the south end will increase the total harvest by 6 coconuts per day, or two more than if he were sent to the north end. So the optimal allocation is 4 people on the south end and 1 on the north end.

		North end	South end
	1	12 coconuts/day	6 coconuts/day
Number	2	16 coconuts/day	12 coconuts/day
of foragers	3	19 coconuts/day	18 coconuts/day
	4	21 coconuts/day	24 coconuts/day

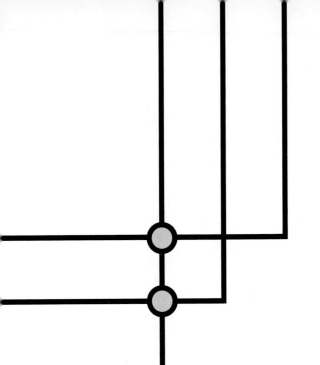

CHAPTER
3

COMPARATIVE ADVANTAGE: THE BASIS FOR EXCHANGE

■

D uring a stint as a Peace Corps Volunteer in rural Nepal, a young economic naturalist employed a cook named Birkhaman, who came from a remote Himalayan village in neighboring Bhutan. Although Birkhaman had virtually no formal education, he was spectacularly resourceful. His primary duties, to prepare food and maintain the kitchen, he performed with competence and dispatch. But he also had many other skills. He could thatch a roof, butcher a goat, and repair shoes. An able tinsmith and a good carpenter, he could sew, fix a broken alarm clock, and plaster walls. On top of all that, he was a local authority on home remedies.

Birkhaman's range of skills was broad even by Nepalese standards. But even the least skilled Nepalese villager could perform a wide range of services that most Americans hire others to perform. Why this difference in skills and employment?

One might be tempted to answer that the Nepalese are simply too poor to hire others to perform these services. Nepal is indeed a poor country, whose income per person is less than one one-hundredth that of the United States. Few Nepalese have spare cash to spend on outside services. But as reasonable as this poverty explanation may seem, the reverse is actually the case. The Nepalese do not perform their own services because they are poor; rather, they are poor largely *because* they perform their own services.

The alternative to a system in which everyone is a jack-of-all-trades is one in which people *specialize* in particular goods and services, then satisfy their needs by trading among themselves. Economic systems based on specialization and the exchange of goods and services are generally far more productive than

Did this man perform most of his own services because he was poor, or was he poor because he performed most of his own services?

those with less specialization. Our task in this chapter is to investigate why this is so. In doing so we will explore why people choose to exchange goods and services in the first place, rather than having each person produce his or her own food, cars, clothing, shelter, and the like.

As this chapter will show, the reason that specialization is so productive is the existence of what economists call *comparative advantage*. Roughly, a person has a comparative advantage at producing a particular good or service, say haircuts, if that person is *relatively* more efficient at producing haircuts than at producing other goods or services. We will see that we can all have more of *every* good and service if each of us specializes in the activities at which we have a comparative advantage.

This chapter will also introduce the *production possibilities curve*, which is a graphical method of describing the combinations of goods and services that an economy can produce. The development of this tool will allow us to see much more precisely how specialization enhances the productive capacity of even the simplest economy.

EXCHANGE AND OPPORTUNITY COST

The scarcity principle (see Chapter 1) reminds us that the opportunity cost of spending more time on any one activity is having less time available to spend on others. As the following example makes clear, this principle helps explain why everyone can do better by concentrating on those activities at which he or she performs best relative to others.

EXAMPLE 3.1

Should Greg Mankiw mow his own lawn?

Professor N. Gregory Mankiw is the author of a best-selling economics textbook for which, according to press accounts, he received an advance payment from his publisher of $1.4 million. A neighborhood high school student offers to mow Professor Mankiw's lawn once each week throughout the summer for a fee of $25 per week. The student takes 2 hours to mow the lawn, a task Professor Mankiw can accomplish in only an hour. Should the professor hire the student to mow his lawn?

With his cash advance in hand, the professor can obviously *afford* to hire the student, but that isn't the question. What we want to know is whether it makes sense for him to do so. And we cannot answer that question from the information given without making a few additional assumptions.

To begin, let's assume the professor can write a book by working at it full time for a year. Let's also suppose, for the sake of simplicity, that he is equally productive during each of his 2,000 working hours per year. If he is free to take on additional writing assignments at the same rate of pay, then the time he devotes to his writing is worth ($1,400,000/year)/(2,000 hours/year) = $700/hour. And if the hour he spends mowing his lawn is time he would have been just as happy to spend writing a book, then the opportunity cost of mowing his own lawn is $700. Because the student is willing to mow the lawn for $25, we know the student's opportunity cost of mowing the lawn cannot be more than that. (If it were, he wouldn't have offered to do the job for that amount.) Given this enormous difference in opportunity costs, the professor would do far better to stick to his writing and hire the student to mow his lawn. This is so even though the professor takes only half as much time to mow the lawn as the student.

absolute advantage one person has an absolute advantage over another if he or she takes fewer hours to perform a task than the other person

comparative advantage One person has a comparative advantage over another if his or her opportunity cost of performing a task is lower than the other person's opportunity cost

In Example 3.1, economists would say the professor has an **absolute advantage** at mowing his lawn but a **comparative advantage** at writing books. He has an absolute advantage at lawn mowing because he can mow his lawn in less time than the student takes. The student has a comparative advantage at mowing lawns because his opportunity cost of mowing lawns is lower than the professor's.

The point of Example 3.1 is not that people whose time is valuable should never mow their own lawns. A pivotal assumption in that example was that the professor was equally happy to spend an hour mowing his lawn or working on his book. But suppose he was tired of working on his book and felt like getting a little exercise. Mowing his own lawn might then have made perfect sense!

THE PRINCIPLE OF COMPARATIVE ADVANTAGE

One of the most important insights of modern economics is that when two people (or two nations) have different opportunity costs of performing various tasks, they can always increase the total value of available goods and services by trading with one another. The following simple example captures the logic behind this insight.

Should Paula update her own web page?

EXAMPLE 3.2

Consider a small community in which Paula is the only bicycle mechanic and Beth is the only hyper-text markup language (HTML) programmer. Paula also happens to be an even better HTML programmer than Beth. If the amount of time each of them takes to perform these tasks is as shown in Table 3.1, and if each regards the two tasks as equally pleasant (or unpleasant), does the fact that Paula can program faster than Beth imply that Paula should update her own web page?

TABLE 3.1
Productivity Information for Paula and Beth

	Time to update a web page	Time to complete a bicycle repair
Paula	20 minutes	10 minutes
Beth	30 minutes	30 minutes

The entries in the table show that Paula has an absolute advantage over Beth in both activities. While Paula, the mechanic, needs only 20 minutes to update a web page, Beth, the programmer, needs 30 minutes. Paula's advantage over Beth is even greater when the task is fixing bikes: She can complete a repair in only 10 minutes, compared to Beth's 30 minutes.

But the fact that Paula is a better programmer than Beth does *not* imply that Paula should update her own web page. As with the professor who writes books instead of mowing lawns, the reason is that Beth has a comparative advantage over Paula at programming: She is *relatively* more productive at programming than Paula. Similarly, Paula has a comparative advantage in bicycle repair. (Remember that a person has a comparative advantage at a given task if his or her opportunity cost of performing that task is lower than another person's.)

What is Beth's opportunity cost of updating a web page? Since she takes 30 minutes to update each page—the same amount of time she takes to fix a bicycle—her opportunity cost of updating a web page is one bicycle repair. In other words, by taking the time to update a web page, Beth is effectively giving up the opportunity to do one bicycle repair. Paula, in contrast, can complete two bicycle repairs in the time she takes to update a single web page. For her, the opportunity cost of updating a web page is two bicycle repairs. Paula's opportunity cost of programming, measured in terms of bicycle repairs forgone, is twice as high as Beth's. Thus Beth has a comparative advantage at programming.

The interesting and important implication of the opportunity cost comparison summarized in Table 3.2 is that the total number of bicycle repairs and web updates accomplished if Paula and Beth both spend part of their time at each

TABLE 3.2
Opportunity Costs for Paula and Beth

	Opportunity cost of updating a web page	Opportunity cost of a bicycle repair
Paula	2 bicycle repairs	0.5 web page update
Beth	1 bicycle repair	1 web page update

activity will always be smaller than the number accomplished if each specializes in the activity in which she has a comparative advantage. Suppose, for example, that people in their community demand a total of 16 web page updates per day. If Paula spent half her time updating web pages and the other half repairing bicycles, an 8-hour workday would yield 12 web page updates and 24 bicycle repairs. To complete the remaining 4 updates, Beth would have to spend 2 hours programming, which would leave her 6 hours to repair bicycles. And since she takes 30 minutes to do each repair, she would have time to complete 12 of them. So when the two women try to be jacks-of-all-trades, they end up completing a total of 16 web page updates and 36 bicycle repairs.

Consider what would have happened had each woman specialized in her activity of comparative advantage. Beth could have updated 16 web pages on her own, and Paula could have performed 48 bicycle repairs. Specialization would have created an additional 12 bicycle repairs out of thin air.

When computing the opportunity cost of one good in terms of another, we must pay close attention to the form in which the productivity information is presented. In Example 3.2, we were told how many minutes each person needed to perform each task. Alternatively, we might be told how many units of each task each person can perform in an hour. Work through the following exercise to see how to proceed when information is presented in this alternative format.

"We're a natural, Rachel. I handle intellectual property, and you're a content-provider."

EXERCISE 3.1

Should Barb update her own web page?

Consider a small community in which Barb is the only bicycle mechanic and Pat is the only HTML programmer. If their productivity rates at the two tasks are as shown in the table, and if each regards the two tasks as equally pleasant (or unpleasant), does the fact that Barb can program faster than Pat imply that Barb should update her own web page?

	Productivity in programming	Productivity in bicycle repair
Pat	2 web page updates per hour	1 repair per hour
Barb	3 web page updates per hour	3 repairs per hour

The principle illustrated by Examples 3.1 and 3.2 is so important that we state it formally as one of the core ideas of the course:

The Principle of Comparative Advantage: Everyone does best when each person (or each country) concentrates on the activities for which his or her opportunity cost is lowest.

Indeed, the gains made possible from specialization based on comparative advantage constitute the rationale for market exchange. They explain why each person does not devote 10 percent of his or her time to producing cars, 5 percent to growing food, 25 percent to building housing, 0.0001 percent to performing brain surgery, and so on. By concentrating on those tasks at which we are relatively most productive, together we can produce vastly more than if we all tried to be self-sufficient.

This insight brings us back to Birkhaman the cook. Though Birkhaman's versatility was marvelous, he was not nearly as good a doctor as someone who has been trained in medical school nor as good a repairman as someone who spends each day fixing things. If a number of people with Birkhaman's native talents had joined together, each of them specializing in one or two tasks, together they would have enjoyed more and better goods and services than each could possibly have produced on his own. Although there is much to admire in the resourcefulness of people who have learned through necessity to rely on their own skills, that path is no route to economic prosperity.

Specialization and its effects provide ample grist for the economic naturalist. Here's an example from the world of sports.

Where have all the .400 hitters gone?

In baseball, a .400 hitter is a player who averages at least four hits every 10 times he comes to bat. Though never common in professional baseball, .400 hitters used to appear reasonably frequently. Early in the twentieth century, for example, a player known as Wee Willie Keeler batted .432, meaning that he got a hit in over 43 percent of his times at bat. But since Ted Williams of the Boston Red Sox batted .406 in 1941, there has not been a single .400 hitter in the major leagues. Why not?

Some baseball buffs argue that the disappearance of the .400 hitter means today's baseball players are not as good as yesterday's. But that claim does not withstand close examination. We can document, for example, that today's players are bigger, stronger, and faster than those of Willie Keeler's day. (Wee Willie himself was just a little over 5 feet 4 inches tall and weighed only 140 pounds.)

The best analysts of baseball history, such as Bill James, argue that the .400 hitter has disappeared because the quality of play in the major leagues has *improved,* not declined. In particular, pitching and fielding standards are higher, which makes batting .400 more difficult.

ECONOMIC NATURALIST 3.1

Why has no major league baseball player batted .400 since Ted Williams did it more than half a century ago?

Why has the quality of play in baseball improved? Although there are many reasons, including better nutrition, training, and equipment, specialization has also played an important role.[1] At one time, pitchers were expected to pitch for the entire game. Now pitching staffs include pitchers who specialize in starting the game ("starters"), others who specialize in pitching two or three innings in the middle of the game ("middle relievers"), and still others who specialize in pitching only the last inning ("closers"). Each of these roles requires different skills and tactics. Pitchers may also specialize in facing left-handed or right-handed batters, in striking batters out, or in getting batters to hit balls on the ground. Similarly, few fielders today play multiple defensive positions; most specialize in only one. Some players specialize in defense (to the sacrifice of their hitting skills); these "defensive specialists" can be brought in late in the game to protect a lead. Even in managing and coaching, specialization has increased markedly. Relief pitchers now have their own coaches, and statistical specialists use computers to discover the weaknesses of opposing hitters. The net result of these increases in specialization is that even the weakest of today's teams plays highly competent defensive baseball. With no "weaklings" to pick on, hitting .400 over an entire season has become a near-impossible task.

SOURCES OF COMPARATIVE ADVANTAGE

At the individual level, comparative advantage often appears to be the result of inborn talent. For instance, some people seem to be naturally gifted at programming computers, while others seem to have a special knack for fixing bikes. But comparative advantage is more often the result of education, training, or experience. Thus we usually leave the design of kitchens to people with architectural training, the drafting of contracts to people who have studied law, and the teaching of physics to people with advanced degrees in that field.

At the national level, comparative advantage may derive from differences in natural resources or from differences in society or culture. The United States, which has a disproportionate share of the world's leading research universities, has a comparative advantage in the design of electronic computing hardware and software. Canada, which has one of the world's highest per capita endowments of farm and forest land, has a comparative advantage in the production of agricultural products. Topography and climate explain why Colorado specializes in ski resorts while Hawaii specializes in ocean resorts.

Seemingly noneconomic factors can also give rise to comparative advantage. For instance, the emergence of English as the de facto world language gives English-speaking countries a comparative advantage over non-English-speaking nations in the production of books, movies, and popular music. Even a country's institutions may affect the likelihood that it will achieve comparative advantage in a particular pursuit. For example, cultures that encourage entrepreneurship will tend to have a comparative advantage in the introduction of new products, whereas those that promote high standards of care and craftsmanship will tend to have a comparative advantage in the production of high-quality variants of established products.

ECONOMIC NATURALIST 3.2

Televisions and videocassette recorders (VCRs) were developed and first produced in the United States, but today the United States accounts for only a minuscule share of the total world production of these products. Why did the United States fail to retain its lead in these markets?

That televisions and VCRs were developed in the United States is explained in part by the country's comparative advantage in technological research, which in turn was supported by the country's outstanding system of higher education. Other contributing

[1]For an interesting discussion of specialization and the decline of the .400 hitter from the perspective of an evolutionary biologist, see Stephen Jay Gould, *Full House*, New York: Three Rivers Press, 1996, part three.

factors were high expenditures on the development of electronic components for the military and a culture that actively encourages entrepreneurship. As for the production of these products, America enjoyed an early advantage partly because the product designs were themselves evolving rapidly at first, which favored production facilities located in close proximity to the product designers. Early production techniques also relied intensively on skilled labor, which is abundant in the United States. In time, however, product designs stabilized, and many of the more complex manufacturing operations were automated. Both these changes gradually led to greater reliance on relatively less skilled production workers. And at that point, factories located in high-wage countries like the United States could no longer compete with those located in low-wage areas overseas.

RECAP   **EXCHANGE AND OPPORTUNITY COST**

Gains from exchange are possible if trading partners have comparative advantages in producing different goods and services. You have a comparative advantage in producing, say, web pages, if your opportunity cost of producing a web page—measured in terms of other production opportunities forgone—is smaller than the corresponding opportunity costs of your trading partners. Maximum production is achieved if each person specializes in producing the good or service in which he or she has the lowest opportunity cost (the principle of comparative advantage). Comparative advantage makes specialization worthwhile even if one trading partner is more productive than others, in absolute terms, in every activity.

COMPARATIVE ADVANTAGE AND PRODUCTION POSSIBILITIES

Comparative advantage and specialization allow an economy to produce more than if each person tries to produce a little of everything. In this section we gain further insight into the advantages of specialization by first examining an imaginary economy with only one person and then noting how economic possibilities change as new people join the economy. Along the way, we will introduce a useful graph called the production possibilities curve, which can be used to describe the combinations of goods and services that a particular economy can produce.

PRODUCTION POSSIBILITIES IN A ONE-PERSON ECONOMY

We begin with a hypothetical economy consisting of a single worker who can produce two goods, coffee and Macadamia nuts. The worker lives on a small island, and "production" consists either of picking coffee beans that grow on small bushes on the island's central valley floor or picking Macadamia nuts that grow on trees on the hillsides overlooking the valley. The more time the worker spends picking coffee, the less time she has available for picking nuts. If she wants to drink more coffee than she does at present, then, she must make do with a smaller amount of nuts. Knowing how productive she is at each activity, we can easily summarize the various combinations of coffee and nuts she can pick each day if she makes full use of her available working time. This menu of possibilities is known as the **production possibilities curve.**

As the following example illustrates, constructing the production possibilities curve for a one-person economy is a straightforward matter.

production possibilities curve
a graph that describes the maximum amount of one good that can be produced for every possible level of production of the other good

EXAMPLE 3.3   **What is the production possibilities curve for an economy in which Susan is the only worker?**

Consider a society consisting only of Susan, who allocates her production time between coffee and nuts. Each hour per day she devotes to picking nuts yields 3 pounds of nuts, and each hour she devotes to picking coffee yields 1.5 pounds of coffee. If Susan works a total of 8 hours per day, describe her production possibilities curve—the graph that displays, for each level of nut production, the maximum amount of coffee that Susan can pick.

The vertical axis in Figure 3.1 shows Susan's daily production of coffee, and the horizontal axis shows her daily production of nuts. Let's begin by looking at two extreme allocations of her time. First, suppose she employs her entire work-

FIGURE 3.1
Susan's Production Possibilities.
For the production relationships given, the production possibilities curve is a straight line.

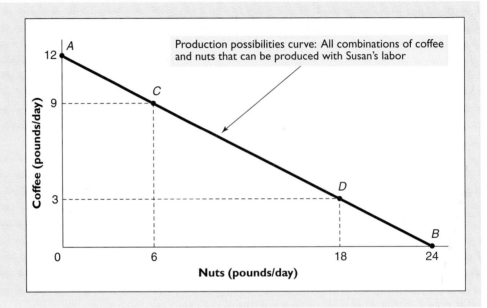

day (8 hours per day) picking coffee. In that case, since she can pick 1.5 pounds of coffee per hour, she would pick (8 hours/day)(1.5 pounds/hour) = 12 pounds per day of coffee and 0 pounds of nuts. That combination of coffee and nut production is represented by point *A* in Figure 3.1, the vertical intercept of Susan's production possibilities curve.

Now suppose, instead, that Susan devotes all her time to picking nuts. Since she can pick 3 pounds of nuts per hour, her total daily production would be (8 hours/day)(3 pounds/hour) = 24 pounds of nuts. That combination is represented by point *B* in Figure 3.1, the horizontal intercept of Susan's production possibilities curve. Because Susan's production of each good is exactly proportional to the amount of time she devotes to that good, the remaining points along her production possibilities curve will lie on the straight line that joins *A* and *B*.

For example, suppose that Susan devotes 6 hours each day to picking coffee and 2 hours to picking nuts. She will then end up with (6 hours/day)(1.5 pounds/hour) = 9 pounds of coffee per day and (2 hours/day)(3 pounds/hour) = 6 pounds of nuts. This is the point labeled *C* in Figure 3.1. Alternatively, if she devotes 2 hours to coffee and 6 hours to nuts, she will get (2 hours/day)(1.5 pounds/hour) = 3 pounds of coffee per day and (6 hours/day)(3 pounds/hour) = 18 pounds of nuts. This alternative combination is represented by point *D* in Figure 3.1.

Since Susan's production possibilities curve (PPC) is a straight line, its slope is constant. The absolute value of the slope of Susan's PPC is the ratio of its vertical intercept to its horizontal intercept: (12 pounds of coffee/day)/(24 pounds of nuts/day) = 1/2 pound of coffee/1 pound of nuts. (Be sure to keep track of the units of measure on each axis when computing this ratio.) *This ratio means that Susan's opportunity cost of an additional pound of nuts is 1/2 pound of coffee.*

Note that Susan's opportunity cost of nuts can also be expressed as the following simple formula:

$$OC_{nuts} = \frac{\text{loss in coffee}}{\text{gain in nuts}},$$

where "loss in coffee" means the amount of coffee given up and "gain in nuts" means the corresponding increase in nuts. Likewise, Susan's opportunity cost of coffee is expressed by this formula:

$$OC_{coffee} = \frac{\text{loss in nuts}}{\text{gain in coffee}}.$$

To say that Susan's opportunity cost of an additional pound of nuts is 1/2 pound of coffee is equivalent to saying that her opportunity cost of 1 pound of coffee is 2 pounds of nuts.

The production possibilities curve shown in Figure 3.1 illustrates the scarcity principle—the idea that because our resources are limited, having more of one good thing generally means having to settle for less of another (see Chapter 1). Susan can have an additional pound of coffee if she wishes, but only if she is willing to give up 2 pounds of nuts. If Susan is the only person in the economy, her opportunity cost of producing a good becomes, in effect, its price. Thus the price she has to pay for an additional pound of coffee is 2 pounds of nuts; or equivalently, the price she has to pay for an additional pound of nuts is 1/2 pound of coffee.

Any point that lies either along the production possibilities curve or within it is said to be an **attainable point,** meaning that it can be produced with currently available resources. In Figure 3.2, for example, points *A, B, C, D,* and *E* are attainable points. Points that lie outside the production possibilities curve are said to be **unattainable,** meaning that they cannot be produced using currently available resources. In Figure 3.2, *F* is an unattainable point because Susan cannot pick 9 pounds of coffee per day *and* 15 pounds of nuts. Points that lie within

attainable point any combination of goods that can be produced using currently available resources

unattainable point any combination of goods that cannot be produced using currently available resources

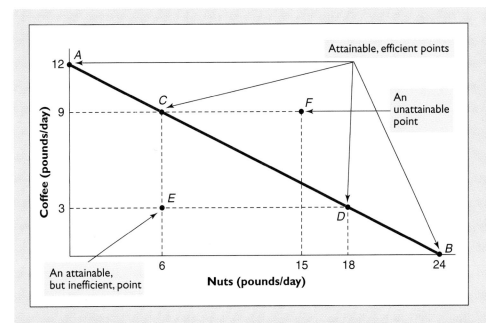

FIGURE 3.2
Attainable and Efficient Points on Susan's Production Possibilities Curve.
Points that lie either along the production possibilities curve (for example, A, C, D, and B) or within it (for example, E) are said to be attainable. Points that lie outside the production possibilities curve (for example, F) are unattainable. Points that lie along the curve are said to be efficient, while those that lie within the curve are said to be inefficient.

inefficient point any combination of goods for which currently available resources enable an increase in the production of one good without a reduction in the production of the other

efficient point any combination of goods for which currently available resources do not allow an increase in the production of one good without a reduction in the production of the other

the curve are said to be **inefficient,** in the sense that existing resources would allow for production of more of at least one good without sacrificing the production of any other good. At *E,* for example, Susan is picking only 3 pounds of coffee per day and 6 pounds of nuts, which means that she could increase her coffee harvest by 6 pounds per day without giving up any nuts (by moving from *E* to *C*). Alternatively, Susan could pick as many as 12 additional pounds of nuts each day without giving up any coffee (by moving from *E* to *D*). An **efficient point** is one that lies along the production possibilities curve. At any such point, more of one good can be produced only by producing less of the other.

FACTORS THAT INFLUENCE THE PRODUCTION POSSIBILITIES CURVE

To see how the slope and position of the production possibilities curve depend on an individual's productivity, let's compare Susan's PPC to that of a person who is less productive in both activities.

EXAMPLE 3.4

How do changes in productivity affect the opportunity cost of nuts?

Suppose Tom can pick 0.75 pound of nuts for each hour he devotes to picking nuts and 0.75 pound of coffee for each hour he spends picking coffee. If Tom is the only person in the economy, describe the economy's production possibilities curve.

We can construct Tom's PPC the same way we did Susan's. Note first that if Tom devotes an entire workday (8 hours/day) to coffee picking, he ends up with (8 hours/day)(0.75 pound/hour) = 6 pounds of coffee per day and 0 pounds of nuts. So the vertical intercept of Tom's PPC is *A* in Figure 3.3. If instead he devotes all his time to picking nuts, he gets (8 hours/day)(0.75 pound/hour) = 6 pounds of nuts per day and no coffee. That means the hor-

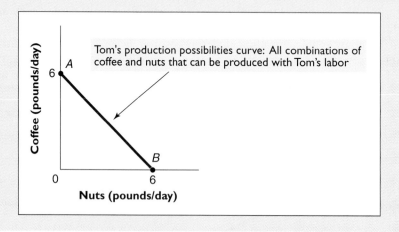

FIGURE 3.3
Tom's Production Possibilities Curve.
The less productive a person is, the closer to the origin is his PPC.

izontal intercept of his PPC is *B* in Figure 3.3. As before, because Tom's production of each good is proportional to the amount of time he devotes to it, the remaining points on his PPC will lie along the straight line that joins these two extreme points.

How does Tom's PPC compare with Susan's? Note that because Tom is less productive than Susan at both activities, the horizontal and vertical intercepts of Tom's PPC lie closer to the origin than do Susan's (see Figure 3.4). For Tom, the opportunity cost of an additional pound of nuts is 1 pound of coffee, which is twice Susan's opportunity cost of nuts. This difference in opportunity costs shows up as a difference in the slopes of their PPCs: the absolute value of the slope of Tom's PPC is 1, whereas Susan's is 1/2.

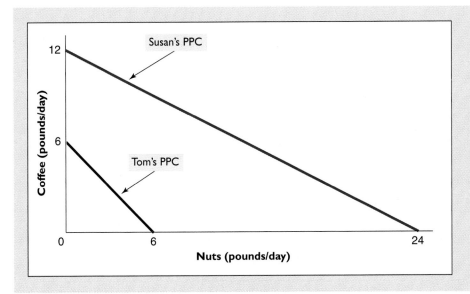

FIGURE 3.4
Individual Production Possibilities Curves Compared.
Though Tom is less productive in both activities than Susan, Tom's opportunity cost of picking coffee is only half Susan's.

But note too that while Tom is absolutely less efficient than Susan at picking coffee, his opportunity cost of coffee is actually only half Susan's. Whereas Susan must give up 2 pounds of nuts to pick an additional pound of coffee, Tom must give up only 1 pound. This difference in opportunity costs is another example of the concept of comparative advantage. Although Tom is *absolutely* less efficient than Susan at picking coffee, he is *relatively* more efficient. That is, Susan has an absolute advantage in picking both coffee and nuts, but Tom has a comparative advantage in picking coffee. Susan's comparative advantage is in picking nuts.

We cannot emphasize strongly enough that the principle of comparative advantage is a relative concept—one that makes sense only when the productivities of two or more people (or countries) are being compared. To cement this idea, work through the following exercise.

EXERCISE 3.2

Suppose Susan can pick 1.5 pounds of coffee per hour or 3 pounds of nuts per hour; Tom can pick 0.75 pound of coffee per hour and 2.25 pounds of nuts per hour. What is Susan's opportunity cost of picking a pound of nuts? What is Tom's opportunity cost of picking a pound of nuts? Where does Susan's comparative advantage now lie?

PRODUCTION POSSIBILITIES IN A TWO-PERSON ECONOMY

Why have we spent so much time defining comparative advantage? As the next examples illustrate, a comparative advantage arising from disparities in individual opportunity costs create gains for everyone.

How does the one-person economy's PPC change when a second person is added?   **EXAMPLE 3.5**

Suppose Susan can pick 1.5 pounds of coffee per hour or 3 pounds of nuts and Tom can pick 0.75 pound of coffee per hour or 0.75 pound of nuts. If Susan and Tom are the only two people in the economy and each works 8 hours per day, describe the production possibilities curve for the economy as a whole.

To construct the PPC for a two-person economy, we use an approach similar to the one we used for a one-person economy. To find the vertical intercept of the PPC, we ask how much coffee we would get if both Susan and Tom worked

FIGURE 3.5
The PPC for a Two-Person Economy.
Initial nut production relies on Susan, whose opportunity cost of nuts is lower than Tom's. Once Susan is fully occupied picking nuts (point *D*), additional nut production must rely on Tom.

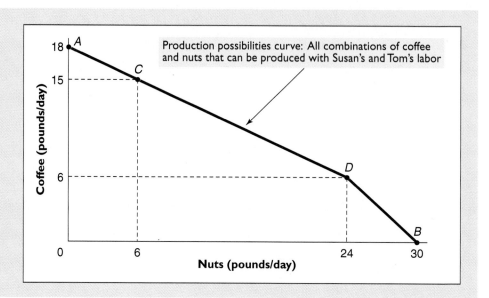

full-time picking coffee. The answer is 18 pounds per day (12 pounds from Susan and 6 pounds from Tom), so point *A* in Figure 3.5 is the vertical intercept of the PPC. Similarly, if Susan and Tom both worked full-time picking nuts, they would make 30 pounds of nuts per day (24 pounds from Susan, and 6 from Tom). Thus point *B* in Figure 3.5 is the horizontal intercept of the PPC.

In contrast to the PPC for the one-person economy, however, the PPC for the two-person economy is not a straight line joining the two extreme points. To see why, suppose Susan and Tom were initially devoting all their time to picking coffee when they decided they would rather have some nuts. How would they launch their nut production effort? Their best bet would be to assign Susan to that task, because her opportunity cost of picking nuts is only half Tom's. Thus, if Susan spent 2 hours picking nuts while Tom continued to devote all his time to picking coffee, they would lose 3 pounds of coffee but gain 6 pounds of nuts each day. Point *C* in Figure 3.5 represents this combination.

If Susan devotes all her time to picking nuts while Tom continues to devote all his time to picking coffee, they will end up at *D* in Figure 3.5, which represents 6 pounds of coffee per day and 24 pounds of nuts. If they want to expand nut production any further, Tom will have to take some of his time away from picking coffee. But in doing so, they gain only one additional pound of nuts for each pound of coffee they lose. Notice in Figure 3.5 how the slope of the PPC changes at point *D*. To the right of point *D*, the slope of the PPC reflects Tom's opportunity cost of picking coffee rather than Susan's.

EXERCISE 3.3

To the left of point *D* in Figure 3.5, what is the slope of the production possibilities curve, and what opportunity cost does this slope represent?

The outward bow shape of the PPC for the two-person economy, then, is a consequence of individual differences in opportunity costs. As the following example shows, this distinctive shape represents expanded opportunities for both Susan and Tom.

EXAMPLE 3.6   **What is the best way to achieve a given production goal?**

Tom and Susan, a married couple, have decided to consume 12 pounds of coffee per day and 12 pounds of nuts. (They are sleepy and have 10 hungry children.)

If their productive abilities are as described in Example 3.5, how should they divide their labor?

Though Tom has a comparative advantage in picking coffee, even if he spends all his time picking coffee, he can pick only (8 hours/day)(0.75 pound/hour) = 6 pounds per day. So Susan will have to pick the additional 6 pounds of coffee to achieve their production target of 12 pounds. Since Susan is capable of picking (8 hours/day)(1.5 pounds/hour) = 12 pounds of coffee per day, she will need only 4 hours per day to pick 6 pounds. She can spend the remaining 4 hours picking nuts, which is exactly the amount of time she needs to pick their production target of 12 pounds. In terms of their two-person production possibilities curve, this allocation of labor puts Susan and Tom at point E in Figure 3.6.

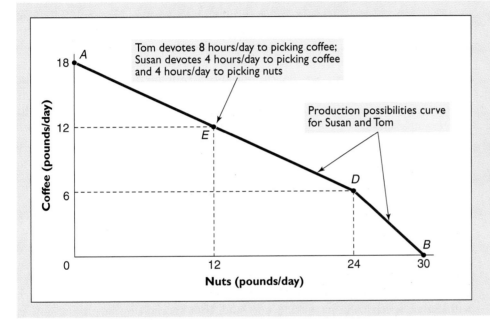

FIGURE 3.6
Optimal Assignment of Production Tasks in a Two-Person Economy.
At the optimal division of labor (point E), Tom specializes completely in picking coffee, and Susan picks only as much coffee as is needed to complete their production target.

Example 3.6 illustrates the general principle that when more than one opportunity is available, we should always exploit the best opportunity first. We call this the low-hanging-fruit principle, in honor of the fruit-picker's rule of picking the most accessible fruit first:

The Principle of Increasing Opportunity Cost (or the Low-Hanging-Fruit Principle): In expanding the production of any good, first employ those resources with the lowest opportunity cost, and only afterward turn to resources with higher opportunity costs.

HOW MUCH DOES SPECIALIZATION MATTER?

In Example 3.6, Tom specialized completely in picking coffee, his area of comparative advantage (lowest opportunity cost). The reason Susan did not specialize completely in picking nuts is that had she done so, the two would have ended up with twice as many nuts (24 pounds) as they wanted to consume (12 pounds). Even so, Tom and Susan still did better through partial specialization than they could have if neither had specialized, as the following example demonstrates.

How much does specialization expand opportunity? (Part 1)

Suppose that in Example 3.6 Susan and Tom had divided their time so that each person's output consisted of half nuts and half coffee. How much worse off would they have been?

EXAMPLE 3.7

Tom can pick equal quantities of both goods by spending 4 hours each day on the production of each, which yields (4 hours/day)(0.75 pound/hour) = 3 pounds of coffee and (4 hours/day)(0.75 pound/hour) = 3 pounds of nuts. Since Susan can pick twice as many pounds of nuts in an hour as she can coffee, to get equal quantities of both goods, she must devote twice as many hours picking coffee as picking nuts. Thus she will need to spend two-thirds of a workday (16/3 hours/day) picking coffee and one-third of a workday (8/3 hours/day) picking nuts. Her output will be (16/3 hours/day)(1.5 pounds/hour) = 8 pounds of coffee per day and (8/3 hours/day)(3 pounds/hour) = 8 pounds of nuts. Their combined daily production will be only 11 pounds of coffee and 11 pounds of nuts—1 pound less of each good than when they specialized.

The relatively small gains from specialization that we saw in Example 3.7 might seem an insufficient explanation for the dramatic differences in the level of wealth across countries. While getting one extra pound of each of two goods by specializing is better than nothing, it is hardly enough to lift a society's standard of living.

This objection is a fair one. But the purpose of Example 3.7 was to demonstrate that specialization produces gains for all, even when one person enjoys an absolute advantage in both tasks, and when differences in opportunity costs are small. As the next example illustrates, the gains from specialization are considerably larger when people are both absolutely *and* relatively more efficient at their respective specialties, and when the differences in opportunity costs are more pronounced.

EXAMPLE 3.8   **How much does specialization of labor expand opportunity? (Part 2)**

Susan can pick 1 pound of coffee or 7 pounds of nuts in an hour. Tom can pick 7 pounds of coffee or 1 pound of nuts in an hour. Draw their combined production possibilities curve. Assuming that the two want to consume coffee and nuts in equal quantities, by how much will specialization increase their consumption?

Susan and Tom's combined PPC is shown in Figure 3.7. By working together, with Susan specializing in picking nuts and Tom specializing in picking coffee, the couple can consume (8 hours/day)(7 pounds/hour) = 56 pounds of coffee and (8 hours/day)(7 pounds/hour) = 56 pounds of nuts each day. If the two had worked separately, each would have been able to pick only 7 pounds of coffee and 7 pounds of nuts each day, for a total of 14 pounds of coffee and 14 pounds of nuts a day—only one-fourth of what they picked when they specialized.

FIGURE 3.7
An Especially Useful Division of Labor.
The gains from specialization are larger when differences in opportunity cost are larger and when individuals enjoy absolute advantage in their respective specialties.

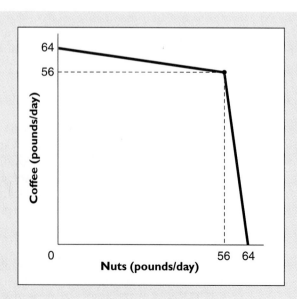

In truth, the gains from specialization will often be far more spectacular than those shown in Example 3.8. One reason is that specialization not only capitalizes on preexisting differences in individual skills but also deepens those skills through practice and experience. It also eliminates many of the switching and start-up costs people incur when they move back and forth among numerous tasks. These gains apply not only to people but also to the tools and equipment they use. Breaking a task down into simple steps, each of which can be performed by a different machine, greatly multiplies the productivity of individual workers.

Even in simple settings, these factors can combine to increase productivity hundredsfold or even thousandsfold. Consider, for instance, Adam Smith's description of work in an eighteenth-century Scottish pin factory:

> One man draws out the wire, another straightens it, a third cuts it, a fourth points it, a fifth grinds it at the top for receiving the head; to make the head requires two or three distinct operations. . . . I have seen a small manufactory of this kind where only ten men were employed . . . [who] could, when they exerted themselves, make among them about twelve pounds of pins in a day. There are in a pound upwards of four thousand pins of middling size. Those ten persons, therefore, could make among them upwards of forty-eight thousand pins in a day. Each person, therefore, making a tenth part of forty-eight thousand pins, might be considered as making four thousand eight hundred pins in a day. But if they had all wrought separately and independently, and without any of them having been educated to this peculiar business, they certainly could not each of them have made twenty, perhaps not one pin in a day. . . .[2]

The gains in productivity that result from specialization are often prodigious. They constitute the single most important explanation for why societies that don't rely heavily on specialization and exchange are rapidly becoming relics of the past.

Of course, the mere fact that specialization boosts productivity does not mean that more specialization is always better than less, for specialization also entails costs. For example, most people appear to enjoy variety in the work they do, but variety tends to be one of the first casualties as workplace tasks become ever more narrowly specialized.

[2]Adam Smith, *The Wealth of Nations*, New York: Everyman's Library, E. P. Dutton, 1910 (1776), book 1, p. 5.

Can specialization proceed too far?

Indeed, one of Karl Marx's central themes was that the fragmentation of workplace tasks often exacts a heavy psychological toll on workers. Thus, he wrote, "[A]ll means for the development of production . . . mutilate the laborer into a fragment of a man, degrade him to the level of an appendage of a machine, destroy every remnant of charm in his work and turn it into hated toil. . . ."[3]

Charlie Chaplin's 1936 film, *Modern Times,* paints a vivid portrait of the psychological costs of repetitive factory work. As an assembly worker, Chaplin's only task, all day every day, is to tighten the nuts on two bolts as they pass before him on the assembly line. Finally he snaps and walks zombielike from the factory, wrenches in hand, tightening every nutlike protuberance he encounters.

Do the extra goods made possible by specialization simply come at too high a price? We must certainly acknowledge at least the *potential* for specialization to proceed too far. Yet specialization need not entail rigidly segmented, mind-numbingly repetitive work. And it is important to recognize that *failure* to specialize entails costs as well. Those who don't specialize must accept low wages or work extremely long hours.

When all is said and done, we can expect to meet life's financial obligations in the shortest time—thereby freeing up more time to do whatever else we wish—if we concentrate at least a significant proportion of our efforts on those tasks for which we have a comparative advantage.

A PRODUCTION POSSIBILITIES CURVE FOR A MANY-PERSON ECONOMY

Most actual economies, of course, consist of millions of workers. Even so, the process of constructing a production possibilities curve for an economy of that size is really no different from the process for a one- or two-person economy. But since each worker's contribution to total output is extremely small in a large economy, production possibilities curves tend not to be kinked like the ones in preceding examples, but smoothly bowed, like the one shown in Figure 3.8.

FIGURE 3.8
Production Possibilities Curve for a Large Economy.
For an economy with millions of workers, the PPC has a gentle outward bow shape.

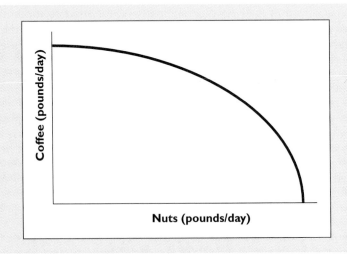

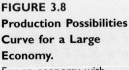

Like all production possibilities curves, the one in Figure 3.8 is downward-sloping, illustrating once again the principle of scarcity and trade-offs. If all available resources are currently engaged in the production of coffee and nuts, the only way to get more nuts is to sacrifice some coffee. Note also that the slope of the production possibilities curve in Figure 3.8 increases as the society moves toward greater production of nuts. Recall the principle of increasing opportunity

[3]Karl Marx, *Das Kapital,* New York: Modern Library, 1936 (1856), pp. 708, 709.

cost (or the low-hanging-fruit principle): In expanding nut production, people turn first to those resources that are relatively efficient at picking nuts. Only when those resources have been deployed do they turn to less efficient resources. As more and more nuts are picked, the opportunity cost of picking additional nuts rises. Note that the principle of increasing opportunity cost applies to both goods shown in Figure 3.8. Thus, as more coffee is picked, the opportunity cost of picking additional coffee rises.

RECAP **COMPARATIVE ADVANTAGE AND PRODUCTION POSSIBILITIES**

For an economy that produces two goods, the production possibilities curve describes the maximum amount of one good that can be produced for every possible level of production of the other good. Attainable points are those that lie on or within the curve, and efficient points are those that lie along the curve. The slope of the production possibilities curve tells us the opportunity cost of producing an additional unit of the good measured along the horizontal axis. The principle of increasing opportunity cost, or the low-hanging-fruit principle, tells us that the slope of the production possibilities curve becomes steeper as we move downward to the right. The greater the differences among individual opportunity costs, the more bow-shaped the production possibilities curve will be, and the more bow-shaped is the production possibilities curve, the greater will be the potential gains from specialization.

COMPARATIVE ADVANTAGE AND INTERNATIONAL TRADE

The same logic that leads the individuals in an economy to specialize and exchange goods with one another also leads nations to specialize and trade among themselves. As with individuals, each trading partner can benefit from exchange, even though one may be more productive than the other in absolute terms.

Can a poor nation prosper by trading with an economic superpower?

Susan and Tom are the only two workers in Islandia, a small island nation, and their production possibilities curve is as shown in Figure 3.9. The only other nation on earth has millions of workers, each of whom can produce 100 pounds

EXAMPLE 3.9

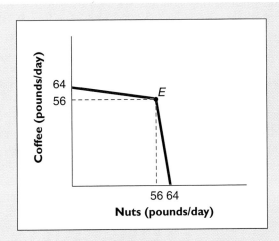

**FIGURE 3.9
Production Possibilities
Curve for a Small Island
Nation.**

of nuts or 100 pounds of coffee per hour. How does the opportunity to trade with the superpower affect consumption opportunities in Islandia?

In the economic superpower, the opportunity cost of a pound of coffee is 1 pound of nuts. The market price of 1 pound of coffee will therefore be 1 pound of nuts. (If someone tried to charge, say, 1.5 pounds of nuts for a pound of coffee, consumers could simply reduce their own nut harvest by a pound and pick an extra pound of coffee instead.) Given the superpower's size relative to the tiny nation of Islandia, in a combined market consisting of the superpower and Islandia, 1 pound of coffee will exchange for exactly 1 pound of nuts. The opportunity to trade with Islandia therefore has no perceptible impact on the citizens of the superpower.

But it has a profound impact on Susan and Tom. Suppose they were initially at point E on their PPC (Figure 3.9). Without the opportunity to trade with the superpower, they would have to give up 7 pounds of nuts to expand their coffee harvest by 1 pound. But with the opportunity to trade, they can purchase 1 pound of coffee in exchange for only 1 pound of nuts. If Islandians started at E and sold their entire 56 pounds of nuts to the superpower, they could buy an addi-

FIGURE 3.10
How Trade Expands the Menu of Possibilities.
The opportunity to trade with an economic superpower greatly expands the consumption opportunities of a smaller nation.

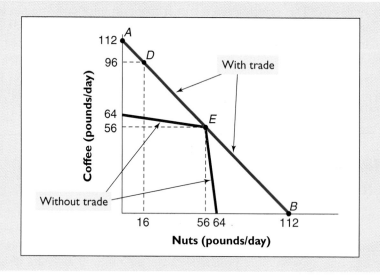

tional 56 pounds of coffee, for a total of $56 + 56 = 112$ pounds of coffee and $56 - 56 = 0$ pounds of nuts. So point A in Figure 3.10 represents their maximum possible daily coffee consumption once they can engage in trade.

Similarly, if they were initially at point E on their PPC, and lacked the opportunity to trade, they would have to sacrifice 7 pounds of coffee to obtain an additional pound of nuts. But if they could trade with the superpower, they could get an extra pound of nuts at a cost of just 1 pound of coffee. If Islandians started at D and sold their entire 56 pounds of coffee to the superpower, they could buy an additional 56 pounds of nuts, for a total of $56 + 56 = 112$ pounds of nuts and $56 - 56 = 0$ pounds of coffee. So point B in Figure 3.10 represents their maximum possible nut consumption once they can engage in trade.

A and B represent the two extreme points on Islandia's new menu of possibilities. By trading lesser quantities of coffee or nuts with the superpower, it is also possible for Islandians to achieve any point along the straight line joining A and B. For example, if Islandians started at point E and sold 40 pounds of nuts to the superpower, they could buy an additional 40 pounds of coffee, which would move them to point D, which has $56 + 40 = 96$ pounds of coffee and $56 - 40 = 16$ pounds of nuts. The opportunity to trade with the superpower thus transforms Islandia's menu of possibilities from the PPC shown in Figure 3.9 to the one labeled AB in Figure 3.10.

EXERCISE 3.4

Refer to Example 3.9. What would Islandia's new menu of possibilities look like if each citizen in the superpower could pick 100 pounds of coffee per day, as before, but only 50 pounds of nuts?

How much does trade benefit the citizens of Islandia? The answer depends on which particular combination of coffee and nuts Islandians most prefer. Suppose, for example, that they most prefer the combination at point E in Figure 3.11: 56 pounds of coffee per day and 56 pounds of nuts. The opportunity to trade with the superpower would then be of no benefit to them, since that combination was available to them before trade became possible (see Figure 3.9).

But suppose that in the absence of trade with the superpower, Islandians would have chosen to pick and consume only 28 pounds of coffee and 60 pounds of nuts per day (point D in Figure 3.11). The opportunity to trade with the superpower would then be very valuable indeed, for it would enable the Islandians

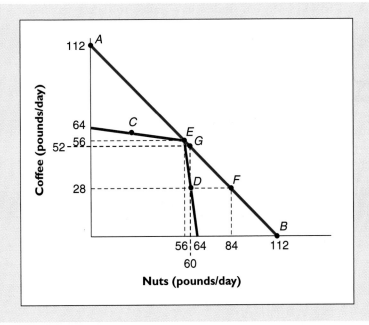

FIGURE 3.11
Gains from International Trade.
If the smaller nation was originally at D on its PPC, the ability to trade with the superpower enables it to increase its consumption of nuts by 24 pounds per day (by moving from D to F). Alternatively, it could increase its consumption of coffee by 24 pounds per day (by moving from D to G).

almost to double their coffee consumption without reducing their nut consumption (by moving from D to G in Figure 3.11). Or they could increase their nut consumption from 60 to 84 pounds per day without giving up any coffee (by moving from D to F in Figure 3.11). The gains from trade would also be valuable if the Islandians had initially chosen to produce at a point at which the opportunity cost of a pound of nuts was less than 1 pound of coffee—say, point C in Figure 3.11.

The patterns displayed in this example are at least roughly indicative of actual patterns of international trade. The volume of trade has grown substantially over time, and with some important exceptions, no single nation produces more than a small fraction of the total supply of any good or service. Thus the price at which one good exchanges for another on the world market is not much influenced by how much a good a nation itself, even an economic superpower like the United States, produces. The greater the difference between domestic opportunity costs and the world opportunity costs, the more a nation benefits from the opportunity to trade with other nations.

DOES EVERYONE BENEFIT FROM TRADE?

If trade between nations is as beneficial as our analysis seems to suggest, then why are free-trade agreements so controversial? One of the most heated issues in the 1996 presidential campaign was President Clinton's support for the North American Free Trade Agreement (NAFTA), a treaty to sharply reduce trade barriers between the United States and its immediate neighbors north and south. The treaty attracted fierce opposition from third-party candidate Ross Perot, who insisted that it would severely reduce the earnings of American workers. If exchange is beneficial, why does anyone oppose it?

The answer is that while reducing barriers to international trade increases the total value of all goods and services produced in each nation, it does not guarantee that each individual citizen will do better. One specific concern regarding NAFTA was that it would help Mexico to exploit a comparative advantage in the production of goods made by unskilled labor. Although U.S. consumers would benefit from reduced prices for such goods, many Americans feared that unskilled workers in the United States would lose their jobs to workers in Mexico.

In the end, NAFTA was enacted over the vociferous opposition of American labor unions. So far, however, studies have failed to detect significant job losses among unskilled workers in the United States. We will look at international trade in much more detail in Chapter 28.

RECAP **COMPARATIVE ADVANTAGE AND INTERNATIONAL TRADE**

Nations, like individuals, can benefit from exchange, even though one trading partner may be more productive than the other in absolute terms. The greater the difference between domestic opportunity costs and world opportunity costs, the more a nation benefits from exchange with other nations. But expansions of exchange do not guarantee that each individual citizen will do better. In particular, unskilled workers in high-wage countries may be hurt in the short run by the reduction of barriers to trade with low-wage nations.

▪ SUMMARY ▪

- One person has an *absolute* advantage over another in the production of a good if she can produce more of that good than the other person. One person has a *comparative* advantage over another in the production of a good if she is relatively more efficient than the other person at producing that good, meaning that her opportunity cost of producing it is lower than her counterpart's. Specialization based on comparative advantage is the basis for economic exchange. When each person specializes in the task at which he or she is relatively most efficient, the economic pie is maximized, making possible the largest slice for everyone.

- At the individual level, comparative advantage may spring from differences in talent or ability or from differences in education, training, and experience. At the national level, sources of comparative advantage include these innate and learned differences, as well as differences in language, culture, institutions, climate, natural resources, and a host of other factors.

- The production possibilities curve is a simple device for summarizing the possible combinations of output that a society can produce if it employs its resources efficiently. In a simple economy that produces only coffee and nuts, the PPC shows the maximum quantity of coffee production (vertical axis) possible at each level of nut production (horizontal axis). The slope of the PPC at any point represents the opportunity cost of nuts at that point, expressed in pounds of coffee.

- All production possibilities curves slope downward because of the scarcity principle, which states that the only way a consumer can get more of one good is to settle for less of another. In economies whose workers have different opportunity costs of picking nuts, the slope of the PPC becomes steeper as consumers move downward along the curve. This change in slope illustrates the principle of increasing opportunity cost (or the low-hanging-fruit principle), which states that in expanding the production of any good, a society should first employ those resources that are relatively efficient at producing that good and only afterward turn to those that are less efficient.

- The same logic that prompts individuals to specialize in their production and exchange goods with one another also leads

nations to specialize and trade with one another. On both levels, each trading partner can benefit from an exchange, even though one may be more productive than the other, in absolute terms, for each good. For both individuals and nations, the benefits of exchange tend to be larger the larger are the differences between the trading partners' opportunity costs.

■ CORE PRINCIPLES ■

The Principle of Comparative Advantage
Everyone does best when each person (or each country) concentrates on the activities for which his or her opportunity cost is lowest.

The Principle of Increasing Opportunity Cost (or The Low-Hanging-Fruit Principle)
In expanding the production of any good, first employ those resources with the lowest opportunity cost and only afterward turn to resources with higher opportunity costs.

■ KEY TERMS ■

absolute advantage (50)
attainable point (57)
comparative advantage (50)

efficient point (58)
inefficient point (58)
production possibilities curve (55)

unattainable point (57)

■ REVIEW QUESTIONS ■

1. Explain what "having a comparative advantage" at producing a particular good or service means. What does "having an absolute advantage" at producing a good or service mean?

2. How will a reduction in the number of hours worked each day affect an economy's production possibilities curve?

3. How will technological innovations that boost labor productivity affect an economy's production possibilities curve?

4. Why does saying that people are poor because they do not specialize make more sense than saying that people perform their own services because they are poor?

5. What factors have helped the United States to become the world's leading exporter of movies, books, and popular music?

■ PROBLEMS ■

1. Consider a society whose only worker is Helen, who allocates her production time between cutting hair and baking bread. Each hour per day she devotes to cutting hair yields 4 haircuts, and each hour she devotes to baking bread yields 8 loaves of bread. If Helen works a total of 8 hours per day, graph her production possibilities curve.

2. Refer to Problem 1. Which of the points listed below is efficient? Which is attainable?
   a. 28 haircuts/day, 16 loaves/day
   b. 16 haircuts/day, 32 loaves/day
   c. 18 haircuts/day, 24 loaves/day

3. Determine whether the following statements are true or false, and briefly explain why.
   a. Toby can produce 5 gallons of apple cider or 2.5 ounces of feta cheese per hour. Kyle can produce 3 gallons of apple cider or 1.5 ounces of feta cheese per hour. Therefore, Toby and Kyle cannot benefit from specialization and trade.
   b. A doctor who can vacuum her office faster and more thoroughly than commercial cleaners should clean her office herself.

c. In an economy in which millions of workers each have different opportunity costs of producing two goods, the low-hanging-fruit principle implies that the slope of the production possibilities curve decreases in absolute value as more of the good on the horizontal axis is produced.

4. Nancy and Bill are auto mechanics. Nancy takes 4 hours to replace a clutch and 2 hours to replace a set of brakes. Bill takes 6 hours to replace a clutch and 2 hours to replace a set of brakes. If Bill and Nancy open a motor repair shop:
   a. Nancy should work only on clutches, and Bill should work only on brakes.
   b. Bill has a comparative advantage at replacing brakes.
   c. Nancy has an absolute advantage at replacing clutches.
   d. Nancy has a comparative advantage at replacing clutches.
   e. All but one of the above statements are correct.

5. Bob and Stella are a married couple. Bob takes 10 minutes to change a lightbulb and 2 minutes to fix a broken fuse. Stella takes 3 minutes to change a lightbulb and 30 seconds to fix a broken fuse. Which of the following statements is true?
   a. Stella has a comparative advantage at fixing fuses, because she can do it faster than Bob.
   b. Stella has a comparative advantage at changing lightbulbs and fixing fuses, because she can do both of them faster than Bob.
   c. Stella has an absolute advantage at changing lightbulbs and fixing fuses, because she can do both of them faster than Bob.
   d. Bob has a comparative advantage at fixing fuses, because Stella has a comparative advantage at changing lightbulbs.
   e. Stella has a comparative advantage at changing lightbulbs.

6. Larry and Harry are stranded together on a desert island. The raw materials on the island are suitable only for making beer and pizza, but their quantities are unlimited. What is scarce is labor. Harry and Larry each spend 10 hours a day making beer or pizza. The following table specifies *how much beer and pizza Harry and Larry can produce per hour.*

	Beer	**Pizza**
Harry	I bottle per hour	0.2 pizza per hour
Larry	0.5 bottle per hour	I.5 pizzas per hour

   a. Draw the daily production possibilities curves (PPCs) for Harry and Larry.
   b. Who has an absolute advantage in making pizza? In brewing beer?
   c. Who has a comparative advantage in making pizza? In brewing beer?
   Now suppose their preferences are as follows: Harry wants 2 beers and as much pizza as he can eat each day; Larry wants 2 pizzas and as much beer as he can drink each day.
   d. If each man is self-reliant, how much beer and pizza will Harry and Larry eat and drink?
   e. Suppose the two men decide to trade with each other. Draw their joint PPC, and give an example of a trade that will make each of them better off.

7. Redo Problem 6 with the following changes:
   a. Each individual's productivity is shown in the table that follows, *which specifies the number of hours each man needs to produce a single unit of beer and pizza.*
   b. Harry wants 6 beers and as much pizza as he can eat each day, while Larry wants 2 pizzas and as much beer as he can drink each day.

	Production time for I beer	**Production time for I pizza**
Harry	5/4 hours	5/3 hours
Larry	5 hours	5/2 hours

8. Given the joint production possibilities curve in Problem 7, what would be the maximum number of pizzas available to Harry and Larry if they could buy or sell in a world market in which 1 beer could be exchanged for 1 pizza? What would be the maximum number of beers available to them?

9. Inlandia and Outlandia both can produce oranges and oil. Inlandia can produce up to 10 million tons of oranges per week or 5 million barrels of oil, or any combination of oil and oranges along a straight-line production possibilities curve linking those two points. Outlandia can produce up to 50 million tons of oranges per week or 1 million barrels of oil, or any combination along a straight-line production possibilities curve linking those points.

  a. Does the low-hanging-fruit principle apply in either of these two economies? Why or why not?

  b. Suppose Outlandia and Inlandia sign a trade agreement in which each country would specialize in the production of either oil or oranges. Which country should specialize in which commodity?

  c. If Inlandia and Outlandia are the only two economies in the world that are open to international trade, what are the maximum and minimum prices that can prevail on the world market for a ton of oranges, in terms of barrels of oil?

10. Jay, Kay, and Dee are marooned alone on the Greek island of Skorpios. They must find a way to provide themselves with food and drinking water. The following table shows how many hours each person takes to produce one unit of food or one unit of water.

	Production time for one unit of food	Production time for one unit of drinking water
Jay	1 hour	2 hours
Kay	2 hours	1 hour
Dee	4 hours	6 hours

  a. If each person can work for 12 hours a day and each person provides for him or herself, draw their individual PPCs.

  b. Suppose Jay, Kay, and Dee decide to produce food and water cooperatively, so they can gain from trade. Draw their combined production possibilities curve.

  c. If the trio wants, in aggregate, to consume 15 units of food and 12 units of water, who should specialize in food production? Who should specialize in water production? Should anyone divide his or her time between food and water production?

  d. If the trio wants, in aggregate, to consume 6 units of water and as much food as possible, who should specialize in food and who should specialize in water? Should anyone divide his or her time between food and water production? How much food will be produced?

  e. Suppose production is as in part c. Dee suggests dividing the output equally among the three of them. Assuming that the amounts of food that Jay and Kay get under this arrangement are exactly what each would have chosen if he or she had lived and worked alone, is each of them strictly better off when they share? Explain.

▪ ANSWERS TO IN-CHAPTER EXERCISES ▪

3.1

	Productivity in programming	Productivity in bicycle repair
Pat	2 web page updates per hour	1 repair per hour
Barb	3 web page updates per hour	3 repairs per hour

The entries in the table tell us that Barb has an absolute advantage over Pat in both activities. While Barb, the mechanic, can update 3 web pages per hour, Pat, the programmer, can update only 2. Barb's absolute advantage over Pat is even greater in the task of fixing bikes—3 repairs per hour versus Pat's 1.

But, as in Example 3.2, the fact that Barb is a better programmer than Pat does not imply that Barb should update her own web page. Barb's opportunity cost of updating a web page is 1 bicycle repair, whereas Pat must give up only half a bicycle repair to update a web page. Pat has a comparative advantage over Barb at programming, and Barb has a comparative advantage over Pat at bicycle repair.

3.2 Susan's opportunity cost of picking a pound of nuts is 1/2 pound of coffee. But Tom's opportunity cost of picking a pound of nuts is now only 1/3 pound of coffee. So Tom has a comparative advantage at picking nuts, and Susan has a comparative advantage at picking coffee.

3.3 The slope to the left of point D (in absolute value) is 1/2 pound of coffee per pound of nuts, which is Susan's opportunity cost of picking nuts.

3.4 In the superpower, the opportunity cost of a pound of nuts is now 2 pounds of coffee, not 1 pound. This means that Islandians can now buy or sell a pound of nuts for 2 pounds of coffee and can buy or sell a pound of coffee for 1/2 pound of nuts. So if Islandians start at point E and sell all 56 pounds of nuts they produce, they can buy an additional 112 pounds of coffee, for a total of 168 pounds of coffee. This would put them at point A in the diagram below. Alternatively, if they start at E and sell all 56 pounds of coffee they produce, they can buy an additional 28 pounds of nuts, for a total of 84 pounds of nuts, which would put them at B. The straight line AB is their new menu of opportunities.

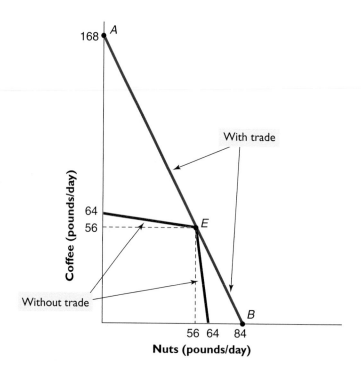

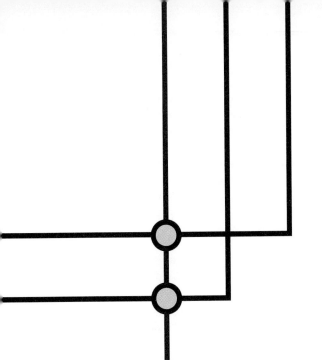

4

SUPPLY AND DEMAND: AN INTRODUCTION

∎

The stock of foodstuffs on hand at any moment in New York City's grocery stores, restaurants, and private kitchens is sufficient to feed the city's 10 million residents for at most a week or so. Since most of these residents have nutritionally adequate and highly varied diets, and since almost no food is produced within the city proper, provisioning New York requires that tens of millions of pounds of food and drink be delivered to locations throughout the city each day.

No doubt many New Yorkers, buying groceries at their favorite local markets or eating at their favorite Italian restaurants, give little or no thought to the nearly miraculous coordination of people and resources that is required to feed city residents on a daily basis. But near-miraculous it is, nevertheless. Even if the supplying of New York City consisted only of transporting a fixed collection of foods to a given list of destinations each day, it would be quite an impressive operation, requiring at least a small army (and a well-managed one) to carry out.

Yet the entire process is astonishingly more complex than that. For example, the system must somehow ensure that not only *enough* food is delivered to satisfy New Yorkers' discriminating palates but also the *right kinds* of food. There mustn't be too much pheasant and not enough smoked eel, or too much bacon and not enough eggs, or too much caviar and not enough canned tuna, and so on. Similar judgments must be made *within* each category of food and drink: There must be the right amount of Swiss cheese and the right amounts of provolone, Gorgonzola, and feta.

But even this doesn't begin to describe the complexity of the decisions and actions required to provide our nation's largest city with its daily bread.

Someone has to decide where each particular type of food gets produced, and how, and by whom. Someone must decide how much of each type of food gets delivered to *each* of the tens of thousands of restaurants and grocery stores in the city. Someone must determine whether the deliveries should be made in big trucks or small ones, arrange that the trucks be in the right place at the right time, and ensure that gasoline and qualified drivers are available.

Thousands of individuals must decide what role, if any, they will play in this collective effort. Some people—just the right number—must choose to drive food delivery trucks, rather than trucks that deliver lumber. Others must become the mechanics who fix these trucks, rather than carpenters who build houses. Others must become farmers, rather than architects or bricklayers. Still others must become chefs in upscale restaurants, or flip burgers at McDonald's, instead of becoming plumbers or electricians.

Yet despite the almost incomprehensible number and complexity of the tasks involved, somehow the supplying of New York City manages to get done remarkably smoothly. Oh, a grocery store will occasionally run out of flank steak, or a diner will sometimes be told that someone else has just ordered the last serving of roast duck. But if episodes like these stick in memory, it is only because they are rare. For the most part, New York's food delivery system—like that of every other city in the country—functions so seamlessly that it attracts virtually no notice.

The situation is strikingly different in New York City's rental housing market. According to one recent estimate, the city needs between 20,000 and 40,000 new housing units each year merely to keep up with population growth and to replace existing housing that is deteriorated beyond repair. The actual rate of new construction in the city, however, is only 6,000 units per year. As a result, America's most densely populated city has been experiencing a protracted housing shortage. Yet, paradoxically, in the midst of this shortage, apartment houses are being demolished; and in the vacant lots left behind, people from the neighborhoods are planting flower gardens!

New York City is experiencing not only a growing shortage of rental housing but also chronically strained relations between landlords and tenants. In one all-too-typical case, for example, a photographer living in a loft on the Lower East Side waged an 8-year court battle with his landlord that generated literally thousands of pages of legal documents. "Once we put up a doorbell for ourselves," the photographer recalled, "and [the landlord] pulled it out, so we pulled out the wires to his doorbell."[1] The landlord, for his part, accused the photographer of obstructing his efforts to renovate the apartment. According to the landlord, the tenant preferred that the apartment remain in substandard condition, since that gave him an excuse to withhold rent payments.

Same city, two strikingly different patterns. In the food industry, a huge variety of goods and services is widely available, and people (at least those with adequate income) are generally satisfied with what they receive and the choices available to them. In contrast, in the rental housing industry, there are chronic shortages and chronic dissatisfaction among both buyers and sellers. Why this difference?

The brief answer is that New York City relies on a complex system of administrative rent regulations to allocate housing units but leaves the allocation of food essentially in the hands of market forces—the forces of supply and demand. Although intuition might suggest otherwise, both theory and experience suggest that the seemingly chaotic and unplanned outcomes of market forces often can do a better job of allocating economic resources than can (for example) a government agency, even if the agency has the best of intentions.

Why does New York City's food distribution system work so much better than its housing market?

[1] Quoted by John Tierney, "The Rentocracy: At the Intersection of Supply and Demand," *The New York Times Magazine,* May 4, 1997, p. 39.

In this chapter we'll explore how markets allocate food, housing, and other goods and services, usually with remarkable efficiency despite the complexity of the tasks. To be sure, markets are by no means perfect, and our stress on their virtues is to some extent an attempt to counteract what most economists view as an underappreciation by the general public of their remarkable strengths. But in the course of our discussion we'll see why markets function so smoothly most of the time and why bureaucratic rules and regulations rarely work as well in solving complex economic problems.

To convey an understanding of how markets work is a major goal of this course, and in this chapter we provide only a brief introduction and overview. As the course proceeds we will discuss the economic role of markets in considerably more detail, paying attention to some of the problems of markets as well as their strengths.

WHAT, HOW, AND FOR WHOM? CENTRAL PLANNING VERSUS THE MARKET

No city, state, or society—irrespective of how it is organized—can escape the need to answer certain basic economic questions. For example, how much of our limited time and other resources should we devote to building housing, how much to the production of food, and how much to providing other goods and services? What techniques should we use to produce each good? Who should be assigned to each specific task? And how should the resulting goods and services be distributed among people?

In the thousands of different societies for which records are available, issues like these have been decided in essentially one of two ways. One approach is for all economic decisions to be made centrally, by an individual or small number of individuals on behalf of a larger group. For example, in many agrarian societies throughout history, families or other small groups consumed only those goods and services that they produced for themselves, and a single clan or family leader made most important production and distribution decisions. On an immensely larger scale, the economic organization of the former Soviet Union (and other communist countries) was also largely centralized. In so-called centrally planned communist nations, a central bureaucratic committee established production targets for the country's farms and factories, developed a master plan for how to achieve the targets (including detailed instructions concerning who was to produce what), and set up guidelines for the distribution and use of the goods and services produced.

Neither form of centralized economic organization is much in evidence today. When implemented on a small scale, as in a self-sufficient family enterprise, centralized decision making is certainly feasible. For the reasons discussed in Chapter 3, however, the jack-of-all-trades approach was doomed once it became clear how dramatically people could improve their living standards by specialization— that is, by having each individual focus his or her efforts on a relatively narrow range of tasks. And with the fall of the Soviet Union and its satellite nations in the late 1980s, there are now only three communist economies left in the world: Cuba, North Korea, and China. The first two of these appear to be on their last legs, economically speaking, and China has by now largely abandoned any attempt to control production and distribution decisions from the center. The major remaining examples of centralized allocation and control now reside in the bureaucratic agencies that administer programs like New York City's rent controls—programs that are themselves becoming increasingly rare.

At the beginning of the twenty-first century we are therefore left, for the most part, with the second major form of economic system, one in which production and distribution decisions are left to individuals interacting in private markets. In the so-called capitalist, or free-market, economies, people decide for themselves which careers to pursue and which products to produce or buy. In fact, there are no *pure* free-market economies today. Modern industrial countries are more properly described as *mixed economies,* meaning that goods and services are allocated by a combination of free markets, regulation, and other forms of collective control. Still, it makes sense to refer to such systems as free-market economies, because people are for the most part free to start businesses, to shut them down, or to sell them. And within broad limits, the distribution of goods and services is determined by individual preferences backed by individual purchasing power, which in most cases comes from the income people earn in the labor market.

In country after country, markets have replaced centralized control for the simple reason that they tend to allocate goods and services so much more effectively. The popular press, and the conventional wisdom, often assert that economists disagree about important issues. (As one wag put it, "If you lay all the economists in the world end to end, they still wouldn't reach a conclusion.") The fact is, however, that there is overwhelming agreement among economists about a broad range of issues, with the great majority accepting the efficacy of markets as means for allocating society's scarce resources. For example, a recent survey found that more than 90 percent of American professional economists believe that rent regulations like the ones implemented by New York City do more harm than good. That the stated aim of these regulations—to make rental housing more affordable for middle- and low-income families—is clearly benign was not enough to prevent them from wreaking havoc on New York City's housing market. To see why, we must explore how goods and services are allocated in private markets and why nonmarket means of allocating goods and services often do not produce the expected results.

MARKETS AND PRICES

Beginning with some simple concepts and definitions, we will explore how the interactions among buyers and sellers in markets determine the prices and quantities of the various goods and services traded in those markets. We begin by defining a market: The **market** for any good consists of all the buyers and sellers of that good. So, for example, the market for hamburgers on a given day in a given place is just the set of people (or other economic actors, like firms) potentially able to buy or sell hamburgers at that time and location.

market the market for any good consists of all buyers or sellers of that good

In the market for hamburgers, sellers comprise the individuals and companies that either do sell—or might, under the right circumstances, sell—hamburgers. Similarly, buyers in this market include all individuals who buy—or might buy—hamburgers.

In most parts of the country a decent hamburger, or some other life-sustaining meal, can still be had for less than $5. Where does the market price of hamburgers come from? Looking beyond hamburgers to the vast array of other goods that are bought and sold every day, we may ask, "Why are some goods cheap and others expensive?" Aristotle had no idea. Nor did Plato, or Copernicus, or Newton. On reflection, it is astonishing that, for almost the entire span of human history, not even the most intelligent and creative minds on earth had any real inkling of how to answer that seemingly simple question. Even Adam Smith, the Scottish moral philosopher whose *Wealth of Nations* launched the discipline of economics in 1776, suffered confusion on this issue.

Smith and other early economists (including Karl Marx) thought that the market price of a good was determined by its cost of production. But although costs surely do affect prices, they cannot explain why one of Pablo Picasso's paintings sells for so much more than one of Jackson Pollock's.

Stanley Jevons and other nineteenth-century economists tried to explain price by focusing on the value people derived from consuming different goods and services. It certainly seems plausible that people will pay a lot for a good they value highly. Yet willingness to pay cannot be the whole story, either. A person deprived of water in the desert, for example, will be dead in a matter of hours, and yet water sells for less than a penny a gallon. By contrast, human beings can get along perfectly well without gold, and yet gold sells for more than $250 an ounce.

Cost of production? Value to the user? Which is it? The answer, which seems obvious to today's economists, is that both matter. Writing in the late nineteenth century, the British economist Alfred Marshall was among the first to show clearly how costs and value interact to determine both the prevailing market price for a good and the amount of it that is bought and sold. Our task in the pages ahead will be to explore Marshall's insights and gain some practice in applying them. As a first step, we introduce the two main components of Marshall's pathbreaking analysis: the supply curve and the demand curve.

Why do Pablo Picasso's paintings sell for so much more than Jackson Pollock's?

THE SUPPLY CURVE

In the market for hamburgers, the **supply curve** of hamburgers is a simple schedule, or graph, that tells us, for each possible price of hamburgers, how many hamburgers all hamburger sellers together would be willing to sell at that price.

What does the supply curve of hamburgers look like? The answer to this question is based on the logical assumption that people should be willing to sell hamburgers as long as the price they receive for them is sufficient to cover their opportunity costs of supplying them. Thus, if what people could earn by selling hamburgers is not sufficient to compensate them for what they could have earned if they had spent their time and invested their money in some other way, they will not sell hamburgers. Otherwise, they will.

supply curve a curve or schedule showing the total quantity of a good that sellers wish to sell at each price

In general, people differ with respect to their opportunity costs of producing and selling hamburgers: For those with limited education and work experience, the opportunity cost of selling hamburgers is relatively low (because such individuals typically do not have a lot of high-paying alternatives). For others, the opportunity cost of selling burgers is of moderate value, and for still others—like rock stars and professional athletes—it is prohibitively high. Because of these differences among people in the opportunity cost of selling hamburgers, the daily supply curve of hamburgers will be *upward-sloping* with respect to the price of hamburgers. As an illustration, see Figure 4.1, which shows a hypothetical supply curve for the hamburger market in the New York

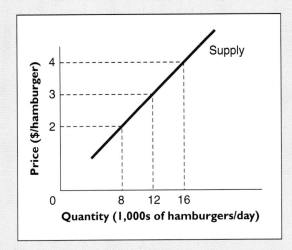

FIGURE 4.1
The Daily Supply Curve of Hamburgers in Greenwich Village.
At higher prices, sellers generally offer more units for sale.

City neighborhood of Greenwich Village on a given day. (Although economists usually refer to demand and supply "curves," we often draw them as straight lines in examples.)

Why is the supply curve for hamburgers upward-sloping? When the price of hamburgers is low—say, $2 per hamburger—only those people whose opportunity cost of selling hamburgers is less than or equal to that amount will offer hamburgers for sale. For the supply curve shown in Figure 4.1, the quantity supplied at a price of $2 will be 8,000 hamburgers per day. In that example, 8,000 hamburgers is the total quantity of hamburgers offered for sale by people whose opportunity cost of selling hamburgers is $2 per hamburger or less. If the price of hamburger were to rise above $2, however, additional sellers would find it worthwhile to offer hamburgers for sale. For example, at a price of $3, Figure 4.1 shows that the quantity of hamburgers supplied is 12,000 per day, while at a price of $4, the quantity supplied is 16,000. The higher the price, the more people find it worthwhile to supply hamburgers.

The fact that the supply curve slopes upward may be seen as a consequence of the low-hanging-fruit principle, discussed in Chapter 3. This principle tells us that as we expand the production of hamburgers, we turn first to those whose opportunity costs of producing hamburgers are lowest and only then to others with higher opportunity costs.

Stated another way, the fact that the supply curve for a good is upward-sloping reflects the fact that the marginal cost of producing the good rises as we produce more of it. If sellers are currently supplying 12,000 hamburgers a day in Figure 4.1, for example, the opportunity cost of the last hamburger produced (including the cost of meat, bun, etc., as well as the value of the supplier's time) must be $3. (If sellers could produce a 12,001st hamburger for less than that, they would have an incentive to supply it, since they can sell it for $3, which is more than it cost them to produce it. And if the cost of producing the 12,000th hamburger were greater than $3, it would not have been offered for sale at that price.) By similar reasoning, when the total quantity of hamburgers is 16,000, the opportunity cost of producing another hamburger must be $4.

THE DEMAND CURVE

The supply curve, by itself, does not tell us how many hamburgers will be sold in Greenwich Village on a given day, or at what price those hamburgers will sell. To find the prevailing price and quantity, we also need the demand curve for hamburgers in this market. The **demand curve** is a graph that tells us the total quantity of hamburgers that buyers wish to buy at various prices.

A fundamental property of the demand curve for a good is that it is downward-sloping with respect to price of that good. For example, the demand curve for hamburgers tells us that the higher the price of hamburgers becomes, the fewer hamburgers buyers as a whole will wish to buy. Thus the daily demand curve for hamburgers in Greenwich Village might look like the curve shown in Figure 4.2.

The demand curve in Figure 4.2 tells us that when the price of hamburgers is low—say, $2 per hamburger—buyers will want to buy 16,000 hamburgers per day, whereas they will want to buy only 12,000 at a price of $3 and only 8,000 at a price of $4. The demand curve for hamburgers—as for any other good—slopes downward for two reasons. First, as hamburgers become more expensive, some people switch to chicken sandwiches, pizza, and other foods that substitute for hamburgers. And second, people simply can't afford to buy as many hamburgers at higher prices as at lower prices.

demand curve a curve or schedule showing the total quantity of a good that buyers wish to buy at each price

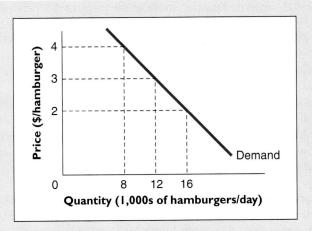

FIGURE 4.2
The Daily Demand Curve for Hamburgers in Greenwich Village.
The demand curve for any good is a downward-sloping function of its price.

MARKET EQUILIBRIUM

The concept of **equilibrium** is employed in both the physical and social sciences and is of central importance in economic analysis. In general, a system is in equilibrium when all forces at work within the system are canceled by others, resulting in a stable, balanced, or unchanging situation. In physics, for example, a ball hanging from a spring is said to be in equilibrium when the spring has stretched sufficiently that the upward force it exerts on the ball is exactly counterbalanced by the downward force of gravity. In economics, a market is said to be in equilibrium when no participant in the market has any reason to alter his or her behavior so that there is no tendency for production or prices in that market to change.

equilibrium a stable, balanced, or unchanging situation in which all forces at work within a system are canceled by others

If we want to determine the final position of a ball hanging from a spring, we need to find the point at which the forces of gravity and spring tension are balanced and the system is in equilibrium. Similarly, if we want to find the price at which a good will sell (which we will call the **equilibrium price**) and the quantity of it that will be sold (the **equilibrium quantity**), we need to find the equilibrium in the market for that good. The basic tools for finding the equilibrium in a market for some good are the supply and demand curves for that good. For reasons that we will explain, the equilibrium price and equilibrium quantity of a good are the price and quantity at which the supply and demand curves for the good intersect. For the hypothetical supply and demand curves for hamburgers in Greenwich Village, the equilibrium price will therefore be $3 per hamburger, and the equilibrium quantity of hamburgers sold will be 12,000 per day, as shown in Figure 4.3.

equilibrium price and equilibrium quantity the price and quantity of a good at the intersection of the supply and demand curves for the good

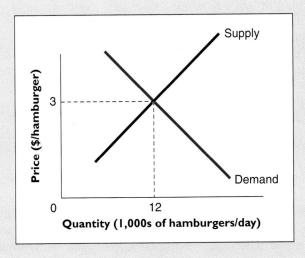

FIGURE 4.3
The Equilibrium Price and Quantity of Hamburgers in Greenwich Village.
The equilibrium quantity and price of a product are the values that correspond to the intersection of the supply and demand curves for that product.

In Figure 4.3, note that at the equilibrium price of $3 per hamburger, both sellers and buyers are "satisfied" in the following sense: Buyers are buying exactly the quantity of hamburgers they wish to buy at that price (12,000 per day), and sellers are selling exactly the quantity of hamburgers they wish to sell (also 12,000 per day). And since they are satisfied in this sense, neither buyers nor sellers face any incentives to change their behavior.

market equilibrium occurs when all buyers and sellers are satisfied with their respective quantities at the market price

Note the limited sense of the term *satisfied* in the definition of **market equilibrium.** It doesn't mean that sellers would not be pleased to receive a price higher than the equilibrium price. Rather, it means only that they're able to sell all they wish to sell at that price. Similarly, to say that buyers are satisfied at the equilibrium price doesn't mean that they would not be happy to pay less than the equilibrium price. Rather, it means only that they're able to buy exactly as many units of the good as they wish to at the equilibrium price.

Note also that if the price of hamburgers in our Greenwich Village market were anything other than $3, either buyers or sellers would not be satisfied. Suppose, for example, that the price of hamburgers were $4, as shown in Figure 4.4. At that price, buyers wish to buy only 8,000 hamburgers per day, but sellers wish

FIGURE 4.4
Excess Supply.
When price exceeds the equilibrium price, there is excess supply, or surplus, the difference between quantity supplied and quantity demanded.

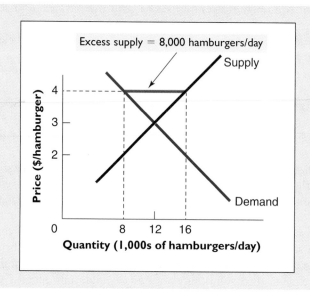

to sell 16,000. And since no one can force someone to buy a hamburger against his or her wishes, this means that buyers will buy only the 8,000 hamburgers they wish to buy. So when the price exceeds the equilibrium price, it is sellers who end up being dissatisfied. At a price of $4 in this example, they are left with an **excess supply, or surplus,** of 8,000 hamburgers per day. (Note that the term *surplus* has a different meaning when used to denote excess supply than when used to denote economic surplus.)

excess supply, or surplus the difference between the quantity supplied and the quantity demanded when the price of a good exceeds the equilibrium price; sellers are dissatisfied when there is excess supply

Conversely, suppose that the price of hamburgers in our Greenwich Village market were less than the equilibrium price, say, $2 per hamburger. As shown in Figure 4.5, buyers want to buy 16,000 hamburgers per day at that price, whereas sellers want to sell only 8,000. And since sellers cannot be forced to sell hamburgers against their wishes, this time it is the buyers who end up being dissatisfied. At a price of $2 in this example, they experience an **excess demand, or shortage,** of 8,000 hamburgers per day.

excess demand, or shortage the difference between the quantity supplied and the quantity demanded when the price of a good lies below the equilibrium price; buyers are dissatisfied when there is excess demand

An extraordinary feature of private markets for goods and services is their automatic tendency to gravitate toward their respective equilibrium prices and quantities. The mechanisms by which this happens are implicit in our definitions of excess supply and excess demand. Suppose, for example, that the price of hamburgers in our hypothetical market was $4, leading to excess supply as shown in Figure 4.4. Because sellers are dissatisfied in the sense of wanting to sell more

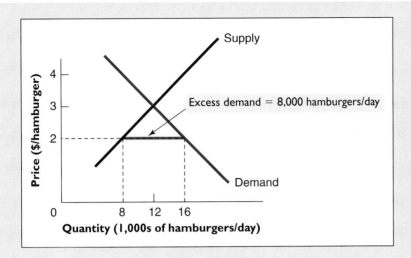

FIGURE 4.5
Excess Demand.
When price lies below the equilibrium price, there is excess demand, the difference between quantity demanded and quantity supplied.

hamburgers than buyers wish to buy, sellers have an incentive to take whatever steps they can to increase their sales. The simplest strategy available to them is to cut their price slightly. Thus, if one seller reduced his price from $4 to, say, $3.95 per hamburger, he would attract many of the buyers who had been paying $4 for hamburgers supplied by other sellers. Those sellers, to recover their lost business, would then have an incentive to match the price cut. But notice that if all sellers lowered their prices to $3.95, there would still be considerable excess supply in the hamburger market. So sellers would face continuing incentives to cut their prices. This pressure to cut prices will not go away until the price falls all the way to $3.

Conversely, suppose that price starts out less than the equilibrium price, say, $2 per hamburger. This time it is buyers who are dissatisfied. A person who can't get all the hamburgers she wants at a price of $2 has an incentive to offer a higher price, hoping to obtain hamburgers that would otherwise have been sold to other buyers. And sellers, for their part, will be only too happy to post higher prices as long as queues of dissatisfied buyers remain.

The upshot is that price has a tendency to gravitate to its equilibrium level under conditions of either excess supply or excess demand. And when price reaches its equilibrium level, both buyers and sellers are satisfied in the technical sense of being able to buy or sell precisely the amounts they choose.

We emphasize that the mere fact that buyers and sellers are satisfied in this sense does not mean that private markets automatically result in the best of all possible worlds. For example, a poor person may be satisfied with the one hamburger he chooses to buy each day at a price of $3, but only in the sense that he *can't* buy a second hamburger without sacrificing other urgent purchases.

Social reformers often fail to understand, however, that the laws of supply and demand cannot simply be repealed by an act of the legislature. And when legislators attempt to prevent markets from reaching their equilibrium prices and quantities, they almost always do more harm than good.

RENT CONTROLS RECONSIDERED

Consider again the market for rental housing units in New York City, and suppose that the demand and supply curves for one-bedroom apartments are as shown in Figure 4.6. This market, left alone, would reach an equilibrium monthly rent of $800, at which 2 million one-bedroom apartments would be rented. Both landlords and tenants would be satisfied, in the sense that they would not wish to rent either more or fewer units at that price.

FIGURE 4.6
An Unregulated Housing Market.
For the supply and demand curves shown, the equilibrium monthly rent is $800, and 2 million apartments will be rented at that price.

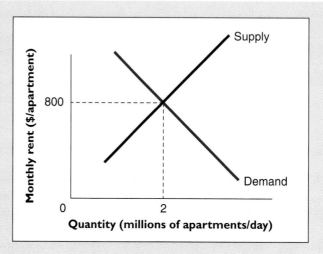

This would not necessarily mean, of course, that all is well and good. Many potential tenants, for example, might simply be unable to afford a rent of $800 per month and thus be forced to remain homeless (or to move out of the city to a cheaper location). Suppose that, acting purely out of benign motives, legislators make it unlawful for landlords to charge more than $400 per month for one-bedroom apartments. Their stated aim in enacting this law was that no person should have to remain homeless because decent housing was unaffordable.

But note in Figure 4.7 that when rents for one-bedroom apartments are prevented from rising above $400 per month, landlords are willing to supply only 1 million apartments per month, 1 million less than at the equilibrium monthly rent of $800. Note also that at the controlled rent of $400 per month, tenants want to rent 3 million one-bedroom apartments per month. (For example, many people who would have decided to live in New Jersey rather than pay $800 a month in New York will now choose to live in the city.) So when rents are prevented from rising above $400 per month, we see an excess demand for one-bedroom apartments of 2 million units each month. Put another way, the rent controls result in a housing shortage of 2 million units each month. What is more, the number of apartments actually available *declines* by 1 million units per month.

If the housing market were completely unregulated, the immediate response to such a high level of excess demand would be for rents to rise sharply. But here the law prevents them from rising above $400. Many other ways exist, however,

FIGURE 4.7
Rent Controls.
When laws prohibit rents from rising to the equilibrium level, the result is excess demand in the housing market.

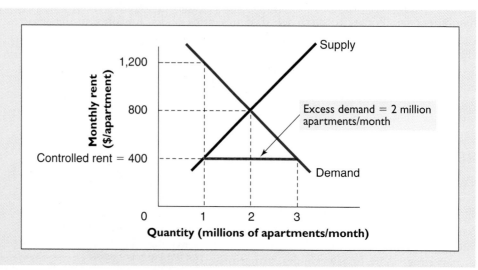

in which the pressures of excess demand can make themselves felt. For instance, owners will quickly learn that they are free to spend less on maintaining the quality of their rental units. After all, if there are scores of renters knocking at the door of each vacant apartment, a landlord has considerable room to maneuver. Leaking pipes, peeling paint, broken furnaces, and other problems are less likely to receive prompt attention—or, indeed, any attention at all—when rents are set well below market-clearing levels.

Nor are reduced availability of apartments and poorer maintenance of existing apartments the only difficulties. With an offering of only 1 million apartments per month, we see in Figure 4.7 that there are renters who would be willing to pay as much as $1,200 per month for an apartment. This pressure almost always finds ways, legal or illegal, of expressing itself. In New York City, for example, it is not uncommon to see "finder's fees" or "key deposits" as high as several thousand dollars. Owners who cannot charge a market-clearing rent for their apartments also have the option of converting them to condominiums or co-ops, which enables them to sell their assets for prices much closer to their true economic value.

Even when rent-controlled apartment owners do not hike their prices in these various ways, serious misallocations result. For instance, ill-suited roommates often remain together despite their constant bickering, because each is reluctant to reenter the housing market. Or a widow might steadfastly remain in her seven-room apartment even after her children have left home, because it is much cheaper than alternative dwellings not covered by rent control. It would be much better for all concerned if she relinquished that space to a larger family. But under rent controls, she has no economic incentive to do so.

Rent controls are not the only instance in which governments have attempted to repeal the law of supply and demand in the interest of helping the poor. During the late 1970s, for example, the federal government tried to

"If you leave me, you know, you'll never see this kind of rent again."

hold the price of gasoline below its equilibrium level out of concern that high gasoline prices imposed unacceptable hardships on low-income drivers. As with controls in the rental housing market, unintended consequences of price controls in the gasoline market made the policy an extremely costly way of trying to aid the poor. For example, gasoline shortages resulted in long lines at the pumps, a waste not only of valuable time but also of gasoline as cars sat idling for extended periods.

In their opposition to rent controls and similar measures, are economists revealing a total lack of concern for the poor? Although this claim is sometimes made by those who don't understand the issues, or who stand to benefit in some way from government regulations, there is little justification for it. *Economists simply realize that there are much more effective ways to help poor people than to give them apartments and other goods at artificially low prices.*

One straightforward approach would be to give the poor additional income and let them decide for themselves how to spend it. True, there are also practical difficulties involved in transferring additional purchasing power into the hands of the poor—most important, the difficulty of targeting cash to the genuinely needy without weakening others' incentives to fend for themselves. But there are practical ways to overcome this difficulty. For example, for far less than the waste caused by price controls, the government could afford generous subsidies to the wages of the working poor and could sponsor a generous program of public-service employment for those who are unable to find jobs in the private sector.

Regulations that peg prices below equilibrium levels have far-reaching effects on market outcomes. The following exercise asks you to consider what happens when a price control is established at a level above the equilibrium price.

EXERCISE 4.1

In the rental housing market whose demand and supply curves are shown below, what will be the effect of a law that prevents rents from rising above $1,200 per month?

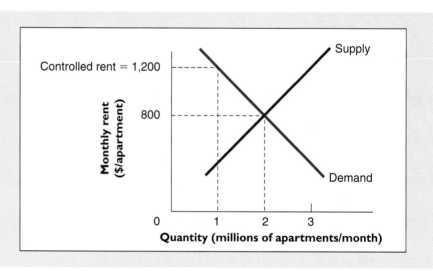

HAMBURGER PRICE CONTROLS?

The sources of the contrast between the rent-controlled housing market and the largely unregulated food markets in New York City can be seen more vividly by trying to imagine what would happen if concern for the poor led the city's leaders to implement price controls on hamburgers. Suppose, for example, that the supply and demand curves for hamburger are as shown in Figure 4.8 and that the city imposes a **price ceiling** of $2 per hamburger, making it unlawful to charge more than $2 for a hamburger. At that price, buyers want to buy 16,000 hamburgers per day, but sellers want to sell only 8,000.

price ceiling a maximum allowable price, specified by law

At a price of $2 per hamburger, every Burger King, every McDonald's, and every other fast-food restaurant in the city will have long queues of buyers trying unsuccessfully to buy hamburgers. Frustrated buyers will behave rudely to clerks, who will respond in kind. Friends of restaurant managers will begin to

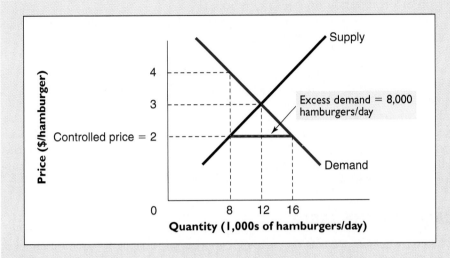

FIGURE 4.8
Price Controls in the Hamburger Market.
A price ceiling below the equilibrium price of hamburgers would result in excess demand for hamburgers.

get preferential treatment. Devious pricing strategies will begin to emerge (such as the $2 hamburger sold in combination with a $2 slice of pickle). Hamburgers will be made from poorer-quality ingredients. Rumors will begin to circulate about sources of black market hamburgers. And so on.

The very idea of not being able to buy a hamburger seems absurd, yet precisely such things happen routinely in markets in which prices are held below the equilibrium levels. For example, in communist countries (prior to their collapse) it was considered normal for people to stand in line for hours to buy basic goods, while the politically connected had first choice of those goods that were available.

RECAP **MARKETS AND PRICES**

The *market* for a good consists of the actual and potential buyers and sellers of that good. For any given price, the *supply curve* shows the total quantity that suppliers of the good would be willing to sell, and the *demand curve* shows the total quantity that demanders would be willing to buy. Suppliers are willing to sell more at higher prices (supply curves slope upward) and demanders are willing to buy less at higher prices (demand curves slope downward).

Market equilibrium, the situation in which all buyers and sellers are satisfied with their respective quantities at the market price, occurs at the intersection of the supply and demand curves. The corresponding price and quantity are called the *equilibrium price* and the *equilibrium quantity*.

Unless prevented by regulation, prices and quantities are driven toward their equilibrium values by the actions of buyers and sellers. If the price is initially too high, resulting in excess supply, dissatisfied sellers will cut their price to sell more. If the price is initially too low, resulting in excess demand, competition among buyers drives the price upward. This process continues until equilibrium is reached.

MARKETS AND SOCIAL WELFARE

Markets represent a highly effective system of allocating resources. When a market for a good is in equilibrium, the equilibrium price conveys important information to potential suppliers about the value that potential demanders place on that good. At the same time, the equilibrium price informs potential demanders about the opportunity cost of supplying the good. This rapid, two-way transmission of information is the reason that markets can coordinate an activity as complex as supplying New York City with food and drink, even though no one person or organization oversees the process.

But are the prices and quantities determined in market equilibrium socially optimal in the sense of maximizing total economic surplus? That is, does equilibrium in unregulated markets always maximize the difference between the total benefits and total costs experienced by market participants? As we see in this section, the answer is "it depends": A market that is out of equilibrium, such as the rent-controlled New York housing market, always creates opportunities for individuals to arrange transactions that will increase their individual economic surplus. However, a market for a good that is in equilibrium maximizes total, societywide economic surplus only when the supply and demand curves in the market fully reflect the costs and benefits associated with the production and consumption of that good.

CASH ON THE TABLE

When a regulation prevents the price of a good from reaching its equilibrium level, it unnecessarily reduces the total economic surplus (economic benefit less opportunity cost) available for buyers and sellers. For example, the demand curve in Figure 4.8 tells us that, with only 8,000 hamburgers being sold, there are buyers who are willing to pay $4 for additional hamburgers. The supply curve, in turn, tells us that the cost of producing additional hamburgers is only $2. The difference—$2 per hamburger—is the additional economic surplus that would result if an additional hamburger were produced and sold. One sold at a price of $3, for example, would result in an additional $1 of economic surplus for both buyer and seller.

When a market is out of equilibrium, it is always possible to identify mutually beneficial exchanges. When people have failed to take advantage of all mutually beneficial exchanges, we often say that there is "cash on the table"—the economist's metaphor for unexploited opportunities. When the price in a market is below the equilibrium price, there is cash on the table, because it will always be possible for a supplier to produce an additional unit at a cost that is lower than buyers are willing to pay for it. In the absence of a law preventing buyers from paying more than $2 per hamburger, restaurant owners would quickly raise their prices and expand their production until the equilibrium price of $3 per hamburger was reached. At that price, buyers would be able to get precisely the 12,000 hamburgers they want to buy each day. All mutually beneficial opportunities for exchange would have been exploited, leaving no more cash on the table.

Buyers and sellers in the marketplace have an uncanny ability to detect the presence of cash on the table. It is almost as if unexploited opportunities give off some exotic scent that sets off neurochemical explosions in the olfactory centers of their brains. The desire to scrape cash off the table and into their pockets is what drives sellers in each of New York City's thousands of individual food markets to work diligently to meet their customers' demands. That they succeed to a far higher degree than participants in the city's rent-controlled housing market is plainly evident. Whatever flaws it might have, the market system moves with considerably greater speed and agility than any centralized allocation mechanisms yet devised. But as we emphasize in the following section, this does not mean that markets *always* lead to the greatest good for all.

SMART FOR ONE, DUMB FOR ALL

The **efficient quantity** of any good is the quantity that maximizes the total economic surplus that results from producing and consuming the good. From the cost-benefit principle, we know that we should keep expanding production of the good as long as its marginal benefit is at least as great as its marginal cost. This means that the efficient quantity is that level for which the marginal cost and marginal benefit of the good are the same.

When the quantity of a good is less than the efficient quantity, a rearrangement boosting its production will increase total economic surplus. By the same token, when the quantity of a good exceeds the efficient quantity, reducing its production will increase total economic surplus. **Economic efficiency, or efficiency,** occurs when all goods and services in the economy are produced and consumed at levels that produce the maximum economic surplus for society.

Efficiency is an important social goal. Failure to achieve efficiency means that total economic surplus is smaller than it could have been. Movements toward efficiency make the total economic pie larger, making it possible for everyone to have a larger slice. The importance of efficiency will be a recurring theme as we move forward, and we state it here as one of the core principles:

The Efficiency Principle: Efficiency is an important social goal, because when the economic pie grows larger, everyone can have a larger slice.

Is the market equilibrium quantity of a good efficient? That is, does it maximize the total economic surplus received by participants in the market for that good? When the private market for a given good is in equilibrium, we can say that the cost *to the seller* of producing an additional unit of the good is the same as the benefit *to the buyer* of having an additional unit. If all costs of producing the good are borne directly by sellers, and if all benefits from the good accrue directly to buyers, it follows that the market equilibrium quantity of the good will equate the marginal cost and marginal benefit of the good. And this implies that the equilibrium quantity also maximizes total economic surplus.

But sometimes the production of a good entails costs that fall on people other than those who sell the good. This will be true, for instance, for goods whose production generates significant levels of environmental pollution. As extra units of these goods are produced, the extra pollution harms other people besides sellers. In the market equilibrium for such goods, the benefit *to buyers* of the last good produced is, as before, equal to the cost incurred by sellers to produce that good. But since producing that good also imposed pollution costs on others, we know that the *full* marginal cost of the last unit produced—the seller's private marginal cost plus the marginal pollution cost borne by others—must be higher than the benefit of the last unit produced. So in this case the market equilibrium quantity of the good will be higher than the socially optimal quantity. Total economic surplus would be higher if output of the good were lower. Yet neither sellers nor buyers have any incentive to alter their behavior.

Another possibility is that people other than those who buy the good may receive significant benefits from it. For instance, when a beekeeper adds an additional hive to his apiary, his neighbor's apple orchard yields a larger crop because of the higher levels of pollination caused by the bees from the extra hive. From the perspective of society as a whole, the best thing to do would be to keep adding hives until their marginal cost became equal to their marginal benefit. The marginal benefit of a hive is the value of the extra honey *plus* the value of the extra apples. Private beekeepers, however, will keep adding hives only up to the point that the cost of an extra hive is equal to the revenue from the extra honey. In this case, then, the market equilibrium quantity of beehives will be smaller than the quantity that maximizes total economic surplus. Yet individual beekeepers and individual consumers of honey have no incentive to alter their behavior.

efficient quantity the efficient quantity of a good is the quantity that results in the maximum possible economic surplus from producing and consuming the good

efficiency, or economic efficiency condition that occurs when all goods and services are produced and consumed at their respective socially optimal levels

Situations like the ones just discussed provide examples of behaviors that we may call "smart for one but dumb for all." In each case, the individual actors are behaving rationally. They are pursuing their goals as best they can, and yet there remain unexploited opportunities for gain from the point of view of the whole society. The difficulty is that these opportunities cannot be exploited by individuals acting alone. In subsequent chapters we will see how people can often organize collectively to exploit such opportunities. For now, we simply summarize this discussion in the form of the following core principle:

The Equilibrium Principle: A market in equilibrium leaves no unexploited opportunities for individuals but may not exploit all gains achievable through collective action.

For the remainder of this chapter, we will confine our attention to markets in which the supply and demand curves capture all relevant costs and benefits. Our focus will be on using supply and demand analysis to predict and explain changes in equilibrium prices and quantities.

RECAP   **MARKETS AND SOCIAL WELFARE**

When the supply and demand curves for a good reflect all significant costs and benefits associated with the production and consumption of that good, the market equilibrium will result in the largest possible economic surplus. But if people other than buyers benefit from the good, or if people other than sellers bear costs because of it, rational behavior on the part of individuals need not maximize economic surplus.

PREDICTING AND EXPLAINING CHANGES IN PRICES AND QUANTITIES

If we know how the factors that govern supply and demand curves are changing, we can make informed predictions about how prices and the corresponding quantities will change. But when describing changing circumstances in the marketplace, we must take care to recognize some important terminological distinctions. For example, we must distinguish between the meanings of the seemingly similar expressions **change in the quantity demanded** and **change in demand**. When we speak of a "change in the quantity demanded," we mean the change in quantity that people wish to buy that occurs in response to a change in price. For instance, Figure 4.9(a) depicts an increase in the quantity demanded that occurs in response to a reduction in the price of tuna. When the price falls from $5 to $4 per can, the quantity demanded rises from 2,000 to 4,000 cans per day. By contrast, when we speak of a "change in demand," we mean a *shift in the entire demand curve*. For example, Figure 4.9(b) depicts an increase in demand, meaning that at every price the quantity demanded is higher than before. In summary, a change in the quantity demanded refers to a movement *along* the demand curve, and a change in demand means a *shift* of the entire curve.

A similar terminological distinction applies on the supply side of the market. A **change in supply** means a shift in the entire supply curve, whereas **a change in the quantity supplied** refers to a movement along the supply curve.

Alfred Marshall's supply and demand model is one of the most useful tools of the economic naturalist. Once we understand the forces that govern the placements of supply and demand curves, we are suddenly in a position to make sense of a host of interesting observations in the world around us.

change in the quantity demanded a movement along the demand curve that occurs in response to a change in price

change in demand a shift of the entire demand curve

change in supply a shift of the entire supply curve

change in the quantity supplied a movement along the supply curve that occurs in response to a change in price

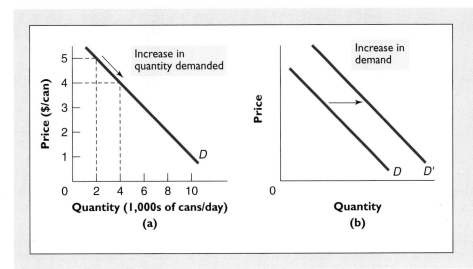

FIGURE 4.9
An Increase in the Quantity Demanded versus an Increase in Demand.
(a) An increase in quantity demanded describes a downward movement along the demand curve as price falls. (b) An increase in demand describes an outward shift of the demand curve.

SHIFTS IN THE SUPPLY CURVE

To get a better feel for how the supply and demand model enables us to predict and explain price and quantity movements, it is helpful to begin with a few simple examples. Because the supply curve is based on costs of production, anything that changes production costs will shift the supply curve and hence will result in a new equilibrium quantity and price.

What will happen to the equilibrium price and quantity of skateboards if the price of fiberglass, an ingredient for making skateboards, rises?

EXAMPLE 4.1

Suppose the initial supply and demand curves for skateboards are as shown by the curves *S* and *D* in Figure 4.10, resulting in an equilibrium price and quantity of $60 per skateboard and 1,000 skateboards per month, respectively. Since fiberglass is one of the ingredients used to produce skateboards, the effect of an increase in the price of fiberglass is to raise the cost of producing skateboards. How will this affect the supply curve of skateboards? Recall that the supply curve is upward-sloping because when the price of skateboards is low, only those potential sellers whose opportunity cost of making skateboards is low can sell boards profitably, whereas at higher prices, those with higher opportunity costs can also enter the market profitably (again, the low-hanging-fruit principle). So if the cost

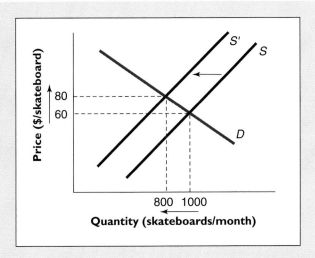

FIGURE 4.10
The Effect on the Skateboard Market of an Increase in the Price of Fiberglass.
When input prices rise, supply shifts left, causing equilibrium price to rise and equilibrium quantity to fall.

of one of the ingredients used to produce skateboards rises, the number of potential sellers who can profitably sell skateboards at any given price will fall. And this, in turn, implies a leftward shift in the supply curve for skateboards. (Note that a "leftward shift" in a supply curve can also be viewed as an "upward shift" in the same curve. We will use these expressions to mean exactly the same thing.) The new supply curve (after the price of fiberglass rises) is the curve labeled S' in Figure 4.10.

Does an increase in the cost of fiberglass have any effect on the demand curve for skateboards? The demand curve tells us how many skateboards buyers wish to purchase at each price. Any given buyer is willing to purchase a skateboard if his or her reservation price for it exceeds its market price. And since each buyer's reservation price, which is based on the benefits of owning a skateboard, does not depend on the price of fiberglass, there should be no shift in the demand curve for skateboards.

In Figure 4.10, we can see what happens when the supply curve shifts leftward and the demand curve remains unchanged. For the illustrative supply curve shown, the new equilibrium price of skateboards, $80, is higher than the original price, and the new equilibrium quantity, 800 per month, is lower than the original quantity. (These new equilibrium values are merely illustrative. There is insufficient information provided in the example to determine their exact values.)

The effects on equilibrium price and quantity run in the opposite direction whenever marginal costs of production decline, as illustrated in the next example.

EXAMPLE 4.2 **What will happen to the equilibrium price and quantity of new houses if the wage rate of carpenters falls?**

Suppose the initial supply and demand curves for new houses are as shown by the curves S and D in Figure 4.11, resulting in an equilibrium price of $120,000 per house and an equilibrium quantity of 40 houses per month. A decline in the wage rate of carpenters reduces the marginal cost of making new houses, and this means that, for any given price of houses, more builders can profitably serve the market than before. Diagrammatically, this means a rightward shift in the supply curve of houses, from S to S'. (A "rightward shift" in the supply curve can also be described as a "downward shift.")

Does a decrease in the wage rate of carpenters have any effect on the demand curve for houses? The demand curve tells us how many houses buyers wish to purchase at each price. Because carpenters are now earning less than before,

FIGURE 4.11
The Effect on the Market for New Houses of a Decline in Carpenters' Wage Rates. When input prices fall, supply shifts right, causing equilibrium price to fall and equilibrium quantity to rise.

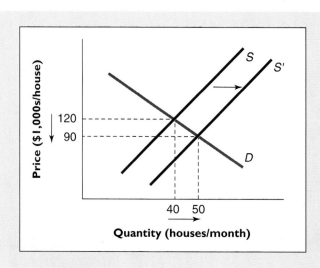

the maximum amount that they are willing to pay for houses may fall, which would imply a leftward shift in the demand curve for houses. But because carpenters make up only a tiny fraction of all potential home buyers, we may assume that this shift is insignificant. Thus, a reduction in carpenters' wages produces a significant rightward shift in the supply curve of houses, but only a negligible shift in the demand curve. We see from Figure 4.11 that the new equilibrium price, $90,000 per house, is lower than the original price, and the new equilibrium quantity, 50 houses per month, is higher than the original quantity.

Both Examples 4.1 and 4.2 involved changes in the cost of an ingredient, or input, in the production of the good in question—fiberglass in the production of skateboards and carpenters' labor in the production of houses. As the following example illustrates, supply curves also shift when technology changes.

Why do Ph.D. dissertations and book manuscripts go through so many more revisions today than in the 1970s?

Graduate students in the dark days before word processors were in widespread use could not make even minor revisions to their Ph.D. dissertations without having to retype their entire manuscripts from scratch. The availability of word-processing technology has, of course, radically changed the picture. Instead of having to retype the entire draft, now only the changes need be entered.

In Figure 4.12, the curves labeled *S* and *D* depict the supply and demand curves for revisions in the days before word processing, and the curve *S'* depicts the supply curve for revisions today. As the diagram shows, the result is not only a sharp decline in the price per revision but also a corresponding increase in the equilibrium number of revisions.

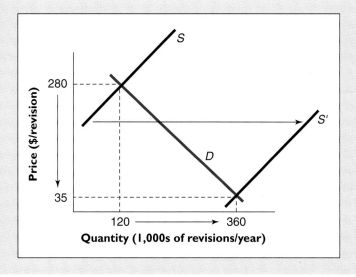

FIGURE 4.12
The Effect of Technical Change on the Market for Manuscript Revisions.
When a new technology reduces the cost of production, supply shifts right, causing equilibrium price to fall and equilibrium quantity to rise.

Changes in input prices and technology are two of the most important factors that give rise to shifts in supply curves. In the case of agricultural commodities, weather may be another important factor, with favorable conditions shifting the supply curves of such products to the right and unfavorable conditions shifting them to the left. (Weather may also affect the supply curves of nonagricultural products through its effects on the national transportation system.) Expectations of future changes in these factors may also shift current supply curves, as when the expectation of poor crops from a current drought causes suppliers to withhold supplies from existing stocks in the hope of selling at higher prices in the future.

SHIFTS IN DEMAND

The preceding examples involved changes that gave rise to shifts in supply curves. Next, we'll look at what happens when demand curves shift. In the following example, the shift in demand results from events outside the particular market itself.

EXAMPLE 4.3

What will happen to the equilibrium price and quantity of tennis balls if court rental fees decline?

complements two goods are complements in consumption if an increase in the price of one causes a leftward shift in the demand curve for the other

Let the initial supply and demand curves for tennis balls be as shown by the curves S and D in Figure 4.13, where the resulting equilibrium price and quantity are $1 per ball and 40 million balls per month, respectively. Tennis courts and tennis balls are what economists call **complements,** goods that are more valuable when used in combination than when used alone. Tennis balls, for example, would be of little value if there were no tennis courts on which to play. (Tennis balls would still have *some* value even without courts—for example, to the parents who pitch them to their children for batting practice.) As tennis courts become cheaper to use, people will respond by playing more tennis, and this will increase their demand for tennis balls. A decline in court rental fees will thus shift

FIGURE 4.13
The Effect on the Market for Tennis Balls of a Decline in Court Rental Fees.
When the price of a complement falls, demand shifts right, causing equilibrium price and quantity to rise.

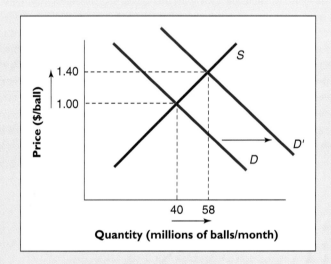

the demand curve for tennis balls rightward to D'. (A "rightward shift" of a demand curve can also be described as an "upward shift.")

Note in Figure 4.13 that for the illustrative demand shift shown, the new equilibrium price of tennis balls, $1.40, is higher than the original price, and the new equilibrium quantity, 58 million balls per month, is higher than the original quantity.

EXAMPLE 4.4

What will happen to the equilibrium price and quantity of overnight letter delivery service as more people gain access to the Internet?

substitutes two goods are substitutes in consumption if an increase in the price of one causes a rightward shift in the demand curve for the other

Suppose that the initial supply and demand curves for overnight letter deliveries are as shown by the curves S and D in Figure 4.14 and that the resulting equilibrium price and quantity are denoted P and Q. E-mail messages and overnight letters are examples of what economists call **substitutes,** meaning that, in many applications at least, the two serve similar functions for people. (Many noneconomists would call them substitutes, too. Economists don't *always* choose obscure terms for important concepts!) When two goods or services are substitutes, a decrease in the effective price of one will cause a leftward shift in the demand curve for the other. (A "leftward shift" in a demand curve can also be described as a "downward shift.") An increase in Internet access is, in effect, a decline in the price of a substitute for overnight delivery for affected users. Diagrammatically, this means a leftward shift in the demand curve for overnight delivery service to D' in Figure 4.14.

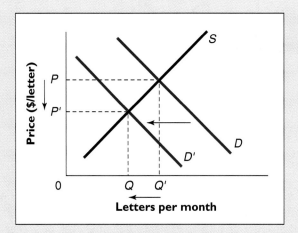

FIGURE 4.14
The Effect on the Market for Overnight Letter Delivery of a Decline in the Price of Internet Access.
When the price of a substitute falls, demand shifts left, causing equilibrium price and quantity to fall.

As the figure shows, both the new equilibrium price P' and the new equilibrium quantity Q' are lower than the initial values P and Q. More widespread Internet access probably won't put Federal Express and UPS out of business, but it will definitely cost them many customers.

To summarize, economists define goods as substitutes if an increase in the price of one causes a rightward shift in the demand curve for the other. By contrast, goods are complements if an increase in the price of one causes a leftward shift in the demand curve for the other.

The concepts of substitutes and complements enable you to answer questions like the one posed in the following exercise.

EXERCISE 4.2

How will a decline in airfares affect bus fares and the price of hotel rooms in resort communities?

Demand curves are shifted not just by changes in the prices of substitutes and complements but also by other factors that change the amounts that people are willing to pay for a given good or service. One of the most important such factors is income.

When the federal government implements a large pay increase for government employees, why do rents for apartments located near Washington Metro Stations go up relative to rents for apartments located far away from Metro Stations?

For the citizens of Washington, D.C., a substantial proportion of whom are government employees, it is more convenient to live in an apartment located 1 block from the nearest subway station than to live in one that is 10 blocks away. These conveniently located apartments thus command relatively high rents. Suppose the initial demand and supply curves for such apartments are as shown in Figure 4.15. Following a federal pay raise, some government employees who live in less convenient apartments will be willing and able to use part of their extra income to bid for more conveniently located apartments, and those who already live in such apartments will be willing and able to pay more to keep them. The effect of the pay raise

ECONOMIC
NATURALIST
4.2

FIGURE 4.15
The Effect of a Federal Pay Raise on the Rent for Conveniently Located Apartments in Washington, D.C.
An increase in income shifts demand for a normal good to the right, causing equilibrium price and quantity to rise.

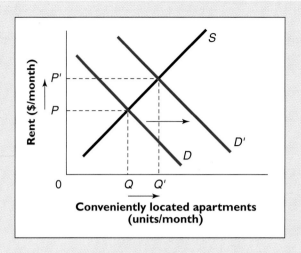

is thus to shift the demand curve for conveniently located apartments to the right, as indicated by the demand curve labeled D' in Figure 4.15. As a result, both the equilibrium price and quantity of such apartments, P' and Q', will be higher than before.

It might seem natural to ask how there could be an increase in the number of conveniently located apartments, which might appear to be fixed by the constraints of geography. But one must never underestimate the ingenuity of sellers when they confront an opportunity to make money by supplying more of something that people want. For example, if rents rose sufficiently, some landlords might respond by converting warehouse space to residential use. Or perhaps people with cars and no pressing need to live near a subway station might sell their apartments to landlords, thereby freeing them up for people eager to rent them.

When incomes increase, the demand curves for most goods will behave like the demand curve for conveniently located apartments, and in recognition of that fact, economists have chosen to call such goods **normal goods.**

normal good a good whose demand curve shifts rightward when the incomes of buyers increase

Nor all goods are normal goods, however. In fact, the demand curves for some goods actually shift leftward when income goes up, and such goods are called **inferior goods.**

When would having more money tend to make you want to buy less of something? In general, this will happen in the case of goods for which there exist attractive substitutes that sell for only slightly higher prices. Apartments in an unsafe, inconveniently located neighborhood are an example. Most residents would choose to move out of such neighborhoods as soon as they could afford to, which means that an increase in income would cause the demand for such apartments to shift leftward.

inferior good a good whose demand curve shifts leftward when the incomes of buyers increase

Ground beef with high fat content is another example of an inferior good. For health reasons, most people prefer grades of meat with low fat content, and when they do buy high-fat meats it is usually a sign of budgetary pressure. When people in this situation receive higher incomes, they usually switch quickly to leaner grades of meat.

EXERCISE 4.3

Normal and inferior goods were defined in terms of how their demand curves were affected by an increase in income. How will a *decrease* in income affect the demand for a normal good? An inferior good?

Preferences, or tastes, are another important factor that determines whether a given good will meet the cost-benefit test. Steven Spielberg's films *Jurassic Park* and *The Lost World* appeared to kindle a powerful, if previously latent, preference among children for toy dinosaurs. In the wake of these films, the demand for such toys shifted sharply to the right. And the same children who couldn't find enough dinosaur toys suddenly seemed to lose interest in toy designs involving horses and other present-day animals, whose respective demand curves shifted sharply to the left.

FOUR SIMPLE RULES

For supply and demand curves that have the conventional slopes (upward-sloping for supply curves, downward-sloping for demand curves), the preceding examples illustrate the four basic rules that govern how shifts in supply and demand affect equilibrium prices and quantities. These rules are summarized in Figure 4.16.

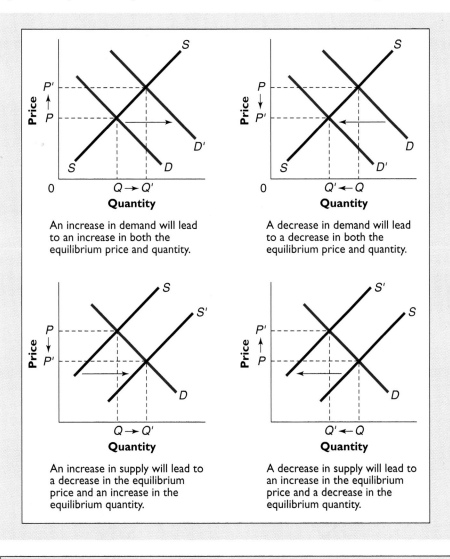

FIGURE 4.16
Four Rules Governing the Effects of Supply and Demand Shifts.

An increase in demand will lead to an increase in both the equilibrium price and quantity.

A decrease in demand will lead to a decrease in both the equilibrium price and quantity.

An increase in supply will lead to a decrease in the equilibrium price and an increase in the equilibrium quantity.

A decrease in supply will lead to an increase in the equilibrium price and a decrease in the equilibrium quantity.

RECAP **FACTORS CAUSING AN INCREASE IN SUPPLY (SUPPLY CURVE SHIFTS RIGHT)**

1. A decrease in the cost of materials, labor, or other inputs used in the production of the good or service
2. An improvement in technology that reduces the cost of producing the good or service

When these factors move in the opposite direction, supply will shift left.

> **RECAP FACTORS CAUSING AN INCREASE IN DEMAND (DEMAND CURVE SHIFTS RIGHT)**
>
> 1. A decrease in the price of complements to the good or service
> 2. An increase in the price of substitutes for the good or service
> 3. An increase in income (for a normal good)
> 4. An increased preference by demanders for the good or service
> 5. An increase in the population of potential buyers
>
> When these factors move in the opposite direction, demand will shift left.

The qualitative rules summarized in Figure 4.16 hold for supply or demand shifts of any magnitude, provided the curves have their conventional slopes. But as the next example demonstrates, when both supply and demand curves shift at the same time, the direction in which equilibrium price or quantity changes will depend on the relative magnitudes of the shifts.

EXAMPLE 4.5

How do shifts in *both* demand and supply affect equilibrium quantities and prices?

What will happen to the equilibrium price and quantity in the corn tortilla chip market if both the following events occur: (1) researchers discover that the oils in which tortilla chips are fried are harmful to human health, and (2) the price of corn harvesting equipment falls?

The discovery regarding the health effects of the oils will shift the demand for tortilla chips to the left, because many people who once bought chips in the belief that they were healthful will now switch to other foods. The decline in the price of harvesting equipment will shift the supply of chips to the right, because additional farmers will now find it profitable to enter the corn market. In Figure 4.17(a) and (b), the original supply and demand curves are denoted by S and D, while the new curves are denoted by S' and D'. Note that in both parts, the shifts lead to a decline in the equilibrium price of chips.

But note also that the effect of the shifts on equilibrium quantity cannot be determined without knowing their relative magnitudes. Taken separately, the demand shift causes a decline in equilibrium quantity, whereas the supply shift causes an increase in equilibrium quantity. The net effect of the two shifts thus depends on which of the individual effects is larger. In Figure 4.17(a), the demand shift dominates, so equilibrium quantity declines. In Figure 4.17(b), the supply shift dominates, so equilibrium quantity goes up.

FIGURE 4.17
The Effects of Simultaneous Shifts in Supply and Demand.
When demand shifts left and supply shifts right, equilibrium price falls, but equilibrium quantity may either rise [part (b)] or fall [part (a)].

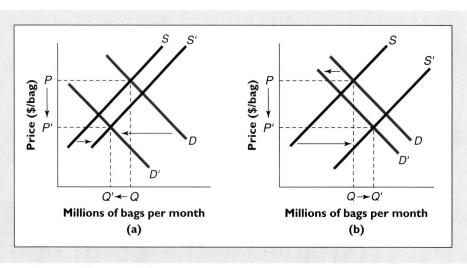

The following exercise asks you to consider a simple variation on the problem posed in Example 4.5.

EXERCISE 4.4

What will happen to the equilibrium price and quantity in the corn tortilla chip market if both the following events occur: (1) researchers discover that a vitamin found in corn helps protect against cancer and heart disease; and (2) a swarm of locusts destroys part of the corn crop?

Why do the prices of some goods, like airline tickets to Europe, go up during the months of heaviest consumption, while others, like sweet corn, go down?

Seasonal price movements for airline tickets are primarily the result of seasonal variations in demand. Thus, ticket prices to Europe are highest during the summer months because the demand for tickets is highest during those months, as shown in Figure 4.18(a) (where the w and s subscripts denote winter and summer values, respectively).

By contrast, seasonal price movements for sweet corn are primarily the result of seasonal variations in supply. The price of sweet corn is lowest in the summer months because its supply is highest during those months [Figure 4.18(b)].

ECONOMIC NATURALIST 4.3

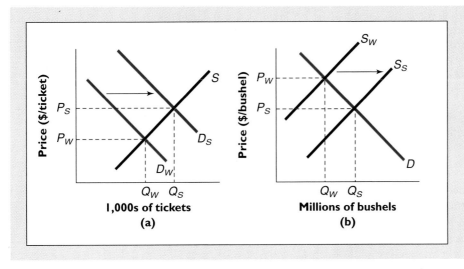

FIGURE 4.18
Seasonal Variation in the Air Travel and Corn Markets.
(a) Prices are highest during the period of heaviest consumption when heavy consumption is the result of high demand. (b) Prices are lowest during the period of heaviest consumption when heavy consumption is the result of high supply.

■ **SUMMARY** ■

- Eighteenth-century economists tried to explain differences in the prices of goods by focusing on differences in their cost of production. But this approach cannot explain why a conveniently located house sells for more than one that is less conveniently located. Early nineteenth-century economists tried to explain price differences by focusing on differences in what buyers were willing to pay. But this approach cannot explain why the price of a lifesaving appendectomy is less than that of a surgical facelift.

- Alfred Marshall's model of supply and demand explains why neither cost of production nor value to the purchaser (as measured by willingness to pay) is, by itself, sufficient to

explain why some goods are cheap and others are expensive. To explain variations in price, we must examine the interaction of cost and willingness to pay. As we saw in this chapter, goods differ in price because of differences in their respective supply and demand curves.

- The supply curve is an upward-sloping line that tells what quantity sellers will offer at any given price. The demand curve is a downward-sloping line that tells what quantity buyers will demand at any given price. Market equilibrium occurs when the quantity buyers demand at the market price is exactly the same as the quantity that sellers offer. The equilibrium price-quantity pair is the one at which the demand and supply curves intersect. In equilibrium, market price measures both the value of the last unit sold to buyers and the cost of the resources required to produce it.

- When the price of a good lies above its equilibrium value, there is an excess supply, or surplus, of that good. Excess supply motivates sellers to cut their prices, and price continues to fall until the equilibrium price is reached. When price lies below its equilibrium value, there is excess demand, or shortage. With excess demand, dissatisfied buyers are motivated to offer higher prices, and the upward pressure on prices persists until equilibrium is reached. A remarkable feature of the market system is that, relying only on the tendency of people to respond in self-interested ways to market price signals, it somehow manages to coordinate the actions of literally billions of buyers and sellers worldwide. When shortages and surpluses do occur, they tend to be small and brief, except in markets where regulations prevent full adjustment of prices.

- When the supply and demand curves for a good reflect all significant costs and benefits associated with the production and consumption of that good, the market equilibrium price will guide people to produce and consume the quantity of the good that results in the largest possible economic surplus. This conclusion does not apply if others, beside buyers, benefit from the good (as when orchard owners benefit from beehives), or if others besides sellers bear costs because of the good (as when its production generates pollution). In such cases, rational behavior on the part of individuals does not result in the greatest gain for all.

- The efficiency of markets in allocating resources does not eliminate social concerns about how goods and services are distributed among different people. For example, we often lament the fact many buyers enter the market with too little income to buy even the most basic goods and services. Concern for the well-being of the poor has motivated many

governments to intervene in a variety of ways to alter the outcomes of market forces. Sometimes these interventions take the form of laws that peg prices below their equilibrium levels. Such laws almost invariably generate harmful, if unintended, consequences. Programs like rent-control laws, for example, lead to severe housing shortages, black marketeering, and a rapid deterioration of the relationship between landlords and tenants.

- If the difficulty is that the poor have too little money, the best solution is to discover ways of boosting their incomes directly. The law of supply and demand cannot be repealed by a legislature. But legislatures do have the capacity to alter the underlying forces that govern the shape and position of supply and demand schedules.

- The basic supply and demand model is a primary tool of the economic naturalist. Changes in the equilibrium price of a good, and in the amount of it traded in the marketplace, can be predicted on the basis of shifts in its supply or demand curves. The following four rules hold for any good with a downward-sloping demand curve and an upward-sloping supply curve:

1. An increase in demand will lead to an increase in equilibrium price and quantity.

2. A reduction in demand will lead to a reduction in equilibrium price and quantity.

3. An increase in supply will lead to a reduction in equilibrium price and an increase in equilibrium quantity.

4. A decrease in supply will lead to an increase in equilibrium price and a reduction in equilibrium quantity.

- Incomes, tastes, population, and the prices of substitutes and complements are among the factors that shift demand schedules. Supply schedules, in turn, are primarily governed by such factors as technology, input prices, and, for agricultural products, the weather.

■ CORE PRINCIPLES ■

The Efficiency Principle
Efficiency is an important social goal, because when the economic pie grows larger, everyone can have a larger slice.

The Equilibrium Principle
A market in equilibrium leaves no unexploited opportunities for individuals but may not exploit all gains achievable through collective action.

■ KEY TERMS ■

change in demand (88)
change in quantity demanded (88)
change in quantity supplied (88)
change in supply (88)
complements (92)

demand curve (78)
economic efficiency (87)
efficiency (87)
efficient quantity (87)
equilibrium (79)

equilibrium price (79)
equilibrium quantity (79)
excess demand (80)
excess supply (80)
inferior good (94)

market (76)
market equilibrium (80)
normal good (94)

price ceiling (85)
shortage (80)
substitutes (92)

supply curve (77)
surplus (80)

■ REVIEW QUESTIONS ■

1. Why isn't knowing how much it costs to produce a good sufficient to predict its market price?

2. Distinguish between the meaning of the expressions "change in demand" and "change in the quantity demanded."

3. Last year a government official proposed that gasoline price controls be imposed to protect the poor from rising gasoline prices. What evidence could you consult to discover whether this proposal was enacted?

4. Explain why, in unregulated markets, the equilibrium principle suggests that excess demand and excess supply tend to be fleeting.

5. Give an example of behavior you have observed that could be described as "smart for one but dumb for all."

■ PROBLEMS ■

1. State whether the following pairs of goods are complements or substitutes. (If you think a pair is ambiguous in this respect, explain why.)
   a. Tennis courts and squash courts
   b. Squash racquets and squash balls
   c. Ice cream and chocolate
   d. Cloth diapers and paper diapers

2. How would each of the following affect the U.S. market supply curve for corn?
   a. A new and improved crop rotation technique is discovered.
   b. The price of fertilizer falls.
   c. The government offers new tax breaks to farmers.
   d. A tornado sweeps through Iowa.

3. Indicate how you think each of the following would affect demand in the indicated market:
   a. An increase in family income on the demand for Adirondack vacations
   b. A study linking beef consumption to heart disease on the demand for hamburgers
   c. A relaxation of immigration laws on the demand for elementary school places
   d. An increase in the price of audiocassettes on the demand for CDs
   e. An increase in the price of CDs on the demand for CDs

4. An Arizona student claims to have spotted a UFO over the desert outside of Tucson. How will his claim affect the supply of binoculars in Tucson stores?

5. What will happen to the equilibrium price and quantity of oranges if the wages paid to farm workers rise?

6. How will an increase in the birthrate affect the equilibrium price of land?

7. What will happen to the equilibrium price and quantity of fish if it is discovered that fish oils help prevent heart disease?

8. What will happen to the equilibrium price and quantity of beef if the price of chicken feed increases?

9. Use supply and demand analysis to explain why hotel room rental rates near your campus during parents' weekend and graduation weekend might differ from the rates charged during the rest of the year.

10. How will a new law mandating an increase in required levels of automobile insurance affect the equilibrium price and quantity in the market for new automobiles?

11. Suppose the current issue of *The New York Times* reports an outbreak of mad cow disease in Nebraska, as well as the discovery of a new breed of chickens that gains more weight than existing breeds from the same amount of food. How will these developments affect the equilibrium price and quantity of chicken sold in the United States?

12. What will happen to the equilibrium quantity and price of potatoes if population increases and a new, higher yielding variety of potato plant is developed?

13. What will happen to the equilibrium price and quantity of apples if apples are discovered to help prevent colds and a fungus kills 10 percent of existing apple trees?

14. What will happen to the equilibrium quantity and price of corn if the price of butter increases and the price of fertilizer decreases?

15. Tofu was available 25 years ago only from small businesses operating in Chinese quarters of large cities. Today tofu has become popular as a high-protein health food and is widely available in supermarkets throughout the United States. At the same time, production has evolved to become factory-based using modern food-processing technologies. Draw a diagram with demand and supply curves depicting the market for tofu 25 years ago and the market for tofu today. Given the information above, what does the demand-supply model predict about changes in the volume of tofu sold in the United States between then and now? What does it predict about changes in the price of tofu?

■ ANSWERS TO IN-CHAPTER EXERCISES ■

4.1 Since landlords are permitted to charge less than the maximum rent established by rent-control laws, a law that sets the maximum rent at $1,200 will have no effect on the rents actually charged in this market, which will settle at the equilibrium value of $800 per month.

4.2 Travel by air and travel by bus are substitutes, so a decline in airfares will shift the demand for bus travel to the left, resulting in lower bus fares and fewer bus trips taken. Travel by air and the use of resort hotels are complements, so a decline in airfares will shift the demand for resort hotel rooms to the right, resulting in higher hotel rates and an increase in the number of rooms rented.

4.3 A decrease in income will shift the demand curve for a normal good to the left and will shift the demand curve for an inferior good to the right.

4.4 The vitamin discovery shifts the demand for chips to the right, and the crop losses shift the supply of chips to the left. Both shifts result in an increase in the equilibrium price of chips. But depending on the relative magnitude of the shifts, the equilibrium quantity of chips may either rise [part (a) of figure] or fall [part (b) of figure].

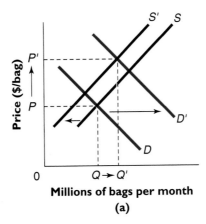

(a)

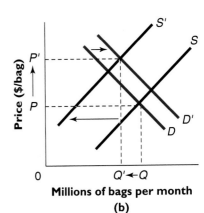

(b)

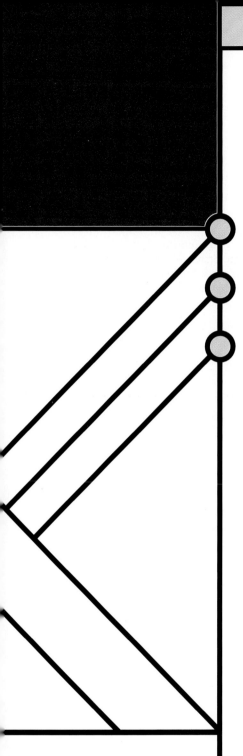

PART

2

COMPETITION AND THE INVISIBLE HAND

■

Having grasped the basic core principles of economics, you are now in a position to sharpen your understanding of how consumers and firms behave. In Part 2 our focus will be on how things work in an idealized perfectly competitive economy in which consumers are perfectly informed and no firm has market power.

In our review of supply and demand in Part 1, we asked you simply to assume the law of demand, which says that demand curves are downward-sloping. In Chapter 5 we will see that this law is a simple consequence of the fact that people spend their limited incomes in rational ways. We will also explore the concept of price elasticity, which describes the sensitivity of purchase decisions to variations in price. In Chapter 6 our focus will shift to the seller's side of the market, where our task will be to see why upward-sloping supply curves are a consequence of production decisions taken by firms whose goal is to maximize profit.

Our agenda in Chapter 7 is to develop more carefully and fully the concept of economic surplus introduced in Part 1 and to investigate the conditions under which unregulated markets generate the largest possible economic surplus. We will also explore why attempts to interfere with market outcomes often lead to unintended and undesired consequences.

Finally, in Chapter 8 we will investigate the economic forces by which the invisible hand of the marketplace guides profit-seeking firms and satisfaction-seeking consumers in ways that, to a surprising degree, serve society's ends. These forces encourage aggressive cost cutting by firms, even though the resulting gains will eventually take the form of lower prices rather than higher profits. We will also see why misunderstanding of competitive forces often results in costly errors, both in everyday decision making and in government policy.

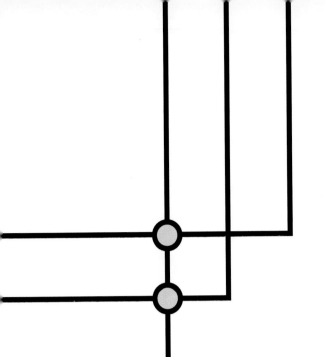

5

DEMAND: THE BENEFIT SIDE OF THE MARKET

Many illicit drug users commit crimes to finance their addiction. The connection between drugs and crime has led to calls for more vigorous efforts to stop the smuggling of illicit drugs. But can such efforts reduce the likelihood that your laptop computer will be stolen in the next month?

If attempts to reduce the supply of illicit drugs are successful, their effect will be to increase the market price of drugs. (From our basic supply and demand analysis, we can see that this increase in price is caused by a leftward shift in the supply curve for drugs.) The law of demand tells us that drug users will respond by consuming a smaller quantity of drugs. But the amount of crime drug users commit depends not on the *quantity* of drugs they consume but rather on their *total expenditure* on drugs. Depending on the specific characteristics of the demand curve for illicit drugs, a price increase might reduce total expenditure on drugs, but it could also raise total expenditure.

Suppose, for example, that extra border patrols shift the supply curve in the market for illicit drugs to the left, as shown in Figure 5.1. As a result, the equilibrium quantity of drugs would fall from 50,000 to 40,000 ounces per day, and the price of drugs would rise from $50 to $80 per ounce. The total amount spent on drugs, which was $2,500,000 per day (50,000 ounces/day times $50/ounce), would rise to $3,200,000 per day (40,000 ounces/day times $80/ounce). In this case, then, efforts to stem the supply of drugs would actually increase the likelihood of your laptop being stolen.

Other benefits from stemming the flow of illicit drugs might still outweigh the resulting increase in crime. But knowing that the policy might increase drug-related crime would clearly be useful to law enforcement authorities.

FIGURE 5.1
The Effect of Extra Border Patrols on the Market for Illicit Drugs.
Extra patrols shift supply leftward and reduce the quantity demanded but may actually increase the total amount spent on drugs.

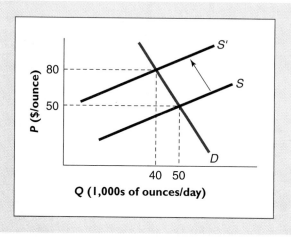

Could reducing the supply of illegal drugs cause an increase in drug-related burglaries?

Our task in this chapter will be to explore the demand side of the market in greater depth than was possible in Chapter 4. There we merely asked you to accept as an intuitively plausible claim that the quantity demanded of a good or service declines as its price rises. This relationship is known as the law of demand, and we will see how it emerges as a simple consequence of the assumption that people spend their limited incomes in rational ways. In the process, we will see more clearly the dual roles of income and substitution as factors that account for the law of demand.

We will also explore the relationship between the price for which a good sells and the total amount that consumers spend on it. In the illicit drug example just considered, the increase in price led to an increase in total spending. In many other cases, an increase in price will lead to a reduction in total spending. Why this difference? The underlying phenomenon that explains this pattern, we will see, is elasticity of demand, a measure of the extent to which quantity demanded responds to variations in price.

NEEDS, WANTS, AND THE LAW OF DEMAND

On the northern border of a large university in the East, a creek widens to form a picturesque lake, fondly remembered by generations of alumni as a popular recreation spot. Over the years, the lake gradually silted in, and by the late 1980s it had become impossible even to paddle a canoe across it. A generous alumnus then sponsored an effort to restore the lake. Heavy dredging equipment hauled out load after load of mud, and months later the lake was finally silt-free.

To mark the occasion, the university held a ceremony. Bands played, the president spoke, a chorus sang, and distinguished visitors applauded the donor's generosity. Hundreds of faculty and students turned out for the festivities. Spotting a good opportunity to promote their product, the proprietors of a local ice cream store set up a temporary stand at the water's edge, with a large sign announcing "Free Ice Cream."

Word spread. Soon scores of people were lined up waiting to try out Vanilla Almond Delight, Hazelnut Cream, and Fudge Faire. The ice cream was plentiful, and because it was free, everyone could obviously afford it. Or so it seemed. In fact, many people who wanted ice cream that day never got any. The reason, of course, was that they found waiting in a long line too steep a price.

When a good or service is scarce, it must somehow be rationed among competing users. In most markets, monetary prices perform that task. But in the case of a stand offering free ice cream, waiting time becomes the effective rationing device. Having to stand in line is a cost, no less so than having to part with some money.

This example drives home the point that although the demand curve is usually described as a relationship between the quantity demanded of a good and its monetary price, the relationship is really much more general. At bottom, the demand curve is a relationship between the quantity demanded and *all* costs—monetary and nonmonetary—associated with acquiring a good. We can thus restate the **law of demand** as follows:

The Law of Demand: **People do less of what they want to do as the cost of doing it rises.**

By stating the law of demand this way, we can see it as a direct consequence of the cost-benefit principle, which says that an activity should be pursued if (and only if) its benefits are at least as great as its costs. Recall that we measure the benefit of an activity by the highest price we'd be willing to pay to pursue it—namely, our reservation price for the activity. When the cost of an activity rises, it is more likely to exceed our reservation price, and we are therefore less likely to pursue that activity.

The law of demand applies to BMWs, cheap key rings, and "free" ice cream, not to mention compact discs, manicures, medical care, and acid-free rain. It stresses that a "cost" is the sum of *all* the sacrifices—monetary and nonmonetary, implicit and explicit—we must make to engage in an activity.

How much are you willing to pay for the latest Alanis Morisette CD? The answer will clearly depend on how you feel about her music. To Morisette's die-hard fans, buying the new release might seem absolutely essential; they'd pay a steep price indeed. But those who don't like Morisette's music may not be willing to buy it at any price.

In everyday language, we distinguish between goods and services people need and ones they merely want. For example, we might say that someone wants a ski vacation in Utah, but what he really needs is a few days off from his daily routine; or that someone wants a house with a view, but what she really needs is shelter from the elements. Likewise, since people need protein to survive, we might say a severely malnourished person needs more protein. But it would strike us as odd to say that anyone—even a malnourished person—needs more prime filet of beef, since health can be restored by consuming far less expensive sources of protein.

Economists like to emphasize that once we have achieved bare subsistence levels of consumption—the amount of food, shelter, and clothing required to maintain our health—we can abandon all reference to needs and speak only in terms of wants. This linguistic distinction helps us think more clearly about the true nature of our choices.

For instance, someone who says "Californians don't have nearly as much water as they need" will tend to think differently about water shortages than someone who says "Californians don't have nearly as much water as they want when the price of water is low." The first person is likely to focus on regulations to prevent people from watering their lawns or on projects to capture additional runoff from the Sierra Nevada mountains. The second person is more likely to focus on the low price of water in California. Whereas remedies of the first sort are often costly and extremely difficult to implement, raising the price of water is both simple and effective.

Why does California experience chronic water shortages? Some might respond that the state must serve the needs of a large population with a relatively low average annual rainfall. Yet other states, like New Mexico, have even less rainfall per person and do not experience water shortages nearly as often as California.

California's problem exists because local governments sell water at extremely low prices, which encourages Californians to use water in ways that make no sense for a state with low rainfall. For instance, rice, which is well suited for conditions in high-rainfall states like South Carolina, requires extensive irrigation in California. But because California farmers can obtain water so cheaply, they plant and flood hundreds of thousands of acres of rice paddies each spring in the Central Valley. It takes 2,000 tons of water to produce 1 ton of rice, but many other grains can be produced with only half that amount. If the price of California water were higher, farmers would simply switch to other grains.

Likewise, cheap water encourages homeowners in Los Angeles and San Diego to plant water-intensive lawns and shrubs, like the ones common in the East and Midwest. By contrast, residents of cities like Santa Fe, New Mexico, where water prices are high, choose native plantings that require little or no watering.

TRANSLATING WANTS INTO DEMAND

The scarcity principle reminds us that although our resources are finite, our appetites for good things are boundless. Even if we had unlimited bank accounts, we'd quickly run out of the time and energy needed to do all the things we wanted to do. Our challenge is to use our limited resources to fulfill our desires to the greatest possible degree. And that leaves us with this practical question: How should we allocate our incomes among the various goods and services that are available? To answer that question, it helps to begin by recognizing that the goods and services we buy are not ends in themselves but rather means for satisfying our desires.

MEASURING WANTS: THE CONCEPT OF UTILITY

Economists use the concept of *utility* to represent the satisfaction people derive from their consumption activities. The assumption is that people try to allocate their incomes so as to maximize their satisfaction, a goal referred to as *utility maximization*.

We begin by imagining that the utility associated with different activities can be measured. The nineteenth-century British economist Jeremy Bentham wrote of a "utilometer," a device that could be used to measure the amount of utility provided by different consumption activities. Such a device doesn't exist, but if it did, we could use it to assign a numerical utility value to every activity—watching a movie, eating a cheeseburger, and so on. The utilometer measures utility in utils, much as a thermometer measures temperature in degrees Fahrenheit or Celsius.

Finally, we make the following plausible assumption: The consumer's goal is to maximize the total number of utils obtained from the goods consumed. The trick is to find that maximum—the combination of goods that provides the most "bang for the buck."

Let's begin with an unusually simple problem, the one facing a consumer who reaches the front of the line at a free ice cream stand. How many cones of ice cream should this person, whom we'll call Lamar, ask for? Table 5.1 shows the relationship between the total number of ice cream cones Lamar eats per hour and the total utility, measured in utils per hour, he derives from them.

Note that the measurements in the table are stated in terms of cones per hour and utils per hour. Why "per hour"? Because without an explicit time dimension, we would have no idea whether a given quantity was a lot or a little. Five ice cream cones in a lifetime isn't much, but five in an hour would be more than most of us would care to eat.

As the entries in Table 5.1 show, Lamar's total utility increases with each cone he eats, up to the fourth cone. Eating 4 cones per hour makes him happier than eating 3, which makes him happier than eating 2, and so on. But beyond 4 cones per hour, consuming more ice cream actually makes Lamar less happy. The fifth cone reduces his total utility from 187 utils per hour to 184 utils per hour.

TABLE 5.1
Lamar's Total Utility from Ice Cream Consumption

Cone quantity (cones/hour)	Total utility (utils/hour)
0	0
1	100
2	150
3	175
4	187
5	184

We can display the utility information in Table 5.1 graphically, as in Figure 5.2. Note in the graph that the more cones per hour Lamar eats, the more utils he gets—but again only up to the fourth cone. Once he moves beyond 4 cones, his total utility begins to decline. Lamar's happiness reaches a maximum of 187 utils when he eats 4 cones per hour. At that point he has no incentive to eat the fifth cone, even though it's absolutely free. Eating the fifth cone actually makes him worse off.

Table 5.1 and Figure 5.2 illustrate another important aspect of the relationship between utility and consumption—namely, that the additional utility from

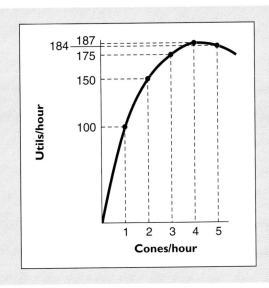

FIGURE 5.2
Lamar's Total Utility from Ice Cream Consumption.
For most goods, utility rises at a diminishing rate with additional consumption.

additional units of consumption declines as total consumption increases. Thus, while 1 cone per hour is a *lot* better—by 100 utils—than zero, 4 cones per hour is just a *little* better than 3 (just 12 utils worth).

The term **marginal utility** denotes the amount by which total utility changes when consumption changes by one unit. In Table 5.2, the third column shows the marginal utility values that correspond to changes in Lamar's level of ice cream consumption. For example, the second entry in column 3 represents the increase in total utility (measured in utils per cone) when Lamar's consumption rises from 1 cone per hour to 2. Note that the marginal utility entries in column 3 are placed midway between the rows of the preceding columns, to indicate that marginal utility corresponds to the movement from one consumption quantity to the next. Thus we would say that the marginal utility of moving from 1 to 2 cones per hour is 20 utils per cone.

marginal utility the additional utility gained from consuming an additional unit of a good

TABLE 5.2
Lamar's Total and Marginal Utility from Ice Cream Consumption

Cone quantity (cones/hour)	Total utility (utils/hour)	Marginal utility (utils/cone)
0	0	
		100
1	100	
		20
2	120	
		10
3	130	
		6
4	136	
		−2
5	134	

> Marginal utility = change in utility ÷ change in consumption
> = (120 utils − 100 utils) ÷ (2 cones − 1 cone)
> = 20 utils/cone

Law of Diminishing Marginal Utility: As consumption of a good increases beyond some point, the additional utility gained from an additional unit of the good tends to decline.

This pattern of diminishing marginal utility holds true not just for Lamar but also for most consumers of most goods. If we have one brownie or one Ferrari, we're happier than we are with none; if we have two, we'll be even happier—but not twice as happy, and so on. Although this pattern is called a law, there are exceptions. Indeed, some consumption activities even seem to exhibit *increasing* marginal utility. For example, an unfamiliar song may seem irritating the first time you hear it, then gradually become more tolerable the next few times you hear it. Before long, you may discover that you *like* the song, and may even find yourself singing it in the shower. Notwithstanding such exceptions, the law of diminishing marginal utility is a plausible characterization of the relationship between utility and consumption for many goods. Unless otherwise stated, we'll assume that it holds for the various goods we discuss.

 What will Lamar do when he gets to the front of the line? At that point, the opportunity cost of the time he spent waiting is a sunk cost and is hence irrelevant to his decision about how many cones to order. And since there is no monetary charge for the cones, the cost of ordering an additional one is zero. According to the cost-benefit criterion, Lamar should therefore continue to order cones as long as the marginal benefit (here, the marginal utility he gets from an additional cone) is greater than or equal to zero. Thus he should order 4 cones.

In this highly simplified example, Lamar's utility-maximization problem is just like the one he'd confront if he were deciding how much water to drink from a public fountain. (Solution: Keep drinking until the marginal utility of water declines to zero.)

ALLOCATING A FIXED INCOME BETWEEN TWO GOODS

Most of us confront considerably more complex purchase decisions than the one Lamar faced. For one thing, we generally must make decisions not just about a single good but about many. Another complication is that the cost of consuming additional units of each good will rarely be zero.

To see how to proceed in more complex cases, suppose Lamar must decide how to spend his fixed income on two different goods each with a positive price. Should he spend all his income on one of the goods or part of it on each? The law of diminishing marginal utility suggests that spending all one's income on a single good isn't a good strategy. Rather than devote more and more money to the purchase of a good we already consume in large quantities (and whose marginal utility is therefore relatively low), we generally do better to spend that money on other goods we don't have many of, whose marginal utility will likely be higher.

The simplest way to illustrate how economists think about the spending decisions of a utility-maximizing consumer is to work through an example like the following.

How many vanilla ice cream cones and chocolate sundaes should Lamar consume?

EXAMPLE 5.1

The free ice cream bonanza is over, and Lamar now has a fixed income of $10 per week to spend at the ice cream parlor. Also, a torn ligament has forced him to resign from the track team, so his appetite for ice cream is considerably smaller than it was. His two favorite choices are vanilla cones and chocolate sundaes. Sundaes sell for $2 and vanilla cones for $1. The number of utils Lamar derives from consuming different amounts of each are as shown in Table 5.3. If Lamar's goal is to maximize the utility he derives from his $10 weekly spending on ice cream, how much of each should he eat?

TABLE 5.3
Utility from Two Types of Ice Cream Consumption

Vanilla cones per week	Utils/week from cones	Chocolate sundaes per week	Utils/week from sundaes
0	0	0	0
1	36	1	50
2	50	2	80
3	60	3	105
4	68	4	120
5	75	5	130
6	80	6	138
7	84	7	144
8	82	8	148
9	81	9	150
10	80	10	151

Lamar wants to maximize the total number of utils he gets from eating two types of ice cream—cones and sundaes—on a $10 weekly budget. His spending limit, or *budget constraint,* is $10. One way Lamar can solve his problem is to list all the combinations of cones and sundaes that cost $10 per week and then choose the one that delivers the highest total utility. Suppose he spends the entire $10 on cones. At $1 apiece, that gives him 10 cones per week, yielding a total utility of 80 utils per week.

Now compare that to what happens if Lamar splits up his budget. Suppose, for example, that he buys only 6 cones, which leaves $4 to spend on sundaes (enough to buy 2 per week). That gives him 80 utils/week from cones + 80 utils/week from sundaes = 160 utils/week, or twice as many utils per week as he got by spending all his income on cones.

Table 5.4 shows the various cone and sundae combinations Lamar can buy without exceeding his $10 weekly budget constraint.

A glance at the table shows that Lamar's *optimal combination* of goods is 4 cones per week and 3 sundaes. His total utility from that combination is 173 utils per week—more than he'd get from any of the other affordable combinations. In other words, the **optimal combination** is the *affordable* combination that delivers *maximum total utility*.

optimal combination of goods
the affordable combination that yields the highest total utility

TABLE 5.4
Affordable Combinations of Cones and Sundaes

Cone/sundae combinations	Total utility (utils/week)
10 cones, 0 sundaes	80 + 0 = 80
8 cones, 1 sundae	82 + 50 = 132
6 cones, 2 sundaes	80 + 80 = 160
4 cones, 3 sundaes	68 + 105 = 173
2 cones, 4 sundaes	50 + 120 = 170
0 cones, 5 sundaes	0 + 130 = 130

EXERCISE 5.1

In Example 5.1, the combination consisting of 8 cones per week and 4 sundaes per week gives a total utility of 202 utils per week. Why isn't that combination Lamar's best choice?

THE RATIONAL SPENDING RULE

If Lamar is to achieve the highest possible utility from the $10 per week he spends on ice cream, he must divide his purchases between the two types so that the marginal utility of the last dollar spent on each good is as large as possible. (If it were not, he could achieve higher total utility by spending his last dollar differently.) Let's see if that condition is satisfied when Lamar buys 4 cones per week and 3 sundaes. Table 5.3A reproduces the utility information given in Example 5.1.

Note that the marginal utility of Lamar's third sundae is 25 utils (the difference between the 105 utils he gets from 3 sundaes and the 80 utils he gets from 2). And since the third sundae costs him $2, his marginal utility per dollar is 25 utils/$2, or 12.5 utils per dollar. Could he have gotten more utils per dollar had he spent $2 on cones instead? Spending $1 more on cones would move him from 4 cones per week to 5, which would increase his total utility from cones by 7 utils per week (the difference between the 75 utils he gets from 5 cones and the 68 utils he gets from 4). Buying a sixth cone would increase his total utility by only 5 utils, for a total increase of 12 utils, significantly less than the 25 utils he would get from an extra sundae. Shifting more money to cones would thus prevent Lamar from achieving the largest possible marginal utility from his last dollars spent on each type.

Note that when Lamar allocates his budget optimally (that is, when he buys 4 cones per week and 3 sundaes), he receives 12.5 utils per dollar from his last purchase of sundaes but only 8 utils per dollar from his last purchase of vanilla cones. If this discrepancy strikes you as a problem, your economic intuition has served you well. Since Lamar is getting more bang for his buck (more utils per dollar) from his last sundae purchase than from his last cone purchase, it would seem that he ought to be spending more heavily on sundaes.

TABLE 5.3A
Utility from Two Types of Ice Cream Consumption

Vanilla cones per week	Utils/week from cones	Chocolate sundaes per week	Utils/week from sundaes
0	0	0	0
1	36	1	50
2	50	2	80
3	60	3	105
4	68	4	120
5	75	5	130
6	80	6	138
7	84	7	144
8	82	8	148
9	81	9	150
10	80	10	151

The way the example is structured, however, Lamar can purchase cones and sundaes *only in whole-number amounts*. Spending more on sundaes would thus require a move from 3 sundaes a week to 4. And because buying a fourth sundae would yield only 7.5 utils per dollar—less than he would get by spending the same amount on cones—Lamar is better off if he stops at 3 sundaes.

In actual experience, the inability to divide goods and services into fractional amounts is seldom an insurmountable problem. After all, if Lamar could do better by consuming, say, 3.2 sundaes per week instead of 3, he could accomplish that by consuming 32 sundaes every 10 weeks (which works out to an average of 3.2 per week).

Whenever goods can be consumed in fractional quantities, we can use the following important rule—the **Rational Spending Rule**—to solve the consumer's allocation problem.

The Rational Spending Rule: Spending should be allocated across goods so that the marginal utility per dollar is the same for each good.

The Rational Spending Rule tells us that if Lamar can purchase ice cream in fractional amounts, he should continue shifting from cones to sundaes until the marginal utility per dollar he obtains from the two goods becomes equal.

The Rational Spending Rule can be expressed in the form of a simple formula. If we use MU_C to denote Lamar's marginal utility from cone consumption (measured in utils per cone) and P_C to denote the price of cones in dollars (measured in dollars per cone), then the ratio MU_C/P_C will represent Lamar's marginal utility per dollar spent on cones. Similarly, if we use MU_S to denote Lamar's marginal utility from sundae consumption, and P_S to denote the price of sundaes, then MU_S/P_S will represent his marginal utility per dollar spent on sundaes. The marginal utility per dollar will be exactly the same for the two types—and hence total utility will be maximized—when the following simple equation is satisfied:

The Rational Spending Rule for Two Goods:

$$\frac{MU_C}{P_C} = \frac{MU_S}{P_S}.$$

The Rational Spending Rule is easily generalized to apply to spending decisions regarding large numbers of goods. In its most general form, it says that the ratio of marginal utility to price must be the same for each good the consumer buys. If the ratio were higher for one good than for another, the consumer could always increase her total utility by buying more of the first good and less of the second.

Notice that we have not chosen to classify the Rational Spending Rule as one of the core principles of economics. We omit it from this list not because the rule is unimportant but because it follows directly from the cost-benefit principle. And as we noted earlier, there is considerable advantage in keeping the list of core principles as small as possible. (If we included 200 principles on this list, there's a good chance you wouldn't remember any of them a few years from now.)

HOW INCOME AND THE PRICES OF SUBSTITUTES AFFECT DEMAND

In Chapter 4 we made the plausible assumption that the demand for any good or service depends on factors like income and the prices of substitutes. As you apply the Rational Spending Rule to work through the following exercises, you'll see more clearly *why* demand depends on factors like these.

EXERCISE 5.2

How should Lamar from Example 5.1 allocate his spending between cones and sundaes if he has $14 per week rather than $10 per week to spend on ice cream?

From among the combinations of goods that are affordable, the utility-maximizing consumer chooses the combination that provides the highest total utility. Extra income stimulates demand by enlarging the set of affordable combinations—by making it possible to buy more of each good than before.

EXERCISE 5.3

Suppose that Lamar again has a budget of $10 per week to allocate between vanilla ice cream cones and chocolate sundaes. The utilities he derives from different quantities of each are again as given in Example 5.1, and chocolate sundaes again sell for $2 apiece. How many units of each type will Lamar buy if the price of vanilla cones is $2 rather than $1?

If you worked through Exercise 5.3 successfully, you saw that a rise in the price of cones caused Lamar to increase his consumption of sundaes. Now consider a more streamlined way of explaining why a change in the price of one good affects demands for other goods. When consumption goods can be purchased in fractional quantities, the Rational Spending Rule requires that the ratio of marginal utility to price be the same for all goods. This means that if the price of one good goes up, the ratio of its current marginal utility to its new price will be lower than for other goods. Consumers can then increase their total utility by devoting smaller proportions of their incomes to that good and larger proportions to others.

> **RECAP   TRANSLATING WANTS INTO DEMAND**
>
> The scarcity principle challenges us to allocate our incomes among the various goods that are available so as to fulfill our desires to the greatest possible degree. The optimal combination of goods is that affordable combination that yields the highest total utility. For goods that are perfectly divisible, the Rational Spending Rule tells us that the optimal combination is one for which the marginal utility per dollar is the same for each good. If this condition were not satisfied, the consumer could increase her utility by spending less on goods for which the marginal utility per dollar was lower and more on goods for which the marginal utility per dollar was higher.

APPLYING THE RATIONAL SPENDING RULE

The real payoff from learning the law of demand and the Rational Spending Rule lies not in working through hypothetical examples but in using these abstract concepts to make sense of the world around you. To encourage you in your efforts to become an economic naturalist, we turn now to a sequence of examples.

SUBSTITUTION AT WORK

In the first of these examples, we focus on the role of substitution. When the price of a good or service goes up, rational consumers generally turn to less expensive substitutes. Can't meet the payments on a new car? Then buy a used one, or rent an apartment on a bus or subway line. French restaurants too pricey? Then go out for Chinese food, or eat at home more often. National Football League tickets too high? Watch the game on television, or read a book. Can't afford a book? Check one out of the library, or download some reading matter from the Internet. Once you begin to see substitution at work, you will be amazed by the number and richness of the examples that confront you every day.

Why do the wealthy in Manhattan live in smaller houses than the wealthy in Seattle?

Microsoft cofounder Paul Allen lives in a 70,000-square-foot house in Seattle, Washington. His house is large even by the standards of Seattle, many of whose wealthy residents live in houses with more than 10,000 square feet of floor space. By contrast, persons of similar wealth in Manhattan rarely live in houses larger than 5,000 square feet. Why this difference?

For people trying to decide how large a house to buy, the most obvious difference between Manhattan and Seattle is the huge difference in housing prices. The cost of land alone is several times higher in Manhattan than in Seattle, and construction costs are also much higher. Although plenty of New Yorkers could *afford* to build a 70,000-square-foot mansion, Manhattan housing prices are so high that they simply choose to live in smaller houses and spend what they save in other ways—on lavish summer homes in eastern Long Island, for instance. New Yorkers also eat out and go to the theater more often than their wealthy counterparts in other U.S. cities.

An especially vivid illustration of substitution occurred during the late 1970s, when fuel shortages brought on by interruptions in the supply of oil from the Middle East led to sharp increases in the price of gasoline and other fuels. In a variety of ways—some straightforward, others remarkably ingenious—consumers changed their behavior to economize on the use of energy. They formed carpools; switched to public transportation; bought four-cylinder cars; moved closer to

ECONOMIC NATURALIST 5.1

work; took fewer trips; turned down their thermostats; installed insulation, storm windows, and solar heaters; and bought more efficient appliances. Many people even moved farther south to escape high winter heating bills.

As the next example points out, consumers not only abandon a good in favor of substitutes when it gets more expensive but also return to that good when real prices return to their original levels.

ECONOMIC
NATURALIST
5.2

Why did people turn to four-cylinder cars in the 1970s, only to shift back to six- and eight-cylinder cars in the 1990s?

In 1973, the price of gasoline was 38 cents per gallon. The following year the price shot up to 52 cents per gallon in the wake of a major disruption of oil supplies. A second disruption in 1979 drove the 1980 price to $1.19 per gallon. These sharp increases in the price of gasoline led to big increases in the demand for cars with four-cylinder engines, which delivered much better fuel economy than the six- and eight-cylinder cars most people had owned. After 1980, however, fuel supplies stabilized, and prices rose only slowly, reaching $1.40 per gallon by 1999. Yet despite the continued rise in the price of gasoline, the switch to smaller engines did not continue. By the late 1980s, the proportion of cars sold with six- and eight-cylinder engines began rising again. Why this reversal?

real price dollar price of a good relative to the average dollar price of all other goods and services

nominal price absolute price of a good in dollar terms

The key to explaining these patterns is to focus on changes in the **real price** of gasoline. When someone decides how big an automobile engine to choose, what matters is not the **nominal price** of gasoline but the price of gasoline *relative* to all other goods. After all, for consumers faced with a decision of whether to spend $1.40 for a gallon of gasoline, the important question is how much utility they could get from other things they could purchase with the same money. Even though the price of gasoline has continued to rise slowly in nominal, or dollar, terms since 1981, it has declined sharply relative to the price of other goods. Indeed, in terms of real purchasing power, the 1999 price was actually slightly lower than the 1973 price. (That is, in 1999, $1.40 bought slightly more goods and services than 38 cents bought in 1973.) It is this decline in the real price of gasoline that accounts for the reversal of the trend toward smaller engines.

A sharp decline in the real price of gasoline also helps account for the explosive growth in sport utility vehicles in the 1990s. More than 4 million SUVs were sold in the United States in 1997, up from only 750,000 in 1990. Some of them—like the Ford Excursion—weigh more than 7,500 pounds (three times as much as a Honda Civic) and get less than 10 miles per gallon on city streets. Vehicles like these would have been dismal failures during the 1970s, but they're by far the hottest sellers in the current cheap-energy environment.

"We motored over to say hi!"

Here's another closely related example of the influence of price on spending decisions.

Why are automobile engines smaller in England than in the United States?

In England, the most popular model of BMW's 5-series car is the 516i, while in the United States it is the 528i. The engine on the 516i is more than 40 percent smaller than the engine on the 528i. Why this difference?

In both countries, BMWs appeal to professionals with roughly similar incomes, so the difference cannot be explained by differences in purchasing power. Rather, it is the direct result of the heavy tax the British levy on gasoline. With tax, a gallon of gasoline sells for almost $6 in England—more than four times the price in the United States. This difference in price encourages the British to choose smaller, more fuel-efficient engines.

ECONOMIC NATURALIST 5.3

THE IMPORTANCE OF INCOME DIFFERENCES

The most obvious difference between the rich and the poor is that the rich have higher incomes. To explain why the wealthy generally buy larger houses than the poor, we need not assume that the wealthy feel more strongly about housing than the poor. A much simpler explanation is that the total utility from housing, as with most other goods, increases with the amount that one consumes.

As the next example illustrates, income influences the demand for not only housing and other goods, but also quality of service.

Why are waiting lines longer in poorer neighborhoods?

As part of a recent promotional campaign, a Baskin-Robbins retailer offered free ice cream at two of its franchise stores. The first store was located in a high-income neighborhood, the second in a low-income neighborhood. Why was the queue for free ice cream longer in the low-income neighborhood?

Residents of both neighborhoods must decide whether to stand in line for free ice cream or go to some other store and avoid the line by paying the usual price. If we make the plausible assumption that people with higher incomes are more willing than others to pay to avoid standing in line, we should expect to see shorter lines in the high-income neighborhood.

ECONOMIC NATURALIST 5.4

Similar reasoning helps explain why lines are shorter in grocery stores that cater to high-income consumers. Keeping lines short at *any* grocery store means hiring more clerks, which means charging higher prices. High-income consumers are more likely than others to be willing to pay for shorter lines.

HOW THE DISTRIBUTION OF INCOME AFFECTS DEMAND

People whose incomes differ substantially spend their incomes in different ways. For example, the proportion of income a person spends on food tends to fall as income rises, whereas the proportion of income spent on foreign travel tends to rise as income rises. This observation suggests that the demand for specific goods may differ from one city to another, not just because of differences in *average* incomes but also because of differences in the way income is distributed among people.

Why does a house with a view cost more in Berkeley than in Hanover?

In many cities, such as Berkeley, California, and Hanover, New Hampshire, a small proportion of homesites are located on hillsides with commanding views. Most homeowners think that having a view is desirable. If lots with views sold for the same price as lots without views, virtually every homeowner would buy a lot with a view. Since homesites with views are in limited supply, however, they command a

ECONOMIC NATURALIST 5.5

significant price premium. But why is this premium more than 50 percent in Berkeley but less than 30 percent in Hanover?

The average income in Hanover is not much lower than in Berkeley, but incomes are much less equally distributed in Berkeley than in Hanover. Berkeley attracts executives and entrepreneurs from the entire San Francisco Bay area, people who earn significantly more than the top earners in Hanover, most of whom work for Dartmouth College. The result is that the effective demand for homesites with views is much stronger in Berkeley than in Hanover. In both cities the houses with views tend to go to the highest earners, but the premium for a view is much higher in Berkeley because its top earners make so much more money.

To illustrate, suppose the supply of homesites with views is essentially fixed in each city, as indicated by the vertical supply curves shown in Figure 5.3, and that people in both cities have identical tastes regarding views. But because the incomes of the top earners in Berkeley are much higher than the incomes of the top earners in Hanover, the demand curve for homesites with views in Berkeley lies significantly to the right of the corresponding demand curve for Hanover. And that explains the significantly higher premium for views in Berkeley.

FIGURE 5.3
The Price for a House with a View.
If the average income level is the same in two cities, then the city in which income is more unequally distributed, as in (a), will have higher demand for luxury goods such as homesites with views.

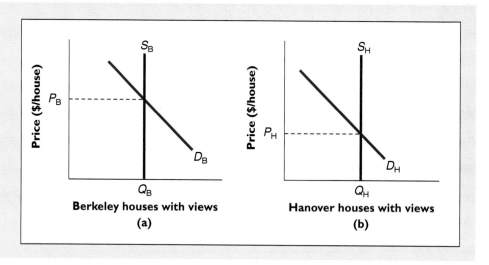

Berkeley houses with views
(a)

Hanover houses with views
(b)

RECAP   **APPLYING THE RATIONAL SPENDING RULE**

Application of the Rational Spending Rule highlights the important roles of income and substitution in explaining differences in consumption patterns—among individuals, among communities, and across time. The rule also highlights the fact that real, as opposed to nominal, prices and income are what matter. The demand for a good falls when the real price of a substitute falls or the real price of a complement rises. Patterns of demand may differ between communities of the same average real-income level if the distributions of income within those communities differ significantly.

INDIVIDUAL AND MARKET DEMAND CURVES

If we know what each individual's demand curve for a good looks like, how can we use that information to construct the market demand curve for the good? We must add together the individual demand curves, a process that is straightforward but requires care.

HORIZONTAL ADDITION

Suppose that there are only two buyers—Smith and Jones—in the market for canned tuna and that their demand curves are as shown in Figure 5.4(a) and (b). To construct the market demand curve for canned tuna, we simply announce a sequence of prices and then add the quantity demanded by each buyer at each price. For example, at a price of $4 per can, Smith demands 8 cans per week [Fig. 5.4(a)] and Jones demands 2 cans per week [Fig. 5.4(b)], for a market demand of 10 cans per week [Fig. 5.4(c)].

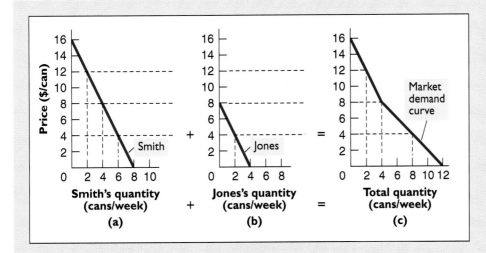

FIGURE 5.4
Individual and Market Demand Curves for Canned Tuna.
The quantity demanded at any price on the market demand curve (c) is the sum of the individual quantities (a) and (b) demanded at that price.

The process of adding individual demand curves to get the market demand curve is known as *horizontal addition,* a term used to emphasize that we are adding quantities, which are measured on the horizontal axes of individual demand curves.

Figure 5.5(a) illustrates the special case in which each of 1,000 consumers in the market has the same demand curve. To get the market demand curve in this case, we simply multiply each quantity on the representative individual demand curve by 1,000 [Fig. 5.5(b)].

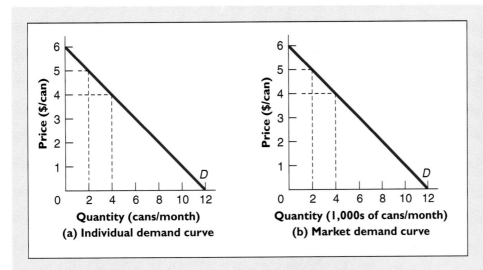

FIGURE 5.5
The Individual and Market Demand Curves When All Buyers Have Identical Demand Curves.
When individual demand curves are identical, we get the market demand curve by multiplying each quantity on the individual demand curve by the number of consumers in the market.

THE STRAIGHT-LINE DEMAND CURVE

The law of demand requires only that the demand curve for a good or service slope downward. It makes no predictions about the specific shape of the curve.

It is often convenient, however, to draw demand curves as downward-sloping straight lines, as we did in Chapter 4.

Market demand curves may be shown not only in graphical form but in two other forms as well. One is to summarize the market demand relationship in the form of a table. For example, the linear market demand curve shown in Figure 5.5(b) may be also represented as Table 5.5.

TABLE 5.5
The Market Demand for Canned Tuna in Tabular Form

Price ($/can)	Quantity (1,000s of cans/month)
0	12
1	10
2	8
3	6
4	4
5	2
6	0

A third alternative—and one especially handy for straight-line demand curves—is to express the market demand curve algebraically. Because economists have adopted the convention of plotting price on the vertical axis and quantity on the horizontal axis, we write the general formula of a straight-line demand curve as follows:

$$P = b - mQ,$$

where P denotes the price of the good, usually measured in dollars per unit; Q denotes the quantity demanded, in physical units per unit of time; b denotes the vertical intercept of the demand curve, and $-m$ represents its slope.

To illustrate, suppose we want to write the equation for the market demand curve shown in Figure 5.6 [which is the same as the one in Figure 5.5(b)].

To begin, we can see from the graph that b, the vertical intercept of the demand curve, is 6. The slope is the ratio of the vertical distance between any

FIGURE 5.6
The Market Demand Curve for Canned Tuna.

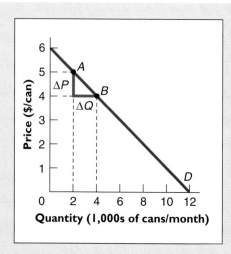

two points on the line (the "rise") to the corresponding horizontal distance (the "run"). For example, if we look at the segment of the demand curve between the points labeled A and B, the rise is $\Delta P = -1$ (since the line falls a vertical distance of 1 unit between A and B), and the corresponding run is $\Delta Q = 2,000$. Thus the slope of the demand curve shown is $-m = \Delta P/\Delta Q = -1/2,000$. Knowing both the slope and vertical intercept of the demand curve, we also know that its equation must be

$$P = 6 - \left(\frac{1}{2,000}\right)Q.$$

To check that this equation is indeed correct, let's see if it works for the two points we started with. Does the equation hold, for example, if we plug in $P = 5$ and $Q = 2,000$? Sure enough, $5 = 6 - (1/2,000)(2,000)$. Similarly, we can verify that $4 = 6 - (1/2,000)(4,000)$.

| EXERCISE 5.4

Find the equation of the linear demand curve for movie tickets shown in the following diagram.

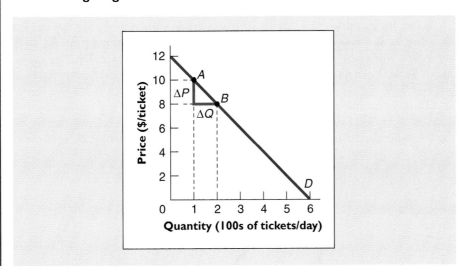

TOTAL EXPENDITURE

Given the market demand curve for a good, the total amount consumers spend on the good will depend on the price for which it is sold. And by definition, the total expenditure on a good per day is simply the number of units bought each day times the price for which it sells.

To illustrate, calculate how much moviegoers will spend on tickets each day if the demand curve is as shown in Figure 5.7 and the price is $2 per ticket. The demand curve tells us that at a price of $2 per ticket, 500 tickets per day will be sold, so total expenditure at that price will be $1,000 per day. If tickets sell not for $2 but for $4 apiece, 400 tickets will be sold each day, so total expenditure at the higher price will be $1,600 per day.

Note that the total amount consumers spend on a product each day must equal the total amount sellers of the product receive. That is, the terms **total expenditure** and **total revenue** are simply two sides of the same coin.

It might seem that an increase in the market price of a product should always result in an increase in the total revenue received by sellers. But although that happened in the case we just saw, it needn't always be so. The law of demand

Total expenditure = total revenue the dollar amount consumers spend on a product is equal to the dollar amount sellers receive

FIGURE 5.7
The Demand Curve for Movie Tickets.
An increase in price from $2 to $4 per ticket increases total expenditure on tickets.

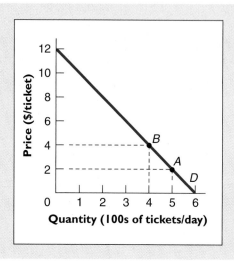

tells us that when the price of a good rises, people will buy less of it. The two factors that govern total revenue—price and quantity—thus will always move in opposite directions. When price goes up and quantity goes down, the product of the two may go either up or down.

Note, for example, that for the demand curve shown in Figure 5.8 (which is the same as the one we just saw in Figure 5.7), a rise in price from $8 to $10 per ticket will cause total expenditure on tickets to go down. Thus people will spend $1,600 per day on tickets at a price of $8, but only $1,000 per day at a price of $10.

The general rule illustrated by these examples is that a price increase will produce an increase in total revenue whenever it is greater, in percentage terms, than the corresponding percentage reduction in quantity demanded. Although the two

FIGURE 5.8
The Demand Curve for Movie Tickets.
An increase in price from $8 to $10 per ticket results in a fall in total expenditure on tickets.

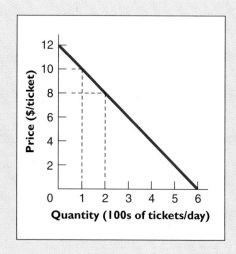

price increases (from $2 to $4 and from $8 to $10) were of the same absolute value—$2 in each case—they are much different when expressed as a percentage of the original price. An increase from $2 to $4 represents a 100 percent increase in price, whereas an increase from $8 to $10 represents only a 25 percent increase in price. And although the quantity reductions caused by the two price increases were equal in absolute terms, they too are very different when expressed as percentages of the quantities originally sold. Thus, although the decline in quantity demanded was 100 tickets per day in each case, it was just a 20 percent reduction in the first case (from 500 units to 400) but a 50 percent reduction in the second (from 200 units to 100). In the second case, the negative effect on total expenditure of the 50 percent quantity reduction outweighed the positive effect of the 25 percent price increase. The reverse happened in the first case: The 100 percent increase in price (from $2 to $4) outweighed the 20 percent reduction in quantity (from 5 units to 4 units).

Example 5.2 provides further insight into the relationship between total revenue and price.

For the demand curve shown in Figure 5.9, draw a separate graph showing how total expenditure varies with the price of movie tickets.

EXAMPLE 5.2

FIGURE 5.9
The Demand Curve for Movie Tickets.

The first step in constructing this graph is to calculate total expenditure for a sample of price points on the demand curve and record the results, as in Table 5.6.

The next step is to plot total expenditure at each of the price points on a graph, as in Figure 5.10. Finally, sketch the curve by joining these points. (If greater accuracy is required, you can use a larger sample of points than the one shown in Table 5.6.)

TABLE 5.6
Total Expenditure as a Function of Price

Price ($/ticket)	Total expenditure ($/day)
12	0
10	1,000
8	1,600
6	1,800
4	1,600
2	1,000
0	0

Note in Figure 5.10 that as the price per ticket increases from 0 to $6, total expenditure increases. But as the price rises from $6 to $12, total expenditure decreases. Total expenditure reaches a maximum of $1,800 per day at a price of $6.

The pattern observed in Example 5.2 holds true in general. For a straight-line demand curve, total expenditure is highest at the price that lies on the mid-point of the demand curve.

FIGURE 5.10
Total Expenditure as a Function of Price.
For a good whose demand curve is a straight line, total expenditure reaches a maximum at the price corresponding to the midpoint of the demand curve.

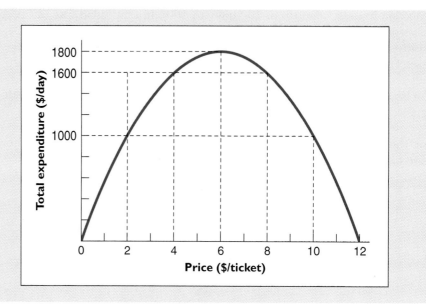

INDIVIDUAL AND MARKET DEMAND CURVES

To generate the market demand curve for a good, we add the individual demand curves of market participants horizontally. Although demand curves for actual goods will seldom be straight lines, they often can be well approximated as straight lines, especially when our concern is with the effects of small variations in quantity or price.

Total expenditure on a good is the product of its price and the quantity bought. Total revenue received by the seller of a good is the product of its price and the quantity sold. Because the quantity bought equals the quantity sold, total revenue must equal total expenditure. For a straight-line demand curve, total expenditure reaches a maximum at the midpoint along the demand curve.

PRICE ELASTICITY OF DEMAND

When the price of a good or service rises, the quantity demanded falls. But as we have seen, to predict the effect of the price increase on total expenditure, we must also know how much quantity will fall. The quantity demanded of some goods, such as salt, is not very sensitive to changes in price. Indeed, even if the price of salt were to double, or to fall by half, most people would alter their consumption of it hardly at all. For other goods, however, the quantity demanded is extremely responsive to changes in price. As we saw earlier, for example, when energy prices rose in the 1970s, gasoline consumption fell sharply.

The **price elasticity of demand** for a good is a measure of the responsiveness of the quantity demanded of that good to changes in its price. Formally, the price elasticity of demand for a good is defined as the percentage change in the quantity demanded that results from a 1 percent change in its price. For example, if the price of beef falls by 1 percent and the quantity demanded rises by 2 percent, then the price elasticity of demand for beef has a value of −2.

Strictly speaking, the price elasticity of demand will always be negative (or zero) because price changes always move in the opposite direction from changes in quantity demanded. So for convenience, we can drop the negative sign and speak of price elasticities in terms of absolute value. The demand for a good is

price elasticity of demand the percentage change in the quantity demanded of a good that results from a 1 percent change in its price

said to be **elastic** with respect to price if the absolute value of its price elasticity is greater than 1. It is said to be **inelastic** if the absolute value of its price elasticity is less than 1. Finally, demand is said to be **unit elastic** if the absolute value of its price elasticity is equal to 1. (See Figure 5.11.)

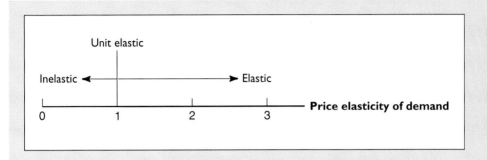

elastic the demand for a good is elastic with respect to price if its price elasticity of demand is greater than 1

FIGURE 5.11
Elastic and Inelastic Demand.
Demand for a good is called elastic, unit elastic, or inelastic with respect to price if the price elasticity is greater than 1, equal to 1, or less than 1, respectively.

ELASTICITY AND TOTAL EXPENDITURE

Sellers of goods and services will often have a strong interest in being able to answer such questions as "Will consumers spend more on my product if I sell more units at a lower price or fewer units at a higher price?" As it turns out, the answer to this question depends critically on the elasticity of demand. Suppose, for example, that the business manager of a rock band knows that 5,000 tickets to the band's weekly summer concerts can be sold if the price is set at $20 per ticket. If the elasticity of demand for tickets is equal to 3.0, will total ticket revenue go up or down in response to a 10 percent increase in the price of tickets?

Total revenue from ticket sales is currently ($20/ticket)(5,000 tickets/week) = $100,000/week. The fact that the price elasticity of demand for tickets is 3 implies that a 10 percent increase in price will produce a 30 percent reduction in the number of tickets sold, which means that ticket sales will fall to 3,500/week. Total expenditure on tickets will therefore fall to (3,500 tickets/week)($22/ticket) = $77,000/week, which is significantly less than the current spending total.

This example illustrates the following important rule regarding the relationship between price elasticity and the effect of a price increase on total expenditure:

For a product whose price elasticity is greater than 1, an increase in price will reduce total expenditure, and a reduction in price will increase total expenditure.

Let's look at the intuition behind this rule. Total expenditure is the product of price and quantity. For an elastically demanded product, the percentage change in quantity will be larger than the corresponding percentage change in price. Thus the change in sales will more than offset the change in revenue per unit sold.

Now let's see how total spending responds to a price increase when demand is *inelastic* with respect to price. Suppose that in the case just considered, the elasticity of demand for tickets is not 3.0 but 0.5. How will total revenue respond to a 10 percent increase in ticket prices? This time the number of tickets sold will fall by only 5 percent to 4,750 tickets/week, which means that total expenditure on tickets will rise to (4,750 tickets/week)($22/ticket) = $104,500/week, or $4,500/week more than the current expenditure level.

As this example illustrates, the effect of a price change on total expenditure when demand is inelastic runs in the opposite direction from the effect when demand is elastic:

inelastic the demand for a good is inelastic with respect to price if its price elasticity of demand is less than 1

unit elastic the demand for a good is unit elastic with respect to price if its price elasticity of demand is equal to 1

For a product whose price elasticity of demand is less than 1, an increase in price will increase total expenditure, and a cut in price will reduce total expenditure.

Again, the intuition behind this rule is straightforward. For a product whose demand is inelastic with respect to price, the percentage change in quantity demanded will be smaller than the corresponding percentage change in price. Thus the change in revenue per unit sold will more than offset the change in the number of units sold.

The relationship between elasticity and the effect of a price change on total revenue are summarized in Table 5.7, where the symbol ϵ is used to denote elasticity.

TABLE 5.7
Elasticity and the Effect of a Price Change on Total Revenue

$\epsilon > 1$	Price increase causes reduction in total revenue.	Price reduction causes increase in total revenue.
$\epsilon < 1$	Price increase causes increase in total revenue.	Price reduction causes reduction in total revenue.

DETERMINANTS OF PRICE ELASTICITY OF DEMAND

What factors determine the price elasticity of demand for a good or service? To answer this question, recall that before a rational consumer buys any product, the product must first pass the cost-benefit test. For instance, consider a good (such as a dorm refrigerator) that, if you buy it at all, you buy only one unit. Suppose that, at the current price, you have decided to buy it. Now imagine that the price goes up by 10 percent. Will a price increase of this magnitude be likely to make you change your mind? The answer will depend on factors such as the following.

Substitution possibilities When the price of a product you want to buy goes up significantly, you are likely to ask yourself, "Is there some other good that can do roughly the same job but for less money?" If the answer is yes, then you can escape the effect of the price increase by simply switching to the substitute product. But if the answer is no, you are more likely to stick with your current purchase.

These observations suggest that the price elasticity of demand will tend to be higher for products for which close substitutes are readily available. Salt, for example, has no close substitutes, which is one reason that the demand for it is highly inelastic. Note, however, that while the quantity of salt people demand is highly insensitive to price, the same cannot be said of the demand for any specific brand of salt. After all, despite what salt manufacturers say about the special advantages of their own labels, consumers tend to regard one brand of salt as a virtually perfect substitute for another. Thus, if Morton were to raise the price of its salt significantly, people would simply switch to some other brand.

If the price of salt were to double, would you use less of it?

The vaccine against rabies is another product for which there are essentially no attractive substitutes. A person who is bitten by a rabid animal and does not take the vaccine faces a certain and painful death. So most people in that position would pay any price they could afford rather than do without the vaccine.

Budget share Suppose the price of key rings suddenly were to double. How would that affect the number of key rings you buy? If you're like most people, it would have no effect at all. Think about it—a doubling of the price of a 25 cent item that you buy only every year or two is simply nothing to worry about.

By contrast, if the price of the new car you were about to buy suddenly doubled, you would definitely want to check out possible substitutes, such as a used car or a smaller new model. You might also consider holding onto your current car a little longer. The larger the share of your budget an item accounts for, the greater is your incentive to look for substitutes when the price of the item rises. Big-ticket items therefore tend to have higher price elasticities of demand.

Time Home appliances come in a variety of models, some more energy-efficient than others. As a general rule, the more efficient an appliance is, the higher its price. If you were about to buy a new air conditioner and the electric rates suddenly rose sharply, it would be in your interest to buy a more efficient machine than you had originally planned. But suppose you had already bought the machine before you learned of the rate increase. In all likelihood, it would not pay you to discard the machine right away and replace it with a more efficient model. Rather, you would wait until the machine wore out, or until you moved, before making the switch.

As this example illustrates, substitution of one product or service for another takes time. Some substitutions occur in the immediate aftermath of a price increase, but many others take place years or even decades later. For this reason, the price elasticity of demand for any good or service will be higher in the long run than in the short run.

An understanding of the factors that govern price elasticity of demand is necessary not only to make sense of consumer behavior but also to design effective public policy. Consider, for example, the debate about how taxes affect teenage smoking.

Will a higher tax on cigarettes curb teenage smoking?

Consultants hired by the tobacco industry have testified in Congress against higher cigarette taxes aimed at curbing teenage smoking. The main reason teenagers smoke is that their friends smoke, these consultants testified, and they concluded that higher taxes would have little effect. Does the consultants' testimony make economic sense?

The consultants are almost certainly right that peer influence is the most important determinant of teen smoking. But that does not imply that a higher tax on cigarettes would have little impact on adolescent smoking rates. Because most teenagers have small disposable incomes (that is, most have little money to spend at their own discretion), cigarettes constitute a significant share of a teenage smoker's budget. The price elasticity of demand is thus likely to be far from negligible. For at least some teenage smokers, a higher tax would make smoking unaffordable. And among those who could afford the higher prices, at least some others would choose to spend their money on other things rather than pay the higher prices.

Given that the tax would affect at least *some* teenage smokers, the consultants' argument begins to unravel. If the tax deters even a small number of smokers directly through its effect on the price of cigarettes, it will also deter others indirectly by reducing the number of peer role models who smoke. And those who refrain because of these indirect effects will in turn no longer influence others to smoke, and so on. So even if the direct effect of higher cigarette taxes on teen smoking is small, the cumulative effects may be extremely large. The mere fact that peer pressure may be the primary determinant of teen smoking therefore does not imply that higher cigarette taxes will have no significant impact on the number of teens who smoke.

ECONOMIC NATURALIST 5.6

CALCULATING PRICE ELASTICITY

We defined price elasticity of demand as the percentage change in quantity demanded that occurs in response to a 1 percent change in price. Another way of phrasing this definition is to say that price elasticity is the proportion by which quantity demanded changes divided by the corresponding proportion by which price changes. For example, if a 5 percent change in price causes quantity demanded to fall by 10 percent, the price elasticity of demand is 10 percent/5 percent = 2.0. By defining elasticity in this way, we can construct a simple formula that enables us to calculate the price elasticity of demand for a product using only minimal information about its demand curve.

Suppose we let P represent the current price of a good and Q the quantity demanded at that price. Similarly, let ΔP represent a small change in the current price and ΔQ the resulting change in quantity demanded. (See Figure 5.12.) The expression $\Delta P/P$ will then stand for the proportion by which price changes when

FIGURE 5.12
A Graphical Interpretation of Price Elasticity of Demand.
Price elasticity of demand at any point along a straight-line demand curve is the ratio of price to quantity at that point times the reciprocal of the slope of the demand curve.

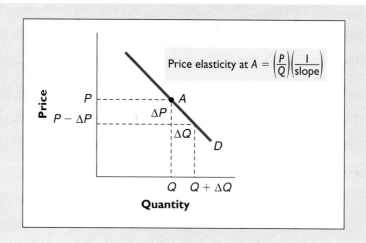

P changes by ΔP, and $\Delta Q/Q$ will stand for the corresponding proportion by which quantity changes. The formula for price elasticity may then be written as

$$\text{Price elasticity} = \epsilon = \left(\frac{\Delta Q}{Q}\right)\bigg/\left(\frac{\Delta P}{P}\right).$$

One attractive feature of this formula for elasticity is that it has a straightforward graphical interpretation. Thus, if we want to calculate the price elasticity of demand at point A on the demand curve shown in Figure 5.12, we can begin by rewriting the right-hand side of the equation as $(P/Q)(\Delta Q/\Delta P)$. And since the slope of the demand curve is equal to $\Delta P/\Delta Q$, $\Delta Q/\Delta P$ is the reciprocal of that slope: $\Delta Q/\Delta P = 1/\text{slope}$. So the price elasticity of demand at point A, denoted ϵ_A, has the following simple formula:

$$\epsilon_A = \left(\frac{P}{Q}\right)\bigg/\left(\frac{1}{\text{slope}}\right).$$

To illustrate how convenient this graphical interpretation of elasticity can be, suppose we want to find the price elasticity of demand at point A on the demand curve in Figure 5.13. The slope of this demand curve is the ratio of its vertical intercept to its horizontal intercept: $20/5 = 4$, so $1/\text{slope} = 1/4$. (Actually, the slope is -4, but we ignore the minus sign for convenience, since price elasticity always has the same sign.) The ratio P/Q at point A is $8/3$, so the price elasticity at point A is equal to $(P/Q)(1/\text{slope}) = (8/3)(1/4) = 2/3$.

EXERCISE 5.5

What is the price elasticity of demand when $P = 4$ on the demand curve in Figure 5.13?

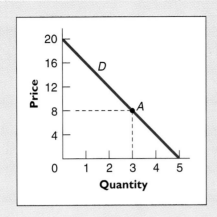

FIGURE 5.13
Calculating Price Elasticity of Demand.
The price elasticity of demand at *A* is given by (*P/Q*)(1/slope) = (8/3)(1/4) = 2/3.

PRICE ELASTICITY CHANGES ALONG A STRAIGHT-LINE DEMAND CURVE

As a glance at our elasticity formula makes clear, price elasticity has a different value at every point along a straight-line demand curve. The slope of a straight-line demand curve is constant, which means that 1/slope is also constant. But the price-quantity ratio, *P/Q*, declines as we move down the demand curve. Thus the elasticity of demand declines steadily as we move downward along a straight-line demand curve.

If we think back to the definition of elasticity as the percentage change in quantity demanded divided by the corresponding percentage change in price, this pattern makes sense. After all, a price movement of a given absolute size is small in percentage terms when it occurs near the top of the demand curve, where price is high, but large in percentage terms when it occurs near the bottom of the demand curve, where price is low. Likewise, a quantity movement of a given absolute value is large in percentage terms when it occurs near the top of the demand curve, where quantity is low, and small in percentage terms when it occurs near the bottom of the curve, where quantity is high.

INCOME ELASTICITY AND CROSS-PRICE ELASTICITY OF DEMAND

The **elasticity of demand** for a good can be defined not only with respect to its own price but also with respect to the prices of substitutes or complements, or even to income. For example, the elasticity of demand for peanuts with respect to the price of cashews—also known as the cross-price elasticity of peanuts with respect to cashew prices—is the percentage by which the quantity of peanuts demanded changes in response to a 1 percent change in the price of cashews.

Unlike the elasticity of demand for a good with respect to its own price, these other elasticities may be either positive or negative, so it is important to note their algebraic signs carefully. The income elasticity of demand for inferior goods, for example, is negative, while the income elasticity of demand for normal goods is positive. When the **cross-price elasticity of demand for two goods** is positive—as in the peanuts-cashews example—the two goods are substitutes. When it is negative, the two goods are complements. The elasticity of demand for tennis racquets with respect to court rental fees, for example, is less than zero.

income elasticity of demand the percentage by which a good's quantity demanded changes in response to a 1 percent change in income

cross-price elasticity of demand for two goods the percentage by which the quantity demanded of the first good changes in response to a 1 percent change in the price of the second

EXERCISE 5.6

If a 10 percent increase in income causes the number of students who choose to attend private universities to go up by 5 percent, what is the income elasticity of demand for private universities?

TWO SPECIAL CASES

There are two important exceptions to the general rule that elasticity declines along straight-line demand curves. Note that the horizontal demand curve Figure 5.14(a) has a slope of zero, which means that the reciprocal of its slope is infi-

FIGURE 5.14
Perfectly Elastic and Perfectly Inelastic Demand Curves.
The horizontal demand curve (a) is perfectly elastic, or infinitely elastic, at every point. Even the slightest increase in price leads consumers to desert the product in favor of substitutes. The vertical demand curve (b) is perfectly inelastic at every point. Consumers do not, or cannot, switch to substitutes even in the face of large increases in price.

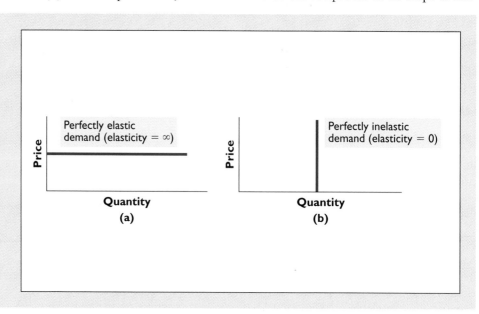

perfectly elastic the demand for a good is perfectly elastic with respect to price if its price elasticity of demand is infinite

perfectly inelastic the demand for a good is perfectly inelastic with respect to price if its price elasticity of demand is zero

nite. Price elasticity of demand is thus infinite at every point along a horizontal demand curve. Such demand curves are said to be **perfectly elastic.**

In contrast, the demand curve in Figure 5.14(b) is vertical, which means that its slope is infinite. The reciprocal of its slope is thus equal to zero. Price elasticity of demand is thus exactly zero at every point along the curve. For this reason, vertical demand curves are said to be **perfectly inelastic.**

RECAP   PRICE ELASTICITY OF DEMAND

The price elasticity of demand for a good is the percentage change in the quantity demanded that results from a 1 percent change in its price. Mathematically, the elasticity of demand at a point along a demand curve is equal to $(P/Q)(1/\text{slope})$, where P and Q represent price and quantity and $(1/\text{slope})$ is the reciprocal of the slope of the demand curve at that point.

For a product whose price elasticity is greater than 1, an increase in price will reduce total expenditure, and a reduction in price will increase total expenditure. For a product whose price elasticity of demand is less than 1, an increase in price will increase total expenditure, and a cut in price will reduce total expenditure.

The price elasticity of demand for a good or service tends to be larger when substitutes for the good are more readily available, when the good's share in the consumer's budget is larger, and when consumers have more time to adjust to a change in price.

When the elasticity of demand for one good with respect to the price of another good is positive, the two goods are substitutes; when this cross-price elasticity of demand is negative, the two goods are complements. A normal good has positive income elasticity of demand, and an inferior good has negative income elasticity of demand.

WHERE DO WANTS COME FROM?

Wants (also called *preferences* or *tastes*) are an important determinant of how much people are willing to pay for specific goods and services. Where do wants come from? Many tastes—such as the taste for water on a hot day or for a comfortable place to sleep at night—are largely biological in origin. But many others are heavily shaped by culture, and even basic cravings may be socially molded. For example, people raised in southern India develop a taste for hot curry dishes, while those raised in England generally prefer milder foods.

Tastes for some items may remain stable for many years, but tastes for others may be highly volatile. Although books about the *Titanic* disaster have been continuously available since the vessel sank in the spring of 1912, not until the appearance of James Cameron's blockbuster film did these books begin to sell in large quantities. In the spring of 1998, 5 of the 15 books on *The New York Times* paperback bestseller list were about the *Titanic* itself or one of the actors in the film. Yet none of these books, or any other book about the *Titanic*, made the bestseller list in 1999. Still, echoes of the film continued to reverberate in the marketplace. In the years since its release, for example, demand for ocean cruises has grown sharply, and several television networks have introduced shows set on cruise ships.

As discussed in the tobacco tax example, peer pressure is another example of how social forces often influence demand. Indeed, it is often the most important single determinant of demand. For instance, if our goal is to predict whether a young man will purchase an illegal recreational drug, knowing how much income he has is not very helpful. Nor does knowing the prices of whiskey and other legal substitutes for illicit drugs. Although these factors do influence purchase decisions, by themselves they are weak predictors. But if we know that most of the young man's best friends are heavy drug users, there is a reasonably good chance that he will use drugs as well.

Another important way in which social forces shape demand is in the relatively common desire to own products that are recognized as the best of their kind. For instance, many people want to hear Luciano Pavorotti sing, not just because of the high quality of his voice, but because he is widely regarded as the world's best—or at least the world's best known—tenor.

Consider, too, the decision of how much to spend on an interview suit. As the employment counselors never tire of reminding us, making a good first impression is extremely important when you go for a job interview. At the very least, it means showing up in a suit that looks good. But looking good is a relative concept. If everyone else shows up in a $200 suit, you'll look good if you show up in a $300 suit. But you won't look as good in that same $300 suit if everyone else shows up in suits costing $1,000. The amount you'll choose to spend on an interview suit, then, clearly depends on how much others in your circle are spending.

■ SUMMARY ■

- The rational consumer allocates income among different goods so that the marginal utility gained from the last dollar spent on each good is the same. This rational spending rule gives rise to the law of demand, which states that people do less of what they want to do as the cost of doing it rises. Here, *cost* refers to the sum of all monetary and non-monetary sacrifices—explicit and implicit—that must be made to engage in the activity.

- The ability to substitute one good for another is an important factor behind the law of demand. Because virtually every good or service has at least some substitutes, economists prefer to speak in terms of wants rather than of needs. We face choices, and describing our demands as needs is misleading because it suggests we have no options.

- The demand curve is a schedule that shows the amounts of a good people want to buy at various prices. Demand curves can be used to summarize the price–quantity relationship for a single individual, but more commonly we employ them to summarize that relationship for an entire market. At any quantity along a demand curve, the corresponding price represents the amount by which the consumer (or consumers) would benefit from having an additional unit of the product. For this reason, the demand curve is sometimes described as a summary of the benefit side of the market.

- The price elasticity of demand is a measure of how strongly buyers respond to changes in price. It is the percentage change in quantity demanded that occurs in response to a 1 percent change in price. The demand for a good is called elastic with respect to price if its price elasticity is more than 1, inelastic if its price elasticity is less than 1, and unit elastic if its price elasticity is equal to 1.

- A cut in price will increase total spending on a good if demand is elastic, but reduce it if demand is inelastic. An increase in price will increase total spending on a good if demand is inelastic but reduce it if demand is elastic. Total expenditure on a good reaches a maximum when price elasticity of demand is equal to 1.

- Goods such as salt, which occupy only a small share of the typical consumer's budget and have few or no good substitutes, tend to have low price elasticity of demand. Goods like new cars of a particular make and model, which occupy large budget shares and have many attractive substitutes, tend to have high price elasticity of demand. Price elasticity of demand is higher in the long run than in the short run because people often need time to adjust to price changes.

- The price elasticity of demand at a point along a demand curve can also be expressed as the formula $\epsilon = (\Delta Q/Q)/(\Delta P/P)$. Here, P and Q represent price and quantity at that point, and ΔQ and ΔP represent small changes in price and quantity. For straight-line demand curves, this formula can also be expressed as $\epsilon = (P/Q)(1/\text{slope})$. These formulations tell us that price elasticity declines in absolute terms as we move down a straight-line demand curve.

■ KEY TERMS ■

cross-price elasticity of demand (127)
elastic (123)
income elasticity of demand (127)
inelastic (123)
law of demand (105)
law of diminishing marginal utility (108)

marginal utility (107)
nominal price (114)
optimal combination of goods (110)
perfectly elastic (128)
perfectly inelastic (128)
price elasticity of demand (122)

rational Spending Rule (111)
real price (114)
total expenditure (119)
total revenue (119)
unit elastic (123)

■ REVIEW QUESTIONS ■

1. Why do economists prefer to speak of demands arising out of "wants" rather than "needs"?

2. Why does the law of diminishing marginal utility encourage people to spread their spending across many different types of goods?

3. Under what conditions will an increase in the price of a product lead to a reduction in total spending for that product?

4. Why do economists pay little attention to the algebraic sign of the elasticity of demand for a good with respect to its own price, yet they pay careful attention to the algebraic sign of the elasticity of demand for a good with respect to another good's price?

5. Why does the elasticity of demand for a good with respect to its own price decline as we move down along a straight-line demand curve?

■ PROBLEMS ■

1. In which type of restaurant do you expect the service to be more prompt and courteous: an expensive gourmet restaurant or an inexpensive diner? Explain your answer.

2. Tom has a weekly allowance of $24, all of which he spends on pizza and movie rentals, whose prices are $6 and $3, respectively. His total utility is the sum of the utility he derives from each of these consumption activities. If these utilities vary with the amounts consumed as shown in the following table, and pizzas and movie rentals are consumable only in integer amounts, how many pizzas and how many movie rentals should Tom consume each week?

Pizzas/week	Utils/week from pizza	Movie rentals/ week	Utils/week from rentals
0	0	0	0
1	20	1	40
2	38	2	46
3	54	3	50
4	68	4	54
5	80	5	56
6	90	6	57
7	98	7	57
8	104	8	57

3. Martha's current marginal utility from consuming orange juice is 75 utils per ounce, and her marginal utility from consuming coffee is 50 utils per ounce. If orange juice costs 25 cents per ounce and coffee costs 20 cents per ounce, is Martha maximizing her total utility from the two beverages? If so, explain how you know. If not, how should she rearrange her spending?

4. The following schedule shows the number of packs of bagels bought in Davis, California, each day at a variety of prices.

Price of bagels ($/pack)	Number of packs purchased per day
6	0
5	3,000
4	6,000
3	9,000
2	12,000
1	15,000
0	18,000

a. Graph the daily demand curve for packs of bagels in Davis.
b. Derive an algebraic expression for the demand schedule you graphed.
c. Calculate the price elasticity of demand at the point on the demand curve where the price of bagels is $3.
d. If all bagel shops increased the price of bagels from $3 to $4, what would happen to total revenue?
e. Calculate the price elasticity of demand at a point on the demand curve where the price of bagels is $2.
f. If bagel shops increased the price of bagels from $2 to $3, what would happen to total revenue?
g. Show on the graph in part a the inelastic and elastic regions of the demand curve.

5. Suppose, while rummaging through your uncle's closet, you found the original painting of *Dogs Playing Poker*, a valuable piece of art. You decided to set up a display in your uncle's garage. The demand curve to see this valuable piece of art is $P = 12 - 2Q$, where P is dollars per visit and Q is the number of visitors per day.
   a. Draw the demand curve for the painting.
   b. How many people would view the painting if you charged them nothing?
   c. What is the price elasticity of demand when the price is $4?

6. Is the demand for a particular brand of car, like a Chevrolet, likely to be more or less price-elastic than the demand for all cars?

7. Among the following groups—senior executives, junior executives, and students— which is likely to have the most and which is likely to have the least price-elastic demand for membership in the Association of Business Professionals?

8. At point *A* on the following demand curve, how will a 1 percent increase in the price of the product affect total expenditure on the product?

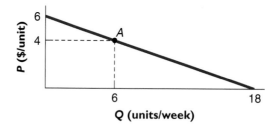

9. Andy is selling Economics Department T-shirts. The vertical axis of his demand curve measures the price of T-shirts in dollars, and the horizontal axis measures the quantity demanded in T-shirts per week. The absolute value of the slope of his demand curve is 2, and if Andy's goal is to maximize revenue from selling the T-shirts, the price he should charge, in dollars, will be:
   a. Half as large as the number of shirts he will sell at that price.
   b. Twice as large as the number of shirts he will sell at that price.
   c. Equal to the number of shirts he will sell at that price.
   d. Low enough to sell as many T-shirts as possible.
   e. There is not enough information here to answer this question.

10. In an attempt to induce citizens to conserve energy, the government enacted regulations requiring that all air conditioners be more efficient in their use of electricity. After this regulation was implemented, government officials were then surprised to discover that people used even more electricity than before. Using the concept of price elasticity, explain how this might have happened.

▪ ANSWERS TO IN-CHAPTER EXERCISES ▪

5.1 To buy 8 cones per week and 4 sundaes would cost $16, which is $2 more than Lamar has to spend.

5.2 Suppose Lamar starts with his previous optimal combination—4 cones per week and 3 sundaes—then allocates his additional $4 one step at a time—either by spending $2 on an additional sundae or by spending that same $2 on 2 more cones. If he buys a fourth sundae for $2, he'll get 15 extra utils, or 7.5 utils per dollar. For the same money, he could buy 2 additional cones, which would give him 12 extra utils, or 6 utils per dollar. Since the first option is better, Lamar should spend the first $2 of his additional $4 weekly ice cream budget on sundaes. That gives him 4 cones and 4 sundaes, with an additional $2 to spend. He can spend it either on a fifth sundae or on 2 more cones. If he buys the fifth sundae, he'll get 10 extra utils, or 5 utils per dollar. If he buys 2 more cones, he'll get 12 extra utils, or 6 utils per dollar. So cones are the better choice this time. Proceeding in this manner, Lamar ends up buying 6 cones per week and 4 sundaes, a combination that yields 200 utils per week. The increase in his income has increased his demands for both cones and more sundaes.

Vanilla cones per week	Utils/week from cones	Chocolate sundaes per week	Utils/week from sundaes
0	0	0	0
1	36	1	50
2	50	2	80
3	60	3	105
4	68	4	120
5	75	5	130
6	80	6	138
7	84	7	144
8	82	8	148
9	81	9	150
10	80	10	151

5.3. As we saw earlier, when the price of cones was $1 apiece, Lamar's best bet was to buy 4 cones per week and 3 sundaes. But with the price of cones now $2 instead of $1, he cannot afford to buy 4 cones and 3 sundaes (whose combined price is $14, or $4 more than his $10 weekly budget). So he needs to cut back, and the best place to start is with the good that delivers less marginal utility per dollar. The marginal utility per dollar delivered by the fourth cone is now only 8 utils/$2 = 4 utils per dollar, much less than the marginal utility per dollar delivered by the third sundae (which is still 12.5 utils per dollar). At 3 cones and 3 sundaes a week, he is still spending $2 too much, and the solution is to reduce consumption of cones still further (since giving up the third cone sacrifices only 5 utils per dollar, or less than he'd lose by giving up a sundae). Having cut back to 2 cones and 3 sundaes, he's spending exactly $10 per week. Now suppose he cuts his cone consumption from 2 to 1. By so doing he'll lose another 14 utils, or 7 utils per dollar saved. And if he then spends that $2 on an additional sundae, he'll gain 15 utils, or 7.5 utils per dollar. So Lamar's best bet this time is to consume 1 cone and 4 sundaes per week, which gives him a total of 156 utils per week.

5.4 The vertical intercept of this demand curve is 12, and its slope is $\Delta P/\Delta Q = -2/100 = -1/50$. So the equation for this demand curve is $P = 12 - (1/50)Q$.

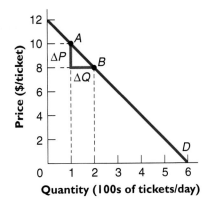

5.5. At point A in the following diagram, $P/Q = 4/4 = 1$. The slope of this demand curve is $20/5 = 4$, so $\epsilon = 1(1/\text{slope}) = 1/4$.

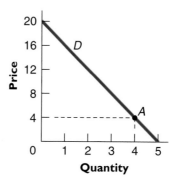

5.6. Income elasticity = percentage change in quantity demanded/(percentage change in income) = 5 percent/10 percent = 0.5.

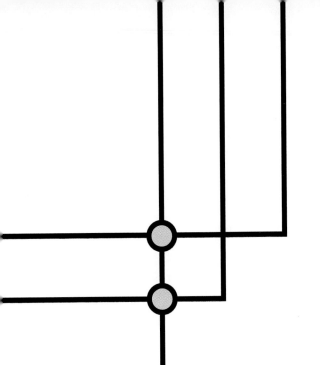

PERFECTLY COMPETITIVE SUPPLY: THE COST SIDE OF THE MARKET

■

Cars that took more than 50 hours to be assembled in the 1970s are now built in less than 8 hours. Similar productivity growth has occurred in many other manufacturing industries. Yet in many service industries, productivity has grown only slowly, if at all. For example, the London Philharmonic Orchestra performs Beethoven's Fifth Symphony with no fewer musicians today than it did in 1850. And it still takes a barber about half an hour to cut someone's hair, just as it always has.

Given the spectacular growth in manufacturing workers' productivity, it is no surprise that their real wages have risen more than fivefold during the last century. But how to explain why real wages for service workers have risen just as much? If barbers and musicians are no more productive than they were at the turn of the century, why are they now paid five times as much?

An answer is suggested by the observation that the opportunity cost of pursuing any given occupation is the most one could have earned in some other occupation. Most people who become barbers or musicians could instead have chosen jobs in manufacturing. If workers in service industries were not paid roughly as much as they could have earned in other occupations, many of them would not have been willing to work in service industries in the first place.

The trajectories of wages in manufacturing and service industries illustrate the intimate link between the prices at which goods and services are offered for sale in the market and the opportunity cost of the resources required to

Why are barbers paid five times as much now as in 1900, even though they can't cut hair any faster than they could then?

produce them. Whereas our focus in Chapter 5 was on the buyer's side of the market, our focus here will be on the seller's side. Earlier, we saw that the demand curve is a schedule that tells how many units buyers wish to purchase at different prices. Our task here is to gain insight into the factors that shape the supply curve, the schedule that tells how many units suppliers wish to sell at different prices.

Although the demand side and the supply side of the market differ in several ways, many of these differences are superficial. Indeed, the behavior of both buyers and sellers is in an important sense fundamentally the same. After all, the two groups confront essentially similar questions—in the buyer's case, "Should I buy another unit?" and in the seller's case, "Should I sell another unit?" What is more, buyers and sellers use the same criterion for answering these questions. Thus a rational consumer will buy another unit if its benefit exceeds its cost, and a rational seller will sell another unit if the cost of making it is less than the extra revenue that results from selling it (the familiar cost-benefit principle again).

THINKING ABOUT SUPPLY

Do you live in a state that requires refundable soft drink container deposits? If so, you've probably noticed that some people always redeem their own containers, while other people pass up this opportunity, leaving their used containers to be recycled by others. The recycling of used containers is a service, and its production obeys the same logic that applies to the production of other goods and services. As the following sequence of recycling examples makes clear, the supply curve for a good or service is rooted in the individual's choice of whether to produce it.

EXAMPLE 6.1   **How much time should Harry spend recycling soft drink containers?**

Harry is trying to decide how to divide his time between his job as a dishwasher in the dining hall, which pays $6/hour for as many hours as he chooses to work, and gathering soft drink containers to redeem for deposit, in which case his pay depends on both the deposit per container and the number of containers he finds. Earnings aside, Harry is indifferent between the two tasks, and the number of containers he will find depends, as shown in the accompanying table, on the number of hours per day he searches:

Search time (hours/day)	Total number of containers found	Additional number of containers found
0	0	
		600
1	600	
		400
2	1,000	
		300
3	1,300	
		200
4	1,500	
		100
5	1,600	

If the containers can be redeemed for 2 cents each, how many hours should Harry spend searching for containers?

For each additional hour Harry spends searching for soft drink containers, he loses the $6 he could have earned as a dishwasher. This is his hourly opportunity cost of searching for soft drink containers. His benefit from each hour spent searching for containers is the number of additional containers he finds (shown in column 3 of the table) times the deposit he collects per container. Since he can redeem each container for 2 cents, his first hour spent collecting containers will yield earnings of 600($0.02) = $12, or $6 more than he could have earned as a dishwasher.

By the cost-benefit principle, then, Harry should spend his first hour of work each day searching for soft drink containers rather than washing dishes. A second hour searching for containers will yield 400 additional containers, for additional earnings of $8, so it too satisfies the cost-benefit test. A third hour spent searching yields 300 additional containers, for 300($0.02) = $6 of additional earnings. Since this is exactly what Harry could have earned washing dishes, he is indifferent between spending his third hour of work each day on one task or the other. For the sake of discussion, however, we'll assume that he resolves ties in favor of searching for containers, in which case he will spend 3 hours each day searching for containers.

What is the lowest redemption price that would induce Harry to spend at least 1 hour per day recycling? Since he will find 600 containers in his first hour of search, a 1 cent deposit on each container would enable him to match his $6/hour opportunity cost. More generally, if the redemption price is p and the next hour spent searching yields ΔQ additional containers, then Harry's additional earnings from searching the additional hour will be $p(\Delta Q)$. This means that the smallest redemption price that will lead Harry to search another hour must satisfy the equation

$$p(\Delta Q) = \$6.$$

How high would the redemption price of containers have to be to induce Harry to search for a second hour? Since he can find $\Delta Q = 400$ additional containers if he searches for a second hour, the smallest redemption price that will lead him to do so must satisfy $p(400) = \$6$, which solves for $p = 1.5$ cents.

EXERCISE 6.1

In Example 6.1, calculate the smallest container redemption prices that will lead Harry to search a third, fourth, and fifth hour.

By searching for soft drink containers, Harry becomes, in effect, a supplier of container-recycling services. In Exercise 6.1, we saw that Harry's reservation prices for his third, fourth, and fifth hours of container search are 2, 3, and 6 cents, respectively. Having calculated these reservation prices, we can now plot his supply curve of container-recycling services. This curve, which plots the redemption price per container on the vertical axis and the number of containers recycled each day on the horizontal axis, is shown in Figure 6.1. Harry's individual supply curve of container-recycling services tells us the number of containers he is willing to recycle at various redemption prices.

Like the supply curves we saw in Chapter 4, the supply curve in Figure 6.1 is upward-sloping. There are exceptions to this general rule, but sellers of most goods will offer higher quantities at higher prices than at lower prices.

The relationship between the individual and market supply curves for a product is analogous to the relationship between the individual and market demand curves. The quantity that corresponds to a given price on the market demand curve is the sum of the quantities demanded at that price by all individual buyers in the market. Likewise, the quantity that corresponds to any given price on the market supply curve is the sum of the quantities supplied at that price by all individual sellers in the market.

FIGURE 6.1
An Individual Supply Curve for Recycling Services.
When the deposit price increases, it becomes attractive to abandon alternative pursuits to spend more time searching for soft drink containers.

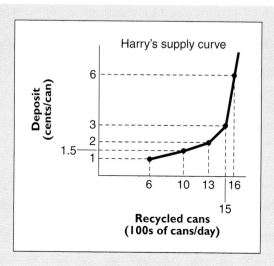

Suppose, for example, that the supply side of the recycling-services market consists only of Harry and his identical twin, Barry, whose individual supply curve is the same as Harry's. To generate the market supply curve, we first put the individual supply curves side by side, as shown in Figure 6.2(a) and (b). We then announce a price, and for that price we add the individual quantities supplied to obtain the total quantity supplied in the market. Thus, at a price of 3 cents/container, both Harry and Barry wish to recycle 1,500 cans/day, so the total market supply at that price is 3,000 cans/day. Proceeding in like manner for a sequence of prices, we generate the market supply curve for recycling services shown in Figure 6.2(c). This is the same process of horizontal summation by which we generated market demand curves from individual demand curves in Chapter 5.

FIGURE 6.2
The Market Supply Curve for Recycling Services.
To generate the market supply curve (c) from the individual supply curves (a) and (b), we add the individual supply curves horizontally.

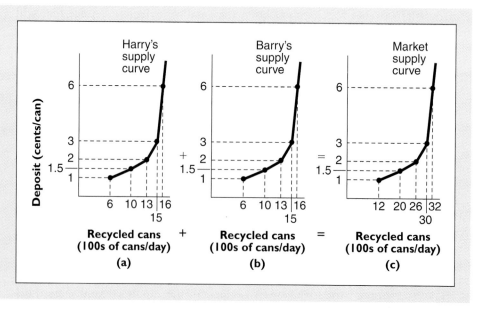

Alternatively, if there were many suppliers with individual supply curves identical to Harry's, we could generate the market supply curve by simply multiplying each quantity value on the individual supply curve by the number of suppliers. For instance, Figure 6.3 shows the supply curve for a market in which there are 1,000 suppliers with individual supply curves like Harry's.

Why do individual supply curves tend to be upward-sloping, at least in the short run? One explanation is suggested by the principle of increasing opportunity cost, or the low-hanging-fruit principle. Container recyclers should always

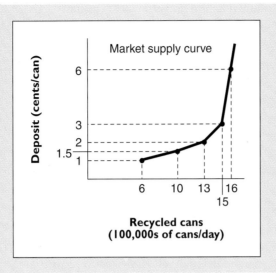

FIGURE 6.3
The Market Supply Curve with 1,000 Identical Sellers.
To generate the market supply curve for a market with 1,000 identical sellers, we simply multiply each quantity value on the individual supply curve by 1,000.

look first for the containers that are easiest to find, such as those in plain view in readily accessible locations. As the redemption price rises, it will pay to incur the additional cost of searching farther from the beaten path.

If all individuals have identical upward-sloping supply curves, the market supply curve will be upward-sloping as well. But there is an important additional reason for the positive slope of market supply curves—namely, that individual suppliers generally differ with respect to their opportunity costs of supplying the product. (The principle of increasing opportunity cost applies not only to each individual searcher but also *across* individuals.) Thus, whereas people facing unattractive employment opportunities in other occupations may be willing to recycle soft drink containers even when the redemption price is low, those with more attractive options will recycle only if the redemption price is relatively high.

In summary then, the upward slope of the supply schedule reflects the fact that costs tend to rise when producers expand production in the short run, partly because each individual exploits her or his most attractive opportunities first, but also because different potential sellers face different opportunity costs.

PROFIT-MAXIMIZING FIRMS AND PERFECTLY COMPETITIVE MARKETS

PROFIT MAXIMIZATION

To explore the nature of the supply curve of a product more fully, we must say more about the goals of the organizations that supply the product and the kind of economic environment in which they operate. In virtually every economy, goods and services are produced by a variety of organizations that pursue a host of different motives. The Red Cross supplies blood because its organizers and donors want to help people in need, the local government fixes potholes because the mayor was elected on a promise to do so, karaoke singers perform because they like public attention, and car wash employees are driven primarily by the hope of making enough money to pay their rent.

Notwithstanding this rich variety of motives, *most* goods and services offered for sale in a market economy are sold by private firms whose main reason for existing is to earn **profit** for their owners. A firm's profit is the difference between the total revenue it receives from the sale of its product and all costs it incurs, both explicit and implicit, in producing it.

profit the total revenue a firm receives from the sale of its product minus all costs—explicit and implicit—incurred in producing it

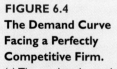

profit-maximizing firm a firm whose primary goal is to maximize the difference between its total revenues and total costs

perfectly competitive market a market in which no individual supplier has significant influence on the market price of the product

price taker a firm that has no influence over the price at which it sells its product

A **profit-maximizing firm** is one whose primary goal is to maximize the amount of profit it earns. The supply curves that economists use in standard supply and demand theory are based on the assumption that goods are sold by profit-maximizing firms in **perfectly competitive markets,** which are markets in which individual firms have no influence over the market prices of the products they sell. Any single firm, being just one of many sellers of the product, cannot hope to charge more than its rivals and has no motive to charge less. Because of their inability to influence market price, perfectly competitive firms are often described as **price takers.**

The market for operating systems for desktop computers, more than 90 percent of which are sold by Microsoft, is not perfectly competitive because Microsoft has enough presence in that market to have significant control over the prices it charges. For example, if Microsoft were to raise the price of its latest edition of its Windows operating system by, say, 20 percent, some consumers might switch to Macintosh or Linux, and others might postpone their next upgrade; but many—perhaps even most—would continue with their plans to buy.

By contrast, if an individual wheat farmer were to charge even just 10 cents more than the current market price for a bushel of wheat, the farmer wouldn't be able to sell any wheat at all. The wheat farmer is a stereotypical example of a perfectly competitive firm—one of a host of essentially similar firms that sell a tiny fraction of their industry's output of a highly standardized product. If any one perfectly competitive seller were to raise its price, buyers would simply switch to another seller.

THE DEMAND CURVE FACING A PERFECTLY COMPETITIVE FIRM

From the perspective of an individual firm in a perfectly competitive market, what does the demand curve for its product look like? Since the firm can sell as much or as little as it wishes at the prevailing market price, the demand curve for its product is perfectly elastic at the market price. Figure 6.4(a) shows the market demand and supply curves intersecting to determine a market price of P_0. Figure 6.4(b) shows the product demand curve D_i as seen by any individual firm in this market, a horizontal line at the market price level P_0.

FIGURE 6.4
The Demand Curve Facing a Perfectly Competitive Firm.
(a) The market demand and supply curves intersect to determine the market price of the product. (b) The individual firm's demand curve (D_i) is a horizontal line at the market price.

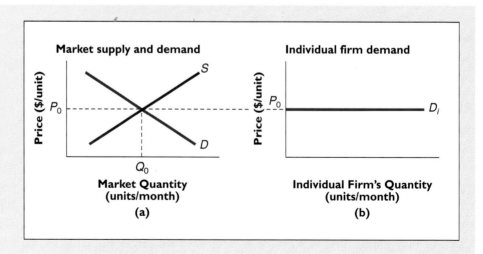

imperfectly competitive firm a firm that has at least some control over the market price of its product

Many of the conclusions of the standard supply and demand model also hold for **imperfectly competitive firms:** those firms, like Microsoft, that have at least some ability to vary their own prices. But certain other conclusions do not, as we will see when we examine the behavior of such firms more closely in Chapter 9.

Since a perfectly competitive firm has no control over the market price of its product, it needn't worry about choosing the level at which to set that price. As we've seen, the equilibrium market price in a competitive market comes from the intersection of the industry supply and demand curves. The challenge confronting the perfectly competitive firm is to choose its output level so that it makes as much profit as it can at that price. As we investigate how the competitive firm responds to this challenge, we'll see once again the pivotal role of our core principle that some costs are more important than others.

PRODUCTION IN THE SHORT RUN

To help gain a deeper understanding of the origins of the supply curve, consider a perfectly competitive firm confronting the decision of how much to produce. The firm in question is a small company that makes glass bottles. To keep things simple, suppose that the silicon required for making bottles is available free of charge from a nearby desert, and that the only costs the firm incurs are the wages it pays its employees and the lease payment on its bottle-making machine. The employees and the machine are the firm's only two **factors of production**—inputs used to produce goods and services. In more complex examples, factors of production might also include land, structures, entrepreneurship, and possibly others, but for the moment we consider only labor and capital.

factor of production an input used in the production of a good or service

When we refer to the **short run,** we mean a period of time during which at least some of the firm's factors of production cannot be varied. (For our bottle maker, the short run is that period of time during which the firm cannot alter the capacity of its bottle-making machine.) By contrast, when we speak of the **long run,** we refer to a time period of sufficient length that all the firm's factors of production are variable.

short run a period of time sufficiently short that at least some of the firm's factors of production are fixed

long run a period of time of sufficient length that all the firm's factors of production are variable

Table 6.1 shows how the company's bottle production depends on the number of hours its employees spend on the job each day.

TABLE 6.1
Employment and Output for a Glass Bottle Maker

Number of bottles/day	Number of employee-hours/day
0	0
100	1
200	2
300	4
400	7
500	11
600	16
700	22

law of diminishing returns a property of the relationship between the amount of a good or service produced and the amount of a variable factor required to produce it; the law says that when some factors of production are fixed, increased production of the good eventually requires ever larger increases in the variable factor

The output-employment relationship described in Table 6.1 exhibits a pattern common to many such relationships. Each time we move down one row in the table, output grows by 100 bottles/day, but note in column 2 that larger and larger increases in the amount of labor are necessary to achieve this increase. Economists refer to this pattern as the **law of diminishing returns,** and it always refers to situations in which at least some factors of production are held fixed. In the current example, the **fixed factor of production** is the bottle-making machine, and the **variable factor of production** is labor. In the context of this example, the law of diminishing returns says simply that

fixed factor of production an input whose quantity cannot be altered in the short run

variable factor of production an input whose quantity can be altered in the short run

successive increases in bottle output require ever larger increases in labor input. The reason for this pattern often entails some form of congestion. For instance, in an office with three secretaries and only a single word processor, we would not expect to get three times as many letters typed per hour as in an office with only one secretary, because only one person can use a word processor at a time.

CHOOSING OUTPUT TO MAXIMIZE PROFIT

Suppose the lease payment for the company's bottle-making machine and the building that houses it is $40/day, and it must be paid whether or not the company makes any bottles. This payment is both a fixed cost (since it does not depend on the number of bottles per day the firm makes) and, for the duration of the lease, a sunk cost. For short, we'll refer to this cost as the company's *capital cost*. In Examples 6.2 to 6.5, we'll explore how the company's decision about how many bottles to make depends on the price of bottles, the wage rate, and the cost of capital.

EXAMPLE 6.2

If bottles sell for $35/hundred and if the employee's wage is $10/hour, how many bottles should the company described above produce each day?

The company's goal is to maximize its profit, which is the difference between the revenue it collects from the sale of bottles and the cost of its labor and capital. Table 6.2 shows how the daily number of bottles produced (denoted Q) is related to the company's revenue, employment, costs, and profit.

TABLE 6.2
Output, Revenue, Costs, and Profit

Q (bottles/ day)	Total revenue ($/day)	Total labor cost ($/day)	Total cost ($/day)	Profit ($/day)
0	0	0	40	−40
100	35	10	50	−15
200	70	20	60	10
300	105	40	80	25
400	140	70	110	30
500	175	110	150	25
600	210	160	200	10
700	245	220	260	−15

To see how the entries in Table 6.2 are constructed, examine the revenue, cost, and profit values that correspond to 200 units of output (row 3). Total revenue is $70, the company's receipts from selling 200 bottles at $35/hundred. To make 200 bottles, the firm's employee had to work 2 hours (see Table 6.1), and at a wage of $10/hour that translates into $20 of total labor cost. When the firm's fixed capital cost of $40/day is added to its total labor cost, we get the total cost entry of $60/day in column 4. The firm's daily profit, finally, is total revenue − total cost = $70 − $60 = $10, the entry in column 5.

From a glance at the final column in Table 6.2, we see that the company's maximum profit, $30/day, occurs when it produces 400 bottles/day.

Same as Example 6.2, except now bottles sell for $45/hundred.

EXAMPLE 6.3

As we see in the entries of Table 6.3, the only consequence of the change in selling price is that total revenue, and hence profit, is now higher than before at every output level. As indicated by the entries of the final column, the company now does best to produce 500 bottles/day, 100 more than when the price was only $35/hundred.

TABLE 6.3
Output, Revenue, Costs, and Profit

Q (bottles/ day)	Total revenue ($/day)	Total labor cost ($/day)	Total cost ($/day)	Profit ($/day)
0	0	0	40	−40
100	45	10	50	−5
200	90	20	60	30
300	135	40	80	55
400	175	70	110	70
500	220	110	150	75
600	270	160	200	70
700	315	220	260	55

Same as Example 6.2, except now the wage rate is $12/hour.

EXAMPLE 6.4

With a higher wage rate, labor costs are higher at every level of output, as shown in column 3, Table 6.4, and maximum profit now occurs when the firm produces 300 bottles/day, or 100 fewer than when the wage rate was $10/hour.

TABLE 6.4
Output, Revenue, Costs, and Profit

Q (bottles/ day)	Total revenue ($/day)	Total labor cost ($/day)	Total cost ($/day)	Profit ($/day)
0	0	0	40	−40
100	35	12	52	−17
200	70	24	64	6
300	105	48	88	17
400	140	84	124	16
500	175	132	172	3
600	210	192	232	−22
700	245	264	304	−59

Consider one final variation:

Same as Example 6.2, except now the capital cost is not $40/day but $70.

EXAMPLE 6.5

The entries in Table 6.5 are just like those in Table 6.2 except that each entry in the total cost column (column 4) is $30 higher than before, with the result that each entry in the profit column (column 5) is $30 lower. Note, however, that the profit-maximizing number of bottles to produce is again 400/day, precisely the same as when capital cost was only $40/day. When the company produces 400 bottles daily, its daily profit is 0, but at any other output level its profit would have been negative; that is, it would have been making a loss.

TABLE 6.5
Output, Revenue, Costs, and Profit

Q (bottles/ day)	Total revenue ($/day)	Total labor cost ($/day)	Total cost ($/day)	Profit ($/day)
0	0	0	70	−70
100	35	10	80	−45
200	70	20	90	−20
300	105	40	110	−5
400	140	70	140	0
500	175	110	180	−5
600	210	160	230	−20
700	245	220	290	−45

PRICE EQUALS MARGINAL COST: THE SELLER'S SUPPLY RULE

The observation that the profit-maximizing quantity for a firm to supply does not depend on its fixed costs is not an idiosyncrasy of this example. That it holds true in general is an immediate consequence of the cost-benefit principle, which says that a firm should increase its output if, and only if, the *extra* benefit exceeds the *extra* cost. If the firm expands production by 100 bottles/day, its benefit is the extra revenue it gets, which in this case is simply the price of 100 bottles. The cost of expanding production by 100 bottles is by definition the marginal cost of producing 100 bottles—the amount by which total cost increases when bottle production rises by 100/day. The cost-benefit principle thus tells us that the perfectly competitive firm should keep expanding production as long as the price of the product is greater than marginal cost.

When the law of diminishing returns applies (that is, when some factors of production are fixed), marginal cost goes up as the firm expands production. Under these circumstances, the firm's best option is to supply that level of output for which price and marginal cost are exactly equal.

Note in Example 6.5 that if the company's capital cost had been any more than $70/day, it would have made a loss at *every* possible level of output. As long as it still had to pay its capital cost, however, its best bet would have been to continue producing 400 bottles/day. It is better, after all, to experience a smaller loss than a larger one. If a firm in that situation expected conditions to remain the same, though, it would want to get out of the bottle business as soon as its equipment lease expired.

A NOTE ON THE FIRM'S SHUTDOWN CONDITION

It might seem that a firm that can sell as much output as it wishes at a constant market price would *always* do best in the short run by producing and selling the output level for which price equals marginal cost. But there are exceptions to this rule. Suppose, for example, that the market price of the firm's product falls so low that its revenue from sales is smaller than its variable cost when price equals marginal cost. The firm should then cease production for the time being. By shutting down, it will suffer a loss equal to its fixed costs. But by remaining open, it would suffer an even larger loss.

EXERCISE 6.2

In Example 6.2, suppose bottles sold not for $35/hundred but for only $5. Calculate the profit corresponding to each level of output, as in Example 6.2, and verify that the firm's best option is to cease operations in the short run.

GRAPHING MARGINAL COST

To plot the marginal cost curve for a specific company, we would need to know how total cost changes for every possible change in output. In Examples 6.2 to 6.5, however, we know the firm's cost for only a small sample of production values. Even with this limited information, though, we can construct a reasonable approximation of the firm's marginal cost curve. For instance, note in Example 6.2 that when the firm expands production from 100 to 200 bottles/day, its increase in cost is $10. When we graph the marginal cost curve, what output level should this $10 marginal cost correspond to? Strictly speaking, it corresponds neither to 100 nor 200 but to the movement between the two. On the graph we thus show the $10 marginal cost value corresponding to an output level midway between 100 and 200 bottles/day, namely, 150 bottles/day, as in Figure 6.5. Similarly, when the firm in Example 6.2 expands from 200 to 300 bottles/day, its costs go up by $20, so we plot a marginal cost of $20 with the output level 250 in Figure 6.5. Proceeding in this fashion, we generate the marginal cost curve shown in the diagram.

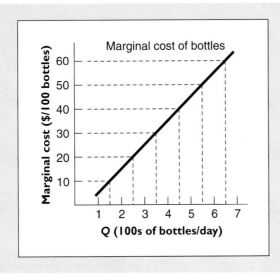

FIGURE 6.5
The Firm's Marginal Cost of Production.
The firm's cost goes up by $10 when it expands production from 100 to 200 bottles/day. The marginal cost of the increased output is thus $10, and by convention we plot that value at a point midway between 100 and 200 bottles/day.

Suppose the market price facing the seller whose marginal cost curve is shown in Figure 6.5 is $25/hundred. If the firm's goal is to make as much profit as possible, how many bottles should it sell? It should sell the quantity for which marginal cost is equal to $25/hundred, and as we see in Figure 6.6, that quantity is 300 bottles/week.

To gain further confidence that 300 must be the profit-maximizing quantity when the price is $25/hundred, first suppose that the firm had sold some amount less than that, say, only 200 bottles/day. Its benefit from expanding output by one bottle would then be the bottle's market price, here 25 cents (since bottles sell

FIGURE 6.6
Price = Marginal Cost:
The Perfectly
Competitive Firm's
Profit-Maximizing Supply
Rule.
If price is less than marginal cost, the firm can increase its profit by expanding production and sales. If price exceeds marginal cost, the firm can increase its profit by producing and selling less output.

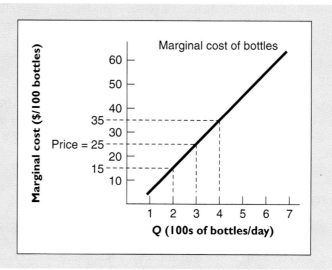

for $25/hundred, each individual bottle sells for 25 cents). The cost of expanding output by one bottle is equal (by definition) to the firm's marginal cost, which at 200 bottles/day is only $15/100 = 15 cents (see Figure 6.6). So by selling the 201st bottle for 25 cents and producing it for an extra cost of only 15 cents, the firm will increase its profit by 25 − 15 = 10 cents/day. Similarly, we can show that for *any* quantity less than the level at which price equals marginal cost, the seller can boost profit by expanding production.

Conversely, suppose the firm is currently selling more than 300 bottles/day—say, 400—at a price of $25/hundred. From Figure 6.6 we see that marginal cost at an output of 400 is $35/100 = 35 cents per bottle. If the firm then contracts its output by one bottle/day, it would cut its costs by 35 cents while losing only 25 cents in revenue. As before, its profit would grow by 10 cents/day. The same argument can be made regarding any quantity larger than 300, so if the firm is currently selling an output at which price is less than marginal cost, it can always do better by producing and selling fewer bottles.

We have thus established that if the firm were selling fewer than 300 bottles/day, it could earn more profit by expanding, and that if it were selling more than 300, it could earn more by contracting. It follows that at a market price of $25/hundred, the seller does best by selling 300 units per week, the quantity for which price and marginal cost are exactly the same.

EXERCISE 6.3

For a bottle price of $25/hundred, calculate the profit corresponding to each level of output, as in Example 6.2, and verify that the profit-maximizing output is 300 bottles/day.

As further confirmation of the claim that the perfectly competitive firm maximizes profit by setting price equal to marginal cost, note in Figure 6.6 that when marginal cost is equal to a price of $35/hundred, the corresponding quantity is 400 bottles/day. This is the same as the profit-maximizing quantity we identified for that price in Table 6.2.

THE "LAW" OF SUPPLY

The law of demand tells us that consumers buy less of a product when its price rises. If there were an analogous law of supply, it would say that producers offer more of a product for sale when its price rises. Is there such a law? We know that supply curves are essentially marginal cost curves, and that because of the law of diminishing returns, marginal cost curves are upward-sloping in the short run. And so there is indeed a law of supply that applies as stated in the short run.

In the long run, however, the law of diminishing returns does not apply. (Recall that it holds only if at least some factors of production are fixed.) Because firms can vary the amounts of *all* factors of production they use in the long run, they can often double their production by simply doubling the amount of each input they use. In such cases costs would be exactly proportional to output, and the firm's marginal cost curve in the long run would be horizontal, not upward-sloping. So for now we'll say only that the "law" of supply holds as stated in the short run but not necessarily in the long run. For both the long run and the short run, however, *the perfectly competitive firm's supply curve is its marginal cost curve.*[1]

Every quantity of output along the market supply curve represents the summation of all the quantities individual sellers offer at the corresponding price. So the correspondence between price and marginal cost exists for the market supply curve as well as for the individual supply curves that lie behind the market supply curve. That is, *for every price-quantity pair along the market supply curve, price will be equal to each seller's marginal cost of production.*

This is why we sometimes say that the supply curve represents the cost side of the market, whereas the demand curve represents the benefit side of the market. At every point along a market demand curve, price represents what buyers would be willing to pay for an additional unit of the product—and this, in turn, is how we measure the amount by which they would benefit by having an additional unit of the product. Likewise, at every point along a market supply curve, price measures what it would cost producers to expand production by one unit.

RECAP **THE COMPETITIVE FIRM'S SUPPLY CURVE**

The perfectly competitive firm faces a horizontal demand curve for its product, meaning that it can sell any quantity it wishes at the market price. In the short run, the firm's goal is to choose the level of output that maximizes its profits. Under a broad range of conditions, it will accomplish this goal by choosing the output level for which its marginal cost is equal to the market price of its product. The perfectly competitive firm's supply curve is its marginal cost curve, which is upward-sloping in the short run because of the law of diminishing returns.

DETERMINANTS OF SUPPLY REVISITED

What factors give rise to changes in supply? (Again, remember that a *change in supply* refers to a shift in the entire supply curve, as opposed to a movement along the curve, which we call a *change in the quantity supplied.*) A seller will offer more units if the benefit of selling extra output goes up relative to the cost of producing it. And since the benefit of selling output in a perfectly competitive market is a fixed market price beyond the seller's control, our search for factors that influence supply naturally focuses on the cost side of the calculation. Examples 6.2 to 6.5 suggest why the following five factors, among others, will affect the likelihood that a product will satisfy the cost-benefit test for a given supplier.

---

[1] Again, this rule holds subject to the provision that total revenue exceeds variable production cost at the output level for which price equals marginal cost.

TECHNOLOGY

Perhaps the most important determinant of production cost is technology. Improvements in technology make it possible to produce additional units of output at lower cost. This shifts each individual supply curve downward and hence shifts the market supply curve downward as well. Over time, the introduction of more sophisticated machinery has resulted in dramatic increases in the number of goods produced per hour of effort expended. Every such development gives rise to an outward shift in the market supply curve.

But how do we know technological change will reduce the cost of producing goods and services? Might not new equipment be so expensive that producers who used it would have higher costs than those who relied on earlier designs? If so, then rational producers simply would not use the new equipment. The only technological changes rational producers will adopt are those that will reduce their cost of production.

INPUT PRICES

Whereas technological change generally (although not always) leads to gradual shifts in supply, changes in the prices of important inputs can give rise to large supply shifts literally overnight. For example, the price of crude oil, which is the most important input in the production of gasoline, rose suddenly in 1979, and the resulting leftward shift in supply caused gasoline prices to rise almost immediately.

Similarly, when wage rates rise, the marginal cost of any business that employs labor also rises, shifting supply curves to the left. When interest rates fall, the opportunity cost of capital equipment also falls, causing supply to shift to the right.

THE NUMBER OF SUPPLIERS

Just as demand curves shift to the right when population grows, supply curves also shift to the right as the number of individual suppliers grows. For example, if container recyclers die or retire at a higher rate than new recyclers enter the industry, the supply curve for recycling services will shift to the left. Conversely, if a rise in the unemployment rate leads more people to recycle soft drink containers (by reducing the opportunity cost of time spent recycling), the supply curve of recycling services will shift to the right.

EXPECTATIONS

Expectations about future price movements can affect how much sellers choose to offer in the current market. Suppose, for example, that recyclers expect the future price of aluminum to be much higher than the current price because of the growing use of aluminum components in cars. The rational recycler would then have an incentive to withhold aluminum from the market at today's lower price, thereby to have more available to sell at the higher future price. Conversely, if recyclers expected next year's price of aluminum to be lower than this year's, their incentive would be to offer more aluminum for sale in today's market.

CHANGES IN PRICES OF OTHER PRODUCTS

Apart from technological change, perhaps the most important determinant of supply is variation in the prices of other goods and services that sellers might produce. Prospectors, for example, search for those precious metals for which the surplus of benefits over costs is greatest. When the price of silver rises, many people stop looking for gold and start looking for silver. Conversely, when the price of platinum falls, many platinum prospectors shift their attention to gold.

APPLYING THE THEORY OF SUPPLY

Whether the activity is producing new soft drink containers or recycling used ones, or indeed any other production activity at all, the same logic governs all supply decisions in perfectly competitive markets (and in any other setting in which sellers can sell as much as they wish to at a constant price): Keep expanding output until marginal cost is equal to the price of the product. This logic helps us understand why recycling efforts are more intensive for some products than others.

When recycling is left to private market forces, why are many more aluminum beverage containers recycled than glass ones?

In both cases, recyclers gather containers until their marginal costs are equal to the containers' respective redemption prices. When recycling is left to market forces, the redemption price for a container is based on what companies can sell it (or the materials in it) for. Aluminum containers can be easily processed into scrap aluminum, which commands a high price, and this leads profit-seeking companies to offer a high redemption price for aluminum cans. By contrast, the glass from which glass containers are made has only limited resale value, and this leads profit-seeking companies to offer very low redemption prices for glass containers.

The high redemption prices for aluminum cans induce many people to track down these cans, whereas the low redemption prices for glass containers leads most people to ignore the containers. If recycling is left completely to market forces, then, we would expect to see aluminum soft drink containers quickly recycled, whereas glass containers would increasingly litter the landscape. This is in fact the pattern we do see in states without recycling laws. (More on how these laws work in a moment.) This pattern is a simple consequence of the fact that the supply curves of container-recycling services are upward-sloping.

The acquisition of valuable raw materials is only one of two important benefits from recycling. The second benefit is that, by removing litter, recycling makes the environment more pleasant for everyone. As the next example suggests, this second benefit might easily justify the cost of recycling substantial numbers of glass containers.

ECONOMIC
NATURALIST
6.1

EXAMPLE 6.6

What is the socially optimal amount of recycling of glass containers?

Suppose that the 60,000 citizens of Burlington, Vermont, collectively would be willing to pay 6 cents for each glass container removed from their local environment.

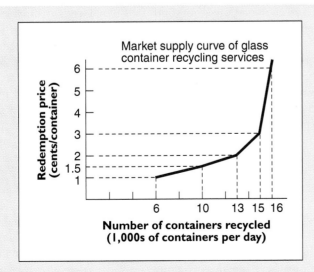

FIGURE 6.7
The Supply Curve of Container Recycling Services for Burlington, Vermont.

If the local market supply curve of glass container recycling services is as shown in Figure 6.7, what is the socially optimal level of glass container recycling?

Suppose the citizens of Burlington authorize their city government to collect tax money to finance litter removal. If the benefit of each glass container removed, as measured by what residents are collectively willing to pay, is 6 cents, the government should offer to pay 6 cents for each glass container recycled. To maximize the total economic surplus from recycling, we should recycle that number of containers for which the marginal cost of recycling is equal to the 6 cent marginal benefit. Given the market supply curve shown, the optimal quantity is 16,000 containers/day, and that is how many will be redeemed when the government offers 6 cents/container.

Although 16,000 containers/day will be removed from the environment in Example 6.6, others will remain. After all, some containers are discarded in remote locations, and a redemption price of 6 cents per container is simply not high enough to induce people to track them all down.

So why not offer an even higher price and get rid of *all* glass container litter? For Example 6.6, the reason is that the marginal cost of removing the 16,001st glass container each day is greater than the benefit of removing it. Total economic surplus is largest when we remove litter only up to the point that the marginal benefit of litter removal is equal to its marginal cost, which occurs when 16,000 containers/day are recycled. To proceed past that point is actually wasteful.

Many people become upset when they first hear economists say that the socially optimal amount of litter is greater than zero. In the minds of these people, the optimal amount of litter is *exactly* zero. But this position completely ignores the scarcity principle. Granted, there would be benefits from reducing litter further, but there would also be costs. Spending more on litter removal therefore means spending less on other useful things. No one would insist that the optimal amount of household dirt is zero. (If someone does make this claim, ask him why he doesn't stay home all day vacuuming the dust that is accumulating in his absence.) If it doesn't pay to remove all the dust from your house, it doesn't pay to remove all the bottles from the environment. Precisely the same logic applies in each case.

If 16,000 containers/day is the optimal amount of litter removal, can we expect the individual spending decisions of private citizens to result in that amount of litter removal? Unfortunately we cannot. The problem is that anyone who paid for litter removal individually would bear the full cost of those services while reaping only a tiny fraction of the benefit. In Example 6.6, the 60,000 citizens of Burlington reaped a total benefit of 6 cents per container removed, which means a benefit of only (6/60,000) = 0.0001 cent per person! Someone who paid 6 cents for someone else to remove a container would thus be incurring a cost 60,000 times greater than her share of the resulting benefit.

Note that the incentive problem here is similar to the one we saw in the case of the beekeeper and orchard owner discussed in Chapter 4. The orchard owner planted too few trees because even though he bore the full cost of planting each tree, part of the extra benefit from extra trees accrued to the beekeeper, whose bees were thereby able to produce extra honey. Similarly, the beekeeper kept too few hives because even though he bore the full cost of each additional hive, part of the benefit of extra hives accrued to the orchard owner, whose trees were thereby more fully pollinated.

In the case of glass container litter, in short, we have an example in which private market forces do not produce the best attainable outcome for society as a whole. Even people who carelessly toss containers on the ground rather than recycle them are often offended by the unsightly landscape to which their own actions contribute. Indeed, this is why they often support laws mandating adequate redemption prices for glass containers.

Is the socially optimal quantity of litter zero?

Activities that generate litter are a good illustration of the equilibrium principle described in Chapter 4. People who litter do so not because they don't care about the environment, but because their private incentives make littering misleadingly attractive. Recycling requires some effort, after all, yet no individual's recycling efforts have a noticeable effect on the quality of the environment. The soft drink-container deposit laws enacted by numerous states were a simple way to bring individual interests more closely into balance with the interests of society as a whole. The vast majority of container litter disappeared almost literally overnight in states that enacted these laws.

EXERCISE 6.4

If the supply curve of glass container recycling services is as shown in the following diagram and each of the city's 60,000 citizens would be willing to pay 0.00005 cent for each glass container removed from the landscape, at what level should the city government set the redemption price for glass containers, and how many containers will be recycled each day?

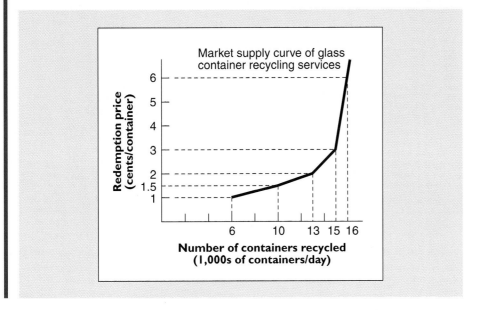

THE PRICE ELASTICITY OF SUPPLY

DEFINING AND CALCULATING ELASTICITY OF SUPPLY

On the buyer's side of the market, we use price elasticity of demand to measure the responsiveness of quantity demanded to changes in price. On the seller's side of the market, the analogous measure is **price elasticity of supply,** which is defined as the percentage change in quantity supplied that occurs in response to a 1 percent change in price. For example, if a 1 percent increase in the redemption price of glass containers leads to a 2 percent increase in the quantity supplied, the price elasticity of supply of recycled glass containers would be 2.0.

The mathematical formula for price elasticity of supply at any point is the same as the corresponding expression for price elasticity of demand:

$$\text{Price elasticity of supply} = \frac{\Delta Q/Q}{\Delta P/P}, \qquad (6.1)$$

where P and Q are the price and quantity at that point, ΔP is a small change in the initial price, and ΔQ is the resulting change in quantity.

price elasticity of supply the percentage change in the quantity supplied that will occur in response to a 1 percent change in the price of a good or service

As with the corresponding expression for price elasticity of demand, Equation 6.1 can be rewritten as $(P/Q)(\Delta Q/\Delta P)$. And since $\Delta Q/\Delta P$ is the reciprocal of the slope of the supply curve, the right-hand side of Equation 6.1 is equal to $(P/Q)(1/slope)$—the same expression we saw for price elasticity of demand. Price and quantity are always positive, as is the slope of the typical short-run supply curve, which implies that price elasticity of supply will be a positive number at every point.

Consider the supply curve in Figure 6.8. The slope of this supply curve is 1/3, so the reciprocal of this slope is 3. Using the formula, this means that the price elasticity of supply at A is $(4/12)(3) = 1$. The corresponding expression at B, $(5/15)(3)$, yields exactly the same value. Indeed, because the ratio P/Q is the same at every point along the supply curve shown, price elasticity of supply will be exactly 1 at every point along this curve. Note the contrast between this result and our earlier finding that price elasticity of demand declines as we move downward along any straight-line demand curve.

FIGURE 6.8
Graphically Calculating the Price Elasticity of Supply.
Price elasticity of supply is $(P/Q)(1/slope)$, which at A is $(4/12)(12/4) = 1$, exactly the same as at B. The price elasticity of supply is equal to 1 at any point along a straight-line supply curve that passes through the origin.

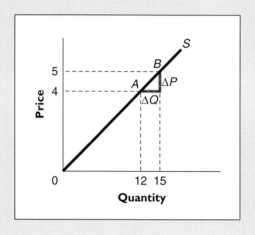

The special property that explains why price elasticity equals 1 at every point in this illustration is that the supply curve was a straight line through the origin. For movements along any such line, both price and quantity always change in exactly the same proportion.

Elasticity is not constant, however, along straight-line supply curves like the one in Figure 6.9, ones that do not pass through the origin. Although the slope of this supply curve is equal to 1 at every point, the ratio P/Q declines as we move to the right along the curve. Elasticity at A is equal to $(4/2)(1) = 2$ and declines to $(5/3)(1) = 5/3$ at B.

FIGURE 6.9
A Supply Curve for Which Price Elasticity Declines As Quantity Rises.
For the supply curve shown, 1/slope is the same at every point, but the ratio P/Q declines as Q increases. So Elasticity = $(P/Q)(1/slope)$ declines as quantity increases.

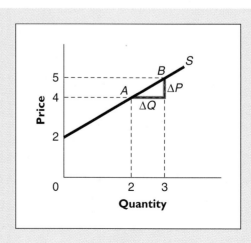

On the buyer's side of the market, two important polar cases were demand curves with infinite price elasticity and zero price elasticity. As Examples 6.7 and 6.8 illustrate, analogous polar cases exist on the seller's side of the market.

EXAMPLE 6.7

What is the elasticity of supply of land within the borough limits of Manhattan?

Land in Manhattan sells in the market for a price, just like aluminum or corn or automobiles or any other product. And the demand for land in Manhattan is a downward-sloping function of its price. For all practical purposes, however, its supply is completely fixed. No matter whether its price is high or low, the same amount of it is available in the market. The supply curve of such a good is vertical, and its price elasticity is zero at every price. Supply curves like the one in Figure 6.10 are said to be **perfectly inelastic**.

perfectly inelastic supply curve a supply curve whose elasticity with respect to price is zero

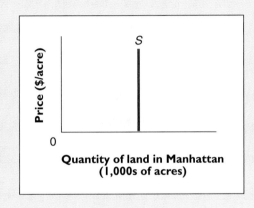

FIGURE 6.10
A Perfectly Inelastic Supply Curve.
Price elasticity of supply is zero at every point along a vertical supply curve.

What is the elasticity of supply of lemonade?

EXAMPLE 6.8

Suppose that the ingredients required to bring a cup of lemonade to market and their respective costs are listed as follows:

Paper cup	2.0 cents
Lemon	3.8 cents
Sugar	2.0 cents
Water	0.2 cents
Ice	1.0 cents
Labor (30 seconds @ $6/hour)	5.0 cents

If these proportions remain the same no matter how many cups of lemonade are made, and the inputs can be purchased in any quantities at the stated prices, draw the supply curve of lemonade and compute its price elasticity.

Since each cup of lemonade costs exactly 14 cents to make, no matter how many cups are made, the supply curve of lemonade is a horizontal line at 14 cents/cup (Figure 6.11). The price elasticity of supply of lemonade is infinite.

Whenever additional units of a good can be produced by using the same combination of inputs, purchased at the same prices, as have been used so far, the supply curve of that good will be horizontal. Such supply curves are said to be **perfectly elastic**.

perfectly elastic supply curve a supply curve whose elasticity with respect to price is infinite

Example 6.8 is a good illustration of how economists use the terms long run and short run. Even though the time span over which lemonade production takes place may be brief, all factors of production were assumed to be variable. By

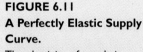

FIGURE 6.11
A Perfectly Elastic Supply Curve.
The elasticity of supply is infinite at every point along a horizontal supply curve.

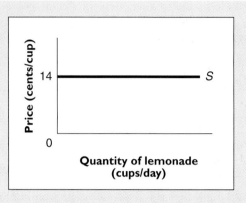

definition, then, the example describes what happens when output changes in the long run, and the law of diminishing returns therefore does not apply. For the specific production process described, the marginal cost curve is constant—at 14 cents/cup—not upward-sloping.

DETERMINANTS OF SUPPLY ELASTICITY

Examples 6.7 and 6.8 suggest some of the factors that govern the elasticity of supply of a good or service. The lemonade case in Example 6.8 was one whose production process was essentially like a cooking recipe. For such cases, we can exactly double our output by doubling each ingredient. If the price of each ingredient remains fixed, the marginal cost of production for such goods will be constant, and hence their horizontal supply curves. Again, when all factors of production can be increased, the law of diminishing returns does not apply, and so the supply curve need not be upward-sloping.

Example 6.7 of land in Manhattan is a contrast in the extreme. The inputs used to produce land in Manhattan—even if we knew what they were—could not be duplicated at any price.

The key to predicting how elastic the supply of a good will be with respect to price is to know the terms on which additional units of the inputs involved in producing that good can be acquired. In general, the more easily additional units of these inputs can be acquired, the higher the price elasticity of supply will be. The following four factors (among others) govern the ease with which additional inputs can be acquired by a producer.

Flexibility of inputs To the extent that production of a good requires inputs that are also useful for the production of other goods, it is relatively easy to lure additional inputs away from their current uses, making supply of that good relatively elastic with respect to price. Thus the fact that lemonade production requires labor with only minimal skills means that a large pool of workers could shift from other activities to lemonade production if a profit opportunity arose. Brain surgery, by contrast, requires elaborately trained and specialized labor, which means that even a large price increase would not increase available supplies, except in the very long run.

Mobility of inputs If inputs can be easily transported from one site to another, an increase in the price of a product in one market will enable a producer in that market to summon inputs from other markets. For example, the supply of agricultural products is made more elastic with respect to price by the fact that thousands of farmworkers are willing to migrate northward during the growing season. The supply of entertainment is similarly made more elastic by the willingness of entertainers to hit the road. Circus performers, lounge singers, comedians, and even exotic dancers often spend a substantial fraction of their time away from home. For instance, according to a 1996 *New York Times* article, the top exotic dancers "basically follow the action, so the same entertainers who worked the Indianapolis 500 now head to Atlanta for the Olympics."

For most goods, the price elasticity of supply increases each time a new canal is dug, or when a new highway is built, or when the telecommunications network improves, or indeed when any other development makes it easier to find and transport inputs from one place to another.

Ability to produce substitute inputs The inputs required to produce finished diamond gemstones include raw diamond crystal, skilled labor, and elaborate cutting and polishing machinery. In time, the number of people with the requisite skills can be increased, as can the amount of specialized machinery. The number of raw diamond crystals buried in the earth is probably fixed in the same way that Manhattan real estate is fixed, but unlike Manhattan real estate, rising prices will encourage miners to spend the effort required to find a larger proportion of those crystals. Still, the supply of natural gemstone diamonds tends to be relatively inelastic because of the difficulty of augmenting the number of diamond crystals.

The day is close at hand, however, when gemstone makers will be able to produce synthetic diamond crystals that are indistinguishable from real ones. Indeed, there are already synthetic crystals that fool even highly experienced jewelers. The introduction of a perfect synthetic substitute for natural diamond crystals would increase the price elasticity of supply of diamonds (or, at any rate, the price elasticity of supply of gemstones that look and feel just like diamonds).

Time Because it takes time for producers to switch from one activity to another and because it takes time to build new capital goods and train additional skilled workers, the price elasticity of supply will be higher for most goods in the long run than in the short run. In the short run, a manufacturer's inability to augment existing stocks of capital equipment and skilled labor may make it impossible to expand output beyond a certain limit. But if a shortage of managers is the bottleneck, new MBAs can be graduated in only 2 years. Or if a shortage of legal staff is the problem, new lawyers can be trained in 3 years. In the long run, firms can always buy new equipment, build new factories, and hire additional skilled workers.

"In six more weeks, these M.B.A.s will be ready for market."

The conditions that gave rise to the perfectly elastic supply curve for lemonade in Example 6.8 are also satisfied for many other products in the long run. If a product can be copied (in the sense that any company can acquire the design and other technological information required to produce it) and if the inputs needed for its production are used in roughly fixed proportions and are available at fixed market prices, then the long-run supply curve for that product will be horizontal. But as we will presently see, many products do not satisfy these conditions, and their supply curves remain steeply upward-sloping, even in the very long run.

UNIQUE AND ESSENTIAL INPUTS: THE ULTIMATE SUPPLY BOTTLENECK

Fans of professional basketball are an enthusiastic bunch. Directly through their purchases of tickets and indirectly through their support of television advertisers, they spend literally billions of dollars each year on the sport. But these dollars are not distributed evenly across all teams. A disproportionate share of all revenues and product endorsement fees accrue to the people associated with consistently winning teams, and at the top of this pyramid generally stands the National Basketball Association's championship team.

Consider the task of trying to produce a championship team in the NBA. What are the inputs you would need? Talented players, a shrewd and dedicated coach and assistants, trainers, physicians, an arena, practice facilities, means for transporting players to away games, a marketing staff, and so on. And whereas some of these inputs can be acquired at reasonable prices in the marketplace, many others cannot. Indeed, the most important input of all— highly talented players—is in extremely limited supply. *This is so because the very definition of a talented player is inescapably relative: Simply put, such a player is one who is better than most others.*

Given the huge payoff that accrues to the NBA championship team, it is no surprise that the bidding for the most talented players has become so intense. If there were a long list of 7-foot 3-inch 325-pound centers, the Los Angeles Lakers wouldn't have had to pay Shaquille O'Neal $120 million over a 7-year contract. But of course the supply of such players is extremely limited. Many hungry organizations would like nothing better than to claim the NBA championship each year, yet no matter how much each is willing to spend, only one can succeed. The supply of NBA championship teams is perfectly inelastic with respect to price even in the very long run.

Sports champions are by no means the only important product whose supply elasticity is constrained by the inability to reproduce unique and essential inputs. In the movie industry, for example, although the supply of movies starring Jim Carrey is not perfectly inelastic, there are only so many films he can make each year. Because his films consistently generate huge box office revenues, scores of film producers want to sign him for their projects. But because there isn't enough of him to go around, his salary per film is more than $20 million.

In the long run, unique and essential inputs are the only truly significant supply bottlenecks. If it were not for the inability to duplicate the services of such inputs, most goods and services would have extremely high price elasticities of supply.

USING THE PRODUCTION POSSIBILITIES CURVE TO GENERATE SUPPLY CURVES

Recall Islandia, the simple economy in Chapter 3, in which Susan and Tom could produce either of two goods: coffee or Macadamia nuts. Our task in this section will be to see how the information implicit in Islandia's production possibilities curve enables us to construct supply curves for each product. To begin, the individual members' productivity information is reproduced in Table 6.6.

TABLE 6.6
Productivity for Two Workers

	Coffee productivity	Nut productivity
Susan	1.5 pounds/hour	3 pounds/hour
Tom	0.75 pound/hour	0.75 pound/hour

As we saw earlier, the opportunity cost of 1 pound of nuts is 1/2 pound of coffee for Susan and 1 pound of coffee for Tom. The production possibilities curve for this economy is reproduced in Figure 6.12.

How can we use the information in the production possibilities curve to construct Islandia's supply curves in world markets for coffee and nuts? Suppose Islandians could sell, or buy, coffee or nuts in the world market at fixed prices. If the price of 1 pound of nuts in the world market were less than 1/2 pound of coffee, the citizens of Islandia simply would not offer any nuts for sale in the world market. To see why, examine what would happen if they did. Suppose, for example, that they could get 1/4 pound of coffee by selling a pound of nuts in the world market and that they were selling 1 pound of nuts/day at that price (picked by Susan, as called for by the low-hanging-fruit principle, since her opportunity cost of picking nuts is lower than Tom's). Why should Islandia continue to make that sale? After all, it can get an extra 1/2 pound of coffee if Susan shifts full-time to picking coffee. As the supply curve in Figure 6.13 indicates, Islandians will supply 0 pounds of nuts to the world market when the price of nuts is lower than 1/2 pound of coffee.

Once the price of nuts rises to 1/2 pound of coffee, however, Susan should no longer pick coffee. At that price, Islandians will offer 24 pounds of nuts/day

FIGURE 6.12

Opportunity Cost of Food at Different Points along the Production Possibilities Curve.

At *A*, the opportunity cost of 1 pound of nuts is 1/2 pound of coffee. At *B*, the opportunity cost of 1 pound of nuts is 1 pound of coffee.

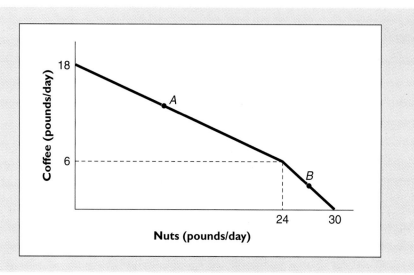

FIGURE 6.13

Islandia's Supply Curve for Nuts.

Since Susan's opportunity cost of producing nuts is only 1/2 pound of coffee, Islandia will supply no nuts when the world price of nuts is less than that. When the price of nuts is above Susan's opportunity cost but below Tom's (1 pound of coffee), Islandia will sell all the nuts Susan can pick. For nut prices larger than 1 pound of coffee, both Tom and Susan will sell all the nuts they can pick.

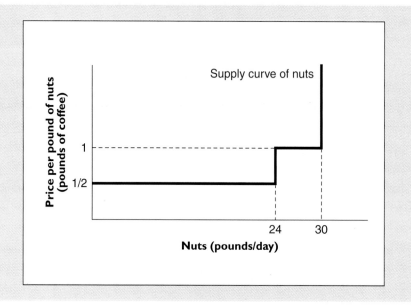

for sale in the world market (the full amount that Susan can pick each day). Similarly, once the price of 1 pound of nuts reaches 1 pound of coffee, Tom should switch from coffee to nut production, which means that Islandians will supply a total of 30 pounds of nuts/day (Susan's 24 pounds plus Tom's 6 pounds) at that price. For nut prices above 1 pound of coffee, the Islandians's supply curve of nuts is perfectly inelastic, since they are unable to supply any more than 30 pounds of nuts/day.

The procedure for constructing Islandia's supply curve for coffee involves essentially parallel reasoning. If the slope of the production possibilities curve at any point represents the opportunity cost of 1 pound of nuts, the reciprocal of that slope represents the opportunity cost of 1 pound of coffee at that point. Thus the opportunity cost of a pound of coffee is 2 pounds of nuts at *A* in Figure 6.12 and 1 pound at *B*.

When the world price of 1 pound of coffee is less than 1 pound of nuts, Islandians will supply no coffee to the world market. Once the price of coffee reaches 1 pound of nuts, Tom should supply 6 pounds of coffee. And for world coffee prices at or above 2 pounds of nuts, Susan should add her offering of 12 pounds of coffee/day, for a total of 18 pounds of coffee/day. Islandia's supply curve for coffee is thus as shown in Figure 6.14.

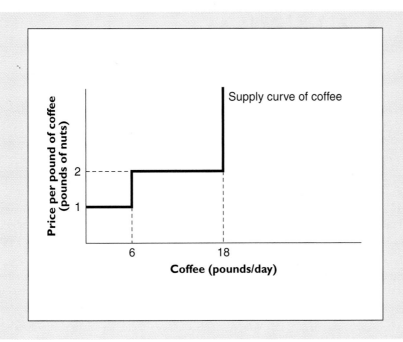

FIGURE 6.14
Islandia's Supply Curve for Coffee.
When the world price of coffee is less than Tom's opportunity cost of picking coffee (1 pound of nuts), Islandia will sell no coffee. When the price of coffee is between Tom's opportunity cost and Susan's (2 pounds of nuts), Islandia will sell all the coffee Tom can pick (6 pounds/day). When the price of coffee is above 2 pounds of nuts, Islandia will sell all the coffee Tom and Susan can pick (18 pounds/day).

▪ SUMMARY ▪

- The supply curve for a good or service is a schedule that for any price tells us the quantity sellers wish to supply at that price. The prices at which goods and services are offered for sale in the market depend, in turn, on the opportunity cost of the resources required to produce them.

- Supply curves tend to be upward-sloping, at least in the short run, partly because of the low-hanging-fruit principle. Generally, rational producers will always take advantage of their best opportunities first, moving on to more difficult or costly opportunities only after their best ones have been exhausted. Reinforcing this tendency is the law of diminishing returns, which says that when some factors of production are held fixed, the amount of additional variable factors required to produce successive increments in output grows larger.

- For perfectly competitive markets—or, more generally, for markets in which individual sellers can sell whatever quantity they wish at constant price—the seller's best option is to sell that quantity of output for which price equals marginal cost. The supply curve for the seller thus coincides with his or her marginal cost curve, the curve that measures the cost of producing additional units of output. This is why we sometimes say the supply curve represents the cost side of the market (in contrast to the demand curve, which represents the benefit side of the market).

- An important terminological distinction from the demand side of the market also applies on the supply side of the market. *A change in supply* means a shift in the entire supply curve, whereas *a change in the quantity supplied* means a movement along the supply curve. The factors that cause supply curves to shift include technology, input prices, the number of sellers, expectations of future price changes, and the prices of other products that firms might produce.

- Price elasticity of supply is defined as the percentage change in quantity supplied that occurs in response to a 1 percent change in price. The mathematical formula for the price elasticity of supply at any point is $(\Delta Q/Q)/(\Delta P/P)$, where P and Q are the price and quantity at that point, ΔP is a small change in the initial price, and ΔQ is the resulting change in quantity. This formula can also be expressed as $(P/Q)(1/\text{slope})$, where 1/slope is the reciprocal of the slope of the supply curve.

- The price elasticity of supply of a good will depend on how difficult or costly it is to acquire additional units of the inputs involved in producing that good. In general, the more easily additional units of these inputs can be acquired, the higher the price elasticity of supply will be. It is easier to expand production of a product if the inputs used to produce that product are similar to inputs used to produce other products, if inputs are relatively mobile, or if an acceptable substitute for existing inputs can be developed. And like the price elasticity of demand, the price elasticity of supply is greater in the long run than in the short run. Except for the existence of unique and essential inputs, all goods and services would have highly elastic supply curves in the long run.

■ KEY TERMS ■

factor of production (141)
fixed factor of production (141)
imperfectly competitive firm (140)
law of diminishing returns (141)
long run (141)

perfectly competitive market (140)
perfectly elastic supply curve (153)
perfectly inelastic supply curve (153)
price elasticity of supply (151)
price taker (140)

profit (139)
profit-maximizing firm (140)
short run (141)
variable factor of production (141)

■ REVIEW QUESTIONS ■

1. Explain why you would expect supply curves to slope upward on the basis of the principle of increasing opportunity cost.

2. Which do you think is more likely to be a fixed factor of production for an ice cream producer during the next 2 months, its factory building or its workers who operate the machines? Explain.

3. Economists often stress that congestion helps account for the law of diminishing returns. With this in mind, explain why it would be impossible to feed all the people on earth with food grown in a single flowerpot, even if unlimited water, labor, seed, fertilizer, sunlight, and other inputs were available.

4. True or false: The perfectly competitive firm should *always* produce the output level for which price equals marginal cost.

5. Why is supply elasticity higher in the long run than in the short run?

■ PROBLEMS ■

1. Zoe is trying to decide how to divide her time between her job as a wedding photographer, which pays $27/hour for as many hours as she chooses to work, and as a fossil collector, in which her pay depends both on the price of fossils and the number of fossils she finds. Earnings aside, Zoe is indifferent between the two tasks, and the number of fossils she can find depends on the number of hours a day she searches, as shown in the following table.

Hours/day	Total fossils/day
1	5
2	9
3	12
4	14
5	15

a. Derive a table with price in dollar increments from $0 to $30 in the first column and the quantity of fossils Zoe is willing to supply per day at that price in the second column.

b. Plot these points in a graph with price on the vertical axis and quantity per day on the horizontal axis. What is this curve called?

2. A price-taking firm makes air conditioners. The market price of one of their new air conditioners is $120. Its total cost information is given in the following table.

Air conditioners/day	Total cost ($/day)
1	100
2	150
3	220
4	310
5	405
6	510
7	650
8	800

How many air conditioners should the firm produce per day if its goal is to maximize its profit?

3. The Paducah Slugger Company makes baseball bats out of lumber supplied to it by Acme Sporting Goods, which pays Paducah $10 for each finished bat. Paducah's only factors of production are lathe operators and a small building with a lathe. The number of bats per day it produces depends on the number of employee-hours per day, as shown in the following table.

Number of bats/day	Number of employee-hours/day
0	0
5	1
10	2
15	4
20	7
25	11
30	16
35	22

a. If the wage is $15/hour and Paducah's daily capital cost for the lathe and building is fixed at $60, what is the profit-maximizing quantity of bats?
b. What would be the profit-maximizing number of bats if the capital cost were not $60/day but only $30?

4. In Problem 3, how would Paducah's profit-maximizing level of output be affected if the government imposed a tax of $10/day on the company? What would Paducah's profit-maximizing level of output be if the government imposed a tax of $2 per bat?

5. Explain how the following would affect supply in the indicated market:
a. An increase in the world price of honey in the market for beeswax candles.
b. An increase in the world price of cauliflower in the market for cabbage. (Assume the demand for cabbage does not shift.)
c. An increase in the world price of ice cream in the market for ice cream.

6. How would each of the following affect the U.S. market supply curve for corn?
a. A new high-yielding genetic strain of corn is discovered.
b. The price of fertilizer falls.
c. The government offers corn farmers a subsidy of $1/bushel.

7. The price elasticity of supply for Basmati rice (an aromatic strain of rice) is likely to be:
a. Higher in the long run than the short run, because farmers cannot easily change their decisions about how much Basmati rice to plant once the current crop has been planted.
b. High, because consumers have a lot of other kinds of rice and other staple foods to choose from.
c. Low in both the long run and short run, because rice farming requires only unskilled labor.

    d. High in both the long run and the short run because the inputs required to produce Basmati rice can easily be duplicated.

8. What are the respective price elasticities of supply at A and B on the supply curve shown in the following figure?

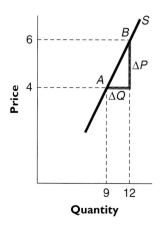

9. The supply curves for the only two firms in a competitive industry are given by $P = 2Q_1$ and $P = 2 + Q_2$, where Q_1 is the output of firm 1 and Q_2 is the output of firm 2. What is the market supply curve for this industry? (*Hint:* Graph the two curves side by side, then add their respective quantities at a sample of different prices.)

10. Jay, Kay, and Dee are marooned on an island in the Bahamas. They must find a way to provide themselves with food and drinking water. The following table shows how many hours it takes each person to produce one unit of food or one unit of water.

	Time to produce one unit of food	Time to produce one unit of water
Jay	1 hour	2 hours
Kay	2 hours	1 hour
Dee	4 hours	6 hours

    a. If each person has 12 hours of daylight available to work, draw the individual production possibility curves when each person provides for himself or herself.

    b. Suppose food and water are also produced on a neighboring island and a boat becomes available at no cost to allow trade between the islands. Draw the supply curve for water on the island inhabited by Jay, Kay, and Dee, where the vertical axis represents the price of water in terms of food. Then draw the supply curve for food on their island, where the vertical axis represents the price of food in terms of water.

■ ANSWERS TO IN-CHAPTER EXERCISES ■

6.1 Since Harry will find 300 containers if he searches a third hour, we find his reservation price for searching a second hour by solving $p(300) = \$6$, for $p = 2$ cents. His reservation prices for additional hours of search are calculated in an analogous way.

Fourth hour: $p(200) = \$6$, so $p = 3$ cents;
Fifth hour: $p(100) = \$6$, so $p = 6$ cents.

6.2 The profit figures corresponding to a price of $5/hundred are as shown in the last column of the following table, where we see that the profit-maximizing output (which here means the loss-minimizing output) is 0 bottles/day. Note that the company actually loses $40/day at that output level. But it would lose even more if it produced any other amount. If the company expects conditions to remain unchanged, it will want to go out of the bottle business as soon as its equipment lease expires.

Q (bottles/day)	Total revenue ($/day)	Total labor cost ($/day)	Total cost ($/day)	Profit ($/day)
0	0	0	40	−40
100	5	10	50	−45
200	10	20	60	−50
300	15	40	80	−65
400	20	70	110	−90
500	25	110	150	−125
600	30	160	200	−170
700	35	220	260	−225

6.3 The profit figures corresponding to a price of $25/hundred are as shown in the last column of the following table, where we see that the profit-maximizing output (which here means the loss-minimizing output) is 300 bottles/day. Note that the company actually loses $5/day at that output level. But as long as it remains committed to its daily lease payment of $40, it would lose even more if it produced any other amount. If the company expects conditions to remain unchanged, it will want to go out of the bottle business as soon as its equipment lease expires.

Q (bottles/day)	Total revenue ($/day)	Total labor cost ($/day)	Total cost ($/day)	Profit ($/day)
0	0	0	40	−40
100	25	10	50	−25
200	50	20	60	−10
300	75	40	80	−5
400	100	70	110	−10
500	125	110	150	−25
600	150	160	200	−50
700	175	220	260	−85

6.4 That each of the city's 60,000 residents is willing to pay 0.00005 cents for each bottle removed means that the collective benefit of each bottle removed is $(60,000)(0.00005) = 3$ cents. So the city should set the redemption price at 3 cents, and from the supply curve we see that 15,000 bottles/day will be recycled at that price.

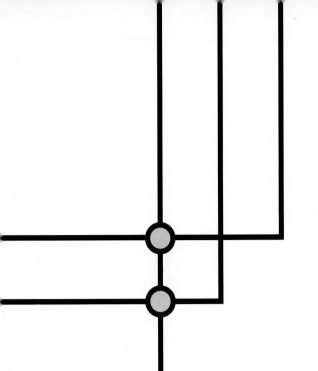

CHAPTER

7

EFFICIENCY AND EXCHANGE

■

Armando Lopez sat watching the Republican National Convention on television one August night as one orator after another extolled the virtues of the free enterprise system. "The greatest engine of progress mankind has ever witnessed," one of the speakers called it. "A rising tide that will lift all boats," said another.

Lopez, however, was skeptical, for although he had worked hard and played by society's rules, his standard of living had been deteriorating rather than improving. Downsized from his draftsman's position at an aircraft plant the year before, Lopez was working as a janitor for a local office-cleaning company, the best job he had been able to find after months of search. He could not afford to repair the leaky roof and faulty plumbing at his house in East Los Angeles. Indeed, his two older children had dropped out of college because he could no longer afford their tuition bills. Although his commute to work was only 6 miles each way, freeway congestion made it a 90-minute trip most mornings. His wife's recurrent asthma attacks, triggered by local air pollution, had recently worsened. Without health insurance, the family's medical bills had been mounting rapidly. And there had been four deaths from drive-by shootings in their neighborhood in the last year.

Given the stark contrast between his own experience and the lofty claims of the orators he was listening to, Lopez's skepticism about the virtues of the free enterprise system was understandable. Yet informed students of the market system understand that it never could have been expected to prevent Lopez's problems in the first place. *In certain domains*—indeed, in very broad domains—markets are every bit as remarkable as even their strongest proponents assert. Yet there are many problems they simply cannot be expected to solve. For example, private markets cannot by themselves guarantee an income distribution that most people regard as fair. Nor can they ensure clean air, uncongested highways, or safe neighborhoods.

"I know we live in troubled times, but I don't seem to be troubled."

But markets do enable society to produce sufficient resources to meet all these goals and more. In virtually all successful societies, however, markets are supplemented by active political coordination in at least some instances. We will almost always achieve our goals more effectively if we know what tasks private markets can do well and then let them perform those tasks. Unfortunately, the discovery that markets cannot solve *every* problem seems to have led some critics to conclude that markets cannot solve *any* problems. This misperception is a dangerous one, because it has prompted attempts to prevent markets from doing even those tasks for which they are ideally suited.

Our task in this chapter will be to explore why many tasks are best left to the market. We will develop more carefully the concept of economic surplus introduced in Chapter 1, and we will explore the conditions under which unregulated markets generate the largest possible economic surplus. We will also discuss why attempts to interfere with market outcomes often lead to unintended and undesired consequences.

MARKET EQUILIBRIUM AND EFFICIENCY

As noted in Chapter 4, the mere fact that markets coordinate the production of such a large and complex list of goods and services is reason enough to marvel at them. But economists make an even stronger claim, namely, that markets not only produce these goods but also produce them as efficiently as possible.

efficient (or Pareto-efficient)
a situation is efficient if no change is possible that will help some people without harming others

The term **efficient**, as economists use it, has a narrow technical meaning. When we say that market equilibrium is efficient, we mean simply this: *If price and quantity take anything other than their equilibrium values, a transaction that will make at least some people better off without harming others can always be found.* This concept of efficiency is also known as **Pareto efficiency**, after Vilfredo Pareto, the nineteenth-century Italian economist who introduced it.

Why is market equilibrium efficient in this sense? The answer to this question involves a straightforward application of the cost-benefit principle. The following examples will illustrate the kinds of welfare-enhancing transactions that become possible whenever a market is out of equilibrium.

Why is holding the price of milk below its equilibrium level inefficient?

EXAMPLE 7.1

Suppose the supply and demand curves for milk are as shown in Figure 7.1 and the current price of milk is $1/gallon. Describe a transaction that will benefit both buyer and seller.

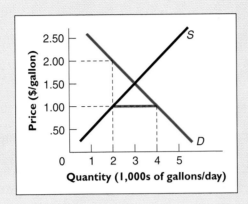

FIGURE 7.1
A Market in Which Price Is Below the Equilibrium Level.
In this market, milk is currently selling for $1/gallon, $0.50 below the equilibrium price of $1.50/gallon.

At a price of $1, sellers offer only 2,000 gallons of milk a day. At that quantity, buyers value an extra gallon of milk at $2 (the price that corresponds to 2,000 gallons a day on the demand curve, which represents what buyers are willing to pay for an additional gallon). We also know that the cost of producing an extra gallon of milk is only $1 (the price that corresponds to 2,000 gallons a day on the supply curve, which equals marginal cost).

Furthermore, a price of $1/gallon leads to excess demand of 2,000 gallons/day, which means that many dissatisfied buyers cannot buy as much milk as they want at the going price. Now suppose a supplier sells an extra gallon of milk to the most eager of these buyers for $1.25, as in Figure 7.2. Since the extra gallon cost only $1 to produce, the seller is $0.25 better off than before. And since the most eager buyer values the extra gallon at $2, that buyer is $0.75 better off than before. In sum, the transaction creates an extra $1 of economic surplus out of thin air!

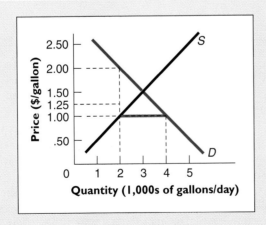

FIGURE 7.2
How Excess Demand Creates an Opportunity for a Surplus-Enhancing Transaction.
At a market price of $1/gallon, the most intensely dissatisfied buyer is willing to pay $2 for an additional gallon, which a seller can produce at a cost of only $1. If this buyer pays the seller $1.25 for the extra gallon, the buyer gains an economic surplus of $0.75 and the seller gains an economic surplus of $0.25.

Note that none of the other buyers or sellers is harmed by this transaction. Thus milk selling for only $1/gallon cannot be efficient. Indeed, if milk sells for *any* price below $1.50/gallon (the market equilibrium price), we can design a transaction in which each participant's benefit exceeds his or her cost, which means that selling milk for any price less than $1.50/gallon cannot be efficient.

EXERCISE 7.1

In Example 7.1, suppose that milk initially sells for 50 cents/gallon. Describe a transaction that will create additional economic surplus for both buyer and seller without causing harm to anyone else.

EXAMPLE 7.2

Why is holding the price of milk above its equilibrium level inefficient?

Suppose the current price of milk is $2/gallon with the same demand and supply curves as in Example 7.1. Describe a transaction that would benefit both buyer and seller.

With the price now above the equilibrium level, we have an excess supply of 2,000 gallons/day (see Figure 7.3). Suppose the most dissatisfied producer sells a gallon of milk for $1.75 to the buyer who values it most highly. This buyer, who would have been willing to pay $2, will be $0.25 better off than before. Likewise the producer, who would have been willing to sell milk for as little as $1/gallon (the marginal cost of production at 2,000 gallons/day), will be $0.75 better

FIGURE 7.3

How Excess Supply Creates an Opportunity for a Surplus-Enhancing Transaction.
At a market price of $2/gallon, dissatisfied sellers can produce an additional gallon of milk at a cost of only $1, which is $1 less than a buyer would be willing to pay for it. If the buyer pays the seller $1.75 for an extra gallon, the buyer gains an economic surplus of $0.25 and the seller gains an economic surplus of $0.75.

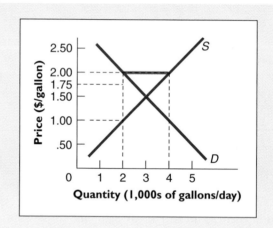

off than before. As in Example 7.1, the new transaction creates $1 of additional economic surplus without harming any other buyer or seller. Since we could design a similar surplus-enhancing transaction at any price above the equilibrium level, selling milk for more than $1.50/gallon cannot be efficient.

Indeed, the market equilibrium price is the *only* price at which buyers and sellers cannot design a surplus-enhancing transaction. In this specific, limited sense, free markets are said to allocate goods and services efficiently.

Actually, to claim that market equilibrium is always efficient even in this limited sense is an overstatement. The claim holds only if buyers and sellers are well informed, if markets are perfectly competitive, and if the demand and supply curves satisfy certain other restrictions. For example, market equilibrium will not be efficient if the individual marginal cost curves that add up to the market supply curve fail to include all relevant costs of producing the product. As we saw in Chapter 4, for example, if production generates pollution that harms others, then the true cost of expanding output will be higher than indicated by the market supply curve. The equilibrium output will be inefficiently large and the equilibrium price inefficiently low.

Likewise, market equilibrium will not be efficient if the individual demand curves that make up the market demand curve do not capture all the relevant benefits of buying additional units of the product. For instance, if a homeowner's willingness to pay for ornamental shrubs is based only on the enjoyment she gains from them, and not on any benefits that may accrue to the neighbors, the market demand curve for shrubs will understate their value to the neighborhood. The equilibrium quantity of ornamental shrubs will be inefficiently small, and the market price for shrubs will be inefficiently low.

We will take up such market imperfections in greater detail in later chapters. For now, we will confine our attention to perfectly competitive markets whose demand curves capture all relevant benefits and whose supply curves capture all relevant costs. For such goods, market equilibrium will always be efficient in the limited sense described earlier.

RECAP   **EQUILIBRIUM AND EFFICIENCY**

When a market is not in equilibrium—either because price is above the equilibrium level or below it—the quantity exchanged is always less than the equilibrium level. At such a quantity, a transaction can always be made in which both buyer and seller benefit from the exchange of an additional unit of output. A market in equilibrium is said to be efficient, or Pareto-efficient, meaning that no reallocation is possible that will benefit some people without harming others.

ECONOMIC SURPLUS

In Chapter 1 we first encountered the concept of economic surplus, which in a buyer's case is the difference between the most she would have been willing to pay for a product and the amount she actually pays for it. The same concept applies to sellers of goods and services, for whom economic surplus is the difference between what they are paid for the goods they sell and the smallest amount they would have been willing to accept. In any given market, **total economic surplus** is the sum of all economic surplus attributable to participation in that market by buyers and sellers. Stated another way, it is a measure of the total amount by which buyers and sellers benefit from their participation in the market.

total economic surplus the total economic surplus in a market is the sum of all the individual economic surpluses gained by buyers and sellers who participate in the market

CALCULATING ECONOMIC SURPLUS

To see how total economic surplus is actually measured, we'll consider a hypothetical market for a good with 11 potential buyers and 11 potential sellers, each of whom can buy or sell a maximum of one unit of the good each day. The first potential seller's marginal cost is $1 per unit, the second potential seller's is $2, the third potential seller's is $3, and so on. Similarly, the first potential buyer's reservation price for the product is $11, the second buyer's reservation price is $10, the third buyer's reservation price is $9, and so on. The supply and demand curves for this market will have the staircase shapes shown in Figure 7.4. We can think of these curves as digital counterparts of the traditional analog demand and supply curves. (If the units shown on the horizontal axis were fine enough, these digital curves would be visually indistinguishable from their analog counterparts.)

The equilibrium price in the market shown in Figure 7.4 is $6/unit, and the equilibrium quantity is 6 units/day. Neither buyer nor seller will receive any surplus from the exchange of the sixth unit, since their respective reservation prices for that unit are exactly $6, the same as its market price. But the first five units yielded surplus for both buyers and sellers. The buyer of the first unit, for

FIGURE 7.4
A Market with "Digital" Supply and Demand Curves.
When a product can be sold only in whole-number amounts, its demand and supply curves have the staircase shapes shown.

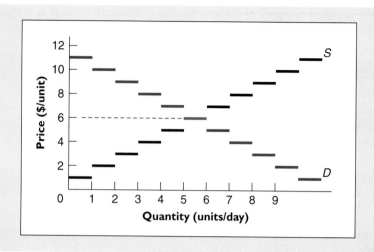

consumer surplus the economic surplus gained by the buyers of a product as measured by the cumulative difference between their respective reservation prices and the price they actually paid.

producer surplus the economic surplus gained by the sellers of a product as measured by the cumulative difference between the price received and their respective reservation prices.

example, would have been willing to pay $11 for it, but since the market price was only $6, the buyer received a surplus of exactly $5. Likewise the seller of the first unit, who would have been willing to supply it for as little as his marginal cost of $1, also received a surplus of $5. The buyer of the second unit, who would have been willing to pay as much as $10, received a surplus of $4, the same as the seller, who would have been willing to sell the unit for $2. For both buyer and seller, the surplus was $3 on the third unit, $2 on the fourth unit, and $1 on the fifth unit.

If we add all the buyers' surpluses, we get a total of $15 of buyers' surplus each day. This total is often referred to as **consumer surplus**. The sum of the corresponding surpluses for sellers is also $15/day. This total is often referred to as **producer surplus**. As we'll see in later examples, the surplus received by buyers and sellers need not always be the same. The total economic surplus for this market is the sum of consumer surplus and producer surplus, or $30/day, which corresponds to the combined blue and green areas in Figure 7.5.

FIGURE 7.5
Consumer and Producer Surplus.
Consumer surplus (blue region) is the cumulative difference between the most that buyers are willing to pay for each unit and the price they actually pay. Producer surplus (green region) is the cumulative difference between the price at which producers sell each unit and the smallest amounts they would be willing to accept.

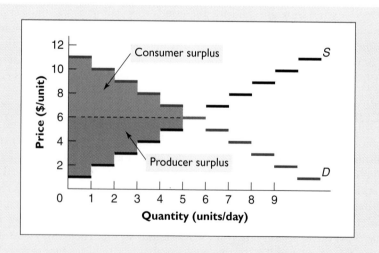

EXERCISE 7.2

Calculate producer surplus and consumer surplus for a market like the one just described, except that the buyers' reservation prices for each unit are $2 higher than before. (That is, how big would the surpluses be if the demand and supply curves were as shown in the following diagram?)

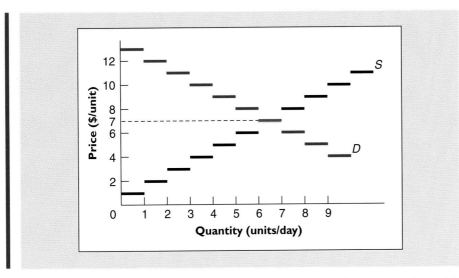

Now suppose we want to measure total economic surplus in a market with conventional straight-line supply and demand curves. As Example 7.3 illustrates, this task is a simple extension of the method used for digital supply and demand curves.

How much do buyers and sellers benefit from their participation in the market for milk?

EXAMPLE 7.3

Consider the market for milk whose demand and supply curves are shown in Figure 7.6, which has an equilibrium price of $2/gallon and an equilibrium quantity of 4,000 gallons/day. How much total economic surplus do the participants in this market reap?

In Figure 7.6, note first that, as in Figure 7.5, the last unit exchanged each day generates no surplus at all, either for buyers or sellers. Note also that for all milk sold up to 4,000 gallons/day, buyers receive consumer surplus and

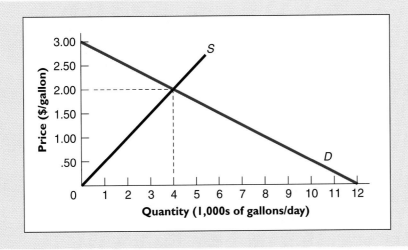

FIGURE 7.6
Supply and Demand in the Market for Milk.
For the supply and demand curves shown, the equilibrium price of milk is $2/gallon and the equilibrium quantity is 4,000 gallons/day.

sellers receive producer surplus, just as in Figure 7.5. For sellers, the surplus is the cumulative difference between market price and marginal cost. For buyers, the surplus is the cumulative difference between the most they would be willing to pay for milk (as measured on the demand curve) and the price they actually pay.

Total consumer surplus received by buyers in the milk market is thus the blue triangle between the demand curve and the market price in Figure 7.7. Note that this area is a right triangle whose vertical arm is h = $1/gallon and whose

FIGURE 7.7
Total Economic Surplus in the Market for Milk.
Consumer surplus is the area of the blue triangle ($2,000/day). Producer surplus is the area of the green triangle ($4,000/day). Total economic surplus is the sum of the two, or $6,000/day.

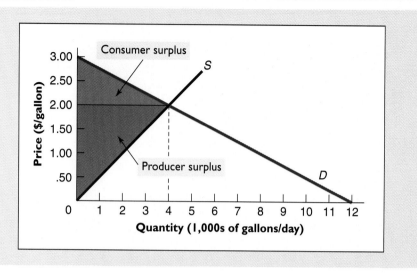

horizontal arm is $b = 4,000$ gallons/day. And since the area of any triangle is equal to $(1/2)bh$, consumer surplus in this market is equal to

$$(1/2)(4,000 \text{ gallons/day})(\$1/\text{gallon}) = \$2,000/\text{day}.$$

Likewise, total producer surplus is the green triangle between the supply curve and the market price. The height of this triangle is $h = \$2/\text{gallon}$ and the base is $b = 4,000$ gallons/day, so producer surplus is equal to

$$(1/2)(4,000 \text{ gallons/day})(\$2/\text{gallon}) = \$4,000/\text{day}.$$

The total economic surplus from this milk market is the sum of consumer and producer surplus, or $6,000/day.

A useful way of thinking about this surplus is to ask what is the highest price consumers and producers would pay, in the aggregate, for the right to continue participating in the milk market. For buyers, the answer is $2,000/day, since that is the amount by which their combined benefits exceed their combined costs. Sellers would pay up to $4,000/day, since that is the amount by which their combined benefits exceed their combined reservation prices. All together, then, buyers and sellers would be willing to pay up to $6,000/day for the right to continue participating in this market.

That economic surplus is the amount by which buyers and sellers benefit from participating in a market sheds further light on the economist's claim that market equilibrium is efficient. At any price other than the equilibrium price, the total economic surplus produced by a market will be less than it would be at the equilibrium price. Stated another way, the equilibrium price and quantity serve to maximize the total economic surplus created by a market.

EFFICIENCY IS NOT THE ONLY GOAL

The fact that market equilibrium maximizes economic surplus is an attractive feature, to be sure. Bear in mind, however, that "efficient" does not mean the same thing as "good." For example, the market for milk may be in equilibrium at a price of $2/gallon, yet many poor families may be unable to afford milk for their children at that price. Still others may not even have a place for their children to sleep.

Efficiency is a concept based on predetermined attributes of buyers and sellers—their incomes, tastes, abilities, knowledge, and so on. Through the combined effects of individual cost-benefit decisions, these attributes give rise to the supply and demand curves for each good produced in an economy. If we are concerned about inequality in the distribution of attributes like income, we should not be surprised to discover that markets do not always yield outcomes we like.

Most of us could agree, for example, that the world would be a better one if poor families had enough income to feed their families adequately. The claim that equilibrium in the market for milk is efficient means simply that *taking people's incomes as given,* the resulting allocation of milk cannot be altered so as to help some people without at the same time harming others.

To this a critic of the market system might respond: So what? As such critics rightly point out, imposing costs on others may be justified if doing so will help those with sufficiently important unmet demands. For example, most people would prefer to fund homeless shelters with their tax dollars rather than let the homeless freeze to death. Arguing in these terms, American policymakers responded to rapid increases in the price of oil in the late 1970s by imposing price controls on home heating oil. And many of us might agree that if the alternative had been to take no action at all, price controls might have been justified in the name of social justice.

But the economist's concept of market efficiency makes clear that there *must* be a better alternative policy. Price controls on oil prevent the market from reaching equilibrium, and as we saw, that means forgoing transactions that would benefit some people without harming others.

WHY EFFICIENCY SHOULD BE THE FIRST GOAL

Efficiency is important not because it is a desirable end in itself but because it enables us to achieve all our other goals to the fullest possible extent. Whenever a market is out of equilibrium, it is always possible to generate additional economic surplus. To gain additional economic surplus is to gain more of the resources we need to do the things we want to do. Whenever any market is out of equilibrium, there is waste, and waste is always a bad thing.

RECAP   ECONOMIC SURPLUS

The economic surplus generated by a market is the total dollar amount by which buyers and sellers benefit from their participation in that market. It is the sum of consumer surplus and producer surplus. Consumer surplus is the cumulative difference between what buyers would have been willing to pay for the product and the price they actually do pay. Graphically it is the area between the demand curve and the market price. Producer surplus is the cumulative difference between the market price and the reservation prices at which producers would have been willing to make their sales. Graphically it is the area between market price and the supply curve.

Total economic surplus in a market is maximized when exchange occurs at the equilibrium price. But the fact that equilibrium is "efficient" in this sense does not mean the same as "good." All markets can be in equilibrium, yet many people may lack sufficient income to buy even basic goods and services. Still, it is important to permit markets to reach equilibrium, because when economic surplus is maximized, it is possible to pursue every goal more fully.

THE COST OF PREVENTING PRICE ADJUSTMENTS

PRICE CEILINGS

price ceiling a law or regulation that prevents sellers from charging more than a specified amount

During 1979, an interruption in oil supplies from the Middle East caused the price of home heating oil to rise by more than 100 percent. Concern about the hardship this sudden price increase would impose on poor families in northern states led the government to impose a **price ceiling** in the market for home heating oil. This price ceiling prohibited sellers from charging more than a specified amount for heating oil.

Example 7.4 illustrates why imposing a price ceiling on heating oil, although well intended, was a bad idea.

EXAMPLE 7.4

How much waste does a price ceiling on heating oil cause?

Suppose the demand and supply curves for home heating oil are as shown in Figure 7.8, in which the equilibrium price is $1.40/gallon. And suppose that at that price, many poor families cannot heat their homes adequately. Out of concern for the poor, legislators pass a law setting the maximum price at $1.00/gallon. How much lost economic surplus does this policy cost society?

FIGURE 7.8

Economic Surplus in an Unregulated Market for Home Heating Oil.

For the supply and demand curves shown, the equilibrium price of home heating oil is $1.40/gallon, and the equilibrium quantity is 3,000 gallons/day. Consumer surplus is the area of the blue triangle ($900/day). Producer surplus is the area of the green triangle (also $900/day).

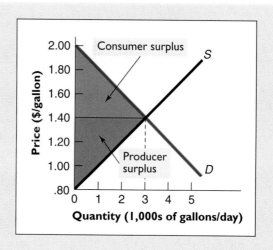

First, let's calculate the surplus without price controls. If this market is not regulated, 3,000 gallons/day will be sold at a price of $1.40/gallon. In Figure 7.8, the economic surplus received by buyers is the area of the blue triangle. Since the height of this triangle is $0.60/gallon and its base is 3,000 gallons/day, its area is equal to (1/2)(3,000 gallons/day)($0.60/gallon) = $900/day. The economic surplus received by producers is the area of the green triangle. Since this triangle also has an area of $900/day, total economic surplus in this market will be $1,800/day.

If the price of heating oil is prevented from rising above $1.00/gallon, only 1,000 gallons/day will be sold, and the total economic surplus will be reduced by the area of the lined triangle in Figure 7.9. Since the height of this triangle is $0.80/gallon, and its base is 2,000 gallons/day, its area is (1/2)(2,000 gallons/day)($0.80/gallon) = $800/day. Producer surplus falls from $900/day in the unregulated market to the area of the green triangle, or (1/2)(1,000 gallons/day)($0.20/gallon) = $100/day, which is a loss of $800/day. Thus the loss in total economic surplus is equal to the loss in producer surplus, which means

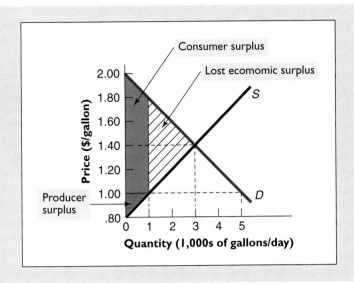

FIGURE 7.9
The Waste Caused by Price Controls.
By limiting output in the home heating oil market to 1,000 gallons/day, price controls cause a loss in economic surplus of $800/day (area of the lined triangle).

that the new consumer surplus must be the same as the original consumer surplus. To verify that, note that consumer surplus under controls is the area of the blue figure, which is again $900/day. (*Hint:* To compute this area, first split the figure into a rectangle and a triangle.) By preventing the home heating oil market from reaching equilibrium, price controls waste $800 of producer surplus per day without creating any additional surplus for consumers!

Defenders of price controls might respond that those poor families who managed to buy some heating oil at the lower price received welcome budget relief. Yes, but the same objective could have been accomplished in a much less costly way, namely, by giving the poor more income with which to buy heating oil. But can the poor, who have limited political power, really hope to receive income transfers that would enable them to heat their homes? On reflection, the answer to this question would seem to be yes, *if the alternative is to impose price controls that would be even more costly than the income transfers.* After all, the price ceiling as implemented ends up costing heating oil sellers $800/day in lost economic surplus. So they ought to be willing to pay some amount less than $800/day in additional taxes to escape the burden of controls. The additional tax revenue could finance income transfers that would be far more beneficial to the poor than price controls.

This point is so important, and so often misunderstood by voters and policymakers, that we will emphasize it by putting it another way. Think of the economic surplus from a market as a pie to be divided among the various market participants. Figure 7.10(a) represents the $1,000/day total economic surplus available to participants in the home heating oil market when the government limits the price of oil to $1/gallon. We have divided this pie into two slices labeled R and P, to denote the surpluses received by rich and poor participants. Figure 7.10(b) represents the $1,800/day total economic surplus available when the price of home heating oil is free to reach its equilibrium level. This pie is divided among rich and poor participants in the same proportion as the pie in part (a).

The important point to notice is this: *Because the pie in the part (b) is larger, both rich and poor participants in the home heating oil market can get a bigger slice of the pie than they would have had under price controls.* Price controls prevent people and firms from engaging in transactions that pass the cost-benefit test. Rather than tinker with the market price of oil, it is in everyone's interest to simply transfer additional income to the poor.

Supporters of price controls may object that income transfers to the poor might weaken people's incentive to work, and thus might prove extremely costly

FIGURE 7.10
When the Pie Is Larger, Everyone Can Have a Bigger Slice.
Any policy that reduces total economic surplus is a missed opportunity to make everyone better off.

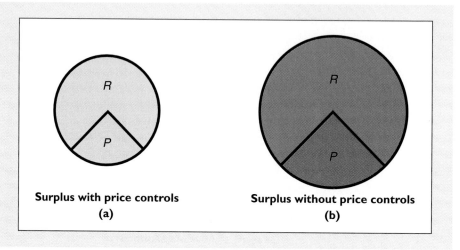

Surplus with price controls
(a)

Surplus without price controls
(b)

in the long run. Difficult issues do indeed arise in the design of programs for transferring income to the poor—issues we will consider in some detail in later chapters. But for now, suffice it to say that ways exist to transfer income without undermining work incentives significantly. One such method is the *earned-income tax credit*, a program that supplements the wages of low-income workers. Given such programs, transferring income to the poor will always be more efficient than trying to boost their living standard through price controls.

Rent controls are another example of a price ceiling. As discussed in Chapter 4, rent controls prevent landlords from charging more than a specified amount for rental housing. Tenants lucky enough to find a rent-controlled apartment often end up paying less than they would have in the absence of rent controls. But rent controls also prevent the housing market from reaching equilibrium and are thus inefficient. As Example 7.5 illustrates, alternatives to rent controls that will do even more for tenants can always be found.

EXAMPLE 7.5   **By how much do rent controls reduce economic surplus in the rental housing market?**

Suppose the supply and demand curves for rental housing units are as shown in Figure 7.11. By how much will a law that prevents rents from exceeding $100/month reduce the total economic surplus of participants in the rental housing market?

Without rent control the equilibrium rent in this market would be $200/month, and the equilibrium quantity would be 4,000 apartments/month. The blue triangle in Figure 7.11 represents the economic surplus for renters. The height of this triangle is $800/apartment, and its base is 4,000 apartments/month, so its area is equal to (1/2)(4,000 apartments/month)($800/apartment) = $1,600,000/month. Economic surplus for landlords is represented by the green triangle in Figure 7.11. This triangle has the same base as the blue triangle, and a height of $200/month, so its area is (1/2)(4,000 apartments/month)($200/month) = $400,000/month. Total economic surplus in this unregulated market—the sum of consumer surplus and producer surplus—is thus $2,000,000/month.

With rents capped at $100/month, however, only 2,000 apartments/month are rented. The reduction in total surplus is equal to the area of the lined triangle in Figure 7.12: (1/2)($500/month)(2,000 apartments/month) = $500,000/month. Producer surplus falls from $400,000/month in the unregulated market to the area of the green triangle: (1/2)($100/month)(2,000 apartments/month) = $100,000/month. Consumer surplus falls from $1,600,000/month in the unregulated market to the area of the blue figure, only $1,400,000. (Again, to calculate the area of the blue figure, first split the figure into a rectangle and a triangle.)

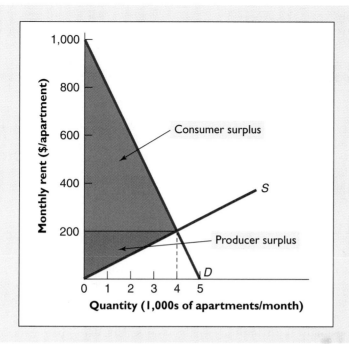

FIGURE 7.11

Economic Surplus in an Unregulated Housing Market.

For the supply and demand curves shown, consumer surplus (area of the blue triangle) is $1,600,000/month and producer surplus (area of the green triangle) is $400,000/month. Total economic surplus is $2,000,000/month.

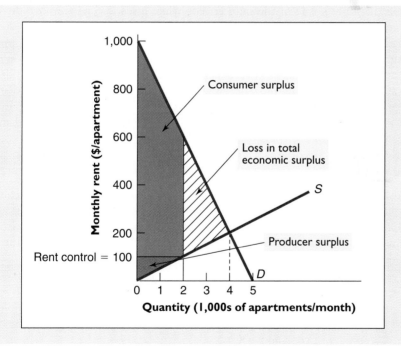

FIGURE 7.12

Lost Surplus from Rent Control.

When rent is prevented from rising above $100/month, the quantity of apartments rented falls from 4,000/month to 2,000/month. The resulting total loss of economic surplus is equal to the area of the lined triangle, $500,000/month.

These reductions in economic surplus constitute pure waste—no different, from the perspective of participants in this market, than if someone had siphoned that much cash out of their bank accounts each month and thrown it into a bonfire.

EXERCISE 7.3

How much total economic surplus would have been lost if the rent ceiling had been set at $150 instead of $100?

Compared to rent control, a much better policy would be to give low-income tenants some additional income and then let them bid for housing on the open market. Those rent control advocates who complain that no one would be willing to give low-income tenants extra money must be asked to explain why people would be willing to tolerate rent controls, which are so much *more* costly than income transfers. Logically, if people are willing to support rent controls, they should be even more eager to support income transfers to low-income tenants.

That is not to say that the poor reap no benefit at all from rent controls. Again, those who are lucky enough to find an apartment that meets their needs often end up paying substantially less than they would in an unregulated market. The point is that more can be done for the poor. Their problem is that they have too little income, so the simplest and best solution is not to regulate the prices of the goods they and others buy but to give them more money.

PRICE FLOORS

price floor a law or regulation that guarantees that suppliers will receive at least a specified amount for their product

Whereas a price ceiling prevents sellers from charging more than a specified amount, a **price floor** guarantees that suppliers will receive at least a specified amount for their product. But unlike a price ceiling, which attempts to hold price below its equilibrium level, a price floor attempts to peg price above its equilibrium level. And unlike the imposition of a price ceiling, in which the government's only responsibility is to impose penalties on sellers who charge too much, the imposition of a price floor requires the government to become an active participant on the buyer's side of the market. For when price is pegged above the equilibrium level, an excess supply develops, which consumers cannot be forced to buy against their wishes.

Agricultural price supports are an example of a price floor. They are another attempt by the government to prevent markets from reaching equilibrium to provide benefits for deserving citizens. But as Example 7.6 demonstrates, price ceilings and price floors do have one fundamental characteristic in common: Both stand in the way of actions that satisfy the cost-benefit test, and both therefore reduce total economic surplus.

EXAMPLE 7.6

By how much do price supports for wheat reduce total economic surplus?

Suppose the supply and demand for wheat are as shown in Figure 7.13. The government offers to buy as much wheat as necessary to clear the market at a price of $40/ton. Assuming that the government then gives the wheat it buys to the consumers who value it most, by how much will price supports reduce the total economic surplus generated in the wheat market?

**FIGURE 7.13
Equilibrium in an Unregulated Wheat Market.**
In the absence of a government price support, 3 million tons of wheat/day are sold at a price of $30/ton.

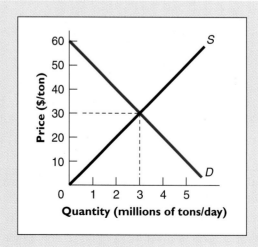

Without the price support, the equilibrium price in this market would be $30/ton. With the price support set at $40/ton, the public purchases 2 million tons/month and the government purchases the remaining 2 million tons offered by farmers at that price. If the government then gives the wheat to the consumers who value it most, the total quantity consumed is 4 million tons/month. The first million pounds that are given away effectively restore the economic surplus that would have been produced had the market been left unregulated (see Figure 7.14), since the cost of producing this wheat is the same as before and the same consumers end up getting it. But the second million pounds the government gives away cost farmers more to produce (as measured by the supply curve) than what buyers were willing to pay for it (as measured by the demand curve). The resulting reduction in economic surplus is represented by the area of the pale blue triangle in Figure 7.14, which is $10 million/month.

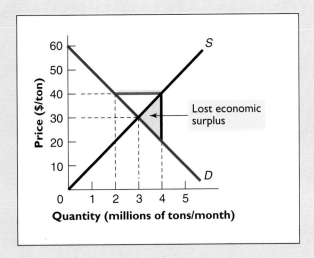

FIGURE 7.14
Lost Surplus from Price Supports for Wheat.
A price support of $40/ton results in 4,000 tons of wheat/month being produced, of which the government buys half and the public buys half. Lost economic surplus from the program is equal to $10 million/month.

Unfortunately, the actual reduction in surplus is likely to be much larger than $10 million/month, because the government is generally unable to give the wheat away to those people who value it most. Indeed, the wheat purchased by the government often spoils or is eaten by rodents before it can be sold or given away. If the government's goal were to help wheat farmers, administrators would have done better to leave the price of wheat alone and simply give farmers some extra money.

EXERCISE 7.4

In Example 7.6, by how much would total economic surplus be reduced by the price support if none of the wheat purchased by the government were given to consumers?

FIRST-COME–FIRST-SERVED POLICIES

Governments are not the only institutions that attempt to promote social goals by preventing markets from reaching equilibrium. Some universities, for example, attempt to protect access by low-income students to concerts and sporting events by selling a limited number of tickets below the market-clearing price on a first-come–first-served basis.

The commercial airline industry was an early proponent of the use of the first-come–first-served allocation method, which it used to ration seats on overbooked flights. Throughout the industry's history, most airlines have routinely

Why are passenger complaints about overbooked flights a thing of the past?

ECONOMIC NATURALIST 7.1

accepted more reservations for their flights than there are seats on those flights. Most of the time, this practice causes no difficulty, because many reservation holders don't show up to claim their seats. Indeed, if airlines did not overbook their flights, most flights would take off with many empty seats, forcing airlines to charge higher ticket prices to cover their costs.

The only real difficulty is that every so often, more people actually do show up for a flight than there are seats on the plane. Until the late 1970s, airlines dealt with this problem by boarding passengers on a first-come–first-served basis. For example, if 120 people showed up for a flight with 110 seats, the last 10 people to arrive were "bumped," or forced to wait for the next available flight.

The bumped passengers often complained bitterly, and no wonder, since many of them ended up missing important business meetings or family events. As the following example illustrates, there was fortunately a simple solution to this problem, one that was almost blocked by a public interest group that failed to appreciate how rich and poor alike can benefit when an efficient policy replaces an inefficient one.

Why does no one complain anymore about being bumped from an overbooked flight?

In 1978, airlines abandoned their first-come–first-served policy in favor of a new procedure. Since then, their practice has been to solicit volunteers to give up their seats on oversold flights in return for a cash payment or free ticket. Now, the only people who give up their seats are those who volunteer to do so in return for compensation. And hence the complete disappearance of complaints about being bumped from overbooked flights.

Example 7.7 illustrates how we might attempt to quantify the loss in surplus that results from first-come–first-served policies.

EXAMPLE 7.7

Which of the two policies—first-come–first-served or compensation for volunteers—is more efficient?

The difficulty with the first-come–first-served policy is that it gives little weight to the interests of passengers with pressing reasons for arriving at their destination on time. Such passengers can sometimes avoid losing their seats by showing up early, but passengers coming in on connecting flights often cannot control when they arrive. And the cost of showing up early is likely to be highest for precisely those people who place the highest value on not missing a flight (such as business executives, whose opportunity cost of waiting in airports is high). How big is the efficiency loss that results from first-come–first served?

For the sake of illustration, suppose that 37 people show up for a flight with only 33 seats. One way or another, four people will have to wait for another flight. Suppose we ask each of them, "What is the most you would be willing to pay to fly now rather than wait?" Typically, different passengers will have different reservation prices for avoiding the wait. Suppose the person who is most willing to pay would pay up to $60 rather than miss the flight; that the person secondmost willing to pay would pay up to $59; that the person thirdmost willing to pay would pay up to $58; and so on. In that case, the person with the smallest reservation price for avoiding the wait would have a reservation price of $24. For the entire group of 37 passengers, the average reservation price for avoiding the wait would be ($60 + $59 + $58 + · · · + $24)/37 = $42.

Given the difficulty of controlling airport arrival times, the passengers who get bumped under the first-come–first-served policy are not likely to differ systematically from others with respect to their reservation price for not missing the flight. On average, then, the total cost imposed on the four bumped passengers would be four times the average reservation price of $42, or $168. As far as those four passengers are concerned, that total is a pure loss of consumer surplus.

How does this cost compare with the cost imposed on bumped passengers when the airline compensates volunteers? Suppose the airline solicits volunteers by conducting an informal auction, increasing its cash compensation offer by $1 increments until it has the desired number of volunteers. As the incentive to stay behind rises, more people will volunteer; those whose reservation prices are the lowest will volunteer first. In this example, offers below $24 would generate no volunteers. An offer of $24 would generate one volunteer; an offer of $25 would generate two volunteers; and so on. A compensation payment of $27 would generate the necessary four volunteers.

What is the net cost of the compensation policy? While the airline pays out (4)($27) = $108 in compensation payments, not all that amount represents lost economic surplus. Thus the passenger whose reservation price for missing the flight is $24 receives a net gain in economic surplus of $3—the difference between the $27 compensation payment and her $24 reservation price. Similarly, those whose reservation prices were $25 and $26 receive a net gain of $2 and $1, respectively. The cost of the cash compensation policy net of these gains is thus $108 − $6 = $102, or $66 less than under the first-come–first-served policy.

The compensation policy is more efficient than the first-come–first-served policy because it establishes a market for a scarce resource that would otherwise be allocated by nonmarket means. Figure 7.15 shows the supply and demand curves for seats under the compensation policy. In this market, the equilibrium price of not having to wait is $27. People who choose not to volunteer at that price incur an opportunity cost of $27 to not miss the flight. The four people who do volunteer accept $27 as ample compensation—indeed, more than ample for three of them.

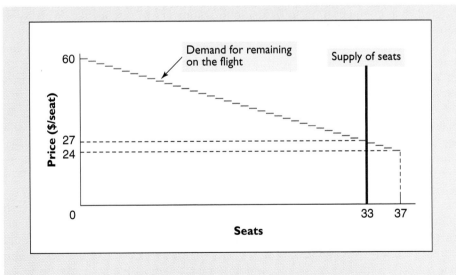

FIGURE 7.15
Equilibrium in the Market for Seats on Oversold Flights.
The demand curve for remaining on the flight is generated by plotting the reservation prices in descending order. The equilibrium compensation payment for volunteers who give up their seats is $27—the price at which four passengers volunteer to wait and the remaining 33 choose not to wait.

An interesting footnote to this example is that the airlines' policy change evoked a fierce protest from the Aviation Consumer Action Project (ACAP), a group that portrayed itself as a watchdog for the interests of airline passengers. ACAP's concern was that the shift to a system of compensation payments would mean that poor people would most often end up waiting for the next flight. This was a curious objection, for several reasons. Although the people who volunteer to wait in return for a compensation payment probably have lower incomes, on average, than those who don't volunteer, the income distributions of the two groups overlap considerably. Many financially comfortable persons with no pressing appointments will gladly volunteer to wait, while many people with lower incomes will choose not to. But more important, the previous policy of first-come–first-served was manifestly less attractive to the poor than the new policy. After all, passengers give up their seats under the volunteer policy only when they find the payment offered sufficient to compensate for the inconvenience of waiting. We may suspect that few poor persons would be grateful if ACAP had succeeded in persuading the government to block the switch to compensation payments.

EXAMPLE 7.8

How should a tennis pro handle the overbooking problem?

Anticipating a high proportion of no-shows, a tennis pro routinely books five people for each of his group lesson slots, even though he is able to teach only three people at a time. One day, all five people show up for their lessons at 10 A.M., the first lesson slot of the morning. Their respective arrival times and the maximum amounts each would be willing to pay to avoid postponing his or her lesson are as given in the following table.

Player	Arrival time	Reservation price
Ann	9:50 A.M.	$ 4
Bill	9:52 A.M.	$ 3
Carrie	9:55 A.M.	$ 6
Dana	9:56 A.M.	$10
Earl	9:59 A.M.	$ 3

If the tennis pro accommodates the players on a first-come–first-served basis, by how much will total economic surplus be smaller than if he had offered cash compensation to induce two volunteers to reschedule? Which system is more efficient?

The result of using a first-come–first-served policy will be that Dana and Earl, the last two to arrive, will have to postpone their lessons. Since the cost of waiting is $10 for Dana and $3 for Earl, the total cost of the first-come–first-served policy is $13.

Suppose that the pro instead had offered cash compensation payments to elicit volunteers. If he offered a payment of $3, both Bill and Earl would be willing to wait. The total cost of the cash compensation policy would therefore be only $6, or $7 less than under the first-come–first-served policy. So the cash compensation policy is more efficient.

You might feel tempted to ask why the tennis pro would bother to offer cash compensation when he has the option of saving the $6 by continuing with his current policy of first-come–first-served. Or why, for that matter, an airline would bother to offer cash compensation to elicit volunteers to wait for the next flight. But from the efficiency principle we know that it is possible for *everyone* to do better under an efficient policy than under an inefficient one. (When the pie is bigger, everyone can have a larger slice.) Exercise 7.5 asks you to design such a transaction for the tennis lesson example.

EXERCISE 7.5

Describe a set of cash transfers in Example 7.7 that would make each of the five students and the tennis pro better off than under the first-come–first-served policy.

In practice, transactions like the one called for in Exercise 7.5 would be cumbersome to administer. Typically, the seller is in a position to solve such problems more easily by offering cash payments to elicit volunteers, and then financing those cash payments by charging slightly higher prices. Buyers, for their part, are willing to pay the higher prices because they value the seller's promise not to cancel their reservations without compensation.

> **RECAP** **THE COST OF BLOCKING PRICE ADJUSTMENTS**
>
> In an effort to increase the economic welfare of disadvantaged consumers, governments often implement policies that attempt to prevent markets from reaching equilibrium. Price ceilings attempt to make housing and other basic goods more affordable for poor families, and price floors attempt to boost the incomes of sellers in distress, typically family farmers. Private organizations also implement policies that prevent markets from reaching equilibrium, such as allocation on a first-come–first-served basis.
>
> Such policies always reduce total economic surplus relative to the alternative of letting prices seek their equilibrium levels. It is always possible to design alternative policies under which rich and poor alike fare better.

TAXES AND EFFICIENCY

WHO PAYS A TAX IMPOSED ON SELLERS OF A GOOD?

Politicians of all stripes seem loath to propose new taxes. But when additional public revenue must be raised, most seem to feel more comfortable proposing taxes paid by sellers than taxes paid by consumers. When pressed to explain this preference, many respond that businesses can more easily afford to pay extra taxes. Yet as Example 7.9 illustrates, the burden of a tax collected from the sellers of a good need not fall exclusively on sellers.

How will the imposition of a tax of $1/pound collected from potato farmers affect the equilibrium price and quantity of potatoes?

EXAMPLE 7.9

Suppose the demand and supply curves for potatoes have the conventional slopes as shown by *D* and *S* in Figure 7.16, resulting in an initial equilibrium price and quantity of $3/pound and 3 million pounds/month, respectively. From the farmers' perspective, the imposition of a tax of $1/pound is essentially the same as a $1 increase in the marginal cost of producing each pound of potatoes, and hence the tax results in an upward shift in the supply curve by $1/pound.

As shown in Figure 7.16, the new equilibrium price (including the tax) will be $3.50, and the new equilibrium quantity will be 2.5 million pounds/month. The net price per pound received by producers is $1 less than the price paid by the consumer, or $2.50. Even though the tax was collected entirely from potato sellers, the burden of the tax fell on both buyers and sellers—on buyers, because they pay $0.50/pound more than before the tax, and on sellers, because they receive $0.50/pound less than before the tax.

The burden of the tax need not fall equally on buyers and sellers, as in Example 7.9. Indeed, as the following example illustrates, a tax levied on sellers may end up being paid almost entirely by buyers.

FIGURE 7.16

The Effect of a Tax on the Equilibrium Quantity and Price of Potatoes.

With no tax, 3 million pounds of potatoes are sold each month at a price of $3/pound. With a tax of $1/pound collected from sellers, consumers end up paying $3.50/pound (including tax), while sellers receive only $2.50/pound (net of tax). Equilibrium quantity falls from 3 million pounds/month to 2.5 million.

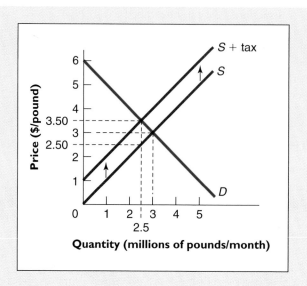

ECONOMIC NATURALIST 7.2

How will a tax on cars affect automobile prices in the long run?

Suppose that, given sufficient time, all the inputs required to produce cars can be acquired in unlimited quantities at fixed market prices. If the inputs required to produce each car cost $10,000, how will the long-run equilibrium price of automobiles be affected if a tax of $100/car is levied on manufacturers?

The fact that all the inputs needed to build cars can be acquired at constant prices suggests that the long-run marginal cost of making cars is constant, or, in other words, that the long-run supply curve of cars is horizontal at $10,000/car. A tax of $100/car effectively raises marginal cost by $100/car and thus shifts the supply curve upward by exactly $100. If the demand curve for cars is as shown by curve D in Figure 7.17, the effect is to raise the equilibrium price of cars by exactly $100, to $10,100. The equilibrium quantity falls from 2 million cars/month to 1.9 million.

Although the long-run supply curve shown in Figure 7.17 is in one sense an extreme case (since its price elasticity is infinite), it is by no means an unrepresentative one. For as we discussed in Chapter 6, the long-run supply curve will tend to be horizontal when it is possible to acquire more of all the necessary inputs at constant prices. As a first approximation, this can be accomplished for many—perhaps even most—goods and services in a typical economy.

FIGURE 7.17

The Effect of a Tax on Sellers of a Good with Infinite Price Elasticity of Supply.

When the supply curve for a good is perfectly elastic, the burden of a tax collected from sellers falls entirely on buyers.

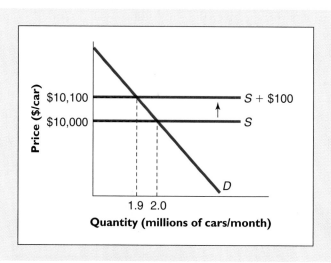

For goods with perfectly elastic supply curves, the entire burden of any tax is borne by the buyer.[1] That is, the increase in the equilibrium price is exactly equal to the tax. For this empirically relevant case, then, there is special irony in the common political practice of justifying taxes on business by saying that businesses have greater ability to pay than consumers.

HOW A TAX COLLECTED FROM A SELLER AFFECTS ECONOMIC SURPLUS

We saw earlier that perfectly competitive markets distribute goods and services efficiently if demand curves reflect all relevant benefits and supply curves reflect all relevant costs. In Example 7.10, we'll consider how the imposition of a tax on a product might affect a market's efficiency.

How does a tax on potatoes affect economic efficiency?

EXAMPLE 7.10

Suppose the supply and demand for potatoes are as shown by the curves *S* and *D* in Figure 7.18. How would the imposition of a tax of $1/pound, collected from potato sellers, affect total economic surplus in the potato market?

In the absence of a tax, 3 million pounds of potatoes/month would be sold at a price of $3/pound, and the resulting total economic surplus would be $9 million/month (the area of the pale blue triangle in Figure 7.18).

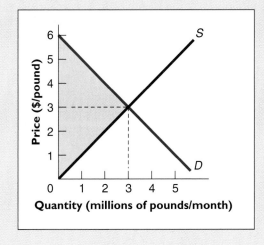

FIGURE 7.18
The Market for Potatoes without Taxes.
Without taxes, total surplus in the potato market equals the area of the pale blue triangle, $9 million/month.

With a tax of $1/pound collected from potato sellers, the new equilibrium price of potatoes would be $3.50/pound (of which sellers receive $2.50, net of tax), and only 2.5 million pounds of potatoes would be sold each month (see Figure 7.19). The total economic surplus reaped by buyers and sellers in the potato market would be the area of the pale blue triangle shown in Figure 7.19, which is $6.25 million/month, or $2.75 million less than before.

This drop in surplus may sound like an enormous loss. But it is a misleading figure, because it fails to take account of the value of the additional tax revenue collected, which is equal to $2.5 million/month ($1/pound on 2.5 million pounds of potatoes). If the government needs to collect no more than a given total amount of tax revenue to pay for the services it provides, then the potato tax revenue should enable it to reduce other taxes by $2.5 million/month. So although buyers and sellers lose $2.75 million/month in economic surplus from their participation in the potato market, they also enjoy a $2.5 million reduction

---

[1]In the example given, the tax was collected from sellers. If you go on to take intermediate microeconomics, you will see that the same conclusions apply when a tax is collected from buyers.

FIGURE 7.19
The Effect of a $1/pound Tax on Potatoes.
A $1/pound tax on potatoes would cause an upward shift in the supply curve by $1. Total surplus would shrink to the area of the pale blue triangle, $6.25 million/month.

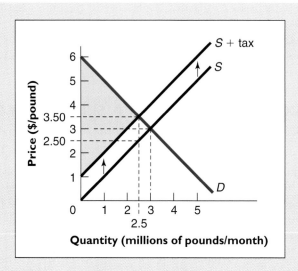

in the other taxes they pay. On balance, then, their net reduction in economic surplus is only $0.25 million.

Graphically, the loss in economic surplus caused by the imposition of the tax can be shown as the area of the small pale blue triangle in Figure 7.20. This loss in surplus is often described as the **deadweight loss** from the tax.

Still, a loss in economic surplus, however small, is something people would prefer to avoid, and taxes like the one just described undoubtedly reduce economic surplus in the markets on which they are imposed. As Federal Reserve Board Chairman Alan Greenspan has remarked, "All taxes are a drag on economic growth. It's only a question of degree."[2]

deadweight loss the deadweight loss caused by a policy is the reduction in economic surplus that results from adoption of that policy

FIGURE 7.20
The Deadweight Loss Caused by a Tax.
For the market shown, the loss in economic surplus caused by a tax of $1/pound of potatoes equals the area of the small pale blue triangle, or $250,000/month.

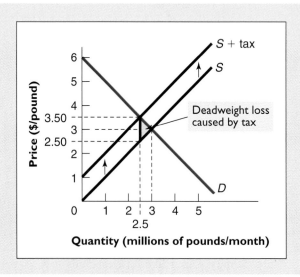

A tax reduces economic surplus because it distorts the basic cost-benefit criterion that would ordinarily guide efficient decisions about production and consumption. In Example 7.10, the cost-benefit test tells us that we should expand potato production up to the point at which the benefit of the last pound of potatoes consumed (as measured by what buyers are willing to pay for it) equals the cost of producing it (as measured by the producer's marginal cost). That condition was satisfied in the potato market before the tax, but it is not satisfied once

[2]*The Wall Street Journal,* March 26, 1997, p. A1.

the tax is imposed. In Figure 7.20, for example, note that when potato consumption is 2.5 million pounds/month, the value of an additional pound of potatoes to consumers is $3.50, whereas the cost to producers is only $2.50, not including the tax. (The cost to producers, including the tax, is $3.50/pound, but again we note that this tax is not a cost to society as a whole because it offsets other taxes that would otherwise have to be collected.)

Is a tax on potatoes necessarily "bad"? (When economists say that a policy, such as a tax, is "bad," they mean that it lowers total economic surplus.) To answer this question, we must first identify the best alternative to taxing potatoes. You may be tempted to say, "Don't tax anything at all!" On a moment's reflection, however, you will realize that this is surely not the best option. After all, a country that taxed nothing could not pay for even the most minimal public services, such as road maintenance, fire protection, and national defense. And a country without at least minimal defense capability could not hope to maintain its independence for long. (In Chapter 15 we will consider why we often empower government to provide public goods.) On balance, if taxing potatoes were the best way to avoid doing without highly valued public services, then a small deadweight loss in the potato market would be a small price indeed.

So the real question is whether there are other things we could tax that would be better than taxing potatoes. The problem with a tax on any activity is that if market incentives encourage people to pursue the "right" amount of the activity (that is, the surplus-maximizing amount), then a tax will encourage them to pursue too little of it. As economists have long recognized, this observation suggests that taxes will cause smaller deadweight losses if they are imposed on goods for which the equilibrium quantity is not highly sensitive to changes in production costs.

TAXES, ELASTICITY, AND EFFICIENCY

Suppose the government put a tax of 50 cents/pound on table salt. How would this affect the amount of salt you and others use? In Chapter 5 we saw that the demand for salt is highly inelastic with respect to price, because salt has few substitutes and occupies only a minuscule share in most family budgets. Because the imposition of a tax on table salt would not result in a significant reduction in the amount of it consumed, the deadweight loss from this tax on would be relatively small. More generally, the deadweight loss from a per-unit tax imposed on the seller of a good will be smaller the smaller is the price elasticity of demand for the good.

Figure 7.21 illustrates how the deadweight loss from a tax declines as the demand for a good becomes less elastic with respect to price. In both parts, the original supply and demand curves yield an equilibrium price of $2/unit and an equilibrium quantity of 24 units/day. The deadweight loss from a tax of $1/unit imposed on the good shown in part (a) is the area of the pale blue triangle in part (a), which is $2.50/day. The demand curve D_2 in part (b) is less elastic at the equilibrium price of $2 than the demand curve D_1 in part (a), which follows from the fact that P/Q is the same in both cases, while 1/slope is smaller in part (b). The deadweight loss from the same $1/unit tax imposed on the good in part (b) is the area of the pale blue triangle in part (b), which is only $1.50/day.

The reduction in equilibrium quantity that results from a tax on a good will also be smaller the smaller is the elasticity of supply of the good. In Figure 7.22, for example, the original supply and demand curves for the markets portrayed in parts (a) and (b) yield an equilibrium price of $2/unit and an equilibrium quantity of 72 units/day. The deadweight loss from a tax of $1/unit imposed on the good shown in part (a) is the area of the pale blue triangle in part (a), which is $7.50/day. The supply curve s_2 in part (b) is less elastic at the equilibrium price than the supply curve s_1 in part (a), again because P/Q is the same in both cases,

FIGURE 7.21
Elasticity of Demand and the Deadweight Loss from a Tax.
At the equilibrium price and quantity, price elasticity of demand is smaller for the good shown in (b) than for the good shown in (a). The area of the deadweight loss triangle in (b) ($1.50/day) is smaller than the area of the deadweight loss triangle in (a) ($2.50/day).

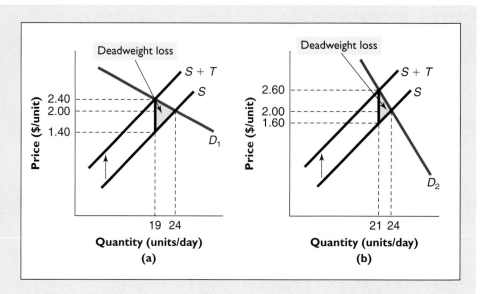

FIGURE 7.22
Elasticity of Supply and the Deadweight Loss from a Tax.
At the equilibrium price and quantity, price elasticity of supply is smaller for the good shown in (b) than for the good shown in (a). The area of the deadweight loss triangle in (b) ($4.50/day) is smaller than the area of the deadweight loss triangle in (a) ($7.50/day).

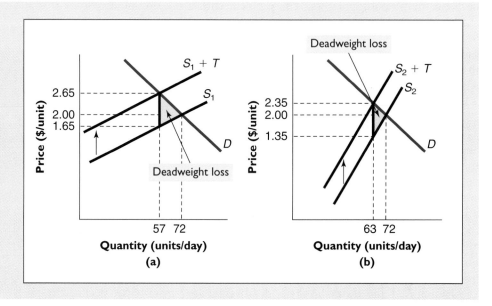

while 1/slope is smaller in part (b). The deadweight loss from the same $1/unit tax imposed on the good in part (b) is the area of the pale blue triangle in part (b), which is only $4.50/day.

The deadweight loss from a tax imposed on a good whose supply curve is perfectly inelastic will be zero. This explains why many economists continue to favor the tax Henry George advocated in the nineteenth century. George proposed that all taxes on labor and goods be abolished and replaced by a single tax on land. Such a tax, he argued, would cause no significant loss in economic surplus because the supply of land is almost perfectly inelastic.

TAXES, EXTERNAL COSTS, AND EFFICIENCY

Even more attractive than taxing land, from an efficiency standpoint, is taxing activities that people tend to pursue to excess. We mentioned activities that generate environmental pollution as one example; in later chapters we will discuss others. Whereas a tax on land does not reduce economic surplus, a tax on pollution can actually increase total economic surplus. Taxes on activities that cause harm to others kill two birds with one stone: They generate revenue to pay for useful public services and at the same time discourage people from pursuing the harmful activities. The notion that taxes always and everywhere constitute an obstacle to efficiency simply does not withstand careful scrutiny.

RECAP   **TAXES AND EFFICIENCY**

A tax levied on the seller of a product has the same effect on equilibrium quantity and price as a rise in marginal cost equal to the amount of the tax. The burden of a tax imposed on sellers will generally be shared among both buyers and sellers. In the extreme case of a good whose elasticity of supply is infinite, the entire burden of the tax is borne by buyers.

A tax imposed on a product whose supply and demand curves embody all relevant costs and benefits associated with its production and use will result in a deadweight loss—a reduction in total economic surplus in the market for the taxed good. Such taxes may nonetheless be justified if the value of the public services financed by the tax outweighs this deadweight loss. In general, the deadweight loss from a tax on a good will be smaller the smaller are the good's price elasticities of supply and demand. Taxes on activities that generate harm to others may produce a net gain in economic surplus, even apart from the value of public services they finance.

■ SUMMARY ■

• When the supply and demand curves for a product capture all the relevant costs and benefits of producing that product, then market equilibrium for that product will be efficient. In such a market, if price and quantity do not equal their equilibrium values, a transaction can be found that will make at least some people better off without harming others.

• Total economic surplus is a measure of the amount by which participants in a market benefit by participating in it. It is the sum of total consumer surplus and total producer surplus in the market. For an individual buyer, the economic surplus from a transaction is the difference between the most the buyer would have been willing to pay and the amount actually paid. For an individual seller, the economic surplus from a transaction is the difference between the revenue received and the lowest amount at which the seller would have been willing to make the sale. Total economic surplus in a market is the sum of all producer and consumer surplus in that market. One of the attractive properties of market equilibrium is that it maximizes the value of total economic surplus.

• Efficiency should not be equated with social justice. If we believe that the distribution of income among people is unjust, we will not like the results produced by the intersection of the supply and demand curves based on that income distribution, even though those results are efficient.

• Even so, we should always strive for efficiency because it enables us to achieve all our other goals to the fullest possi-

ble extent. Whenever a market is out of equilibrium, the economic pie can be made larger. And with a larger pie, everyone can have a larger slice.

• Regulations or policies that prevent markets from reaching equilibrium—such as rent controls, price supports for agricultural products, and first-come–first-served allocation schemes—are often defended on the grounds that they help the poor. But such schemes reduce economic surplus, meaning that we can find alternatives under which both rich and poor would be better off. The main difficulty of the poor is that they have too little income. Rather than try to control the prices of the goods they buy, we could do better to enact policies that raise the incomes of the poor, and then let prices seek their equilibrium levels. Those who complain that the poor lack the political power to obtain the income transfers they need must explain why the poor have the power to impose regulations that are far more costly than income transfers.

• Critics often complain that taxes make the economy less efficient. A tax will indeed reduce economic surplus if the supply and demand curves in the market for the taxed good reflect all the relevant costs and benefits of its production and consumption. But this decline in surplus may be more than offset by the increase in economic surplus made possible by public goods financed with the proceeds of the tax. The best taxes are ones imposed on activities that would otherwise be pursued to excess, such as activities that generate environmental pollution. Such taxes not only do not reduce economic surplus, they actually increase it.

■ KEY TERMS ■

consumer surplus (170)
deadweight loss (186)
efficient (or Pareto-efficient) (166)

price ceiling (174)
price floor (178)
producer surplus (170)

total economic surplus (169)

■ REVIEW QUESTIONS ■

1. Why do economists emphasize efficiency as an important goal of public policy?

2. You are a senator considering how to vote on a policy that would reduce the economic surplus of workers by $100 million/year but increase the economic surplus of retirees by $1 million/year. What additional measure might you combine with the policy to assure that the overall result is a better outcome for everyone?

3. Why does the loss in total economic surplus directly experienced by participants in the market for a good that is taxed overstate the overall loss in economic surplus that results from the tax?

4. Why is compensating volunteers to relinquish their seats on overbooked flights more efficient than a policy of first-come–first-served?

5. Why do price supports reduce economic surplus?

■ PROBLEMS ■

1. Calculate the producer and consumer surplus for the market whose demand and supply curves are shown as follows.

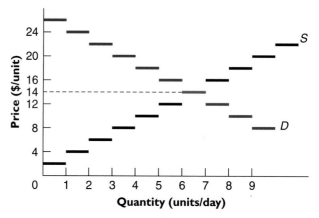

2. Suppose the weekly demand curve for wristwatches in Lincoln, Nebraska, is given by the equation $P = 12 - 0.25Q$, and the weekly supply of wristwatches is given by the equation $P = 6 + 0.75Q$, where P is the dollar price of a wristwatch. Sketch the weekly demand and supply curves in Lincoln, and calculate:
   a. The weekly consumer surplus
   b. The weekly producer surplus
   c. The maximum weekly amount that producers and consumers in Lincoln would be willing to pay to be able to buy and sell wristwatches in any given week

3. Refer to Problem 2. Suppose a coalition of students from Lincoln High School succeeds in persuading the local government to impose a price ceiling of $7.50 on wristwatches, on the grounds that local suppliers are taking advantage of teenagers by charging exorbitant prices.
   a. Calculate the weekly shortage of wristwatches that will result from this policy.
   b. Calculate the total economic surplus lost every week as a result of the price ceiling.
   c. In the face of the price ceiling, describe a transaction that would benefit both a buyer and a seller of wristwatches.

4. The Kubak crystal caves are renowned for their stalactites and stalagmites. The warden of the caves offers a tour each afternoon at 2 P.M. sharp. Only four people per day can see the caves without disturbing their fragile ecology. Occasionally, however, more than four people want to see the caves on the same day. The following table shows the list of people who wanted to see the caves on September 24, 2001, together with their respective times of arrival and reservation prices for taking the tour that day.

	Arrival time	Reservation price ($)
Herman	1:48	20
Jon	1:50	14
Kate	1:53	30
Jack	1:56	15
Penny	1:57	40
Fran	1:59	12
Faith	2:00	17

   a. If the tour is "free" and the warden operates it on a first-come–first-served basis, what will the total consumer surplus be for the four people who get to go on the tour on that day?
   b. Suppose the warden solicits volunteers to postpone their tour by offering increasing amounts of cash compensation until only four people still wish to see the caves that day. If he gives each volunteer the same compensation payment, how much money will he have to offer to generate the required number of volunteers? What is the total economic surplus under this policy?
   c. Why is the compensation policy more efficient than the first-come-first-served policy?
   d. Describe a way of financing the warden's compensation payments that will make everyone, including the warden, either better off or no worse off than under the first-come–first-served approach.

5. Suppose the weekly demand for a certain good, in thousands of units, is given by the equation $P = 8 - Q$, and the weekly supply of the good by the equation $P = 2 + Q$, where P is the price in dollars.
   a. Calculate the total weekly economic surplus generated at the market equilibrium.
   b. Suppose a per-unit tax of $2, to be collected from sellers, is imposed in this market. Calculate the direct loss in economic surplus experienced by participants in this market as a result of the tax.
   c. How much government revenue will this tax generate each week? If the revenue is used to offset other taxes paid by participants in this market, what will be their net reduction in total economic surplus?

6. A price support for milk will lead to a loss of economic efficiency because:
   a. It will raise the marginal cost of milk above the marginal benefit of milk to consumers.
   b. It will cause a reduction in economic surplus.
   c. It will lead consumers to buy less milk than they would otherwise have bought.
   d. All of the above.

7. The government of Islandia, a small island nation, imports heating oil at a price of $2/gallon and makes it available to citizens at a price of $1/gallon. If Islandians' demand curve for heating oil is given by $P = 6 - Q$, where P is the price per gallon in dollars and Q is the quantity in millions of gallons per year, how much economic surplus is lost as a result of the government's policy?

8. Refer to Problem 7. Suppose each of the 1 million Islandian households has the same demand curve for heating oil.
   a. What is the household demand curve?
   b. How much consumer surplus would each household lose if it had to pay $2/gallon instead of $1/gallon for heating oil, assuming there were no other changes in the household budget?

    c. With the money saved by not subsidizing oil, by how much could the Islandian government afford to cut each family's annual taxes?

    d. If the government abandoned its oil subsidy and implemented the tax cut, by how much would each family be better off?

    e. How does the resulting total gain for the 6 million families compare with your calculation of the lost surplus in Problem 7?

9. Phil's demand curve for visits to the Gannett walk-in medical clinic is given by $P = 48 - 8Q$, where P is the price per visit in dollars and Q is the number of visits per semester. The marginal cost of providing medical services at Gannett is $24/visit. Phil has a choice between two health policies, A and B. Both policies cover all the costs of any serious illness from which Phil might suffer. Policy A also covers the cost of visits to the walk-in clinic, while policy B does not. Thus if Phil chooses policy B, he must pay $24/visit to the walk-in clinic.

    a. If the premiums the insurance company charges for policies A and B must cover their respective costs, by how much will the two premiums differ, and what will be the difference in Phil's total expenditure for medical care under the two policies?

    b. Which policy will Phil choose?

    c. What is the most Phil would be willing to pay for the right to continue buying that policy?

10. Is a company's producer surplus the same as its profit? (*Hint:* A company's total cost is equal to the sum of all marginal costs incurred in producing its output, plus any fixed costs.)

■ ANSWERS TO IN-CHAPTER EXERCISES ■

7.1 At a price of 50 cents/gallon, there is excess demand of 4,000 gallons/day. Suppose a seller produces an extra gallon of milk (marginal cost = 50 cents) and sells it to the buyer who would value it most (reservation price = $2.50) for $1.50. Both buyer and seller will gain an additional economic surplus of $1, and no other buyers or sellers will be hurt by the transaction.

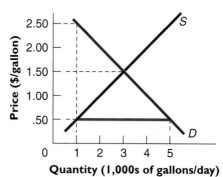

7.2 The new equilibrium price becomes $7/unit. Consumer surplus is now $(13 - 7) + (12 - 7) + (11 - 7) + (10 - 7) + (9 - 7) + (8 - 7) = \$21$. Producer surplus is $(7 - 1) + (7 - 2) + (7 - 3) + (7 - 4) + (7 - 5) + (7 - 6) = \$21$. Total economic surplus is $42.

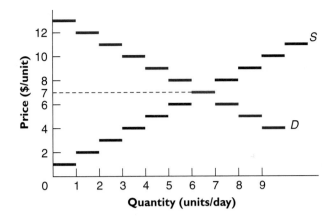

7.3 The new lost surplus is the area of the lined triangle in the following figure: (1/2)($250/month)(1,000 apartments/month) = $125,000/month.

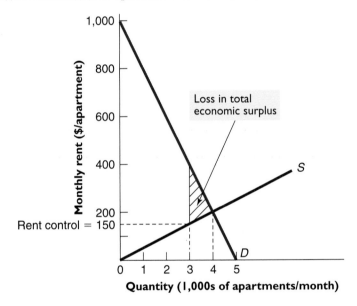

7.4 With the price support set at $40/ton, the public again purchases 2 million tons/month, and the government purchases the remaining 2 million tons farmers offer at that price. If none of the wheat purchased by the government goes to consumers, it will generate no benefit. So compared to the case without price supports, the lost benefit is equal to the area under the demand curve between 2 and 3 million tons/month. The cost of producing the extra 1 million tons/month, which is the area under the supply curve between 3 and 4 million tons/month, is also lost. The total loss in economic surplus caused by the price support is thus the area of the pale blue region shown in the following diagram, which is $70 million/month.

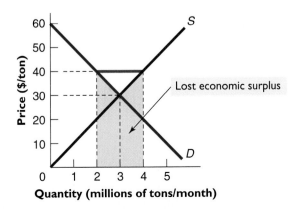

7.5 Under first-come–first-served, Dana will have to postpone his lesson. Since Dana would be willing to pay up to $10 to avoid postponing it, he will be better off if we charge him, say, $8, and let him take Bill's place at the scheduled time. We could then give $4 to Bill, which would make him $1 better off than if he had not postponed his lesson. The remaining $4 of Dana's payment could be distributed by giving $1 each to Ann, Carrie, Earl, and the tennis pro.

Player	Arrival time	Reservation price ($)
Ann	9:50 A.M.	$ 4
Bill	9:52 A.M.	3
Carrie	9:55 A.M.	6
Dana	9:56 A.M.	10
Earl	9:59 A.M.	3

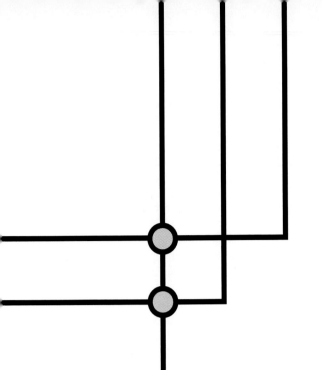

THE QUEST FOR PROFIT AND THE INVISIBLE HAND

■

The market for ethnic cuisine in Ithaca, New York, offered few choices in the mid-1970s: The city had one Japanese, two Greek, four Italian, and three Chinese restaurants. But now, some 25 years later and with essentially the same population, Ithaca has one Sri Lankan, two Indian, one Spanish, three Thai, two Korean, two Vietnamese, four Mexican, three Greek, seven Italian, and eight Chinese restaurants. In at least some of the city's other markets, however, the range of available choices has narrowed. For example, several companies provided telephone answering service in 1972, but only one does so today.

Rare indeed is the marketplace in which the identities of the buyers and sellers remain static for extended periods. New businesses enter, established ones leave. There are more body-piercing studios in Ithaca now and fewer watch repair shops, more marketing consultants and fewer intercity bus companies; and more appliances in stainless steel or black finishes, fewer in avocado or coppertone.

Driving these changes is the businessowner's quest for profit. Businesses migrate to industries and locations in which profit opportunities abound and desert those whose prospects appear bleak. In perhaps the most widely quoted passage from his landmark treatise, *The Wealth of Nations*, Adam Smith wrote:

> It is not from the benevolence of the butcher, the brewer, or the baker that we expect our dinner, but from their regard of their own interest. We address ourselves not to their humanity, but to

Why do most American cities now have more tattoo parlors and fewer watch repair shops than in 1972?

their self-love, and never talk to them of our necessities, but of their advantage.[1]

Smith went on to argue that although the entrepreneur "intends only his own gain," he is "led by an invisible hand to promote an end which was no part of his intention." As Smith saw it, even though self-interest is the prime mover of economic activity, the end result is an allocation of goods and services that serves society's collective interests remarkably well. If producers are offering "too much" of one product and "not enough" of another, profit opportunities immediately alert entrepreneurs to that fact and provide incentives for them to take remedial action. All the while, the system exerts relentless pressure on producers to hold the price of each good close to its cost of production, and indeed to reduce that cost in any ways possible.

Our task in this chapter is to gain deeper insight into the nature of the forces that guide the invisible hand. What exactly does "profit" mean? How is it measured, and how does the quest for it serve society's ends? And if competition holds price close to the cost of production, why do so many entrepreneurs become fabulously wealthy? We will also discuss cases in which misunderstanding of Smith's theory results in costly errors, both in everyday decision making and in the realm of government policy.

THE CENTRAL ROLE OF ECONOMIC PROFIT

The economic theory of business behavior is built on the assumption that the firm's goal is to maximize its profit. So we must be clear at the outset about what, exactly, profit means.

THREE TYPES OF PROFIT

explicit costs the actual payments a firm makes to its factors of production and other suppliers

accounting profit the difference between a firm's total revenue and its explicit costs

implicit costs all the firm's opportunity costs of the resources supplied by the firm's owners

economic profit the difference between a firm's total revenue and the sum of its explicit and implicit costs; also called excess profit

The economist's understanding of profit is different from the accountant's, and the distinction between the two is important in understanding how the invisible hand works. Accountants define the annual profit of a business as the difference between the revenue it takes in over the year and its **explicit costs** for the period, which are the actual payments the firm makes to its factors of production and other suppliers. Profit thus defined is called **accounting profit**.

$$\text{Accounting profit} = \text{Total revenue} - \text{Explicit costs.}$$

Accounting profit is the most familiar profit concept in everyday discourse. It is the one that companies use, for example, when they provide statements about their profits in press releases or annual reports.

Economists, by contrast, define profit as the difference between the firm's total revenue and not just its explicit costs but also its **implicit costs,** which are the opportunity costs of all the resources supplied by the firm's owners. Profit thus defined is called **economic profit,** or **excess profit.**

$$\text{Economic profit} = \text{Total revenue} - \text{Explicit costs} - \text{Implicit costs.}$$

To illustrate the difference between accounting profit and economic profit, consider a firm with $400,000 in total annual revenue whose only explicit costs are workers' salaries that total $250,000/year. The owners of this firm have supplied machines and other capital equipment with a total market value of $1 million. This firm's accounting profit, then, is the difference between its total revenue of $400,000/year and its explicit costs of $250,000/year, or $150,000/year.

[1]Adam Smith, *The Wealth of Nations,* New York: Everyman's Library, E. P. Dutton, 1910 (1776), book 1.

To calculate the firm's economic profit, we must first calculate the opportunity cost of the resources supplied by the firm's owners. Suppose the current annual interest rate on savings accounts is 10 percent. Had owners not invested in capital equipment, they could have earned an additional $100,000/year interest by depositing their $1 million in a savings account. So the firm's economic profit is $400,000/year – $250,000/year – $100,000/year = $50,000/year.

Note that this economic profit is smaller than the accounting profit by exactly the amount of the firm's implicit costs—the $100,000/year opportunity cost of the resources supplied by the firm's owners. This difference between a business's accounting profit and its economic profit is called its **normal profit.** Normal profit is simply the opportunity cost of the resources supplied to a business by its owners.

Figure 8.1 illustrates the difference between accounting and economic profit. Part (a) represents a firm's total revenues, while parts (b) and (c) show how these revenues are apportioned among the various cost and profit categories.

normal profit the opportunity cost of the resources supplied by the firm's owners; Normal profit = Accounting profit – Economic profit

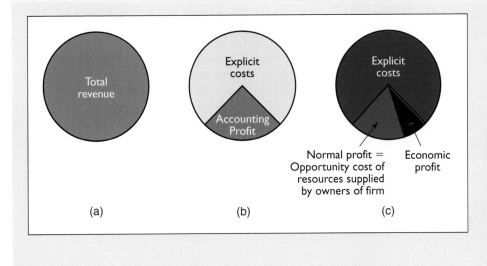

Normal profit =
Opportunity cost of
resources supplied
by owners of firm

Economic
profit

(a)   (b)   (c)

FIGURE 8.1
The Difference between Accounting Profit and Economic Profit.
(a) A firm's total revenues.
(b) Accounting profit is the difference between total revenue and explicit costs.
(c) Normal profit is the opportunity cost of all resources supplied by firm's owners. Economic profit is the difference between total revenue and all costs, explicit and implicit (also equal to the difference between accounting profit and normal profit).

*"All I know, Harrison, is that I've been on the board forty
years and have yet to see an excess profit."*

Examples 8.1 to 8.5 illustrate why the distinction between accounting and economic profit is so important.

EXAMPLE 8.1   **Should Pudge Buffet stay in the farming business?**

Pudge Buffet is a corn farmer who lives near Lincoln, Nebraska. His payments for land and equipment rental and other supplies come to $10,000/year. The only input he supplies is his own labor, and he considers farming just as attractive as his only other employment opportunity, managing a retail store at a salary of $11,000/year. Apart from the matter of pay, Pudge is indifferent between farming and being a manager. Corn sells for a constant price per bushel in an international market too large to be affected by changes in one farmer's corn production. Pudge's revenue from corn sales is $22,000/year. What is his accounting profit? His economic profit? His normal profit? Should he remain a corn farmer?

As shown in Table 8.1, Pudge's accounting profit is $12,000/year, the difference between his $22,000 annual revenue and his $10,000 yearly payment for land, equipment, and supplies. His economic profit is that amount less the opportunity cost of his labor, which is the $11,000/year he could have earned as a store manager. Thus he is making an economic profit of $1,000/year. Finally, his normal profit is the $11,000 opportunity cost of the only resource he supplies, namely, his labor. Since Pudge likes the two jobs equally well, he will be better off by $1,000/year if he remains in farming.

TABLE 8.1
Revenue, Cost, and Profit Summary for Example 8.1

Total revenue ($/year)	Explicit costs ($/year)	Implicit costs ($/year)	Accounting profit (= Total revenue − Explicit costs) ($/year)	Economic profit (= Total revenue − Explicit costs − Implicit costs) ($/year)	Normal profit (= Implicit costs) ($/year)
22,000	10,000	11,000	12,000	1,000	11,000

EXAMPLE 8.2   **If Pudge's annual revenue falls by $2,000, should he stay in farming?**

Refer to Example 8.1. How will Pudge's economic profit change if his annual revenue from corn production is not $22,000 but $20,000? Should he continue to farm?

As shown in Table 8.2, Pudge's accounting profit is now $10,000, the difference between his $20,000 annual revenue and his $10,000/year payment for land, equipment, and supplies. His economic profit is that amount minus the opportunity cost of his labor—again, the $11,000/year he could have earned as a store manager. So Pudge is now earning a negative economic profit, −$1,000/year.

TABLE 8.2
Revenue, Cost, and Profit Summary for Example 8.2

Total revenue ($/year)	Explicit costs ($/year)	Implicit costs ($/year)	Accounting profit (= Total revenue − Explicit costs) ($/year)	Economic profit (= Total revenue − Explicit costs − Implicit costs) ($/year)	Normal profit (= Implicit costs) ($/year)
20,000	10,000	11,000	10,000	−1,000	11,000

As before, his normal profit is the $11,000/year opportunity cost of his labor. Although an accountant would say Pudge is making an annual profit of $10,000, that amount is less than a normal profit for his activity. An economist would therefore say that he is making an **economic loss** of $1,000/year. Since Pudge likes the two jobs equally well, he will be better off by $1,000/year if he leaves farming to become a manager.

economic loss an economic profit that is less than zero

EXERCISE 8.1

Refer to Example 8.1. Pudge can now be not only a farmer or a store manager, he can also choose to be a ski instructor at $8,000/year. If the store manager's salary were $13,000/year, Pudge would be indifferent between being a ski instructor and being a store manager. (At a manager's salary less than $13,000/year, he would prefer to be a ski instructor.) Should Pudge remain in farming?

You might think that if Pudge could just save enough money to buy his own land and equipment, his best option would be to remain a farmer. But as Example 8.3 makes clear, that impression is based on a failure to perceive the difference between accounting profit and economic profit.

Does owning one's own land make a difference?

EXAMPLE 8.3

Refer to Example 8.2. Suppose Pudge's Uncle Warren, who owns the farmland Pudge has been renting, dies and leaves Pudge that parcel of land. If the land could be rented to some other farmer for $6,000/year, should Pudge remain in farming?

As shown in Table 8.3, if Pudge continues to farm his own land, his accounting profit will be $16,000/year, or $6,000 more than before. But his economic profit will be the same as before——$1,000/year—because Pudge must deduct the $6,000/year opportunity cost of farming his own land. If other farmers have tastes like Pudge's and face similar outside employment opportunities, the normal profit from owning and operating a farm like his will be $17,000/year, the opportunity cost of the land and labor provided by the farmer. But since Pudge earns an accounting profit of only $16,000, he will again do better to abandon farming for the managerial job.

TABLE 8.3
Revenue, Cost, and Profit Summary for Example 8.3

Total revenue ($/year)	Explicit costs ($/year)	Implicit costs ($/year)	Accounting profit (= Total revenue − Explicit costs) ($/year)	Economic profit (= Total revenue − Explicit costs − Implicit costs) ($/year)	Normal profit (= Implicit costs) ($/year)
20,000	4,000	17,000	16,000	−1,000	17,000

Needless to say, Pudge would be wealthier as an owner than he was as a renter. But the question of whether to remain a farmer is answered the same way whether Pudge rents his farmland or owns it.

What would happen if *all* farmers in Lincoln earned less than normal profit?

EXAMPLE 8.4

Suppose the conditions confronting Pudge Buffet in Example 8.2 are essentially the same as those confronting all other farmers in Lincoln, Nebraska; that is, all earn less than a normal profit. What economic changes will result?

If all farmers in Lincoln are earning a negative economic profit, some farmers will begin switching to other activities. As they abandon farming, however, the market price for farmland—and hence its opportunity cost—will begin to fall. It will continue to fall until farmers in Lincoln can once again earn a normal profit. Specifically, the price of land will fall until the yearly rental for a farm like Pudge's is only $5,000, for at that rent the accounting profit of those who farmed their own land would be $16,000/year, exactly the same as normal profit. Their economic profit would be zero.

EXAMPLE 8.5   **What will happen if all farmers earn *more* than a normal profit?**

Suppose corn growers farm 80 acres of their own land, which sells for $1,000/acre. Each farm's revenue from corn sales is $20,000/year. Equipment and other supplies cost $4,000/year, and the current annual interest rate on savings accounts is 5 percent. Farmers can earn $11,000/year in alternative jobs that they like equally well as farming. What is normal economic profit for these farmers? How much accounting profit will they earn? How much economic profit? Is their economic situation stable? If not, how is it likely to change?

As shown in Table 8.4, accounting profit—the difference between the $20,000 annual revenue and the $4,000 annual expense for equipment and supplies—is $16,000/year, as in Example 8.3. Normal profit is the opportunity cost of the farmer's time and land—$11,000 for his time and $4,000 for his land (since had he sold the land for $80,000 and put the money in the bank at 5 percent interest, he would have earned $4,000/year in interest)—for a total of $15,000. Accounting profit thus exceeds normal profit by $1,000/year, which means that farmers are earning an economic profit of $1,000/year.

TABLE 8.4
Revenue, Cost, and Profit Summary for Example 8.5

Total revenue ($/year)	Explicit costs ($/year)	Implicit costs ($/year)	Accounting profit (= Total revenue − Explicit costs) ($/year)	Economic profit (= Total revenue − Explicit costs − Implicit costs) ($/year)	Normal profit (= Implicit costs) ($/year)
20,000	4,000	15,000	16,000	1,000	15,000

To see whether this situation is stable, we must ask whether people have an incentive to change their behavior. Consider the situation from the perspective of a manager who is earning $11,000/year. To switch to farming, he would need to borrow $80,000 to buy land, which would mean interest payments of $4,000/year. With $20,000/year in revenue from corn sales and $4,000/year in expenses for supplies and equipment, in addition to $4,000/year in interest payments, the manager would earn an accounting profit of $12,000/year. And since that amount is $1,000/year more than the opportunity cost of the manager's time, he will want to switch to farming. Indeed, *all* managers will want to switch to farming. At current land prices, there is cash on the table in farming.

As we know from the equilibrium principle, however, such situations are not stable. There is only so much farmland to go around, so as demand for farmland increases, its price will begin to rise. The price will keep rising until there is no longer any incentive for managers to switch to farming.

How much must the price of land rise to eliminate the incentive to switch? If 80 acres of land sold for $100,000 (that is, if land sold for $1,250/acre), the interest on the money borrowed to buy a farm would be $5,000/year, an amount that would make workers indifferent between farming or being a manager. But if land sells for anything less than $1,250/acre, there will be excess demand for farmland.

THE EFFECT OF MARKET FORCES ON ECONOMIC PROFIT

A firm's normal profit is just a cost of doing business. Thus the owner of a firm that earns no more than a normal profit has managed only to recover the opportunity cost of the resources invested in the firm. By contrast, the owner of a firm that makes a positive economic profit earns more than the opportunity cost of the invested resources; the owner earns a normal profit and then some. Naturally, everyone would be delighted to earn more than a normal profit, and no one wants to earn less. The result is that those markets in which firms are earning an economic profit tend to attract additional resources, whereas markets in which firms are experiencing economic losses tend to lose resources.

In Examples 8.1 to 8.5 discussed in the last section, we assumed that the price of corn was set in a world market too large to be influenced by the amount of corn produced in any one locality. More generally, however, we need to consider the effects of supply shifts on price.

Consider first the effect of an influx of resources in a market in which firms are currently earning an economic profit. As new firms enter the market, the supply curve will shift to the right, causing a reduction in the price of the product (see Figure 8.2).

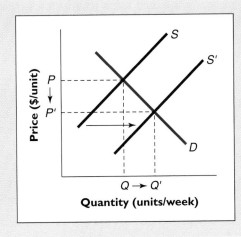

FIGURE 8.2
The Effect of Positive Economic Profit on Entry.
A market in which firms earn a positive economic profit will attract new firms from other markets. The resulting increase in supply will lead to a reduction in market price.

If firms continue to earn a positive economic profit at the new, lower price P', additional firms will enter, causing the market price to fall still further. The process will continue until economic profit is driven down to zero—that is, until price is just sufficient to cover all costs, including a normal profit.

Now consider the effect of resources moving out of a market in which businesses are currently experiencing an economic loss. As firms leave, the market supply curve shifts to the left, causing the price of the product to rise, as shown in Figure 8.3. Firms will continue to exit until the price rises to cover all resource costs—including the opportunity cost of the resources that owners have invested in their firms. The economic loss firms have been sustaining will be eliminated.

FIGURE 8.3
The Effect of Economic Losses on Market Exit.
Firms tend to leave a market when they experience an economic loss. The result is a leftward shift in the supply curve and a corresponding increase in price. Firms will continue to leave the market until the price rises enough to cover all costs, including the opportunity cost of resources supplied by a firm's owners.

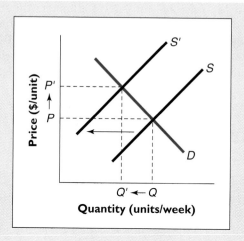

The net result of these resource movements is that in the long run all firms will tend to earn zero economic profit. Their *goal* is not to earn zero profit. Rather, the zero-profit tendency is a consequence of the dynamics of their entry into and exit from the market. As the equilibrium principle predicts, when people confront an opportunity for gain, they are almost always quick to exploit it.

ECONOMIC NATURALIST 8.1

Why do supermarket checkout lines all tend to be roughly the same length?

Pay careful attention the next few times you go grocery shopping, and you'll notice that the lines at all the checkout stations tend to be roughly the same length. Suppose you saw one line that was significantly shorter than the others as you wheeled your cart toward the checkout area. Which line would you choose? The shorter one, of course; and because most shoppers would do the same, the short line seldom remains shorter for long.

EXERCISE 8.2

Use the equilibrium principle to explain why all lanes on a crowded, multi-lane freeway move at about the same speed.

RECAP   **THE CENTRAL ROLE OF ECONOMIC PROFIT**

A firm's accounting profit is the difference between its revenue and the sum of all explicit costs it incurs. Economic profit is the difference between the firm's revenue and *all* costs it incurs—both explicit and implicit. Normal profit is the opportunity cost of the resources supplied by the owners of the firm. When a firm's accounting profit is exactly equal to the opportunity cost of the inputs supplied by the firm's owners, the firm's economic profit is zero. Industries in which firms earn a positive economic profit tend to attract new firms, shifting industry supply to the right. Firms tend to leave industries in which they sustain an economic loss, shifting supply curves to the left. In each case, the supply movements continue until economic profit reaches zero.

THE INVISIBLE HAND THEORY

TWO FUNCTIONS OF PRICE

In the free enterprise system, market prices serve two important and distinct functions. The first, the **rationing function of price**, is to distribute scarce goods among potential claimants, assuring that those who get them are the ones who value them most. Thus, if three people want the only antique clock for sale at an auction, the clock goes home with the person who bids the most for it. The second function, the **allocative function of price**, is to direct productive resources to different sectors of the economy. Resources leave markets in which price cannot cover the cost of production and enter those in which price exceeds the cost of production.

Both the allocative and rationing functions of price underlie Adam Smith's celebrated **theory of the invisible hand** of the market. Recall that Smith thought the market system channels the selfish interests of individual buyers and sellers so as to promote the greatest good for society. The carrot of economic profit and the stick of economic loss, he argued, were the only forces necessary to assure not only that existing supplies in any market would be allocated efficiently, but also that resources would be allocated across markets to produce the most efficient possible mix of goods and services.

We must emphasize that Smith's invisible hand theory does not mean that market allocation of resources is optimal in every way. It simply means that markets are efficient in the limited technical sense discussed in Chapter 7. Thus, if the current allocation differs from the market equilibrium allocation, the invisible hand theory implies that we can reallocate resources in a way that makes some people better off without harming others. We can gain additional insight into Smith's theory by working through a series of simple examples.

rationing function of price distributes scarce goods to those consumers who value them most highly

allocative function of price directs resources away from overcrowded markets and toward markets that are underserved

invisible hand theory a theory stating that the actions of independent, self-interested buyers and sellers will often result in the most efficient allocation of resources

EXAMPLE 8.6

What happens in a city with "too many" hairstylists and "not enough" aerobics instructors?

According to the invisible hand theory, the right number of haircuts and aerobics classes for a community are determined by the intersections of the respective supply and demand curves. For a specific community, suppose that means 50 haircuts/day and 20 aerobics classes/day, as shown in Figure 8.4. Why,

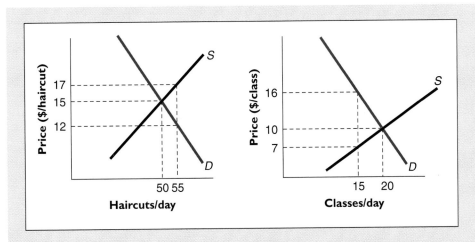

FIGURE 8.4
An Imbalance in the Markets for Haircuts and Aerobics Classes.
In a market for too many haircuts and not enough aerobics classes, hairstylists will suffer economic losses and aerobics instructors will enjoy economic profits. Eventually, stylists will leave haircutting for other occupations, and others will become aerobics instructors. The shift in resources will continue until all economic profits and losses are eliminated.

according to Adam Smith, would 55 haircuts/day and 15 aerobics classes be worse? What resource movements would occur in response to those production levels?

Note that when the market for haircuts is in equilibrium, the $15 value that buyers receive from the last haircut purchased is exactly equal to the $15 cost of producing it, which includes a salary sufficient to cover the stylist's opportunity cost. If instead stylists offer 55 haircuts/day, the last haircut will fail the cost-benefit test: Its value ($12) will be less than the stylist's marginal cost of producing it ($17). By contrast, if aerobics instructors offer five fewer aerobics classes than the market equilibrium number, the value of the last lesson ($16) will be far higher than the instructor's marginal cost of producing it ($7).

By definition, a situation in which there are "too many" hairstylists and "too few" aerobics instructors is one in which stylists earn less than the opportunity cost of their time, while aerobics instructors earn more than the opportunity cost of theirs. Stated another way, stylists earn an economic loss and aerobics instructors earn an economic profit. Over time, economic losses will induce some stylists to leave the haircutting market, and economic profits will lure new instructors to the aerobics teaching market. These resource movements will continue until there are only enough stylists to provide 50 haircuts/day and enough aerobics instructors to provide 20 classes/day—the equilibrium output levels in the two markets.

Those people who leave the haircutting market will not necessarily enter the aerobics teaching market, however. Indeed, given the sheer number of occupations a former hairstylist might choose to pursue, the likelihood of such a switch is low. Nor does the invisible hand theory imply an immediate adjustment of resources. In some markets, especially labor markets, the required movements might take months or even years. But if the supply and demand curves remain stable, the markets will eventually reach equilibrium prices and quantities.

THE IMPORTANCE OF FREE ENTRY AND EXIT

The allocative function of price cannot operate unless firms can enter new markets and leave existing ones at will. If new firms could not enter a market in which existing firms were making a large economic profit, economic profit would not tend to fall to zero over time, and price would not tend to gravitate toward the cost of production.

barrier to entry any force that prevents firms from entering a new market

Forces that inhibit firms from entering new markets are sometimes called **barriers to entry**. In the book publishing market, for example, the publisher of a book enjoys copyright protection granted by the government. Copyright law forbids other publishers from producing and selling their own editions of protected works. This barrier allows the price of a popular book to remain significantly above its cost of production for an extended period, all the while generating an economic profit for its publisher. (A copyright provides no *guarantee* of a profit, and indeed most new books actually generate an economic loss for their publishers.)

Barriers to entry may result from practical constraints as well as legal ones. Some economists, for example, have argued that the compelling advantages of product compatibility have created barriers to entry in the computer software market. Since more than 90 percent of new desktop computers come with Microsoft's Windows software already installed, rival companies have difficulty selling other operating systems, whose use would prevent most users from exchanging files with friends and colleagues. This fact, more than any other, explains Microsoft's spectacular profit history.

No less important than the freedom to enter a market is the freedom to leave. When the airline industry was regulated by the federal government, air carriers were often required to serve specific markets, even though they were losing money in them. When firms discover that a market, once entered, is difficult or impossible to leave, they become reluctant to enter these new markets. Barriers to exit thus become barriers to entry. Without reasonably free entry and exit, then, the implications of Adam Smith's invisible hand theory cannot be expected to hold.

All things considered, however, producers enjoy a high degree of freedom of entry in most U.S. markets. Because free entry is one of the defining characteristics of a perfectly competitive market, unless otherwise stated, we will assume its existence.

ECONOMIC RENT VERSUS ECONOMIC PROFIT

Microsoft chairman Bill Gates is the wealthiest man on the planet, largely because the problem of compatibility prevents rival suppliers from competing effectively in the many software markets dominated by his company. Yet numerous people have become fabulously rich even in markets with no conspicuous barriers to entry. If market forces push economic profit toward zero, how can that happen?

The answer to this question hinges on the distinction between economic profit and **economic rent**. Most people think of rent as the payment they make to a landlord or the supplier of a dorm refrigerator, but the term *economic rent* has a different meaning. Economic rent is that portion of the payment for an input that is above the supplier's reservation price for that input. Suppose, for example, that a landowner's reservation price for an acre of land is $100/year. That is, suppose he would be willing to lease it to a farmer as long as he received an annual payment of at least $100, but for less than that amount he would rather leave it fallow. If a farmer gives him an annual payment not of $100 but of $1,000, the landowner's economic rent from that payment will be $900/year.

economic rent that part of the payment for a factor of production that exceeds the owner's reservation price, the price below which the owner would not supply the factor

Economic profit is like economic rent in that it, too, may be seen as the difference between what someone is paid (the businessowner's total revenue) and her reservation price for remaining in business (the sum of all her costs, explicit and implicit). But whereas competition pushes economic profit toward zero, it has no such effect on the economic rent for inputs that cannot be replicated easily. For example, although the lease payments for land may remain substantially above the landowner's reservation price, year in and year out, new land cannot come onto the market to reduce or eliminate the economic rent through competition. There is, after all, only so much land to be had.

As Example 8.7 illustrates, economic rent can accrue to people as well as land.

How much economic rent will a talented chef get?

A community has 100 restaurants, 99 of which employ chefs of normal ability at a salary of $30,000/year, the same as the amount they could earn in other occupations that are equally attractive to them. But the 100th restaurant has an unusually talented chef. Because of her reputation, diners are willing to pay 50 percent more for the meals she cooks than for those prepared by ordinary chefs. Owners of the 99 restaurants with ordinary chefs each collect $300,000/year in revenue, which is just enough to assure that each earns exactly a normal profit. If the talented chef's opportunities outside the restaurant industry are the same as those of ordinary chefs, how much will she be paid by her employer at equilibrium? How much of her pay will be economic rent? How much economic profit will her employer earn?

Because diners are willing to pay 50 percent more for meals cooked by the talented chef, the owner who hires her will take in total receipts not of $300,000/year but of $450,000. In the long run, competition should assure that the talented chef's total pay each year will be $180,000/year, the sum of the $30,000 that ordinary chefs get and the $150,000 in extra revenues for which she is solely responsible. Since the talented chef's reservation price is the amount she could earn outside the restaurant industry—by assumption, $30,000/year, the same as for ordinary chefs—her economic rent is $150,000/year. The economic profit of the owner who hires her will be exactly zero.

EXAMPLE 8.7

Since the talented chef's opportunities outside the restaurant industry are no better than an ordinary chef's, why is it necessary to pay the talented chef so much? Suppose her employer were to pay her only $60,000, which they both would consider a generous salary, since it is twice what ordinary chefs earn. The employer would then earn an economic profit of $120,000/year, since his annual revenue would be $150,000 more than that of ordinary restaurants, but his costs would be only $30,000 more.

But this economic profit would create an opportunity for the owner of some other restaurant to bid the talented chef away. For example, if the owner of a competing restaurant were to hire the talented chef at a salary of $70,000, the chef would be $10,000/year better off, and the rival owner would earn an economic profit of $110,000/year rather than his current economic profit of zero. Furthermore, if the talented chef is the sole reason that a restaurant earns a positive economic profit, the bidding for that chef should continue as long as any economic profit remains. Some other owner will pay her $80,000, still another $90,000, and so on. Equilibrium will be reached only when the talented chef's salary has been bid up to the point that no further economic profit remains—in Example 8.7, at an annual paycheck of $180,000.

This bidding process assumes, of course, that the reason for the chef's superior performance is that she possesses some personal talent that cannot be copied. If instead it were the result of, say, training at a culinary institute in France, then her privileged position would erode over time as other chefs sought similar training.

THE EFFECT OF COST-SAVING INNOVATIONS

When economists speak of perfectly competitive firms, they have in mind businesses whose contribution to total market output is too small to have a perceptible impact on market price. As explained in Chapter 6, such firms are often called price takers: They take the market price of their product as given and then produce that quantity of output for which marginal cost equals that price.

This characterization of the competitive firm gives the impression that the firm is essentially a passive actor in the marketplace. Yet for most firms, that is anything but the case. As Example 8.8 illustrates, even those firms that cannot hope to influence the market prices of their products have very powerful incentives to develop and introduce cost-saving innovations.

EXAMPLE 8.8   **How do cost-saving innovations affect economic profit in the short run? In the long run?**

Forty merchant marine companies operate supertankers that carry oil from the Middle East to the United States. The cost per trip, including a normal profit, is $500,000. An engineer at one of these companies develops a more efficient propeller design that results in fuel savings of $20,000/trip. How will this innovation affect the company's accounting and economic profits? Will these changes persist in the long run?

In the short run, the reduction in a single firm's costs will have no impact on the market price of transoceanic shipping services. The firm with the more efficient propeller will thus earn an economic profit of $20,000/trip (since its total revenue will be the same as before, while its total costs are now $20,000/trip lower). As other firms learn about the new design, however, they will begin to adopt it, causing their individual supply curves to shift downward (since the marginal cost per trip at these firms will drop by $20,000). The shift in these individual supply curves will cause the market supply curve to shift, which in turn will result in a lower market price for shipping and a decline in economic profit at the firm where the innovation originated. When all firms have adopted the new efficient design, the long-run supply curve for the industry will have shifted downward by $20,000/trip, and each company will again be earning only a normal profit. At that point, any firm that did *not* adopt the new propeller design would suffer an economic loss of $20,000/trip.

The incentive to come up with cost-saving innovations to reap economic profit is one of the most powerful forces on the economic landscape. Its beauty, in terms of the invisible hand theory, is that competition among firms assures that the resulting cost savings will be passed along to consumers in the long run.

RECAP THE INVISIBLE HAND THEORY

In market economies, the allocative and rationing functions of prices guide resources to their most highly valued uses. Prices influence how much of each type of good gets produced (the allocative function). Firms enter those industries in which prices are sufficiently high to sustain an economic profit and leave those in which low prices result in an economic loss. Prices also direct existing supplies of goods to the buyers who value them most (the rationing function).

Economic rent is the amount by which the payment to a factor of production exceeds the supplier's reservation price. Unlike economic profit, which is driven toward zero by competition, economic rent may persist for extended periods, especially in the case of factors with special talents that cannot easily be duplicated.

Early adopters of cost-saving innovations enjoy temporary economic profits. But as additional firms adopt the innovations, the resulting downward supply shift causes price to fall. In the long run, economic profit returns to zero, and all cost savings are passed on to consumers.

THE INVISIBLE HAND IN ACTION

To help develop your intuition about how the invisible hand works, we will examine how it helps us gain insight into patterns we observe in a variety of different contexts.

THE INVISIBLE HAND IN REGULATED MARKETS

The carrot of economic profit and the stick of economic loss guide resource movements in regulated markets no less than in unregulated ones. Consider the taxi industry, which many cities regulate by licensing cabs. These licenses are often called medallions, because they are issued in the form of a metal shield that must be affixed to the hood of the cab, where enforcement officials can easily see it. Cities that regulate cabs in this fashion typically issue fewer medallions than the equilibrium number of taxicabs in similar markets that are not regulated. Officials then allow the medallions to be bought and sold in the marketplace. As the next example demonstrates, the issuance of taxi medallions alters the equilibrium quantity of taxicabs but does not change the fundamental rule that resources flow in response to profit and loss signals.

ECONOMIC
NATURALIST
8.2

Why do New York City taxicab medallions sell for more than $250,000?

Because New York City issues far fewer taxi medallions than would-be taxi owners could operate profitably, the equilibrium passenger fare is higher than the direct cost of operating a taxicab. Suppose the cost of operating a cab full-time—including car, fuel, maintenance, depreciation, and the opportunity cost of the driver's time, but excluding the purchase price of a medallion—is $40,000/year, and a cab in full-time operation will collect $60,000/year in fares. If the annual interest rate on savings accounts is 8 percent, how much will a medallion cost at equilibrium? Will the owner of a medallion earn an economic profit?

If the medallion were free and could not be sold to others, its owner would earn an economic profit of $20,000/year, the difference between $60,000 in fares and $40,000 in operating cost. But the equilibrium principle tells us that the lure of this economic profit would induce outsiders to enter the taxi industry, which could be done by purchasing an owner's medallion.

How much would the entrant be willing to pay for a medallion? If one were available for, say, $100,000, would it be a good buy? Since $100,000 in the bank would earn only $8,000/year in interest, but would bring $20,000 in earnings if used to purchase a taxi medallion, the answer must be yes. In fact, when the annual interest rate is 8 percent, a rational buyer's reservation price for a stream of economic profits of $20,000/year is the amount of money the buyer would have to put in the bank to earn that much interest each year—namely, $250,000. At any amount less than that, medallions would be underpriced.

Clearly, the owner of a $250,000 medallion has a valuable asset. The opportunity cost of using it to operate a taxi is forgone interest of $20,000/year. So the medallion owner who takes in $60,000 in fares actually covers only the cost of the resources invested in the operation. The owner's economic profit is zero. From the perspective of the medallion owner, the $20,000 difference between the owner's fares and explicit costs is an economic rent.

EXERCISE 8.3

How much would the medallion in the preceding example sell for if the annual interest rate were not 8 percent but 4 percent?

Another regulated market in which the invisible hand was very much in evidence was the regulated commercial airline industry. Until late 1978, airlines were heavily regulated by the Civil Aeronautics Board (CAB), an agency of the federal government. Carriers could not provide air service between two cities unless they were given explicit permission to do so. The CAB also prescribed what fares carriers could charge. The standard practice was to set fares well above the cost of providing service on most routes, and then require carriers to use some of the resulting economic profit to pay for service on sparsely traveled routes. But as the following example illustrates, the CAB failed to reckon with the invisible hand.

ECONOMIC
NATURALIST
8.3

Why did major commercial airlines install piano bars on the upper decks of Boeing 747s in the 1970s?

At the high airfares the CAB established on the New York to Los Angeles and other large transcontinental routes in the 1970s, any air carrier that managed to fill a flight with passengers would have earned tens of thousands of dollars in economic profit on that one flight alone. The invisible hand theory tells us that resources will flow into any market in which economic profit is positive and out of any market in which economic profit is negative, eventually driving economic profit to zero. But although an influx of resources will normally cause prices to fall in an unregulated market, the CAB's rules prevented fares from falling. The rules could not prohibit carriers from competing with one another in other ways, however. Because passengers care not only about fares but also about the frequency of service, a carrier can steal business from rivals simply by adding another flight. Carriers did so, adding flights to their routes until economic profit disappeared. The CAB's goal of generating surplus revenue to pay for service on sparsely traveled routes was doomed from the start.

Adding insult to injury, the policy of setting high fares on heavily traveled routes was wasteful, insofar as it resulted in so many flights on those routes that each left with a substantial number of empty seats. Carrier executives quickly realized that they could fill many of those seats by offering service enhancements that would lure passengers away from other airlines. For instance, one carrier converted the upper deck of its 747s to a piano bar, and other airlines quickly followed suit. Others offered elaborate meals. Recognizing this difficulty, the CAB responded by trying to regulate the kinds of food carriers could serve, leading in one case to a protracted legal squabble over the definition of a sandwich.

The problem is not that the extra amenities carriers offered were of *no* value whatever to passengers. Piano bars and more frequent flights were obviously of value to many travelers. But for efficiency's sake, additional amenities should be offered only if their benefit exceeds their cost, and most passengers would not voluntarily have paid for the high level of amenities air carriers offered in the 1970s. Evidence for this claim comes from the operations of several intrastate airlines, which were exempt from federal regulation. Unregulated carriers in California provided service on the San Francisco to San Diego route for about half the fare charged by regulated carriers on the Washington to Boston route of the same distance. Though the California carriers were free to offer more frequent service and more elaborate in-flight amenities, passengers voted with their dollars to sacrifice those amenities for lower airfares.

THE INVISIBLE HAND IN ANTIPOVERTY PROGRAMS

As Example 8.9 shows, failure to understand the logic of the invisible hand can lead not only to inefficient government regulation but also to antipoverty programs that are doomed to fail.

How will an irrigation project affect the incomes of poor farmers?

EXAMPLE 8.9

Suppose unskilled workers must choose between working in a textile mill at $8,000/year and growing rice on a rented parcel of farmland. One worker can farm an 80-acre rice parcel, which rents for $5,000/year. Such farms yield $16,000/year in revenue, and the total nonlabor costs of bringing the crop to market are $3,000/year. The net incomes of rice farmers are thus $8,000/year, the same as those of textile workers. A state legislator has introduced a bill to fund an irrigation project that would double the output of rice on farms operated by tenant farmers. If the state's contribution to the total supply of rice is too small to affect the price, how will the project affect the incomes of tenant farmers over the long run?

The direct effect of the project will be to double rice yields, which means that each farmer will sell $32,000 worth of rice per year rather than $16,000. If nothing else changed, farmers' incomes would rise from $8,000/year to $24,000/year. But the equilibrium principle tells us that farmers cannot sustain this income level. From the perspective of textile workers, there is cash on the table in farming. Seeing an opportunity to triple their incomes, many will want to switch to farming. But since the supply of land is fixed, farm rents will rise as textile workers begin bidding for them. They will continue to rise as long as farmers can earn more than textile workers. The long-run effect of the project, then, will be to raise the rent on rice farms, from $5,000/year to $21,000/year (since at the higher rent the incomes of rice farmers and textile workers will again be the same). Thus the irrigation project will increase the wealth of landowners but will have no long-run effect on the incomes of tenant farmers.

THE INVISIBLE HAND IN THE STOCK MARKET

One of the most competitive markets in the world is the market for stocks and bonds on Wall Street in New York. And as we will see, public understanding of how the invisible hand works in this market is often no better than the state legislator's understanding of how the rice market works.

Calculating the Value of a Share of Stock

A share of stock in a company is a claim to a share of the current and future accounting profits of that company. Thus, if you own 1 percent of the total number of shares of a company's stock, you effectively own 1 percent of the company's annual accounting profit, both now and in the future. (We say "effectively" because companies generally do not distribute their accounting profit to shareholders each year; many reinvest their earnings in the company's operations. Such reinvestment benefits the stockholder by enlarging the company and increasing its future accounting profit.) The price of a share of stock depends not only on a company's accounting profit, however, but also on the market rate of interest, as Example 8.10 illustrates.

EXAMPLE 8.10

How much will a share of stock sell for?

Suppose we know with certainty that a company's accounting profit will be $1 million this year and every year. If the company has issued a total of 1,000 shares of stock and the annual interest rate is 5 percent, at what price will each share sell?

Because there are 1,000 shares of stock, each share entitles its owner to one one-thousandth of the company's annual accounting profit, or $1,000/year. Owning this stock is like having a bank deposit that earns $1,000/year in interest. To calculate the economic value of the stock, therefore, we need only ask how much an investor would need to deposit in the bank at 5 percent interest to generate an annual interest payment of $1,000. The answer is $20,000, and that is the price that each share will command in the stock market.

Calculating the Present Value of Future Costs and Benefits

Someone who is trying to estimate how much a business is worth must take into account that earnings received in the future are less valuable than earnings received today. Consider a company whose only accounting profit, $14,400, will occur exactly 2 years from now. At all other times its accounting profit will be exactly zero. How much is ownership of this company worth?

To answer this question, we need to employ the concept of the *time value of money*, which we first encountered in Chapter 2. Our goal is to compute what economists call the **present value** of a $14,400 payment to be received in 2 years. We can think of this present value as the amount that would have to be deposited in an interest-bearing bank account today to generate a balance 2 years from today of $14,400. Let PV denote present value, and let r be the market rate of interest, measured as a fraction. (For example, an annual interest rate of 10 percent would correspond to $r = 0.10$.) If we put PV in the bank today at the interest rate r, we will have $PV(1 + r)$ 1 year from now and $PV(1 + r)^2$ 2 years from now. So to find the present value of a $14,400 payment to be received 2 years from now we simply solve the equation $14,400 = PV(1 + r)^2$ and get $PV = 14,400/(1 + r)^2$. If the interest rate is 20 percent, then $PV = \$14,400(1.2)^2 = \$10,000$. To verify this answer, note that $10,000 deposited at 20 percent interest today would grow to $\$10,000(1 + 0.2) = \$12,000$ by the end of 1 year, and that amount left on deposit for a second year would grow to $\$12,000(1 + 0.2) = \$14,400$.

More generally, when the interest rate is r, the present value of a payment M to be received T years from now is given by the equation $PV = M/(1 + r)^T$.

present value when the annual interest rate is r, the present value (PV) of a payment M to be received T years from now is the amount that would have to be deposited today at an annual interest rate r to generate a balance of M after T years: $PV = M/(1 + r)^T$

EXERCISE 8.4

What is the present value of a payment of $1,728 to be received 3 years from now if the annual interest rate is 20 percent?

The Efficient Markets Hypothesis

In practice, of course, no one knows with certainty what a company's future profits will be. So the current price of a share of stock will depend not on the actual amount of future profits but on investors' estimates of them. These estimates incorporate information about current profits, prospects for the company's industry, the state of the economy, demographic trends, and a host of other factors. As this information changes, investors' estimates of future profits change with it, along with the prices of a share of stock.

How fast does new information affect the price of a stock? With blazing speed, according to the **efficient markets hypothesis.** The theory says that the current price of a stock incorporates all available information relevant to the company's earnings.

The plausibility of this theory is evident if we think for a moment about what might happen if it were false. Suppose, for example, that at 9:00 A.M. on Monday, October 14, some investors acquire new information to the effect that the company in Example 8.10 will realize accounting profits not of $1 million/year but $2 million. That information implies that the new equilibrium price for each share of its stock should be $40,000. Now suppose that the price were to remain at its current level ($20,000) for 24 hours before rising gradually to $40,000 over the next 2 weeks. If so, an investor privy to this information could double her wealth in 2 weeks without working hard, taking any risk, or even being lucky. All she would have to do is invest all her wealth in the stock at today's price of $20,000/share.

We may safely assume that there is no shortage of investors who would be delighted to double their wealth without having to work hard or take risks. But in the example just described, they would have to buy shares of the stock within 24 hours of learning of the new profit projections. As eager investors rushed to buy the stock, its price would rise quickly so that those who waited until the end of the day to buy would miss much of the opportunity for gain. To get the full advantage of the new information, they would have to make their purchases earlier in the day. As more and more investors rushed to buy shares, the window of opportunity would grow narrower and narrower. In the end, the duration of the opportunity to profit from the new information may be just a few minutes long.

In practice, of course, new information often takes time to interpret, and different investors may have different beliefs about exactly what it means. Early information may signal an impending change that is far from certain. As time passes, events may confirm or contradict the implications of the earlier information. The usual pattern is for information to emerge in bits and pieces and for stock prices to adjust in small increments as each new bit of information emerges. But this does not mean that the price of a stock adjusts gradually to new information. Rather, it means that new information usually emerges gradually. And as each piece of new information emerges, the market reacts almost instantly.

For instance, when a Florida jury awarded a lung cancer patient $750,000 in damages in July of 1996, the price of tobacco stocks plummeted roughly 20 percent *within minutes*. The award broke a long series of legal precedents in which tobacco companies were not held liable for the illnesses suffered by smokers. When the verdict was announced, no one knew whether it would be reversed on appeal, or whether it would influence future verdicts in such cases. Yet investors who had been monitoring the case carefully knew instantly when the verdict was announced that the industry faced the possibility of massive new financial liabilities. To the extent that further court decisions confirm that possibility, the price of tobacco stocks will fall still further.

efficient markets hypothesis the theory that the current price of stock in a corporation reflects all relevant information about its current and future earnings prospects

Despite such persuasive evidence in favor of the efficient markets hypothesis, many investors seem to believe that information about the next sure investment bonanza is as close as their broker's latest newsletter. Securities salespersons in New York routinely call investors to offer the latest tips on how to invest their money. The difficulty is that by the time information reaches investors in this way, days, weeks, or even months will have gone by, and the information will have been already incorporated into any stock prices for which it might have been relevant.

The Wall Street Journal publishes a feature in which a group of leading investment advisors predicts which stocks will increase most in price during the coming months. The *Journal* then compares the forecasts with the performance of a randomly selected set of stocks. The usual finding is that the randomly selected portfolios perform little differently from the ones chosen by the "experts." Some of the experts do better than average, others worse. This pattern is consistent with the economist's theory that the invisible hand moves with unusual speed to eliminate profit opportunities in financial markets.

Why isn't a stock portfolio consisting of America's "best-managed companies" a good investment?

Each year *Fortune* magazine asks executives at the nation's largest companies to list those U.S. firms, excluding their own, that are managed most efficiently. Imagine that you see the results of this survey and immediately purchase 100 shares of stock in each of the top 10 companies on the list. How well might you expect those stocks to perform relative to a randomly selected portfolio?

A stock is said to "perform well" if its price rises more rapidly than the prices of other stocks. Changes in the price of a company's stock depend not on investors' current beliefs about the company's accounting profit but on changes in those beliefs. Suppose, for the sake of argument, that the "best-managed" companies had higher accounting profits than other companies at the time of the Fortune survey. Because the prices you paid for their stocks would have reflected those higher earnings, there would be no reason to expect their prices to rise more rapidly than those of other stocks.

But won't the accounting profits of a well-managed company be likely to grow more rapidly than those of other companies? Perhaps, but even so, beliefs to that effect would also be reflected in current stock prices. Indeed, the stocks of many software, biotechnology, and Internet commerce companies sell at high prices years before they ever post their first dollar of accounting profit.

An understanding of the invisible hand theory might even lead us to question whether a "well-managed" company will have higher accounting profit than other companies. After all, if an unusually competent manager were known to be the reason a company consistently posted a positive economic profit, other companies could be expected to bid for the manager's services, causing her salary to rise. And the market for the manager's services will not reach equilibrium until her salary has captured all the gains for which her talent is responsible.

We must stress that our point in the preceding examples is *not* that good management doesn't matter. Good management is obviously better than bad management, for it increases total economic surplus. The point is that the reward for good performance tends to be captured by those who provide that performance. And that is a good thing, insofar as it provides powerful incentives for everyone to perform well.

RECAP   **THE INVISIBLE HAND IN ACTION**

The quest for advantage guides resources not only in perfectly competitive markets but also in heavily regulated ones. Firms can almost always find ways to expand sales in markets in which the regulated price permits an economic profit or to withdraw service from markets in which the regulated price results in an economic loss.

An understanding of the invisible hand theory is also important for the design of antipoverty programs. An irrigation program that makes land more productive, for example, will raise the incomes of tenant farmers only temporarily. In the long run, the gains from such projects tend to be captured as rents to landowners.

The efficient markets hypothesis says that the price of a firm's stock at any moment reflects all available information that is relevant for predicting the firm's future earnings. This hypothesis identifies several common beliefs as false—among them that stocks in well managed companies perform better than stocks in poorly managed ones, and that ordinary investors can make large financial gains by trading stocks on the basis of information reported in the news media.

THE DISTINCTION BETWEEN AN EQUILIBRIUM AND A SOCIAL OPTIMUM

NO CASH ON THE TABLE

The examples discussed in the preceding section illustrate the equilibrium principle, which tells us that when a market reaches equilibrium, no further opportunities for gain are available to individuals. This principle implies that the market prices of resources that people own will eventually reflect their economic value. (As we will see in later chapters, the same cannot be said of resources that are not owned by anyone, such as fish in international waters.)

The equilibrium principle is sometimes misunderstood to mean that there are *never* any valuable opportunities to exploit. For example, the story is told of two economists on their way to lunch when they spot what appears to be a $100 bill lying on the sidewalk. When the younger economist stoops to pick up the bill, his older colleague restrains him, saying, "That can't be a $100 dollar bill." "Why not?" asks the younger colleague. "If it were, someone would have picked it up by now," the older economist replies.

The equilibrium principle means not that there *never* are any unexploited opportunities but that there are none when the market is *in equilibrium*. Occasionally a $100 bill does lie on the sidewalk, and the person who first spots it and picks it up gains a windfall. Likewise, when a company's earnings prospects improve, *somebody* must be the first to recognize the opportunity, and that person can make a lot of money by purchasing the stock quickly.

Still, the equilibrium principle is important. It tells us, in effect, that there are only three ways to earn a big payoff: to work especially hard, to have some unusual skill, talent, or training, or simply to be lucky. The person who finds a big bill on the sidewalk is lucky, as are many of the investors whose stocks perform better than average. Other investors whose stocks do well achieve their gains through hard work or special talent. For example, the legendary investor Warren Buffett, whose portfolio has grown in value at almost three times the stock market average for the last 40 years, spends long hours studying annual financial reports and has a remarkably keen eye for the telling detail. Thousands of others work just as hard, yet never even match the market averages.

It is important to stress, however, that a market being in equilibrium implies only that no additional opportunities are available *to individuals.* It does not imply that the resulting allocation is necessarily best from the point of view of society as a whole.

SMART FOR ONE, DUMB FOR ALL

Adam Smith's profound insight was that the individual pursuit of self-interest often promotes the broader interests of society. But unlike some of his modern disciples, Smith was under no illusion that *always* is the case. Note, for example, Smith's elaboration on his description of the entrepreneur led by the invisible hand "to promote an end which was no part of his intention":

> Nor is it *always* the worse for society that it was no part of it. By pursuing his own interest he *frequently* promotes that of society more effectively than when he really intends to promote it. [Italics supplied.][2]

As Smith was well aware, the individual pursuit of self-interest often does not coincide with society's interest. In Chapter 4 we cited activities that generate environmental pollution as an example of conflicting economic interests, noting that behavior in those circumstances may be described as smart for one, but dumb for all. As the following example suggests, extremely high levels of investment in earnings forecasts can also be smart for one, dumb for all.

ECONOMIC NATURALIST 8.5

Are there "too many" smart people working as corporate earnings forecasters?

Stock analysts use complex mathematical models to forecast corporate earnings. The more analysts invest in the development of these models, the more accurate the models become. Thus the analyst whose model produces a reliable forecast sooner than others can reap a windfall buying stocks whose prices are about to rise. Given the speed with which stock prices respond to new information, however, the results of even the second-fastest forecasting model may come too late to be of much use. Individual stock analysts thus face a powerful incentive to invest more and more money in their models in the hope of generating the fastest forecast. Does this incentive result in the socially optimal level of investment in forecast models?

Beyond some point, increased speed of forecasting is of little benefit to society as a whole, whose interests suffer little when the price of a stock moves to its proper level a few hours more slowly. If *all* stock analysts spent less money on their forecasting models, *someone's* model would still produce the winning forecast, and the resources that might otherwise be devoted to fine-tuning the models could be put to more valued uses. Yet if any one individual spends less, she can be sure the winning forecast will not be hers.

The invisible hand went awry in the situation just described because the benefit of an investment to the individual who made it was larger than the benefit of that investment to society as a whole. In later chapters we will discuss a broad class of investments with this property. In general, the efficacy of the invisible hand depends on the extent to which the individual costs and benefits of actions

[2]Adam Smith, *The Wealth of Nations,* New York: Everyman's Library, E. P. Dutton, 1910 (1776), book 1.

taken in the marketplace coincide with the respective costs and benefits of those actions to society. These exceptions notwithstanding, some of the most powerful forces at work in competitive markets clearly promote society's interests.

RECAP   **EQUILIBRIUM VERSUS SOCIAL OPTIMUM**

A market in equilibrium is one in which no additional opportunities for gain remain available to individual buyers or sellers. The equilibrium principle describes powerful forces that help push markets toward equilibrium. But even if all markets are in equilibrium, the resulting allocation of resources need not be socially optimal. Equilibrium will not be socially optimal when the costs or benefits to individual participants in the market differ from those experienced by society as a whole.

■ SUMMARY ■

- Accounting profit is the difference between a firm's revenue and its explicit expenses. It differs from economic profit, which is the difference between revenue and the sum of the firm's explicit and implicit costs. Normal profit is the difference between accounting profit and economic profit. It is the opportunity cost of the resources supplied to a business by its owners.

- The quest for economic profit is the invisible hand that drives resource allocation in market economies. Markets in which businesses earn an economic profit tend to attract additional resources, whereas markets in which businesses experience an economic loss tend to lose resources. If new firms enter a market with economic profits, that market's supply curve shifts to the right, causing a reduction in the price of the product. Prices will continue to fall until economic profits are eliminated. By contrast, the departure of firms from markets with economic losses causes the supply curve in such markets to shift left, increasing the price of the product. Prices will continue to rise until economic losses are eliminated. In the long run, market forces drive economic profits and losses toward zero.

- When market supply and demand curves reflect the underlying costs and benefits to society of the production of a good or service, the quest for economic profit assures not only that existing supplies are allocated efficiently among individual buyers but also that resources are allocated across markets in the most efficient way possible. In any other allocation than the one generated by the market, resources could be rearranged so as to benefit some people without harming others.

- Economic rent is the portion of the payment for an input that exceeds the reservation price for that input. If a professional baseball player is willing to play for as little as $100,000/year, but is paid $15 million, he earns an economic rent of $14,900,000/year. While the invisible hand

drives economic profit toward zero over the long run, economic rent can persist indefinitely, because replicating the services of players like Ken Griffey, Jr., is impossible. Talented individuals who are responsible for the superior performance of a business will tend to capture the resulting financial gains as economic rents.

- Failure to understand the logic of Adam Smith's invisible hand often compromises the design of regulatory programs. For instance, when regulation prevents firms from lowering prices to capture business from rivals, firms generally find other ways in which to compete. Thus, if airline regulators set passenger fares above cost, air carriers will try to capture additional business by offering extra amenities and more frequent service. Likewise, many antipoverty programs have been compromised by failure to consider how incentives change people's behavior.

- A share of stock in a company is a claim to a share of the current and future accounting profits of that company. The price of a share of stock depends not only on its accounting profits but on the market rate of interest, since the interest rate affects the present value of future costs and benefits. When the annual interest rate is r, the present value (PV) of a payment M to be received (or paid) T years from now is the amount that would have to be deposited in an account today at interest rate r to generate a balance of M after T years: $PV = M/(1 + r)^T$.

- According to the efficient markets hypothesis, the market price of a stock incorporates all currently available information that is relevant to that company's earnings. If this hypothesis were untrue, people could earn large sums of money without working hard, having talent, or being lucky.

- The equilibrium principle implies that if someone owns a valuable resource, the market price of that resource will fully reflect its economic value. The implication of this principle is not that lucrative opportunities never exist but rather that such opportunities cannot exist when markets are in equilibrium.

- Exceptions to the invisible hand theory arise when the benefit of an investment to an individual differs from its benefit to society as a whole. Such conflicting incentives give rise to

behavior that is smart for one but dumb for all. But despite such exceptions, the invisible hand of the market works remarkably well much of the time. One of the market system's most important contributions to social well-being is the pressure it creates to adopt cost-saving innovations. Competition among firms assures that the resulting cost savings get passed along to consumers in the long run.

■ KEY TERMS ■

accounting profit (196)
allocative function of price (203)
barrier to entry (204)
economic loss (199)
economic profit (196)

economic rent (205)
efficient markets hypothesis (211)
explicit costs (196)
implicit costs (196)
invisible hand theory (203)

normal profit (197)
present value (210)
rationing function of price (203)

■ REVIEW QUESTIONS ■

1. Why do most cities in the United States now have more radios but fewer radio repair shops than they did in 1960?

2. How can a businessowner who earns $10 million/year from his or her business credibly claim to earn zero economic profit?

3. Why do market forces drive economic profit but not economic rent toward zero?

4. Why did airlines that once were regulated by the government generally fail to earn an economic profit, even on routes with relatively high fares?

5. Why is a payment of $10,000 to be received 1 year from now more valuable than a payment of $10,000 to be received 2 years from now?

■ PROBLEMS ■

1. True or false: Explain why the following statements are true or false:
   a. The economic maxim "There's no cash on the table" means that there are never any unexploited economic opportunities.
   b. Firms in competitive environments make no accounting profit when the market is in long-run equilibrium.
   c. Firms that can introduce cost-saving innovations can make an economic profit in the short run.

2. Explain why new software firms that give away their software products at a short-run economic loss are nonetheless able to sell their stock at positive prices.

3. John Jones owns and manages a café in Collegetown whose annual revenue is $5,000. Annual expenses are shown in the following list:

Labor	$2,000
Food and drink	500
Electricity	100
Vehicle lease	150
Rent	500
Interest on loan for equipment	1,000

   a. Calculate John's annual accounting profit.
   b. John could earn $1,000/year as a recycler of aluminum cans. However, he prefers to run the café. In fact, he would be willing to pay up to $275/year to run the café rather than to recycle. Is the café making an economic profit? Should John stay in the café business? Explain.

number of units produced increases. For example, in the generation of electricity, the use of larger generators lowers the unit cost of production. The markets for such products tend to be served by a single seller, or perhaps only a few sellers, because having a large number of sellers would result in significantly higher costs. A monopoly that results from economies of scale is called a **natural monopoly.**

natural monopoly a monopoly that results from economies of scale

PATENTS

Patents give the inventors or developers of new products the exclusive right to sell those products for a specified period of time. By insulating sellers from competition for an interval, patents enable innovators to charge higher prices to recoup their product's development costs. Pharmaceutical companies, for example, spend millions of dollars on research in the hope of discovering new drug therapies for serious illnesses. The drugs they discover are insulated from competition for an interval—currently 17 years in the United States—by government patents. For the life of the patent, only the patent holder may legally sell the drug. This protection enables the patent holder to set a price above the marginal cost of production to recoup the cost of the research on the drug. In the same way, copyrights protect the authors of published works.

GOVERNMENT LICENSES OR FRANCHISES

The Yosemite Concession Services Corporation has an exclusive license from the U.S. government to run the lodging and concession operations at Yosemite National Park. One of the government's goals in granting this monopoly was to preserve the wilderness character of the area to the greatest degree possible. And indeed, the inns and cabins offered by the Yosemite Concession Services Company blend nicely with the valley's scenery. No garish neon signs mar the national park as they do in places where rivals compete for the tourist's dollars.

By far the most important and enduring of these four sources of market power is economies of scale. Lured by economic profit, firms almost always find substitutes for exclusive inputs. Thus, real estate developer Donald Trump has proposed a building taller than the Sears Tower, to be built on the west side of Manhattan. Likewise, firms can often evade patent laws by making slight changes in design of products. Patent protection is only temporary, in any case. Finally, governments grant very few franchises each year. But economies of scale are both widespread and enduring.

ECONOMIES OF SCALE AND THE IMPORTANCE OF FIXED COSTS

As we saw in Chapter 2, variable costs are those that vary with the level of output produced, while fixed costs are independent of output. Strictly speaking, there are no fixed costs in the long run, because all inputs can be varied. But as a practical matter, start-up costs often loom large for the duration of a product's useful life. Most of the costs involved in the production of computer software, for example, are fixed costs of this sort, one-time costs incurred in writing and testing the software. Once those tasks are done, additional copies of the software can be produced at a very low marginal cost. A good such as software, whose production entails large fixed costs and low variable costs, will be subject to significant economies of scale. Because by definition fixed costs don't increase as output increases, the average cost of production for such goods will decline sharply as output increases.

To illustrate, consider a production process for which total cost is given by the equation $TC = F + MQ$, where F is fixed cost, M is marginal cost (assumed constant in this illustration), and Q is the level of output produced. For the produc-

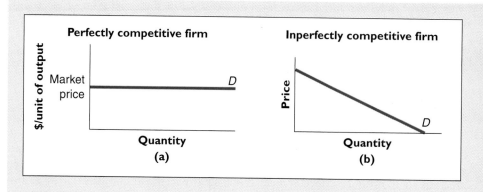

FIGURE 9.1
The Demand Curves Facing Perfectly and Imperfectly Competitive Firms.
(a) The demand curve confronting a perfectly competitive firm is perfectly elastic at the market price.
(b) The demand curve confronting an imperfectly competitive firm is downward-sloping.

RECAP   **IMPERFECT COMPETITION**

Perfect competition is an ideal case, at best only approximated in actual industries. Economists study three other types of market structure that differ in varying degrees from perfect competition: monopoly, an industry with only one seller of a unique product; oligopoly, an industry with only a few sellers; and monopolistic competition, an industry in which many firms sell products that are close, but imperfect, substitutes for one another. The demand curve confronting a perfectly competitive firm is perfectly elastic at the market price, while the demand curve confronting an imperfectly competitive firm is downward-sloping.

If the Sunoco station at State and Meadow Streets raised its gasoline prices by 3 cents/gallon, would all its customers shop elsewhere?

FOUR SOURCES OF MARKET POWER

Firms that confront downward-sloping demand curves are sometimes said to enjoy **market power,** a term that refers to their ability to set the prices of their products. A common misconception is that a firm with market power can sell any quantity at any price it wishes. It cannot. All it can do is pick a price-quantity combination along its demand curve. If the firm chooses to raise its price, it must settle for reduced sales.

Why do some firms have market power while others do not? Since market power often carries with it the ability to charge a price above the cost of production, such power tends to arise from factors that limit competition. In practice, the following four factors often confer such power: exclusive control over inputs, economies of scale, patents, and government licenses or franchises.

EXCLUSIVE CONTROL OVER IMPORTANT INPUTS

If a single firm controls an input essential to the production of a given product, that firm will have market power. For example, to the extent that some tenants are willing to pay a premium for office space in the country's tallest building, the Sears Tower, the owner of that building has market power.

ECONOMIES OF SCALE (NATURAL MONOPOLIES)

When a firm doubles all its factors of production, what happens to its output? If output exactly doubles, the firm's production process is said to exhibit **constant returns to scale.** If output more than doubles, the production process is said to exhibit **increasing returns to scale,** or **economies of scale.** When production is subject to economies of scale, the average cost of production declines as the

market power a firm's ability to raise the price of a good without losing all its sales

constant returns to scale a production process is said to have constant returns to scale if, when all inputs are changed by a given proportion, output changes by the same proportion

increasing returns to scale a production process is said to have increasing returns to scale if, when all inputs are changed by a given proportion, output changes by more than that proportion; also called *economies of scale*

Why do Magic Cards sell for 10 times as much as ordinary playing cards, even though they cost no more to produce?

price setter or imperfectly competitive firm a firm with at least some latitude to set its own price

pure monopoly the only supplier of a unique product with no close substitutes

oligopolist a firm that produces a product for which only a few rival firms produce close substitutes

monopolistically competitive firm one of a large number of firms that produce slightly differentiated products that are reasonably close substitutes for one another

absolute. We'll also see how some imperfectly competitive firms manage to earn an economic profit, even in the long run, and even without government protections like copyright. And we'll explore why Adam Smith's invisible hand is less in evidence in a world served by imperfectly competitive firms.

IMPERFECT COMPETITION

The perfectly competitive market is an ideal; the actual markets we encounter in everyday life differ from the ideal in varying degrees. In a classification scheme whose arbitrariness most economists would feel hard pressed to defend, economics texts usually distinguish among three types of imperfectly competitive market structures.

DIFFERENT FORMS OF IMPERFECT COMPETITION

Farthest from the perfectly competitive ideal is the **pure monopoly,** a market in which a single firm is the lone seller of a unique product. The producer of Magic Cards is a pure monopolist, as are many providers of electric power. If the residents of Miami don't buy their electricity from the Florida Power and Light Company, they simply do without.

Somewhat closer to the perfectly competitive ideal is **oligopoly,** the market structure in which only a few firms sell a given product. Examples include the market for long-distance telephone service, in which firms like AT&T, Sprint, and MCI are the principal providers. Closer still to perfect competition is the industry structure known as **monopolistic competition,** which typically consists of a relatively large number of firms that sell the same product with slight differentiations. Examples of this structure include local gasoline stations, which differ not so much in the gas they sell as in their physical locations.

As we'll see in the next section, the essential characteristic that differentiates imperfectly competitive firms from perfectly competitive firms is the same in each of the three cases. So for convenience, we'll use the term *monopolist* to refer to any of the three types of imperfectly competitive firms.

THE ESSENTIAL DIFFERENCE BETWEEN PERFECTLY AND IMPERFECTLY COMPETITIVE FIRMS

In advanced economics courses, professors generally devote much attention to the analysis of subtle differences in the behavior of different types of imperfectly competitive firms. Far more important for our purposes, however, will be to focus on the single, common feature that differentiates all imperfectly competitive firms from their perfectly competitive counterparts—namely, that *whereas the perfectly competitive firm faces a perfectly elastic demand curve for its product, the imperfectly competitive firm faces a downward-sloping demand curve.*

In the perfectly competitive industry, the supply and demand curves intersect to determine an equilibrium market price. At that price, the perfectly competitive firm can sell as many units as it wishes. It has no incentive to charge more than the market price, because it won't sell anything if it does so. Nor does it have any incentive to charge less than the market price, because it can sell as many units as it wants to at the market price. The perfectly competitive firm's demand curve is thus a horizontal line at the market price, as we saw in Chapter 6.

By contrast, if a local gasoline retailer—an imperfect competitor—charges a few pennies more than its rivals for a gallon of gas, some of its customers may desert it. But others will remain, perhaps because they are willing to pay a little extra to continue stopping at their most convenient location. An imperfectly competitive firm thus faces a negatively sloped demand curve. Figure 9.1 summarizes this contrast between the demand curves facing perfectly competitive and imperfectly competitive firms.

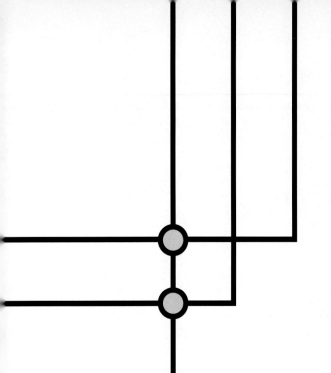

9

MONOPOLY AND OTHER FORMS OF IMPERFECT COMPETITION

■

Several years ago, schoolchildren around the country became obsessed with the game of Magic. To play, you need a deck of Magic Cards, available only from the creators of the game. But unlike ordinary playing cards, which can be bought in most stores for only a dollar or two, a deck of Magic Cards sells for upward of $10. And since Magic Cards cost no more to manufacture than ordinary playing cards, their producer earns an enormous economic profit.

In a normal competitive market, entrepreneurs would see this economic profit as cash on the table. It would entice them to offer Magic Cards at slightly lower prices so that eventually the cards would sell for roughly their cost of production, just as ordinary playing cards do. But Magic Cards have been on the market for several years now, and that hasn't happened. The reason is that the cards are copyrighted, which means the government has granted the creators of the game an exclusive license to sell them.

The holder of a copyright is an example of an **imperfectly competitive firm,** or **price setter,** that is, a firm with at least some latitude to set its own price. The competitive firm, by contrast, is a price taker, a firm with no influence over the price of its product.

Our focus in this chapter will be on the ways in which markets served by imperfectly competitive firms differ from those served by perfectly competitive firms. One salient difference is the imperfectly competitive firm's ability, under certain circumstances, to charge more than its cost of production. But if the producer of Magic Cards could charge any price it wished, why does it charge only $10? Why not $100, or even $1,000? We'll see that even though such a company may be the only seller of its product, its pricing freedom is far from

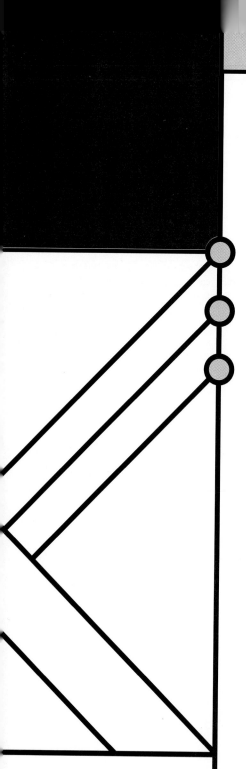

PART

3

MARKET IMPERFECTIONS

We now abandon Adam Smith's frictionless world to investigate what happens when people and firms interact in markets plagued by a variety of imperfections. Not surprisingly, the invisible hand that served society so well in the perfectly competitive world often goes astray in this new environment.

Our focus in Chapter 9 will be on how markets served by only one or a small number of firms differ from those served by perfectly competitive firms. We will see that although monopolies often escape the pressures that constrain the profits of their perfectly competitive counterparts, the two types of firms also have many important similarities.

In Chapter 10 we will investigate how the allocation of resources is affected when activities generate costs or benefits that accrue to people not directly involved in those activities. We will see that if parties cannot easily negotiate with one another, the self-serving actions of individuals usually will not lead to efficient outcomes.

In Chapters 1 to 10 economic decision makers confronted an environment that was essentially fixed. In Chapter 11, however, we will discuss cases in which people can expect their actions to alter the behavior of others, as when a firm's decision to advertise or launch a new product induces a rival to follow suit. Interdependencies of this sort are the rule rather than the exception, and we will explore how to take them into account using simple theories of games.

Although the invisible hand theory assumes that buyers and sellers are perfectly informed about all relevant options, this assumption is almost never satisfied in practice. In Chapter 12 we will explore how basic economic principles can help imperfectly informed individuals and firms make the best use of the limited information they possess.

▪ ANSWERS TO IN-CHAPTER EXERCISES ▪

8.1 Since Pudge is indifferent between being a ski instructor or a store manager if the store manager's salary is $13,000/year, his economic surplus as a ski instructor at $8,000/year is $2,000/year higher than as a manager at $11,000/year. Thus his economic surplus as a ski instructor is $1,000/year higher than it would be if he stayed in farming. Pudge should become a ski instructor.

8.2 If each lane did not move at about the same pace, any driver in a slower lane could reduce his or her travel time by simply switching to a faster one. People will exploit these opportunities until each lane moves at about the same pace.

8.3 If the taxi medallion were available for free, it would still command an economic profit of $20,000/year. So its value is still the answer to the question "How much would you need to put in the bank to generate interest earnings of $20,000/year?" When the interest rate is 4 percent/year, the answer is $500,000, or twice what the medallion was worth at an interest rate of 8 percent.

8.4 $PV = \$1,728/(1.2)^3 = \$1,000.$

c. Suppose the café's revenues and expenses remain the same, but recyclers' earnings rise to $1,100/year. Is the café still making an economic profit? Explain.

d. Suppose John had not had to get a $10,000 loan at an annual interest rate of 10 percent to buy equipment, but instead he had invested $10,000 of his own money in equipment. How would your answers to parts a and b change?

e. If John can earn $1,000/year as a recycler and he likes recycling just as well as running the café, how much additional revenue would the café have to collect each year to earn a normal profit?

4. The city of New Orleans has 200 advertising companies, 199 of which employ designers of normal ability at a salary of $100,000/year. Paying this salary, each of the 199 firms makes a normal profit on $500,000 in revenue. However, the 200th company employs Janus Jacobs, an unusually talented designer. This company collects $1,000,000 in revenues because of Jacobs's talent.

a. How much will Jacobs earn? What proportion of his annual salary will be economic rent?

b. Why won't the advertising company for which Jacobs works be able to earn an economic profit?

5. Explain carefully why, in the absence of a patent, a technical innovation invented and pioneered in one tofu factory will cause the supply curve for the entire tofu industry to shift to the right. What will finally halt the rightward shift?

6. The government of the Republic of Self-Reliance has decided to limit imports of machine tools to encourage development of locally made machine tools. To do so, the government offers to sell a small number of machine tool import licenses. To operate a machine tool import business costs $30,000, excluding the cost of the import license. An importer of machine tools can expect to earn $50,000/year. If the annual interest rate is 10 percent, for how much will the government be able to auction the import licenses? Will the owner of a license earn an economic profit?

7. Unskilled workers in a poor cotton-growing region must choose between working in a factory for $6,000/year or being a tenant cotton farmer. One farmer can work a 120-acre farm, which rents for $10,000/year. Such farms yield $20,000 worth of cotton each year. The total nonlabor cost of producing and marketing the cotton is $4,000/year. A local politician whose motto is "working people come first" has promised that if he is elected, his administration will fund a fertilizer, irrigation, and marketing scheme that will triple cotton yields on tenant farms at no charge to tenant farmers.

a. If the market price of cotton would be unaffected by this policy and no new jobs would be created in the cotton-growing industry, how would the project affect the incomes of tenant farmers in the short run? In the long run?

b. Who would reap the benefit of the scheme in the long run? How much would they gain each year?

8. You have a friend who is a potter. He holds a permanent patent on an indestructible teacup whose sale generates $30,000/year more revenue than production costs. If the annual interest rate is 20 percent, what is the market value of his patent?

9. You have an opportunity to buy an apple orchard that produces $25,000/year in total revenue. To run the orchard, you would have to give up your current job, which pays $10,000/year. If you would find both jobs equally satisfying, and the annual interest rate is 10 percent, what is the highest price you would be willing to pay for the orchard?

10. Louisa, a renowned chef, owns one of the 1,000 spaghetti restaurants in Sicily. Each restaurant serves 100 plates of spaghetti a night at $5/plate. Louisa knows she can develop a new sauce at the same cost as the current sauce, which would be so tasty that all 100,000 spaghetti eaters would buy her spaghetti at $10/plate. There are two problems: Developing the new sauce would require some experimental cost, and the other spaghetti producers could figure out the recipe after 1 day.

a. What is the highest experimental cost Louisa would be willing to incur?

b. How would your answer change if Louisa could enforce a year-long patent on her new sauce? (Assume that the interest rate is zero.)

80 percent of the cost of a computer was in its hardware (which has relatively high marginal cost); the remaining 20 percent was in its software. But by 1990 those proportions were reversed. Fixed cost now accounts for about 85 percent of total costs in the computer software industry, whose products are included in a growing share of ordinary manufactured goods.

Why does Intel sell the overwhelming majority of all microprocessors used in personal computers?

The fixed investment required to produce a new leading-edge microprocessor such as the Intel Pentium chip currently runs upward of $2 billion. But once the chip has been designed and the manufacturing facility built, the marginal cost of producing each chip is only pennies. This cost pattern explains why Intel currently sells more than 80 percent of all microprocessors.

ECONOMIC NATURALIST 9.1

As fixed cost becomes more and more important, the perfectly competitive pattern of many small firms, each producing only a small share of its industry's total output, becomes less common. For this reason, we must develop a clear sense of how the behavior of firms with market power differs from that of the perfectly competitive firm.

RECAP **FOUR SOURCES OF MARKET POWER**

A firm's power to raise its price without losing its entire market stems from its exclusive control of important inputs, patents, government licenses, or economies of scale. By far the most important and enduring of these is economies of scale. For a firm that enjoys economies of scale, the average cost per unit of output declines as output grows. This cost advantage explains why many industries are dominated by either a single firm or a small number of firms.

PROFIT MAXIMIZATION FOR THE MONOPOLIST

Regardless of whether a firm is a price taker or a price setter, economists assume that its basic goal is to maximize its profit. Another commonality is that the operational decision confronting both types of firm is to select the output level that results in the greatest possible difference between total revenue and total cost. But there are some important differences in how the two types of firm carry out this decision. To help focus attention on these differences, we begin with a brief review of how the perfectly competitive firm chooses the profit-maximizing level of output.

THE PERFECTLY COMPETITIVE FIRM'S DECISION RULE: A REVIEW

Recall from Chapter 6 that a perfectly competitive firm is typically one among many firms that produce products that are essentially perfect substitutes for one another. As the following example reminds us, the competitive firm maximizes profit by selling that quantity of output at which marginal cost equals the market price.

EXAMPLE 9.3

How many watermelons should a farmer produce?

Consider a perfectly competitive watermelon farmer whose marginal cost is shown in Figure 9.3. If this grower can sell as many tons of melons as he chooses at a price of $200/ton, how many tons should he sell to maximize his profit?

FIGURE 9.3
The Profit-Maximizing Output Level for a Perfectly Competitive Watermelon Farmer.
At a market price of $200/ton, the perfectly competitive farmer maximizes profit by selling 18 tons of watermelon a year, the quantity for which price equals marginal cost.

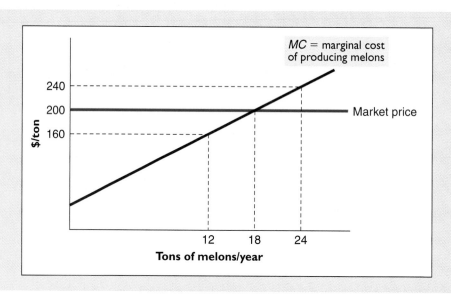

A competitive firm, or a monopolist for that matter, should expand its production if and only if the benefit of doing so exceeds the cost. If the farmer in this example were producing only 12 tons/year, his marginal cost would be $160/ton, while his benefit from expanding production would be the market price for which he can sell the melons, $200/ton. So this farmer should expand his production of melons until he reaches 18 tons/year, the quantity at which marginal cost exactly equals the market price.

For both the perfectly competitive firm and the monopolist, the marginal benefit of expanding output is the additional revenue the firm will receive if it sells one additional unit of output. In both cases, this marginal benefit is called the firm's **marginal revenue.** For the perfectly competitive firm, marginal revenue is exactly equal to the market price of the product.

marginal revenue the change in a firm's total revenue that results from a one-unit change in output

MARGINAL REVENUE FOR THE MONOPOLIST

The logic of profit maximization is precisely the same for the monopolist as for the perfectly competitive firm. In both cases, the firm keeps expanding output as long as the benefit of doing so exceeds the cost. The calculation of marginal cost is also precisely the same for the monopolist as for the perfectly competitive firm. *The only significant difference between the two cases concerns the calculation of marginal revenue.*

As we have seen, marginal revenue for a competitive firm is simply the market price. If that price is $6, then the marginal benefit of selling an extra unit is exactly $6. *To a monopolist, in contrast, the marginal benefit of selling an additional unit is strictly less than the market price.* As Examples 9.4 to 9.6 make clear, the reason is that while the perfectly competitive firm can sell as many units as it wishes at the market price, the monopolist can sell an additional unit only if it cuts the price—and it must do so not just for the additional unit but for the units it is currently selling.

How much extra revenue would a monopolist get by expanding output?

EXAMPLE 9.4

A monopolist with the demand curve shown in Figure 9.4 is currently selling 2 units of output at a price of $6/unit. What would be its marginal benefit from selling an additional unit?

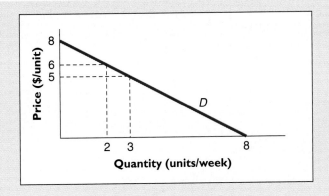

FIGURE 9.4
The Monopolist's Benefit from Selling an Additional Unit.
The monopolist shown receives $12/week in total revenue by selling 2 units/week at a price of $6 each. This monopolist could earn $15/week by selling 3 units/week at a price of $5 each. In that case, the benefit from selling the third unit would be $15 − $12 = $3, less than its selling price of $5.

This monopolist's total revenue from the sale of 2 units/week is ($6/unit)(2 units/week) = $12/week. Its total revenue from the sale of 3 units/week would be $15/week. The difference—$3/week—is the marginal revenue from the sale of the third unit each week. Note that this amount is not only smaller than the original price ($6) but smaller than the new price ($5) as well.

EXERCISE 9.2

Calculate marginal revenue for the monopolist in Example 9.4 as it expands output from 3 to 4 units/week, and then from 4 to 5 units/week.

Consider again the monopolist whose demand curve is shown in Figure 9.4. In Example 9.4 and Exercise 9.1, we saw that a sequence of increases in output—from 2 to 3, from 3 to 4, and from 4 to 5—could yield marginal revenue of $3, $1, and −$1, respectively. We can display these results in tabular form, as in Table 9.4.

TABLE 9.4
Marginal Revenue for a Monopolist ($/unit)

Quantity	Marginal revenue
2	
	3
3	
	1
4	
	−1
5	

Note in the table that the marginal revenue values are displayed in between the two quantity figures to which they correspond. For example, when the firm expanded its output from 2 units/week to 3, its marginal revenue was $3/unit. Strictly speaking, this marginal revenue corresponds to neither quantity but to the movement between those quantities, hence its placement in the table. Likewise, in moving from 3 to 4 units/week, the firm earned marginal revenue of $1/unit so that figure is placed midway between the quantities of 3 and 4, and so on.

To graph marginal revenue as a function of quantity, we would plot the marginal revenue for the movement from 2 to 3 units of output per week ($3) at a quantity value of 2.5, because 2.5 lies midway between 2 and 3. Similarly, we would plot the marginal revenue for the movement from 3 to 4 units/week ($1) at a quantity of 3.5 units/week, and the marginal revenue for the movement from 4 to 5 units/week (−$1) at a quantity of 4.5. The resulting marginal revenue curve *MR*, is shown in Figure 9.5.

FIGURE 9.5
Marginal Revenue in Graphical Form.
Because a monopolist must cut price to sell an extra unit, not only for the extra unit sold but also for all existing units, marginal revenue from the sale of the extra unit is less than its selling price.

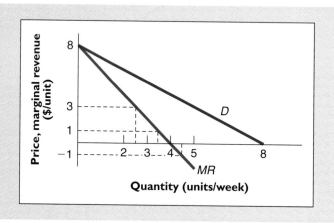

More generally, consider a monopolist with a straight-line demand curve whose vertical intercept is a and whose horizontal intercept is Q_0, as shown in Figure 9.6. This monopolist's marginal revenue curve will also have a vertical intercept of a, and it will be twice as steep as the demand curve. Thus its horizontal intercept will be not Q_0, but $Q_0/2$, as shown in Figure 9.6.

Marginal revenue curves can also be expressed algebraically. If the formula for the monopolist's demand curve is $P = a - bQ$, then the formula for its marginal revenue curve will be $MR = a - 2bQ$. If you have had calculus, this relationship is easy to derive,[1] but even without calculus you can verify it by working through a few numerical examples. First, translate the formula for the

---

[1]For those who have had an introductory course in calculus, marginal revenue can be expressed as the derivative of total revenue with respect to output. If $P = a - bQ$, then total revenue will be given by $TR = PQ = aQ - bQ^2$, which means that $MR = dTR/dQ = a - 2bQ$.

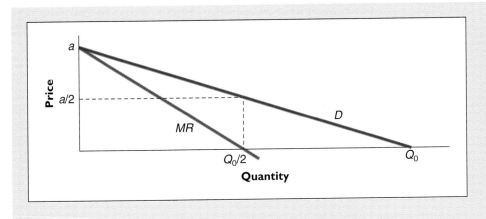

FIGURE 9.6
The Marginal Revenue Curve for a Monopolist with a Straight-Line Demand Curve.
For a monopolist with the demand curve shown, the corresponding marginal revenue curve has the same vertical intercept as the demand curve, and a horizontal intercept only half as large as that of the demand curve.

demand curve into a diagram, and then construct the corresponding marginal revenue curve graphically. Reading from the graph, write the formula for that marginal revenue curve.

What is the marginal revenue curve that corresponds to a specific demand curve?

EXAMPLE 9.5

Find the formula for the marginal revenue curve for the monopolist whose demand curve is given by $P = 10 - (1/2)Q$.

Figure 9.7(a) shows the demand curve for this monopolist. In Figure 9.7(b), we use the fact that the marginal revenue curve has the same vertical intercept as the demand curve and a horizontal intercept half as large as the demand curve's horizontal intercept. Since the demand curve has a slope of $-1/2$ and since the marginal revenue curve is twice as steep as the demand curve, the slope of the marginal revenue curve must be -1. And since the marginal revenue curve has the same vertical intercept as the demand curve, its formula must be $MR = 10 - Q$, as shown in Figure 9.7(b).

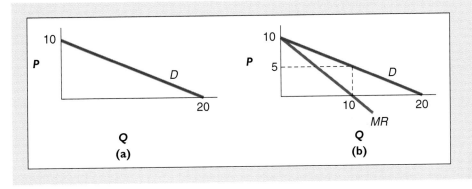

FIGURE 9.7
The Marginal Revenue Curve for a Specific Demand Curve.
If the formula for the monopolist's demand curve is $P = a - bQ$, the formula for the corresponding marginal revenue curve is $MR = a - 2bQ$.

THE MONOPOLIST'S PROFIT-MAXIMIZING DECISION RULE

Having derived the monopolist's marginal revenue curve, we are now in a position to describe how the monopolist chooses the output level that maximizes profit. As in the case of the perfectly competitive firm, the cost-benefit principle says that the monopolist should continue to expand output as long as the gain from doing so exceeds the cost. At the current level of output, the benefit from expanding output is the marginal revenue value that corresponds to that output level. The cost of expanding output is the marginal cost at that level of output. Whenever marginal revenue exceeds marginal cost, the firm should expand.

Conversely, whenever marginal revenue falls short of marginal cost, the firm should reduce its output. *Profit is maximized at the level of output for which marginal revenue precisely equals marginal cost.*

When the monopolist's profit-maximizing rule is stated in this way, we can see that the perfectly competitive firm's rule is actually a special case of the monopolist's rule. When the perfectly competitive firm expands output by one unit, its marginal revenue exactly equals the product's market price (because the perfectly competitive firm can expand sales by a unit without having to cut the price of existing units). So when the perfectly competitive firm equates price with marginal cost, it is also equating marginal revenue with marginal cost.

EXAMPLE 9.6

What is the monopolist's profit-maximizing output level?

Consider a monopolist with the demand and marginal cost curves shown in Figure 9.8. If this firm is currently producing 12 units/week, should it expand or contract production? What is the profit-maximizing level of output?

FIGURE 9.8
The Demand and Marginal Cost Curves for a Monopolist.
At the current output level of 12 units/week, price equals marginal cost. Since the monopolist's price is always greater than marginal revenue, marginal revenue must be less than marginal cost, which means this monopolist should produce less.

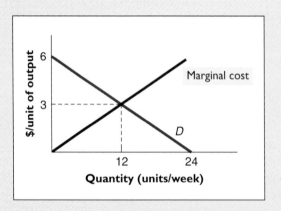

In Figure 9.9, we begin by constructing the marginal revenue curve that corresponds to the monopolist's demand curve. It has the same vertical intercept as the demand curve, and its horizontal intercept is half as large. Note that the monopolist's marginal revenue at 12 units/week is zero, which is clearly less than its marginal cost of $3/unit. This monopolist will therefore earn a higher profit by contracting production until marginal revenue equals marginal cost, which occurs at an output level of 8 units/week. At this profit-maximizing output level, and the firm will charge $4/unit, the price that corresponds to 8 units/week on the demand curve.

FIGURE 9.9
The Monopolist's Profit-Maximizing Output Level.
This monopolist maximizes profit by selling 8 units/week, the output level at which marginal revenue equals marginal cost. The profit-maximizing price is $4/unit, the price that corresponds to the profit-maximizing quantity on the demand curve.

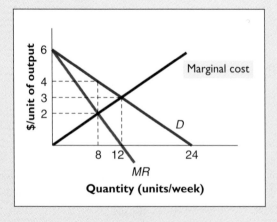

EXERCISE 9.3

Find the profit-maximizing price and level of output for a monopolist with the demand curve $P = 12 - Q$ and the marginal cost curve $MC = 2Q$, where P is the price of the product in dollars per unit and Q is output in units per week.

> **RECAP** **PROFIT MAXIMIZATION FOR THE MONOPOLIST**
>
> Both the perfectly competitive firm and the monopolist maximize profit by choosing the output level at which marginal revenue equals marginal cost. But whereas marginal revenue equals market price for the perfectly competitive firm, it is always less than market price for the monopolist.

WHY THE INVISIBLE HAND BREAKS DOWN UNDER MONOPOLY

In our discussion of equilibrium in perfectly competitive markets in Chapter 7, we saw conditions under which the self-serving pursuits of consumers and firms were consistent with the broader interests of society as a whole. Let's explore whether the same conclusion holds true for the case of imperfectly competitive firms.

Consider the monopolist in Example 9.6. Is this firm's profit-maximizing output level efficient from society's point of view? For any given level of output, the corresponding price on the demand curve indicates the amount buyers would be willing to pay for an additional unit of output. When the monopolist is producing 8 units/week, the marginal benefit to society of an additional unit of output is thus $4 (see Figure 9.9.) And since the marginal cost of an additional unit at that output level is only $2 (again, see Figure 9.9), society would gain a net benefit of $2/unit if the monopolist were to expand production by one unit above the profit-maximizing level. Because this economic surplus is not realized, the profit-maximizing monopolist is socially inefficient.

Recall that the existence of inefficiency means that the economic pie is smaller than it might be. If that is so, why doesn't the monopolist simply expand production? The answer is that the monopolist would gladly do so, if only there were some way to maintain the price of existing units and cut the price of only the extra units. As a practical matter, however, that is not always possible.

Consider again the monopolist in Example 9.6, whose demand and marginal cost curves are reproduced in Figure 9.10. For the market served by this monopolist, what is the socially efficient level of output?

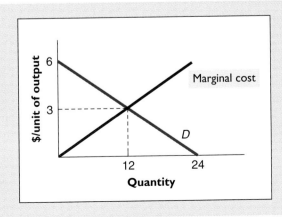

FIGURE 9.10
The Demand and Marginal Cost Curves for a Monopolist.
The socially optimal output level is 12 units/week, the quantity for which the marginal benefit *to the public* is exactly the same as marginal cost.

At any output level, the cost to society of an additional unit of output is the same as the cost to the monopolist, namely, the amount shown on the monopolist's marginal cost curve. The marginal benefit *to society* (not to the monopolist) of an extra unit of output is simply the amount people are willing to pay for it, which is the amount shown on the monopolist's demand curve. To achieve social efficiency, the monopolist should expand production until the marginal benefit to society equals the marginal cost, which in this case occurs at a level of 12 units/week. Social efficiency is thus achieved at the output level at which the market demand curve intersects the monopolist's marginal cost curve.

The fact that marginal revenue is less than price for the monopolist results in a deadweight loss. For the monopolist just discussed, the size of this deadweight loss is equal to the area of the pale blue triangle in Figure 9.11, which is (1/2)($2/unit)(4 units/week) = $4/week. That is the amount by which total economic surplus is reduced because the monopolist produces too little.

FIGURE 9.11
The Deadweight Loss from Monopoly.
A loss in economic surplus results because the profit-maximizing level of output (8 units/week) is less than the socially optimal level of output (12 units/week). This deadweight loss is the area of the pale blue triangle, $4/week.

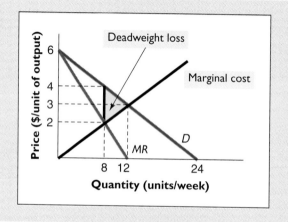

For a monopolist, profit maximization occurs when marginal cost equals marginal revenue. Since the monopolist's marginal revenue is always less than price, the monopolist's profit-maximizing output level is always below the socially efficient level. Under perfect competition, by contrast, profit maximization occurs when marginal cost equals the market price—the same criterion that must be satisfied for social efficiency. This difference explains why the invisible hand of the market is less evident in monopoly markets than in perfectly competitive markets.

If perfect competition is socially efficient and monopoly is not, why isn't monopoly against the law? The nation's legislators have in fact tried to limit the extent of monopoly through the antitrust laws. But even the most enthusiastic proponents of those laws recognize the limited utility of the legislative approach, since the alternatives to monopoly often entail problems of their own.

Suppose, for example, that a monopoly results from a patent that prevents all but one firm from manufacturing some highly valued product. Would society be better off without patents? Probably not, because eliminating such protection would discourage innovation. Virtually all successful industrial nations grant some form of patent protection, which gives firms a chance to recover the research and development costs without which new products would seldom reach the market.

Or suppose that the market in question is a natural monopoly—one that, because of economies of scale, is most cheaply served by a single firm. Would society do better to require this market to be served by many small firms, each with significantly higher average costs of production? Such a requirement would merely replace one form of inefficiency with another.

In short, we live in an imperfect world. Monopoly is socially inefficient, and that, needless to say, is bad. But the alternatives to monopoly aren't perfect, either.

> **RECAP** **WHY THE MONOPOLIST PRODUCES "TOO LITTLE" OUTPUT**
>
> The monopolist maximizes profit at the output level for which marginal revenue equals marginal cost. Because its profit-maximizing price exceeds marginal revenue, and hence also marginal cost, the benefit to society of the last unit produced (the market price) must be less than the cost of the last unit produced (the marginal cost). So the output level for an industry served by a profit-maximizing monopolist is smaller than the socially optimal level of output.

USING DISCOUNTS TO EXPAND THE MARKET

The source of inefficiency in monopoly markets is the fact that the benefit to the monopolist of expanding output is less than the corresponding benefit to society. From the monopolist's point of view, the price reduction the firm must grant existing buyers to expand output is a loss. But from the point of view of those buyers, each dollar of price reduction is a gain—one dollar more in their pockets.

Note the tension in this situation, which is similar to the tension that exists in all other situations in which the economic pie is smaller than it might otherwise be. As the efficiency principle reminds us, when the economic pie grows larger, everyone can have a larger slice. To say that monopoly is inefficient means that steps could be taken to make some people better off without harming others. If people have a healthy regard for their own self-interest, why doesn't someone take those steps? Why, for example, doesn't the monopolist from the earlier examples sell 8 units of output at a price of $4, and then once those buyers are out the door, cut the price for more price-sensitive buyers?

PRICE DISCRIMINATION DEFINED

Sometimes the monopolist does precisely that. Charging different buyers different prices for the same good or service is a practice known as **price discrimination.** Examples of price discrimination include senior citizens' and children's discounts on movie tickets, supersaver discounts on air travel, and rebate coupons on retail merchandise.

Attempts at price discrimination seem to work effectively in some markets, but not in others. Buyers are not stupid, after all; if the monopolist periodically offered a 50 percent discount on the $8 list price, those who were paying $8 might anticipate the next price cut and postpone their purchases to take advantage of it. In some markets, however, buyers may not know, or simply may not take the trouble to find out, how the price they pay compares to the prices paid by other buyers. Alternatively, the monopolist may be in a position to prevent some groups from buying at the discount prices made available to others. In such cases, the monopolist can price-discriminate effectively.

price discrimination the practice of charging different buyers different prices for essentially the same good or service

Why do many movie theaters offer discount tickets to students?

Whenever a firm offers a discount, the goal is to target that discount to buyers who would not purchase the product without it. People with low incomes generally have lower reservation prices for movie tickets than people with high incomes. Because students generally have lower disposable incomes than working adults, theater owners can expand their audiences by charging lower prices to students than to adults. Student discounts are one practical way of doing so. Offering student discounts also entails no risk of some people buying the product at a low price and then reselling it to others at a higher price.

ECONOMIC NATURALIST 9.2

HOW PRICE DISCRIMINATION AFFECTS OUTPUT

In Examples 9.7 to 9.9 we will see how the ability to price-discriminate affects the monopolist's profit-maximizing level of output. First we will consider a baseline case in which the monopolist must charge the same price to every buyer.

EXAMPLE 9.7   **How many manuscripts should Carla edit?**

Carla supplements her income as a teaching assistant by editing term papers for undergraduates. There are eight students/week for whom she might edit, each with a reservation price as given in the following table.

Student	Reservation price
A	$40
B	38
C	36
D	34
E	32
F	30
G	28
H	26

Carla is a profit maximizer. If the opportunity cost of her time to edit each paper is $29 and she must charge the same price to each student, how many papers should she edit? How much economic profit will she make? How much accounting profit?

Table 9.5 summarizes Carla's total and marginal revenue at various output levels. To generate the amounts in the total revenue column, we simply multiplied the corresponding reservation price by the number of students whose reservation prices were at least that high. For example, to edit 4 papers/week (for

TABLE 9.5
Total and Marginal Revenue from Editing

Student	Reservation price ($/paper)	Total revenue ($/week)	Marginal revenue ($/paper)
			40
A	40	40	
			36
B	38	76	
			32
C	36	108	
			28
D	34	136	
			24
E	32	160	
			20
F	30	180	
			16
G	28	196	
			12
H	26	208	

students *A*, *B*, *C*, and *D*), Carla must charge a price no higher than *D*'s reservation price ($34). So her total revenue when she edits 4 papers/week is (4)($34) = $136/week. Carla should keep expanding the number of students she serves as long as her marginal revenue exceeds the opportunity cost of her time. Marginal revenue, or the difference in total revenue that results from adding another student, is shown in the last column of Table 9.5.

Note that if Carla were editing 2 papers/week, her marginal revenue from editing a third paper would be $32. Since that amount exceeds her $29 opportunity cost, she should take on the third paper. But since the marginal revenue of taking on a fourth paper would be only $28, Carla should stop at 3 papers/week. The total opportunity cost of the time required to edit the 3 papers is (3)($29) = $87, so Carla's economic profit is $108 − $87 = $21/week. Since Carla incurs no explicit costs, her accounting profit will be $108/week.

What is the socially efficient number of papers for Carla to edit?

EXAMPLE 9.8

Again, suppose that Carla's opportunity cost of editing is $29/paper and that she could edit as many as 8 papers/week for students whose reservation prices are again as listed in the following table.

Student	Reservation price
A	$40
B	38
C	36
D	34
E	32
F	30
G	28
H	26

What is the socially efficient number of papers for Carla to edit? If she must charge the same price to each student, what will her economic and accounting profits be if she edits the socially efficient number of papers?

Students *A* to *F* are willing to pay more than Carla's opportunity cost, so serving these students is socially efficient. But students *G* and *H* are unwilling to pay at least $29 for Carla's services. The socially efficient outcome, therefore, is for Carla to edit 6 papers/week. To attract that number, she must charge a price no higher than $30/paper. Her total revenue will be (6)($30) = $180/week, slightly more than her total opportunity cost of (6)($29) = $174/week. Her economic profit will thus be only $6/week. Again, because Carla incurs no explicit costs, her accounting profit will be the same as her total revenue, $180/week.

If Carla can price-discriminate, how many papers should she edit?

EXAMPLE 9.9

Suppose Carla is a shrewd judge of human nature. After a moment's conversation with a student, she can discern that student's reservation price. The reservation prices of her potential customers are again as given in the following table. If Carla confronts the same market as before, but can charge students their respective reservation prices, how many papers should she edit, and how much economic and accounting profit will she make?

Student	Reservation price
A	$40
B	38
C	36
D	34
E	32
F	30
G	28
H	26

Carla will edit papers for students *A* to *F* and charge each exactly his or her reservation price. Because students *G* and *H* have reservation prices below $29, Carla will not edit their papers. Carla's total revenue will be $40 + $38 + $36 + $34 + $32 + $30 = $210/week, which is also her accounting profit. Her total opportunity cost of editing 6 papers is (6)($29) = $174/week, so her economic profit will be $210 − $174 = $36/week, $30/week more than when she was constrained to charge each customer the same price.

perfectly discriminating monopolist a firm that charges each buyer exactly his or her reservation price

A monopolist who can charge each buyer exactly his or her reservation price is called a **perfectly discriminating monopolist**. Notice that when Carla was discriminating among customers in this way, her profit-maximizing level of output was exactly the same as the socially efficient level of output: 6 papers/week. With a perfectly discriminating monopoly, there is no loss of efficiency. All buyers who are willing to pay a price high enough to cover marginal cost will be served.

Note that although total economic surplus is maximized by a perfectly discriminating monopolist, consumers would have little reason to celebrate if they found themselves dealing with such a firm. After all, consumer surplus is exactly zero for the perfectly discriminating monopolist. In this instance, total economic surplus and producer surplus are one and the same.

In practice, of course, perfect price discrimination can never occur, because no seller knows each and every buyer's precise reservation price. But even if some sellers did know, practical difficulties would stand in the way of their charging a separate price to each buyer. For example, in many markets the seller could not prevent buyers who bought at low prices from reselling to other buyers at higher prices, capturing some of the seller's business in the process. Despite these difficulties, price discrimination is widespread. But it is generally *imperfect price discrimination*, that is, price discrimination in which at least some buyers are charged less than their reservation prices.

THE HURDLE METHOD OF PRICE DISCRIMINATION

The profit-maximizing seller's goal is to charge each buyer the highest price that buyer is willing to pay. Two primary obstacles prevent sellers from achieving this goal. First, sellers don't know exactly how much each buyer is willing to pay. And second, they need some means of excluding those who are willing to pay a high price from buying at a low price. These are formidable problems, which no seller can hope to solve completely.

hurdle method of price discrimination the practice by which a seller offers a discount to all buyers who overcome some obstacle

One common method by which sellers achieve a crude solution to both problems is to require buyers to overcome some obstacle to be eligible for a discount price. This method is called the **hurdle method of price discrimination**. For example, the seller might sell a product at a standard list price and offer a rebate to any buyer who takes the trouble to mail in a rebate coupon.

The hurdle method solves both the seller's problems, provided that buyers with low reservation prices are more willing than others to jump the hurdle. Because the decision to jump the hurdle is subject to the cost-benefit test, such a link seems to exist. As noted earlier, buyers with low incomes are more likely than others to have low reservation prices (at least in the case of normal goods). Because of the low opportunity cost of their time, they are more likely than others to take the trouble to send in rebate coupons. Rebate coupons thus target a discount toward those buyers whose reservation prices are low and who therefore might not buy the product otherwise.

A **perfect hurdle** is one that separates buyers precisely according to their reservation prices, and in the process imposes no cost on those who jump the hurdle. With a perfect hurdle, the highest reservation price among buyers who jump the hurdle will be lower than the lowest reservation price among buyers who choose not to jump the hurdle. In practice, perfect hurdles do not exist. Some buyers will always jump the hurdle, even though their reservation prices are high. And hurdles will always exclude at least some buyers with low reservation prices. Even so, many commonly used hurdles do a remarkably good job of targeting discounts to buyers with low reservation prices. In the examples that follow, we will assume for convenience that the seller is using a perfect hurdle.

perfect hurdle one that completely segregates buyers whose reservation prices lie above some threshold from others whose reservation prices lie below it, imposing no cost on those who jump the hurdle

How much should Carla charge for editing if she uses a perfect hurdle?

EXAMPLE 9.10

Suppose Carla again has the opportunity to edit as many as 8 papers/week for the students whose reservation prices are as given in the following table. This time she can offer a rebate coupon that gives a discount to any student who takes the trouble to mail it back to her. Suppose further that students whose reservation prices are at least $36 never mail in the rebate coupons, while those whose reservation prices are below $36 always do so.

Student	Reservation price
A	$40
B	38
C	36
D	34
E	32
F	30
G	28
H	26

If Carla's opportunity cost of editing each paper is again $29, what should her list price be, and what amount should she offer as a rebate? Will her economic profit be larger or smaller than when she lacked the discount option (Example 9.7)?

The rebate coupon allows Carla to divide her original market into two submarkets in which she can charge two different prices. The first submarket consists of students A, B, and C, whose reservation prices are at least $36, and who therefore will not bother to mail in a rebate coupon. The second submarket consists of students D to H, whose lower reservation prices indicate a willingness to use rebate coupons.

In each submarket, Carla must charge the same price to every buyer, just like an ordinary monopolist. She should therefore keep expanding output in each submarket as long as marginal revenue in that market exceeds her marginal cost. The relevant data for the two submarkets are displayed in Table 9.6.

On the basis of the entries in the marginal revenue column for the list price submarket, we see that Carla should serve all three students *(A, B,* and *C)*, since marginal revenue for each exceeds $29. Her profit-maximizing price in the list price submarket is $36, the highest price she can charge in that market and still sell her services to students *A, B,* and *C.* For the discount price submarket, marginal revenue exceeds $29 only for the first two students *(D* and *E).* So the profit-maximizing price in this submarket is $32, the highest price Carla can charge and still sell her services to *D* and *E.* (A discount price of $32 means that students who mail in the coupon will receive a rebate of $4 on the $36 list price.)

Note that the rebate offer enables Carla to serve a total of five students/week, compared to only three without the offer (see Example 9.7). Carla's combined total revenue for the two markets is (3)($36) + 2($32) = $172/week. Since her opportunity cost is $29/paper, or a total of (5)($29) = $145/week, her economic profit is $172/week − $145/week = $27/week, $6 more than when she did not offer the rebate.

TABLE 9.6
Price Discrimination with a Perfect Hurdle

	List Price Submarket		
Student	Reservation price ($/paper)	Total revenue ($/week)	Marginal revenue ($/paper)
A	40	40	
			40
B	38	76	
			36
C	36	108	
			32
	Discount Price Submarket		
D	34	34	
			34
E	32	64	
			30
F	30	90	
			26
G	28	112	
			22
H	26	130	
			18

EXERCISE 9.4

Refer to Example 9.10. How much should Carla charge in each submarket if she knows that only those students whose reservation prices are below $34 will use rebate coupons?

IS THE HURDLE METHOD EFFICIENT?

We are so conditioned to think of discrimination as bad that we may be tempted to conclude that price discrimination must run counter to the public interest. In Example 9.10, however, both consumer and producer surplus were actually enhanced by the monopolist's use of the hurdle method of price discrimination. To show this, we compare consumer and producer surplus when Carla employs the hurdle method (Example 9.10) to the corresponding values when she charges the same price to all buyers (Example 9.7).

When Carla had to charge the same price to every customer, she edited only the papers of students A, B, and C, each of whom paid a price of $36. We can tell at a glance that the total surplus must be larger under the hurdle method, because not only are students A, B, and C served at the same price ($36), but also students E and F are now served at a price of $32.

To confirm this intuition, we can calculate the exact amount of the surplus. For any student who hires Carla to edit her paper, consumer surplus is the difference between her reservation price and the price actually paid. In both the single price and discount price examples, student A's consumer surplus is thus $40 − $36 = $4; student B's consumer surplus is $38 − $36 = $2; and student C's consumer surplus is $36 − $36 = 0. Total consumer surplus in the list price submarket is thus $4 + $2 = $6/week, which is the same as total consumer surplus in Example 9.7. But now the discount price submarket generates additional consumer surplus. Specifically, student D receives $2/week of consumer surplus, since this student's reservation price of $34 is $2 more than the discount price of $32. So total consumer surplus is now $6 + $2 = $8/week, or $2/week more than before.

Carla's producer surplus also increases under the hurdle method. For each paper she edits, her producer surplus is the price she charges minus her reservation price ($29). In the single price case, Carla's surplus was (3)($36 − $29) = $21/week. When she offers a rebate coupon, she earns the same producer surplus as before from students A, B, and C, and an additional (2)($32 − $29) = $6/week from students D and E. Total producer surplus with the discount is thus $21 + $6 = $27/week. Adding that amount to the total consumer surplus of $8/week, we get a total economic surplus of $35/week with the rebate coupons, $8/week more than without the rebate.

Note, however, that even with the rebate, the final outcome is not socially efficient, because Carla does not serve student F, even though this student's reservation price of $30 exceeds her opportunity cost of $29. But though the hurdle method is not perfectly efficient, it is still more efficient than charging a single price to all buyers.

EXAMPLES OF THE HURDLE METHOD

Once you grasp the principle behind the hurdle method of price discrimination, you will begin to see examples of it all around you. Next time you visit a grocery, hardware, or appliance store, for instance, notice how many different product promotions include cash rebates. Temporary sales are another illustration of the hurdle method. Most of the time, stores sell most of their merchandise at the "regular" price but periodically offer special sales at a significant discount. The hurdle in this instance is taking the trouble to find out when and where the sales occur and then going to the store during that period. This technique works because buyers who care most about price (mainly, those with low reservation prices) are more likely to monitor advertisements carefully and buy only during sale periods.

To give another example, book publishers typically launch a new book in hardcover form at a price from $20 to $30, and a year later they bring out a paperback edition priced between $5 and $15. In this instance, the hurdle involves having to wait the extra year and accepting a slight reduction in the quality of the finished product. People who are strongly concerned about price end up waiting for the paperback edition, while those with high reservation prices usually spring for the hardback.

Or take the example of automobile producers, who typically offer several different models with different trim and accessories. Although GM's actual cost of producing a Cadillac may be only $2,000 more than its cost of producing a Chevrolet, the Cadillac's selling price may be $10,000 to $15,000 higher than the Chevrolet's. Buyers with low reservation prices purchase the Chevrolet, while those with high reservation prices are more likely to choose the Cadillac.

Commercial air carriers have perfected the hurdle method to an extent matched by almost no other seller. Their supersaver fares are often less than half their regular coach fares. To be eligible for these discounts, travelers must purchase their tickets 7 to 21 days in advance, and their journey must include a Saturday night stayover. Vacation travelers can more easily satisfy these restrictions than business travelers, whose schedules often change at the last moment and whose trips seldom involve Saturday stayovers. And—no surprise—the business traveler's reservation price tends to be much higher than the vacation traveler's.

Many sellers employ not just one hurdle but several by offering deeper discounts to buyers who jump successively more difficult hurdles. For example, movie producers release their major films to first-run theaters at premium prices, then several months later to neighborhood theaters at a few dollars less. Still later they make the films available on pay-per-view cable channels, then release them on video, and finally permit them to be shown on network television. Each successive hurdle involves waiting a little longer, and in the case of the televised versions, accepting lower quality. These hurdles are remarkably effective in segregating moviegoers according to their reservation prices.

Recall that the efficiency loss from single-price monopoly occurs because to the monopolist the benefit of expanding output is smaller than the benefit to society as a whole. The hurdle method of price discrimination reduces this loss by giving the monopolist a practical means of cutting prices for price-sensitive buyers only. In general, the more finely the monopolist can partition a market using the hurdle method, the smaller the efficiency loss. Hurdles are not perfect, however, and some degree of efficiency will inevitably be lost.

Why might an appliance retailer instruct its clerks to hammer dents into the sides of its stoves and refrigerators?

The Sears "Scratch 'n' Dent Sale" is another example of how retailers use quality differentials to segregate buyers according to their reservation prices. Many Sears stores hold an annual sale in which they display appliances with minor scratches and blemishes in the parking lot at deep discounts. People who don't care much about price are unlikely to turn out for these events, but those with very low reservation prices often get up early to be first in line. Indeed, these sales have proven so popular that it might even be in a retailer's interest to put dents in some of its sale items deliberately.

ECONOMIC NATURALIST 9.5

Would a profit-maximizing appliance retailer ever deliberately damage its own merchandise?

RECAP   USING DISCOUNTS TO EXPAND THE MARKET

A price-discriminating monopolist is one who charges different prices to different buyers for essentially the same good or service. A common method of price discrimination is the hurdle method, which involves granting a discount to buyers who jump over a hurdle, such as mailing in a rebate coupon. An effective hurdle is one that is more easily cleared by buyers with low reservation prices than by buyers with high reservation prices. Such a hurdle enables the monopolist to expand output and thereby reduce the deadweight loss from monopoly pricing.

■ SUMMARY ■

- Our concern in this chapter was the conduct and performance of the imperfectly competitive firm, a firm that has at least some latitude to set its own price. Economists often distinguish among three different types of imperfectly competitive firms: the pure monopolist, the lone seller of a product in a given market; the oligopolist, one of only a few sellers of a given product; and the monopolistic competitor, one of a relatively large number of firms that sell similar though slightly differentiated products.

- Although advanced courses in economics devote much attention to differences in the behavior among these three types of firms, our focus was on the common feature that differentiates them from perfectly competitive firms. Whereas the perfectly competitive firm faces an infinitely elastic demand curve for its product, the imperfectly competitive firm faces a downward-sloping demand curve. For convenience, we use the term *monopolist* to refer to any of the three types of imperfectly competitive firms.

- Monopolists are sometimes said to enjoy market power, a term that refers to their power to set the price of their product. Market power stems from exclusive control over important inputs, from economies of scale, and from patents and government licenses or franchises. The most important and enduring of these four sources of market power is economies of scale.

- Unlike the perfectly competitive firm, for which marginal revenue exactly equals market price, the monopolist realizes a marginal revenue that is always less than its price. This shortfall reflects the fact that to sell more output, the monopolist must cut the price not only to additional buyers but to existing buyers as well. For the monopolist with a straight-line demand curve, the marginal revenue curve has the same vertical intercept and a horizontal intercept that is half as large as the intercept for the demand curve.

- Whereas the perfectly competitive firm maximizes profit by producing at the level at which marginal cost equals the market price, the monopolist maximizes profit by equating marginal cost with marginal revenue, which is significantly lower than the market price. The result is an output level that is best for the monopolist but smaller than the level that would be best for society as a whole. At the profit-maximizing level of output, the benefit of an extra unit of output (the market price) is greater than its cost (the marginal cost). At the socially efficient level of output, where the monopolist's marginal cost curve intersects the demand curve, the benefit and cost of an extra unit are the same.

- Both the monopolist and its potential customers can do better if the monopolist can grant discounts to price-sensitive buyers. The extreme example is the perfectly discriminating monopolist, who charges each buyer exactly his or her reservation price. Such producers are socially efficient, because they sell to every buyer whose reservation price is at least as high as the marginal cost.

- One common method of targeting discounts toward price-sensitive buyers is the hurdle method of price discrimination, in which the buyer becomes eligible for a discount only after overcoming some obstacle, such as mailing in a rebate coupon. This technique works well because those buyers who care most about price are more likely than others to jump the hurdle. While the hurdle method reduces the efficiency loss associated with single-price monopoly, it does not completely eliminate it.

■ KEY TERMS ■

constant returns to scale (223)
economies of scale (223)
hurdle method of price discrimination (238)
imperfectly competitive firm (221)
increasing returns to scale (223)

marginal revenue (228)
market power (223)
monopolistically competitive firm (222)
natural monopoly (224)
oligopolist (222)

perfect hurdle (239)
perfectly discriminating monopolist (238)
price discrimination (235)
price setter (221)
pure monopoly (222)

■ REVIEW QUESTIONS ■

1. What important characteristic do all three types of imperfectly competitive firm share?

2. True or false: A firm with market power can sell whatever quantity it wishes at whatever price it chooses.

3. Why do most successful industrial societies offer patents and copyright protection, even though these protections enable sellers to charge higher prices?

4. Why is marginal revenue always less than price for a monopolist but equal to price for a perfectly competitive firm?

5. True or false: Because a natural monopolist charges a price greater than marginal cost, it necessarily earns a positive economic profit.

▪ PROBLEMS ▪

1. Two car manufacturers, Saab and Volvo, have fixed costs of $1 billion and marginal costs of $10,000/car. If Saab produces 50,000 cars/year and Volvo produces 200,000, calculate the average production cost for each company. On the basis of these costs, which company's market share do you think will grow in relative terms?

2. State whether the following statements are true or false, and explain why.
   a. In a perfectly competitive industry the industry demand curve is horizontal, whereas for a monopoly it is downward-sloping.
   b. Perfectly competitive firms have no control over the price they charge for their product.
   c. For a natural monopoly, average cost declines as the number of units produced increases over the relevant output range.

3. A single-price profit-maximizing monopolist:
   a. Causes excess demand, or shortages, by selling too few units of a good or service.
   b. Chooses the output level at which marginal revenue begins to increase.
   c. Always charges a price above the marginal cost of production.
   d. Also maximizes marginal revenue.
   e. None of the above statements is true.

4. If a monopolist could perfectly price-discriminate:
   a. The marginal revenue curve and the demand curve would coincide.
   b. The marginal revenue curve and the marginal cost curve would coincide.
   c. Every consumer would pay a different price.
   d. Marginal revenue would become negative at some output level.
   e. The resulting pattern of exchange would still be socially inefficient.

5. Explain why price discrimination and the existence of slightly different variants of the same product tend to go hand in hand. Give an example from your own experience.

6. What is the socially desirable price for a natural monopoly to charge? Why will a natural monopoly that attempts to charge the socially desirable price invariably suffer an economic loss?

7. TotsPoses, Inc., a profit-maximizing business, is the only photography business in town that specializes in portraits of small children. George, who owns and runs TotsPoses, expects to encounter an average of eight customers per day, each with a reservation price shown in the following table.

Customer	Reservation price ($/photo)
A	50
B	46
C	42
D	38
E	34
F	30
G	26
H	22

   a. If the total cost of each photoportrait is $12, how much should George charge if he must charge a single price to all customers? At this price, how many portraits will George produce each day? What will be his economic profit?
   b. How much consumer surplus is generated each day at this price?
   c. What is the socially efficient number of portraits?
   d. George is very experienced in the business and knows the reservation price of each of his customers. If he is allowed to charge any price he likes to any consumer, how many portraits will he produce each day, and what will his economic profit be?

e. In this case, how much consumer surplus is generated each day?

f. Suppose George is permitted to charge two prices. He knows that customers with a reservation price above $30 never bother with coupons, whereas those with a reservation price of $30 or less always use them. At what level should George set the list price of a portrait? At what level should he set the discount price? How many photoportraits will he sell at each price?

g. In this case, what is George's economic profit, and how much consumer surplus is generated each day?

8. Suppose that the University of Michigan Cinema is a local monopoly whose demand curve for adult tickets on Saturday night is $P = 12 - 2Q$, where P is the price of a ticket in dollars and Q is the number of tickets sold in hundreds. The demand for children's tickets on Sunday afternoon is $P = 8 - 3Q$, and for adult tickets on Sunday afternoon, $P = 10 - 4Q$. On both Saturday night and Sunday afternoon, the marginal cost of an additional patron, child or adult, is $2.

a. What is the marginal revenue curve in each of the three submarkets?

b. What price should the cinema charge in each of the three markets if its goal is to maximize profit?

9. Suppose you are a monopolist in the market for a specific video game. Your demand curve is given by $P = 80 - Q/2$, and your marginal cost curve is $MC = Q$. Your fixed costs equal $400.

a. Graph the demand and marginal cost curve.

b. Derive and graph the marginal revenue curve.

c. Calculate and indicate on the graph the equilibrium price and quantity.

d. What is your profit?

e. What is the level of consumer surplus?

10. Beth is a second-grader who sells lemonade on a street corner in your neighborhood. Each cup of lemonade costs Beth 20 cents to produce; she has no fixed costs. The reservation prices for the 10 people who walk by Beth's lemonade stand each day are listed in the following table.

Person	A	B	C	D	E	F	G	H	I	J
Reservation Price	$1.00	$0.90	$0.80	$0.70	$0.60	$0.50	$0.40	$0.30	$0.20	$0.10

Beth knows the distribution of reservation prices (that is, she knows that one person is willing to pay $1, another $0.90, and so on), but she does not know any specific individual's reservation price.

a. Calculate the marginal revenue of selling an additional cup of lemonade. (Start by figuring out the price Beth would charge if she produced only one cup of lemonade, and calculate the total revenue; then find the price Beth would charge if she sold two cups of lemonade; and so on.)

b. What is Beth's profit-maximizing price?

c. At that price, what are Beth's economic profit and total consumer surplus?

d. What price should Beth charge if she wants to maximize total economic surplus?

e. Now suppose Beth can tell the reservation price of each person. What price would she charge each person if she wanted to maximize profit? Compare her profit to the total surplus calculated in part d.

■ ANSWERS TO IN-CHAPTER EXERCISES ■

9.1 The relevant cost figures are as shown in the following table, which shows that the Sega's unit-cost advantage is now $50.20 − $5.20 = $45.00.

	Nintendo	Sega
Annual production	200,000	2,000,000
Fixed cost	$10,000,000	$10,000,000
Variable cost	$40,000	$400,000
Total cost	$10,040,000	$10,400,000
Average cost per game	$50.20	$5.20

9.2   When the monopolist expands from 3 to 4 units/week, total revenue rises from $15 to $16/week, which means that the marginal revenue from the sale of the fourth unit is only $1/week. When the monopolist expands from 4 to 5 units/week, total revenue drops from $16 to 15/week, which means that the marginal revenue from the sale of the fifth unit is actually negative, or −$1/week.

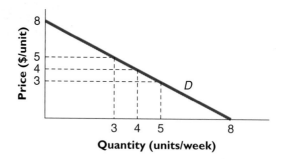

9.3   For the demand curve $P = 12 - Q$, the corresponding marginal revenue curve is $MR = 12 - 2Q$. Equating MR and MC, we solve the equation $12 - 2Q = 2Q$ for $Q = 3$. Substituting $Q = 3$ into the demand equation, we solve for the profit-maximizing price, $P = 12 - 3 = 9$.

9.4   As the marginal revenue column in the following table shows, Carla should again serve students A, B, and C in the list price submarket (at a price of $36), and only student E in the discount submarket (at a price of $32).

Student	Reservation price ($/paper)	Total revenue ($/week)	Marginal revenue ($/paper)
List Price Submarket			
			40
A	40	40	
			36
B	38	76	
			32
C	36	108	
			28
D	34	136	
Discount Price Submarket			
			32
E	32	32	
			28
F	30	60	
			24
G	28	84	
			20
H	26	104	

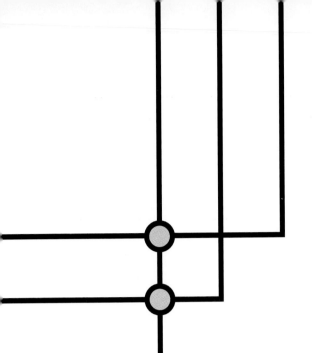

CHAPTER

THINKING
STRATEGICALLY

■

At a Christmas Eve dinner party in 1997, actor Robert DeNiro pulled singer Tony Bennett aside for a moment. "Hey Tony—there's a film I want you in," DeNiro said. He was referring to the project that became the 1999 Warner Brothers hit comedy *Analyze This,* in which the troubled head of a crime family, played by DeNiro, seeks the counsel of a psychotherapist, played by Billy Crystal. In the script, both the mob boss and his therapist are big fans of Bennett's music.

Bennett heard nothing further about the project for almost a year. Then his son and financial manager, Danny Bennett, got a phone call from Warner Brothers, in which the studio offered Tony $15,000 to sing "Got the World on a String" in the movie's final scene. As Danny described the conversation, ". . . they made a fatal mistake. They told me they had already shot the film. So I'm like: 'Hey, they shot the whole film around Tony being the end gag and they're offering me $15,000?'"[1]

Warner Brothers wound up paying $200,000 for Bennett's performance.

In business negotiations, as in life, timing can be everything. If executives at Warner Brothers had thought the problem through carefully, they would have negotiated with Bennett *before* shooting the movie. At that point Bennett would have realized that the script could be rewritten if he asked too high a fee. By waiting, studio executives left themselves with no other option than to pay Bennett's price.

[1]As quoted by Geraldine Fabrikant, "Talking Money with Tony Bennett," *The New York Times,* May 2, 1999, Money & Business, p. 1.

The payoff to many actions depends not only on the actions themselves but also on when they are taken and how they relate to actions taken by others. In previous chapters, economic decision makers confronted an environment that was essentially fixed. This chapter will focus on cases in which people must consider the effect of their behavior on others. For example, an imperfectly competitive firm will want to weigh the likely responses of rivals when deciding whether to cut prices or to increase the advertising budget. Interdependencies of this sort are the rule rather than the exception in economic and social life. To make sense of the world we live in, then, we must take these interdependencies into account.

THE THEORY OF GAMES

In chess, tennis, or any other game, the payoff to a given move depends on what your opponent does in response. In choosing your move, therefore, you must anticipate your opponent's responses, how you might respond, and what further moves your own response might elicit. To analyze such situations, in which the payoffs to different actors depend on the actions their opponents take, economists and other behavioral scientists have devised the mathematical theory of games.

THE THREE ELEMENTS OF A GAME

basic elements of a game the players, the strategies available to each player, and the payoffs each player receives for each possible combination of strategies

Any game has three **basic elements**: the players, the list of possible actions (or strategies) each player can choose from, and the payoffs the players receive for each combination of strategies. How these elements combine to form the basis of a theory of behavior will become clear in the context of the following illustrative examples.

EXAMPLE 10.1

Should United Airlines spend more money on advertising?

Suppose that United Airlines and TWA are the only air carriers that serve the Chicago–St. Louis market. Each currently earns an economic profit of $6,000/flight on this route. If United increases its advertising spending in this market by $1,000/flight and TWA spends no more on advertising than it does now, United's profit will rise to $8,000/flight and TWA's will fall to $2,000. If both spend $1,000 more on advertising, each will earn an economic profit of $5,500/flight. These payoffs are symmetric, so if United stands pat while TWA increases its spending by $1,000, United's economic profit will fall to $2,000/flight and TWA's will rise to $8,000. If each must decide independently whether to increase spending on advertising, what should United do?

Think of this situation as a game. What are its three elements? The players are the two airlines, each of which must choose one of two strategies: to raise spending by $1,000 or to leave it the same. The payoffs are the economic profits that correspond to the four possible scenarios resulting from their choices. One way to summarize the relevant information about this game is to display the players, strategies, and payoffs in the form of a simple table called a **payoff matrix** (see Table 10.1).

payoff matrix a table that describes the payoffs in a game for each possible combination of strategies

Confronted with the payoff matrix in Table 10.1, what should United Airlines do? The essence of strategic thinking is to begin by looking at the situation from the other party's point of view. Suppose TWA assumes that United will raise its spending on advertising (the top row in Table 10.1). In that case, TWA's best bet would be to follow suit (the left column in Table 10.1). Why is the left column TWA's best response when United chooses the top row? TWA's economic profits, given in the upper left cell of Table 10.1, will be $5,500 as compared to only $2,000 if it keeps spending level (see the upper right cell).

TABLE 10.1
The Payoff Matrix for an Advertising Game

		TWA	
		Raise ad spending	Leave ad spending the same
United	Raise ad spending	$5,500 for United / $5,500 for TWA	$8,000 for United / $2,000 for TWA
	Leave ad spending the same	$2,000 for United / $8,000 for TWA	$6,000 for United / $6,000 for TWA

Alternatively, suppose TWA assumes that United will keep its ad spending level (that is, United will choose the bottom row in Table 10.1). In that case, TWA would still do better to increase spending, because it would earn $8,000 (the lower left cell) as compared to only $6,000 if it keeps spending level (lower right cell). In this particular game, no matter which strategy United chooses, TWA will earn a higher economic profit by increasing its spending on advertising. And since this game is perfectly symmetric, a similar conclusion holds for United: No matter which strategy TWA chooses, United will do better by increasing its spending on ads.

When one player has a strategy that yields a higher payoff no matter which choice the other player makes, that player is said to have a **dominant strategy**. Not all games involve dominant strategies, but both players in this game have one, and that is to increase spending on ads. For both players, to leave ad spending the same is a **dominated strategy**—one that leads to a lower payoff than an alternative choice, regardless of the other player's choice.

Notice, however, that when each player chooses the dominant strategy, the resulting payoffs are smaller than if each had left spending unchanged. When United and TWA increase their spending on ads, each earns only $5,500 in economic profits as compared to the $6,000 each would have earned without the increase. (We'll say more below about this apparent paradox.)

dominant strategy one that yields a higher payoff no matter what the other players in a game choose

dominated strategy any other strategy available to a player who has a dominant strategy

NASH EQUILIBRIUM

A game is said to be in equilibrium if each player's strategy is the best he or she can choose, given the other players' strategies. This definition of equilibrium is sometimes called a **Nash equilibrium**, after the Nobel laureate John Nash, who developed the concept in the early 1950s. When a game is in equilibrium, no player has any incentive to deviate from his or her current strategy.

If each player in a game has a dominant strategy, as in Example 10.1, equilibrium occurs when each player follows that strategy. But even in games in which not every player has a dominant strategy, we can often identify an equilibrium outcome. Consider, for instance, the following variation on the advertising game in Example 10.1.

Nash equilibrium any combination of strategies in which each player's strategy is his or her best choice, given the other players' strategies

Should TWA spend more money on advertising?

Suppose United Airlines and TWA are the only carriers that serve the Chicago–St. Louis market. Their payoff matrix for advertising decisions is shown in Table 10.2. Does United have a dominant strategy? Does TWA? If each firm does the best it can, given the incentives facing the other, what will be the outcome of this game?

EXAMPLE 10.2

TABLE 10.2
Equilibrium When One Player Lacks a Dominant Strategy

		TWA	
		Raise ad spending	Leave ad spending the same
United	Raise ad spending	$3,000 for United $8,000 for TWA	$8,000 for United $4,000 for TWA
	Leave ad spending the same	$4,000 for United $5,000 for TWA	$5,000 for United $2,000 for TWA

In this game, no matter what United does, TWA will do better to raise its ad spending, so raising the advertising budget is a dominant strategy for TWA. United, however, does not have a dominant strategy. If TWA raises its spending, United will do better to stand pat; if TWA stands pat, however, United will do better to spend more. But even though United does not have a dominant strategy, we can still predict what is likely to happen in this game. After all, United's managers know what the payoff matrix is, so they can predict that TWA will spend more on ads (since that is TWA's dominant strategy). Thus the best strategy for United, given the prediction that TWA will spend more on ads, is to keep its own spending level. If both players do the best they can, taking account of the incentives each faces, this game will end in the lower left cell of the payoff matrix: TWA will raise its spending on ads and United will not. (Note that when both players are positioned in the lower left cell, neither has any incentive to change its strategy.)

EXERCISE 10.1

What should United and TWA do if their payoff matrix is modified as follows?

		TWA	
		Raise ad spending	Leave ad spending the same
United	Raise ad spending	$3,000 for United $8,000 for TWA	$4,000 for United $5,000 for TWA
	Leave ad spending the same	$8,000 for United $4,000 for TWA	$5,000 for United $2,000 for TWA

RECAP **THE THEORY OF GAMES**

The three elements of any game are the players, the list of strategies from which they can choose, and the payoffs to each combination of strategies. Players in some games have a dominant strategy, one that yields a higher payoff regardless of the strategies chosen by other players.

Equilibrium in a game occurs when each player's strategy choice yields the highest payoff available, given the strategies chosen by other players. Such a combination of strategies is called a Nash equilibrium.

THE PRISONER'S DILEMMA

The game in Example 10.1 belongs to an important class of games called the **prisoner's dilemma**. In the prisoner's dilemma, when each player chooses his dominant strategy, the result is unattractive to the group of players as a whole.

THE ORIGINAL PRISONER'S DILEMMA

Example 10.3 recounts the original scenario from which the prisoner's dilemma drew its name.

Should the prisoners confess?

Two prisoners, Horace and Jasper, are being held in separate cells for a serious crime that they did in fact commit. The prosecutor, however, has only enough hard evidence to convict them of a minor offense, for which the penalty is a year in jail. Each prisoner is told that if one confesses while the other remains silent, the confessor will go scot-free and the other will spend 20 years in prison. If both confess, they will get an intermediate sentence of years. (These payoffs are summarized in Table 10.3.) The two prisoners are not allowed to communicate with one another. Do they have a dominant strategy? If so, what is it?

prisoner's dilemma a game in which each player has a dominant strategy, and when each plays it, the resulting payoffs are smaller than if each had played a dominated strategy

EXAMPLE 10.3

TABLE 10.3
The Payoff Matrix for a Prisoner's Dilemma

		Jasper	
		Confess	Remain silent
Horace	Confess	5 years for each	0 years for Horace 20 years for Jasper
	Remain silent	20 years for Horace 0 years for Jasper	1 year for each

In this game, the dominant strategy for each prisoner is to confess. No matter what Jasper does, Horace will get a lighter sentence by speaking out. If Jasper confesses, Horace will get 5 years (upper left cell) instead of 20 (lower left cell). If Jasper remains silent, Horace will go free (upper right cell) instead of spending a year in jail (lower right cell). Because the payoffs are perfectly symmetric, Jasper will also do better to confess, no matter what Horace does. The difficulty is that when each follows his dominant strategy and confesses, both will do worse than if each had shown restraint. When both confess, they each get 5 years (upper left cell) instead of the 1 year they would have gotten by remaining silent (lower right cell). Hence the name of this game, the prisoner's dilemma.

EXERCISE 10.2

GM and Chrysler must both decide whether to invest in a new process. Games 1 and 2 below show how their profits depend on the decisions they might make. Which of these games is a prisoner's dilemma?

	Game 1				Game 2	
	Chrysler				Chrysler	
	Don't invest	Invest			Don't invest	Invest
GM — Don't invest	10 for each	4 for GM / 12 for Chrysler		GM — Don't invest	4 for GM / 12 for Chrysler	5 for each
GM — Invest	12 for GM / 4 for Chrysler	5 for each		GM — Invest	10 for each	12 for GM / 4 for Chrysler

The prisoner's dilemma is one of the most powerful metaphors in all of human behavioral science. Countless social and economic interactions have pay-off structures analogous to the one confronted by the two prisoners. Some of those interactions occur between only two players, as in the examples just discussed; many others involve larger groups. But regardless of the number of players involved, the common thread is one of conflict between the narrow self-interest of individuals and the broader interests of larger communities.

PRISONER'S DILEMMAS CONFRONTING IMPERFECTLY COMPETITIVE FIRMS

cartel a coalition of firms that agrees to restrict output for the purpose of earning an economic profit

A **cartel** is any coalition of firms that conspires to restrict production for the purpose of earning an economic profit. As we will see in the next example, the problem confronting oligopolists who are trying to form a cartel is a classic illustration of the prisoner's dilemma.

Why are cartel agreements notoriously unstable?

Consider a market for bottled water served by only two firms, Aquapure and Mountain Spring. Each firm can draw water free of charge from a mineral spring located on its own land. Customers supply their own bottles. Rather than compete with one another, the two firms decide to collude by selling water at the price a profit-maximizing pure monopolist would charge. Under their agreement (which constitutes a cartel), each firm would produce and sell half the quantity of water demanded by the market at the monopoly price (see Figure 10.1). The agreement is not legally enforceable, however, which means that each firm has the option of charging less than the agreed price. If one firm sells water for less than the other firm, it will capture the entire quantity demanded by the market at the lower price.

FIGURE 10.1
The Market Demand for Mineral Water.
Faced with the demand curve shown, a monopolist with zero marginal cost would produce 1,000 bottles/day (the quantity at which marginal revenue equals zero) and sell them at a price of $1.00/bottle.

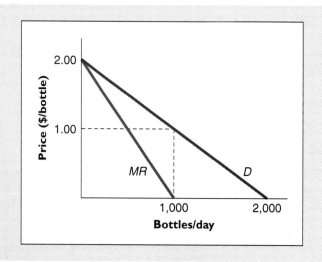

Why is this agreement likely to collapse?

Since the marginal cost of mineral water is zero, the profit-maximizing quantity for a monopolist with the demand curve shown in Figure 10.1 is 1,000 bottles/day, the quantity for which marginal revenue equals marginal cost. At that quantity, the monopoly price is $1/bottle. If the firms abide by their agreement, each will sell half the market total, or 500 bottles/day at a price of $1/bottle, for an economic profit of $500/day.

But suppose Aquapure reduced its price to $0.90/bottle. By underselling Mineral Spring, it would capture the entire quantity demanded by the market, which as shown in Figure 10.2 is 1,100 bottles/day. Aquapure's economic profit would rise from $500/day to ($0.90/bottle)(1,100 bottles/day) = $990/day, almost twice as much as before. In the process, Mountain Spring's economic profit would fall from $500/day to zero. Rather than see its economic profit disappear, Mountain Spring would match Aquapure's price cut, recapturing its original 50 percent share of the market. But when each firm charges $0.90/bottle and sells 550 bottles/day, each earns an economic profit of ($0.90/bottle)(550 bottles/day) = $495/day, or $5/day less than before.

Suppose we view the cartel agreement as an economic game in which the two available strategies are to sell for $1/bottle or to sell for $0.90/bottle. The payoffs are the economic profits that result from these strategies. Table 10.4 shows the payoff matrix for this game. Each firm's dominant strategy is to sell at the lower price, yet in following that strategy, each earns a lower profit than if each had sold at the higher price.

The game does not end with both firms charging $0.90/bottle. Each firm knows that if it cuts the price a little further, it can recapture the entire market, and in the process earn a substantially higher economic profit. At every step the rival firm will match any price cut, until the price falls all the way to the marginal cost—in this example, zero.

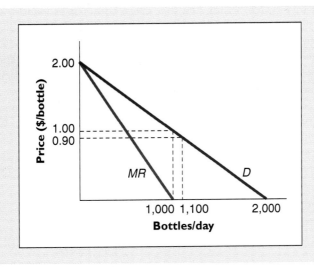

FIGURE 10.2
The Temptation to Violate a Cartel Agreement.
By cutting its price from $1/bottle to $0.90/bottle, Aquapure can sell the entire market quantity demanded at that price, 1,100 bottles/day, rather than half the monopoly quantity of 1,000 bottles/day.

TABLE 10.4
The Payoff Matrix for a Cartel Agreement

		Mountain Spring	
		Charge $1/bottle	Charge $0.90/bottle
Aquapure	Charge $1/bottle	$500/day for each	0 for Aquapure $990/day for Mt. Spring
	Charge $0.90/bottle	$990/day for Aquapure 0 for Mt. Spring	$495/day for each

Cartel agreements confront participants with the economic incentives inherent in the prisoner's dilemma, which explains why such agreements have historically been so unstable. Usually a cartel involves not just two firms, but several, an arrangement that can make retaliation against price cutters extremely difficult. In many cases, discovering which parties have broken the agreement is difficult. For example, the Organization of Petroleum Exporting Countries (OPEC), a cartel of oil producers formed in the 1970s to restrict oil production, has no practical way to prevent member countries from secretly pumping oil offshore in the dead of night.

ECONOMIC NATURALIST 10.2

How did Congress unwittingly solve the television advertising dilemma confronting cigarette producers?

In 1970, Congress enacted a law making cigarette advertising on television illegal after January 1, 1971. As evidenced by the steadily declining proportion of Americans who smoke, this law seems to have achieved its stated purpose of protecting citizens against a proven health hazard. But the law also had an unintended effect, which was to increase the economic profit of cigarette makers, at least in the short run. In the year before the law's passage, manufacturers spent more than $300 million on advertising, about $60 million more than they spent during the year after the law was enacted. Much of the saving in advertising expenditures in 1971 was reflected in higher cigarette profits at year-end. But if eliminating television advertising made companies more profitable, why didn't the manufacturers eliminate the ads on their own?

When an imperfectly competitive firm advertises its product, its demand curve shifts rightward, for two reasons. First, people who have never used that type of product learn about it, and some buy it. Second, people who consume a different brand of the product may switch brands. The first effect boosts sales industrywide; the second merely redistributes existing sales.

Although advertising produces both effects in the cigarette industry, its primary effect is brand switching. Thus the decision of whether to advertise confronts the individual firm with a prisoner's dilemma. Table 10.5 shows the payoffs facing a pair of cigarette producers trying to decide whether to advertise. If both firms advertise on TV (upper left cell), each earns a profit of only $10 million/year as compared to a profit of $20 million/year for each if neither advertises (lower right cell). Clearly, both will benefit if neither advertises.

Yet note the powerful incentive that confronts each firm. RJR sees that if Philip Morris doesn't advertise, RJR can earn higher profits by advertising ($35 million/year)

TABLE 10.5
Cigarette Advertising as a Prisoner's Dilemma

		Philip Morris	
		Advertise on TV	Don't advertise on TV
RJR	Advertise on TV	$10 million/year for each	$35 million/year for RJR $5 million/year for Philip Morris
	Don't advertise on TV	$5 million/year for RJR $35 million/year for Philip Morris	$20 million/year for each

than by not advertising ($20 million/year). RJR also sees that if Philip Morris does advertise, RJR will again earn more by advertising ($10 million/year) than by not advertising ($5 million/year). Thus RJR's dominant strategy is to advertise. And because the payoffs are symmetric, Philip Morris's dominant strategy is also to advertise. So when each firm behaves rationally from its own point of view, the two together do worse than if they had both shown restraint. The Congressional ad ban forced cigarette manufacturers to do what they could not have accomplished on their own.

PRISONER'S DILEMMAS IN EVERYDAY LIFE

As the following examples make clear, the prisoner's dilemma helps the economic naturalist to make sense of human behavior not only in the world of business, but in other domains of life as well.

Why do people often stand at concerts, even though they can see just as well when everyone sits?

A few years ago, an economic naturalist went with friends to hear Diana Ross sing. They bought good seats, some 20 rows from the stage. But before Ross had finished her first song, several people in front of them rose to their feet, presumably to get a better view. In doing so, they blocked the line of sight for others behind them, forcing those people to stand to see better. Before long, the entire crowd was standing. Then a few people in the front rows climbed atop their seats, blocking the views of those behind them and forcing them to stand on their seats too. The seats had fold-up bottoms, so from time to time someone who stood too close to the pivot point would tumble as the seat popped into its vertical position. All things considered, the outcome was far less satisfactory than if everyone had remained seated. Why this pattern of self-defeating behavior?

To understand what happened at the concert, note that standing is self-defeating only when viewed from the group's perspective. From the individual's perspective, however, standing passes the cost-benefit test. No matter what others do, an individual sees better by standing than by sitting. Suppose for the sake of discussion that you and other members of the audience would be willing to pay $2 to avoid standing and $3 to get a better view (or avoid having a worse one). In this multiperson prisoner's dilemma, you are one player and the rest of the audience is the other. The two strategies are to stand or to sit. Suppose everyone is seated to begin with. The payoffs you and others face will depend on the combination of strategies that you and others choose, as shown Table 10.6.

The payoff of 0 in the lower right cell of the payoff matrix reflects the fact that when everyone remains seated, everyone is just as well off as before. Your payoff of −$3 in the lower left cell reflects the fact that if you sit while others stand, you will have a worse view. Your payoff of −$2 in the upper left cell reflects the fact that when

Since standing is tiring and the view is no better when everyone stands than when everyone sits, why do people often stand at concerts?

TABLE 10.6
Standing Versus Sitting at a Concert as a Prisoner's Dilemma

		Others	
		Stand	Sit
You	Stand	−$2 for each	$1 for you −$3 for others
	Sit	−$3 for you $1 for others	0 for each

ECONOMIC NATURALIST 10.3

you and others stand, you must endure the $2 cost of standing, even though you don't get a better view. Finally, your $1 payoff in the upper right cell represents the difference between your $3 benefit and your $2 cost of standing when you stand while others sit.

These payoffs mean that your dominant strategy is to stand. If others stand, you will get −$2 by standing, which is better than the −$3 you will get by sitting. If others sit, you will get $1 by standing, which is better than the $0 you will get by sitting. Since this game is symmetric, the dominant strategy for others is also to stand. Yet when everyone stands, everyone gets a payoff of −$2, which is $2 worse than if everyone had remained seated. As in all prisoner's dilemmas, the choice that is more attractive from the perspective of the individual turns out to be less attractive from the perspective of the group.

ECONOMIC NATURALIST 10.4

Why do people shout at parties?

Whenever large numbers of people gather for conversation in a closed space, the ambient noise level rises sharply. After attending such gatherings, people often complain of sore throats and hoarse voices. If everyone spoke at a normal volume at parties, the overall noise level would be lower, and people would hear just as well. So why do people shout?

Again the problem involves the difference between individual incentives and group incentives. Suppose everyone starts by speaking at a normal level. But because of the crowded conditions, conversation partners have difficulty hearing one another, even when no one is shouting. The natural solution, from the point of view of the individual, is to simply raise one's voice a bit. But that is also the natural solution for everyone else. And when everyone speaks more loudly, the ambient noise level rises, so no one hears any better than before.

No matter what others do, the individual will do better by speaking more loudly. Doing so is a dominant strategy for everyone, in fact. Yet when everyone follows the dominant strategy, the result is worse (no one can hear well) than if everyone had continued to speak normally. While shouting is wasteful, individuals acting alone have no better option. If anyone were to speak softly while others shout, that person wouldn't be heard. No one wants to go home with raw vocal cords, but people apparently prefer that cost to the alternative of not being heard at all.

RECAP **THE PRISONER'S DILEMMA**

The prisoner's dilemma is a game in which each player has a dominant strategy, and in which the payoff to each player when each chooses that strategy is smaller than if each had chosen a dominated strategy. Incentives analogous to those found in the prisoner's dilemmas help to explain a broad range of behavior in business and everyday life—among them, excessive spending on advertising, cartel instability, standing at concerts, and shouting at parties.

GAMES IN WHICH TIMING MATTERS

In the games discussed so far, players were assumed to choose their strategies simultaneously, and which player moved first didn't particularly matter. For example, in the prisoner's dilemma, players would follow their dominant strategies even if they knew in advance what strategies their opponents had chosen. But in other situations, such as the negotiations between Warner Brothers and Tony Bennett described at the beginning of this chapter, timing is of the essence.

THE ULTIMATUM BARGAINING GAME

Another such game is illustrated in Example 10.4.

Should Michael accept Tom's offer?

EXAMPLE 10.4

Tom and Michael are subjects in an experiment. The experimenter begins by giving $100 to Tom, who must then propose how to divide the money between himself and Michael. Tom can propose any division he chooses, provided the proposed amounts are whole dollars and he offers Michael at least $1. Suppose Tom proposes X for himself and $(100 − X)$ for Michael, where X is a whole number no larger than 99. Michael must then say whether he accepts the proposal. If he does, each will get the proposed amount. But if Michael rejects the proposal, each player will get zero, and the $100 will revert to the experimenter. If Tom and Michael know they will play this game only once, and each wants to make as much money for himself as possible, what should Tom propose?

A payoff matrix is not a useful way to summarize the information in this game, because it says nothing about the timing of each player's move. For games in which timing matters, a **decision tree**, or **game tree**, is more useful. This type of diagram describes the possible moves in the sequence in which they may occur and lists the final payoffs for each possible combination of moves.

decision tree (or game tree) a diagram that describes the possible moves in a game in sequence and lists the payoffs that correspond to each possible combination of moves

The decision tree for the game in Example 10.4 is shown in Figure 10.3. At A, Tom begins the game by making his proposal. At B, Michael responds to Tom's proposal. If he accepts (the top branch of the tree), Tom will get X and Michael will get $(100 − X)$. If he refuses (the bottom branch of the tree), both will get nothing.

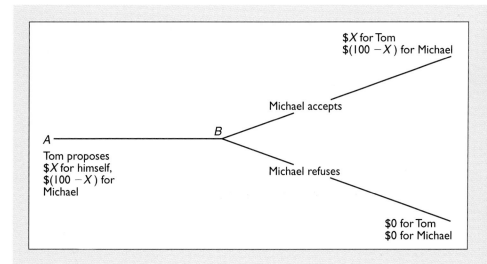

FIGURE 10.3
Decision Tree for Example 10.4.
This decision tree shows the possible moves and payoffs for the game in Example 10.4 in the sequence in which they may occur.

In thinking strategically about this game, the key for Tom is to put himself in Michael's shoes and imagine how he might react to various proposals. Because he knows Michael's goal is to make as much money as possible, he knows that Michael will accept his offer no matter how small, because the alternative is to reject it and get nothing. For instance, suppose Tom proposes $99 for himself and only $1 for Michael (see Figure 10.4). At B, Michael's best option is to accept the offer. This is a Nash equilibrium, because neither player has any incentive to deviate from the strategy he chose.

This type of game has been called the **ultimatum bargaining game**, because of the power of the first player to confront the second player with a take-it-or-leave-it offer. Michael could refuse a one-sided offer from Tom, but doing so would make him worse off than if he accepted it.

ultimatum bargaining game one in which the first player has the power to confront the second player with a take-it-or-leave-it offer

FIGURE 10.4
Tom's Best Strategy in an Ultimatum Bargaining Game.
Because Tom can predict that Michael will accept any positive offer, Tom's income-maximizing strategy at A is to offer Michael the smallest positive amount possible, $1.

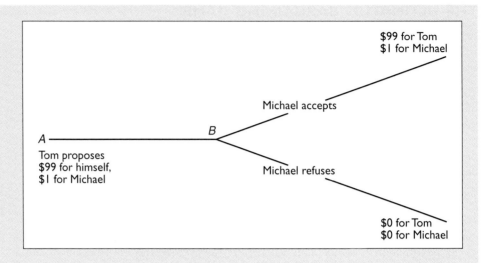

Example 10.5 illustrates the importance of the timing of moves in determining the outcome of the ultimatum bargaining game.

EXAMPLE 10.5   **What should Michael's acceptance threshold be?**

Suppose we change the rules of the ultimatum bargaining game slightly so that Michael has the right to specify *in advance* the smallest offer he will accept. Once Michael announces this number, he is bound by it. If Tom's task is again to propose a division of the $100, what amount should Michael specify?

This seemingly minor change in the rules completely alters the game. Once Michael announces that Y is the smallest offer he will accept, his active role in the game is over. If Y is $60 and Tom proposes X for himself and $(100 − X)$ for Michael, his offer will be rejected automatically if X exceeds 40. The decision tree for this game is shown in Figure 10.5.

When Michael announces that Y is the smallest offer he will accept, the best Tom can do is to propose $(100 − Y)$ for himself and Y for Michael. If he proposes any amount less than Y for Michael, both will get nothing at all. Since this reasoning holds for any value of Y less than 100, Michael's best bet is to announce an acceptance threshold of $99—the largest whole number that is less

FIGURE 10.5
The Ultimatum Bargaining Game with an Acceptance Threshold.
If Michael can commit himself to a minimum acceptable offer threshold at A, he will fare dramatically better than in the standard ultimatum bargaining game.

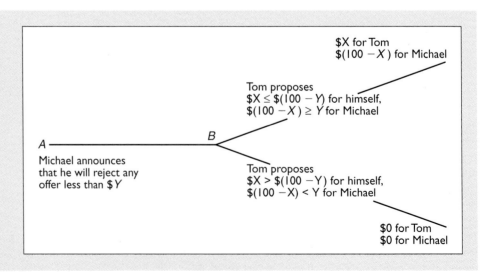

than $100. The equilibrium outcome of the game will then be $99 for Michael and only $1 for Tom, exactly the opposite of the outcome when Tom had the first move.

CREDIBLE THREATS AND PROMISES

Why couldn't Michael have threatened to refuse a one-sided offer in the original version of the game? While nothing prevented him from doing so, such a threat would not have been credible. In the language of game theory, a **credible threat** is one that is in the threatener's interest to carry out when the time comes to act. The problem in the original version of the game is that Michael would have no reason to carry out his threat to reject a one-sided offer in the event he actually received one. Once Tom announced such an offer, refusing it would not pass the cost-benefit test.

credible threat a threat to take an action that is in the threatener's interest to carry out

The concept of a credible threat figured prominently in the negotiations between Warner Brothers managers and Tony Bennett over the matter of Mr. Bennett's fee for performing in *Analyze This*. Once most of the film had been shot, managers knew they couldn't threaten credibly to refuse Mr. Bennett's salary demand, because at that point adapting the film to another singer would have been prohibitively costly. In contrast, a similar threat made before production of the movie had begun would have been credible.

"Listen to me, John. Tell them this is our final offer. Let 'em know we'll take an option at twenty-five million over five years—not a penny more, not a minute longer! If they balk, stall them for time and get back to me."

Here is another example in which one person suffers as a result of the inability to make a credible threat.

Is it safe to steal Veronica's briefcase?

EXAMPLE 10.6

When Veronica travels out of town on business, she usually brings along an expensive briefcase. A stranger takes a liking to her briefcase and assumes that because Veronica is an economist, she must be a self-interested, rational person. If the cost to Veronica of pressing charges in the event her briefcase is stolen exceeds the value of the briefcase, can the stranger safely steal it?

Provided the thief's assumptions about Veronica are correct, he can get away with his crime. To press charges once her briefcase has been stolen, Veronica must call the police, and will probably miss her flight home. Months later, she will have to return to testify at the thief's trial, and she may have to endure hostile cross-examination by the thief's attorney. Since these costs clearly exceed the value of the briefcase, a rational, self-interested person would simply write off the briefcase. But if Veronica could somehow have made a credible threat to press charges in the event her briefcase was stolen, she could have deterred the thief. The problem is that the thief knows the cost of retaliation will exceed the benefit, so the threat is not credible.

credible promise a promise to take an action that is in the promiser's interest to keep

Just as in some games credible threats are impossible to make, in others **credible promises** are impossible. A credible promise is one that is in the interests of the promiser to keep when the time comes to act. In Example 10.7, both players suffer because of their inability to make a credible promise.

EXAMPLE 10.7

Will the kidnapper release his victim?

A kidnapper who has seized a hostage for ransom suddenly changes his mind. He wants to set his victim free but is afraid that the victim will go to the police. Although the victim promises not to do so, both realize that he will have no incentive to keep his promise once he is free. The victim also realizes that the kidnapper would still pose a threat to him, out of fear that the victim may change his mind and go to the police. So if only to protect himself from the possibility of further harm, the victim has a powerful incentive to go to the police once he is free. Finally, if the victim goes to the police, the kidnapper will be caught and executed. The kidnapper desperately wants to set his victim free, but he prefers survival to execution. What will the kidnapper do?

The decision tree for the situation in Example 10.7 is shown in Figure 10.6. At *A,* the victim promises not to go to the police. He knows his life depends on the credibility of his promise, and at the moment he makes it, he sincerely means to keep it.

At *B* the kidnapper must decide what to do. If he sets his victim free (top branch at *B*), they reach *C,* where the victim must decide whether to go to the police. If the victim keeps his promise to remain silent (bottom branch at *C*), the kidnapper survives as a continuing threat to the victim. But if the victim goes to the police (top branch at *C*), the kidnapper will be caught and executed, and the victim will be safe. Since the victim prefers the second outcome, he will go to the police if freed. *And since the kidnapper can anticipate what will happen if the*

FIGURE 10.6
Decision Tree for the Kidnapper Game.
Both the kidnapper and the victim want to see the victim freed, but because the victim's promise to remain silent is not credible, the kidnapper kills him.

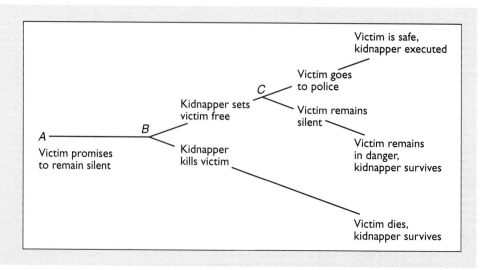

game reaches C, he cannot let the game reach that point. His only hope of survival is to choose the bottom branch at *B*. The irony is that both he and the victim strongly prefer the alternative in which he sets the victim free and the victim remains silent.

Here is another instance in which both parties suffer because of the inability to make a credible promise.

Should the businessowner open a remote office?

EXAMPLE 10.8

The owner of a thriving business wants to start up an office in a distant city. If she hires someone to manage the new office, she can afford to pay a weekly salary of $1,000—a premium of $500 over what the manager would otherwise be able to earn—and still earn a weekly economic profit of $1,000 for herself. The owner's concern is that she will not be able to monitor the manager's behavior. The owner knows that by managing the remote office dishonestly, the manager can boost his take-home pay to $1,500 while causing the owner an economic loss of $500/week. If the owner believes that all managers are selfish income maximizers, will she open the new office?

The decision tree for the remote office game is shown in Figure 10.7. At *A*, the managerial candidate promises to manage honestly, which brings the owner to *B*, where she must decide whether to open the new office. If she opens it, they reach *C*, where the manager must decide whether to manage honestly. If the manager's only goal is to make as much money as he can, he will manage dishonestly (bottom branch at *C*), since that way he will earn $500 more than by managing honestly (top branch at *C*).

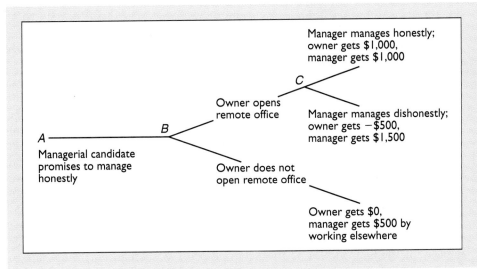

FIGURE 10.7
Decision Tree for the Remote Office Game.
The best outcome is for the manager to open the office at *B* and for the manager to manage the office honestly at *C*. But if the manager is purely self-interested and the owner knows it, this path will not be an equilibrium outcome.

So if the owner opens the new office, she will end up with an economic loss of $500. If she had not opened the office (bottom branch at *B*), she would have realized an economic profit of zero. Since zero is better than −$500, the owner will choose not to open the remote office. In the end, the opportunity cost of the manager's inability to make a credible promise is $1,500: the manager's forgone $500 salary premium and the owner's forgone $1,000 return.

EXERCISE 10.3

Smith and Jones are playing a game in which Smith has the first move at *A* in the following decision tree. Once Smith has chosen either the top or bottom branch at *A*, Jones, who can see what Smith has chosen, must

choose the top or bottom branch at *B* or *C*. If the payoffs at the end of each branch are as shown, what is the equilibrium outcome of this game? If before Smith chose, Jones could make a credible commitment to choose either the top or bottom branch when his turn came, what would he do?

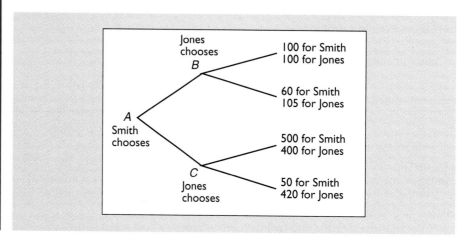

COMMITMENT PROBLEMS

Games like the one in Exercise 10.3, as well as the prisoner's dilemma, the cartel game, the ultimatum bargaining game, the kidnapper game, and the remote office game, confront players with a **commitment problem**, a situation in which they have difficulty achieving the desired outcome because they cannot make credible threats or promises. If both players in the prisoner's dilemma (Example 10.3) could make a binding promise to remain silent, both would be assured of a shorter sentence. Hence the logic of the underworld code of *omerta*, under which the family of anyone who provides evidence against a fellow mob member is killed. A similar logic explains the adoption of military arms control agreements, in which opponents sign an enforceable pledge to curtail weapons spending.

The commitment problem in the kidnapper game (Example 10.7) could be solved if the victim could find some way of committing himself to remain silent once released. The economist Thomas Schelling suggests the following way out of the dilemma: "If the victim has committed an act whose disclosure could lead to blackmail, he may confess it; if not, he might commit one in the presence of his captor, to create a bond that will ensure his silence."[2] (Perhaps the victim could allow the kidnapper to photograph him in the process of some unspeakable act.) The blackmailable act serves as a **commitment device**, something that provides the victim with an incentive to keep his promise. Doing so will be unpleasant for him once he is freed, but clearly less so than not being able to make a credible promise.

Businessowners seem well aware of commitment problems in the workplace and have adopted a variety of commitment devices to solve them. Consider, for example, the problem confronting the owner of a restaurant. She wants her table staff to provide good service so that customers will enjoy their meals and come back in the future. And since good service is valuable to her, she would be willing to pay waiters extra for it. For their part, waiters would be willing to provide good service in return for the extra pay. The problem is that the owner cannot always monitor whether the waiters do provide good service. Her concern is that, having been paid extra for it, the waiters may slack off when she isn't looking. Unless the owner can find some way to solve this problem, she will not pay

commitment problem a situation in which people cannot achieve their goals because of an inability to make credible threats or promises

commitment device a way of changing incentives so as to make otherwise empty threats or promises credible

[2]Thomas Schelling, *The Strategy of Conflict*, Cambridge, Mass.: Harvard University Press, 1960, pp. 43, 44.

extra, the waiters will not provide good service, and she, they, and the diners will suffer. A better outcome for all concerned would be for the waiters to find some way to commit themselves to good service.

Restaurateurs in many countries have tried to solve this commitment problem by encouraging diners to leave tips at the end of their meals. The attraction of this solution is that the diner is *always* in a good position to monitor service quality. The diner should be happy to reward good service with a generous tip, since doing so will help to ensure good service in the future. And the waiter has a strong incentive to provide good service, because he knows that the size of his tip may depend on it.

The various commitment devices just discussed—the underworld code of *omerta*, military arms control agreements, the tip for the waiter—all work because they change the material incentives facing the decision makers. But as Example 10.9 illustrates, changing incentives in precisely the desired way is not always practical.

Will leaving a tip at an out-of-town restaurant affect the quality of service you receive?

EXAMPLE 10.9

Will Sylvester leave a tip when dining on the road?

Sylvester has just finished a $100 steak dinner at a restaurant on Interstate 81, some 500 miles from home. The waiter provided good service. If Sylvester cares only about himself, will he leave a tip?

Once the waiter has provided good service, there is no way for him to take it back if the diner fails to leave a tip. In restaurants patronized by local diners, failure to tip is not a problem, because the waiter can simply provide poor service the next time a nontipper comes in. But the waiter lacks that leverage with out-of-town diners. Having already received good service, Sylvester must choose between paying $100 or $115 for his meal. If he is an essentially selfish person, the former choice may be a compelling one.

RECAP   **GAMES IN WHICH TIMING MATTERS**

The outcomes in many games depend on the timing of each player's move. For such games, the payoffs are best summarized by a decision tree rather than a payoff matrix.

The inability to make credible threats and promises often prevents people from achieving desired outcomes in many games. Games with this property are said to confront players with commitment problems. Such problems can sometimes be solved by employing commitment devices—ways of changing incentives to facilitate making credible threats or promises.

THE STRATEGIC ROLE OF PREFERENCES

In all the games we have discussed so far, players were assumed to care only about obtaining the best possible outcome for themselves. Thus each player's goal was to get the highest monetary payoff, the shortest jail sentence, the best chance of survival, and so on. The irony, in most of these games, is that players do not attain the best outcomes. Better outcomes can sometimes be achieved by altering the material incentives selfish players face, but not always.

If altering the relevant material incentives is not possible, commitment problems can sometimes be solved by altering people's psychological incentives. As Example 10.10 illustrates, in a society in which people are strongly conditioned to develop moral sentiments—feelings of guilt when they harm others, feelings of sympathy for their trading partners, feelings of outrage when they are treated unjustly—commitment problems arise less often than in more narrowly self-interested societies.

EXAMPLE 10.10   **In a moral society, will the businessowner open a remote office?**

Consider again the owner of the thriving business who is trying to decide whether to open an office in a distant city (Example 10.8). Suppose the society in which she lives is one in which all citizens have been strongly conditioned to behave honestly. Will she open the remote office?

Suppose, for instance, that the managerial candidate would suffer guilt pangs if he embezzled money from the owner. Most people would be reluctant to assign a monetary value to guilty feelings. But for the sake of discussion, let's suppose that those feelings are so unpleasant that the manager would be willing to pay at least $10,000 to avoid them. On this assumption, the manager's payoff if he manages dishonestly will not be $1,500 but $1,500 − $10,000 = −$8,500. The new decision tree is shown in Figure 10.8.

FIGURE 10.8

The Remote Office Game with an Honest Manager.

If the owner can identify a managerial candidate who would choose to manage honestly at C, she will hire that candidate at B and open the remote office.

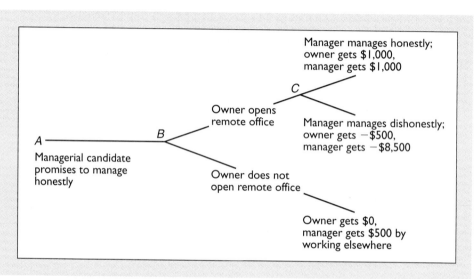

Manager manages honestly; owner gets $1,000, manager gets $1,000

C

Owner opens remote office

Manager manages dishonestly; owner gets −$500, manager gets −$8,500

A

B

Managerial candidate promises to manage honestly

Owner does not open remote office

Owner gets $0, manager gets $500 by working elsewhere

In this case, the best choice for the owner at B will be to open the remote office, because she knows that at C the manager's best choice will be to manage honestly. The irony, of course, is that the honest manager in this example ends up richer than the selfish manager in Example 10.8, who earned only a normal salary.

ARE PEOPLE FUNDAMENTALLY SELFISH?

As Example 10.10 suggests, the assumption that people are self-interested in the narrow sense of the term does not always capture the full range of motives that govern choice in strategic settings. Think, for example, about the last time you had a meal at an out-of-town restaurant. Did you leave a tip? If so, your behavior was quite normal. Researchers have found that tipping rates in restaurants patronized mostly by out-of-town diners are essentially the same as in restaurants patronized mostly by local diners.

Reflect also on how you would behave in some of the other games we have discussed. In the ultimatum game, what would you do if your partner proposed $99 for himself and only $1 for you? Would you reject the offer? If so, you are not alone. Two findings of extensive laboratory studies of the ultimatum bargaining game challenge the assumption that most players are narrowly self-interested. First, the most common proposal by the first player in this game is not a 99-1 split, but a 50-50 split. And second, on the few occasions when the first player does propose a highly one-sided split, the second player almost always rejects it. Subjects who reject the offer often mention the satisfaction they experienced at having penalized the first player for an "unfair" offer.

Indeed, there are many exceptions to the outcomes predicted on the basis of the assumption that people are self-interested in the most narrow sense of the term. People who have been treated unjustly often seek revenge even at ruinous cost to themselves. Every day people walk away from profitable transactions whose terms they believe to be "unfair." And the British spent vast sums to defend the desolate Falkland Islands, even though they had little empire left against which to deter future aggression. (The Argentine writer Jorge Luis Borges likened the Falklands war to two bald men fighting over a comb.) In these and countless other ways, people do not seem to be pursuing self-interest narrowly defined. And if motives beyond narrow self-interest are significant, we must take them into account in attempting to predict and explain human behavior.

PREFERENCES AS SOLUTIONS TO COMMITMENT PROBLEMS

Economists tend to view preferences as ends in themselves. Taking them as given, they calculate what actions will best serve those preferences. This approach to the study of behavior is widely used by other social scientists and by game theorists, military strategists, philosophers, and others. In its standard form, it assumes purely self-interested preferences for present and future consumption goods of various sorts, leisure pursuits, and so on. Concerns about fairness, guilt, honor, sympathy, and the like typically play no role.

Preferences clearly affect the choices people make in strategic interactions. Sympathy for one's trading partner can make a businessperson trustworthy even when material incentives favor cheating. A sense of justice can prompt a person to incur the costs of retaliation, even when incurring those costs will not undo the original injury. It can also induce people to reject one-sided offers, even when their wealth would be increased by accepting them.

Note, however, that although preferences can clearly shape behavior in these ways, that alone does not solve commitment problems. The solution to such problems requires not only that a person *have* certain preferences, but also that others have some way of *discerning* them. Unless the businessowner can identify the trustworthy employee, that employee cannot land a job whose pay is predicated on trust. Unless the predator can identify a potential victim whose character will motivate retaliation, that person is likely to become a victim. And unless a person's potential trading partners can identify him as someone predisposed to reject one-sided offers, he will not be able to deter such offers.

From among those whom we might engage in ventures requiring trust, can we identify reliable partners? If people could make *perfectly* accurate character judgments, they could always steer clear of dishonest persons. That people continue to be victimized at least occasionally by dishonest persons suggests that perfectly reliable character judgments are either impossible to make or prohibitively expensive.

Vigilance in the choice of trading partners is an essential element in solving (or avoiding) commitment problems, for if there is an advantage in being honest and being perceived as such, there is an even greater advantage in only *appearing* to be honest. After all, a liar who appears trustworthy will have better opportunities than one who glances about furtively, sweats profusely, and has difficulty making eye contact. Indeed, the liar will have the same opportunities as an honest person but will get higher payoffs because the liar will exploit them to the fullest.

In the end, the question of whether people can make reasonably accurate character judgments is an empirical one. Experimental studies have shown that even on the basis of brief encounters involving strangers, subjects are adept at predicting who will cooperate and who will defect in prisoner's dilemma games. For example, in one experiment in which only 26 percent of subjects defected, the accuracy rate of predicted defections was more than 56 percent. One might expect that predictions regarding those we know well would be even more accurate.

Do you know someone who would return an envelope containing $1,000 in cash to you if you lost it at a crowded concert? If so, then you accept the claim that personal character helps people to solve commitment problems. As long as honest individuals can identify at least some others who are honest, and can interact selectively with them, honest individuals can prosper in a competitive environment.

RECAP **THE STRATEGIC ROLE OF PREFERENCES**

Most applications of the theory of games assume that players are self-interested in the narrow sense of the term. In practice, however, many choices, such as leaving tips in out-of-town restaurants, appear inconsistent with this assumption.

The fact that people seem driven by a more complex range of motives makes behavior more difficult to predict but also creates new ways of solving commitment problems. Psychological incentives can often serve as commitment devices when changing players' material incentives is impractical. For example, people who are able to identify honest trading partners and interact selectively with them are able to solve commitment problems that arise from lack of trust.

■ SUMMARY ■

- Economists use the mathematical theory of games to analyze situations in which the payoffs of one's actions depend on the actions taken by others. Games have three basic elements: the players; the list of possible actions, or strategies, from which each player can choose; and the payoffs the players receive for those strategies. The payoff matrix is the most useful way to summarize this information in games in which the timing of the players' moves is not decisive. In games in which the timing of moves does matter, a decision tree provides a much more useful summary of the information.

- A dominant strategy is one that yields a higher payoff regardless of the strategy chosen by the other player. In some games, such as the prisoner's dilemma, each player has a dominant strategy. The equilibrium occurs in such games when each player chooses his or her dominant strategy. In other games, not all players have a dominant strategy.

- Although the equilibrium outcome of any game is any combination of choices in which each player does the best he

can, given the choices made by others, the result is often unattractive from the perspective of players as group. The prisoner's dilemma has this feature. The incentive structure of this game helps explain such disparate social dilemmas as excessive advertising, military arms races, and failure to reap the potential benefits of interactions requiring trust.

- Individuals can often resolve these dilemmas if they can make binding commitments to behave in certain ways. Some commitments, such as those involved in military arms control agreements, are achieved by altering the material incentives confronting the players. Other commitments can be achieved by relying on psychological incentives to counteract material payoffs. Moral sentiments like guilt, sympathy, and a sense of justice often foster better outcomes than can be achieved by narrowly self-interested players. For this type of commitment to work, the relevant moral sentiments must be discernible by one's potential trading partners.

■ KEY TERMS ■

▪ REVIEW QUESTIONS ▪

---

1. Explain why a military arms race is an example of a prisoner's dilemma.

2. Why did Warner Brothers make a mistake by waiting until the filming of *Analyze This* was almost finished before negotiating with Tony Bennett to perform in the final scene?

3. Suppose General Motors is trying to hire a small firm to manufacture the door handles for Pontiac sedans. The task requires an investment in expensive capital equipment that cannot be used for any other purpose. Why might the president of the small firm refuse to undertake this venture without a long-term contract fixing the price of the door handles?

4. Would you be irrational to refuse a one-sided offer in an ultimatum bargaining game if you knew that you would be playing that game many times with the same partner?

5. Describe the commitment problem that narrowly self-interested diners and waiters would confront at restaurants located on interstate highways. Given that in such restaurants tipping does seem to assure reasonably good service, do you think people are always selfish in the narrowest sense?

▪ PROBLEMS ▪

---

1. In studying for his economics final, Sam is concerned about only two things: his grade and the amount of time he spends studying. A good grade will give him a benefit of 20; an average grade, a benefit of 5; and a poor grade, a benefit of 0. By studying a lot, Sam will incur a cost of 10; by studying a little, a cost of 6. Moreover, if Sam studies a lot and all other students study a little, he will get a good grade and they will get poor ones. But if they study a lot and he studies a little, they will get good grades and he will get a poor one. Finally, if he and all other students study the same amount of time, everyone will get average grades. Other students share Sam's preferences regarding grades and study time.

   a. Model this situation as a two-person prisoner's dilemma in which the strategies are to study a little and to study a lot, and the players are Sam and all other students. Include the payoffs in the matrix.

   b. What is the equilibrium outcome in this game? From the students' perspective, is it the best outcome?

2. Consider the following "dating game," which has two players, *A* and *B,* and two strategies, to buy a movie ticket or a baseball ticket. The payoffs, given in points, are as shown in the following matrix. Note that the highest payoffs occur when both *A* and *B* attend the same event.

		B	
		Buy movie ticket	Buy baseball ticket
A	Buy movie ticket	2 for *A* 3 for *B*	0 for *A* 0 for *B*
	Buy baseball ticket	I for *A* I for *B*	3 for *A* 2 for *B*

Assume that players *A* and *B* buy their tickets separately and simultaneously. Each must decide what to do knowing the available choices and payoffs but not what the other has actually chosen. Each player believes the other to be rational and self-interested.

   a. Does either player have a dominant strategy?

   b. How many potential equilibriums are there? (*Hint:* To see whether a given combination of strategies is an equilibrium, ask whether either player could get a higher payoff by changing his or her strategy.)

   c. Is this game a prisoner's dilemma? Explain.

d. Suppose player *A* gets to buy his or her ticket first. Player *B* does not observe *A*'s choice but knows that *A* chose first. Player *A* knows that player *B* knows he or she chose first. What is the equilibrium outcome?

e. Suppose the situation is similar to part d, except that player B chooses first. What is the equilibrium outcome?

3. Blackadder and Baldrick are rational, self-interested criminals imprisoned in separate cells in a dark medieval dungeon. They face the prisoner's dilemma displayed in the following matrix.

		Blackadder	
		Confess	Deny
Baldrick	Confess	5 years for each	0 years for Baldrick 20 years for Blackadder
	Deny	0 years for Blackadder 20 years for Baldrick	1 year for each

Assume that Blackadder is willing to pay $1,000 for each year by which he can reduce his sentence below 20 years. A corrupt jailer tells Blackadder that before he decides whether to confess or deny the crime, she can tell him Baldrick's decision. How much is this information worth to Blackadder?

4. The owner of a thriving business wants to open a new office in a distant city. If he can hire someone who will manage the new office honestly, he can afford to pay that person a weekly salary of $2,000 ($1,000 more than the manager would be able to earn elsewhere) and still earn an economic profit of $800. The owner's concern is that he will not be able to monitor the manager's behavior and that the manager would therefore be in a position to embezzle money from the business. The owner knows that if the remote office is managed dishonestly, the manager can earn $3,100 while causing the owner an economic loss of $600/week.

a. If the owner believes that all managers are narrowly self-interested income maximizers, will he open the new office?

b. Suppose the owner knows that a managerial candidate is a devoutly religious person who condemns dishonest behavior and who would be willing to pay up to $15,000 to avoid the guilt she would feel if she were dishonest. Will the owner open the remote office?

5. Imagine yourself sitting in your car in a campus parking lot that is currently full, waiting for someone to pull out so that you can park your car. Somebody pulls out, but at the same moment a driver who has just arrived overtakes you in an obvious attempt to park in the vacated spot before you can. Suppose this driver would be willing to pay up to $10 to park in that spot and up to $30 to avoid getting into an argument with you. (That is, the benefit of parking is $10, and the cost of an argument is $30.) At the same time the other driver guesses, accurately, that you too would be willing to pay up to $30 to avoid a confrontation and up to $10 to park in the vacant spot.

a. Model this situation as a two-stage decision tree in which the other driver's bid to take the space is the opening move and your strategies are (1) to protest and (2) not to protest. If you protest (initiate an argument), the rules of the game specify that the other driver has to let you take the space. Show the payoffs at the end of each branch of the tree.

b. What is the equilibrium outcome?

c. What would be the advantage of being able to be able to communicate credibly to the other driver that your failure to protest would be a significant psychological cost to you?

6. Newfoundland's fishing industry has recently declined sharply due to overfishing, even though fishing companies were supposedly bound by a quota agreement. If all fishing companies had abided by the agreement, yields could have been maintained at high levels.

a. Model this situation as a prisoner's dilemma in which the players are Company *A* and Company *B* and the strategies are to keep the quota and break the quota. Include appropriate payoffs in the matrix. Explain why overfishing is inevitable in the absence of effective enforcement of the quota agreement.

b. Provide another environmental example of a prisoner's dilemma.

c. In many potential prisoner's dilemmas, a way out of the dilemma for a would-be cooperator is to make reliable character judgments about the trustworthiness of potential partners. Explain why this solution is not available in many situations involving degradation of the environment.

7. Consider the following game, called matching pennies, which you are playing with a friend. Each of you has a penny hidden in your hand, facing either heads up or tails up (you know which way the one in your hand is facing). On the count of "three" you simultaneously show your pennies to each other. If the face-up side of your coin matches the face-up side of your friend's coin, you get to keep the two pennies. If the faces do not match, your friend gets to keep the pennies.

a. Who are the players in this game? What are each player's strategies? Construct a payoff matrix for the game.

b. Is there a dominant strategy? If so, what?

c. Is there an equilibrium? If so, what?

8. Consider the following game. Harry has four quarters. He can offer Sally from one to four of them. If she accepts his offer, she keeps the quarters Harry offered her and Harry keeps the others. If Sally declines Harry's offer, they both get nothing ($0). They play the game only once, and each cares only about the amount of money he or she ends up with.

a. Who are the players? What are each player's strategies? Construct a decision tree for this ultimatum bargaining game.

b. Given their goal, what is the optimal choice for each player?

9. Two airplane manufacturers are considering the production of a new product, a 150-passenger jet. Both are deciding whether to enter the market and produce the new plane. The payoff matrix is as shown (payoff values are in millions of dollars).

		Airbus	
		Produce	Don't produce
Boeing	Produce	−5 for each	100 for Boeing 0 for Airbus
	Don't produce	0 for Boeing 100 for Airbus	0 for each

The implication of these payoffs is that the market demand is large enough to support only one manufacturer. If both firms enter, both will sustain a loss.

a. Identify two possible equilibrium outcomes in this game.

b. Consider the effect of a subsidy. Suppose the European Union decides to subsidize the European producer, Airbus, with a check for $25 million if it enters the market. Revise the payoff matrix to account for this subsidy. What is the new equilibrium outcome?

c. Compare the two outcomes (pre- and post-subsidy). What qualitative effect does the subsidy have?

10. Jill and Jack both have two pails that can be used to carry water down from a hill. Each makes only one trip down the hill, and each pail of water can be sold for $5. Carrying the pails of water down requires considerable effort. Both Jill and Jack would be willing to pay $2 each to avoid carrying one bucket down the hill and an additional $3 to avoid carrying a second bucket down the hill.

a. Given market prices, how many pails of water will each child fetch from the top of the hill?

b. Jill and Jack's parents are worried that the two children don't cooperate enough with one another. Suppose they make Jill and Jack share their revenues from selling the water equally. Given that both are self-interested, construct the payoff matrix for the decisions Jill and Jack face regarding the number of pails of water each should carry. What is the equilibrium outcome?

■ ANSWERS TO IN-CHAPTER EXERCISES ■

10.1 In game 1, no matter what Chrysler does, GM will do better to invest, and no matter what GM does, Chrysler will do better to invest. Each has a dominant strategy, but in following it, each does worse that if it had not invested. So game 1 is a prisoner's dilemma. In game 2, no matter what Chrysler does, GM again will do better to invest; but no matter what GM does, Chrysler will do better *not* to invest. Each has a dominant strategy, and in following it, each gets a payoff of 10—5 more than if each had played its dominated strategy. So game 2 is not a prisoner's dilemma.

Game 1

GM	Chrysler Don't invest	Chrysler Invest
Don't invest	10 for each	4 for GM / 12 for Chrysler
Invest	12 for GM / 4 for Chrysler	5 for each

Game 2

GM	Chrysler Don't invest	Chrysler Invest
Don't invest	4 for GM / 12 for Chrysler	5 for each
Invest	10 for each	12 for GM / 4 for Chrysler

10.2 No matter what TWA does, United will do better to leave ad spending the same. No matter what United does, TWA will do better to raise ad spending. So each player will play its dominant strategy: TWA will raise its ad spending, and United will leave its ad spending the same.

United	TWA Raise ad spending	TWA Leave ad spending the same
Raise ad spending	$3,000 for United / $8,000 for TWA	$4,000 for United / $5,000 for TWA
Leave ad spending the same	$8,000 for United / $4,000 for TWA	$5,000 for United / $2,000 for TWA

10.3 Smith assumes that Jones will choose the branch that maximizes his payoff, which is the bottom branch at either *B* or *C*. So Jones will choose the bottom branch when his turn comes, no matter what Smith chooses. Since Smith will do better (60) on the bottom branch at *B* than on the bottom branch at *C* (50), Smith will choose the top branch at *A*. So the equilibrium in this game is for Smith to choose the top branch at *A* and Jones to choose the bottom branch at *B*. Smith gets 60, and Jones gets 105. If Jones could make a credible commitment to choose the top branch no matter what, both would do better. Smith would choose the bottom branch at *A* and Jones would choose the top branch at *C*, giving Smith 500 and Jones 400.

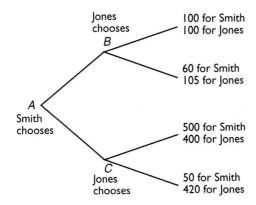

A
Smith
chooses

Jones
chooses
B

100 for Smith
100 for Jones

60 for Smith
105 for Jones

500 for Smith
400 for Jones

C
Jones
chooses

50 for Smith
420 for Jones

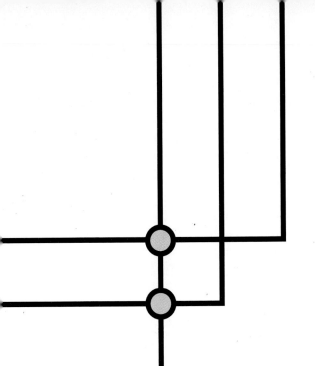

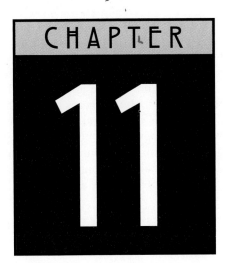

CHAPTER 11

EXTERNALITIES
AND PROPERTY RIGHTS

■

A droll television ad for a British brand of pipe tobacco opens with a distinguished looking gentleman sitting quietly on a park bench, smoking his pipe and reading a book of poetry. Before him lies a pond, unrippled except for a mother duck swimming peacefully with her ducklings. Suddenly a raucous group of teenage boys bursts onto the scene with a remote-controlled toy warship. Yelling and chortling, they launch their boat and maneuver it in aggressive pursuit of the terrified ducks.

Interrupted from his reverie, the gentleman looks up from his book and draws calmly on his pipe as he surveys the scene before him. He then reaches into his bag, pulls out a remote control of his own, and begins manipulating the joystick. The scene shifts underwater, where a miniature submarine rises from the depths of the pond. Once the boys' boat is in the sub's sights, the gentleman pushes a button on his remote control. Seconds later, the boat is blown to smithereens by a torpedo. The scene fades to a close-up of the tobacco company's label.

EXTERNAL COSTS AND BENEFITS

Many activities generate costs or benefits that accrue to people not directly involved in those activities. These effects are generally unintended. They are called **external costs** and **benefits—externalities,** for short. From the pipe smoker's point of view, the noise generated by the marauding boys was an external cost. And had others been disturbed by the boys' rowdiness, they may well have regarded the pipe smoker's retaliatory gesture as an external benefit.

***external cost (or negative
externality)*** a cost of an
activity that falls on people
other than those who pursue
the activity

***external benefit (or positive
externality)*** a benefit of an
activity received by people other
than those who pursue the
activity

externality an external cost or
benefit of an activity

This chapter focuses on how externalities affect the allocation of resources. Adam Smith's theory of the invisible hand applies to an ideal marketplace in which externalities do not exist. In such situations, Smith argued, the self-interested actions of individuals would lead to socially efficient outcomes. We will see that when the parties affected by externalities can easily negotiate with one another, the invisible hand will still produce an efficient outcome.

But in many cases, such as the scene depicted in the tobacco ad, negotiation is impractical. In those cases, the self-serving actions of individuals simply will not lead to efficient outcomes. Because externalities are widespread, the attempt to forge solutions to the problems they cause is one of the most important rationales, not only for the existence of government but for a variety of other forms of collective action as well.

HOW EXTERNALITIES AFFECT RESOURCE ALLOCATION

The way in which externalities distort the allocation of resources can be seen clearly in the next several examples.

EXAMPLE II.I

Does the honeybee keeper face the right incentives? (Part I)

Phoebe earns her living as a keeper of honeybees. Her neighbors on all sides grow apples. Because bees pollinate apple trees as they forage for nectar, the more hives Phoebe keeps, the larger the harvests will be in the surrounding orchards. If Phoebe takes only her own costs and benefits into account in deciding how many hives to keep, will she keep the socially optimal number of hives?

For the orchard owners, Phoebe's hives constitute an external benefit, or a positive externality. If she takes only her own personal costs and benefits into account, she will add hives only until the added revenue she gets from the last hive just equals the cost of adding it. But since the orchard owners also benefit from additional hives, the total benefit of adding another hive at that point will be greater than its cost. Phoebe, then, will keep too few hives.

EXAMPLE II.2

Does the honeybee keeper face the right incentives? (Part 2)

As in Example 11.1, Phoebe earns her living as a keeper of honeybees. But now her neighbors are not apple growers but an elementary school and a nursing home. The more hives Phoebe keeps, the more students and nursing home residents will be stung by bees. If Phoebe takes only her own costs and benefits into account in deciding how many hives to keep, will she keep the socially optimal number of hives?

For the students and nursing home residents, Phoebe's hives constitute an external cost, or a negative externality. If she considers only her own costs and benefits in deciding how many hives to keep, she will continue to add hives until the added revenue from the last hive is just enough to cover its cost. But since Phoebe's neighbors also incur costs when she adds a hive, the benefit of the last hive at that point will be smaller than its cost. Phoebe, in other words, will keep too many hives.

Every activity involves costs and benefits. When all the relevant costs and benefits of an activity accrue directly to the person who carries it out—that is, when the activity generates no externalities—the level of the activity that is best for the individual will be best for society as a whole. But when an activity generates externalities, be they positive or negative, individual self-interest does not produce the best allocation of resources. Individuals who consider only their own costs and benefits will tend to engage too much in activities that generate negative externalities and too little in activities that generate positive externalities. When an activity generates both positive and negative externalities, private and social interests will coincide only in the unlikely event that the opposing effects offset one another exactly.

THE GRAPHICAL PORTRAYAL OF EXTERNALITIES

The effects of externalities on resource allocation can be portrayed graphically, as in Figure 11.1. In part (a), Private MC (for marginal cost) is the supply curve of a product whose production is accompanied by an external cost of XC per unit. The market equilibrium level of output is Q_{pvt}, the output level at which the demand curve D intersects Private MC. Note that Q_{pvt} is larger than the socially optimal level of output, Q_{soc}, the output level at which the demand curve intersects Social MC. Social MC, the socially optimal supply curve of the product, is the result of adding the external cost XC to every value along Private MC.

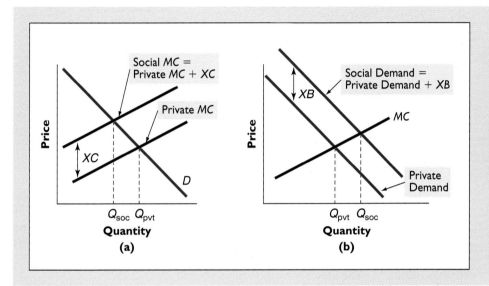

FIGURE 11.1
How External Costs and Benefits Affect Resource Allocation.
The market equilibrium level of output (Q_{pvt}) is larger than the socially optimal level (Q_{soc}) for products accompanied by external costs [part (a)] but smaller than the socially optimal level for products accompanied by external benefits [part (b)].

In Figure 11.1(b), Private Demand is the demand curve for a product whose production generates an external benefit of XB per unit. The market equilibrium quantity of this good, Q_{pvt}, is the output level at which Private Demand intersects the supply curve of the product *(MC)*. This time Q_{pvt} is smaller than the socially optimal level of output, Q_{soc}. Q_{soc} is the output level at which MC intersects the socially optimal demand curve (Social Demand), which is the result of adding the external benefit XB to every value along Private Demand.

Externalities thus distort the allocation of resources in an otherwise efficient market. When externalities are present, the individual pursuit of self-interest will not result in the largest possible economic surplus. And when it does not, the outcome is by definition inefficient.

THE COASE THEOREM

To say that a situation is inefficient means that it can be rearranged in a way that would make at least some people better off without harming others. Such situations, we have seen, are a source of creative tension. The existence of inefficiency, after all, means that there is cash on the table, which usually triggers a race to see who can capture it. For example, we saw that because monopoly pricing results in an inefficiently low output level, the potential for gain gave monopolists an incentive to make discounts available to price-sensitive buyers. As the next examples illustrate, the inefficiencies that result from externalities create similar incentives for remedial action.

EXAMPLE 11.3

Will Abercrombie dump toxins in the river? (Part 1)

Abercrombie's factory produces a toxic waste by-product. If Abercrombie dumps it in the river, he causes damage to Fitch, a fisherman located downstream. The toxins are short-lived and cause no damage to anyone other than Fitch. At a cost, Abercrombie can filter out the toxins, in which case Fitch will suffer no damage at all. The relevant gains and losses for the two individuals are listed in Table 11.1.

TABLE 11.1
Costs and Benefits of Eliminating Toxic Waste (Part 1)

	With filter	Without filter
Gains to Abercrombie	$100/day	$130/day
Gains to Fitch	$100/day	$50/day

If the law does not penalize Abercrombie for dumping toxins in the river, and if Abercrombie and Fitch cannot communicate with one another, will Abercrombie operate with or without a filter? Is that choice socially efficient?

Since Abercrombie earns $30/day more without a filter than with one, his natural incentive is to operate without one. But the outcome when he does so is socially inefficient. Thus, when Abercrombie operates without a filter, the total daily gain to both parties is only $130 + $50 = $180, compared to $100 + $100 = $200 if Abercrombie had operated with a filter. The daily cost of the filter to Abercrombie is only $130 − $100 = $30, which is smaller than its daily benefit to Fitch of $100 − $50 = $50. The fact that Abercrombie does not install the filter implies a squandered daily surplus of $20.

EXAMPLE 11.4

Will Abercrombie dump toxins in the river? (Part 2)

Suppose the costs and benefits of using the filter are as in Example 11.3 except that Abercrombie and Fitch can now communicate with one another at no cost. Even though the law does not require him to do so, will Abercrombie use a filter?

This time, Abercrombie will use a filter. Recall from Chapter 7 the observation that when the economic pie grows larger, everyone can have a larger slice. Because use of a filter would result in the largest possible economic surplus, it would enable both Abercrombie and Fitch to have a larger net gain than before. Fitch thus has an incentive to *pay* Abercrombie to use a filter. For example, suppose Fitch offers Abercrombie $40/day to compensate him for operating with a filter. Both Abercrombie and Fitch will then be exactly $10/day better off than before, for a total daily net gain of $20.

EXERCISE 11.1

In Example 11.4, what is the largest whole-dollar amount by which Fitch could compensate Abercrombie for operating with a filter and still be better off than before?

Ronald Coase, a professor at the University of Chicago Law School, was the first to see clearly that if people can negotiate with one another at no cost over the right to perform activities that cause externalities, they will always arrive at an efficient solution. This insight, which is often called the **Coase theorem**, is a profoundly important idea, for which Coase (rhymes with "dose") was awarded the 1991 Nobel Prize in Economics.

Why, you might ask, should Fitch pay Abercrombie to filter out toxins that would not be there in the first place if not for Abercrombie's factory? The rhetorical force of this question is undeniable. Yet Coase points out that externalities are reciprocal in nature. The toxins do harm Fitch, to be sure, but preventing Abercrombie from emitting them would penalize Abercrombie, by exactly $30/day. Why should Fitch necessarily have the right to harm Abercrombie? Indeed, as Example 11.5 illustrates, even if Fitch had that right, he would exercise it only if filtering the toxins proved the most efficient outcome.

Will Abercrombie dump toxins in the river? (Part 3)

Suppose the law says that Abercrombie may *not* dump toxins in the river unless he has Fitch's permission. If the relevant costs and benefits of filtering the toxins are as shown in Table 11.2, and if Abercrombie and Fitch can negotiate with one another at no cost, will Abercrombie filter the toxins?

TABLE 11.2
Costs and Benefits of Eliminating Toxic Waste (Part 3)

	With filter	Without filter
Gains to Abercrombie	$100/day	$150/day
Gains to Fitch	$100/day	$70/day

Note that this time the most efficient outcome is for Abercrombie to operate without a filter, for the total daily surplus in that case will be $220 as compared to only $200 with a filter. Under the law, however, Fitch has the right to insist that Abercrombie use a filter. We might expect him to exercise that right, since his own gain would rise from $70 to $100/day if he did so. But because this outcome would be socially inefficient, we know that each party can do better.

Suppose, for example, that Abercrombie gives Fitch $40/day in return for Fitch's permission to operate without a filter. Each would then have a net daily gain of $110, which is $10 better for each of them than if Fitch had insisted that Abercrombie use a filter. Abercrombie's pollution harms Fitch, sure enough. But failure to allow the pollution would have caused even greater harm to Abercrombie.

These examples drive home the point that when externalities are a source of inefficiency, the affected parties will search for the outcome with the highest total economic surplus. And that is precisely what will happen, provided they can negotiate with one another at no cost.

Externalities are hardly rare and isolated occurrences. On the contrary, finding examples of actions that are altogether free of them is difficult. And because externalities can distort the allocation of resources, recognizing them and dealing intelligently with them are important. Consider the following example of an externality that arises because of shared living arrangements.

Will Ann and Betty share an apartment?

Ann and Betty can live together in a two-bedroom apartment for $600/month, or separately in 2 one-bedroom apartments, each for $400/month. If the rent paid

Coase theorem if at no cost people can negotiate the purchase and sale of the right to perform activities that cause externalities, they can always arrive at efficient solutions to the problems caused by externalities

EXAMPLE 11.5

EXAMPLE 11.6

were the same for both alternatives, the two women would be indifferent between living together or separately, except for one problem: Ann talks constantly on the telephone. Ann would pay up to $250/month for this privilege. Betty, for her part, would pay up to $150/month to have better access to the phone. If the two cannot install a second phone line, should they live together or separately?

Ann and Betty should live together only if the benefit of doing so exceeds the cost. The benefit of living together is the reduction in their rent. Since 2 one-bedroom apartments would cost a total of $800/month, compared to $600 for a two-bedroom unit, their benefit from living together is $200/month. Their cost of living together is the least costly accommodation they can make to Ann's objectionable telephone habits. Since Ann would be willing to pay up to $250/month to avoid changing her behavior, the $200 rent saving is too small to persuade her to change. But Betty is willing to put up with Ann's behavior for a compensation payment of only $150/month. Since that amount is smaller than the total saving in rent, the least costly solution to the problem is for Betty to live with Ann and simply put up with her behavior.

Table 11.3 summarizes the relevant costs and benefits of this shared living arrangement. The cost-benefit principle tells us that Ann and Betty should live together if and only if the benefit of living together exceeds the cost. The cost of the shared living arrangement is not the sum of all possible costs but the least costly accommodation to the problem (or problems) of shared living. Since the $200/month saving in rent exceeds the least costly accommodation to the phone problem, Ann and Betty can reap a total gain in economic surplus of $50/month by sharing their living quarters.

TABLE 11.3
The Gain in Surplus from Shared Living Arrangements

Benefits of Shared Living		
Total cost of separate apartments	Total cost of shared apartment	Rent savings from sharing
(2)($400/month) = $800/month	$600/month	$200/month

Costs of Shared Living			
Problem	Ann's cost of solving problem	Betty's cost of solving problem	Least costly solution to the problem
Ann's phone usage	Curtailed phone usage: $250/month	Tolerate phone usage: $150/month	Betty tolerates Ann's phone usage: $150/month

Gain in Surplus from Shared Living		
Rent savings ($200/month) −	Least costly accommodation to shared living problems ($150/month) =	Gain in surplus: $50/month

Some people might conclude that Ann and Betty should not live together, because if the two share the rent equally, Betty will end up paying $300/month—which when added to the $150 cost of putting up with Ann's phone behavior comes to $50 more than the cost of living alone. As persuasive as that argument may sound, however, it is mistaken. The source of the error, as Example 11.7 makes clear, is the assumption that the two must share the rent equally.

What is the highest rent Betty would be willing to pay for the two-bedroom apartment?

EXAMPLE 11.7

In Example 11.6, what is the highest rent Betty would be willing to pay to share an apartment with Ann?

Betty's alternative is to live alone, which would mean paying $400/month, her reservation price for a living arrangement with no phone problem. Since the most she would be willing to pay to avoid the phone problem is $150/month, the highest monthly rent she would be willing to pay for the shared apartment is $400 − $150 = $250. If she pays that amount, Ann will have to pay the difference, namely, $350/month, which is clearly a better alternative for Ann than paying $400 to live alone.

How much should Ann and Betty pay if they agree to split their economic surplus equally?

EXAMPLE 11.8

If Ann and Betty agree to live together and split the resulting gain in economic surplus equally, how much rent will each of them pay?

As we saw in Table 11.3, the total rent saving from the shared apartment is $200, and since the least costly solution to the phone problem is $150, the monthly gain in economic surplus is $50. We know that Ann's reservation price for living together is $400/month and Betty's is $250 (see Example 11.7). So if the two women want to split the $50 monthly surplus equally, each should pay $25 less than her reservation price. Ann's monthly rent will thus be $375 and Betty's, $225. The result is that each is $25/month better off than if she had lived alone.

EXERCISE 11.2

As in Example 11.6, Ann and Betty can live together in a two-bedroom apartment for $600/month or separately in 2 one-bedroom apartments, each for $400/month. Ann would pay up to $250/month rather than moderate her telephone habits, and Betty would pay up to $150/month to achieve reasonable access to the telephone. But Betty would also be willing to pay up to $60/month to avoid the loss of privacy that comes with shared living space. Should the two women live together?

LEGAL REMEDIES FOR EXTERNALITIES

We have seen that efficient solutions to externalities can be found whenever the affected parties can negotiate with one another at no cost. But negotiation is not always practical. A motorist with a noisy muffler, for example, imposes costs on others, yet they cannot flag him down and offer him a compensation payment to fix his muffler. In recognition of this difficulty, most governments simply require that cars have working mufflers. Indeed, the explicit or implicit purpose of a large share—perhaps the lion's share—of laws is to solve problems caused by externalities. The goal of such laws is to help people achieve the solutions they might have reached had they been able to negotiate with one another.

When negotiation is costless, the task of adjustment generally falls on the party who can accomplish it at the lowest cost. For instance, in Example 11.6, Betty put up with Ann's annoying phone habits because doing so was less costly than asking Ann to change her habits. Many municipal noise ordinances also place the burden of adjustment on those who can accomplish it at lowest cost. Consider, for example, the restrictions on loud party music, which often take effect at a later hour on weekends than on weekdays. This pattern reflects both the fact that the gains from loud music tend to be larger on weekends and the fact that such music is more likely to disturb people on weekdays. By setting the noise curfew at different hours on different days of the week, the law places the burden on partygoers during the week and on sleepers during the weekend. Similar logic explains why noise ordinances allow motorists to honk their horns in most neighborhoods, but not in the immediate vicinity of a hospital.

As the following examples demonstrate, economic naturalists can hone their craft by focusing on laws whose purpose is to solve the problems caused by externalities.

What is the purpose of speed limits and other traffic laws?

A motorist driving a car at high speed endangers not just her own life and property but also the lives and property of others. Speed limits, no-passing zones, right-of-way rules, and a host of other traffic laws may be seen as reasoned attempts to limit the harm one party inflicts on another. Many jurisdictions even have laws requiring that motorists install snow tires on their cars by November 1. These laws promote not just safety but also the smooth flow of traffic: A single motorist who can't get up a snow-covered hill delays not only herself but also the motorists behind her.

ECONOMIC NATURALIST 11.2

Why do most communities have zoning laws?

Most communities restrict the kinds of activities that take place in various parts of the city. Because many residents place a high value on living in an uncongested neighborhood, some cities have enacted zoning laws specifying minimum lot sizes. In places like Manhattan, where a shortage of land encourages developers to build very large and tall buildings, zoning laws limit both a building's height and the proportion of a lot it may occupy. Such restrictions recognize that the taller a building is, and the greater the proportion of its lot that it occupies, the more it blocks sunlight from reaching surrounding properties. The desire to control external costs also helps to explain why many cities establish separate zones for business and residential activity. Even within business districts, many cities limit certain kinds of commercial activity. For example, in an effort to revitalize the Times Square neighborhood, New York City enacted a zoning law banning adult bookstores and pornographic movie theaters from the area.

Why do many governments enact laws that limit the discharge of environmental pollutants?

Limitations on the discharge of pollutants into the environment are perhaps the clearest examples of laws aimed at solving problems caused by externalities. The details of these laws reflect the cost-benefit principle. The discharge of toxic wastes into rivers, for example, tends to be most strictly regulated on those waterways whose commercial fishing or recreational uses are most highly valued. On other waterways, the burden of adjustment is likely to fall more heavily on fishermen, recreational boaters, and swimmers. Similarly, air quality regulations tend to be strictest in the most heavily populated regions of the country, where the marginal benefit of pollution reduction is the greatest.

What is the purpose of free speech laws?

The First Amendment's protection of free speech and the pattern of exceptions to that protection are another illustration of how legal remedies are used to solve the problems caused by externalities. The First Amendment acknowledges the decisive value of open communication, as well as the practical difficulty of identifying and regulating acts of speech that cause more harm than good. Yet it does allow some important exceptions. For instance, it does not allow someone to yell "fire" in a crowded theater if there is no fire, nor does it allow someone to advocate the violent overthrow of the government. In those instances, the external benefits of free speech are far too small to justify the external costs.

Why does government subsidize activities that generate positive externalities?

The laws discussed in the preceding examples are meant to regulate activities that generate negative externalities. But government also uses the law to encourage activities that generate positive externalities. The planting of trees on hillsides, for example, benefits not just the landowner but also his neighbors by limiting the danger of flooding. In recognition of this fact, many jurisdictions subsidize the planting of trees. Similarly, Congress budgets millions of dollars each year in support of basic research, an implicit acknowledgment of the positive externalities associated with the generation of new knowledge.

ECONOMIC NATURALIST 11.5

THE OPTIMAL AMOUNT OF NEGATIVE EXTERNALITIES IS NOT ZERO

Curbing pollution and other negative externalities entails both costs and benefits. As we saw in Chapter 6, the best policy is to curtail pollution until the cost of further abatement just equals the marginal benefit. In general, the marginal cost of abatement rises with the amount of pollution eliminated. (Following the low-hanging-fruit principle, polluters use the cheapest cleanup methods first and then turn to more expensive ones.) And the law of diminishing marginal utility suggests that beyond some point, the marginal benefit of pollution reduction tends to fall as more pollution is removed. As a result, the marginal cost and marginal benefit curves almost always intersect at less than the maximum amount of pollution reduction.

The intersection of the two curves marks instead the socially optimal level of pollution reduction. If pollution is curtailed by any less than that amount, society will gain more than it will lose by pushing the cleanup effort a little further. But if regulators push beyond the point at which the marginal cost and benefit curves intersect, society will incur costs that exceed the benefits. The existence of a socially optimal level of pollution reduction implies the existence of a socially optimal level of pollution, and that level will almost always be greater than zero.

As we saw in Chapter 6, because people have been conditioned to think of pollution as bad, many cringe when they hear the phrase "socially optimal level of pollution." How can any positive level of pollution be socially optimal? But to speak of a socially optimal level of pollution is not the same as saying that pollution is good. It is merely to recognize that society has an interest in cleaning up the environment, but only up to a certain point. The underlying idea is no different from the idea of an optimal level of dirt in an apartment. After all, even if you spent the whole day, every day, vacuuming your apartment, there would be *some* dirt left in it. And because you have better things to do than vacuum all day, you probably tolerate substantially more than the minimal amount of dirt. A dirty apartment is not good, nor is pollution in the air you breathe. But in both cases, the cleanup effort should be expanded only until the marginal benefit equals the marginal cost.

RECAP **EXTERNAL COSTS AND BENEFITS**

Externalities occur when the costs or benefits of an activity accrue to people other than those directly involved in the activity. The Coase theorem says that when affected parties can negotiate with one another without cost, activities will be pursued at efficient levels, even in the presence of positive or negative externalities. But when negotiation is prohibitively costly, inefficient behavior generally results. Activities that generate negative externalities are pursued to excess, while those that generate positive externalities are pursued too little. Laws and regulations are often adopted in an effort to alter inefficient behavior that results from externalities.

PROPERTY RIGHTS AND THE TRAGEDY OF THE COMMONS

People who grow up in the industrialized nations tend to take the institution of private property for granted. Our intuitive sense is that people have the right to own any property they acquire by lawful means and to do with that property much as they see fit. In reality, however, property laws are considerably more complex in terms of the rights they confer and the obligations they impose.

THE PROBLEM OF UNPRICED RESOURCES

To understand the laws that govern the use of property, we must begin by asking why societies created the institution of private property in the first place. The following examples, which show what happens to property that nobody owns, suggest an answer.

EXAMPLE 11.9   **How many steers will villagers send onto the commons?**

A village has five residents, each of whom has accumulated savings of $100. Each villager can use the money to buy a government bond that pays 13 percent interest per year or to buy a year-old steer, send it onto the commons to graze, and sell it after 1 year. The price the villager will get for the 2-year-old steer depends on the amount of weight it gains while grazing on the commons, which in turn depends on the number of steers sent onto the commons, as shown in Table 11.4.

The price of a 2-year-old steer declines with the number of steers grazing on the commons, because the more steers, the less grass available to each. The villagers make their investment decisions one at a time, and the results are public. If each villager decides how to invest individually, how many steers will be sent onto the commons, and what will be the village's total income?

TABLE 11.4
The Relationship between Herd Size and Steer Price

Number of steers on the commons	Price per 2-year-old steer ($)	Income per steer ($/year)
1	126	26
2	119	19
3	116	16
4	113	13
5	111	11

If a villager buys a $100 government bond, he will earn $13 of interest income at the end of 1 year. Thus he should send a steer onto the commons if and only if that steer will command a price of at least $113 as a 2-year-old. When each villager chooses in this self-interested way, we can expect four villagers to send a steer onto the commons. (Actually, the fourth villager would be indifferent between investing in a steer or buying a bond, since he would earn $13 either way. For the sake of discussion, we'll assume that in the case of a tie, people choose to be cattlemen.) The fifth villager, seeing that he would earn only $11 by sending a fifth steer onto the commons, will choose instead to buy a government bond. As a result of these decisions, the total village income will be $65/year—$13 for the one bondholder and 4($13) = $52 for the four cattlemen.

Has Adam Smith's invisible hand produced the most efficient allocation of these villagers' resources? We can tell at a glance that it has not, since their total village income is only $65—precisely the same as it would have been had the possibility of cattle raising not existed. The source of the difficulty will become evident in Example 11.10.

What is the socially optimal number of steers to send onto the commons?

EXAMPLE 11.10

Suppose the five villagers in Example 11.9 confront the same investment opportunities as before, except that this time they are free to make their decisions as a group rather than individually. How many steers will they send onto the commons, and what will be their total village income?

This time the villagers' goal is to maximize the income received by the group as a whole. When decisions are made from this perspective, the criterion is to send a steer onto the commons only if its marginal contribution to village income is at least $13, the amount that could be earned from a government bond. As the entries in the last column of Table 11.5 indicate, the first steer clearly meets this criterion, since it contributes $26 to total village income. But the second steer does not. Sending that steer onto the commons raises the village's income from cattle raising from $26 to $38, a gain of just $12. The $100 required to buy the second steer would thus have been better invested in a government bond. Worse, the collective return from sending a third steer is only $10; from a fourth, only $4; and from a fifth, only $3.

TABLE 11.5
Marginal Income and the Socially Optimal Herd Size

Number of steers on the commons	Price per 2-year-old steer ($)	Income per steer ($/year)	Total village income ($/year)	Marginal income ($/year)
				26
1	126	26	26	
				12
2	119	19	38	
				10
3	116	16	48	
				4
4	113	13	52	
				3
5	111	11	55	

In sum, when investment decisions are made with the goal of maximizing total village income, the best choice is to buy four government bonds and send only a single steer onto the commons. The resulting village income will be $78: $26 from sending the single steer and $52 from the four government bonds. That amount is $13 more than the total income that resulted when villagers made their investment decisions individually. Once again, the reward from moving from an inefficient allocation to an efficient one is that the economic pie grows larger. And when the pie grows larger, everyone can get a larger slice. For instance, if the villagers agree to pool their income and share it equally, each will get $15.60, or $2.60 more than before.

EXERCISE 11.3

How would your answers to Examples 11.9 and 11.10 differ if the interest rate were not 13 percent but 11 percent/year?

Why do the villagers in Examples 11.9 and 11.10 do better when they make their investment decisions collectively? The answer is that when individuals decide alone, they ignore the fact that sending another steer onto the commons will cause existing steers to gain less weight. Their failure to consider this effect makes the return from sending another steer seem misleadingly high to them.

tragedy of the commons the tendency for a resource that has no price to be used until its marginal benefit falls to zero

The grazing land on the commons is a valuable economic resource. When no one owns it, no one has any incentive to take the opportunity cost of using it into account. And when that happens, people will tend to use it until its marginal benefit is zero. This problem, and others similar to it, are known as the **tragedy of the commons.** The essential cause of the tragedy of the commons is the fact that one person's use of commonly held property imposes an external cost on others by making the property less valuable. The tragedy of the commons also provides a vivid illustration of the equilibrium principle (see Chapter 4). Each individual villager behaves rationally by sending an additional steer onto the commons, yet the overall outcome falls far short of the attainable ideal.

THE EFFECT OF PRIVATE OWNERSHIP

As Example 11.11 illustrates, one solution to the tragedy of the commons is to place the village grazing land under private ownership.

EXAMPLE 11.11

How much will the right to control the village commons sell for?

Suppose the five villagers face the same investment opportunities as before, except that this time they decide to auction off the right to use the commons to the highest bidder. Assuming that villagers can borrow as well as lend at an annual interest rate of 13 percent, what price will the right to use the commons fetch? How will the owner of that property right use it, and what will be the resulting village income?

To answer these questions, simply ask yourself what you would do if you had complete control over how the grazing land were used. As we saw in Example 11.10, the most profitable way to use this land is to send only a single steer to graze on it. If you do so, you will earn a total of $26/year. Since the opportunity cost of the $100 you spent on the single yearling steer is the $13 in interest you could have earned from a bond, your economic profit from sending a single steer onto the commons will be $13 per year, provided you can use the land for free. But you cannot; to finance your purchase of the property right, you must borrow money (since you used your $100 savings to buy a year-old steer).

What is the most you should pay for the right to use the commons? Since its use generates an income of $26/year, or $13 more than the opportunity cost of your investment in the steer, the most you should pay is $100 (because that amount used to purchase a bond that pays 13 percent interest would also generate income of $13/year). If the land were sold at auction, $100 is precisely the amount you would have to pay. Your annual earnings from the land would be exactly enough to pay the $13 interest on your loan and cover the opportunity cost of not having put your savings into a bond.

Note that when the right to use the land is auctioned to the highest bidder, the village achieves a more efficient allocation of its resources, because the owner has a strong incentive to take the opportunity cost of more intensive grazing fully into account. Total village income in this case will again be $78. If the annual interest on the $100 proceeds from selling the land rights is shared equally among the five villagers, each will again have an annual investment income of $15.60.

The logic of economic surplus maximization helps to explain why the most economically successful nations have all been ones with well-developed private property laws. Property that belongs to everyone belongs, in effect, to no one. Not only is its potential economic value never fully realized, it usually ends up being of no value at all.

Bear in mind, however, that in most countries the owners of private property are not free to do *precisely* as they wish with it. For example, local zoning laws may give the owner of a residential building lot the right to build a three-story house but not a six-story house. Here, too, the logic of economic surplus maximization applies, for a fully informed and rational legislature would define property rights so as to create the largest possible total economic surplus. In practice, of course, such ideal legislatures never really exist. Yet the essence of politics is the cutting of deals that make people better off. If a legislator could propose a change in the property laws that would enlarge the total economic surplus, she could also propose a scheme that would give each of her constituents a larger slice, thus enhancing her chances for reelection.

As an economic naturalist, challenge yourself to use this framework when thinking about the various restrictions you encounter in private property laws: zoning laws that constrain what you can build and what types of activities you can conduct on your land; traffic laws that constrain what you can do with your car; employment and environmental laws that constrain how you can operate your business. Your understanding of these and countless other laws will be enhanced by the insight that everyone can gain when the private property laws are defined so as to create the largest total economic surplus.

WHEN PRIVATE OWNERSHIP IS IMPRACTICAL

Do not be misled into thinking that the law provides an *ideal* resolution of all problems associated with externalities and the tragedy of the commons. Defining and enforcing efficient property rights entails costs, after all, and sometimes, as in the following examples, the costs outweigh the gains.

Why are shared milkshakes drunk too quickly?

Why do blackberries in public parks get picked too soon?

Wild blackberries grow profusely at the edge of a wooded area in a crowded city park. The blackberries will taste best if left to ripen fully, but they still taste reasonably good if picked and eaten a few days early. Will the blackberries be left to ripen fully?

Obviously, the costs of defining and enforcing the property rights to blackberries growing in a public park are larger than the potential gains, so the blackberries will remain common property. That means that whoever picks them first gets them. Even though everyone would benefit if people waited until the berries were fully ripe, everyone knows that those who wait are likely to end up with no berries at all. And that means that the berries will be eaten too soon.

ECONOMIC NATURALIST 11.6

Why are shared milkshakes consumed too quickly?

Sam and Stan are identical twins who have been given a chocolate milkshake to share. If each has a straw and each knows that the other is self-interested, will the twins consume the milkshake at an optimal rate?

Because drinking a milkshake too quickly chills the taste buds, the twins will enjoy their shake more if they drink it slowly. Yet each knows that the other will drink any part of the milkshake he doesn't finish himself. The result is that each will consume the shake at a faster rate than he would if he had half a shake all to himself.

ECONOMIC NATURALIST 11.7

Here are some further examples of the type of tragedy of the commons that is not easily solved by defining private ownership rights.

Harvesting timber on remote public land On remote public lands, enforcing restrictions against cutting down trees may be impractical. Each tree cutter knows that a tree that is not harvested this year will be bigger, and hence more valuable, next year. But he also knows that if he doesn't cut the tree down this year, someone else will. In contrast, private companies that grow trees on their own land have no incentive to harvest timber prematurely and a strong incentive to prevent outsiders from doing so.

Harvesting whales in international waters Each individual whaler knows that harvesting an extra whale reduces the breeding population, and hence the size of the future whale population. But the whaler also knows that any whale that is not harvested today will be taken by some other whaler. The solution would be to define and enforce property rights to whales. But the oceans are vast, and the behavior of whalers is hard to monitor. And even if their behavior could be monitored, the concept of national sovereignty would make the international enforcement of property rights problematic.

Controlling multinational environmental pollution Each individual polluter may know that if he and all others pollute, the damage to the environment will be greater than the cost of not polluting. But if the environment is common property into which all are free to dump, each has a powerful incentive to pollute. If all polluters live under the jurisdiction of a single government, enforcing laws and regulations that limit the discharge of pollution may be practical. But if polluters come from many different countries, solutions are much more difficult to implement. Thus the Mediterranean Sea has long suffered serious pollution, because none of the many nations that border it has an economic incentive to consider the effects of its discharges on other countries.

As the world's population continues to grow, the absence of an effective system of international property rights will become an economic problem of increasing significance.

RECAP   PROPERTY RIGHTS AND THE TRAGEDY OF THE COMMONS

When a valuable resource has a price of zero, people will continue to exploit it as long as its marginal benefit remains positive. The tragedy of the commons describes situations in which valuable resources are squandered because users are not charged for them. In many cases, an efficient remedy for such waste is to define and enforce rights to the use of valuable property. But this solution is difficult to implement for resources such as the oceans and the atmosphere, because no single government has the authority to enforce property rights for these resources.

POSITIONAL EXTERNALITIES

Steffi Graf received more than $1.6 million in tournament winnings in 1992; her endorsement and exhibition earnings totaled several times that amount. By any reasonable measure, the quality of her play was outstanding, yet she consistently lost to archrival Monica Seles. But in April of 1993, Seles was stabbed in the back by a deranged fan and forced to withdraw from the tour. In the ensuing months, Graf's tournament winnings accumulated at almost double her 1992 pace, despite little change in the quality of her play.

PAYOFFS THAT DEPEND ON RELATIVE PERFORMANCE

In professional tennis and a host of other competitive situations, the rewards people receive typically depend not only on how they perform in absolute terms but also on how they perform relative to their closest rivals. In these situations, competitors have an incentive to take actions that will increase their odds of winning. For example, tennis players can increase their chances of winning by hiring personal fitness trainers and sports psychologists to travel with them on the tour. Yet the simple mathematics of competition tells us that the sum of all individual payoffs from such investments will be larger than the collective payoff. In any tennis match, for example, each contestant will get a sizable payoff from money spent on fitness trainers and sports psychologists, yet each match will have exactly one winner and one loser, no matter how much players spend. The overall gain to tennis spectators is likely to be small, and the overall gain to players as a group must be zero. To the extent that each contestant's payoff depends on his or her relative performance, then, the incentive to undertake such investments will be excessive, from a collective point of view.

Consider the following example.

Why do football players take anabolic steroids?

The offensive linemen of many National Football League teams currently average more than 330 pounds. In the 1970s, by contrast, offensive linemen in the league averaged barely 280 pounds, and the all-decade linemen of the 1940s averaged only 229 pounds. One reason that today's players are so much heavier is that players' salaries have escalated sharply over the last two decades, which has intensified competition for the positions. Size and strength are the two cardinal virtues of an offensive lineman, and other things being equal, the job will go to the larger and stronger of two rivals.

Size and strength, in turn, can be enhanced by the consumption of anabolic steroids. But if all players consume these substances, the rank ordering of players by size and strength—and hence the question of who lands the jobs—will be largely unaffected. And since the consumption of anabolic steroids entails potentially serious long-term health consequences, as a group football players are clearly worse off if they consume these drugs. So why do football players take steroids?

The problem here is that contestants for starting berths on the offensive line confront a prisoner's dilemma, like the ones analyzed in Chapter 10. Consider two closely matched rivals—Smith and Jones—who are competing for a single position. If neither takes steroids, each has a 50 percent of winning the job and a starting salary of $1 million/year. If both take steroids, each again has a 50 percent chance of winning the job. But if one takes steroids and the other doesn't, the first is sure to win the job. The loser ends up selling insurance for $30,000/year. Neither likes the fact that the drugs may have adverse health consequences, but each would be willing to take that risk in return for a shot at the big salary. Given these choices, the two competitors face a payoff matrix like the one shown in Table 11.6.

TABLE 11.6
Payoff Matrix for Steroid Consumption

		Jones	
		Don't take steroids	Take steroids
Smith	Don't take steroids	Second best for each	Best for Jones / Worst for Smith
	Take steroids	Best for Smith / Worst for Jones	Third best for each

ECONOMIC NATURALIST 11.8

Clearly, the dominant strategy for both Smith and Jones is to take steroids. Yet when they so, each gets the only the third-best outcome, whereas they could have gotten the second-best outcome by not taking the drugs. Hence the attraction of rules that forbid the consumption of anabolic steroids.

POSITIONAL ARMS RACES

positional externality occurs when an increase in one person's performance reduces the expected reward of another's in situations in which reward depends on relative performance

The steroid problem is an example of a **positional externality.** Whenever the pay-offs to one contestant depend at least in part on how he or she performs relative to a rival, any step that improves one side's relative position must necessarily worsen the other's. The standing-at-concerts example discussed in Chapter 10 (Economic Naturalist 10.3) is another instance of a positional externality. Just as the invisible hand of the market is weakened by the presence of standard externalities, it is also weakened by positional externalities.

"I don't know why McGillicuddy is so pleased with himself. We're <u>all</u> wee, darlin' men here."

Here is another example of a positional externality.

Why do many grocery stores stay open all night, even in small towns?

Ithaca, New York, has seven large supermarkets, five of which are open 24 hours a day. The convenience of all-night shopping could be maintained at lower cost if all but one of the stores were to close during late-night hours. Why do many remain open?

Most people do the bulk of their shopping at a single store. If other relevant factors—price, location, merchandise quality, and so on—are essentially the same, people will choose the store with the most convenient hours. Suppose the two leading stores, Tops and Wegmans, currently close at midnight and are considering whether to stay open until 1 A.M. If one does so and the other doesn't, the store that is open longer will capture the lion's share of all business, not just from midnight to 1 A.M. but during other hours as well, because most people will do most of their shopping at the store with the most attractive offering. But suppose the benefit the public receives when each store stays open an extra hour—as measured by the higher prices people will pay—is smaller than the cost to both stores of staying open the extra hour. Each store will then face a payoff matrix like the one shown in Table 11.7.

TABLE 11.7
Payoff Matrix for Extended Shopping Hours

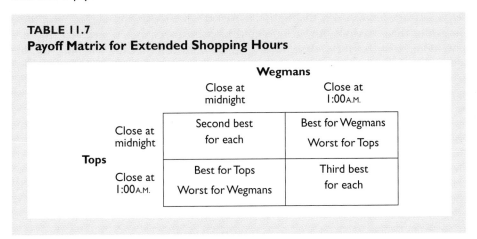

		Wegmans	
		Close at midnight	Close at 1:00 A.M.
Tops	Close at midnight	Second best for each	Best for Wegmans Worst for Tops
	Close at 1:00 A.M.	Best for Tops Worst for Wegmans	Third best for each

In this situation, the dominant strategy for each store is to remain open an extra hour, even though each would be better off if both closed at midnight. And of course, the rivalry does not stop there, for if both stay open until 1 A.M., each will see an opportunity to better its rival by staying open until 2. As long as the cost of staying open another hour is small relative to the gains received, all stores will stay open 24 hours a day. But though consumers do gain when stores remain open longer, beyond some point, the benefit to consumers is small relative to the costs borne by merchants. The problem is that for any individual merchant who fails to match a rival's hours, the costs will be even larger.

In such situations, the public might be well served by an amendment to the antitrust laws that permits stores to cooperate to limit their hours, perhaps through an agreement calling for each store to serve in rotation as the only all-night grocery. Local statutes that limit business hours might serve the same purpose. Such statutes, often called *blue laws,* remain on the books in many jurisdictions.

We have seen that positional externalities often lead contestants to engage in an escalating series of mutually offsetting investments in performance enhancement. We call such spending patterns **positional arms races.**

POSITIONAL ARMS CONTROL AGREEMENTS

Because positional arms races produce inefficient outcomes, people have an incentive to curtail them. Steps taken to reduce positional arms races, such as blue laws and rules against anabolic steroids, may therefore be thought of as **positional arms control agreements.**

Once you become aware of positional arms races, you will begin to see examples of them almost everywhere. You can hone your skills as an economic naturalist by asking these questions about every competitive situation you observe: What form do the investments in performance enhancement take? What steps have contestants taken to limit these investments? Sometimes positional arms control agreements are achieved by the imposition of formal rules, or by the signing of legal contracts. Some examples of this type of agreement follow.

Campaign spending limits In the United States, presidential candidates routinely spend more than $100 million on advertising. Yet if both candidates double their spending on ads, each one's odds of winning will remain essentially the

positional arms race a series of mutually offsetting investments in performance enhancement that is stimulated by a positional externality

positional arms control agreement an agreement in which contestants attempt to limit mutually offsetting investments in performance enhancement

same. Recognition of this pattern led Congress to adopt strict spending limits for presidential candidates. (That those regulations have proved difficult to enforce does not call into question the logic behind the legislation.)

Roster limits   Major League Baseball permits franchises to have only 25 players on the roster during the regular season. The National Football League sets its roster limit at 49; the National Basketball Association at 12. Why these limits? In their absence, any team could increase its chance of winning by simply adding players. Inevitably, other teams would follow suit. On the plausible assumption that, beyond some point, larger rosters do not add much to the entertainment value for fans, roster limits are a sensible way to deliver sports entertainment at a more reasonable cost.

Arbitration agreements   In the business world, contracting parties often sign a binding agreement that commits them to arbitration in the event of a dispute. By doing so, they sacrifice the option of pursuing their interests as fully as they might wish to later, but they also insulate themselves from costly legal battles. Other parties in the legal system may sometimes take steps to limit spending on litigation. For example, a federal judge in South Dakota recently announced—presumably to the approval of litigants—that he would read only the first 15 pages of any brief submitted to his court.

Mandatory starting dates for kindergarten   A child who is a year or so older than most of her kindergarten classmates is likely to perform better, in relative terms, than if she had entered school with children her own age. And since most parents are aware that admission to prestigious universities and eligibility for top jobs upon graduation depend largely on *relative* academic performance, many are tempted to keep their children out of kindergarten a year longer than necessary. Yet there is no social advantage in holding *all* children back an extra year, since their relative performance would essentially be unaffected. In most jurisdictions, therefore, the law requires children who reach their fifth birthday before December 1 of a given year to start kindergarten the same year.

SOCIAL NORMS AS POSITIONAL ARMS CONTROL AGREEMENTS

In some cases, social norms may take the place of formal agreements to curtail positional arms races. Some familiar examples follow.

Nerd norms   Some students care more—in the short run, at least—about the grades they get than how much they actually learn. When such students are graded on the curve—that is, on the basis of their performance relative to other students—a positional arms race ensues, because if all students were to double the amount of time they studied, the distribution of grades would remain essentially the same. Students who find themselves in this situation are often quick to embrace "nerd norms," which brand as social misfits those who "study too hard."

Fashion norms   Social norms regarding dress and fashion often change quickly because of positional competitions. Consider, for instance, the person who wishes to be on the cutting edge of fashion. In some American social circles during the 1950s, that goal could be accomplished by having pierced ears. But as more and more people adopted the practice, it ceased to communicate avant-garde status. At the same time, those who wanted to make a conservative fashion statement gradually became freer to have their ears pierced.

For a period during the 1960s and 1970s, one could be on fashion's cutting edge by wearing two earrings in one earlobe. But by the 1990s multiple ear piercings had lost much of their social significance, the threshold of cutting-edge status having been raised to upward of a dozen piercings of each ear, or a smaller number of piercings of the nose, eyebrows, or other body parts. A similar escalation has taken place in the number, size, and placement of tattoos.

The increase in the required number of tattoos or body piercings has not changed the value of avant-garde fashion status to those who desire it. Being on the outer limits of fashion has much the same meaning now as it once did. So to the extent that there are costs associated with body piercings, tattoos, and other steps required to achieve avant-garde status, the current fashions are wasteful compared to earlier ones. In this sense, the erosion of social norms against tattoos and body piercings has produced a social loss. Of course, the costs associated with this loss are small in most cases. Yet since each body piercing entails a small risk of infection, the costs will continue to rise with the number of piercings. And once those costs reach a certain threshold, support may mobilize on behalf of social norms that discourage body mutilation.

Norms of taste Similar cycles occur with respect to behaviors considered to be in bad taste. In the 1950s, for example, prevailing norms prevented major national magazines from accepting ads that featured nude photographs. Naturally, advertisers had a powerful incentive to chip away at such norms in an effort to capture the reader's limited attention. And indeed, taboos against nude photographs have eroded in the same way as taboos against body mutilation.

Consider, for instance, the evolution of perfume ads. First came the nude silhouette; then, increasingly well-lighted and detailed nude photographs; and more recently, photographs of what appear to be group sex acts. Each innovation achieved just the desired effect: capturing the reader's instant and rapt attention. Inevitably, however, other advertisers followed suit, causing a shift in our sense of what is considered attention-grabbing. Photographs that once would have shocked readers now often draw little more than a bored glance.

Is being on fashion's cutting edge more valuable now than in the 1950s?

"We're looking for the kind of bad taste that will grab—but not appall."

Opinions differ, of course, about whether this change is an improvement. Many believe that the earlier, stricter norms were ill-advised, the legacy of a more prudish and repressive era. Yet even people who take that view are likely to believe that *some* kinds of photographic material ought not to be used in magazine advertisements. Obviously, what is acceptable will differ from person to person, and each person's threshold of discomfort will depend in part on current standards. But as advertisers continue to break new ground in their struggle to capture attention, the point may come when people begin to mobilize in favor of stricter standards of "public decency." Such a campaign would provide yet another example of a positional arms control agreement.

Norms against vanity Cosmetic and reconstructive surgery has produced dramatic benefits for many people, enabling badly disfigured accident victims to recover a normal appearance. It has also eliminated the extreme self-consciousness felt by people born with strikingly unusual features. Such surgery, however, is by no means confined to the conspicuously disfigured. Increasingly, "normal" people are seeking surgical improvements to their appearance. Some 2 million cosmetic "procedures" were done in 1991—six times the number just a decade earlier[1]—and demand has continued to grow steadily in the years since. Once a carefully guarded secret, these procedures are now offered as prizes in southern California charity raffles. And morticians have begun to complain that the noncombustible silicon implants used in breast and buttocks augmentation are clogging their crematoria.

In individual cases, cosmetic surgery may be just as beneficial as reconstructive surgery is for accident victims. Buoyed by the confidence of having a straight nose or a wrinkle-free complexion, patients sometimes go on to achieve much more than they ever thought possible. But the growing use of cosmetic surgery has also had an unintended side effect: It has altered the standards of normal appearance. A nose that once would have seemed only slightly larger than average may now seem jarringly big. The same person who once would have looked like an average 55-year-old may now look nearly 70. And someone who once would have tolerated slightly thinning hair or an average amount of cellulite may now feel compelled to undergo hair transplantation or liposuction. Because such procedures shift people's frame of reference, their payoffs to individuals are misleadingly large. From a social perspective, therefore, reliance on them is likely to be excessive.

Legal sanctions against cosmetic surgery are difficult to imagine. But some communities have embraced powerful social norms against cosmetic surgery, heaping scorn and ridicule on the consumers of face-lifts and tummy tucks. In individual cases, such norms may seem cruel. Yet without them, many more people might feel compelled to bear the risk and expense of cosmetic surgery.

■ SUMMARY ■

- Externalities are the costs and benefits of activities that accrue to people who are not directly involved in those activities. When all parties affected by externalities can negotiate with one another at no cost, the invisible hand of the market will produce an efficient allocation of resources. According to the Coase theorem, the allocation of resources is efficient in such cases because the parties affected by externalities can compensate others for taking remedial action.

- Negotiation over externalities is often impractical, however. In these cases, the self-serving actions of individuals typically will not lead to an efficient outcome. The attempt to forge solutions to the problems caused by externalities is one of the most important rationales for collective action. Sometimes collective action takes the form of laws and government regulations that alter the incentives facing those who generate, or are affected by, externalities. Such remedies work best when they place the burden of accommodation on the

[1]*The Economist*, January 11, 1992, p. 25.

parties who can accomplish it at the lowest cost. Traffic laws, zoning laws, environmental protection laws, and free speech laws are examples.

- Curbing pollution and other negative externalities entails costs as well as benefits. The optimal amount of pollution reduction is the amount for which the marginal benefit of further reduction just equals the marginal cost. In general, this formula implies that the socially optimal level of pollution, or of any other negative externality, is greater than zero.

- When grazing land and other valuable resources are owned in common, no one has an incentive to take the opportunity cost of using those resources into account. This problem is known as the tragedy of the commons. Defining and enforcing of private rights governing the use of valuable resources is often an effective solution to the tragedy of the commons. Not surprisingly, most economically successful nations have well-developed institutions of private property. Property that belongs to everyone belongs, in effect, to no one. Not only is its potential economic value never fully realized; it usually ends up having no value at all.

- The difficulty of enforcing property rights in certain situations explains a variety of inefficient outcomes, such as the excessive harvest of whales in international waters and the premature harvest of timber on remote public lands. The excessive pollution of seas that are bordered by many countries also results from a lack of enforceable property rights.

- Situations in which people's rewards depend on how well they perform in relation to their rivals give rise to positional externalities. In these situations, any step that improves one side's relative position necessarily worsens the other's. Positional externalities tend to spawn positional arms races—escalating patterns of mutually offsetting investments in performance enhancement. Collective measures to curb positional arms races are known as positional arms control agreements. These collective actions may take the form of formal regulations or rules, such as rules against anabolic steroids in sports, campaign spending limits, and binding arbitration agreements. Informal social norms can also curtail positional arms races.

▪ KEY TERMS ▪

Coase theorem (277)
external benefit (273)
external cost (273)
externality (273)

negative externality (274)
positional arms control agreement (289)
positional arms race (289)

positional externality (288)
positive externality (274)
tragedy of the commons (284)

▪ REVIEW QUESTIONS ▪

1. What incentive problem explains why the freeways in cities like Los Angeles suffer from excessive congestion?

2. How would you explain to a friend why the optimal amount of freeway congestion is not zero?

3. If Congress could declare any activity that imposes external costs on others illegal, would such legislation be advisable?

4. Why does the Great Salt Lake, which is located wholly within the state of Utah, suffer lower levels of pollution than Lake Erie, which is bordered by several states and Canada?

5. Explain why the wearing of high-heeled shoes might be viewed as the result of a positional externality.

▪ PROBLEMS ▪

1. Determine whether the following statements are true or false, and briefly explain why:
   a. A given total emission reduction in a polluting industry will be achieved at the lowest possible total cost when the cost of the last unit of pollution curbed is equal for each firm in the industry.
   b. In an attempt to lower their costs of production, firms sometimes succeed merely in shifting costs to outsiders.

2. Phoebe keeps a bee farm next door to an apple orchard. She chooses her optimal number of beehives by selecting the honey output level at which her private marginal benefit from beekeeping equals her private marginal cost.
   a. Assume that Phoebe's private marginal benefit and marginal cost curves from beekeeping are normally shaped. Draw a diagram of them.

  b. Phoebe's bees help to pollinate the blossoms in the apple orchard, increasing the fruit yield. Show the social marginal benefit from Phoebe's beekeeping in your diagram.
  c. Phoebe's bees are Africanized killer bees that aggressively sting anyone who steps into their flight path. Phoebe, fortunately, is naturally immune to the bees' venom. Show the social marginal cost curve from Phoebe's beekeeping in your diagram.
  d. Indicate the socially optimal quantity of beehives on your diagram. Is it higher or lower than the privately optimal quantity? Explain.

3. Suppose the supply curve of boom box rentals in Golden Gate Park is given by $P = 5 + 0.1Q$, where P is the daily rent per unit in dollars and Q is the volume of units rented in hundreds per day. The demand curve for boom boxes is $20 - 0.2Q$. If each boom box imposes $3/day in noise costs on others, by how much will the equilibrium number of boom boxes rented exceed the socially optimal number?

4. Refer to Problem 3. How would the imposition of a tax of $3/unit on each daily boom box rental affect efficiency in this market?

5. Suppose the law says that Jones may *not* emit smoke from his factory unless he gets permission from Smith, who lives downwind. If the relevant costs and benefits of filtering the smoke from Jones's production process are as shown in the following table, and if Jones and Smith can negotiate with one another at no cost, will Jones emit smoke?

	Jones emits smoke	Jones does not emit smoke
Surplus for Jones	$200	$160
Surplus for Smith	400	420

6. John and Karl can live together in a two-bedroom apartment for $500/month, or each can rent a single-bedroom apartment for $350/month. Aside from the rent, the two would be indifferent between living together and living separately, except for one problem: John leaves dirty dishes in the sink every night. Karl would be willing to pay up to $175/month to avoid John's dirty dishes. John, for his part, would be willing to pay up to $225 to be able to continue his sloppiness. Should John and Karl live together? If they do, will there be dirty dishes in the sink? Explain.

7. How, if at all, would your answer to Problem 6 differ if John would be willing to pay up to $30/month to avoid giving up his privacy by sharing quarters with Karl?

8. Barton and Statler are neighbors in an apartment complex in downtown Manhattan. Barton is a concert pianist, and Statler is a poet working on an epic poem. Barton rehearses his concert pieces on the baby grand piano in his front room, which is directly above Statler's study. The following matrix shows the monthly payoffs to Barton and Statler when Barton's front room is and is not soundproofed. The soundproofing will be effective only if it is installed in Barton's apartment.

	Soundproofed	Not soundproofed
Gains to Barton	$100/month	$150/month
Gains to Statler	$120/month	$ 80/month

  a. If Barton has the legal right to make any amount of noise he wants and he and Statler can negotiate with one another at no cost, will Barton install and maintain soundproofing? Explain. Is his choice socially efficient?

b. If Statler has the legal right to peace and quiet and can negotiate with Barton at no cost, will Barton install and maintain soundproofing? Explain. Is his choice socially efficient?

c. Does the attainment of an efficient outcome depend on whether Barton has the legal right to make noise, or Statler the legal right to peace and quiet?

9. Refer to Problem 8. Barton decides to buy a full-sized grand piano. The new payoff matrix is as follows:

	Soundproofed	Not soundproofed
Gains to Barton	$100/month	$150/month
Gains to Statler	$120/month	$ 60/month

a. If Statler has the legal right to peace and quiet and Barton and Statler can negotiate at no cost, will Barton install and maintain soundproofing? Explain. Is this outcome socially efficient?

b. Suppose that Barton has the legal right to make as much noise as he likes and that negotiating an agreement with Barton costs $15/month. Will Barton install and maintain soundproofing? Explain. Is this outcome socially efficient?

c. Suppose Statler has the legal right to peace and quiet, and it costs $15/month for Statler and Barton to negotiate any agreement. (Compensation for noise damage can be paid without incurring negotiation cost.) Will Barton install and maintain soundproofing? Is this outcome socially efficient?

d. Why does the attainment of a socially efficient outcome now depend on whether Barton has the legal right to make noise?

10. A village has six residents, each of whom has accumulated savings of $100. Each villager can use this money either to buy a government bond that pays 15 percent interest per year or to buy a year-old llama, send it onto the commons to graze, and sell it after 1 year. The price the villager gets for the 2-year-old llama depends on the quality of the fleece it grows while grazing on the commons. That in turn depends on the animal's access to grazing, which depends on the number of llamas sent to the commons, as shown in the following table:

Number of llamas on the commons	Price per 2-year-old llama ($)
1	122
2	118
3	116
4	114
5	112
6	109

The villagers make their investment decisions one after another, and their decisions are public.

a. If each villager decides individually how to invest, how many llamas will be sent onto the commons, and what will be the resulting net village income?

b. What is the socially optimal number of llamas for this village? Why is that different from the actual number? What would net village income be if the socially optimal number of llamas were sent onto the commons?

c. The village committee votes to auction the right to graze llamas on the commons to the highest bidder. Assuming villagers can both borrow and lend at 15 percent annual interest, how much will the right sell for at auction? How will the new owner use the right, and what will be the resulting village income?

■ ANSWERS TO IN-CHAPTER EXERCISES ■

11.1 Since Fitch gains $50/day when Abercrombie operates with a filter, he could pay Abercrombie as much as $49/day and still come out ahead.

11.2 If the two were to live together, the most efficient way to resolve the telephone problem would be as before, for Betty to give up reasonable access to the phone. But on top of that cost, which is $150, Betty would also bear a $60 cost from the loss of her privacy. The total cost of their living together would thus be $210/month. Since that amount is greater than the $200 saving in rent, the two should live separately.

11.3 The income figures from the different levels of investment in cattle would remain as before, as shown in the table. What is different is the opportunity cost of investing in each steer, which is now $11/year instead of $13. The last column of the table shows that the socially optimal number of steers is now 2 instead of 1. And if individuals still favor holding cattle, all other things being equal, they will now send 5 steers onto the commons instead of 4, as shown in the middle column.

Number of steers on the commons	Price per 2-year-old steer ($)	Income per steer ($/year)	Total village income ($/year)	Marginal income ($/year)
				26
1	126	26	26	
				12
2	119	19	38	
				10
3	116	16	48	
				4
4	113	13	52	
				3
5	111	11	55	

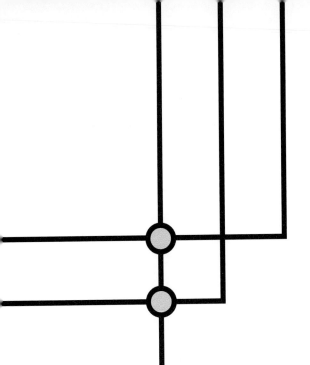

THE ECONOMICS OF INFORMATION

∎

Years ago, a naive young economist spent a week in Kashmir on a houseboat on scenic Dal Lake, outside the capital city of Srinigar. Kashmir is renowned for its woodcarvings, and one afternoon a man in a gondola stopped by to show the economist some of his wooden bowls. When the economist expressed interest in one of them, the woodcarver quoted a price of 200 rupees. The economist had lived in that part of Asia long enough to realize that the price was more than the woodcarver expected to get, so he made a counteroffer of 100 rupees.

The woodcarver appeared to take offense, saying that he couldn't possibly part with the bowl for less than 175 rupees. Suspecting that the woodcarver was merely feigning anger, the young economist held firm. The woodcarver appeared to become even angrier, but quickly retreated to 150 rupees. The economist politely restated his unwillingness to pay more than 100 rupees. The woodcarver then tried 125 rupees, and again the economist replied that 100 was his final offer. Finally, they struck a deal at 100 rupees, and with cash in hand, the woodcarver left in a huff.

Pleased with his purchase, the economist showed it to the houseboat's owner later that evening. "It's a lovely bowl," he agreed, and asked how much the economist had paid for it. The economist told him, expecting praise for his negotiating prowess. The host's failed attempt at suppressing a giggle was the economist's first clue that he had paid too much. When asked how much such a bowl would normally sell for, the houseboat owner was reluctant to respond. But the economist pressed him, and the host speculated that the seller had probably hoped for 30 rupees at most.

Adam Smith's invisible hand theory presumes that buyers are fully informed about the myriad ways in which they might spend their money—what goods and services are available, what prices they sell for, how long they last, how frequently they break down, and so on. But of course no one is ever really *fully* informed about anything. And sometimes, as in the transaction with the woodcarver, people are completely ignorant of even the most basic information. Still, life goes on, and most people muddle through somehow.

Consumers employ a variety of strategies for gathering information, some of which are better than others. They read *Consumer Reports,* talk to family and friends, visit stores, kick the tires on used cars, and so on. But one of the most important aspects of choosing intelligently without having complete information is having at least some idea of the extent of one's ignorance. Someone once said that there are two kinds of consumers in the world: those who don't know what they're doing and those who don't know that they don't know what they're doing. As in the case of the wooden bowl, the people in the second category are the ones who are most likely to choose foolishly.

Basic economic principles can help you in identifying those situations in which additional information is most likely to prove helpful. In this chapter, we will explore what those principles tell us about how much information to acquire and how to make the best use of limited information.

HOW THE MIDDLEMAN ADDS VALUE

One of the most common problems consumers confront is the need to choose among different versions of a product whose many complex features they do not fully understand. As Example 12.1 illustrates, in such cases consumers can sometimes rely on the knowledge of others.

EXAMPLE 12.1

How should a consumer decide which pair of skis to buy?

You need a new pair of skis, but the technology has changed considerably since you bought your last pair, and you don't know which of the current brands and models would be best for you. Skis R Us has the largest selection, so you go there and ask for advice. The salesperson appears to be well informed; after asking about your experience level and how aggressively you ski, he recommends the Salomon X-Scream 9. You buy a pair for $600, then head back to your apartment and show them to your roommate, who says that you could have bought them on the Internet for only $400. How do you feel about your purchase? Are the different prices charged by the two suppliers related to the services they offer? Were the extra services you got by shopping at Skis R Us worth the extra $200?

Internet retailers can sell for less because their costs are so much lower than those of full-service retail stores. Those stores, after all, must hire knowledgeable salespeople, put their merchandise on display, rent space in expensive shopping malls, and so on. Internet retailers and mail-order houses, by contrast, typically employ unskilled telephone clerks, and they store their merchandise in cheap warehouses. But if you are a consumer who doesn't know which is the right product for you, the extra expense of shopping at a specialty retailer is likely to be a good investment. Spending $600 on the right skis is smarter than spending $400 on the wrong ones.

Many people believe that wholesalers, retailers, and other agents who assist manufacturers in the sale of their products play a fundamentally different economic role from the one played by those who actually make the products. In this view, the production worker is the ultimate source of economic value added. Sales agents are often disparaged as mere middlemen, parasites on the efforts of others who do the real work.

"On the one hand, eliminating the middleman would result in lower costs, increased sales, and greater consumer satisfaction; on the other hand, we're the middleman."

On a superficial level, this view might seem to be supported by the fact that many people will go to great lengths to avoid paying for the services of sales agents. Many manufacturers cater to them by offering consumers a chance to "buy direct" and sidestep the middleman's commission. But on closer examination, we can see that the economic role of sales agents is essentially the same as that of production workers. Consider Example 12.2.

How does better information affect economic surplus?

Ellis has just inherited a rare Babe Ruth baseball card issued during the great slugger's rookie year. He'd like to keep the card but has reluctantly decided to sell it to pay some overdue bills. His reservation price for the card is $300, but he is hoping to get significantly more for it. He has two ways of selling it: He can place a classified ad in the local newspaper for $5, or he can list the card on eBay, the Internet auction service. If he sells the card on eBay, the fee will be 5 percent of the winning bid.

Because Ellis lives in a small town with few potential buyers of rare baseball cards, the local buyer with the highest reservation price is willing to pay $400 at most. If Ellis lists the card on eBay, however, a much larger number of potential buyers will see it. If the two eBay shoppers who are willing to pay the most for Ellis's card have reservation prices of $900 and $800, respectively, by how much will the total economic surplus be larger if Ellis sells his card on eBay? (For the sake of simplicity, assume that the eBay commission and the classified ad fee equal the respective costs of providing those services.)

In an eBay auction, each bidder reports his or her reservation price for an item. When the auction closes, the bidder with the highest reservation price wins, and the price he or she pays is the reservation price of the second highest bidder. So in this example, the Babe Ruth baseball card will sell for $800 if Ellis lists it on eBay. Net of the $40 eBay commission, Ellis will receive a payment of $760, or $460 more than his reservation price for the card. Ellis's economic surplus will thus be $460. The winning bidder's surplus will be $900 − $800 = $100, so the total surplus from selling the card on eBay will be $560.

If Ellis instead advertises the card in the local newspaper and sells it to the local buyer whose reservation price is $400, then Ellis's surplus (net of the newspaper's $5 fee) will be only $95, and the buyer's surplus will be $0. Thus total economic surplus will be $560 − $95 = $465 larger if Ellis sells the card on eBay than if he lists it in the local newspaper.

eBay provides a service by making information available to people who can make good use of it. A real increase in economic surplus results when an item ends up in the hands of someone who values it more highly than the person who otherwise would have bought it. That increase is just as valuable as the increase in surplus that results from manufacturing cars, growing corn, or any other productive activity.

> **RECAP**   **HOW THE MIDDLEMAN ADDS VALUE**
>
> In a world of incomplete information, sales agents and other middlemen add genuine economic value by increasing the extent to which goods and services find their way to the consumers who value them most. When a sales agent causes a good to be purchased by a person who values it by $20,000 more than the person who would have bought it in the absence of a sales agent, that agent augments total economic surplus by $20,000, an achievement on a par with the production of a $20,000 car.

THE OPTIMAL AMOUNT OF INFORMATION

Without a doubt, having more information is better than having less. But information is generally costly to acquire. In most situations, the value of additional information will decline beyond some point. And because of the low-hanging-fruit principle, people tend to gather information from the cheapest sources first before turning to more costly ones. Typically, then, the marginal benefit of information will decline, and its marginal cost will rise, as the amount of information gathered increases.

THE COST-BENEFIT TEST

Information gathering is an activity like any other. The cost-benefit principle tells us that a rational consumer will continue to gather information as long as its marginal benefit exceeds its marginal cost. If the relevant marginal cost and marginal benefit curves are as shown in Figure 12.1, a rational consumer will acquire I^* units of information, the amount for which the marginal benefit of information equals its marginal cost.

Another way to think about Figure 12.1 is that it shows the optimal level of ignorance. When the cost of acquiring information exceeds its benefits, acquiring additional information simply does not pay. If information could be acquired free,

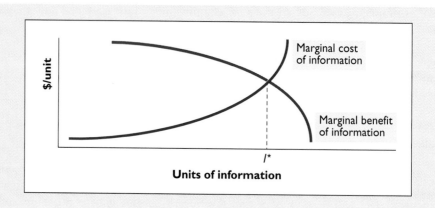

FIGURE 12.1
The Optimal Amount of Information.
For the marginal cost and benefit curves shown, the optimal amount of information is I^*. Beyond that point, information costs more to acquire than it is worth.

decision makers would, of course, be glad to have it. But when the cost of acquiring the information exceeds the gain in value from the decision it will facilitate, people are better off to remain ignorant.

THE FREE-RIDER PROBLEM

Does the invisible hand assure that the optimal amount of advice will be made available to consumers in the marketplace? The next example suggests one reason that it might not.

Why is finding a knowledgeable salesclerk often difficult?

People can choose for themselves whether to bear the extra cost of retail shopping. Those who value advice and convenience can pay slightly higher prices, while those who know what they want can buy for less from a mail-order house. True or false: It follows that private incentives lead to the optimal amount of retail service.

The market would provide the optimal level of retail service except for one practical problem, namely, that consumers can make use of the services offered by retail stores without paying for them. After benefiting from the advice of informed salespersons and after inspecting the merchandise, the consumer can return home and buy the same item from an Internet retailer or mail-order house. Not all consumers do so, of course. But the fact that customers can benefit from the information provided by retail stores without paying for it is an example of the **free-rider problem,** an incentive problem that results in *too little of a good or service being produced.* Because retail stores have difficulty recovering the cost of providing information, private incentives are likely to yield less than the socially optimal level of retail service. So the statement above is false.

ECONOMIC NATURALIST 12.1

free-rider problem an incentive problem in which too little of a good or service is produced because nonpayers cannot be excluded from using it

Why did Rivergate Books, the last bookstore in Lambertville, New Jersey, recently go out of business?

Small independent bookstores often manage to survive competition from large chains like Borders and Barnes and Noble by offering more personalized service. Janet Holbrooke, the proprietor of Rivergate Books, followed this strategy successfully for more than a decade before closing her doors in 1999. What finally led her to quit?

According to Mrs. Holbrooke, a retired English teacher, "When Barnes and Noble came in, a few people were curious, went to look, and bought some books. But they came back and said they wanted to be able to find things more easily and have clerks that had an idea of what their grandchildren might like to read, and we held our own."[1] Customers were also drawn in by special events, such as readings and book signings by authors. But during one of these events, Mrs. Holbrooke saw that her store's days were numbered:

ECONOMIC NATURALIST 12.2

> I found out that Gerald Stern, who won the National Book Award for poetry, was a Lambertville man, and I asked him if he would come in and do a reading. He gave a wonderful presentation, and we had a good turnout, but we sold very few books, and then I overheard one of the women who were presenting a book for his signature say that she had bought hers through Amazon.com. Here I thought we were bringing something special to the town. But if people are going to bring in books that they got from the Internet, then we don't have a chance."[2]

[1]Quoted by Iver Peterson, "A Bookseller Quits Battle With Internet," *The New York Times,* June 27, 1999, p. 21.
[2]Ibid.

"In reply to your inquiry regarding the Burke garden hoe, please visit our Worldwide Web home page at: http://www.burke1903.com."

EXERCISE 12.1

Apart from its possible contribution to free-rider problems, how is increased access to the Internet likely to affect total economic surplus?

TWO GUIDELINES FOR RATIONAL SEARCH

In practice, of course, the exact value of additional information is difficult to know, so the amount of time and effort one should invest in acquiring it is not always obvious. But as Examples 12.3 and 12.4 suggest, the cost-benefit principle provides a strong conceptual framework for thinking about this problem.

EXAMPLE 12.3   **Should a person living in Paris, Texas, spend more or less time searching for an apartment than someone living in Paris, France?**

Suppose that rents for one-bedroom apartments in Paris, Texas, vary between $300 and $500/month, with an average rent of $400/month. Rents for similar one-bedroom apartments in Paris, France, vary between $2,000 and $3,000/month, with an average rent of $2,500. In which city should a rational person expect to spend a longer time searching for an apartment?

In both cities, visiting additional apartments entails a cost, largely, the opportunity cost of one's time. In both cities, the more apartments someone visits, the more likely it is that he or she will find one near the lower end of the rent distribution. But because rents are higher and are spread over a broader range in Paris, France, the expected saving from further time spent searching will be greater there than in Paris, Texas. And so a rational person will expect to spend more time searching for an apartment in France.

Example 12.3 illustrates the principle that spending additional search time is more likely to be worthwhile for expensive items than for cheap ones. For example, one should spend more time searching for a good price on a diamond engagement ring than for a good price on a stone made of cubic zirconium; more time searching for a low fare to Sydney, Australia, than for a low fare to Sidney, New York; and more time searching for a car than for a bicycle. By extension, hiring an agent—someone who can assist with a search—is more likely to be a good investment in searching for something expensive than for something cheap. For example, people typically engage real estate agents to help them find a house, but they seldom hire agents to help them buy a gallon of milk.

Who should expect to search longer for a good price on a used piano?

EXAMPLE 12.4

Both Tom and Tim are shopping for a used upright piano. To examine a piano listed in the classified ads, they must travel to the home of the piano's current owner. If Tom has a car and Tim does not and both are rational, which one should expect to examine fewer pianos before making his purchase?

The benefits of examining an additional piano are the same in both cases, namely, a better chance of finding a good instrument for a low price. But because it is more costly for Tim to examine pianos, he should expect to examine fewer of them than Tom.

Example 12.4 makes the point that when searching becomes more costly, we should expect to do less of it. And as a result, the prices we expect to pay will be higher when the cost of a search is higher.

THE GAMBLE INHERENT IN SEARCH

Suppose you are in the market for a one-bedroom apartment and have found one that rents for $400 per month. Should you rent it or search further in hopes of finding a cheaper apartment? Even in a large market with many vacant apartments, there is no guarantee that searching further will turn up a cheaper or better apartment. Searching further entails a cost, which might outweigh the gain. In general, someone who engages in further search must accept certain costs in return for unknown benefits. Thus further search invariably carries an element of risk.

In thinking about whether to take any gamble, a helpful first step is to compute its **expected value**—the average amount you would win (or lose) if you played that gamble an infinite number of times. To calculate the expected value of a gamble with more than one outcome, we first multiply each outcome by its corresponding probability of occurring, and then add. For example, suppose you win $1 if a coin flip comes up heads and lose $1 if it comes up tails. Since 1/2 is the probability of heads (and also the probability of tails), the expected value of this gamble is $(1/2)(\$1) + (1/2)(-\$1) = 0$. A gamble with an expected value of zero is called a **fair gamble.** If you played this gamble a large number of times, you wouldn't expect to make money, but you also wouldn't expect to lose money.

A **better-than-fair gamble** is one with a positive expected value. (For example, a coin flip in which you win $2 for heads and lose $1 for tails is a better-than-fair gamble.) A **risk-neutral** person is someone who would accept any gamble that is fair or better. A **risk-averse** person is someone who would refuse to take any fair gamble.

expected value of a gamble the sum of the possible outcomes of the gamble multiplied by their respective probabilities

fair gamble a gamble whose expected value is zero

better-than-fair gamble one whose expected value is positive

risk-neutral person someone who would accept any gamble that is fair or better

risk-averse person someone who would refuse any fair gamble

EXERCISE 12.2

Consider a gamble in which you win $4 if you flip a coin and it comes up heads and lose $2 if it comes up tails. What is the expected value of this gamble? Would a risk-neutral person accept it?

In Example 12.5 we apply these concepts to the decision of whether to search further for an apartment.

EXAMPLE 12.5

Should you search further for an apartment?

You have arrived in San Francisco for a 1-month summer visit and are searching for a one-bedroom sublet for the month. There are only two kinds of one-bedroom apartments in the neighborhood in which you wish to live, identical in every respect except that one rents for $400 and the other for $360. Of the vacant apartments in this neighborhood, 80 percent are of the first type and 20 percent are of the second type. The only way you can discover the rent for a vacant apartment is to visit it in person. The first apartment you visit is one that rents for $400. If you are risk-neutral and your opportunity cost of visiting an additional apartment is $6, should you visit another apartment or rent the one you've found?

If you visit one more apartment, you have a 20 percent chance of it being one that rents for $360 and an 80 percent chance of it being one that rents for $400. If the former, you'll save $40 in rent, but if the latter, you'll face the same rent as before. Since the cost of a visit is $6, visiting another apartment is a gamble with a 20 percent chance to win $40 − $6 = $34 and an 80 percent chance of losing $6 (which means "winning" −$6). The expected value of this gamble is thus (0.20)($34) + (0.80)(−$6) = $2. Visiting another apartment is a better-than-fair gamble, and since you are risk-neutral, you should take it.

EXERCISE 12.3

Refer to Example 12.5. Suppose you visit another apartment and discover it is one that rents for $400. If you are risk-neutral, should you visit a third apartment?

THE COMMITMENT PROBLEM WHEN SEARCH IS COSTLY

When most people search for an apartment, they want a place to live not for just a month but for a year or more. Most landlords, for their part, are also looking for long-term tenants. Similarly, few people accept a full-time job in their chosen field unless they expect to hold the job for several years. Firms, too, generally prefer employees who will stay for extended periods. Finally, when most people search for mates, they are looking for someone with whom to settle down.

Because in all these cases search is costly, examining every possible option will never make sense. Apartment hunters don't visit every vacant apartment, nor do landlords interview every possible tenant. Job seekers don't visit every employer, nor do employers interview every job seeker. And not even the most determined searcher can manage to date every eligible mate. In these and other cases, people are rational to end their searches, even though they know a more attractive option surely exists out there somewhere.

But herein lies a difficulty. What happens when, by chance, a more attractive option comes along after the search has ceased? Few people would rent an apartment if they thought the landlord would kick them out the moment another tenant came along who was willing to pay higher rent. Few landlords would be willing to rent to a tenant if they expected her to move out the moment she discovers a cheaper apartment. Employers, job seekers, and people who are looking for mates would have similar reservations about entering relationships that could be terminated once a better option happened to come along.

This potential difficulty in maintaining stable matches between partners in ongoing relationships would not arise in a world of perfect information. In such a world, everyone would end up in the best possible relationship, so no one would be tempted to renege. But when information is costly and the search must be limited, there will always be the potential for existing relationships to dissolve.

In most contexts, people solve this problem not by conducting an exhaustive search (which is usually impossible, in any event) but by committing themselves to remain in a relationship once a mutual agreement has been reached to terminate the search. Thus landlords and tenants sign a lease that binds them to one another for a specified period, usually 1 year. Employees and firms enter into employment contracts, either formal or informal, under which each promises to honor his obligations to the other, except under extreme circumstances. And in most countries a marriage contract penalizes those who abandon their spouses. Entering into such commitments limits the freedom to pursue one's own interests. Yet most people freely accept such restrictions, because they know the alternative is failure to solve the search problem.

RECAP   **THE OPTIMAL AMOUNT OF INFORMATION**

Additional information creates value, but it is also costly to acquire. A rational consumer will continue to acquire information until its marginal benefit equals its marginal cost. Beyond that point, it is rational to remain uninformed.

Markets for information do not always function perfectly. Free-rider problems often hinder retailers' efforts to provide information to consumers.

Search inevitably entails an element of risk, because costs must be incurred without any assurance that search will prove fruitful. A rational consumer can minimize this risk by concentrating search efforts on goods for which the variation in price or quality is relatively high and on those for which the cost of search is relatively low.

ASYMMETRIC INFORMATION

One of the most common information problems occurs when the participants in a potential exchange are not equally well informed about the product or service that is offered for sale. For instance, the owner of a used car may know that the car is in excellent mechanical condition, but potential buyers cannot know that merely by inspecting it or taking it for a test drive. Economists use the term **asymmetric information** to describe situations in which buyers and sellers are not equally well informed about the characteristics of products or services. In these situations, sellers are typically much better informed than buyers, but sometimes the reverse will be true.

asymmetric information situations in which buyers and sellers are not equally well informed about the characteristics of goods and services for sale in the marketplace

As Example 12.6 illustrates, the problem of asymmetric information can easily prevent exchanges that would benefit both parties.

EXAMPLE 12.6

Will Jane sell her car to Tom?

Jane's 1995 Miata has 70,000 miles on the odometer, but most of these are highway miles driven during weekend trips to see her boyfriend in Toronto. (Highway driving causes less wear and tear on a car than city driving.) Moreover, Jane has maintained the car precisely according to the manufacturer's specifications. In short, she knows her car to be in excellent condition. Because she is about to start graduate school in Boston, however, Jane wants to sell the car. 1995 Miatas sell for an average price of $8,000, but because Jane knows her car to be in excellent condition, her reservation price for it is $10,000.

Tom wants to buy a used Miata. He would be willing to pay $13,000 for one that is in excellent condition but only $9,000 for one that is not in excellent condition. Tom has no way of telling whether Jane's Miata is in excellent condition. (He could hire a mechanic to examine the car, but doing so is expensive, and many problems cannot be detected even by a mechanic.) Will Tom buy Jane's car? Is this outcome efficient?

Because Jane's car looks no different from other 1995 Miatas, Tom will not pay $10,000 for it. After all, for only $8,000, he can buy some other 1995 Miata that is in just as good condition, as far as he can tell. Tom therefore will buy someone else's Miata, and Jane's will go unsold. This outcome is not efficient. If Tom had bought Jane's Miata for, say, $11,000, his surplus would have been $2,000 and Jane's another $1,000. Instead, Tom ends up buying a Miata that is in average condition (or worse), and his surplus is only $1,000. Jane gets no economic surplus at all.

THE LEMONS MODEL

We can't be sure, of course, that the Miata Tom ends up buying will be in worse condition than Jane's—since *someone* might have a car in perfect condition that must be sold even if the owner cannot get what it is really worth. Even so, the economic incentives created by asymmetric information suggest that most used cars that are put up for sale will be of lower-than-average quality. One reason is that people who mistreat their cars, or whose cars were never very good to begin with, are more likely than others to want to sell them. Buyers know from experience that cars for sale on the used car market are more likely to be "lemons" than cars that are not for sale. This realization causes them to lower their reservation prices for a used car.

But that's not the end of the story. Once used car prices have fallen, the owners of cars that are in good condition have an even stronger incentive to hold onto them. That causes the average quality of the cars offered for sale on the used car market to decline still further. Berkeley economist George Akerlof was the first to explain the logic behind this downward spiral.[3] Economists use the term **lemons model** to describe Akerlof's explanation of how asymmetric information affects the average quality of the used goods offered for sale.

As Example 12.7 suggests, the lemons model has important practical implications for consumer choice.

lemons model George Akerlof's explanation of how asymmetric information tends to reduce the average quality of goods offered for sale

EXAMPLE 12.7

Should you buy your aunt's car?

You want to buy a used Honda Accord. Your Aunt Germaine buys a new car every 4 years, and she has a 4-year-old Accord that she is about to trade in. You believe her report that the car is in good condition, and she is willing to sell it to you for $10,000, which is the current blue book value for 4-year-old Accords. (The blue book value of a car is the average price for which cars of that age and model sell in the used car market.) Should you buy your aunt's Honda?

Akerlof's lemons model tells us that cars for sale in the used car market will be of lower average quality than cars of the same vintage that are not for sale. If you believe your aunt's claim that her car is in good condition, then being able to buy it for its blue book value is definitely a good deal for you, since the blue book price is the equilibrium price for a car that is of lower quality than your aunt's.

Examples 12.8 and 12.9 illustrate the conditions under which asymmetric information about product quality results in a market in which *only* lemons are offered for sale.

[3]George Akerlof, "The Market for Lemons," *Quarterly Journal of Economics*, 84: 488–500, 1970.

What price will a used car fetch?

EXAMPLE 12.8

Consider a world with only two kinds of cars, good ones and lemons. An owner knows with certainty which type of car she has, but potential buyers cannot distinguish between the two types. Ten percent of all new cars produced are lemons. Good used cars are worth $10,000 to their owners, but lemons are worth only $6,000. Consider a naive consumer who believes that the used cars currently for sale have the same quality distribution as new cars (i.e., 90 percent good, 10 percent lemons). If this consumer is risk-neutral, how much would he be willing to pay for a used car?

Buying a car of unknown quality is a gamble, but a risk-neutral buyer would be willing to take the gamble provided it is fair. If the buyer can't tell the difference between a good car and a lemon, the probability that he will end up with a lemon is simply the proportion of lemons among the cars from which he chooses. The buyer believes he has a 90 percent chance of getting a good car and a 10 percent chance of getting a lemon. Given the prices he is willing to pay for the two types of car, his expected value of the car he buys will thus be $0.90(\$10,000) + 0.10(\$6,000) = \$9,600$. And since he is risk-neutral, that is his reservation price for a used car.

EXERCISE 12.4

How would your answer to the question posed in Example 12.8 differ if the proportion of new cars that are lemons had been not 10 percent but 20 percent?

Who will sell a used car for what the naive buyer is willing to pay?

EXAMPLE 12.9

Refer to Example 12.8. If you were the owner of a good used car, what would it be worth to you? Would you sell it to a naive buyer? What if you owned a lemon?

Since you know your car is good, it is worth $10,000 to you, by assumption. But since a naive buyer would be willing to pay only $9,600, neither you nor any other owner of a good car would be willing to sell to that buyer. If you had a lemon, of course, you would be happy to sell it to a naive buyer, since the $9,600 the buyer is willing to pay is $3,600 more than the lemon would be worth to you. So the only used cars for sale will be lemons. In time, buyers will revise their naively optimistic beliefs about the quality of the cars for sale on the used car market. In the end, all used cars will sell for a price of $6,000, and all will be lemons.

In practice, of course, the mere fact that a car is for sale does not guarantee that it is a lemon, because the owner of a good car will sometimes be forced to sell it, even at a price that does not reflect its condition. The logic of the lemons model explains this owner's frustration. The first thing sellers in this situation want a prospective buyer to know is the reason they are selling their cars. For example, classified ads often announce, "Just had a baby, must sell my 1999 Corvette" or "Transferred to Germany, must sell my 2000 Toyota Camry." Any time you pay the blue book price for a used car that is for sale for some reason unrelated to its condition, you are beating the market.

THE CREDIBILITY PROBLEM IN TRADING

Why can't someone with a high-quality used car simply *tell* the buyer about the car's condition? The difficulty is that buyers' and sellers' interests tend to conflict. Sellers of used cars, for example, have an economic incentive to overstate the quality of their products. Buyers, for their part, have an incentive to understate the

Why do new cars lose a significant fraction of their value as soon as they are driven from the showroom?

amount they are willing to pay for used cars and other products. Potential employees may be tempted to overstate their qualifications for a job. And people searching for mates have been known to engage in deception.

That is not to say that most people *consciously* misrepresent the truth in communicating with their potential trading partners. But people do tend to interpret ambiguous information in ways that promote their own interests. Thus, 92 percent of factory employees surveyed in one study rated themselves as more productive than the average factory worker. Psychologists call this phenomenon the "Lake Wobegon effect," after Garrison Keillor's mythical Minnesota homestead, where "all the children are above average."

Notwithstanding the natural tendency to exaggerate, the parties to a potential exchange can often gain if they can find some means to communicate their knowledge truthfully. In general, however, mere statements of relevant information will not suffice. People have long since learned to discount the used car salesman's inflated claims about the cars he is trying to unload. But as the next examples illustrate, though communication between potential adversaries may be difficult, it is not impossible.

EXAMPLE 12.10

How can a used car seller signal high quality credibly?

Jane knows her Miata to be in excellent condition, and Tom would be willing to pay considerably more than her reservation price if he could be confident of getting such a car. What kind of signal about the car's quality would Tom find credible?

Again, the potential conflict between Tom's and Jane's interests suggests that mere statements about the car's quality may not be persuasive. But suppose Jane offers a warranty, under which she agrees to remedy any defects the car develops over the next 6 months. Jane can afford to extend such an offer because she knows her car is unlikely to need expensive repairs. In contrast, the person who knows his car has a cracked engine block would never extend such an offer. The warranty is a credible signal that the car is in good condition. It enables Tom to buy the car with confidence, to both his and Jane's benefit.

THE COSTLY-TO-FAKE PRINCIPLE

costly-to-fake principle to communicate information credibly to a potential rival, a signal must be costly or difficult to fake

The preceding examples illustrate the **costly-to-fake principle**, which holds that if parties whose interests potentially conflict are to communicate credibly with one another, the signals they send must be costly or difficult to fake. If the seller of a defective car could offer an extensive warranty just as easily as the seller of a good car, a warranty offer would communicate nothing about the car's quality. But warranties entail costs that are significantly higher for defective cars than for good cars—hence their credibility as a signal of product quality.

To the extent that sellers have an incentive to portray a product in the most flattering light possible, their interests conflict with those of buyers, who want the most accurate assessment of product quality possible. Note that in the following example, the costly-to-fake principle applies to a producer's statement about the quality of a product.

ECONOMIC NATURALIST 12.3

Why do firms insert the phrase "As advertised on TV" when they advertise their products in magazines and newspapers?

Company A sponsors an expensive national television advertising campaign on behalf of its compact disc player, claiming it has the clearest sound and the best repair record of any CD player in the market. Company B makes similar claims in a sales brochure but does not advertise its product on television. If you had no additional information to go on, which company's claim would you find more credible? Why do you suppose Company A mentions its TV ads when it advertises its CD player in print media?

Accustomed as we are to discounting advertisers' inflated claims, the information given might seem to provide no real basis for a choice between the two products. On closer examination, however, we see that a company's decision to advertise its product on national television constitutes a credible signal about the product's quality. The cost of a national television campaign can run well into the millions of dollars, a sum a company would be foolish to spend on an inferior product.

For example, in 1996 Pizza Hut spent some $50 million to launch a new cheese-stuffed TripleDecker pizza. In that year, a single 30-second TV spot on the *Seinfeld* show cost advertisers $450,000, and the same spot during the Super Bowl cost $1.3 million. National TV ads can attract the potential buyers' attention and persuade a small fraction of them to try a product. But these huge investments pay off only if the resulting initial sales generate other new business—either repeat sales to people who tried the product and liked it or sales to others who heard about the product from a friend.

Because ads cannot persuade buyers that a bad product is a good one, a company that spends millions of dollars advertising a bad product is wasting its money. An expensive national advertising campaign is therefore a credible signal that the producer *thinks* its product is a good one. Of course, the ads don't guarantee that a product *is* a winner, but in an uncertain world, they provide one more piece of information. Note, however, that the relevant information lies in the expenditure on the advertising campaign, not in what the ads themselves say.

These observations may explain why some companies mention their television ads in their print ads. Advertisers understand the costly-to-fake principle and hope that consumers will understand it as well.

As the next example illustrates, the costly-to-fake principle is also well known to many employers.

Why do many companies care so much about elite educational credentials?

Microsoft is looking for a hardworking, smart person for an entry-level managerial position in a new technical products division. Two candidates, Cooper and Duncan, seem alike in every respect but one: Cooper graduated with the highest honors from MIT, while Duncan graduated with a C+ average from Somerville College. Whom should Microsoft hire?

If you want to persuade prospective employers that you are both hardworking and intelligent, there is perhaps no more credible signal than to have graduated with distinction from a highly selective educational institution. Most people would like potential employers to think of them as hardworking and intelligent. But unless you actually have both those qualities, graduating with the highest honors from a school like MIT will be extremely difficult. The fact that Duncan graduated from a much less selective institution and earned only a C+ average is not proof positive that he is not diligent and talented, but companies are forced to play the percentages. In this case the odds strongly favor Cooper.

CONSPICUOUS CONSUMPTION AS A SIGNAL OF ABILITY

Some individuals of high ability are not highly paid. (Remember the best elementary school teacher you ever had.) And some people, such as the multibillionaire investor Warren Buffet, earn a lot, yet spend very little. But such cases run counter to general tendencies. In competitive markets, the people with the most ability tend to receive the highest salaries. And as suggested by the cost-benefit principle, the more someone earns, the more he or she is likely to spend on high-quality goods and services. As the following example suggests, these tendencies often lead us to infer a person's ability from the amount and quality of the goods he consumes.

Why do many clients seem to prefer lawyers who wear expensive suits?

You have been unjustly accused of a serious crime and are looking for an attorney. Your choice is between two lawyers who appear identical in all respects except for the things they buy. One of them wears a cheap polyester suit and arrives at the courthouse in a 10-year-old rust-eaten Dodge Colt. The other wears an impeccably tailored suit and drives a new BMW 740i. If this were the *only* information available to you at the time you chose, which lawyer would you hire?

The correlation between salary and the abilities buyers value most is particularly strong in the legal profession. A lawyer whose clients usually prevail in court will be much more in demand than one whose clients generally lose, and their fees will reflect the difference. The fact that one of the lawyers consumes much more than the other does not *prove* that he is the better lawyer, but if that is the only information you have, you can ill afford to ignore it.

If the less able lawyer loses business because of the suits he wears and the car he drives, why doesn't he simply buy better suits and a more expensive car? His choice is between saving for retirement or spending more on his car and clothing. In one sense, he cannot afford to buy a more expensive car, but in another sense, he cannot afford *not* to. If his current car is discouraging potential clients from hiring him, buying a better one may simply be a prudent investment. But because *all* lawyers have an incentive to make such investments, their effects tend to be mutually offsetting.

When all is said and done, the things people consume will continue to convey relevant information about their respective ability levels. The costly-to-fake principle tells us that the BMW 740i is an effective signal precisely because the lawyer of low ability cannot afford one, no matter how little he saves for retirement. Yet from a social perspective, the resulting spending pattern is inefficient, for the same reason that other positional arms races are inefficient (see Chapter 11). Society would be better off if everyone spent less and saved more for retirement.

The problem of conspicuous consumption as an ability signal does not arise with equal force in every environment. In small towns, where people tend to know one another well, a lawyer who tries to impress people by spending beyond her means is likely to succeed only in demonstrating how foolish she is. Thus the wardrobe a professional person "needs" in towns like Dubuque, Iowa, or Athens, Ohio, costs less than half as much as the wardrobe the same person would need in Manhattan or Los Angeles.

STATISTICAL DISCRIMINATION

In a competitive market with perfect information, the buyer of a service would pay the seller's cost of providing the service. In many markets, however—the market for fire insurance is one example—the seller does not know the exact cost of serving each individual buyer.

In such cases, the missing information has an economic value. If the seller can come up with even a rough estimate of the missing information, she can improve her position. As the following examples illustrate, firms often do so by imputing characteristics to individuals on the basis of the groups to which they belong.

Why do males under 25 years of age pay more than other drivers for auto insurance?

Gerald is 23 years old and is an extremely careful and competent driver. He has never had an accident, or even a moving traffic violation. His twin sister Geraldine has had two accidents, one of them serious, in the last 3 years and has accumulated three speeding tickets during that same period. Why does Gerald pay $1,600/year for auto insurance, while Geraldine pays only $800?

The expected cost to an insurance company of insuring any given driver depends on the probability that the driver will be involved in an accident. No one knows what that probability is for any given driver, but insurance companies can estimate rather precisely the proportion of drivers in specific groups who will be involved in an accident in any given year. Males under 25 are much more likely than older males and females of any age to become involved in auto accidents. (Testosterone seems to have something to do with it.) Gerald pays more than his sister because even those males under 25 who have never had an accident are more likely to have one than females the same age who have had several accidents.

Of course, females who have had two accidents and accumulated several tickets in the last 3 years are more likely to have an accident than a female with a spotless driving record. The insurance company knows that and has increased Geraldine's premium accordingly. Yet it is still less than her brother's premium. That does not mean that Gerald is in fact more likely to have an accident than Geraldine. Indeed, given the twins' respective driving skills, Geraldine clearly poses the higher risk. But because insurance companies lack such detailed information, they are forced to set rates according to the information they possess.

To remain in business, an insurance company must collect enough money from premiums to cover the cost of the claims it pays out, plus whatever administrative expenses it incurs. Consider an insurance company that charges lower rates for young males with clean driving records than for females with blemished ones. Given that the former group is more likely to have accidents than the latter, the company cannot break even unless it charges females more, and males less, than the respective costs of insuring them. But if it does so, rival insurance companies will see cash on the table: They can offer females slightly lower rates and lure them away from the first company. The first company will end up with only young male policyholders and thus will suffer an economic loss at the low rates it charges. That is why, in equilibrium, young males with clean driving records pay higher insurance rates than young females with blemished records.

The insurance industry's policy of charging high rates to young male drivers is an example of **statistical discrimination.** Other examples include the common practice of paying higher salaries to people with college degrees than to people without them and the policy of favoring college applicants with high SAT scores. Statistical discrimination occurs whenever people or products are judged on the basis of the groups to which they belong.

Even though everyone *knows* that the characteristics of specific individuals can differ markedly from those of the group to which they belong, competition promotes statistical discrimination. For example, insurance companies know perfectly well that *some* young males are careful and competent drivers. But unless they can identify *which* males are the better drivers, competitive pressure forces them to act on their knowledge that as a group young males are more likely than others to generate insurance claims.

Similarly, employers know that many people with only a high school diploma are more productive than the average college graduate. But because employers usually cannot tell in advance who those people are, competitive pressure leads them to offer higher wages to college graduates, who are more productive, on average, than high school graduates. Universities, too, realize that many applicants with low SAT scores will earn higher grades than applicants with high scores. But if two applicants look equally promising except for their SAT scores, competition forces universities to favor the applicant with higher scores since, on average, that applicant will perform better than the other.

Statistical discrimination is the *result* of observable differences in group characteristics, not the cause of those differences. Young males, for example, do not generate more insurance claims because of statistical discrimination. Rather, statistical discrimination occurs because insurance companies know that young males generate more claims. Nor does statistical discrimination cause young

statistical discrimination the practice of making judgments about the quality of people, goods, or services based on the characteristics of the groups to which they belong

males to pay insurance rates that are high in relation to the claims they generate. Among any group of young male drivers, some are careful and competent, and others are not. Statistical discrimination means the more able males will pay high rates relative to the volume of claims they generate, but it also means the less able male drivers will pay low rates relative to the claims they generate. On average, the group's rates will be appropriate to the claims its members generate.

Still, these observations do little to ease the frustration of the young male who knows himself to be a careful and competent driver, or the high school graduate who knows herself to be a highly productive employee. Competitive forces provide firms an incentive to identify such individuals and treat them more favorably whenever practical. When firms succeed in this effort, however, they have often discovered some other relevant information on group differences. For example, many insurance companies offer lower rates to young males who belong to the National Honor Society or make the dean's list at school. Members of those groups generate fewer claims, on average, than other young males. But even these groups include risky drivers, and the fact that companies offer discounts to their members means that that all other young males must pay higher rates.

ADVERSE SELECTION

adverse selection the pattern in which insurance tends to be purchased disproportionately by those who are most costly for companies to insure

Although insurance companies routinely practice statistical discrimination, each individual within a group pays the same rate, even though individuals within the group often differ sharply in terms of their likelihood of filing claims. Within each group, buying insurance is thus most attractive to those individuals with the highest likelihood of filing claims. As a result, high-risk individuals are more likely to buy insurance than low-risk individuals, a pattern known as **adverse selection**. Adverse selection forces insurance companies to raise their premiums, which makes buying insurance even less attractive to low-risk individuals, which raises still further the average risk level of those who remain insured. In some cases, only those individuals faced with extreme risks may continue to find insurance an attractive purchase.

RECAP   **ASYMMETRIC INFORMATION**

Asymmetric information describes situations in which not all parties to a potential exchange are equally well informed. In the typical case, the seller of a product will know more about its quality than the potential buyers. Such asymmetries often stand in the way of mutually beneficial exchange in the markets for high-quality goods, because buyers' inability to identify high quality makes them unwilling to pay a commensurate price.

Information asymmetries and other communication problems between potential exchange partners can often be solved through the use of signals that are costly or difficult to fake. Product warranties are such a signal, because the seller of a low-quality product would find them too costly to offer.

Buyers and sellers also respond to asymmetric information by attempting to judge the qualities of products and people on the basis of the groups to which they belong. A young male may know he is a good driver, but auto insurance companies must nonetheless charge him high rates because they know only that he is a member of a group that is frequently involved in accidents.

DISAPPEARING POLITICAL DISCOURSE

An intriguing illustration of statistical discrimination arises when a politician decides what to say about controversial public issues. Politicians have an interest in supporting the positions they genuinely believe in, but they also have an interest in winning reelection. As the next examples illustrate, the two motives often conflict, especially when a politician's statements about one subject convey information about her beliefs on other subjects.

ECONOMIC NATURALIST 12.7

Why do opponents of the death penalty often remain silent?

Quite apart from the question of whether execution of convicted criminals is morally legitimate, there are important practical arguments against capital punishment. For one thing, it is extremely expensive relative to the alternative of life without parole. Execution is costly because of judicial safeguards against execution of innocent persons. In each capital case prosecuted in the United States, these safeguards consume thousands of person-hours from attorneys and other officers of the court, at a cost that runs well into the millions of dollars.[4] Such efforts notwithstanding, the record is replete with examples of executed persons who are later shown to be innocent. Another argument against capital punishment is that many statistical studies find that it does not deter people from committing capital crimes. Though many political leaders in both parties find these and other arguments against capital punishment compelling, few politicians voice their opposition to capital punishment publicly. Why not?

A possible answer to this puzzle is suggested by the theory of statistical discrimination. Voters in both parties are concerned about crime and want to elect politicians who take the problem seriously. Suppose there are two kinds of politicians, some who in their heart of hearts take the crime issue seriously and others who merely pay lip service to it. Suppose also that voters classify politicians in a second way: those who publicly favor the death penalty or remain silent, and those who publicly oppose it. Some politicians will oppose the death penalty for the reasons just discussed, but others will oppose it because they are simply reluctant to punish criminals—perhaps because they believe that crime is ultimately more society's fault than the criminal's. (Politicians in the latter category are the ones voters think of as being "not serious about crime"; they are the ones most voters want to get rid of.) These two possible motives for opposing the death penalty suggest that the proportion of death penalty opponents who take the crime issue seriously, in the public's view, will be somewhat smaller than the corresponding proportion among proponents of the death penalty. For the sake of discussion, imagine that 95 percent of politicians who favor the death penalty and only 80 percent of politicians who oppose the death penalty are "serious about crime."

If you are a voter who cares about crime, how will your views about a politician be affected by hearing that he opposes the death penalty? If you knew nothing about that politician to begin with, your best guess on hearing his opposition to the death penalty would be that there is an 80 percent chance that he is serious about crime. Had he instead voiced support for the death penalty, your best guess would be that there is a 95 percent chance that he is serious about crime. And since voters are looking for politicians who are serious about crime, the mere act of speaking out against the death penalty will entail a small loss of political support even for those politicians who are extremely serious about crime.

Knowing this tendency on the part of voters, some politicians who are only marginally opposed to the death penalty may prefer to keep their views to themselves. As a result, the composition of the group that speaks out publicly against the death penalty will change slightly so that it is more heavily weighted with people reluctant to punish criminals in any way. Suppose, for example, that the proportion of death penalty oppo-

[4]See Philip J. Cook and Donna B. Slawson, "The Costs of Processing Murder Cases in North Carolina," The Sanford Institute of Public Policy, Duke University, Durham, N.C., 1993.

nents who are serious about crime falls from 80 to 60 percent. Now the political cost of speaking out against the death penalty rises, leading still more opponents to remain silent. Once the dust settles, very few opponents of capital punishment will risk stating their views publicly. In their desire to convince voters that they are tough on crime, some may even become proponents of the death penalty. In the end, public discourse will strongly favor capital punishment. But that is no reason to conclude that most leaders—or even most voters—genuinely favor it.

disappearing political discourse the theory that people who support a position may remain silent, because speaking out would create a risk of being misunderstood

The economist Glen Loury was the first to call attention to the phenomenon described in the preceding example. We call it the problem of **disappearing political discourse.** Once you understand it, you will begin to notice examples not just in the political sphere but in everyday discourse as well.

ECONOMIC NATURALIST 12.8

Why do proponents of legalized drugs remain silent?

That addictive drugs like heroine, cocaine, and methamphetamines cause enormous harm is not a matter of dispute. The clear intent of laws that ban commerce in these drugs is to prevent that harm. But the laws also entail costs. By making the drugs illegal, they substantially increase their price, leading many addicts to commit crimes to pay for drugs. The high incomes of illicit drug dealers also divert many people from legitimate careers and result in turf battles that often have devastating consequences for both participants and bystanders. If these drugs were legal, drug-related crime would vanish completely. Drug use would also rise, how significantly we do not know. In short, it is at least *conceivable* that legalizing addictive drugs might be sound public policy. Why, then, do virtually no politicians publicly favor such a policy?

Many politicians may simply believe that legalizing drugs is simply a bad idea. Theoretically, legalization could lead to such a steep rise in drug consumption that the cost of the policy might far outweigh its benefits. This concern, however, is not supported by experience in countries such as England and the Netherlands, which have tried limited forms of legalization. A second explanation is that politicians who favor legalization are reluctant to speak out for fear that others will misinterpret them. Suppose that some people favor legalization based on careful analysis of the costs and benefits, while other proponents are merely crazy. If the proportion of crazies is higher among supporters than among opponents of legalization, someone who speaks out in favor of legalization may cause those who do not know her to increase their estimate of the likelihood she is crazy. This possibility deters some proponents from speaking out, which raises the proportion of crazies among the remaining public supporters of legalization—and so on in a downward spiral, until most of the remaining public supporters really are crazy.

Why did the task of reestablishing normal diplomatic relations with China fall to President Richard Nixon, the lifelong communist basher?

The disappearing political discourse problem helps to explain why the United States had difficulty reestablishing normal diplomatic relations with China, which were severed in the wake of the communist revolution. One could oppose communist expansionism and yet still favor normalized relations with China on the grounds that war is less likely when antagonists communicate openly. In the Cold War environment, however, American politicians were under enormous pressure to demonstrate their steadfast opposition to communism at every opportunity. Fearing that support for the normalization of relations with China would be misinterpreted as a sign of softness toward communism, many supporters of the policy remained silent. Not until Richard Nixon—whose anticommunist credentials no one could question—was elected President were diplomatic relations with China finally reopened.

The problem of disappearing discourse also helps explain the impoverished state of public debate on issues such as the reform of Social Security, Medicare, and other entitlement programs.

■ SUMMARY ■

- Virtually every market exchange takes place on the basis of less than complete information. More information is beneficial both to buyers and to sellers, but information is costly to acquire. The rational individual therefore acquires information only up to the point at which its marginal benefit equals its marginal cost. Beyond that point one is rational to remain ignorant.

- Retailers and other sales agents are important sources of information. To the extent that they enable consumers to find the right products and services, they add economic value. In that sense they are no less productive than the workers who manufacture goods or perform services directly. Unfortunately, the free-rider problem often prevents firms from offering useful product information.

- Several principles govern the rational search for information. Searching more intensively makes sense when the cost of a search is low, when quality is highly variable, or when prices vary widely. Further search is always a gamble. A risk-neutral person will search whenever the expected gains outweigh the expected costs. A rational search will always terminate before all possible options have been investigated. Thus in a search for a partner in an ongoing bilateral relationship, there is always the possibility that a better partner will turn up after the search is over. In most contexts, people deal with this problem by entering into contracts that commit them to their partners once they have mutually agreed to terminate the search.

- Many potentially beneficial transactions are prevented from taking place by asymmetric information—the fact that one party lacks information that the other has. For example, the owner of a used car knows whether it is in good condition, but potential buyers do not. Even though a buyer may be willing to pay more for a good car than the owner of such a car would require, the fact that the buyer cannot be sure he is getting a good car often discourages the sale. More generally, asymmetric information often prevents sellers from supplying the same quality level that consumers would be willing to pay for.

- Both buyers and sellers can often gain by finding ways of communicating what they know to one another. But because of the potential conflict between the interests of buyers and sellers, mere statements about the relevant information may not be credible. For a signal between potential trading partners to be credible, it must be costly to fake. For instance, the owner of a high-quality used car can credibly signal the car's quality by offering a warranty—an offer that the seller of a low-quality car could not afford to make.

- Firms and consumers often try to estimate missing information by making use of what they know about the groups to which people or things belong. For example, insurance firms estimate the risk of insuring individual young male drivers on the basis of the accident rates for young males as a group. This practice is known as statistical discrimination. Other examples include paying college graduates more than high school graduates and charging higher life insurance rates to 60-year-olds than to 20-year-olds. Statistical discrimination helps to explain the phenomenon of disappearing political discourse, which occurs when opponents of a practice such as the death penalty remain silent when the issue is discussed publicly.

■ KEY TERMS ■

adverse selection (312)
asymmetric information (305)
better-than-fair gamble (303)
costly-to-fake principle (308)

disappearing political discourse (314)
expected value of a gamble (303)
fair gamble (303)
free-rider problem (301)

lemons model (306)
risk-averse person (303)
risk-neutral person (303)
statistical discrimination (311)

■ REVIEW QUESTIONS ■

1. Can it be rational for a consumer to buy a Chevrolet without having first taken test drives in competing models built by Ford, Chrysler, Honda, Toyota, and others?

2. Explain why a gallery owner who sells a painting might actually create more economic surplus than the artist who painted it.

3. Explain why used cars offered for sale are different, on average, from used cars not offered for sale.

4. Explain why the used-car market would be likely to function more efficiently in a community in which moral norms of honesty are strong than in a community in which such norms are weak.

5. Why might leasing a new Porsche be a good investment for an aspiring Hollywood film producer, even though he can't easily afford the monthly payments?

▪ PROBLEMS ▪

1. State whether the following are true or false, and briefly explain why:
   a. Companies spend billions of dollars advertising their products on network TV primarily because the texts of their advertisements persuade consumers that the advertised products are of high quality.
   b. You may not get the optimal level of advice from a retail shop when you go in to buy a lamp for your bike, because of the free-rider problem.
   c. If you need a lawyer, and all your legal expenses are covered by insurance, you should *always* choose the best-dressed lawyer with the most expensive car and the most ostentatiously furnished office.
   d. The benefit of searching for a spouse is affected by the size of the community you live in.

2. Consumers know that some fraction x of all new cars produced and sold in the market are defective. The defective ones cannot be identified except by those who own them. Cars do not depreciate with use. Consumers are risk-neutral and value non-defective cars at $10,000 each. New cars sell for $5,000 and used ones for $2,500. What is the fraction x?

3. Carlos is risk-neutral and has an ancient farmhouse with great character for sale in Slaterville Springs. His reservation price for the house is $130,000. The only possible local buyer is Whitney, whose reservation price for the house is $150,000. The only other houses on the market are modern ranch houses that sell for $125,000, which is exactly equal to each potential buyer's reservation price for such a house. Suppose that if Carlos does not hire a realtor, Whitney will learn from her neighbor that Carlos's house is for sale, and will buy it for $140,000. However, if Carlos hires a realtor, he knows that the realtor will put him in touch with an enthusiast for old farmhouses who is willing to pay up to $300,000 for the house. Carlos also knows that if he and this person negotiate, they will agree on a price of $250,000. If realtors charge a commission of 5 percent of the selling price and all realtors have opportunity costs of $2,000 for negotiating a sale, will Carlos hire a realtor? If so, how will total economic surplus be affected?

4. Ann and Barbara are computer programmers in Nashville who are planning to move to Seattle. Each owns a house that has just been appraised for $100,000. But whereas Ann's house is one of hundreds of highly similar houses in a large, well-known suburban development, Barbara's is the only one that was built from her architect's design. Who will benefit more by hiring a realtor to assist in selling her house, Ann or Barbara?

5. For each pair of occupations listed, identify the one for which the kind of car a person drives is more likely to be a good indication of how good she is at her job.
   a. Elementary school teacher, real estate agent
   b. Dentist, municipal government administrator
   c. Engineer in the private sector, engineer in the military

6. Brokers who sell stocks over the Internet can serve many more customers than those who transact business by mail or over the phone. How will the expansion of Internet access affect the average incomes of stockbrokers who continue to do business in the traditional way?

7. Whose income do you predict will be more affected by the expansion of Internet access:
   a. Stockbrokers or lawyers?
   b. Doctors or pharmacists?
   c. Bookstore owners or the owners of galleries that sell original oil paintings?

8. How will growing Internet access affect the number of film actors and musicians who have active fan clubs?

9. Fred, a retired accountant, and Jim, a government manager, are 63-year-old identical twins who collect antique pottery. Each has an annual income of $100,000 (Fred's from a pension, Jim's from salary). One buys most of his pottery at local auctions,

and the other buys most of his from a local dealer. Which brother is more likely to buy at an auction, and does he pay more or less than his brother who buys from the local dealer?

10. Female heads of state (e.g., Israel's Golda Meir, India's Indira Gandhi, Britain's Margaret Thatcher) have often been described as more bellicose in foreign policy matters than the average male head of state. Using Loury's theory of disappearing discourse, suggest an explanation for this pattern.

■ ANSWERS TO IN-CHAPTER EXERCISES ■

12.1 Internet search is a cheap way to acquire information about many goods and services, so the effect of increased Internet access will be a downward shift in the supply curve of information. In equilibrium, people will acquire more information, and the goods and services they buy will more closely resemble those they would have chosen in an ideal world with perfect information. These effects will cause total economic surplus to grow. Some of these gains, however, might be offset if the Internet makes the free-rider problem more serious.

12.2 The probability of getting heads is 0.5, the same as the probability of getting tails. Thus the expected value of this gamble is $(0.5)(\$4) + (0.5)(-\$2) = \$1$. Since the gamble is better than fair, a risk-neutral person would accept it.

12.3 Since you still have a 20 percent chance of finding a cheaper apartment if you make another visit, the expected outcome of the gamble is again \$2, and you should search again. The bad outcome of any previous search is a sunk cost and should not influence your decision about whether to search again.

12.4 The expected value of a new car will now be $0.8(\$10,000) + 0.2(\$6,000) = \$9,200$. Any risk-neutral consumer who believed that the quality distribution of used cars for sale was the same as the quality distribution of new cars off the assembly line would be willing to pay \$9,200 for a used car.

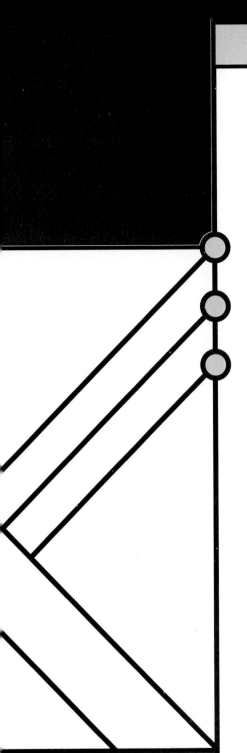

PART

4

LABOR MARKETS AND THE PUBLIC SECTOR

■

The market imperfections discussed in Part 3 help explain why no country on earth leaves all important economic decisions entirely in the hands of market forces. But income disparities among individuals are perhaps an even more important source of government involvement in modern economic life. In Chapter 13 we will explore why some people earn so much more than others. We will discuss the human capital model, which emphasizes the importance of differences in personal characteristics. But our focus will be on why people with similar personal characteristics often earn sharply different incomes.

In Chapter 14 we will explore examples in which careful application of basic economic principles can help society design policies that mitigate the market imperfections discussed in Part 3. The thread uniting these examples is the problem of scarcity. In each case we will explore how intelligent application of the cost-benefit principle can help resolve the resulting trade-offs in ways that expand the economic pie.

In Chapter 15 we will tackle such questions as how big government should be, what sorts of goods and services it should provide, and how it should raise the revenue to pay for them. We will also explore why rational citizens might empower government to constrain their behavior in various ways, and how such powers should be apportioned among local, state, and federal levels.

Finally, in Chapter 16 we will investigate why poverty and income inequality have become issues of central concern to all democratically elected governments. Because government programs to redistribute income have costs as well as benefits, policymakers must compare an imperfect status quo with the practical consequences of imperfect government remedies. We will explore why policies that would expand the economic pie often cannot be adopted unless steps are simultaneously taken to assure that everyone will end up with a larger slice.

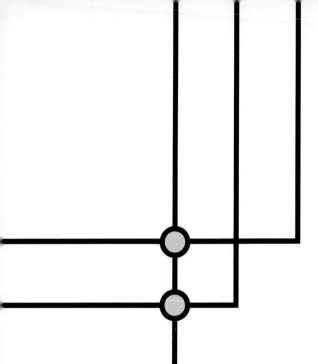

LABOR MARKETS

■

By only the slimmest of margins, Mary Lou Retton won the individual all-around gold medal in women's gymnastics at the Los Angeles Summer Olympic Games in 1984. In the years since, she has remained in the spotlight, continuing to earn millions of dollars from product endorsements and motivational speeches. In contrast, the silver medalist from 1984 has dropped completely from view. (Can you name her?) She is Ecaterina Szabo, one of the most talented Romanian gymnasts of her era, and although she came within a hairsbreadth of beating Retton, wealth and international recognition were not to be hers.

Many physicians in Szabo's homeland are likewise every bit as talented and hardworking as physicians here in the United States. But while American physicians earn an average annual income of almost $200,000, Romanian physicians earn so little that some of them supplement their incomes by cleaning the Bucharest apartments of expatriate Americans for just $10 a day.

Why do some people earn so much more than others? No other single question in economics has stimulated nearly as much interest and discussion. American citizenship, of course, is neither necessary nor sufficient for receiving high income. Many of the wealthiest people in the world come from extremely poor countries, and hundreds of thousands of Americans are homeless and malnourished.

Our aim in this chapter will be to employ simple economic principles in an attempt to explain why different people earn different salaries. We'll discuss the human capital model, which emphasizes the importance of differences in personal characteristics. But our focus will be on why people with similar personal characteristics often earn sharply different incomes. Among the factors we will consider are labor unions, winner-take-all markets, discrimination, and the effect of nonwage conditions of employment.

Why do small differences in performance sometimes translate into enormous differences in pay?

WAGE AND SALARY DETERMINATION IN COMPETITIVE LABOR MARKETS

In some respects, the sale of human labor is profoundly different from the sale of other goods and services. For example, although someone may legally relinquish all future rights to the use of her television set by selling it, the law does not permit people to sell themselves into slavery. The law does, however, permit us to "rent out" our services to employers. And in many ways the rental market for labor services functions much like the market for most other goods and services. Each specific category of labor has a demand curve and a supply curve. These curves intersect to determine both the equilibrium wage and the equilibrium quantity of employment for each category of labor.

What is more, shifts in the relevant demand and supply curves produce changes analogous to those produced by shifts in the demand and supply curves for other goods and services. For example, an increase in the demand for a specific category of labor will generally increase both the equilibrium wage and the equilibrium quantity of employment in that category. By the same token, an increase in the supply of labor to a given occupation will tend to increase the level of employment and lower the wage rate in that occupation.

As in our discussions of other markets, our strategy for investigating how the labor market works will be to go through a series of examples that shed light on different parts of the picture. In the first example, we focus on how the equilibrium principle helps us to understand how wages will differ among workers with different levels of productive ability.

EXAMPLE 13.1

How much will the potters earn?

Mackintosh Pottery Works is one of numerous identical companies that hire potters who mold clay into pots. These companies sell the pots for $1.10 each to a finishing company that glazes and fires them and then sells them in the retail marketplace. Clay, which is available free of charge in unlimited quantities, is the only input used by the potters. Rennie and Laura are currently the only two potters who work for Mackintosh, whose only cost other than potters' salaries is a 10 cent handling cost for each pot it delivers to the finisher. Rennie delivers 100 pots/week and Laura delivers 120. If the labor market for potters is perfectly competitive, how much will each be paid?

In this example, we assume that Rennie and Laura have decided to work full-time as potters, so our focus is not on how much they will work but on how much they will be paid. After taking handling costs into account, the value of the pots that Rennie delivers is $100/week, and that is the amount Mackintosh will pay him. To pay him less would risk having him bid away by a competitor. For example, if Mackintosh paid Rennie only $90/week, the company would then enjoy an economic profit of $10/week as a result of hiring him. Seeing this cash on the table, a rival firm could then offer Rennie $91 and would earn additional economic profit of $9/week by bidding him away from Mackintosh. So under the bidding pressure from rival employers, Mackintosh will have difficulty keeping Rennie if it pays him less than $100/week. And the company would suffer an economic loss if it paid him more than $100/week. Similarly, the value of the pots delivered each week by Laura is $120, and this will be her competitive equilibrium wage.

In Example 13.1, the number of pots each potter delivered each week was that potter's **marginal physical product**, or **marginal product (MP)** for short. More generally, a worker's marginal product is the extra output the firm gets as a result of hiring that worker. When we multiply a worker's marginal product by the net price for which each unit of the product sells, we get that worker's **value of**

marginal product of labor (MP) the additional output a firm gets by employing one additional unit of labor

marginal product, or *VMP*. (In Example 13.1 the "net price" of each pot was $1.00—the difference between the $1.10 sale price and the $0.10 handling charge.) The general rule in competitive labor markets is that *a worker's pay in long-run equilibrium will be equal to his or her VMP—the net contribution he or she makes to the employer's revenue.* Employers would be delighted to pay workers less than their respective *VMPs*, to be sure. But if labor markets are truly competitive, they cannot get away with doing so for long.

In Example 13.1, each worker's *VMP* was independent of the number of other workers employed by the firm. In such cases, we cannot predict how many workers a firm will hire. Mackintosh could break even with 2 potters, with 10, or even with 1,000 or more. In many other situations, however, we can predict exactly how many workers a firm will hire. Consider Example 13.2.

value of marginal product of labor (VMP) the dollar value of the additional output a firm gets by employing one additional unit of labor

How many workers should Adirondack hire? (Part 1)

EXAMPLE 13.2

The Adirondack Woodworking Company hires workers in a competitive labor market at a wage of $350/week to make kitchen cutting boards. If the boards sell for $20 each and the company's weekly output varies with the number of workers hired as shown in Table 13.1, how many workers should Adirondack hire?

TABLE 13.1
Employment and Productivity in a Woodworking Company (When Cutting Boards Sell for $20 Each)

Number of workers	Total number of cutting boards/week	MP (extra cutting boards/week)	VMP ($/week)
0	0		
		30	600
1	30		
		25	500
2	55		
		21	420
3	76		
		18	360
4	94		
		14	280
5	108		

In Example 13.1 our focus was on wage differences for employees whose productive abilities differed. In contrast, we assume here that all workers are equally productive and the firm faces a fixed market wage for each. The fact that the marginal product of labor declines with the number of workers hired is a consequence of the law of diminishing returns. (As discussed in Chapter 6, the law of diminishing returns says that when a firm's capital and other productive inputs are held fixed in the short run, adding workers beyond some point results in ever-smaller increases in output.) The third column of the table reports the marginal product for each additional worker, and the last column reports the value of each successive worker's marginal product—the number of cutting boards he or she adds times the selling price of $20. Adirondack should keep hiring as long as the next worker's *VMP* is at least $350/week (the market wage). The first four workers have *VMPs* larger than $350, so Adirondack should hire them. But since hiring the fifth worker would add only $280 to weekly revenue, Adirondack should not hire that worker.

Note the similarity between the perfectly competitive firm's decision about how many workers to hire and the perfectly competitive firm's output decision we considered in Chapter 6. When labor is the only variable factor of production, the two decisions are essentially the same. Because of the unique correspondence between the firm's total output and the total number of workers it hires, deciding how many workers to hire is the same as deciding how much output to supply.

As Examples 13.3 and 13.4 illustrate, the worker's attractiveness to the employer depends not only on how many cutting boards he or she produces but also on the price of cutting boards and on the wage rate.

EXAMPLE 13.3

How many workers should Adirondack hire? (Part 2)

Refer to Example 13.2. Suppose that the price of cutting boards rises from $20 to $30. If the wage rate and marginal physical products are as before, how many workers should Adirondack hire?

As shown in the last column of Table 13.2, the 14 cutting boards produced by the fifth worker now add (14)($30) = $420 to weekly revenue, and since his wage is only $350, the company should hire him.

TABLE 13.2
The Effect of a Price Increase on Employment

Number of workers	Total number of cutting boards/week	MP (extra cutting boards/week)	VMP ($/week)
0	0		
		30	900
1	30		
		25	750
2	55		
		21	630
3	76		
		18	540
4	94		
		14	420
5	108		

EXERCISE 13.1

In Example 13.3, what is the lowest cutting board price at which Adirondack should hire two workers?

EXAMPLE 13.4

How many workers should Adirondack hire? (Part 3)

Now suppose that cutting boards again sell for their original price of $20 but that the wage rate of workers is not $350/week but $370. If the company's weekly output of cutting boards again varies with the number of workers as shown in Table 13.3, how many workers should it hire?

This time note that although the fourth worker was an attractive hire at a wage of $350/week, he will not be worth hiring at a wage of $370. His *VMP* is now smaller than his wage, so the company should hire only three workers.

TABLE 13.3
The Effect of a Wage Increase on Employment

Number of workers	Total number of cutting boards/week	MP (extra cutting boards/week)	VMP ($/week)
0	0		
		30	600
1	30		
		25	500
2	55		
		21	420
3	76		
		18	360
4	94		
		14	280
5	108		

EXERCISE 13.2

In Example 13.4, how many workers would Adirondack hire if the wage rate were $275/week?

RECAP   **WAGE AND SALARY DETERMINATION IN COMPETITIVE LABOR MARKETS**

In competitive labor markets, employers face pressure to pay each worker the value of his or her marginal product. When a firm can hire as many workers as it wishes at a given market wage, it should expand employment as long as the value of marginal product of labor exceeds the market wage.

MONOPSONY: THE LONE EMPLOYER IN A LABOR MARKET

In perfectly competitive product markets, sellers have no control over product prices. Market supply and demand curves intersect, and firms take the resulting prices as given. Similarly, in perfectly competitive labor markets, firms have no control over wage rates. The wage in each market is determined by supply and demand. In Examples 13.2 to 13.4, Adirondack Woodworking was a buyer in a perfectly competitive labor market, and viewed the market wage accordingly. The supply curve of labor facing such an employer is perfectly elastic—a horizontal line at the market wage.

But now suppose that Adirondack is a **monopsony**—the only buyer of labor services in its local labor market. The labor supply curve facing the company is now the labor supply curve for the market as a whole. There is no market wage per se. Workers get paid whatever Adirondack chooses to offer. But Adirondack is not free to offer just any wage, for if its offer is extremely low, workers may decide to relocate, or they may stop working and go on welfare. Even so, Adirondack now has some discretion about the wage it pays. In general, the more

monopsony a market with only a single buyer

workers the company wishes to hire, the more it will have to pay. How much should it pay its workers?

In many ways, the problem facing the monopsonist is similar to the one facing a monopolist in the market for a product. Because the monopolist's demand curve is the same as the product demand curve for the market as a whole, the only way the monopolist can expand sales is by cutting price. Similarly, because the supply curve of labor confronting the monopsonist is the supply curve for the labor market as a whole, the only way the monopsonist can hire additional workers is by offering higher wages. But raising the wage to an additional worker generally means also having to raise the wage for the workers hired thus far. And as Example 13.5 illustrates, the monopsonist has an incentive to limit employment, much as the monopolist has an incentive to limit output.

EXAMPLE 13.5

How many workers should Adirondack hire? (Part 4)

The Adirondack Woodworking Company is the only employer in a small town in the mountains of upstate New York. It sells kitchen cutting boards for $20 each, and its weekly output again varies with the number of workers as shown in Table 13.4. If there are five workers in town whom Adirondack might hire, with reservation wages as shown in Table 13.5, and if Adirondack must pay each worker the same wage, how many should it hire? (An individual's reservation wage for a job is the smallest payment for which she or he would be willing to accept the job.)

TABLE 13.4
Output and Employment for a Monopsonist

Number of workers	Total number of cutting boards/week	MP (extra cutting boards/week)	VMP ($/week)
0	0		
		30	600
1	30		
		25	500
2	55		
		21	420
3	76		
		18	360
4	94		
		14	280
5	108		

For the monopolist in the product market, recall that the decision rule is to sell another unit if marginal revenue (the amount by which its total revenue goes up when it sells an extra unit) exceeds marginal cost. For the monopsonist in the labor market, the corresponding rule is to hire another worker if that worker's *VMP* exceeds **marginal labor cost**—the amount by which the monopsonist's total wage bill would go up if it hired the extra worker. Marginal labor cost in this example is shown in the last column of Table 13.6. (Again, we assume that the monopsonist does not know each worker's reservation wage and must therefore pay each worker the same wage.)

marginal labor cost the amount by which a monopsonist's total wage bill goes up if it hires an extra worker

If Adirondack offers a wage of $200, the only worker it will attract is Alice. If the company also wants to hire a second worker (Bert), it must not only pay him $50/week more than it is currently paying Alice, but it must also raise Alice's

TABLE 13.5
Reservation Wages for the Monopsonist's Potential Employees

Worker	Reservation wage ($/week)
Alice	200
Bert	250
Carrie	300
Donna	350
Ernie	400

TABLE 13.6
Calculating Marginal Labor Cost for the Monopsonist

Worker	Reservation wage ($/week)	Total labor cost ($/week)	Marginal labor cost ($/week)
			200
Alice	200	200	
			300
Bert	250	500	
			400
Carrie	300	900	
			500
Donna	350	1,400	
			600
Ernie	400	2,000	

pay to $250/week. Because the company's total labor cost will go from $200 to $500/week in the process, the marginal labor cost of hiring Bert is $300/week. But since Bert's *VMP* is $500/week, hiring him is clearly in Adirondack's interest. Carrie, too, is a worthwhile hire because her marginal labor cost of $400/week is less than her *VMP* of $420. But Donna's marginal labor cost of $500/week is considerably more than her $360 *VMP*. So even though Donna's reservation wage of $350 is less than her *VMP*, the cost-benefit principle tells us that Adirondack will do better by not hiring her. Thus the company will hire only three workers—Alice, Carrie, and Bert—and will pay each a wage of $300/week.

EXERCISE 13.3

In Example 13.5, how many workers should Adirondack hire if cutting boards sold not for $20 but for $30?

In Chapter 9, we saw that a monopolist in the product market produces too little output because price exceeds marginal revenue. A similar inefficiency occurs with a monopsonist in the labor market. In Example 13.5, note that Adirondack the monopsonist has the same *VMP* schedule (Table 13.4) as its perfectly competitive counterpart in Example 13.2 (Table 13.1). In both cases, the company *could* hire four workers at a wage of $350/week. Yet the monopsonist hires one less worker than its perfectly competitive counterpart in Example 13.2. With only three workers on the monopsonist's payroll, the *social* cost of adding another worker is just the fourth worker's reservation wage, namely, $350. Because the fourth worker would add 18 cutting boards to the weekly production total, for a gain in revenue of $360, society would thus gain output worth $10 more than the social cost of hiring the fourth worker. Yet the monopsonist will not hire a fourth worker, because the private cost (marginal labor cost) of doing so is $500.

The monopsonist produces too little because the private cost of an additional hire is greater than the social cost of that hire. The reason for the discrepancy is that the new hire necessitates paying existing workers more, which the monopsonist understandably views as a real cost, but which from society's perspective is merely a transfer from the monopsonist to the existing workers.

Monopsony was once far more common than it is today. One reason for the decline is that a much greater proportion of workers now live in cities, giving them a broad choice of employers within driving distance of their homes. Another reason is that geographic mobility is greater now than in the past. Thus even those who live in small communities dominated by a single employer are more likely to have the option of seeking employment elsewhere. And with the continuing rise of telecommuting, the significance of monopsony in the labor market will diminish still further. Most economists believe that today's labor markets are highly competitive and that firms must be highly aggressive if they are to recruit and retain the capable workers they need.

RECAP **MONOPSONY**

Unlike the perfectly competitive employer, who can hire as much labor as he wishes at the market wage, the monopsonist can expand employment only by offering higher wages. And unlike the perfectly competitive employer, who continues hiring only until *VMP* equals the market wage, the monopsonist continues hiring until *VMP* equals marginal labor cost, which exceeds the market wage. The profit-maximizing employment level for the monopsonist is lower than the level that would maximize total economic surplus.

EQUILIBRIUM IN THE LABOR MARKET

An employer's reservation price for a worker is the most the employer could pay without suffering a decline in profit. As discussed, this reservation price for the employer in a perfectly competitive labor market is simply *VMP*, the value of the worker's marginal product. Because of the law of diminishing returns, we know that the marginal product of labor, and hence *VMP*, declines in the short run as the quantity of labor rises. The individual employer's demand curve for labor in any particular occupation—say, computer programmers—may thus be shown, as in Figure 13.1(a), as a downward-sloping function of the wage rate. Suppose firm 1 [part (a)] and firm 2 [part (b)] are the only two firms that employ programmers in a given community. The demand for programmers in that community will then be the horizontal sum of the individual firm demands [part (c)].

What does the supply curve of labor for a specific occupation look like? Will more labor be offered at high wage rates than at low wage rates? For the economy as a whole during the past several centuries, the workweek has been declining and real wages have been rising. This pattern might seem to suggest that the supply curve of labor is downward-sloping, and for the economy as a whole it may be. Yet the supply of labor *to any particular occupation* is almost surely upward-sloping, because wage differences among occupations influence occupational choice. It is no accident, for example, that many more people are choosing jobs as computer programmers now than in 1970. Wages of programmers have risen sharply during the past several decades, which has led many people to forsake other career paths in favor of programming.

Curve *S* in Figure 13.2 represents the supply curve of computer programmers. As more tasks have become computerized in recent decades, the demand for pro-

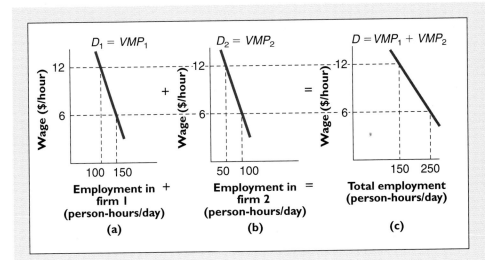

FIGURE 13.1
The Occupational Demand for Labor.
If firm 1 and firm 2 are the only firms that employ labor in a given occupation, we generate the demand curve for labor in that occupation by adding the individual demand curves horizontally.

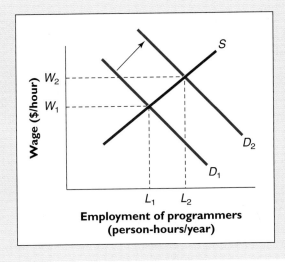

FIGURE 13.2
The Effect of an Increase in the Demand for Computer Programmers.
An increase in the demand for programmers from D_1 to D_2 results in an increase in the equilibrium level of employment (from L_1 to L_2) and an increase in the equilibrium wage (from W_1 to W_2).

grammers has grown, as shown by the shift from D_1 to D_2 in Figure 13.2. Equilibrium in the market for computer programmers occurs at the intersection of the relevant supply and demand curves. The increase in demand has led to an increase in the equilibrium level of programmers from L_1 to L_2 and a rise in the equilibrium wage from W_1 to W_2.

As discussed in Chapter 8, the market for stocks and other financial assets reaches equilibrium very quickly in the wake of shifts in the underlying supply and demand curves. Labor markets are often much slower to adjust. When the demand for workers in a given profession increases, shortages may remain for months or even years, depending on how long it takes people to acquire the skills and training needed to enter the profession.

<table>
<tr><td>

RECAP   **EQUILIBRIUM IN THE LABOR MARKET**

The demand for labor in a perfectly competitive labor market is the horizontal sum of each employer's *VMP* curve. The supply curve of labor for an individual labor market is upward-sloping, even though the supply curve of labor for the economy as a whole may be vertical, or even downward-sloping. In each labor market, the demand and supply curves intersect to determine the equilibrium wage and level of employment.

</td></tr>
</table>

EXPLAINING DIFFERENCES IN EARNINGS

The theory of competitive labor markets tells us that differences in pay reflect differences in the corresponding *VMP*s. Thus, in Example 13.1, Laura earned 20 percent more than Rennie because she made 20 percent more pots each week than he did. This difference in productivity may have resulted from an underlying difference in talent or training, or perhaps Laura simply worked harder than Rennie.

Yet often we see large salary differences even between people who appear equally talented and hardworking. Why, for example, do lawyers earn so much more than plumbers who are just as smart and work just as hard? And why do surgeons earn so much more than general practitioners? These wage differences might seem to violate the no-cash-on-the-table principle, which says that only differences in talent, luck, or hard work can account for long-run differences in earnings. For example, if plumbers could earn more by becoming lawyers, why don't they just switch occupations? Likewise, if general practitioners could boost their incomes by becoming surgeons, why didn't they become surgeons in the first place?

HUMAN CAPITAL THEORY

human capital theory a theory of pay determination that says a worker's wage will be proportional to his or her stock of human capital

human capital an amalgam of factors such as education, training, experience, intelligence, energy, work habits, trustworthiness, initiative, and others that affect the value of a worker's marginal product

Answers to these questions are suggested by the **human capital theory**, which holds that an individual's *VMP* is proportional to his or her stock of **human capital**—an amalgam of factors such as education, experience, training, intelligence, energy, work habits, trustworthiness, initiative, and so on. According to this theory, some occupations pay better than others because they require larger stocks of human capital. For example, a general practitioner could become a surgeon, but only by extending her formal education by several more years. An even larger additional investment in education is required for a plumber to become a lawyer.

In general, a decision to invest in human capital, like decisions to invest in other assets, requires comparing costs incurred in the present with benefits received in the future. As Example 13.6 illustrates, intelligent decisions of this sort require us to make use of the present value concept we encountered in Chapter 8.

EXAMPLE 13.6   **Should Betsy get an MBA?**

Betsy has a bachelor's degree and 2 years of experience as a branch manager of a small business. If she continues along her present career path, she will be promoted to positions of greater managerial responsibility, and the present value of her lifetime earnings in those positions will be $350,000. If instead she takes 2 years off and completes an MBA degree, she will be assigned to positions of significantly higher responsibility. The present value of her lifetime earnings in those positions will be $393,000. The only expenses of attending business school are two tuition payments—a $22,000 payment now and another $22,000 payment 1 year from now. Suppose that apart from monetary considerations, Betsy is indifferent between these two life courses. If the annual interest rate is 10 percent, should she go for her MBA?

The benefit of the MBA is the resulting increase in the present value of Betsy's lifetime earnings, which is $393,000 − $350,000 = $43,000. The cost of the MBA is the present value of her tuition payments, which is $22,000 + $22,000/1.10 = $42,000. (The opportunity cost of her lost earnings while getting the degree is reflected in the present value of her lifetime earnings with the degree.) Since the benefit of getting her MBA exceeds the cost by $1,000, Betsy should get the degree.

Someone who compared the salaries of managers with MBAs to those of managers without MBAs might be tempted to conclude that the MBAs had reaped an enormous windfall. But their advantage appears less dramatic once we include the cost of acquiring the additional human capital.

EXERCISE 13.4

Refer to Example 13.6. If Betsy had been indifferent between getting an MBA or not at an interest rate of 10 percent, which option should she choose if the interest rate is 12 percent? (*Hint:* An increase in the interest rate will change the present value of the cost of obtaining the degree by a different amount than it will change the present value of the benefit.)

Differences in demand can result in some kinds of human capital being more valuable than others. Consider again the increase in demand for computer programmers that has been occurring for the past several decades. During that same time period, the demand for the services of tax accountants has fallen as more and more taxpayers have used tax-preparation software in lieu of hiring accountants to help them with their taxes. Both occupations require demanding technical training, but the training received by computer programmers now yields a higher return in the labor market.

LABOR UNIONS

Two workers with the same amount of human capital may earn different wages if one of them belongs to a **labor union** and the other does not. A labor union is an organization through which workers attempt to bargain collectively with employers for better wages and working conditions.

Many economists believe that unions affect labor markets in much the same way that cartels affect product markets. To illustrate, consider a simple economy with two labor markets, neither of which is unionized initially. Suppose the total supply of labor to the two markets is fixed at $S_0 = 200$ workers/day and that the demand curves are as shown by VMP_1 and VMP_2 in Figure 13.3(a) and (b). The sum of the two demand curves, $VMP_1 + VMP_2$ [Figure 13.3(c)], intersects the supply curve to determine an equilibrium wage of $9/hour. At that wage, firms in market 1 hire 125 workers/day [part (a)], and firms in market 2 hire 75 [part (b)].

Now suppose workers in market 1 form a union and refuse to work for less than $12/hour. Because demand curves for labor are downward-sloping, employers of unionized workers reduce employment from 125 workers/day to 100 [Figure 13.4(a)]. The 25 displaced workers in the unionized market would, of course, be delighted to find other jobs in that market at $12/hour. But they cannot and so are forced to seek employment in the nonunionized market. The result is an excess supply of 25 workers in the nonunion market at the original wage of $9/hour. In time, wages in that market decline to $W_N = \$6$/hour, the level at which 100 workers can find jobs in the nonunionized market [Figure 13.4(b)].

labor union a group of workers who bargain collectively with employers for better wages and working conditions

FIGURE 13.3
An Economy with Two Nonunionized Labor Markets.
Supply and demand intersect to determine a market wage of $9/hour in part (c). At that wage, employers in market 1 hire 125 workers/day, and employers in market 2 hire 75 workers/day. The *VMP* is $9 in each market.

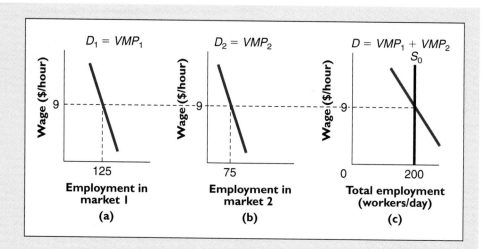

FIGURE 13.4
The Effect of a Union Wage above the Equilibrium Wage.
When the unionized wage is pegged at $W_U = \$12$/hour [part (a)], 25 workers are discharged. When these workers seek employment in the nonunionized market, the wage in that market falls to $W_N = \$6$/hour.

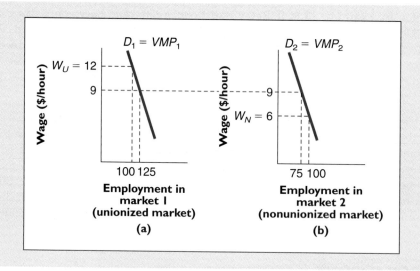

It might seem that the gains of the unionized workers are exactly offset by the losses of nonunionized workers. On closer inspection, however, we see that pegging the union wage above the equilibrium level actually reduces the value of total output. Recall from Chapter 2 that the condition for allocating a resource between two activities efficiently is for the marginal benefit of the resource to be the same in each activity. Here, the two activities are production in the unionized market and production in the nonunionized market; the marginal benefit of the resource in each market is the labor's *VMP* in that market. With the wage set initially at $9/hour in both markets, the condition for efficient allocation was met, because labor's *VMP* was $9/hour in both markets. But because the collective bargaining process drives wages in the two markets apart, the value of total output is no longer maximized. To verify this claim, note that if a worker is taken out of the nonunionized market, the reduction in the value of output there will be only $6/hour, which is less than the $12/hour gain in the value of output when that same worker is added to the unionized market.

EXERCISE 13.5

In Figure 13.4, by how much would the value of total output be increased if the wage rate were $9/hour in each market?

If unionized firms have to pay more, how do they manage to survive in the face of competition from their nonunionized counterparts?

In fact, nonunionized firms sometimes do drive unionized firms out of business, as when the American textile industry moved to the south to escape the burden of high union wages in New England. Even so, unionized and nonunionized firms often manage to compete head-to-head for extended periods. If their costs are significantly higher, how do the unionized firms manage to survive?

Wages paid to workers in a unionized firm are sometimes 50 percent or more above the wages paid to their nonunionized counterparts. But this difference actually overstates the difference between the labor costs of the two types of firms. Because the higher union wage attracts an excess supply of workers, unionized employers can adopt more stringent hiring requirements than their nonunionized counterparts. As a result, unionized workers tend to be more experienced and skilled than nonunionized workers. Studies estimate that the union wage premium for workers with the same amount of human capital is only about 10 percent.

Another factor is that unions may actually boost the productivity of workers with any given amount of human capital, perhaps by improving communication between management and workers. Similarly, the implementation of formal grievance procedures, in combination with higher pay, may boost morale among unionized workers, leading to higher productivity. Labor turnover is also significantly lower in unionized firms, which reduces hiring and training costs. Studies suggest that union productivity may be sufficiently high to compensate for the premium in union wages. So even though wages are higher in unionized firms, these firms may not have significantly higher labor costs per unit of output than their nonunionized counterparts.

Only one in six American workers currently belongs to a labor union, about half the union membership rate during the 1950s. Because the union wage premium is small and applies to only a small fraction of the labor force, union membership in the United States is probably not an important explanation for why workers with similar qualifications often earn sharply different incomes.

WINNER-TAKE-ALL MARKETS

Differences in human capital do much to explain observed differences in earnings. Yet earnings differentials have also grown sharply in many occupations within which the distribution of human capital among workers seems essentially unchanged. Consider the following example.

Why does Kathleen Battle earn millions more than singers of only slightly lesser ability?

Although the best sopranos have always earned more than others with slightly lesser talents, the earnings gap is sharply larger now than it was in the last century. Today, top singers like Kathleen Battle earn millions of dollars per year, hundreds or even thousands of times what sopranos only marginally less talented earn. Given that listeners in blind hearings often have difficulty identifying the most highly paid singers, why is this earnings differential so large?

The answer lies in a fundamental change in the way we consume most of our music. In the nineteenth century, virtually all professional musicians delivered their services in concert halls in front of live audiences. (In 1900, the state of Iowa alone had more than 1,300 concert halls!) Audiences of that day would have been delighted to listen to the world's best soprano, but no one singer could hope to perform in more than a tiny fraction of the world's concert halls. Today, in contrast, most of the music we hear comes in recorded form, which enables the best soprano to be literally everywhere at once. As soon as the master recording has been made, Kathleen Battle's performance can be burned onto compact discs at the same low cost as for a slightly less talented singer's.

ECONOMIC NATURALIST 13.1

ECONOMIC NATURALIST 13.2

Tens of millions of buyers worldwide are willing to pay a few cents extra to hear the most talented performers. Recording companies would be delighted to hire those singers at modest salaries, for by so doing they would earn an enormous economic profit. But that would unleash bidding by rival recording companies for the best singers. Such bidding assures that the top singers will earn multimillion dollar annual salaries (most of which constitute economic rents, as discussed in Chapter 8). Slightly less talented singers earn much less, because the recording industry simply does not need those singers.

winner-take-all labor market
one in which small differences in human capital translate into large differences in pay

The market for sopranos is an example of a **winner-take-all market,** one in which small differences in ability or other dimensions of human capital translate into large differences in pay. Long familiar in entertainment and professional sports, this reward pattern is becoming more common in other professions, as technology enables the most talented individuals to serve broader markets. A winner-take-all market does not mean a market with literally only one winner. Indeed, hundreds of professional musicians earn multimillion dollar annual salaries. Yet tens of thousands of others, many of them nearly as good, struggle to pay their bills.

One consequence of the spread of winner-take-all markets has been the sharp increase in the pay of top earners relative to others. Compensation of the chief executives of America's largest companies, for example, is now more than 400 times the salary of the average American production worker, up from a multiple of 42 in 1980. These executives now average roughly $4 million/year, and the highest paid among them earn considerably more.

The top earners on Wall Street have also fared well. For example, roughly 1,000 Wall Street professionals received bonuses in excess of $1 million in 1997–1998. Goldman Sachs alone made roughly $3 billion in fiscal 1997, the bulk of which was apportioned among its 190 most senior directors. In terms of their "current compensation," these directors typically earn less than $4 million annually, but many took home nearly four times that amount in bonus money. One layer down in the hierarchy, Goldman's 215 managing directors received an average of $1.5 million in 1998 bonus money.

A similar earnings explosion has taken place in publishing, where even six-figure advances for works of hardcover fiction were rare just two decades ago. For authors, the watershed event was the $5 million paid in 1985 by William Morrow for the rights to James Clavel's novel *Whirlwind*. Five years later, NAL/Viking paid Stephen King $40 million for the rights to his next four novels, and Dell/Delacourt paid Danielle Steel $60 million for her next five books.

Big winners have also become increasingly common in show business and professional sports. Both Mel Gibson and Adam Sandler now command approximately $25 million per film. In his final year of play, Chicago Bulls star Michael Jordan was paid about $30 million, and he earned a considerably larger sum for his various product endorsements.

Some social critics view the escalating salaries of top earners as a signal that labor markets are no longer effectively competitive. Yet competitive pressures in domestic and international labor markets have never been more intense than they are today. The role of growing competition in the rise of top performers' salaries is clearly evident in the salary trajectory of professional baseball players.

Why did professional baseball players' salaries remain stagnant until 1975, despite the large influx of television revenue that began in the 1950s?

Baseball as a whole grew much more lucrative in the 1950s to 1970s with the influx of national and local television revenues (another example of how new technology enables top performers to serve broader markets). Why, then, were players' salaries little higher in 1975 than in 1950?

Until 1975, contract restrictions prevented players from selling their services to the highest bidder. They had to play for their current teams or not play at all. Under such restrictions, the predictions of a competitive labor market theory simply do not apply. Two important court decisions, one in 1975, the other in 1976, ushered in the modern era of free agency, in which players are essentially free to play for whichever teams they choose. As Figure 13.5 shows, player salaries began escalating sharply in the aftermath of those court decisions. The pace of salary growth escalated further with the signing of the $1 billion CBS television contract in 1988.

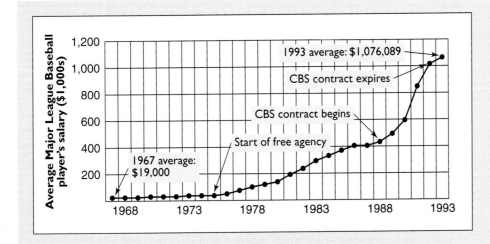

FIGURE 13.5
Salary Growth in Professional Baseball.
The value of baseball players' services rose sharply in the 1950s, when nationally televised games dramatically increased the size of the audience. But this increase in value was not reflected in salaries until 1975, when players won the right to sell their services to any team they chose. (SOURCE: Major League Baseball Players Association.)

Many critics have complained that the rapid escalation of players' salaries is a sure signal that team owners have lost their senses. This charge, too, misses the mark. The New York Yankees offered star center fielder Bernie Williams an $87 million contract in 1998 not because team owner George Steinbrenner was stupid but because Williams's presence helped fill the stands, land a more lucrative TV contract, and win the World Series. Williams was a free agent when he signed with the Yankees, and a smaller offer would have risked losing him to a rival bidder.

Why have the salaries of corporate executives been rising so rapidly?

As noted earlier, the chief executive officers of America's 200 largest companies made 42 times as much as the average production worker in 1980 but now earn more than 400 times as much. Why this dramatic increase?

Growth in productivity of the top performers and the more open bidding for their services have occurred for different reasons in different markets. In broad terms, however, the story has been much the same in the market for executive talent as in the market for professional baseball players. As a corporation's local markets have expanded into regional, then national, and finally global markets, the value of good decisions at the top of the organization has grown rapidly. But as in baseball, contributing a lot to the organization's bottom line does not guarantee a commensurate salary. There must also be open competition for the services of top performers. The almost universal practice once was to promote business executives from within the company, which often enabled firms to retain top executives for less than one-tenth of today's salaries. As recently as 1984, the business community arched its collective eyebrow when Apple Computer hired a new chief executive with a background in soft drink marketing.

But interfirm and interindustry boundaries have become increasingly permeable in the years since. As shown in Figure 13.6, for example, the number of chief executives hired from outside the company grew almost 50 percent between 1970 and 1992. This greater mobility has been accompanied by explosive growth in executive salaries.

ECONOMIC NATURALIST 13.4

FIGURE 13.6
Percentage of CEOs with Less than 3 Years' Tenure at Time of Hire.
The number of CEOs hired from outside the company grew almost 50 percent between 1990 and 1992, a factor that helped the rapid growth of CEO pay.
(SOURCE: Robert H. Frank and Philip J. Cook, *The Winner-Take-All Society,* New York: The Free Press, 1995.)

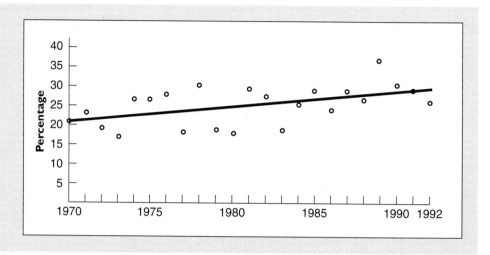

Disney CEO Michael Eisner was paid more than $500 million in 1997 not because he duped shareholders but because he delivered an unprecedented increase in the company's value at a time when the mobility of chief executives had made them increasingly like the free agents of professional sports.

The fact that small differences in human capital often give rise to extremely large differences in pay might seem to contradict human capital theory. Note, however, that the winner-take-all reward pattern is completely consistent with the competitive labor market theory's claim that individuals are paid in accordance with the contributions they make to the employer's net revenue. The leverage of technology often amplifies small performance differentials into very large ones.

COMPENSATING WAGE DIFFERENTIALS

If people are paid the value of what they produce, why do garbage collectors earn more than lifeguards? Picking up the trash is important, to be sure, but is it more valuable than saving the life of a drowning child? Similarly, we need not question the value of a timely plumbing repair to wonder why plumbers get paid more than fourth grade teachers. Is replacing faucet washers really more valuable than educating children? As the next examples illustrate, the wage for a particular job depends not only on the value of what workers produce but also on how attractive they find its working conditions.

Why do garbage collectors earn more than lifeguards?

ECONOMIC NATURALIST 13.5

There are two summer jobs open to the 20 Wisconsin undergraduates who live in a small northeastern city: lifeguards at the local beach (10 positions) and garbage collectors for the municipal sanitation department (10 positions). All 20 summer job seekers possess the requisite skills for each job, and all view the lifeguard job as the more desirable of the two. What will happen if the city posts the same wage rate for the two jobs?

Because lifeguarding is generally regarded as pleasant work and garbage collecting is generally regarded as unpleasant, we may expect 20 applicants for the lifeguard job and none for the garbage job. If city employment directors respond in the usual way to this imbalance in supply and demand, they will keep raising the wage of garbage collectors and keep lowering the wage for lifeguards until both labor markets reach equilibrium.

Other things being equal, jobs with attractive working conditions will pay less than jobs with less attractive conditions. Wage differences associated with differences in working conditions are known as **compensating wage differentials.** Economists have identified compensating differentials for a host of different specific working conditions. Studies have found, for example, that safe jobs tend to pay less than otherwise similar jobs that entail greater risks to health and safety. Studies have also found that wages vary in accord with the attractiveness of the work schedule. For instance, working night shifts commands a wage premium, and teachers must accept lower wages because those with children value having hours that coincide with the school calendar.

As the next example illustrates, we see compensating wage differentials even for such hard-to-measure characteristics as the degree of social approval associated with different jobs.

compensating wage differential a difference in the wage rate—negative or positive—that reflects the attractiveness of a job's working conditions

Why do some advertising copywriters earn more than others?

Suppose you plan to pursue a career in advertising. You have two job offers, one to write ad copy for the American Cancer Society, the other to write copy for Camel Cigarette ads aimed at the youth market. Except for the subject matter of the ads, working conditions are identical in the two jobs. If the two jobs paid the same salary, which would you choose?

This question and several similar ones were recently posed to a sample of seniors about to graduate from Cornell University, who were told that the jobs in each of the six matched pairs described in Table 13.7 pay $30,000/year and have the same prospects for advancement. Suppose the same questions were put to you: Imagine, for example, that you could be an accountant for a large petrochemical company or an accountant for a large art museum, with identical salaries, offices, tasks, promotion prospects, and so on. Which would you choose? Would you choose to be a language teacher for the CIA or a language teacher for a local high school? A recruiter for Exxon or a recruiter for the Peace Corps? And so on.

ECONOMIC NATURALIST 13.6

Do tobacco company CEOs get paid extra for testifying that cigarette smoking does not cause cancer?

TABLE 13.7
Job Pairs Requiring Similar Ability and Experience

Ad copywriter for Camel Cigarettes	Ad copywriter for the American Cancer Society
Accountant for a large petrochemical company	Accountant for a large art museum
Language teacher for the CIA	Language teacher for a local high school
Recruiter for Exxon	Recruiter for the Peace Corps
Lawyer for the National Rifle Association	Lawyer for the Sierra Club
Chemist for Union Carbide	Chemist for Dow Chemical

After students reported which job they would choose from each pair in Table 13.7, they were asked to report the minimum pay premium they would require for switching to the job they hadn't chosen. Table 13.8 reports the percentage of students who chose jobs in the right column of Table 13.7 and the median and average pay premiums they required for switching in each case.

Conversations with these students confirmed the impression that the favored jobs were chosen at least in part because they were more likely to command the social approval of others. This does not imply, necessarily, that there is anything morally questionable about the jobs that students tended not to choose. The Dow versus Union Carbide example is especially instructive in this regard. In the early 1970s, Dow was widely seen as an "evil" company because it manufactured the napalm that was dropped on villages during the Vietnam war. But memories of this association are no longer fresh. In contrast, many people still recall vividly the disaster in which poisonous methyl cyanate gas leaked from a Union Carbide chemical plant in Bhopal, India, killing and maiming tens of thousands of sleeping villagers. Despite the fact that subsequent

TABLE 13.8
Compensating Wage Differentials for Social Approval

Job chosen	Percentage choosing	Median pay premium for switching	Average pay premium for switching
American Cancer Society	88.2	$15,000/year	$24,333/year
Art museum	79.4	$ 5,000/year	$14,185/year
High school	82.4	$ 8,000/year	$18,679/year
Peace Corps	79.4	$ 5,000/year	$13,037/year
Sierra Club	94.1	$10,000/year	$37,129/year*
Dow Chemical	79.4	$ 2,000/year	$11,796/year

*Excludes one response of $1 trillion/year.

evidence suggested the accident resulted from negligence by Union Carbide's Indian partner, the company is only now beginning to recover from the damage the incident caused to its reputation.

Faced with two otherwise equally attractive jobs, most people will choose the employer whose mission they feel best about. How else can we explain why, in the years since it gained notoriety as a napalm manufacturer, Dow has invested millions of dollars on a national advertising campaign aimed at persuading the public that Dow's employees perform services that benefit humanity?

As the next example illustrates, employers can sometimes gain advantage by offering nonwage conditions that have special appeal to the types of workers they want.

ECONOMIC NATURALIST 13.7

Why did a telecommunications equipment manufacturer recently offer "free" BMW sedans to employees with more than 1 year of service?

Arcnet, Inc., which designs and builds wireless telecommunications systems, recently started giving a "free" BMW sedan to every employee with at least 1 year of service. The cars are not really free, of course. Each one costs the company about $9,000 a year in leasing and insurance fees, and employees who get one must declare that amount as additional income each year to the Internal Revenue Service. So we're left with a puzzle: If the company had given not the car but an additional $9,000 a year in salary instead, no one should have been worse off and at least some should have been better off. After all, any worker who really wanted a BMW could have spent the extra cash to lease one. Others who happen not to want a BMW would have come out ahead by having $9,000 a year extra to spend on other things. So why give cars instead of cash?

Essentially the same question is raised by ordinary gift exchanges among family and friends. Why give someone a necktie he might never wear when you know you could trust him to spend the same money on something he really wants? Some would answer that giving cash is just too easy and is hence a less effective way of demonstrating affection than taking the time and trouble to shop for a gift. That explanation might work for small gifts, but it is surely a stretch for luxury cars.

A more promising tack was suggested by the economist Richard Thaler, who observed that the best gifts are often things we don't dare buy for ourselves. Why, for example, is a man happy when his wife gives him a $1,000 set of titanium golf clubs paid for out of their joint checking account? Perhaps he really wanted those clubs but couldn't quite justify spending so much.

The plausibility of this way of thinking about gift giving is affirmed by the advice it suggests for gift givers. For example, consider this thought experiment: Among each of the following pairs of items costing the same amounts, which item would be the more suitable gift for a close friend?

- $20 worth of Macadamia nuts (1 pound) or $20 worth of peanuts (10 pounds)?

- A $75 gift certificate for Lespinasse (one lunch) or a $75 gift certificate for McDonald's (15 lunches)?

- $30 worth of wild rice (3 pounds) versus $30 worth of Uncle Ben's converted rice (50 pounds)?

For most people, the first item in each pair is almost surely the safer choice.

Arcnet and other employers in the fast lane may be giving away BMWs for essentially similar reasons. An employee might find it awkward to explain to his depression-era parents why he had bought a car costing almost twice as much as a Honda Accord. Or he may worry that buying a new BMW might make his neighbors think he was putting on airs. Or perhaps he really wants to buy the new BMW, but his wife insists on remodeling the kitchen instead. A gift car from his employer wipes away all these concerns and more.

Is the American labor market headed for a full-fledged barter system? Not likely, because the Arcnet strategy would make little sense for many employers. Burger King owners, for example, probably won't dangle used Ford Escorts the next time they find themselves short of counter help. They and other employers of unskilled labor are more likely to stick with the time-honored strategy of paying higher wages.

But in-kind compensation is almost certain to spread further among employers of the most highly skilled workers. It is these employers who have faced consistent labor shortages, and it's the people they are trying to hire and retain who have been so responsive to the new luxury offerings.

As the trend unfolds, the gifts are likely to change. The new strategy depends on the gift's ability to generate excitement. And excitement, always and everywhere, depends on context. Most readers were astonished when the young lawyer in John Grisham's 1991 novel *The Firm* was given a new German luxury sedan as a signing bonus, and the same tactic attracts media attention even today. As more and more companies adopt this tactic, however, it will inevitably lose much of its punch.

To achieve the same impact, employers will have to raise the stakes. Can anyone doubt that talented consultants and software developers will eventually snub any employer who dares offer less than a Porsche 911?

RECAP   **EXPLAINING DIFFERENCES IN EARNINGS**

Earnings differ among people in part because of differences in their human capital, an amalgam of personal characteristics that affect productivity. Two people with the same amount of human capital may earn different wages if one belongs to a labor union and the other does not. Their earnings may also differ because a given amount of human capital has greater leverage in some contexts than others. The world's most talented soprano is far more valuable, for example, if people can listen to her music not just in live performances but on compact discs as well. Earnings may also differ between equally productive individuals because of compensating wage differentials—positive or negative wage differentials attributable to differences in working conditions.

DISCRIMINATION IN THE LABOR MARKET

Women and minorities continue to receive lower wage rates, on average, than white males with similar measures of human capital. This pattern poses a profound challenge to standard theories of competitive labor markets, which hold that competitive pressures will eliminate wage differentials not based on differences in productivity. Defenders of standard theories attribute the wage gap to unmeasured differences in human capital. Critics of these theories, who reject the idea that labor markets are effectively competitive, attribute the gap to various forms of discrimination.

DISCRIMINATION BY EMPLOYERS

employer discrimination an arbitrary preference by the employer for one group of workers over another

Employer discrimination is the term used to describe wage differentials that arise from an arbitrary preference by the employer for one group of workers over another. An example occurs if two labor force groups, such as males and females, are equally productive, on average, yet some employers ("discriminators") prefer hiring males and are willing to pay higher wages to do so.

Most consumers are not willing to pay more for a product produced by males than for an identical one produced by females (if indeed they even *know* which type of worker produced the product). If product price is unaffected by the composition of the workforce that produces the product, a firm's profit will be smaller the more males it employs, because males cost more yet are no more productive. Thus the most profitable firms will be ones that employ only females.

Arbitrary wage gaps are an apparent violation of the equilibrium principle. The initial wage differential provides an opportunity for employers who hire mostly females to grow at the expense of their rivals. Because such firms make an economic profit on the sale of each unit of output, their incentive is to expand as rapidly as they possibly can. And to do that, they would naturally want to continue hiring only the cheaper females.

But as profit-seeking firms continue to pursue this strategy, the supply of females at the lower wage rate will run out. The short-run solution is to offer females a slightly higher wage. But this strategy works only if other firms do not pursue it. Once they too start offering a higher wage, females will again be in short supply. The only stable outcome will occur when the wage of females reaches parity with the wage of males. The wage for both males and females will thus settle at the common value of their *VMP*.

Any employer who wants to voice a preference for hiring males must now do so by paying males a wage in excess of their *VMP*. Employers can discriminate against females if they wish, but only if they are willing to pay premium wages to males out of their own profits. Not even the harshest critics of the competitive model seem willing to impute such behavior to the owners of capitalist enterprises.

DISCRIMINATION BY OTHERS

customer discrimination the willingness of consumers to pay more for a product produced by members of a favored group, even if the quality of the product is unaffected

If employer discrimination is not the primary explanation of the wage gap, what is? In some instances, **discrimination by customers** may provide a plausible explanation. For example, if people believe that juries and clients are less likely to take female or minority attorneys seriously, members of these groups will face a reduced incentive to attend law school, and law firms will face a reduced incentive to hire those who do.

Another possible source of persistent wage gaps is discrimination and socialization within the family. For example, families may provide less education for their female children, or they may socialize them to believe that lofty career ambitions are not appropriate.

OTHER SOURCES OF THE WAGE GAP

Family location constraints provide another possible explanation of wage differentials by sex. In two-career couples, the best job opportunities for both spouses are unlikely to be in the same local labor market. For spouses who wish to live together, one or both usually accept something less than the best available job offer. Compromises of this sort tend to be more costly the more human capital someone has.

Because women marry men who, on average, are several years older and have more education and experience than they do, the burden of those compromises tends to fall more heavily on wives. The historical pattern was that family location was dictated by the husband's best offer, and wives took the best job they could find in that particular labor market. Even within local markets, wives may be relatively more constrained in their choice of jobs by their desire to be closer to home and children's schools. Such constraints imply that part of the sex differential in wages is attributable to the fact that males can utilize their human capital more fully than females.

Related to location constraints are differences in preferences for other non-wage elements of the compensation package. Jobs that involve exposure to physical risk, for example, command higher wages, and if men are relatively more willing to accept such risks, they will earn more than females with otherwise identical stocks of human capital. (The same difference would result if employers felt constrained by social forces not to assign female employees to risky jobs.)

Elements of human capital that are difficult to measure may also help to explain earnings differentials. For example, productivity is influenced not only by the quantity of education an individual has, which is easy to measure, but also by its quality, which is much harder to measure. Part of the black-white differential in wages may thus be due to the fact that schools in black neighborhoods have not been as good, on average, as those in white neighborhoods. Differences in the courses people take in college appear to have similar implications for differences in productivity. For instance, students in math, engineering, or business—male or female—tend to earn significantly higher salaries than those who concentrate in the humanities. The fact that males are disproportionately represented in the former group gives rise to a male wage premium that is unrelated to employer discrimination.

"English lit—how about you?"

Wage differentials may also result from behavioral choices that affect productivity. As discussed earlier, for example, people earn less when they choose jobs, such as those commonly seen in the nonprofit sector, that provide a measure of moral satisfaction in exchange for smaller monetary compensation. When males choose such jobs, they earn the same low wages that women do. But women are much more likely than males to choose such jobs, and this difference further reduces the previously unexplained sex-differential in wages.

Wage rates depend not only on the total amount of experience someone has but also on the manner in which that experience accumulates. Continuous labor force participation results in significantly higher wages than intermittent labor force participation, for males and females. But because women are also more likely than men to specialize in childrearing, their labor force participation is more likely to be intermittent. Wage differentials that stem from differences in labor force participation patterns also cannot be attributed to employer discrimination.

Despite concerted efforts to explain sex and race differentials in wages, significant gaps remain. One recent survey, for example, reported that almost 40 percent of the wage gap between men and women with a high school education could not be explained by the usual human capital variables. Studies of wage differentials by race report similar findings. Debate about discrimination in the workplace will continue until the causes of these differentials are more fully understood.

COMPARABLE WORTH POLICIES: A COSTLY REMEDY?

comparable worth legislation
legislation that would set wages for a job not by market forces but by collective judgments about the social value of the job

Many social critics bemoan the fact that bond traders and personal-injury lawyers earn millions of dollars annually, while the salaries of teachers and librarians stagnate. Concern with such inequities has led some people to favor **comparable worth legislation**—statutes that would shift wage determination from private market forces to committees of government bureaucrats. The goal of those committees would be to assure that workers are paid in accord with the social value of what they produce. For example, if the committee decided that a good fourth grade teacher, or a brave soldier, is worth more to society than a good corporate tax specialist, it would set their respective salaries accordingly.

Regardless of one's views about the social concerns that motivated the comparable worth movement, there are good reasons to be skeptical about the proposed remedy. As discussed earlier, many people value employment that offers a chance to contribute to society's well-being. In perfectly competitive markets, workers in such jobs tend to earn lower wages—a compensating wage differential for morally satisfying work. Now suppose, as in Example 13.7, that a government regulation tried to prohibit compensating differentials for jobs that command social approval.

EXAMPLE 13.7

What would be the consequence of a law requiring that ad copywriters for the United Way be paid more than ad copywriters for the Philip Morris Tobacco Company?

Suppose the demand and supply curves for ad copywriters in the two settings are as shown in Figure 13.7. By how much will total economic surplus be reduced if the government says that ad copywriters for the United Way must be paid at least $60,000/year and that those who are employed by Philip Morris cannot be paid more?

In the unregulated case, ad copywriters who choose employment with the United Way will earn only $40,000/year [Figure 13.7(a)], while those who choose Philip Morris will earn $80,000/year. If comparable worth legislation then pegs the salary at $60,000/year for both employers, employment of copywriters will decline at each company: from 1,000 to 500 at United Way and from 1,000 to 750 at Philip Morris, as shown in Figure 13.8. The resulting reduction in total economic surplus is equal to the sum of the areas of the two pale blue triangles. The lost surplus at the United Way is $(1/2)(\$40,000)(500) = \$10$ million/year [part (a)]. The lost surplus at Philip Morris is $(1/2)(\$30,000)(250) = \$3.75$ million/year [part (b)].

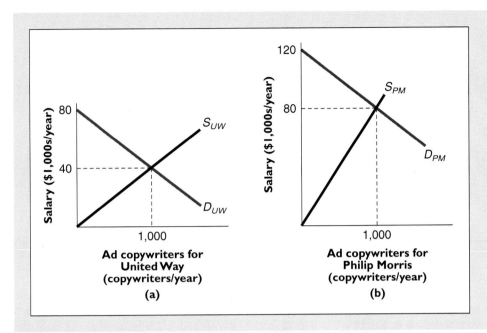

FIGURE 13.7
Equilibrium in Unregulated Markets for Ad Copywriters.
Because many ad copywriters prefer employment with the United Way to employment with Philip Morris, the equilibrium wage for copywriters will be higher at Philip Morris, part (b), than at the United Way, part (a).

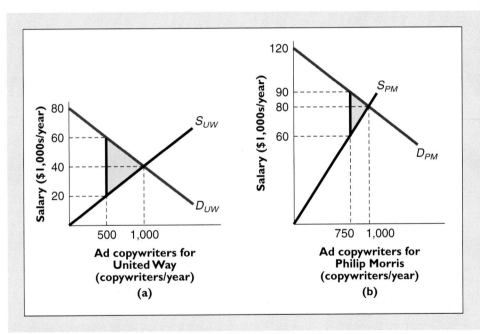

FIGURE 13.8
The Reduction in Economic Surplus Caused by Comparable Worth Legislation.
A comparable worth law that requires all ad copywriters to be paid $60,000 results in lost surplus of $10 million at United Way [area of the pale blue triangle, part (a)] and $3.75 million at Philip Morris [area of the pale blue triangle, part (b)].

Despite their manifestly benign intent, comparable worth statutes make the economic pie smaller by preventing markets from reaching equilibrium. Comparable worth legislation is thus similar in its effects to other laws that attempt to regulate prices. Any problem with an existing market equilibrium is best solved, as the efficiency principle reminds us, by altering the forces that produced that equilibrium in the first place. Any other approach inevitably results in failure to maximize total economic surplus.

> **RECAP**   **DISCRIMINATION IN THE LABOR MARKET**
>
> Critics of the theory of competitive labor markets have offered a variety of theories of discrimination to explain why women and minorities continue to receive lower wages than would be predicted by standard human capital models. The theory of employer discrimination holds that the observed wage gaps are the result of prejudice against women and minorities on the part of employers. The theory of customer discrimination attributes the same wage gaps to prejudice on the part of customers. Comparable worth policies attempt to reduce wage gaps by imposing collective restraints on the amounts that different employees may be paid.

■ SUMMARY ■

- A worker's long-run equilibrium pay in a competitive labor market will be equal to the value of her marginal product (*VMP*)—the market value of whatever goods and services she produces for her employer. The law of diminishing returns says that when a firm's capital and other productive inputs are held fixed in the short run, adding workers beyond some point results in ever-smaller increases in output. Firms that purchase labor in competitive labor markets face a constant wage, and they will hire labor up to the point at which *VMP* equals the market wage.

- Human capital theory says that an individual's *VMP* is proportional to his stock of human capital—an amalgam of education, experience, training, intelligence, and other factors that influence productivity. According to this theory, some occupations pay better than others simply because they require larger stocks of human capital.

- Wages often differ between individuals whose stocks of human capital appear nearly the same, as when one belongs to a labor union and the other does not. Technologies that allow the most productive individuals to serve broader markets can translate even small differences in performance into enormous differences in pay. Such technologies give rise to winner-take-all markets, which have long been common in sports and entertainment and which are becoming common in other professions.

- Compensating wage differentials—wage differences associated with differences in working conditions—are another important explanation for why some earn more than oth-

ers. They help to explain why garbage collectors earn more than lifeguards and, more generally, why individuals with a given stock of human capital tend to earn more in jobs that have less attractive working conditions.

- Many firms pay members of certain groups—notably blacks and females—less than they pay white males with similar personal characteristics. If such wage gaps are the result of employer discrimination, their existence implies profit opportunities for firms that do not discriminate. Several other factors, including discrimination by customers and institutions other than firms, may explain at least part of the observed wage gaps.

- Proponents of comparable worth legislation have proposed that wages be based not on market forces but instead on government assessments of social value. Such proposals would reduce economic surplus by preventing employers and workers from making mutually advantageous exchanges.

- Competitive labor markets do a remarkable job of creating order out of chaos. Driven only by the usual mix of human motives, people sort themselves surprisingly well into the jobs that interest them most and make the most productive use of their talents and training. In the process, most workers manage to support themselves and their families without government assistance. But the labor market is not immune from the imperfections that plague product markets. Monopsonists tend to hire too few workers, just as monopolists tend to produce too little output.

■ KEY TERMS ■

comparable worth legislation (342)
compensating wage differential (336)
customer discrimination (340)
employer discrimination (340)
human capital (330)

human capital theory (330)
labor union (331)
marginal labor cost (326)
marginal product of labor (322)
monopsony (325)

value of marginal product (*VMP*) (323)
winner-take-all market (334)

■ REVIEW QUESTIONS ■

1. You are an aide to a senator who wants advice about how to vote on a proposal that would outlaw paying truck drivers more than librarians. Can you suggest a more efficient way to promote the objective of the proposal, which is to increase the salary of librarians relative to other workers?

2. Why is the supply curve of labor for any specific occupation likely to be upward-sloping, even if, for the economy as a whole, people work fewer hours when wage rates increase?

3. True or false: If the human capital possessed by two workers is nearly the same, their wage rates will be nearly the same. Explain.

4. Congress periodically holds hearings to examine the effects of smoking on health. The witnesses who testify at those hearings under the sponsorship of the Tobacco Institute (a cigarette industry organization) are generally thought to have weaker scientific reputations than the witnesses who testify under the sponsorship of the American Cancer Society. Why, then, do the former witnesses get paid much more than the latter?

5. True or false: Economic surplus would be larger if a profit-maximizing monopsonist in the labor market were required to hire one more worker than it otherwise would have chosen to. Explain.

■ PROBLEMS ■

1. Mountain Breeze supplies air filters to the retail market and hires workers to assemble the components. An air filter sells for $26, and Mountain Breeze can buy the components for each filter for $1. Sandra and Bobby are two workers for Mountain Breeze. Sandra can assemble 60 air filters per month, and Bobby can assemble 70. If the labor market is perfectly competitive, how much will Sandra and Bobby be paid?

2. Stone, Inc., owns a clothing factory and hires workers in a competitive labor market to cut and sew denim fabric into jeans. The fabric required to make each pair of jeans costs $5. The company's weekly output of finished jeans varies with the number of workers hired, as shown in the following table:

Number of workers	Jeans (pairs/week)
0	0
1	25
2	45
3	60
4	72
5	80
6	85

  a. If the jeans sell for $35/pair, and the competitive market wage is $250/week, how many workers should Stone hire? How many pairs of jeans will the company produce each week?
  b. Suppose the Clothing Workers Union now sets a weekly minimum acceptable wage of $230/week. All the workers Stone hires belong to the union. How does the minimum wage affect Stone's decision about how many workers to hire?
  c. If the minimum wage set by the union had been $400/week, how would the minimum wage affect Stone's decision about how many workers to hire?
  d. If Stone again faces a market wage of $250/week, but the price of jeans rises to $45/week, how many workers will the company now hire?

3. The Rainflower Cactus Nursery is the only employer in a small town in Nevada. It sells potted cacti at $5 each, and its weekly output of cacti varies with the number of workers, as shown in the following table:

Number of workers	Potted cacti/week
0	0
1	50
2	90
3	120
4	140
5	150
6	155

There are six people in town potentially available to work at Rainflower. The six people, together with their reservation wages, are shown in the following table:

Worker	Reservation wage ($/week)
Jon	75
Joe	80
Jenny	85
Jeff	90
Jessica	100
Luke	150

    a. If Rainflower must pay the same wage to all workers, how many workers will the firm hire? What wage will it pay?

    b. What is the socially optimal number of workers to hire?

    c. If Rainflower could pay each worker exactly his or her reservation wage, how many workers would the company hire?

4. Acme, Inc., supplies rocket ships to the retail market and hires workers to assemble the components. A rocket ship sells for $30,000, and Acme can buy the components for each rocket ship for $25,000. Wiley and Sam are two workers for Acme. Sam can assemble one-fifth rocket ship per month, and Wiley can assemble one-tenth. If the labor market is perfectly competitive and rocket components are Acme's only other cost, how much will Sam and Wiley be paid?

5. Carolyn owns a soda factory and hires workers in a competitive labor market to bottle the soda. Her company's weekly output of bottled soda varies with the number of workers hired, as shown in the following table:

Number of workers	Cases/week
0	0
1	200
2	360
3	480
4	560
5	600

    a. If each case sells for $10 more than the cost of the materials used in producing it and the competitive market wage is $1,000/week, how many workers should Carolyn hire? How many cases will be produced per week?

b. Suppose the Soda Bottlers Union now sets a weekly minimum acceptable wage of $1,500/week. All the workers Carolyn hires belong to the union. How does the minimum wage affect Carolyn's decision about how many workers to hire?

c. If the wage is again $1,000/week but the price of soda rises to $15/case, how many workers will Carolyn now hire?

6. Laura has a nursing degree and 2 years of experience working at George Washington University Hospital. If she continues along her present career path, the present value of her lifetime earnings will be $200,000. If she takes 2 years off and completes a midwifery degree, the present value of her lifetime earnings will be $221,000. However, she must make two tuition payments for the midwifery course, one now and one a year from now, both of $10,500. Apart from her salary, Laura is indifferent between nursing and midwifery. If the interest rate is 5 percent, should Laura go to midwifery college? Explain.

7. Stefano is thinking about getting a law degree. If he continues along his present career path, the present value of his lifetime earnings will be $500,000. If instead he takes 3 years off and gets the law degree, the present value of his lifetime earnings will be $550,000. However, he must make annual tuition payments of $20,000 at the beginning of each academic year. Apart from his salary, Stefano is indifferent between his current occupation and a career in law. If the interest rate is 20 percent, should Stefano go to law school? Explain.

8. A simple economy has two labor markets for carpenters: one for residential houses, the other for commercial buildings. The demand for residential carpenters is given by $W_R = 40 - 10L_R$, where W_R is the wage of residential carpenters in dollars per hour and L_R is the number of residential carpenters in hundreds per day. The demand for commercial carpenters is given by $W_C = 40 - 5L_C$, where W_C is the wage of commercial carpenters in dollars per hour and L_C is the number of commercial carpenters in hundreds per day. The economy has 300 carpenters, each of whom has the skills required to be either a residential or a commercial carpenter, and each of whom wants to work full-time in whichever type of carpentry pays best. What will be the equilibrium wage and employment level for each type? (*Hint:* To find the total demand curve for carpenters, first graph the two demand curves side by side and then add them horizontally.)

9. In Problem 8, suppose commercial carpenters form a union and announce that they will not work for less than $30/hour. Any union member who cannot find work in the commercial market will work in the residential market. How many carpenters work in each market, and what is the wage in the residential market?

10. Refer to Problem 9. By how much does the formation of the commercial carpenter's union reduce the total value of carpenters' services provided each hour?

■ ANSWERS TO IN-CHAPTER EXERCISES ■

13.1 Adirondack will hire a second worker only if the *VMP* with two workers is at least 300. Since $VMP = (P)(MP)$, and since the marginal product of the second worker is 25 cutting boards, the lowest P for which the company will hire two workers is found by solving $(P)(25) = 300$ for $P = 12$.

13.2 Since the *VMP* of each worker exceeds $275, Adirondack will now hire five workers.

13.3 As shown in the following table, *VMP* for each of the first four workers now exceeds marginal labor cost, so Adirondack should now hire four workers.

Number of workers	Total number of cutting boards/week	MP (extra cutting boards/week)	VMP ($/week)	Marginal labor cost
0	0			
		30	900	200
1	30			
		25	750	300
2	55			
		21	632	400
3	76			
		18	540	500
4	94			
		14	420	600
5	108			

13.4 A higher interest rate reduces the present value of both the cost of an MBA degree and the resulting higher earnings. But the cost of getting an MBA occurs during the next 2 years, while the salary increase is spread out over many years. The higher interest rate will therefore reduce the present value of the benefit of the degree by more than it will reduce the present value of its cost. Since Betsy was indifferent at an interest rate of 10 percent, she should not get the degree if the interest rate is 12 percent.

13.5 When the wage rate is $9/hour in each market, 25 fewer workers will be employed in the nonunionized market and 25 more in the unionized market. The loss in output from removing 25 workers from the nonunionized market is the sum of the VMPs of those workers, which is the pale blue area in part (b) of the following figure. This area is $187.50/hour. (*Hint:* To calculate this area, first break the figure into a rectangle and a triangle.) The gain in output from adding 25 workers to the unionized market is the pale blue area in part (a), which is $262.50/hour. The net increase in output is thus $262.50 − $187.50 = $75/hour.

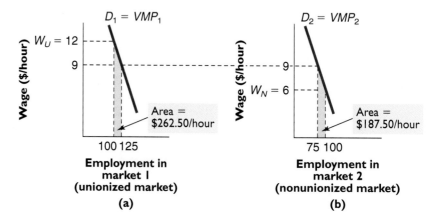

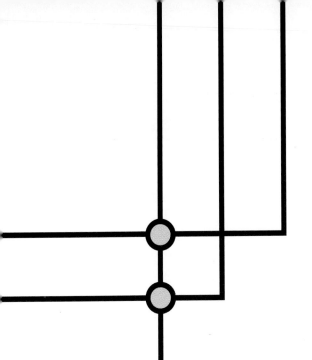

THE ECONOMICS OF PUBLIC POLICY

■

I n 1979, in the wake of the second major oil supply interruption in a decade, officials in the Carter administration met to discuss policies for reducing U.S. dependence on foreign oil. The proposal they ultimately put forward was a gasoline tax of 50 cents per gallon. Anticipating objections that the tax would impose an unacceptable hardship on the poor, policymakers proposed to return the revenues from the tax to the citizenry by reducing the payroll tax, the tax on wages that supports the Social Security system.

Proponents of the gasoline tax argued that in addition to reducing the nation's dependence on foreign oil, the tax would reduce air pollution and ease highway congestion. But critics ridiculed the proposal, charging that if the revenues from the tax were returned to the people, the quantity of gasoline demanded would remain essentially the same. Their argument tipped the debate, and officials never managed to implement the proposal.

But whatever the ultimate merits of the administration's proposal, there was no merit at all in the argument the critics used to attack it. True, the proposed tax rebate meant that people *could* have bought just as much gasoline as before the tax. Yet the tax would have given them a powerful incentive not to do so. As we saw in Chapter 5, the cost-benefit principle leads consumers to change their behavior to escape the effects of a steep rise in the after-tax price of gasoline: by switching to cars with smaller, more fuel-efficient engines, forming carpools, and so on. Such changes free up money to spend on other goods and services, which become relatively more attractive because they are not taxed.

No society can hope to formulate and implement intelligent economic policies unless its citizens and leaders share an understanding of basic economic principles. Our aim in this chapter will be to explore how careful application of these principles can help us design policies that both expand the economic pie and make everyone's slice larger. We will begin with a discussion of government policy toward natural monopoly, and then we will explore a seemingly unrelated collection of policy issues, including the pricing of public services, health care delivery, environmental regulation, and crime control. The unifying thread running through these issues is the problem of scarcity. In each case, we will explore how the cost-benefit principle can help to resolve the resulting trade-offs.

PUBLIC POLICY TOWARD NATURAL MONOPOLY

Monopoly is problematic not only because of the loss in efficiency associated with restricted output but also because the monopolist earns an economic profit at the buyer's expense. Many people are understandably uncomfortable about having to purchase from the sole provider of any good or service. For this reason, voters in many societies have empowered government to adopt policies aimed at controlling natural monopolists.

There are several ways to achieve this aim. A government may assume ownership and control of a natural monopoly, or it may merely attempt to regulate the prices it charges. In some cases government solicits competitive bids from private firms to produce natural monopoly services. In still other cases, governments attempt to dissolve natural monopolies into smaller entities that compete with one another. But many of these policies create economic problems of their own. In each case, the practical challenge is to come up with the solution that yields the greatest surplus of benefits over costs. Natural monopoly may be inefficient and unfair, but the alternatives to natural monopoly are far from perfect.

STATE OWNERSHIP AND MANAGEMENT

Recall from Chapter 9 that a natural monopoly is inefficient because the monopolist's profit-maximizing price is greater than its marginal cost. But even if the natural monopolist *wanted* to set price equal to marginal cost, it could not do so and hope to remain in business. After all, the defining feature of a natural monopoly is economies of scale in production, which means that marginal cost will always be less than average cost. Setting price equal to marginal cost would fail to cover average production cost, which implies an economic loss.

Consider the case of a local cable television company. Once an area has been wired for cable television, the marginal cost of adding an additional subscriber is very low. For the sake of efficiency, all subscribers should pay a price equal to that marginal cost. Yet a cable company that priced in this manner would never be able to recover the fixed cost of setting up the network. This same problem applies not just to cable television companies but to all other natural monopolies. Even if such firms wanted to set price equal to marginal cost (which, of course, they do not, since they will earn more by setting marginal revenue equal to marginal cost), they cannot do so without suffering an economic loss.

One way to attack the efficiency and fairness problems is for the government to take over the industry, set price equal to marginal cost, and then absorb the resulting losses out of general tax revenues. This approach has been followed with good results in the state-owned electric utility industry in France, whose efficient pricing methods have set the standard for electricity pricing worldwide.

But state ownership and efficient management do not always go hand in hand. Granted, the state-owned natural monopoly is free to charge marginal cost, while the private natural monopoly is not. Yet private natural monopolies often face a much stronger incentive to cut costs than their government-owned counterparts. When the private monopolist figures out a way to cut $1 from the cost of production, its profit goes up by $1. But when the government manager of a state-owned monopoly cuts $1 from the cost of production, the government typically cuts the monopoly's budget by $1. Think back to your last visit to the Department of Motor Vehicles. Did it strike you as an efficiently managed organization?

Whether the efficiency that is gained by being able to set price equal to marginal cost outweighs the inefficiency that results from a weakened incentive to cut costs is an empirical question.

STATE REGULATION OF PRIVATE MONOPOLIES

In the United States, the most common method of curbing monopoly profits is for government merely to regulate the natural monopoly rather than own it. Most states, for example, take this approach with electric utilities, natural gas providers, local telephone companies, and cable television companies. The standard procedure in these cases is called **cost-plus regulation:** Government regulators gather data on the monopolist's explicit costs of production and then permit the monopolist to set prices that cover those costs, plus a markup to assure a normal return on the firm's investment.

cost-plus regulation a method of regulation under which the regulated firm is permitted to charge a price equal to its explicit costs of production plus a markup to cover the opportunity cost of resources provided by the firm's owners

While it may sound reasonable, cost-plus regulation has several pitfalls. First, it generates costly administrative proceedings in which regulators and firms quarrel over which of the firm's expenditures can properly be included in the costs it is allowed to recover. This question is difficult to answer even in theory. Consider a firm like Pacific Telesis, whose local telephone service is subject to cost-plus regulation but whose other products and services are unregulated. Many Pacific Telesis employees, from the president on down, are involved in both regulated and unregulated activities. How should their salaries be allocated between the two? The company has a strong incentive to argue for greater allocation to the regulated activities, which allows it to capture more revenue from captive customers in the local telephone market.

A second problem with cost-plus regulation is that it blunts the firm's incentive to adopt cost-saving innovations, for when it does, regulators require the firm to cut its rates. The firm gets to keep its cost savings in the current period, which is a stronger incentive to cut costs than the one facing a government-owned monopoly. But the incentive to cut costs would be stronger still if the firm could retain its cost savings indefinitely. Furthermore, in cases in which regulators set rates by allowing the monopolist to add a fixed markup to costs incurred, the regulated monopolist may actually have an incentive to *increase* costs rather than reduce them. Outrageous though the thought may be, the monopolist may earn a higher profit by installing gold-plated faucets in the company rest rooms.

Finally, cost-plus regulation does not solve the natural monopolist's basic problem, the inability to set price equal to marginal cost without losing money. Although these are all serious problems, governments seem to be in no hurry to abandon cost-plus regulation.

EXCLUSIVE CONTRACTING FOR NATURAL MONOPOLY

One of the most promising methods for dealing with natural monopoly is for the government to invite private firms to bid for the natural monopolist's market. The government specifies in detail the service it wants—cable television, fire protection, garbage collection—and firms submit bids describing how much they will charge for the service. The low bidder wins the contract.

The incentive to cut costs under such an arrangement is every bit as powerful as that facing ordinary competitive firms. Competition among bidders should also eliminate any concerns about the fairness of monopoly profits. And if the government is willing to provide a cash subsidy to the winning bidder, exclusive contracting even allows the monopolist to set price equal to marginal cost.

Contracting has been employed with good results in municipal fire protection and garbage collection. Communities that employ private companies to provide these services often spend only half as much as adjacent communities served by municipal fire and sanitation departments.

Despite these attractive features, however, exclusive contracting is not without problems, especially when the service to be provided is complex or requires a large fixed investment in capital equipment. In such cases, contract specifications may be so detailed and complicated that they become tantamount to regulating the firm directly. And in cases involving a large fixed investment—electric power generation and distribution, for example—officials face the question of how to transfer the assets if a new firm wins the contract. The winning firm naturally wants to acquire the assets as cheaply as possible, but the retiring firm is entitled to a fair price for them. What, in such cases, is a fair price?

Fire protection and garbage collection are simple enough that the costs of contracting out these functions is not prohibitive. But in other cases, such costs might easily outweigh any savings made possible by exclusive contracting.

VIGOROUS ENFORCEMENT OF ANTITRUST LAWS

The nineteenth century witnessed the accumulation of massive private fortunes, the likes of which had never been seen in the industrialized world. Public sentiment ran high against the so-called robber barons of the period—the Carnegies, Rockefellers, Mellons, and others. In 1890, Congress passed the Sherman Act, which declared illegal any conspiracy "to monopolize, or attempt to monopolize . . . any part of the trade or commerce among the several States . . ." And in 1914, Congress passed the Clayton Act, whose aim was to prevent corporations from acquiring shares in a competitor if the transaction would "substantially lessen competition or create a monopoly."

Antitrust laws have helped to prevent the formation of cartels, or coalitions of firms that collude to raise prices above competitive levels. But they have also caused some harm. For example, federal antitrust officials spent more than a decade trying to break up the IBM Corporation in the belief that it had achieved an unhealthy dominance in the computer industry. That view was proved comically wrong by IBM's subsequent failure to foresee and profit from the rise of the personal computer. By breaking up large companies and discouraging mergers between companies in the same industry, antitrust laws may help to promote competition, but they may also prevent companies from achieving economies of scale.

A final possibility is simply to ignore the problem of natural monopoly: to let the monopolist choose the quantity to produce and sell it at whatever price the market will bear. The obvious objections to this policy are the two we began with, namely, that a natural monopoly is not only inefficient but also unfair. But just as the hurdle method of price discrimination mitigates efficiency losses (see Chapter 9), it also lessens the concern about taking unfair advantage of buyers.

Consider first the source of the natural monopolist's economic profit. This firm, recall, is one with economies of scale, which means that its average production cost declines as output increases. Efficiency requires that price be set at marginal cost, but because the natural monopolist's marginal cost is lower than its average cost, it cannot charge all buyers the marginal cost without suffering an economic loss.

The depth and prevalence of discount pricing suggests that whatever economic profit a natural monopolist earns generally will not come out of the discount buyer's pocket. Although discount prices are higher than the monopolist's marginal cost of production, in most cases they are lower than the average cost. Thus the monopolist's economic profit, if any, must come from buyers who pay list price. And since those buyers have the option, in most cases, of jumping a hurdle and paying a discount price, their contribution, if not completely voluntary, is at least not strongly coerced.

So much for the source of the monopolist's economic profit. What about its disposition? Who gets it? A large chunk—some 35 percent, in many cases—goes to the federal government via the corporate income tax. The remainder is paid out to shareholders, some of whom are wealthy and some of whom are not. These shareholder profits are also taxed by state and even local governments. In the end, two-thirds or more of a monopolist's economic profit may fund services provided by governments of various levels.

Both the source of the monopolist's economic profit (the list price buyer) and the disposition of that profit (largely, to fund public services) cast doubt on the claim that monopoly profit constitutes a social injustice on any grand scale. Nevertheless, the hurdle method of differential pricing cannot completely eliminate the fairness and efficiency problems that result from monopoly pricing. In the end, then, we are left with a choice among imperfect alternatives. As the cost-benefit principle emphasizes, the best choice is the one for which the balance of benefits over costs is largest. But which choice that is will depend on the circumstances at hand.

> **RECAP** **PUBLIC POLICY TOWARD NATURAL MONOPOLY**
>
> The natural monopolist sets price above marginal cost, resulting in too little output from society's point of view (the efficiency problem). The natural monopolist may also earn an economic profit at buyers' expense (the fairness problem). Policies for dealing with the efficiency and fairness problems include state ownership and management, state regulation, exclusive contracting, and vigorous enforcement of antitrust laws. Each of these remedies entails problems of its own.

MARGINAL COST PRICING OF PUBLIC SERVICES

Suppose the government has decided to become the provider of a natural monopoly good or service. How much should it charge its customers? The theory of competitive supply, normally applied to perfectly competitive firms that can sell any quantity they choose at a constant market price (see Chapter 6), helps to answer this question. Consider Example 14.1, in which a local government supplies water to its residents.

What is the marginal cost of water in Gainesville?

EXAMPLE 14.1

The municipal water supply company in Gainesville, Florida, has three potential sources of water: an underground spring, a nearby lake, and the Atlantic Ocean. The spring can supply up to 1 million gallons/day at a cost of 0.2 cent/gallon. The lake can supply an additional 2 million gallons/day at a cost of 0.8 cent/gallon. Additional water must be distilled from the ocean at a cost of 4.0 cents/gallon. Draw the marginal cost curve for water in Gainesville.

The low-hanging-fruit principle tells us that the city will use the cheapest source of water first (the spring). Only when the quantity demanded exceeds the spring's capacity will the city turn to the next least expensive source, the lake; and only when the lake's capacity is exhausted will the city supply water from the ocean. The marginal cost curve will thus be as shown in Figure 14.1.

FIGURE 14.1
The Marginal Cost Curve for Water.
The current marginal cost of water is the cost of producing an extra gallon by means of the most expensive production source currently in use.

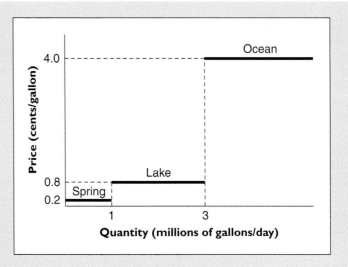

EXAMPLE 14.2

How much should the government charge for water?

In Example 14.1, suppose that if the price of water were 4.0 cents/gallon, citizens of Gainesville would consume 4 million gallons/day. Given the marginal cost curve shown in Figure 14.1, how much should the city charge a citizen whose water comes from the underground spring? How much should it charge someone whose water comes from the lake?

The citizens of Gainesville will enjoy the largest possible economic surplus if the price they pay for water exactly equals the marginal cost of providing it. Since the total amount of water demanded at 4.0 cents/gallon exceeds 3 million gallons/day, the city will have to supply at least some households with water distilled from the Atlantic Ocean, at a cost of 4.0 cents/gallon. At 4 million gallons/day, the marginal cost of water is thus 4.0 cents/gallon, and *that is true no matter where the water comes from.* As long as the city must get *some* of its water from the ocean, the marginal cost of water taken from the underground spring is 4.0 cents/gallon. Water taken from the lake also has a marginal cost of 4.0 cents/gallon.

This statement might seem to contradict the claim that water drawn from the spring costs only 0.2 cent/gallon, water drawn from the lake, only 0.8 cent/gallon. But there is no contradiction. To see why, ask yourself how much the city would save if a family that currently gets its water from the spring were to reduce its consumption by 1 gallon/day. The cutback would enable the city to divert that gallon of spring water to some other household that currently gets its water from the ocean, and that in turn would reduce consumption of ocean water by 1 gallon. So if a family currently served by the spring were to reduce its daily consumption by 1 gallon, the cost savings would be exactly 4.0 cents. And that, by definition, is the marginal cost of water.

To encourage the efficient use of water, the city should charge every household 4.0 cents/gallon for all the water it consumes. Charging any household less than that would encourage households to use water whose marginal benefit is less than its marginal cost. For example, suppose the city charged households who get their water from the spring only 0.2 cent/gallon. Those households would then expand their use of water until the benefit they received from the last gallon used equaled 0.2 cent. Because that gallon could have been used to serve someone who is currently using water distilled from the ocean, for whom the value of the marginal gallon is 4 cents, its use would entail a loss in economic surplus of 3.8 cents.

EXERCISE 14.1

Suppose that at a price of 0.8 cent/gallon the citizens of Gainesville would consume a total of only 2 million gallons/day. How much should the city charge for water? Should that same charge apply to people who get their water from the spring?

The general rule is that a public utility maximizes economic surplus by charging its customers the marginal cost of the goods or services it provides. Example 14.3 provides another illustration of this principle.

How should electric rates charged by a Vermont utility vary by season?

EXAMPLE 14.3

A government-owned electric utility in Vermont has two sources of power, a hydroelectric generator and a coal-burning steam generator. Electricity from the hydroelectric facility can be delivered to households at a cost of 2 cents/kilowatthour for any amount up to 4 million kilowatthours/day. Additional electricity can be produced in unlimited quantities by the steam generator, at a cost of 6 cents/kilowatthour. The company's daily demand curve for electricity during the summer months is $P = 4 - 2Q$, where P is the price in cents per kilowatthour and Q is the quantity demanded, in millions of kilowatthours per day. The demand curve for electricity in the winter months is $P = 12 - Q$. How much should this utility charge for electricity during the summer months? During the winter months? Should a family that receives its power directly from the hydroelectric generator during the winter months pay less than a family that receives its power from the steam generator?

As before, the efficient pricing rule is to set price equal to marginal cost, which depends on how much energy the utility produces each day. As shown in Figure 14.2, marginal cost *(MC)* is 2 cents/kilowatthour when production is between 0 and 4 million kilowatthours/day and 6 cents/kilowatthour when production levels exceed 4 million kilowatthours/day. To sell power efficiently, the utility should view this marginal cost curve as its supply curve and charge the market-clearing price for each season. During the winter months, demand intersects marginal cost at a price of 6 cents/kilowatthour, so that is the price the utility should charge in the winter. During the summer months, demand intersects marginal cost at a price of 2 cents/kilowatthour, so that is the optimal price during the summer months.

Note that the optimal price during the winter months is 6 cents/kilowatthour for *all* families, even those whose electricity is supplied by the hydroelectric generator. If you were the public relations spokesperson for this utility, how would

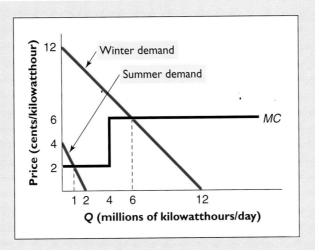

FIGURE 14.2
Seasonal Differences in Electric Rates.
The efficient price in each season is the one that equates marginal cost with seasonal demand. Given the two seasonal demand curves shown, the utility should charge 2 cents/kilowatthour in the summer months and 6 cents/kilowatthour in the winter months.

you respond to a family that complained it was being overcharged for the power it received from the hydroelectric generator in the winter? You might begin by pointing out how much the utility would save if it no longer had to supply power to this family. It could allocate the hydroelectric capacity this family used to some other family that would otherwise have been served by the steam generator, for a savings of 6 cents/kilowatthour. Whenever the utility has to supply more electricity than it can produce with the hydroelectric generator, the marginal cost of serving every user is 6 cents/kilowatthour.

EXERCISE 14.2

How would your answer to the question posed in Example 14.3 have differed if the winter demand curve had been $P = 8 - 2Q$?

> **RECAP** **MARGINAL COST PRICING OF PUBLIC SERVICES**
>
> For a good or service—private or public—to be allocated efficiently, its price must equal its marginal cost of production. This principle tells us that when a public utility supplies water or electricity from several different sources, each with different costs, all users should pay a price equal to the highest-cost source in current use.

HEALTH CARE DELIVERY

In the United States, real health care expenditures per capita have grown more rapidly than real income per capita for as long as the relevant data have been available. As a share of national income, health care costs have risen from only 4 percent in 1940 to roughly 14 percent today. Part of this increase is the result of costly new health care technologies and procedures. Diagnostic tests have grown more expensive and sophisticated, and procedures like coronary bypass surgery and organ transplantation have grown far more common. Yet a great deal of medical expenditure inflation has nothing to do with these high-tech developments. Rather, it is the result of fundamental changes in the way we pay for medical services.

The most important change has been the emergence of the so-called third-party payment system. Earlier in this century, many people insured themselves against catastrophic illness but purchased routine medical care out of their own pockets. But starting after World War II, and increasingly since the mid-1960s, people have come to depend on insurance for even routine medical services. Some of this insurance is provided privately by employers; some, by the government. In the latter category, Medicaid covers the medical expenses of the poor, and Medicare those of the elderly and disabled.

The spread of medical insurance, especially government-financed medical insurance, owes much to the belief that an inability to pay should not prevent people from receiving medical care they need. Indeed, medical insurance has surely done much to shelter people from financial hardship. The difficulty is that in its most common form, medical insurance has also spawned literally hundreds of billions of dollars of waste each year.

APPLYING THE COST-BENEFIT CRITERION

To understand the nature of this waste, we must recognize that although medical services differ from other services in many ways, they are in one fundamental respect the same—namely, that the cost-benefit test is the only sensible criterion for deciding which services ought to be performed. The fact that a medical procedure has *some* benefit does not, by itself, imply that the procedure should be performed. Rather, it should be performed only if its benefit, broadly construed, exceeds its cost.

The costs of medical procedures are relatively easy to measure, using the same methods applied to other goods and services. But the usual measure of the benefit of a good or service, a person's willingness to pay, may not be acceptable in the case of medical services. For example, most of us would not conclude that a lifesaving appendectomy that costs $2,000 is unjustified merely because the person who needs it can afford to pay only $1,000. When someone lacks the resources to pay for what most of us would consider an essential medical service, society has at least some responsibility to help. Hence the proliferation of government-sponsored medical insurance.

Many other medical expenditures are not as pressing as an emergency appendectomy, however. Following such surgery, for example, the patient requires a period of recuperation in the hospital. How long should that period last: 2 days? 5? 10? The cost-benefit principle is critically important to thinking intelligently about such questions. But as Example 14.4 illustrates, the third-party payment system has virtually eliminated cost-benefit thinking from the medical domain.

How long should David stay in the hospital?

To eliminate recurrent sore throats, David plans to have his tonsils removed. His surgeon tells him that the average hospital stay after this procedure is 2 days (some people stay only 1 day, while others stay 3, 4, or even 5 days). Hospital rooms cost $300/day. If David's demand curve for days in the hospital is as shown in Figure 14.3, how many days will he stay if he must pay for his hospital room himself? How many days will he stay if his medical insurance fully covers the cost of his hospital room?

EXAMPLE 14.4

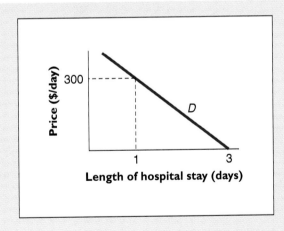

FIGURE 14.3
The Demand for Hospital Care.
The demand curve for postoperative hospital care is downward-sloping, just like any other demand curve. At higher prices, people choose shorter hospital stays, not because there is no benefit to a longer stay, but because they prefer to spend their money in other ways.

If David must pay for his hospital room himself, his best option will be to stay for just 1 day. But if the cost of his hospital room is completely covered by insurance, the marginal cost *to him* will be zero. In that case he will stay for 3 days.

Should we be concerned that people choose longer hospital stays when their expenses are fully insured? The cost-benefit principle tells us that a hospital stay should be extended another day only if the benefit of doing so would be at least as great as the cost of the resources required to extend the stay. But when hospital costs are fully covered by insurance, the decision maker sees a marginal cost of zero, when in fact the marginal cost is several hundred dollars. According to the cost-benefit criterion, then, full insurance coverage leads to wastefully long hospital stays. That is not to say that the additional days in the hospital do no good at all. Rather, their benefit is less than their cost. As Example 14.5 illustrates, a shorter hospital stay would increase total economic surplus.

EXAMPLE 14.5

How much waste does full insurance coverage cause?

Using the demand and cost information from Example 14.4, calculate how much waste results from full insurance coverage of David's hospital room.

If the marginal cost of an additional day in the hospital is $300, the supply curve of hospital room days in an open market would be horizontal at $300. If David had to pay that price, he would choose a 1-day stay, which would result in the largest possible economic surplus. If he extends his stay past 1 day, cost continues to accumulate at the rate of $300/day, but the benefit of additional care—as measured by his demand curve—falls below $300. If he stays 3 days, as he will if he has full insurance coverage, the extra 2 days cost society $600 but benefit David by only $300 (the area of the pale blue triangle under David's demand curve in Figure 14.4). The amount by which the extra cost exceeds the extra benefit will thus be $300 (the area of the dark blue triangle).

FIGURE 14.4
The Waste Resulting from Full Insurance Coverage.
The area of the pale blue triangle ($300) represents the benefit of extending the hospital stay from 1 to 3 days. Since the cost of the extra 2 days is $600, the area of the dark blue triangle ($300) represents the loss in economic surplus that results from the longer stay.

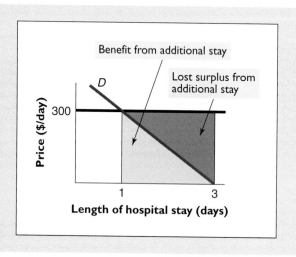

EXERCISE 14.3

Refer to Example 14.4. How much waste would be caused by an insurance policy that reimbursed hospital room expenses at the rate of $150/day?

DESIGNING A SOLUTION

In circumstances in which economic surplus has not been maximized, a transaction can always be found that will make both the patient *and* the insurance company better off. Suppose, for example, that the insurance company in Example 14.5 gives David a cash payment of $700 toward hospital expenses and lets him decide for himself how long to stay in the hospital. Confronted with a price of $300/day, David would choose to stay only a single day. The $400 cash he would have left after paying his hospital bill is $100 more than enough to compensate him for the benefit he would lose by not staying an extra 2 days. (Again, that benefit is $300, the area of the pale blue triangle in Figure 14.4.) A $700 cash payment would also leave his insurance company better off by $200 than if it had provided unlimited hospital coverage at no extra charge (since David would have stayed 3 days in that case). And since no one else is harmed by this transaction, it represents a *Pareto improvement* over unlimited coverage, meaning a change that makes some people better off without harming others (see Chapter 7).

The amount of waste caused by full insurance coverage depends on the price elasticity of demand for medical services—the more elastic the demand, the greater the waste. Proponents of full coverage believe that the demand for medical services is almost completely inelastic with respect to price and that the resulting waste is therefore negligible. Critics of full coverage argue that the demand for medical services is actually quite sensitive to price and that the resulting waste is significant.

Who is right? One way to tell is to examine whether people who lack full insurance coverage spend significantly less than those who have it. The economist W. G. Manning and several coauthors did so by performing an experiment in which they assigned subjects randomly to one of two different kinds of medical insurance policies.[1] The first group of subjects received **first-dollar insurance coverage**, meaning that 100 percent of their medical expenses were covered by insurance. The second group got "$1,000 deductible" coverage, meaning that only expenses beyond the first $1,000 a year were covered. (For example, subjects with $1,200 of medical bills would receive $1,200 from their insurance company if they belonged to the first group but only $200 if they belonged to the second.) In effect, since most people incur less than $1,000 a year in medical expenses, most subjects in the second group effectively paid full price for their medical services, while subjects in the first group paid nothing. Manning and his colleagues found that *people with $1,000 deductible policies spent between 40 and 50 percent less on health care than subjects with first-dollar coverage. More important, there were no measurable differences in health outcomes between the two groups.*

Taken at face value, the results of the Manning study suggest that a large share of the inflation in medical expenditures since World War II has been caused by growth in first-dollar medical insurance. Why not simply abandon first-dollar coverage in favor of high deductibles? People would still be protected against financial catastrophe but would have a strong incentive to avoid medical services whose benefit does not exceed their cost.

Some would say that Medicaid and Medicare should not carry high deductibles because they would impose too great a burden on poor families. But as in other instances in which concern for the poor is offered in defense of an inefficient policy, an alternative can be designed that is better for rich and poor alike. For example, all health insurance could be written to include high deductibles, and the poor could be given an annual stipend to defray the initial medical expenses not covered by insurance. At year's end, any unspent stipend would be theirs to keep. Here again, the efficiency principle reminds us that concern for the well-being of the poor is simply no reason for not adopting the most efficient policy.

first-dollar insurance coverage insurance that pays all expenses generated by the insured activity

THE HMO REVOLUTION

During the 1990s, the high cost of conventional health insurance led many people to switch to a **health maintenance organization (HMO)**. An HMO is a group of physicians that provides its patients with medical services in return for a fixed annual fee. As the next example illustrates, the incentive to provide any given medical service is weaker under the standard HMO contract than under conventional health insurance.

health maintenance organization (HMO) a group of physicians that provides health services to individuals and families for a fixed annual fee

[1]W. G. Manning, J. P. Newhouse, E. B. Keeler, A. Liebowitz, and M. S. Marquis, "Health Insurance and the Demand for Medical Care," *American Economic Review* 77: 251–277, June 1987.

Why is a patient with a sore knee more likely to receive a magnetic resonance imaging (MRI) exam if he has conventional health insurance than if he belongs to a health maintenance organization?

When a patient visits his physician complaining of a sore knee, the physician has several options. After hearing the patient describe his symptoms and examining the knee manually, the physician may prescribe anti-inflammatory drugs and advise the patient to abstain from vigorous physical activity for a period, or she may advise the patient to undergo an (MRI) exam, a costly diagnostic procedure that generates images of the inner workings of the injured joint. The physician in an HMO receives no additional revenue if she orders the MRI exam, because all services are covered by the patient's fixed annual fee. Under conventional health insurance, in contrast, the physician will be reimbursed at a fixed rate, usually well above her marginal cost, for each additional service performed.

"Well, Bob, it looks like a paper cut, but just to be sure let's do lots of tests."

In many instances, the most prudent course of treatment is unambiguous, and in such cases physicians will make the same recommendation despite this striking difference in incentives. But in many other cases, it may not be obvious which decision is best. And in these cases, HMO physicians are much less likely to order expensive tests.

People who switch to HMOs pay less for their health plans than those who stick with conventional health insurance, because the HMO contract provides a strong incentive for doctors not to prescribe nonessential services. Many people fear, however, that the very same incentive may sometimes result in their not receiving valuable care. These concerns have led to proposed legislation granting patients rights of appeal when they are denied care by an HMO.

PAYING FOR HEALTH INSURANCE

It is troubling, but perhaps not surprising, that access to medical care is extremely limited in many of the world's poorest nations. After all, citizens of those nations lack enough income to buy adequate food, shelter, and many other basic goods and services. What *is* surprising, however, is that despite the movement to less expensive HMO plans, some 45 million Americans had no health coverage of any kind in 2000, almost 5 million more than in 1993. Politicians in both parties agree that something must be done to expand health coverage. But before an intelligent solution to this problem can be implemented, we must first understand why so many people are without coverage in the first place.

In the richest country on earth, experiencing the longest sustained economic boom in its history, why do the ranks of the uninsured keep swelling?

Although the incomes of most Americans are higher than ever, millions of American families continue to experience day-to-day financial distress. In 1998, for example, one of every 68 families filed for bankruptcy, more than the number of families with children graduating from college that year. Under the circumstances, it is easy to see why many families in generally good health might be tempted to press their luck. After all, health coverage for a family of four with no preexisting medical conditions costs upward of $4,000 a year, which is almost always far more than what such a family spends on medical services. The extra cash could help pay for a move into a better school district, for example, or at least keep creditors at bay.

As more people cancel their health coverage, going without insurance becomes more socially acceptable. Parents who didn't buy health insurance for their families were once viewed as irresponsible, but this stigma loses some of its sting as the number of uninsured grows. Making matters worse is the changing composition of the pool of the insured. As more healthy families forgo coverage, those left tend to be sicker and more costly to treat, forcing up premiums (an example of *adverse selection,* discussed in Chapter 12). In short, our health insurance system is in a death spiral. And as more people become uninsured, the problem will get worse, because the costs borne by those who remain insured will continue to escalate.

ECONOMIC NATURALIST 14.2

Government could eliminate the downward spiral by simply reimbursing each family up to $4,000 a year for health insurance. Government bureaucrats would not need to prescribe which doctors we see or micromanage any of the other details. They would simply process insurance receipts and send out reimbursement checks. This plan sounds expensive but would actually be less costly than the current system. The principal savings would come from delivering more cost-effective care to those who are now uninsured.

As it stands now, the untreated minor illnesses of the uninsured often develop into major illnesses, which are far more costly to treat. And when such illnesses befall the uninsured, we almost always treat them, often in costly emergency rooms. The resulting burden on hospitals leads to higher fees and increased government support—both of which now come largely out of the pockets of high-income taxpayers with health insurance.

The total budget needed to finance a $4,000 health insurance reimbursement for every American family—some $250 billion a year—would obviously require higher taxes. But for those whose employers currently provide health insurance, these taxes would be offset by an increase in salaries. After all, companies offer insurance not because they are charitable, but because they find doing so an effective way to compete for workers. Any company that did not offer higher salaries to previously insured workers would risk losing them to a company that did.

A universal reimbursement program would impose no net burden on taxpayers because of both salary adjustments and reductions in the high cost of care for the uninsured. And by providing a powerful incentive for all families to buy insurance, it would reverse the current downward spiral.

Critics of health care reform will say that if some people want to save money by going without health insurance, that's their problem or their choice. Perhaps, but it's a problem for the rest of society as well, one that if left untended will grow steadily worse.

> **RECAP HEALTH CARE DELIVERY**
>
> The rapid escalation in medical expenditures since World War II is attributable in large part to the spread of first-dollar insurance coverage, which encourages people to behave as if medical services were free of charge. Total economic surplus would be larger if we switched to insurance coverage with high deductibles, because such policies provide an incentive to use only those services whose benefit exceeds their cost.
>
> The switch to HMOs addresses this problem, because the standard HMO contract provides a strong incentive for physicians not to prescribe nonessential services. Some voice concern, however, that HMO contracts may lead physicians to withhold services that satisfy the cost-benefit test.
>
> Mounting insurance premiums have caused many people in good health to do without health coverage, resulting in higher premiums for those who remain insured. Government reimbursement for health coverage is one way to stop the downward spiral in health coverage.

ENVIRONMENTAL REGULATION

As we saw in Chapter 11, goods whose production generates negative externalities, such as atmospheric pollution, tend to be overproduced whenever negotiation among private parties is costly. Suppose we decide, as a society, that the best attainable outcome would be to have half as much pollution as would occur under completely unregulated conditions. In that case, how should the cleanup effort be distributed among those firms that currently discharge pollution into the environment?

The most efficient—and hence best—distribution of effort is the one for which each polluter's marginal cost of abatement is exactly the same. To see why, imagine that under current arrangements, the cost to one firm of removing a ton of pollution from the air is larger than the cost to another firm. Society could then achieve the same total reduction in pollution at lower cost by having the first firm discharge 1 ton more into the air and the second firm 1 ton less.

Unfortunately, government regulators seldom have detailed information on how the cost of reducing pollution varies from one firm to another. Many pollution laws therefore require all polluters simply to cut back their emissions by the same proportion, or to meet the same absolute emissions standards. If different polluters have different marginal costs of pollution abatement, however, those approaches will not be efficient.

TAXING POLLUTION

Fortunately, alternative policies can distribute the cleanup more efficiently, even if the government does not know firms' costs. One method is to tax pollution and allow firms to decide for themselves how much pollution to emit. The logic of this approach is illustrated in Example 14.6.

EXAMPLE 14.6   **What is the least costly way to cut pollution by half?**

Two firms, Sludge Oil and Northwest Lumber, have access to five production processes, each of which has a different cost and produces a different amount of pollution. The daily costs of the processes and the number of tons of smoke emitted are shown in Table 14.1. Pollution is currently unregulated, and negotiation between the firms and those who are harmed by pollution is impossible, which means that each firm uses process *A*, the least costly of the five. Each firm emits 4 tons of pollution/day, for a total of 8 tons of pollution/day.

TABLE 14.1
Costs and Emissions for Different Production Processes

Process (smoke)	A (4 tons/day)	B (3 tons/day)	C (2 tons/day)	D (1 ton/day)	E (0 tons/day)
Cost to Sludge Oil ($/day)	100	200	600	1,300	2,300
Cost to Northwest Lumber ($/day)	300	320	380	480	700

The government is considering two options for reducing total emissions by half. One is to require each firm to curtail its emissions by half. The other is to set a tax of $T on each ton of smoke emitted each day. How large must T be to curtail emissions by half? What would be the total cost to society under each alternative?

If each firm is required to cut pollution by half, each must switch from process A to process C. The result will be 2 tons/day of pollution for each firm. The cost of the switch for Sludge Oil will be $600/day − $100/day = $500/day. The cost to Northwest Lumber will be $380/day − $300/day = $80/day, for a total cost of $580/day.

Consider now how each firm would react to a tax of $T/ton of pollution. If a firm can cut pollution by 1 ton/day, it will save $T/day in tax payments. Whenever the cost of cutting a ton of pollution is less than $T, then, each firm has an incentive to switch to a cleaner process. For example, if the tax were set at $40/ton, Sludge Oil would stick with process A, because switching to process B would cost $100/day but would save only $40/day in taxes. Northwest Lumber, however, would switch to process B, because the $40 saving in taxes would be more than enough to cover the $20 cost of switching.

The problem is that a $40/day tax on each ton of pollution results in a reduction of only 1 ton/day, 3 tons short of the 4-ton target. Suppose instead that the government imposed a tax of $101/ton. Sludge Oil would then adopt process B, because the $100 daily cost of doing so would be less than the $101 saved in taxes. Northwest Lumber would adopt process D, because for every process up to and including D, the cost of switching to the next process would be less than the resulting tax saving.

Overall, then, a tax of $101/ton would result in the desired pollution reduction of 4 tons/day. The total cost of the reduction would be only $280/day ($100/day for Sludge Oil and $180/day for Northwest Lumber), or $300/day less than when each firm was required to cut its pollution by half. (The taxes paid by the firms do not constitute a cost of pollution reduction, because the money can be used to reduce whatever taxes would otherwise need to be levied on citizens.)

The advantage of the tax approach is that it concentrates pollution reduction in the hands of the firms that can accomplish it at least cost. Requiring each firm to cut emissions by the same proportion ignores the fact that some firms can reduce pollution much more cheaply than others. Note that under the tax approach, the cost of the last ton of smoke removed is the same for each firm, so the efficiency condition is satisfied.

One problem with the tax approach is that unless the government has detailed knowledge about each firm's cost of reducing pollution, it cannot know how high to set the pollution tax. A tax that is too low will result in too much pollution, while a tax that is too high will result in too little. Of course, the government could start by setting a low tax rate and gradually increase the rate until pollution is reduced to the target level. But because firms often incur substantial sunk costs when they switch from one process to another, that approach might be even more wasteful than requiring all firms to cut their emissions by the same proportion.

AUCTIONING POLLUTION PERMITS

Another alternative is to establish a target level for pollution and then auction off permits to emit that level of pollution. The virtues of this approach will become clear in Example 14.7.

EXAMPLE 14.7

How much will pollution permits sell for?

Two firms, Sludge Oil and Northwest Lumber, have access to the five different production processes described in Example 14.6. The government's goal is to cut the current level of pollution, 8 tons/day, by half. To do so, the government auctions off four permits, each one of which entitles the bearer to emit 1 ton of smoke/day. No smoke may be emitted without a permit. What price will the pollution permits fetch at auction, how many permits will each firm buy, and what will be the total cost of the resulting pollution reduction?

Process (smoke)	A (4 tons/day)	B (3 tons/day)	C (2 tons/day)	D (1 ton/day)	E (0 tons/day)
Cost to Sludge Oil ($/day)	100	200	600	1,300	2,300
Cost to Northwest Lumber ($/day)	300	320	380	480	700

If Sludge Oil has no permits, it must use process E, which costs $2,300/day to operate. If it had one permit it could use process D, which would save it $1,000/day. Thus, the most Sludge Oil would be willing to pay for a single 1-ton pollution permit is $1,000/day. With a second permit, Sludge Oil could switch to process C and save another $700/day; with a third permit, it could switch to process B and save another $400; and with a fourth permit, it could switch to process A and save another $100. Using similar reasoning, we can see that Northwest Lumber would pay up to $220 for one permit, up to $100 for a second, up to $60 for a third, and up to $20 for a fourth.

Suppose the government starts the auction at a price of $90. Sludge Oil will then demand four permits and Northwest Lumber will demand two, for a total demand of six permits. Since the government wishes to sell only four permits, it will keep raising the price until the two firms together demand a total of only four permits. Once the price reaches $101, Sludge Oil will demand three permits and Northwest Lumber will demand only one, for a total demand of four permits. Compared to the unregulated alternative, in which each firm used process A, the daily cost of the auction solution is $280: Sludge Oil spends $100 switching from process A to process B, and Northwest Lumber spends $180 switching from A to D. This total is $300 less than the cost of the original alternative, requiring each firm to reduce its emissions by half. (Again, the permit fees paid by the firms do not constitute a cost of cleanup, because the money can be used to reduce taxes that would otherwise have to be collected.)

The auction method has the same virtue as the tax method—namely, that of concentrating pollution reduction in the hands of those firms that can accomplish it at the lowest cost. But the auction method also has other attractive features that the tax approach does not. First, it does not induce firms to commit themselves to costly investments that they will have to abandon if the cleanup falls short of the target level. And second, it allows private citizens a direct voice in determining where the emission level will be set. For example, any group that believes the pollution target is too lenient could raise money to buy permits at auction. By keeping those permits locked away in a safe, the group could assure that they will not be used to emit pollution.

Several decades ago, when economists first proposed the auctioning of pollution permits, reactions of outrage were widely reported in the press. Most of those reactions amounted to the charge that the proposal would "permit rich firms to pollute to their hearts' content." Such an assertion betrays a total misunderstanding of the forces that generate pollution. Firms pollute not because they *want* to pollute, but because dirty production processes are cheaper than clean ones. Society's only real interest is in keeping the total amount of pollution from becoming excessive, not in *who* actually does the polluting. And in any event, the firms that do most of the polluting under an auction system will not be rich firms but those for whom pollution reduction is most costly.

Economists have argued patiently against these misinformed objections to the auction system, and their efforts have finally borne fruit. The sale of pollution permits is now common in several parts of the United States, and there is growing interest in the approach in other countries. Sound ideas may not always triumph over wrongheaded ones, especially in the short run, but in this instance economic education has helped society move forward.

RECAP   **ENVIRONMENTAL REGULATION**

An efficient program for reducing pollution is one for which the marginal cost of abatement is the same for all polluters. Taxing pollution has this desirable property, as does the auction of pollution permits. The auction method has the advantage that regulators can achieve a desired abatement target without having detailed knowledge of the abatement technologies available to polluters.

WORKPLACE SAFETY REGULATION

Most industrialized countries have laws that attempt to limit the extent to which workers are exposed to health and safety risks on the job. Those laws have often been described as necessary to protect workers against exploitation by employers with market power. Given the working conditions we saw in the early stages of the industrial revolution, the idea that such exploitation pervades unregulated private markets has intuitive appeal. Witness Upton Sinclair's vivid account of life in the Chicago meatpacking factories at the turn of the twentieth century:

> Some worked at the stamping machines, and it was very seldom that one could work long there at the pace that was set, and not give out and forget himself, and have a part of his hand chopped off. There were the hoisters, as they were called, whose task it was to press the lever which lifted the dead cattle off the floor. They ran along a rafter, peering down through the damp and the steam; and as old Durham's architects had not built the killing room for the convenience of the hoisters, at every few feet they would have to stoop under a beam, say four feet above the one they ran on; which got them into the habit of stooping, so that in a few years they would be walking like chimpanzees. Worst of any, however, were the fertilizer men, and those who served in the cooking rooms. These people could not be shown to the visitors—for the odor of the fertilizer-man would scare any ordinary visitor at a hundred yards, and as for the other men, who worked in tank-rooms full of

steam, and in which there were open vats near the level of the floor, their peculiar trouble was that they fell into the vats; and when they were fished out, there was never enough of them left to be worth exhibiting—sometimes they would be overlooked for days, till all but the bones of them had gone out to the world as Durham's Pure Leaf Lard.[2]

The miserable conditions of factory workers, juxtaposed with the often opulent lifestyle enjoyed by factory owners, seemed to affirm the idea that owners were exploiting workers. But given that conditions in the factories were in fact too dangerous, how much safer should they have been?

Consider the question of whether to install a specific safety device, say, a guardrail on a lathe. Many people are reluctant to employ the cost-benefit principle to answer such a question. To them, safety is an absolute priority, so the guardrail should be installed regardless of its cost. Yet most of us do not make personal decisions about our own health and safety that way. No one you know, for example, gets the brakes on his car checked every day, even though doing so would reduce the likelihood of being killed in an accident. The reason, obviously, is that daily brake inspections would be very costly and would not reduce the probability of an accident much compared to annual or semiannual inspections.

The same logic can be applied to installing a guardrail on a lathe. If the amount one is willing to pay to reduce the likelihood of an accident exceeds the cost of the guardrail, it should be installed; otherwise, it should not be. And no matter how highly we value reducing the odds of an accident, we will almost surely settle for less than perfect safety. After all, to reduce the risk of an accident to nearly zero, one would have to enclose the lathe in a thick plexiglass case and operate it with remote-controlled mechanical arms. Faced with the prohibitive cost of such an alternative, most of us would decide that the best approach is to add safety equipment whose benefit exceeds its cost, and then use caution while operating the machine.

But will unregulated employers offer the level of workplace safety suggested by the cost-benefit principle? Most nations appear to have decided that they will not. As noted, virtually every industrial country now has comprehensive legislation mandating minimum safety standards in the workplace—laws usually described as safeguards against exploitation of workers.

Yet explaining safety regulation as an antidote for exploitation raises troubling questions. One difficulty stems from the economist's argument that competition for workers prods firms to provide the socially optimal level of amenities. For example, if an amenity—say, a guardrail on a lathe—costs $50/month to install and maintain and workers value it at $100/month, then the firm must install the device or risk losing workers to a competitor that does. After all, if a competing firm were to pay workers $60/month less than they currently earn, it could cover the cost of the device with $10 to spare, while providing a compensation package that is $40/month more attractive than the first employer's.

To this argument, critics respond that in practice there is very little competition in the labor market. They argue that incomplete information, worker immobility, and other frictions create situations in which workers have little choice but to accept whatever conditions employers offer. But even if a firm were the *only* employer in the market, it would still have an incentive to install a $50 safety device that is worth $100 to the worker. Failure to do so would be to leave cash on the table.

Other defenders of regulation suggest that workers may not know about safety devices they lack. But that explanation, too, is troubling, because competing firms would have a strong incentive to call the devices to workers' attention.

Is safety regulation needed to protect workers from exploitation?

[2]Upton Sinclair, *The Jungle,* Sinclair, 1906, p. 106.

If the problem is that workers cannot move to the competing firm's location, then the firm can set up a branch near the exploited workers. Collusive agreements to restrain such competition have proved difficult to maintain, because each firm can increase its profit by cheating on the agreement.

In fact, worker mobility between firms is high, as is entry by new firms into existing markets; cartel agreements have always been notoriously unstable. Information may not be perfect, but if a new employer in town is offering a better deal, sooner or later word gets around.

Finally, if, despite these checks, some firms still manage to exploit their workers, we should expect those firms to earn a relatively high profit. But in fact we observe just the opposite. Year in and year out, firms that pay the *highest* wages are the most profitable. And so we are left with a puzzle. The fear of exploitation by employers with market power has led governments to adopt sweeping and costly safety regulations; yet the evidence suggests that exploitation cannot be a major problem. As Example 14.8 suggests, however, safety regulation might prove useful even in a perfectly competitive environment with complete information.

Will Don and Michael choose the optimal amount of safety?

EXAMPLE 14.8

Suppose Don and Michael are the only two members of a hypothetical community. They get satisfaction from three things: their income, safety on the job, and their position on the economic ladder. Suppose Don and Michael must both choose between two jobs, a safe job that pays $50/week and a risky job that pays $80/week. The value of safety to each is $40/week. Having more income than one's neighbor is worth $40/week to each; having less income than one's neighbor means a $40/week reduction in satisfaction. (Having the same income as one's neighbor means no change in satisfaction.) Will Don and Michael make the best job choices possible in this situation?

Viewed in isolation, each person's decision should be to take the safe job. Granted, it pays $30/week less than the risky job, but the extra safety it offers is worth $40/week. So aside from the issue of relative income, the value of the safe job is $90/week (its $50 salary plus $40 worth of safety), or $10/week more than the risky job.

Once we incorporate concerns about relative income, however, the logic of the decision changes in a fundamental way. Now the attractiveness of each job depends on the job chosen by the other. The four possible combinations of choices and their corresponding levels of satisfaction are shown in Table 14.2. If each man chooses a safe job, he will get $50 of income, $40 worth of satisfaction from safety, and—because each will have the same income—zero satisfaction from relative income. So if each man chooses the safe job, each will get a total of $90

TABLE 14.2
The Effect of Concern about Relative Income on Worker Choices Regarding Safety

		Michael	
		Safe job at $50/week	Risky job at $80/week
Don	Safe job at $50/week	$90 each	$50 for Don $120 for Michael
	Risky job at $80/week	$120 for Don $50 for Michael	$80 each

worth of satisfaction. If instead each man chooses the risky job, each will get $80 of income, zero satisfaction from safety, and because each has the same income as the other, zero satisfaction from relative income. If we compare the upper left cell of the table to the lower right cell, then, we can say unequivocally that Don and Michael would be happier if each took a safe job at lower income than if each chose a risky job with more income.

But consider how the choice plays out once the two men recognize their interdependency. Suppose, for example, that Michael chooses the safe job. If Don then chooses the unsafe job, he ends up with a total of $120 of satisfaction: $80 in salary plus $40 from having more income than Michael. Michael, for his part, ends up with only $50 worth of satisfaction: $50 in salary plus $40 from safety, minus $40 from having a lower income than Don. Alternatively, suppose Michael chooses the risky job. Then Don will again do better to accept the risky job, for by doing so he gets $80 worth of satisfaction rather than $50.

In short, no matter which job Michael chooses, Don will get more satisfaction by choosing the risky job. Likewise, no matter which job Don chooses, Michael will do better by choosing the risky job. Yet when each follows his dominant strategy, they end up in the lower right cell of the table, which provides only $80/week of satisfaction to each—$10 less than if each had chosen the safe job. Thus their job safety choice confronts them with a prisoner's dilemma (see Chapter 10). As in all such situations, when the players choose independently, they fail to make the most of their opportunities.

EXERCISE 14.4

How would your answer to the question posed in Example 14.8 have differed if the value of safety had been not $40/week but $20?

Example 14.8 suggests an alternative explanation for safety regulation, one that is not based on the need to protect workers from exploitation. If Don and Michael could choose collectively, they would pick the safe job and maximize their combined satisfaction. Thus each might support legislation that establishes safety standards in the workplace.

We stress that concern about relative income need not mean that people care only about having more or better goods than their neighbors. In our society, a person's relative income is important for reasons that everyone recognizes. For example, if you want to send your child to a good school, you must buy a house in a good school district. But who gets a house in a good school district? Those who have high relative income. Similarly, if you want a house with a view, and only 10 percent of homesites have views, who gets them? The people in the top 10 percent of the income distribution, of course, and only those people. Many important outcomes in life depend on where a person stands on the economic ladder. And when people care about their relative income, rational, self-interested actions will not always lead to efficient outcomes in the labor market.

That is not to say that regulation always improves matters. The labor market may not be perfect, but government regulators aren't perfect, either. Safety in the workplace is overseen by the Occupational Safety and Health Administration (OSHA), an agency that has drawn considerable criticism, much of it justified. Consider, for example, the following passage on safety requirements for ladders, taken verbatim from an early OSHA manual:

> The general slope of grain in flat steps of minimum dimension shall not be steeper than 1 in 12, except that for ladders under 10 feet in length the slope shall not be steeper than 1 in 10. The slope of grain in areas of local deviation shall not be steeper than 1 in 12 or 1 in 10 as specified above. For all ladders, cross grain not steeper than 1 in 10 are permitted in lieu of 1 in 12, provided the size is

increased to afford at least 15 percent greater strength than for ladders built to minimum dimensions. Local deviations of grain associated with otherwise permissible irregularities are permitted.[3]

This befogged passage appears in a section devoted to ladders that is 30 pages long, two columns to the page. One can easily imagine the managers of a firm deciding that their best course of action is simply to abandon any activities requiring ladders.

As an alternative to OSHA-style prescriptive safety regulation, many economists favor programs that increase employers' financial incentives to reduce workplace injuries. The **workers' compensation** system provides a mechanism through which such a change might be achieved. Workers' compensation is a government insurance system that provides benefits to workers who are injured in the workplace. As currently administered, the program does not adjust each individual employer's premiums fully to reflect the claims generated by its workers. Employers with low injury rates thus pay premiums higher than needed to cover the claims generated by their workers, while those with high injury rates pay premiums too small to cover the claims generated by their workers.

workers' compensation a government insurance system that provides benefits to workers who are injured on the job

Economists argue that revising insurance premiums to reflect the full social cost of the injuries sustained by each employer's workers would provide the optimal incentive to curtail injuries in the workplace. In effect, premiums set at this level would be an optimal tax on injuries and would be efficient for the same reason that a properly chosen tax on pollution is efficient. An injury tax set at the marginal cost of injury would encourage employers to adopt all safety measures whose benefit exceeds their cost.

As in other domains, we are far more likely to achieve optimal safety levels in the workplace if we choose among policies on practical cost-benefit grounds rather than on the basis of slogans about the merits or flaws of the free market.

Why does the government require safety seats for infants who travel in cars but not for infants who travel in airplanes?

A mother cannot legally drive her 6-month-old son to a nearby grocery store without first strapping him into a government-approved safety seat. Yet she can fly with him from Miami to Seattle with no restraining device at all. Why this difference?

In case of an accident—whether in a car or an airplane—an infant who is strapped into a safety seat is more likely to escape injury or death than one who is unrestrained. But the probability of being involved in a serious accident is hundreds of times higher when traveling by car than when traveling by air, so the benefit of having safety seats is greater for trips made by car. Using safety seats is also far more costly on plane trips than on car trips. Whereas most cars have plenty of extra room for a safety seat, parents might need to purchase an extra ticket to use one on an airplane. Most parents appear unwilling to pay $600 more per trip for a small increment in safety, either for themselves or their children.

ECONOMIC NATURALIST 14.3

RECAP **SAFETY REGULATION**

Most countries regulate safety in the workplace, a practice often defended as needed to protect workers from being exploited by employers with market power. Yet safety regulation might be attractive even in perfectly competitive labor markets, because the social payoff from investment in safety often exceeds the private payoff. An injury tax set at the marginal cost of injury would encourage optimal investment in workplace safety.

---

[3]Quoted by Robert S. Smith, "Compensating Wage Differentials and Public Policy: A Review," *Industrial and Labor Relations Review,* **32:**339–352, 1977.

CRIME CONTROL

Because police and other law enforcement officials are charged with protecting our lives and personal safety, political leaders are often reluctant to discuss expenditures on law enforcement in cost-benefit terms. But because we live in a world of scarcity, we cannot escape the fact that spending more on law enforcement means spending less on other things of value. Crimes, like accidents, are costly to prevent. The socially optimal amount to spend on avoiding any specific type of crime is that amount for which the marginal benefit of reducing that crime exactly equals its marginal cost. As the next example illustrates, the cost-benefit principle helps to explain why society invests so much more heavily in preventing some crimes than in preventing others.

ECONOMIC NATURALIST 14.4

Should college professors receive Secret Service protection when they give out-of-town lectures?

Why do more Secret Service agents guard the President than the Vice President, and why do no Secret Service agents guard college professors?

When the President of the United States flies to Cleveland to give a speech, hundreds of federal agents are assigned to protect him against attack by an assassin. But when the Vice President flies to Cleveland to give a speech, many fewer agents are assigned, and when a college professor goes to Cleveland for the same purpose, no agents are assigned at all. Why this difference?

According to the cost-benefit principle, the government should keep assigning agents in each case until the cost of an additional agent equals the value of the extra protection provided. In each of the three cases, the marginal cost of assigning agents is essentially the same. As shown in Figure 14.5, marginal cost (MC) is likely to be upward-sloping, because of the low-hanging fruit principle, according to which the most effective agents should be assigned first.

The important difference among these three cases lies in the value of assigning additional agents. The marginal benefit of an agent assigned to the President [MB_P, (a)] is much higher than the marginal benefit of an agent assigned to the Vice President [MB_{VP}, (b)], for at least two reasons. First, opponents of the government have a stronger motive to attack the President than the Vice President, because the President's role is so much more important than the Vice President's. Thus assigning an additional agent to the President is more likely to prevent an attack. And second, the benefit of preventing an attack against the President is much higher than that of preventing an attack against the Vice President, again, because the President's role is so much more important. These observations imply that the optimal number of agents to assign to the President [N_P, part (a)] is much greater than the optimal number of agents to assign to the Vice President [N_{VP}, part (b)]. Finally, the optimal number of agents to assign to a trav-

FIGURE 14.5
Differential Investment in Crime Prevention.
Because of differences in the marginal benefit of protection, more Secret Service agents are assigned to protect the President [part (a)] than to protect the Vice President [part (b)], and none are assigned to protect an ordinary citizen [part (c)].

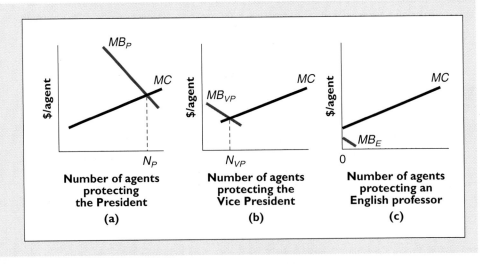

eling professor is zero [part (c)], because the marginal benefit of such an assignment [MB_E, part (c)] is so small. After all, few people have any reason to attack a professor, and in the unlikely event of an attack, the consequences would be far less serious than if a prominent government leader were attacked.

Many critics of the cost-benefit approach complain that when applied in examples like the one just discussed, it gives short shrift to the dignity of human life. On closer inspection, however, this complaint is difficult to support. The recommendation to assign no Secret Service agents to protect a traveling college professor does not imply that the lives of ordinary citizens are not to be cherished. Rather, it simply acknowledges that even without Secret Service protection, not even a single traveling professor is likely to be assassinated in the course of the next hundred years. For the same money that we would spend to send agents on largely pointless assignments, we could install guardrails on dangerous mountain roads, purchase additional mobile emergency units, or make any number of other investments that would save thousands of lives. The logic of the scarcity principle does not cease to apply whenever the choices we must make involve human health or safety.

RECAP **CRIME CONTROL**

The cost-benefit principle applies in crime policy just as in other areas of public policy. Society's efforts to curb crime should be expanded only to the point at which the marginal benefit from crime reduction equals its marginal cost.

LEGALIZED GAMBLING

Before 1964, lotteries were illegal in every state in America. Recent years, however, have witnessed the steady proliferation of legalized gambling. State lotteries now exist in 37 states and the District of Columbia, and most citizens now live within hours of the nearest legal casino.[4]

Proponents of legalization call gambling a victimless crime. They argue that since neither bettors nor casino operators can be *forced* to gamble, any gambling that occurs must be a voluntary exchange that benefits all parties. In this view, gambling is just like any other form of entertainment; to prohibit it is like prohibiting the sale of tickets to basketball games.

Why, then, did most states originally enact laws to prohibit gambling? The apparent explanation is similar to the one for bans on the sale of heroin, cocaine, and other mood-altering drugs. Although many people—perhaps most people—appear to be capable of gambling in moderation, for a small minority gambling is a highly addictive activity. When the opportunity to gamble is freely available, many of these people will gamble to excess, jeopardizing their psychological health and, more important from the state's point of view, their ability to support and care for their families.

Prior to 1970, although gambling was officially against the law, the authorities made little attempt to prosecute people who gambled discreetly. At that time, virtually all gambling occurred surreptitiously. People who really wanted to gamble could still find ways to do it, but those who wanted to avoid the temptation

---

[4]See Charles Clotfelter, Philip Cook, Julie Edell, and Marian Moore, "State Lotteries at the Turn of the Century: Report to the National Gambling Impact Study Commission," June 1, 1999, mimeograph.

could easily steer clear. As legalized gambling has proliferated, however, problem gamblers have experienced more difficulty staying out of trouble. Casinos advertise heavily, and states themselves often promote their lotteries with sophisticated multimillion dollar advertising campaigns. In New York State, for example, television commercials portrays people's fantasies about winning the lottery ("I'd buy the company and fire my boss!").

An average of 55 percent of the adults living in states that have lotteries bought at least one ticket during 1998. Most of them enjoyed the experience enough to justify the few dollars they spent. Since only about half the revenue from ticket sales is paid out in prizes, legalized gambling brings in additional revenue to pay for public services. Yet for a significant minority, the expanded gambling opportunities have not been welcome. New chapters of Gamblers Anonymous, a support group much like Alcoholics Anonymous, are forming at record rates.

Should gambling be outlawed again? Although the task of measuring the relevant costs and benefits is too complex to attempt here, one thing is clear: Any state that attempted to outlaw gambling on its own would have serious difficulty. Residents of a state that did not sponsor a lottery could still patronize lotteries in neighboring states. The lottery-free state would then lose much of its tax revenue yet fail to re-create a nongambling environment. On a state-by-state basis, each state confronts a decision to ban gambling much like the prisoner's dilemma discussed in Chapter 10.

■ SUMMARY ■

- Our aim in this chapter was to apply basic microeconomic principles to a variety of government policy questions. We began by looking at the various policies governments employ to mitigate concerns about fairness and efficiency losses arising from natural monopolies. Such policies include state ownership and management of natural monopolies, state regulation, private contracting, and vigorous enforcement of antitrust laws. Each of these remedies entails costs as well as benefits. In some cases, a combination of policies will produce a better outcome than simply allowing natural monopolists to do as they please. But in other cases, a hands-off policy may be the best available option.

- Basic economic principles can help to determine the optimal pricing policy when government is the direct provider of a service. We saw that the total economic surplus from the provision of a service will be largest if each user is charged the marginal cost of providing the service. In the case of public utilities, such a policy often entails charging different rates for similar services provided at different times. Economic principles can also help to show how different methods of paying for health care affect the efficiency with which medical services are delivered. In the case of health care, the gains from marginal cost pricing can often be achieved through insurance policies with large deductibles.

- An understanding of the forces that give rise to environmental pollution can help to identify those policy measures that will achieve a desired reduction in pollution at the lowest possible cost. Both the taxing of pollution and the sale of

transferable pollution rights promote this goal. Each distributes the environmental cleanup effort so that the marginal cost of pollution abatement is the same for all polluters.

- A perennially controversial topic is the application of the cost-benefit principle to policies involving health and safety. Many critics feel that the use of cost-benefit analysis in this domain is not morally legitimate, because it involves putting a monetary price on human life. Yet the fundamental principle of scarcity applies to health and safety, just as it does to other issues. Spending more on health and safety necessarily means spending less on other things of value. Failure to weigh the relevant costs and benefits, then, means that society will be less likely to achieve its stated goals in law enforcement, health care, workplace safety, and pollution abatement.

- Until the 1960s most states had laws against gambling but did not vigorously enforce them. The implicit aim of those laws may have been to shield potentially vulnerable citizens from the temptation to gamble excessively, without preventing gambling entirely. In recent decades most states have repealed their gambling laws, and now actively promote the sale of tickets in state-sponsored lotteries. One result has been a steep increase in compulsive gambling, which has led to renewed calls to declare gambling illegal. But the decision to ban gambling confronts states with a prisoner's dilemma. Any state that unilaterally outlawed it would lose substantial tax revenue without reducing gambling, for many citizens would simply patronize lotteries in neighboring states.

▪ KEY TERMS ▪

cost-plus regulation (351)
first-dollar insurance coverage (359)

health maintenance organization
(HMO) (359)

workers' compensation (369)

▪ REVIEW QUESTIONS ▪

1. Since natural monopolists tend to produce less than the socially optimal level of output, does this mean that we should always try to break up natural monopolists into several smaller firms?

2. Why do economists believe that pollution taxes and effluent permits are a more efficient way to curb pollution than laws mandating across-the-board cutbacks?

3. Why is first-dollar health care coverage inefficient?

4. How would you explain to a skeptical bank manager why the socially optimal number of bank robberies is not zero?

5. Does it make sense for the Federal Aviation Administration to require more sophisticated and expensive safety equipment in large commercial passenger jets than in small private planes?

▪ PROBLEMS ▪

1. In Charlotte, North Carolina, citizens can get their electric power from two sources: a hydroelectric generator and a coal-fired steam generator. The hydroelectric generator can supply up to 100 units of power/day at a constant marginal cost of 1 cent/unit. The steam generator can supply any additional power that is needed at a constant marginal cost of 10 cents/unit. When electricity costs 10 cents/unit, residents of Charlotte demand 200 units/day.
   a. Draw the marginal cost curve of electric power production in Charlotte.
   b. How much should the city charge for electric power? Explain. Should it charge the same price for a family whose power comes from the hydroelectric generator as it does for a family whose power comes from the steam generator?

2. The municipal waterworks of Cortland draws water from two sources, an underground spring and a nearby lake. Water from the spring costs 2 cents/100 gallons to deliver, and the spring has a capacity of 1 million gallons/day. Water from the lake costs 4 cents/100 gallons to deliver and is available in unlimited quantities. The demand for water in the summer months in Cortland is $P = 20 - 0.001Q$, where P is the price of water in cents per hundred gallons and Q is quantity demanded in hundreds of gallons per day. The demand curve for water in the winter months is $P = 10 - 0.001Q$. If the waterworks wants to encourage efficient water use, how much should it charge for water in the summer months? In the winter months?

3. Refer to Problem 2. By how much would daily total economic surplus go down if, in response to complaints from summer residents, the Cortland city council passed a law requiring all water to be sold at 3 cents/100 gallons throughout the year.

4. In the event he requires an appendectomy, David's demand for hospital accommodations is as shown in the following diagram. David's current insurance policy fully covers the cost of hospital stays. The marginal cost of providing a hospital room is $150/day.

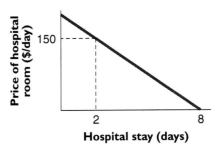

a. If David's only illness this year results in an appendectomy, how many days will he choose to stay in the hospital?

b. By how much would total economic surplus have been higher this year if David's hospital insurance covered only the cost of hospital stays that exceed $1,000 per illness?

5. Refer to Problem 4. Suppose David's employer adopts a new health care plan that pays 50 percent of all medical expenses up to $1,000 per illness, with full coverage thereafter. How will economic surplus under this plan compare with economic surplus with the policy in Problem 4b?

6. Two firms, Sludge Oil and Northwest Lumber, have access to five production processes, each one of which has a different cost and gives off a different amount of pollution. The daily costs of the processes and the corresponding number of tons of smoke emitted are as shown in the following table.

Process (smoke)	A (4 tons/day)	B (3 tons/day)	C (2 tons/day)	D (1 ton/day)	E (0 tons/day)
Cost to Sludge Oil ($/day)	50	70	120	200	500
Cost to Northwest Lumber ($/day)	100	180	500	1,000	2,000

a. If pollution is unregulated, which process will each firm use, and what will be the daily smoke emission?

b. The city council wants to curb smoke emissions by 50 percent. To accomplish this, it requires each firm to curb its emissions by 50 percent. What will be the total cost to society of this policy?

7. The city council in Problem 6 again wants to curb emissions by half. This time, it sets a tax of $T on each ton of smoke emitted per day. How large will T have to be to effect the desired reduction? What is the total cost to society of this policy?

8. Refer to Problem 7. Instead of taxing pollution, the city council decides to auction off four permits, each of which entitles the bearer to emit 1 ton of smoke/day. No smoke may be emitted without a permit. Suppose the government conducts the auction by starting at $1 and asking how many permits each firm wants to buy at that price. If the total is more than four, it then raises the price by $1, and asks again, and so on, until the total quantity of permits demanded falls to four. How much will each permit sell for in this auction? How many permits will each firm buy? What will be the total cost to society of this reduction in pollution?

9. Tom and Al are the only two members of a household. Each gets satisfaction from three things: his income, his safety at work, and his income relative to his roommate's income. Suppose Tom and Al must each choose between two jobs: a safe job that pays $100/week and a risky job that pays $130/week. The value of safety to each is $40/week. Each person evaluates relative income as follows: Having more income than his roommate provides the equivalent of $30/week worth of satisfaction, having less implies a reduction of $30/week worth of satisfaction, and earning the same income as his roommate means no change in satisfaction. Will Tom and Al choose optimally between the two jobs?

10. Refer to Problem 9. If Tom and Al could negotiate binding agreements with one another at no cost, which job would they choose? Suppose that negotiation is impractical and that the only way Tom and Al can achieve greater workplace safety is for the government to adopt safety regulations. If enforcement of the regulations costs $25/week, would Tom and Al favor their adoption?

▪ ANSWERS TO IN-CHAPTER EXERCISES ▪

14.1 At a consumption level of 2 million gallons/day, the marginal source of water is the lake, which has a marginal cost of 0.8 cent/gallon. The city should charge everyone 0.8 cent/gallon, including those who get their water from the spring.

14.2 If winter demand were $P = 8 - 2Q$, all winter power could be provided by the hydroelectric generator, and the marginal cost of producing electricity would be 2 cents/kilowatthour during both the winter and summer months.

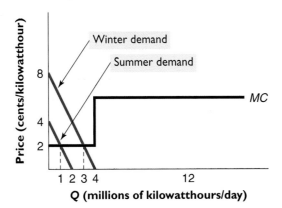

14.3 The optimal stay is still 1 day. If insurance reimburses $150/day, then the marginal charge seen by David will be the remaining $150/day, so he will stay 2 days. The cost to society of the additional day is $300, and the benefit to David of the extra day is only $225 (the area of the pale blue figure). The loss in surplus from the additional day's stay is thus $75.

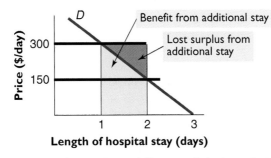

14.4 The payoff matrix would now be as follows, and the best choice, both individually and collectively, would be the risky job.

		Michael	
		Safe job at $50/week	Risky job at $80/week
Don	Safe job at $50/week	$70 each	$30 for Don $120 for Michael
	Risky job at $80/week	$120 for Don $30 for Michael	$80 each

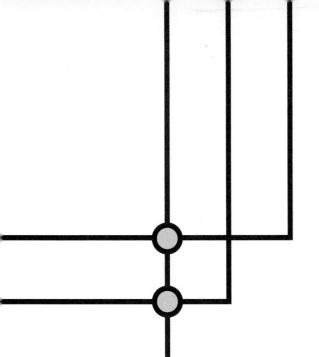

PUBLIC GOODS AND TAXATION

■

Government has the power to tax. Unlike a private business, which can get our money only if we voluntarily buy its product, the government can take our money even if we don't want the particular mix of goods and services provided.

Government also has a monopoly on the legitimate use of force. If people break the law, government has the power to restrain them, using force if necessary. It also has the power to deprive lawbreakers of their liberty for extended periods, and, in some places, even to execute them. Government can draft law-abiding citizens into the armed forces and send them into situations in which they must kill others and risk being killed themselves.

These are awesome powers. And although they are often used in the pursuit of noble ends, the historical record abounds with illustrations of their abuse. Voters and politicians of both parties are keenly aware of these abuses. Indeed, contemporary political rhetoric almost invariably entails criticism of bloated, out-of-control government bureaucracy. Even mainstream Democrats—ostensibly the party of activist government in the United States—have conceded the need to curb government's role. For example, as President Clinton remarked in his 1996 State of the Union Message, "the era of big government is over."

Others advocate even more radical retrenchment. For instance, Harry Browne, the 1996 Libertarian Party presidential candidate, called for abolition of the Internal Revenue Service, the agency responsible for collecting the federal income tax. This step would be tantamount to abolishing the federal government itself, for without tax revenues, there would be no way to pay for public goods and services.

Browne is right, of course, that a sure way to prevent government abuse of power is simply to have no government. But since virtually no society on earth lacks a government, we may suspect that governments, on balance, do more good than harm.

But how big, exactly, should government be? What goods and services should it provide? How should it raise the revenue to pay for them? What other powers should it have to constrain the behavior of its citizens? And how should the various powers we assign to government be apportioned among local, state, and federal levels? Our goal in this chapter will be to employ the principles of microeconomics in an attempt to answer these pragmatic questions.

GOVERNMENT PROVISION OF PUBLIC GOODS

public good a good or service that, to at least some degree, is both nonrival and nonexcludable

One of the primary tasks of government is to provide what economists call **public goods,** such as national defense and the criminal justice system.

PUBLIC GOODS VERSUS PRIVATE GOODS

nonrival good a good whose consumption by one person does not diminish its availability for others

nonexcludable good a good that is difficult, or costly, to exclude nonpayers from consuming

Public goods are those goods or services that are, in varying degrees, **nonrival** and **nonexcludable.** A nonrival good is one whose consumption by one person does not diminish its availability for others. For example, if the military prevents a hostile nation from invading your city, your enjoyment of that protection does not diminish its value to your neighbors. A good is nonexcludable if it is difficult to exclude nonpayers from consuming it. For instance, even if your neighbors don't pay their share of the cost of maintaining an army, they will still enjoy its protection.

Another example of a nonrival and nonexcludable good is an over-the-air broadcast of the *David Letterman Show.* The fact that you tune in one evening does not make the program any less available to others, and once the broadcast has been beamed out over the airwaves, it is difficult to prevent anyone from tuning in. Similarly, when the City of New York puts on a fireworks display in New York harbor to celebrate the Fourth of July, it cannot charge admission, because the harbor may be viewed from so many different locations in the city. And the fact that additional persons view the display does not in any way diminish its value to other potential viewers.

In contrast, the typical private good is diminished one-for-one by any individual's consumption of it. For instance, when you eat a cheeseburger, it is no longer available for anyone else. Moreover, people can be easily prevented from consuming cheeseburgers they don't pay for.

EXERCISE 15.1

Which of the following, if any, is nonrival?
a. The website of the Bureau of Labor Statistics at 3 A.M.
b. The World Cup Soccer championship game watched in person.
c. The World Cup Soccer championship game watched on television.

pure public good a good or service that, to a high degree, is both nonrival and nonexcludable

Goods that are both highly nonexcludable and nonrival are often called **pure public goods.** Two reasons favor government provision of such goods. First, for-profit private companies would have obvious difficulty recovering their cost of production. Many people might be willing to pay enough to cover the cost of producing the good, but if it is nonexcludable, the company cannot easily charge for it (an example of the free-rider problem discussed in Chapter 12). And second, if the marginal cost of serving additional users is zero once the good has been produced, then charging for the good would be inefficient, even if there were some practical way to do so. This inefficiency often characterizes the provision of **collective goods**—nonrival goods for which it is possible to exclude nonpayers. Pay-per-view cable television is an example. People who don't pay don't get to watch, a restriction that excludes many viewers who would have benefited from watching. Since the marginal cost to society of their tuning in is literally zero, excluding these viewers is wasteful.

A **pure private good** is one from which nonpayers can easily be excluded and for which one person's consumption creates a one-for-one reduction in the good's availability for others. The theory of perfectly competitive supply developed in Chapter 6 applies to pure private goods, of which basic agricultural products are perhaps the best examples. A **pure commons good** is a rival good that is also nonexcludable, so-called because goods with this combination of properties almost always result in a tragedy of the commons (see Chapter 11). Fish in ocean waters are an example.

The classification scheme defined by the nonrival and nonexcludable properties is summarized in Table 15.1. The columns of the table indicate the extent to which one person's consumption of a good fails to diminish its availability for others. Goods in the right column are nonrival, and those in the left column are not. The rows of the table indicate the difficulty of excluding nonpayers from consuming the good. Goods in the top row are nonexcludable, those in the bottom row, excludable. Private goods (lower left cell) are rival and excludable. Public goods (upper right cell) are nonrival and nonexcludable. The two hybrid categories are commons goods (upper left cell), which are rival but nonexcludable, and collective goods (lower right cell), which are excludable but nonrival.

collective good a good or service that, to at least some degree, is nonrival but excludable

pure private good one for which nonpayers can easily be excluded and for which each unit consumed by one person means one less unit available for others

pure commons good one for which nonpayers cannot easily be excluded and for which each unit consumed by one person means one less unit available for others

TABLE 15.1
Private, Public, and Hybrid Goods

		Nonrival	
		Low	High
Nonexcludable	High	Commons good (fish in the ocean)	Public good (national defense)
	Low	Private good (wheat)	Collective good (pay-per-view TV)

Collective goods are sometimes provided by government, sometimes by private companies. Most pure public goods are provided by government, but even private companies can sometimes find profitable ways of producing goods that are both nonrival *and* nonexcludable. An example is broadcast radio and television, which covers its costs by selling airtime to advertisers.

The mere fact that a good is a pure public good does not necessarily mean that government ought to provide it. On the contrary, the only public goods the government should even *consider* providing are those whose benefits exceed their costs. The cost of a public good is simply the sum of all explicit and implicit costs incurred to provide it. The benefit of a public good is measured by asking how much people would be willing to pay for it. Although that sounds similar to the way we measure the benefit of a private good, an important distinction exists. The benefit of an additional unit of a private good, such as a cheeseburger, is the highest sum that any individual buyer would be willing to pay for it. In contrast, the benefit of an additional unit of a public good, such as an additional broadcast episode of *Sesame Street,* is the sum of the reservation prices of all people who will watch that episode.

Even if the amount that all beneficiaries of a public good would be willing to pay exceeds its cost, government provision of that good makes sense only if there is no other less costly way of providing it. For example, whereas city governments often pay for fireworks displays, they almost invariably hire private companies to put on these events. Finally, if the benefit of a public good does not exceed its cost, we are better off without it.

PAYING FOR PUBLIC GOODS

Not everyone benefits equally from the provision of a given public good. For example, some people find fireworks displays highly entertaining, but others simply don't care about them, and still others actively dislike them. Ideally, it might seem that the most equitable method of financing a given public good would be to tax people in proportion to their willingness to pay for the good. To illustrate this approach, suppose Jones values a public good at $100, Smith values the same good at $200, and the cost of the good is $240. Jones would then be taxed $80, and Smith would be taxed $160. The good would be provided, and each taxpayer in this example would reap a surplus equal to 25 percent of his tax payment: $20 for Jones, $40 for Smith.

In practice, however, government officials usually lack the information they would need to tax people in proportion to their willingness to pay for specific public goods. (Think about it: If an IRS agent asked you how much you would be willing to pay to have a new freeway and you knew you would be taxed in proportion to the amount you responded, what would you say?) Examples 15.1 to 15.3 illustrate some of the problems that arise in financing public goods and suggests possible solutions to these problems.

EXAMPLE 15.1

Will Prentice and Wilson buy a water filter?

Prentice and Wilson own adjacent summer cottages along an isolated stretch of shoreline on Cayuga Lake. Because of a recent invasion of zebra mussels, each must add chlorine to his water intake valve each week to prevent it from becoming clogged by the tiny mollusks. A manufacturer has introduced a new filtration device that eliminates the nuisance of weekly chlorination. The cost of the device, which has the capacity to serve both houses, is $1,000. Both owners feel equally strongly about having the filter. But because Wilson earns twice as much as Prentice, Wilson is willing to pay up to $800 to have the filter, whereas its value to Prentice, a retired schoolteacher, is only $400. Would either person be willing to purchase the device individually? Is it efficient for them to share its purchase?

Neither will purchase the filter individually because each has a reservation price that is below its selling price. But because the two together value the filter at $1,200, sharing its use would be socially efficient. If they were to do so, total economic surplus would be $200 higher than if they did not buy the filter.

Since sharing the filter is the efficient outcome, we might expect that Prentice and Wilson would quickly reach agreement to purchase it. Unfortunately, however, the joint purchase and sharing of facilities is often easier proposed than accomplished. One hurdle is that people must incur costs merely to get together to discuss joint purchases. With only two people involved, those costs might not be significant. But if hundreds or thousands of people were involved, communication costs could be prohibitive.

With large numbers of people, the free-rider problem also emerges (see Chapter 12). After all, everyone knows that the project will either succeed or fail independently of any one person's contribution to it. Everyone thus has an incentive to withhold contributions—or get a free ride—in the hope that others will give.

Finally, even when only a few people are involved, reaching agreement on a fair sharing of the total expense may be difficult. For example, Prentice and Wilson might be reluctant to disclose their true reservation prices to one another for the same reason that you might be reluctant to disclose your reservation price for a public good to an IRS agent.

These practical concerns may lead us to empower government to buy public goods on our behalf. But as Example 15.2 makes clear, this approach does not eliminate the need to reach political agreement on how public purchases are to be financed.

Will government buy the water filter if there is an "equal tax" rule?

Suppose Prentice and Wilson from Example 15.1 could ask the government to help broker the water filter purchase. And suppose that the government's tax policy must follow a "nondiscrimination" rule that prohibits charging any citizen more than his or her neighbor for a public good. Another rule is that public goods can be provided only if a majority of citizens approve of them. Will a government bound by these rules provide the filter that Prentice and Wilson want?

A tax that collects the same amount from every citizen is called a **head tax.** If the government must rely on a head tax, it must raise $500 from Prentice and $500 from Wilson. But since the device is worth only $400 to Prentice, he will vote against the project, thus denying it a majority. So a democratic government cannot provide the water filter if it must rely on a head tax.

A head tax is an example of a **regressive tax,** one for which the proportion of a taxpayer's income that is paid in taxes declines as the taxpayer's income rises.

The point illustrated by Example 15.2 is not confined to the specific public good considered. It applies whenever taxpayers place significantly different valuations on public goods, as will almost always happen whenever people earn significantly different incomes. An equal tax rule under these circumstances will almost invariably rule out the provision of many worthwhile public goods.

As Example 15.3 suggests, one solution to this problem is to allow taxes to vary by income.

EXAMPLE 15.2

head tax a tax that collects the same amount from every taxpayer

regressive tax a tax under which the proportion of income paid in taxes declines as income rises

EXAMPLE 15.3

proportional income tax one under which all taxpayers pay the same proportion of their incomes in taxes

ECONOMIC NATURALIST 15.1

progressive tax one in which the proportion of income paid in taxes rises as income rises

Will the government buy the filter if there is a proportional tax on income?

Suppose that Prentice proposes that the government raise revenue by imposing a proportional tax on income to finance the provision of the water filter described in Example 15.1. Will Wilson, who earns twice as much as Prentice, support this proposal?

A **proportional income tax** is one under which all taxpayers pay the same percentage of their incomes in taxes. Under such a tax, Wilson would support Prentice's proposal, because if he didn't, each would fail to enjoy a public good whose benefit exceeds his share of its cost. Under the proportional tax on income, Prentice would contribute $333 toward the $1,000 purchase price of the filter and Wilson would contribute $667. The government would buy the filter, resulting in additional surpluses of $67 for Prentice and $133 for Wilson.

The following example makes the point that just as equal contributions are often a poor way to pay for public goods, they are also often a poor way to share expenses within the household.

Why don't most married couples contribute equally to joint purchases?

Suppose Hillary earns $2,000,000 per year while her husband Bill earns only $20,000. Given her income, Hillary as an individual would want to spend much more than Bill would on housing, travel, entertainment, education for their children, and the many other items they consume jointly. What will happen if the couple adopts a rule that each must contribute an equal amount toward the purchase of such items?

This rule would constrain the couple to live in a small house, take only inexpensive vacations, and skimp on entertainment, dining out, and their children's education. It is therefore easy to see why Hillary might find it attractive to pay considerably more than 50 percent for jointly consumed goods, because doing so would enable *both* of them to consume in the manner their combined income permits.

Public goods and jointly consumed private goods are different from individually consumed private goods in the following important way: *Different individuals are free to consume whatever quantity and quality of most private goods they choose to buy, but jointly consumed goods must be provided in the same quantity and quality for all persons.*

As in the case of private goods, people's willingness to pay for public goods is generally an increasing function of income. Wealthy individuals tend to assign greater value to public goods than low-income people, not because the wealthy have different tastes but because they have more money. A head tax would result in high-income persons getting smaller amounts of public goods than they want. By increasing the total economic surplus available for all to share, a tax system that assigns a larger share of the tax burden to people with higher incomes makes possible a better outcome for both rich and poor alike. Indeed, virtually all industrialized nations have tax systems that are at least mildly **progressive,** which means that the proportion of income that is taxed actually rises with a family's income.

Progressive taxation and even proportional taxation have often been criticized as being unfair to the wealthy, who are forced to pay more than others for public goods that all consume in common. The irony in this charge, however, is that exclusive reliance on head taxes, or even proportional taxes, would curtail the provision of public goods and services that are of greatest value to high-income families. Studies have shown, for example, that the income elasticity of demand for public goods such as parks and recreation facilities, clean air and water, public safety, uncongested roads, and aesthetically pleasing public spaces is substantially greater than 1. Failure to rely on progressive taxation would result in gross underprovision of such public goods and services.

PUBLIC GOODS

A public good is both nonrival and nonexcludable. Private firms typically cannot recover the costs of producing such goods because they cannot exclude nonpayers from consuming them. Nor would charging for a public good promote efficiency, since one person's consumption of the good does not diminish its availability for others.

Both obstacles can be overcome by creating a government with the power to levy taxes. Even high-income citizens often favor progressive taxes, because proportional or regressive taxes may generate insufficient revenue to pay for the public goods those taxpayers favor.

THE OPTIMAL QUANTITY OF A PUBLIC GOOD

In the examples considered thus far, the question was whether to provide a particular public good and, if so, how to pay for it. In practice, we often confront additional questions about what level and quality of a public good to provide.

Standard cost-benefit logic also applies to these questions. For example, New York City should add another rocket to its Fourth of July fireworks display if and only if the amount that citizens would collectively be willing to pay to see the rocket is at least as great as its cost.

THE DEMAND CURVE FOR A PUBLIC GOOD

To calculate the socially optimal quantity of a public good, we must first construct the demand curve for that public good. The process for doing so differs in an important way from the one we use to generate the market demand curve for a private good.

For a private good, all buyers face the same price and each chooses the quantity he or she wishes to purchase at that price. Recall that to construct the demand curve for a private good from the demand curves for individual consumers, we place the individual demand curves side by side and add them horizontally. That is, for each of a series of fixed prices, we add the resulting quantities demanded on the individual demand curves. In Figure 15.1, for example, we add the individual demand curves for a private good, D_1 and D_2 [parts (a) and (b)], horizontally to obtain the market demand curve for the good D [part (c)].

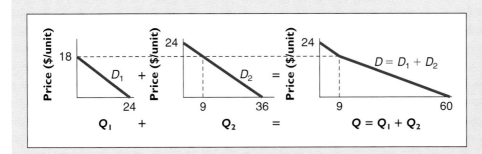

FIGURE 15.1
Generating the Market Demand Curve for a Private Good.
To construct the market demand curve for a private good [part (c)], we add the individual demand curves [parts (a) and (b)] horizontally.

For a public good, all buyers necessarily consume the same quantity, although each may differ in terms of willingness to pay for additional units of the good. Constructing the demand curve for a public good thus entails not horizontal summation of the individual demand curves but vertical summation. That is, for each of a series of quantity values, we must add the prices that individuals are willing to pay for an additional unit of the good. The curves D_1 and D_2 in Figure 15.2

(c) and (b) show individual demand curves for a public good by two different people. At each quantity, these curves tell how much the individual would be willing to pay for an additional unit of the public good. If we add D_1 and D_2 vertically, we obtain the total demand curve D for the public good [part (a)].

FIGURE 15.2
Generating the Demand Curve for a Public Good.
To construct the demand curve for a public good [part (a)], we add the individual demand curves [parts (c) and (b)] vertically.

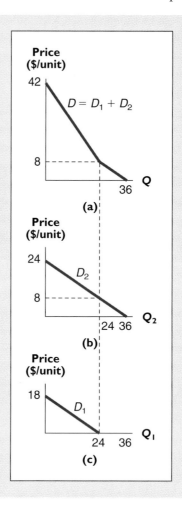

EXERCISE 15.2

Bill and Tom are the only demanders of a public good. If Bill's demand curve is $P_B = 6 - 0.5Q$ and Tom's is $P_T = 12 - Q$, construct the demand curve for this public good.

In Example 15.4, we see how the demand curve for a public good might be used in conjunction with information about costs to determine the optimal level of parkland in a city.

EXAMPLE 15.4   **What is the optimal quantity of urban parkland?**

The city government of a new planned community must decide how much parkland to provide. The marginal cost curve and the public demand curve for urban parkland are as shown in Figure 15.3. Why is the marginal cost curve upward-sloping and the demand curve downward-sloping? Given these curves, what is the optimal quantity of parkland?

The marginal cost schedule for urban parkland is upward-sloping because of the low-hanging-fruit principle: The city acquires the cheapest parcels of land first, and only then turns to more expensive parcels. Likewise, the marginal will-

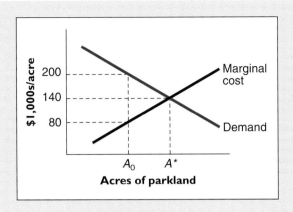

FIGURE 15.3
The Optimal Quantity of Parkland.
The optimal number of acres of urban parkland is A^*, the quantity at which the public's willingness to pay for additional parkland is equal to the marginal cost of parkland.

ingness-to-pay curve is downward-sloping because of the law of diminishing marginal utility. Just as people are generally willing to pay less for their fifth hot dog than for their first, they are also willing to pay less for the 101st acre of parkland than for the 100th acre. Given these curves, A^* is the optimal quantity of parkland. For any quantity less than A^*, the benefit of additional parkland exceeds its cost, which means that total economic surplus can be made larger by expanding the amount of parkland. For example, at A_0, the community would be willing to pay \$200,000 for an additional acre of urban parkland, but its cost is only \$80,000. Similarly, for any quantity of parkland in excess of A^*, the community would gain more than it would lose by selling off some parkland.

PRIVATE PROVISION OF PUBLIC GOODS

One advantage of using the government to provide public goods is that once a tax collection agency has been established to finance a single public good, it can be expanded at relatively low cost to generate revenue for additional public goods. Another advantage is that because government has the power to tax, it can summarily assign responsibility for the cost of a public good without endless haggling over who bears what share of the burden. And in the case of goods for which nonpayers cannot be excluded, the government may be the only feasible provider.

But exclusive reliance on government also entails disadvantages. Most fundamentally, the government's one-size-fits-all approach invariably requires many people to pay for public goods they don't want, while others end up having to do without public goods they want desperately. For example, many people vehemently oppose the provision of *any* sex education in the public schools, while others fervently believe that far more such instruction should be provided than is currently offered in most current public school curriculums. In addition, mandatory taxation strikes many people as coercive, even if they approve of the particular public goods being provided.

It is no surprise, then, that governments are not the exclusive providers of public goods in any society. Indeed, many public goods are routinely provided through private channels. The challenge, in each case, is to devise a scheme for raising the required revenues. Here are some methods that seem to work.

Funding by donation In 1998 Americans gave almost \$175 billion to private charities, many of which provide public goods to their communities. People also volunteer their time on behalf of organizations that provide public goods. When you paint your house, mow your lawn, or plant a flower garden, you are enhancing the quality of life in your neighborhood, and in that sense you are voluntarily providing a public good to your neighbors.

Development of new means to exclude nonpayers New electronic technology makes it possible to exclude nonpayers from many goods that in the past could not be thus restricted. For instance, broadcast television stations now have the ability to scramble their signals, making them available only to those consumers who purchase descrambling devices.

Private contracting More than 8 million Americans now live in gated private communities—private homeowners' associations that wall off contiguous properties and provide various services to residents. Many of these associations provide security services, schools, and fire protection and in other ways function much like ordinary local governments. Recognizing that individual incentives may not be strong enough to assure socially optimal levels of maintenance and landscaping, these associations often bill homeowners for those services directly. Many of the rules imposed by these associations are even more restrictive than those imposed by local governments, a distinction that is defended on the grounds that people are always free to choose some other neighborhood if they don't like the rules of any particular homeowners' association. Many people would be reluctant to tolerate a municipal ordinance that prevents people from painting their houses purple, yet such restrictions are common in the bylaws of homeowners' associations.

Sale of by-products Many public goods are financed by the sale of rights or services that are generated as by-products of the public goods. For instance, as noted earlier, radio and television programming is a public good that is paid for in many cases by the sale of advertising messages. Internet services are also underwritten in part by commercial messages that appear in the headers or margins of web pages.

Given the quintessentially voluntary nature of privately provided public goods, it might seem that reliance on private provision might be preferred whenever it proved feasible. But as the following example makes clear, private provision often entails problems of its own.

ECONOMIC NATURALIST 15.2

Why do television networks favor Jerry Springer over *Masterpiece Theater*?

In a given time slot, a television network faces the alternative of broadcasting either the *Jerry Springer Show* or *Masterpiece Theater*. If it chooses *Springer,* it will win 20 percent of the viewing audience, but only 18 percent if it chooses *Masterpiece Theater.* Suppose those who would choose *Springer* would collectively be willing to pay $10 million for the right to see that program, while those who choose *Masterpiece Theater* would be willing to pay $30 million. And suppose, finally, that the time slot is to be financed by a detergent company. Which program will the network choose? Which program would be socially optimal?

A detergent maker cares primarily about the number of people who will see its advertisements and will thus choose the program that will attract the largest audience—here, the *Springer Show.* The fact that those who prefer *Masterpiece Theater* would be willing to pay a lot more to see it is of little concern to the sponsor. But to identify the optimal result from society's point of view, we must take this difference into account. Because the people who prefer *Masterpiece Theater* could pay the *Springer* viewers more than enough to compensate them for relinquishing the time slot, *Masterpiece Theater* is the efficient outcome. But unless its supporters happen to buy more soap in total than the *Springer* viewers, the latter will prevail. In short, reliance on advertising and other indirect mechanisms for financing public goods provides no assurance that the goods chosen will maximize economic surplus.

Of course, the fact that the programs that best suit advertisers' needs may not be socially optimal does not mean that government decisions would necessarily be better. One can imagine, for example, a cultural affairs ministry that would choose television programming that would be "good for us" but that few of us would want to watch.

One way to avoid the inefficiency that arises when advertisers choose programming is to employ pay-per-view methods of paying for television programming. These methods allow viewers to register not just which programs they prefer but also the strength of their preferences, as measured by how much they are willing to pay.

But although pay-per-view TV is more likely to select the programs the public most values, it is also less efficient than broadcast TV in one important respect. As noted earlier, charging each household a fee for viewing discourages some households from tuning in. And since the marginal social cost of serving an additional household is exactly zero, limiting the audience in this way is inefficient. Which of the two inefficiencies is more important—free TV's inefficiency in choosing among programs or pay TV's inefficiency in excluding potential beneficiaries—is an empirical question.

In any event, the mix between private and public provision of public goods and services differs substantially from society to society and from arena to arena within any given society. These differences depend on the nature of available technologies for delivering and paying for public goods, and also on people's preferences.

Why do detergent companies care more about audience size than about how much people would be willing to pay to see the programs they sponsor?

By how much is economic surplus reduced by a pay-per-view charge?

EXAMPLE 15.5

If *Mystery Theater* is shown on pay-per-view television at 10 P.M. on Thursdays, the demand curve for each episode is given by $P = 20 - Q$, where P is the price per household in dollars and Q is the number of households who choose to watch the program (in millions). If the regulated pay-per-view charge is $10 per household, by how much would economic surplus rise if the same episode were shown instead on "free" broadcast public TV?

With a fee of $10 per episode, 10 million households will watch (see Figure 15.4). But if the same episode were shown instead on broadcast public TV, 20 million households would watch. The additional economic surplus reaped by the extra 10 million households is the area of the blue triangle, which is $50 million. The marginal cost of permitting these additional households to watch the episode is zero, so the total gain in surplus is $50 million.

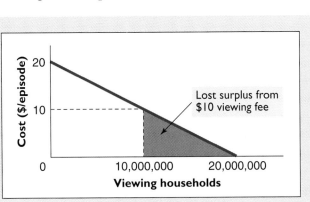

FIGURE 15.4
The Loss in Surplus from a Pay-per-View Fee.
Twice as many households would watch the program if its price were zero instead of $10. The additional economic surplus is the area of the blue triangle, or $50 million.

In general, charging a positive price for a good whose marginal cost is zero will result in a loss in surplus. As we saw in Chapter 7, the size of the loss that results when price is set above marginal cost depends on the price elasticity of demand. When demand is more elastic, the loss in surplus is greater. Exercise 15.3 provides an opportunity to see that principle at work.

EXERCISE 15.3

How would your answer to Example 15.5 have been different if the demand curve had been given instead by $P = 15 - 2Q$?

RECAP **THE OPTIMAL QUANTITY OF A PUBLIC GOOD**

Because the quantity of a public good must be the same for every consumer, the total demand curve for a public good is constructed by adding individual demand curves vertically. Optimal production of a public good occurs at the quantity for which the demand curve intersects the marginal cost curve for the public good.

Government need not always be the best way to provide public goods. Such goods can be provided by private organizations that rely on charitable contributions or the sale of by-products. Private for-profit companies can also become providers when new technologies such as pay-per-view television convert public goods into collective goods.

ADDITIONAL FUNCTIONS OF GOVERNMENT

The provision of public goods is not the only rationale for the existence of government. Government also creates and enforces the rules without which the efficient production of private goods would not be possible.

EXTERNALITIES AND PROPERTY RIGHTS

As we saw in Chapter 11, for example, externalities often stand in the way of socially optimal resource allocation in private activities. We saw, too, that optimal allocations are unlikely to result whenever property rights are poorly defined (for example, the tragedy of the commons). These observations suggest the existence of two additional important roles for government: namely, the regulation of activities that generate externalities and the definition and enforcement of property rights.

These rationales for government action explain why most governments regulate activities that generate pollution, subsidize education (on the grounds that an educated public creates positive externalities), control access to fishing waters and public timber lands, and enforce zoning laws. Most laws, in fact, represent attempts to define property rights or to control externalities. The law requiring motorists to drive on the right, for example, is an attempt to prevent the activities of one motorist from causing harm to others.

Proponents of minimalist government often object that the government unjustly curtails our freedom when it uses zoning laws to limit the size of the houses we build or imposes fines on motorists who violate highway speed limits. Yet the justification for such regulations is precisely the same as for the laws that prohibit your fist from occupying the same physical space as your neighbor's nose. You are free to swing your fists as you please, provided you cause no harm to others. But if your fist strikes your neighbor's nose, you become a violator of the law and subject to punishment. If the proponents of minimalist government approve of restricting behavior in this way, why do they disapprove of other attempts to discourage behaviors that cause harm to others?

Perhaps their fear is that because externalities are so pervasive, governments that were empowered to regulate them might quickly get out of control. This is by no means an idle fear, and we emphasize that the mere fact that an externality exists does not necessarily mean that the best outcome is for the government to regulate it. As we will see in the next section, regulation entails costs of its own. The ultimate question is therefore a practical one: Will government regulation of the externality in question do more good than harm? Slogans about being free to live without government interference provide little help in answering such questions.

LOCAL, STATE, OR FEDERAL?

Framers of the American Constitution were deeply skeptical of centralized government power. In drafting the Constitution, therefore, they explicitly tried to limit the powers of the federal government as much as possible, delegating most important powers to the states, who in turn delegated many of their powers to governments at the local level.

That the dangers of remote, centralized government ranked high among founding fathers' concerns is no surprise. After all, fresh in their memories was the autocratic treatment received by the American colonies at the hands of the monarchy in England. The founding fathers recognized that government will be more responsive the shorter the distance between officeholders and the voters who elect them.

Another obvious advantage of giving as much authority to local governments as possible is that different communities often have markedly different preferences about how much to spend on public goods, and even on what kinds of public goods to provide. When such decisions are made at the local level, people can shop for a community whose voters' preferences largely coincide with their own. Those who like high levels of public goods and services can band together and authorize high taxes to pay for them. Others who place less value on public services can choose communities in which both services and taxes are lower.

Why, given the many attractions of decisions made at the local level, did the founding fathers create federal and state governments at all? One reason is economies of scale in defense. For a country to survive politically, it must be able to deter aggression by hostile governments. A country consisting only of, say, Concord, New Hampshire, would be ill-equipped to do that. Large, well-equipped armies and navies cost a lot of money, and countries without sufficient population simply cannot afford them.

Defense, however, is not the only reason to empower governments beyond the local or state level. As discussed in Chapter 14, for example, no individual state has the authority required to significantly reduce the extent of legalized gambling in the current environment. Similarly, the problem of pollution is difficult to solve when the various sources of pollution are not subject to regulatory control by a single government. Much of the acid rain experienced in Canada, for example, is the result of sulfur dioxide emissions from industrial sources in the upper midwest of the United States. These emissions are beyond the reach of Canadian environmental regulations. In many instances, as with the discharge of greenhouse gases, not even a coalition of all the governments in North, Central, and South America would have power to take effective action. Carbon dioxide emitted anywhere on the planet disperses to uniform concentrations around the globe in a matter of months.

The choice between different levels of government, then, often confronts us with difficult trade-offs. Ceding the power of taxation to a federal government often entails painful compromises for voters in individual states. But the loss of political autonomy is an even less attractive option. Similarly, nations are understandably reluctant to cede any of their sovereign powers to a higher authority, but failure to take such steps may entail unacceptable environmental costs in the long run.

RECAP **ADDITIONAL FUNCTIONS OF GOVERNMENT**

Government creates economic surplus not only by providing public goods but also by regulating activities that generate externalities and by defining and enforcing property rights. These rationales explain why most governments regulate pollution, subsidize education, control access to fishing waters and public timber lands, and enforce zoning laws.

> Although the framers of the Constitution disliked centralized government power, they recognized that some government functions are not best performed at the local or even state level. Economies of scale argue for provision of defense at the national level. Externalities that transcend local boundaries provide an additional rationale for national or even international government.

SOURCES OF INEFFICIENCY IN THE POLITICAL PROCESS

In most countries, expenditures on public goods, tax policy, and laws regulating behavior are determined in large part by the votes of democratically elected representatives. This process is far from perfect. (Winston Churchill called democracy "the worst form of government, except for any other.") Inefficiencies often arise in the public sphere not because of incompetent or ignorant legislators but because of structural incentive problems.

PORK BARREL LEGISLATION

The following example, drawn not from the public sector but from everyday private life, illustrates one of the important incentive gaps.

ECONOMIC NATURALIST 15.3

Why does check-splitting make the total restaurant bill higher?

Sven Torvaldsen and nine friends are having dinner at la Maison de la Casa House, a four-star restaurant in Minneapolis. To simplify the task of paying for their meal, they have agreed in advance to split the cost of their meal equally, with each paying one-tenth of the total check. Having cleared the entree dishes, the waiter arrives with the dessert menu, on which Sven's two favorite items are pumpkin bread pudding ($10) and chocolate mousse ($6). Sven's reservation prices for these items are $4 and $3, respectively. Will he order dessert, and, if so, which one? Would he order dessert if he were dining by himself?

When Sven and his friends split the total check equally, Sven's payment goes up by one-tenth of the menu price of any dessert he orders. Thus the prices—to him—of the bread pudding and chocolate mousse are $1 and 60 cents, respectively. Because he gets $4 − $1 = $3 of consumer surplus from the bread pudding and only $3 − $0.60 = $2.40 from the chocolate mousse, he will order the bread pudding. If Sven were dining alone, however, his bill would increase dollar for dollar with the menu price of any dessert he ordered. And since the menu prices exceed his corresponding reservation prices, he would not order dessert at all.

The irony, of course, is that if Sven's nine friends have the same preferences regarding dessert, each will order bread pudding and each person's share of the total bill will rise not by $1 but by the full $10. Compared to the alternative of no one having dessert, each diner suffers a $6 loss in consumer surplus. Still, it made sense for each to order bread pudding, since failure to do so would have reduced each diner's bill by only $1.

EXERCISE 15.4

In the preceding example, would Sven have ordered dessert if there had been only five people splitting the check instead of 10?

Alert readers will have noticed the similarity between the problem posed in the preceding example and the one posed in Economic Naturalist 11.6, in which identical twins had a single milkshake to share with two straws. The same incentive problem leads to the inefficient outcome in both cases.

The following example illustrates how the very same incentive problem rears its head in the legislative process.

Why do legislators often support one another's pork barrel spending programs?

Pork barrel programs are government programs that benefit local areas but are of questionable value from a national perspective. Why do voters seem to support legislators who initiate such projects even when the total effect of all such projects on local tax bills far exceeds the local benefits?

Consider a voter in a congressional district that contains one one-hundredth of the country's taxpayers. Suppose that voter's representative is able to deliver a public project that generates benefits of $100 million for the district but that costs the federal government $150 million. Since the district's share of the tax bill for the project will be only $150 million/100 = $1.5 million, residents of the district are $98.5 million better off with the project than without it. And that explains why so many voters favor legislators with a successful record of "bringing home the bacon."

But why would legislator A support such a project in legislator B's home district? After all, B's project will cause A's constituents' taxes to rise—albeit by a small amount—yet they will get no direct benefit from the project. The answer is that if A does not support B's project, then B will not support A's. The practice whereby legislators support one another's pet projects is known as **logrolling**. This practice creates a bias toward excessive spending, much like the bias created when a dinner check is split equally.

RENT-SEEKING

A related source of inefficiency in the public sphere occurs because the gains from government projects are often concentrated in the hands of a few beneficiaries, while the costs are spread among many. This means that beneficiaries often have a powerful incentive to organize and lobby in favor of public projects. Individual taxpayers, by contrast, have little at stake in any public project and therefore have little incentive to incur the cost of mobilizing themselves in opposition.

Suppose, for example, that a price support bill for sugar will raise the price of sugar by 10 cents per pound and that the average American family currently consumes 100 pounds of sugar per year. How will this legislation affect the average family's consumption of sugar? Recall from Chapter 5 that a good, such as salt or sugar, whose share in most family budgets is small is likely to have a low price elasticity of demand. Hence each family's sugar consumption will decline only slightly as a result of the 10 cent price hike. The resulting increase in each family's annual expenditures on sugar—slightly less than $10—is scarcely a noticeable burden, and surely not enough to induce many people to complain to their representatives. The same legislation, however, will raise sugar industry revenues by nearly $1 billion annually. With a sum that large at stake, it is certain that the industry will lobby vigorously in its favor.

Why don't citizens vote those legislators who support such bills out of office? One reason is the problem of rational ignorance, discussed in Chapter 12. Most voters have no idea that a price support bill for sugar and other special-interest bills even exist, much less how individual legislators vote on them. If all voters became well-informed about such bills, the resulting increase in the quality of legislation might well be sufficient to compensate each voter for the cost of becoming informed. But because of the free-rider problem, each voter knows that the outcome of votes in Congress will not be much affected by whether he becomes well-informed.

ECONOMIC NATURALIST 15.4

pork barrel spending a public expenditure that is larger than the total benefit it creates but that is favored by a legislator because his or her constituents benefit from the expenditure by more than their share of the resulting extra taxes

logrolling the practice whereby legislators support one another's legislative proposals

Still other sources of inefficiency arise even in the case of projects whose benefits exceed their costs. Several years ago, for example, the federal government announced its decision to build a $25 billion high-energy physics research facility (the "superconducting supercollider"), which ignited an intense competition among more than 20 states vying to be chosen as the site for this facility. Hundreds of millions of dollars was spent on proposal preparation, consultants' fees, and various other lobbying activities. Such investments are known as **rent-seeking**, and they tend to be inefficient for the same reason that investments by contestants in other positional arms races are inefficient (see Chapter 11).

Efforts devoted to rent-seeking are socially unproductive because of the simple incentive problem illustrated in Example 15.6.

rent-seeking the socially unproductive efforts of people or firms to win a prize

EXAMPLE 15.6

Why would anyone pay $50 for a $20 bill?

Suppose a $20 bill is to be auctioned off to the highest bidder. The rules of this particular auction require an initial bid of at least 50 cents, and succeeding bids must exceed the previous high bid by at least 50 cents. When the bidding ceases, both the highest bidder and the second-highest bidder must give the amounts they bid to the auctioneer. The highest bidder then receives the $20, and the second-highest bidder gets nothing. For example, if the highest bid is $11 and the second-highest bid is $10.50, the winner earns a net payment of $20 − $11 = $9, and the runner-up loses $10.50. How high will the winning bid be, on average?

Auctions like this one have been extensively studied in the laboratory. And although subjects in these experiments have ranged from business executives to college undergraduates, the pattern of bidding is almost always the same. Following the opening bid, offers proceed quickly to $10, or half the amount being auctioned. A pause then occurs as the subjects appear to digest the fact that with the next bid the sum of the two highest bids will exceed $20, thus taking the auctioneer off the hook. At this point, the second-highest bidder, whose bid stands at $9.50, invariably offers $10.50, apparently preferring a shot at winning $9.50 to a sure loss of $9.50.

In most cases, all but the top two bidders drop out at this point, and the top two quickly escalate their bids. As the bidding approaches $20, a second pause occurs, this time as the bidders appear to recognize that even the highest bidder is likely to come out behind. The second-highest bidder, at $19.50, is understandably reluctant to offer $20.50. But consider the alternative. If he drops out, he will lose $19.50 for sure. But if he offers $20.50 and wins, he will lose only 50 cents. So as long as he thinks there is even a small chance that the other bidder will drop out, it makes sense to continue. Once the $20 threshold has been crossed, the pace of the bidding quickens again, and from then on it is a war of nerves between the two remaining bidders. It is common for the bidding to reach $50 before someone finally yields in frustration.

One might be tempted to think that any intelligent, well-informed person would know better than to become involved in an auction whose incentives so strongly favor costly escalation. But many of the subjects in these auctions have been experienced business professionals; many others have had formal training in the theory of games and strategic interaction. For example, the psychologist Max Bazerman reports that during the past 10 years he has earned more than $17,000 by auctioning $20 bills to his MBA students at Northwestern University's Kellogg Graduate School of Management, which is consistently among the top-rated MBA programs in the world. In the course of almost 200 of his auctions, the top two bids never totaled less than $39, and in one instance they totaled $407.

As Example 15.7 shows, the incentives that confront participants in the $20 bill auction are strikingly similar to those that confront companies that are vying for lucrative government contracts.

How much will cellular phone companies bid for an exclusive license?   **EXAMPLE 15.7**

The State of Wyoming has announced its intention to grant an exclusive license to provide cellular phone services within its borders. Two firms have met the deadline for applying for this license. The franchise lasts for exactly 1 year, during which time the franchisee can expect to make an economic profit of $20 million. The state legislature will choose the applicant that spends the most money lobbying legislators. If the applicants cannot collude, how much will each spend on lobbying?

If both spend the same, each will have a 50-50 chance at the $20 million prize, which means an expected profit of $10 million minus the amount spent lobbying. If the lobbyists could collude, each would agree to spend the same small, token amount on lobbying. But in the absence of a binding agreement, each will be strongly tempted to try to outspend the other. Once each firm's spending reaches $10 million, each will have an expected profit of zero (a 50-50 chance to earn $20 million, minus the $10 million spent on lobbying).

Further bidding would guarantee an expected loss. And yet, if one firm spent $10,000,001 while the other stayed at $10 million, the first firm would get the franchise for sure and earn an economic profit of $9,999,999. The other firm would have an economic loss of $10 million. Rather than face a sure loss of $10 million, it may be tempted to bid $10,000,002. But then, of course, its rival would face a similar incentive to respond to that bid. No matter where the escalation stops, it is sure to dissipate much of the gains that could have been had from the project. And perhaps, as in the $20 bill auction, the total amount dissipated will be even more than the value of the franchise itself.

From the individual perspective, it is easy to see why firms might lobby in this fashion for a chance to win government benefits. From society's perspective, however, this activity is almost purely wasteful. Lobbyists are typically intelligent, well-educated, and socially skilled. The opportunity cost of their time is high. If they were not lobbying government officials on behalf of their clients, they could be producing other goods or services of value. Governments can discourage such waste by selecting contractors not according to the amount they spend lobbying but on the basis of the price they promise to charge for their services. Society will be more successful the more its institutions encourage citizens to pursue activities that create wealth rather than activities that merely transfer existing wealth from one person or company to another.

STARVE THE GOVERNMENT?

The Nobel laureate Milton Friedman has said that no bureaucrat spends taxpayers' money as carefully as those taxpayers themselves would have. And indeed, there can be little doubt that many government expenditures are wasteful. Beyond the fact that logrolling often results in pork barrel programs that would not satisfy the cost-benefit test, we must worry that government employees may not always face strong incentives to get the most for what they spend. The Pentagon, for example, once purchased a coffeemaker for $7,600 and on another occasion paid $600 for a toilet seat. Such expenditures may have been aberrations, but there seems little doubt that private contractors often deliver comparable services at substantially lower costs than their public counterparts.

In their understandable outrage over government waste, many critics have urged major cutbacks in the volume of public goods and services. These critics reason that if we let the government spend more money, there will be more waste. This is true, of course, but only in the trivial sense that there would be more of *everything* the government does—good and bad—if public spending were higher. One of our most extensive experiences with the consequences of major reductions in government spending comes from the Proposition 13 movement in California. This movement began with the passage of State Proposition 13 in 1978, which mandated large reductions in property taxes. As Californians have belatedly recognized, this remedy for government waste is like trying to starve a tapeworm by not eating. Fasting does harm the tapeworm, sure enough, but it harms the host even more. Residents of the Golden State, who once proudly sent their children to the nation's best schools, are now sending them to some of its worst.

The physician treats an infected patient by prescribing drugs that are toxic to the parasite but not to the host. A similar strategy should guide our attack on government waste. For example, we might consider the adoption of campaign-finance reform laws that would prevent legislators from accepting campaign contributions from the tobacco industry and other special interests whose government subsidies they support.

The question, then, isn't whether bureaucrats know best how to spend our money. Rather, it's "How much of our money do *we* want to spend on public services?" Although we must remain vigilant against government waste, we must also remember that many public services deliver good value for our money.

RECAP **SOURCES OF INEFFICIENCY IN THE POLITICAL PROCESS**

Government does much to help the economy function more efficiently, but it can also be a source of waste. For example, legislators may support pork barrel projects, which do not satisfy the cost-benefit criterion but which benefit constituents by more than their share of the extra taxes required to pay for the projects.

Rent-seeking, a second important source of inefficiency, occurs when individuals or firms use real resources in an effort to win favors from the government. Voters often fail to discipline legislators who abet rent-seeking, because the free-rider problem gives rise to rational ignorance on the part of many voters.

Concern about government waste has led many to conclude that the best government is necessarily the smallest one. The solution favored by these critics is to starve government by reducing the amount of money it can collect in taxes. Yet starving the government reduces one kind of waste only to increase another by curtailing public services whose benefit exceeds their cost.

WHAT SHOULD WE TAX?

Although the primary purpose of the tax system is to generate the revenue needed to fund public goods and other government expenditures, taxes also have many other consequences, some intended, others not. For example, taxes alter the relative costs and benefits of engaging in different activities. They also affect the distribution of real purchasing power in the economy. The best tax system is one that raises the needed revenues while at the same time having the most beneficial, or least deleterious, side effects.

On the first criterion, the federal tax system has not performed particularly well. Although the federal budget began to show a modest surplus in the late 1990s, until then it had been in continuous deficit since 1969, during which time the federal government had to borrow trillions of dollars to pay its bills.

crowding out occurs when private firms cancel planned investment projects because of higher interest rates caused by government borrowing

The fact that governments and private corporations borrow money in the same capital market explains the phenomenon economists call **crowding out**. When government increases its demand in the market for borrowed funds, interest rates rise, causing firms to cancel some of their planned investment projects. When the government fails to raise enough revenue from taxes to cover the amount it spends on public goods and services, it thus diverts funds from investments that would have helped the economy to grow.

What about the effect of taxes on incentives? As discussed in Chapter 7, taxes will hold production and consumption below socially optimal levels in markets in which the private costs and benefits coincide exactly with all relevant social costs and benefits. Suppose, for example, that the long-run private marginal cost of producing cars is $10,000/unit and that the demand curve for cars is as shown in Figure 15.5. The equilibrium quantity and price will be 6 million/year and $10,000, respectively. If no externalities accompany the production or consumption of cars, these will be the socially optimal levels for quantity and price. But if we now add a tax of $2,000/car, the new equilibrium price and quantity will be $12,000 and 4 million, respectively. The loss in economic surplus will be equal to the area of the blue triangle ($1 billion/year), which is the cumulative sum of the differences between what excluded buyers would have been willing to pay for extra cars and the marginal cost of producing those cars.

Economists who write for the popular press have long focused on the loss in surplus caused by taxes like the one shown in Figure 15.5. These economists argue that the economy would perform better if taxes were lower and total government expenditures were smaller.

But arguments for that claim are far from compelling. As discussed in Chapter 7, for example, even if a tax in a market like the one shown in Figure 15.5 did produce a loss in surplus for participants in that market, it might nonetheless be justified if it led to an even larger gain in surplus from the public expenditures it financed. We also saw in Chapter 7 that the deadweight loss from taxing a good (or activity) will be smaller the smaller is the elasticity of demand or supply for the good. This principle suggests that deadweight losses could be minimized by concentrating taxes on goods with highly inelastic supply or demand curves.

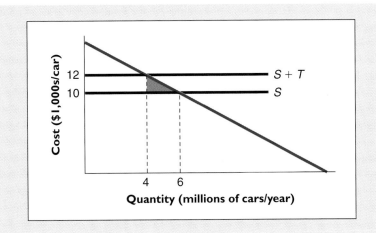

FIGURE 15.5
The Loss in Surplus from a Tax on Cars.
If the supply and demand curves for cars embody all relevant cost benefits of producing and consuming cars, then placing a tax on cars will lead to underproduction of them and a corresponding reduction in economic surplus.

Another difficulty with the argument that taxes harm the economy is more fundamental—namely, that taxes need not cause any loss in surplus at all, even in the markets in which they are directly applied. Suppose, for example, that in the market for cars considered earlier, private marginal cost is again $10,000 but that the production and use of cars now generates air pollution and congestion, negative externalities that sum to $2,000/car each year. The socially optimal quantity of cars would then be not 6 million/year but only 4 million (see Figure 15.5). Without a tax on cars, the market would reach equilibrium at a price of $10,000 and a quantity of 6 million/year. But with a tax of $2,000/car, the equilibrium quantity would shrink to 4 million/year, precisely the socially optimal number.

Here, the direct effect of the tax is not only not to reduce total economic surplus but actually to augment it by $1 billion/day. To that amount we would then add the additional daily surplus made possible by the additional $8 billion worth of public goods financed by the tax.

Could we raise enough tax revenue to run the government if we limited ourselves to taxing only those activities that generate negative externalities? No one knows for sure, but it might be possible, for the list of such activities is a long one.

For instance, when someone enters a congested freeway, he creates additional delays for the motorists already there. Existing technology would enable us to levy road-use taxes that reflect these congestion externalities. Each time fossil fuels are burned, they emit greenhouse gases into the atmosphere, which will accelerate the trend toward global warming. A tax on carbon would increase economic surplus by causing decision makers to take this external cost into account. Taxes on other forms of air and water pollution would have similarly benign effects on resource allocation. Recent experience with refundable taxes on food and beverage containers demonstrates that taxes like these can raise needed revenue while at the same time contributing to a cleaner environment.

▪ SUMMARY ▪

- Our aim in this chapter was to apply principles of microeconomics to the study of the government's role in modern society. One of government's principal tasks is to provide public goods, such as national defense and the criminal justice system. Such goods are, in varying degrees, nonrival and nonexcludable. The first property describes goods for which one person's consumption does not diminish the amount available for others, while the second refers to the difficulty of preventing nonpayers from consuming certain goods.

- Goods that are both highly nonexcludable and nonrival are often called pure public goods. A collective good—such as pay-per-view cable television—is nonrival but excludable. Commons goods are goods that are rival but nonexcludable.

- Because not everyone benefits equally from the provision of any given public good, charging all taxpayers equal amounts for the provision of public goods will generally not be either feasible or desirable. As in the case of private goods, people's willingness to pay for public goods generally increases with income, and most governments therefore levy higher taxes on the rich than on the poor. Tax systems with this property have been criticized on the grounds that they are unfair to the wealthy, but this criticism ignores the fact that alternative tax schemes generally lead to worse outcomes for both rich and poor alike.

- The criterion for providing the optimal quantity or quality of a public good is to keep increasing quantity or quality as long as the marginal benefit of doing so exceeds the marginal cost. One advantage of using the government to provide public goods is that once a tax collection agency has been established to finance a single public good, it can be expanded at relatively low cost to generate revenue to fi-

nance additional public goods. A second advantage is that because government has the power to tax, it can easily assign responsibility for the cost of a public good. And in the case of goods for which nonpayers simply cannot be excluded, the government may be the only feasible provider.

- One disadvantage to exclusive reliance on government for public goods provision is the element of coercion inherent in the tax system, which makes some people pay for public goods they don't want, while others do without public goods they do want. Many public goods are provided through private channels, with the necessary funding provided by donations, sale of by-products, by development of new means to exclude nonpayers, and in many cases by private contract. A loss in surplus results, however, whenever monetary charges are levied for the consumption of a nonrival good.

- In addition to providing public goods, government serves two other important roles: the regulation of activities that generate externalities and the definition and enforcement of property rights. Despite a general view that government is more responsive the shorter the distance between citizens and their elected representatives, factors such as economies of scale in the provision of public goods and externalities with broad reach often dictate the assignment of important functions to state or national governments.

- Although history has shown that democracy is the best form of government, it is far from perfect. For example, practices such as logrolling and rent-seeking, common in most democracies, often result in the adoption of laws and public projects whose costs exceed their benefits.

- To finance public goods and services, governments at all levels must tax. But a tax on any activity not only generates revenue, it also creates an incentive to reduce the activity. If the activity would have been pursued at the optimal level in the absence of a tax, taxing it will result in too little of the activity. This observation has led many critics to denounce all taxes as harmful to the economy. Yet the negative effects of taxes on incentives must be weighed against the benefits of the public goods and services financed by tax revenue. Furthermore, taxes on inelastically supplied or demanded activities may generate only small deadweight losses, while taxes on activities that create negative externalities may actually increase economic efficiency.

▪ KEY TERMS ▪

collective good (379)
crowding out (394)
head tax (381)
logrolling (391)
nonexcludable good (378)

nonrival good (378)
pork barrel spending (391)
progressive tax (382)
proportional income tax (382)
public good (378)

pure commons good (379)
pure private good (379)
pure public good (378)
regressive tax (381)
rent-seeking (392)

▪ REVIEW QUESTIONS ▪

1. a. Which of the following goods are nonrival?
   Apples
   Stephen King novels
   Street lighting on campus
   NPR radio broadcasts
   b. Which of these goods are nonexcludable?

2. Give examples of goods that are, for the most part:
   a. Rival but nonexcludable
   b. Nonrival but excludable
   c. Both nonrival and nonexcludable

3. Why might even a wealthy person prefer a proportional income tax to a head tax?

4. True or false: A tax on an activity that generates negative externalities will improve resource allocation in the private sector and also generate revenue that could be used to pay for useful public goods. Explain.

5. Consider a good that would be provided optimally by private market forces. Why is the direct loss in surplus that would result from a tax on this good an overstatement of the loss in surplus caused by the tax?

▪ PROBLEMS ▪

1. Jack and Jill are the only two residents in a neighborhood, and they would like to hire a security guard. The value of a security guard is $50/month to Jack and $150/month to Jill. Irrespective of who pays the guard, the guard will protect the entire neighborhood.
   a. What is the most a guard can charge per month and still be assured of being hired by at least one of them?
   b. Suppose the competitive wage for a security guard is $120/month. The local government proposes a plan whereby Jack and Jill each pay 50 percent of this monthly fee, and asks them to vote on this plan. Will the plan be voted in? Would economic surplus be higher if the neighborhood had a guard?

2. Refer to Problem 1. Suppose Jack earns $1,000/month and Jill earns $11,000/month.
   a. Suggest a proportional tax on income that would be accepted by majority vote and would pay for the security guard.
   b. Suppose instead that Jack proposes a tax scheme under which Jack and Jill would each receive the same net benefit from hiring the guard. How much would Jack and Jill pay now? Would Jill agree to this scheme?
   c. What is the practical problem that prevents ideas like the one in part b from working in real-life situations?

3. The following table shows all the marginal benefits for each voter in a small town whose town council is considering a new swimming pool with capacity for at least three citizens. The cost of the pool would be $18 per week and would not depend on the number of people who actually used it. The interest rate is 1 percent per week.

Voter	Marginal benefit ($/week)
A	12
B	5
C	2

a. If the pool must be financed by a weekly head tax levied on all voters, will the pool be approved by majority vote? Is this outcome socially efficient? Explain.

b. The town council instead decides to auction a franchise off to a private monopoly to build and maintain the pool. If it cannot find such a firm willing to operate the pool, then the pool project will be scrapped. If all such monopolies are constrained by law to charge a single price to users, will the franchise be sold, and if so, how much will it sell for? Is this outcome socially efficient? Explain.

4. Refer to Problem 3. Suppose now that all such monopolies can perfectly price-discriminate.

a. Will the franchise be sold, and if so, how much will it sell for? Is this outcome socially efficient? Explain.

b. The town council decides that, rather than auction off the franchise, it will give it away to the firm that spends the most money lobbying council members. If there are four identical firms in the bidding and they cannot collude, what will happen?

5. Two consumers, Smith and Jones, have the following demand curves for Podunk Public Radio broadcasts of recorded opera on Saturdays:

$$\text{Smith:} \quad P_S = 12 - Q$$
$$\text{Jones:} \quad P_J = 12 - 2Q,$$

where P_S and P_J represent marginal willingness to pay values for Smith and Jones, respectively, and Q represents the number of hours of opera broadcast each Saturday.

a. If Smith and Jones are the only public radio listeners in Podunk, construct the demand curve for opera broadcasts.

b. If the marginal cost of opera broadcasts is $15 per hour, what is the socially optimal number of hours of broadcast opera?

6. Suppose the demand curves for hour-long episodes of the *Jerry Springer Show* and *Masterpiece Theater* are as shown in the following diagram. A television network is considering whether to add one or both programs to its upcoming fall lineup. The only two time slots remaining are sponsored by Colgate, which is under contract to pay the network 10 cents for each viewer who watches the program, out of which the network would have to cover its production costs of $400,000 per episode. (Viewership can be estimated accurately with telephone surveys.) Any time slot the network does not fill with *Springer* or *Masterpiece Theater* will be filled by infomercials for a weight-loss program, for which the network incurs no production costs and for which it receives a fee of $500,000. Viewers will receive $5 million in economic surplus from watching each installment of the infomercial.

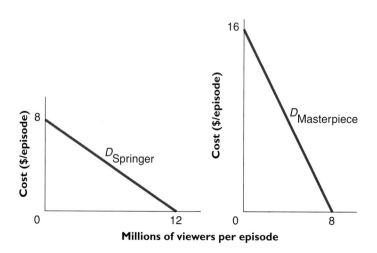

a. How will the network fill the two remaining slots in its fall lineup?

b. Is this outcome socially efficient?

7. Refer to Problem 6. By how much would total economic surplus be higher if each episode of *Masterpiece Theater* were shown on PBS free of charge than if it were shown by a profit-maximizing pay-per-view network?

8. When a TV company chooses a pay-per-view scheme to pay for programming, which of the following statements is true? Explain.

a. The outcome is socially efficient.

b. The programs selected will maximize advertising revenue.

c. The marginal cost to an additional viewer of watching the programs is lower than when advertising is used to finance programming.

d. The outcome is always more socially efficient than when advertising is used to finance programming.

e. The variety of programs provided is likely to rise.

9. When a group of people must decide whether to buy a shared public good or service, the free-rider problem frequently occurs because:

a. People have an incentive to understate how much the facility is really worth to them if they have to pay taxes to finance it.

b. Each individual's needed contribution is an insignificant amount of the total required.

c. People have an incentive to overstate how much the facility is worth to them if they don't have to pay taxes to finance it.

d. People hope that others will value the facility enough to pay for it entirely.

e. Only one of the above statements is not a reason for the existence of the free-rider problem.

10. The town of Smallsville is considering building a museum. The interest on the money Smallsville will have to borrow to build the museum will be $1,000 per year. Each citizen's marginal benefit from the museum is shown in the following table, and this marginal benefit schedule is public information.

a. Assuming each citizen voted his or her private interests, would a referendum to build the museum and raise each citizen's annual taxes by $200 pass?

b. A citizen proposes that the city let a private company build the museum and charge the citizens a lump-sum fee each year to view it as much as they like. Only citizens who paid the fee would be allowed to view the museum. If the private company were allowed to set a single fee, would any company offer to build the museum?

c. A second citizen proposes allowing the private company to charge different prices to different citizens and auctioning the right to build the museum to the highest bidding company. Again, only the citizens who pay the fee may view the museum. What is the highest bid a private company would make to supply the museum to Smallsville?

Citizen	Marginal benefit from museum ($/year)
Anita	340
Brandon	290
Carlena	240
Dallas	190
Eloise	140

■ ANSWERS TO IN-CHAPTER EXERCISES ■

15.1 a. The BLS web site at 3 in the morning has the capacity to serve far more users than it attracts, so an additional user calling up the site does not prevent some other user from doing so. Other web sites, however do not show the nonrival property, at least during certain hours, because they attract more users than their servers can accommodate.

b. The stadium at the championship game is always full, so anyone who watches the game in person prevents someone else from doing so.

c. Additional people can watch the game on television without diminishing the availability of the telecast for others.

15.2 To construct the demand curve [part (a)], we first graph Bill's demand curve [part (c)] and Tom's demand curve [part (b)] and then add the two individual demand curves vertically. The equation for the demand curve is $P = 18 - 1.5Q$.

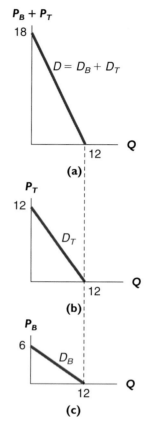

15.3 Whereas elasticity of demand was 1 at a price of $10 on the original demand curve, it is 1.5 on the new demand curve. As a result, the $10 fee now excludes 20 million viewers, and the resulting loss in surplus (again the area of the blue triangle) is now $100 million.

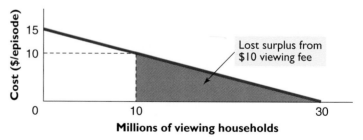

15.4 If Sven orders bread pudding, his share of the bill would now go up by $2 instead of $1. If he orders chocolate mousse, his share of the bill would go up by $1.20 instead of $0.60. So he would still order the bread pudding (surplus = $4 − $2 = $2) rather than the chocolate mousse (surplus = $3 − $1.20 = $1.80).

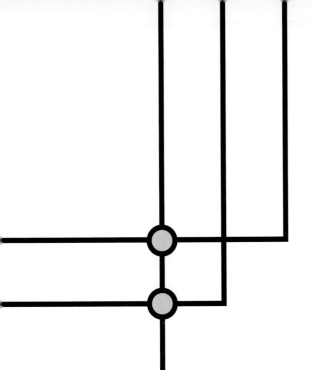

CHAPTER

16

INCOME
REDISTRIBUTION

■

P atek Philippe's Calibre '89 is perhaps the most remarkably elaborate and accurate mechanical watch ever built. Among its many features is a "tourbillon," a gyroscope that turns about once each minute, whose purpose is to offset the distortionary effects of the earth's gravitational field. Yet despite its $2.7 million price tag and formidable engineering wizardry, the Calibre '89 is actually less accurate than a battery-powered quartz watch costing less than $20. The earth's gravitational field, it turns out, doesn't affect the accuracy of an electronic watch.

Accurate or not, top-of-the line mechanical wristwatches are selling briskly. A Patek Philippe watch priced at $45,000, for example, is available only on backorder, and sales of watches costing more than $2,000 are growing at almost 13 percent a year. The men who purchase these mechanical wristwatches (women almost never buy them) often own several, which confronts them with a problem: Although the watches are self-winding, they will stop if put aside for a few days. So the owner of several of these watches must often reset each one before wearing it.

One could hardly expect men of means to tolerate such a problem for long. And sure enough, there is now a ready solution. On display in Asprey & Garrard showrooms, discerning buyers will find a finely tooled calfskin-covered box with a golden clasp, whose doors open to reveal six mechanical wrists that rotate just often enough to keep the mechanical wristwatches they hold running smoothly. The price? Only $5,700.

Many people might think that if the government were to tax buyers of $50,000 wristwatches more heavily and use the proceeds to buy school lunches for poor children, the world would a better place. Yet this proposition remains a remarkably controversial one. Our aim in this chapter will be to explore whether income inequality is something society should be concerned about, and, if so, whether practical remedies exist. As we will see, government programs to redistribute income have costs as well as benefits. As always, policymakers must employ the cost-benefit principle to compare an imperfect status quo with the practical consequences of imperfect government remedies.

RECENT TRENDS IN INEQUALITY AND CONSUMER SPENDING

The period from the end of World War II until the early 1970s was one of balanced income growth in the United States. During that period, incomes grew at almost 3 percent a year for rich, middle-class, and poor Americans alike.

In the ensuing years, however, the pattern of income growth has been dramatically different. In the first row of Table 16.1, for example, notice that families in the bottom 20 percent of the income distribution saw their real incomes actually decline by more than 4 percent from 1978 to 1998. The third row of the table indicates that the real incomes of families in the middle quintile grew by less than 10 percent during the same 20-year period (a growth rate of less than one-half of 1 percent per year). But while the real incomes of middle-class and poor families were stagnant or declining, families with the highest earnings experienced much bigger gains than in the immediate postwar decades. Thus real incomes jumped more than 40 percent for families in the top quintile between 1978 and 1998, while those for families in the top 5 percent jumped by more than 68 percent.

TABLE 16.1
Mean Income Received by Families in Each Income Quintile and by the Top 5 Percent of Families, 1968–1998 (1998 dollars)

Quintile	1978	1988	1998
Bottom 20 percent	$ 13,103	$ 12,256	$ 12,526
Second 20 percent	28,415	28,541	29,482
Middle 20 percent	42,667	44,414	46,662
Fourth 20 percent	58,786	63,785	68,430
Top 20 percent	99,754	117,035	140,846
Top 5 percent	146,178	182,863	246,520

SOURCE: Census Bureau. www.census.gov/hhes/income/histinc/f03.html.

The result has been a significant shift in the overall distribution of earnings among American families. Table 16.2, for example, shows how the shares of total earnings have evolved for the different groups between 1968 and 1998. Note that the lowest three quintiles each had a significantly smaller share of the national income in 1998 than in 1968, while the share of the fourth quintile was essentially unchanged. But note in the final two rows of the table that the share of the top quintile rose more than 17 percent, and the share of the top 5 percent rose almost 33 percent.

Recent earnings growth has been even greater for those higher up the income ladder. Thus real earnings of the top 1 percent of U.S. workers have more than doubled since 1979, and those near the top of the income ladder have taken home paychecks that might have seemed unimaginable just two decades ago. For

TABLE 16.2
Share of Aggregate Income Received by Each Quintile and by the Top 5 Percent of Families, 1968–1998

Quintile	1968	1978	1988	1998
Bottom 20 percent	5.6	5.4	4.6	4.2
Second 20 percent	12.4	11.7	10.7	9.9
Middle 20 percent	17.7	17.6	16.7	15.7
Fourth 20 percent	23.7	24.2	24.0	23.0
Top 20 percent	40.6	41.1	44.0	47.3
Top 5 percent	15.6	15.1	17.2	20.7

SOURCE: Census Bureau. www.census.gov/hhes/income/histinc/f02.html.

example, though no American CEO earned as much as $1 million in 1978, Disney's CEO Michael Eisner took home more than $565 million in 1997 (including gains from exercising his stock options).

Recent decades also witnessed dramatic growth and increased concentration of personal wealth. Wealth holdings for the richest 1 percent of Americans have roughly doubled since 1980, and the combined wealth of this group now exceeds the combined wealth of Americans below the 95th percentile. The Forbes Four Hundred—the celebrated list of the 400 richest people in America—included 243 billionaires in 1998, up from 170 just a year earlier. In 1982 the list contained just 13 billionaires—five of them children of Texas oil tycoon H. L. Hunt. Together the Forbes 400 are worth more than $1 trillion, nearly one-eighth the national income of the United States, and more than the national income of China, a country of more than 1 billion people.

The recent gains in wealth have not been confined to those who were already worth hundreds of millions. For example, more than 4 million American households had a net worth of at least $1 million in 1998, 20 percent more than in 1995. Some 274,000 households had a net worth of at least $10 million in 1998, up from 190,400 households in 1995.

In sum, to say that recent changes in the distributions of income and wealth have produced a fundamental shift in the American economic landscape is hardly an exaggeration. People who had a lot of money to begin with have considerably more now, and many more people have a lot of money now than in the past.

These fortunate people have been buying more and better things, just as people with extra cash in their pockets have always done. Sales trends in the wristwatch industry are like those in virtually every other product category. For example, while total car sales in the United States went down 3 percent in 1997, Porsche sales rose 79 percent, Mercedes sales 35 percent, and BMW sales 16 percent. And while overall wine sales are down slightly from their peak in 1986, sales of ultrapremium wines have been growing more than 20 percent a year since 1980.

Houses with more than 20,000 square feet of living space are currently being constructed in record numbers. A typical house of that size has 10 or more large bedrooms, each with its own bath; an informal living room and a formal living room; a ballroom; a 500-square-foot kitchen with separate pantry; a dining room; a media room; a library; maid's quarters; and a five- or six-car garage. Many have squash courts and bowling alleys.

Suffice it to say that in purely economic terms, those near the top of the income ladder are prospering as never before. In contrast, those farther down the ladder have seen their living standards grow much more slowly, or even decline.

> **RECAP** **RECENT TRENDS IN INEQUALITY AND CONSUMER SPENDING**
>
> From 1945 until the mid-1970s, incomes grew at almost 3 percent a year for rich, middle-class, and poor families alike. In contrast, most of the income growth since the mid-1970s has been concentrated among top earners. The real earnings of low-income families have actually declined since the mid-1970s. Changes in wealth concentration have followed the same patterns. Higher income and wealth at the top of the economic pyramid has stimulated large increases in spending on luxury consumption goods.

MORAL CONCERNS RAISED BY INCOME INEQUALITY

In the United States, as in most other market economies, the vast majority of citizens receive most of their income from the sale of their own labor. An attractive feature of the free-market system, in both moral and practical terms, is that it rewards initiative, effort, and risk taking. The harder, longer, and more effectively a person works, the more she will be paid. And if she risks her capital on a venture that happens to succeed, she will reap a handsome dividend indeed.

Yet relying on the marketplace to distribute income also entails a moral drawback—namely, that those who do well often end up with vastly more money than they can spend, while those who fail often cannot afford even basic goods and services. Hundreds of thousands of American families are homeless, and still larger numbers go to bed hungry each night. Many distinguished philosophers have argued that such poverty in the midst of plenty is impossible to justify on moral grounds.

JUSTICE AS FAIRNESS

Inequality might be easier to accept if it were strictly the result of differences in effort, but it is not. Talent plays an important role in most endeavors, and although it can be nurtured and developed in those who have it, having it in the first place is essentially a matter of luck.

Yet having abundant talent is no guarantee of doing well. To become wealthy, one must have the *right* talent. Being able to hit a baseball 400 feet with consistency will earn an athlete millions annually, but being the best fourth grade teacher in the nation will earn an educator little. The baseball star earns so much more not because he works harder or has more talent, but because he is lucky enough to be good at something people are willing to pay a premium for.

John Rawls, a moral philosopher at Harvard University, has constructed a cogent ethical critique of the marginal productivity system, one based heavily on the economic theory of choice itself.[1] In thinking about what constitutes a just distribution of income, Rawls asks us to imagine ourselves meeting to choose the rules for distributing income. The meeting takes place behind a "veil of ignorance," which conceals from participants any knowledge of what talents and abilities each has. Because no individual knows whether he is smart or dull, strong or weak, fast or slow, no one knows which rules of distribution would work to his own advantage.

Rawls argues that the rules people would choose in such a state of ignorance would necessarily be fair, and if the rules are fair, the income distribution to which they give rise will also be fair.

[1]John Rawls, *A Theory of Justice,* Cambridge, Mass.: Harvard University Press, 1971.

What sort of rules would people choose from behind a veil of ignorance? If the national income were a fixed amount, most people would probably give everyone an equal share. That scenario is likely, Rawls argues, because most people are strongly risk-averse. Since an unequal income distribution would involve not only a chance of doing well but a chance of doing poorly, most people would prefer to eliminate the risk by choosing an equal distribution. Imagine, for example, that you and two friends have been told that an anonymous benefactor has donated $300,000 to divide among you. How would you split it? If you are like most people, you would immediately propose an equal division, or $100,000 for each of you.

Yet despite the obvious attraction of equality, it is far from absolute. Indeed, the goal of absolute equality is quickly trumped by other concerns when we make the rules for distributing wealth in modern market economies. Wealth, after all, generally doesn't come from anonymous benefactors; we must produce it. In a large economy, if each person were guaranteed an equal amount of income, few would invest in education or the development of special talents, and as Example 16.1 illustrates, the incentive to work would be sharply reduced.

Does income sharing affect labor supply?

EXAMPLE 16.1

Sue is offered a job reshelving books in the University of Montana library from noon until 1 P.M. each Friday. Her reservation wage for this task is $10/hour. If the library director offers Sue $100/hour, how much economic surplus will she enjoy as a result of accepting the job? Now suppose the library director announces that the earnings from the job will be divided equally among the 400 students who live in Sue's dormitory. Will Sue still accept?

When the $100/hour is paid directly to Sue, she accepts the job and enjoys an economic surplus of $100 − $10 = $90. If the $100 were divided equally among the 400 residents of Sue's dorm, however, each resident's share would be only 25 cents. Accepting the job would thus mean a negative surplus for Sue of $0.25 − $10 = −$9.75, so she will not accept the job.

EXERCISE 16.1

What is the largest dorm population for which Sue would accept the job on a pay-sharing basis?

In a country without rewards for hard work and risk taking, national income would be dramatically smaller than in a country with such rewards. Of course, material rewards for effort and risk taking necessarily lead to inequality. Rawls argues, however, that people would be willing to accept a certain degree of inequality as long as these rewards produced a sufficiently large increase in the total amount of output available for distribution.

But how much inequality would people accept? Much less than the amount produced by purely competitive markets, Rawls argues. The idea is that behind the veil of ignorance, each person would fear being put in a disadvantaged position, so each would choose rules that would produce a more equal distribution of income than exists under the marginal productivity system. And since such choices *define* the just distribution of income, he argues, fairness requires at least some attempt to reduce the inequality produced by the market system.

THE UTILITARIAN ARGUMENT

The branch of moral philosophy called **utilitarianism** holds that the right course of action is the one that results in the highest total level of utility. Utilitarians argue against income inequality on the grounds that the marginal utility of income is typically smaller for a wealthy person than for a poor person. In their view,

utilitarianism a moral theory in which the right course of action is the one that results in the highest total utility

transferring $1,000 of income from a rich person to a poor person is justified because the extra happiness experienced when the poor person received the money would far outweigh the decline in happiness when the rich person gave it up.

Although some have objected to this argument, saying that no one knows for sure how gains and losses affect the well-being of people in different circumstances, most people accept the claim that an extra dollar generally meets more pressing demands for a poor person than for a rich person. But even utilitarians do not argue for complete equalization on these grounds. With Rawls, they recognize that a regime of complete equality would so weaken incentives that it would not, in fact, produce the greatest utility for all.

THE PSYCHOLOGICAL COSTS OF INEQUALITY

Many modern disciples of Adam Smith appear reluctant to introduce concerns about inequality into discussions of economic policy. Yet as Smith himself recognized, such concerns are a basic component of human nature. Writing more than two centuries ago, he introduced the important idea that local consumption standards influence the goods and services that people consider essential (or "necessaries," as Smith called them). In the following passage, for example, Smith described the factors that influence the amount an individual must spend on clothing in order to be able appear in public "without shame."

> By necessaries I understand not only the commodities which are indispensably necessary for the support of life, but whatever the custom of the country renders it indecent for creditable people, even of the lowest order, to be without. A linen shirt, for example, is, strictly speaking, not a necessary of life. The Greeks and Romans lived, I suppose, very comfortably though they had no linen. But in the present times, through the greater part of Europe, a creditable day-labourer would be ashamed to appear in public without a linen shirt, the want of which would be supposed to denote that disgraceful degree of poverty which, it is presumed, nobody can well fall into without extreme bad conduct. Custom, in the same manner, has rendered leather shoes a necessary of life in England. The poorest creditable person of either sex would be ashamed to appear in public without them.[2]

The absolute standard of living in the United States today is vastly higher than it was in Adam Smith's eighteenth-century Scotland. Yet Smith's observations apply with equal force to contemporary industrial societies. Consider, for instance, the journalist Dirk Johnson's recent account of the experiences of Wendy Williams, a middle school student from a low-income family in Dixon, Illinois.

> Watching classmates strut past in designer clothes, Wendy Williams sat silently on the yellow school bus, wearing a cheap belt and rummage-sale slacks. One boy stopped and yanked his thumb, demanding her seat.
>
> "Move it, trailer girl," he sneered.
>
> It has never been easy to live on the wrong side of the tracks. But in the economically robust 1990's, with sprawling new houses and three-car garages sprouting like cornstalks on the Midwestern prairie, the sting that comes with scarcity gets rubbed with an extra bit of salt. . . .
>
> To be without money, in so many ways, is to be left out.
>
> "I told this girl: 'That's a really awesome shirt. Where did you get it?'" said Wendy, explaining that she knew it was out of her price

[2]Adam Smith, *The Wealth of Nations*, New York: Everyman's Library, E. P. Dutton, 1910 (1776), book 1.

range, but that she wanted to join the small talk. "And she looked at me and laughed and said, 'Why would you want to know?'"

A lanky, soft-spoken girl with large brown eyes, Wendy pursed her lips to hide a slight overbite that got her the nickname Rabbit, a humiliation she once begged her mother and father to avoid by sending her to an orthodontist.

For struggling parents, keenly aware that adolescents agonize over the social pecking order, the styles of the moment and the face in the mirror, there is no small sense of failure in telling a child that she cannot have what her classmates take for granted.

"Do you know what it's like?" asked Wendy's mother, Veronica Williams, "to have your daughter come home and say, 'Mom, the kids say my clothes are tacky,' and then walk off with her head hanging low."[3]

An adolescent in eighteenth-century Scotland would not have been much embarrassed by having a slight overbite, because not even the wealthiest members of society wore braces on their teeth then. Rising living standards have altered the frame of reference that defines an acceptable standard of cosmetic dentistry. The toll that inequality takes on individuals like Wendy Williams is no less important because it occurs in psychological rather than explicit monetary terms.

RECAP   **MORAL CONCERNS RAISED BY INCOME INEQUALITY**

High levels of income inequality have drawn moral objections on several grounds. John Rawls has argued that the degree of inequality typical of unregulated market systems is unfair because people would favor substantially less inequality if they chose distributional rules from behind a veil of ignorance. Utilitarians favor reducing inequality because the marginal utility of income is smaller for wealthy persons than for poor persons. Others have objected to extreme inequality because it imposes significant psychological costs.

PRACTICAL CONCERNS RAISED BY POVERTY AND INCOME INEQUALITY

Even if we set moral concerns completely aside, compelling practical reasons to limit poverty and inequality would remain. One concern is that poverty imposes many costs on those who are not poor. Another is that growing income inequality raises the price of achieving many important family goals.

THE EFFECT OF POVERTY ON THE NONPOOR

The productivity of any member of a team depends on the productivity of other team members. For example, the amount by which the efforts of skilled engineers or managers contribute to national income will be many times greater in an economy with a highly skilled workforce than in one with a poorly trained workforce. Those at the top of the productivity ladder gain by working with people of the highest caliber. Yet beyond some point, poverty may inhibit those near the bottom of the income ladder from developing their skills to the fullest. For example, low-income parents often cannot afford after-school lesson programs for their

---

[3]Dirk Johnson, "When Money Is Everything, Except Hers," *The New York Times*, October 28, 1998, p. A1.

children, who are often forced to drop out of school prematurely. Low-income parents may also fail to learn about training programs for themselves or may lack transportation to get to those programs.

Even the psychological burden of being poor can result in missed opportunities. For instance, when a teacher asked Wendy Williams, the Illinois middle school student, to join an advanced class in algebra, she declined, saying "I get picked on for my clothes and living in the trailer park. I don't want to get picked on for being a nerd, too."[4] No matter what its cause, the undeveloped potential of low-income persons works not just to their own disadvantage but also to the disadvantage of those at the top.

Low-income persons are also less likely to be well nourished and less likely to obtain preventive medical care on a routine basis. Compounding these problems, the psychological stresses of living in poverty are known to foster a variety of physical illnesses. Poor people get sick more often than others, and their illnesses tend to be more serious.

These illnesses not only harm the poor but also impose costs on others. As noted in Chapter 15, some 45 million Americans currently lack health insurance. When uninsured people become seriously ill, they often receive medical care at public expense, imposing an additional tax burden on healthy people. The unpaid medical bills of the uninsured also force doctors and hospitals to increase their fees, raising the insurance premiums of those who remain insured. To the extent that illness prevents people from achieving their full potential, healthy people will miss many of the indirect benefits that spring from working with more productive colleagues.

Finally, because poverty prevents some people from capitalizing on legitimate career opportunities, it also increases the attractiveness of crime. Total U.S. spending on private security currently runs about $60 billion a year, and private security firms now employ some 1.5 million persons—more than 2 1/2 times the number in public law enforcement. When people are occupied in either committing crimes or trying to avoid them, they are diverted from producing legitimate goods and services. This pattern is profoundly wasteful from the perspective of both rich and poor.

THE EFFECT OF A WIDENING INCOME GAP ON THE MIDDLE CLASS

Since Ronald Reagan's administration, presidential aspirants have urged voters to ask themselves whether they are better off now than they were 4 years ago. At any time from 1945 to the early 1970s, the answer for most Americans would have been a resounding yes, for as noted earlier, incomes were growing at about 3 percent a year during that period for families in every income class.

Today, however, Reagan's question is more difficult to answer. Does the fact that median family income is slightly higher, in real terms, than it was in the 1970s mean that the typical middle-class family is better off now? If we measure economic well-being by the amount of goods and services such a family can buy, the answer would appear to be yes. Many respected economists have argued to that effect, invoking the Pareto criterion (see Chapter 7). According to that criterion, a change in circumstances must be counted as an improvement if it makes at least some people better off without harming others.

Yet "having more income" and "being better off" do not have exactly the same meaning. Indeed, increased spending at the top of the income distribution has caused tangible harm to families in the middle by raising the cost of achieving goals that almost every family cherishes. Few middle-income parents, for example, would be comfortable knowing that their children were attending below-average schools. But since the quality of public schools is closely linked to

[4]Johnson, ibid.

local property taxes, which in turn are closely linked to local real estate prices, people cannot send their children to a public school of even average quality if they buy a home in a school district in which house prices are well below average. The relationship between school quality and housing prices creates a problem for middle-income families, because the average new home built in the United States today, which has some 2,200 square feet of living space, is roughly 50 percent larger than the average new home built in 1970. So today's middle-income family cannot send its children to schools of average quality unless it carries a much larger mortgage than its counterparts in 1970.

Increased income inequality is the reason the average house has grown so much bigger. The process begins when higher incomes prompt top earners to build larger homes. Perhaps your parents didn't care whether your neighbors had bigger homes than yours. Yet many people *do* care about relative home size. Thus when top earners build 20,000-square-foot houses, others just below the top income level find their 10,000-square-foot houses no longer adequate. This process of comparison repeats itself all the way down the income ladder.

If an average earner doesn't envy his neighbor's larger house, couldn't he simply buy the same size house that average earners bought in 1970? He could, but then he would have to send his children to below-average schools. Rather than do that, he might prefer to buy the bigger house, even if he doesn't care about the extra space. Worse still, he might end up buying an existing 1,500-square-foot house whose price has been bid up sharply because of its location in a good school district.

Increased spending at the top also imposes other costs on those below. A soccer mom who buys a typical 3,000-pound sedan will incur risks that didn't exist in the 1970s, since she must now share the road with 6,000-pound Lincoln Navigators and 7,500-pound Ford Excursions. So in self-defense, she may want to spend more for a bulkier vehicle. And if her family does manage to buy a home in a good school district, she may need to spend more on her children's clothes or else share the embarrassment they experience at not measuring up to wealthier classmates. The clothing she and her husband buy might have to come up a notch as well. After all, others are wearing more expensive clothes now, and in job interviews they will want to make a good impression. Even the gifts they must give will be affected by the greater affluence of top earners.

The pressures that stem from increased spending at the top may help to explain why American families now carry an average of more than $5,000 in credit card debt. Those same pressures may explain why American families at the turn of the millennium were filing for personal bankruptcy at seven times the rate they did in 1980, even though the unemployment rate was at a 29-year low. The point is not that Americans should somehow turn back the clock to the 1970s. Rather, it is that the expanding income and wealth gaps appear to have caused tangible harm, even to middle-class people who earn a little more than they used to.

RECAP   **PRACTICAL CONCERNS RAISED BY POVERTY AND INCOME INEQUALITY**

Apart from moral concerns about income inequality, practical reasons would argue for limiting the gap between the rich and poor. One is that poverty imposes costs on the nonpoor. High-income persons benefit from having highly skilled people to work with, and poverty often limits the extent to which people can develop their skills. Poverty also fosters illness and crime, both of which burden the nonpoor. Even in the absence of absolute poverty, extreme income inequality raises the price of pursuing many basic goals, as when the growing gap between the rich and the middle class drives up the price of a house in a good school district.

METHODS OF INCOME REDISTRIBUTION

As we have seen, both moral and practical concerns provide grounds for reducing income inequality. But attempts to limit inequality are also fraught with practical difficulties. The challenge is to find ways to raise the incomes of those who cannot fend well enough for themselves, without at the same time undermining their incentive to work and without using scarce resources to subsidize those who are not poor.

Recall that in the absence of externalities and various other market imperfections, total economic surplus is largest when price is set at the level for which supply and demand curves intersect (see Chapter 7). Nevertheless, most governments disregard the efficiency principle by taking at least some steps to protect the poor by keeping the prices in certain markets from reaching market-clearing levels. Rent controls on apartments and price controls on home heating oil are familiar examples. In such cases, rich and poor alike would fare better if government simply gave the poor some more money. As we will see, a similar objection applies to legislation that sets minimum wages in the labor market.

MINIMUM WAGES

The United States and many other industrialized countries have sought to ease the burden of the working poor by enacting minimum wage legislation—laws that prohibit employers from paying workers less than a specified hourly wage. The federal minimum wage in the United States is currently set at \$5.15/hour, and several states have set minimum wage levels significantly higher. Massachusetts, for example, increased its minimum wage to \$6.75/hour in early 2000.

How does a minimum wage affect the market for low-wage labor? In Figure 16.1, note that when the law prevents employers from paying less than W_{min}, employers hire fewer workers (a decline from L_0 to L_1). Unemployment results. The L_1 workers who keep their jobs earn more than before, but the $L_0 - L_1$ workers who lose their jobs earn nothing. Whether workers together earn more or less than before thus depends on the elasticity of demand for labor. If elasticity of demand is less than 1, workers as a group will earn more than before. If it is more than 1, workers as a group will earn less.

At one point, economists were almost unanimous in their opposition to minimum wage laws, arguing that those laws reduce total economic surplus, much like other regulations that prevent markets from reaching equilibrium. In recent years, however, some economists have softened their opposition to minimum wage laws, citing studies that have failed to show significant reductions in employment following increases in minimum wage levels. These studies may well

FIGURE 16.1

The Effect of Minimum Wage Legislation on Employment.

If minimum wage legislation requires employers to pay more than the equilibrium wage, the result will be a decline in employment for low-wage workers.

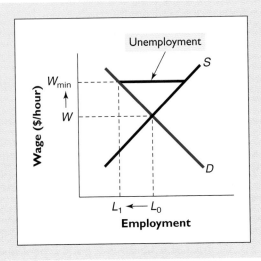

imply that as a group low-income workers are better off with minimum wage laws than without them. But as we saw in Chapter 7, any policy that prevents a market from reaching equilibrium causes a reduction in total economic surplus, which means society ought to be able to find a more effective policy for helping low-wage workers.

THE EARNED-INCOME TAX CREDIT

One such policy is the **earned-income tax credit (EITC)**, which gives low-wage workers a credit on their federal income tax each year. First proposed by President Richard Nixon, the EITC was enacted into law in 1975, and in the years since it has drawn praise from both liberals and conservatives. The program is essentially a wage subsidy in the form of a credit against the amount a family owes in federal income taxes. For example, a family of four with total earned income of $18,000 in 1999 would have received an annual tax credit of about $2,500 under this program. That is, the program would have reduced the annual federal income tax payment of this family by roughly that amount. Families who earned less would have received a larger tax credit, and those who earned more would have received a smaller one. Families whose tax credit exceeded the amount of tax owed actually would have received a check from the government for the difference. (We will see more clearly how the EITC works when we discuss a closely related program in a moment.)

Like the minimum wage, the EITC puts extra income into the hands of workers who are employed at low-wage levels. But unlike the minimum wage, the earned-income tax credit creates no incentive for employers to lay off low-wage workers.

Examples 16.2 to 16.4 illustrate how switching from a minimum wage to an earned-income tax credit can produce gains for both employers and workers.

earned-income tax credit (EITC) a policy under which low-income workers receive credits on their federal income tax

By how much will a minimum wage reduce total economic surplus?

EXAMPLE 16.2

Suppose the demand for unskilled labor in the Cedar Falls labor market is given by $W = 10 - 0.001L$, where W is the wage rate in dollars per hour and L is the quantity of labor demanded in person-hours per day. If the supply curve of unskilled labor in Cedar Falls is given by $W = 0.001L$, by how much will the imposition of a minimum wage at $7/hour reduce total economic surplus? By how much do worker surplus and employer surplus change as a result of adopting the minimum wage?

In the absence of a minimum wage, the equilibrium wage for Cedar Falls would be $5/hour, and employment would be 5,000 person-hours/day (see Figure 16.2). Both employers and workers would enjoy economic surplus equal to the area of the shaded triangles, $12,500/day.

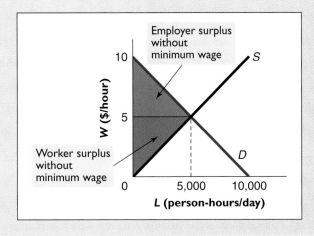

FIGURE 16.2
Worker and Employer Surplus in an Unregulated Labor Market.
For the demand and supply curves shown, worker surplus is the area of the green triangle, $12,500/day, the same as employer surplus (blue triangle).

FIGURE 16.3
The Effect of a Minimum Wage on Economic Surplus.
A minimum wage of $7/hour reduces employment in this market by 2,000 person-hours/day, for a reduction in total economic surplus of $4,000/day (area of the light blue triangle). Employer surplus falls to $4,500/day (area of cross-hatched triangle), while worker surplus rises to $16,500/day (green area).

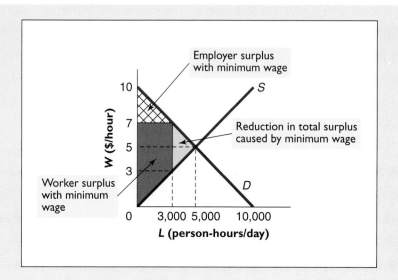

With a minimum wage set at $7/hour, employer surplus is the area of the cross-hatched triangle in Figure 16.3, $4,500/day, and worker surplus is the area of the four-sided green figure, $16,500/day. The minimum wage thus reduces employer surplus by $8,000/day and increases worker surplus by $4,000/day. The net reduction in surplus is the area of the blue triangle shown in Figure 16.3, $4,000/day.

EXERCISE 16.2

In Example 16.2, by how much would total economic surplus have been reduced by the $7 minimum wage if labor demand in Cedar Falls had been perfectly inelastic at 5,000 person-hours/day?

EXAMPLE 16.3

Refer to Example 16.2. How much would it cost the government each day to provide an earned-income tax credit under which workers as a group receive the same economic surplus as they do under the $7/hour minimum wage? (Assume for simplicity that the earned-income tax credit has no effect on labor supply.)

With an earned-income tax credit in lieu of a minimum wage, employment will be 5,000 person-hours/day at $5/hour, just as in the unregulated market. Since worker surplus in the unregulated market was $4,000/day less than under the minimum wage, the government would have to offer a tax credit worth $0.80/hour for each of the 5,000 person-hours of employment to restore worker surplus to the level obtained under the $7 minimum wage.

EXAMPLE 16.4

Can you propose an earned-income tax credit that would win unanimous support from employers and workers?

Suppose that the status quo is the unregulated labor market described in Example 16.2 and that employers and workers in that market are risk-neutral. Labor unions have sufficient political power to induce Congress to enact a minimum wage law. The President's chief economist has urged the President to persuade unions to drop their demand for a minimum wage in favor of an earned-income tax credit. Suppose neither workers nor employers would support the switch unless the expected value of each party's economic surplus under the earned-income tax credit would be at least as great as under the minimum wage. Describe an earned-income tax credit (and a tax that would raise enough money to pay for it) that would receive unanimous support from both workers and employers in the Cedar Falls labor market.

Because employer surplus is $8,000/day lower under the minimum wage than under the earned-income tax credit, employers would be willing to pay a tax up to that amount to secure the policy switch. And since worker surplus would be only $4,000/day smaller in the absence of a minimum wage, $8,000/day is more than enough to finance a tax credit that workers would support. For example, a tax of $6,000 levied on employers could be used to fund an earned-income tax credit of $1.20/hour, which would make both employers and workers better off than under the minimum wage.

The moral, as in similar examples, is that when the economic pie grows larger, everyone can have a bigger slice.

WELFARE PAYMENTS AND IN-KIND TRANSFERS

If price controls and minimum wages are inefficient, why do so many governments use them? Why don't they just transfer additional resources directly to the poor? In fact, such transfers are at the forefront of antipoverty efforts around the globe. Virtually all governments employ them, both in the form of cash transfers (such as welfare payments and EITC payments) and **in-kind transfers.**

in-kind transfer a payment made not in the form of cash but in the form of a good or service

Historically, the most important welfare program has been Aid to Families with Dependent Children (AFDC), which in most cases provides cash payments to poor single-parent households. In-kind transfers are direct transfers of goods or services to low-income individuals or families, such as food stamps, public housing, subsidized school lunches, and Medicaid.

Why did many critics charge that the AFDC program undermined family stability?

As administered in many states, a poor mother was ineligible for AFDC payments if her husband or other able-bodied adult male lived with her and her children. This provision confronted many long-term unemployed fathers with an agonizing choice. They could leave their families, making them eligible for public assistance, or they could remain, making them ineligible. Even many who deeply loved their families understandably chose to leave.

ECONOMIC NATURALIST 16.1

In most places, the extent of cash and in-kind transfers to the poor is limited, because of fear that higher transfers would weaken people's incentive to find work and support themselves. Of course, some people simply cannot work or cannot find work that pays enough to live on. In a world of perfect information, the government could make generous cash payments to those people and withhold support from those who can fend for themselves. In practice, however, the two groups are often hard to distinguish from each other.

Current welfare programs are **means-tested:** The more income one has, the smaller the benefits. The purpose of means testing is to avoid paying benefits to those who don't really need them. But because of the way welfare programs are administered, means testing often has a pernicious effect on work incentives, as Example 16.5 illustrates.

means-tested a benefit program is means-tested if its benefit level declines as the recipient earns additional income

How will earning an extra dollar affect Smith's standard of living?

Smith is an unemployed participant in four welfare programs: Food stamps, rent stamps, energy stamps, and day care stamps. Each program gives him $100 worth

EXAMPLE 16.5

of stamps per month, which he is then free to spend on food, rent, energy, and day care. If Smith gets a job, his benefits in each program are reduced by 50 cents for each dollar he earns. How will his net weekly income change if he accepts a job that pays $50/week?

Smith will lose $25 in weekly benefits from each of the four welfare programs, for a total benefit reduction of $100/week. Taking the job thus leaves him $50/week worse off than before.

Low-income persons need no formal training in economics to realize that under the current welfare system, seeking gainful employment often does not pay. What is more, the system is extremely costly to administer. If the government were to eliminate all existing welfare and social service agencies, the resulting savings would be enough to raise every poor person above the poverty line. One proposal to do precisely that is the negative income tax.

THE NEGATIVE INCOME TAX

negative income tax a system under which the government would grant every citizen a cash payment each year, financed by an additional tax on earned income

Nobel laureate Milton Friedman has proposed that current welfare programs be replaced by a single program called the **negative income tax** (**NIT**). Under the NIT, every man, woman, and child—rich or poor—receives a substantial income tax credit. The NIT is thus just like the earned-income tax credit except that it also applies to people who are not employed and hence have no earned income. A person who earns no income would receive the credit in cash. People who earn income would be taxed at some rate less than 100 percent.

breakeven income level under a negative income tax, the level of before-tax income at which a family's tax liability exactly offsets its initial tax credit

Under a negative income tax, the initial credit and the tax rate would combine to determine a **breakeven income level** at which a person's tax liability exactly offsets his initial tax credit. People earning below that level would receive a net benefit payment from the government; people earning above it would make a net tax payment. Example 16.6 illustrates how the breakeven income level would be calculated.

EXAMPLE 16.6

What is the breakeven level of earned income in an NIT program?

Consider a negative income tax program with a tax credit of $6,000/year and a tax rate of 50 percent. At what income level would an individual in this program neither pay a tax nor receive a benefit? How large a net benefit would a person earning $6,000/year receive? How large a net tax payment would a person earning $18,000/year owe?

The horizontal axis of Figure 16.4 shows an individual's before-tax income, while the vertical axis measures after-tax income. With the credit payment set

FIGURE 16.4
A Hypothetical Negative Income Tax Program.
Under this negative income tax program, each person starts with a cash grant of $6,000/year, which is reduced at the rate of 50 cents for each dollar of income earned during the year. The breakeven income level is $12,000/year.

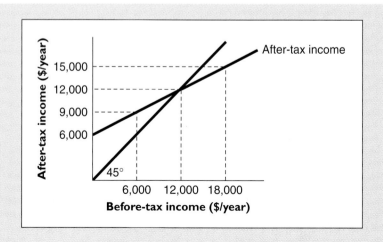

at $6,000/year, someone with a before-tax income of $0 would end up with an after-tax income of $6,000/year. From that point, his income would rise by 50 cents for each dollar earned, as shown by the red line labeled "After-tax income," until at some point it equaled his before-tax income. The 45° line shows all the points at which after-tax income equals before-tax income. In this program, the breakeven level of income is the before-tax income level at which the two lines intersect, which is $12,000/year. A person who earned $6,000/year would receive an after-tax income of $9,000, which implies that the government would send that person a check for $3,000. A person who earned $18,000/year would receive an after-tax income of $15,000, which implies that he would pay $3,000 in taxes.

EXERCISE 16.3

In Example 16.6, what would the breakeven income level have been if the tax credit had been not $6,000/year but $4,000?

The negative income tax would do much less than current programs to weaken work incentives, because unlike current programs, it would assure that someone who earned an extra dollar would keep at least a portion of it. And because the program would be administered by the existing Internal Revenue Service, administrative costs would be far lower than under the current welfare system.

Despite these advantages, however, the negative income tax is by no means a perfect solution to the income-transfer problem. Although the incentive problem would be less severe under a negative income tax than under current welfare programs, it would remain a serious difficulty. To see why, note that if the negative income tax were the *sole* means of insulating people against poverty, the payment to people with no earned income would need to be at least as large as the government's official poverty threshold.

The **poverty threshold** is the annual income level below which a family is officially classified as "poor" by the government. The threshold is based on government estimates of the cost of the so-called economy food plan, the least costly of four nutritionally adequate food plans designed by the Department of Agriculture. The department's 1955 Household Food Consumption Survey found that families of three or more people spent approximately one-third of their after-tax income on food, so the government pegs the poverty threshold at three times the cost of the economy food plan. In 1998, that threshold was $16,600 for a family of four.

For a family of four living in a city, $16,600 a year is scarcely enough to make ends meet. But suppose a group of, say, eight families were to pool their negative tax payments and move to the mountains of northern New Mexico. With a total of $132,800/year to spend, plus the fruits of their efforts at gardening and animal husbandry, such a group could live very nicely indeed.

Once a small number of experimental groups demonstrated the possibility of quitting their jobs and living well on the negative income tax, others would surely follow suit. Two practical difficulties would ensue. First, as more and more people left their jobs to live at government expense, the program would eventually become prohibitively costly. And second, the political cost of the program would almost surely force supporters to abandon it long before that point. Reports of people living lives of leisure at taxpayer expense would be sure to appear on the nightly news. People who worked hard at their jobs all day long would wonder why their tax dollars were being used to support those who were capable of holding paying jobs, yet chose not to work. If the resulting political backlash did not completely eliminate the negative income tax program, it would

poverty threshold the level of income below which the federal government classifies a family as poor

force policymakers to cut back the payment so that members of rural communes could no longer afford to live comfortably. And that would mean the payment would no longer support an urban family.

PUBLIC EMPLOYMENT FOR THE POOR

An alternative method of transferring income to the poor would completely eliminate the problem with work incentives. Government-sponsored jobs could pay wages to the poor for useful work. With public service employment, the specter of people living lives of leisure at public expense simply does not arise.

But public service employment has difficulties of its own. Evidence shows that if government jobs pay the same wages as private jobs, many people will leave their private jobs in favor of government jobs, apparently because they view government jobs as being more secure. Such a migration would make public service employment extremely expensive. Other worrisome possibilities are that such jobs might involve meaningless make-work tasks and that they would prompt an expansion in government bureaucracy. By themselves, government-sponsored jobs for the poor probably are not an adequate solution to the income-transfer problem.

A COMBINATION OF METHODS

Although neither the negative income tax nor public service employment can completely solve the income-transfer problem, a combination of the two might do so. Such a program would consist of a cash grant that is far too small for anyone to live on, supplemented if necessary by a public service job at below minimum wage. Keeping the wage in public service jobs well below the minimum wage would eliminate the risk of a large-scale exodus from private jobs. And while living well on either the negative income tax or the public service wage would be impossible, the two programs together could lift people out of poverty (see Figure 16.5).

To prevent an expansion of the bureaucracy, the government could solicit bids from private management companies to oversee the public service employment program. The fear that this program would inevitably become a make-work project is allayed by evidence that unskilled workers can, with proper supervision, perform many valuable tasks that would not otherwise be performed in the private sector. They can, for example, do landscaping and maintenance in public parks, provide transportation for the elderly and handicapped, fill potholes in city streets and replace burned-out street lamps, transplant seedlings in erosion control projects, remove graffiti from public places and

Can unskilled workers perform useful public service jobs?

FIGURE 16.5
Income by Source in a Combination NIT/Jobs Program.
Together, a small negative income tax and a public job at below minimum wage would provide a family enough income to escape poverty, without weakening work incentives significantly.

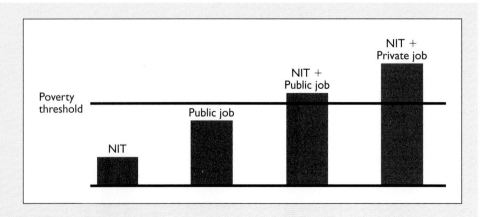

paint government buildings, recycle newspapers and containers, and staff day care centers.

This combination of a small negative income tax payment and public service employment at a subminimum wage would not be cheap. But the direct costs of existing welfare programs are also extremely large, and the indirect costs, in the form of perverse work incentives and misguided attempts to control prices, are even larger. In economic terms, dealing intelligently with the income-transfer problem may in fact prove relatively inexpensive, once society recognizes the enormous opportunity cost of failing to deal intelligently with it.

If the current approach to dealing with income transfers is highly inefficient, then there must be cash on the table that could be made available for productive uses. Yet skeptical readers may ask: If the combination of income-transfer programs just proposed would be so effective, why haven't governments around the world adopted it? Perhaps the economic logic of the proposal requires a bit of time to sink in. Such was the case with economists' proposal to auction pollution licenses, which was greeted with great hostility at first and was not adopted until decades later (see Chapter 14). In fact, many governments have shown interest in the earned-income tax credit, which was first adopted in the United States. As noted, the EITC is essentially the same as the negative income tax, except that people who are not employed are ineligible for benefits. And many cities and states have begun experiments with public service employment.

BENEFIT LEVELS: A STATE OR FEDERAL QUESTION?

An issue of current debate concerns the proper level of government for setting the welfare payments received by poor families. One side in this debate maintains that the decision is best made at the state level, because when states are free to experiment, society is more likely to discover an effective solution to the poverty problem.

Others, however, counter that allowing states to set their own welfare levels creates a budgetary prisoner's dilemma. The problem is that a state that sets its support level higher than other states will attract welfare beneficiaries, placing a greater burden on taxpayers. Compounding the problem, high-income taxpayers will be less likely to move into that state, and its current high-income taxpayers will be more likely to move out. For states that offer below-average support levels, the reverse will happen. Low-income families will be more likely to leave or not move in, and high-income families more likely to remain or move in. Thus the fear is that allowing states to set their own welfare levels will cause a race to the bottom. The end result may be a level of public assistance far too low to solve any of the important problems of poverty.

Both sides in this debate have powerful arguments. But for the time being, Congress has delegated public assistance to state governments. In 1996, it passed the **Personal Responsibility Act,** which abolished the federal government's commitment to provide cash assistance to low-income families. The new law requires the federal government to make lump-sum cash grants to the states, who are then free to spend it on AFDC benefits or other income-support programs of their own design. For each welfare recipient, the new law also sets a 5-year lifetime limit on receipt of benefits under the AFDC program.

Supporters of the Personal Responsibility Act argue that it has already reduced the nation's welfare rolls substantially and that it will encourage greater self-reliance over the long run. Skeptics fear that denial of benefits may impose severe hardships on poor children if overall economic conditions deteriorate even temporarily. This debate is unlikely to be resolved before the economy experiences its next significant downturn.

Personal Responsibility Act the 1996 federal law that transferred responsibility for welfare programs from the federal level to the state level and placed a 5-year lifetime limit on payment of AFDC benefits to any given recipient

> **RECAP**   **METHODS OF INCOME REDISTRIBUTION**
>
> Minimum wage laws reduce total economic surplus by contracting employment. The earned-income tax credit boosts the incomes of the working poor without that drawback, but neither policy provides benefits for those who are not employed.
>
> Other instruments in the battle against poverty include in-kind transfers such as food stamps, subsidized school lunches, Medicaid, and public housing; and cash transfers such as Aid to Families with Dependent Children. Because benefits under most of these programs are means-tested, beneficiaries often experience a net decline in income when they accept paid employment.
>
> The negative income tax is an expanded version of the earned-income tax credit that includes those who are not employed. Combining this program with access to public service jobs would enable government to assure adequate living standards for the poor without significantly undermining work incentives.
>
> Assigning states the responsibility of managing their own welfare programs encourages experimentation and diversity but creates an incentive for a possibly destructive competition among states to avoid attracting welfare recipients.

PAYING FOR INCOME-SUPPORT PROGRAMS: EQUITY VERSUS EFFICIENCY?

Policymakers must choose not only which policies to employ in the effort to reduce poverty and income inequality but also how to pay for them. A common proposal is to make the federal income tax more progressive. Proponents contend that such a change would not only finance additional transfers to low-income families but would also reduce the gap between the after-tax incomes of wealthy and middle-class families. Opponents of this proposal worry about the unintended side effects of increasing top tax rates.

ADVERSE EFFECTS ON INCENTIVES

Most liberals, and even many conservatives, have always considered a more progressive tax structure to be desirable on the grounds of equity. Yet many fear that steeply progressive taxes might kill the proverbial goose that lays the golden egg. Thus, as John Rawls emphasized, sufficiently high tax rates on top earners could weaken their incentive to work hard and take risks. But most empirical evidence suggests that modest increases from current tax rates would not seriously undermine the incentive to work. If tax rates at the top rose slightly, the 40 vice presidents in a large corporation who aspire to become CEO probably would not start taking Fridays off to play golf.

Another concern is that raising top marginal tax rates might compromise economic efficiency by channeling talent and effort from productive work into tax avoidance and tax evasion. Several economists saw indirect evidence for this claim when the reduction in top U.S. tax rates that was enacted in 1986 was followed by a large increase in the amount of income reported by top earners.

Without doubt, the payoff from a dollar invested in tax avoidance is higher when tax rates are high than when they are low. But although the Tax Reform Act of 1986 cut top tax rates, it also broadened the tax base significantly by eliminating a large number of deductions and exemptions. If rational tax avoiders know about a legal deduction or exemption, they will almost surely claim it whether their tax rate is 40 percent (the current top federal tax rate on income) or 60 percent. They may spend a little more effort searching out exemptions when the tax rate is higher, but their tax consultants are unlikely to advise them differently in the two cases. Thus the post-1986 increase in reported income appears more plausibly explained by the act's elimination of many existing loopholes.

Another potential efficiency loss is that higher tax rates also provide greater incentives for corporations to compensate executives with expensive perks. For instance, when top British marginal tax rates were higher than 90 percent, some companies provided top executives with chauffeur-driven Rolls Royces. For each executive, this perk might cost the company $50,000 per year, an amount most executives would hardly see fit to spend out of their own pockets. But since the after-tax value of an extra $50,000 in pay would have been less than $5,000 for these executives, a company-provided Rolls might nonetheless have seemed an attractive option.

Policymakers should weigh each of these costs carefully as they deliberate among alternative tax structures. But as we will see in the next section, a modest increase in the tax rates on top earners might also help to eliminate existing sources of economic waste.

TAX POLICY AND OCCUPATIONAL CHOICE

One way in which higher tax rates at the top could actually stimulate the economy stems from their effect on occupational choice. When an individual's reward in an occupation depends only on his or her absolute performance, the invisible hand of the market works reasonably well. That is, self-interested career choices tend to be socially efficient. But as we saw in Chapter 13, the modern economy is increasingly permeated by markets in which small differences in *relative* performance translate into large differences in reward. Given the incentives inherent in such markets, the career choices of rational individuals may not produce the largest possible economic surplus.

Increasingly, young people pursue careers in law, finance, consulting, and other professions in the hope of landing a limited number of extremely high-paying positions at the top of these professions. In the process, they forsake other careers in which pay scales at the top are less spectacular but in which additional infusions of talent appear to yield large benefits. One study estimated, for example, that while a doubling of enrollments in engineering would cause national income to grow by an additional half a percentage point each year, a doubling of enrollments in law would reduce the annual growth rate by three-tenths of a point. Other studies show that higher-quality teachers and smaller class sizes significantly increase the number of students who graduate from high school and go on to college, which would also increase the economy's growth rate. Yet average class size rose and SAT scores of entering public school teachers declined significantly between 1970 and 1990, a period during which the number of new lawyers admitted to the bar each year more than doubled.

If some labor markets attract too many contestants for a limited number of high-paying positions while other markets suffer shortages of talent, one might hope that the imbalances would fade as wages are bid up in the latter markets and driven down in the former ones. Indeed recent data show a decline in the number of law school applicants.

For two reasons, however, such adjustments are likely to fall short, even in the long run. The first is an informational problem. An intelligent decision about whether to pit one's skills against a largely unknown field of contestants for a superstar position requires a well-informed estimate of the odds of winning. Yet people's assessments of these odds tend to be notoriously inaccurate. Surveys consistently show, for example, that more than 90 percent of subjects polled think

"You will like Mr. Woofard. He has an attention-deficit disorder."

they are better than average drivers, and that more than 90 percent of workers think they are more productive than their colleagues.

Psychologists call this tendency the "Lake Wobegon Effect," after Garrison Keillor's mythical Minnesota town in which "all the children are above average." Its importance to this discussion is that it leads people to overestimate their odds of landing a superstar position. Indeed, overconfidence is likely to be especially strong in the realm of career choice, because the biggest winners are so conspicuous. Seven-figure NBA stars appear on television several times each week, but the many thousands of players who fail to make the league never attract a moment's notice. When people overestimate their chances of winning, the number of people who forsake productive occupations in traditional markets to compete in winner-take-all markets is larger than can be justified on traditional cost-benefit grounds.

The second reason for persistent overcrowding in many labor markets is a structural incentive problem we encountered in Chapter 11, the tragedy of the commons. This problem, recall, accounts for overfishing of coastal waters, overgrazing of common pastureland, and overcutting of public forests. As the next example illustrates, the same problem also accounts for why too many people crowd into certain kinds of labor markets.

Why are there too many singers and not enough teachers?

A small village has five residents, each of whom can earn a living in one of two ways: by singing or by teaching in a nearby town. Teachers are paid $12,000/year, but only one person receives a recording contract. The singer who is awarded this contract is paid in accordance with the quality of his or her performance, but in all cases considerably more than $12,000. The only requirement for entering the competition for a recording contract is to devote 1 year to an unpaid singing tournament. At the end of the tournament, the singer whose recording is chosen as the winner receives a payment and the losing contestants receive nothing. Thereafter, all contestants return to work as teachers.

At the beginning of the tournament, no one knows how well his or her voice compares with the voices of the other contestants, so all contestants perceive the same likelihood of winning. On average, the quality of the winning contestant's voice will be higher the more people who enter the contest (just as the fastest runner in a big high school is faster, on average, than the fastest runner in a small high school). The winning singer thus expects to receive a higher payoff when more people enter the tournament (see column 2 of Table 16.3), because a larger field of contestants generally yields a better singer. Note, however, that the expected payoff *to each contestant* decreases as the number of contestants increases, as shown in column 3 of Table 16.3. For example, with three people competing for the recording contract, each has a one-third chance of receiving a payment of $42,000, which translates into an expected payoff of (1/3)($42,000) = $14,000. With four people competing, the expected payoff per contestant falls to $12,000. If villagers have the same tastes and are risk-neutral, how many will compete for the recording contract? What is the socially optimal number of contestants?

TABLE 16.3
The Relationship between the Number of Contestants in a Contest and the Expected Payoff

Number of contestants	Expected payment to the winner ($1,000s)	Expected payoff per contestant ($1,000s)
1	20	20
2	32	16
3	42	14
4	48	12
5	50	10

Competing for the recording contract is like buying a lottery ticket. The cost of the ticket is $12,000, the opportunity cost of not working as a teacher. The value of winning, as in many other lotteries, goes up with the number of people who enter. But whereas the prize in many lotteries rises in proportion to the number of tickets sold, the payment in this contest rises at a diminishing rate (just as the fastest runner's time improves at a diminishing rate as the size of the school increases).

By counting the number of people who are trying out for the recording contract, people can estimate their chances of winning and decide whether to enter the contest. Imagine yourself trying to choose between singing and teaching. The two occupations are equally attractive to you except for differences in the expected rate of compensation. (In other words, if both had the same expected salary, you would be indifferent between singing and teaching.) If no one else was competing for the recording contract, you would be sure to win $20,000 if you entered the contest, which is obviously better than the $12,000 you would earn as a teacher. If one other person were competing, you would get $32,000 if you won, but your chance of winning would be halved. With a 50 percent chance of winning $32,000 and a 50 percent chance of winning nothing, your expected payoff from competing in the contest would be (1/2)$32,000 = $16,000, or $4,000 more than you could earn as a teacher. Being one of two singing contestants is therefore better than a fair gamble. Armed with the cost-benefit principle, a risk-neutral person would gladly become the second contestant.

If two contestants had already announced their intention to compete for the recording contract, your entry would bring the total to three, and you would have a one-third chance of winning $42,000, or an expected payoff of $14,000. With four contestants, you would have a one-fourth chance of winning $48,000, or an expected payoff of $12,000. Finally, if all five villagers entered, you would have a one-fifth chance of winning $50,000, or an expected payoff of $10,000.

Since each villager is willing to accept a fair gamble, their decision rule will be to enter the contest as long as the expected payoff per contestant is at least equal to their $12,000 opportunity cost. In this example, a $12,000 expected payoff occurs when there are four contestants, so we would expect four people to compete for the recording contract.

With four people competing and only one working as a teacher, total village income will be $60,000/year ($48,000 for the winning singer and $12,000 for the lone teacher). That is the same as the total income the economy would have if the singer's position did not exist. Note the similarity between this result and the result in the cattle-grazing example in Chapter 11 (see Example 11.11). Indeed, the payoff structure in the singing contest is identical to the payoff structure in the tragedy of the commons. Just as the entire potential gain from the cattle industry was dissipated by excessive grazing, the entire prize in the singing contest is dissipated by the competition to obtain it.

Note too that the villagers would have generated more income if more people had become teachers and fewer had competed for the recording contract. For instance, if only two people had competed in the contest, the economy's total income would have been $68,000/year ($32,000 for the winning singer plus $36,000 for the three teachers). Two is the socially optimal number of contestants, for if a third were to enter, total income would fall to $66,000/year ($42,000 for the winning singer and $24,000 for the two teachers).

EXERCISE 16.4

In the preceding example, how many people would compete for the recording contract if the winning singer's prize increased by 20 percent?

In the singing tournament just discussed, market incentives result in a higher-quality singer than society would enjoy if labor were allocated in the socially optimal way. Thus, with four contestants (the market equilibrium number), the best singer's performance fetches $48,000 in the world recording market compared to only $32,000 with the socially optimal number, just two contestants. But the fact that total income is higher with two contestants than with four means that the market equilibrium quality of singing is too high from society's perspective. Noneconomists sometimes find such a statement jarring. ("Hey, Marge, get this: Some economist thinks the singers are too good!") But their reaction ignores the fact that the opportunity cost of higher quality in one sector of the economy is reduced output in other sectors. Society's interest would be served best by allocating additional resources to the recording sector only up to the point at which the incremental value of the resulting improvement in quality just equals the corresponding reduction in the value of other output. In the example considered, that point is reached when there are two contestants.

Once again, note the similarities between this example and the tragedy of the commons. In the cattle-grazing example, each villager decided whether to send a steer onto the commons by comparing the individual reward of doing so with the interest income forgone. Similarly, in the singing tournament example, each person decided whether to compete for the recording contract by comparing the expected reward with the teacher's salary forgone. In the commons example, the source of inefficiency was that each villager ignored the fact that sending another steer onto the commons would cause existing cattle to gain less weight. Similarly, the source of inefficiency in the singing contest is that each contestant ignores the fact that his or her entry will reduce everyone else's chances of winning. The difficulty in both the cattle and recording industries is that their payoff structures are more attractive to individuals than to society as a whole. The result is that both industries will attract too many resources.

But if misallocations arising from winner-take-all reward structures are in fact a serious problem, the solution is surely not to empower government to tell people which careers they can enter. When the rewards of competing in a market are larger for individuals than for society as a whole, the simplest solution, as Example 16.7 suggests, may be to alter the individual rewards.

How will higher taxes on top earners affect national income?

EXAMPLE 16.7

In the singing tournament described in the preceding example, how many contestants will enter the contest for a recording contract if the winning singer's income is taxed at a rate of 25 percent?

This tax is a progressive income tax, because it taxes only the winning singer's income, not the incomes of teachers. The third column in Table 16.4 shows the after-tax payment to the winning singer, and the fourth column, the expected after-tax payoff per contestant. For example, with three contestants in the contest, the winning singer will get $42,000, which means an after-tax payment of only $31,500. And since each contestant has a one-third chance to be the winner, the expected after-tax payoff is $(1/3)(\$31,500) = \$10,500$ per contestant.

TABLE 16.4
A Progressive Income Tax as a Remedy for Occupational Overcrowding

Number of contestants	Expected before-tax payment to winner ($1,000s)	Expected after-tax payment to winner ($1,000s)	Expected after-tax payoff per contestant ($1,000s)
1	20	15	15
2	32	24	12
3	42	31.50	10.50
4	48	36	9
5	50	47.50	7.50

As before, an individual will enter the contest for the recording contract as long as the expected payoff is at least as large as a teacher's income, which is not taxed. That means that an individual will enter the singing contest if the after-tax expected payoff is at least $12,000. Thus the entries in the last column of Table 16.4 suggest that only two people will enter the contest—and that, recall, is the socially optimal number. Note that total income for the economy, which was $60,000 when the winning singer's income was not taxed, rises to $68,000— $36,000 for the three teachers plus $32,000 for the winning singer. (The $8,000 in income tax received by the government is included in national income because it can be used to purchase goods and services or to reduce other taxes.)

Misleading incentives like the ones in these examples confront potential contestants in a host of other high-end markets. For instance, beyond some point, an increase in the number of aspiring mergers-and-acquisitions lawyers produces much less than a proportional increase in the commissions to be had from such transactions. One law student's good fortune in landing a position in a leading Wall Street firm is largely offset by her rival's failure to land the same position. The result is an incentive gap similar to the one that encouraged too many people to compete for the recording contract: in each case, aspiring superstars tend to ignore the fact that their presence reduces other contestants' chances.

Whether misallocations of the sort just described are a serious practical problem in modern economies remains an open question. Certainly the high salaries in top law and investment banking firms appear to have lured a steadily growing number of the best and brightest into competition for those positions. And as noted, the academic qualifications of people who choose teaching as a career have been declining steadily.

To the extent that economic incentives matter at all (and economic theory tells us they do), higher taxes on top earners would discourage some people from competing for the limited number of top positions in many high-end labor markets. Moreover, those with the smallest odds of making it into the winner's circle would be the ones most likely to drop out. Thus the value of what is produced in those markets would not be reduced much by higher taxes, and any reductions would tend to be more than offset by increased output in traditional markets. Accordingly, a more progressive tax structure might help to bring about not only greater equality but also higher economic growth.

A PROGRESSIVE CONSUMPTION TAX?

Critics have also objected to progressive income taxation on the grounds that high tax rates on top earners might slow economic growth by weakening the incentive to save and invest. This is a serious concern. One way to ameliorate it is by switching from our current progressive income tax to a progressive consumption tax.

Such a tax would be straightforward to administer: Each family would pay tax not on its income but on its total spending—as measured by the simple difference between its annual income and its annual savings. And because the rich usually save and invest so much more than the poor, fairness would require that tax rates on the highest spenders be significantly higher than the current top tax rates on incomes.

For example, the current 40 percent top tax rate on income might translate into a 60 percent top rate on consumption expenditure. As shown in Table 16.5, a large standard deduction and a progressive rate structure could be employed to make sure that the tax burden of the poor and middle class remained as low as, or lower than, under the current system.

TABLE 16.5
An Illustrative Progressive Consumption Tax

Taxable consumption = Income (as currently reported to the IRS) − Annual savings − $30,000 (standard deduction for family of four)	Tax rate on each additional dollar of taxable consumption
0 – $ 39,999	20 percent
$40,000 – $ 59,999	24 percent
$60,000 – $ 79,999	28 percent
$80,000 – $ 99,999	32 percent
$100,000 – $149,999	36 percent
$150,000 – $199,999	40 percent
$200,000 – $399,999	46 percent
$400,000 – $999,999	52 percent
$1 million or more	60 percent

Under the tax shown in the table, a family of four with an annual income of $50,000 and annual savings of $5,000 would have taxable consumption of $50,000 − $5,000 − $30,000 = $15,000, and its annual tax bill would be (0.20)($15,000) = $3,000. A family of four with an annual income of $1 million and annual savings of $270,000 would have taxable consumption of $700,000, of which the first $40,000 would be taxed at 20 percent, the next $20,000 at 24 percent, and so on, for a tax bill of $306,800.

In 1943 Milton Friedman proposed a tax essentially like the one shown in Table 16.5. The federal government at that time desperately needed to raise additional revenue to finance the war effort, and Friedman argued that a progressive consumption tax was the most efficient way to do so.

To see why Friedman found this tax so attractive, note that a disproportionate share of its revenue would come from people who spend at the highest levels on consumption. Would the tax cause these people to curtail their spending? It might seem that the wealthiest individuals would simply ignore the tax, since people with billions of dollars in personal wealth could not spend it all during their lifetimes in any event. But as we saw in Chapter 5, the high prices of real estate in Manhattan induce even the city's billionaires to live in smaller houses. Would a tax that leads people to postpone building a bigger mansion cause hardship? Apparently not, and *in that fact lies a striking advantage of the progressive consumption tax.* Evidence suggests that when everyone's mansion grows a little larger, the primary effect is simply to set a new standard for how big a mansion wealthy people feel they need. Thus the current trend toward larger mansions entails an element of waste. As an individual, failure to keep pace with this trend might trigger embarrassment on social occasions, or raise troubling questions about the health of one's business. But if *everyone* postponed building a bigger mansion, such concerns would not arise.

Slowing the rate at which mansions grow larger would also generate indirect benefits for middle- and low-income families. If the biggest houses grew more slowly, so would the next biggest, and so on, all the way down. A progressive consumption tax would thus slow the rate of growth in average house size, a clear benefit to the middle-income family that already has difficulty meeting its mortgage payments.

Another beneficial effect of exempting savings from tax would be to counteract the reduction in saving that has occurred as an unintended side effect of government programs. For example, because the Social Security System replaces a significant fraction of people's earnings during retirement, they are rational to save considerably less than they would in the absence of this program. Yet Social Security is not a true savings program at all. Rather, workers pay taxes on their earnings, and the receipts are used to write checks to retirees. In the absence of Social Security, rational individuals would save much more.

Other programs such as Medicare, Medicaid, and unemployment insurance have a similar effect. Many people would save more if not for the protections these programs provide against unforeseen financial emergencies. Exempting savings from taxation can thus be justified as a way to promote saving levels closer to the ones rational consumers would have chosen under free-market conditions.

Finally, switching from a progressive income tax to a progressive consumption tax would also reduce the incentive for tax avoidance and tax evasion. Under a progressive consumption tax, a family that wants to avoid paying tax on some of its income need not participate in costly or legally questionable tax shelters. It can simply deposit that money in a savings account or mutual fund.

In sum, many of the concerns associated with the progressive income tax are reduced or eliminated by switching to a progressive consumption tax.

THE LEGISLATOR'S DILEMMA

Throughout this book, we have emphasized how the cost-benefit principle can identify ways of increasing total economic surplus. Whenever a public policy, a personal purchase, a pollution control measure, or any other action fails the cost-benefit test, an alternative can always be found that makes some people better off without harming others.

Yet government consistently implements policies that fail the cost-benefit test, especially in the realm of income redistribution. If rent controls, sugar price supports, price controls on gasoline and home heating oil, minimum wage laws, and a host of other policies reduce total economic surplus, why don't legislators replace them with more efficient measures?

A possible answer is that price and wage controls can be implemented without having to raise taxes. Thus, while policies like a negative income tax or public service employment would require funding out of general tax revenue, minimum wages and rent controls do not. Because voters fear additional tax dollars will be used to support pork barrel projects and other forms of government waste (see Chapter 15), legislators who vote for higher taxes jeopardize their political survival. Yet the mere fact that most of the costs of price and wage controls do not appear in government budgets does not make those costs any less real. Indeed, our recurring theme has been that the cost of attacking poverty with such measures is far higher than the cost of transferring income to the poor directly. The legislator's dilemma is that such inefficiencies cannot be eliminated unless the public is willing to support the necessary taxes.

REDISTRIBUTION AND COST-BENEFIT ANALYSIS

A related paradox is the question of why advocates for the poor have often been among the most vociferous opponents of cost-benefit analysis. Their objection is that because willingness to pay is based on income, cost-benefit analysis is biased in favor of high-income persons. Critics presumably have the interests of the poor in mind when they press this objection. *Yet a rational poor person would not want policy decisions to be made on any basis other than willingness to pay.*

This point is of central importance. We review the logic that supports it with the following simple example. Consider a community consisting of three voters: one rich, the other two poor. Up for decision is a proposal to switch the local public radio station from an all-music format to an all-talk format. The rich voter would be willing to pay $1,000 to see this change enacted, while the poor voters would be willing to pay $100 each to prevent it. If each voter's interests are weighted equally, the switch will not be adopted. Yet, in cost-benefit terms, failure to switch results in a net loss of $800.

Under the circumstances, little ingenuity is required to design a proposal that would command unanimous support. The programming switch could be made conditional, for example, on the rich voter paying an additional $500 in taxes, which could then be used to reduce the taxes on each poor voter by $250. This arrangement would make the rich voter $500 better off and each poor voter $150 better off than if the switch had been prevented.

Critics may respond that although such transfers would be fine in principle, the poor lack the political muscle to assure they are carried out. In an imperfect world, they argue, we get better results by resolving such issues on a one-person–one-vote basis. But this response does not withstand scrutiny. If the poor lack the political power to bargain for compensation in return for supporting a policy that harms them, what gives them the power to block that policy in the first place? Alternatively, if they have that power—and it appears they do—they necessarily have the power to bargain for compensation. After all, any policy that passes the cost-benefit test but creates net losses for the poor can be transformed into a Pareto improvement simply by making the tax system more progressive.

Critics of cost-benefit analysis are correct that measuring benefits by willingness to pay virtually assures a mix of public programs that are slanted in favor of high-income persons. But rather than abandon cost-benefit analysis, we have a better alternative. We can employ willingness-to-pay measures without apology and then use the welfare and tax system to compensate low-income families for any resulting injury. The compensation need not—indeed cannot—occur after the fact on a case-by-case basis. Rather, low-income persons could simply be granted the welfare and tax breaks required by distributive justice, *plus* additional concessions to offset their expected loss from the implementation of cost-benefit analysis using willingness to pay to measure benefits.

Rich and poor alike have an interest in making the economic pie as large as possible. Any policy that passes the cost-benefit test makes the economic pie larger. And as the efficiency principle reminds us, when the pie is larger, everyone can have a larger slice.

RECAP   **PAYING FOR INCOME-SUPPORT PROGRAMS: EQUITY VERSUS EFFICIENCY?**

Poverty is more effectively attacked by transferring additional income to the poor than by trying to regulate prices and wages. Yet many fear that the higher taxes on top earners needed to pay for such transfers will reduce effort and investment and stimulate wasteful tax avoidance. Tax avoidance can be curtailed by making the tax code simpler, and moderate increases in current top tax rates probably would not cause significant reductions in effort. The more serious concern is that higher taxes on top earners might reduce savings and investment, a danger that could be avoided by taxing consumption instead of income.

Higher tax rates on top earners have positive effects on efficiency as well as negative ones. Individuals with the highest earnings are often the winning contestants in labor markets with limited numbers of positions at the top. Such markets tend to attract too many contestants for the same reason that villagers tend to send too many cattle onto commonly owned pastureland. Higher taxes on top earners would steer marginal contestants from such markets to others in which their services would yield greater value.

Because cost-benefit analysis uses willingness to pay to measure benefits, many of its recommendations will be slanted in favor of high-income families. A democratically elected government will be unable to employ cost-benefit analysis unless it compensates low-income persons for the losses associated with that bias. Income transfers to the poor are thus a precondition for efficient economic policies.

■ SUMMARY ■

- Although incomes grew at almost 3 percent a year for all income classes during the three decades following World War II, the lion's share of income growth in the years since has been concentrated among top earners. Low-income families now have less purchasing power than in the mid-1970s.

- Apart from moral concerns about income inequality, practical reasons argue for limiting the gap between rich and poor. Poverty promotes illness and crime, both of which increase the burden on the nonpoor. Large income gaps also harm the middle class by raising the cost of pursuing basic goals.

- Policies and programs for reducing poverty include minimum wage laws, the earned-income tax credit, food stamps, subsidized school lunches, Medicaid, public housing, and Aid to Families with Dependent Children. Of

these, all but the earned-income tax credit fail to maximize total economic surplus, either by interfering with work incentives or by preventing markets from reaching equilibrium.

- The negative income tax works much like the earned-income tax credit, except that it includes those who are not employed. A combination of a small negative income tax and access to public service jobs at subminimum wages would assure adequate living standards for the poor without significantly undermining work incentives.

- Many fear that the higher taxes needed to finance such programs could curtail economic growth. This concern can be addressed by switching from the current progressive income tax to a progressive consumption tax.

▪ KEY TERMS ▪

---

breakeven income level (414)
earned-income tax credit (EITC) (411)
in-kind transfer (413)

means-tested (413)
negative income tax (NIT) (414)
Personal Responsibility Act (417)

poverty threshold (415)
utilitarianism (405)

▪ REVIEW QUESTIONS ▪

---

1. What costs does greater concentration of income among top earners impose on middle-class families?

2. Why does John Rawls believe that policies to redistribute income would command unanimous support behind a veil of ignorance?

3. Mention two self-interested reasons that a top earner might favor policies to redistribute income.

4. Why is exclusive reliance on the negative income tax unlikely to constitute a long-term solution to the poverty problem?

5. Describe the externality that makes the decision to become a contestant in a winner-take-all labor market similar to the decision to send an additional steer onto commonly owned grazing land.

▪ PROBLEMS ▪

---

1. Harold is one of 1,000 employees in a new start-up company. In lieu of being paid a salary, he and his coworkers were each given an equal number of shares in the company's stock. Together they own half of all stock in the company. If Harold works hard at home on company projects each evening and on weekends for the next year, the present value of the company's current and future accounting profit will grow by $1 million. How much of that gain will Harold receive? (*Hint:* As we saw in Chapter 8, a change in the present value of accounting profit will produce an equal change in the total value of the company's stock.)

2. Refer to Problem 1. If Harold's reservation price for working evenings and weekends for the next year is $10,000, what fraction of the company's stock would he have to own to induce him to put in the extra effort? On the basis of your answer, do you think the widely touted incentive effects of employee stock ownership plans may have been exaggerated?

3. Suppose the demand for unskilled labor in the Corvallis labor market is given by $W = 20 - 0.001L$, where W is the wage rate in dollars per hour and L is the quantity of labor demanded in person-hours per day. If the supply curve of unskilled labor in Corvallis is given by $W = 0.001L$, by how much will the imposition of a minimum wage at $12/hour reduce total economic surplus? Calculate the amounts by which employer surplus and worker surplus change as a result of the minimum wage.

4. Refer to Problem 3. How much would it cost the government each day to provide an earned-income tax credit under which workers as a group receive the same economic surplus as they do under the $12/hour minimum wage? (Assume for simplicity that the earned-income tax credit has no effect on labor supply.)

5. Suppose employers and workers are risk-neutral and Congress is about to enact the $12/hour minimum wage described in Problem 3. Congressional staff economists have urged legislators to consider adopting an earned-income tax credit instead. Suppose neither workers nor employers would support that proposal unless the expected value of each party's economic surplus would be at least as great as under the minimum wage. Describe an earned-income tax credit (and a tax that would raise enough money to pay for it) that would receive unanimous support from both workers and employers.

6. Suppose the equilibrium wage for unskilled workers in New Jersey is $7/hour. How will the wages and employment of unskilled workers in New Jersey change if the state legislature raises the minimum wage from $5.15/hour to $6/hour?

7. Jones, who is currently unemployed, is a participant in three means-tested welfare programs: food stamps, rent stamps, and day care stamps. Each program grants him $150/month in stamps, which can be used like cash to purchase the good or service they cover.
   a. If benefits in each program are reduced by 40 cents for each additional dollar Jones earns in the labor market, how will Jones's economic position change if he accepts a job paying $120/week?
   b. In light of your answer to part a, explain why means testing for welfare recipients has undesirable effects on work incentives.

8. What is the breakeven level of before-tax earned income in a negative income tax program with a tax credit of $5,000/year and a tax rate of 40 percent? How large a net benefit would be received by a person earning $6,000/year? How large a net tax would be paid by someone earning $15,000/year?

9. Enfield is a small economy consisting of five identical people who can earn a living in either of two ways: by acting or by growing corn. A corn farmer can earn $10,000, and the best actor in Enfield will be chosen for a film contract that pays in accordance with the performer's acting ability. The only audition requirement is to be filmed working as an unpaid actor in a theater on Broadway, which means being unable to work as a farmer. From among the filmed performances, a winner is chosen and paid. All contestants perceive the same likelihood of being chosen, and the payment to the winner increases with the number of contestants in the manner shown in the following table.

Number of contestants	Expected payment to the winner ($1,000s)	Expected payoff per contestant ($1,000s)
1	21	21
2	34	17
3	45	15
4	50	12.5
5	55	11

   a. If all villagers have the same tastes and are risk-neutral, how many will compete to become an actor? What will be the total income of the residents of Enfield?
   b. What is the socially optimal number of villagers to enter the competition? How much would village income be if only the optimal number entered?

10. Refer to Problem 9. What is the smallest lump-sum tax on the winner's earnings that would ensure that the optimal number of villagers entered the competition?

■ ANSWERS TO IN-CHAPTER EXERCISES ■

16.1 Since Sue's reservation wage is $10/hour, she must be paid at least that amount before she will accept the job. The largest dorm population for which she will accept is thus 10 residents, since her share in that case would be exactly $10/hour.

16.2 With perfectly inelastic demand, employment would remain at 5,000 person-hours/day, so the minimum wage would cause no reduction in economic surplus.

16.3 The breakeven level falls from $12,000/year to $8,000.

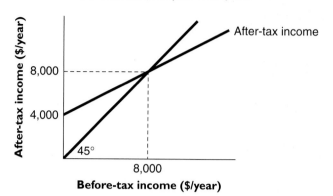

16.4 With a 20 percent increase in the winning singer's pay, the payoffs and expected payoffs are now as shown in the following table. Contestants will continue to enter as long as the expected payoff is at least $12,000, so five contestants will now compete for the recording contract.

Number of contestants	Expected payment to the winner ($1,000s)	Expected payoff per contestant ($1,000s)
1	24	24
2	38.4	19.2
3	50.4	16.8
4	57.6	14.4
5	60	12

PART

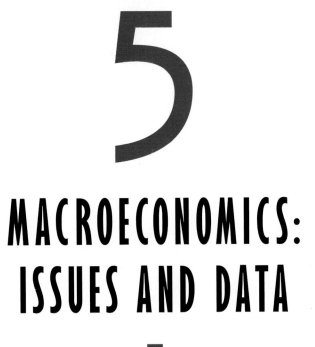

5

MACROECONOMICS: ISSUES AND DATA

■

Physical scientists study the world at many different scales, ranging from the inner workings of the atom to the vast dimensions of the cosmos. Although the laws of physics are thought to apply at all scales, scientists find that some phenomena are best understood "in the small" and some "in the large." Although the range of scales they must deal with is much more modest than in physics, economists also find it useful to analyze economic behavior at both the small-scale, or "micro-" level, and the large-scale, or "macro-" level. This section introduces you to *macroeconomics*, the study of the performance of national economies. Unlike *microeconomics*, which focuses on the behavior of individual households, firms, and markets, macroeconomics takes a bird's-eye view of the economy. So, while a microeconomist might study the determinants of consumer spending on personal computers, macroeconomists analyze the factors that determine aggregate, or total, consumer spending. Experience has shown that, for many issues, the macroeconomic perspective is the more useful.

Chapter 17 begins our discussion of macroeconomics by introducing you to some of the key macroeconomic issues and questions. These include the search for the factors that cause economies to grow, productivity to improve, and living standards to rise over long periods of time. Macroeconomists also study shorter-term fluctuations in the economy (called recessions and expansions), unemployment, inflation, and the economic interdependence among nations, among other topics. Macroeconomic policies—government actions to improve the performance of the economy—are of particular concern to macroeconomists, as the quality of macroeconomic policymaking is a major determinant of a nation's economic health.

To study phenomena like economic growth scientifically, economists must have accurate measurements. Chapters 18 and 19 continue the introduction to macroeconomics by discussing how some key macroeconomic concepts are measured and interpreted. Chapter 18 discusses two important measures of the level of economic activity, the gross domestic product and the unemployment rate. Besides describing how these variables are constructed in practice, this chapter also discusses the issue of how these measures are related to the economic well-being of the typical person. Chapter 19 concerns the measurement of the price level and inflation and includes a discussion of the costs that inflation imposes on the economy. When you have completed Part 5, you will be familiar not only with the major questions that macroeconomists ask but also with some of the most important tools that they use to try to find the answers.

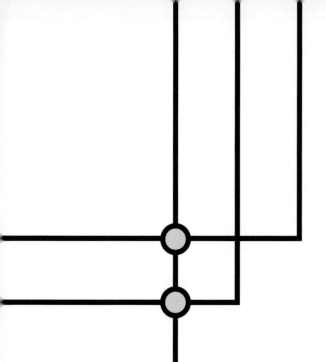

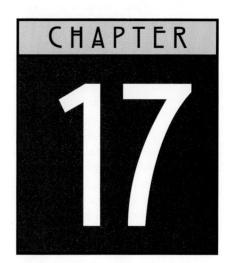

MACROECONOMICS: THE BIRD'S-EYE VIEW OF THE ECONOMY

■

In 1929 the economy of the United States slowed dramatically. Between August of 1929 and the end of 1930, the nation's factories and mines, facing sharp declines in sales, cut their production rates by a remarkable 31 percent. These cutbacks led in turn to mass layoffs: Between 1929 and 1930, the number of people without jobs almost tripled, from about 3 percent of the workforce to nearly 9 percent.[1] Financial markets were equally shaky. The stock market crashed in October 1929, and stocks lost nearly a third of their value in just 3 weeks.

At first, policymakers and the general public (except for those people who had put their life savings into the stock market) were concerned but not panic-stricken. Americans remembered that the nation had experienced a similar slowdown only 8 years earlier, in 1921–1922. That episode had ended quickly, apparently on its own, and the decade that followed (popularly known as the roaring twenties) had been one of unparalleled prosperity. But the fall in production and the rise in unemployment that began in 1929 continued into 1931. In the spring of 1931 the economy seemed to stabilize briefly, and President Herbert Hoover optimistically proclaimed that

[1]The source for these and most other pre-1960 statistics cited in this chapter is the U.S. Bureau of the Census, *Historical Statistics of the United States: Colonial Times to 1970,* Washington, 1975.

"prosperity is just around the corner." But in mid-1931 the economy went into an even steeper dive. What historians now call the Great Depression had begun in earnest.

Labor statistics tell the story of the Great Depression from the worker's point of view. Unemployment was extremely high throughout the 1930s, despite government attempts to reduce it through large-scale public employment programs. At the worst point of the Depression, in 1933, one out of every four American workers was unemployed. Joblessness declined gradually to 17 percent of the workforce by 1936 but remained stuck at that level through 1939. Of those lucky enough to have jobs, many were able to work only part-time, while others worked for near-starvation wages.

In some other countries conditions were even worse. In Germany, which had never fully recovered from its defeat in World War I, nearly a third of all workers were without jobs, and many families lost their savings as major banks collapsed. Indeed, the desperate economic situation was a major reason for Adolf Hitler's election as Chancellor of Germany in 1933. Introducing extensive government control over the economy, Hitler rearmed the country and ultimately launched what became the most destructive war in history, World War II.

How could such an economic catastrophe have happened? One often-heard hypothesis is that the Great Depression was caused by wild speculation on Wall Street, which provoked the stock market crash. But though stock prices may have been unrealistically high in 1929, there is little evidence to suggest that the fall in stock prices was a major cause of the Depression. A similar crash in October 1987, when stock prices fell a record 23 percent in 1 day—an event comparable in severity to the crash of October 1929—did not slow the economy significantly. Another reason to doubt that the 1929 stock market crash caused the Great Depression is that, far from being confined to the United States, the Depression was a worldwide event, affecting countries that did not have well-developed stock markets at the time. The more reasonable conclusion is that the onset of the Depression probably caused the stock market crash, rather than the other way round.

Another explanation for the Depression, suggested by some economists in the 1930s, was that free-market economies like those of the United States and Germany are "naturally" unstable, prone to long periods of low production and high unemployment. But this idea too has fallen out of favor, since the period after World War II has generally been one of prosperity and economic growth throughout the industrialized world.

What *did* cause the Great Depression, then? Today most economists who have studied the period blame *poor economic policymaking* both in the United States and in other major industrialized countries. Of course, policymakers did not set out to create an economic catastrophe. Rather, they fell prey to misconceptions of the time about how the economy worked. In other words, the Great Depression, far from being inevitable, *could have been avoided*—if only the state of economic knowledge had been better. From today's perspective, the Great Depression was to economic policymaking what the voyage of the *Titanic* was to ocean navigation.

One of the few benefits of the Great Depression was that it forced economists and policymakers of the 1930s to recognize that there were major gaps in their understanding of how the economy works. This recognition led to the development of a new subfield within economics, called macroeconomics. Recall from Chapter 1 that *macroeconomics* is the study of the performance of national economies and the policies governments use to try to improve that performance.

This chapter will introduce the subject matter and some of the tools of macroeconomics. Although understanding episodes like the Great Depression remains an important concern of macroeconomists, the field has expanded to include the analysis of many other aspects of national economies. Among the issues macroeconomists study are the sources of long-run economic growth and development,

Could better economic policies have prevented the Great Depression?

the causes of high unemployment, and the factors that determine the rate of inflation. Appropriately enough in a world in which economic "globalization" preoccupies businesspeople and policymakers, macroeconomists also study how national economies interact. Since the performance of the national economy has an important bearing on the availability of jobs, the wages workers earn, the prices they pay, and the rates of return they receive on their saving, it's clear that macroeconomics addresses bread-and-butter issues that affect virtually everyone.

In light of the nation's experience during the Great Depression, macroeconomists are particularly concerned with understanding how *macroeconomic policies* work and how they should be applied. **Macroeconomic policies** are government actions designed to affect the performance of the economy as a whole (as opposed to policies intended to affect the performance of the market for a particular good or service, such as sugar or haircuts). The hope is that by understanding more fully how government policies affect the economy, economists can help policymakers do a better job—and avoid serious mistakes, such as those that were made during the Great Depression. On an individual level, educating people about macroeconomic policies and their effects will make for a better-informed citizenry, capable of making well-reasoned decisions in the voting booth.

macroeconomic policies
government actions designed to affect the performance of the economy as a whole

THE MAJOR MACROECONOMIC ISSUES

We have defined macroeconomics as the study of the performance of the national economy as well as the policies used to improve that performance. Let's now take a closer look at some of the major economic issues that macroeconomists study.

ECONOMIC GROWTH AND LIVING STANDARDS

Although the wealthy industrialized countries (such as the United States, Canada, Japan, and the countries of Western Europe) are certainly not free from poverty, hunger, and homelessness, the typical person in those countries enjoys a standard of living better than at any previous time or place in history. By *standard of living* we mean the degree to which people have access to goods and services that make their lives easier, healthier, safer, and more enjoyable. People with a high living standard enjoy more and better consumer goods: sports utility vehicles, camcorders, cellular phones, and the like. But they also benefit from a longer life expectancy and better general health (the result of high-quality medical care, good nutrition, and good sanitation), from higher literacy rates (the result of greater access to education), from more time and opportunity for cultural enrichment and recreation, from more interesting and fulfilling career options, and from better working conditions. Of course, the *scarcity principle* will always apply—even for the citizen of a rich country, having more of one good thing means having less of another. But higher incomes make these choices much less painful than they would be otherwise. Choosing between a larger apartment and a nicer car is much easier than choosing between feeding your children adequately and sending them to school, the kind of hard choice people in the poorest nations face.

Americans sometimes take their standard of living for granted, or even as a "right." As a Paul Simon lyric proclaims, "God bless our standard of living—let's keep it that way!" But we should realize that the way we live today is radically different from the way people have lived throughout most of history. The current standard of living in the United States is the result of several centuries of sustained *economic growth,* a process of steady increase in the quantity and quality of the goods and services the economy can produce. The basic equation is simple: The more we can produce, the more we can consume. Though not everyone in a society shares equally in the fruits of economic growth, in most cases growth brings an improvement in the average person's standard of living.

To get a sense of the extent of economic growth over time, examine Figure 17.1, which shows how the output of the U.S. economy has increased since 1900. (We discuss the measure of output used here, real gross domestic product, in Chapter 18.) Although output fluctuates at times, the overall trend has been unmistakably upward. Indeed, in 1999 the output of the U.S. economy was nearly 25 times what it was in 1900 and more than 5 times its level in 1950. What caused this remarkable economic growth? Can it continue? Should it? These are some of the questions macroeconomists try to answer.

FIGURE 17.1
Output of the U.S. Economy, 1900–1999.
The output of the U.S. economy has increased by nearly 25 times since 1900 and by more than 5 times since 1950.

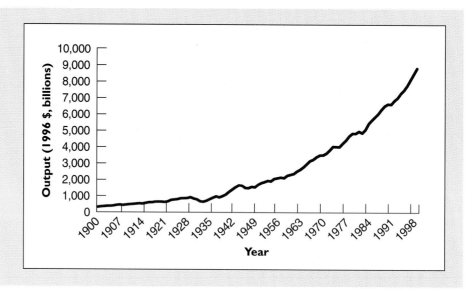

One reason for the growth in U.S. output over the past century has been the rapid growth of the U.S. population, and hence the number of workers available. Because of population growth, increases in *total* output cannot be equated with improvements in the general standard of living. Although increased output means that more goods and services are available, increased population implies that more people are sharing those goods and services. Because the population changes over time, output *per person* is a better indicator of the average living standard than total output.

Figure 17.2 shows output per person in the United States since 1900 (the blue line). Note that the long-term increase in output per person is smaller than the increase in total output shown in Figure 17.1 because of population growth. Nevertheless, the gains made over this long period are still impressive: In 1999 a typical U.S. resident consumed nearly seven times the quantity of goods and services available to a typical resident at the beginning of the century. To put this increase into perspective, according to recent estimates more than 50 million U.S. households now own two or more automobiles; only about 10 million U.S. households (many of them located in cities, with good access to public transportation) have no car. A remarkable 98 percent of U.S. households own a television—95 percent a color television—and two-thirds subscribe to cable. And as of 1999 more than one-third of adults in the United States were regular users of the Internet, a number that has certainly climbed since then.

Nor has the rise in output been reflected entirely in increased availability of consumer goods. For example, as late as 1960, only 41 percent of U.S. adults over age 25 had completed high school, and less than 8 percent had completed 4 years of college. Today, over 80 percent of the adult population have at least a high school diploma, and about 25 percent have a college degree. Over half the students currently leaving high school will go on to college. Higher incomes, which allow young people to continue their schooling rather than work to support themselves and their families, are a major reason for these increases in educational levels.

More than 50 million American households own two or more automobiles.

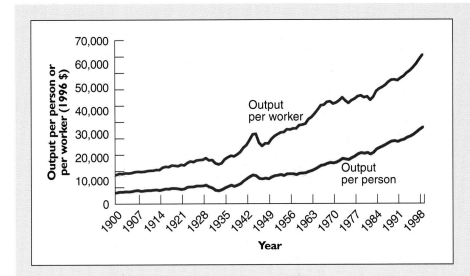

FIGURE 17.2
Output per Person and per Worker in the U.S. Economy, 1900–1999.
The red line shows the output per worker in the U.S. economy since 1900, and the blue line shows output per person. Both have risen substantially. Relative to 1900, output per person today is nearly seven times greater, and output per worker is more than five times greater.

PRODUCTIVITY

While growth in output per person is closely linked to changes in what the typical person can *consume,* macroeconomists are also interested in changes in what the average worker can *produce.* Figure 17.2 shows how output per employed worker (that is, total output divided by the number of people working) has changed since 1900 (red line). The figure shows that in 1999 a U.S. worker could produce more than five times the quantity of goods and services produced by a worker at the beginning of the century, despite the fact that the workweek is now much shorter than it was 100 years ago.

Economists refer to output per employed worker as **average labor productivity.** As Figure 17.2 shows, average labor productivity and output per person are closely related. This relationship makes sense—as we noted earlier, the more we can produce, the more we can consume. Because of this close link to the average living standard, average labor productivity and the factors that cause it to increase over time are of major concern to macroeconomists.

average labor productivity
output per employed worker

Although the long-term improvement in output per worker is impressive, the *rate* of improvement has slowed somewhat since the 1970s. Between 1950 and 1973 in the United States, output per employed worker increased by 2.1 percent per year. But from 1973 to 1999 the average rate of increase in output per worker was less than 1 percent per year, although in the past few years the pace of productivity growth seems to have picked up again. Slowing productivity growth leads to less rapid improvement in living standards, since the supply of goods and services cannot grow as quickly as it does during periods of rapid growth in productivity. Identifying the causes of productivity slowdowns and speedups is thus an important challenge for macroeconomists.

The current standard of living in the United States is not only much higher than in the past but also much higher than in many other nations today. Why have many of the world's countries, including both the developing nations of Asia, Africa, and Latin America and some formerly communist countries of Eastern Europe not enjoyed the same rates of economic growth as the industrialized countries? How can the rate of economic growth be improved in these countries? Once again, these are questions of keen interest to macroeconomists.

Productivity and living standards in China and the United States

EXAMPLE 17.1

In 1997 the value of the output of the U.S. economy was about $8,300 billion. In the same year, the estimated value of the output of the People's Republic of China was $902 billion (U.S). The populations of the United States and China in

1997 were about 268 million and 1,236 million, respectively, while the number of employed workers in the two countries were approximately 130 million and 696 million.

Find output per person and average labor productivity for the United States and China in 1997. What do the results suggest about comparative living standards in the two countries?

Output per person is simply total output divided by the number of people in an economy, and average labor productivity is output divided by the number of employed workers. Doing the math we get the following results for 1997:

	United States	**China**
Output per person	$30,970	$ 730
Average labor productivity	$63,846	$1,296

Note that, although the total output of the Chinese economy is more than 10 percent of that of the U.S. output, output per person and average labor productivity in China are each only about 2.5 and 2 percent, respectively, of what they are in the United States. Thus, though the Chinese economy may someday rival the U.S. economy in total output, for the time being there remains a large gap in productivity. This gap translates into striking differences in the living standard between the two countries—in access to consumer goods, health care, transportation, education, and other benefits of affluence.

RECESSIONS AND EXPANSIONS

Economies do not always grow steadily; sometimes they go through periods of unusual strength or weakness. A look back at Figure 17.1 shows that although output generally grows over time, it does not always grow smoothly. Particularly striking is the decline in output during the Great Depression of the 1930s, followed by the sharp increase in output during World War II (1941–1945). But the figure shows many more moderate fluctuations in output as well.

Slowdowns in economic growth are called *recessions;* particularly severe economic slowdowns, like the one that began in 1929, are called *depressions*. In the United States, major recessions occurred in 1973–1975 and 1981–1982 (find those recessions in Figure 17.1). A more modest downturn occurred in 1990–1991. During recessions economic opportunities decline: Jobs are harder to find, people with jobs are less likely to get wage increases, profits are lower, and more companies go out of business. Recessions are particularly hard on economically disadvantaged people, who are most likely to be thrown out of work and have the hardest time finding new jobs.

Sometimes the economy grows unusually quickly. These periods of rapid economic growth are called *expansions,* and particularly strong expansions are called *booms*. During an expansion, jobs are easier to find, more people get raises and promotions, and most businesses thrive.

The alternating cycle of recessions and expansions raises some questions that are central to macroeconomics. What causes these short-term fluctuations in the rate of economic growth? Can government policymakers do anything about them? Should they try?

UNEMPLOYMENT

The *unemployment rate,* the fraction of people who would like to be employed but can't find work, is a key indicator of the state of the labor market. When the unemployment rate is high, work is hard to find, and people who do have jobs typically find it harder to get promotions or wage increases.

Figure 17.3 shows the unemployment rate in the United States since 1900. Unemployment rises during recessions—note the dramatic spike in unemployment during the Great Depression, as well as the increases in unemployment during the 1973–1975 and 1981–1982 recessions. But even in the so-called good times, such as the 1960s and the 1990s, some people are unemployed. Why does unemployment rise so sharply during periods of recession? And why are there always unemployed people, even when the economy is booming?

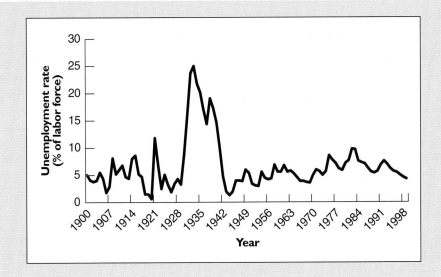

FIGURE 17.3
The U.S. Unemployment Rate, 1900–1999.
The unemployment rate is the percentage of the labor force that is out of work. Unemployment spikes upward during recessions and depressions, but the unemployment rate is always above zero, even in good times.

Increases in unemployment during recessions

EXAMPLE 17.2

Using monthly data on the national civilian unemployment rate, find the increase in the unemployment rate between the onset of recession in November 1973, January 1980, and July 1990 and the peak unemployment rate in the following 3 years. Compare these increases in unemployment to the increase during the Great Depression.

Unemployment data are collected by the U.S. Bureau of Labor Statistics (BLS) and can be obtained from the BLS home page (http://stats.bls.gov/datahome.htm). Hard copy sources include the *Survey of Current Business*, the *Federal Reserve Bulletin*, and *Economic Indicators*. Monthly data from the BLS home page yield the following comparisons:

Unemployment rate at beginning of recession (%)	Peak unemployment rate (%)	Increase in unemployment rate (%)
4.8 (Nov. 1973)	9.0 (May 1975)	+4.2
6.3 (Jan. 1980)	10.8 (Nov./Dec. 1982)	+4.5
5.5 (July 1990)	7.8 (June 1992)	+2.3

Unemployment increased significantly following the onset of each recession, although the impact of the 1990 recession on the labor market was clearly less serious than that of the 1973 and the 1980 recessions. (Actually, the 1980 recession was a "double dip"—a short recession in 1980, followed by a longer one in 1981–82.) In comparison, during the Great Depression the unemployment rate rose from about 3 percent in 1929 to about 25 percent in 1933, as we mentioned in the introduction to this chapter. Clearly, the 22 percentage point change in the unemployment rate that Americans experienced in the Great Depression dwarfs the effects of the three postwar recessions.

One question of great interest to macroeconomists is why unemployment rates sometimes differ markedly from country to country. For the past two decades unemployment rates in Western Europe have more often than not been measured in the "double digits." On average, more than 10 percent of the European workforce has been out of a job during this period, a rate roughly double that in the United States. The high unemployment is particularly puzzling, because during the 1950s and 1960s, European unemployment rates were generally much lower than those in the United States. What explains these differences in the unemployment rate in different countries at different times?

EXERCISE 17.1

Find the most recent unemployment rates for France, Germany, and the United Kingdom, and compare them to the most recent unemployment rate for the United States. A useful source is the home page of the Organization for Economic Cooperation and Development (OECD), an organization of industrialized countries (http://www.oecd.org/). See also the OECD's publication, *Main Economic Indicators*. Is unemployment still lower in the United States than in Western Europe?

INFLATION

Another important economic statistic is the rate of *inflation*, which is the rate at which prices in general are increasing over time. As we discuss in Chapter 19, inflation imposes a variety of costs on the economy. And when the inflation rate is high, people on fixed incomes, such as pensioners who receive a fixed dollar payment each month, can't keep up with the rising cost of living.

In recent years inflation has been relatively low in the United States, but that has not always been the case (see Figure 17.4 for data on U.S. inflation since 1900). During the 1970s, inflation was a major problem; in fact, many people told poll takers that inflation was "public enemy number one." Why was inflation high in the 1970s, and why is it relatively low today? What difference does it make to the average person?

FIGURE 17.4
The U.S. Inflation Rate, 1900–1999.
The U.S. inflation rate has fluctuated over time. Inflation was high in the 1970s but has been quite low recently.

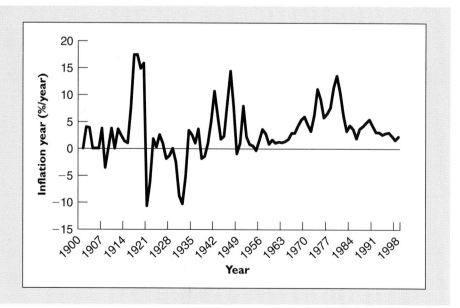

As with unemployment rates, the rate of inflation can differ markedly from country to country. For example, in 1995 the inflation rate was less than 3 percent in the United States but more than 400 percent in the Ukraine. (Since 1995, the Ukraine has brought its inflation rate down to the single digits.) What accounts for such large differences in inflation rates between countries?

Inflation and unemployment are often linked together in policy discussions. One reason for this linkage is the oft-heard argument that unemployment can be reduced only at the cost of higher inflation and that inflation can be reduced only at the cost of higher unemployment. Must the government accept a higher rate of inflation to bring down unemployment, and vice versa?

ECONOMIC INTERDEPENDENCE AMONG NATIONS

National economies do not exist in isolation but are increasingly interdependent. The United States, because of its size and the wide variety of goods and services it produces, is one of the most self-sufficient economies on the planet. Even so, in 1999 the United States exported about 10.8 percent of all the goods and services it produced and imported from abroad 13.3 percent of the goods and services that Americans used.

Sometimes international flows of goods and services become a matter of political and economic concern. In 1999, exports to the United States of very low priced Russian steel threatened the jobs of U.S. steelworkers. Ross Perot, the Texas businessman and presidential candidate, predicted such problems when he opposed the adoption of the North American Free Trade Agreement (NAFTA) and similar agreements designed to promote international trade in goods and services. (Perot made famous the phrase "giant sucking sound" to describe what he thought free trade would do to American jobs.) Are free trade agreements, in which countries agree not to tax or otherwise block the international flow of goods and services, a good or bad thing?

"I don't know what the hell happened—one minute I'm at work in Flint, Michigan, then there's a giant sucking sound and suddenly here I am in Mexico."

A related issue is the phenomenon of *trade imbalances*, which occur when the quantity of goods and services that a country sells abroad (its *exports*) differs significantly from the quantity of goods and services its citizens buy from abroad (its *imports*). Figure 17.5 shows U.S. exports and imports since 1900, measured as a percentage of the economy's total output. Prior to the 1970s the United States generally exported more than it imported. (Notice the major export booms that occurred after both world wars, when the United States was helping to reconstruct Europe.) Since the 1970s, however, imports to the United States have outstripped exports, creating a situation called a *trade deficit*. Other

FIGURE 17.5

Exports and Imports as a Share of U.S. Output, 1900–1999.

The blue line shows U.S. exports as a percentage of U.S. output. The red line shows U.S. imports relative to U.S. output. For much of its history the United States has exported more than it imported, but over the past two decades imports have greatly outstripped exports.

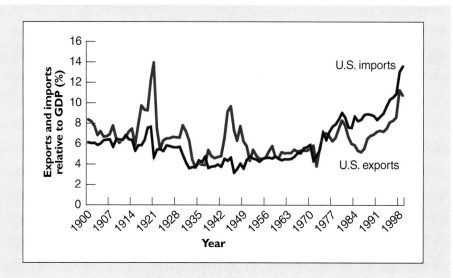

countries—Japan, for example—export much more than they import. In 1998, for example, Japan exported more than 23 percent of its output but imported goods and services equaling less than 19 percent of its output. A country such as Japan is said to have a *trade surplus*. What causes trade deficits and surpluses? Are they harmful or helpful?

RECAP   **THE MAJOR MACROECONOMIC ISSUES**

- *Economic growth and living standards.* Over the past century the industrialized nations have experienced remarkable economic growth and improvements in living standards. Macroeconomists study the reasons for this extraordinary growth and try to understand why growth rates vary markedly among nations.

- *Productivity. Average labor productivity,* or output per employed worker, is a crucial determinant of living standards. Macroeconomists ask, What causes slowdowns and speedups in the rate of productivity growth?

- *Recessions and expansions.* Economies experience periods of slower growth (recessions) and more rapid growth (expansions). Macroeconomists examine the sources of these fluctuations and the government policies that attempt to moderate them.

- *Unemployment.* The unemployment rate is the fraction of people who would like to be employed but can't find work. Unemployment rises during recessions, but there are always unemployed people even during good times. Macroeconomists study the causes of unemployment, including the reasons why it sometimes differs markedly across countries.

- *Inflation.* The inflation rate is the rate at which prices in general are increasing over time. Questions macroeconomists ask about inflation include, Why does inflation vary over time and across countries? Must a reduction in inflation be accompanied by an increase in unemployment, or vice versa?

- *Economic interdependence among nations.* Modern economies are highly interdependent. Related issues studied by macroeconomists include the desirability of free trade agreements and the causes and effects of trade imbalances.

MACROECONOMIC POLICY

We have seen that macroeconomists are interested in why different countries' economies perform differently and why a particular economy may perform well in some periods and poorly in others. Although many factors contribute to economic performance, government policy is surely among the most important. Understanding the effects of various policies and helping government officials develop better policies are important objectives of macroeconomists.

TYPES OF MACROECONOMIC POLICY

We have defined macroeconomic policies as government policies that affect the performance of the economy as a whole, as opposed to the market for a particular good or service. There are three major types of macroeconomic policy: *monetary policy, fiscal policy,* and *structural policy.*

The term **monetary policy** refers to the determination of the nation's money supply. (Cash and coin are the basic forms of money, although as we will see, modern economies have other forms of money as well.) For reasons that we will discuss in later chapters, most economists agree that changes in the money supply affect important macroeconomic variables, including national output, employment, interest rates, inflation, stock prices, and the international value of the dollar. In virtually all countries, monetary policy is controlled by a government institution called the *central bank.* The Federal Reserve System, often called the Fed for short, is the central bank of the United States.

Fiscal policy refers to decisions that determine the government's budget, including the amount and composition of government expenditures and government revenues. The balance between government spending and taxes is a particularly important aspect of fiscal policy. When government officials spend more than they collect in taxes, the government runs a *deficit,* and when they spend less, the government's budget is in *surplus.* As with monetary policy, economists generally agree that fiscal policy can have important effects on the overall performance of the economy. For example, many economists believe that the large deficits run by the federal government during the 1980s were harmful to the nation's economy. Likewise, many would say that the balancing of the federal budget that occurred during the 1990s contributed to the nation's strong economic performance during that decade.

monetary policy determination of the nation's money supply

fiscal policy decisions that determine the government's budget, including the amount and composition of government expenditures and government revenues

EXERCISE 17.2

The Congressional Budget Office (CBO) is the government agency that is charged with projecting the federal government's surpluses or deficits. From the CBO's home page (http://www.cbo.gov/), find the most recent value of the federal government's surplus or deficit and the CBO's projected values for the next 5 years. How do you think these projections are likely to affect congressional deliberations on taxation and government spending?

Finally, the term **structural policy** includes government policies aimed at changing the underlying structure, or institutions, of the nation's economy. Structural policies come in many forms, from minor tinkering to ambitious overhauls of the entire economic system. The move away from government control of the economy and toward a more market-oriented approach in many formerly communist countries, such as Poland, the Czech Republic, and Hungary, is a large-scale example of structural policy. Many developing countries have tried similar structural reforms. Supporters of structural policy hope that, by changing the basic characteristics of the economy or by remaking its institutions, they can stimulate economic growth and improve living standards.

structural policy government policies aimed at changing the underlying structure, or institutions, of the nation's economy

POSITIVE VERSUS NORMATIVE ANALYSES OF MACROECONOMIC POLICY

Macroeconomists are frequently called upon to analyze the effects of a proposed policy. For example, if Congress is debating a tax cut, economists in the Congressional Budget Office or the Treasury may be asked to prepare an analysis of the likely effects of the tax cut on the overall economy, as well as on specific industries, regions, or income groups. An objective analysis aimed at determining only the economic consequences of a particular policy—not whether those consequences are desirable—is called a **positive analysis.** In contrast, a **normative analysis** includes recommendations on whether a particular policy *should* be implemented. While a positive analysis is supposed to be objective and scientific, a normative analysis involves the *values* of the person or organization doing the analysis—conservative, liberal, or middle-of-the-road.

positive analysis addresses the economic consequences of a particular event or policy, not whether those consequences are desirable

normative analysis addresses the question of whether a policy *should* be used; normative analysis inevitably involves the values of the person doing the analysis

While pundits often joke that economists cannot agree among themselves, the tendency for economists to disagree is exaggerated. When economists do disagree, the controversy often centers on normative judgments (which relate to economists' personal values) rather than on positive analysis (which reflects objective knowledge of the economy). For example, liberal and conservative economists might agree that a particular tax cut would increase the incomes of the relatively wealthy (positive analysis). But they might vehemently disagree on whether the policy *should* be enacted, reflecting their personal views about whether wealthy people deserve a tax break (normative analysis).

The next time you hear or read about a debate over economic issues, try to determine whether the differences between the two positions are primarily *positive* or *normative*. If the debate focuses on the actual effects of the event or policy under discussion, then the disagreement is over positive issues. But if the main question has to do with conflicting personal opinions about the *desirability* of those effects, the debate is normative. The distinction between positive and normative analyses is important, because objective economic research can help to resolve differences over positive issues. When people differ for normative reasons, however, economic analysis is of less use.

EXAMPLE 17.3

Positive and normative judgments in an editorial

In the summer of 1999 the Republican-controlled Congress, responding to large projected budget surpluses (see Exercise 17.2), passed a sweeping tax cut. A *New York Times* editorial (7/31/99) on the tax cut read, in part, as follows:

An Irresponsible Tax Cut

> The House and Senate have now passed unreasonably large tax cuts that provide huge benefits for the rich and would assure that the current era of budget surpluses will be a brief one. Whatever bill emerges from a House-Senate conference committee deserves a veto.
>
> Economically, the case for a tax cut is very weak. The economy is booming, and the Federal Reserve may need to raise interest rates again to keep inflation from rising. Applying fiscal stimulus through a tax cut now would be likely to bring on even higher interest rates.
>
> In the longer term, the argument that the money will be available for large tax cuts is based on optimistic economic forecasts and on completely unrealistic estimates of government spending. . . . If there is to be a tax cut, it should be relatively modest, allowing for the possibility that the economic forecasts will prove too rosy. A good bill would concentrate relief on lower- and middle-income taxpayers and would encourage them to save more money. . . . Congress should embrace a modified version of the Clinton Administration's Universal Savings Accounts, as Vice

President Al Gore suggested yesterday. Those accounts would provide subsidies to encourage savings by those who will need the money the most....

Which arguments in this editorial are predominantly positive? Which are predominantly normative?

This editorial is a mixture of positive and normative statements. In the first paragraph, the assertions that the tax cuts are "unreasonably large," that the benefits for the rich are "huge" (with no quantification), and that the bill "deserves a veto" are based largely on the writer's personal values and thus are normative. However, the forecast that the tax cuts would quickly end the budget surplus is a positive statement, because it addresses the likely consequences of a policy.

There are several positive statements in the second paragraph, including the assertion that the Federal Reserve may need to raise interest rates to keep inflation from rising and the statement that a tax cut might lead to higher interest rates. Both statements addressed the likely consequences of the proposed policy; their truth or falsehood does not depend on the writer's values. Similarly, the assertions that the government's economic forecasts are too optimistic and that its projections of government spending are not realistic (third paragraph) are positive statements, since time will tell if the forecasts are true or false.

Finally, the sentence beginning "A good bill would . . ." (third paragraph) is purely normative, being based on the writer's personal beliefs that lower- and middle-income taxpayers are most deserving of a tax cut and that this group should be encouraged to save more. However, the argument that Universal Savings Accounts would encourage savings is a positive assertion, since it predicts the effects of a specific policy.

In thinking about whether they agree with an editorial like this one, careful readers ask two questions: First, are the positive claims the writer has made factually correct, or at least plausible? Second, are the writer's normative arguments consistent with their own personal values?

EXERCISE 17.3

Which of the following statements are positive and which are normative? How can you tell?

a. **A tax increase is likely to lead to lower interest rates.**

b. **Congress should increase taxes to reduce the inappropriately high level of interest rates.**

c. **A tax increase would be acceptable if most of the burden fell on those with incomes over $100,000.**

d. **Higher tariffs (taxes on imports) are needed to protect American jobs.**

e. **An increase in the tariff on imported steel would increase employment of American steelworkers.**

RECAP **MACROECONOMIC POLICY**

Macroeconomic policies affect the performance of the economy as a whole. The three types of macroeconomic policy are monetary policy, fiscal policy, and structural policy. *Monetary policy,* which in the United States is under the control of the Federal Reserve System, refers to the determination of the nation's money supply. *Fiscal policy* involves decisions about the government budget, including its expenditures and tax collections. *Structural policy* refers to government actions to change the underlying structure, or institutions, of the economy. Structural policy can range from minor tinkering to a major overhaul of the economic system, as with the formerly communist countries that are attempting to convert to market-oriented systems.

The analysis of a proposed policy can be positive or normative. A *positive analysis* addresses the policy's likely economic consequences, but not whether those consequences are desirable. A *normative analysis* addresses the question of whether a proposed policy *should* be used. Debates about normative conclusions inevitably involve personal values and thus generally cannot be resolved by objective economic analysis alone.

AGGREGATION

In Chapter 1 we discussed the difference between macroeconomics, the study of national economies, and microeconomics, the study of individual economic entities, such as households and firms, and the markets for specific goods and services. The main difference between the fields is one of perspective: Macroeconomists take a "bird's-eye view" of the economy, ignoring the fine details to understand how the system works as a whole. Microeconomists work instead at "ground level," studying the economic behavior of individual households, firms, and markets. Both perspectives are useful—indeed essential—to understand what makes an economy work.

Although macroeconomics and microeconomics take different perspectives on the economy, the basic tools of analysis are much the same. In the chapters to come you will see that macroeconomists apply the same core principles as microeconomists (see Chapters 1 to 4) in their efforts to understand and predict economic behavior. Even though a national economy is a much bigger entity than a household or even a large firm, the choices and actions of individual decision makers ultimately determine the performance of the economy as a whole. So, for example, to understand saving behavior at the national level, the macroeconomist must first consider what motivates an individual family or household to save. The core principles introduced in Chapters 1 to 4 prove very useful for attacking such questions.

EXERCISE 17.4

Which of the following questions would be studied primarily by macroeconomists? By microeconomists? Explain.

a. **Does increased government spending lower the unemployment rate?**

b. **Does Microsoft Corporation's dominance of the software industry harm consumers?**

c. **Would a school voucher program improve the quality of education in the United States? (Under a voucher program, parents are given a fixed amount of government aid, which they may use to send their children to any school, public or private.)**

d. **Should government policymakers aim to reduce inflation still further?**

e. **Why is the average rate of household saving low in the United States?**

f. **Does the increase in the number of consumer products being sold over the Internet threaten the profits of conventional retailers?**

While macroeconomists use the core principles of economics to understand and predict individual economic decisions, they need a way to relate millions of individual decisions to the behavior of the economy as a whole. One important tool they use to link individual behavior to national economic performance is **aggregation,** the adding up of individual economic variables to obtain economy-wide totals.

aggregation the adding up of individual economic variables to obtain economywide totals

For example, macroeconomists don't care whether consumers drink Pepsi or Coke, go to the movie theater or rent videos, drive a convertible or a sports utility vehicle. These individual economic decisions are the province of microeconomics. Instead, macroeconomists add up consumer expenditures on all goods and services during a given period to obtain *aggregate,* or total, consumer expenditure. Similarly, a macroeconomist would not focus on plumbers' wages versus electricians' but would concentrate instead on the average wage of all workers. By focusing on aggregate variables, like total consumer expenditures or the average wage, macroeconomists suppress the mind-boggling details of a complex modern economy to see broad economic trends.

Aggregation (1): A national crime index

EXAMPLE 17.4

To illustrate not only why aggregation is needed but also some of the problems associated with it, consider an issue that is only partly economic: crime. Suppose policymakers want to know whether *in general* the problem of crime in the United States is getting better or worse. How could an analyst obtain a statistical answer to that question?

Police keep detailed records of the crimes reported in their jurisdictions, so in principle a researcher could determine precisely how many purse snatchings occurred last year on New York City subways. But data on the number of crimes of each type in each jurisdiction would produce stacks of computer output. Is there a way to add up, or aggregate, all the crime data to get some sense of the national trend?

Law enforcement agencies such as the FBI use aggregation to obtain national *crime rates,* which are typically expressed as the number of "serious" crimes committed per 100,000 population. For example, the FBI reported that in 1998 some 12.5 million serious crimes (both violent crimes and property crimes) occurred in the United States (http://www.fbi.gov). Dividing the number of crimes by the U.S. population in 1998, which was about 270 million, and multiplying by 100,000 yields the crime rate for 1998, equal to about 4,600 crimes per 100,000 people. This rate represented a substantial drop from the crime rate in 1992, which was nearly 5,700 crimes per 100,000 people. So aggregation (the adding up of many different crimes into a national index) indicates that, in general, serious crime decreased in the United States between 1992 and 1998. (Interestingly enough, the unemployment rate also declined between 1992 and 1998—see Figure 17.3. The fact that periods of low unemployment tend to coincide with periods of reduced crime is probably not a coincidence.)

Although aggregation of crime statistics reveals the "big picture," it may obscure important details. The FBI crime index lumps together relatively minor crimes such as theft with very serious crimes such as murder and rape. Most people would agree that murder and rape do far more damage than a typical theft, so adding together these two very different types of crimes might give a false picture of crime in the United States. For example, although the U.S. crime rate fell 19.3 percent between 1992 and 1998, the murder rate fell 31.5 percent. Since murder is the most serious of crimes, the reduction in crime between 1992 and 1998 was probably more significant than the change in the overall crime rate indicates. The aggregate crime rate glosses over other important details, such as the fact that the most dramatic reductions in crime have occurred in urban areas. This loss of detail is a cost of aggregation, the price analysts pay for the ability to look at broad economic or social trends.

EXAMPLE 17.5   **Aggregation (2): U.S. exports**

The United States exports a wide variety of products and services to many different countries. Kansas farmers sell grain to Russia, Silicon Valley programmers sell software to France, and Hollywood movie studios sell entertainment the world over. Suppose macroeconomists want to compare the total quantities of American-made goods sold to various regions of the world. How could such a comparison be made?

Economists can't add bushels of grain, lines of code, and movie tickets—the units aren't comparable. But they can add the *dollar values* of each—the revenue farmers earned from foreign grain sales, the royalties programmers received for their exported software, and the revenues studios reaped from films shown abroad. By comparing the dollar values of U.S. exports to Europe, Asia, Africa, and other regions in a particular year, economists are able to determine which regions are the biggest customers for American-made goods.

RECAP   **AGGREGATION**

Macroeconomics, the study of national economies, differs from microeconomics, the study of individual economic entities (such as households and firms) and the markets for specific goods and services. Macroeconomists take a "bird's-eye view" of the economy. To study the economy as a whole, macroeconomists make frequent use of *aggregation*, the adding up of individual economic variables to obtain economywide totals. For example, a macroeconomist is more interested in the determinants of total U.S. exports, as measured by total dollar value, than in the factors that determine the exports of specific goods. A cost of aggregation is that the fine details of the economic situation are often obscured.

STUDYING MACROECONOMICS: A PREVIEW

This chapter introduced many of the key issues of macroeconomics. In the chapters to come we will look at each of these issues in more detail. The next two chapters (Chapters 18 and 19) cover the *measurement* of economic performance, including key variables like the level of economic activity, the extent of unemployment, and the rate of inflation. Obtaining quantitative measurements of the economy, against which theories can be tested, is the crucial first step in answering basic macroeconomic questions like those raised in this chapter.

In Part 6 we will study economic behavior over relatively long periods of time. Chapter 20 examines economic growth and productivity improvement, the fundamental determinants of the average standard of living in the long run. Chapter 21 discusses the long-run determination of employment, unemployment, and wages. In Chapter 22 we study saving and its link to the creation of new capital goods, such as factories and machines. The role played in the economy by money and financial markets is covered in Chapter 23, which also introduces the Federal Reserve, the central bank of the United States.

John Maynard Keynes, a celebrated British economist, once wrote that "In the long run, we are all dead." Keynes's statement was intended as an ironic comment on the tendency of economists to downplay short-run economic problems on the grounds that "in the long run," the operation of the free market will always restore economic stability. Keynes, who was particularly active and influential during the Great Depression, correctly viewed the problem of massive unemployment, whether "short run" or not, as the most pressing economic issue of the time.

So why start our study of macroeconomics with the long run? Keynes's comment notwithstanding, long-run economic performance is extremely important, accounting for most of the substantial differences in living standards and economic well-being the world over. Furthermore, studying long-run economic behavior provides important background for understanding short-term fluctuations in the economy.

We turn to those short-term fluctuations in Part 7. Chapter 24 provides background on what happens during recessions and expansions, as well as some historical perspective. Chapter 25 discusses one important source of short-term economic fluctuations, variations in aggregate spending. The chapter also shows how, by influencing aggregate spending, fiscal policy may be able to moderate economic fluctuations. The second major policy tool for stabilizing the economy, monetary policy, is the subject of Chapter 26. Chapter 27 brings inflation into the analysis and discusses the circumstances under which macroeconomic policymakers may face a short-term trade-off between inflation and unemployment.

The international dimension of macroeconomics is the focus of Part 8, beginning with a discussion of international trade and financial investments in Chapter 28. Finally, Chapter 29 introduces exchange rates between national currencies. We will discuss how exchange rates are determined and how they affect the workings of the economy and macroeconomic policy.

■ SUMMARY ■

- Macroeconomics is the study of the performance of national economies and of the policies governments use to try to improve that performance. Some of the broad issues macroeconomists study are:

  Sources of economic growth and improved living standards

  Trends in *average labor productivity,* or output per employed worker

  Short-term fluctuations in the pace of economic growth (recessions and expansions)

  Causes and cures of unemployment and inflation

  Economic interdependence among nations

- To help explain differences in economic performance among countries, or in economic performance in the same country at different times, macroeconomists study the implementation and effects of macroeconomic policies. *Macroeconomic policies* are government actions designed to affect the performance of the economy as a whole. Macroeconomic policies include *monetary policy* (the

determination of the nation's money supply), *fiscal policy* (relating to decisions about the government's budget), and *structural policy* (aimed at affecting the basic structure and institutions of the economy).

- In studying economic policies, economists apply both *positive analysis* (an objective attempt to determine the consequences of a proposed policy) and *normative analysis* (which addresses whether a particular policy *should* be adopted). Normative analysis involves the values of the person doing the analysis.

- Macroeconomics is distinct from microeconomics, which focuses on the behavior of individual economic entities and specific markets. Macroeconomists make heavy use of *aggregation,* which is the adding up of individual economic variables into economywide totals. Aggregation allows macroeconomists to study the "big picture" of the economy, while ignoring fine details about individual households, firms, and markets.

▪ KEY TERMS ▪

aggregation (447)

average labor productivity (437)

fiscal policy (443)

macroeconomic policies (435)

monetary policy (443)

normative analysis (444)

positive analysis (444)

structural policy (443)

▪ REVIEW QUESTIONS ▪

1. How did the experience of the Great Depression motivate the development of the field of macroeconomics?

2. Generally, how does the standard of living in the United States today compare to the standard of living in other countries? To the standard of living in the United States a century ago?

3. Why is average labor productivity a particularly important economic variable?

4. True or false, and explain: Economic growth within a particular country generally proceeds at a constant rate.

5. True or false, and explain: Differences of opinion about economic policy recommendations can always be resolved by objective analysis of the issues.

6. Baseball statistics, such as batting averages, are calculated and reported for each individual player, for each team, and for the league as a whole. What purposes are served by doing this? Relate to the idea of aggregation in macroeconomics.

7. What type of macroeconomic policy (monetary, fiscal, structural) might include each of the following actions:
   a. A broad government initiative to reduce the country's reliance on agriculture and promote high-technology industries
   b. A reduction in income tax rates
   c. Provision of additional cash to the banking system
   d. An attempt to reduce the government budget deficit by reducing spending
   e. A decision by a developing country to reduce government control of the economy and to become more market-oriented

▪ PROBLEMS ▪

1. Over the next 50 years the Japanese population is expected to decline, while the fraction of the population that is retired is expected to increase sharply. What are the implications of these population changes for total output and average living standards in Japan, assuming that average labor productivity continues to grow? What if average labor productivity stagnates?

2. Is it possible for average living standards to rise during a period in which average labor productivity is falling? Discuss, using a numerical example for illustration.

3. The Bureau of Economic Analysis, or BEA, is a government agency that collects a wide variety of statistics about the U.S. economy. From the BEA's home page (http://www.bea.doc.gov) find data for the most recent year available on U.S. exports and imports of goods and services. Is the United States running a trade surplus or deficit? Calculate the ratio of the surplus or deficit to U.S. exports.

4. Which of the following statements are positive and which are normative?
   a. If the Federal Reserve raises interest rates, demand for housing is likely to fall.
   b. The Federal Reserve should raise interest rates to keep inflation at an acceptably low level.
   c. Stock prices are likely to fall over the next year as the economy slows.
   d. A reduction in the capital gains tax (the tax on profits made in the stock market) would lead to a 10 to 20 percent increase in stock prices.
   e. Congress should not reduce capital gains taxes without also providing tax breaks for lower-income people.

5. Which of the following would be studied by a macroeconomist? By a microeconomist?
   a. The worldwide operations of General Motors
   b. The effect of government subsidies on sugar prices
   c. Factors affecting average wages in the U.S. economy
   d. Inflation in developing countries
   e. The effects of tax cuts on consumer spending

▪ ANSWERS TO IN-CHAPTER EXERCISES ▪

17.1 No answer given.

17.2 No answer given.

17.3 a. Positive. This is a prediction of the effect of a policy, not a value judgment on whether the policy should be used.
   b. Normative. Words like *should* and *inappropriately* express value judgments about the policy.
   c. Normative. The statement is about the desirability of certain types of policies, not their likely effects.
   d. Normative. The statement is about desirability of a policy.
   e. Positive. The statement is a prediction of the likely effects of a policy, not a recommendation on whether the policy should be used.

17.4 a. Macroeconomists. Government spending and the unemployment rate are aggregate concepts pertaining to the national economy.
   b. Microeconomists. Microsoft, though large, is an individual firm.
   c. Microeconomists. The issue relates to the supply and demand for a specific service, education.
   d. Macroeconomists. Inflation is an aggregate, economywide concept.
   e. Macroeconomists. Average saving is an aggregate concept.
   f. Microeconomists. The focus is on a relatively narrow set of markets and products rather than on the economy as a whole.

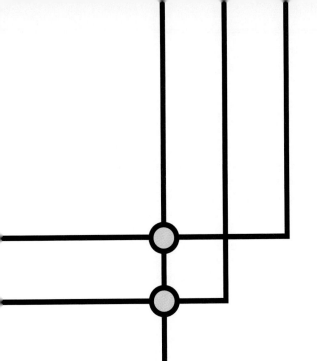

MEASURING ECONOMIC ACTIVITY: GDP AND UNEMPLOYMENT

"Nonfarm payrolls grew at a 2 percent rate in the third quarter . . ."

"The Dow Jones stock market index closed up 93 points yesterday in moderate trading . . ."

"Inflation appears subdued as the consumer price index registered an increase of only 0.2 percent last month . . .

"The unemployment rate last month fell to 4.1 percent, its lowest level since . . ."

News reports like these fill the airwaves—some TV and radio stations carry nothing else. In fact, all kinds of people are interested in economic data. The average person hopes to learn something that will be useful in a business decision, a financial investment, or a career move. The professional economist depends on economic data in much the same way that a doctor depends on a patient's vital signs—pulse, blood pressure, and temperature—to make an accurate diagnosis. To understand economic developments and to be able to give useful advice to policymakers, businesspeople, and financial investors, an economist simply must have up-to-date, accurate data. Political leaders and policymakers also need economic data to help them in their decisions and planning.

Interest in measuring the economy, and attempts to do so, date back as far as the mid-seventeenth century, when Sir William Petty (1623–1687) conducted a detailed survey of the land and wealth of Ireland. The British government's purpose in commissioning the survey was to determine the capacity of the Irish people to pay taxes to the Crown. But Petty used the opportunity to measure a variety of social and economic variables and went on to conduct pioneering studies of wealth, production, and population in several other countries. A firm believer in the idea that scientific progress depends first and foremost on accurate measurement, he once interrupted a meeting of the British Royal Society (a distinguished association of scientists, of which Petty was a founding member) to correct a speaker who had used the phrase "considerably bigger." A rule should be passed barring such vague terms, Petty proposed, so that "no word might be used but what marks either number, weight, or measure."[1]

Not until the twentieth century, though, did economic measurement come into its own. World War II was an important catalyst for the development of accurate economic statistics, since its very outcome was thought to depend on the mobilization of economic resources. Two economists, Simon Kuznets in the United States and Richard Stone in the United Kingdom, developed comprehensive systems for measuring a nation's output of goods and services, which were of great help to Allied leaders in their wartime planning. Kuznets and Stone each received a Nobel prize in economics for their work, which became the basis for the economic accounts used today by almost all the world's countries. The governments of the United States and many other countries now collect and publish a wealth of statistics covering all aspects of their economies.

In this chapter and the next we will talk about how economists measure three basic macroeconomic variables that arise in almost any discussion of the economy: the *gross domestic product*, or *GDP*, the *rate of unemployment*, and the *rate of inflation*. The focus of this chapter is on the first two of these statistics, GDP and the unemployment rate, which both measure the overall level of economic activity in a country.

Measuring economic activity might sound like a straightforward and uncontroversial task, but that is not the case. Indeed, the basic measure of a nation's output of goods and services, the gross domestic product or GDP, has been criticized on many grounds. Some critics have complained that GDP does not adequately reflect factors such as the effect of economic growth on the environment or the rate of resource depletion. Because of problems like these, they charge, policies based on GDP statistics are likely to be flawed. Unemployment statistics have also been the subject of some controversy. By the end of this chapter you will understand how official measures of output and unemployment are constructed and used and will have gained some insight into these debates over their accuracy. Understanding the strengths and limitations of economic data is the first critical step toward becoming an intelligent user of economic statistics, as well as a necessary background for the economic analysis in the chapters to come.

GROSS DOMESTIC PRODUCT: MEASURING THE NATION'S OUTPUT

Chapter 17 emphasized the link between an economy's output of goods and services and its living standard. We noted that high levels of output per person, and per worker, are typically associated with a high standard of living. But what, exactly, does "output" mean? To study economic growth and productivity scientifically, we need to be more precise about how economists define and measure an economy's output.

The most commonly used measure of an economy's output is called the *gross domestic product*, or *GDP*. GDP is intended to measure how much an economy

---

[1]This story is reported by Charles H. Hull, "Petty's Place in the History of Economic Theory," *Quarterly Journal of Economics*, May 14, 1900, pp. 307–340.

produces in a given period, such as a quarter (3 months) or a year. More precisely, **gross domestic product (GDP)** is the market value of the final goods and services produced in a country during a given period. To understand this definition, let's take it apart and examine each of its parts separately. The first key phrase in the definition is "market value."

gross domestic product (GDP) the market value of the final goods and services produced in a country during a given period

MARKET VALUE

A modern economy produces many different goods and services, from dental floss (a good) to acupuncture (a service). Macroeconomists are not interested in this kind of detail, however; rather, their goal is to understand the behavior of the economy as a whole. For example, a macroeconomist might ask, Has the overall capacity of the economy to produce goods and services increased over time? If so, by how much?

To be able to talk about concepts like the "total output" or "total production"—as opposed to the production of specific items like dental floss—economists need to *aggregate* the quantities of the many different goods and services into a single number. They do so by adding up the *market values* of the different goods and services the economy produces. A simple example will illustrate the process. In the imaginary economy of Orchardia, total production is 4 apples and 6 bananas. To find the total output of Orchardia, we could add the number of apples to the number of bananas and conclude that total output is 10 pieces of fruit. But what if this economy also produced three pairs of shoes? There really is no sensible way to add apples and bananas to shoes.

Suppose though that we know that apples sell for $0.25 each, bananas for $0.50 each, and shoes for $20.00 a pair. Then the market value of this economy's production, or its GDP, is equal to

$$(4 \text{ apples} \times \$0.25/\text{apple}) + (6 \text{ bananas} \times \$0.50/\text{banana}) + (3 \text{ pairs of shoes} \times \$20.00/\text{pair}) = \$64.00.$$

Notice that when we calculate total output this way, the more expensive items (the shoes) receive a higher weighting than the cheaper items (the apples and bananas). In general, the amount people are willing to pay for an item is an indication of the economic benefit they expect to receive from it (see Chapter 4). For this reason higher-priced items should count for more in a measure of aggregate output.

Orchardia's GDP

Suppose Orchardia were to produce 3 apples, 3 bananas, and 4 pairs of shoes at the same prices as in the preceding text. What is its GDP now?

Now the Orchardian GDP is equal to

$$(3 \text{ apples} \times \$0.25/\text{apple}) + (3 \text{ bananas} \times \$0.50/\text{banana}) + (4 \text{ pairs of shoes} \times \$20.00/\text{pair}) = \$82.25.$$

Notice that Orchardian GDP is higher in Example 18.1 than in the previous text, even though two of the three goods (apples and bananas) are being produced in smaller quantities than before. The reason is that the good whose production has increased (shoes) is much more valuable than the goods whose production has decreased (apples and bananas).

EXAMPLE 18.1

EXERCISE 18.1

Suppose Orchardia produces the same quantities of the three goods as originally at the same prices (see text preceding Example 18.1). In addition, it produces 5 oranges at $0.30 each. What is the GDP of Orchardia now?

EXERCISE 18.2

Following are data for a recent month on U.S. production of passenger cars and other light vehicles (a category that includes minivans, light trucks, and sports utility vehicles). The data are broken down into two categories: U.S. auto producers (GM, Ford, and Chrysler, now Daimler-Chrysler) and foreign-owned plants (such as Honda, Toyota, and BMW). The average selling price is $17,000 for passenger cars and $25,000 for other light vehicles.

	Passenger cars	Other light vehicles
U.S. producers	471,000	714,000
Foreign-owned plants	227,000	63,000

Compare the output of U.S. producers to that of foreign-owned plants in terms of both the total number of vehicles produced and their market values (contribution to GDP). Explain why the two measures give different impressions of the relative importance of production by U.S.-owned and foreign-owned plants.

Market values provide a convenient way to add together, or aggregate, the many different goods and services produced in a modern economy. A drawback of using market values, however, is that not all economically valuable goods and services are bought and sold in markets. For example, the unpaid work of a homemaker, although it is of economic value, is not sold in markets and so isn't counted in GDP. But paid housekeeping and child care services, which are sold in markets, do count. This distinction can create some pitfalls, as Example 18.2 shows.

EXAMPLE 18.2

Women's labor force participation and GDP measurement

The percentage of adult American women working outside the home has increased dramatically in the past four decades, from less than 40 percent in 1960 to about 60 percent today (see Figure 18.1). This trend has led to a substantial increase in the demand for paid day care and housekeeping services, as working wives and mothers require more help at home. How have these changes affected measured GDP?

FIGURE 18.1

Percentages of American Men and Women over Age 16 Working Outside the Home, 1960–1999.

The fraction of American women working outside the home has risen by about 20 percentage points since 1960, while the fraction of men working outside the home has declined slightly.

[SOURCE: *Economic Report of the President,* February 2000 (http://w3.access.gpo.gov/eop/index.html)].

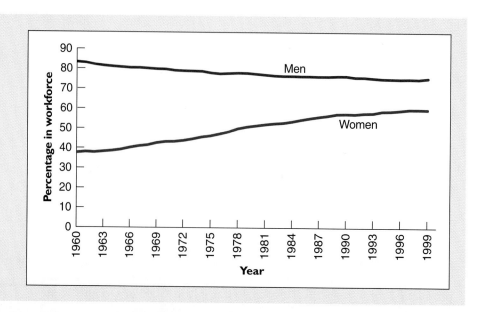

The entry of many women into the labor market has raised measured GDP in two ways. First, the goods and services that women produce in their new jobs have contributed directly to increasing GDP. Second, the fact that paid workers took over previously unpaid housework and child care duties has increased measured GDP by the amount paid to those workers. The first of these two changes represents a genuine increase in economic activity, but the second reflects a transfer of existing economic activities from the unpaid sector to the market sector. Overall, then, the increase in measured GDP associated with increased participation in the labor force by women probably overstates the actual increase in economic activity.

Why has female participation in the labor market increased by so much? What explains the trends illustrated in Figure 18.1?

In a world governed only by economic principles—without social conventions, customs, or traditions—homemaking tasks like cleaning, cooking, and child rearing would be jobs like any other. As such, they would be subject to the principle of comparative advantage: Those people (either men or women) whose comparative advantage lay in performing homemaking tasks would specialize in them, freeing people whose comparative advantage lies elsewhere to work outside the home. In other words, homemaking tasks would be done by those with the lowest opportunity cost in those tasks. In such a world, to see a woman with a medical degree doing housework would be very unusual—her opportunity cost of doing housework would be too high.

But of course we don't live in a world driven only by economic considerations. Traditionally, social custom has severely limited the economic opportunities of women (and in some societies still does). However, social restrictions on women have weakened considerably over the past century, particularly in the industrialized countries, as a result of the increased educational attainment of women, the rise of the feminist movement, and other factors. As traditional social restraints on women have loosened, domestic arrangements have moved in the direction dictated by comparative advantage—to an increasing degree, homemaking tasks are now performed by paid specialists, while the majority of women (and men) work outside the home.

Although homemaking activities are excluded from measured GDP, in a few cases goods and services that are not sold in markets are included in GDP. By far the most important are the goods and services provided by federal, state, and local governments. The protection provided by the army and navy, the transportation convenience of the interstate highway system, and the education provided by the public school system are examples of publicly provided goods and services that are not sold in markets. As market prices for publicly provided goods and services do not exist, economic statisticians add to the GDP the *costs* of providing those goods and services as rough measures of their economic value. For example, to include public education in the GDP, the statisticians add to GDP the salaries of teachers and administrators, the costs of textbooks and supplies, and the like. Similarly, the economic value of the national defense establishment is approximated, for the purposes of measuring GDP, by the *costs* of defense: the pay earned by soldiers and sailors, the costs of acquiring and maintaining weapons, and so on.

With a few exceptions, like publicly provided goods and services, GDP is calculated by adding up market values. However, not all goods and services that have a market value are counted in GDP. As we will see next, GDP includes only those goods and services that are the end products of the production process, called *final goods and services*. Goods and services that are used up in the production process are not counted in GDP.

FINAL GOODS AND SERVICES

Many goods are used in the production process. Before a baker can produce a loaf of bread, grain must be grown and harvested, then the grain must be ground

ECONOMIC NATURALIST 18.1

Why is the female labor force participation rate now more than 50 percent greater than in the 1960s?

final goods or services goods or services consumed by the ultimate user; because they are the end products of the production process, they are counted as part of GDP

intermediate goods or services goods or services used up in the production of final goods and services and therefore not counted as part of GDP

into flour, and, together with other ingredients, baked into bread. Of the three major goods that are produced during this process—the grain, the flour, and the bread—only the bread is used by consumers. Because producing the bread is the ultimate purpose of the process, the bread is called a *final good*. In general, a **final good or service** is the end product of a process, the product or service that consumers actually use. The goods or services produced on the way toward making the final product—here, the grain and the flour—are called **intermediate goods or services**.

Since we are interested in measuring only those items that are of direct economic value, *only final goods and services are included in GDP*. Intermediate goods and services are *not* included. To illustrate, suppose that the grain from the previous example has a market value of $0.50 (the price the milling company paid for the grain). The grain is then ground into flour, which has a market value of $1.20 (the price the baker paid for the flour). Finally, the flour is made into a loaf of fine French bread, worth $2.00 at the local store. In calculating the contribution of these activities to GDP, would we want to add together the values of the grain, the flour, and the bread? No, because the grain and flour are intermediate goods, valuable only because they can be used to make bread. So in this example, the total contribution to GDP is $2.00, the value of the loaf of bread, the final product.

Example 18.3 illustrates the same distinction but this time with a focus on services.

EXAMPLE 18.3

The barber and his assistant

Your barber charges $10 for a haircut. In turn, the barber pays his assistant $2 per haircut in return for sharpening the scissors, sweeping the floor, and other chores. For each haircut given, what is the total contribution of the barber and his assistant, taken together, to GDP?

The answer to this problem is $10, the price, or market value, of the haircut. The haircut is counted in GDP because it is the final service, the one that actually has value to the final user. The services provided by the assistant have value only because they contribute to the production of the haircut; thus they are not counted in GDP.

Example 18.4 illustrates that the same good can be either intermediate or final, depending on how it is used.

EXAMPLE 18.4

A good that can be either intermediate or final

Farmer Brown produces $100 worth of milk. He sells $40 worth of milk to his neighbors and uses the rest to feed his pigs, which he sells to his neighbors for $120. What is Farmer Brown's contribution to the GDP?

The final goods in this example are the $40 worth of milk and the $120 worth of pigs sold to the neighbors. Adding $40 and $120, we get $160, which is Farmer Brown's contribution to the GDP. Note that part of the milk Farmer Brown produced serves as an intermediate good and part as a final good. The $60 worth of milk that is fed to the pigs is an intermediate good, and so it is not counted in GDP. The $40 worth of milk sold to the neighbors is a final good, and so it is counted.

capital good a long-lived good, which is itself produced and used to produce other goods and services

A special type of good that is difficult to classify as intermediate or final is a capital good. A **capital good** is a long-lived good, which is itself produced and used to produce other goods and services. Factories and machines are examples of capital goods. Capital goods do not fit the definition of final goods, since their purpose is to produce other goods. On the other hand, they are not used up during the production process, except over a very long period, so they are not exactly intermediate goods either. For purposes of measuring GDP, economists have agreed to classify newly produced capital goods as final goods. Otherwise, a country that invested in its future by building modern factories and buying new machines would be counted as having a lower GDP than a country that devoted all its resources to producing consumer goods.

We have established the rule that only final goods and services (including newly produced capital goods) are counted in GDP. Intermediate goods and services, which are used up in the production of final goods and services, are not counted. In practice, however, this rule is not easy to apply, because the production process often stretches over several periods. To illustrate, recall the earlier example of the grain that was milled into flour, which in turn was baked into a loaf of French bread. The contribution of the whole process to GDP is $2, the value of the bread (the final product). Suppose, though, that the grain and the flour were produced near the end of the year 2000 and the bread was baked early the next year in 2001. In this case, should we attribute the $2 value of the bread to the GDP for the year 2000 or to the GDP for the year 2001?

Neither choice seems quite right, since part of the bread's production process occurred in each year. Part of the value of the bread should probably be counted in the year 2000 GDP and part in the year 2001 GDP. But how should we make the split? To deal with this problem, economists determine the market value of final goods and services indirectly, by adding up the *value added* by each firm in the production process. The **value added** by any firm equals the market value of its product or service minus the cost of inputs purchased from other firms. As we'll see, summing the value added by all firms (including producers of both intermediate and final goods and services) gives the same answer as simply adding together the value of final goods and services. But the value-added method eliminates the problem of dividing the value of a final good or service between two periods.

value added for any firm, the market value of its product or service minus the cost of inputs purchased from other firms

To illustrate this method, let's revisit the example of the French bread, which is the result of multiple stages of production. We have already determined that the total contribution of this production process to GDP is $2, the value of the bread. Let's show now that we can get the same answer by summing value added. Suppose that the bread is the ultimate product of three corporations: ABC Grain Company, Inc., produces grain; General Flour produces flour; and Hot'n'Fresh Baking produces the bread. If we make the same assumptions as before about the market value of the grain, the flour, and the bread, what is the value added by each of these three companies?

ABC Grain Company produces $0.50 worth of grain, with no inputs from other companies, so ABC's value added is $0.50. General Flour uses $0.50 worth of grain from ABC to produce $1.20 worth of flour. The value added by General Flour is thus the value of its product ($1.20) less the cost of purchased inputs ($0.50), or $0.70. Finally, Hot'n'Fresh Baking buys $1.20 worth of flour from General Flour and uses it to produce $2.00 worth of bread. So the value added by Hot'n'Fresh is $0.80. These calculations are summarized in Table 18.1.

TABLE 18.1
Value Added in Bread Production

Company	Revenues − Cost of purchased inputs = Value added		
ABC Grain	$0.50	$0.00	$0.50
General Flour	$1.20	$0.50	$0.70
Hot'n'Fresh	$2.00	$1.20	$0.80
Total			$2.00

You can see that summing the value added by each company gives the same contribution to GDP, $2.00, as the method based on counting final goods and services only. Basically, the value added by each firm represents the portion of the value of the final good or service that the firm creates in its stage of production. Summing the value added by all firms in the economy yields the total value of final goods and services, or GDP.

You can also see now how the value-added method solves the problem of production processes that bridge two or more periods. Suppose that the grain and flour are produced during the year 2000 but the bread is not baked until 2001. Using the value-added method, the contribution of this production process to the year 2000 GDP is the value added by the grain company plus the value added by the flour company, or $1.20. The contribution of the production process to the year 2001 GDP is the value added by the baker, which is $0.80. Thus part of the value of the final product, the bread, is counted in the GDP for each year, reflecting the fact that part of the production of the bread took place in each year.

EXERCISE 18.3

Amy's card shop receives a shipment of Valentine's Day cards in December 2000. Amy pays the wholesale distributor of the cards a total of $500. In February 2001 she sells the cards for a total of $700. What are the contributions of these transactions to GDP in the years 2000 and 2001?

We have now established that GDP is equal to the market value of final goods and services. Let's look at the last part of the definition, "produced within a country during a given period."

PRODUCED WITHIN A COUNTRY DURING A GIVEN PERIOD

The word *domestic* in the term *gross domestic product* tells us that GDP is a measure of economic activity within a given country. Thus, only production that takes place within the country's borders is counted. For example, the GDP of the United States includes the market value of *all* cars produced within U.S. borders, even if they are made in foreign-owned plants (recall Exercise 18.2). However, cars produced in Mexico by a U.S.-based company like General Motors are *not* counted.

We have seen that GDP is intended to measure the amount of production that occurs during a given period, such as the calendar year. For this reason, only goods and services that are actually produced during a particular year are included in the GDP for that year. Example 18.5 and Exercise 18.4 illustrate.

EXAMPLE 18.5   **The sale of a house and GDP**

A 20-year-old house is sold to a young family for $100,000. The family pays the real estate agent a 6 percent commission. What is the contribution of this transaction to GDP?

Because the house was not produced during the current year, its value is *not* counted in this year's GDP. (The value of the house was included in the GDP 20 years earlier, the year the house was built.) In general, purchases and sales of existing assets, such as old houses or used cars, do not contribute to the current year's GDP. However, the $6,000 fee paid to the real estate agent represents the market value of the agent's services in helping the family find the house and make the purchase. Since those services were provided during the current year, the agent's fee *is* counted in current-year GDP.

EXERCISE 18.4

Lotta Doe sells 100 shares of stock in Benson Buggywhip for $50 per share. She pays her broker a 2 percent commission for executing the sale. How does Lotta's transaction affect the current-year GDP?

RECAP **MEASURING GDP**

Gross domestic product (GDP) equals

the market value
GDP is an aggregate of the market values of the many goods and services produced in the economy.

Goods and services that are not sold in markets, such as unpaid housework, are not counted in GDP. An important exception is goods and services provided by the government, which are included in GDP at the government's cost of providing them.

of final goods and services
Final goods and services (which include capital goods, such as factories and machines) are counted in GDP. Intermediate goods and services, which are used up in the production of final goods and services, are not counted.

In practice, the value of final goods and services is determined by the value-added method. The value added by any firm equals the firm's revenue from selling its product minus the cost of inputs purchased from other firms. Summing the value added by all firms in the production process yields the value of the final good or service.

produced in a country during a given period.
Only goods and services produced within a nation's borders are included in GDP.

Only goods and services produced during the current year (or the portion of the value produced during the current year) are counted as part of the current-year GDP.

THE EXPENDITURE METHOD FOR MEASURING GDP

GDP is a measure of the quantity of goods and services *produced* by an economy. But any good or service that is produced will also be *purchased* and used by some economic agent—a consumer buying Christmas gifts or a firm investing in new machinery, for example. For many purposes, knowing not only how much is produced, but who uses it and how, is important.

Economic statisticians divide the users of the final goods and services that make up the GDP for any given year into four categories: *households, firms, governments,* and the *foreign sector* (that is, foreign purchasers of domestic products). They assume that all the final goods and services that are produced in a country in a given year will be purchased and used by members of one or more of these four groups. Furthermore, the amounts that purchasers spend on various goods and services should be equal to the market values of those goods and services. As a result, GDP can be measured with equal accuracy by either of two methods: (1) adding up the market values of all the final goods and

TABLE 18.2
Expenditure Components of U.S. GDP, 1999 (billions of dollars)

Consumption		6,254.9
Durable goods	758.1	
Nondurable goods	1,841.1	
Services	3,655.7	
Investment		1,621.6
Business fixed investment	1,166.5	
Residential investment	410.9	
Inventory investment	44.3	
Government purchases		1,628.7
Net exports		−256.8
Exports	996.3	
Imports	1,253.1	
Total: Gross domestic product		9,248.4

SOURCE: *Economic Report of the President,* February 2000.

services that are produced domestically, or (2) adding up the total amount spent by each of the four groups on final goods and services and subtracting spending on imported goods and services. The values obtained by the two methods will be the same.

Corresponding to the four groups of final users are four components of expenditure: consumption, investment, government purchases, and net exports. That is, households consume, firms invest, governments make government purchases, and the foreign sector buys the nation's exports. Table 18.2 gives the dollar values for each of these components for the U.S. economy in 1999. As the table shows, GDP for the United States in 1999 was about $9.25 trillion, roughly $34,000 per person. Detailed definitions of the components of expenditure, and their principal subcomponents, follow. As you read through them, refer to Table 18.2 to get a sense of the relative importance of each type of spending.

consumption expenditure, or consumption spending by households on goods and services, such as food, clothing, and entertainment

Consumption expenditure, or simply *consumption,* is spending by households on goods and services such as food, clothing, and entertainment. Consumption expenditure is subdivided into three subcategories:

- *Consumer durables* are long-lived consumer goods such as cars and furniture. Note that new houses are not treated as consumer durables but as part of investment.

- *Consumer nondurables* are shorter-lived goods like food and clothing.

- *Services,* a large component of consumer spending, include everything from haircuts and taxi rides to legal, financial, and educational services.

investment spending by firms on final goods and services, primarily capital goods and housing

Investment is spending by firms on final goods and services, primarily capital goods and housing. Investment is divided into three subcategories:

- *Business fixed investment* is the purchase by firms of new capital goods such as machinery, factories, and office buildings. (Remember that for the purposes of calculating GDP, long-lived capital goods are treated as final goods rather than as intermediate goods.) Firms buy capital goods to increase their capacity to produce.

- *Residential investment* is construction of new homes and apartment buildings. For GDP accounting purposes, residential investment is treated as an investment by the business sector, which then sells the homes to households.

■ *Inventory investment* is the addition of unsold goods to company inventories. In other words, the goods that a firm produces but doesn't sell during the current period are treated, for accounting purposes, as if the firm had bought those goods from itself. (This convention guarantees that production equals expenditure.) Inventory investment can take a negative value, if the value of inventories on hand falls over the course of the year.

People often refer to purchases of financial assets, such as stocks or bonds, as "investments." That use of the term is different from the definition we give here. If someone buys a share of a company's stock, they acquire partial ownership of the *existing* physical and financial assets controlled by the company. A stock purchase does not usually correspond to the creation of *new* physical capital, however, and so is not investment in the sense we are using the term in this chapter. We will generally refer to purchases of financial assets, such as stocks and bonds, as "financial investments," to distinguish them from a firm's investments in new capital goods, such as factories and machines.

Government purchases are purchases by federal, state, and local governments of final goods, such as fighter planes, and services, such as teaching in public schools. Government purchases do *not* include *transfer payments*, which are payments made by the government in return for which no current goods or services are received. Examples of transfer payments (which, again, are *not* included in government purchases) are Social Security benefits, unemployment benefits, pensions paid to government workers, and welfare payments. Interest paid on the government debt is also excluded from government purchases.

Net exports equal exports minus imports.

■ *Exports* are domestically produced final goods and services that are sold abroad.

■ *Imports* are purchases by domestic buyers of goods and services that were produced abroad. Imports are subtracted from exports to find the net amount of spending on domestically produced goods and services.

government purchases purchases by federal, state, and local governments of final goods and services; government purchases do *not* include *transfer payments,* which are payments made by the government in return for which no current goods or services are received, nor do they include interest paid on the government debt

net exports exports minus imports

A country's net exports reflect the net demand by the rest of the world for its goods and services. Net exports can be negative, since imports can exceed exports in any given year. As Table 18.2 shows, the United States had significantly greater imports than exports in 1999.

RECAP **EXPENDITURE COMPONENTS OF GDP**

GDP can be expressed as the sum of expenditures on domestically produced final goods and services. The four types of expenditure that are counted in the GDP, and the economic groups that make each type of expenditure, are as follows:

Who makes the expenditure?	Type of expenditure	Examples
Households	Consumption	Food, clothes, haircuts, new cars
Business firms	Investment	New factories and equipment, new houses, increases in inventory stocks
Governments	Government purchases	New school buildings, new military hardware, salaries of soldiers and government officials
Foreign sector	Net exports, or exports minus imports	Exported manufactured goods, legal or financial services provided by domestic residents to foreigners

---

The relationship between GDP and expenditures on goods and services can be summarized by an equation. Let

$$Y = \text{gross domestic product, or output}$$
$$C = \text{consumption expenditure}$$
$$I = \text{investment}$$
$$G = \text{government purchases}$$
$$NX = \text{net exports.}$$

Using these symbols, we can write that GDP equals the sum of the four types of expenditure algebraically as

$$Y = C + I + G + NX.$$

EXAMPLE 18.6 **Measuring GDP by production and by expenditure**

An economy produces 1,000,000 automobiles valued at $15,000 each. Of these, 700,000 are sold to consumers, 200,000 are sold to businesses, 50,000 are sold to the government, and 25,000 are sold abroad. No automobiles are imported. The automobiles left unsold at the end of the year are held in inventory by the auto producers. Find GDP in terms of (a) the market value of production and (b) the components of expenditure. You should get the same answer both ways.

The market value of the production of final goods and services in this economy is 1,000,000 autos times $15,000 per auto, or $15 billion.

To measure GDP in terms of expenditure, we must add spending on consumption, investment, government purchases, and net exports. Consumption is 700,000 autos times $15,000, or $10.5 billion. Government purchases are 50,000 autos times $15,000, or $0.75 billion. Net exports are equal to exports (25,000 autos at $15,000, or $0.375 billion) minus imports (zero), so net exports are $0.375 billion.

But what about investment? Here we must be careful. The 200,000 autos that are sold to businesses, worth $3 billion, count as investment. But notice too that the auto companies produced 1,000,000 automobiles but sold only 975,000 (700,000 + 200,000 + 50,000 + 25,000). Hence 25,000 autos were unsold at the end of the year and were added to the automobile producers' inventories. This addition to producer inventories (25,000 autos at $15,000, or $0.375 billion) counts as inventory investment, which is part of total investment. Thus total investment spending equals the $3 billion worth of autos sold to businesses plus the $0.375 billion in inventory investment, or $3.375 billion.

Recapitulating, in this economy consumption is $10.5 billion, investment (including inventory investment) is $3.375 billion, government purchases equal $0.75 billion, and net exports are $0.375 billion. Summing these four components of expenditure yields $15 billion—the same value for GDP that we got by calculating the market value of production.

EXERCISE 18.5

Extending Example 18.6, suppose that 25,000 of the automobiles purchased by households are imported rather than domestically produced. Domestic production remains at 1,000,000 autos valued at $15,000 each. Once again, find GDP in terms of (a) the market value of production and (b) the components of expenditure.

GDP AND THE INCOMES OF CAPITAL AND LABOR

The GDP can be thought of equally well as a measure of total production or as a measure of total expenditure—either method of calculating the GDP gives the same final answer. There is yet a third way to think of the GDP, which is as the *incomes of capital and labor.*

Whenever a good or service is produced or sold, the revenue from the sale is distributed to the workers and the owners of the capital involved in the production of the good or service. Thus, except for some technical adjustments that we will ignore, GDP also equals labor income plus capital income. *Labor income* (equal to about 75 percent of GDP) comprises wages, salaries, and the incomes of the self-employed. *Capital income* (about 25 percent of GDP) is made up of payments to owners of physical capital (such as factories, machines, and office buildings) and intangible capital (such as copyrights and patents). The components of capital income include items such as profits earned by businessowners, the rents paid to owners of land or buildings, interest received by bondholders, and the royalties received by the holders of copyrights or patents. Both labor income and capital income are to be understood as measured prior to payment of taxes; ultimately, of course, a portion of both types of income is captured by the government in the form of tax collections.

Figure 18.2 may help you visualize the three equivalent ways of thinking about GDP: the market value of production, the total value of expenditure, and the sum of labor income and capital income. The figure also roughly captures the relative importance of the expenditure and income components. About 65 percent of expenditure is consumption spending, about 20 percent is government purchases, and the rest is investment spending and net exports. (Actually, as Table 18.2 or Figure 17.5 shows, net exports have been negative in recent years, reflecting the U.S. trade deficit.) As we mentioned, labor income is about 75 percent of total income, with capital income making up the rest.

FIGURE 18.2
The Three Faces of GDP.
The GDP can be expressed equally well as (1) the market value of production, (2) total expenditure (consumption, investment, government purchases, net exports), or (3) total income (labor income and capital income).

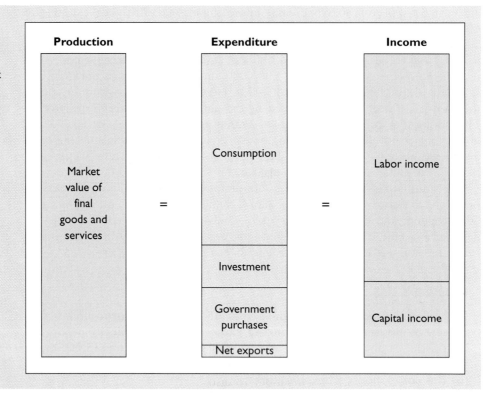

NOMINAL GDP VERSUS REAL GDP

As a measure of the total production of an economy over a given period, such as a particular year, GDP is useful in comparisons of economic activity in different places. For example, GDP data for the year 2000, broken down state by state, could be used to compare aggregate production in New York and California during that year. However, economists are interested in comparing levels of economic activity not only in different *locations* but *over time* as well. For example, a President who is running for reelection on the basis of successful economic policies might want to know by how much output in the U.S. economy had increased during his term.

Using GDP to compare economic activity at two different points in time may give misleading answers, however, as the following example shows. Suppose for the sake of illustration that the economy produces only pizzas and calzones. The prices and quantities of the two goods in the years 1996 and 2000, the beginning and end of the President's term, are shown in Table 18.3. If we calculate GDP in each year as the market value of production, we find that the GDP for 1996 is (10 pizzas × $10/pizza) + (15 calzones × $5/calzone) = $175. The GDP for 2000 is (20 pizzas × $12/pizza) + (30 calzones × $6/calzone) = $420. Comparing the GDP for the year 2000 to the GDP for the year 1996, we might conclude that it is 2.4 times greater ($420/$175).

TABLE 18.3
Prices and Quantities in 1996 and 2000

	Quantity of pizzas	Price of pizzas	Quantity of calzones	Price of calzones
1996	10	$10	15	$5
2000	20	$12	30	$6

But look more closely at the data given in Table 18.3. Can you see what is wrong with this conclusion? The quantities of both pizzas and calzones produced in the year 2000 are exactly twice the quantities produced in the year 1996. If economic activity, as measured by actual production of both goods, exactly doubled over the 4 years, why do the calculated values of GDP show a greater increase?

The answer, as you also can see from the table, is that prices as well as quantities rose between 1996 and 2000. Because of the increase in prices, the *market value* of production grew more over those 4 years than the *physical volume* of production. So in this case, GDP is a misleading gauge of economic growth during the President's term, since the physical quantities of the goods and services produced in any given year, not the dollar values, are what determine people's economic well-being. Indeed, if the prices of pizzas and calzones had risen 2.4 times between 1996 and 2000, GDP would have risen 2.4 times as well, with no increase in physical production! In that case, the claim that the economy's (physical) output had more than doubled during the President's term would obviously be wrong.

As this example shows, if we want to use GDP to compare economic activity at different points in time, we need some method of excluding the effects of price changes. In other words, we need to adjust for inflation. To do so, economists use a common set of prices to value quantities produced in different years. The standard approach is to pick a particular year, called the *base year,* and use the prices from that year to calculate the market value of output. When GDP is calculated using the prices from a base year, rather than the current year's prices, it is called **real GDP**, to indicate that it is a measure of real physical production. Real GDP is GDP adjusted for inflation. To distinguish real GDP, in which quantities produced are valued at base-year prices, from GDP valued at current-year prices, economists refer to the latter measure as **nominal GDP.**

real GDP a measure of GDP in which the quantities produced are valued at the prices in a base year rather than at current prices; real GDP measures the actual *physical volume* of production

nominal GDP a measure of GDP in which the quantities produced are valued at current-year prices; nominal GDP measures the *current dollar value of production*

Calculating the change in real GDP over the President's term

EXAMPLE 18.7

Using data from Table 18.3 and assuming that 1996 is the base year, find real GDP for the years 2000 and 1996. By how much did real output grow between 1996 and 2000?

To find real GDP for the year 2000, we must value the quantities produced that year using the prices in the base year, 1996. Using the data in Table 18.3:

Year 2000 real GDP = (year 2000 quantity of pizzas × year 1996 price of
                     pizzas) + (year 2000 quantity of calzones × year
                     1996 price of calzones)
                   = (20 × \$10) + (30 × \$5)
                   = \$350.

The real GDP of this economy in the year 2000 is \$350. What is the real GDP for 1996?

By definition, the real GDP for 1996 equals 1996 quantities valued at base-year prices. The base year in this example happens to be 1996, so real GDP for 1996 equals 1996 quantities valued at 1996 prices, which is the same as nominal GDP for 1996. In general, in the base year, real GDP and nominal GDP are the same. We already found nominal GDP for 1996, \$175, so that is also the real GDP for 1996.

We can now determine how much real production has actually grown over the 4-year period. Since real GDP was \$175 in 1996 and \$350 in 2000, the physical volume of production doubled between 1996 and 2000. This conclusion makes good sense, since Table 18.3 shows that the production of both pizzas and calzones exactly doubled over the period. By using real GDP, we have eliminated the effects of price changes and obtained a reasonable measure of the actual change in physical production over the 4-year span.

Of course, the production of all goods will not necessarily grow in equal proportion, as in Example 18.7. Exercise 18.6 asks you to find real GDP when pizza and calzone production grow at different rates.

EXERCISE 18.6

Suppose production and prices of pizza and calzone in 1996 and 2000 are as follows:

	Quantity of pizzas	Price of pizzas	Quantity of calzones	Price of calzones
1996	10	$10	15	$5
2000	30	$12	30	$6

These data are the same as those in Table 18.3, except that pizza production has tripled rather than doubled between 1996 and 2000. Find real GDP in 2000 and 1996, and calculate the growth in real output over the 4-year period. (Continue to assume that 1996 is the base year.)

If you complete Exercise 18.6, you will find that the growth in real GDP between 1996 and 2000 reflects a sort of average of the growth in physical production of pizzas and calzones. Real GDP therefore remains a useful measure of overall physical production, even when the production of different goods and services grows at different rates.

The method of calculating real GDP just described was followed for many decades by the Bureau of Economic Analysis (BEA), the U.S. government agency responsible for GDP statistics. However, in recent years the BEA has adopted a more complicated procedure of determining real GDP, called *chain weighting*. The new procedure makes the official real GDP data less sensitive to the particular base year chosen. However, the chain-weighting and traditional approaches share the basic idea of valuing output in terms of base-year prices, and the results obtained by the two methods are generally similar.

RECAP **NOMINAL GDP VERSUS REAL GDP**

Real GDP is calculated using the prices of goods and services that prevailed in a base year rather than in the current year. Nominal GDP is calculated using current-year prices. Real GDP is GDP adjusted for inflation; it may be thought of as measuring the physical volume of production. Comparisons of economic activity at different times should always be done using real GDP, not nominal GDP.

REAL GDP IS NOT THE SAME AS ECONOMIC WELL-BEING

Government policymakers pay close attention to real GDP, often behaving as if the greater the GDP, the better. However, real GDP is *not* the same as economic well-being. At best, it is an imperfect measure of economic well-being because, for the most part, it captures only those goods and services that are priced and sold in markets. Many factors that contribute to people's economic well-being are not priced and sold in markets and thus are largely or even entirely omitted from GDP. Maximizing real GDP is not, therefore, always the right goal for government policymakers. Whether or not policies that increase GDP will also make people better off has to be determined on a case-by-case basis.[2]

To understand why an increase in real GDP does not always promote economic well-being, let's look at some factors that are not included in GDP but do affect whether people are better off.

LEISURE TIME

Most Americans (and most people in other industrialized countries as well) work many fewer hours than their great-grandparents did 100 years ago. Early in the twentieth century some industrial workers—steelworkers, for example—worked as many as 12 hours a day, 7 days a week. Today, the 40-hour workweek is typical. Today, Americans also tend to start working later in life (after college or graduate school), and, in many cases, they are able to retire earlier. The increased leisure time available to workers in the United States and other industrialized countries—which allows them to pursue many worthwhile activities, including being with family and friends, participating in sports and hobbies, and pursuing cultural and educational activities—is a major benefit of living in a wealthy society. These extra hours of leisure are not priced in markets, however, and therefore are not reflected in GDP.

Why do people work fewer hours today than their great-grandparents did?

Americans start work later in life, retire earlier, and in many cases work fewer hours per week than people of 50 or 100 years ago. What accounts for these trends?

The *opportunity cost* of working less—retiring earlier, for example, or working fewer hours per week—is the earnings you forgo by not working. If you can make $400 per week at a summer job in a department store, for example, then leaving the job 2 weeks early to take a trip with some friends has an opportunity cost of $800. The fact that people are working fewer hours today suggests that their opportunity cost of forgone earnings is lower than their grandparents' and great-grandparents' opportunity cost. Why this difference?

Over the past century, rapid economic growth in the United States and other industrialized countries has greatly increased the purchasing power of the average worker's wages (see Chapter 21). In other words, the typical worker today can buy more goods and services with his or her hourly earnings than ever before. This fact would seem to suggest that the opportunity cost of forgone earnings (measured in terms of what those earnings can buy) is greater, not smaller, today than in earlier times. But because the buying power of wages is so much higher today than in the past, Americans can achieve a reasonable standard of living by working fewer hours than they did in the past. Thus, while your grandparents may have had to work long hours to pay the rent or put food on the table, today the extra income from working long hours is more likely to buy relative luxuries, like nicer clothes or a fancier car. Because such discretionary purchases are easier to give up than basic food and shelter, the true opportunity cost of forgone earnings is lower today than it was 50 years ago. As the opportunity cost of leisure has fallen, Americans have chosen to enjoy more of it.

NONMARKET ECONOMIC ACTIVITIES

Not all economically important activities are bought and sold in markets; with a few exceptions, such as government services, nonmarket economic activities are omitted from GDP. We mentioned earlier the example of unpaid housekeeping

ECONOMIC NATURALIST 18.2

---

[2]For a critique of the use of GDP as a measure of economic well-being, see Clifford Cobb, Ted Halstead, and Jonathan Rowe, "If the GDP Is Up, Why Is America Down?" *The Atlantic Monthly*, October 1995.

services. Another example is volunteer services, such as the volunteer fire and rescue squads that serve many small towns. The fact that these unpaid services are left out of GDP does *not* mean that they are unimportant. The problem is that, because there are no market prices and quantities for unpaid services, estimating their market values is very difficult.

How far do economists go wrong by leaving nonmarket economic activities out of GDP? The answer depends on the type of economy being studied. Although nonmarket economic activities exist in all economies, they are particularly important in poor economies. For example, in rural villages of developing countries, people commonly trade services with each other or cooperate on various tasks without exchanging any money. Families in these communities also tend to be relatively self-sufficient, growing their own food and providing many of their own basic services (recall the many skills of the Nepalese cook Birkhaman, described in Chapter 3). Because such nonmarket economic activities are not counted in official statistics, GDP data may substantially understate the true amount of economic activity in the poorest countries. In 1998 the official GDP per person in Nepal was about $210, an amount that seems impossibly low. Part of the explanation for this figure is that because the Nepalese seldom use formal markets, many economic activities that would ordinarily be included in GDP are excluded from it in Nepal.

Closely related to nonmarket activities is what is called the *underground economy*, which includes transactions that are never reported to government officials and data collectors. The underground economy encompasses both legal and illegal activities, from informal babysitting jobs to organized crime. For instance, some people pay temporary or part-time workers like housecleaners and painters in cash, which allows these workers to avoid paying taxes on their income. Economists who have tried to estimate the value of such services by studying how much cash the public holds have concluded that these sorts of transactions are quite important, even in advanced industrial economies.

ENVIRONMENTAL QUALITY AND RESOURCE DEPLETION

China has recently experienced tremendous growth in real GDP. But in expanding its manufacturing base, it has also suffered a severe decline in air and water quality. Increased pollution certainly detracts from the quality of life, but because air and water quality are not bought and sold in markets, the Chinese GDP does not reflect this downside of their economic growth.

The exploitation of finite natural resources also tends to be overlooked in GDP. When an oil company pumps and sells a barrel of oil, GDP increases by the value of the oil. But the fact that there is one less barrel of oil in the ground, waiting to be pumped sometime in the future, is not reflected in GDP.

A number of efforts have been made to incorporate factors like air quality and resource depletion into a comprehensive measure of GDP. Doing so is difficult, since it often involves placing a dollar value on intangibles, like having a clean river to swim in instead of a dirty one. But the fact that the benefits of environmental quality and resource conservation are hard to measure in dollars and cents does not mean that they are unimportant.

QUALITY OF LIFE

What makes a particular town or city an attractive place in which to live? Some desirable features you might think of are reflected in GDP: spacious, well-constructed homes, good restaurants and stores, a variety of entertainment, and high-quality medical services. However, other indicators of the good life are not sold in markets and so may be omitted from GDP. Examples include a low crime rate, minimal traffic congestion, active civic organizations, and open space. Thus, citizens of a rural area may be justified in opposing the construction of a new shopping center because of its presumed negative effect on the quality of life— even though the new center may increase GDP.

POVERTY AND ECONOMIC INEQUALITY

GDP measures the *total* quantity of goods and services produced and sold in an economy, but it conveys no information about who gets to enjoy those goods and services. Two countries may have identical GDPs but differ radically in the distribution of economic welfare across the population. Suppose, for example, that in one country—call it Equalia—most people have a comfortable middle-class existence; both extreme poverty and extreme wealth are rare. But in another country, Inequalia—which has the same real GDP as Equalia—a few wealthy families control the economy, and the majority of the population lives in poverty. While most people would say that Equalia has a better economic situation overall, that judgment would not be reflected in the GDPs of the two countries, which are the same.

In the United States absolute poverty has been declining. Today, many families whose income is below today's official "poverty line" (in 1999, $16,700 for a family of four) own a television, a car, and in some cases their own home. Some economists have argued that people who are considered poor today live as well as many middle-class people did in the 1950s.

But, though absolute poverty seems to be decreasing in the United States, inequality of income has generally been rising. The chief executive officer of a large U.S. corporation may earn hundreds of times what the typical worker in the same firm receives. Psychologists tell us that people's economic satisfaction depends not only on their absolute economic position—the quantity and quality of food, clothing, and shelter they have—but on what they have compared to what others have. If you own an old, beat-up car but are the only person in your neighborhood to have a car, you may feel privileged. But if everyone else in the neighborhood owns a luxury car, you are likely to be less satisfied. To the extent that such comparisons affect people's well-being, inequality matters as well as absolute poverty. Again, because GDP focuses on total production rather than on the distribution of output, it does not capture the effects of inequality.

BUT GDP IS RELATED TO ECONOMIC WELL-BEING

You might conclude from the list of important factors omitted from the official figures that GDP is useless as a measure of economic welfare. Indeed, numerous critics have made that claim. Clearly, in evaluating the effects of a proposed economic policy, considering only the likely effects on GDP is not sufficient. Planners must also ask whether the policy will affect aspects of economic well-being that are not captured in GDP. Environmental regulations may reduce production of steel, for example, which reduces the GDP. But that fact is not a sufficient basis on which to decide whether such regulations are good or bad. The right way to decide such questions is to apply the *cost-benefit principle* (see Chapter 1). Are the benefits of cleaner air worth more to people than the costs the regulations impose in terms of lost output and lost jobs? If so, then the regulations should be adopted; otherwise, they should not.

While looking at the effects of a proposed policy on real GDP is not a good enough basis on which to evaluate a policy, nevertheless real GDP per person *does* tend to be positively associated with many things people value, including a high material standard of living, better health and life expectancies, and better education. We discuss next some of the ways in which a higher real GDP implies greater economic well-being.

AVAILABILITY OF GOODS AND SERVICES

Obviously, citizens of a country with a high GDP are likely to possess more and better goods and services (after all, that is what GDP measures). On average, people in high-GDP countries enjoy larger, better-constructed, and more comfortable homes, higher-quality food and clothing, a greater variety of entertainment and cultural opportunities, better access to transportation and travel, better communications and sanitation, and other advantages. While social commentators may question the value of material consumption—and we agree that riches do not necessarily bring happiness or peace of mind—the majority of people in the world place great importance on achieving material prosperity. Throughout history people have made tremendous sacrifices and taken great risks to secure a higher standard of living for themselves and their families. In fact, to a great extent the United States was built by people who were willing to leave their native lands, often at great personal hardship, in hopes of bettering their economic condition.

HEALTH AND EDUCATION

Beyond an abundance of consumer goods, a high GDP brings other more basic advantages. Table 18.4 shows the differences between rich and poor countries with regard to some important indicators of well-being, including life expectancy, infant and child mortality rates, number of doctors, measures of nutrition, and educational opportunity. Three groups of countries are compared: (1) developing countries as a group (total population, 4.5 billion); (2) the least developed countries (25 countries with a total population of about 600 million); and (3) the industrialized countries (25 countries, including the United States, Canada, the Western

TABLE 18.4
GDP and Basic Indicators of Well-Being

Indicator	All developing countries	Least developed countries	Industrialized countries
GDP per person (U.S. dollars)	1,294	274	25,879
Life expectancy at birth (years)	64.4	51.7	77.7
Infant mortality rate (per 1,000 live births)	64	104	6
Under-5 mortality rate (per 1,000 live births)	94	162	7
Doctors (per 100,000 people)	76	14	253
Daily calories per person	2,628	2,095	3,377
Daily protein per person (grams)	66.4	51.4	104.8
Primary enrollment rate (as % of age group)	85.7	60.4	99.9
Secondary enrollment rate (as % of age group)	60.4	31.2	96.2
Adult literacy rate (%)	70.4	49.2	98.6

SOURCE: United Nations, *Human Development Report*, 1999, available at http://www.undp.org/hdro. All data are for 1997, except doctors per 100,000 people (1993), calorie consumption (1996), and the adult literacy rate (1995).

European countries, and Japan, with a total population of 850 million). As the first row of Table 18.4 shows, these three groups of countries have radically different levels of GDP per person. Most notably, GDP per person in the industrialized countries is more than 90 times that of the least developed countries.

How do these large differences in GDP relate to other measures of well-being? Table 18.4 shows that on some of the most basic measures of human welfare, the developing countries fare much worse than the industrial countries. A child born in one of the least developed countries has greater than a 10 percent (104/1,000) chance of dying before its first birthday and more than a 16 percent (162/1,000) chance of dying before its fifth birthday. The corresponding figures for the industrialized countries are 0.6 percent (6/1000) and 0.7 percent (7/1000), respectively. A child born in an industrialized country has a life expectancy of about 78 years, compared to about 52 years for a child born in one of the least developed countries. Superior nutrition, sanitation, and medical services in the richer countries account for these large discrepancies in basic welfare, differences that are shown clearly in the data of Table 18.4. For example, the table shows that people in industrialized countries consume half again as many calories and twice as much protein per day as people in the least developed countries. For treatment of the sick, industrialized countries have about 253 doctors per 100,000 people, compared to 14 doctors per 100,000 people in the least developed countries.

On another important dimension of human well-being, literacy and education rates, high-GDP countries also have the advantage. As Table 18.4 shows, in the industrialized countries the percentage of adults who can read and write exceeds 98 percent, about twice the percentage (49 percent) in the poorest developing countries. The percentage of children of primary-school age who are enrolled in school is virtually 100 percent in industrialized countries, compared to about 60 percent in the least developed countries. At the secondary (high school) level the difference is even greater, with about 96 percent of children enrolled in industrialized countries and 31 percent enrolled in the poorest countries. Furthermore, enrollment rates do not capture important differences in the quality of education available in rich and poor countries, as measured by indicators such as the educational backgrounds of teachers and student-teacher ratios. Once again, the average person in an industrialized country seems to be better off than the average person in a poor developing country.

A child born in one of the least developed countries has a 16 percent chance of dying before its fifth birthday.

Why do far fewer children complete high school in poor countries than in rich countries?

One possible explanation is that people in poor countries place a lower priority on getting an education than people in rich countries. But immigrants from poor countries often put a heavy emphasis on education—though it may be that people who emigrate from poor countries are unrepresentative of the population as a whole.

An economic naturalist's explanation for the lower schooling rates in poor countries would rely not on cultural differences but on differences in *opportunity cost.* In poor societies, most of which are heavily agricultural, children are an important source of labor. Beyond a certain age, sending children to school imposes a high opportunity cost on the family. Children who are in school are not available to help with planting, harvesting, and other tasks that must be done if the family is to survive. In addition, the cost of books and school supplies imposes a major hardship on poor families. In rich, nonagricultural countries, school-age children have few work opportunities, and their potential earnings are small relative to other sources of family income. The low opportunity cost of sending children to school in rich countries is an important reason for the higher enrollment rates in those countries.

ECONOMIC NATURALIST 18.3

In Chapter 20 we will discuss the costs and benefits of economic growth—which in practice means growth in real GDP per person—in greater depth. In that context we will return to the question of whether a growing real GDP is necessarily equated with greater economic well-being.

> **RECAP** | **REAL GDP AND ECONOMIC WELL-BEING**
>
> Real GDP is at best an imperfect measure of economic well-being. Among the factors affecting well-being omitted from real GDP are the availability of leisure time, nonmarket services such as unpaid homemaking and volunteer services, environmental quality and resource conservation, and quality-of-life indicators such as a low crime rate. The GDP also does not reflect the degree of economic inequality in a country. Because real GDP is not the same as economic well-being, proposed policies should not be evaluated strictly in terms of whether or not they increase the GDP.
>
> Although GDP is not the same as economic well-being, it is positively associated with many things that people value, including a higher material standard of living, better health, longer life expectancies, and higher rates of literacy and educational attainment. This relationship between real GDP and economic well-being has led many people to emigrate from poor nations in search of a better life and has motivated policymakers in developing countries to try to increase their nations' rates of economic growth.

THE UNEMPLOYMENT RATE

In assessing the level of economic activity in a country, economists look at a variety of statistics. Besides real GDP, one statistic that receives a great deal of attention, both from economists and from the general public, is the rate of unemployment. The unemployment rate is a sensitive indicator of conditions in the labor market. When the unemployment rate is low, jobs are secure and relatively easier to find. Low unemployment is often associated with improving wages and working conditions as well, as employers compete to attract and retain workers.

We will discuss labor markets and unemployment in detail in Chapter 21. This chapter will explain how the unemployment rate and some related statistics are defined and measured. It will close with a discussion of the costs of unemployment, both to the unemployed and to the economy as a whole.

MEASURING UNEMPLOYMENT

In the United States, defining and measuring unemployment is the responsibility of the Bureau of Labor Statistics, or BLS. Each month the BLS surveys about 60,000 randomly selected households. Each person in those households who is 16 years or older is placed in one of three categories:

1. *Employed.* A person is employed if he or she worked full-time or part-time (even for a few hours) during the past week or is on vacation or sick leave from a regular job.

2. *Unemployed.* A person is unemployed if he or she did not work during the preceding week but made some effort to find work (for example, by going to a job interview) in the past 4 weeks.

3. *Out of the labor force.* A person is considered to be out of the labor force if he or she did not work in the past week and did not look for work in the past 4 weeks. In other words, people who are neither employed nor unemployed (in the sense of looking for work but not being able to find it) are "out of the labor force." Full-time students, unpaid homemakers, retirees, and people unable to work because of disabilities are examples of people who are out of the labor force.

Based on the results of the survey, the BLS estimates how many people in the whole country fit into each of the three categories.

To find the unemployment rate, the BLS must first calculate the size of the *labor force*. The **labor force** is defined as the total number of employed and unemployed people in the economy (the first two categories of respondents to the BLS survey). The **unemployment rate** is then defined as the number of unemployed people divided by the labor force. Notice that people who are out of the labor force (because they are in school, have retired, or are disabled, for example) are not counted as unemployed and thus do not affect the unemployment rate. In general, a high rate of unemployment indicates that the economy is performing poorly.

Another useful statistic is the **participation rate,** or the percentage of the working-age population in the labor force (that is, the percentage that is either employed or looking for work). Figure 18.1 showed participation rates for American women and men since 1960. The participation rate is calculated by dividing the labor force by the working-age (16+) population.

Table 18.5 illustrates the calculation of key labor market statistics, using data based on the BLS survey for February 2000. In that month unemployment was at the unusually low level of 4.1 percent of the labor force. The participation rate was 67.6 percent; that is, about two out of every three adults had a job or were looking for work. Figure 18.3 shows the U.S. unemployment rate since 1960. Unemployment rates were exceptionally low—just above 4 percent—in the late 1960s and the late 1990s. By this measure, the latter part of the 1990s was an exceptionally good time for American workers.

labor force the total number of employed and unemployed people in the economy

unemployment rate the number of unemployed people divided by the labor force

participation rate the percentage of the working-age population in the labor force (that is, the percentage that is either employed or looking for work)

TABLE 18.5
U.S. Employment Data, February 2000 (in millions)

Employed	135.36
Plus:	
Unemployed	5.80
Equals: Labor force	141.16
Plus:	
Not in labor force	67.74
Equals:	
Working-age (over 16) population	208.90

Unemployment rate = unemployed/labor force = 5.80/141.16 = 4.1%
Participation rate = labor force/working-age population = 141.16/208.90 = 67.6%

SOURCE: Bureau of Labor Statistics, http://stats.bls.gov/.

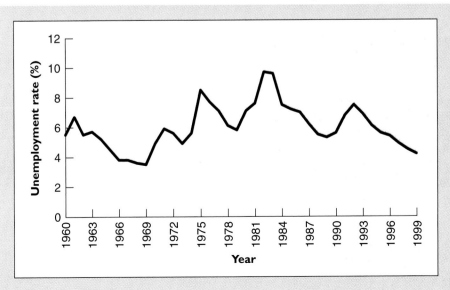

FIGURE 18.3
The U.S. Unemployment Rate since 1960.
The unemployment rate— the fraction of the U.S. labor force that is unemployed— was just above 4 percent in the late 1990s, the lowest recorded rate since the latter part of the 1960s.

EXERCISE 18.7

African-Americans generally have higher unemployment rates than the population as the whole. In February 2000, BLS statistics for the African-American population were:

Employed	15.164 million
Unemployed	1.359 million
Not in the labor force	8.534 million

Find the labor force, the working-age population, the unemployment rate, and the participation rate.

THE COSTS OF UNEMPLOYMENT

Unemployment imposes *economic, psychological,* and *social* costs on a nation. From an economic perspective, the main cost of unemployment is the output that is lost because the workforce is not fully utilized. Much of the burden of the reduced output is borne by the unemployed themselves, whose incomes fall when they are not working and whose skills may deteriorate from lack of use. However, society at large also bears part of the economic cost of unemployment. For example, workers who become unemployed are liable to stop paying taxes and start receiving government support payments, such as unemployment benefits. This net drain on the government's budget is a cost to all taxpayers.

The *psychological* costs of unemployment are felt primarily by unemployed workers and their families. Studies show that lengthy periods of unemployment can lead to a loss of self-esteem, feelings of loss of control over one's life, depression, and even suicidal behavior.[3] The unemployed worker's family is likely to feel increased psychological stress, compounded by the economic difficulties created by the loss of income.

The *social* costs of unemployment are a result of the economic and psychological effects. People who have been unemployed for a while tend not only to face severe financial difficulties but also to feel anger, frustration, and despair. Not surprisingly, increases in unemployment tend to be associated with increases in crime, domestic violence, alcoholism, drug abuse, and other social problems. The costs created by these problems are borne not only by the unemployed but by society in general, as more public resources must be spent to counteract these problems—for example, by hiring more police to control crime.

THE DURATION OF UNEMPLOYMENT

In assessing the impact of unemployment on jobless people, economists must know how long individual workers have been without work. Generally, the longer a person has been out of work, the more severe are the economic and psychological costs that person will face. People who are unemployed for only a few weeks, for example, are not likely to suffer a serious reduction in their standard of living, since for a short period they can draw upon their savings and perhaps on government benefits. Nor would we expect someone who is unemployed for only a short time to experience psychological problems such as depression or loss of self-esteem, at least not to the extent as someone who has been out of work for months or years.

---

[3]For a survey of the literature on the psychological effects of unemployment, see William Darity, Jr., and Arthur H. Goldsmith, "Social Psychology, Unemployment and Macroeconomics," *Journal of Economic Perspectives,* 10:121–140, Winter 1996.

In its surveys, therefore, the BLS asks respondents how long they have been unemployed. A period during which an individual is continuously unemployed is called an **unemployment spell**; it begins when the worker becomes unemployed and ends when the worker either finds a job or leaves the labor force. (Remember, people outside the labor force are not counted as unemployed.) The length of an unemployment spell is called its **duration**. The duration of unemployment rises during recessions, reflecting the greater difficulty of finding work during those periods.

At any given time a substantial fraction of unemployed workers has been unemployed for 6 months or more; we will refer to this group as the *long-term unemployed*. Long-term unemployment creates the highest economic, psychological, and social costs, both for the unemployed themselves and for society as a whole.

Although long-term unemployment is a serious problem, many unemployment spells are quite short. For example, in June 1999, nearly 43 percent of the unemployed had been out of work for just 5 weeks or less, and another 29 percent had been unemployed for 5 to 14 weeks. In other words, only about 28 percent of the unemployed had been without a job for as long as 14 weeks (about 3 months). These statistics are a bit deceptive, however, because short unemployment spells can arise from two very different patterns of labor-market experience. Some people have short unemployment spells that end in their finding a stable long-term job. For the most part, these workers, whom we will refer to as the *short-term unemployed,* do not bear a high cost of unemployment. But other workers have short unemployment spells that typically end either in their withdrawal from the labor force or in a short-term or temporary job that soon leaves the worker unemployed again. Workers whose unemployment spells are broken up by brief periods of employment or withdrawal from the labor force are referred to as the *chronically unemployed*. In terms of the costs of unemployment, the experience of these workers is similar to that of the long-term unemployed.

unemployment spell a period during which an individual is continuously unemployed

duration the length of an unemployment spell

THE UNEMPLOYMENT RATE VERSUS "TRUE" UNEMPLOYMENT

Like GDP measurement, unemployment measurement has its critics. Most of them argue that the official unemployment rate understates the true extent of unemployment. They point in particular to two groups of people who are not counted among the unemployed: so-called *discouraged workers* and *involuntary part-time workers.*

Discouraged workers are people who say they would like to have a job but have not made an effort to find one in the past 4 weeks. Often, discouraged workers tell the survey takers that they have not searched for work because they have tried without success in the past, or because they are convinced that labor-market conditions are such that they will not be able to find a job. Because they have not sought work in the past 4 weeks, discouraged workers are counted as being out of the labor force rather than unemployed. Some observers have suggested that treating discouraged workers as unemployed would provide a more accurate picture of the labor market.

Involuntary part-time workers are people who say they would like to work full-time but are able to find only part-time work. Because they do have jobs, involuntary part-time workers are counted as employed rather than unemployed. Some economists have suggested that these workers should be counted as partially unemployed.

In response to these criticisms, in recent years the BLS has released special unemployment rates that include estimates of the number of discouraged workers and involuntary part-time workers. In February 2000, when the official unemployment rate was 4.1 percent (see Table 18.5), the BLS calculated that if both

discouraged workers people who say they would like to have a job but have not made an effort to find one in the past 4 weeks

discouraged workers and involuntary part-time workers were counted as unemployed, the unemployment rate would have been 7.6 percent. So the problem of discouraged and underemployed workers appears to be fairly significant.

Whether in an official or adjusted version, the unemployment rate is a good overall indicator of labor-market conditions. A high unemployment rate tends to be bad news even for those people who are employed, since raises and promotions are hard to come by in a "slack" labor market. We will discuss the causes and cures of unemployment at some length in Chapter 21 and subsequent chapters.

■ SUMMARY ■

- The basic measure of an economy's output is *gross domestic product (GDP)*, the market value of the final goods and services produced in a country during a given period. Expressing output in terms of market values allows economists to aggregate the millions of goods and services produced in a modern economy.

- Only *final goods and services* (which include *capital goods*) are counted in GDP, since they are the only goods and services that directly benefit final users. *Intermediate goods and services,* which are used up in the production of final goods and services, are not counted in GDP, nor are sales of existing assets, such as a 20-year-old house. Summing the value added by each firm in the production process is a useful method of determining the value of final goods and services.

- GDP can also be expressed as the sum of four types of expenditure: *consumption, investment, government purchases,* and *net exports.* These four types of expenditure correspond to the spending of households, firms, the government, and the foreign sector, respectively.

- To compare levels of GDP over time, economists must eliminate the effects of inflation. They do so by measuring the market value of goods and services in terms of the prices in a base year. GDP measured in this way is called *real GDP,* while GDP measured in terms of current-year prices is called *nominal GDP.* Real GDP should always be used in making comparisons of economic activity over time.

- Real GDP per person is an imperfect measure of economic well-being. With a few exceptions, notably government purchases of goods and services (which are included in GDP at their cost of production), GDP includes only those goods and services sold in markets. It excludes important factors that affect people's well-being, such as the amount of leisure time available to them, the value of unpaid or volunteer services, the quality of the environment, quality of life indicators such as the crime rate, and the degree of economic inequality.

- Real GDP is still a useful indicator of economic well-being, however. Countries with a high real GDP per person not only enjoy high average standards of living, they also tend to have higher life expectancies, low rates of infant and child mortality, and high rates of school enrollment and literacy.

- The unemployment rate, perhaps the best-known indicator of the state of the labor market, is based on surveys conducted by the Bureau of Labor Statistics. The surveys classify all respondents over age 16 as employed, unemployed, or not in the labor force. The *labor force* is the sum of employed and unemployed workers—that is, people who have a job or are looking for one. The *unemployment rate* is calculated as the number of unemployed workers divided by the labor force. The *participation rate* is the percentage of the working-age population that is in the labor force.

- The costs of employment include the economic cost of lost output, the psychological costs borne by unemployed workers and their families, and the social costs associated with problems like increased crime and violence. The greatest costs are imposed by long *unemployment spells* (periods of unemployment). Critics of the official unemployment rate argue that it understates "true" unemployment by excluding *discouraged workers* and involuntary part-time workers.

■ KEY TERMS ■

capital good (458)	government purchases (463)	nominal GDP (467)
consumption expenditure (462)	gross domestic product (GDP) (455)	participation rate (475)
discouraged workers (477)	intermediate goods and services (462)	real GDP (467)
duration (of an unemployment spell) (477)	investment (462)	unemployment rate (475)
	labor force (475)	unemployment spell (477)
final goods and services (458)	net exports (463)	value added (459)

▪ REVIEW QUESTIONS ▪

1. Why do economists use market values when calculating GDP? What is the economic rationale for giving high-value items more weight in GDP than low-value items?

2. A large part of the agricultural sector in developing countries is subsistence farming, in which much of the food that is produced is consumed by the farmer and the farmer's family. Discuss the implications of this fact for the measurement of GDP in poor countries.

3. Give examples of each of the four types of aggregate expenditure. Which of the four represents the largest share of GDP in the United States? Can an expenditure component be negative? Explain.

4. Al's Shoeshine Stand shined 1,000 pairs of shoes last year and 1,200 pairs this year. He charged $4 for a shine last year and $5 this year. If last year is taken as the base year, find Al's contribution to both nominal GDP and real GDP in both years. Which measure would be better to use if you were trying to measure the change in Al's productivity over the past year? Why?

5. Would you say that real GDP per person is a useful measure of economic well-being? Defend your answer.

6. True or false, and explain: A high participation rate in an economy implies a low unemployment rate.

7. What are the costs of a high unemployment rate? Do you think providing more generous government benefits to the unemployed would increase these costs, reduce these costs, or leave them unchanged? Discuss.

▪ PROBLEMS ▪

1. George and Al, stranded on an island, use clamshells for money. Last year George caught 300 fish and five wild boars. Al grew 200 bunches of bananas. In the two-person economy that George and Al set up, fish sell for 1 clamshell each, boars sell for 10 clamshells each, and bananas go for 5 clamshells a bunch. George paid Al a total of 30 clamshells for helping him to dig bait for fishing, and he also purchased five of Al's mature banana trees for 30 clamshells each. What is the GDP of George's and Al's island in terms of clamshells?

2. How would each of the following transactions affect the GDP of the United States?
   a. The U.S. government pays $1 billion in salaries for government workers.
   b. The U.S. government pays $1 billion to Social Security recipients.
   c. The U.S. government pays a U.S. firm $1 billion for newly produced airplane parts.
   d. The U.S. government pays $1 billion in interest to holders of U.S. government bonds.
   e. The U.S. government pays $1 billion to Saudi Arabia for crude oil to add to U.S. official oil reserves.

3. Intelligence Incorporated produces 100 computer chips and sells them for $200 each to Bell Computers. Using the chips and other labor and materials, Bell produces 100 personal computers. Bell sells the computers, bundled with software that Bell licenses from Macrosoft at $50 per computer, to PC Charlie's for $800 each. PC Charlie's sells the computers to the public for $1,000 each. Calculate the total contribution to GDP using the value-added method. Do you get the same answer by summing up the market values of final goods and services?

4. For each of the following transactions, state the effect both on U.S. GDP and on the four components of aggregate expenditure.
   a. Your mother-in-law buys a new car from a U.S. producer.
   b. Your mother-in-law buys a new car imported from Sweden.
   c. Your mother-in-law's car rental business buys a new car from a U.S. producer.
   d. Your mother-in-law's car rental business buys a new car imported from Sweden.
   e. The U.S. government buys a new, domestically produced car for the use of your mother-in-law, who has been appointed the ambassador to Sweden.

5. Here are some data for an economy. Find its GDP. Explain your calculation.

Consumption expenditures	$600
Exports	75
Government purchases of goods and services	200
Construction of new homes and apartments	100
Sales of existing homes and apartments	200
Imports	50
Beginning-of-year inventory stocks	100
End-of-year inventory stocks	125
Business fixed investment	100
Government payments to retirees	100
Household purchases of durable goods	150

6. The nation of Potchatoonie produces hockey pucks, cases of root beer, and back rubs. Here are data on prices and quantities of the three goods in the years 2000 and 2005.

Year	Pucks		Root beer		Back rubs	
	Quantity	Price	Quantity	Price	Quantity	Price
2000	100	$5	300	$20	100	$20
2005	125	$7	250	$20	110	$25

Assume that 2000 is the base year. Find nominal GDP and real GDP for both years.

7. The government is considering a policy to reduce air pollution by restricting the use of "dirty" fuels by factories. In deciding whether to implement the policy, how, if at all, should the likely effects of the policy on real GDP be taken into account? Discuss.

8. Here is a report from a not-very-efficient BLS survey taker: "There were 65 people in the houses I visited, 10 of them children under 16 and 10 retired; 25 people had full-time jobs, and 5 had part-time jobs. There were 5 full-time homemakers, 5 full-time students over age 16, and 2 people who were disabled and cannot work. The remaining people did not have jobs but all said they would like one. One of these people had not looked actively for work for 3 months, however."

    Find the labor force, the unemployment rate, and the participation rate implied by the survey taker's report.

9. Ellen is downloading labor market data for the most recent month, but her connection is slow and so far this is all she has been able to get:

Unemployment rate	5.0%
Participation rate	62.5%
Not in the labor force	60 million

Find the labor force, the working-age population, the number of employed workers, and the number of unemployed workers.

10. The towns of Sawyer and Thatcher each have a labor force of 1,200 people. In Sawyer, 100 people were unemployed for the entire year, while the rest of the labor force was employed continuously. In Thatcher every member of the labor force was unemployed for 1 month and employed for 11 months.
    a. What is the average unemployment rate over the year in each of the two towns?
    b. What is the average duration of unemployment spells in each of the two towns?
    c. In which town do you think the costs of unemployment are higher? Explain.

■ ANSWERS TO IN-CHAPTER EXERCISES ■

18.1 In the text, GDP was calculated to be $64.00. If in addition Orchardia produces five oranges at $0.30 each, GDP is increased by $1.50 to $65.50.

18.2 Plants owned by U.S. companies produced a total of 1,185,000 vehicles, or 4.09 times the 290,000 vehicles produced by foreign-owned plants. In market value terms, with passenger cars valued at $17,000 and other light vehicles at $25,000, plants owned by U.S. companies produced (471,000 × $17,000) + (714,000 × $25,000), = $25,857,000 worth of vehicles. Foreign-owned plants produced (227,000 × $17,000) + (63,000 × $25,000) = $5,434,000 worth of vehicles. In market value terms U.S.-owned plants outproduced the foreign-owned plants by a ratio of 4.76 to 1. The U.S. producers have a greater advantage when output is compared in market value terms instead of in terms of number of vehicles because the U.S. companies produce relatively more of the higher-value types of vehicles than the foreign companies do.

18.3 The value added of the wholesale distributor together with the ultimate producers of the cards is $500. Amy's value added—her revenue less her payments to other firms—is $200. Since the cards were produced and purchased by Amy during the year 2000 (we assume), the $500 counts toward year 2000 GDP. The $200 in value added originating in Amy's card shop counts in year 2001 GDP, since Amy actually sold the cards in that year.

18.4 The sale of stock represents a transfer of ownership of part of the assets of Benson Buggywhip, not the production of new goods or services. Hence the stock sale itself does not contribute to GDP. However, the broker's commission of $100 (2 percent of the stock sale proceeds) represents payment for a current service and is counted in GDP.

18.5 As in Example 18.6, the market value of domestic production is 1,000,000 autos times $15,000 per auto, or $15 billion.

   Also as in Example 18.6, consumption is $10.5 billion and government purchases are $0.75 billion. However, because 25,000 of the autos that are purchased are imported rather than domestic, the domestic producers have unsold inventories at the end of the year of 50,000 (rather than 25,000 as in Example 18.6). Thus inventory investment is 50,000 autos times $15,000, or $0.75 billion, and total investment (autos purchased by businesses plus inventory investment) is $3.75 billion. Since exports and imports are equal (both are 25,000 autos), net exports (equal to exports minus imports) are zero. Notice that since we subtract imports to get net exports, it is unnecessary also to subtract imports from consumption. Consumption is defined as total purchases by households, not just purchases of domestically produced goods.

   Total expenditure is $C + I + G + NX$ = $10.5 billion + $3.75 billion + $0.75 billion + 0 = $15 billion, the same as the market value of production.

18.6 Real GDP in the year 2000 equals the quantities of pizzas and calzones produced in the year 2000, valued at the market prices that prevailed in the base year 1996. So real GDP in 2000 = (30 pizzas × $10/pizza) + (30 calzones × $5/calzone) = $450.

   Real GDP in 1996 equals the quantities of pizzas and calzones produced in 1996, valued at 1996 prices, which is $175. Notice that since 1996 is the base year, real GDP and nominal GDP are the same for that year.

   The real GDP in the year 2000 is $450/$175, or about 2.6 times what it was in 1996. Hence the expansion of real GDP lies between the threefold increase in pizza production and the doubling in calzone production that occurred between 1996 and 2000.

18.7   Labor force = Employed + Unemployed
              = 15.164 million + 1.359 million = 16.523 million

   Working-age population = Labor force + Not in labor force
              = 16.523 million + 8.534 million = 25.057 million

$$\text{Unemployment rate} = \frac{\text{Unemployed}}{\text{Labor force}}$$

$$= \frac{1.359 \text{ million}}{16.523 \text{ million}} = 8.2\%$$

$$\text{Participation rate} = \frac{\text{Labor force}}{\text{Working-age population}}$$

$$= \frac{16.523 \text{ million}}{25.057 \text{ million}} = 65.9\%$$

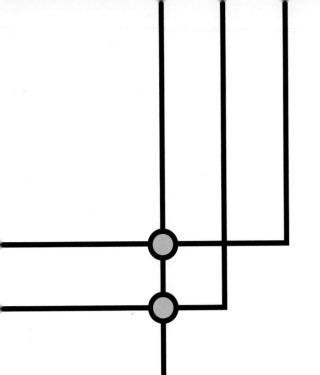

CHAPTER

19

MEASURING THE PRICE LEVEL
AND INFLATION

■

There is a story about a Wall Street investor, call her Lotta Doe, who was the first volunteer for an experiment in suspended animation. A team of scientists put Lotta into a deep sleep. Thirty years later she awoke, not having aged a day. Lotta's first action upon awakening was to run to a pay phone to call her broker. When the now-aged broker picked up the phone, Lotta asked how much her portfolio of financial investments, left to grow these 30 years, was now worth. "As of this morning," the broker replied, "your net worth is approximately $100 million."

Lotta was, of course, thrilled with this news. But at that moment the operator's voice broke into the call, and Lotta heard, "Please deposit $5 million for the next 3 minutes."

The story illustrates a simple but very important point, which is that the value of money depends entirely on the prices of the goods and services one wants to buy. A $100 million nest egg is a substantial fortune at the prices prevailing in the United States today, but it is only a pittance if a phone call costs $5 million. Likewise, high and sustained inflation—a rapid and ongoing increase in the prices of most goods and services—can radically reduce the buying power of a given amount of money. Apparently, there had been quite a lot of inflation during the 30 years Lotta Doe was in suspended animation.

Inflation can make a comparison of economic conditions at different points in time quite difficult. We remember being able to buy both a comic book and a chocolate sundae for a quarter. Today the same two items might cost $4 or $5. You might conclude from this fact that kids were much better off in "the good old days," but were they really? Without more information, we can't tell, for though the prices of comic books and sundaes have gone up, so have allowances. The real question is whether young people's spending money has increased as much as or more than the prices of the things they want to buy. If so, then they are no worse off today than we were when we were young and candy bars cost a nickel.

Inflation also creates uncertainty when we try to look into the future, to ask questions such as, "How much should I plan to save for retirement?" The answer to this question depends on how much inflation is likely to occur before one retires (and thus how much heating oil, food, and clothing will cost). Inflation can pose similar problems for policymakers. For example, to plan long-term government spending programs they must estimate how much the government's purchases will cost several years in the future.

An important benefit of studying macroeconomics is learning how to avoid the confusion inflation interjects into comparisons of economic conditions over time or projections for the future. In this chapter, a continuation of our study of the construction and interpretation of economic data, we will see how both prices and inflation are measured and how dollar amounts, such as the price of a comic book, can be "adjusted" to eliminate the effects of inflation. Quantities that are measured in dollars (or other currency units) and then adjusted for inflation are called *real* quantities (recall, for example, the concept of real GDP in Chapter 18). By working with real quantities, economists can avoid the kind of confusion that beset Lotta Doe.

More important than the complications inflation creates for economic measurement are the costs that it imposes on the economy. In this chapter we will see why high inflation can significantly impair an economy's performance, to the extent that economic policymakers claim a low and stable rate of inflation as one of their chief objectives. We will conclude the chapter by showing how inflation is linked to another key economic variable, the rate of interest on financial assets.

THE CONSUMER PRICE INDEX: MEASURING THE PRICE LEVEL

consumer price index (CPI) for any period, measures the cost in that period of a standard basket of goods and services relative to the cost of the same basket of goods and services in a fixed year, called the *base year*

The basic tool economists use to measure the price level and inflation in the U.S. economy is the *consumer price index,* or CPI for short. The CPI is a measure of the "cost of living" during a particular period. Specifically, the **consumer price index (CPI)** for any period measures the cost in that period of a standard set, or basket, of goods and services *relative* to the cost of the same basket of goods and services in a fixed year, called the *base year*.

To illustrate how the CPI is constructed, suppose the government has designated 1995 as the base year. Assume for the sake of simplicity that in 1995 a typical American family's monthly household budget consisted of spending on just three items: rent on a two-bedroom apartment, hamburgers, and movie tickets. In reality, of course, families purchase hundreds of different items each month, but the basic principles of constructing the CPI are the same no matter how many items are included. Suppose too that the family's average monthly expenditures in 1995, the base year, were as shown in Table 19.1.

TABLE 19.1
Monthly Household Budget of the Typical Family in 1995 (Base Year)

Item	Cost (in 1995)
Rent, two-bedroom apartment	$500
Hamburgers (60 at $2.00 each)	120
Movie tickets (10 at $6.00 each)	60
Total Expenditure	$680

Now let's fast-forward to the year 2000. Over that period, the prices of various goods and services are likely to have changed; some will have risen and some fallen. Let's suppose that by the year 2000 the rent that our family pays for their two-bedroom apartment has risen to $630. Hamburgers now cost $2.50 each, and the price of movie tickets has risen to $7.00 each. So, in general, prices have been rising.

By how much did the family's cost of living increase between 1995 and 2000? Table 19.2 shows that if the typical family wanted to consume the *same basket of goods and services* in the year 2000 as they did in the year 1995, they would have to spend $850 per month, or $170 more than the $680 per month they spent in 1995. In other words, to live the same way in the year 2000 as they did in the year 1995, the family would have to spend 25 percent more ($170/$680) each month. So, in this example, the cost of living for the typical family rose 25 percent between 1995 and 2000.

TABLE 19.2
Cost of Reproducing the 1995 (Base-Year) Basket of Goods and Services in Year 2000

Item	Cost (in 2000)	Cost (in 1995)
Rent, two-bedroom apartment	$630	$500
Hamburgers (60 at $2.50 each)	150	120
Movie tickets (10 at $7.00 each)	70	60
Total Expenditure	$850	$680

The government—actually, the Bureau of Labor Statistics (BLS), the same agency that is responsible for determining the unemployment rate—calculates the official consumer price index (CPI) using essentially the same method. The first step in deriving the CPI is to pick a base year and determine the basket of goods and services that were consumed by the typical family during that year. In practice, the government learns how consumers allocate their spending through a detailed survey, called the Consumer Expenditure Survey, in which randomly selected families record every purchase they make and the price they paid over a given month. (Quite a task!) Let's call the basket of goods and services that results the *base-year basket*. Then, each month BLS employees visit thousands of stores and conduct numerous interviews to determine the current prices of the goods and services in the base-year basket. The CPI in any given year is computed using this formula:

$$CPI = \frac{\text{Cost of base-year basket of goods and services in current year}}{\text{Cost of base-year basket of goods and services in base year}}.$$

Returning to the example of the typical family that consumes three goods, we can calculate the CPI in the year 2000 as

$$CPI \text{ in year } 2000 = \frac{\$850}{\$680} = 1.25.$$

In other words, in this example the cost of living in the year 2000 is 25 percent higher than it was in 1995, the base year. Notice that the base-year CPI is always equal to 1.00, since in that year the numerator and the denominator of the CPI formula are the same. The CPI for a given period (such as a month or year) measures the cost of living in that period *relative* to what it was in the base year.

Often news reporters multiply the CPI by 100 to get rid of the decimal point. If we were to do that here, the year 2000 CPI would be expressed as 125 rather than 1.25, and the base-year CPI would be expressed as 100 rather than 1.00. However, some calculations we will do later in the chapter are simplified if the CPI is stated in decimal form, so we will not adopt the convention of multiplying it by 100.

EXAMPLE 19.1

Measuring the typical family's cost of living

Suppose that in addition to the three goods and services the typical family consumed in 1995 they also bought four sweaters at $30 each. In the year 2000 the same sweaters cost $50 each. The prices of the other goods and services in 1995 and 2000 were the same as in Table 19.2. Find the change in the family's cost of living between 1995 and 2000.

In the example in the text, the cost of the base-year (1995) basket was $680. Adding four sweaters at $30 each raises the cost of the base-year basket to $800. What does this same basket (including the four sweaters) cost in 2000? The cost of the apartment, the hamburgers, and the movie tickets is $850, as before. Adding the cost of the four sweaters at $50 each raises the total cost of the basket to $1050. The CPI equals the cost of the basket in 2000 divided by the cost of the basket in 1995 (the base year), or $1050/$800 = 1.31. We conclude that the family's cost of living rose 31 percent between 1995 and 2000.

EXERCISE 19.1

Returning to the three-good example in Tables 19.1 and 19.2, find the year 2000 CPI if the rent on the apartment falls from $500 in 1995 to $400 in 2000. The prices for hamburgers and movie tickets in the 2 years remain the same as in the two tables.

price index a measure of the average price of a given class of goods or services relative to the price of the same goods and services in a base year

The CPI is not itself the price of a specific good or service; it is a *price index*. A **price index** measures the average price of a class of goods or services relative to the price of those same goods or services in a base year. The CPI is an especially well-known price index, one of many economists use to assess economic trends. For example, because manufacturers tend to pass on increases in the prices of raw materials to their customers, economists use indexes of raw materials' prices to try to forecast changes in the prices of manufactured goods. Other indexes are used to study the rate of price change in energy, food, health care, and other major sectors.

EXERCISE 19.2

The consumer price index captures the cost of living for the "typical" or average family. Suppose you were to construct a personal price index to measure changes in your own cost of living over time. In general, how would you go about constructing such an index? Why might changes in your personal price index differ from changes in the CPI?

INFLATION

rate of inflation the annual percentage rate of change in the price level, as measured, for example, by the CPI

The CPI provides a measure of the average *level* of prices relative to prices in the base year. *Inflation*, in contrast, is a measure of how fast the average price level is *changing* over time. The **rate of inflation** is defined as the annual percentage rate of change in the price level, as measured, for example, by the CPI. Suppose, for example, that the CPI has a value of 1.25 in the year 2000 and a value of 1.30 in the year 2001. The rate of inflation between 2000 and 2001 is the percentage increase in the price level, or the increase in the price level (.05) divided by the initial price level (1.25), which is equal to 4 percent.

Calculating inflation rates: 1972–1976

EXAMPLE 19.2

The CPIs for the years 1972 through 1976 are shown below. Find the rates of inflation between 1972 and 1973, 1973 and 1974, 1974 and 1975, and 1975 and 1976.

Year	CPI
1972	0.418
1973	0.444
1974	0.493
1975	0.538
1976	0.569

The inflation rate between 1972 and 1973 is the percentage increase in the price level between those years, or $(0.444 - 0.418)/0.418 = 0.026/0.418 = 0.062 = 6.2$ percent. Do the calculations on your own to confirm that inflation during each of the next 3 years was 11.0, 9.1, and 5.8 percent, respectively. During the 1970s, inflation rates were much higher than the 2 to 3 percent inflation rates that have prevailed in recent years.

EXERCISE 19.3

Below are CPIs for the years 1929 through 1933. Find the rates of inflation between 1929 and 1930, 1930 and 1931, 1931 and 1932, and 1932 and 1933.

Year	CPI
1929	0.171
1930	0.167
1931	0.152
1932	0.137
1933	0.130

How did inflation rates in the 1930s differ from those of the 1970s?

The results of the calculations for Exercise 19.3 include some examples of *negative* inflation rates. A situation in which the prices of most goods and services are falling over time so that inflation is negative is called **deflation**. The early 1930s was the last time the United States experienced significant deflation. Japan experienced relatively mild deflation during the 1990s.

deflation a situation in which the prices of most goods and services are falling over time so that inflation is negative

ADJUSTING FOR INFLATION

The CPI is an extremely useful tool. Not only does it allow us to measure changes in the cost of living, it can also be used to adjust economic data to eliminate the effects of inflation. In this section we will see how the CPI can be used to convert quantities measured at current dollar values into real terms, a process called *deflating*. We will also see that the CPI can be used to convert real quantities into current-dollar terms, a procedure called *indexing*. Both procedures are useful not only to economists but to anyone who needs to adjust payments, accounting measures, or other economic quantities for the effects of inflation.

DEFLATING A NOMINAL QUANTITY

nominal quantity a quantity that is measured in terms of its current dollar value

An important use of the CPI is to adjust **nominal quantities**—quantities measured at their current dollar values—for the effects of inflation. To illustrate, suppose we know that the typical family in a certain metropolitan area had a total income of $20,000 in 1995 and $22,000 in the year 2000. Was this family economically better off in the year 2000 than in 1995?

Without any more information than this we might be tempted to say yes. After all, their income has risen by 10 percent over the 5-year period. But prices might also have been rising, as fast or faster than the family's income. Suppose the prices of the goods and services the family consumes have risen 25 percent over the same period. Since the family's income rose only 10 percent, we would have to conclude that the family is worse off, in terms of the goods and services they can afford to buy, despite the increase in their *nominal,* or current-dollar, income.

real quantity a quantity that is measured in physical terms—for example, in terms of quantities of goods and services

We can make a more precise comparison of the family's purchasing power in 1995 and 2000 by calculating their incomes in those years in *real* terms. In general, a **real quantity** is one that is measured in terms of physical terms—for example, in terms of quantities of goods and services. To convert a nominal quantity into a real quantity, we must divide the nominal quantity by a price index for the period, as shown in Table 19.3. The calculations in the table show that in *real* or purchasing power terms, the family's income actually *decreased* by $2,400, or 12 percent of their initial real income of $20,000, between 1995 and 2000.

TABLE 19.3
Comparing the Real Values of a Family's Income in 1995 and 2000

Year	Nominal family income	CPI	Real family income = Nominal family income/CPI
1995	$20,000	1.00	$20,000/1.00 = $20,000
2000	$22,000	1.25	$22,000/1.25 = $17,600

deflating (a nominal quantity) the process of dividing a nominal quantity by a price index (such as the CPI) to express the quantity in real terms

The problem for this family is that though their income has been rising in nominal (dollar) terms, it has not kept up with inflation. Dividing a nominal quantity by a price index to express the quantity in real terms is called **deflating** the nominal quantity. (Be careful not to confuse the idea of deflating a nominal quantity with deflation, or negative inflation. The two concepts are different.)

Dividing a nominal quantity by the current value of a price index to measure it in real or purchasing power terms is a very useful tool. It can be used to eliminate the effects of inflation from comparisons of any nominal quantity—workers' wages, health care expenditures, the components of the federal budget—over time. Why does this method work? In general, if you know both how many dollars you have spent on a given item and the item's price, you can figure out how many of the item you bought (by dividing your expenditures by the price). For example, if you spent $100 on hamburgers last month and hamburgers cost $2.50 each, you can determine that you purchased 40 hamburgers. Similarly, if you divide a family's dollar income or expenditures by a price index, which is a measure of the average price of the goods and services they buy, you will obtain a measure of the real quantity of goods and services they purchased. Such real quantities are sometimes referred to as *inflation-adjusted* quantities.

EXAMPLE 19.3

Home run hitters drive Cadillacs

In 1930 the great baseball player Babe Ruth earned a salary of $80,000. When it was pointed out to him that he had earned more than President Hoover, Ruth replied, with some justification, "I had a better year than he did." In 1998 St. Louis Cardinals slugger Mark McGwire earned approximately $8.3 million in the process of breaking both Ruth's and Roger Maris's single-season home run records. Adjusting for inflation, who earned more, Ruth or McGwire?

To answer this question, we need to know that the CPI (using the average of 1982–1984 as the base year) was 0.167 in 1930 and 1.64 in 1998. Dividing Babe Ruth's salary by 0.167, we obtain approximately $479,000, which is Ruth's salary "in 1982–1984 dollars." In other words, to enjoy the same purchasing power during the 1982–1984 period as in 1930, the Babe would have needed a salary of $479,000. Dividing Mark McGwire's 1998 salary by the 1998 CPI, 1.64, yields a salary of $5.06 million in 1982–1984 dollars. We can now compare the salaries of the two power hitters. Although adjusting for inflation brings the two figures closer together (since part of McGwire's higher salary compensates for the increase in prices between 1930 and 1998), in real terms McGwire still earned more than 10 times Ruth's salary. Incidentally, McGwire also earned about 40 times what President Clinton earned.

real wage the wage paid to workers measured in terms of real purchasing power; the real wage for any given period is calculated by dividing the nominal (dollar) wage by the CPI for that period

Clearly, in comparing wages or earnings at two different points in time, we must adjust for changes in the price level. Doing so yields the **real wage**—the wage measured in terms of real purchasing power. The real wage for any given period is calculated by dividing the nominal (dollar) wage by the CPI for that period.

EXAMPLE 19.4

Real wages of U.S. production workers

Production workers are nonsupervisory workers, such as those who work on factory assembly lines. According to the Bureau of Labor Statistics, http://stats.bls.gov, the average U.S. production worker earned $3.23/hour in 1970 and $10.01/hour in 1990. Compare the real wages for this group of workers in the 2 years.

To find the real wage in 1970 and 1990, we need to know that the CPI was 0.388 in 1970 and 1.307 in 1990 (again using the 1982–1984 average as the base period). Dividing $3.23 by 0.388, we find that the real wage in 1970 was $8.32. Dividing $10.01 by 1.307, we find that the real wage in 1990 was only $7.66. In real or purchasing power terms, manufacturing workers' wages fell between 1970 and 1990, despite the fact that the nominal or dollar wage more than tripled.

Figure 19.1 shows nominal wages and real wages for U.S. production workers for the period 1960–1999. Notice the dramatic difference between the two

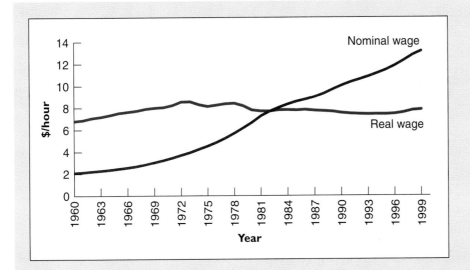

FIGURE 19.1
Nominal and Real Wages for Production Workers, 1960–1999.
Though nominal wages of production workers have risen dramatically since 1960, real wages have stagnated.

trends. Looking only at nominal wages, one might conclude that production-line workers were much better paid in 1999 than in 1960. But once wages are adjusted for inflation, we see that in terms of buying power production-line workers' wages have stagnated since the early 1970s. This example illustrates the crucial importance of adjusting for inflation when comparing dollar values over time.

EXERCISE 19.4

In 1950 the minimum wage prescribed by federal law was $0.75/hour. In 1997 the minimum wage was raised to $5.15/hour. How does the real minimum wage in 1950 compare to that of 1997? The CPI was 0.241 in 1950 and 1.61 in 1997.

INDEXING TO MAINTAIN BUYING POWER

The consumer price index can also be used to convert real quantities to nominal quantities. Suppose, for example, that in the year 1995 the government paid certain Social Security recipients $1,000 per month in benefits. Let's assume that Congress would like the buying power of these benefits to remain constant over time so that the recipients' standard of living is unaffected by inflation. To achieve that goal, at what level should Congress set the monthly Social Security benefit in the year 2000?

The nominal, or dollar, benefit Congress should pay in the year 2000 to maintain the purchasing power of retired people depends on how much inflation has taken place between 1995 and 2000. Suppose once again that the CPI has risen 25 percent between 1995 and 2000. That is, on average the prices of the goods and services consumers buy have risen 25 percent over that period. For Social Security recipients to "keep up" with inflation, their benefit in the year 2000 must be $1,250 per month, or 25 percent more than it was in 1995. In general, to keep purchasing power constant, the dollar benefit must be increased each year by the percentage increase in the CPI.

indexing the practice of increasing a nominal quantity each period by an amount equal to the percentage increase in a specified price index. Indexing prevents the purchasing power of the nominal quantity from being eroded by inflation

The practice of increasing a nominal quantity according to changes in a price index to prevent inflation from eroding purchasing power is called **indexing**. In the case of Social Security, federal law provides for the automatic indexing of benefits. Each year, without any action by Congress, benefits increase by an amount equal to the percentage increase in the CPI. Some labor contracts are indexed as well so that wages are adjusted fully or partially for changes in inflation (see Example 19.5).

EXAMPLE 19.5

An indexed labor contract

A labor contract provides for a first-year wage of $12.00/hour and specifies that the real wage will rise by 2 percent in the second year of the contract and by another 2 percent in the third year. The CPI is 1.00 in the first year, 1.05 in the second year, and 1.10 in the third year. Find the dollar wage that must be paid in the second and third years.

Because the CPI is 1.00 in the first year, both the nominal wage and the real wage are $12.00. Let W_2 stand for the nominal wage in the second year. Deflating by the CPI in the second year, we can express the real wage in the second year as $W_2/1.05$. The contract says that the second-year real wage must be 2 percent higher than the real wage in the first year, so $W_2/1.05 = \$12.00 \times 1.02 = \$12.24$. Multiplying through by 1.05 to solve for W_2, we get $W_2 = \$12.85$, the nominal wage required by the contract in the second year. In the third year the nominal wage W_3 must satisfy the equation $W_3/1.10 = \$12.24 \times 1.02 = \$12.48$. (Why?) Solving this equation for W_3 yields $13.73 as the nominal wage that must be paid in the third year.

EXERCISE 19.5

The minimum wage is not indexed to inflation, but suppose it had been when it was introduced in 1950. What would the nominal minimum wage have been in 1997? See Exercise 19.4 for the data necessary to answer the question.

Every few years there is a well-publicized battle in Congress over whether the minimum wage should be raised. Why do these heated legislative debates recur so regularly?

Because the minimum wage is not indexed to inflation, its purchasing power falls as prices rise. Congress must therefore raise the nominal minimum wage periodically to keep the real value of the minimum wage from eroding. Ironically, despite the public's impression that Congress has raised the nominal minimum wage steeply over the years, the real minimum wage has fallen about one-third since 1970.

Why doesn't Congress index the minimum wage to the CPI and eliminate the need to reconsider it so often? Evidently, some members of Congress prefer to hold a highly publicized debate on the issue every few years—perhaps because it mobilizes both advocates and opponents of the minimum wage to make campaign donations to those members who represent their views.

ECONOMIC NATURALIST 19.1

RECAP   METHODS TO ADJUST FOR INFLATION

Deflating. To correct a nominal quantity, such as a family's dollar income, for changes in the price level, divide it by a price index such as the CPI. This process, called *deflating* the nominal quantity, expresses the nominal quantity in terms of real purchasing power. If nominal quantities from two different years are deflated by a price index with the same base year, the purchasing power of the two deflated quantities can be compared.

Indexing. To ensure that a nominal payment, such as a Social Security benefit, represents a constant level of real purchasing power, increase the nominal quantity each year by a percentage equal to the rate of inflation for that year (a procedure known as *indexing*).

DOES THE CPI MEASURE "TRUE" INFLATION?

You may have concluded that measuring inflation is straightforward, but as with GDP and the unemployment rate, the issue is not free from controversy. Indeed the question of whether U.S. inflation is properly measured has been the subject of serious debates in recent years. Because the CPI is one of the most important U.S. economic statistics, the issue is far from academic. Policymakers pay close attention to the latest inflation numbers when deciding what actions to take. Furthermore, because of the widespread use of indexing, changes in the CPI directly impact the government's budget. For example, if the CPI rises by 3 percent during a given year, by law Social Security benefits—which are a significant part of federal government spending—increase automatically by 3 percent. Many other government payments and private contracts, such as union labor contracts, are indexed to the CPI as well.

When a 1996 report concluded that changes in the CPI are a poor measure of "true" inflation, therefore, a major controversy ensued. The report, prepared by a commission headed by Michael Boskin, formerly the chief economic adviser to President Bush, concluded that the official CPI inflation rate *overstates* the true inflation rate by as much as one to two percentage points a year. In other words, if the official CPI inflation rate is reported to be 3 percent, the "true" inflation rate might be 2 percent, or even 1 percent.

If this assessment is in fact correct, the indexing of Social Security and other government benefits to the CPI could be costing the federal government billions of dollars more than necessary every year. In addition, an overstated rate of inflation would lead to an underestimation of the true improvement in living standards over time. If the typical family's nominal income increases by 3 percent per year, and inflation is reported to be 3 percent per year, economists would conclude that American families are experiencing no increase in their real income. But if the "true" inflation rate is really 2 percent per year, then the family's real income is actually rising by 1 percent per year (the 3 percent increase in nominal income minus 2 percent inflation).

The Boskin Commission gave a number of reasons why the official inflation rate, based on the CPI, may overestimate the true rate of inflation. Two are particularly important. First, in practice government statisticians cannot always adjust adequately for changes in the *quality* of goods and services. Suppose a new personal computer has 20 percent more memory, computational speed, and data storage capacity than last year's model. Suppose too for the sake of illustration that its price is 20 percent higher. Has there been inflation in computer prices? Economists would say no; although consumers are paying 20 percent more for a computer, they are getting a 20 percent better machine. The situation is really no different from paying 20 percent more for a pizza that is 20 percent bigger. However, because quality change is difficult to measure precisely and because they have many thousands of goods and services to consider, government statisticians often miss or understate changes in quality. In general, whenever statisticians fail to adjust adequately for improvements in the quality of goods or services, they will tend to overstate inflation. This type of overstatement is called *quality adjustment bias.*

An extreme example of quality adjustment bias can occur whenever a totally new good becomes available. For example, the introduction of the first effective AIDS drugs significantly increased the quality of medical care received by AIDS patients. In practice, however, quality improvements that arise from totally new products are likely to be poorly captured by the CPI, if at all. The problem is that since the new good was not produced in the base year, there is no base-year price with which to compare the current price of the good. Government statisticians use various approaches to correct for this problem, such as comparing the cost of the new drug to the cost of the next-best therapies. But such methods are necessarily imprecise and open to criticism.

The second problem emphasized by the Boskin Commission arises from the fact that the CPI is calculated for a fixed basket of goods and services. This procedure does not allow for the possibility that consumers can switch from products whose prices are rising to those whose prices are stable or falling. Ignoring the fact that consumers can switch from more expensive to less expensive goods leads statisticians to overestimate the true increase in the cost of living.

Suppose, for instance, that people like coffee and tea equally well and in the base year consumed equal amounts of each. But then a frost hits a major coffee-producing nation, causing the price of coffee to double. The increase in coffee prices encourages consumers to forgo coffee and drink tea instead—a switch that doesn't make them much worse off, since they like coffee and tea equally well. However the CPI, which measures the cost of buying the base-year basket of goods and services, will rise significantly when the price of coffee doubles. This rise in the CPI, which ignores the fact that people can substitute tea for coffee without being made significantly worse off, exaggerates the true increase in the cost of living. This type of overstatement of inflation is called *substitution bias.*

Substitution bias

EXAMPLE 19.6

Suppose the CPI basket for 1995, the base year, is as follows:

Item	Expenditure
Coffee (50 cups at $1/cup)	$ 50.00
Tea (50 cups at $1/cup)	50.00
Scones (100 at $1 each)	100.00
Total	$200.00

Assume that consumers are equally happy to drink coffee or tea with their scones. In 1995, coffee and tea cost the same, and the average person drinks equal amounts of coffee and tea.

In the year 2000, coffee has doubled in price to $2/cup. Tea remains at $1/cup, and scones are $1.50 each. What has happened to the cost of living as measured by the CPI? How does this result compare to the true cost of living?

To calculate the value of the CPI for the year 2000, we must first find the cost of consuming the 1995 basket of goods in that year. At year 2000 prices, 50 cups each of coffee and tea and 100 scones cost $(50 \times \$2) + (50 \times \$1) + (100 \times \$1.50) = \$300$. Since consuming the same basket of goods cost $200 in 1995, the base year, the CPI in 2000 is $300/$200, or 1.50. This calculation leads us to conclude that the cost of living has increased 50 percent between 1995 and 2000.

However, we have overlooked the possibility that consumers can substitute a cheaper good (tea) for the more expensive one (coffee). Indeed, since consumers like coffee and tea equally well, when the price of coffee doubles they will shift entirely to tea. Their new consumption basket—100 cups of tea and 100 scones—is just as enjoyable to them as their original basket. If we allow for the substitution of less expensive goods, how much has the cost of living really increased? The cost of 100 cups of tea and 100 scones in the year 2000 is only $250, not $300. From the consumer's point of view, the true cost of living has risen by only $50, or 25 percent. The 50 percent increase in the CPI therefore overstates the increase in the cost of living as the result of substitution bias.

The Boskin Commission's findings have been controversial. While quality adjustment bias and substitution bias undoubtedly distort the measurement of inflation, estimating precisely how much of an overstatement they create is difficult. (If economists knew exactly how big these biases were, they could simply correct the data.) But the Bureau of Labor Statistics (the agency responsible for calculating the CPI) has recently made significant efforts to improve the quality of its data as a result of the Commission's report.

Why is inflation in the health care sector apparently high?

Government statisticians report inflation rates for different categories of goods and services, as well as for the overall consumer basket. According to the official measures, over recent decades the prices of medical services have tended to rise much more rapidly than the prices of other goods and services. Why is inflation in the health care sector apparently high?

Although inflation rates in the health care sector are high, some economists have argued that reported rates greatly overstate the true rate of inflation in that sector. The reason, claim critics, is the quality adjustment bias. Health care is a dynamic sector of the economy, in which ongoing technological change has significantly improved the quality of care. To the extent that official data fail to account for improvements in the quality of medical care, inflation in the health care sector will be overstated.

ECONOMIC
NATURALIST
19.2

Economists Matthew Shapiro and James Wilcox[1] illustrated the problem with the example of changes in the treatment of cataracts, a cloudiness in the lens of the eye that impairs vision. The lens must still be removed surgically, but there have been important improvements in the procedure over the past 30 years. First, surgeons can now replace the defective lens with an artificial one, which improves the patient's vision considerably without contact lenses or thick glasses. Second, the techniques for making and closing the surgical incision have been substantially improved. Besides reducing complications and therefore follow-up visits, the new techniques can be performed in the physician's office, with no hospital stay (older techniques frequently required 3 nights in the hospital). Thus the new technologies have both improved patient outcomes and reduced the number of hours doctors and nurses spend on the procedure.

Shapiro and Wilcox point out that official measures of health care inflation are based primarily on data such as the doctor's hourly rate or the cost of a night in the hospital. They do not take into account either the reduction in a doctor's time or the shorter hospital stay now needed for procedures such as cataract surgery. Furthermore, Shapiro and Wilcox argue, official measures do not take adequate account of improvements in patient outcomes, such as the improved vision cataract patients now enjoy. Because of the failure to adjust for improvements in the quality of procedures, including increased productivity of medical personnel, official measures may significantly overstate inflation in the health care sector.

THE COSTS OF INFLATION: NOT WHAT YOU THINK

In the late 1970s, when inflation was considerably higher than it is now, the public told poll takers that they viewed it as "public enemy number one"—that is, as the nation's most serious problem. Although U.S. inflation rates have not been very high in recent years, today many Americans remain concerned about inflation or the threat of inflation. Why do people worry so much about inflation? Detailed opinion surveys often find that many people are confused about the meaning of inflation and its economic effects. Before describing the true economic costs of inflation, which are real and serious, let's examine this confusion people experience about inflation and its costs.

price level a measure of the overall level of prices at a particular point in time as measured by a price index such as the CPI

relative price the price of a specific good or service *in comparison to* the prices of other goods and services

We need first to distinguish between the *price level* and the *relative price* of a good or service. The **price level** is a measure of the overall level of prices at a particular point in time as measured by a price index such as the CPI. Recall that the inflation rate is the percentage change in the price level from year to year. In contrast, a **relative price** is the price of a specific good or service *in comparison to* the prices of other goods and services. For example, if the price of oil were to rise by 10 percent while the prices of other goods and services were rising on average by 3 percent, the relative price of oil would increase. But if oil prices rise by 3 percent while other prices rise by 10 percent, the relative price of oil would decrease. That is, oil would become cheaper relative to other goods and services, even though it has not become cheaper in absolute terms.

Public opinion surveys suggest that many people are confused about the distinction between inflation, or an increase in the overall *price level*, and an increase in a specific *relative price*. Suppose that hostilities in the Middle East were to double the price of gas at the pump, leaving other prices unaffected. Appalled by the increase in gasoline prices, people might demand that the government do something about "this inflation." But while the increase in gas prices hurts consumers, is it an example of inflation? Gasoline is only one item in a consumer's budget, one of the thousands of goods and services that people buy every day. Thus the increase in the price of gasoline might affect the overall price level, and hence the inflation rate, only slightly. In this example, inflation is not the real problem. What upsets consumers is the change in the *relative price* of oil, particularly compared to the price of labor (wages). By increasing the cost of using a car, the increase in the relative price of oil reduces the income people have left over to spend on other things.

Again, changes in relative prices do *not* necessarily imply a significant amount of inflation. For example, increases in the prices of some goods could well be counterbalanced by decreases in the prices of other goods, in which case the price level and the inflation rate would be largely unaffected. Conversely, inflation can be high without affecting relative prices. Imagine, for example, that all prices in the economy, including wages and salaries, go up exactly 10 percent each year. The inflation rate is 10 percent, but relative prices are not changing. Indeed, because wages (the price of labor) are increasing by 10 percent per year, people's ability to buy goods and services is unaffected by the inflation.

These examples show that changes in the average price level (inflation) and changes in the relative prices of specific goods are two quite different issues. The public's tendency to confuse the two is important, because the remedies for the two problems are different. To counteract changes in relative prices, the government would need to implement policies that affect the supply and demand for specific goods. In the case of an increase in oil prices, for example, the government could try to restore supplies by mediating the peace process in the Middle East. To counteract inflation, however, the government must resort (as we will see) to changes in macroeconomic policies, such as monetary or fiscal policies. If, in confusion, the public forces the government to adopt anti-inflationary policies when the real problem is a relative price change, the economy could actually be hurt by the effort. Here is an example of why economic literacy is important, both to policymakers and the general public.

The price level, relative prices, and inflation

EXAMPLE 19.7

Suppose the value of the CPI is 1.20 in the year 2000, 1.32 in 2001, and 1.40 in 2002. Assume also that the price of oil increases 8 percent between 2000 and 2001 and another 8 percent between 2001 and 2002. What is happening to the price level, the inflation rate, and the relative price of oil?

The price level can be measured by the CPI. Since the CPI is higher in 2001 than in 2000 and higher still in 2002 than in 2001, the price level is rising throughout the period. The inflation rate is the *percentage increase* in the CPI. Since the CPI increases by 10 percent between 2000 and 2001, the inflation rate between those years is 10 percent. However, the CPI increases only about 6 percent between 2001 and 2002 ($1.40/1.32 \approx 1.06$), so the inflation rate decreases to about 6 percent between those years. The decline in the inflation rate implies that although the price level is still rising, it is doing so at a slower pace than the year before.

The price of oil rises 8 percent between 2000 and 2001. But because the general inflation over that period is 10 percent, the relative price of oil—that is, its price *relative to all other goods and services*—falls by about 2 percent ($8\% - 10\% = -2\%$). Between 2001 and 2002 the price of oil rises by another 8 percent, while the general inflation rate is about 6 percent. Hence the relative price of oil rises between 2001 and 2002 by about 2 percent ($8\% - 6\%$).

THE TRUE COSTS OF INFLATION

Having dispelled the common confusion between inflation and relative price changes, we are now free to address the true economic costs of inflation. There are a variety of such costs, each of which tends to reduce the efficiency of the economy. Five of the most important are discussed here.

"SHOE-LEATHER" COSTS

As all shoppers know, cash is convenient. Unlike checks, which are not accepted everywhere, and credit cards, for which a minimum purchase is often required, cash can be used in almost any routine transaction. Businesses, too, find cash convenient to hold. Having plenty of cash on hand facilitates transactions with customers and reduces the need for frequent deposits and withdrawals from the bank.

Inflation raises the cost of holding cash to consumers and businesses. Consider a miser with $10,000 in $20 bills under his mattress. What happens to the buying power of his hoard over time? If inflation is zero so that on average the prices of goods and services are not changing, the buying power of the $10,000 does not change over time. At the end of a year the miser's purchasing power is the same as it was at the beginning of the year. But suppose the inflation rate is 10 percent. In that case, the purchasing power of the miser's hoard will fall by 10 percent each year. After a year, he will have only $9,000 in purchasing power. In general, the higher the rate of inflation, the less people will want to hold cash because of the loss of purchasing power that they will suffer.

Technically, currency is a debt owed by the government to the currency holder. So when currency loses value, the losses to holders of cash are offset by gains to the government, which now owes less in real terms to currency holders. Thus, from the point of view of society as a whole, the loss of purchasing power is not in itself a cost of inflation, because it does not involve wasted resources. (Indeed, no real goods or services were used up when the miser's currency hoard lost part of its value.) However, when faced with inflation, people are not likely to accept a loss in purchasing power but instead will take actions to try to "economize" on their cash holdings. For example, instead of drawing out enough cash for a month the next time they visit the bank, they will draw out only enough to last a week. The inconvenience of visiting the bank more often to minimize one's cash holdings is a real cost of inflation. Similarly, businesses will reduce their cash holdings by sending employees to the bank more frequently, or by installing computerized systems to monitor cash usage. To deal with the increase in bank transactions required by consumers and businesses trying to use less cash, banks will need to hire more employees and expand their operations.

The costs of more frequent trips to the bank, new cash management systems, and expanded employment in banks are real costs. They use up resources, including time and effort, that could be used for other purposes. Traditionally, the costs of economizing on cash have been called *shoe-leather costs*—the idea being that shoe leather is worn out during extra trips to the bank. Shoe-leather costs probably are not a significant problem in the United States today, where inflation is only 2 to 3 percent per year. But in economies with high rates of inflation, they can become quite significant.

| EXAMPLE 19.8 | **Shoe-leather costs at Woodrow's Hardware** |

Woodrow's Hardware needs $5,000 cash per day for customer transactions. Woodrow has a choice between going to the bank first thing on Monday morning to withdraw $25,000—enough cash for the whole week—or going to the bank first thing every morning for $5,000 each time. Woodrow puts the cost of going to the bank, in terms of inconvenience and lost time, at $4 per trip. Assume that funds left in the bank earn precisely enough interest to keep their purchasing power unaffected by inflation.

If inflation is zero, how often will Woodrow go to the bank? If it is 10 percent? In this example, what are the shoe-leather costs of a 10 percent inflation rate?

If inflation is zero, there is no cost to holding cash. Woodrow will go to the bank only once a week, incurring a shoe-leather cost of $4 per week. But if inflation is 10 percent, Woodrow may need to change his banking habits. If he continues to go to the bank only on Monday mornings, withdrawing $25,000 for the week, what will be Woodrow's average cash holding over the week? At the beginning of each day, his cash holding will be as follows:

Monday	$25,000
Tuesday	20,000
Wednesday	15,000
Thursday	10,000
Friday	5,000

Averaging the holdings on those 5 days, we can calculate that Woodrow's average cash holding at the beginning of each day is $75,000/5 = $15,000. If inflation is 10 percent a year, over the course of a year the cost to Woodrow of holding an average of $15,000 in cash equals 10 percent of $15,000, or $1,500.

On the other hand, if Woodrow goes to the bank every day, his average cash holding at the beginning of the day will be only $5,000. In that case, his losses from inflation will be $500 (10 percent of $5,000) a year. Will Woodrow start going to the bank every day when inflation reaches 10 percent? The *benefit* of changing his banking behavior is a loss of only $500 per year to inflation, rather than $1,500, or $1,000 saved. The *cost* of going to the bank every day is $4 per trip. Assuming Woodrow's store is open 50 weeks a year, going to the bank 5 days a week instead of 1 day a week adds 200 trips per year, at a total cost of $800. Since the $800 cost is less than the $1,000 benefit, Woodrow will begin going to the bank more often.

To repeat, the shoe-leather costs of a high inflation rate are the extra costs incurred to avoid holding cash. In this example they are the additional $800 per year associated with Woodrow's daily trips to the bank.

"NOISE" IN THE PRICE SYSTEM

In Chapter 4 we described the remarkable economic coordination that is necessary to provide the right amount and the right kinds of food to New Yorkers every day. This feat is not orchestrated by some Food Distribution Ministry staffed by bureaucrats. It is done much better than a Ministry ever could by the workings of free markets, operating without central guidance.

How do free markets transmit the enormous amounts of information necessary to accomplish complex tasks like the provisioning of New York City? The answer, as we saw in Chapter 4, is through the price system. When the owners of French restaurants in Manhattan cannot find sufficient quantities of chanterelles, a particularly rare and desirable mushroom, they bid up its market price. Specialty food suppliers notice the higher price for chanterelles and realize that they can make a profit by supplying more chanterelles to the market. At the same time, price-conscious diners will shift to cheaper, more available mushrooms. The market for chanterelles will reach equilibrium only when there are no more unexploited opportunities for profit, and both suppliers and demanders are satisfied at the market price (the *equilibrium principle*). Multiply this example a million times, and you will gain a sense of how the price system achieves a truly remarkable degree of economic coordination.

When inflation is high, however, the subtle signals that are transmitted through the price system become more difficult to interpret, much in the way that static, or "noise," makes a radio message harder to interpret. In an economy with little or no inflation, the supplier of specialty foodstuffs will immediately recognize the increase in chanterelle prices as a signal to bring more to market. If inflation is high, however, the supplier must ask whether a price increase represents a true increase in the demand for chanterelles or is just a result of the general

Inflation adds static to the information conveyed by changes in prices.

inflation, which causes all food prices to rise. If the price rise reflects only inflation, the price of chanterelles *relative to other goods and services* has not really changed. The supplier therefore should not change the quantity of mushrooms he brings to market.

In an inflationary environment, to discern whether the increase in chanterelle prices is a true signal of increased demand, the supplier needs to know not only the price of chanterelles but also what is happening to the prices of other goods and services. Since this information takes time and effort to collect, the supplier's response to the change in chanterelle prices is likely to be slower and more tentative.

In summary, price changes are the market's way of communicating information to suppliers and demanders. An increase in the price of a good or service, for example, tells demanders to economize on their use of the good or service and suppliers to bring more of it to market. But in the presence of inflation, prices are affected not only by changes in the supply and demand for a product but by changes in the general price level. Inflation creates static, or "noise," in the price system, obscuring the information transmitted by prices and reducing the efficiency of the market system. This reduction in efficiency imposes real economic costs.

DISTORTIONS OF THE TAX SYSTEM

Just as some government expenditures, such as Social Security benefits, are indexed to inflation, many taxes are also indexed. In the United States, people with higher incomes pay a higher *percentage* of their income in taxes. Without indexing, an inflation that raises people's nominal incomes would force them to pay an increasing percentage of their income in taxes, even though their *real* incomes may not have increased. To avoid this phenomenon, which is known as *bracket creep*, Congress has indexed income tax brackets to the CPI. The effect of this indexation is that a family whose nominal income is rising at the same rate as inflation does not have to pay a higher percentage of income in taxes.

Although indexing has solved the problem of bracket creep, many provisions of the tax code have not been indexed, either because of lack of political support or because of the complexity of the task. As a result, inflation can produce unintended changes in the taxes people pay, which in turn may cause them to change their behavior in economically undesirable ways.

To illustrate, an important provision in the business tax code for which inflation poses problems is the *capital depreciation allowance,* which works as follows. Suppose a firm buys a machine for $1,000, expecting it to last for 10 years. Under U.S. tax law, the firm can take one-tenth of the purchase price, or $100, as a deduction from its taxable profits in each of the 10 years. By deducting a fraction of the purchase price from its taxable profits, the firm reduces its taxes. The exact amount of the yearly tax reduction is the tax rate on corporate profits times $100.

The idea behind this provision of the tax code is that the wearing out of the machine is a cost of doing business that should be deducted from the firm's profit. Also, in giving firms a tax break for investing in new machinery, Congress intended to encourage firms to modernize their plants. Yet capital depreciation allowances are not indexed to inflation. Suppose that, at a time when the inflation rate is high, a firm is considering purchasing a $1,000 machine. The managers know that the purchase will allow them to deduct $100 per year from taxable profits for the next 10 years. But that $100 is a fixed amount that is not indexed to inflation. Looking forward, managers will recognize that 5, 6, or 10 years into the future, the real value of the $100 tax deduction will be much lower than at present because of inflation. They will have less incentive to buy the machine and may decide not to make the investment at all. Indeed, many studies have found that a high rate of inflation can significantly reduce the rate at which firms invest in new factories and equipment.

Because the complex U.S. tax code contains hundreds of provisions and tax rates that are not indexed, inflation can seriously distort the incentives provided by the tax system for people to work, save, and invest. The resulting adverse effects on economic efficiency and economic growth represent a real cost of inflation.

UNEXPECTED REDISTRIBUTION OF WEALTH

Yet another concern about inflation is that it may arbitrarily redistribute wealth from one group to another. Consider a group of union workers who have signed a contract setting their wages for the next 3 years. If those wages are not indexed to inflation, then the workers will be vulnerable to upsurges in the price level. Suppose, for example, that inflation is much higher than expected over the 3 years of the contract. In that case the buying power of the workers' wages—their real wages—will be less than anticipated when they signed the contract.

From society's point of view, is the buying power that workers lose to inflation really "lost"? The answer is no; the loss in their buying power is exactly matched by an unanticipated gain in the employer's buying power, because the real cost of paying the workers is less than anticipated. In other words, the effect of the inflation is not to *destroy* purchasing power but to *redistribute* it, in this case from the workers to the employer. If inflation had been *lower* than expected, the workers would have enjoyed greater purchasing power than they anticipated and the employer would have been the loser.

Another example of the redistribution caused by inflation takes place between borrowers (debtors) and lenders (creditors). Suppose one of the authors of this book wants to buy a house on a lake and borrows $150,000 from the bank to pay for it. Shortly after signing the mortgage agreement, he learns that inflation is likely to be much higher than expected. How should he react to the news? Perhaps as a public-spirited macroeconomist the author should be saddened to hear that inflation has risen, but as a consumer he should be pleased. In real terms, the dollars with which he will repay his loan in the future will be worth much less than expected. The loan officer should be distraught, because the dollars the bank will receive from the author will be worth less, in purchasing power terms, than expected at contract signing. Once again, no real wealth is "lost" to the inflation; rather, the borrower's gain is just offset by the lender's loss. *In general, unexpectedly high inflation rates help borrowers at the expense of lenders*, because borrowers are able to repay their loans in less valuable dollars. Unexpectedly low inflation rates, in contrast, help lenders and hurt borrowers by forcing borrowers to repay in dollars that are worth more than expected when the loan was made.

Although redistributions caused by inflation do not directly destroy wealth, but only transfer it from one group to another, they are still bad for the economy. Our economic system is based on incentives. For it to work well, people must know that if they work hard, save some of their income, and make wise financial investments, they will be rewarded in the long run with greater real wealth and a better standard of living. Some observers have compared a high-inflation economy to a casino, in which wealth is distributed largely by luck—that is, by random fluctuations in the inflation rate. In the long run, a "casino economy" is likely to perform poorly, as its unpredictability discourages people from working and saving. (Why bother if inflation can take away your savings overnight?) Rather, a high-inflation economy encourages people to use up resources in trying to anticipate inflation and protect themselves against it.

INTERFERENCE WITH LONG-RUN PLANNING

The fifth and final cost of inflation we will examine is its tendency to interfere with the long-run planning of households and firms. Many economic decisions take place within a long time horizon. Planning for retirement, for example, may begin when workers are in their twenties or thirties. And firms develop long-run investment and business strategies that look decades into the future.

Clearly, high and erratic inflation can make long-term planning difficult. Suppose, for example, that you want to enjoy a certain standard of living when you retire. How much of your income do you need to save to make your dreams a reality? That depends on what the goods and services you plan to buy will cost 30 or 40 years from now. With high and erratic inflation, even guessing what your chosen lifestyle will cost by the time you retire is extremely difficult. You may end up saving too little and having to compromise on your retirement plans; or you may save too much, sacrificing more than you need to during your working years. Either way, inflation will have proved costly.

In summary, inflation damages the economy in a variety of ways. Some of its effects are difficult to quantify and are therefore controversial. But most economists agree that a low and stable inflation rate is instrumental in maintaining a healthy economy.

RECAP **THE TRUE COSTS OF INFLATION**

The public sometimes confuses changes in relative prices (such as the price of oil) with inflation, which is a change in the overall level of prices. This confusion can cause problems, because the remedies for undesired changes in relative prices and for inflation are different.

There are a number of true costs of inflation, which together tend to reduce economic growth and efficiency. These include:

- Shoe-leather costs, or the costs of economizing on cash (for example, by making more frequent trips to the bank or installing a computerized cash management system)

- "Noise" in the price system, which occurs when general inflation makes it difficult for market participants to interpret the information conveyed by prices

- Distortions of the tax system, for example, when provisions of the tax code are not indexed

- Unexpected redistributions of wealth, as when inflation higher than expected hurts wage earners to the benefit of employers or hurts creditors to the benefit of debtors

- Interference with long-term planning, arising because people find it difficult to forecast prices over long periods.

HYPERINFLATION

Although there is some disagreement about whether an inflation rate of, say, 5 percent per year imposes important costs on an economy, few economists would question the fact that an inflation rate of 500 percent or 1,000 percent per year disrupts economic performance. A situation in which the inflation rate is extremely high is called **hyperinflation**. While there is no official threshold above which inflation becomes hyperinflation, inflation rates in the range of 500 to 1,000 percent per year would surely qualify. In the past few decades episodes of hyperinflation have occurred in several Latin American countries (including Bolivia, Argentina, and Brazil), in Israel, and in several countries attempting to make the transition from communism to capitalism, including Russia. The United States has never experienced hyperinflation, although the short-lived Confederate States of America suffered severe inflation during the Civil War. Between 1861 and 1865 prices in the Confederacy rose to 92 times their prewar levels.

Hyperinflation greatly magnifies the costs of inflation. For example, shoe-leather costs—a relatively minor consideration in times of low inflation—become quite important during hyperinflation, when people may visit the bank two or three times per day to hold money for as short a time as possible. With prices changing daily or even hourly, markets work quite poorly, slowing economic growth. Massive redistributions of wealth take place, impoverishing many. Not surprisingly, episodes of hyperinflation rarely last more than a few years; they are so disruptive that they quickly lead to public outcry for relief.

hyperinflation a situation in which the inflation rate is extremely high

Why is shopping with U.S. dollars easy in Buenos Aires?

American visitors to Argentina find that they can use U.S. dollars freely in making purchases and often receive dollars in change. Argentina has its own currency, called the peso, so why are U.S. dollars usable everywhere in that nation, even in official transactions?

In 1991 Argentina introduced a system called a *currency board*. Under this system, the Argentine government stands ready to trade U.S. dollars for Argentine pesos, or pesos for dollars, at a one-to-one rate. Because dollars and pesos are legally interchangeable, people use and accept either in making transactions.

Why did Argentina introduce this system? During the 1980s Argentina suffered several episodes of hyperinflation, which proved highly destructive to its economy. By introducing a system of one-to-one convertibility between dollars and pesos, the Argentine government hoped to ensure that their currency would be "as strong as the dollar," with the same low inflation rate as in the United States. So far this approach has been successful; inflation has come down and remained low in Argentina. Some economists have suggested that Argentina should take the next logical step and abandon the peso in favor of using U.S. dollars exclusively, a policy referred to as "dollarization."

INFLATION AND INTEREST RATES

So far we have focused on the measurement and economic costs of inflation. Another important aspect of inflation is its close relationship to other key macroeconomic variables. For example, economists have long realized that during periods of high inflation interest rates tend to be high as well. We will close this chapter with a look at the relationship between inflation and interest rates, which will provide a useful background in the chapters to come.

INFLATION AND THE REAL INTEREST RATE

Earlier in our discussion of the ways in which inflation redistributes wealth, we saw that inflation tends to hurt creditors and help debtors by reducing the value of the dollars with which debts are repaid. The effect of inflation on debtors and

ECONOMIC NATURALIST 19.3

Why are U.S. dollars legal currency in Argentina?

creditors can be explained more precisely using an economic concept called the *real interest rate*. An example will illustrate.

Suppose that there are two neighboring countries, Alpha and Beta. In Alpha, whose currency is called the alphan, the inflation rate is zero and is expected to remain at zero. In Beta, where the currency is the betan, the inflation rate is 10 percent and is expected to remain at that level. Bank deposits pay 2 percent annual interest in Alpha and 10 percent annual interest in Beta. In which countries are bank depositors getting a better deal?

You may answer "Beta," since interest rates on deposits are higher in that country. But if you think about the effects of inflation, you will recognize that Alpha, not Beta, offers the better deal to depositors. To see why, think about the change over a year in the real purchasing power of deposits in the two countries. In Alpha, someone who deposits 100 alphans in the bank on January 1 will have 102 alphans on December 31. Because there is no inflation in Alpha, on average prices are the same at the end of the year as they were at the beginning. Thus the 102 alphans the depositor can withdraw represent a 2 percent increase in buying power.

In Beta, the depositor who deposits 100 betans on January 1 will have 110 betans by the end of the year—10 percent more than she started with. But the prices of goods and services in Beta, we have assumed, will also rise by 10 percent. Thus the Beta depositor can afford to buy precisely the same amount of goods and services at the end of the year as she could at the beginning; she gets no increase in buying power. So the Alpha depositor has the better deal, after all.

real interest rate the annual percentage increase in the purchasing power of a financial asset; the real interest rate on any asset equals the nominal interest rate on that asset minus the inflation rate

Economists refer to the annual percentage increase in the *real* purchasing power of a financial asset as the **real interest rate,** or the *real rate of return,* on that asset. In our example, the real purchasing power of deposits rises by 2 percent per year in Alpha and by 0 percent per year in Beta. So the real interest rate on deposits is 2 percent in Alpha and 0 percent in Beta. The real interest rate should be distinguished from the more familiar market interest rate, also called the *nominal interest rate*. The **nominal interest rate** is the annual percentage increase in the nominal, or dollar, value of an asset.

nominal interest rate (or market interest rate) the annual percentage increase in the nominal value of a financial asset

As the example of Alpha and Beta illustrates, we can calculate the real interest rate for any financial asset, from a checking account to a government bond, by subtracting the rate of inflation from the market or nominal interest rate on that asset. So in Alpha, the real interest rate on deposits equals the nominal interest rate (2 percent) minus the inflation rate (0 percent), or 2 percent. Likewise in Beta, the real interest rate equals the nominal interest rate (10 percent) minus the inflation rate (10 percent), or 0 percent.

We can write this definition of the real interest rate in mathematical terms:

$$r = i - \pi,$$

where

$$r = \text{the real interest rate,}$$

$$i = \text{the nominal, or market, interest rate,}$$

$$\pi = \text{the inflation rate.}$$

EXAMPLE 19.9   **Real interest rates in the 1970s, 1980s, and 1990s**

Following are interest rates on government bonds for selected years in the 1970s, 1980s, and 1990s. In which of these years did the financial investors who bought government bonds get the best deal? The worst deal?

Year	Interest rate (%)	Inflation rate (%)
1970	6.5	5.7
1975	5.8	9.1
1980	11.5	13.5
1985	7.5	3.6
1990	7.5	5.4
1995	5.5	2.8
1999	4.7	2.5

Financial investors and lenders do best when the real (not the nominal) interest rate is high, since the real interest rate measures the increase in their purchasing power. We can calculate the real interest rate for each year by subtracting the inflation rate from the nominal interest rate. The results are 0.8 percent for 1970, −3.3 percent for 1975, −2.0 percent for 1980, 3.9 percent for 1985, 2.1 percent for 1990, 2.7 percent for 1995, and 2.2 percent for 1999. For purchasers of government bonds, the best of these years was 1985, when they enjoyed a real return of 3.9 percent. The worst year was 1975, when their real return was actually negative. In other words, despite receiving 5.8 percent nominal interest, financial investors ended up losing buying power in 1975, as the inflation rate exceeded the interest rate earned by their investments.

Figure 19.2 shows the real interest rate in the United States since 1960 as measured by the nominal interest rate paid on the federal government's debt minus the inflation rate. Note that the real interest rate was negative in the 1970s but reached historically high levels in the mid-1980s.

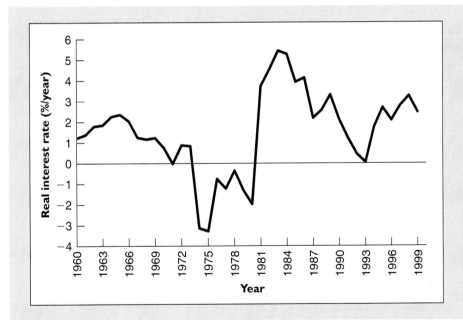

FIGURE 19.2
The Real Interest Rate in the United States, 1960–1999.
The real interest rate is the nominal interest rate—here the interest rate on funds borrowed by the federal government for a term of 3 months—minus the rate of inflation. In the United States, the real interest rate was negative in the 1970s but reached historically high levels in the mid-1980s. (SOURCE: *Economic Report of the President,* February 2000, and authors' calculations.)

EXERCISE 19.6

You have some funds to invest but are unimpressed with the low interest rates your bank offers. You consult a broker, who suggests a bond issued by the government of a small island nation. The broker points out that these bonds pay 25 percent interest—much more than your bank—and that the island's government has never failed to repay its debts. What should be your next question?

The concept of the real interest rate helps to explain more precisely why an unexpected surge in inflation is bad for lenders and good for borrowers. For any given nominal interest rate that the lender charges the borrower, the higher the inflation rate, the lower the real interest rate the lender actually receives. So unexpectedly high inflation leaves the lender worse off. Borrowers, on the other hand, are better off when inflation is unexpectedly high, because their real interest rate is lower than anticipated.

Although unexpectedly high inflation hurts lenders and helps borrowers, a high rate of inflation that is *expected* may not redistribute wealth at all, because expected inflation can be built into the nominal interest rate. Suppose, for example, that the lender requires a real interest rate of 2 percent on new loans. If the inflation rate is confidently expected to be zero, the lender can get a 2 percent real interest rate by charging a nominal interest rate of 2 percent. But if the inflation rate is expected to be 10 percent, the lender can still ensure a real interest rate of 2 percent by charging a nominal interest rate of 12 percent. Thus high inflation, if it is *expected*, need not hurt lenders—as long as the lenders can adjust the nominal interest they charge to reflect the expected inflation rate.

EXERCISE 19.7

What is the real rate of return to holding cash? (*Hint:* Does cash pay interest?) Does this real rate of return depend on whether or not the rate of inflation is correctly anticipated? How does your answer relate to the idea of shoe-leather costs?

THE FISHER EFFECT

Earlier we mentioned the observation that interest rates tend to be high when inflation is high and low when inflation is low. This relationship can be seen in Figure 19.3, which shows both the U.S. inflation rate and a nominal interest rate (the rate at which the government borrows for short periods) from 1960 to the present. Notice that nominal interest rates have tended to be high in periods of high inflation, such as the late 1970s, and relatively low in periods of low inflation, such as the early 1960s and the late 1990s.

Why do interest rates tend to be high when inflation is high? Our discussion of real interest rates provides the answer. Suppose inflation has recently been high,

FIGURE 19.3
Inflation and Interest Rates in the United States, 1960–1999.
Nominal interest rates tend to be high when inflation is high and low when inflation is low, a phenomenon called the Fisher effect. (SOURCE: *Economic Report of the President,* February 2000.)

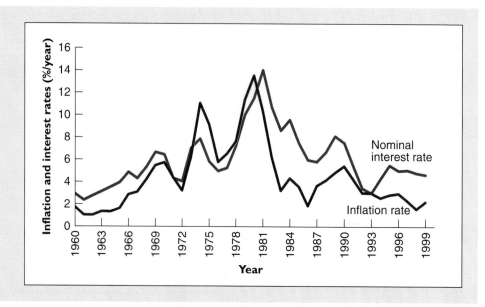

so borrowers and lenders anticipate that it will be high in the near future. We would expect lenders to raise their nominal interest rate so that their real rate of return will be unaffected. For their part, borrowers are willing to pay higher nominal interest rates when inflation is high, because they understand that the higher nominal interest rate only serves to compensate the lender for the fact that the loan will be repaid in dollars of reduced real value—in real terms, their cost of borrowing is unaffected by an equal increase in the nominal interest rate and the inflation rate. Conversely, when inflation is low, lenders do not need to charge so high a nominal interest rate to ensure a given real return. Thus nominal interest rates will be high when inflation is high and low when inflation is low. This tendency for nominal interest rates to follow inflation rates is called the **Fisher effect,** after the early twentieth-century American economist Irving Fisher, who first pointed out the relationship.

Fisher effect the tendency for nominal interest rates to be high when inflation is high and low when inflation is low

▪ SUMMARY ▪

- The basic tool for measuring inflation is the *consumer price index,* or CPI. The CPI measures the cost of purchasing a fixed basket of goods and services in any period relative to the cost of the same basket of goods and services in a base year. The *inflation rate* is the annual percentage rate of change in the price level as measured by a *price index* such as the CPI.

- The official U.S. inflation rate, based on the CPI, may overstate the true inflation rate for two reasons: First, it may not adequately reflect improvements in the quality of goods and services. Second, the method of calculating the CPI ignores the fact that consumers can substitute cheaper goods and services for more expensive ones.

- A *nominal quantity* is a quantity that is measured in terms of its current dollar value. Dividing a nominal quantity, such as a family's income or a worker's wage in dollars, by a price index such as the CPI expresses that quantity in terms of real purchasing power. This procedure is called *deflating* the nominal quantity. If nominal quantities from two different years are deflated by a common price index, the purchasing power of the two quantities can be compared. To ensure that a nominal payment, such as a Social Security benefit, represents a constant level of real purchasing power, the nominal payment should be increased each year by a percentage equal to the inflation rate. This method of adjusting nominal payments to maintain their purchasing power is called *indexing.*

- The public sometimes confuses increases in the *relative prices* for specific goods or services with inflation, which is an increase in the general price level. Since the remedies for a change in relative prices are different from the remedies for inflation, this confusion can cause problems.

- Inflation imposes a number of true costs on the economy, including "shoe-leather" costs, which are the real resources that are wasted as people try to economize on cash holdings; "noise" in the price system; distortions of the tax system; unexpected redistributions of wealth; and interference with long-run planning. Because of these costs, most economists agree that sustained economic growth is more likely if inflation is low and stable. *Hyperinflation,* a situation in which the inflation rate is extremely high, greatly magnifies the costs of inflation and is highly disruptive to the economy.

- The *real interest rate* is the annual percentage increase in the purchasing power of a financial asset. It is equal to the *nominal,* or *market, interest rate* minus the inflation rate. When inflation is unexpectedly high, the real interest rate is lower than anticipated, which hurts lenders but benefits borrowers. When inflation is unexpectedly low, lenders benefit and borrowers are hurt. To obtain a given real rate of return, lenders must charge a high nominal interest rate when inflation is high and a low nominal interest rate when inflation is low. The tendency for nominal interest rates to be high when inflation is high and low when inflation is low is called the *Fisher effect.*

▪ KEY TERMS ▪

■ REVIEW QUESTIONS ■

1. Explain why changes in the cost of living for any particular individual or family may differ from changes in the official cost-of-living index, the CPI.

2. What is the difference between the *price level* and the *rate of inflation* in an economy?

3. Why is it important to adjust for inflation when comparing nominal quantities (for example, workers' average wages) at different points in time? What is the basic method for adjusting for inflation?

4. Describe how indexation might be used to guarantee that the purchasing power of the wage agreed to in a multi-year labor contract will not be eroded by inflation.

5. Give two reasons why the official inflation rate may understate the "true" rate of inflation. Illustrate by examples.

6. "It's true that unexpected inflation redistributes wealth, from creditors to debtors, for example. But what one side of the bargain loses, the other side gains. So from the perspective of the society as a whole, there is no real cost." Do you agree? Discuss.

7. How does inflation affect the real return on holding cash?

8. True or false, and explain: If both the potential lender and the potential borrower correctly anticipate the rate of inflation, inflation will not redistribute wealth from the creditor to the debtor.

■ PROBLEMS ■

1. Government survey takers determine that typical family expenditures each month in the year designated as the base year are as follows:

   20 pizzas at $10 each
   Rent of apartment, $600 per month
   Gasoline and car maintenance, $100
   Phone service (basic service plus 10 long-distance calls), $50

   In the year following the base year, the survey takers determine that pizzas have risen to $11 each, apartment rent is $640, gasoline and maintenance has risen to $120, and phone service has dropped in price to $40.
   a. Find the CPI in the subsequent year and the rate of inflation between the base year and the subsequent year.
   b. The family's nominal income rose by 5 percent between the base year and the subsequent year. Are they worse off or better off in terms of what their income is able to buy?

2. Here are values of the CPI (multiplied by 100) for each year in the decade of the 1990s. For each year beginning with 1991, calculate the rate of inflation from the previous year. What happened to inflation rates over the 1990s?

1990	130.7
1991	136.2
1992	140.3
1993	144.5
1994	148.2
1995	152.4
1996	156.9
1997	160.5
1998	163.0
1999	166.2

3. According to the U.S. Census Bureau, nominal income for the typical family of four in the United States (median income) was $24,332 in 1980, $32,777 in 1985, $41,451 in 1990, and $53,350 in 1997. In purchasing power terms, how did family income compare in each of those 4 years? You will need to know that the CPI (multiplied by 100, 1982–1984 = 100) was 82.4 in 1980, 107.6 in 1985, 130.7 in 1990, and 160.5 in 1997. In general terms, how would your answer be affected if the Boskin Commission's conclusions about the CPI were confirmed?

4. A recent report found that the real entry-level wage for college graduates declined by 8 percent between 1990 and 1997. The nominal entry-level wage in 1997 was $13.65 per hour. Assuming that the findings are correct, what was the nominal entry-level wage in 1990? You will need to use data from Problem 2 above.

5. Here is a hypothetical income tax schedule, expressed in nominal terms, for the year 2000:

Family income	Taxes due (percent of income)
≤$20,000	10
$20,001–$30,000	12
$30,001–$50,000	15
$50,001–$80,000	20
>$80,000	25

The legislature wants to ensure that families with a given real income are not pushed up into higher tax brackets by inflation. The CPI (times 100) is 175 in 2000 and 185 in 2001. How should the income tax schedule above be adjusted for the year 2001 to meet the legislature's goal?

6. The typical consumer's food basket in the base year, 2000, is as follows:

   30 chickens at $3.00 each
   10 hams at $6.00 each
   10 steaks at $8.00 each

   A chicken feed shortage causes the price of chickens to rise to $5.00 each in the year 2001. Hams rise to $7.00 each, and the price of steaks is unchanged.
   a. Calculate the change in the "cost-of-eating" index between 2000 and 2001.
   b. Suppose that consumers are completely indifferent between two chickens and one ham. For this example, how large is the substitution bias in the official "cost-of-eating" index?

7. Here are the actual per-gallon prices for unleaded regular gasoline for June of each year between 1978 and 1986, together with the values of the CPIs for those years. For each year from 1979 to 1986, find the CPI inflation rate and the change in the relative price of gasoline, both from the previous year. Would it be fair to say that most of the changes in gas prices during this period were due to general inflation, or were factors specific to the oil market playing a role as well?

Year	Gasoline price ($/gallon)	CPI (1982–1984 = 1.00)
1978	0.663	0.652
1979	0.901	0.726
1980	1.269	0.824
1981	1.391	0.909
1982	1.309	0.965
1983	1.277	0.996
1984	1.229	1.039
1985	1.241	1.076
1986	0.955	1.136

8. Repeat Example 19.8 from the text (Shoe leather costs at Woodrow's Hardware). Calculate shoe leather costs (relative to the original situation, in which Woodrow goes to the bank once a week) assuming
   a. that inflation is 5 percent rather than 10 percent.
   b. that inflation is 5 percent and Woodrow's trips to the banks cost $2 each.
   c. that inflation remains at 10 percent and a trip to the bank costs $4, but Woodrow needs $10,000 per day to transact with customers.

9. On January 1, 2000, Albert invested $1,000 at 6 percent interest/year for 3 years. The CPI on January 1, 2000, stood at 100. On January 1, 2001, the CPI (times 100) was 105, on January 1, 2002, it was 110, and on January 1, 2003, the day Albert's investment matured, the CPI was 118. Find the real rate of interest earned by Albert in each of the 3 years and his total real return over the 3-year period. Assume that interest earnings are reinvested each year and themselves earn interest.

10. Frank is lending $1,000 to Sarah for 2 years. Frank and Sarah agree that Frank should earn a 2 percent real return per year.
    a. The CPI (times 100) is 100 at the time that Frank makes the loan. It is expected to be 110 in 1 year and 121 in 2 years. What nominal rate of interest should Frank charge Sarah?
    b. Suppose Frank and Sarah are unsure about what the CPI will be in two years. Show how Frank and Sarah could index Sarah's annual repayments to ensure that Frank gets an annual 2 percent real rate of return.

11. (More difficult) The Bureau of Labor Statistics has found that the base-year expenditures of the typical consumer break down as follows:

Food and beverages	17.8 percent
Housing	42.8 percent
Apparel and upkeep	6.3 percent
Transportation	17.2 percent
Medical care	5.7 percent
Entertainment	4.4 percent
Other goods, services	5.8 percent
Total	100.0 percent

Suppose that since the base year the prices of food and beverages have increased by 10 percent, the price of housing has increased by 5 percent, and the price of medical care has increased by 10 percent. Other prices are unchanged. Find the CPI for the current year.

■ ANSWERS TO IN-CHAPTER EXERCISES ■

19.1 The cost of the family's basket in 1995 remains at $680, as in Table 19.1. If the rent on their apartment falls to $400 in 2000, the cost of reproducing the 1995 basket of goods and services in 2000 is $620 ($400 for rent + $150 for hamburgers + $70 for movie tickets). The CPI for 2000 is accordingly $620/$680, or 0.912. So in this example, the cost of living has fallen nearly 9 percent between 1995 and 2000.

19.2 To construct your own personal price index, you would need to determine the basket of goods and services that you personally purchased in the base year. Your personal price index in each period would then be defined as the cost of your personal basket in that period relative to its cost in the base year. To the extent that your mix of purchases differs from that of the typical American consumer, your cost-of-living index will differ from the official CPI. For example, if in the base year you spent a higher share of your budget than the typical American on goods and services that have risen relatively rapidly in price, your personal inflation rate will be higher than the CPI inflation rate.

19.3 The percentage changes in the CPI in each year from the previous year are as follows:

1930	−2.3 percent = (0.167 − 0.171)/0.171
1931	−9.0 percent
1932	−9.9 percent
1933	−5.1 percent

Negative inflation is called deflation. The experience of the 1930s, when prices were falling, contrasts sharply with the 1970s, during which prices rose rapidly.

19.4 The real minimum wage in 1950 is $0.75/0.241, or $3.11 in 1982–1984 dollars. The real minimum wage in 1997 is $5.15/1.61, or $3.20 in 1982–1984 dollars. So the real minimum wage in 1997 is only slightly higher than what it was in 1950.

19.5 The increase in the cost of living between 1950 and 1997 is reflected in the ratio of the 1997 CPI to the 1950 CPI, or 1.61/0.241 = 6.68. That is, the cost of living in 1997 was 6.68 times what it was in 1950. If the minimum wage were indexed to preserve its purchasing power, it would have been 6.68 times higher in 1997 than in 1950, or 6.68 × $0.75 = $5.01. Since the actual minimum wage in 1997 was $5.15, the effect of formal indexation in this case would not have been very significant.

19.6 You should be concerned about the real return on your investment, not your nominal return. To calculate your likely real return, you need to know not only the nominal interest paid on the bonds of the island nation but also the prevailing inflation rate in that country. So your next question should be, "What is the rate of inflation in this country likely to be over the period that I am holding these bonds?"

19.7 The real rate of return to cash, as with any asset, is the nominal interest rate less the inflation rate. But cash pays no interest; that is, the nominal interest rate on cash is zero. Therefore the real rate of return on cash is just minus the inflation rate. In other words, cash loses buying power at a rate equal to the rate of inflation. This rate of return depends on the actual rate of inflation and does not depend on whether the rate of inflation is correctly anticipated.

   If inflation is high so that the real rate of return on cash is very negative, people will take actions to try to reduce their holdings of cash, such as going to the bank more often. The costs associated with trying to reduce holdings of cash are what economists call shoe-leather costs.

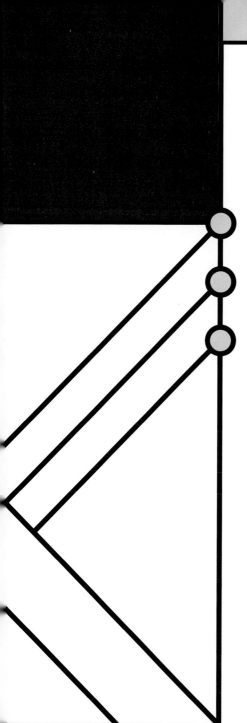

PART

6

THE ECONOMY IN THE LONG RUN

■

For millennia the great majority of the world's inhabitants eked out a spare existence by tilling the soil. Only a small proportion of the population lived above the level of subsistence, learned to read and write, or traveled more than a few miles from their birthplaces. Large cities grew up, serving as imperial capitals and centers of trade, but the great majority of urban populations lived in dire poverty, subject to malnutrition and disease.

Then, about three centuries ago, a fundamental change occurred. Spurred by technological advances and entrepreneurial innovations, a process of economic growth began. Sustained over many years, this growth in the economy's productive capacity has transformed almost every aspect of how we live—from what we eat and wear to how we work and play. What caused this economic growth? And why have some countries enjoyed substantially greater rates of growth than others? As Nobelist Robert E. Lucas, Jr., put it in a classic article on economic development, "The consequences for human welfare involved in questions like these are simply staggering: Once one starts to think about them, it is hard to think about anything else." Although most people would attach less significance to these questions than Lucas did, they are undoubtedly of very great importance.

The subject of Part 6 is the behavior of the economy in the long run, including the factors that cause the economy to grow and develop. Chapter 20 begins by tackling directly the causes and consequences of economic growth. A key conclusion of the chapter is that improvements in average labor productivity are the primary source of rising living standards; hence, policies to improve living standards should focus on stimulating productivity. Chapter 21 studies long-term trends in the labor market, analyzing the long-run effects of economic growth on real wages and employment opportunities. As the creation of new capital goods is an important factor underlying rising productivity, Chapter 22 examines the processes of saving and capital formation. Finally, Chapter 23 looks at the financial side of the saving-investment process, considering the role of banks, bond markets, and stock markets in allocating saving to productive uses. Chapter 23 also introduces the Federal Reserve System, which plays an important role in ensuring the stability of the economy.

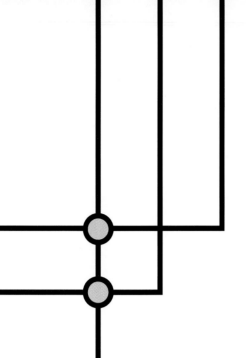

CHAPTER

20

ECONOMIC GROWTH, PRODUCTIVITY, AND LIVING STANDARDS

■

One of us once attended a conference on the effects of economic growth and development on society. A speaker at the conference posed the following question: "Which would you rather be? An ordinary, middle-class American living today, or the richest person in America at the time of George Washington?"

A member of the audience spoke out immediately: "I can answer that question in one word. Dentistry."

The answer drew a laugh, perhaps because it reminded people of George Washington's famous wooden teeth. But it was a good answer. Dentistry in early America—whether the patient was rich or poor—was a primitive affair. Most dentists simply pulled a patient's rotten teeth, with a shot of whiskey for anesthetic.

Other types of medical care were not much better than dentistry. Eighteenth-century doctors had no effective weapons against tuberculosis, typhoid fever, diphtheria, influenza, pneumonia, and other communicable diseases. Such illnesses, now quite treatable, were major killers in Washington's time. Infants and children were particularly susceptible to deadly infectious diseases, especially whooping cough and measles. Even a well-to-do family often lost two or three children to these illnesses. Washington, an unusually large and

Would you rather be a rich person living in the eighteenth century or a middle-class person living in the twenty-first century?

vigorous man, lived to the age of 67, but the average life expectancy during his era was probably not much more than 40 years.

Medical care is not the only aspect of ordinary life that has changed drastically over the past two centuries. Author Stephen Ambrose, in his account of the Lewis and Clark expedition, described the limitations of transportation and communication in early America:

> A critical fact in the world of 1801 was that nothing moved faster than the speed of a horse. No human being, no manufactured item, no bushel of wheat, no side of beef (or any beef on the hoof for that matter), no letter, no information, no idea, order, or instruction of any kind moved faster, and, as far as Jefferson's contemporaries were able to tell, nothing ever would.
>
> And except on a racetrack, no horse moved very fast. Road conditions in the United States ranged from bad to abominable, and there weren't very many of them. The best highway in the country ran from Boston to New York; it took a light stagecoach . . . three full days to make the 175-mile journey. The hundred miles from New York to Philadelphia took two full days. . . .[1]

Today New Yorkers can go to Philadelphia by train in an hour and a half. What would George Washington have thought of that? And how would nineteenth-century pioneers, who crossed the continent by wagon train, have reacted to the idea that their great-grandchildren would be able to have breakfast in New York and lunch the same day in San Francisco?

No doubt you can think of other enormous changes in the way average people live, even over the past few decades. Computer technologies and the Internet have changed the ways people work and study in just a few years, for example. Though these changes are due in large part to scientific advances, such discoveries *by themselves* usually have little effect on most people's lives. New scientific knowledge leads to widespread improvements in living standards only when it is commercially applied. Better understanding of the human immune system, for example, has little impact unless it leads to new therapies or drugs. And a new drug will do little to help unless it is affordable to those who need it.

A tragic illustration of this point is the AIDS epidemic in Africa. Although some new drugs will moderate the effects of the virus that causes AIDS, they are so expensive that they are of little practical value in poverty-stricken African nations grappling with the disease. But even if the drugs were affordable, they would have limited benefit without modern hospitals, trained health professionals, and adequate nutrition and sanitation. In short, most improvements in a nation's living standard are the result not just of scientific and technological advances but of an economic system that makes the benefits of those advances available to the average person.

In this chapter we will explore the sources of economic growth and rising living standards in the modern world. We will begin by reviewing the remarkable economic growth in the industrialized countries, as measured by real GDP per person. Since the mid-nineteenth century (and earlier in some countries), a radical transformation in living standards has occurred in these countries. What explains this transformation? The key to rising living standards is a *continuing increase in average labor productivity,* which depends on several factors, from the skills and motivation workers bring to their jobs to the legal and social environment in which they work. We will analyze each of these factors and discuss its implications for government policies to promote growth. We will also discuss the costs of rapid economic growth and consider whether there may be limits to the amount of economic growth a society can achieve.

---

[1]Stephen E. Ambrose, *Undaunted Courage: Meriwether Lewis, Thomas Jefferson, and the Opening of the American West,* New York: Touchstone (Simon & Schuster), 1996, p. 52.

THE REMARKABLE RISE IN LIVING STANDARDS: THE RECORD

The advances in health care and transportation mentioned in the beginning of this chapter illustrate only a few of the impressive changes that have taken place in people's material well-being over the past two centuries, particularly in industrialized countries like the United States. To study the factors that affect living standards systematically, however, we must go beyond anecdotes and adopt a specific measure of economic well-being in a particular country and time.

In Chapter 18 we introduced the concept of real GDP as a basic measure of the level of economic activity in a country. Recall that, in essence, real GDP measures the physical volume of goods and services produced within a country's borders during a specific period, such as a quarter or a year. Consequently, real GDP *per person* provides a measure of the quantity of goods and services available to the typical resident of a country at a particular time. Although real GDP per person is certainly not a perfect indicator of economic well-being, as we saw in Chapter 18, it is positively related to a number of pertinent variables, such as life expectancy, infant health, and literacy. Lacking a better alternative, economists have focused on real GDP per person as a key measure of a country's living standard and stage of economic development.

Figure 17.2 showed the remarkable growth in real GDP per person that occurred in the United States between 1900 and 1999. For comparison, Table 20.1 shows real GDP per person in eight major countries in selected years from 1870 to 1998. Figure 20.1 displays the same data graphically for five of the eight countries.

The data in Table 20.1 and Figure 20.1 tell a dramatic story. For example, in the United States (which was already a relatively wealthy industrialized country in 1870), real GDP per person grew more than 10-fold between 1870 and 1998. In Japan, real GDP per person grew more than 25 times over the same period. Underlying these statistics is an amazingly rapid process of economic growth and transformation, through which in just a few generations relatively poor agrarian societies became highly industrialized economies—with average standards of living

TABLE 20.1

Real GDP per Person in Selected Countries, 1870–1998 (in 1990 U.S. Dollars)

Country	1870	1913	1950	1979	1998	Annual % change 1870–1998	Annual % change 1950–1998
Australia	4,280	5,618	7,274	13,719	18,089	1.1	1.9
Canada	1,928	4,563	7,377	16,468	19,406	1.8	2.0
France	1,933	3,783	5,200	15,302	18,334	1.8	2.6
Germany	1,016	1,957	4,222	15,195	18,723	2.3	3.1
Italy	1,853	2,611	3,332	10,989	17,329	1.7	3.4
Japan	774	1,466	1,780	13,576	19,379	2.5	5.0
United Kingdom	2,875	4,414	6,433	12,230	16,674	1.4	2.0
United States	2,352	5,581	9,864	18,601	25,340	1.9	2.0

SOURCES: Derived from Angus Maddison, *Phases of Capitalist Development*, Oxford: Oxford University Press, reprinted 1988, Tables A2, B2–B4. Rebased to 1990 and updated to 1998 by the authors using OECD *Quarterly National Accounts* (real GDP), *International Financial Statistics* (population), and the *Economic Report of the President* (U.S. data). "Germany" refers to West Germany in 1950 and 1979.

FIGURE 20.1

Real GDP per Person in Five Industrialized Countries, 1870–1998. Economic growth has been especially rapid since the 1950s, particularly in Japan.

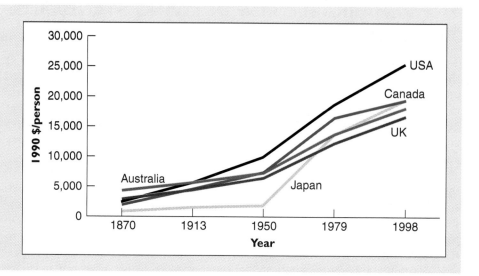

that could scarcely have been imagined in 1870. As Figure 20.1 shows, a significant part of this growth has occurred since 1950, particularly in Japan.

A note of caution is in order. The farther back in time we go, the less precise are historical estimates of real GDP. Most governments did not keep official GDP statistics until after World War II; production records from earlier periods are often incomplete or of questionable accuracy. Comparing economic output over a century or more is also problematic because many goods and services that are produced today were unavailable—indeed, inconceivable—in 1870. How many nineteenth-century horse-drawn wagons, for example, would be the economic equivalent of a BMW 328i automobile or a Boeing 757 jet? Despite the difficulty of making precise comparisons, however, we can say with certainty that the variety, quality, and quantity of available goods and services increased enormously in industrialized countries during the nineteenth and twentieth centuries, a fact reflected in the data on real GDP per capita.

WHY "SMALL" DIFFERENCES IN GROWTH RATES MATTER

The last two columns of Table 20.1 show the annual growth rates of real GDP per person, both for the entire 1870–1998 period and the more recent years, 1950–1998. At first glance these growth rates don't seem to differ much from country to country. For example, for the period 1870–1998, the highest growth rate is 2.5 percent (Japan) and the lowest is 1.1 percent (Australia). But consider the long-run effect of this seemingly "small" difference in annual growth rates. In 1870, in terms of output per person, Australia was by far the richest of the eight countries listed in Table 20.1, with a real GDP per person nearly six times that of Japan. Yet by 1998 Japan had not just caught up to but exceeded Australia. This remarkable change in economic fortunes is the result of the apparently small difference between a 1.1 percent growth rate and a 2.5 percent growth rate, maintained over 128 years.

The fact that what seem to be small differences in growth rates can have large long-run effects results from what is called the *power of compound interest.*

EXAMPLE 20.1

Compound interest (1)

In 1800 your great-great-grandfather deposited $10.00 in a checking account at 4 percent interest. Interest is compounded annually (so that interest paid at the end of each year receives interest itself in later years). Great-Grandpa's will specified that the account be turned over to his most direct descendant (you) in the year 2000. When you withdraw the funds in that year, how much is the account worth?

The account was worth $10.00 in 1800; $10.00 × 1.04 = $10.40 in 1801; $10.00 × 1.04 × 1.04 = $10.00 × $(1.04)^2$ = $10.82 in 1802; and so on. Since 200 years have elapsed between 1800, when the deposit was made, and the year 2000, when the account is closed, the value of the account in the year 2000 is $10.00 × $(1.04)^{200}$, or $10.00 × 1.04 to the 200th power. Using a calculator, you will find that $10.00 times 1.04 to the 200th power is $25,507.50—a good return for a $10.00 deposit!

Compound interest—an arrangement in which interest is paid not only on the original deposit but on all previously accumulated interest—is distinguished from *simple interest,* in which interest is paid only on the original deposit. If your great-grandfather's account had been deposited at 4 percent simple interest, it would have accumulated only 40 cents each year (4 percent of the original $10.00 deposit), for a total value of $10.00 + 200 × $0.40 = $90.00 after 200 years. The tremendous growth in the value of his account came from the compounding of the interest—hence the phrase "the power of compound interest."

compound interest the payment of interest not only on the original deposit but on all previously accumulated interest

Compound interest (2)

EXAMPLE 20.2

Refer to Example 20.1. What would your great-grandfather's $10.00 deposit have been worth after 200 years if the annual interest rate had been 2 percent? 6 percent?

At 2 percent interest the account would be worth $10.00 in 1800; $10.00 × 1.02 = $10.20 in 1801; $10.00 × $(1.02)^2$ = $10.40 in 1802; and so on. In the year 2000 the value of the account would be $10.00 × $(1.02)^{200}$, or $524.85. If the interest rate were 6 percent, after 200 years the account would be worth $10.00 × $(1.06)^{200}$, or $1,151,259.04. Let's summarize the results of Examples 20.1 and 20.2:

Interest rate (%)	Value of $10 after 200 years
2	$524.85
4	$25,507.50
6	$1,151,259.04

The power of compound interest is that even at relatively low rates of interest, a small sum, compounded over a long enough period, can greatly increase in value. A more subtle point, illustrated by this example, is that small differences in interest rates matter a lot. The difference between a 2 percent and a 4 percent interest rate doesn't seem tremendous, but over a long period of time it implies large differences in the amount of interest accumulated on an account. Likewise, the effect of switching from a 4 percent to a 6 percent interest rate is enormous, as our calculations show.

Economic growth rates are similar to compound interest rates. Just as the value of a bank deposit grows each year at a rate equal to the interest rate, so the size of a nation's economy expands each year at the rate of economic growth. This analogy suggests that even a relatively modest rate of growth in output per person—say, 1 to 2 percent per year—will produce tremendous increases in average living standard over a long period. And relatively small *differences* in growth rates, as in the case of Australia versus Japan, will ultimately produce very different living standards. Over the long run, then, the rate of economic growth is an extremely important variable. Hence, government policy changes or other factors that affect the long-term growth rate even by a small amount will have a major economic impact.

EXERCISE 20.1

Suppose that real GDP per capita in the United States had grown at 2.5 percent per year, as Japan's did, instead of the actual 1.9 percent per year, from 1870 to 1998. How much larger would real GDP per person have been in the United States in 1998?

WHY NATIONS BECOME RICH: THE CRUCIAL ROLE OF AVERAGE LABOR PRODUCTIVITY

What determines a nation's economic growth rate? To get some insight into this vital question, we will find it useful to express real GDP per person as the product of two terms: average labor productivity and the share of the population that is working.

To do this, let Y equal total real output (as measured by real GDP, for example), N equal the number of employed workers, and POP equal the total population. Then real GDP per person can be written as Y/POP; average labor productivity, or output per employed worker, equals Y/N; and the share of the population that is working is N/POP. The relationship between these three variables is

$$\frac{Y}{POP} = \frac{Y}{N} \times \frac{N}{POP},$$

which, as you can see by canceling out N on the right-hand side of the equation, always holds exactly. In words, this basic relationship is

Real GDP per person = Average labor productivity ×
Share of population employed.

This expression for real GDP per person tells us something very basic and intuitive: The quantity of goods and services that each person can consume depends on (1) how much each worker can produce and (2) how many people (as a fraction of the total population) are working. Furthermore, because real GDP per person equals average labor productivity times the share of the population that is employed, real GDP per person can *grow* only to the extent that there is *growth* in worker productivity and/or the fraction of the population that is employed.

Figures 20.2 and 20.3 show the U.S. figures for the three key variables in the relationship above for the period 1960–1999. Figure 20.2 shows both real GDP per person and real GDP per worker (average labor productivity). Figure 20.3 shows the portion of the entire U.S. population (not just the working-age population) that was employed during that period. Once again, we see that the expansion in output per person in the United States has been impressive. Between 1960 and 1999, real GDP per person in the U.S. grew by 149 percent. Thus in 1999, the average American enjoyed about 2 1/2 times as many goods and services as in 1960. Figures 20.2 and 20.3 show that increases in both labor productivity and the share of the population holding a job contributed to this rise in living standard.

Let's look a bit more closely at these two contributing factors, beginning with the share of the population that is employed. As Figure 20.3 shows, between 1960 and 1999 the number of people employed in the United States rose from 36 to 49 percent of the entire population, a remarkable increase. The growing tendency of women to work outside the home (see Economic Naturalist 18.1) was the most important reason for this rise in employment. Another factor leading to higher rates of employment was an increase in the share of the general population that

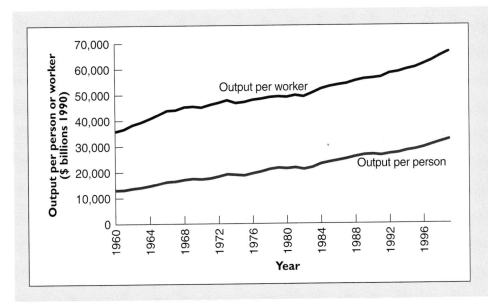

FIGURE 20.2
Real GDP per Person and Average Labor Productivity in the United States, 1960–1999.
Real output per person in the United States grew 149 percent between 1960 and 1999, and real output per worker (average labor productivity) grew by 85 percent.

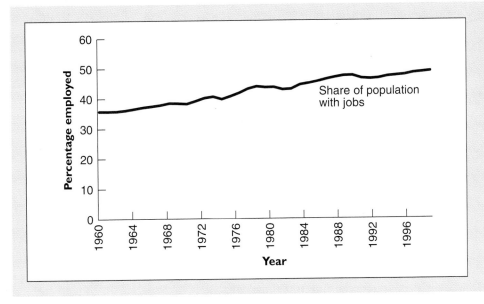

FIGURE 20.3
Share of the U.S. Population Employed, 1960–1999.
The share of the U.S. population holding a job increased from 36 percent in 1960 to 49 percent in 1999.

is of working age (ages 16 to 65). The coming of age of the "baby boom" generation, born in the years after World War II, and to a lesser extent the immigration of young workers from other countries, helped cause this growth in the workforce.

Although the rising share of the U.S. population with jobs contributed significantly to the increase in real GDP per person during the past four decades, this trend almost certainly will not continue in the future. Women's participation in the labor force seems unlikely to continue rising at the same rate as in the past four decades. More important, the baby boom generation, now in its prime years of employment, will begin to reach retirement age around the year 2010. As more and more baby boomers retire, the fraction of the population that is employed will begin to drop, probably significantly. In the long run, then, the improvement in living standards brought about by the rising share of Americans with jobs will likely prove transitory.

What about the other factor that determines output per person, average labor productivity? As Figure 20.2 shows, between 1960 and 1999, average labor productivity in the United States increased by 85 percent, accounting for a sizable share of the overall increase in GDP per person. In other periods, the link between average labor productivity and output per person in the United States has often been even stronger, since in most earlier periods the share of the population holding jobs was more stable than it has been recently. (See Figure 17.2 for the behavior of real GDP per person and average labor productivity in the United States over the period 1900–1999.)

This quick look at recent data supports a more general conclusion. *In the long run, increases in output per person arise primarily from increases in average labor productivity.* In simple terms, the more people can produce, the more they can consume. To understand why economies grow, then, we must understand the reasons for increased labor productivity.

RECAP   **ECONOMIC GROWTH AND PRODUCTIVITY**

Real GDP per person, a basic indicator of living standards, has grown dramatically in the industrialized countries. This growth reflects the *power of compound interest:* Even a modest growth rate, if sustained over a long period of time, can lead to large increases in the size of the economy.

Output per person equals average labor productivity times the share of the population that is employed. Since 1960 the share of the U.S. population with jobs has risen significantly, but this variable is likely to decline in coming decades. In the long run, increases in output per person and hence living standards arise primarily from increases in average labor productivity.

THE DETERMINANTS OF AVERAGE LABOR PRODUCTIVITY

What determines the productivity of the average worker in a particular country at a particular time? Popular discussions of this issue often equate worker productivity with the willingness of workers of a given nationality to work hard. Everything else being equal, a culture that promotes hard work certainly tends to increase worker productivity. But intensity of effort alone cannot explain the huge differences in average labor productivity that we observe around the world. For example, average labor productivity in the United States is about 24 times what it is in Indonesia and 100 times what it is in Bangladesh, though there is little doubt that Indonesians and Bangladeshis work very hard.

In this section we will examine six factors that appear to account for the major differences in average labor productivity, both between countries and between generations. Later in the chapter we will discuss how economic policies can influence these factors to spur productivity and growth.

HUMAN CAPITAL

To illustrate the factors that determine average labor productivity, we introduce two prototypical assembly line workers, Lucy and Ethel.

EXAMPLE 20.3   **Lucy and Ethel on the assembly line**

Lucy and Ethel have jobs wrapping chocolate candies and placing them into boxes. Lucy, a novice wrapper, can wrap only 100 candies/hour. Ethel, who has had on-the-job training, can wrap 300 candies/hour. Lucy and Ethel each work 40 hours/week. Find average labor productivity, in terms of candies wrapped per week and candies wrapped per hour, (a) for Lucy, (b) for Ethel, and (c) for Lucy and Ethel as a team.

We have defined average labor productivity in general terms as output per worker. Note, though, that the measurement of average labor productivity depends on the time period that is specified. For example, the data presented in Figure 20.2 tell us how much the average worker produces *in a year.* In this example we are concerned with how much Lucy and Ethel can produce *per hour* of work or *per week* of work. Any one of these ways of measuring labor productivity is equally valid, as long as we are clear about the time unit we are using.

Lucy and Ethel's hourly productivities are given in the problem: Lucy can wrap 100 candies/hour and Ethel can wrap 300. Lucy's weekly productivity is (40 hours/week) × (100 candies wrapped/hour) = 4,000 wrapped candies/week. Ethel's weekly productivity is (40 hours/week) × (300 candies wrapped/hour), or 12,000 candies/week.

Together Lucy and Ethel can wrap 16,000 candies/week. As a team, their average weekly productivity is (16,000 candies wrapped)/(2 weeks of work), or 8,000 candies/week. Their average hourly productivity as a team is (16,000 candies wrapped)/(80 hours of work) = 200 candies/hour. Notice that, taken as a team, the two women's productivity lies midway between their individual productivities.

How productive are these workers?

Ethel is more productive than Lucy because she has had on-the-job training, which has allowed her to develop her candy-wrapping skills to a higher level than Lucy's. Because of her training, Ethel can produce more than Lucy can in a given number of hours.

EXERCISE 20.2

Suppose Ethel attends additional classes in candy wrapping and learns how to wrap 500 candies/hour. Find the output per week and output per hour for Lucy and Ethel, both individually and as a team.

Economists would explain the difference in the two women's performance by saying that Ethel has more human capital than Lucy. *Human capital* comprises the talents, education, training, and skills of workers. Workers with a large stock of human capital are more productive than workers with less training. For example, a secretary who knows how to use a word processing program will be able to type more letters than one who doesn't; an auto mechanic who is familiar with computerized diagnostic equipment will be able to fix engine problems that less well-trained mechanics could not.

Why did West Germany and Japan recover so successfully from the devastation of World War II?

Germany and Japan sustained extensive destruction of their cities and industries during World War II and entered the postwar period impoverished. Yet within 30 years both countries had not only been rebuilt but had become worldwide industrial and economic leaders. What accounts for these "economic miracles"?

Many factors contributed to the economic recovery of West Germany and Japan from World War II, including the substantial aid provided by the United States to Europe under the Marshall Plan and to Japan during the U.S. occupation. Most economists agree, however, that high levels of *human capital* played a crucial role in both countries.

At the end of the war Germany's population was exceptionally well educated, with a large number of highly qualified scientists and engineers. The country also had (and still does today) an extensive apprentice system that provided on-the-job training to young workers. As a result, Germany had a skilled industrial workforce. In addition, the area that became West Germany benefited substantially from an influx of skilled workers from East Germany and the rest of Soviet-controlled Europe, including 20,000

ECONOMIC NATURALIST 20.1

trained engineers and technicians. Beginning as early as 1949, this concentration of human capital contributed to a major expansion of Germany's technologically sophisticated, highly productive manufacturing sector. By 1960 West Germany was a leading exporter of high-quality manufactured goods, and its citizens enjoyed one of the highest standards of living in Europe.

Japan, which probably sustained greater physical destruction in the war than Germany, also began the postwar period with a skilled and educated labor force. In addition, occupying American forces restructured the Japanese school system and encouraged all Japanese to obtain a good education. Even more so than the Germans, however, the Japanese emphasized on-the-job training. As part of a lifetime employment system, under which workers were expected to stay with the same company their entire career, Japanese firms invested extensively in worker training. The payoff to these investments in human capital was a steady increase in average labor productivity, particularly in manufacturing. By the 1980s Japanese manufactured goods were among the most advanced in the world and Japan's workers among the most skilled.

Although high levels of human capital were instrumental in the rapid economic growth of West Germany and Japan, human capital alone cannot create a high living standard. A case in point is Soviet-dominated East Germany, which had a level of human capital similar to West Germany's after the war but did not enjoy the same economic growth. For reasons we will discuss later in the chapter (see Economic Naturalist 20.3), the communist system imposed by the Soviets utilized East Germany's human capital far less effectively than the economic systems of Japan and West Germany.

Human capital is analogous to physical capital (such as machines and factories) in that it is acquired primarily through the investment of time, energy, and money. For example, to learn how to use a word processing program, a secretary might need to attend a technical school at night. The cost of going to school includes not only the tuition paid but also the *opportunity cost* of the secretary's time spent attending class and studying. The benefit of the schooling is the increase in wages the secretary will earn when the course has been completed. We know by the *cost-benefit principle* that the secretary should learn word processing only if the benefits exceed the costs, including the opportunity costs. In general, then, we would expect to see people acquire additional education and skills when the difference in the wages paid to skilled and unskilled workers is significant.

PHYSICAL CAPITAL

Workers' productivity depends not only on their skills and effort but on the tools they have to work with. Even the most skilled surgeon cannot perform open-heart surgery without sophisticated equipment, and an expert computer programmer is of limited value without a computer. These examples illustrate the importance of *physical capital*, such as factories and machines. More and better capital allows workers to produce more efficiently, as Example 20.4 shows.

EXAMPLE 20.4   **Lucy and Ethel get automated**

Refer to Example 20.3. Lucy and Ethel's boss has acquired an electric candy-wrapping machine, which is designed to be operated by one worker. Using this machine, an untrained worker can wrap 500 candies/hour. What are Lucy and Ethel's hourly and weekly outputs now? Will the answer change if the boss gets a second machine? A third?

Suppose for the sake of simplicity that a candy-wrapping machine must be assigned to one worker only. (This assumption rules out sharing arrangements, in which one worker uses the machine on the day shift and another on the night shift.) If the boss buys just one machine, she will assign it to Lucy. (Why? See Exercise 20.3.) Now Lucy will be able to wrap 500 candies/hour, while Ethel can wrap only 300/hour. Lucy's weekly output will be 20,000 wrapped candies (40 hours × 500 candies wrapped/hour). Ethel's weekly output is still 12,000 wrapped candies (40 hours × 300 candies wrapped/hour). Together they can now wrap 32,000 candies/week, or 16,000 candies/week each. On an hourly basis, average labor productivity for the two women taken together is 32,000 candies wrapped/80 hours of work, or 400 candies wrapped/hour—twice their average labor productivity before the boss bought the machine.

With two candy-wrapping machines available, both Lucy and Ethel could use a machine. Each could wrap 500 candies/hour, for a total of 40,000 wrapped candies/week. Average labor productivity for both women taken together would be 20,000 wrapped candies/week, or 500 wrapped candies/hour.

What would happen if the boss purchased a third machine? With only two workers, a third machine would be useless: it would add nothing to either total output or average labor productivity.

EXERCISE 20.3

Using the assumptions made in Examples 20.3 and 20.4, explain why the boss should give the single available candy-wrapping machine to Lucy rather than Ethel. (Hint: Use the principle of increasing opportunity cost, introduced in Chapter 3.)

The candy-wrapping machine is an example of a *capital good,* which was defined in Chapter 18 as a long-lived good, which is itself produced and used to produce other goods and services. Capital goods include machines and equipment (such as computers, earthmovers, or assembly lines) as well as buildings (such as factories or office buildings).

Capital goods like the candy-wrapping machine enhance workers' productivity. Table 20.2 summarizes the results from Examples 20.3 and 20.4. For each number of machines the boss might acquire (column 1), Table 20.2 gives the total weekly output of Lucy and Ethel taken together (column 2), the total number of hours worked by the two women (column 3), and average output per hour (column 4), equal to total weekly output divided by total weekly hours.

Table 20.2 demonstrates two important points about the effect of additional capital on output. First, for a given number of workers, adding more capital generally increases both total output and average labor productivity. For example, adding the first candy-wrapping machine increases weekly output (column 2) by 16,000 candies and average labor productivity (column 4) by 200 candies wrapped/hour.

The second point illustrated by Table 20.2 is that the more capital is already in place, the smaller the benefits of adding extra capital. Notice that the first

TABLE 20.2
Capital, Output, and Productivity in the Candy-Wrapping Factory

(1) Number of machines (capital)	(2) Total number of candies wrapped each week (output)	(3) Total hours worked per week	(4) Candies wrapped per hour worked (productivity)
0	16,000	80	200
1	32,000	80	400
2	40,000	80	500
3	40,000	80	500

machine adds 16,000 candies to total output, but the second machine adds only 8,000. The third machine, which cannot be used since there are only two workers, does not increase output or productivity at all. This result illustrates a general principle of economics, called *diminishing returns to capital*. According to the principle of **diminishing returns to capital**, if the amount of labor and other inputs employed is held constant, then the greater the amount of capital already in use, the less an additional unit of capital adds to production. In the case of the candy-wrapping factory, diminishing returns to capital implies that the first candy-wrapping machine acquired adds more output than the second, which in turn adds more output than the third.

> **diminishing returns to capital** if the amount of labor and other inputs employed is held constant, then the greater the amount of capital already in use, the less an additional unit of capital adds to production

Diminishing returns to capital are a natural consequence of firms' incentive to use each piece of capital as productively as possible. To maximize output, managers will assign the first machine that a firm acquires to the most productive use available, the next machine to the next most productive use, and so on—an illustration of the *principle of increasing opportunity cost,* or *low-hanging fruit principle* (Chapter 3). When many machines are available, all the highly productive ways of using them already have been exploited. Thus, adding yet another machine will not raise output or productivity by very much. If Lucy and Ethel are already operating two candy-wrapping machines, there is little point to buying a third machine, except perhaps as a replacement or spare.

The implications of Table 20.2 can be applied to the question of how to stimulate economic growth. First, increasing the amount of capital available to the workforce will tend to increase output and average labor productivity. The more adequately equipped workers are, the more productive they will be. Second, the degree to which productivity can be increased by an expanding stock of capital is limited. Because of diminishing returns to capital, an economy in which the quantity of capital available to each worker is already very high will not benefit much from further expansion of the capital stock.

Is there empirical evidence that giving workers more capital makes them more productive? Figure 20.4 shows the relationship between average labor productivity (real GDP per worker) and the amount of capital per worker in 15 major countries, including the 8 industrialized countries listed in Table 20.1. The figure shows a strong relationship between the amounts of capital per worker and productivity, consistent with the theory. Note, though, that the relationship between capital and productivity is somewhat weaker for the richest

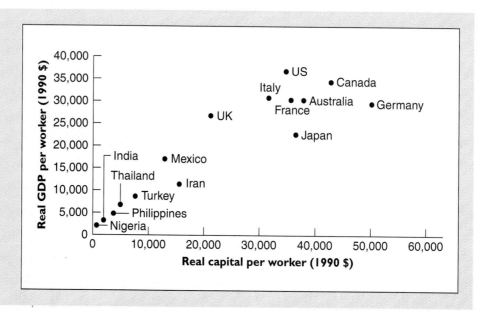

FIGURE 20.4

Average Labor Productivity and Capital per Worker in 15 Countries, 1990.

Countries with large amounts of capital per worker also tend to have high average labor productivity, as measured by real GDP per worker. (SOURCE: Penn World Tables [www.nber.org]. Countries included are those listed in Table 20.1, plus all countries with populations of 40 million or more for which data are available.)

countries. For example, Germany has more capital per worker than the United States, but German workers are less productive than American workers on average. Diminishing returns to capital may help to explain the weakening of the relationship between capital and productivity at high levels of capital. In addition, Figure 20.4 does not account for many other differences among countries, such as differences in economic systems or government policies. Thus we should not expect to see a perfect relationship between the two variables.

LAND AND OTHER NATURAL RESOURCES

Besides capital goods, other inputs to production help to make workers more productive, among them land, energy, and raw materials. Fertile land is essential to agriculture, and modern manufacturing processes make intensive use of energy and raw materials.

In general, an abundance of natural resources increases the productivity of the workers who use them. For example, a farmer can produce a much larger crop in a land-rich country like the United States or Australia than in a country where the soil is poor or arable land is limited in supply. With the aid of modern farm machinery and great expanses of land, today's American farmers are so productive that even though they constitute less than 3 percent of the population, they provide enough food not only to feed the country but to export to the rest of the world.

Although there are limits to a country's supply of arable land, many other natural resources, such as petroleum and metals, can be obtained through international markets. Because resources can be obtained through trade, countries need not possess large quantities of natural resources within their own borders to achieve economic growth. Indeed, a number of countries have become rich without substantial natural resources of their own, including Japan, Hong Kong, Singapore, and Switzerland. Just as important as possessing natural resources is the ability to use them productively—for example, by means of advanced technologies.

TECHNOLOGY

Besides human capital, physical capital, and natural resources, a country's ability to develop and apply new, more productive technologies will help to determine its productivity. Consider just one industry, transportation. Two centuries ago, as suggested by the quote from Steven Ambrose in the beginning of the chapter, the horse and wagon was the primary means of transportation—a slow and costly method indeed. But in the nineteenth century, technological advances such as the steam engine supported the expansion of riverborne transportation and the development of a national rail network. In the twentieth century, the invention of the internal combustion engine and the development of aviation, supported by the construction of an extensive infrastructure of roads and airports, have produced increasingly rapid, cheap, and reliable transport. Technological change has clearly been a driving force in the transportation revolution.

New technologies can improve productivity in industries other than the one in which they are introduced. Once farmers could sell their produce only in their local communities, for example. Now the availability of rapid shipping and refrigerated transport allows farmers to sell their products virtually anywhere in the world. With a broader market in which to sell, farmers can specialize in those products best suited to local land and weather conditions. Similarly, factories can obtain their raw materials wherever they are cheapest and most abundant, produce the goods they are most efficient at manufacturing, and sell their products wherever they will fetch the best price. Both these examples illustrate *the principle of comparative advantage,* that overall productivity increases when producers concentrate on those activities at which they are relatively most efficient (see Chapter 3).

Numerous other technological developments led to increased productivity, including advances in communication and medicine and the introduction of computer technology. All indications are that the Internet will have a major impact on the U.S. economy, not just in retailing but in many other sectors. In fact, *most economists would probably agree that new technologies are the single most important source of productivity improvement,* and hence of economic growth in general.

However, economic growth does not automatically follow from breakthroughs in basic science. To make the best use of new knowledge, an economy needs entrepreneurs who can exploit scientific advances commercially, as well as a legal and political environment that encourages the practical application of new knowledge.

EXERCISE 20.4

A new kind of wrapping paper has been invented that makes candy-wrapping quicker and easier. The use of this paper *increases* the number of candies a person can wrap by hand by 200 per hour, and the number of candies a person can wrap by machine by 300 per hour. Using the data from Examples 20.3 and 20.4, construct a table like Table 20.2 that shows how this technological advance affects average labor productivity. Do diminishing returns to capital still hold?

ENTREPRENEURSHIP AND MANAGEMENT

entrepreneurs people who create new economic enterprises

The productivity of workers depends in part on the people who help to decide what to produce and how to produce it: entrepreneurs and managers. **Entrepreneurs** are people who create new economic enterprises. Because of the new products, services, technological processes, and production methods they introduce, entrepreneurs are critical to a dynamic, healthy economy. In the late nineteenth and early twentieth centuries, individuals like Henry Ford and Alfred Sloan (automobiles), Andrew Carnegie (steel), John D. Rockefeller (oil), and J. P. Morgan (finance) played central roles in the development of American industry—and, not incidentally, amassed huge personal fortunes in the process. These people and others like them (including contemporary entrepreneurs like Bill Gates) have been criticized for some of their business practices, in some cases with justification. Clearly, though, they and dozens of other prominent business leaders of the past century have contributed significantly to the growth of the U.S. economy. Henry Ford, for example, developed the idea of mass production, which lowered costs sufficiently to bring automobiles within reach of the average American family. Ford began his business in his garage, a tradition that has been maintained by thousands of innovators ever since.

Entrepreneurship, like any form of creativity, is difficult to teach, although some of the supporting skills, like financial analysis and marketing, can be learned in college or business school. How, then, does a society encourage entrepreneurship? History suggests that the entrepreneurial spirit will always exist; the challenge to society is to channel entrepreneurial energies in economically productive ways. For example, economic policymakers need to ensure that taxation is not so heavy, and regulation not so inflexible, that small businesses—some of which will eventually become big businesses—cannot get off the ground. Sociological factors may play a role as well. Societies in which business and commerce are considered to be beneath the dignity of refined, educated people are less likely to produce successful entrepreneurs (see Economic Naturalist 20.2). In the United States, for the most part, business has been viewed as a respectable activity. Overall, a social and economic milieu that allows entrepreneurship to flourish appears to promote economic growth and rising productivity, perhaps especially so in high-technology eras like our own.

Lucy and Ethel get discovered

A television producer "discovers" Lucy and Ethel working on the production line at the candy factory and makes them stars of their own TV series. The show is a huge success and is seen by millions. How does the producer's discovery of Lucy and Ethel affect their average labor productivity?

Because Lucy and Ethel are so popular, and because television advertising fees are based on the number of people who watch a show, Lucy and Ethel are likely to increase the TV network's revenues by many millions of dollars. This increase in revenues is a measure of Lucy and Ethel's contribution to GDP. Their average labor productivity (in per-hour terms) is their contribution to GDP divided by the number of hours they work on the show. Clearly, Lucy's and Ethel's average labor productivity as TV stars will be many times what it was when they were candy wrappers.

This example illustrates the importance of creative entrepreneurship: If not for the TV producer's entrepreneurial skills, Lucy and Ethel would still be working on the assembly line, where their average labor productivity would be much lower.

Why did medieval China stagnate economically?

The Sung period in China (960–1270 A.D.) was one of considerable technological sophistication; its inventions included paper, waterwheels, water clocks, gunpowder, and possibly the compass. Yet no significant industrialization occurred, and in subsequent centuries Europe saw more economic growth and technological innovation than China. Why did medieval China stagnate economically?

According to research by economist William Baumol,[2] the main impediment to industrialization during the Sung period was a social system that inhibited entrepreneurship. Commerce and industry were considered low-status activities, not fit for an educated person. In addition, the emperor had the right to seize his subjects' property and to take control of their business enterprises—a right that greatly reduced his subjects' incentives to undertake business ventures. The most direct path to status and riches in medieval China was to go through a system of demanding civil service examinations given by the government every 3 years. The highest scorers on these national examinations were granted lifetime positions in the imperial bureaucracy, where they wielded much power and often became wealthy, in part through corruption. Not surprisingly, medieval China did not develop a dynamic entrepreneurial class, and consequently its scientific and technological advantages did not translate into sustained economic growth. China's experience shows why scientific advances alone cannot guarantee economic growth; to have economic benefits, scientific knowledge must be commercially applied through new products and new, more efficient means of producing goods and services.

EXAMPLE 20.5

ECONOMIC NATURALIST 20.2

Although entrepreneurship may be more glamorous, managers—the people who run businesses on a daily basis—also play an important role in determining average labor productivity. Managerial jobs span a wide range of positions, from the supervisor of the loading dock to the CEO (chief executive officer) at the helm of a *Fortune* 500 company. Managers work to satisfy customers, deal

[2]"Entrepreneurship: Productive, Unproductive, and Destructive," *Journal of Political Economy,* October 1990, pp. 893–921.

with suppliers, organize production, obtain financing, assign workers to jobs, and motivate them to work hard and effectively. Such activities enhance labor productivity. For example, in the 1970s and 1980s, Japanese managers introduced new production methods that greatly increased the efficiency of Japanese manufacturing plants. Among them was the *just-in-time* inventory system, in which suppliers deliver production components to the factory just when they are needed, eliminating the need for factories to stockpile components. Japanese managers also pioneered the idea of organizing workers into semi-independent production teams, which allowed workers more flexibility and responsibility than the traditional assembly line. Managers in the United States and other countries studied the Japanese managerial techniques closely and adopted many of them.

THE POLITICAL AND LEGAL ENVIRONMENT

So far we have emphasized the role of the private sector in increasing average labor productivity. But government too has a role to play in fostering improved productivity. One of the key contributions government can make is to provide a *political and legal environment* that encourages people to behave in economically productive ways—to work hard, save and invest wisely, acquire useful information and skills, and provide the goods and services that the public demands.

One specific function of government that appears to be crucial to economic success is the establishment of *well-defined property rights*. Property rights are well defined when the law provides clear rules for determining who owns what resources (through a system of deeds and titles, for example) and how those resources can be used. Imagine living in a society in which a dictator, backed by the military and the police, could take whatever he wanted, and regularly did so. In such a country, what incentive would you have to raise a large crop or to produce other valuable goods and services? Very little, since much of what you produced would likely be taken away from you. Unfortunately, in many countries of the world today, this situation is far from hypothetical.

Political and legal conditions affect the growth of productivity in other ways, as well. Political scientists and economists have documented the fact that *political instability* can be detrimental to economic growth. This finding is reasonable, since entrepreneurs and savers are unlikely to invest their resources in a country whose government is unstable, particularly if the struggle for power involves civil unrest, terrorism, or guerrilla warfare. On the other hand, a political system that promotes the *free and open exchange of ideas* will speed the development of new technologies and products. For example, some economic historians have suggested that the decline of Spain as an economic power was due in part to the advent of the Spanish Inquisition, which permitted no dissent from religious orthodoxy. Because of the Inquisition's persecution of those whose theories about the natural world contradicted Church doctrine, Spanish science and technology languished, and Spain fell behind more tolerant nations like the Netherlands.

EXERCISE 20.5

A Bangladeshi worker who immigrates to America is likely to find that his average labor productivity is much higher in the United States than it was at home. The worker is, of course, the same person he was when he lived in Bangladesh. How can the simple act of moving to the United States increase the worker's productivity? What does your answer say about the incentive to immigrate?

Why did communism fail?

For more than 70 years, from the Russian revolution in 1917 until the collapse of the Soviet Union in 1991, communism was believed by many to pose a major challenge to market-based economic systems. Yet, by the time of the Soviet Union's breakup, the poor economic record of communism had become apparent. Indeed, low living standards in communist countries, compared to those achieved in the West, were a major reason for the popular discontent that brought down the communist system. Economically speaking, why did communism fail?

The poor growth records of the Soviet Union and other communist countries did not reflect a lack of resources or economic potential. The Soviet Union had a highly educated workforce; a large capital stock; a vast quantity of natural resources, including land and energy; and access to sophisticated technologies. Yet, at the time of its collapse, output per person in the Soviet Union was probably less than one-seventh what it was in the United States.

Most observers would agree that the political and legal environment that established the structure of the communist economic system was a major cause of its ultimate failure. The economic system of the Soviet Union and other communist countries had two main elements: First, the capital stock and other resources were owned by the government rather than by individuals or private corporations. Second, most decisions regarding production and distribution were made and implemented by a government planning agency rather than by individuals and firms interacting through markets. This system performed poorly, we now understand, for several reasons.

One major problem was *the absence of private property rights.* With no ability to acquire a significant amount of private property, Soviet citizens had little incentive to behave in economically productive ways. The owner of an American or Japanese firm is strongly motivated to cut costs and to produce goods that are highly valued by the public, because the owner's income is determined by the firm's profitability. In contrast, the performance of a Soviet firm manager was judged on whether the manager produced the quantities of goods specified by the government's plan—irrespective of the quality of the goods produced or whether consumers wanted them. Soviet managers had little incentive to reduce costs or produce better, more highly valued products, as any extra profits would accrue to the government and not to the manager; nor was there any scope for entrepreneurs to start new businesses. Likewise, workers had little reason to work hard or effectively under the communist system, as pay rates were determined by the government planning agency rather than by the economic value of what the workers produced.

A second major weakness of the communist system was the *absence of free markets.* In centrally planned economies, markets are replaced by detailed government plans that specify what should be produced and how. But, as we saw in the example of New York City's food supply (Chapter 4), the coordination of even relatively basic economic activities can be extremely complex and require a great deal of information, much of which is dispersed among many people. In a market system, changes in prices both convey information about the goods and services people want and provide suppliers the incentives to bring these goods and services to market. Indeed, as we know from the *equilibrium principle,* a market in equilibrium leaves individuals with no unexploited opportunities. Central planners in communist countries proved far less able to deal with this complexity than decentralized markets. As a result, under communism consumers suffered constant shortages and shoddy goods.

After the collapse of communism, many formerly communist countries began the difficult transition to a market-oriented economic system. Changing an entire economic system (the most extreme example of a *structural policy*) is a slow and difficult task, and many countries saw economic conditions worsen at first rather than improve. *Political instability* and the absence of a modern *legal framework,* particularly laws applying to commercial transactions, have often hampered the progress of reforms. However, a number of formerly communist countries, including Poland, the Czech Republic, and the former East Germany, have succeeded in implementing Western-style market systems and have begun to achieve significant economic growth.

RECAP **DETERMINANTS OF AVERAGE LABOR PRODUCTIVITY**

Key factors determining average labor productivity in a country include:

- The skills and training of workers, called *human capital*

- The quantity and quality of *physical capital*—machines, equipment, and buildings

- The availability of land and other *natural resources*

- The sophistication of the *technologies* applied in production

- The effectiveness of *management* and *entrepreneurship*

- The broad *social and legal environment*

THE WORLDWIDE PRODUCTIVITY SLOWDOWN—AND RECOVERY?

During the 1950s and 1960s most of the major industrialized countries saw rapid growth in real GDP and average labor productivity. In the 1970s, however, productivity growth began to slow around the world. Slower growth in real GDP and in average living standards followed.

The slowdown in the growth of labor productivity is documented in Table 20.3, which gives data for the same eight industrialized countries included in Table 20.1. Note the sharp decline in productivity growth in all eight countries during 1973–1979 compared to 1960–1973. Japan's case was particularly striking: Its productivity growth rate fell from 8.4 percent per year in 1960–1973 to 2.8 percent in 1973–1979. In the United States, annual productivity growth fell from 2.6 percent before 1973 to just 0.3 percent per year during 1973–1979. During the period 1979–1997, productivity growth improved somewhat in the United States and the United Kingdom, but in all eight countries, the rate of productivity improvement since 1979 has been much slower than it was prior to 1973.

The sudden decline in worldwide productivity growth around 1973 is puzzling to economists and policymakers alike. What might have caused it? Some analysts have suggested answers that are specific to the United States, such as the

---

TABLE 20.3
Average Labor Productivity Growth Rates in Selected Countries, 1960–1997

Country	Percentage growth, annual rates		
	1960–1973	1973–1979	1979–1997
Australia	3.0	2.5	1.5
Canada	2.5	1.1	1.0
France	5.3	2.9	2.2
Germany	4.5	3.1	2.2
Italy	6.4	2.8	2.0
Japan	8.4	2.8	2.3
United Kingdom	4.0	1.6	2.0
United States	2.6	0.3	0.9

SOURCE: Growth rates of labor productivity in the business sector, OECD *Economic Outlook*, December 1998, Annex Table 59.

perceived decline in the quality of public education. However, such explanations are not very convincing, since they do not explain why so many other countries had the same problem. In the 1970s and 1980s many economists thought that the fourfold increase in oil prices that followed the Arab-Israeli war (1973) might have caused the slowdown. However, oil prices (relative to the prices of other goods) have long since returned to pre-1973 levels, yet productivity growth has not. Thus oil prices are no longer thought to have played a critical role in the slowdown.

One view of the slowdown in productivity since 1973 is that (at least in part) it is not a real phenomenon but the result of *poor measurement of productivity growth*. According to this argument, many of the productivity improvements that occur in modern services-oriented economies are difficult to capture in economic statistics. For example, the computerization of inventories allows supermarkets to offer customers a wider variety of products, with less chance that a particular product will be out of stock. ATM machines allow people to make banking transactions 24 hours a day, not just when the bank is open. And many medical procedures can be done far more quickly, safely, and painlessly today than just a few years ago (see Economic Naturalist 19.2). In theory, all these improvements in the quality of services should be captured in real GDP, and hence in productivity measures. In reality, accurate measurement of improvements in quality is difficult, as we saw when discussing biases in the CPI in Chapter 19, and some improvements may be missed. If the productivity slowdown is not real but reflects only poor measurement, then economists need not worry about it.

Another explanation, which is not mutually exclusive with the first, has been called the *technological depletion hypothesis*.[3] According to this hypothesis, the high rates of productivity in the 1950s and 1960s reflected an unusual period of "catch-up" after the Depression and the Second World War. Although scientific and technical advances continued to be made during the 1930s and 1940s (many of which arose from military research), depression and war prevented them from being adapted to civilian use. During the 1950s and 1960s, the backlog of technological breakthroughs was applied commercially, producing high rates of productivity growth at first and then a sharp decline in new technological opportunities. Once the catch-up period was over, productivity growth slowed. According to this hypothesis, then, the slowdown in productivity growth since the 1970s reflects a dearth of technological opportunities relative to the immediate postwar period. From this perspective, the 1950s and 1960s were the exception, and the period since the 1970s represents a return to more normal rates of productivity growth.

Although the rate of productivity growth over the past two decades has generally been low, in recent years there have been some hints of a possible recovery in productivity, particularly in the United States (see Figure 20.2). Between 1993 and 1999, U.S. productivity growth averaged nearly 2.1 percent per year, close to the rate achieved prior to 1973. Will this increase in productivity growth be sustained? Optimists argue that the United States is currently leading a new technological revolution, sparked by advances in computers, communications, genetics, and other fields, which will allow productivity to continue to grow indefinitely. Others are more cautious, arguing that the long-run commercial value of the new technologies has yet to be proven. A great deal is riding on which view will turn out to be correct.

THE COSTS OF ECONOMIC GROWTH

Both this chapter and Chapter 18 emphasized the positive effects of economic growth on the average person's living standard. But should societies always strive for the highest possible rate of economic growth? The answer is no. Even if we

[3]See, for example, William Nordhaus, "Economic Policy in the Face of Declining Productivity Growth," *European Economic Review*, May/June 1982, pp. 131–158.

accept for the moment the idea that increased output per person is always desirable, attaining a higher rate of economic growth does impose costs on society.

What are the costs of increasing economic growth? The most straightforward is the cost of creating new capital. We know that by expanding the capital stock we can increase future productivity and output. But, to increase the capital stock, we must divert resources that could otherwise be used to increase the supply of consumer goods. For example, to add more robot-operated assembly lines, a society must employ more of its skilled technicians in building industrial robots and fewer in designing video games. To build new factories, more carpenters and lumber must be assigned to factory construction and less to finishing basements or renovating family rooms. In short, high rates of investment in new capital require people to tighten their belts, consume less, and save more—a real economic cost.

Should a country undertake a high rate of investment in capital goods at the sacrifice of consumer goods? The answer depends on the extent that people are willing and able to sacrifice consumption today to have a bigger economic pie tomorrow. In a country that is very poor, or is experiencing an economic crisis, people may prefer to keep consumption relatively high and savings and investment relatively low. The midst of a thunderstorm is not the time to be putting something aside for a rainy day! But in a society that is relatively well off, people may be more willing to make sacrifices to achieve higher economic growth in the future.

Consumption sacrificed to capital formation is not the only cost of achieving higher growth. In the United States in the nineteenth and early twentieth centuries, periods of rapid economic growth were often times in which many people worked extremely long hours at dangerous and unpleasant jobs. While those workers helped to build the economy that Americans enjoy today, the costs were great in terms of reduced leisure time and, in some cases, workers' health and safety.

Other costs of growth include the cost of the research and development that is required to improve technology and the costs of acquiring training and skill (human capital). The fact that a higher living standard tomorrow must be purchased at the cost of current sacrifices is an example of the *scarcity principle,* that having more of one good thing usually means having less of another. Because achieving higher economic growth imposes real economic costs, we know from the *cost-benefit principle* that higher growth should be pursued only if the benefits outweigh the costs.

PROMOTING ECONOMIC GROWTH

If a society decides to try to raise its rate of economic growth, what are some of the measures that policymakers might take to achieve this objective? Here is a short list of suggestions, based on our discussion of the factors that contribute to growth in average labor productivity and, hence, output per person.

POLICIES TO INCREASE HUMAN CAPITAL

Because skilled and well-educated workers are more productive than unskilled labor, governments in most countries try to increase the human capital of their citizens by supporting education and training programs. In the United States, government provides public education through high school and grants extensive support to post-secondary schools, including technical schools, colleges, and universities. Publicly funded early-intervention programs like Head Start also attempt to build human capital by helping disadvantaged children prepare for school. To a lesser degree than some other countries, the U.S. government also funds job training for unskilled youths and retraining for workers whose skills have become obsolete.

Why do almost all countries provide free public education?

All industrial countries provide their citizens free public education through high school, and most subsidize college and other post-secondary schools. Why?

Americans are so used to the idea of free public education that this question may seem odd. But why should the government provide free education when it does not provide even more essential goods and services, such as food or medical care, for free, except to the most needy? Furthermore, educational services can be, and indeed commonly are, supplied and demanded on the private market, without the aid of the government.

An important argument for free or at least subsidized education is that the private demand curve for educational services does not include all the social benefits of education. (Recall the *equilibrium principle* of Chapter 4, which states in part that a market in equilibrium may not exploit all gains achievable from collective action). For example, the democratic political system relies on an educated citizenry to operate effectively—a factor that an individual demander of educational services has little reason to consider. From a narrower economic perspective, we might argue that individuals do not capture the full economic returns from their schooling. For example, people with high human capital, and thus high earnings, pay more taxes—funds that can be used to finance government services and aid the less fortunate. Because of income taxation, the private benefit to acquiring human capital is less than the social benefit, and the demand for education on the private market may be less than optimal from society's viewpoint. Similarly, educated people are more likely than others to contribute to technological development, and hence to general productivity growth, which may benefit many other people besides themselves. Finally, another argument for public support of education is that poor people who would like to invest in human capital may not be able to do so because of insufficient income.

The Nobel laureate Milton Friedman, among many economists, has suggested that these arguments may justify government grants, called educational *vouchers,* to help citizens purchase educational services in the private sector, but they do *not* justify the government providing education directly, as through the public school system. Defenders of public education, on the other hand, argue that the government should have some direct control over education in order to set standards and monitor quality. What do you think?

Why do almost all countries provide free public education?

POLICIES THAT PROMOTE SAVING AND INVESTMENT

Average labor productivity increases when workers can utilize a sizable and modern capital stock. To support the creation of new capital, government can encourage high rates of saving and investment in the private sector. Many provisions in the U.S. tax code are designed expressly to stimulate households to save and firms to invest. For example, a household that opens an Individual Retirement Account (IRA) is able to save for retirement without paying taxes on either the funds deposited in the IRA or the interest earned on the account. (However, taxes are due when the funds are withdrawn at retirement.) The intent of IRA legislation is to make saving more financially attractive to American households. Similarly, at various times Congress has instituted an investment tax credit, which reduces the tax bills of firms that invest in new capital. Private-sector saving and investment are discussed in greater detail in Chapter 22.

Government can contribute directly to capital formation through *public investment,* or the creation of government-owned capital. Public investment includes the building of roads, bridges, airports, dams, and, in some countries, energy and communications networks. The construction of the U.S. interstate highway system, begun during the administration of President Eisenhower, is often cited as an example of successful public investment. The interstate system substantially reduced long-haul transportation costs in the United States, improving productivity throughout the economy. Today, the web of computers and communications links we call the Internet is having a similar effect. This project, too, received crucial government funding in its early stages. Many research studies have confirmed that government investment in the *infrastructure,* the public capital that supports private-sector economic activities, can be a significant source of growth.

POLICIES THAT SUPPORT RESEARCH AND DEVELOPMENT

Productivity is enhanced by technological progress, which in turn requires investment in research and development (R&D). In many industries private firms have adequate incentive to conduct research and development activities. There is no need, for example, for the government to finance research for developing a better underarm deodorant. But some types of knowledge, particularly basic scientific knowledge, may have widespread economic benefits that cannot be captured by a single private firm. The developers of the silicon computer chip, for example, were instrumental in creating huge new industries, yet they received only a small portion of the profits flowing from their inventions. Because society in general, rather than the individual inventors, may receive much of the benefit from basic research, government may need to support basic research, as it does through agencies such as the National Science Foundation. The federal government also sponsors a great deal of applied research, particularly in military and space applications. To the extent that national security allows, the government can increase growth by sharing the fruits of such research with the private sector. For example, the Global Positioning System (GPS), which was developed originally for military purposes, is now available in private passenger vehicles, helping drivers find their way.

THE LEGAL AND POLITICAL FRAMEWORK

Although economic growth comes primarily from activities in the private sector, the government plays an essential role in providing the framework within which the private sector can operate productively. We have discussed the importance of secure property rights and a well-functioning legal system, of an economic environment that encourages entrepreneurship, and of political stability and the free and open exchange of ideas. Government policymakers should also consider the potential effects of tax and regulatory policies on activities that increase productivity, such as investment, innovation, and risk taking. Policies that affect the legal and political framework are examples of *structural macroeconomic policies* (see Chapter 17).

THE POOREST COUNTRIES: A SPECIAL CASE?

Radical disparities in living standards exist between the richest and poorest countries of the world (see Table 18.4 for some data). Achieving economic growth in the poorest countries is thus particularly urgent. Are the policy prescriptions of this section relevant to those countries, or are very different types of measures necessary to spur growth in the poorest nations?

To a significant extent, the same factors and policies that promote growth in richer countries apply to the poorest countries as well. Increasing human capital by supporting education and training, increasing rates of saving and investment, investing in public capital and infrastructure, supporting research and development, and encouraging entrepreneurship are all measures that will enhance economic growth in poor countries.

However, to a much greater degree than in richer countries, most poor countries need to improve the legal and political environment that underpins their economies. For example, many developing countries have poorly developed or corrupt legal systems, which discourage entrepreneurship and investment by creating uncertainty about property rights. Taxation and regulation in developing countries are often heavy-handed and administered by inefficient bureaucracies, to the extent that it may take months or years to obtain the approvals needed to start a small business or expand a factory. Regulation is also used to suppress market forces in poor countries; for example, the government, rather than the market, may determine the allocation of bank credit or the prices for agricultural products. Structural policies that aim to ameliorate these problems are important preconditions for generating growth in the poorest countries. But probably most important—and most difficult, for some countries—is establishing political stability and the rule of law. Without political stability, domestic and foreign savers will be reluctant to invest in the country, and economic growth will be difficult if not impossible to achieve.

Can rich countries help poor countries to develop? Historically, richer nations have tried to help by providing financial aid through loans or grants from individual countries (foreign aid) or by loans made by international agencies, such as the World Bank. Experience has shown, however, that financial aid to countries that do not undertake structural reforms, such as reducing excessive regulation or improving the legal system, are of limited value. To make their foreign aid most effective, rich countries should help poor countries achieve political stability and undertake the necessary reforms to the structure of their economies.

ARE THERE LIMITS TO GROWTH?

Earlier in this chapter we saw that even relatively low rates of economic growth, if sustained for a long period, will produce huge increases in the size of the economy. This fact raises the question of whether economic growth can continue indefinitely without depleting natural resources and causing massive damage to the global environment. Does the basic truth that we live in a finite world of finite resources imply that, ultimately, economic growth must come to an end?

The concern that economic growth may not be sustainable is not a new one. An influential 1972 book, *The Limits to Growth,*[4] reported the results of computer simulations that suggested that unless population growth and economic expansion were halted, the world would soon be running out of natural resources, drinkable water, and breathable air. This book, and later works in the same vein, has raised some fundamental questions that cannot be done full justice here. However, in some ways its conclusions are misleading.

One problem with the "limits to growth" thesis lies in its underlying concept of economic growth. Those who emphasize the environmental limits on growth assume implicitly that economic growth will always take the form of more of what we have now—more smoky factories, more polluting cars, more fast-food restaurants. If that were indeed the case, then surely there would be limits to the growth the planet can sustain. But growth in real GDP does not necessarily take such a form. Increases in real GDP can also arise from new or higher-quality products. For example, not too long ago tennis rackets were relatively simple items made primarily of wood. Today they are made of newly invented synthetic materials and designed for optimum performance using sophisticated computer simulations. Because these new high-tech tennis rackets are more valued by consumers than the old wooden ones, they increase the real GDP. Likewise, the introduction of new pharmaceuticals has contributed to economic growth, as have the expanded number of TV channels, digital sound, and Internet-based sales. Thus, economic growth need not take the form of more and

---

[4]Donella H. Meadows, Dennis L. Meadows, Jørgen Randers, and William W. Behrens, III, *The Limits to Growth*, New York: New American Library, 1972.

more of the same old stuff; it can mean newer, better, and perhaps cleaner and more efficient goods and services.

A second problem with the "limits to growth" conclusion is that it overlooks the fact that increased wealth and productivity expand society's capacity to take measures to safeguard the environment. In fact, the most polluted countries in the world are not the richest but those that are in a relatively early stage of industrialization (see Economic Naturalist 20.5). At this stage countries must devote the bulk of their resources to basic needs—food, shelter, health care—and continued industrial expansion. In these countries, clean air and water may be viewed as a luxury rather than a basic need. In more economically developed countries, where the most basic needs are more easily met, extra resources are available to keep the environment clean. Thus continuing economic growth may lead to less, not more, pollution.

A third problem with the pessimistic view of economic growth is that it ignores the power of the market and other social mechanisms to deal with scarcity. During the oil-supply disruptions of the 1970s, newspapers were filled with headlines about the energy crisis and the imminent depletion of world oil supplies. Yet 25 years later, the world's known oil reserves are actually *greater* than they were in the 1970s.

Today's energy situation is so much better than was expected 25 years ago because the market went to work. Reduced oil supplies led to an increase in prices that changed the behavior of both demanders and suppliers. Consumers insulated their homes, purchased more energy-efficient cars and appliances, and switched to alternative sources of energy. Suppliers engaged in a massive hunt for new reserves, opening up major new sources in Latin America, China, and the North Sea. In short, market forces solved the energy crisis.

In general, shortages in any resource will trigger price changes that induce suppliers and demanders to deal with the problem. Simply extrapolating current economic trends into the future ignores the power of the market system to recognize shortages and make the necessary corrections. Government actions spurred by political pressures, such as the allocation of public funds to preserve open space or reduce air pollution, can be expected to supplement market adjustments.

Despite the shortcomings of the "limits to growth" perspective, most economists would agree that not all the problems created by economic growth can be dealt with effectively through the market or the political process. Probably most important, global environmental problems, such as the possibility of global warming or the ongoing destruction of rain forests, are a particular challenge for existing economic and political institutions. Environmental quality is not bought and sold in markets and thus will not automatically reach its optimal level through market processes (recall the *equilibrium principle*). Nor can local or national governments effectively address problems that are global in scope. Unless international mechanisms are established for dealing with global environmental problems, these problems may become worse as economic growth continues.

Why is the air quality so poor in Mexico City?

Developing countries like Mexico, which are neither fully industrialized nor desperately poor, often have severe environmental problems. Why?

One concern about economic growth is that it will cause ever-increasing levels of environmental pollution. Empirical studies show, however, that the relationship between pollution and real GDP per person is more like an inverted U (see Figure 20.5). In other words, as countries move from very low levels of real GDP per person to "middle-income" levels, most measures of pollution tend to worsen, but environmental quality improves as real GDP per person rises even further. One study of the relationship between air quality and real GDP per person found that the level of real GDP per person at which air quality is the worst—indicated by point A in Figure 20.5—is roughly

ECONOMIC NATURALIST 20.5

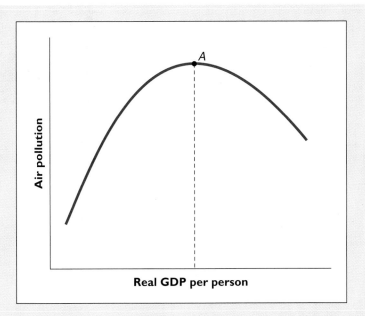

FIGURE 20.5
The Relationship between Air Pollution and Real GDP per Person.
Empirically, air pollution increases with real GDP per person up to a point and then begins to decline. Maximum air pollution (point A) occurs at a level of real GDP per person roughly equal to that of Mexico.

equal to the average income level in Mexico.[5] And indeed, the air quality in Mexico City is exceptionally poor, as any visitor to that sprawling metropolis can attest.

That pollution may worsen as a country industrializes is understandable, but why does environmental quality improve when real GDP per person climbs to very high levels? There are a variety of explanations for this phenomenon. Compared to middle-income economies, the richer economies are relatively more concentrated in "clean," high-value services like finance and software production as opposed to pollution-intensive industries like heavy manufacturing. Rich economies are also more likely to have the expertise to develop sophisticated and cost-effective antipollution technologies. But the main reason the richer economies tend to be cleaner is the same reason that the homes of rich people are generally cleaner and in better condition than the homes of the poor. As income rises above the level necessary to fulfill basic needs, more resources remain to dedicate to "luxuries" like a clean environment (the *scarcity principle*). For the rich family, the extra resources will pay for a cleaning service; for the rich country, they will pay for pollution control devices in factories and on automobiles. Indeed, antipollution laws are generally tougher and more strictly enforced in rich countries than in middle-income and poor countries.

■ SUMMARY ■

- Over the past two centuries the industrialized nations saw enormous improvements in living standards, as reflected in large increases in real GDP per person. Because of the power of *compound interest*, relatively small differences in growth rates, if continued over long periods, can produce large differences in real GDP per person and average living standards. Thus, the rate of long-term economic growth is an economic variable of critical importance.

- Real GDP per person is the product of average labor productivity (real GDP per employed worker) and the share of the population that is employed. Growth in real GDP per person can occur only through growth in average labor productivity, in the share of the population that is working, or both. In the period since 1960, increases in the share of the U.S. population holding a job contributed significantly to rising real GDP per person. But in the past

[5]Gene M. Grossman and Alan B. Krueger, "Environmental Impacts of a North American Free Trade Agreement," in Peter Garber, ed., *The Mexico–U.S. Free Trade Agreement*, Cambridge, MA: MIT Press, 1993. See also Grossman and Krueger, "Economic Growth and the Environment," *Quarterly Journal of Economics*, May 1995, pp. 353–78; and World Bank, *World Development Report: Development and the Environment*, 1992.

four decades, as in most periods, the main source of the increase in real GDP per person was rising average labor productivity.

- Among the factors that determine labor productivity are the talents, education, training, and skills of workers, or human capital; the quantity and quality of the physical capital that workers use; the availability of land and other natural resources; the application of technology to the production and distribution of goods and services; the effectiveness of *entrepreneurs* and managers; and the broad social and legal environment. Because of *diminishing returns to capital,* beyond a certain point expansion of the capital stock is not the most effective way to increase average labor productivity. Economists generally agree that new technologies are the most important single source of improvements in productivity.

- Since the 1970s the industrial world has experienced a slowdown in productivity growth. Some economists have suggested that the "slowdown" is more the result of an inability to measure increases in the quality of output than of any real economic change. Others have suggested that the exploitation of a backlog of technological opportunities following the Great Depression and World War II led to unusually high growth rates in the 1950s and 1960s, a view called the technological depletion hypothesis. In this view, the slower growth in U.S. productivity since about 1970 in fact reflects a return to a more normal rate of growth. U.S. productivity growth has picked up since about 1993; it is too early to tell if this increased growth will be sustained.

- Economic growth has costs as well as benefits. Prominent among them is the need to sacrifice current consumption to achieve a high rate of investment in new capital goods; other costs of growing more quickly include extra work effort and the costs of research and development. Thus more economic growth is not necessarily better; whether increased economic growth is desirable depends on whether the benefits of growth outweigh the costs.

- Among the ways in which government can stimulate economic growth are by adopting policies that encourage the creation of human capital; that promote saving and investment, including public investment in infrastructure; that support research and development, particularly in the basic sciences; and that provide a legal and political framework that supports private-sector activities. The poorest countries, with poorly developed legal, tax, and regulatory systems, are often in the greatest need of an improved legal and political framework and increased political stability.

- Are there limits to growth? Arguments that economic growth must be constrained by environmental problems and the limits of natural resources ignore the fact that economic growth can take the form of increasing quality as well as increasing quantity. Indeed, increases in output can provide additional resources for cleaning up the environment. Finally, the market system, together with political processes, can solve many of the problems associated with economic growth. On the other hand, global environmental problems, which can be handled neither by the market nor by individual national governments, have the potential to constrain economic growth.

■ KEY TERMS ■

compound interest (517)   diminishing returns to capital (524)   entrepreneur (526)

■ REVIEW QUESTIONS ■

1. What has happened to real GDP per person in the industrialized countries over the past century? What implications does this have for the average person?

2. Why do economists consider growth in average labor productivity to be the key factor in determining long-run living standards?

3. What is *human capital*? Why is it economically important? How is new human capital created?

4. You have employed five workers of varying physical strength to dig a ditch. Workers without shovels have zero productivity in ditchdigging. How should you assign shovels to workers if you don't have enough shovels to go around? How should you assign any additional shovels that you obtain? Using this example, discuss (a) the relationship between the availability of physical capital and average labor productivity and (b) the concept of diminishing returns to capital.

5. Discuss how talented entrepreneurs and effective managers can enhance average labor productivity.

6. What major contributions can the government make to the goal of increasing average labor productivity?

7. What explanations have been offered for the slowdown in productivity growth observed in industrial countries since the early 1970s?

8. Discuss the following statement: "Because the environment is fragile and natural resources are finite, ultimately economic growth must come to an end."

▪ PROBLEMS ▪

1. Richland's real GDP per person is $10,000, and Poorland's real GDP per person is $5,000. However, Richland's real GDP per person is growing at 1% per year and Poorland's is growing at 3% per year. Compare real GDP per person in the two countries after ten years and after twenty years. Approximately how many years will it take Poorland to catch up to Richland?

2. Refer to Table 20.3 for growth rates of average labor productivity over the periods 1960–1973, 1973–1979, and 1979–1997. Suppose that growth of average labor productivity in the United States had continued at its 1960–1973 rate until 1997. Proportionally, how much higher would U.S. average labor productivity in 1997 have been, compared to its actual value? (*Note:* You do not need to know the actual values of average labor productivity in any year to solve this problem.) Does your answer shed light on why economists consider the post-1973 productivity slowdown to be an important issue?

3. The "graying of America" will substantially increase the fraction of the population that is retired in the decades to come. To illustrate the implications for U.S. living standards, suppose that over the 39 years following 1999 the share of the population that is working returns to its 1960 level, while average labor productivity increases by as much as it did during 1960–1999. Under this scenario, what would be the net change in real GDP per person between 1999 and 2038? The following data will be useful:

	Average labor productivity	Share of population employed
1960	$35,836	36.4%
1999	$66,381	48.9%

4. Here are data for Canada, Germany, and Japan on the ratio of employment to population in 1979 and 1998:

	1979	1998
Canada	.45	.46
Germany	.34	.33
Japan	.47	.51

   Using data from Table 20.1, find average labor productivity for each country in 1979 and in 1998. How much of the increase in output per person in each country over the 1979–1998 period is due to increased labor productivity? To increased employment relative to population?

5. Joanne has just completed high school and is trying to determine whether to go to junior college for 2 years or go directly to work. Her objective is to maximize the savings she will have in the bank 5 years from now. If she goes directly to work she will earn $20,000 per year for each of the next 5 years. If she goes to junior college, for each of the next 2 years she will earn nothing—indeed, she will have to borrow $6,000 each year to cover tuition and books. This loan must be repaid in full 3 years after graduation. If she graduates from junior college, in each of the subsequent 3 years her wages will be $38,000 per year. Joanne's total living expenses and taxes, excluding tuition and books, equal $15,000 per year.
   a. Suppose for simplicity that Joanne can borrow and lend at 0 percent interest. On purely economic grounds, should she go to junior college or work?
   b. Does your answer to part a change if she can earn $23,000 per year with only a high school degree?
   c. Does your answer to part a change if Joanne's tuition and books cost $8,000 per year?

d. (More difficult) Suppose that the interest rate at which Joanne can borrow and lend is 10 percent per year, but other data are as in part a. Savings are deposited at the end of the year they are earned and receive (compound) interest at the end of each subsequent year. Similarly, the loans are taken out at the end of the year in which they are needed, and interest does not accrue until the end of the subsequent year. Now that the interest rate has risen, should Joanne go to college or go to work?

6. The Good'n'Fresh Grocery Store has two checkout lanes and four employees. Employees are equally skilled, and all are able either to operate a register (checkers) or bag groceries (baggers). The store owner assigns one checker and one bagger to each lane. A lane with a checker and a bagger can check out 40 customers per hour. A lane with a checker only can check out 25 customers per hour.
   a. In terms of customers checked out per hour, what is total output and average labor productivity for the Good'n'Fresh Grocery Store?
   b. The owner adds a third checkout lane and register. Assuming that no employees are added, what is the best way to reallocate the workers to tasks? What is total output and average labor productivity (in terms of customers checked out per hour) now?
   c. Repeat part b for the addition of a fourth checkout lane, and a fifth. Do you observe diminishing returns to capital in this example?

7. Harrison, Carla, and Fred are housepainters. Harrison and Carla can paint 100 square feet per hour using a standard paintbrush, and Fred can paint 80 square feet per hour. Any of the three can paint 200 square feet per hour using a roller.
   a. Assume Harrison, Carla, and Fred have only paintbrushes at their disposal. What is the average labor productivity, in terms of square feet per painter-hour, for the three painters taken as a team? Assume that the three painters always work the same number of hours.
   b. Repeat part a for the cases in which the team has one, two, three, or four rollers available. Are there diminishing returns to capital?
   c. An improvement in paint quality increases the area that can be covered per hour (by either brushes or rollers) by 20%. How does this technological improvement affect your answers to part b? Are there diminishing returns to capital? Does the technological improvement increase or reduce the economic value of an additional roller?

8. Hester's Hatchery raises fish. At the end of the current season she has 1,000 fish in the hatchery. She can harvest any number of fish that she wishes, selling them to restaurants for $5 apiece. Because big fish make little fish, for every fish that she leaves in the hatchery this year she will have two fish at the end of next year. The price of fish is expected to be $5 each next year as well. Hester relies entirely on income from current fish sales to support herself.
   a. How many fish should Hester harvest if she wants to maximize the growth of her stock of fish from this season to next season?
   b. Do you think maximizing the growth of her fish stock is an economically sound strategy for Hester? Why or why not? Relate to the text discussion on the costs of economic growth.
   c. How many fish should Hester harvest if she wants to maximize her current income? Do you think this is a good strategy?
   d. Explain why Hester is unlikely to harvest either all or none of her fish, but instead will harvest some and leave the rest to reproduce.

9. "For advances in basic science to translate into improvements in standards of living, they must be supported by favorable economic conditions." True or false, and discuss. Use concrete examples where possible to illustrate your arguments.

10. (Essay question) Write a short essay evaluating the U.S. economy in terms of each of the six determinants of average labor productivity discussed in the text. Are there any areas in which the U.S. is exceptionally strong, relative to other countries? Areas where the U.S. is less strong than some other countries? Illustrate your arguments with numbers from the *Statistical Abstract of the United States* (available online at www.census.gov/statab/www/) and other sources, as appropriate.

■ ANSWERS TO IN-CHAPTER EXERCISES ■

20.1 If the United States had grown at the Japanese rate for the period 1870–1998, real GDP per person in 1998 would have been ($2,352) $\times$ (1.025^{128}) = $55,474. Actual GDP per person in the United States in 1998 was $25,340, so at the higher rate of growth output per person would have been $55,474/$25,340 = 2.19 times higher.

20.2 As before Lucy can wrap 4,000 candies/week, or 100 candies/hour. Ethel can wrap 500 candies/hour, and working 40 hours weekly she can wrap 20,000 candies/week. Together Lucy and Ethel can wrap 24,000 candies/week. Since they work a total of 80 hours between them, their output per hour as a team is 24,000 candies wrapped/80 hours = 300 candies wrapped/hour, midway between their hourly productivities as individuals.

20.3 Because Ethel can wrap 300 candies/hour by hand, the benefit of giving Ethel the machine is 500 − 300 = 200 additional candies wrapped/hour. Because Lucy wraps only 100 candies/hour by hand, the benefit of giving Lucy the machine is 400 additional candies wrapped/hour. So the benefit of giving the machine to Lucy is greater than of giving it to Ethel. Equivalently, if the machine goes to Ethel, then Lucy and Ethel between them can wrap 500 + 100 = 600 candies/hour, but if Lucy uses the machine the team can wrap 300 + 500 = 800 candies/hour. So output is increased by letting Lucy use the machine.

20.4 Now, working by hand, Lucy can wrap 300 candies/hour and Ethel can wrap 500 candies/hour. With a machine, either Lucy or Ethel can wrap 800 candies/hour. As in Exercise 20.3, the benefit of giving a machine to Lucy (500 candies/hour) exceeds the benefit of giving a machine to Ethel (300 candies/hour), so if only one machine is available Lucy should use it.

The table analogous to Table 20.2 now looks like this:

Relationship of Capital, Output, and Productivity in the Candy-Wrapping Factory

Number of machines (K)	Candies wrapped per week (Y)	Total hours worked (N)	Average hourly labor productivity (Y/N)
0	32,000	80	400
1	52,000	80	650
2	64,000	80	800
3	64,000	80	800

Comparing this table with Table 20.2, you can see that technological advance has increased labor productivity for any value of K, the number of machines available.

Adding one machine increases output by 20,000 candies wrapped/week, adding the second machine increases output by 12,000 candies wrapped/week, and adding the third machine does not increase output at all (because there is no worker available to use it). So diminishing returns to capital still holds after the technological improvement.

20.5 Although the individual worker is the same person he was in Bangladesh, by coming to the U.S. he gains the benefit of factors that enhance average labor productivity in this country, relative to his homeland. These include more and better capital to work with, more natural resources per person, more advanced technologies, sophisticated entrepreneurs and managers, and a political-legal environment that is conducive to high productivity. It is not guaranteed that the value of the immigrant's human capital will rise (it may not, for example, if he speaks no English and has no skills applicable to the U.S. economy), but normally it will.

Since increased productivity leads to higher wages and living standards, on economic grounds the Bangladeshi worker has a strong incentive to immigrate to the United States if he is able to do so.

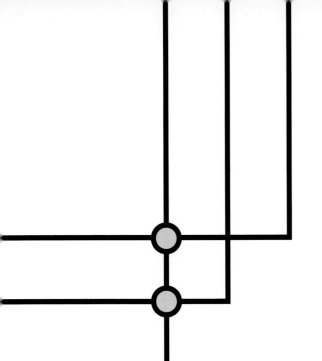

WORKERS, WAGES, AND UNEMPLOYMENT IN THE MODERN ECONOMY

■

A book by *The New York Times* columnist Thomas L. Friedman about the changing world economy, *The Lexus and the Olive Tree*,[1] contains a remarkable photograph. Taken in Jerusalem near the end of 1998, the photo shows an orthodox Jew, Shimon Biton, praying at the Western Wall, one of Judaism's most sacred places. Mr. Biton's devotions are not unusual—indeed thousands of Jews pray at the Wall every day. What *is* unusual about the photograph is that it shows Mr. Biton holding a cell phone up against the Wall. Through the cell phone, a relative of Mr. Biton's in France is fulfilling his religious obligation to pray "at" the Western Wall.

The photograph nicely illustrates the theme of Friedman's book, that one of the most striking features of the modern world is the close juxtaposition of rapid economic and technological change with traditional values and customs. The photograph suggests that Mr. Biton is quite comfortable combining the traditional and the modern, but as Friedman's book emphasizes, not everyone is so comfortable. In many countries, the conflicting pulls of modernization and traditional ways of life have created enormous social conflicts.

---

[1]New York: Farrar, Straus, & Giroux, 1999.

© Nati Harnik/AP Photo

Economically, Friedman argues, the powerful forces of modernization have widened the gap between the "haves"—those who can take advantage of rapid technological and economic change—and the "have-nots"—those who are unable or unwilling to do so.

In Chapter 20 we examined the remarkable economic growth and increased productivity that have occurred in the industrialized world over the past two centuries. These developments have greatly increased the quantity of goods and services that the economy can produce. But we have not yet discussed how the fruits of economic growth are distributed. Has everyone in the industrial countries benefited equally from economic growth and increased productivity? Or as Friedman's thesis would suggest, is the population divided between those who have caught the "train" of economic modernization, enriching themselves in the process, and those who have been left at the station?

To understand how economic growth and change affect different groups, we must turn to the labor market. Except for retirees and others receiving government support, most people rely almost entirely on wages and salaries to pay their bills and put something away for the future. Hence it is in the labor market that most people will see the benefits of the economic growth and increasing productivity. This chapter describes and explains some important trends in the labor markets of industrial countries. Using a supply and demand model of the labor market, we focus first on several important trends in real wages and employment. In the second part of the chapter we turn to the problem of unemployment, especially long-term unemployment. We will see that two key factors contributing to recent trends in wages, employment, and unemployment are the *globalization* of the economy, as reflected in the increasing importance of international trade, and ongoing *technological change*. By the end of the chapter, you will better understand the connection between these macroeconomic developments and the economic fortunes of workers and their families.

FIVE IMPORTANT LABOR MARKET TRENDS

In recent decades, at least five trends have characterized the labor markets of the industrialized world. We divide these trends into two groups: those affecting real wages and those affecting employment and unemployment.

TRENDS IN REAL WAGES

1. Over the twentieth century, all industrial countries have enjoyed substantial growth in real wages.

In the United States in 1999, the average worker's yearly earnings could command nearly twice as many goods and services as in 1960 and about four times as much as in 1929, just prior to the Great Depression. Similar trends have prevailed in other industrialized countries.

2. Since the early 1970s, however, the rate of real wage growth has slowed.

Though the post-World War II period has seen impressive increases in real wages, the fastest rates of increase occurred during the 1960s and early 1970s. In the 13 years between 1960 to 1973 the buying power of workers' incomes rose at a rate of 2.57 percent per year, a strong rate of increase. But from 1973 to 1996, real yearly earnings grew at only 0.93 percent per year. The good news is that, from 1996 to 1999, real earnings grew at 3.33 percent per year, reflecting robust economic growth. However, annual earnings growth for the whole 1973–1999 period, at 1.20 percent per year, remained well below what was achieved prior to 1973.

3. Furthermore, recent decades have brought a pronounced increase in wage inequality in the United States.

A growing gap in real wages between skilled and unskilled workers has been of particular concern. Indeed, the real wages of the least skilled, least educated workers have actually *declined* since the early 1970s, by as much as 25 to 30 percent according to some studies. At the same time, the best-educated, highest-skilled workers have enjoyed continuing gains in real wages. Data for a recent year showed that, in the United States, the typical worker with a master's degree earned twice the income of a high school graduate and four times the income of a worker with less than 9 years of schooling. Many observers worry that the United States is developing a "two-tier" labor market: plenty of good jobs at good wages for the well-educated and highly skilled, but less and less opportunity for those without schooling or skills.

Outside the United States, particularly in Western Europe, the trend toward wage inequality has been much less pronounced. But, as we will see, employment trends in Europe have not been as encouraging as in the United States. Let's turn now to the trends in employment and unemployment.

TRENDS IN EMPLOYMENT AND UNEMPLOYMENT

4. In the United States, the number of people with jobs has grown substantially in recent decades.

In 1970, about 57 percent of the over-16 population in the United States had jobs. By 1999, total U.S. employment exceeded 133 million people, more than 64 percent of the over-16 population. Between 1980 and 1999, the U.S. economy created more than 34 million new jobs—an increase in total employment of 34 percent—while the over-16 population grew only 24 percent. Similar job growth has *not* occurred in most other industrialized countries, however. In particular:

5. Western European countries have been suffering high rates of unemployment for almost two decades.

In France, for example, 11.1 percent of the workforce was unemployed in 1999, compared to just 4.2 percent in the United States. Except for the period 1989–1991, when unemployment averaged just over 9 percent of the French workforce, the unemployment rate has been in "double digits" in France since 1984. (Figure 21.9, page 566, shows recent unemployment rates in four Western European countries.) Consistent with the high rates of unemployment, rates of job creation in Western Europe have been exceptionally weak.

Given the trend toward increasing wage inequality in the United States and the persistence of high unemployment in Europe, we may conclude that a significant fraction of the industrial world's labor force has not been sharing in the recent economic growth and prosperity. While in the United States the problem takes the form of low and falling real wages for unskilled workers, in Europe work is often simply unavailable for the unskilled and sometimes even for the skilled.

What explains these trends in employment and wages? In the remainder of the chapter we will show that a supply and demand analysis of the labor market can help to explain these important developments.

> **RECAP** **IMPORTANT LABOR MARKET TRENDS**
>
> 1. Over a long period, average real wages have risen substantially both in the United States and in other industrialized countries.
>
> 2. Despite the long-term upward trend in real wages, real wage growth has slowed significantly in the United States since the early 1970s.
>
> 3. In the United States wage inequality has increased dramatically in recent decades. The real wages of most unskilled workers have actually declined, while the real wages of skilled and educated workers have continued to rise.
>
> 4. Employment has grown substantially—indeed, much faster than the working-age population—in the United States in recent decades.
>
> 5. Since about 1980 Western European nations have experienced very high rates of unemployment and low rates of job creation.

SUPPLY AND DEMAND IN THE LABOR MARKET

In Chapter 4 we saw how supply and demand analysis can be used to determine equilibrium prices and quantities for individual goods and services. The same approach is equally useful for studying labor market conditions. In the market for labor, the "price" is the wage paid to workers in exchange for their services. The wage is expressed per unit of time, for example, per hour or per year. The "quantity" is the amount of labor firms use, which in this book we will generally measure by number of workers employed. Alternatively, we could state the quantity of labor in terms of the number of hours worked; the choice of units is a matter of convenience.

Who are the demanders and suppliers in the labor market? Firms and other employers demand labor in order to produce goods and services. Virtually all of us supply labor during some phase of our lives. Whenever people work for pay, they are supplying labor services at a price equal to the wage they receive. In this chapter, we will discuss both the supply of and demand for labor, with an emphasis on the demand side of the labor market. Changes in the demand for labor turn out to be key in explaining the aggregate trends in wages and employment described in the preceding section.

Because the supply of and demand for labor was also covered in Chapter 13, we will keep this discussion relatively brief. The focus of Chapter 13 was on microeconomic issues such as the determination of wages for specific jobs or individuals. In this chapter we take a macroeconomic approach and examine factors that affect economywide trends in employment and wages.

WAGES AND THE DEMAND FOR LABOR

Let's start by thinking about what determines the number of workers employers want to hire at any given wage, that is, the demand for labor. As we will see, the demand for labor depends both on the productivity of labor and the price that the market sets on workers' output. The more productive workers are, or the more valuable the goods and services they produce, the greater the number of workers an employer will want to hire at any given wage.

Table 21.1 shows the relationship between output and the number of workers employed at the Banana Computer Company (BCC), which builds and sells computers. Column 1 of the table shows some different possibilities for the number of technicians BCC could employ in its plant. Column 2 shows how many computers the company can produce each year, depending on the number of workers

TABLE 21.1
Production and Marginal Product for Banana Computers

(1) Number of workers	(2) Computers produced per year	(3) Marginal product	(4) Value of marginal product (at $3,000/computer)
0	0		
		25	$75,000
1	25		
		23	69,000
2	48		
		21	63,000
3	69		
		19	57,000
4	88		
		17	51,000
5	105		
		15	45,000
6	120		
		13	39,000
7	133		
		11	33,000
8	144		

employed. The more workers, the greater the number of computers BCC can produce. For the sake of simplicity, we will assume that only workers are needed to build computers, not other inputs such as capital, energy, and raw materials.

Column 3 of Table 21.1 shows the *marginal product* of each worker, the extra production that is gained by adding one more worker. Note that each additional worker adds less to total production than the previous worker did. The tendency for marginal product to decline as more and more workers are added is called *diminishing returns to labor*. The principle of **diminishing returns to labor** states that if the amount of capital and other inputs in use is held constant, then the greater the quantity of labor already employed, the less each additional worker adds to production.

diminishing returns to labor if the amount of capital and other inputs in use is held constant, then the greater the quantity of labor already employed, the less each additional worker adds to production

The principle of diminishing returns to labor is analogous to the principle of diminishing returns to capital discussed in Chapter 20. The economic basis for these principles is the same, namely the *principle of increasing opportunity cost,* also known as the *low-hanging fruit principle.* As we saw in Chapter 20, a firm's managers want to use their available inputs in the most productive way possible. Hence, an employer who has one worker will assign that worker to the most productive job. If she hires a second worker, she will assign that worker to the second most productive job. The third worker will be given the third most productive job available, and so on. The greater the number of workers already employed, the lower the marginal product of adding another worker, as shown in Table 21.1.

If BCC computers sell for $3,000 each, then column 4 of Table 21.1 shows the *value of the marginal product* of each worker. The value of a worker's marginal product is the amount of extra revenue that the worker generates for the firm. Specifically, the value of the marginal product of each BCC worker is that worker's marginal product, stated in terms of the number of additional computers produced, multiplied by the price of output, here $3,000/computer. We now have all the information necessary to find BCC's demand for workers.

BCC's demand for labor

EXAMPLE 21.1

Suppose that the going wage for computer technicians is $60,000 per year. BCC managers know that this is the wage being offered by all their competitors, so they cannot hired qualified workers for less. How many technicians will BCC hire? What would the answer be if the wage were $50,000 per year?

BCC will hire an extra worker if and only if the value of that worker's marginal product (which equals the extra revenue the worker creates for the firm) exceeds the wage BCC must pay. The going wage for computer technicians, which BCC takes as given, is $60,000 per year. Table 21.1 shows that the value of the marginal product of the first, second, and third workers each exceeds $60,000. Hiring these workers will be profitable for BCC because the extra revenue each generates exceeds the wage that BCC must pay. However, the fourth worker's marginal product is worth only $57,000. If BCC's managers hired a fourth worker, they would be paying $60,000 in extra wages for additional output that is worth only $57,000. Since hiring the fourth worker is a money-losing proposition, BCC will hire only three workers. Thus the quantity of labor BCC demands when the going wage is $60,000 per year is three technicians.

If the market wage for computer technicians were $50,000 per year instead of $60,000, the fourth technician would be worth hiring, since the value of his marginal product, $57,000, would be $7,000 more than his wages. The fifth technician would also be worth hiring, since the fifth worker's marginal product is worth $51,000—$1,000 more than the going wage. The value of the marginal product of a sixth technician, however, is only $45,000, so hiring a sixth worker would not be profitable. When wages are $50,000 per year then, BCC's labor demand is five technicians.

EXERCISE 21.1

How many workers will BCC hire if the going wage for technicians is $35,000 per year?

The lower the wage a firm must pay, the more workers it will hire. Thus the demand for labor is like the demand for other goods or services in that the quantity demanded rises as the price (in this case, the wage) falls. Figure 21.1 shows a hypothetical labor demand curve for a firm or industry, with the wage on the vertical axis and employment on the horizontal axis. All else being equal, the higher the wage, the fewer workers a firm or industry will demand.

In our example thus far we have discussed how labor demand depends on the *nominal,* or dollar, wage, and the *nominal* price of workers' output. Equivalently, we could have expressed the wage and the price of output in *real* terms, that is, measured relative to the average price of goods and services. The wage measured relative to the general price level is the *real wage*; as we saw in Chap-

FIGURE 21.1
The Demand Curve for Labor.
The demand curve for labor is downward-sloping. The higher the wage, the fewer workers employers will hire.

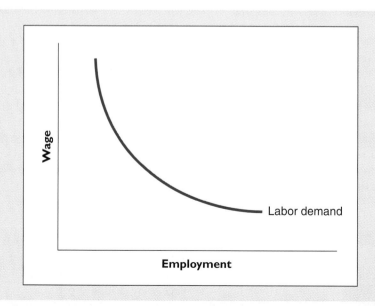

ter 19, the real wage expresses the wage in terms of its purchasing power. The price of a specific good or service measured relative to the general price level is called the *relative price* of that good or service. Because our main interest is in real rather than nominal wages, from this point on we will analyze the demand for labor in terms of the real wage and the relative price of workers' output, rather than in terms of nominal variables.

SHIFTS IN THE DEMAND FOR LABOR

The number of workers that BCC will employ at any given real wage depends on the value of their marginal product, as shown in column 4 of Table 21.1. Changes in the economy that increase the value of workers' marginal product will increase the value of extra workers to BCC, and thus BCC's demand for labor at any given real wage. In other words, any factor that raises the value of the marginal product of BCC's workers will shift BCC's labor demand curve to the right.

Two main factors could increase BCC's labor demand: (1) an increase in the relative price of the company's output (computers) and (2) an increase in the productivity of BCC's workers. Example 21.2 illustrates the first of these possibilities; Example 21.3, the second.

The relative price of computers and BCC's demand for labor

EXAMPLE 21.2

Suppose an increase in the demand for BCC's computers raises the relative price of its computers to $5,000 each. How many technicians will BCC hire now, if the real wage is $60,000 per year? If the real wage is $50,000?

The effect of the increase in computer prices is shown in Table 21.2. Columns 1 to 3 of the table are the same as in Table 21.1. The number of computers a given number of technicians can build (column 2) has not changed; hence, the marginal product of particular technicians (column 3) is the same. But because computers can now be sold for $5,000 each instead of $3,000, the *value* of each worker's marginal product has increased by two-thirds (compare column 4 of Table 21.2 with column 4 of Table 21.1).

How does the increase in the relative price of computers affect BCC's demand for labor? Recall from Example 21.1 that when the price of computers was

TABLE 21.2
Production and Marginal Product for Banana Computers after an Increase in Computer Prices

(1) Number of workers	(2) Computers produced per year	(3) Marginal product	(4) Value of marginal product ($5,000/computer)
0	0		
		25	$125,000
1	25		
		23	115,000
2	48		
		21	105,000
3	69		
		19	95,000
4	88		
		17	85,000
5	105		
		15	75,000
6	120		
		13	65,000
7	133		
		11	55,000
8	144		

$3,000 and the going wage for technicians was $60,000, BCC's demand for labor was three workers. But now, with computers selling for $5,000 each, the value of the marginal product of each of the first seven workers exceeds $60,000 (Table 21.2). So if the real wage of computer technicians is still $60,000, BCC would increase its demand from three workers to seven.

Suppose instead that the going real wage for technicians is $50,000. In Example 21.1, when the price of computers was $3,000 and the wage was $50,000, BCC demanded five workers. But if computers sell for $5,000, we can see from column 4 of Table 21.2 that the value of the marginal product of even the eighth worker exceeds the wage of $50,000. So if the real wage is $50,000, the increase in computer prices raises BCC's demand for labor from five workers to eight.

EXERCISE 21.2

How many workers will BCC hire if the going real wage for technicians is $100,000 per year and the relative price of computers is $5,000? Compare your answer to the demand for technicians at a wage of $100,000 when the price of computers is $3,000.

The general conclusion to be drawn from Example 21.2 is that *an increase in the relative price of workers' output increases the demand for labor,* shifting the labor demand curve to the right, as shown in Figure 21.2. A higher relative price for workers' output makes workers more valuable, leading employers to demand more workers at any given real wage.

FIGURE 21.2
A Higher Relative Price of Output Increases the Demand for Labor.
An increase in the relative price of workers' output increases the value of their marginal product, shifting the labor demand curve to the right.

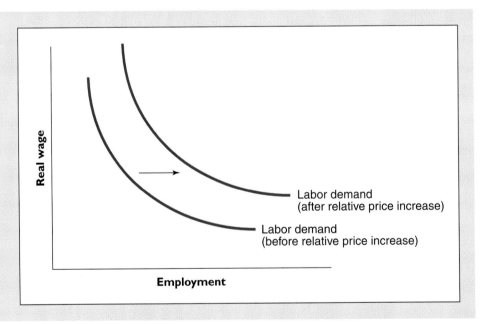

The second factor that affects the demand for labor is worker productivity. Since an increase in productivity increases the value of a worker's marginal product, it also increases the demand for labor, as Example 21.3 shows.

EXAMPLE 21.3   **Worker productivity and BCC's demand for labor**

Suppose BCC adopts a new technology that reduces the number of components to be assembled, permitting each technician to build 50 percent more machines per year. Assume that the relative price of computers is $3,000 per machine. How many technicians will BCC hire if the real wage is $60,000 per year?

TABLE 21.3
Production and Marginal Product for Banana Computers after an Increase in Worker Productivity

(1) Number of workers	(2) Computers produced per year	(3) Marginal product	(4) Value of marginal product ($3,000/computer)
0	0		
		37.5	$112,500
1	37.5		
		34.5	103,500
2	72		
		31.5	94,500
3	103.5		
		28.5	85,500
4	132		
		25.5	76,500
5	157.5		
		22.5	67,500
6	180		
		19.5	58,500
7	199.5		
		16.5	49,500
8	216		

Table 21.3 shows workers' marginal products and the value of their marginal products after the 50 percent increase in productivity, assuming that computers sell for $3,000 each.

Before the productivity increase, BCC would have demanded three workers at a wage of $60,000 (Table 21.1). After the productivity increase, however, the value of the marginal product of the first six workers exceeds $60,000 (see Table 21.3, column 4). So at a wage of $60,000, BCC's demand for labor increases from three workers to six.

EXERCISE 21.3

How many workers will BCC hire after the 50 percent increase in productivity if the going real wage for technicians is $50,000 per year? Compare this figure to the demand for workers at a $50,000 wage before the increase in productivity.

In general, an increase in worker productivity increases the demand for labor, shifting the labor demand curve to the right, as in Figure 21.3 on the next page.

THE SUPPLY OF LABOR

We have discussed the demand for labor by employers; to complete the story we need to consider the supply of labor. The suppliers of labor are workers and potential workers. At any given real wage, potential suppliers of labor must decide if they are willing to work. The total number of people who are willing to work at each real wage is the supply of labor.

FIGURE 21.3
Higher Productivity Increases the Demand for Labor.
An increase in productivity raises workers' marginal product and—assuming no change in the price of output—the value of their marginal product. Since a productivity increase raises the value of marginal product, employers will hire more workers at any given real wage, shifting the labor demand curve to the right.

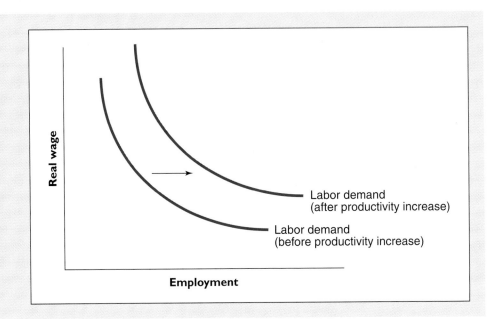

EXAMPLE 21.3

Will you clean your neighbor's basement or go to the beach?

You were planning to go to the beach today, but your neighbor asks you to clean out his basement. You like the beach a lot more than fighting cobwebs. Do you take the job?

Unless you are motivated primarily by neighborliness, your answer to this job offer would probably be "It depends on how much my neighbor will pay." You probably would not be willing to take the job for $10 or $20, unless you have a severe and immediate need for cash. But if your neighbor were wealthy and eccentric enough to offer you $500 (to take an extreme example), you would very likely say yes. Somewhere between $20 and the unrealistic figure of $500 is the minimum payment you would be willing to accept to tackle the dirty basement. This minimum payment, the *reservation price* you set for your labor, is the compensation level that leaves you just indifferent between working and not working.

In economic terms, deciding whether to work at any given wage is a straightforward application of the *cost-benefit principle*. The cost to you of cleaning out the basement is the opportunity cost of your time (you would rather be surfing) plus the cost you place on having to work in unpleasant conditions. You can measure this total cost in dollars simply by asking yourself, "What is the minimum amount of money I would take to clean out the basement instead of going to the beach?" The minimum payment that you would accept is the same as your reservation price. The benefit of taking the job is measured by the pay you receive, which will go toward that new DVD player you want. You should take the job only if the promised pay (the benefit of working) exceeds your reservation price (the cost of working).

In this example, your willingness to supply labor is greater the higher the wage. In general, the same is true for the population as a whole. Certainly people work for many reasons, including personal satisfaction, the opportunity to develop skills and talents, and the chance to socialize with coworkers. Still, for most people, income is one of the principal benefits of working, so the higher the real wage, the more willing they are to sacrifice other possible uses of their time. The fact that people are more willing to work when the wage they are offered is higher is captured in the upward slope of the supply curve of labor (see Figure 21.4).

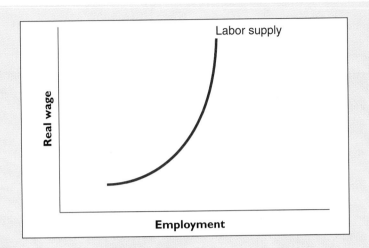

FIGURE 21.4
The Supply of Labor.
The labor supply curve is upward-sloping because, in general, the higher the real wage, the more people are willing to work.

EXERCISE 21.4

You want to make a career in broadcasting. The local radio station is offering an unpaid summer internship that would give you valuable experience. Your alternative to the internship is to earn $3,000 working in a car wash. How would you decide which job to take? Would a decision to take the internship contradict the conclusion that the labor supply curve is upward-sloping?

SHIFTS IN THE SUPPLY OF LABOR

Any factor that affects the quantity of labor offered at a given real wage will shift the labor supply curve. At the macroeconomic level, the most important factor affecting the supply of labor is the size of the working-age population, which is influenced by factors such as the domestic birthrate, immigration and emigration rates, and the ages at which people normally first enter the workforce and retire. All else being equal, an increase in the working-age population raises the quantity of labor supplied at each real wage, shifting the labor supply curve to the right. Changes in the percentage of people of working age who seek employment—for example, as a result of social changes that encourage women to work outside the home—can also affect the supply of labor.

Now that we have discussed both the demand for and supply of labor, we are ready to apply supply and demand analysis to real-world labor markets. But first, try your hand at using supply and demand analysis to answer the following question.

Might accepting a job that pays no salary ever be a good career move?

EXERCISE 21.5

Labor unions typically favor tough restrictions on immigration, while employers tend to favor more liberal rules. Why? (*Hint:* How is an influx of potential workers likely to affect real wages?)

| RECAP | SUPPLY AND DEMAND IN THE LABOR MARKET |

The demand for labor The extra production gained by adding one more worker is the *marginal product* of that worker. The *value of the marginal product* of a worker is that worker's marginal product times the relative price of the firm's output. A firm will employ a worker only if the worker's value of marginal product, which is the same as the extra revenue the worker generates for the firm, exceeds the real wage that the firm must pay. The lower the real wage, the more workers the firm will find it profitable to employ. Thus the labor demand curve, like most demand curves, is downward-sloping.

For a given real wage, any change that increases the value of workers' marginal products will increase the demand for labor and shift the labor demand curve to the right. Examples of factors that increase labor demand are an increase in the relative price of workers' output and an increase in productivity.

The supply of labor An individual is willing to supply labor if the real wage that is offered is greater than the opportunity cost of the individual's time. Generally, the higher the real wage, the more people are willing to work. Thus the labor supply curve, like most supply curves, is upward-sloping.

For a given real wage, any factor that increases the number of people available and willing to work increases the supply of labor and shifts the labor supply curve to the right. Examples of facts that increase labor supply include an increase in the working-age population or an increase in the share of the working-age population seeking employment.

EXPLAINING THE TRENDS IN REAL WAGES AND EMPLOYMENT

We are now ready to analyze the important trends in real wages and employment discussed earlier in the chapter. We will do so in a series of Economic Naturalist boxes.

ECONOMIC NATURALIST 21.1

Why have real wages increased by so much in the industrialized countries?

As we discussed, real annual earnings in the United States have quadrupled since 1929, and other industrialized countries have experienced similar gains. These increases have greatly improved the standard of living of workers in these countries. Why have real wages increased by so much in the United States and other industrialized countries?

The large increase in real wages results from the sustained growth in productivity experienced by the industrialized countries during the twentieth century. (Figure 17.2, page 437, shows the growth of output per worker in the United States since 1900.) As illustrated by Figure 21.5, increased productivity raises the demand for labor, increasing employment and the real wage.

FIGURE 21.5
An Increase in Productivity Raises the Real Wage.
An increase in productivity raises the demand for labor, shifting the labor demand curve from D to D'. The real wage rises from w to w', and employment rises from N to N'.

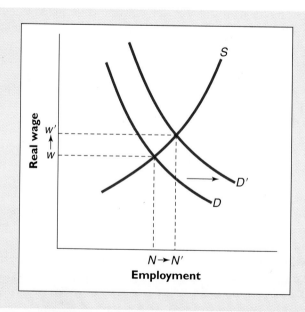

Of the factors contributing to productivity growth in the industrialized countries, two of the most important were (1) the dramatic technological progress that occurred during the twentieth century and (2) large increases in capital stocks, which provided workers with more and better tools with which to work. Labor supply increased during the century as well, of course (not shown in the diagram). However, the increases in labor demand, driven by rapidly expanding productivity, have been so great as to overwhelm the depressing effect on real wages of increased labor supply.

Since the 1970s, real wage growth in the United States has slowed, while employment has expanded rapidly. What accounts for these trends?

With the exception of a short period at the end of the 1990s, rates of real wage growth after 1973 in the United States have been significantly lower than in previous decades. But over much of the recent period the economy has created new jobs at a record rate. What accounts for these trends?

Let's begin with the slowdown in real wage growth since the early 1970s. Supply and demand analysis tells us that a slowdown in real wage growth must result from slower growth in the demand for labor, more rapid growth in the supply of labor, or both. On the demand side, recall from Chapter 20 that since the early 1970s the United States and other industrialized nations have experienced a slowdown in productivity growth. Thus, one possible explanation for the slowdown in the growth of real wages since the early 1970s is the decline in the pace of productivity gains.

Some evidence for a relationship between productivity and real wages is given in Table 21.4, which shows the average annual growth rates in labor productivity and real annual earnings for the 1960s, 1970s, 1980s, and 1990s. You can see that the growth in productivity decade by decade corresponds closely to the growth in real earnings. Particularly striking is the rapid growth of both productivity and wages during the 1960s. Since the 1970s, growth in both productivity and real wages has been significantly slower, although some improvement is apparent in the 1990s.

ECONOMIC NATURALIST 21.2

TABLE 21.4
Growth Rates in Productivity and Real Earnings

	Annual Growth Rate (%)	
	Productivity	Real Earnings
1960–1970	2.33	2.89
1970–1980	0.84	0.79
1980–1990	1.38	1.15
1990–1999	1.85	1.84

SOURCE: *Economic Report of the President*, 2000 (www.access.gpo.gov/eop/index.html). Productivity is real GDP divided by civilian employment; real earnings equal total compensation of employees divided by civilian employment and deflated by the GDP deflator.

While the effects of the slowdown in productivity on the demand for labor are an important reason for declining real wage growth, they can't be the whole story. We know this because, with labor supply held constant, slower growth in labor demand would lead to reduced rates of employment growth, as well as reduced growth in real wages. But job growth in the United States has been rapid in recent decades. Large increases in employment in the face of slow growth of labor demand can only be explained by simultaneous increases in the supply of labor (see Exercise 21.6).

Labor supply in the United States does appear to have grown rapidly recently. As we saw in Chapter 18, for example, increased participation in the labor market by women has increased the U.S. supply of labor since the mid-1970s. Other factors, including the coming of age of the baby boomers and high rates of immigration, also help to explain the increase in the supply of labor. The combination of slower growth in labor demand (the result of the productivity slowdown) and accelerated growth in labor supply (the result of increased participation by women in the workforce, together with other factors) helps to explain why real wage growth has been sluggish for many years in the United States, even as employment has grown rapidly.

What about the future? As we saw in Chapter 20, labor supply growth is likely to slow as the baby boomers retire and the percentage of women in the labor force stabilizes. Productivity has recently grown more quickly, reflecting the benefits of new technologies, among other factors (Chapter 20). So there seems a good chance that the more rapid increases in real wages that began around 1996 will continue in years to come.

EXERCISE 21.6

According to Economic Naturalist 21.2, relatively weak growth in productivity and relatively strong growth in labor supply after about 1973 can explain (1) the slowdown in real wage growth and (2) the more rapid expansion in employment after about 1973. Show this point graphically by drawing two supply and demand diagrams of the labor market, one corresponding to the period 1960–1972 and the other to 1973–1996. Assuming that productivity growth was strong but labor supply growth was modest during 1960–1972, show that we would expect to see rapid real wage growth but only moderate growth in employment in that period. Now apply the same analysis to 1973–1996, assuming that productivity growth is weaker but labor supply growth stronger than in 1960–1972. What do you predict for growth in the real wage and employment in 1973–1996 relative to the earlier period?

INCREASING WAGE INEQUALITY: THE EFFECTS OF GLOBALIZATION

Another important trend in U.S. labor markets is increasing inequality in wages, especially the tendency for the wages of the less-skilled and less-educated to fall further and further behind those of better-trained workers. We next discuss two reasons for this increasing inequality: (1) globalization and (2) technological change.

Why has the gap between the wages of skilled and unskilled workers widened in recent years? (1) Globalization

ECONOMIC NATURALIST 21.3

In recent years the real wages of more-skilled and educated workers have continued to rise, while the real wages of less-skilled workers have stagnated or even declined. Does the "globalization" of the world economy have anything to do with this trend?

Many commentators have blamed the increasing divergence between the wages of skilled and unskilled workers on the phenomenon of "globalization." This popular term refers to the fact that to an increasing extent, the markets for many goods and services are becoming international, rather than national or local in scope. While Americans have long been able to buy products from all over the world, the ease with which goods and services can cross borders is increasing rapidly. In part this trend is the result of international trade agreements, such as the North American Free Trade Agreement (NAFTA), which reduced taxes on goods and services traded among Canada, the United States, and Mexico. However, technological advances such as the Internet have also promoted globalization. A recent TV commercial showed a small auto parts manufacturer in Texas bidding over the Internet for a contract from a Japanese auto firm.

The main economic benefit of globalization is increased specialization and the efficiency that it brings. Instead of each country trying to produce everything its citizens consume, each can concentrate on producing those goods and services at which it is relatively most efficient. As implied by the *principle of comparative advantage* (Chapter 3), the result is that consumers of all countries enjoy a greater variety of goods and services, of better quality and at lower prices, than they would without international trade.

The effects of globalization on the *labor* market are mixed, however, which explains why many politicians opposed free trade agreements. Expanded trade means that consumers stop buying certain goods and services from domestic producers and switch to foreign-made products. Consumers would not make this switch unless the foreign products were better, cheaper, or both, so expanded trade clearly makes them better off. But the workers and firm owners in the domestic industries that lose business may well suffer from the increase in foreign competition.

The effects of increasing trade on the labor market can be analyzed using Figure 21.6. The figure contrasts the supply and demand for labor in two different industries, (a) textiles and (b) computer software. Imagine that, initially, there is little or no international trade in these two goods. Without trade, the demand for workers in each industry is indicated by the curves marked $D_{textiles}$ and $D_{software}$, respectively. Wages and employment in each industry are determined by the intersection of the demand curves and the labor supply curves in each industry. As we have drawn the figure, initially, the real wage is the same in both industries, equal to w. Employment is $N_{textiles}$ in textiles and $N_{software}$ in software.

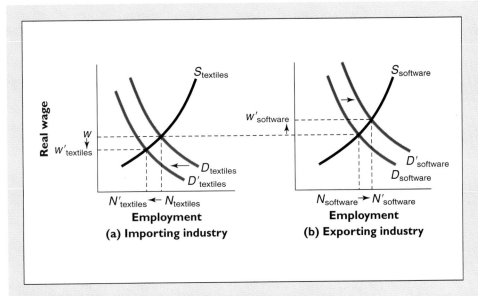

FIGURE 21.6
The Effect of Globalization on the Demand for Workers in Two Industries.
Initially, real wages in the two industries are equal at w. After an increase in trade, (a) demand for workers in the importing industry (textiles) declines, lowering real wages and employment, while (b) demand for workers in the exporting industry (software) increases, raising real wages and employment in that industry.

What will happen when this economy is opened up to trade, perhaps because of a free trade agreement? Under the agreement, countries will begin to produce for export those goods or services at which they are relatively more efficient and to import goods or services that they are relatively less efficient at producing. Suppose the country in this example is relatively more efficient at producing software than manufacturing textiles. With the opening of trade, the country gains new foreign markets for its software and begins to produce for export as well as for domestic use. Meanwhile, because the country is relatively less efficient at producing textiles, consumers begin to purchase foreign-made textiles, which are cheaper or of higher quality, instead of the domestic product. In short, software becomes an exporting industry and textiles an importing industry.

These changes in the demand for domestic products are translated into changes in the demand for labor. The opening of export markets increases the demand for domestic software, raising its relative price. The higher price for domestic software, in turn, raises the value of the marginal products of software workers, shifting the labor demand curve in the software industry to the right, from $D_{software}$ to $D'_{software}$ in Figure 21.6(b). Wages in the software industry rise, from w to $w'_{software}$, and employment in the industry rises as well. In the textile industry the opposite happens. Demand for domestic textiles falls as consumers switch to imports. The relative price of domestic textiles falls with demand, reducing the value of the marginal product of textile workers and hence the demand for their labor, to $D'_{textiles}$ in Figure 21.6(a). Employment in the textile industry falls, and the real wage falls as well, from w to $w'_{textiles}$.

In sum, Figure 21.6 shows how globalization can contribute to increasing wage inequality. Initially, we assumed that software workers and textile workers received the same wage. However, the opening up of trade raised the wages of workers in the "winning" industry (software) and lowered the wages of workers in the "losing" industry (textiles), increasing inequality.

In practice, the tendency of trade to increase wage inequality may be even worse than depicted in the example, because the great majority of the world's workers, particularly those in developing countries, have relatively low skill levels. Thus, when industrialized countries like the United States open up trade with developing countries, the domestic industries that are likely to face the toughest international competition are those that use mostly low-skilled labor. Conversely, the industries that are likely to do the best in international competition are those that employ mostly skilled workers. Thus increased trade may lower the wages of those workers who are already poorly paid and increase the wages of those who are well paid.

The fact that increasing trade may exacerbate wage inequality explains some of the political resistance to globalization, but in general it does not justify attempts to reverse the trend. Increasing trade and specialization is a major source of improvement in living standards, both in the United States and abroad, so trying to stop the process is counterproductive. Indeed, the economic forces behind globalization—primarily, the desire of consumers for better and cheaper products and of producers for new markets—are so powerful that the process would be hard to stop even if government officials were determined to do so.

Rather than trying to stop globalization, helping the labor market to adjust to the effects of globalization is probably a better course. To a certain extent, indeed, the economy will adjust on its own. Figure 21.6 showed that, following the opening to trade, real wages and employment fall in (a) textiles and rise in (b) software. At that point, wages and job opportunities are much more attractive in the software industry than in textiles. Will this situation persist? Clearly, there is a strong incentive for workers who are able to do so to leave the textile industry and seek employment in the software industry.

worker mobility the movement of workers between jobs, firms, and industries

The movement of workers between jobs, firms, and industries is called **worker mobility.** In our example, worker mobility will tend to reduce labor supply in textiles and increase it in software, as workers move from the contracting industry to the growing one. This process will reverse some of the increase in wage inequality by raising wages in textiles and lowering them in software. It will also shift workers from a less competitive sector to a more competitive sector. To some extent, then, the labor market can adjust on its own to the effects of globalization.

Of course, there are many barriers to a textile worker becoming a software engineer. So there may also be a need for *transition aid* to workers in the affected sectors. Ideally, such aid helps workers train for and find new jobs. If that is not possible or desirable—say, because a worker is nearing retirement—transition aid can take the form of government payments to help the worker maintain his or her standard of living. Because trade and specialization increase the total economic pie, the "winners" from globalization can afford the taxes necessary to finance aid and still enjoy a net benefit from increased trade.

INCREASING WAGE INEQUALITY: TECHNOLOGICAL CHANGE

A second source of increasing wage inequality is ongoing technological change that favors more-skilled or educated workers. Economic Naturalist 21.4 examines the effect of technological change on the labor market.

Why has the gap between the wages of less-skilled and higher-skilled workers widened in recent years? (2) Technological change

How has the pattern of technological change contributed to increasing inequality of wages?

As we have seen, new scientific knowledge and the technological advances associated with it are a major source of improved productivity and economic growth. Increases in worker productivity are in turn a driving force behind wage increases and higher average living standards. In the long run and on average, technological progress is undoubtedly the worker's friend.

This sweeping statement is not true at all times and in all places, however. Whether a particular technological development is good for a particular worker depends on the effect of that innovation on the worker's value of marginal product and, hence, on his or her wage. For example, at one time the ability to add numbers rapidly and accurately was a valuable skill; a clerk with that skill could expect advancement and higher wages. However, the invention and mass production of the electronic calculator has rendered human calculating skills less valuable, to the detriment of those who have that skill.

History is replete with examples of workers who opposed new technologies out of fear that their skills would become less valuable. In England in the early nineteenth century, rioting workmen destroyed newly introduced labor-saving machinery. The name of the workers' reputed leader, Ned Ludd, has been preserved in the term *Luddite,* meaning a person who is opposed to the introduction of new technologies. The same theme appears in American folk history in the tale of John Henry, the mighty pile-driving man who died in an attempt to show that a human could tunnel into a rock face more quickly than a steam-powered machine.

How do these observations bear on wage inequality? According to some economists, many recent technological advances have taken the form of **skill-biased technological change,** that is, technological change that affects the marginal product of higher-skilled workers differently from that of lower-skilled workers. Specifically, technological developments in recent decades appear to have favored more-skilled and educated workers. Developments in automobile production are a case in point. The advent of mass production techniques in the 1920s provided highly paid work for several generations of relatively low-skilled autoworkers. But in recent years automobile production, like the automobiles themselves, has become considerably more sophisticated. The simplest production jobs have been taken over by robots and computer-controlled machinery, which require skilled operatives who know how to use and maintain the new equipment. Consumer demands for luxury features and customized options has also raised the automakers' demand for highly skilled craftsmen. Thus, in general, the skill requirements for jobs in automobile production have risen. Similarly, few office workers today can escape the need to use computer applications, such as word processing and spreadsheets. And in many places, elementary school teachers are expected to know how to set up a web page or use the Internet.

Figure 21.7 illustrates the effects of technological change that favors skilled workers. Figure 21.7(a) shows the market for unskilled workers; Figure 21.7(b) shows the market for skilled workers. The demand curves labeled $D_{unskilled}$ and $D_{skilled}$ show the demand for each type of worker before a skill-biased technical change. Wages and employment for each type of worker are determined by the intersection of the demand and supply curves in each market. Figure 21.7 shows that, even before the technological change, unskilled workers received lower real wages than skilled workers ($w_{unskilled} < w_{skilled}$), reflecting the lower marginal products of the unskilled.

Now suppose that a new technology—computer-controlled machinery, for example—is introduced. This technological change is biased toward skilled workers, which means that it raises their marginal productivity relative to unskilled workers. We will assume in this example that the new technology also lowers the marginal productivity of unskilled workers, perhaps because they are unable to use the new technology, but all that is necessary for our conclusions is that they benefit less than skilled workers. Figure 21.7 shows the effect of this change in marginal products. In part (b) the

ECONOMIC NATURALIST 21.4

skill-biased technological change technological change that affects the marginal products of higher-skilled workers differently from those of lower-skilled workers

Unimpressed by new technology

FIGURE 21.7

The Effect of Skill-Biased Technological Change on Wage Inequality.

The figure shows the effects of a skill-biased technological change that increases the marginal product of skilled workers and reduces the marginal product of unskilled workers. The resulting increase in the demand for skilled workers raises their wages [part (b)], while the decline in demand for unskilled workers reduces their wages [part (a)]. Wage inequality increases.

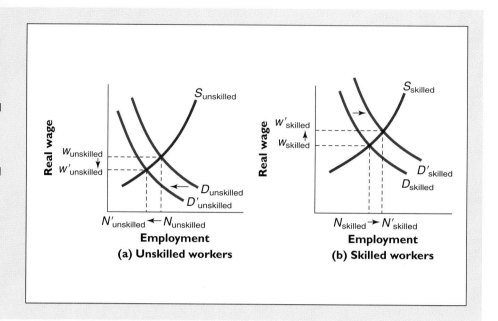

increase in the marginal productivity of skilled workers raises the demand for those workers; the demand curve shifts rightward to $D'_{skilled}$. Accordingly, the real wages and employment of skilled workers also rise. In contrast, because they have been made less productive by the technological change, the demand for unskilled workers shifts leftward to $D'_{unskilled}$ [Figure 21.7(a)]. Lower demand for unskilled workers reduces their real wages and employment.

In summary, this analysis supports the conclusion that technological change that is biased in favor of skilled workers will tend to increase the wage gap between the skilled and unskilled. Empirical studies have confirmed the role of skill-biased technological change in recent increases in wage inequality.

Because new technologies that favor skilled workers increase wage inequality, should government regulators act to block them? As in the case of globalization, most economists would argue against trying to block new technologies, since technological advances are necessary for economic growth and improved living standards. If the Luddites had somehow succeeded in preventing the introduction of labor-saving machinery in Great Britain, economic growth and development over the past few centuries might have been greatly reduced.

The remedies for the problem of wage inequalities caused by technological change are similar to those for wage inequalities caused by globalization. First among them is worker mobility. As the pay differential between skilled and unskilled work increases, unskilled workers will have a stronger incentive to acquire education and skills, to everyone's benefit. A second remedy is transition aid. Government policymakers should consider programs that will help workers to re-train if they are able, or provide income support if they are not.

RECAP **EXPLAINING THE TRENDS IN REAL WAGES AND EMPLOYMENT**

The long-term increase in real wages enjoyed by workers in industrial countries results primarily from large productivity gains, which have raised the demand for labor. Technological progress and an expanded and modernized capital stock are two important reasons for these long-term increases in productivity.

The slowdown in real-wage growth that began in the 1970s resulted in part from the slowdown in productivity growth (and, hence, the slower growth in labor demand) that occurred at about the same time. Increased labor supply, arising from such factors as the increased participation of women and the coming of age of the baby boom generation, depressed real wages further while also expanding employment. In the latter part of the 1990s, resurgence in productivity growth was accompanied by an increase in real-wage growth.

Both globalization and skill-biased technological change contribute to wage inequality. Globalization raises the wages of workers in exporting industries by raising the demand for those workers, while reducing the wages of workers in importing industries. Technological change that favors more skilled workers increases the demand for such workers, and hence their wages, relative to the wages of less skilled workers.

Attempting to block either globalization or technological change is not the best response to the problem of wage inequality. To some extent, worker mobility (movement of workers from low-wage to high-wage industries) will offset the inequality created by these forces. Where mobility is not practical, transition aid—government assistance to workers whose employment prospects have worsened—may be the best solution.

UNEMPLOYMENT

The concept of the unemployment rate was introduced in Chapter 18. To review, government survey takers classify adults as employed (holding a job), unemployed (not holding a job, but looking for one), or not in the labor force (not holding a job and not looking for one—retirees, for example). The labor force consists of the employed and the unemployed. The unemployment rate is the percentage of the labor force that is unemployed.

Unemployment rates differ markedly from country to country. In the United States, unemployment rates have recently reached historic lows—slightly above 4 percent of the labor force (Figure 18.3, page 475, shows the U.S. unemployment rate since 1960). In Canada and many Western European countries, unemployment rates for many years have been two to three times the U.S. rate. In Europe, unemployment is exceptionally high among young people. Supposedly, high school guidance counselors in Britain once gave high school seniors a pamphlet titled "Leaving School: How to Apply for Unemployment Benefits."

As we saw in Chapter 18, a high unemployment rate has serious economic, psychological, and social costs. Understanding the causes of unemployment and finding ways to reduce it are therefore major concerns of macroeconomists. In the remainder of this chapter we discuss the causes and costs of three types of unemployment, and we will also consider some features of labor markets that may exacerbate the problem.

TYPES OF UNEMPLOYMENT AND THEIR COSTS

Economists have found it useful to think of unemployment as being of three broad types: *frictional* unemployment, *structural* unemployment, and *cyclical* unemployment. Each type of unemployment has different causes and imposes different economic and social costs.

Frictional unemployment The function of the labor market is to match available jobs with available workers. If all jobs and workers were the same, or if the set of jobs and workers were static and unchanging, this matching process would be quick and easy. But the real world is more complicated. In practice, both jobs and workers are highly *heterogeneous*. Jobs differ in their location, in the skills they require, in their working conditions and hours, and in many other ways. Workers differ in their career aspirations, their skills and experience, their preferred working hours, their willingness to travel, and so on.

The real labor market is also *dynamic,* or constantly changing and evolving. On the demand side of the labor market, technological advances, globalization, and changing consumer tastes spur the creation of new products, new firms, and even new industries, while outmoded products, firms, and industries disappear. Thus, CD players have replaced record players, and word processors have replaced typewriters. As a result of this upheaval, new jobs are constantly being created, while some old jobs cease to be viable. The workforce in a modern economy is equally dynamic. People move, gain new skills, leave the labor force for a time to rear children or go back to school, and even change careers.

Because the labor market is heterogeneous and dynamic, the process of matching jobs with workers often takes time. For example, a software engineer who loses or quits her job in Silicon Valley may take weeks or even months to find an appropriate new job. In her search she will probably consider alternative areas of software development or even totally new challenges. She may also want to think about different regions of the country in which software companies are located, such as North Carolina's Research Triangle or New York City's Silicon Alley. During the period in which she is searching for a new job, she is counted as unemployed.

Short-term unemployment that is associated with the process of matching workers with jobs is called **frictional unemployment.** The *costs* of frictional unemployment are low and may even be negative; that is, frictional unemployment may be economically beneficial. First, frictional unemployment is short-term, so its psychological effects and direct economic losses are minimal. Second, to the extent that the search process leads to a better match between worker and job, a period of frictional unemployment is actually productive, in the sense that it leads to higher output over the long run. Indeed, a certain amount of frictional unemployment seems essential to the smooth functioning of a rapidly changing, dynamic economy.

frictional unemployment the short-term unemployment associated with the process of matching workers with jobs

Structural unemployment A second major type of unemployment is **structural unemployment,** or the long-term and chronic unemployment that exists even when the economy is producing at a normal rate. Several factors contribute to structural unemployment. First, a *lack of skills, language barriers, or discrimination* keeps some workers from finding stable, long-term jobs. Migrant farmworkers and unskilled construction workers who find short-term or temporary jobs from time to time, but never stay in one job for very long, fit the definition of chronically unemployed.

structural unemployment the long-term and chronic unemployment that exists even when the economy is producing at a normal rate

Second, economic changes sometimes create a *long-term mismatch* between the skills some workers have and the available jobs. The U.S. steel industry, for example, has declined over the years, while the computer industry has grown rapidly. Ideally, steelworkers who lose their jobs would be able to find new jobs in computer firms (worker mobility), so their unemployment would only be frictional in nature. In practice, of course, many ex-steelworkers lack the education, ability, or interest necessary to work in the computer industry. Since their skills are no longer in demand, these workers may drift into chronic or long-term unemployment.

Finally, structural unemployment can result from *structural features of the labor market* that act as barriers to employment. Examples of such barriers include unions and minimum wage laws, both of which may keep wages above their market-clearing level, creating unemployment. We will discuss some of these structural features shortly.

"The one single thought that sustains me is that the fundamentals are good."

The *costs* of structural unemployment are much higher than those of frictional unemployment. Because structurally unemployed workers do little productive work over long periods, their idleness causes substantial economic losses both to the unemployed workers and to society. Structurally unemployed workers also lose out on the opportunity to develop new skills on the job, and their existing skills wither from disuse. Long spells of unemployment are also much more difficult for workers to handle psychologically than the relatively brief spells associated with frictional unemployment.

Cyclical unemployment The third type of unemployment occurs during periods of recession (that is, periods of unusually low production) and is called **cyclical unemployment.** The sharp peaks in unemployment shown in Figure 18.3 reflect the cyclical unemployment that occurs during recessions. Increases in cyclical unemployment, although they are relatively short-lived, are associated with significant declines in real GDP and are therefore quite costly economically. We will study the cyclical unemployment in more detail later in the chapters dealing with booms and recessions.

cyclical unemployment the extra unemployment that occurs during periods of recession

In principle, frictional, structural, and cyclical unemployment add up to the total unemployment rate. In practice, sharp distinctions often cannot be made between the different categories, so any breakdown of the total unemployment rate into the three types of unemployment is necessarily subjective and approximate.

IMPEDIMENTS TO FULL EMPLOYMENT

In discussing structural unemployment, we mentioned that structural features of the labor market may contribute to long-term and chronic unemployment. Let's discuss a few of those features.

Minimum wage laws[2] The federal government and most states have minimum wage laws, which prescribe the lowest hourly wage that employers may pay to workers. Basic supply and demand analysis shows that if the minimum wage law has any effect at all, it must raise the unemployment rate. Figure 21.8 shows why. The figure shows the demand and supply curves for low-skilled workers, to whom the minimum wage is most relevant. The market-clearing real wage, at which the quantity of labor demanded equals the quantity of labor supplied, is w, and the corresponding level of employment of low-skilled workers is N. Now suppose there is a legal minimum wage w_{min} that exceeds the market-clearing wage w, as shown in Figure 21.8. At the minimum wage, the number of people who want jobs, N_B, exceeds the number of workers that employers are willing to hire, N_A. The result is unemployment in the amount $N_B - N_A$, also equal to the length of the line segment AB in the figure. If there were no minimum wage, this unemployment would not exist, since the labor market would clear at wage w.

FIGURE 21.8
A Legal Minimum Wage May Create Unemployment.

If the minimum wage w_{min} exceeds the market-clearing wage w for low-skilled workers, it will create unemployment equal to the difference between the number of people who want to work at the minimum wage, N_B, and the number of people that employers are willing to hire, N_A.

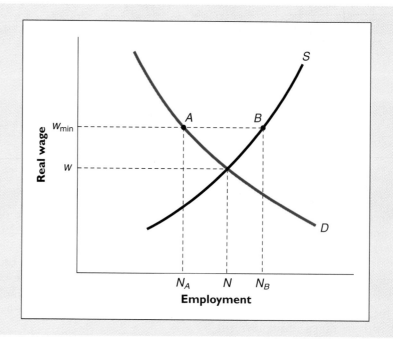

If minimum wages create unemployment, why are they politically popular? A minimum wage creates two classes of workers: those who are lucky enough to find jobs at the minimum wage and those who are shut out because the minimum wage exceeds the market-clearing wage. Workers who do find jobs at the minimum wage will earn more than they would have otherwise, because the minimum wage is higher than the market-clearing wage. If the minimum wage were put to a vote, the number of workers who benefit from the legislation, and who could thus be expected to support it, might well exceed the number of workers who are hurt by it. In creating groups of "winners" and "losers," minimum wage legislation resembles rent control legislation (see Chapter 4). But like rent controls, minimum wages create economic inefficiency. Thus, other methods of attacking poverty, such as direct grants to the working poor, might prove more effective.

Labor unions Labor unions are organizations that negotiate with employers on behalf of workers. Among the issues that unions negotiate, which are embodied in the contracts they draw up with employers, are the wages workers earn,

[2]Minimum wages are also discussed Chapter 13.

rules for hiring and firing, the duties of different types of workers, working hours and conditions, and procedures for resolving disputes between workers and employers. Unions gain negotiating power by their power to call a strike—that is, to refuse work until a contract agreement has been reached.

Through the threat of a strike, a union can usually get employers to agree to a wage that is higher than the market-clearing wage. Thus Figure 21.8 could represent conditions in a unionized industry if w_{min} is interpreted as the union wage instead of the legal minimum wage. As in the case of a minimum wage, a union wage that is higher than the market-clearing wage leads to unemployment, in the amount $N_B - N_A$ in Figure 21.8. Furthermore, a high union wage creates a trade-off similar to the one created by a minimum wage. Those workers who are lucky enough to get jobs as union members will be paid more than they would be otherwise. Unfortunately, their gain comes at the expense of other workers who are unemployed as a result of the artificially high union wage.

Are labor unions good for the economy? That is a controversial, emotionally charged question. Early in the twentieth century, some employers who faced little local competition for workers—coal-mining companies in Appalachia, for example—exploited their advantage by forcing workers to toil long hours in dangerous conditions for low pay. Through bitter and sometimes bloody confrontations with these companies, labor organizations succeeded in eliminating many of the worst abuses. Unions also point with pride to their historic political role in supporting progressive labor legislation, such as laws that banned child labor. Finally, union leaders often claim to increase productivity and promote democracy in the workplace by giving workers some voice in the operations of the firm.

Opponents of unions, while acknowledging that these organizations may have played a positive role in the past, question their value in a modern economy. Today, more and more workers are professionals or semiprofessionals, rather than production workers, so they can move relatively easily from firm to firm. Indeed, many labor markets have become national or even international, so today's workers have numerous potential employers. Thus the forces of competition—the fact that employers must persuade talented workers to work for them—should provide adequate protection for workers. Indeed, opponents would argue that unions are becoming increasingly self-defeating, since firms that must pay artificially high union wages and abide by inflexible work rules will not be able to compete in a global economy. The ultimate effect of such handicaps will be the failure of unionized firms and the loss of union jobs. Indeed, unions are in decline in the United States and now represent less than 15 percent of the workforce—a large fraction of which are government workers, such as public school teachers and the police.

Unemployment insurance Another structural feature of the labor market that may increase the unemployment rate is the availability of *unemployment insurance,* or government transfer payments to unemployed workers. Unemployment insurance provides an important social benefit in that it helps the unemployed to maintain a decent standard of living while they are looking for a job. But because its availability allows the unemployed to search for longer or less intensively for a job, it may lengthen the average amount of time the typical unemployed worker is without a job.

Most economists would argue that unemployment insurance should be generous enough to provide basic support to the unemployed but not so generous as to remove the incentive to actively seek work. Thus, unemployment insurance should last for only a limited time, and its benefits should not be as high as the income a worker receives when working.

Other government regulations Besides minimum wage legislation, many other government regulations bear on the labor market. They include, for example, *health and safety regulations,* which establish the safety standards employers must follow, and rules that prohibit racial or gender-based discrimination in hiring. Many of these regulations are beneficial (see Chapter 13 for further discussion). In some cases, however, the costs of complying with regulations may exceed the benefits they provide. Further, to the extent that regulations increase employer costs and reduce productivity, they depress the demand for labor, lowering real wages and contributing to unemployment. For maximum economic efficiency, legislators should use the *cost-benefit criterion* when deciding what regulations to impose on the labor market.

The points raised in this section can help us to understand one of the important labor market trends discussed earlier in the chapter, namely, the persistence of high unemployment in Western Europe.

ECONOMIC NATURALIST 21.5

Why are unemployment rates so high in Western Europe?

For more than two decades, unemployment has been exceptionally high in the major countries of Western Europe, as Figure 21.9 shows. In 1999, the unemployment rate was 9 percent in Germany and greater than 11 percent in France and Italy, compared with a U.S. unemployment rate that was just above 4 percent. In the 1950s, 1960s, and 1970s, Western Europe consistently enjoyed very low unemployment rates. Why has European unemployment been so stubbornly high for the past two decades?

One explanation for the high unemployment in major Western European countries is the existence of structural "rigidities" in their labor markets. Relative to the United States, European labor markets are highly regulated. European governments set rules in matters ranging from the number of weeks of vacation workers must receive to the reasons for which a worker can be dismissed. Minimum wages in Europe are high, and unemployment benefits are much more generous than in the United States. European unions are also far more powerful than those in the United States; their wage agreements are often extended by law to all firms in the industry, whether or not they are unionized. This lack of flexibility in labor markets—which some observers refer to as *Eurosclerosis*—causes higher frictional and structural unemployment.

FIGURE 21.9
Unemployment Rates in Western Europe, 1980–1999.
In the major Western European countries, unemployment rates have been high for more than two decades. (SOURCE: Standardized unemployment rates from OECD, *Economic Outlook.*)

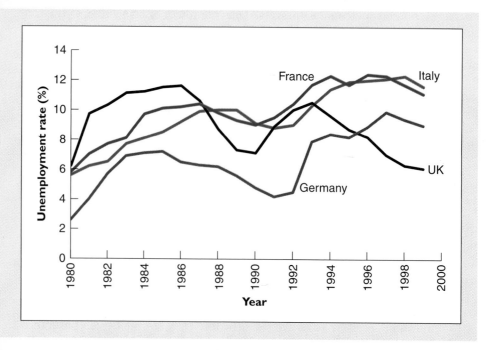

If European labor markets are so dysfunctional, why has serious European unemployment emerged only in the past two decades? One explanation turns on the increasing pace of *globalization* and *skill-biased technological change*. As we saw, these two factors decrease the demand for less-skilled labor relative to the demand for skilled labor. In the United States, falling demand has depressed the wages of the less skilled, increasing wage inequality. But in Western Europe, high minimum wages, union contracts, generous unemployment insurance, and other factors may have created a floor for the wage that firms could pay or that workers would accept. As the marginal productivity of the less skilled dropped below that floor, firms no longer found it profitable to employ those workers, swelling the ranks of the unemployed. Thus the combination of labor market rigidity and the declining marginal productivity of low-skilled workers may be responsible for the European unemployment problem.

Evidence for the idea that inflexible labor markets have contributed to European unemployment comes from the United Kingdom, where the government of Prime Minister Margaret Thatcher instituted a series of reforms beginning in the early 1980s. Britain has since largely deregulated its labor market so that it functions much more like that in the United States. Figure 21.9 shows that unemployment in Britain has gradually declined and is now lower than in other Western European countries. Labor market reforms like those in Britain are examples of *structural policies*.

RECAP   **UNEMPLOYMENT**

Economists distinguish among three broad types of unemployment. *Frictional unemployment* is the short-term unemployment that is associated with the process of matching workers with jobs. *Structural unemployment* is the long-term or chronic unemployment that occurs even when the economy is producing at a normal rate. *Cyclical unemployment* is the extra unemployment that occurs during periods of recession. Frictional unemployment may be economically beneficial, as improved matching of workers and jobs may increase output in the long run. Structural and cyclical unemployment impose heavy economic costs on workers and society, as well as psychological costs on workers and their families.

Structural features of the labor market may cause structural unemployment. Examples of such features are legal minimum wages or union contracts that set wages above market-clearing levels, unemployment insurance, which allows unemployed workers to search longer or less intensively for a job, and government regulations that impose extra costs on employers. Regulation of the labor market is not necessarily undesirable, but it should be subject to the cost-benefit criterion. Heavy labor market regulation and high unionization rates in Western Europe help to explain the persistence of high unemployment rates in those countries.

▪ SUMMARY ▪

- For the average person, the most tangible result of economic growth and increasing productivity is the availability of "good jobs at good wages." Over the long run the U.S. economy has for the most part delivered on this promise, as both real wages and employment have grown strongly. But while growth in employment has recently been rapid, two worrisome trends dog the U.S. labor market: a slowdown since the early 1970s in the growth of real wages and increasing wage inequality. Western Europe has experienced less wage inequality but significantly higher rates of unemployment than the United States.

- Trends in real wages and employment can be studied using a supply and demand model of the labor market. The productivity of labor and the relative price of workers' output determine the demand for labor. Employers will hire workers only as long as the value of the marginal product of the

last worker hired equals or exceeds the wage the firm must pay. Because of *diminishing returns to labor,* the more workers a firm employs, the less additional product will be obtained by adding yet another worker. The lower the going wage, the more workers will be hired; that is, the demand for labor curve slopes downward. Economic changes that increase the value of labor's marginal product, such as an increase in the relative price of workers' output or an increase in productivity, shift the labor demand curve to the right. Conversely, changes that reduce the value of labor's marginal product shift the labor demand curve to the left.

- The supply curve for labor shows the number of people willing to work at any given real wage. Since more people will work at a higher real wage, the supply curve is upward-sloping. An increase in the working-age population, or a social change that promotes labor market participation (like increased acceptance of women in the labor force) will raise labor supply and shift the labor supply curve to the right.

• Improvements in productivity, which raise the demand for labor, account for the bulk of the increase in U.S. real wages over the last century. The slowdown in real wage growth that has occurred in recent decades is the result of slower growth in labor demand, which was caused in turn by a slowdown in the rate of productivity improvement, and of more rapid growth in labor supply. Rapid growth in labor supply, caused by such factors as immigration and increased labor force participation by women, has also contributed to the continued expansion of employment. Recently, there has been some improvement in the rate of growth of productivity and real wages.

• Two reasons for the increasing wage inequality in the United States are economic globalization and *skill-biased technological change*. Both have increased the demand for, and hence the real wages of, relatively skilled and educated workers. Attempting to block globalization and technological change is counterproductive, however, since both factors are essential to economic growth and increased productivity. To some extent, the movement of workers from lower-paying to higher-paying jobs or industries (*worker mobility*) will counteract the trend toward wage inequality. A policy of providing transition aid and training for workers with obsolete skills is a more useful response to the problem.

• There are three broad types of unemployment: frictional, structural, and cyclical. *Frictional unemployment* is the short-term unemployment associated with the process of matching workers with jobs in a dynamic, heterogeneous labor market. *Structural unemployment* is the long-term and chronic unemployment that exists even when the economy is producing at a normal rate. It arises from a variety of factors, including language barriers, discrimination, structural features of the labor market, lack of skills, or long-term mismatches between the skills workers have and the available jobs. *Cyclical unemployment* is the extra unemployment that occurs during periods of recession. The costs of frictional unemployment are low, as it tends to be brief and to create more productive matches between workers and jobs. But structural unemployment, which is often long-term, and cyclical unemployment, which is associated with significant reductions in real GDP, are relatively more costly.

• Structural features of the labor market that may contribute to unemployment include minimum wage laws, which discourage firms from hiring low-skilled workers; labor unions, which can set wages above market-clearing levels; unemployment insurance, which reduces the incentives of the unemployed to find work quickly; and other government regulations, which—although possibly conferring benefits—increase the costs of employing workers. The labor market "rigidity" created by government regulations and union contracts is more of a problem in Western Europe than in the United States, which may account for Europe's high unemployment rates.

▪ KEY TERMS ▪

cyclical unemployment (563)
diminishing returns to labor (547)

frictional unemployment (562)
skill-biased technological change (559)

structural unemployment (562)
worker mobility (558)

▪ REVIEW QUESTIONS ▪

1. List and discuss the five important labor market trends given in the first section of the chapter. How do these trends either support or qualify the proposition that increasing labor productivity leads to higher standards of living?

2. Alice is very skilled at fixing manual typewriters. Would you expect her high productivity to result in a high real wage for her? Why or why not?

3. Acme Corporation is considering hiring Jane Smith. Based on her other opportunities in the job market, Jane has told Acme that she will work for them for $40,000 per year. How should Acme determine whether they should employ her?

4. Why have real wages risen by so much in the United States in the past century? Why has real wage growth

slowed since the early 1970s? What has been happening to real wages recently?

5. What are two major factors contributing to increased inequality in wages? Briefly, why do these factors raise wage inequality? Contrast possible policy responses to increasing inequality in terms of their effects on economic efficiency.

6. List three types of unemployment and their causes. Which of these types is economically and socially the least costly? Explain.

7. Describe some of the structural features of European labor markets that have helped to keep European unemployment rates high. If these structural features create unemployment, why don't European governments just eliminate them?

▪ PROBLEMS ▪

1. Data on the average earnings of people of different education levels are available from the Bureau of the Census (try online at www.census.gov/population/socdemo/education/tablea-03.txt). Using these data prepare a table showing the earnings of college graduates relative to high school graduates and of college graduates relative to those with less than a high school degree. Show the data for the latest year available, for every fifth year going back to the earliest data available. What are the trends in relative earnings?

2. Production data for Bob's Bicycle Factory are as follows:

Numer of workers	Bikes assembled/day
1	10
2	18
3	24
4	28
5	30

Other than wages, Bob has costs of $100 (for parts and so on) for each bike assembled.
a. Bikes sell for $130 each. Find the marginal product and the value of the marginal product for each worker (don't forget about Bob's cost of parts).
b. Make a table showing Bob's demand curve for labor.
c. Repeat part b for the case in which bikes sell for $140 each.
d. Repeat part b for the case in which worker productivity increases by 50 percent. Bikes sell for $130 each.

3. The marginal product of a worker in a lightbulb factory equals $30 - N$ bulbs per hour, where N is the total number of workers employed. Lightbulbs sell for $2 each, and there are no costs to producing them other than labor costs.
a. The going hourly wage for factory workers is $20 per hour. How many workers should the factory manager hire? What if the wage is $30 per hour?
b. Graph the factory's demand for labor.
c. Repeat part b for the case in which lightbulbs sell for $3 each.
d. Suppose the supply of factory workers in the town in which the lightbulb factory is located is 20 workers (in other words, the labor supply curve is vertical at 20 workers). What will be the equilibrium real wage for factory workers in the town if lightbulbs sell for $2 each? If they sell for $3 each?

4. How would each of the following likely affect the real wage and employment of unskilled workers on an automobile plant assembly line?
a. Demand for the type of car made by the plant increases.
b. A sharp increase in the price of gas causes many commuters to switch to mass transit.
c. Because of alternative opportunities, people become less willing to do factory work.
d. The plant management introduces new assembly-line methods that increase the number of cars unskilled workers can produce per hour, while reducing defects.
e. Robots are introduced to do most basic assembly line tasks.
f. The workers unionize.

5. How would each of the following factors be likely to affect the economywide supply of labor?
a. The mandatory retirement age is increased.
b. Increased productivity causes real wages to rise.
c. War preparations lead to the institution of a national draft, and many young people are called up.
d. More people decide to have children (consider both short-run and long-run effects).
e. Social Security benefits are made more generous.

6. Either skilled or unskilled workers can be used to produce a small toy. The marginal product of skilled workers, measured in terms of toys produced per day, equals $200 - N^s$, where N^s is the number of skilled workers employed. Similarly, the marginal product of unskilled workers is $100 - N^u$, where N^u is the number of unskilled workers employed. The toys sell for $3 each.
   a. Assume that there are 100 skilled workers and 50 unskilled workers available (and the labor supply curves for each group are vertical). In dollars, what will be the equilibrium wage for each type of worker? (*Hint:* What are the marginal products and the values of marginal product for each type of worker when all workers are employed?)
   b. Electronic equipment is introduced that increases the marginal product of skilled workers (who can use the equipment) to $300 - N^s$. The marginal products of unskilled workers are unaffected. Now what are the equilibrium wages for the two groups?
   c. Suppose that unskilled workers find it worthwhile to acquire skills when the wage differential between skilled and unskilled workers is $300 per day or greater. Following the introduction of the electronic equipment, how many unskilled workers will become skilled? (*Hint:* How many workers would have to shift from the unskilled to the skilled category to make the equilibrium difference in wages precisely equal to $300 per day?) What are equilibrium wages for skilled and unskilled workers after some unskilled workers acquire training?

7. An economy with no foreign trade produces sweaters and dresses. There are 14 workers in the sweater industry and 26 workers in the dress industry. The marginal product of workers in the sweater industry, measured in sweaters produced per day, is $20 - NS$, where NS is the number of workers employed in the sweater industry. The marginal product of workers in the dress industry, measured in dresses produced per day, is $30 - ND$, where ND is the number of workers employed in the dress industry.
   a. Initially, sweaters sell for $40 apiece and dresses are $60 apiece. Find the equilibrium wage in each industry.
   b. The economy opens up to trade. Foreign demand for domestically produced sweaters is strong, raising the price of sweaters to $50 each. But foreign competition reduces demand for domestically produced dresses so that they now sell for $50 each. Assuming that workers cannot move between industries, what are wages in each industry now? Who has been hurt and who has been helped by the opening up to trade?
   c. Now suppose that workers can move freely from one industry to the other, and will always move to the industry that pays the higher wage. In the long run, how many of the 40 workers in the economy will be in each industry? What wages will they receive? In the long run, are domestic workers hurt or helped by the opening up to foreign trade? Assume that sweaters and dresses continue to sell for $50.

8. For each of the following scenarios, state whether the unemployment is frictional, structural, or cyclical. Justify your answer.
   a. Ted lost his job when the steel mill closed down. He lacks the skills to work in another industry and so has been unemployed over a year.
   b. Alice was laid off from her job at the auto plant because the recession has reduced the demand for cars. She expects to get her job back when the economy picks up.
   c. Lance is an unskilled worker who works for local moving companies during their busy seasons. The rest of the year he is unemployed.
   d. Gwen had a job as a clerk but quit when her husband was transferred to another state. She looked for a month before finding a new job that she liked.
   e. Tao looked for a job for 6 weeks after finishing college. He turned down a couple of offers because they didn't let him use the skills he had acquired in college, but now he has a job in the area that he trained for.
   f. Karen, a software engineer, lost her job when the start-up company she was working for went bankrupt. She interviewed at five companies before accepting a new job in another firm in the same industry.

9. The demand for and supply of labor in a certain industry are given by the equations

$$N^d = 400 - 2w$$
$$N^s = 240 + 2w$$

where N^d is the number of workers employers want to hire, N^s is the number of people willing to work, and both labor demand and labor supply depend on the real wage w, which is measured in dollars per day.

a. Find employment and the real wage in labor market equilibrium.

b. Suppose the minimum wage is $50 per day. Find employment and unemployment. Is anyone made better off by the minimum wage? Worse off? In answering the last part of the question, consider not only workers but employers and other people in the society, such as consumers and taxpayers.

c. Repeat part b except now assume that a union contract requires that workers be paid $60 per day.

d. Repeat part b but, instead of a minimum wage, suppose there is an unemployment benefit that pays $50 per day. Workers are indifferent between earning a wage of $50 per day and remaining unemployed and collecting the benefit.

e. Repeat part b, assuming that the minimum wage is $50 per day. However, assume that the cost of complying with government regulations on workplace safety reduces labor demand to $N^d = 360 - 2w$.

10. The *Economic Report of the President* (ERP), put out annually by the President's Council of Economic Advisers, is available in the library or online (www.access.gpo.gov/eop/index.html). ERP includes both useful articles on recent economic developments and a statistical section that provides historical data on many macro variables.

   From the ERP or some other source, find data for the most recent year on the percentage of the unemployed who were out of work less than 5 weeks, between 5 and 14 weeks, and over 26 weeks. What do these data suggest about the relative importance of frictional and structural unemployment in the economy?

   Compare the data you found for the most recent year to similar data for the recession years 1981–1982 and 1990–1991, plus the 2 years following each of the two recessions. How do recessions change the proportion of unemployment that is short term and long term?

▪ ANSWERS TO IN-CHAPTER EXERCISES ▪

21.1 The value of the marginal product of the seventh worker is $39,000, and the value of the marginal product of the eighth worker is $33,000. So the seventh but not the eighth worker is profitable to hire at a wage of $35,000.

21.2 With the computer price at $5,000, it is profitable to hire three workers at a wage of $100,000, since the third worker's value of marginal product ($105,000) exceeds $100,000 but the fourth worker's value of marginal product ($95,000) is less than $100,000. At a computer price of $3,000, we can refer to Table 21.1 to find that not even the first worker has a value of marginal product as high as $100,000, so at that computer price BCC will hire no workers. In short, at a wage of $100,000, the increase in the computer price raises the demand for technicians from zero to three.

21.3 The seventh but not the eighth worker's value of marginal product exceeds $50,000 (Table 21.3), so it is profitable to hire seven workers if the going wage is $50,000. From Table 21.1, before the increase in productivity, the first five workers have values of marginal product greater than $50,000, so the demand for labor at a given wage of $50,000 is five workers. Thus the increase in productivity raises the quantity of labor demanded at a wage of $50,000 from five workers to seven workers.

21.4 Even though you are receiving no pay, the valuable experience you gain as an intern is likely to raise the pay you will be able to earn in the future, so it is an investment in human capital. You also find working in the radio station more enjoyable than working in a car wash, presumably. To decide which job to take, you should ask yourself, "Taking into account both the likely increase in my future earnings and my greater enjoyment from working in the radio station, would I be willing to pay $3,000 to work in the radio station rather than in the car wash?" If the answer is yes, then you should work in the radio station, otherwise you should go to the car wash.

A decision to work in the radio station does not contradict the idea of an upward-sloping labor supply curve, if we are willing to think of the total compensation for that job as including not just cash wages but such factors as the value of the training that you receive. Your labor supply curve is still upward-sloping in the sense that the greater the value you place on the internship experience, the more likely you are to accept the job.

21.5 Immigration to a country raises labor supply—indeed, the search for work is one of the most powerful factors drawing immigrants in the first place. As shown in the accompanying figure, an increase in labor supply will tend to lower the wages that employers have to pay (from w to w'), while raising overall employment (from N to N'). Because of its tendency to reduce real wages, labor unions generally oppose large-scale immigration, while employers support it.

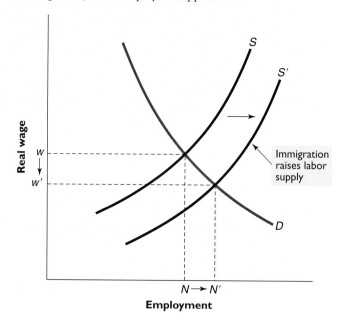

Although the figure shows the overall, or aggregate, supply of labor in the economy, the specific effects of immigration on wages depend on the skills and occupations of the immigrants. Current U.S. immigration policy makes the reunification of families the main reason for admitting immigrants, and for the most part immigrants are not screened by their education or skills. The U.S. also has a good deal of illegal immigration, made up largely of people looking for economic opportunity. These two factors create a tendency for new immigrants to the United States to be relatively low-skilled. Since immigration tends to increase the supply of unskilled labor by relatively more, it depresses wages of domestic low-skilled workers more than it does the wages of domestic high-skilled workers. Some economists, such as George Borjas of Harvard University, have argued that low-skilled immigration is another important factor reducing the wages of less-skilled workers relative to workers with greater skills and education. Borjas argues that the United States should adopt the approach used by Canada and give preference to potential immigrants with relatively higher levels of skills and education.

21.6 Part (a) of the accompanying figure shows the labor market in 1960–1972; part (b) shows the labor market in 1973–1996. For comparability, we set the initial labor supply (S) and demand (D) curves the same in both parts, implying the same initial values of the real wage (w) and employment (N). In part (a) we show the effects of a large increase in labor demand (from D to D'), the result of rapid productivity growth, and a relatively small increase in labor supply (from S to S'). The real wage rises to w' and employment rises to N'. In part (b) we observe the effects of a somewhat smaller increase in labor demand (from D to D'') and a larger increase in labor supply (from S to S''). Part (b), corresponding to the 1973–1996 period, shows a smaller increase in the real wage and a larger increase in employment than part (a), corresponding to 1960–1972. These results are consistent with actual developments in the U.S. labor market over these two periods.

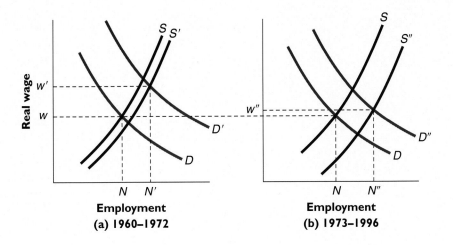

Employment
(a) 1960–1972

Employment
(b) 1973–1996

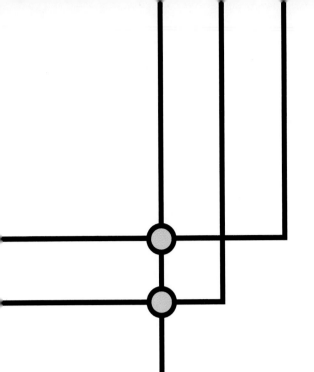

CHAPTER

22

SAVING AND CAPITAL FORMATION

■

On your mother's or father's knee you probably heard the fable of the ant and the grasshopper. All summer the ant worked hard laying up food for the winter. The grasshopper mocked the ant's efforts and contented himself with basking in the sunshine, ignoring the ant's earnest warnings. When winter came the ant was well-fed, while the grasshopper starved. Moral: When times are good, the wise put aside something for the future.

Of course, there is also the modern ending to the fable, in which the grasshopper breaks his leg by tripping over the anthill, sues the ant for negligence, and ends up living comfortably on the ant's savings. (Nobody knows what happened to the ant.) Moral: Saving is risky; live for today.

The pitfalls of modern life notwithstanding, saving is important, both to individuals and to nations. People need to save to provide for their retirement and for other future needs, such as their children's education or a new home. An individual's or a family's savings can also provide a crucial buffer in the event of an economic emergency, such as the loss of a job or unexpected medical bills. At the national level, the production of new capital goods—factories, equipment, and housing—is an important factor promoting economic growth and higher living standards. As we will see in this chapter, the resources necessary to produce new capital come primarily from a nation's collective saving.

Because adequate saving is so important both to ensuring families' financial security and creating new capital goods, many people expressed concern in the fall of 1998, when the U.S. government reported that the saving rate of American households had turned *negative*, in other words, that aggregate household spending had exceeded household income. Data revisions later reversed the conclusion that the household saving rate had reached negative territory, but there is no doubt that recently household saving has been exceptionally low. Figure 22.1 shows the U.S. household saving rate (the percentage of after-tax household income that is saved) since 1960. Never very high by international standards, the U.S. household saving rate declined sharply in the mid-1980s and fell again in the mid-1990s, reaching 2.4 percent in 1999 (according to revised data).

FIGURE 22.1
Household Saving Rate in the United States, 1960–1999.
The U.S. household saving rate, declining since the mid-1980s, fell to 2.4 percent in 1999. (SOURCE: *Economic Report of the President,* February 2000.)

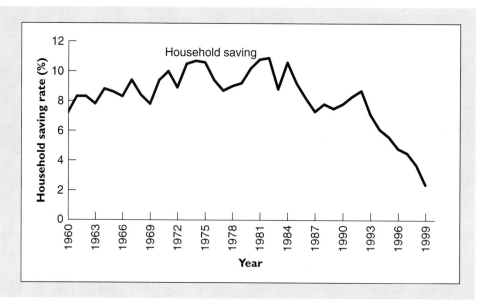

What was the significance of this precipitous decline? Alarmists saw the data as evidence of "grasshopperish" behavior, and a threat to Americans' future prosperity. The reality, as we will see, is more complex. Many American families do save very little, a choice that is likely to exact a toll on their economic well-being in the long run. On the other hand, household saving is only one part of the total saving of the U.S. economy, as businesses and governments also save. In fact, the total saving of the U.S. economy, called *national saving,* has not declined significantly in recent years. Thus, if the United States is suffering a "savings shortfall," it is much less severe than might be suggested by the figures on household saving only.

In this chapter we will look at saving and its links to the formation of new capital. We begin by defining the concepts of saving and wealth and exploring the connection between them. We will consider why people choose to save, rather than spending all their income. We then turn to national saving—the collective saving of households, businesses, and government. Because national saving determines the capacity of an economy to create new capital, it is the more important measure of saving from a macroeconomic perspective.

We next discuss capital formation. Most decisions to invest in new capital are made by firms. As we will see, a firm's decision to invest is in many respects analogous to its decision about whether to increase employment; firms will choose to expand their capital stocks when the benefits of doing so exceed the costs. We end the chapter by showing how national saving and capital formation are related, using a supply and demand approach.

SAVING AND WEALTH

saving current income minus spending on current needs

In general, the **saving** of an economic unit—whether a household, a business, a university, or a nation—may be defined as its *current income* minus its *spending on current needs.* For example, if Consuelo earns $300 per week, spends $280 weekly on living expenses such as rent, food, clothes, and entertainment, and deposits the remaining $20 in the bank, her saving is $20 per week. The **saving rate** of any economic unit is its saving divided by its income. Since Consuelo saves $20 of her weekly income of $300, her saving rate is $20/$300, or 6.7 percent.

The saving of an economic unit is closely related to its **wealth,** or the value of its assets minus its liabilities. **Assets** are anything of value that one *owns,* either *financial* or *real.* Examples of financial assets that you or your family might own include cash, a checking account, stocks, and bonds. Examples of real assets include a home or other real estate, jewelry, consumer durables like cars, and valuable collectibles. **Liabilities,** on the other hand, are the debts one *owes.* Examples of liabilities are credit card balances, student loans, and mortgages.

Accountants list the assets and liabilities of a family, a firm, a university, or any other economic unit on a *balance sheet.* Comparing the values of the assets and liabilities helps them to determine the economic unit's wealth, also called its *net worth.*

saving rate saving divided by income

wealth the value of *assets* minus *liabilities*

assets anything of value that one *owns*

liabilities the debts one *owes*

Consuelo constructs her balance sheet

To take stock of her financial position, Consuelo lists her assets and liabilities on a balance sheet. The result is shown in Table 22.1. What is Consuelo's wealth?

EXAMPLE 22.1

TABLE 22.1
Consuelo's Balance Sheet

Assets		Liabilities	
Cash	$ 80	Student loan	$3,000
Checking account	1,200	Credit card balance	250
Shares of stock	1,000		
Car (market value)	3,500		
Furniture (market value)	500		
Total	$6,280		$3,250
		Net worth	$3,030

Consuelo's financial assets are the cash in her wallet, the balance in her checking account, and the current value of some shares of stock her parents gave her. Together her financial assets are worth $2,280. She also lists $4,000 in real assets, the sum of the market values of her car and her furniture. Consuelo's total assets, both financial and real, come to $6,280. Her liabilities are the student loan she owes the bank and the balance due on her credit card, which total $3,250. Consuelo's wealth, or net worth, then, is the value of her assets ($6,280) minus the value of her liabilities ($3,250), or $3,030.

EXERCISE 22.1

What would Consuelo's net worth be if her student loan were for $6,500 rather than $3,000? Construct a new balance sheet for her.

Saving and wealth are related, because saving contributes to wealth. To understand this relationship better, we must distinguish between *stocks* and *flows.*

STOCKS AND FLOWS

Saving is an example of a **flow,** a measure that is defined *per unit of time.* For example, Consuelo's saving is $20 *per week.* Wealth, in contrast, is a **stock,** a measure that is defined *at a point in time.* Consuelo's wealth of $3,030, for example, is her wealth on a particular date—say, January 1, 2000.

flow a measure that is defined *per unit of time*

stock a measure that is defined *at a point in time*

The flow of saving increases the stock of wealth in the same way that the flow of water through the faucet increases the amount of water in the tub.

To visualize the difference between stocks and flows, think of water running into a bathtub. The amount of water in the bathtub at any specific moment—for example, 40 gallons at 7:15 P.M.—is a stock, because it is measured at a specific point in time. The rate at which the water flows into the tub—for example, 2 gallons per minute—is a flow, because it is measured per unit of time. In many cases, a flow is the *rate of change* in a stock: If we know that there are 40 gallons of water in the tub at 7:15 P.M., for example, and that water is flowing in at 2 gallons per minute, we can easily determine that the stock of water will be changing at the rate of 2 gallons per minute and will equal 42 gallons at 7:16 P.M., 44 gallons at 7:17 P.M., and so on, until the bathtub overflows.

EXERCISE 22.2

Continuing the example of the bathtub: If there are 40 gallons of water in the tub at 7:15 P.M. and water is being *drained* at the rate of 3 gallons per minute, what will be the stock and flow at 7:16 P.M.? At 7:17 P.M.? Does the flow still equal the rate of change in the stock?

The relationship between saving (a flow) and wealth (a stock) is similar to the relationship between the flow of water into a bathtub and the stock of water in the tub in that the *flow* of saving causes the *stock* of wealth to change at the same rate. Indeed, as Example 22.2 illustrates, every dollar that a person saves adds a dollar to his or her wealth.

EXAMPLE 22.2

The link between saving and wealth

Consuelo saves $20 per week. How does this saving affect her wealth? Does the change in her wealth depend on whether Consuelo uses her saving to accumulate assets or to pay down her liabilities?

Consuelo could use the $20 she saved this week to increase her assets—for example, by adding the $20 to her checking account—or to reduce her liabilities—for example, by paying down her credit card balance. Suppose she adds the $20 to her checking account, increasing her assets by $20. Since her liabilities are unchanged, her wealth also increases by $20, to $3,050 (see Table 22.1).

If Consuelo decides to use the $20 she saved this week to pay down her credit card balance, she reduces it from $250 to $230. That action would reduce her liabilities by $20, leaving her assets unchanged. Since wealth equals assets minus liabilities, reducing her liabilities by $20 increases her wealth by $20, to $3,050. Thus, saving $20 per week raises Consuelo's stock of wealth by $20 a week, irrespective of whether she uses her saving to increase her assets or reduce her liabilities.

The close relationship between saving and wealth explains why saving is so important to an economy. Higher rates of saving today lead to faster accumulation of wealth, and the wealthier a nation is, the higher its standard of living. Thus a high rate of saving today contributes to an improved standard of living in the future.

CAPITAL GAINS AND LOSSES

Though saving increases wealth, it is not the only factor that determines wealth. Wealth can also change because of changes in the values of the real or financial assets one owns. Suppose Consuelo's shares of stock rise in value, from $1,000 to $1,500. This increase in the value of Consuelo's stock raises her total assets by $500 without affecting her liabilities. As a result, Consuelo's wealth rises by $500, from $3,030 to $3,530 (see Table 22.2).

TABLE 22.2
Consuelo's Balance Sheet after an Increase in the Value of Her Stocks

Assets		Liabilities	
Cash	$ 80	Student loan	$3,000
Checking account	1,200	Credit card balance	250
Shares of stock	1,500		
Car (market value)	3,500		
Furniture (market value)	500		
Total	**$6,780**		**$3,250**
		Net worth	**$3,530**

Changes in the value of existing assets are called **capital gains** when an asset's value increases and **capital losses** when an asset's value decreases. Just as capital gains increase wealth, capital losses decrease wealth. Capital gains and losses are not counted as part of saving, however. Instead, the change in a person's wealth during any period equals the saving done during the period plus capital gains or minus capital losses during that period. In terms of an equation,

capital gains increases in the value of existing assets

capital losses decreases in the values of existing assets

$$\text{Change in wealth} = \text{Saving} + \text{Capital gains} - \text{Capital losses}$$

EXERCISE 22.3

How would each of the following actions or events affect Consuelo's *saving* and her *wealth*?

a. Consuelo deposits $20 in the bank at the end of the week as usual. She also charges $50 on her credit card, raising her credit card balance to $300.

b. Consuelo uses $300 from her checking account to pay off her credit card bill.

c. Consuelo's old car is recognized as a classic. Its market value rises from $3,500 to $4,000.

d. Consuelo's furniture is damaged and as a result falls in value from $500 to $200.

Capital gains and losses can have a major effect on one's overall wealth, as Economic Naturalist 22.1 illustrates.

The bull market and household wealth

On the whole, Americans felt very prosperous during the 1990s: Measures of household wealth during this period showed enormous gains. One study found that U.S. household wealth increased by an amount equal to approximately half of after-tax household income in 1997 and again in 1998,[1] and the wealth increase in 1999 was perhaps even greater. Yet, as Figure 22.1 shows, saving by U.S. households was quite low in all three of those years. How did American households get rich in the 1990s while saving very little?

During the 1990s an increasing number of Americans acquired stocks, either directly through purchases or indirectly through their pension and retirement funds. At the same time, stock prices rose at record rates (see Figure 22.2). The strongly rising

ECONOMIC NATURALIST 22.1

[1] William G. Gale and John Sabelhaus, "The Saving Crisis: In the Eye of the Beholder?" *The Milken Institute Review,* Third Quarter 1999, pp. 46–56, Table 5.

"bull market," which increased the prices of most stocks, enabled many Americans to enjoy significant capital gains and increased wealth without saving much, if anything. Indeed, some economists argue that the low household saving rate of the 1990s is partially *explained* by the bull market; because capital gains increased household wealth by so much, many people saw no need to save.

FIGURE 22.2
The Bull Market of the 1990s.
Stock prices rose sharply during the 1990s, greatly increasing the wealth of households that held stocks. This figure shows the Standard & Poor 500 index of stock prices, divided by the CPI to correct for inflation, for the period 1960–1999.

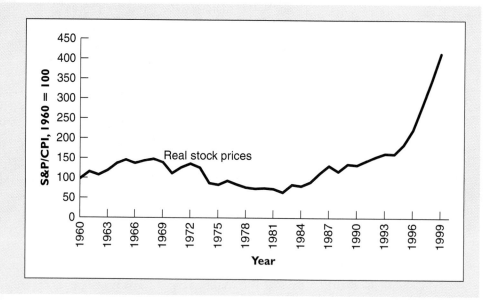

We have seen how saving is related to the accumulation of wealth. To understand why people choose to save, however, we need to examine their motives for saving.

RECAP   SAVING AND WEALTH

In general, *saving* is current income minus spending on current needs. *Wealth* is the value of assets—anything of value that one owns—minus liabilities—the debts one owes. Saving is measured per unit of time (for example, dollars per week) and thus is a *flow*. Wealth is measured at a point in time and thus is a *stock*. In the same way the flow of water through the faucet increases the stock of water in a bathtub, the flow of saving increases the stock of wealth.

Wealth can also be increased by *capital gains* (increases in the value of existing assets) or reduced by *capital losses* (decreases in asset values). The capital gains afforded stockholders by the bull market of the 1990s allowed many families to increase their wealth significantly while doing very little saving.

WHY DO PEOPLE SAVE?

Why do people save part of their income instead of spending everything they earn? Economists have identified at least three broad reasons for saving. First, people save to meet certain long-term objectives, such as a comfortable retirement. By putting away part of their income during their working years, they can live better after retirement than they would if they had to rely solely on Social Security and their company pensions. Other long-term objectives might include college tuition for one's children and the purchase of a new home or car. Since many of these needs occur at fairly predictable stages in one's life, economists call this type of saving **life-cycle saving.**

life-cycle saving saving to meet long-term objectives, such as retirement, college attendance, or the purchase of a home

A second reason to save is to protect oneself and family against unexpected setbacks—the loss of a job, for example, or a costly health problem. Personal financial advisors typically suggest that families maintain an emergency reserve (a "rainy-day fund") equal to 3 to 6 months' worth of income. Saving for protection against potential emergencies is called **precautionary saving**.

precautionary saving saving for protection against unexpected setbacks, such as the loss of a job or a medical emergency

"Fortunately, you have the life savings of a man three times your age."

A third reason to save is to accumulate an estate to leave to one's heirs, usually one's children but possibly a favorite charity or other worthy cause. Saving for the purpose of leaving an inheritance, or bequest, is called **bequest saving**. Bequest saving is done primarily by people at the higher end of the income ladder. But because these people control a large share of the nation's wealth, bequest saving is an important part of overall saving.

bequest saving saving done for the purpose of leaving an inheritance

To be sure, people usually do not mentally separate their saving into these three categories; rather, all three reasons for saving motivate most savers to varying degrees. The Economic Naturalist 22.2 shows how the three reasons for saving can explain the high rate of household saving in Japan.

Why do Japanese households save so much?

Japanese households save about 20 percent of their income, an unusually high rate. Although cultural factors are often cited as a reason for their propensity to save, the high saving rate is a relatively recent phenomenon; the Japanese were not especially big savers prior to World War II. Why do the Japanese save so much, then?

Among the reasons for saving we discussed, *life-cycle* reasons are clearly important in Japan. The Japanese have long life expectancies, and many retire relatively early. With a long period of retirement to finance, Japanese families must save a great deal during their working years. Second, even though the Japanese real estate market crashed at the beginning of the 1990s, land and housing prices remain extremely high in Japan compared to other countries. In addition, down payment requirements are typically quite high. Young people must therefore save a great deal, or borrow their parents' savings, to buy their first homes in Japan.

ECONOMIC NATURALIST 22.2

Studies have also found that *bequest saving* is important in Japan. Many older people live with their children after retirement. In return for support and attention during their later years, parents feel they must provide substantial inheritances for their children.

Precautionary saving is probably lower in Japan than in some other countries, however. Although Japan's recent economic troubles have reduced the practice of *lifetime employment,* Japanese firms still make extensive use of the system, which essentially guarantees a job for life to workers who join a firm after graduating from college. This type of job security, coupled with Japan's traditionally low unemployment rate, reduces the need for precautionary saving.

Although most people are usually motivated to save for at least one of the three reasons we have discussed, the amount they choose to save may depend on the economic environment. One economic variable that is quite significant in saving decisions is the real interest rate.

SAVING AND THE REAL INTEREST RATE

Most people don't save by putting cash in a mattress. Instead, they make financial investments that they hope will provide a good return on their saving. For example, a checking account may pay interest on the account balance. More sophisticated financial investments, such as government bonds or shares of stock in a corporation (see Chapter 23), also pay returns in the form of interest payments, dividends, or capital gains. High returns are desirable, of course, because the higher the return, the faster one's savings will grow.

The rate of return that is most relevant to saving decisions is the *real interest rate,* denoted r. Recall from Chapter 19 that the real interest rate is the rate at which the real purchasing power of a financial asset increases over time. The real interest rate equals the market, or nominal, interest rate (i) minus the inflation rate (π).

The real interest rate is relevant to savers because it is the "reward" for saving. Suppose you are thinking of increasing your saving by $1,000 this year, which you can do if you give up your habit of eating out once a week. If the real interest rate is 5 percent, then in a year your extra saving will give you extra purchasing power of $1,050, measured in today's dollars. But if the real interest rate were 10 percent, your sacrifice of $1,000 this year would be rewarded by $1,100 in purchasing power next year. Obviously, all else being equal, you would be more willing to save today if you knew the reward next year would be greater. In either case the *cost* of the extra saving—giving up your weekly night out—is the same. But the *benefit* of the extra saving, in terms of increased purchasing power next year, is higher if the real interest rate is 10 percent rather than 5 percent.

EXAMPLE 22.3

By how much does a high savings rate enhance a family's future living standard?

The Spends and the Thrifts are similar families, except that the Spends save 5 percent of their income each year and the Thrifts save 20 percent. The two families began to save in 1980 and plan to continue to save until their respective breadwinners retire in the year 2015. Both families earn $40,000 a year in real terms in the labor market, and both put their savings in a mutual fund that has yielded a real return of 8 percent per year, a return they expect to continue into the future. Compare the amount that the two families consume in each year from 1980 to 2015, and compare the families' wealth at retirement.

In the first year, 1980, the Spends saved $2,000 (5 percent of their $40,000 income) and consumed $38,000 (95 percent of $40,000). The Thrifts saved

$8,000 in 1980 (20 percent of $40,000) and hence consumed only $32,000 in that year, $6,000 less than the Spends. In 1981, the Thrifts' income was $40,640, the extra $640 representing the 8 percent return on their $8,000 savings. The Spends saw their income grow by only $160 (8 percent of their savings of $2,000) in 1981. With an income of $40,640, the Thrifts consumed $32,512 in 1981 (80 percent of $40,640) compared to $38,152 (95 percent of $40,160) for the Spends. The consumption gap between the two families, which started out at $6,000, thus fell to $5,640 after 1 year.

Because of the more rapid increase in the Thrifts' wealth and hence interest income, each year the Thrifts' income grew faster than the Spends'; each year the Thrifts continued to save 20 percent of their higher incomes compared to only 5 percent for the Spends. Figure 22.3 shows the paths followed by the consumption spending of the two families. You can see that the Thrifts' consumption, though starting at a lower level, grows relatively more quickly. By

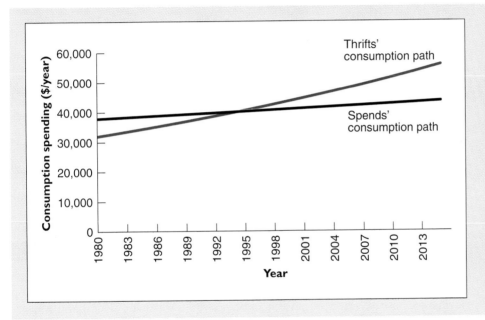

FIGURE 22.3
Consumption Trajectories of the Thrifts and the Spends.
The figure shows consumption spending in each year by two families, the Thrifts and the Spends. Because the Thrifts save more than the Spends, their annual consumption spending rises relatively more quickly. By the time of retirement in the year 2015, the Thrifts are both consuming significantly more each year than the Spends and also have a retirement nest egg that is five times larger.

1995 the Thrifts had overtaken the Spends, and from that point onward, the amount by which the Thrifts outspent the Spends grew with each passing year. Even though the Spends continued to consume 95 percent of their income each year, their income grew so slowly that by 2000, they were consuming nearly $3,000 a year less than the Thrifts ($41,158 a year versus $43,957). And by the time the two families retire, in 2015, the Thrifts will be consuming more than $12,000 per year more than the Spends ($55,774 versus $43,698). Even more striking is the difference between the retirement nest eggs of the two families. Whereas the Spends will enter retirement with total accumulated savings of just over $77,000, the Thrifts will have more than $385,000, five times as much.

These dramatic differences depend in part on the assumption that the real rate of return is 8 percent—lower than the actual return to mutual funds since 1980 but still a relatively high rate of return from a historical perspective. On the other hand, the Spend family in our example actually saves more than typical U.S. households, many of which carry $5,000 or more in credit card debt at high rates of interest and have no significant savings at all. The point of the example, which remains valid under alternative assumptions about the real interest rate and saving rates, is that, because of the power of compound interest, a high rate of saving pays off handsomely in the long run.

"Someday, son, all this will be mine."

While a higher real interest rate increases the reward for saving, which tends to strengthen people's willingness to save, another force counteracts that extra incentive. Recall that a major reason for saving is to attain specific goals: a comfortable retirement, a college education, or a first home. If the goal is a specific amount—say, $25,000 for a down payment on a home—then a higher rate of return means that households can save *less* and still reach their goal, because funds that are put aside will grow more quickly. For example, to accumulate $25,000 at the end of 5 years, at a 5 percent interest rate a person would have to save about $4,309 per year. At a 10 percent interest rate, reaching the $25,000 goal would require saving only about $3,723 per year. To the extent that people are *target savers* who save to reach a specific goal, higher interest rates actually decrease the amount they need to save.

In sum, a higher real interest rate has both positive and negative effects on saving—a positive effect because it increases the reward for saving and a negative effect because it reduces the amount people need to save each year to reach a given target. Empirical evidence suggests that, in practice, higher real interest rates lead to modest increases in saving.

SAVING, SELF-CONTROL, AND DEMONSTRATION EFFECTS

The reasons for saving we just discussed are based on the notion that people are rational decision makers who will choose their saving rates to maximize their welfare over the long run. Yet many psychologists, and some economists, have argued instead that people's saving behavior is based as much on psychological as on economic factors. For example, psychologists stress that many people lack the *self-control* to do what they know is in their own best interest. People smoke or eat greasy food, despite the known long-term health risks. Similarly, they may have good intentions about saving but lack the self-control to put aside as much as they ought to each month.

One way to strengthen self-control is to remove temptations from the immediate environment. A person who is trying to quit smoking will make a point of not having cigarettes in the house, and a person with a weight problem will avoid going to a bakery. Similarly, a person who is not saving enough might arrange to use a payroll savings plan, through which a predetermined amount is deducted from each paycheck and set aside in a special account from which withdrawals are not permitted until retirement. Making saving automatic and withdrawals difficult eliminates the temptation to spend all of current earnings or squander accumulated savings. Payroll savings plans have helped many people to increase the amount that they save for retirement or other purposes.

An implication of the self-control hypothesis is that consumer credit arrangements that make borrowing and spending easier may reduce the amount that people save. For example, in recent years banks have encouraged people to borrow against the *equity* in their homes, that is, the value of the home less the value of the outstanding mortgage. Such financial innovations, by increasing the temptation to spend, may have reduced the household saving rate. The increased availability of credit cards with high borrowing limits is another temptation.

Downward pressure on the saving rate may also occur when additional spending by some consumers stimulates additional spending by others. Such *demonstration effects* arise when people use the spending of others as a yardstick by which to measure the adequacy of their own living standards. For example, a family in an upper-middle-class American suburb in which the average house has 3,000 square feet of living space might regard a 1,500-square-foot house as being uncomfortably small—too cramped, for example, to entertain friends in the manner to which community members have become accustomed. In contrast, a similar family living in a low-income neighborhood might find the very same house luxuriously large.

The implication of demonstration effects for saving is that families who live among others who consume more than they do may be strongly motivated to increase their own consumption spending. When satisfaction depends in part on *relative* living standards, an upward spiral may result in which household spending is higher, and saving lower, than would be best for either the individual families involved or for the economy as a whole.

Why do U.S. households save so little?

Household saving in the United States, which has always been comparatively low, dropped nearly to zero in the late 1990s (Figure 22.1). Surveys show that a significant fraction of American households live from paycheck to paycheck with very little saving. Why do U.S. households save so little?

Economists do not agree on the reasons for low household saving in the United States, although many hypotheses have been suggested.

One possible reason for low saving is the availability of generous government assistance to the elderly. From a *life-cycle* perspective, an important motivation for saving is to provide for retirement. In general, the U.S. government provides a less comprehensive "social safety net" than other industrialized countries; that is, it offers relatively fewer programs to assist people in need. To the extent that the U.S. government does provide income support, however, it is heavily concentrated on the older segment of the population. Together the Social Security and Medicare programs, both of which are designed primarily to assist retired people, constitute a major share of the federal government's expenditures. These programs have been very successful; indeed they have virtually wiped out poverty among the elderly. To the extent that Americans believe that the government will ensure them an adequate living standard in retirement, however, their incentive to save for the future is reduced.

Another important life-cycle objective is buying a home. We have seen that the Japanese must save a great deal to purchase a home because of high house prices and down-payment requirements. The same is true in many other countries. But in the United States, with its highly developed financial system, people can buy homes with down payments of 10 percent or even 5 percent of the purchase price. The ready availability of mortgages with low down payments reduces the need to save for the purchase of a home.

What about *precautionary saving*? Unlike Japan and Europe, which had to rebuild after World War II, the United States has not known sustained economic hardship since the Great Depression of the 1930s (which fewer and fewer Americans are alive to

ECONOMIC NATURALIST 22.3

remember). Perhaps the nation's prosperous past has led Americans to be more confident about the future and hence less inclined to save for economic emergencies than other people, even though the United States does not offer the level of employment security found in Japan or in Europe.

U.S. household saving is not only low by international standards, it is declining. The decline in U.S. household saving in the 1980s and 1990s is probably due at least in part to the sharp increase in stock prices, as well as the prices of other household assets like housing (see Economic Naturalist 22.1). As long as Americans are enjoying capital gains, they will see their wealth increase almost without effort, and their incentive to save will be reduced.

Psychological factors may also explain Americans' saving behavior. For example, unlike in most countries, U.S. homeowners can easily borrow against their home equity. This ability, made possible by the highly developed U.S. financial markets, may exacerbate *self-control* problems by increasing the temptation to spend. Finally, *demonstration effects* may have depressed saving in recent decades. Chapter 21 discussed the phenomenon of increasing wage inequality, which has improved the relative position of more skilled and educated workers. Increased spending by households at the top of the earnings scale on houses, cars, and other consumption goods may have led those just below them to spend more as well, and so on. Middle-class families that were once content with medium-priced cars may now feel they need Volvos and BMWs to keep up with community standards. To the extent that demonstration effects lead families to spend beyond their means, they reduce their saving rate.

RECAP   **WHY DO PEOPLE SAVE?**

Motivations for saving include saving to meet long-term objectives, such as retirement (*life-cycle saving*), saving for emergencies (*precautionary saving*), and saving to leave an inheritance or bequest (*bequest saving*). The amount that people save also depends on macroeconomic factors, such as the real interest rate. A higher real interest rate stimulates saving by increasing the reward for saving, but it can also depress saving by making it easier for savers to reach a specific savings target. On net, a higher real interest rate appears to lead to modest increases in saving.

Psychological factors may also affect saving rates. If people have *self-control* problems, then financial arrangements (such as automatic payroll deductions) that make it more difficult to spend will increase their saving. People's saving decisions may also be influenced by *demonstration effects*, as when people feel compelled to spend at the same rate as their neighbors, even though they may not be able to afford to do so.

NATIONAL SAVING AND ITS COMPONENTS

Thus far we have been examining the concepts of saving and wealth from the individual's perspective. But macroeconomists are interested primarily in saving and wealth for the country as a whole. In this section we will study *national saving*, or the aggregate saving of the economy. National saving includes the saving of business firms and the government as well as that of households. Later in the chapter we will examine the close link between national saving and the rate of capital formation in an economy.

THE MEASUREMENT OF NATIONAL SAVING

To define the saving rate of a country as a whole, we will start with a basic accounting identity that was introduced in Chapter 18. According to this identity, for the economy as a whole, production (or income) must equal total expenditure. In symbols, the identity is

$$Y = C + I + G + NX,$$

where Y stands for either production or aggregate income (which must be equal), C equals consumption expenditure, I equals investment spending, G equals government purchases of goods and services, and NX equals net exports.

For now, let's assume that net exports *(NX)* is equal to zero, which would be the case if a country did not trade at all with other countries or if its exports and imports were always balanced. (We'll reintroduce the foreign sector in Chapter 28.) With net exports set at zero, the condition that output equals expenditure becomes

$$Y = C + I + G.$$

To determine how much saving is done by the nation as a whole, we can apply the general definition of saving. As for any other economic unit, a nation's saving equals its *current income* less its *spending on current needs*. The current income of the country as a whole is its GDP, or Y, that is, the value of the final goods and services produced within the country's borders during the year.

Identifying the part of total expenditure that corresponds to the nation's spending on current needs is more difficult than identifying the nation's income. The component of aggregate spending that is easiest to classify is investment spending I. We know that investment spending—the acquisition of new factories, equipment, and other capital goods, as well as residential construction—is done to expand the economy's future productive capacity or provide more housing for the future, not to satisfy current needs. So investment spending clearly is *not* part of spending on current needs.

Deciding how much of consumption spending by households, C, and government purchases of goods and services, G, should be counted as spending on current needs is less straightforward. Certainly most consumption spending by households—on food, clothing, utilities, entertainment, and so on—is for current needs. But consumption spending also includes purchases of long-lived *consumer durables,* such as cars, furniture, and appliances. Consumer durables are only partially used up during the current year; they may continue to provide service, in fact, for years after their purchase. So household spending on consumer durables is a combination of spending on current needs and spending on future needs.

As with consumption spending, most government purchases of goods and services are intended to provide for current needs. However, like household purchases, a portion of government purchases is devoted to the acquisition or construction of long-lived capital goods, such as roads, bridges, schools, government buildings, and military hardware. And like consumer durables, these forms of *public capital* are only partially used up during the current year; most will provide useful services far into the future. So, like consumption spending, government purchases are in fact a mixture of spending on current needs and spending on future needs.

Although in reality not all spending by households and the government is for current needs, in practice, determining precisely how much of such spending is for current needs and how much is for future needs is extremely difficult. For this reason, for a long time U.S. government statistics have treated *all* of both consumption expenditures (C) and government purchases (G) as spending on current needs.[2] For simplicity's sake, in this book we will follow the same practice.

---

[2]Recently, however, the official data have begun to distinguish investment in public capital from the rest of government purchases.

But keep in mind that because consumption spending and government purchases do in fact include some spending for future rather than current needs, treating all of C and G as spending on current needs will understate the true amount of national saving.

If we treat all consumption spending and government purchases as spending on current needs, then the nation's saving is its income Y less its spending on current needs, C + G. So we can define **national saving** S as

$$S = Y - C - G. \tag{22.1}$$

national saving the saving of the entire economy, equal to GDP less consumption expenditures and government purchases of goods and services, or Y − C − G

Figure 22.4 shows the U.S. national saving rate (national saving as a percentage of GDP) for the years 1960 through 1999. Since 1960 the U.S. national saving rate has fluctuated between 13 and 18 percent. Like household saving, national saving declined somewhat in the second half of the 1980s and the early 1990s, though by comparing Figures 22.4 and 22.1 you can see that the decline in national saving has been far more modest. Furthermore, unlike household saving, national saving recovered in the latter 1990s. As we will see next, the reason for these differences between the behavior of national saving and household saving is that saving done by business firms and, more recently, by the government has been substantial.

FIGURE 22.4
U.S. National Saving Rate, 1960–1999.
Since 1960, U.S. national saving has fluctuated between 13 and 18 percent of GDP.

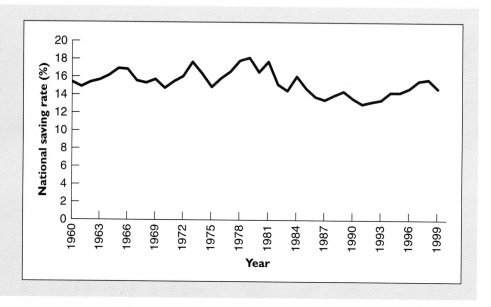

PRIVATE AND PUBLIC COMPONENTS OF NATIONAL SAVING

To understand national saving better, we will divide it into two major components: private saving, which is saving done by households and businesses, and public saving, which is saving done by the government.

To see how national saving breaks down into public and private saving, we work with the definition of national saving, S = Y − C − G. To distinguish private-sector income from public-sector income, we must expand this equation to incorporate taxes as well as payments made by the government to the private sector. Government payments to the private sector include both *transfers* and *interest* paid to individuals and institutions who hold government bonds. **Transfer payments** are payments the government makes to the public for which it receives no current goods or services in return. Social Security benefits, welfare (AFDC) payments, farm support payments, and pensions to government workers are transfer payments.

transfer payments payments the government makes to the public for which it receives no current goods or services in return

Let T stand for taxes paid by the private sector to the government *less* transfer payments and interest payments made by the government to the private sector. Since T equals private-sector tax payments minus the various benefits and interest payments the private sector receives from the government, we can think of T as net taxes. If we add and then subtract T from the definition of national saving, $S = Y - C - G$, we get

$$S = Y - C - G + T - T.$$

Rearranging this equation and grouping terms, we obtain

$$S = (Y - T - C) + (T - G). \tag{22.2}$$

This equation splits national saving S into two parts, *private saving*, or $Y - T - C$, and *public saving*, $T - G$.

Private saving, $Y - T - C$, is the saving of the private sector of the economy. Why is $Y - T - C$ a reasonable definition of private saving? Remember that saving equals current income minus spending on current needs. The income of the private (nongovernmental) sector of the economy is the economy's total income Y less net taxes paid to the government, T. The private sector's spending on current needs is its consumption expenditures C. So private-sector saving, equal to private-sector income less spending on current needs, is $Y - T - C$. Letting S_{private} stand for private saving, we can write the definition of private saving as

$$S_{\text{private}} = Y - T - C.$$

Private saving can be further broken down into saving done by households and business firms. *Household saving*, also called personal saving, is saving done by families and individuals. Household saving corresponds to the familiar image of families putting aside part of their incomes each month, and it is the focus of much attention in the media. But businesses are important savers as well—indeed business saving makes up the bulk of private saving in the United States. Businesses use the revenues from their sales to pay workers' salaries and other operating costs, to pay taxes, and to provide dividends to their shareholders. The funds remaining after these payments have been made are equal to *business saving*. A business firm's savings are available for the purchase of new capital equipment or the expansion of its operations. Alternatively, a business can put its savings in the bank for future use.

Public saving, $T - G$, is the saving of the government sector, including state and local governments as well as the federal government. Net taxes T are the income of the government. Government purchases G represent the government's spending on current needs (remember that, for the sake of simplicity, we are ignoring the investment portion of government purchases). Thus $T - G$ fits our definition of saving, in this case by the public sector. Letting S_{public} stand for public saving, we can write out the definition of public saving as

$$S_{\text{public}} = T - G.$$

Using Equation 22.2 and the definitions of private and public saving, we can rewrite national saving as

$$S = S_{\text{private}} + S_{\text{public}}. \tag{22.3}$$

This equation confirms that national saving is the sum of private saving and public saving. Since private saving can be broken down in turn into household and business saving, we see that national saving is made up of the saving of three groups: households, businesses, and the government.

private saving the saving of the private sector of the economy is equal to the after-tax income of the private sector minus consumption expenditures $(Y - T - C)$; private saving can be further broken down into household saving and business saving

public saving the saving of the government sector is equal to net tax payments minus government purchases $(T - G)$

PUBLIC SAVING AND THE GOVERNMENT BUDGET

Although the idea that households and businesses can save is familiar to most people, the fact that the government can also save is less widely understood. Public saving is closely linked to the government's decisions about spending and taxing. Governments finance the bulk of their spending by taxing the private sector. If taxes and spending in a given year are equal, the government is said to have a *balanced budget*. If in any given year the government's spending exceeds its tax collections, the difference is called the **government budget deficit**. If the government runs a deficit, it musts make up the difference by borrowing from the public through issuance of government bonds. Algebraically, the government budget deficit can be written as $G - T$, or government purchases minus net tax collections.

government budget deficit the excess of government spending over tax collections ($G - T$)

In some years the government may spend less than it collects in taxes. The excess of tax collections over government spending is called the **government budget surplus**. When a government has a surplus, it uses the extra funds to pay down its outstanding debt to the public. Algebraically, the government budget surplus may be written as $T - G$, or net tax collections less government purchases.

government budget surplus the excess of government tax collections over government spending ($T - G$); the government budget surplus equals public saving

If the algebraic expression for the government budget surplus, $T - G$, looks familiar, that is because it is also the definition of public saving, as we saw earlier. Thus, *public saving is identical to the government budget surplus*. In other words, when the government collects more in taxes than it spends, public saving will be positive. When the government spends more than it collects in taxes so that it runs a deficit, public saving will be negative.

Example 22.4 illustrates the relationships among public saving, the government budget surplus, and national saving.

EXAMPLE 22.4

Government saving

Following are data on U.S. government revenues and expenditures for 1999, in billions of dollars. Find (a) the federal government's budget surplus or deficit, (b) the budget surplus or deficit of state and local governments, and (c) the contribution of the government sector to national saving.

Federal government:	
Receipts	1,865.8
Expenditures	1,754.9
State and local governments:	
Receipts	1,138.1
Expenditures	1,089.0

The federal government's receipts minus its expenditures were 1,865.8 − 1,754.9 = 110.9, so the federal government ran a budget surplus of $110.9 billion in 1999. State and local government receipts minus expenditures were 1,138.1 − 1,089.0 = 49.1, so state and local governments ran a collective budget surplus of $49.1 billion. The budget surplus of the entire government sector—that is, the federal surplus plus the state and local surplus—was 110.9 + 49.1 = 160.0, or $160.0 billion. So the contribution of the government sector to U.S. national saving in 1999 was $160.0 billion, out of total national saving in that year of $1,364.8 billion.

EXERCISE 22.4

Continuing Example 22.4, here are the analogous data on government revenues and expenditures for 1995, in billions of dollars. Again, find (a) the federal government's budget surplus or deficit, (b) the budget surplus or deficit of state and local governments, and (c) the contribution of the government sector to national saving.

Federal government:	
Receipts	1,460.3
Expenditures	1,634.7
State and local governments:	
Receipts	997.7
Expenditures	886.0

If you did Exercise 22.4 correctly, you found that the government sector's contribution to national saving in 1995 was *negative*. The reason is that the federal, state, and local governments taken together ran a budget deficit in that year, reducing national saving by the amount of the budget deficit.

Figure 22.4 showed the U.S. national saving rate since 1960. Figure 22.5 shows the behavior since 1960 of the three components of national saving: household saving, business saving, and public saving, each measured as a percentage of GDP. Note that business saving played a major role in national saving during these years, while the role of household saving was relatively modest. As we saw in Figure 22.1, household saving has been declining since the mid-1980s.

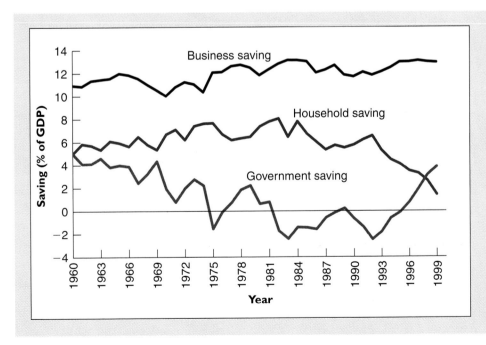

FIGURE 22.5
The Three Components of National Saving, 1960–1999.
Of the three components of national saving, business saving is the most important. In recent years increased public saving has offset a decline in household saving.

The contribution of public saving has varied considerably over time. Until the early 1970s, the federal, state, and local governments ran a combined surplus, making a positive contribution to national saving. But by the 1980s and 1990s, public saving had turned negative, reflecting large budget deficits, particularly at the federal level. In those two decades, the government was a net drain on national saving. Recently, however, government budgets have moved back into surplus and are projected to remain in surplus for the near future. The recent increase in public saving partially offsets the recent decline in household saving.

IS LOW HOUSEHOLD SAVING A PROBLEM?

Figure 22.1 showed that saving by U.S. households, never high by international standards, fell substantially during the 1990s. This decline in the household saving rate received much attention from the media. Is the United States' low household saving rate as much of a problem as the media suggest?

From a macroeconomic perspective, the problem posed by low household saving has probably been overstated. The key fact often overlooked in media reports is that national saving, not household saving, determines the capacity of an economy to invest in new capital goods and to achieve continued improvement in living standards. Although household saving is low, saving by business firms has been significant. Furthermore, public saving increased substantially during the 1990s, as government budgets moved from deficit to surplus. Overall, U.S. national saving has been reasonably stable, despite the sharp decline in the household saving rate shown in Figure 22.1. Although U.S. national saving is somewhat low compared to that of other industrialized countries, it has been sufficient to allow the United States to become one of the world's most productive economies.

From a microeconomic perspective, however, the low household saving rate does signal a problem, which is the large and growing inequality in wealth among U.S. households. Saving patterns tend to increase this inequality, since the economically better-off households tend not only to save more but, as businessowners or shareholders, are also the ultimate beneficiaries of the saving done by businesses. Thus the wealth of these households, including both personal assets and the value of the businesses, is great. In contrast, lower-income families, many of whom save very little and do not own a business or shares in a corporation, have very little wealth—in many cases, their life savings are less than $5,000. These households have little protection against setbacks such as chronic illness or job loss and must rely almost entirely on government support programs such as Social Security to fund their retirement. For this group, the low household saving rate is definitely a concern.

RECAP   **NATIONAL SAVING AND ITS COMPONENTS**

National saving, the saving of the nation as a whole, is defined by $S = Y - C - G$, where Y is GDP, C is consumption spending, and G is government purchases of goods and services. National saving is the sum of public saving and private saving: $S = S_{private} + S_{public}$.

Private saving, the saving of the private sector, is defined by $S_{private} = Y - T - C$, where T is net tax payments. Private saving can be broken down further into household saving and business saving.

Public saving, the saving of the government, is defined by $S_{public} = T - G$. Public saving equals the government budget surplus, $T - G$. When the government budget is in surplus, government saving is positive; when the government budget is in deficit, public saving is negative.

INVESTMENT AND CAPITAL FORMATION

From the point of view of the economy as a whole, the importance of national saving is that it provides the funds needed for investment. Investment—the creation of new capital goods and housing—is critical to increasing average labor productivity and improving standards of living.

What factors determine whether and how much firms choose to invest? Firms acquire new capital goods for the same reason they hire new workers: They expect that doing so will be profitable. We saw in Chapter 21 that the profitability of employing an extra worker depends primarily on two factors: the cost of employing the worker and the value of the worker's marginal product. In the same way, firms' willingness to acquire new factories and machines depends on the expected *cost* of using them and the expected *benefit*, equal to the value of the marginal product that they will provide.

EXAMPLE 22.5

Should Larry buy a riding lawn mower?

Larry is thinking of going into the lawn care business. He can buy a $4,000 riding mower by taking out a loan at 6 percent annual interest. With this mower and his own labor Larry can net $6,000 per summer, after deduction of costs such as gasoline and maintenance. Of the $6,000 net revenues, 20 percent must be paid to the government in taxes. Assume that Larry could earn $4,400 after taxes by working in an alternative job. Assume also that the lawn mower can always be resold for its original purchase price of $4,000. Should Larry buy the lawn mower?

To decide whether to invest in the capital good (the lawn mower), Larry should compare the financial benefits and costs. With the mower he can earn revenue of $6,000, net of gasoline and maintenance costs. However, 20 percent of that, or $1,200, must be paid in taxes, leaving Larry with $4,800. Larry could earn $4,400 after taxes by working at an alternative job, so the financial benefit to Larry of buying the mower is the difference between $4,800 and $4,400, or $400; $400 is the value of the marginal product of the lawn mower.

Since the mower does not lose value over time and since gasoline and maintenance costs have already been deducted, the only remaining cost Larry should take into account is the interest on the loan for the mower. Larry must pay 6 percent interest on $4,000, or $240 per year. Since this financial cost is less than the financial benefit of $400, the value of the mower's marginal product, Larry should buy the mower.

Larry's decision might change if the costs and benefits of his investment in the mower change, as Example 22.6 shows.

EXAMPLE 22.6

Should Larry buy a riding lawn mower? (continued)

With all other assumptions the same as in Example 22.5, decide whether Larry should buy the mower:

a. If the interest rate is 12 percent rather than 6 percent

b. If the purchase price of the mower is $7,000 rather than $4,000

c. If the tax rate on Larry's net revenues is 25 percent rather than 20 percent

d. If the mower is less efficient than Larry originally thought so that his net revenues will be $5,500 rather than $6,000.

In each case, Larry must compare the financial costs and benefits of buying the mower.

a. If the interest rate is 12 percent, then the interest cost will be 12 percent of $4,000, or $480, which exceeds the value of the mower's marginal product ($400). Larry should not buy the mower.

b. If the cost of the mower is $7,000, then Larry must borrow $7,000 instead of $4,000. At 6 percent interest, his interest cost will be $420—too high to justify the purchase, since the value of the mower's marginal product is $400.

c. If the tax rate on net revenues is 25 percent, then Larry must pay 25 percent of his $6,000 net revenues, or $1,500, in taxes. After taxes, his revenues from mowing will be $4,500, which is only $100 more than he could make

594 CHAPTER 22 SAVING AND CAPITAL FORMATION

working at an alternative job. Furthermore, the $100 will not cover the $240 in interest that Larry would have to pay. So again, Larry should not buy the mower.

d. If the mower is less efficient than originally expected so that Larry can earn net revenues of only $5,500, Larry will be left with only $4,400 after taxes—the same amount he could earn by working at another job. So in this case, the value of the mower's marginal product is zero. At any interest rate greater than zero, Larry should not buy the mower.

EXERCISE 22.5

Repeat Example 22.5, but assume that, over the course of the year, wear and tear reduces the resale value of the lawn mower from $4,000 to $3,800. Should Larry buy the mower?

The examples involving Larry and the lawn mower illustrate the main factors firms must consider when deciding whether to invest in new capital goods. On the cost side, two important factors are the *price of capital goods* and the *real interest rate*. Clearly, the more expensive new capital goods are, the more reluctant firms will be to invest in them. Buying the mower was profitable for Larry when its price was $4,000, but not when its price was $7,000.

Why is the real interest rate an important factor in investment decisions? The most straightforward case is when a firm has to borrow (as Larry did) to purchase its new capital. The real interest rate then determines the real cost to the firm of paying back its debt. Since financing costs are a major part of the total cost of owning and operating a piece of capital, much as mortgage payments are a major part of the cost of owning a home, increases in the real interest rate make the purchase of capital goods less attractive to firms, all else being equal.

Even if a firm does not need to borrow to buy new capital—say, because it has accumulated enough profits to buy the capital outright—the real interest rate remains an important determinant of the desirability of an investment. If a firm does not use its profits to acquire new capital, most likely it will use those profits to acquire financial assets such as bonds, which will earn the firm the real rate of interest. If the firm uses its profits to buy capital rather than to purchase a bond, it forgoes the opportunity to earn the real rate of interest on its funds. Thus the real rate of interest measures the *opportunity cost* of a capital investment. Since an increase in the real interest rate raises the opportunity cost of investing in new capital, it lowers the willingness of firms to invest, even if they do not literally need to borrow to finance new machines or equipment.

On the benefit side, the key factor in determining business investment is the *value of the marginal product* of the new capital, which should be calculated net of both operating and maintenance expenses and taxes paid on the revenues the capital generates. The value of the marginal product is affected by several factors. For example, a technological advance that allows a piece of capital to produce more goods and services would increase the value of its marginal product, as would lower taxes on the revenues produced by the new capital. An increase in the relative price of the good or service that the capital is used to produce will also increase the value of the marginal product and, hence, the desirability of the investment. For example, if the going price for lawn-mowing services were to rise, then all else being equal, investing in the mower would become more profitable for Larry.

RECAP   **FACTORS THAT AFFECT INVESTMENT**

Any of the following factors will increase the willingness of firms to invest in new capital:

1. A decline in the price of new capital goods

2. A decline in the real interest rate

3. Technological improvement that raises the marginal product of capital

4. Lower taxes on the revenues generated by capital

5. A higher relative price for the firm's output

Why has investment in computers increased so much in recent decades?

Since about 1980, investment in new computer systems by U.S. firms has risen sharply (see Figure 22.6). Purchases of new computers and software by firms now exceed 2.5 percent of GDP and amount to about 15 percent of all private nonresidential investment. Why has investment in computers increased so much?

Investment in computers has increased by much more than other types of investment. Hence, the factors that affect all types of investment (such as the real interest rate and the tax rate) are not likely to be responsible for the boom. The two main causes of increased investment in computers appear to be the declining price of computing power and the increase in the value of the marginal product of computers. In

ECONOMIC NATURALIST 22.4

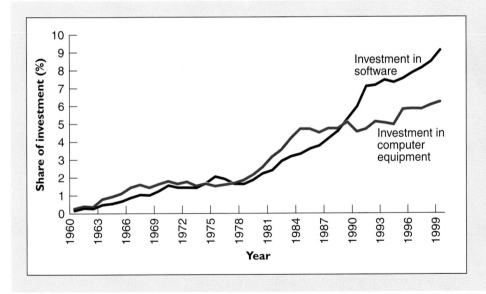

FIGURE 22.6
Investment in Computers and Software, 1960–1999.
Shown is investment in computer equipment and software since 1960 as a percentage of private nonresidential investment. Computer-related investments by U.S. firms have risen sharply since about 1980.

recent years, the price of computing power has fallen at a precipitous rate. An industry rule of thumb is that the amount of computing power that is obtainable at a given price doubles every 18 months. As the price of computing power falls, an investment in computers becomes more and more likely to pass the *cost-benefit* test.

On the benefit side, for some years after the beginning of the computer boom economists were unable to associate the technology with significant productivity gains. Defenders of investment in computer systems argued that the improvements in goods and services computers create are particularly hard to measure. How does one quantify the value to consumers of 24-hour-a-day access to cash or of the ability to make airline reservations on line? Critics responded that the expected benefits of the computer revolution may have proved illusory because of problems such as user-unfriendly software and poor technical training. However, U.S. productivity has increased notice-ably in recent years (see Chapter 20), and many people are now crediting the improve-ment to investment in computers and computer-related technologies like the Internet. As more firms become convinced that computers do add significantly to productivity and profits, the boom in computer investment can be expected to continue.

SAVING, INVESTMENT, AND FINANCIAL MARKETS

Saving and investment are determined by different forces. Ultimately, though, in an economy without international borrowing and lending, national saving must equal investment. The supply of savings (by households, firms, and the govern-ment) and the demand for savings (by firms that want to purchase or construct new capital) are equalized through the workings of *financial markets*. Figure 22.7 illustrates this process. Quantities of national saving and investment are mea-sured on the horizontal axis; the real interest rate is shown on the vertical axis. As we will see, in the market for saving, the real interest rate functions as the "price."

FIGURE 22.7
The Supply of and Demand for Savings.
Savings are supplied by households, firms, and the government and demanded by borrowers wishing to invest in new capital goods. The supply of saving (S) increases with the real interest rate, and the demand for saving by investors (I) decreases with the real interest rate. In financial market equilibrium, the real interest rate takes the value that equates the quantity of saving supplied and demanded.

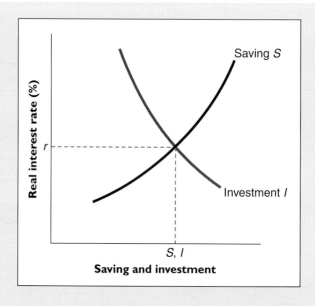

In the figure the supply of savings is shown by the upward-sloping curve marked S. This curve shows the quantity of national saving that households, firms, and the government are willing to supply at each value of the real interest rate. The saving curve is upward-sloping because empirical evidence suggests that increases in the real interest rate stimulate saving. The demand for saving is given by the downward-sloping curve marked I. This curve shows the quantity of investment in new capital that firms would choose and hence the amount they would need to borrow in financial markets, at each value of the real interest rate. Because higher real interest rates raise the cost of borrowing and reduce firms' willingness to invest, the demand for saving curve is downward-sloping.

Putting aside the possibility of borrowing from foreigners (to be discussed in Chapter 28), a country can invest only those resources that its savers make avail-able. In equilibrium, then, desired investment (the demand for savings) and desired national saving (the supply of savings) must be equal. As Figure 22.7 sug-gests, desired saving is equated with desired investment through adjustments in the real interest rate, which functions as the "price" of saving. The movements of the real interest rate clear the market for savings in much the same way that the price of apples clears the market for apples. In Figure 22.7, the real interest rate that clears the market for saving is r, the real interest rate that corresponds to the intersection of the supply and demand curves.

The forces that push the real interest rate toward its equilibrium level are similar to the forces that lead to equilibrium in any other supply and demand situation. Suppose, for example, that the real interest rate exceeded r. At a higher real interest rate, savers would provide more funds than firms would want to invest. As lenders (savers) competed among themselves to attract borrowers (investors), the real interest rate would be bid down. The real interest rate would fall until it equaled r, the only interest rate at which both borrowers and lenders are satisfied, and no opportunities are left unexploited in the financial market (recall Chapter 4's *equilibrium principle*). What would happen if the real interest rate were *lower* than r?

Changes in factors *other than the real interest rate* that affect the supply of or demand for saving will shift the curves, leading to a new equilibrium in the financial market. Changes in the real interest rate cannot shift the supply or demand curves, just as a change in the price of apples cannot shift the supply or demand for apples, because the effects of the real interest rate on savings are already incorporated in the slopes of the curves. A few examples will illustrate the use of the supply and demand model of financial markets.

The effects of new technology

EXAMPLE 22.7

Exciting new technologies have been introduced in recent years, ranging from the Internet to new applications of genetics. A number of these technologies appear to have great commercial potential. How does the introduction of new technologies affect saving, investment, and the real interest rate?

The introduction of any new technology with the potential for commercial application creates profit opportunities for those who can bring the fruits of the technology to the public. In economists' language, the technical breakthrough raises the marginal product of new capital. Figure 22.8 shows the effects of a technological breakthrough, with a resulting increase in the marginal product of capital. At any given real interest rate, an increase in the marginal product of capital makes firms more eager to invest. Thus, the advent of the new technology causes the demand for saving to shift upward and to the right, from I to I'.

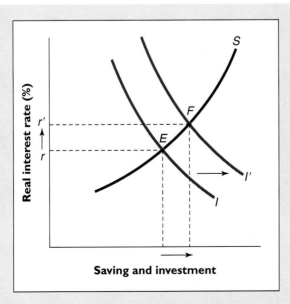

FIGURE 22.8
The Effects of a New Technology on National Saving and Investment.
A technological breakthrough raises the marginal product of new capital goods, increasing desired investment and the demand for savings. The real interest rate rises, as do national saving and investment.

Saving and investment

At the new equilibrium point *F*, investment and national saving are higher than before, as is the real interest rate, which rises from *r* to *r'*. The rise in the real interest rate reflects the increased demand for funds by investors as they race to apply the new technologies. Because of the incentive of higher real returns, saving increases as well. Indeed, the real interest rate in the United States was relatively high in the late 1990s (Figure 19.2), as was the rate of investment, reflecting the opportunities created by new technologies.

Example 22.8 examines the effect of changing fiscal policies on the market for saving.

EXAMPLE 22.8

An increase in the government budget deficit

Suppose the government increases its spending without raising taxes, thereby increasing its budget deficit (or reducing its budget surplus). How will this decision affect national saving, investment, and the real interest rate?

National saving includes both private saving (saving by households and businesses) and public saving, which is equivalent to the government budget surplus. An increase in the government budget deficit (or a decline in the surplus) reduces public saving. Assuming that private saving does not change, the reduction in public saving will reduce national saving as well.

Figure 22.9 shows the effect of the increased government budget deficit on the market for saving and investment. At any real interest rate, a larger deficit

FIGURE 22.9

The Effects of an Increase in the Government Budget Deficit on National Saving and Investment.

An increase in the government budget deficit reduces the supply of saving, raising the real interest rate and lowering investment. The tendency of increased government deficits to reduce investment in new capital is called *crowding out*.

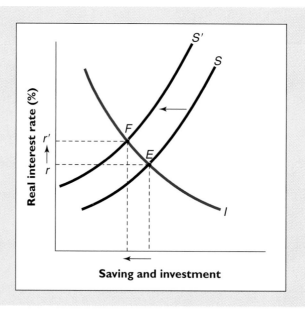

reduces national saving, causing the saving curve to shift to the left, from *S* to *S'*. At the new equilibrium point *F*, the real interest rate is higher at *r'*, and both national saving and investment are lower. In economic terms, the government has dipped further into the pool of private savings to borrow the funds to finance its budget deficit. The government's extra borrowing forces investors to compete for a smaller quantity of available saving, driving up the real interest rate. The higher real interest rate makes investment less attractive, assuring that investment will decrease along with national saving.

crowding out the tendency of increased government deficits to reduce investment spending

The tendency of government budget deficits to reduce investment spending is called **crowding out**. Reduced investment spending implies slower capital formation, and thus lower economic growth, as we saw in Chapter 20. This adverse effect of budget deficits on economic growth is probably the most important cost of deficits, and a major reason why economists advise governments to minimize their deficits.

EXERCISE 22.6

Suppose the general public becomes more "grasshopper-like" and less "ant-like" in their saving decisions, becoming less concerned about saving for the future. How will the change in public attitudes affect the country's rate of capital formation and economic growth?

▪ SUMMARY ▪

- In general, *saving* equals current income minus spending on current needs; the *saving rate* is the percentage of income that is saved. *Wealth*, or net worth, equals the market value of assets (real or financial items of value) minus liabilities (debts). Saving is a *flow*, being measured in dollars per unit of time, while wealth is a *stock*, measured in dollars at a point in time. As the amount of water in a bathtub changes according to the rate at which water flows in, the stock of wealth increases at the saving rate. Wealth also increases if the value of existing assets rises (*capital gains*) and decreases if the value of existing assets falls (*capital losses*).

- Individuals and households save for a variety of reasons, including *life-cycle* objectives, as saving for retirement or a new home; the need to be prepared for an emergency (*precautionary saving*); and the desire to leave an inheritance (*bequest saving*). The amount people save is also affected by the real interest rate, which is the "reward" for saving. Evidence suggests that higher real interest rates lead to modest increases in saving. Saving can also be affected by psychological factors, such as the degree of self-control and the desire to consume at the level of one's neighbors (*demonstration effects*).

- The saving of an entire country is *national saving S*. National saving is defined by $S = Y - C - G$, where Y represents total output or income, C equals consumption spending, and G equals government purchases of goods and services. National saving can be broken up into private saving, or $Y - T - C$, and public saving, or $T - G$, where T stands for taxes paid to the government less transfer payments and interest paid by the government to the private sector. Private saving can be further broken down into household saving and business saving. In the United States, the bulk of private saving is done by businesses.

- Public saving is equivalent to the government budget surplus, $T - G$; if the government runs a budget deficit, then public saving is negative. The U.S. national saving rate is low relative to other industrialized countries, but it is higher and more stable than U.S. household saving.

- Investment is the purchase or construction of new capital goods, including housing. Firms will invest in new capital goods if the benefits of doing so outweigh the costs. Two factors that determine the cost of investment are the price of new capital goods and the real interest rate. The higher the real interest rate, the more expensive it is to borrow, and the less likely firms are to invest. The benefit of investment is the value of the marginal product of new capital, which depends on factors such as the productivity of new capital goods, the taxes levied on the revenues they generate, and the relative price of the firm's output.

- In the absence of international borrowing or lending, the supply of and demand for national saving must be equal. The supply of national saving depends on the saving decisions of households and businesses and the fiscal policies of the government (which determine public saving). The demand for saving is the amount business firms want to invest in new capital. The real interest rate, which is the "price" of borrowed funds, changes to equate the supply of and demand for national saving. Factors that affect the supply of or demand for saving will change saving, investment, and the equilibrium real interest rate. For example, an increase in the government budget deficit will reduce national saving and investment and raise the equilibrium real interest rate. The tendency of government budget deficits to reduce investment is called *crowding out*.

▪ KEY TERMS ▪

▪ REVIEW QUESTIONS ▪

1. Explain the relationship between saving and wealth, using the concepts of flows and stocks. Is saving the only means by which wealth can increase? Explain. What was the major reason for the increased wealth of U.S. households during the 1990s?

2. Give three basic motivations for saving. Illustrate each with an example. What other factors would psychologists cite as being possibly important for saving?

3. Define *national saving,* relating your definition to the general concept of saving. Why does the standard U.S. definition of national saving potentially understate the true amount of saving being done in the economy?

4. Household saving rates in the U.S. are very low. Is this fact a problem for the U.S. economy? Why or why not?

5. Why do increases in real interest rates reduce the quantity of saving demanded? (*Hint:* Who are the "demanders" of saving?)

6. Name one factor that could increase the supply of saving and one that could increase the demand for saving. Show the effects of each on saving, investment, and the real interest rate.

▪ PROBLEMS ▪

1. a. Corey has a mountain bike worth $300, a credit card debt of $150, $200 in cash, a Sandy Koufax baseball card worth $400, $1,200 in a checking account, and an electric bill due for $250. Construct Corey's balance sheet and calculate his net worth. For each remaining part, explain how the event affects Corey's assets, liabilities, and wealth.
   b. Corey goes to a baseball card convention and finds out that his baseball card is a worthless forgery.
   c. Corey uses $150 from his paycheck to pay off his credit card balance. The remainder of his earnings is spent.
   d. Corey writes a $150 check on his checking account to pay off his credit card balance.
   Of the events in the previous three parts, which, if any, corresponds to saving on Corey's part?

2. State whether each of the following is a stock or a flow, and explain.
   a. The gross domestic product
   b. National saving
   c. The value of the U.S. housing stock on January 1, 2001
   d. The amount of U.S. currency in circulation as of this morning
   e. The government budget deficit
   f. The quantity of outstanding government debt on January 1, 2001

3. Ellie and Vince are a married couple, both with college degrees and jobs. How would you expect each of the following events to affect the amount they save each month? Explain your answers in terms of the basic motivations for saving.
   a. Ellie learns she is pregnant.
   b. Vince reads in the paper about possible layoffs in his industry.
   c. Vince had hoped that his parents would lend financial assistance toward the couple's planned purchase of a house, but he learns that they can't afford it.
   d. Ellie announces that she would like to go to law school in the next few years.
   e. A boom in the stock market greatly increases the value of the couple's retirement funds.
   f. Vince and Ellie agree that they would like to leave a substantial amount to local charities in their wills.

4. Individual Retirement Accounts, or IRAs, were established by the U.S. government to encourage saving. An individual who deposits part of current earnings in an IRA does not have to pay income taxes on the earnings deposited, nor are any income taxes charged on the interest earned by the funds in the IRA. However, when the funds are

withdrawn from the IRA, the full amount withdrawn is treated as income and is taxed at the individual's current income tax rate. In contrast, an individual depositing in a non-IRA account has to pay income taxes on the funds deposited and on interest earned in each year but does not have to pay taxes on withdrawals from the account. Another feature of IRAs which is different from a standard saving account is that funds deposited in an IRA cannot be withdrawn prior to retirement, except upon payment of a substantial penalty.

a. Greg, who is 5 years from retirement, receives a $10,000 bonus at work. He is trying to decide whether to save this extra income in an IRA account or in a regular savings account. Both accounts earn 5 percent nominal interest, and Greg is in the 30 percent tax bracket in every year (including his retirement year). Compare the amounts that Greg will have in 5 years under each of the two saving strategies, net of all taxes. Is the IRA a good deal for Greg?

b. Would you expect the availability of IRAs to increase the amount that households save? Discuss in light of (1) the response of saving to changes in the real interest rate and (2) psychological theories of saving.

5. In each part below, use the economic data given to find national saving, private saving, public saving, and the national saving rate.

a. Household saving = 200   Business saving = 400
   Government purchases of goods and services = 100
   Government transfers and interest payments = 100
   Tax collections = 150   GDP = 2,200

b. GDP = 6,000   Tax collections = 1,200
   Government transfers and interest payments = 400
   Consumption expenditures = 4,500
   Government budget surplus = 100

c. Consumption expenditures = 4,000   Investment = 1,000
   Government purchases = 1,000   Net exports = 0
   Tax collections = 1,500
   Government transfers and interest payments = 500

6. Obtain a recent copy of the *Survey of Current Business,* published by the Bureau of Economic Analysis, in the library or on line at www.bea.doc.gov/bea/pubs.htm. In the national data portion of the *Survey,* find nominal data on GDP, consumption, government purchases of goods and services, total government expenditures, and total government receipts for the most recent quarter available (see Tables 1.1 and 3.1). Calculate national saving, private saving, public saving, and the national saving rate. How does the government's contribution to national saving in the most recent period compare to 1999 (see Example 22.4 in the text)?

7. Ellie and Vince are trying to decide whether to purchase a new home. The house they want is priced at $200,000. Annual expenses such as maintenance, taxes, and insurance equal 4 percent of the home's value. If properly maintained, the house's real value is not expected to change. The real interest rate in the economy is 6 percent, and Ellie and Vince can qualify to borrow the full amount of the purchase price (for simplicity, assume no down payment) at that rate. Ignore the fact that mortgage interest payments are tax-deductible in the United States.

a. Ellie and Vince would be willing to pay $1,500 monthly rent to live in a house of the same quality as the one they are thinking about purchasing. Should they buy the house?

b. Does the answer to part a change if they were willing to pay $2,000 monthly rent?

c. Does the answer to part a change if the real interest rate is 4 percent instead of 6 percent?

d. Does the answer to part a change if the developer offers to sell Ellie and Vince the house for $150,000?

e. Why do home-building companies dislike high interest rates?

8. The builder of a new movie theater complex is trying to decide how many screens she wants. Below are her estimates of the number of patrons the complex will attract each year, depending on the number of screens available.

Number of screens	Total number of patrons
1	40,000
2	75,000
3	105,000
4	130,000
5	150,000

After paying the movie distributors and meeting all other noninterest expenses, the owner expects to net $2.00 per ticket sold. Construction costs are $1,000,000 per screen.

   a. Make a table showing the value of marginal product for each screen from the first through the fifth. What property is illustrated by the behavior of marginal products?

   b. How many screens will be built if the real interest rate is 5.5 percent?

   c. If the real interest rate is 7.5 percent?

   d. If the real interest rate is 10 percent?

   e. If the real interest rate is 5.5 percent, how far would construction costs have to fall before the builder would be willing to build a five-screen complex?

9. For each of the following scenarios, use supply and demand analysis to predict the resulting changes in the real interest rate, national saving, and investment. Show all your diagrams.

   a. The legislature passes a 10 percent investment tax credit. Under this program, for every $100 that a firm spends on new capital equipment, it receives an extra $10 in tax refunds from the government.

   b. A reduction in military spending moves the government's budget from deficit into surplus.

   c. A new generation of computer-controlled machines becomes available. These machines produce manufactured goods much more quickly and with fewer defects.

   d. The government raises its tax on corporate profits. Other tax changes are also made, such that the government's deficit remains unchanged.

   e. Concerns about job security raise precautionary saving.

   f. New environmental regulations increase firms' costs of operating capital.

▪ ANSWERS TO IN-CHAPTER EXERCISES ▪

22.1 If Consuelo's student loan were for $6,500 instead of $3,000, her liabilities would be $6,750 (the student loan plus the credit card balance) instead of $3,250. The value of her assets, $6,280, is unchanged. In this case Consuelo's wealth is negative, since assets of $6,280 less liabilities of $6,750 equals −$470. Negative wealth or net worth means one owes more than one owns.

22.2 If water is being drained from the tub, the flow is negative, equal to −3 gallons/minute. There are 37 gallons in the tub at 7:16 P.M. and 34 gallons at 7:17 P.M. The rate of change of the stock is −3 gallons/minute, which is the same as the flow.

22.3 a. Consuelo has set aside her usual $20, but she has also incurred a new liability of $50. So her net saving for the week is *minus* $30. Since her assets (her checking account) have increased by $20 but her liabilities (her credit card balance) have increased by $50, her wealth has also declined by $30.

   b. In paying off her credit card bill, Consuelo reduces her assets by $300 by drawing down her checking account and reduces her liabilities by the same amount by reducing her credit card balance to zero. Thus there is no change in her wealth. There is also no change in her saving (note that Consuelo's income and spending on current needs have not changed).

   c. The increase in the value of Consuelo's car raises her assets by $500. So her wealth also rises by $500. Changes in the value of existing assets are not treated as part of saving, however, so her saving is unchanged.

   d. The decline in the value of Consuelo's furniture is a capital loss of $300. Her assets and wealth fall by $300. Her saving is unchanged.

22.4 The federal government had expenditures greater than receipts, so it ran a deficit. The federal deficit equaled expenditures of 1,634.7 minus revenues of 1,460.3, or $174.4 billion. Equivalently, the federal budget surplus was *minus* $174.4 billion. State and local governments had a surplus, equal to receipts of 997.7 minus expenditures of 886.0, or $111.7 billion. The entire government sector ran a deficit of $62.7 billion, as the federal deficit of 174.4 outweighed the state and local surplus of 111.7. (You can also find this answer by adding federal to state and local expenditures and comparing this number to the sum of federal and state-local receipts.) The government sector's contribution to national saving in 1995 was negative, equal to −$62.7 billion.

22.5 The loss of value of $200 over the year is another financial cost of owning the mower, of which Larry should take into account in making his decision. His total cost is now $240 in interest costs plus $200 in anticipated loss of value of the mower (known as depreciation), or $440. This exceeds the value of marginal product, $400, and so now Larry should not buy the mower.

22.6 Household saving is part of national saving. A decline in household saving, and hence national saving, at any given real interest rate shifts the saving supply curve to the left. The results are as in Figure 22.9. The real interest rate rises and the equilibrium values of national saving and investment fall. Lower investment is the same as a lower rate of capital formation, which would be expected to slow economic growth.

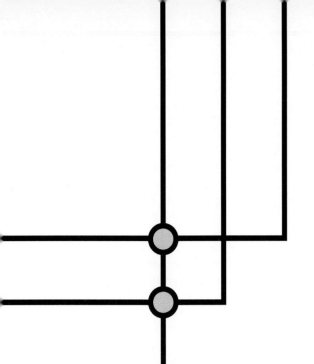

CHAPTER 95

FINANCIAL MARKETS, MONEY, AND THE FEDERAL RESERVE

■

A recent television ad for an online trading company showed an office worker, call him Ed, sitting in front of his computer. Instead of working, Ed is checking the prices of the stocks he bought over the Internet. Suddenly his eyes widen, as on the computer screen a graph shows the price of his stock shooting up like a rocket. With a whoop Ed heads down to his boss's office, delivers a few well-chosen insults, and quits his job. Unfortunately, when Ed returns to his desk to pack up his belongings, the computer screen shows that the price of his stock has fallen as quickly as it rose. The last we hear of Ed are his futile attempts to convince his boss that he was only kidding.

The 1990s were a boom period in the United States, with strong economic growth, record low unemployment rates, and almost nonexistent inflation. This prosperity was mirrored in the spectacular performance of the stock market. In 1999 the Dow Jones index, a popular measure of stock prices, broke 10,000 and then 11,000 for the first time—almost triple the value of the index 5 years earlier. Prices of stocks of start-up companies, particularly high-technology and Internet companies, rose to stunning levels, making billionaires of some entrepreneurs still in their twenties. Nor were the benefits of rising stock prices confined to the very rich or the very nerdy. Stock ownership among the general population—including both direct ownership of stocks and indirect ownership

Would investors have spent $5.3 billion to build the Shoreham Nuclear Power Plant if they had known that regulators would never certify it as safe enough to operate?

through mutual funds and pension plans—reached record levels, with many middle-class families sharing in the bonanza created by the rising market (Economic Naturalist 22.1).

During periods such as the 1990s, people often begin to think of the stock market as a place to gamble and, maybe, to strike it rich. Some people do get rich playing the market, and some people, like Ed, lose everything. But the stock market, as well as other financial markets, play a crucial role in the economy that is not shared by the gambling establishments in Las Vegas or Atlantic City. That role is to ensure that national saving is devoted to the most productive uses.

In Chapter 22 we discussed the importance of national saving. Under most circumstances, a high rate of national saving permits a high rate of capital formation, which both economic logic and experience predict will tend to increase labor productivity and living standards. However, creating new capital does not *guarantee* a richer and more productive economy. History is full of examples of "white elephants," capital projects in which millions, and even billions, of dollars were invested with little economic benefit: nuclear power plants that were never opened, massive dams whose main effect was to divert water supplies and disrupt the local agriculture, new technologies that just didn't work as planned.

A healthy economy not only saves adequately but also invests those savings in a productive way. In market economies, like that of the United States, channeling society's savings into the best possible capital investments is the role of the financial system: banks, stock markets, bond markets, and other financial markets and institutions. For this reason, many economists have argued that the development of well-functioning financial markets is a crucial precursor to sustained economic growth. In the first part of this chapter we discuss some major financial markets and institutions and their role in directing saving to productive uses.

Savers hold a variety of financial assets, including stocks and bonds. However, the most widely held group of assets is referred to by economists as *money*. Money comprises those financial assets, such as cash or checking accounts, that can be used in making purchases. Money is closely tied to the financial system, particularly the banking sector, and also plays an important role in macroeconomic policy. Indeed, as we mentioned in Chapter 17, one of the three main types of macroeconomic policy, monetary policy, relates primarily to decisions about how much money should be allowed to circulate in the economy. In the second part of this chapter, we introduce the idea of money and discuss how the quantity of money in the economy is determined.

A common thread between financial markets and monetary policy is the crucial role played by the Federal Reserve, the central bank of the United States. The Federal Reserve's two primary responsibilities are to determine the supply of money in the economy—that is, to make monetary policy—and to help ensure the smooth functioning of financial markets. In the last section of the chapter we introduce the Federal Reserve and discuss some of the policy tools at its disposal. The policies of the Fed, as it is called, will receive a great deal more attention in the chapters to come.

THE FINANCIAL SYSTEM AND THE ALLOCATION OF SAVING TO PRODUCTIVE USES

We have emphasized the importance of high rates of saving and capital formation for economic growth and increased productivity. High rates of saving and investment by themselves are not sufficient, however. A case in point is the former Soviet Union, which had very high rates of saving and investment but often used its resources very inefficiently, for example, by constructing massive but poorly designed factories that produced inferior goods at high cost. A successful economy not only saves but also uses its savings wisely by applying these limited funds to the investment projects that seem likely to be the most productive.

In the Soviet Union, a centralized bureaucracy made decisions about the allocation of saving to alternative uses. Because the bureaucrats in Moscow had relatively poor information and because they allowed themselves to be influenced by noneconomic considerations such as political favoritism, they often made poor decisions. In a market economy like that of the United States, in contrast, savings are allocated by means of a decentralized, market-oriented financial system. The U.S. financial system consists both of financial institutions, like banks, and financial markets, such as bond markets and stock markets.

The financial system of countries like the United States improves the allocation of savings in at least two distinct ways. First, the financial system provides *information* to savers about which of the many possible uses of their funds are likely to prove most productive and hence pay the highest return. By evaluating the potential productivity of alternative capital investments, the financial system helps to direct savings to its best uses. Second, financial markets help savers to *share the risks* of individual investment projects. Sharing of risks protects individual savers from bearing excessive risk, while at the same time making it possible to direct savings to projects, such as the development of new technologies, which are risky but potentially very productive as well.

In this section we briefly discuss three key components of the financial system: the banking system, the bond market, and the stock market. In doing so we elaborate on the role of the financial system as a whole in providing information about investment projects and in helping savers to share the risks of lending.

THE BANKING SYSTEM

The banking system consists of commercial banks, of which there are thousands in the United States. Commercial banks are privately owned firms that accept deposits from individuals and businesses and use those deposits to make loans. Banks are the most important example of a class of institutions called **financial intermediaries,** firms that extend credit to borrowers using funds raised from savers. Other examples of financial intermediaries are savings and loan associations and credit unions.

financial intermediaries firms that extend credit to borrowers using funds raised from savers

Why are financial intermediaries such as banks, which "stand between" savers and investors, necessary? Why don't individual savers just lend directly to borrowers who want to invest in new capital projects? The main reason is that, through specialization, banks and other intermediaries develop a *comparative advantage* in evaluating the quality of borrowers—the information-gathering function that we referred to a moment ago. Most savers, particularly small savers, do not have the time or the knowledge to determine for themselves which borrowers are likely to use the funds they receive most productively. In contrast, banks and other intermediaries have gained expertise in performing the information-gathering activities necessary for profitable lending, including checking out the borrower's background, determining whether the borrower's business plans make sense, and monitoring the borrower's activities during the life of the loan. Because banks specialize in evaluating potential borrowers, they can perform this function at a much lower cost, and with better results, than individual savers could on their own. Banks also reduce the costs of gathering information about potential borrowers by pooling the savings of many individuals to make large loans. Each large loan needs to be evaluated only once, by the bank, rather than separately by each of the hundreds of individuals whose savings may be pooled to make the loan.

Banks help savers by eliminating their need to gather information about potential borrowers and by directing their savings toward higher-return, more productive investments. Banks help borrowers as well, by providing access to

"O.K., folks, let's move along. I'm sure you've all seen someone qualify for a loan before."

credit that might otherwise not be available. Unlike a *Fortune 500* corporation, which typically has many ways to raise funds, a small business that wants to buy a copier or remodel its offices will have few options other than going to a bank. Because the bank's lending officer has developed expertise in evaluating small-business loans, and may even have an ongoing business relationship with the small-business owner, the bank will be able to gather the information it needs to make the loan at a reasonable cost. Likewise, consumers who want to borrow to finish a basement or add a room to a house will find few good alternatives to a bank. In sum, banks' expertise at gathering information about alternative lending opportunities allows them to bring together small savers, looking for good uses for their funds, and small borrowers with worthwhile investment projects.

In addition to being able to earn a return on their savings, a second reason that people hold bank deposits is to make it easier to make payments. Most bank deposits allow the holder to write a check against them or draw on them using a debit card or ATM card. For many transactions, paying by check or debit card is more convenient than using cash. For example, it is safer to send a check through the mail than to send cash, and paying by check gives you a record of the transaction, while a cash payment does not. We will further discuss the role of bank deposits in making transactions later in this chapter.

How did the 1990s banking crisis in Japan affect the Japanese economy?

During the 1980s, real estate and stock prices soared in Japan. Japanese banks made many loans to real estate developers, and the banks themselves acquired stock in corporations. (Unlike in the United States, in Japan it is legal for commercial banks to own stock.) However, in the early 1990s land prices plummeted in Japan, leading many bank borrowers to default on their loans. Stock prices also came down sharply, reducing the value of banks' shareholdings. The net result was that most Japanese banks fell into severe financial trouble, with many large banks near bankruptcy. What was the effect of this crisis, which lasted more than a decade, on the Japanese economy?

ECONOMIC NATURALIST 23.1

Relative to the United States, which has more developed stock and bond markets, Japan has traditionally relied very heavily on banks to allocate its savings. Thus, when the severe financial problems of the banks prevented them from operating normally, many borrowers found it unusually difficult to obtain credit—a situation known as a "credit crunch." Smaller borrowers, such as small- and medium-sized businesses, had been particularly dependent on banks for credit and thus suffered disproportionately.

The Japanese economy, after many years of robust growth, suffered a severe recession throughout the 1990s. Many factors contributed to this sharp slowdown. However, the virtual breakdown of the banking system certainly did not help the situation, as credit shortages interfered with smaller firms' ability to make capital investments and, in some cases, to purchase raw materials and pay workers. The Japanese government recognized the problem but responded very slowly. Not until 1999 did the government institute a large-scale attempt to restore the banking system to health.

BONDS AND STOCKS

Large and well-established corporations that wish to obtain funds for investment will sometimes go to banks. Unlike the typical small borrower, however, a larger firm usually has alternative ways of raising funds, notably through the corporate bond market and the stock market. We first discuss some of the mechanics of bonds and stocks, then return to the role of bond and stock markets in allocating saving.

Bonds A **bond** is a legal promise to repay a debt, usually including both the **principal amount,** which is the amount originally lent, and regular interest payments. The promised interest rate when a bond is issued is called the **coupon rate.** The regular interest payments made to the bondholder are called coupon payments. The **coupon payment** of a bond that pays interest annually equals the coupon rate times the principal amount of the bond. For example, if the principal amount of a bond is $1,000,000 and its coupon rate is 5 percent, then the annual coupon payment made to the holder of the bond is (0.05)($1,000,000), or $50,000.

Corporations and governments frequently raise funds by issuing bonds and selling them to savers. The coupon rate that a newly issued bond has to promise in order to be attractive to savers depends on a number of factors, including the bond's term, its credit risk, and its tax treatment. The *term* of a bond is the length of time before the debt it represents is fully repaid, a period that can range from 30 days to 30 years or more. Generally lenders will demand a higher interest rate to lend for a longer term. *Credit risk* is the risk that the borrower will go bankrupt and thus not repay the loan. A borrower that is viewed as risky will have to pay a higher interest rate to compensate lenders for taking the chance of losing all or part of their financial investment. For example, so-called high-yield bonds, less formally known as "junk bonds," are bonds issued by firms judged to be risky by credit-rating agencies; these bonds pay higher interest rates than bonds issued by companies thought to be less risky.

Bonds also differ in their *tax treatment.* For example, interest paid on bonds issued by local governments, called municipal bonds, is exempt from federal taxes, while interest on other types of bonds is treated as taxable income. Because of this tax advantage, lenders are willing to accepting a lower interest rate on municipal bonds.

Bondholders are not required to hold bonds until *maturity,* the time at which they are supposed to be repaid by the issuer, but are always free to sell their bonds in the *bond market,* an organized market run by professional bond traders. The market value of a particular bond at any given point in time is called the *price* of the bond. As it turns out, there is a close relationship between the price of a bond at a given point of time and the interest rate prevailing in financial markets at that time, illustrated by Example 23.1.

bond a legal promise to repay a debt, usually including both the principal amount and regular interest payments

principal amount the amount originally lent

coupon rate the interest rate promised when a bond is issued

coupon payments regular interest payments made to the bondholder

EXAMPLE 23.1 **Bond prices and interest rates**

On January 1, 2000, Tanya purchases a newly issued, 2-year government bond with a principal amount of $1,000. The coupon rate on the bond is 5 percent, paid annually. Hence Tanya, or whoever owns the bond at the time, will receive a coupon payment of $50 (5 percent of $1,000) on January 1, 2001, and $1,050 (a $50 coupon payment plus repayment of the original $1,000 lent) on January 1, 2002.

On January 1, 2001, after receiving her first year's coupon payment, Tanya decides to sell her bond to raise the funds to take a vacation. She offers her bond for sale in the bond market. How much can she expect to get for her "used" bond if the prevailing interest rate in the bond market is 6 percent? If the prevailing interest rate is 4 percent?

As we mentioned, the price of a "used" bond at any point in time depends on the prevailing interest rate. Suppose first that, on January 1, 2001, when Tanya takes her bond to the bond market, the prevailing interest rate on newly issued 1-year bonds is 6 percent. Would another saver be willing to pay Tanya the full $1,000 principal amount of her bond? No, because the purchaser of Tanya's bond will receive $1,050 in 1 year, when the bond matures; whereas if he uses his $1,000 to buy a new 1-year bond paying 6 percent interest, he will receive $1,060 ($1,000 principal repayment plus $60 interest) in 1 year. So Tanya's bond is not worth $1,000 to another saver.

How much would another saver be willing to pay for Tanya's bond? Since newly issued 1-year bonds pay a 6 percent return, he will buy Tanya's bond only at a price that allows him to earn at least that return. As the holder of Tanya's bond will receive $1,050 ($1,000 principal plus $50 interest) in 1 year, the price for her bond that allows the purchaser to earn a 6 percent return must satisfy the equation

$$\text{Bond price} \times 1.06 = \$1{,}050.$$

Solving the equation for the bond price, we find that Tanya's bond will sell for $1,050/1.06, or just under $991. To check this result, note that in 1 year the purchaser of the bond will receive $1,050, or $59 more than he paid. His rate of return is $59/$991, or 6 percent, as expected.

What if the prevailing interest rate had been 4 percent rather than 6 percent? Then the price of Tanya's bond would satisfy the relationship bond price × 1.04 = $1,050, implying that the price of her bond would be $1,050/1.04, or almost $1,010.

What happens if the interest rate when Tanya wants to sell is 5 percent, the same as it was when she originally bought the bond? You should show that in this case the bond would sell at its face value of $1,000.

This example illustrates a general principle, that *bond prices and interest rates are inversely related*. When the interest rate being paid on newly issued bonds rises, the prices financial investors are willing to pay for existing bonds falls, and vice versa.

EXERCISE 23.1

Three-year government bonds are issued at a face value (principal amount) of 100 and a coupon rate of 7 percent, interest payable at the end of each year. One year prior to the maturation of these bonds, a newspaper headline reads, "Bad Economic News Causes Prices of Bonds to Plunge," and the story reveals that these 3-year bonds have fallen in price to 96. What has happened to interest rates? What is the 1-year interest rate at the time of the newspaper story?

Issuing bonds is one means by which a corporation or a government can obtain funds from savers. Another important way of raising funds, but one restricted to corporations, is by issuing stock to the public.

Stocks A share of **stock** (or *equity*) is a claim to partial ownership of a firm. For example, if a corporation has 1 million shares of stock outstanding, ownership of one share is equivalent to ownership of one-millionth of the company. Stockholders receive returns on their financial investment in two forms. First, stockholders receive a regular payment called a **dividend** for each share of stock they own. Dividends are determined by the firm's management and usually depend on the firm's recent profits. Second, stockholders receive returns in the form of *capital gains* when the price of their stock increases (we discussed capital gains and losses in Chapter 22).

Prices of stocks are determined through trading on a stock exchange, such as the New York Stock Exchange. A stock's price rises and falls as the demand for the stock changes. Demand for stocks in turn depends on factors such as news about the prospects of the company. For example, the stock price of a pharmaceutical company that announces the discovery of an important new drug is likely to rise on the announcement, even if actual production and marketing of the drug is some time away, because financial investors expect the company to become more profitable in the future. Example 23.2 gives a numerical illustration of some key factors that affect stock prices.

stock (or equity) a claim to partial ownership of a firm

dividend a regular payment received by stockholders for each share that they own

How much should you pay for a share of FortuneCookie.com?

EXAMPLE 23.2

You have the opportunity to buy shares in a new company called FortuneCookie.com, which plans to sell gourmet fortune cookies over the Internet. Your stockbroker estimates that the company will pay $1.00 per share in dividends a year from now, and that in a year the market price of the company will be $80.00 per share. Assuming that you accept your broker's estimates as accurate, what is the most that you should be willing to pay today per share of FortuneCookie.com? How does your answer change if you expect a $5.00 dividend? If you expect a $1.00 dividend but an $84.00 stock price in 1 year?

Based on your broker's estimates, you conclude that in 1 year each share of FortuneCookie.com you own will be worth $81.00 in your pocket—the $1.00 dividend plus the $80.00 you could get by reselling the stock. Finding the maximum price you would pay for the stock today therefore boils down to asking how much would you invest today to have $81.00 a year from today. Answering this question in turn requires one more piece of information, which is the expected rate of return that you require in order to be willing to buy stock in this company.

How would you determine your required rate of return to hold stock in FortuneCookie.com? For the moment, let's imagine that you are not too worried about the potential riskiness of the stock, either because you think that it is a "sure thing" or because you are a devil-may-care type who is not bothered by risk. In that case, your required rate of return to hold FortuneCookie.com should be about the same as you can get on other financial investments, such as government bonds. The available return on other financial investments gives the *opportunity cost* of your funds. So for example if the interest rate currently being offered by government bonds is 6 percent, you should be willing to accept a 6 percent return to hold FortuneCookie.com as well. In that case, the maximum price you would pay today for a share of FortuneCookie satisfies the equation

$$\text{Stock price} \times 1.06 = \$81.00.$$

This equation defines the stock price you should be willing to pay if you are willing to accept a 6 percent return over the next year. Solving this equation yields stock price = $81.00/1.06 = $76.42. If you buy FortuneCookie.com for $76.42, then your return over the year will be ($81.00 − $76.42)/$76.42 = $4.58/$71.42 = 6 percent, which is the rate of return you required to buy the stock.

If instead the dividend is expected to be $5.00, then the total benefit of holding the stock in 1 year, equal to the expected dividend plus the expected price, is $5.00 + $80.00, or $85.00. Assuming again that you are willing to accept a 6 percent return to hold FortuneCookie.com, the price you are willing to pay for the stock today satisfies the relationship stock price × 1.06 = $85.00. Solving this equation for the stock price yields stock price = $85.00/1.06 = $80.19. Comparing with the previous case we see that a higher expected dividend in the future increases the value of the stock today. That's why good news about the future prospects of a company—such as the announcement by a pharmaceutical company that it has discovered a useful new drug—affects its stock price immediately.

If the expected future price of the stock is $84.00, with the dividend at $1.00, then the value of holding the stock in 1 year is once again $85.00, and the calculation is the same as the previous one. Again, the price you should be willing to pay for the stock is $80.19.

These examples show that an increase in the future dividend or in the future expected stock price raises the stock price today, whereas an increase in the return a saver requires to hold the stock lowers today's stock price. Since we expect required returns in the stock market to be closely tied to market interest rates, this last result implies that increases in interest rates tend to depress stock prices as well as bond prices.

Our examples also took the future stock price as given. But what determines the future stock price? Just as today's stock price depends on the dividend shareholders expect to receive this year and the stock price a year from now, the stock price a year from now depends on the dividend expected for next year and the stock price 2 years from now, and so on. Ultimately, then, today's stock price is affected not only by the dividend expected this year but future dividends as well. A company's ability to pay dividends depends on its earnings. Thus, as we noted in the example of the pharmaceutical company that announces the discovery of a new drug, news about future earnings—even earnings quite far in the future—is likely to affect a company's stock price immediately.

EXERCISE 23.2

As in Example 23.2, you expect a share of FortuneCookie.com to be worth $80.00 per share in 1 year, and also to pay a dividend of $1.00 in 1 year. What should you be willing to pay for the stock today if the prevailing interest rate, equal to your required rate of return, is 4 percent? What if the interest rate is 8 percent? In general, how would you expect stock prices to react if economic news arrives that implies that interest rates will rise in the very near future?

In Example 23.2 we assumed that you were willing to accept a return of 6 percent to hold FortuneCookie.com, the same return that you could get on a government bond. However, financial investments in the stock market are quite risky in that returns to holding stocks can be quite variable and unpredictable. For example, although you expect a share of FortuneCookie.com to be worth $80.00 in 1 year, you also realize that there is a chance it might sell as low as $50.00 or as high as $110.00 per share. Most financial investors dislike risk and unpredictability and thus have a higher required rate of return for holding risky assets like stocks than for holding relatively safe assets like government bonds. The difference between the required rate of return to hold risky assets and the rate of return on safe assets, like government bonds, is called the **risk premium**. Example 23.3 illustrates the effect of financial investors' dislike of risk on stock prices.

risk premium the rate of return that financial investors require to hold risky assets minus the rate of return on safe assets

EXAMPLE 23.3

Riskiness and stock prices

Continuing Example 23.2, suppose that FortuneCookie.com is expected to pay a $1.00 dividend and have a market price of $80.00 per share in 1 year. The interest rate on government bonds is 6 percent per year. However, to be willing to hold a risky asset like a share of FortuneCookie.com, you require an expected return four percentage points higher than the rate paid by safe assets like government bonds (a risk premium of 4 percent). Hence you require a 10 percent expected return to hold FortuneCookie.com. What is the most you would be willing to pay for the stock now? What do you conclude about the relationship between perceived riskiness and stock prices?

As a share of FortuneCookie.com is expected to pay $81.00 in 1 year and the required return is 10 percent, we have stock price $\times$ 1.10 = $81.00. Solving for the stock price, we find the price to be $81.00/1.10 = $73.64, less than the price of $76.42 we found when there was no risk premium and the required rate of return was 6 percent (Example 23.2). We conclude that financial investors' dislike of risk, and the resulting risk premium, lowers the prices of risky assets like stocks.

RECAP **FACTORS AFFECTING STOCK PRICES**

1. An increase in expected future dividends or in the expected future market price of a stock raises the current price of the stock.

2. An increase in interest rates, implying an increase in the required rate of return to hold stocks, lowers the current price of stocks.

3. An increase in perceived riskiness, as reflected in an increase in the risk premium, lowers the current price of stocks.

BOND MARKETS, STOCK MARKETS, AND THE ALLOCATION OF SAVINGS

Like banks, bond markets and stock markets provide a means of channeling funds from savers to borrowers with productive investment opportunities. For example, a corporation that is planning a capital investment but does not want to borrow from a bank has two other options: It can issue new bonds, to be sold to savers in the bond market, or it can issue new shares in itself, which are then sold in the stock market. The proceeds from the sales of new bonds or stocks are then available to the firm to finance its capital investment.

How do stock and bond markets help to ensure that available savings are devoted to the most productive uses? As we mentioned earlier, two important functions served by these markets are gathering information about prospective borrowers and helping savers to share the risks of lending.

The informational role of bond and stock markets Savers and their financial advisors know that to get the highest possible returns on their financial investments, they must find the potential borrowers with the most profitable opportunities. This knowledge provides a powerful incentive to scrutinize potential borrowers carefully.

For example, companies considering a new issue of stocks or bonds know that their recent performance and plans for the future will be carefully studied by professional analysts on Wall Street and other financial investors. If the analysts and other potential purchasers have doubts about the future profitability of the firm, they will offer a relatively low price for the newly issued shares or they will demand a high interest rate on newly issued bonds. Knowing this, a company will be reluctant to go to the bond or stock market for financing unless its management is confident that it can convince financial investors that the firm's planned use of the funds will be profitable. Thus the ongoing search by savers and their financial advisors for high returns leads the bond and stock markets to direct funds to the uses that appear most likely to be productive.

Risk sharing and diversification Many highly promising investment projects are also quite risky. The successful development of a new drug to lower cholesterol could create billions of dollars in profits for a drug company, for example; but if the drug turns out to be less effective than some others on the market, none of the development costs will be recouped. An individual who lent his or her life savings to help finance the development of the anticholesterol drug might enjoy a handsome return but also takes the chance of losing everything. Savers are generally reluctant to take large risks, so without some means of reducing the risk faced by each saver it might be very hard for the company to find the funds to develop the new drug.

diversification the practice of spreading of one's wealth over a variety of different financial investments to reduce overall risk

Bond and stock markets help reduce risk by giving savers a means to *diversify* their financial investments. **Diversification** is the practice of spreading one's wealth over a variety of different financial investments to reduce overall risk. The idea of diversification follows from the adage that "you shouldn't put all your eggs in one basket." Rather than putting all of his or her savings in one very risky project, a financial investor will find it much safer to allocate a small amount of savings to each of a large number of stocks and bonds. That way, if some financial assets fall in value, there is a good chance that others will rise in value, with gains offsetting losses. Example 23.4 illustrates the benefits of diversification.

EXAMPLE 23.4

The benefits of diversification

Vikram has $1,000 to invest and is considering two stocks, the Smith Umbrella Company and the Jones Suntan Lotion Company. The price of Smith Umbrella stock will rise by 10 percent if it rains but will remain unchanged if the weather is sunny. The price of Jones Suntan stock is expected to rise by 10 percent if it is sunny but will remain unchanged if there is rain. The chance of rain is 50 percent, and the chance of sunshine is 50 percent. How should Vikram invest his $1,000?

If Vikram were to invest all his $1,000 in Smith Umbrella, he has a 50 percent chance of earning a 10 percent return, in the event that it rains, and a 50 percent chance of earning zero, if the weather is sunny. His average return is 50 percent times 10 percent plus 50 percent times zero, or 5 percent. Similarly, an investment in Jones Suntan yields 10 percent return half the time, when it's sunny, and 0 percent return the other half the time, when it rains, for an average return of 5 percent.

Although Vikram can earn an *average* return of 5 percent in either stock, investing in only one stock or the other is quite risky, since the actual return he receives varies widely depending on whether there is rain or shine. Can Vikram *guarantee* himself a 5 percent return, avoiding the uncertainty and risk? Yes, all he has to do is put $500 into each of the two stocks. If it rains, he will earn $50 on his Smith Umbrella stock and nothing on his Jones Suntan. If it's sunny, he will earn nothing on Smith Umbrella but $50 on Jones Suntan. Rain or shine, he is guaranteed to earn $50—a 5 percent return—without risk.

The existence of bond markets and stock markets make it easy for savers to diversify by putting a small amount of their savings into each of a wide variety of different financial assets, each of which represents a share of a particular company or investment project. From society's point of view, diversification makes it possible for risky but worthwhile projects to obtain funding, without individual savers having to bear too much risk.

For the typical person, a particularly convenient way to diversify is to buy bonds and stocks indirectly through mutual funds. A **mutual fund** is a financial intermediary that sells shares in itself to the public, then uses the funds raised to buy a wide variety of financial assets. Holding shares in a mutual fund thus amounts to owning a little bit of many different financial assets, which helps to achieve diversification. The advantage of mutual funds is that it is usually less costly and time consuming to buy shares in one or two mutual funds than to buy many different stocks and bonds directly. Over the past decade mutual funds have become increasingly popular in the United States.

mutual fund a financial intermediary that sells shares in itself to the public, then uses the funds raised to buy a wide variety of financial assets

Why did the U.S. stock market boom in the 1990s?

Stock prices soared during the 1990s in the United States. The Standard & Poor 500 index, which summarizes the stock price performance of 500 major companies, rose 60 percent between 1990 and 1995, then more than doubled between 1995 and 1999. Why did the U.S. stock market boom in the 1990s?

The prices of stocks depend on financial investors' expectations about future dividends and stock prices and on the rate of return required by potential stockholders. The required rate of return in turn equals the interest rate on safe assets plus the risk premium. In principle, a rise in stock prices could be the result of increased optimism about future dividends, a fall in the required return, or some combination.

Dividends grew rapidly in the 1990s, reflecting the strong overall performance of the U.S. economy. However, neither the increase in dividends nor plausible expectations of future dividend growth seem to have been nearly large enough to justify the enormous gains in the market. Interest rates on safe assets actually rose over the decade, which is the "wrong" direction to explain the boom in the market. That leaves changes in the risk premium as the remaining possible explanation. A significant drop in the risk premium, by lowering the required rate of return to hold stocks, might explain the stock market's performance.

Although the idea is controversial, a number of economists have argued that the risk premium did fall during the 1990s and that its decline is an important explanation of the rise in stock prices. Why would the risk premium have fallen? One explanation is increased diversification. Recent years have seen an explosion in the number and variety of mutual funds available. Millions of Americans have invested in these funds, including many who either had never owned stock before or had owned stock in only a few companies. This increase in the diversification of the typical stock market investor may have lowered the perceived risk of owning stocks, which in turn reduced the risk premium and raised stock prices.

ECONOMIC NATURALIST 23.2

Although many Americans own stocks and bonds, a far greater percentage own a type of financial asset that economists refer to as *money*. Money consists of financial assets, such as currency and checking accounts, that can be used in making purchases. As we will see in the chapters to come, money plays a central role both in financial markets and in macroeconomic policymaking. As necessary background, much of the remainder of this chapter focuses on money and the factors that determine the amount of money that circulates in the economy.

MONEY: A SPECIAL FINANCIAL ASSET

In deciding what financial assets to hold, savers generally seek out higher returns. For example, given the choice between two bonds of equal risk, maturity, and tax treatment, a saver would generally choose the bond that pays the highest interest rate. By putting their wealth in high-return assets, savers increase their future buying power. There is one class of financial assets, however, that is held by virtually every saver, despite the fact that this type of asset usually pays a low return. This special type of financial asset is called *money*. In this section we discuss why money is useful, how economists measure money in practice, and how money is created.

MONEY AND ITS USES

money any asset that can be used in making purchases

In everyday language, people use the word *money* to mean "income" or "wealth," as in "That job pays good money" or "I wish I had as much money as she does." Economists, however, give a much more specific meaning to the term. To the economist, **money** is any asset that can be used in making purchases.

Common examples of money are currency and coin. A checking account balance represents another asset that can be used in making payments (as when you write a check to pay for your weekly groceries) and so is also counted as money. In contrast, shares of stock, for example, cannot be used directly in most transactions. Stock must first be sold—that is, converted into cash or a checking account deposit—before further transactions, such as buying your groceries, can be made.

Historically, a wide variety of objects have been used as money, ranging from gold and silver coins to shells, beads, feathers, and, on the Island of Yap, large, immovable boulders. Prior to the use of metallic coins, by far the most common form of money was the cowrie, a type of shell found in the South Pacific. Cowries were used as money in some parts of Africa until very recently, being officially accepted for payment of taxes in Uganda until the beginning of the twentieth century. Today money can be virtually intangible, as in the case of your checking account balance, which exists only in the form of an entry in your bank's computer.

Why do people use money? Money has three principal uses: a *medium of exchange*, a *unit of account*, and a *store of value*.

medium of exchange an asset used in purchasing goods and services

Money serves as a **medium of exchange** when it is used to purchase goods and services, as when you pay cash for a newspaper or write a check to cover your utilities bill. This is perhaps money's most crucial function. Think about how complicated daily life would become if there were no money. Without money, all economic transactions would have to be in the form of **barter**, which is the direct trade of goods or services for other goods or services.

barter the direct trade of goods or services for other goods or services

Barter is highly inefficient because it requires that both parties to a trade have something that the other party wants, a so-called double coincidence of wants. For example, under a barter system, a musician could get her dinner only by finding someone willing to trade food for a musical performance. Finding such a match of needs, where both parties happen to want exactly what the other person has to offer, would be difficult to do on a regular basis. In a world with money, the musician's problem is considerably simpler. First, she must find someone who is willing to pay money for her musical performance. Then, with the money received, she can purchase the food and other goods and services that she needs. In a society that uses money, it is not necessary that the person who wants to hear music and the person willing to provide food to the musician be one and the same. In other words, there need not be a double coincidence of wants for trades of goods and services to take place.

By eliminating the problem of having to find a double coincidence of wants in order to trade, the use of money in a society permits individuals to specialize in producing particular goods or services, as opposed to having every family or village produce most of what it needs. Specialization greatly increases economic efficiency and material standards of living, as we discussed in Chapter 3 (*the principle of comparative advantage*). This usefulness of money in making transactions

In a world without money, she could eat only by finding someone willing to trade food for a musical performance.

explains why savers hold money, even though money generally pays a low rate of return. Cash, for example, pays no interest at all, and the balances in checking accounts usually pay a lower rate of interest than could be obtained in alternative financial investments.

Money's second function is as a *unit of account*. As a **unit of account,** money is the basic yardstick for measuring economic value. In the United States virtually all prices—including the price of labor (wages) and the prices of financial assets, such as shares of General Motors stock—are expressed in dollars. Expressing economic values in a common unit of account allows for easy comparisons. For example, grain can be measured in bushels and coal in tons, but to judge whether 20 bushels of grain is economically more or less valuable than a ton of coal, we express both values in dollar terms. The use of money as a unit of account is closely related to its use as a medium of exchange; because money is used to buy and sell things, it makes sense to express prices of all kinds in money terms.

unit of account a basic measure of economic value

As a **store of value,** its third function, money is a way of holding wealth. For example, the miser who stuffs cash in his mattress or buries gold coins under the old oak tree at midnight is holding wealth in money form. Likewise, if you regularly keep a balance in your checking account, you are holding part of your wealth in the form of money. Although money is usually the primary medium of exchange or unit of account in an economy, it is not the only store of value. There are numerous other ways of holding wealth, such as owning stocks, bonds, or real estate.

store of value an asset that serves as a means of holding wealth

For most people, money is not a particularly good way to hold wealth, apart from its usefulness as a medium of exchange. Unlike government bonds and other types of financial assets, most forms of money pay no interest, and there is always the risk of cash being lost or stolen. However, cash has the advantage of being anonymous and difficult to trace, making it an attractive store of value for smugglers, drug dealers, and others who want their assets to stay out of the view of the Internal Revenue Service.

Private money: Ithaca Hours and LETS

Since money is such a useful tool, why is money usually issued only by governments? Are there examples of privately issued money?

Money is usually issued by the government, not private individuals, but in part this reflects legal restrictions on private money issuance. Where the law allows, private moneys do sometimes emerge.[1] For example, privately issued currencies circulate in more than 30 U.S. communities. In Ithaca, New York, a private currency known as "Ithaca Hours" has circulated since 1991. Instituted by town resident Paul Glover, each Ithaca Hour is equivalent to $10, the average hourly wage of workers in the county. The bills, printed with specially developed inks to prevent counterfeiting, honor local people and the environment. An estimated 1,600 individuals and businesses have earned and spent Hours. Founder Paul Glover argues that the use of Hours, which can't be spent elsewhere, induces people to do more of their shopping in the local economy.

A more high-tech form of private money is associated with computerized trading systems called LETS, for local electronic trading system. These are quite popular in Australia, New Zealand, and Great Britain (the United States has about 10 of them). Participants in a LETS post a list of goods and services they would like to buy or sell. When transactions are made, the appropriate number of "computer credits" is subtracted from the buyer's account and added to the seller's account. People are allowed to have negative balances in their accounts, so participants have to trust other members not to abuse the system by buying many goods and services

ECONOMIC NATURALIST 23.3

[1]Barbara A. Good, "Private Money: Everything Old Is New Again," Federal Reserve Bank of Cleveland, *Economic Commentary,* April 1, 1998.

and then quitting. LETS credits exist in the computer only and are never in the form of paper or metal. In this respect LETS may foreshadow the electronic monetary systems of the future.

What do Ithaca Hours and LETS credits have in common? By functioning as a medium of exchange, each facilitates trade within a community.

MEASURING MONEY

How much money, defined as financial assets usable for making purchases, is there in the U.S. economy at any given time? This question is not simple to answer because in practice it is not easy to draw a clear distinction between those assets that should be counted as money and those that should not. Dollar bills are certainly a form of money, and a van Gogh painting certainly is not. However, brokerage firms now offer accounts that allow their owners to combine financial investments in stocks and bonds with check-writing and credit card privileges. Should the balances in these accounts, or some part of them, be counted as money? It is difficult to tell.

Economists skirt the problem of deciding what is and isn't money by using several alternative definitions of money, which vary in how broadly the concept of money is defined. A relatively "narrow" definition of the amount of money in the U.S. economy is called M1. **M1** is the sum of currency outstanding and balances held in checking accounts. A broader measure of money, called **M2**, includes all the assets in M1 plus some additional assets that are usable in making payments, but at greater cost or inconvenience than currency or checks. Table 23.1 lists the components of M1 and M2 and also gives the amount of each type of asset outstanding as of February 2000. For most purposes, however, it is sufficient to think of money as the sum of currency outstanding and balances in checking accounts, or M1.

M1 sum of currency outstanding and balances held in checking accounts

M2 All the assets in M1 plus some additional assets that are usable in making payments but at greater cost or inconvenience than currency or checks

TABLE 23.1
Components of M1 and M2, February 2000

M1		1,105.0
Currency	518.1	
Demand deposits	338.2	
Other checkable deposits	240.6	
Travelers' checks	8.1	
M2		4,683.6
M1	1,105.0	
Savings deposits	1,751.3	
Small-denomination time deposits	966.7	
Money market mutual funds	860.6	

NOTES: Billions of dollars, adjusted for seasonal variations. In M1, currency refers to cash and coin. Demand deposits are non-interest-bearing checking accounts, and "other checkable deposits" includes checking accounts that bear interest. M2 includes all the components of M1, balances in savings accounts, "small-denomination" (under $100,000) deposits held at banks for a fixed term, and money market mutual funds (MMMFs). MMMFs are organizations that sell shares, use the proceeds to buy safe assets (like government bonds), and often allow their shareholders some check-writing privileges.

SOURCE: Federal Reserve Bank of St. Louis, FRED database, www.stls.frb.org/research/aggreg.html, or Federal Reserve release H.6.

> **RECAP** **MONEY: A SPECIAL FINANCIAL ASSET**
>
> *Money* is any asset that can be used in making purchases, such as currency or a checking account. Money serves as a *medium of exchange* when it is used to purchase goods and services. The use of money as a medium of exchange eliminates the need for *barter* and the difficulties of finding a "double coincidence of wants." Money also serves as a *unit of account* and a *store of value*.
>
> In practice, two basic measures of money are *M1* and *M2*. *M1*, a more narrow measure, is made up primarily of currency and balances held in checking accounts. The broader measure, *M2*, includes all the assets in *M1* plus some additional assets usable in making payments.

COMMERCIAL BANKS AND THE CREATION OF MONEY

What determines the amount of money in the economy? If the economy's supply of money consisted entirely of currency, the answer would be simple: The supply of money would just be equal to the value of the currency created and circulated by the government. However, as we have seen, in modern economies the money supply consists not only of currency but also of deposit balances held by the public in commercial, that is private, banks. The determination of the money supply in a modern economy thus depends in part on the behavior of commercial banks and their depositors.

To see how the existence of commercial banks affects the money supply, we will use the example of a fictional country, the Republic of Gorgonzola. Initially, we assume, Gorgonzola has no commercial banking system. To make trading easier and eliminate the need for barter, the government directs the central bank of Gorgonzola to put into circulation a million identical paper notes, called guilders. The central bank prints the guilders and distributes them to the populace. At this point the Gorgonzolan money supply is a million guilders.

However, the citizens of Gorgonzola are unhappy with a money supply made up entirely of paper guilders, since the notes may be lost or stolen. In response to the demand for safekeeping of money, some Gorgonzolan entrepreneurs set up a system of commercial banks. At first, these banks are only storage vaults where people can deposit their guilders. When people need to make a payment they can either physically withdraw their guilders or, more conveniently, write a check on their account. Checks give the banks permission to transfer guilders from the account of the person paying by check to the account of the person to whom the check is made out. With a system of payments based on checks the paper guilders need never leave the banking system, although they flow from one bank to another as a depositor of one bank makes a payment to a depositor in another bank. Deposits do not pay interest in this economy; indeed, the banks can make a profit only by charging depositors fees in exchange for safeguarding their cash.

Let's suppose for now that people prefer bank deposits to cash and so deposit all of their guilders with the commercial banks. With all guilders in the vaults of banks, the balance sheet of all of Gorgonzola's commercial banks taken together is as shown in Table 23.2.

The *assets* of the commercial banking system in Gorgonzola are the paper guilders sitting in the vaults of all the individual banks. The banking system's *liabilities* are the deposits of the banks' customers, since checking account balances represent money owed by the banks to the depositors.

Cash or similar assets held by banks are called **bank reserves**. In this example, bank reserves, for all the banks taken together, equal 1,000,000 guilders—the

bank reserves cash or similar assets held by commercial banks for the purpose of meeting depositor withdrawals and payments

TABLE 23.2
Consolidated Balance Sheet of Gorgonzolan Commercial Banks (Initial)

Assets		Liabilities	
Currency	1,000,000 guilders	Deposits	1,000,000 guilders

currency listed on the asset side of the consolidated balance sheet. Banks hold reserves to meet depositors' demands for cash withdrawals or to pay checks drawn on their depositors' accounts. In this example, the bank reserves of 1,000,000 guilders equal 100 percent of banks' deposits, which are also 1,000,000 guilders. A situation in which bank reserves equal 100 percent of bank deposits is called **100 percent reserve banking.**

Bank reserves are held by banks in their vaults, rather than circulated among the public, and thus are *not* counted as part of the money supply. However, bank deposit balances, which can be used in making transactions, *are* counted as money. So, after the introduction of "safekeeper" banks in Gorgonzola, the money supply, equal to the value of bank deposits, is 1,000,000 guilders, which is the same as it was prior to the introduction of banks.

After a while, to continue the story, the commercial bankers of Gorgonzola begin to realize that keeping 100 percent reserves against deposits is not necessary. True, a few guilders flow in and out of the typical bank as depositors receive payments or write checks, but for the most part the stacks of paper guilders just sit there in the vaults, untouched and unused. It occurs to the bankers that they can meet the random inflow and outflow of guilders to their banks with reserves that are less than 100 percent of their deposits. After some observation, the bankers conclude that keeping reserves equal to only 10 percent of deposits is enough to meet the random ebb and flow of withdrawals and payments from their individual banks. The remaining 90 percent of deposits, the bankers realize, can be lent out to borrowers to earn interest.

So the bankers decide to keep reserves equal to 100,000 guilders, or 10 percent of their deposits. The other 900,000 guilders they lend out at interest to Gorgonzolan cheese producers who want to use the money to make improvements to their farms. After the loans are made, the balance sheet of all of Gorgonzola's commercial banks taken together has changed, as shown in Table 23.3.

TABLE 23.3
Consolidated Balance Sheet of Gorgonzolan Commercial Banks after One Round of Loans

Assets		Liabilities	
Currency (= reserves)	100,000 guilders	Deposits	1,000,000 guilders
Loans to farmers	900,000 guilders		

reserve-deposit ratio bank reserves divided by deposits

fractional-reserve banking system a banking system in which bank reserves are less than deposits so that the reserve-deposit ratio is less than 100 percent

100 percent reserve banking a situation in which banks' reserves equal 100 percent of their deposits

After the loans are made, the banks' reserves of 100,000 guilders no longer equal 100 percent of the banks' deposits of 1,000,000 guilders. Instead, the **reserve-deposit ratio,** which is bank reserves divided by deposits, is now equal to 100,000/1,000,000, or 10 percent. A banking system in which banks hold fewer reserves than deposits so that the reserve-deposit ratio is less than 100 percent is called a **fractional-reserve banking system.**

Notice that 900,000 guilders have flowed out of the banking system (as loans to farmers) and are now in the hands of the public. But we have assumed that private citizens prefer bank deposits to cash for making transactions. So ultimately people will redeposit the 900,000 guilders in the banking system. After these deposits are made, the consolidated balance sheet of the commercial banks is as in Table 23.4.

TABLE 23.4
Consolidated Balance Sheet of Gorgonzolan Commercial Banks after Guilders Are Redeposited

Assets		Liabilities	
Currency (= reserves)	1,000,000 guilders	Deposits	1,900,000 guilders
Loans to farmers	900,000 guilders		

Notice that bank deposits, and hence the economy's money supply, now equal 1,900,000 guilders. In effect, the existence of the commercial banking system has permitted the creation of new money. These deposits, which are liabilities of the banks, are balanced by assets of 1,000,000 guilders in reserves and 900,000 guilders in loans owed to the banks.

The story does not end here. On examining their balance sheets, the bankers are surprised to see that they once again have "too many" reserves. With deposits of 1,900,000 guilders and a 10 percent reserve-deposit ratio, they need only 190,000 guilders in reserves. But they have 1,000,000 guilders in reserves—810,000 too many. Since lending out their excess guilders is always more profitable than leaving them in the vault, the bankers proceed to make another 810,000 guilders in loans. Eventually these loaned-out guilders are redeposited in the banking system, after which the consolidated balance sheet of the banks is as shown in Table 23.5.

TABLE 23.5
Consolidated Balance Sheet of Gorgonzolan Commercial Banks after Two Rounds of Loans and Redeposits

Assets		Liabilities	
Currency (= reserves)	1,000,000 guilders	Deposits	2,710,000 guilders
Loans to farmers	1,710,000 guilders		

Now the money supply has increased to 2,710,000 guilders, equal to the value of bank deposits. Despite the expansion of loans and deposits, however, the bankers find that their reserves of 1,000,000 guilders *still* exceed the desired level of 10 percent of deposits, which are 2,710,000 guilders. And so yet another round of lending will take place.

EXERCISE 23.3

Determine what the balance sheet of the banking system of Gorgonzola will look like after a third round of lending to farmers and redeposits of guilders into the commercial banking system. What is the money supply at that point?

The process of expansion of loans and deposits will only end when reserves equal 10 percent of bank deposits, because as long as reserves exceed 10 percent of deposits the banks will find it profitable to lend out the extra reserves. Since reserves at the end of every round equal 1,000,000 guilders, for the reserve-deposit ratio to equal 10 percent total deposits must equal 10,000,000 guilders. Further, since the balance sheet must balance, with assets equal to liabilities, we know as well that at the end of the process loans to cheese producers must equal 9,000,000 guilders. If loans equal 9,000,000 guilders, then bank assets, the sum of loans and reserves (1,000,000 guilders) will equal 10,000,000 guilders, which is the same as bank liabilities (bank deposits). The final consolidated balance sheet is as shown in Table 23.6.

TABLE 23.6
Final Consolidated Balance Sheet of Gorgonzolan Commercial Banks

Assets		Liabilities	
Currency (= reserves)	1,000,000 guilders	Deposits	10,000,000 guilders
Loans to farmers	9,000,000 guilders		

The money supply, which is equal to total deposits, is 10,000,000 guilders at the end of the process. We see that the existence of a fractional-reserve banking system has multiplied the money supply by a factor of 10, relative to the economy with no banks or the economy with 100 percent reserve banking. Put another way, with a 10 percent reserve-deposit ratio, each guilder deposited in the banking system can "support" 10 guilders worth of deposits.

To find the money supply in this example more directly, we observe that deposits will expand through additional rounds of lending as long as the ratio of bank reserves to bank deposits exceeds the reserve-deposit ratio desired by banks. When the actual ratio of bank reserves to deposits equals the desired reserve-deposit ratio, the expansion stops. So ultimately, deposits in the banking system satisfy the following relationship:

$$\frac{\text{Bank reserves}}{\text{Bank deposits}} = \text{desired reserve-deposit ratio}.$$

This equation can be rewritten to solve for bank deposits:

$$\text{Bank deposits} = \frac{\text{bank reserves}}{\text{desired reserve-deposit ratio}}. \qquad (23.1)$$

In Gorgonzola, since all the currency in the economy flows into the banking system, bank reserves equal 1,000,000 guilders. The reserve-deposit ratio desired by banks is 0.10. Therefore, using Equation 23.1, we find that bank deposits equal (1,000,000 guilders)/0.10, or 10 million guilders, the same answer as we found in the consolidated balance sheet of the banks, Table 23.6.

EXERCISE 23.4

Find deposits and the money supply in Gorgonzola if the banks' desired reserve-deposit ratio is 5 percent rather than 10 percent. What if the total amount of currency circulated by the central bank is 2,000,000 guilders and the desired reserve-deposit ratio remains at 10 percent?

THE MONEY SUPPLY WITH BOTH CURRENCY AND DEPOSITS

In the example of Gorgonzola we assumed that all money is held in the form of deposits in banks. In reality, of course, people keep only part of their money holdings in the form of bank accounts and hold the rest in the form of currency.

Fortunately, allowing for the fact that people hold both currency and bank deposits does not greatly complicate the determination of the money supply, as Example 23.5 shows.

The money supply with both currency and deposits

EXAMPLE 23.5

Suppose that the citizens of Gorgonzola choose to hold a total of 500,000 guilders in the form of currency and to deposit the rest of their money in banks. Banks keep reserves equal to 10 percent of deposits. What is the money supply in Gorgonzola?

The money supply is the sum of currency in the hands of the public and bank deposits. Currency in hands of the public is given as 500,000 guilders. What is the quantity of bank deposits? Since 500,000 of the 1,000,000 guilders issued by the central bank are being used by the public in the form of currency, only the remaining 500,000 guilders is available to serve as bank reserves. We know that deposits equals bank reserves divided by the reserve-deposit ratio, so deposits are 500,000 guilders/0.10 = 5,000,000 guilders. The total money supply is the sum of currency in the hands of the public (500,000 guilders) and bank deposits (5,000,000 guilders), or 5,500,000 guilders.

We can write a general relationship that captures the reasoning of Example 23.5. First, let's write out the fact that the money supply equals currency plus bank deposits:

$$\text{Money supply} = \text{Currency held by the public} + \text{Bank deposits.}$$

We also know that bank deposits equal bank reserves divided by the reserve-deposit ratio that is desired by commercial banks (Equation 23.1). Using that relationship to substitute for bank deposits in the expression for the money supply, we get

$$\text{Money supply} = \text{Currency held by public} + \frac{\text{Bank reserves}}{\text{Desired reserve-deposit ratio}}. \quad (23.2)$$

We can use Equation 23.2 to confirm our answer to Example 23.5. In that example, currency held by the public is 500,000 guilders, bank reserves are 500,000 guilders, and the desired reserve-deposit ratio is 0.10. Plugging these values into Equation 23.2, we get that the money supply equals 500,000 + 500,000/0.10 = 5,500,000, the same answer we found before.

The money supply at Christmas

EXAMPLE 23.6

During the Christmas season people choose to hold unusually large amounts of currency for shopping. With no action by the central bank, how would this change in currency holding affect the national money supply?

To illustrate with a numerical example, suppose that initially bank reserves are 500, the amount of currency held by the public is 500, and the desired reserve-deposit ratio in the banking system is 0.2. Inserting these values into Equation 23.2, we find that the money supply equals 500 + 500/0.2 = 3,000.

Now suppose that because of Christmas shopping needs, the public increases its currency holdings to 600 by withdrawing 100 from commercial banks. These withdrawals reduce bank reserves to 400. Using Equation 23.2 we find now that the money supply is 600 + 400/0.2 = 2,600. So the public's increased holdings of currency have caused the money supply to drop, from 3,000 to 2,600. The reason for the drop is that with a reserve-deposit ratio of 20 percent, every dollar in the vaults of banks can "support" $5 of deposits and hence $5 of money supply. However, the same dollar in the hands of the public becomes $1 of currency, contributing only $1 to the total money supply. So when the public withdraws cash from the banks, the overall money supply declines. (We will see in the next section, however, that in practice the central bank has means to offset the impact of the public's actions on the money supply.)

RECAP **COMMERCIAL BANKS AND THE CREATION OF MONEY**

Part of the money supply consists of deposits in private commercial banks. Hence the behavior of commercial banks and their depositors help to determine the money supply.

Cash or similar assets held by banks are called *bank reserves*. In modern economies, banks' reserves are less than their deposits, a situation called *fractional-reserve banking*. The ratio of bank reserves to deposits is called the *reserve-deposit ratio*; in a fractional-reserve banking system, this ratio is less than 1.

The portion of deposits not held as reserves can be lent out by the banks to earn interest. Banks will continue to make loans and accept deposits as long as the reserve-deposit ratio exceeds its desired level. This process stops only when the actual and desired reserve-deposit ratios are equal. At that point, total bank deposits equal bank reserves divided by the desired reserve-deposit ratio, and the money supply equals the currency held by the public plus bank deposits (see Equation 23.2).

THE FEDERAL RESERVE SYSTEM

Federal Reserve System (or Fed) the central bank of the United States

For participants in financial markets and the average citizen as well, one of the most important branches of the government is the **Federal Reserve System,** often called the Fed. The Fed is the *central bank* of the United States. Like central banks in other countries, the Fed has two main responsibilities.

First, it is responsible for monetary policy, which means that the Fed determines how much money circulates in the economy. As we will see in later chapters, changes in the supply of money can affect many important macroeconomic variables, including interest rates, inflation, unemployment, and exchange rates. Because of its ability to affect key variables, particularly financial variables such as interest rates, financial market participants pay close attention to Fed actions and announcements. As a necessary first step in understanding how Fed policies have the effects that they do, in this chapter we will focus on the basic question of how the Fed affects the supply of money, leaving for later the explanation of why changes in the money supply affect the economy.

Second, along with other government agencies, the Federal Reserve bears important responsibility for the oversight and regulation of financial markets. The Fed also plays a major role during periods of crisis in financial markets. To lay the groundwork for discussing how the Fed carries out its responsibilities, we first briefly review the history and structure of the Federal Reserve System.

THE HISTORY AND STRUCTURE OF THE FEDERAL RESERVE SYSTEM

The Federal Reserve System was created by the Federal Reserve Act, passed by Congress in 1913, and began operations in 1914. Like all central banks, the Fed is a government agency. Unlike commercial banks, which are private businesses whose principal objective is making a profit, central banks like the Fed focus on promoting public goals such as economic growth, low inflation, and the smooth operation of financial markets.

"I'm sorry, sir, but I don't believe you know us well enough to call us the Fed."

The Federal Reserve Act established a system of 12 regional Federal Reserve banks, each associated with a geographical area called a Federal Reserve district. Congress hoped that the establishment of Federal Reserve banks around the country would ensure that different regions were represented in the national policy-making process. In fact, the regional Feds regularly assess economic conditions in their districts and report this information to policymakers in Washington. Regional Federal Reserve banks also provide various services, such as check-clearing services, to the commercial banks in their district.

At the national level, the leadership of the Federal Reserve System is provided by its **Board of Governors.** The Board of Governors, together with a large professional staff, is located in Washington, D.C. The Board consists of seven governors, who are appointed by the President of the United States to 14-year terms. The terms are staggered so that one governor comes up for reappointment every other year. The President also appoints one of these Board members to serve as Chairman of the Board of Governors for a term of 4 years. The Fed Chairman, along with the Secretary of the Treasury, is probably one of the two most powerful economic policymakers in the United States government, after the President. Recent Chairmen, such as Paul Volcker and Alan Greenspan, have been highly regarded and influential.

Decisions about monetary policy are made by a 12-member committee called the **Federal Open Market Committee** (or **FOMC**). The FOMC consists of the seven Fed governors, the president of the Federal Reserve Bank of New York, and four of the presidents of the other regional Federal Reserve banks, who serve on a rotating basis. The FOMC meets approximately eight times a year to review the state of the economy and to determine monetary policy.

Board of Governors the leadership of the Fed, consisting of seven governors appointed by the President to staggered 14-year terms

Federal Open Market Committee (or FOMC) the committee that makes decisions concerning monetary policy

CONTROLLING THE MONEY SUPPLY: OPEN-MARKET OPERATIONS

The Fed's primary responsibility is making monetary policy, which involves decisions about the appropriate size of the nation's money supply. As we saw in the previous section, central banks in general, and the Fed in particular, do not control the money supply directly. However, they can control the money supply indirectly by changing the supply of reserves held by commercial banks.

The Fed has several ways of affecting the supply of bank reserves. By far the most important of these are *open-market operations*. Suppose that the Fed wants to increase bank reserves, with the ultimate goal of increasing bank deposits and the money supply. To accomplish this the Fed buys financial assets, usually government bonds, from the public. To simplify the actual procedure a bit, think of the Fed as paying for the bonds it acquires with newly printed money. Assuming that the public is already holding all the currency that it wants, they will deposit the cash they receive as payment for their bonds in commercial banks. Thus, the reserves of the commercial banking system will increase by an amount equal to the value of the bonds purchased by the Fed. The increase in bank reserves will lead in turn, through the process of lending and redeposit of funds described in the previous section, to an expansion of bank deposits and the money supply, as summarized by Equation 23.2. The Fed's purchase of government bonds from the public, with the result that bank reserves and the money supply are increased, is called an **open-market purchase**.

open-market purchase the purchase of government bonds from the public by the Fed for the purpose of increasing the supply of bank reserves and the money supply

To reduce bank reserves and hence the money supply, the Fed reverses the procedure. It sells some of the government bonds that it holds (acquired in previous open-market purchases) to the public. Assume that the public pays for the bonds by writing checks on their accounts in commercial banks. Then, when the Fed presents the checks to the commercial banks for payment, reserves equal in value to the government bonds sold by the Fed are transferred from the commercial banks to the Fed. The Fed retires these reserves from circulation, lowering the supply of bank reserves and, hence, the overall money supply. The sale of government bonds by the Fed to the public for the purpose of reducing bank reserves and hence the money supply is called an **open-market sale**. Open-market purchases and sales together are called **open-market operations**. Open-market operations are the most convenient and flexible tool that the Federal Reserve has for affecting the money supply and are employed on a regular basis.

open-market sale the sale by the Fed of government bonds to the public for the purpose of reducing bank reserves and the money supply

open-market operations open-market purchases and open-market sales

EXAMPLE 23.7   Increasing the money supply by open-market operations

In a particular economy, currency held by the public is 1,000 shekels, bank reserves are 200 shekels, and the desired reserve-deposit ratio is 0.2. What is the money supply? How is the money supply affected if the central bank prints 100 shekels and uses this new currency to buy government bonds from the public? Assume that the public does not wish to change the amount of currency it holds.

As bank reserves are 200 shekels and the reserve-deposit ratio is 0.2, bank deposits must equal 200 shekels/0.2, or 1,000 shekels. The money supply, equal to the sum of currency held by the public and bank deposits, is therefore 2,000 shekels, a result you can confirm using Equation 23.2.

The open-market purchase puts 100 more shekels into the hands of the public. We assume that the public continues to want to hold 1,000 shekels in currency, so they will deposit the additional 100 shekels in the commercial banking system, raising bank reserves from 200 to 300 shekels. As the desired reserve-deposit ratio is 0.2, multiple rounds of lending and redeposit will eventually raise the level of bank deposits to 300 shekels/0.2, or 1,500 shekels. The money supply, equal to 1,000 shekels held by the public plus bank deposits of 1,500 shekels, equals 2,500 shekels. So the open-market purchase of 100 shekels, by raising bank reserves by 100 shekels, has increased the money supply by 500 shekels. Again, you can confirm this result using Equation 23.2.

EXERCISE 23.5

Continuing Example 23.7, suppose that instead of an open-market purchase of 100 shekels the central bank conducts an open-market sale of 50 shekels' worth of government bonds. What happens to bank reserves, bank deposits, and the money supply?

CONTROLLING THE MONEY SUPPLY: DISCOUNT WINDOW LENDING

A second means by which the Fed can affect bank reserves and thus the money supply is by what is called *discount window lending*. When individual commercial banks are short of reserves, they may choose to borrow reserves from the Fed. For historical reasons, lending of reserves by the Federal Reserve to commercial banks is called **discount window lending**. The interest rate that the Fed charges commercial banks that borrow reserves is called the **discount rate**. Loans of reserves by the Fed directly increase the quantity of reserves in the banking system, leading ultimately to increases in bank deposits and the money supply.

discount window lending the lending of reserves by the Federal Reserve to commercial banks

discount rate the interest rate that the Fed charges commercial banks to borrow reserves

CONTROLLING THE MONEY SUPPLY: CHANGING RESERVE REQUIREMENTS

As Equation 23.2 shows, the economy's money supply depends on three factors: the amount of currency the public chooses to hold, the supply of bank reserves, and the reserve-deposit ratio maintained by commercial banks. For given quantities of currency held by the public and of reserves held by the banks, an increase in the reserve-deposit ratio reduces the money supply, as you can see from Equation 23.2. A higher reserve-deposit ratio implies that banks lend out a smaller share of their deposits in each of the rounds of lending and redeposit described earlier, limiting the overall expansion of loans and deposits.

Within a certain range, commercial banks are free to set the reserve-deposit ratio they want to maintain. However, Congress granted the Fed the power to set minimum values of the reserve-deposit ratio for commercial banks. The legally required values of the reserve-deposit ratio set by the Fed are called **reserve requirements.**

Changes in reserve requirements can be used to affect the money supply, although the Fed does not usually use them in this way. For example, suppose that commercial banks are maintaining a 3 percent reserve-deposit ratio, and the Fed wants to contract the money supply. By raising required reserves to, say, 5 percent of deposits, the Fed could force commercial banks to raise their reserve-deposit ratio, at least until it reached 5 percent. As you can see from Equation 23.2, an increase in the reserve-deposit ratio lowers deposits and the money supply. Similarly, a reduction in required reserves by the Fed might allow at least some banks to lower their ratio of reserves to deposits. A decline in the economywide reserve-deposit ratio would in turn cause the money supply to rise.

reserve requirements set by the Fed, the minimum values of the ratio of bank reserves to bank deposits that commercial banks are allowed to maintain

THE FED'S ROLE IN STABILIZING FINANCIAL MARKETS: BANKING PANICS

Besides controlling the money supply, the Fed also has the responsibility (together with other government agencies) of ensuring that financial markets operate smoothly. Indeed, the creation of the Fed in 1913 was prompted by a series of financial market crises that disrupted both the markets themselves and the U.S. economy as a whole. The hope of the Congress was that the Fed would be able to eliminate or at least control such crises.

banking panic an episode in which depositors, spurred by news or rumors of the imminent bankruptcy of one or more banks, rush to withdraw their deposits from the banking system

Historically, in the United States, *banking panics* were perhaps the most disruptive type of recurrent financial crisis. In a **banking panic,** news or rumors of the imminent bankruptcy of one or more banks leads bank depositors to rush to withdraw their funds. We close the chapter by discussing banking panics and the Fed's attempts to control them.

Why do banking panics occur? An important factor that helps make banking panics possible is the existence of fractional-reserve banking. In a fractional-reserve banking system, like that of the United States and all other industrialized countries, bank reserves are less than deposits, which means that banks do not keep enough cash on hand to pay off their depositors if they were all to decide to withdraw their deposits. Normally this is not a problem, as only a small percentage of depositors attempt to withdraw their funds on any given day. But if a rumor circulates that one or more banks are in financial trouble and may go bankrupt, depositors may panic, lining up to demand their money. Since bank reserves are less than deposits, a sufficiently severe panic could lead even financially healthy banks to run out of cash, forcing them into bankruptcy and closure.

The Federal Reserve was established in response to a particularly severe banking panic that occurred in 1907. The Fed was equipped with two principal tools to try to prevent or moderate banking panics. First, the Fed was given the power to supervise and regulate banks. It was hoped that the public would have greater confidence in banks, and thus be less prone to panic, if people knew that the Fed was keeping a close watch on bankers' activities. Second, the Fed was allowed to make loans to banks through the discount window, discussed earlier. The idea was that, during a panic, banks could borrow cash from the Fed with which to pay off depositors, avoiding the need to close.

There were no banking panics between 1914, when the Fed was established, and 1930. However, between 1930 and 1933 the United States experienced the worst and most protracted series of banking panics in its history. Economic historians agree that much of the blame for this panic should be placed on the shoulders of the Fed, which did not appreciate the severity of the problem nor act aggressively enough to contain it.

ECONOMIC NATURALIST 23.4

The banking panics of 1930–1933 and the money supply

The worst banking panics ever experienced in the United States occurred during the early stages of the Great Depression, between 1930 and 1933. During this period approximately one-third of the banks in the United States were forced to close. This near-collapse of the banking system was probably an important reason that the Depression was so severe. With many fewer banks in operation it was very difficult for small businesses and consumers during the early 1930s to obtain credit. Another important effect of the banking panics was to greatly reduce the nation's money supply. Why should banking panics reduce the national money supply?

During a banking panic people are afraid to keep deposits in a bank because of the risk that the bank will go bankrupt and their money will be lost (this was prior to the introduction of federal deposit insurance, discussed below). During the 1930–1933 period, many bank depositors withdrew their money from banks, holding currency instead. These withdrawals reduced bank reserves. Each extra dollar of currency held by the public adds $1 to the money supply; but each extra dollar of bank reserves translates into several dollars of money supply, because in a fractional-reserve banking system each dollar of reserves can "support" several dollars in bank deposits. Thus the public's withdrawals from banks, which increased currency holdings by the public but reduced bank reserves by an equal amount, led to a net decrease in the total money supply (currency plus deposits).

In addition, fearing banking panics and the associated withdrawals by depositors, banks increased their reserve-deposit ratios, which reduced the quantity of deposits that could be supported by any given level of bank reserves. This change in reserve-deposit ratios also tended to reduce the money supply.

Data on currency holdings by the public, the reserve-deposit ratio, bank reserves, and the money supply for selected dates are shown in Table 23.7. Notice the increase over the period in the amount of currency held by the public and in the reserve-deposit ratio, as well as the decline in bank reserves after 1930. The last column shows that the U.S. money supply dropped by about one-third between December 1929 and December 1933.

TABLE 23.7
Key U.S. Monetary Statistics, 1929–1933

	Currency held by public	Reserve-deposit ratio	Bank reserves	Money supply
December 1929	3.85	0.075	3.15	45.9
December 1930	3.79	0.082	3.31	44.1
December 1931	4.59	0.095	3.11	37.3
December 1932	4.82	0.109	3.18	34.0
December 1933	4.85	0.133	3.45	30.8

NOTE: Data on currency, the monetary base, and the money supply are in billions of dollars.

SOURCE: Milton Friedman and Anna J. Schwartz, *A Monetary History of the United States, 1863–1960*, Princeton, N.J.: Princeton University Press, 1963, Table A-1.

Using Equation 23.2, we can see that increases in currency holdings by the public and increases in the reserve-deposit ratio both tend to reduce the money supply. These effects were so powerful in 1930–1933 that the nation's money supply, shown in the fourth column of Table 23.7, dropped precipitously, even though currency holdings and bank reserves, taken separately, actually rose during the period.

EXERCISE 23.6

Using the data from Table 23.7, confirm that the relationship between the money supply and its determinants is consistent with Equation 23.2. Would the money supply have fallen in 1931–1933 if the public had stopped withdrawing deposits after December 1930 so that currency held by the public had remained at its December 1930 level?

EXERCISE 23.7

According to Table 23.7, the U.S. money supply fell from $44.1 billion to $37.3 billion over the course of 1931. The Fed did use open-market purchases during 1931 to replenish bank reserves in the face of depositor withdrawals. Find (a) the quantity of reserves that the Fed injected into the economy in 1931, and (b) the quantity of reserves the Fed would have had to add to the economy to keep the money supply unchanged from 1930, assuming that public currency holdings and reserve-deposit ratios for each year remained as reported in the table. Why has the Fed been criticized for being too timid in 1931?

When the Fed failed to stop the banking panics of the 1930s, policymakers decided to look at other strategies for controlling panics. In 1934 Congress instituted a system of deposit insurance. Under a system of **deposit insurance**, the government guarantees depositors—specifically, under current rules, those with deposits of less than $100,000—that they will get their money back even if the bank goes bankrupt. Deposit insurance eliminates the incentive for people to

deposit insurance a system under which the government guarantees that depositors will not lose any money even if their bank goes bankrupt

withdraw their deposits when rumors circulate that the bank is in financial trouble, which nips panics in the bud. Indeed, since deposit insurance was instituted, the United States has had no significant banking panics.

Unfortunately, deposit insurance is not a perfect solution to the problem of banking panics. An important drawback is that when deposit insurance is in force, depositors know they are protected no matter what happens to their bank, and they become completely unconcerned about whether their bank is making prudent loans. This situation can lead to reckless behavior by banks or other insured intermediaries. For example, during the 1980s many savings and loan associations in the United States went bankrupt, in part because of reckless lending and financial investments. Like banks, savings and loans have deposit insurance, so the U.S. government had to pay savings and loans depositors the full value of their deposits. This action ultimately cost U.S. taxpayers hundreds of billions of dollars.

To this point in the book we have discussed a variety of issues relating to the long-run performance of the economy, including economic growth, the sources of increasing productivity and improved living standards, the determination of real wages, and the determinants of saving and capital formation. Beginning with the next chapter we will take a more short-run perspective, examining first the causes of recessions and booms in the economy and then turning to policy measures that can be used to affect these fluctuations.

■ SUMMARY ■

- Besides balancing saving and investment in the aggregate, financial markets and institutions play the important role of allocating saving to the most productive investment projects. The financial system improves the allocation of saving in two ways: First, it provides information to savers about which of the many possible uses of their funds are likely to prove must productive, and hence pay the highest return. For example, *financial intermediaries* such as banks develop expertise in evaluating prospective borrowers, making it unnecessary for small savers to do that on their own. Similarly, stock and bond analysts evaluate the business prospects of a company issuing shares of stock or bonds, which determines the price the stock will sell for or the interest rate the company will have to offer on its bond. Second, financial markets help savers share the risks of lending by permitting them to *diversify* their financial investments. Individual savers often hold stocks through *mutual funds*, a type of financial intermediary that reduces risk by holding many different financial assets. By reducing the risk faced by any one saver, financial markets allow risky but potentially very productive projects to be funded.

- Corporations that do not wish to borrow from banks can obtain finance by issuing bonds or stocks. A *bond* is a legal promise to repay a debt, including both the *principal amount* and regular interest payments. The prices of existing bonds decline when interest rates rise. A share of *stock* is a claim to partial ownership of a firm. The price of a stock depends positively on the *dividend* the stock is expected to pay and on the expected future price of the stock and negatively on the rate of return required by financial investors to hold the stock. The required rate of return

in turn is the sum of the return on safe assets and the additional return required to compensate financial investors for the riskiness of stocks, called the *risk premium*.

- *Money* is any asset that can be used in making purchases, such as currency and checking account balances. Money has three main functions: It is a *medium of exchange*, which means that it can be used in transactions. It is a *unit of account*, in that economic values are typically measured in units of money (e.g., dollars). And it is a *store of value*, a means by which people can hold wealth. In practice it is difficult to measure the money supply, since many assets have some moneylike features. A relatively narrow measure of money is M1, which includes currency and checking accounts. A broader measure of money, M2, includes all the assets in M1 plus additional assets that are somewhat less convenient to use in transactions than those included in M1.

- Because bank deposits are part of the money supply, the behavior of commercial banks and of bank depositors affects the amount of money in the economy. A key factor is the *reserve-deposit ratio* chosen by banks. *Bank reserves* are cash or similar assets held by commercial banks, for the purpose of meeting depositor withdrawals and payments. The reserve-deposit ratio is bank reserves divided by deposits in banks. A banking system in which all deposits are held as reserves practices *100 percent reserve banking*. Modern banking systems have reserve-deposit ratios less than 100 percent, and are called *fractional-reserve banking systems*.

- Commercial banks create money through multiple rounds of lending and accepting deposits. This process of lending and increasing deposits comes to an end when banks' reserve-deposit ratios equal their desired levels. At that point, bank deposits equal bank reserves divided by the desired reserve-deposit ratio. The money supply equals currency held by the public plus deposits in the banking system.

- The central bank of the United States is called the *Federal Reserve System,* or the Fed for short. The Fed's two main responsibilities are making monetary policy, which means determining how much money will circulate in the economy, and overseeing and regulating financial markets, especially banks. Created in 1913, the Fed is headed by a *Board of Governors* made up of seven governors appointed by the President. One of these seven governors is appointed Chairman. The *Federal Open Market Committee,* which meets about eight times a year to determine monetary policy, is made up of the seven governors and five of the presidents of the regional Federal Reserve banks.

- The Fed can affect the money supply indirectly through its control of the supply of bank reserves. The Fed has two ways to change bank reserves: through *open-market opera-tions,* in which the Fed buys or sells government securities in exchange for currency held by banks or the public, or through *discount window lending,* which is the Fed's lending of reserves to commercial banks. In addition the Fed can affect the money supply by changing legal *reserve requirements,* which influences banks' reserve-deposit ratios and hence deposits.

- One of the original purposes of the Federal Reserve was to help eliminate or control banking panics. A *banking panic* is an episode in which depositors, spurred by news or rumors of the imminent bankruptcy of one or more banks, rush to withdraw their deposits from the banking system. Because banks do not keep enough reserves on hand to pay off all depositors, even a financially healthy bank can run out of cash during a panic and be forced to close. The Federal Reserve failed to contain banking panics during the Great Depression, which led to sharp declines in the money supply. The adoption of a system of *deposit insurance* in the United States eliminated banking panics. A disadvantage of deposit insurance is that if banks or other insured intermediaries make bad loans or financial investments, the taxpayers may be responsible for covering the losses.

■ KEY TERMS ■

bank reserves (619)
banking panic (628)
barter (616)
Board of Governors of the Federal
  Reserve System (625)
bond (609)
coupon payments (609)
coupon rate (609)
deposit insurance (629)
discount rate (627)
discount window lending (627)
diversification (614)

dividend (611)
Federal Open Market Committee
  (FOMC) (625)
Federal Reserve System (the Fed)
  (624)
financial intermediaries (607)
fractional-reserve banking system
  (620)
M1 (618)
M2 (618)
medium of exchange (616)
money (616)

mutual fund (615)
100 percent reserve banking (620)
open-market operations (626)
open-market purchase (626)
open-market sale (626)
principal amount (609)
reserve-deposit ratio (620)
reserve requirements (627)
risk premium (613)
stock (equity) (611)
store of value (617)
unit of account (617)

■ REVIEW QUESTIONS ■

1. Give two ways that the financial system helps to improve the allocation of savings. Illustrate with examples.

2. Arjay plans to sell a bond that matures in 1 year and has a principal value of $1,000. Can he expect to receive $1,000 in the bond market for the bond? Explain.

3. Suppose you are much less concerned about risk than the typical person. Are stocks a good financial investment for you? Why or why not?

4. Stock prices surge but the prices of government bonds remain stable. What can you infer from the behavior of bond prices about the possible causes of the increase in stock values?

5. What is *money?* Why do people hold money even though it pays a lower return than other financial assets?

6. Suppose that the public switches from doing most of its shopping with currency to using checks instead. If the Fed takes no action, what will happen to the national money supply? Explain.

7. The Fed wants to reduce the U.S. money supply. Describe the various actions it might take, and explain how each action would accomplish the Fed's objective.

8. What is a *banking panic?* Prior to the introduction of deposit insurance, why might even a bank that had made sound loans have reason to fear a panic?

▪ PROBLEMS ▪

---

1. Simon purchases a bond, newly issued by the Amalgamated Corporation, for $1,000. The bond pays $60 to its holder at the end of the first and second years and pays $1,060 upon its maturity at the end of the third year.
    a. What are the principal amount, the term, the coupon rate, and the coupon payment for Simon's bond?
    b. After receiving the second coupon payment (at the end of the second year), Simon decides to sell his bond in the bond market. What price can he expect for his bond if the 1-year interest rate at that time is 3 percent? 8 percent? 10 percent?
    c. Can you think of a reason that the price of Simon's bond after 2 years might fall below $1,000, even though the market interest rate equals the coupon rate?

2. Shares in Brothers Grimm, Inc., manufacturers of gingerbread houses, are expected to pay a dividend of $5.00 in 1 year and to sell for $100 per share at that time. How much should you be willing to pay today per share of Grimm:
    a. If the safe rate of interest is 5 percent and you believe that investing in Grimm carries no risk?
    b. If the safe rate of interest is 10 percent and you believe that investing in Grimm carries no risk?
    c. If the safe rate of interest is 5 percent but your risk premium is 3 percent?
    d. Repeat parts a to c, assuming that Grimm is not expected to pay a dividend but the expected price is unchanged.

3. Your financial investments consist of U.S. government bonds maturing in 10 years and shares in a start-up company doing research in pharmaceuticals. How would you expect the each of the following news items to affect the value of your assets? Explain.
    a. Interest rates on newly issued government bonds rise.
    b. Inflation is forecasted to be much lower than previously expected (*Hint:* Recall the Fisher effect from Chapter 18.) Assume for simplicity that this information does *not* affect your forecast of the dollar value of the pharmaceutical company's future dividends and stock price.
    In parts c to f, interest rates on newly issued government bonds are assumed to remain unchanged.
    c. Large swings in the stock market increase financial investors' concerns about market risk.
    d. The start-up company whose stock you own announces the development of a valuable new drug. However, the drug will not come to market for at least 5 years.
    e. The pharmaceutical company announces that it will not pay a dividend next year.
    f. The federal government announces a system of price controls on prescription drugs.

4. You have $1,000 to invest and are considering buying some combination of the shares of two companies, DonkeyInc and ElephantInc. Shares of DonkeyInc will pay a 10 percent return if the Democrats are elected, an event you believe to have a 40 percent probability; otherwise the shares pay a zero return. Shares of ElephantInc will pay 8 percent if the Republicans are elected (a 60 percent probability), zero otherwise. Either the Democrats or the Republicans will be elected.
    a. If your only concern is maximizing your average expected return, with no regard for risk, how should you invest your $1,000?
    b. What is your expected return if you invest $500 in each stock? (*Hint:* Consider what your return will be if the Democrats win and if the Republicans win, then weight each outcome by the probability that that event occurs.)
    c. The strategy of investing $500 in each stock does *not* give the highest possible average expected return. Why might you choose it anyway?
    d. Devise an investment strategy that guarantees at least a 4.4 percent return, no matter which party wins.
    e. Devise an investment strategy that is riskless, that is, one in which the return on your $1,000 does not depend at all on which party wins.

5. During World War II, an Allied soldier named Robert Radford spent several years in a large German prisoner-of-war camp. At times more than 50,000 prisoners were held in the camp, with some freedom to move about within the compound. Radford later wrote an account of his experiences. He described how an economy developed in the

camp, in which prisoners traded food, clothing, and other items. Services, such as barbering, were also exchanged. Lacking paper money, the prisoners began to use cigarettes (provided monthly by the Red Cross) as money. Prices were quoted, and payments made, using cigarettes.

    a. In Radford's POW camp, how did cigarettes fulfill the three functions of money?

    b. Why do you think the prisoners used cigarettes as money, as opposed to other items of value such as squares of chocolate or pairs of boots?

    c. Do you think a nonsmoking prisoner would have been willing to accept cigarettes in exchange for a good or service in Radford's camp? Why or why not?

6. Obtain recent data on *M*1, *M*2, and their components. (For an online source, see Table 23.1). By what percentage have the two monetary aggregates grown over the past year? Which components of the two aggregates have grown the most quickly?

7. Redo the example of Gorgonzola in the text (see Tables 23.2 to 23.6), assuming that (a) initially, the Gorgonzolan central bank puts 5,000,000 guilders into circulation, and (b) commercial banks desire to hold reserves of 20 percent of deposits. As in the text, assume that the public holds no currency. Show the consolidated balance sheets of Gorgonzolan commercial banks after the initial deposits (compare to Table 23.2), after one round of loans (compare to Table 23.3), after the first redeposit of guilders (compare to Table 23.4), and after two rounds of loans and redeposits (Table 23.5). What are the final values of bank reserves, loans, deposits, and the money supply?

8. a. Bank reserves are 100, the public holds 200 in currency, and the desired reserve-deposit ratio is 0.25. Find deposits and the money supply.

    b. The money supply is 500, and currency held by the public equals bank reserves. The desired reserve-deposit ratio is 0.25. Find currency held by the public and bank reserves.

    c. The money supply is 1,250, of which 250 is currency held by the public. Bank reserves are 100. Find the desired reserve-deposit ratio.

9. When a central bank increases bank reserves by $1, the money supply rises by more than $1. The amount of extra money created when the central bank increases bank reserves by $1 is called the *money multiplier.*

    a. Explain why the money multiplier is generally greater than 1. In what special case would it equal 1?

    b. The initial money supply is $1,000, of which $500 is currency held by the public. The desired reserve-deposit ratio is 0.2. Find the increase in money supply associated with increases in bank reserves of $1, $5, and $10. What is the money multiplier in this economy?

    c. Find a general rule for calculating the money multiplier.

    d. Suppose the Fed wanted to reduce the money multiplier, perhaps because it believes that change would give it more precise control over the money supply. What action could the Fed take to achieve its goal?

10. Refer to Table 23.7. Suppose that the Fed had decided to set the U.S. money supply in December 1932 and in December 1933 at the same value as in December 1930. Assuming that the values of currency held by the public and the reserve-deposit ratio had remained as given in the table, by how much more should the Fed have increased bank reserves at each of those dates to accomplish that objective?

▪ ANSWERS TO IN-CHAPTER EXERCISES ▪

23.1 Since bond prices fell, interest rates must have risen. To find the interest rate, note that bond investors are willing to pay only 96 today for a bond that will pay back 107 (a coupon payment of 7 plus the principal amount of 100) in 1 year. To find the 1-year return, divide 107 by 96 to get 1.115. Thus the interest rate must have risen to 11.5 percent.

23.2 The share of stock will be worth $81.00 in 1 year—the sum of its expected future price and the expected dividend. At an interest rate of 4 percent, its value today is $81.00/1.04 =$77.88. At an interest rate of 8 percent, the stock's current value is $81.00/1.08 = $75.00. Recall from Example 23.2 that when the interest rate is 6 percent, the value of a share of FortuneCookie.com is $76.42. Since higher interest rates imply lower stock values, news that interest rates are about to rise should cause the stock market to fall.

23.3 Table 23.5 shows the balance sheet of banks after two rounds of lending and rede-posits. At that point deposits are 2,710,000 guilders and reserves are 1,000,000 guilders. Since banks have a desired reserve-deposit ratio of 10 percent, they will keep 271,000 guilders (10 percent of deposits) as reserves and lend out the remain-ing 729,000 guilders. Loans to farmers are now 2,439,000 guilders. Eventually the 729,000 guilders lent to the farmers will be redeposited into the banks, giving the banks deposits of 3,439,000 guilders and reserves of 1,000,000 guilders. The bal-ance sheet is as shown in the accompanying table.

Assets		Liabilities	
Currency (= reserves)	1,000,000 guilders	Deposits	3,439,000 guilders
Loans to farmers	2,439,000 guilders		

Notice that assets equal liabilities. The money supply equals deposits, or 3,439,000 guilders. Currency held in the banks as reserves does not count in the money supply.

23.4 Because the public holds no currency, the money supply equals bank deposits, which in turn equal bank reserves divided by the reserve-deposit ratio (Equation 23.1). If bank reserves are 1,000,000 and the reserve-deposit ratio is 0.05, then deposits equal 1,000,000/0.05 = 20,000,000 guilders, which is also the money supply. If bank reserves are 2,000,000 guilders and the reserve-deposit ratio is 0.10, then the money supply and deposits are again equal to 20,000,000 guilders, or 2,000,000/0.10.

23.5 If the central bank sells 50 shekels of government bonds in exchange for currency, the immediate effect is to reduce the amount of currency in the hands of the pub-lic by 50 shekels. To restore their currency holding to the desired level of 1,000 shekels, the public will withdraw 50 shekels from commercial banks, reducing bank reserves from 200 shekels to 150 shekels. The desired reserve-deposit ratio is 0.2, so ultimately deposits must equal 150 shekels in reserves divided by 0.2, or 750 shekels. (Note that to contract deposits, the commercial banks will have to "call in" loans, reducing their loans outstanding.) The money supply equals 1,000 shekels in currency held by the public plus 750 shekels in deposits, or 1,750 shekels. Thus the open-market purchase has reduced the money supply from 2,000 to 1,750 shekels.

23.6 Verify directly for each date in Table 23.7 that

$$\text{Money supply} = \text{Currency} + \frac{\text{Bank reserves}}{\text{Desired reserve-deposit ratio}}$$

For example, for December 1929 we can check that 45.9 = 3.85 + 3.15/0.075.

Suppose that the currency held by the public in December 1933 had been 3.79, as in December 1930, rather than 4.85, and that the difference (4.85 − 3.79 = 1.06) had been left in the banks. Then bank reserves in December 1933 would have been 3.45 + 1.06 = 4.51, and the money supply would have been 3.79 + 4.51/0.133 = 37.7. So the money supply would still have fallen between 1930 and 1933 if peo-ple had not increased their holdings of currency, but only by about half as much.

23.7 Over the course of 1931, currency holdings by the public rose by $0.80 billion but bank reserves fell overall by only $0.20 billion. Thus the Fed must have replaced $0.60 billion of lost reserves during the year through open-market purchases or dis-count window lending.

Currency holdings at the end of 1931 were $4.59 billion. To have kept the money supply at the December 1930 value of $44.1 billion, the Fed would have had to ensure that bank deposits equaled $44.1 billion − $4.59 billion, or $39.51 billion. As the reserve-deposit ratio in 1931 was 0.095, this would have required bank reserves of 0.095 × $39.51 billion, or $3.75 billion, compared to the actual value in December 1931 of $3.11 billion. Thus, to keep the money supply from falling, the Fed would have had to increase bank reserves by $0.64 billion more than it did. The Fed has been criticized for increasing bank reserves by only about half what was needed to keep the money supply from falling.

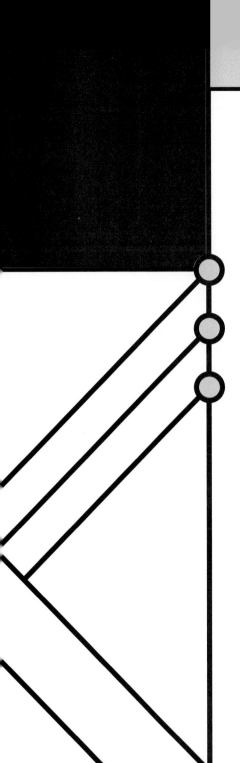

7

THE ECONOMY
IN THE SHORT RUN

■

A sign in Redwood City, California, boasts that the Bay Area town has the world's best climate. Redwood City's mean annual temperature and rainfall are similar to that of many other U.S. cities, so on what basis do Redwood City's boosters make their claim? The weather in Redwood City is attractive to many people because it varies so little over the year, being almost equally comfortable and temperate in winter and in summer. A city with the same average yearly temperature as Redwood City, but where the winters are freezing and the summers unbearably hot, would not be nearly so pleasant a place to live.

An analogous idea applies to the performance of the economy. As we saw, over a period of decades or more, the economy's average rate of growth is the crucial determinant of average living standards. But short-term fluctuations of the economy's growth rate around its long-run average matter for economic welfare as well. In particular, periods of slow or negative economic growth, known as *recessions,* may create significant economic hardship and dissatisfaction. In Part 7 we will explore the causes of short-term fluctuations in key economic variables, including output, unemployment, and inflation, and we will discuss the options available to government policymakers for stabilizing the economy.

Chapter 24 provides some necessary background for our study of short-term fluctuations by describing their key characteristics and reviewing the historical record of fluctuations in the U.S. economy. In Chapters 25 through 27 we develop a framework for the analysis of short-term fluctuations and the alternative policy responses. Chapter 25 shows how fluctuations in spending, or *aggregate demand,* may lead to short-run fluctuations in output and employment. That chapter also explains how changes in fiscal policy—policies relating to government spending and taxation—can be used to stabilize spending and output. Chapter 26 focuses on monetary policy, a second tool for stabilizing output and employment. Finally, Chapter 27 incorporates inflation into the analysis discussing both the sources of inflation and the policies that can be used to control it.

CHAPTER

24

SHORT-TERM ECONOMIC FLUCTUATIONS: AN INTRODUCTION

■

I n early 1991, following the defeat of Iraq in the Gulf War by the United States and its allies, polls showed that 90 percent of the American public approved of the job George Bush was doing as president. The Gulf War victory followed a number of other foreign policy successes for the Bush administration, including the ouster of the corrupt leader General Manuel Noriega from Panama in December 1989, the electoral defeat of the leftist Sandinistas in Nicaragua in 1990, improved relations with China, progress in Middle East peace talks, and the end of apartheid in South Africa. The collapse of the Soviet Union in December 1991—a stunning event that signaled the end of the Cold War—also occurred during Bush's term. Yet despite these politically popular developments, in the months following the Gulf War, Bush's sky-high approval rating declined sharply. According to one poll, by the time of the Republican national convention in 1992, only 29 percent of the public approved of Bush's performance. Although the President's ratings improved during the campaign, Bush and his running mate, Dan Quayle, lost the 1992 general election to Bill Clinton and Al Gore, receiving only 39 million of the 104 million votes cast. A third-party candidate, Ross Perot, received nearly 20 million votes.

What caused this turnaround in President Bush's political fortunes? Despite his foreign policy successes, the President's domestic economic policies were widely viewed as ineffective. Bush received much criticism for breaking his campaign pledge not to raise taxes. More important, the economy weakened significantly in 1990–1991, then recovered only slowly. Although inflation was low, by mid-1992 unemployment had reached 7.8 percent of the labor force—2.5 percent higher than in the first year of Bush's term and the highest level since 1984. As suggested by a sign in Bill Clinton's 1992 campaign headquarters, "It's the economy, stupid," Clinton realized the importance of the nation's economic problems and pounded away at the Republican administration's inability to pull the country out of the doldrums. Clinton's focus on the economy, including his proposals for tax cuts and health care reform, was the key to his election.

Clinton's ability to parlay criticism of economic conditions into electoral success is not unusual in U.S. political history. Weakness in the economy played a decisive role in helping Franklin D. Roosevelt to beat Herbert Hoover in 1932, John F. Kennedy to best Richard Nixon in 1960, and Ronald Reagan to defeat Jimmy Carter in 1980. Strong economic conditions have helped incumbents (or the incumbent's party) to retain office, including Nixon in 1972, Reagan in 1984, and Clinton in 1996. Indeed, a number of empirical studies have suggested that economic performance in the year preceding the election is among the most important determinants of whether an incumbent President is likely to win reelection.

In Part 6 we discussed the factors that determine long-run economic growth. Over the broad sweep of history, those factors determine how economically successful a society is, for as we saw in Chapter 20, over a span of 30, 50, or 100 years, small differences in the rate of economic growth can have an enormous effect on the average person's standard of living. But even though the economic "climate" (long-run economic conditions) is the ultimate determinant of living standards, changes in the economic "weather" (short-run fluctuations in economic conditions) are also important. A good long-run growth record is not much consolation to a worker who has lost her job due to a recession. The bearing that short-term macroeconomic performance has on election results is one indicator of the importance the average person attaches to it.

In this part of the book we study short-term fluctuations in economic activity, commonly known as *recessions* and *expansions*. We will start, in this chapter, with some background on the history and characteristics of these economic ups and downs. However, the main focus of this part is the *causes* of short-term fluctuations, as well as the available *policy responses*. Because the analysis of short-term economic fluctuations can become complex and even controversial, we will proceed in a step-by-step fashion. In Chapter 25 we will introduce a basic, and oversimplified, model of booms and recessions, which we will refer to as the *basic Keynesian model* in honor of its principal originator, the British economist John Maynard Keynes. The basic Keynesian model focuses on the components of aggregate spending, such as consumption spending by households and investment spending by firms, and the effects of changes in spending on total real GDP.

Though this model is a useful starting point, it leaves out important features of the economy. First, the basic Keynesian model says nothing about the determinants of inflation. Second, because it focuses on the very short run, this model does not give adequate attention to the economy's natural tendency to eliminate deviations from full employment over the longer run. Because the basic Keynesian model does not take into account the "self-correcting" tendencies of the economy, it tends to overstate the need for government intervention. In Chapters 26 and 27 we will add new features to the model to make it more realistic. The objective of Part 7 is to convey the major causes of short-term economic fluctuations as well as the options policymakers have in responding to them.

Hoover
© Bettmann/Corbis

Carter
© Bettmann/Corbis

Bush
© Wally McNamee/Corbis

Victims of recession.

RECESSIONS AND EXPANSIONS

As background to the study of short-term economic fluctuations, let's review the historic record of the fluctuations in the U.S. economy. Figure 24.1 shows the path of real GDP in the United States since 1920. (Figure 17.1 provided an even longer data series.) As you can see, the growth path of real GDP is not always smooth; the bumps and wiggles correspond to short periods of faster or slower growth.

A period in which the economy is growing at a rate significantly below normal is called a **recession,** or a *contraction*. An extremely severe or protracted recession is called a **depression.** You should be able to pick out the Great Depression in Figure 24.1, particularly the sharp initial decline between 1929 and 1933. But you can also see that the U.S. economy was volatile in the mid-1970s and the early 1980s, with serious recessions in 1973–1975 and 1981–1982. A moderate recession (but not moderate enough for George Bush) occurred in 1990–1991.

recession (or contraction) a period in which the economy is growing at a rate significantly below normal

depression a particularly severe or protracted recession

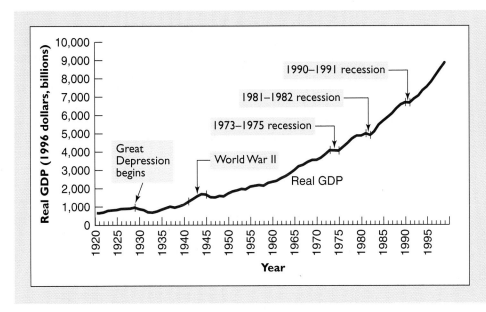

FIGURE 24.1
Fluctuations in U.S. Real GDP, 1920–1999.
Real GDP does not grow smoothly but has speedups (expansions or booms) and slowdowns (recessions or depressions). Note the contraction from 1929 to 1933 (the first phase of the Great Depression), the boom in 1941–1945 (World War II), and the recessions of 1973–1975, 1981–1982, and 1990–1991.

"Please stand by for a series of tones. The first indicates the official end of the recession, the second indicates prosperity, and the third the return of the recession."

A more informal definition of a recession, one that is often cited by the media, is a period during which real GDP falls for at least two consecutive quarters. This definition is not a bad rule of thumb, as real GDP usually does fall during recessions. However, many economists would argue that periods in which real GDP growth is well below normal, though not actually negative, should be counted as recessions. The "two-consecutive-quarters" rule does not classify such slow-growth episodes as recessions.

Table 24.1 lists the beginning and ending dates of U.S. recessions since 1929, as well as the *duration* (length, in months) of each. The table also gives the highest unemployment rate recorded during each recession and the percentage change in real GDP. (Ignore the last column of the table for now.) The beginning of a recession is called the **peak,** because it represents the high point of economic activity prior to a downturn. The end of a recession, which marks the low point of economic activity prior to a recovery, is called the **trough.** The dates of peaks and troughs reported in Table 24.1 were determined by the National Bureau of Economic Research (NBER), a nonprofit organization of economists that has been a major source of research on short-term economic fluctuations since its founding in 1920.

Table 24.1 shows that since 1929, by far the longest and most severe recession in the United States was the 43-month economic collapse that began in August 1929 and lasted until March 1933, initiating what became known as the Great Depression. Between 1933 and 1937 the economy grew fairly rapidly, so technically the period was not a recession, although unemployment remained very high at close to 20 percent of the workforce. In 1937–1938 the nation was hit by another significant recession. Full economic recovery from the Depression did not come until U.S. entry into World War II at the end of 1941. The economy boomed from 1941 to 1945 (see Figure 24.1), reflecting the enormous wartime production of military equipment and supplies.

In sharp contrast to the 1930s, U.S. recessions since World War II have generally been short—between 6 and 16 months, from peak to trough. As Table

peak the beginning of a recession, the high point of economic activity prior to a downturn

trough the end of a recession, the low point of economic activity prior to a recovery

TABLE 24.1
U.S. Recessions since 1929

Peak date (beginning)	Trough date (end)	Duration (months)	Highest unemployment rate (%)	% change in real GDP	Duration of subsequent expansion (months)
Aug. 1929	Mar. 1933	43	24.9	−28.8	50
May 1937	June 1938	13	19.0	−5.5	80
Feb. 1945	Oct. 1945	8	3.9	−8.5	37
Nov. 1948	Oct. 1949	11	5.9	−1.4	45
July 1953	May 1954	10	5.5	−1.2	39
Aug. 1957	Apr. 1958	8	6.8	−1.7	24
Apr. 1960	Feb. 1961	10	6.7	2.3	106
Dec. 1969	Nov. 1970	11	5.9	0.1	36
Nov. 1973	Mar. 1975	16	8.5	−1.1	58
Jan. 1980	July 1980	6	7.6	−0.3	12
July 1981	Nov. 1982	16	9.7	−2.1	92
July 1990	Mar. 1991	8	7.5	−0.9	>106

NOTES: Peak and trough dates from the National Bureau of Economic Research. Unemployment and real GDP data from *Historical Statistics of the United States* and the *Economic Report of the President.* Unemployment rate is the annual rate for the trough year or the subsequent year, whichever is higher. Change in annual real GDP is measured from the peak year to the trough year, except that the entry for the 1945 recession is the 1945–1946 change in real GDP and the entry for the 1980 recession is the 1979–1980 change.

24.1 shows, the two most severe postwar recessions, 1973–1975 and 1981–1982, lasted just 16 months. Although unemployment rates during these recessions were high by today's standards, they were low compared to the Great Depression. As of this writing, the U.S. economy has been relatively recession-free since 1982, with only one 8-month recession (in 1990–1991). While this record might tempt you to conclude that recessions are a thing of the past, history suggests that such a conclusion would be premature. Indeed, many commentators made the same claim during the long expansion of the 1960s, only to see the economy go into a moderate decline in 1969 and a deep downturn in 1973. Recently, other industrialized countries, such as Japan, have experienced severe recessions.

The opposite of a recession is an **expansion,** a period in which the economy is growing at a rate that is significantly *above* normal. A particularly strong and protracted expansion is called a **boom.** In the United States, strong expansions occurred during 1933–1937, 1961–1969, 1982–1990, and most of the 1990s (see Figure 24.1). On average, expansions have been much longer than recessions. The final column of Table 24.1 shows the duration, in months, of U.S. expansions since 1929. As you can see in the table, the 1961–1969 expansion lasted 106 months; the 1982–1990 expansion, 92 months. The longest expansion of all began in March 1991, at the trough of the 1990–1991 recession. In February 2000 this boom broke the all-time record for the duration of a U.S. economic expansion, 107 months, or nearly 9 years.

expansion a period in which the economy is growing at a rate significantly above normal

boom a particularly strong and protracted expansion

EXERCISE 24.1

Update Table 24.1 using the National Bureau of Economic Research web site (go to www.nber.org and click on *recession dates*). Is the U.S. economy currently in recession or expansion? How much time has elapsed since the last peak or trough?

CHARACTERISTICS OF SHORT-TERM FLUCTUATIONS

Although Figure 24.1 and Table 24.1 show only twentieth-century data, periods of expansion and recession have been a feature of industrial economies since at least the late eighteenth century. Karl Marx and Friedrich Engels referred to these fluctuations, which they called "commercial crises," in their Communist Manifesto (1848). In the United States, economists have been studying short-term fluctuations for at least a century. The traditional term for these fluctuations is *business cycles,* and they are still often referred to as *cyclical fluctuations.* Neither term is very accurate though, since as Figure 24.1 shows, economic fluctuations are not "cyclical" at all in the sense that they recur at predictable intervals but instead are quite *irregular in their length and severity.* This irregularity makes the dates of peaks and troughs extremely hard to predict, despite the fact that professional forecasters have devoted a great deal of effort and brainpower to the task.

Expansions and recessions usually are not limited to a few industries or regions but are *felt throughout the economy.* Indeed, the largest fluctuations may have a global impact. For instance, the Great Depression of the 1930s affected nearly all the world's economies, and the 1973–1975 and 1981–1982 recessions were also widely felt outside the United States. When East Asia suffered a major slowdown in the late 1990s, the effects of that slowdown spilled over into many other regions (although not so much in the United States).

Unemployment is a key indicator of short-term economic fluctuations. The unemployment rate typically rises sharply during recessions and recovers (although

Recessions are very difficult to forecast.

more slowly) during expansions. Figure 18.3 showed the U.S. unemployment rate since 1960. You should be able to identify the recessions that began in 1960, 1969, 1973, 1981, and 1990 by noting the sharp peaks in the unemployment rate in those years. Recall from Chapter 21 that the part of unemployment that is associated with recessions is called *cyclical unemployment*. Beyond this increase in unemployment, labor market conditions become less favorable to workers during recessions. For example, real wages grow more slowly or even decline, and workers are less likely to receive promotions or bonuses during a recession than during expansionary periods.

FIGURE 24.2
U.S. Inflation, 1960–1999.
U.S. inflation since 1960 is measured by the change in the CPI, and periods of recession are indicated by the blue bars. Note that inflation declined after the recessions of 1960–1961, 1969–1970, 1973–1975, 1981–1982, and 1990–1991 and rose prior to many of those recessions.

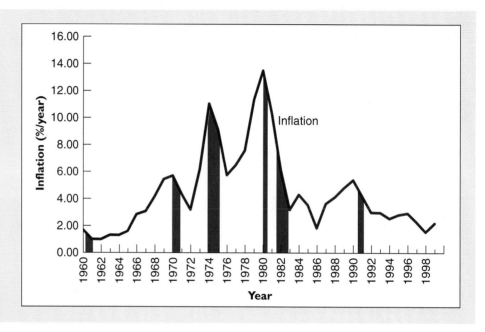

Like unemployment, *inflation* follows a typical pattern in recessions and expansions, though it is not so sharply defined. Figure 24.2 shows the U.S. inflation rate since 1960; in the figure, periods of recession are indicated by blue bars. As you can see, recessions tend to be followed soon after by a decline in the rate of inflation. For example, the recessions of 1980 and 1981–1982 were followed by a sharp reduction in inflation. Furthermore, many—though not all—postwar recessions have been preceded by increases in inflation, as Figure 24.2 shows. The behavior of inflation during expansions and recessions will be discussed more fully in Chapter 27.

Generally, industries that produce *durable goods*, such as cars, houses, and capital equipment, are more affected than others by recessions and booms. In contrast, industries that provide *services* and *nondurable goods* like food are much less sensitive to short-term fluctuations. Thus an automobile worker or a construction worker is far more likely to lose his or her job in a recession than a barber or a baker.

Unemployment among construction workers rises substantially during recessions.

RECAP   **CHARACTERISTICS OF SHORT-TERM FLUCTUATIONS**

■ Short-term economic fluctuations are irregular in length and severity and thus are difficult to predict.

■ Expansions and recessions have widespread (and sometimes global) impacts, affecting most regions and industries.

■ Unemployment rises sharply during a recession and falls, usually more slowly, during an expansion.

■ Recessions tend to be followed by a decline in inflation and are often preceded by an increase in inflation.

■ Durable goods industries are more affected by expansions and recessions than other industries. Services and nondurable goods industries are less sensitive to ups and downs in the economy.

MEASURING FLUCTUATIONS: OUTPUT GAPS AND CYCLICAL UNEMPLOYMENT

If policymakers are to respond appropriately to recessions and expansions, and economists are to study them, knowing whether a particular economic fluctuation is "big" or "small" is essential. Intuitively, a "big" recession or expansion is one in which output and the unemployment rate deviate significantly from their normal or trend levels. In this section we will attempt to be more precise about this idea, in preparation for our analysis of the causes and cures of short-run fluctuations. Specifically, we will introduce the concept of the *output gap,* which measures how far output is from its normal level at a particular time, and we will revisit the idea of *cyclical unemployment,* or the deviation of unemployment from its normal level. Finally, we will examine how these two concepts are related.

POTENTIAL OUTPUT AND THE OUTPUT GAP

The concept of *potential output* is a useful starting point for thinking about the measurement of expansions and recessions. **Potential output,** also called *potential GDP* or *full-employment output,* is the amount of output (real GDP) that an economy can produce when using its resources, such as capital and labor, at normal rates. Potential output is not a fixed number but grows over time, reflecting increases in both the amounts of available capital and labor and their productivity. We discussed the sources of growth in potential output (the economy's productive capacity) at some length in Chapter 20. We will use the symbol Y^* to signify the economy's potential output at a given point in time.

A recession, as we have seen, is a period in which the economy is growing significantly below its normal rate. What causes this slow growth? Logically, there are two possibilities. First, a recession could be a period in which actual output equals potential output, but potential output itself is growing very slowly. Severe soil erosion, for example, would reduce the rate of growth in an agricultural economy, and a decline in the rate of technological innovation might reduce the rate of potential output growth in an industrial economy. Similarly, new technologies, increased capital investment, or a surge in immigration that swells the labor force could produce unusually brisk growth in potential output, and hence an economic boom.

Undoubtedly, changes in the rate of growth of potential output are part of the explanation for expansions and recessions. In the United States, for example, the sustained boom of the 1990s was propelled in part by new information technologies, such as the Internet. And the slowdown in Japan during the same period reflected, in part, slower growth in potential output (see Economic Naturalist 24.1). When changes in the rate of GDP growth reflect changes in the growth rate of potential output, the appropriate policy responses are those discussed in Chapter 20. In particular, when a recession results from slowing growth in potential output, the government's best response is to try to promote saving, investment, technological innovation, human capital formation, and other activities that support growth.

A second possible explanation for short-term economic fluctuations is that *actual output does not always equal potential output.* For example, potential

potential output (or potential GDP or full-employment output) the amount of output (real GDP) that an economy can produce when using its resources, such as capital and labor, at normal rates

output may be growing normally, but for some reason the economy's capital and labor resources may not be fully utilized, so actual output falls below potential output (a recession). Alternatively, capital and labor may be working harder than usual, so actual output expands beyond potential output (a boom). In either of these scenarios, policymakers face a new problem, which is how to return actual output to potential. In the next three chapters we will discuss policies for *stabilizing* the economy, that is, bringing actual output into line with potential output.

At any point in time, the difference between potential output and actual output is called the **output gap.** Recalling that Y^* is the symbol for potential output and that Y stands for actual output (real GDP), we can express the output gap as $Y^* - Y$. A positive output gap—when actual output is below potential and resources are not being fully utilized—is called a **recessionary gap.** A negative output gap—when actual output is above potential and resources are being utilized at above-normal rates—is referred to as an **expansionary gap.**

How do output gaps arise? Why doesn't the economy always produce at its potential? Is there anything policymakers can do about output gaps? These are fundamental questions we will return to frequently in subsequent chapters.

output gap (or $Y^* - Y$) the difference between the economy's potential output and its actual output at a point in time

recessionary gap a positive output gap, which occurs when potential output exceeds actual output

expansionary gap a negative output gap, which occurs when actual output is higher than potential output

"Ed, this is Art Simbley over at Hollis, Bingham, Cotter & Krone. What did you get for thirty-four across, 'Persian fairy,' four letters?"

ECONOMIC NATURALIST 24.1

The Japanese slump of the 1990s

As we noted in Chapter 20, the Japanese economy has enjoyed a remarkable record of long-term growth. During the 1960s Japanese real GDP grew at the stunning rate of 10.2 percent per year. Growth was slower in the 1970s (4.6 percent per year) and 1980s (3.8 percent per year) but still well above the rates in other industrial countries. During the 1990s, however, the Japanese economy slowed markedly, averaging only 1.5 percent growth in real GDP per year and less than 1 percent real GDP growth per year from 1992 to the end of the decade. What underlay the Japanese economic slump of the 1990s?

A first step in explaining this slowdown—and in finding policies to address it—is to determine how much of the slump reflected slower growth in the Japanese economy's normal productive capacity (its potential GDP) and how much reflected under-utilization of that productive capacity (an output gap). The International Monetary Fund

(IMF), an international agency that has as one of its functions the monitoring of world economic conditions, prepares estimates of potential output and output gaps for the major industrial countries. Figure 24.3 shows the IMF's estimates of Japan's actual and

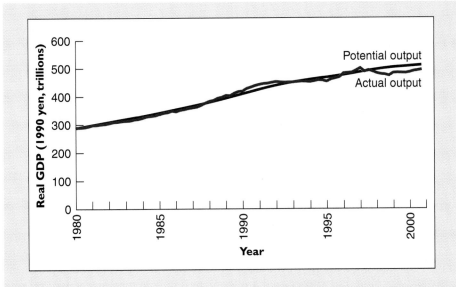

FIGURE 24.3
Actual and Potential Output in Japan, 1980–2000.
The vertical distance between potential GDP (red line) and actual real GDP (blue line) represents Japan's output gap in the last two decades of the twentieth century. Japan experienced a significant recessionary gap in the 1990s, with real GDP falling more than 4 percent below potential by the end of the decade. Growth in potential output also slowed in the 1990s. (SOURCE: International Monetary Fund.)

potential GDP for the period 1980–2000. Because calculating potential GDP requires estimates of both the normal utilization rates of capital and labor and the underlying trend in productivity, in practice, these estimates are subject to error. But if we take the IMF's estimates at face value, Figure 24.3 suggests that the Japanese economic slump resulted from *both* slower growth in potential output and a significant output gap.

The red line in the figure shows that growth in potential GDP slowed significantly in the 1990s, falling from 3.6 percent per year in the 1980s to 2.2 percent per year in the 1990s. According to the IMF, slower growth in Japan's capital stock (due to reduced rates of investment), its labor force (due to slow population growth), and its productivity all contributed to this decline in the growth of potential GDP. But though growth in potential output slipped to 2.2 percent per year in the 1990s, it cannot account for the entire decline in actual output growth, which as we noted was only 1.5 percent per year during that decade. Indeed, as Figure 24.3 shows, a growing output gap played a major role in the slump. At the beginning of 1990, Japan had an expansionary gap of 2.4 percent (that is, actual output was 2.4 percent greater than potential). Throughout much of the decade, however, actual output was below potential. According to IMF estimates, at the end of 1999 actual output was 4.3 percent below potential—a highly significant output gap.

We conclude that the Japanese economic slump of the 1990s reflected *both* a slowdown in the growth of potential output and a significant underutilization of existing resources (an output gap). To restore growth, then, Japanese policymakers must address two separate problems: first, how to reinvigorate Japan's rate of long-term economic growth, and second, how to end the recession that has sunk Japanese GDP well below potential.

THE NATURAL RATE OF UNEMPLOYMENT AND CYCLICAL UNEMPLOYMENT

Whether recessions arise because of slower growth in potential output or because actual output falls below potential, they bring bad times. In either case output falls (or at least grows more slowly), implying reduced living standards. Recessionary output gaps are particularly frustrating for policymakers, however, because they imply that the economy has the *capacity* to produce more but for some reason is not fully utilizing available resources. Recessionary gaps are *inefficient* in that they unnecessarily reduce the total economic "pie," making the typical person worse off.

An important indicator of the low utilization of resources during recessions is the unemployment rate. In general, a high unemployment rate means that labor resources are not being fully utilized, so output has fallen below potential (a recessionary gap). By the same logic, an unusually low unemployment rate implies that labor is being utilized at a rate greater than normal, so actual output exceeds potential output (an expansionary gap).

To better understand the relationship between the output gap and unemployment, recall from Chapter 21 the three broad types of unemployment: frictional, structural, and cyclical. *Frictional unemployment* is the short-term unemployment that is associated with the matching of workers and jobs. *Structural unemployment* is the long-term and chronic unemployment that occurs even when the economy is producing at its normal rate. *Cyclical unemployment* is the extra unemployment that occurs during periods of recession. Unlike cyclical unemployment, which is present only during recessions, frictional unemployment and structural unemployment are always present in the labor market, even when the economy is operating normally. Economists call the part of the total unemployment rate that is attributable to frictional and structural unemployment the **natural rate of unemployment**. Put another way, the natural rate of unemployment is the unemployment rate that prevails when cyclical unemployment is zero, so the economy has neither a recessionary nor an expansionary output gap. We will denote the natural rate of unemployment as u^*.

Cyclical unemployment, which is the difference between the total unemployment rate and the natural rate, can thus be expressed as $u - u^*$, where u is the actual unemployment rate and u^* denotes the natural rate of unemployment. In a recession, the actual unemployment rate u exceeds the natural unemployment rate u^*, so cyclical unemployment $u - u^*$ is positive. When the economy experiences an expansionary gap, in contrast, the actual unemployment rate is lower than the natural rate, so cyclical unemployment is negative. Negative cyclical unemployment corresponds to a situation in which labor is being used more intensively than normal, so actual unemployment has dipped below its usual frictional and structural levels.

natural rate of unemployment (or u*) the part of the total unemployment rate that is attributable to frictional and structural unemployment; equivalently, the unemployment rate that prevails when cyclical unemployment is zero, so the economy has neither a recessionary nor an expansionary output gap.

ECONOMIC NATURALIST 24.2

Why is the natural rate of unemployment so low in the United States today?

According to the Congressional Budget Office, which regularly estimates the natural rate of unemployment in the United States, the natural rate has fallen steadily since about 1979, from 6.3 percent of the labor force to about 5.2 percent.[1] Some economists, noting that unemployment remained close to 4 percent for several years around the turn of the millennium, have argued for an even lower natural rate, perhaps 4.5 percent or lower. Why is the U.S. natural rate of unemployment apparently so much lower today than it was 20 years ago?

The natural rate of unemployment may have fallen because of reduced frictional unemployment, reduced structural unemployment, or both. A variety of ideas has been advanced to explain declines in both types of unemployment. One promising suggestion is based on the changing age structure of the U.S. labor force.[2] The average age of U.S. workers is rising, reflecting the aging of the baby boomer generation. Indeed, over the past 20 years the share of the labor force aged 16 to 24 has fallen from about

---

[1]Congressional Budget Office, *Economic and Budget Outlook: Fiscal Years 2001–2010*, Table F-1, available online at www.cbo.gov/.

[2]See Robert Shimer, "Why Is the U.S. Unemployment Rate So Much Lower?" in B. Bernanke and J. Rotemberg, eds., *NBER Macroeconomics Annual*, 1998.

25 percent to about 16 percent. Since young workers are more prone to unemployment than older workers, the aging of the labor force may help to explain the overall decline in unemployment.

Why are young workers more likely to be unemployed? Compared to teenagers and workers in their twenties, older workers are much more likely to hold long-term, stable jobs. In contrast, younger workers tend to hold short-term jobs, perhaps because they are not ready to commit to a particular career, or because their time in the labor market is interrupted by schooling or military service. Because they change jobs more often, younger workers are more prone than others to frictional unemployment. They also have fewer skills, on average, than older workers, so they may experience more structural unemployment. As workers age and gain experience, however, their risk of unemployment declines.

Another possible explanation for the declining natural rate of unemployment is that labor markets have become more efficient at matching workers with jobs, thereby reducing both frictional and structural unemployment. For example, agencies that arrange temporary help have become much more commonplace in the United States in recent years. Although the placements these agencies make are intended to be temporary, they often become permanent when an employer and worker discover that a particularly good match has been made. Online job services, which allow workers to search for jobs nationally and even internationally, are also becoming increasingly important. By reducing the time people must spend in unemployment and by creating more lasting matches between workers and jobs, temporary help agencies, online job services, and similar innovations may have reduced the natural rate of unemployment.[3]

OKUN'S LAW

What is the relationship between an output gap and the amount of cyclical unemployment in the economy? We have already observed that by definition, cyclical unemployment is positive when the economy has a recessionary gap, negative when there is an expansionary gap, and zero when there is no output gap. A more quantitative relationship between cyclical unemployment and the output gap is given by a rule of thumb called *Okun's law*, after Arthur Okun, one of President Kennedy's chief economic advisers. According to **Okun's law**, each extra percentage point of cyclical unemployment is associated with about a 2 percentage point increase in the output gap, measured in relation to potential output.[4] So, for example, if cyclical unemployment increases from 1 to 2 percent of the labor force, the recessionary gap will increase from 2 to 4 percent of potential GDP. Example 24.1 illustrates further.

Okun's law states that each extra percentage point of cyclical unemployment is associated with about a 2 percentage point increase in the output gap, measured in relation to potential output

Okun's law and the output gap in the U.S. economy

EXAMPLE 24.1

Following are the actual unemployment rate, the natural unemployment rate (as estimated by the Congressional Budget Office), and potential real GDP, in billions of 1992 dollars (estimated by the IMF), for the U.S. economy in three selected years. Using Okun's law, estimate the output gap in each year, in billions of 1992 dollars.

Year	u	u^*	Y^*
1982	9.7%	6.1%	4,957
1991	6.8%	5.9%	6,286
1998	4.5%	5.6%	7,561

---

[3]For a detailed analysis of factors affecting the natural rate, see Lawrence Katz and Alan Krueger, "The High-Pressure U.S. Labor Market of the 1990s," *Brookings Papers on Economic Activity*, 1:1–88, 1999.

[4]This relationship between unemployment and output has weakened over time. When Arthur Okun first formulated his law in the 1960s, he suggested that each extra percentage point of unemployment was associated with about a 3 percentage point increase in the output gap.

In 1982 cyclical unemployment $u - u^*$ was 9.7% − 6.1%, or 3.6 percent of the labor force. According to Okun's law, the output gap for that year would be twice that percentage, or 7.2 percent of potential output. Since potential output in 1982 was $4,957 billion, the value of the output gap for that year in 1992 dollars would be 7.2 percent times $4,957 billion, or $357 billion.

In 1991 cyclical unemployment was 6.8% − 5.9%, or 0.9 percent of the labor force. According to Okun's law, the output gap for 1991 would be twice 0.9 percent, or 1.8 percent of potential GDP. Since potential GDP in 1991 was $6,286 billion, the output gap in that year should have been 1.8 percent of $6,286, or $113 billion.

Both 1982 and 1991 were recession years, so the output gaps were recessionary gaps. In contrast, 1998 was a year of expansion, in which unemployment was below the natural rate and the economy experienced an expansionary gap. Cyclical unemployment in 1998 was 4.5% − 5.6%, or *minus* 1.1 percent. The output gap in 1998 should therefore have been about −2.2 percent of the potential GDP of $7,561 billion, or −$166 billion. In other words, in 1998 real GDP was about $166 billion greater than potential GDP.

The output losses sustained in recessions, calculated according to Okun's law, are quite significant. In Example 24.1 we found the U.S. output gap in 1982 to be $357 billion, in 1992 dollars. The U.S. population in 1982 was about 230 million. Hence the output loss per person in that year equaled the total output gap of $357 billion divided by 230 million people, or about $1,550—more than $6,000 for a family of four. This calculation implies that output gaps and cyclical unemployment have significant costs—a conclusion that is consistent with the observation discussed in the introduction to this chapter that a recession can severely damage a president's prospects for reelection.

RECAP **OUTPUT GAPS, CYCLICAL UNEMPLOYMENT, AND OKUN'S LAW**

Potential output is the amount of output (real GDP) that an economy can produce when using its resources, such as capital and labor, at normal rates. The *output gap* $Y^* - Y$ is the difference between potential output Y^* and actual output Y. When actual output is below potential, the resulting output gap is called a *recessionary gap*. When actual output is above potential, the difference is called an *expansionary gap*.

The *natural rate of unemployment* u^* is the sum of the frictional and structural unemployment rates. It is the rate of unemployment that is observed when the economy is operating at a normal level, with no output gap.

Cyclical unemployment $u - u^*$ is the difference between the actual unemployment rate u and the natural rate of unemployment u^*. Cyclical unemployment is positive when there is a recessionary gap, negative when there is an expansionary gap, and zero when there is no output gap.

Okun's law relates cyclical unemployment and the output gap. According to this rule of thumb, each percentage point increase in cyclical unemployment is associated with about a 2 percentage point increase in the output gap, measured in relation to potential output.

WHY DO SHORT-TERM FLUCTUATIONS OCCUR? A PREVIEW AND A PARABLE

What causes periods of recession and expansion? In the previous section we discussed two possible reasons for slowdowns and speedups in real GDP growth. First, growth in potential output itself may slow down or speed up, reflecting changes in the growth rates of available capital and labor and in the pace of technological progress. Second, even if potential output is growing normally, actual output may be higher or lower than potential output; that is, expansionary or recessionary output gaps may develop. Earlier in this book we discussed some of the reasons that growth in potential output can vary and the options that policymakers have for stimulating growth in potential output. But we have not yet addressed the question of how output gaps can arise or what policymakers should do in response. The causes and cures of output gaps will be a major topic of the next three chapters. Here is a brief preview of the main conclusions of those chapters:

1. In a world in which prices adjusted immediately to balance the quantities supplied and demanded for all goods and services, output gaps would not exist. However, for many goods and services, the assumption that prices will adjust immediately is not realistic. Instead, many firms adjust the prices of their output only periodically. In particular, rather than changing prices with every variation in demand, firms tend to adjust to changes in demand in the short run by varying the quantity of output they produce and sell. This type of behavior is known as "meeting the demand" at a preset price.

2. Because in the short run firms tend to meet the demand for their output at preset prices, changes in the amount that customers decide to spend will affect output. When total spending is low for some reason, output may fall below potential output; conversely, when spending is high, output may rise above potential output. In other words, *changes in economywide spending are the primary cause of output gaps.* Thus, government policies can help to eliminate output gaps by influencing total spending. For example, the government can affect total spending directly simply by changing its own level of purchases.

3. Although firms tend to meet demand in the short run, they will not be willing to do so indefinitely. If customer demand continues to differ from potential output, firms will eventually adjust their prices so as to eliminate output gaps. If demand exceeds potential output (an expansionary gap), firms will raise their prices aggressively, spurring inflation. If demand falls below potential output (a recessionary gap), firms will raise their prices less aggressively or even cut prices, reducing inflation.

4. Over the longer run, price changes by firms eliminate any output gap and bring production back into line with the economy's potential output. Thus the economy is "self-correcting" in the sense that it operates to eliminate output gaps over time. Because of this self-correcting tendency, in the long run actual output equals potential output, so output is determined by the economy's productive capacity rather than by the rate of spending. In the long run, total spending influences only the rate of inflation.

These ideas will become clearer as we proceed through the next chapters. Before plunging into the details of the analysis, though, let's consider an example that illustrates the links between spending and output in the short and long run.

Al's ice cream store produces gourmet ice cream on the premises and sells it directly to the public. What determines the amount of ice cream that Al produces on a daily basis? The productive capacity, or potential output, of the shop is one important factor. Specifically, Al's potential output of ice cream depends on the amount of capital (number of ice cream makers) and labor (number of workers) that he employs and on the productivity of that capital and labor. Although Al's potential output usually changes rather slowly, on occasion it can fluctuate significantly—for example, if an ice cream maker breaks down or Al contracts the flu.

The main source of day-to-day variations in Al's ice cream production, however, is not changes in potential output but fluctuations in the demand for ice cream by the public. Some of these fluctuations in spending occur predictably over the course of the day (more demand in the afternoon than in the morning, for example), the week (more demand on weekends), or the year (more demand in the summer). Other changes in demand are less regular—more demand on a hot day than on a cool one, or when a parade is passing by the store. Some changes in demand are hard for Al to interpret: For example, a surge in demand for rocky road ice cream on one particular Tuesday could reflect a permanent change in consumer tastes, or it might just be a random, one-time event.

How should Al react to these ebbs and flows in the demand for ice cream? The basic supply and demand model that we introduced in Chapter 4, if applied to the market for ice cream, would predict that the price of ice cream should change with every change in the demand for ice cream. For example, prices should rise just after the movie theater next door to Al's shop lets out on Friday night, and should fall on unusually cold, blustery days, when most people would prefer a hot cider to an ice cream cone. Indeed, taken literally, the supply and demand model of Chapter 4 predicts that ice cream prices should change almost moment to moment. Imagine Al standing in front of his shop like an auctioneer, calling out prices in an effort to determine how many people are willing to buy at each price!

Of course, we do not expect to see this behavior by an ice cream storeowner. Price setting by auction does in fact occur in some markets, such as the market for grain or the stock market, but it is not the normal procedure in most retail markets, such as the market for ice cream. Why this difference? The basic reason is that sometimes the economic benefits of hiring an auctioneer and setting up an auction exceeds the costs of doing so, and sometimes they do not. In the market for grain, for example, many buyers and sellers gather together in the same place at the same time to transact large volumes of standardized goods (bushels of grain). In that kind of situation, an auction is an efficient way to determine prices and balance the quantities supplied and demanded. In an ice cream store, by contrast, customers come in by twos and threes at random times throughout the day. Some want shakes, some cones, and some sodas. With small numbers of customers and a low sales volume at any given time, the costs involved in selling ice cream by auction are much greater than the benefits of allowing prices to vary with demand.

So how does Al the ice cream store manager deal with changes in the demand for ice cream? Observation suggests that he begins by setting prices based on the best information he has about the demand for his product and the costs of production. Perhaps he prints up a menu or makes a sign announcing the prices. Then, over a period of time, he will keep his prices fixed and serve as many customers as want to buy (up to the point where he runs out of ice cream or room in the store at these prices). This behavior is what we call "meeting the demand" at preset prices, and it implies that *in the short run,* the amount of ice cream Al produces and sells is determined by the demand for his products.

However, *in the long run* the situation is quite different. Suppose, for example, that Al's ice cream earns a citywide reputation for its freshness and flavor. Day after day Al observes long lines in his store. His ice cream maker is overtaxed, as are his employees and his table space. There can no longer be any doubt that at current prices, the quantity of ice cream the public wants to consume exceeds what Al is able and willing to supply on a normal basis (his potential output). Expanding the store is an attractive possibility, but not one (we assume) that is immediately feasible. What will Al do?

Certainly one thing Al can do is raise his prices. At higher prices, Al will earn higher profits. Moreover, raising ice cream prices will bring the quantity of ice cream demanded closer to Al's normal production capacity—his potential output. Indeed, when the price of Al's ice cream finally rises to its equilibrium level, the shop's actual output will equal its potential output. Thus, over the long run, ice cream prices adjust to their equilibrium level, and the amount that is sold is determined by potential output.

This example illustrates in a simple way the links between spending and output—except, of course, that we must think of this story as applying to the whole economy, not to a single business. The key point is that there is an important difference between the short run and the long run. In the short run, producers often choose not to change their prices but rather to meet the demand at preset prices. Because output is determined by demand, in the short run total spending plays a central role in determining the level of economic activity. Thus, Al's ice cream store enjoys a boom on an unusually hot day, when the demand for ice cream is strong, while an unseasonably cold day brings an ice cream recession. But in the long run, prices adjust to their market-clearing levels, and output equals potential output. Thus, the quantities of inputs, and the productivity with which they are used, are the primary determinants of economic activity in the long run, as we saw in Chapter 20. Although total spending affects output in the short run, in the long run its main effects are on prices.

Why did the Coca-Cola Company test a vending machine that "knows" when the weather is hot?

ECONOMIC NATURALIST 24.3

According to *The New York Times* (Oct. 28, 1999, p. C-1), the Coca-Cola Company has quietly tested a soda vending machine that includes a temperature sensor. Why would Coca-Cola want a vending machine that "knows" when the weather is hot?

When the weather is hot, the demand for refreshing soft drinks rises, increasing their market-clearing price. To take advantage of this variation in consumer demand, the vending machines that Coca-Cola tested were equipped with a computer chip that gave them the capability to raise soda prices automatically when the temperature climbs. The company's chairman and chief executive, M. Douglas Ivester, described in an interview how the desire for a cold drink increases during a sports championship final held in the summer heat. "So it is fair that it should be more expensive," Mr. Ivester was quoted as saying. "The machine will simply make this process automatic." Company officials suggested numerous other ways in which vending machine prices could be made dependent on demand. For example, machines could be programmed to reduce prices during off-peak hours or at low-traffic machines.

In traditional vending machines, cold drinks are priced in a way analogous to the way Al prices his ice cream: A price is set, and demand is met at the preset price, until the machine runs out of soda. The weather-sensitive vending machine illustrates how technology may change pricing practices in the future. Indeed, increased computing power and access to the Internet have already allowed some firms, such as airline companies, to change prices almost continuously in response to variations in demand. Conceivably, the practice of meeting demand at a preset price may someday be obsolete.

On the other hand, Coca-Cola's experiments with "smart" vending machines also illustrate the barriers to fully flexible pricing in practice. First, the new vending machines are more costly than the standard model. In deciding whether to use them, the company must decide whether the extra profits from variable pricing justify the extra cost of the machines. Second, in early tests many consumers reacted negatively to the new machines, complaining that they take unfair advantage of thirsty customers. In practice, customer complaints and concerns about "fairness" make companies less willing to vary prices sensitively with changing demand.

■ SUMMARY ■

- Real GDP does not grow smoothly. Periods in which the economy is growing at a rate significantly below normal are called *recessions;* periods in which the economy is growing at a rate significantly above normal are called *expansions.* A severe or protracted recession, like the long decline that occurred between 1929 and 1933, is called a *depression,* while a particularly strong expansion is called a *boom.*

- The beginning of a recession is called the *peak,* because it represents the high point of economic activity prior to a downturn. The end of a recession, which marks the low point of economic activity prior to a recovery, is called the *trough.* Since World War II, U.S. recessions have been much shorter on average than booms, lasting between 6 and 16 months. The longest boom period in U.S. history began with the end of the 1990–1991 recession in March 1991.

- Short-term economic fluctuations are irregular in length and severity and are thus hard to forecast. Expansions and recessions are typically felt throughout the economy and may even be global in scope. Unemployment rises sharply during recessions (the phenomenon of cyclical unemployment), while inflation tends to fall during or shortly after a recession. Durable goods industries tend to be particularly sensitive to recessions and booms, while services and nondurable goods industries are less sensitive.

- *Potential output,* also called potential GDP or full-employment output, is the amount of output (real GDP) that an economy can produce when it is using its resources, such as capital and labor, at normal rates. The difference between potential output and actual output is the *output gap.* When output is below potential, the gap is called a *recessionary gap;* when output is above potential, the difference is called an *expansionary gap.* Recessions can occur either because potential output is growing unusually slowly or because actual output is below potential.

- The *natural rate of unemployment* is the part of the total unemployment rate that is attributable to frictional and structural unemployment. Equivalently, the natural rate of unemployment is the rate of unemployment that exists when the output gap is zero. Cyclical unemployment, the part of unemployment that is associated with recessions and expansions, equals the total unemployment rate less the natural unemployment rate. Cyclical unemployment is related to the output gap by *Okun's law,* which states that each extra percentage point of cyclical unemployment is associated with about a 2 percentage point increase in the output gap, measured in relation to potential output.

- In the next several chapters our study of recessions and expansions will focus on the role of economywide spending. If firms adjust prices only periodically, and in the meantime produce enough output to meet demand, then fluctuations in spending will lead to fluctuations in output over the short run. During that short-run period, government policies that influence aggregate spending may help to eliminate output gaps. In the long run, however, firms' price changes will eliminate output gaps—that is, the economy will "self-correct"—and total spending will influence only the rate of inflation.

■ KEY TERMS ■

---

boom (641)
depression (639)
expansion (641)
expansionary gap (644)
natural rate of unemployment (646)

Okun's law (647)
output gap (or $Y^* - Y$) (644)
peak (640)
potential output (or potential GDP or full-employment output) (643)

recession (or contraction) (639)
recessionary gap (644)
trough (640)

■ REVIEW QUESTIONS ■

---

1. Define *recession* and *expansion.* What are the beginning and ending points of a recession called? In the postwar United States, which have been longer on average, recessions or expansions?

2. Why is the traditional term *business cycles* a misnomer? How does your answer relate to the ease or difficulty of forecasting peaks and troughs?

3. Which firm is likely to see its profits reduced the most in a recession: an automobile producer, a manufacturer of boots and shoes, or a barbershop? Which is likely to see its profits reduced by the least? Explain.

4. How is each of the following likely to be affected by a recession: the natural unemployment rate, the cyclical unemployment rate, the inflation rate?

5. Define *potential output.* Is it possible for an economy to produce an amount greater than potential output? Explain.

6. True or false, and explain: All recessions are the result of output gaps.

7. True or false, and explain: When output equals potential output, the unemployment rate is zero.

8. If the natural rate of unemployment is 5 percent, what is the overall rate of unemployment if output is 2 percent below potential output? What if output is 2 percent above potential output?

▪ PROBLEMS ▪

---

1. Using Table 24.1, find the average duration, the minimum duration, and the maximum duration of expansions in the United States since 1929. Are expansions getting longer or shorter on average over time? Is there any tendency for long expansions to be followed by long recessions?

2. Given below are data on real GDP and potential GDP for the United States for the years 1988–1993, in billions of 1992 dollars. For each year calculate the output gap as a percentage of potential GDP, and state whether the gap is a recessionary gap or an expansionary gap. Also calculate the year-to-year growth rates of real GDP. Can you identify the recession that occurred during this period?

Year	Real GDP	Potential GDP
1988	5,844	5,788
1989	6,056	5,943
1990	6,172	6,102
1991	6,075	6,265
1992	6,214	6,432
1993	6,360	6,604

SOURCE: International Monetary Fund.

3. From the home page of the Bureau of Labor Statistics, stats.bls.gov/, obtain the most recent available data on the unemployment rate for workers aged 16–19 and workers aged 20 or over. How do they differ? What are some of the reasons for the difference? How does this difference relate to the decline in the overall natural rate of unemployment since 1980?

4. Using Okun's law, fill in the four pieces of missing data in the following table.

Year	Real GDP	Potential GDP	Natural unemployment rate (%)	Actual unemployment rate (%)
2001	7,840	8,000	(1)	6
2002	8,100	(2)	5	5
2003	(3)	8,200	4.5	4
2004	8,415	8,250	5	(4)

▪ ANSWERS TO IN-CHAPTER EXERCISE ▪

24.1 The answer depends on current data.

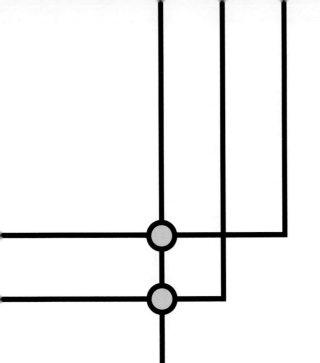

AGGREGATE DEMAND AND OUTPUT IN THE SHORT RUN

∎

When one of the authors of this book was a small boy, he used to spend some time every summer with his grandparents, who lived a few hours from his home. A favorite activity of his during these visits was to spend a summer evening on the front porch with his grandmother, listening to her stories. For some reason Grandma's recounting of her own life was particularly fascinating to her grandson.

Grandma had spent the early years of her marriage in New England during the worst part of the Great Depression. In one of her reminiscences she remarked that at that time, in the mid-1930s, it had been a satisfaction to her to be able to buy her children a new pair of shoes every year. In the small town where she and her family lived, many children had to wear their shoes until they fell apart, and a few unlucky boys and girls went to school barefoot. Her grandson thought this was scandalous: "Why didn't their parents just buy them new shoes?" he demanded.

"They couldn't," said Grandma. "They didn't have the money. Most of the fathers had lost their jobs because of the Depression."

"What kind of jobs did they have?"

"They worked in the shoe factories, which had to close down."

"Why did the factories close down?"

"Because," Grandma explained, "nobody had any money to buy shoes."

The grandson was only 6 or 7 years old at the time, but even he could see that there was something badly wrong with Grandma's logic. On the one side were boarded-up shoe factories and shoe workers with no jobs; on the other, children without shoes. Why couldn't the shoe factories just open and

produce the shoes the children so badly needed? He made his point quite firmly, but Grandma just shrugged and said it didn't work that way.

The story of the closed-down shoe factories illustrates in a microcosm the cost to society of an output gap. In an economy with a recessionary gap, available resources that could in principle be used to produce valuable goods and services are instead allowed to lie fallow. This waste of resources lowers the economy's output and economic welfare, compared to its potential.

Grandma's account also suggests how such an unfortunate situation might come about. Suppose factory owners and other producers, being reluctant to accumulate unsold goods on their shelves, produce just enough output to satisfy the demand for their products. And suppose that for some reason the public's willingness or ability to spend declines. If spending declines, factories will respond by cutting their production (because they don't want to produce goods they can't sell) and by laying off workers who are no longer needed. And because the workers who are laid off will lose most of their income—a particularly serious loss in the 1930s, in the days before government-sponsored unemployment insurance—they must reduce their own spending. As their spending declines, factories will reduce their production again, laying off more workers, who in turn reduce their spending, and so on, in a vicious circle. In this scenario, the problem is not a lack of productive capacity—the factories have not lost their ability to produce—but rather *insufficient spending* to support the normal level of production.

The idea that a decline in aggregate spending may cause output to fall below potential output was one of the key insights of John Maynard Keynes, a highly influential British economist of the first half of the twentieth century. Box 25.1 gives a brief account of Keynes's life and ideas. The goal of this chapter is to

---

BOX 25.1: JOHN MAYNARD KEYNES AND THE KEYNESIAN REVOLUTION

John Maynard Keynes (1883–1946), perhaps the most influential economist of the twentieth century, was a remarkable individual who combined a brilliant career as an economic theorist with an active life in diplomacy, finance, journalism, and the arts. Keynes (pronounced "canes") first came to prominence at the end of World War I when he attended the Versailles peace conference as a representative of the British Treasury. He was appalled by the shortsightedness of the diplomats at the conference, particularly their insistence that the defeated Germans make huge compensatory payments (called reparations) to the victorious nations. In his widely read book *The Economic Consequences of the Peace* (1919), Keynes argued that the reparations imposed on Germany were impossibly large and that attempts to extract the payments would prevent Germany's economic recovery and perhaps lead to another war. Unfortunately for the world, he turned out to be right.

In the period between the two world wars, Keynes held a professorship at Cambridge, where his father had taught economics. Keynes's early writings had been on mathematics and logic, but after his experience in Versailles he began to work primarily on economics, producing several well-regarded books. He developed an imposing intellectual reputation, editing Great Britain's leading scholarly journal in economics, writing articles for newspapers and magazines, advising the government, and playing a major role in the political and economic debates of the day. On the side, Keynes made fortunes both for himself and for King's College (a part of Cambridge University) by speculating in international currencies and commodities. He was also an active member of the Bloomsbury Group, a circle of leading artists, performers, and writers that included E. M. Forster and Virginia

develop a model of how recessions and expansions may arise from fluctuations in aggregate spending, along the lines first suggested by Keynes. This model, which we call the *basic Keynesian model*, is also known as the *Keynesian cross*, after the diagram that is used to illustrate the theory. In the body of the chapter we will emphasize a numerical and graphical approach to the basic Keynesian model. The appendix to this chapter provides a more general algebraic analysis.

We will begin with a brief discussion of the key assumptions of the basic Keynesian model. We will then turn to the important concept of *aggregate demand*, or total planned spending in the economy. We will show how, in the short run, aggregate demand helps to determine the level of output, which can be greater than or less than potential output. In other words, depending on the level of spending, the economy may develop an output gap. "Too little" spending leads to a recessionary output gap, while "too much" creates an expansionary output gap.

An implication of the basic Keynesian model is that government policies that affect the level of spending can be used to reduce or eliminate output gaps. Policies used in this way are called *stabilization policies*. Keynes himself argued for the active use of fiscal policy—policy relating to government spending and taxes—to eliminate output gaps and stabilize the economy. In the latter part of this chapter we will show why Keynes thought fiscal policy could help to stabilize the economy, and we will discuss the usefulness of fiscal policy as a stabilization tool.

As we foreshadowed in Chapter 24, the basic Keynesian model is not a complete or entirely realistic model of the economy, since it applies only to the short period during which firms do not adjust their prices but instead meet the demand forthcoming at preset prices. Furthermore, by treating prices as fixed, the basic Keynesian model presented in this chapter does not address the determination of

© Bettman/Corbis

Woolf. In 1925 Keynes married the glamorous Russian ballerina Lydia Lopokova. Theirs was by all accounts a very successful marriage, and Keynes devoted significant energies to managing his wife's career and promoting the arts in Britain.

Like other economists of the time, Keynes struggled to understand the Great Depression that gripped the world in the 1930s. His work on the problem led to the publication in 1936 of *The General Theory of Employment, Interest, and Money*. In *The General Theory*, Keynes tried to explain how economies can remain at low levels of output and employment for protracted periods. He stressed a number of factors, most notably that aggregate spending may be too low to permit full employment during such periods. Keynes recommended increases in government spending as the most effective way to increase aggregate spending and restore full employment.

The General Theory is a difficult book, reflecting Keynes's own struggle to understand the complex causes of the Depression. In retrospect, some of *The General Theory*'s arguments seem unclear or even inconsistent. Yet the book is full of fertile ideas, many of which had a worldwide impact and eventually led to what has been called the *Keynesian revolution*. Over the years many economists have added to or modified Keynes's conception, to the point that Keynes himself, were he alive today, probably would not recognize much of what is now called Keynesian economics. But the ideas that insufficient aggregate spending can lead to recession and that government policies can help to restore full employment are still critical to Keynesian theory.

In 1937 a heart attack curtailed Keynes's activities, but he remained an important figure on the world scene. In 1944 he led the British delegation to the international conference in Bretton Woods, New Hampshire, which established the key elements of the postwar international monetary and financial system, including the International Monetary Fund and the World Bank. Keynes died in 1946.

inflation. Nevertheless, this model is a key building block of current theories of short-run economic fluctuations and stabilization policies. In subsequent chapters we will extend the basic Keynesian model to incorporate inflation and other important features of the economy.

THE BASIC KEYNESIAN MODEL

The basic Keynesian model, on which we will focus in this chapter, is built on two key assumptions, given below. Of these two assumptions, the second—that, in the short run, firms meet the demand for their products at preset prices—is the crucial one. As we will see in this chapter, if firms respond to changes in demand primarily by changing their production levels instead of their prices, then changes in aggregate spending will have a powerful effect on aggregate output.

KEY ASSUMPTIONS OF THE BASIC KEYNESIAN MODEL

1. **Aggregate demand fluctuates.** Total planned spending in an economy, called *aggregate demand,* depends on the prevailing level of real GDP as well as other factors. Changes in either real GDP or in other factors that affect total spending will cause aggregate demand to fluctuate.

2. **In the short run, firms meet the demand for their products at preset prices.** Firms do not respond to every change in the demand for their products by changing their prices. Instead, they typically set a price for some period, then *meet the demand* at that price. By "meeting the demand," we mean that firms produce just enough to satisfy their customers.

The assumption that over short periods of time firms will meet the demand for their products at preset prices is generally realistic. Think of the stores where you shop: The price of a pair of jeans does not fluctuate with the number of customers who enter the store or the latest news about the price of denim. Instead, the store posts a price and sells jeans to any customer who wants to buy at that price, at least until the store runs out of stock. Similarly, the corner pizza restaurant may leave the price of its large pie unchanged for months or longer, allowing its pizza production to be determined by the number of customers who want to buy at the preset price.

menu costs the costs of changing prices

Firms do not change their prices frequently because doing so would be costly. Economists refer to the costs of changing prices as **menu costs.** In the case of the pizza restaurant, the menu cost is literally just that—the cost of printing up a new menu when prices change. Similarly, the clothing store faces the cost of re-marking all its merchandise if the manager changes prices. But menu costs may also include other kinds of costs, including, for example, the cost of doing a market survey to determine what price to charge and the cost of informing customers about price changes.

Menu costs will not prevent firms from changing their prices indefinitely. As we saw in Chapter 24 for the case of Al's ice cream store, too great an imbalance between demand and supply, as reflected by a difference between sales and potential output, will eventually lead to a change in price. If no one is buying jeans, for example, at some point the clothing store will mark down their jeans prices. Or if the pizza restaurant becomes the local hot spot, with a line of customers stretching out the door, eventually the manager will raise the price of a large pie. Like other economic decisions, the decision to change prices reflects a *cost-benefit comparison*: Prices should be changed if the benefit of doing so—the fact that sales will be brought more nearly in line with the firm's normal production capacity—outweighs the menu costs associated with making the change. As we have stressed, the basic Keynesian model developed in this chapter ignores the fact that prices will eventually adjust, and should therefore be interpreted as applying to the short run.

AGGREGATE DEMAND

In the Keynesian theory discussed in this chapter, output at each point in time is determined by the amount that people want to spend—what economists call *aggregate demand*. Specifically, **aggregate demand** (*AD*) is total planned spending on final goods and services.

aggregate demand (AD) total planned spending on final goods and services

The four components of total, or aggregate, spending on final goods and services were introduced in Chapter 18:

1. *Consumer expenditure,* or simply *consumption* (C), is spending by households on final goods and services. Examples of consumer expenditure are spending on food, clothes, and entertainment, and on consumer durable goods like automobiles and furniture.

2. *Investment* (I) is spending by firms on new capital goods, such as office buildings, factories, and equipment. Spending on new houses and apartment buildings (residential investment) and increases in inventories (inventory investment) are also included in investment.

3. *Government purchases* (G) is spending by governments (federal, state, and local) on goods and services. Examples of government purchases include new schools and hospitals, military hardware, equipment for the space program, and the services of government employees, such as soldiers, police, and government office workers. Recall from Chapter 18 that *transfer payments,* such as Social Security benefits and unemployment insurance, and *interest on the government debt* are *not* included in government purchases.

4. *Net exports* (NX) equals exports minus imports. Exports are sales of domestically produced goods and services to foreigners; imports are purchases by domestic residents of goods and services produced abroad. Net exports represents the net demand for domestic goods by foreigners.

Together these four types of spending—by households, firms, the government, and the rest of the world—sum to total, or aggregate, spending.

PLANNED SPENDING VERSUS ACTUAL SPENDING

Aggregate demand, we have just noted, equals total *planned* spending. Could *planned* spending ever differ from *actual* spending? The answer is yes. The most important case is that of a firm that sells either less or more of its product than expected. As was noted in Chapter 18, additions to the stocks of goods sitting in a firm's warehouse are treated in official government statistics as inventory investment by the firm. In effect, government statisticians assume that the firm buys its unsold output from itself; they then count those purchases as part of the firm's investment spending.[1]

Suppose, then, that a firm's actual sales are less than expected so that part of what it had planned to sell remains in the warehouse. In this case, the firm's actual investment, including the unexpected increases in its inventory, is greater than its planned investment, which did not include added inventory. Suppose we agree to let I^p equal the firm's planned investment, including planned inventory investment. A firm that sells less of its output than planned, and therefore adds more to its inventory than planned, will find that its actual investment (including unplanned inventory investment) exceeds its planned investment so that $I > I^p$.

---

[1]For the purposes of measuring GDP, treating unsold output as being purchased by its producer has the virtue of ensuring that actual production and actual expenditure are equal.

What about a firm that sells more of its output than expected? In that case, the firm will add less to its inventory than it planned, so actual investment will be less than planned investment, or $I < I^p$. Example 25.1 gives a numerical illustration.

EXAMPLE 25.1

Actual and planned investment

The Fly-by-Night Kite Company produces $5,000,000 worth of kites during the year. It expects sales of $4,800,000 for the year, leaving $200,000 worth of kites to be stored in the warehouse for future sale. During the year, Fly-by-Night adds $1,000,000 in new production equipment as part of an expansion plan. Find Fly-by-Night's actual investment I and its planned investment I^p if actual kite sales turn out to be $4,600,000. What if sales are $4,800,000? What if they are $5,000,000?

Fly-by-Night's planned investment I^p equals its purchases of new production equipment ($1,000,000) plus its planned additions to inventory ($200,000), for a total of $1,200,000 in planned investment. The company's planned investment does not depend on how much it actually sells.

If Fly-by-Night sells only $4,600,000 worth of kites, it will add $400,000 in kites to its inventory instead of the $200,000 worth originally planned. In this case, actual investment equals the $1,000,000 in new equipment plus the $400,000 in inventory investment, so $I = \$1,400,000$. We see that when the firm sells less output than planned, actual investment exceeds planned investment ($I > I^p$).

If Fly-by-Night has $4,800,000 in sales, then it will add $200,000 in kites to inventory, just as planned. In this case, actual and planned investment are the same: $I = I^p = \$1,200,000$.

Finally, if Fly-by-Night sells $5,000,000 worth of kites, it will have no output to add to inventory. Its inventory investment will be zero, and its total actual investment (including the new equipment) will equal $1,000,000, which is less than its planned investment of $1,200,000 ($I < I^p$).

Because firms that are meeting the demand for their product or service at preset prices cannot control how much they sell, their actual investment (including inventory investment) may well differ from their planned investment. However, for households, the government, and foreign purchasers, we may reasonably assume that actual spending and planned spending are the same. Thus, from now on we will assume that for consumption, government purchases, and net exports, actual spending equals planned spending.

With these assumptions, we can define aggregate demand by the equation

$$AD = C + I^p + G + NX. \quad \text{Definition of aggregate demand} \quad (25.1)$$

Equation 25.1 says that aggregate demand equals the economy's total planned spending, which in turn is the sum of planned spending by households, firms, governments, and foreigners. We use a superscript p to distinguish planned investment spending by firms I^p from actual investment spending I. However, because planned spending equals actual spending for households, the government, and foreigners, we do not need to use superscripts for consumption, government purchases, or net exports.

DETERMINING AGGREGATE DEMAND: THE CONSUMPTION FUNCTION

When we study the demand for a particular good or service, say Danish pastries, our first task is to specify the factors that determine how much people want to spend on it—factors such as the price of pastries, the incomes of pastry-loving consumers, the prices of competing items like cinnamon buns, the health effects of carbohydrate consumption, and so on. In the same way, to study aggregate demand we need to specify the factors that determine how much households plan to consume, how much firms plan to invest, and so on.

The largest component of aggregate demand—nearly two-thirds of total spending—is consumption spending, or C. What determines how much people plan to spend on consumer goods and services in a given period? While many factors may be relevant, a particularly important determinant of the amount people plan to consume is their after-tax, or *disposable,* income. All else being equal, households and individuals with higher disposable incomes will consume more than those with lower disposable incomes. Keynes himself stressed the importance of disposable income in determining household consumption decisions, claiming a "psychological law" that people would tie their spending closely to their incomes.

Recall from Chapter 22 that the disposable income of the private sector is the total production of the economy, Y, less net taxes (taxes minus transfers), or T. So we can assume that consumption spending (C) increases as disposable income ($Y - T$) increases. As already mentioned, other factors may also affect consumption, such as the real interest rate, also discussed in Chapter 22. For now we will ignore those other factors, returning to some of them later.

An equation that captures the link between consumption and the private sector's disposable income is

$$C = \overline{C} + c(Y - T). \qquad (25.2)$$

This equation, which we will dissect in a moment, is known as the *consumption function*. The **consumption function** relates consumption spending to its determinants, such as disposable (after-tax) income.

Let's look at the consumption function, Equation 25.2, more carefully. The right side of the equation contains two terms, $\overline{C}$ and $c(Y - T)$. The first term, $\overline{C}$, is a constant term in the equation that is intended to capture factors *other than disposable income* that affect consumption. For example, suppose consumers were to become more optimistic about the future so that they desire to consume more and save less at any given level of their current disposable incomes. An increase in desired consumption at any given level of disposable income would be represented in the consumption function, Equation 25.2, as an increase in the term $\overline{C}$.

The second term on the right side of Equation 25.2, $c(Y - T)$, reflects the effect of disposable income $Y - T$ on consumption. The parameter c, a fixed number, is called the *marginal propensity to consume*. The **marginal propensity to consume**, or MPC, is the amount by which consumption rises when current disposable income rises by \$1. Presumably, if people receive an extra dollar of income, they will consume part of the dollar and save the rest. In other words, their consumption will increase but by less than the full dollar of extra income. Thus we assume that the marginal propensity to consume is greater than 0 (an increase in income leads to an increase in consumption), but less than 1 (the increase in consumption will be less than the full increase in income). These assumptions can be written symbolically as $0 < c < 1$.

Figure 25.1 shows a hypothetical consumption function, with consumption spending (C) on the vertical axis and disposable income ($Y - T$) on the horizontal axis. The intercept of the consumption function on the vertical axis equals the constant term $\overline{C}$, and the slope of the consumption function equals the marginal propensity to consume c.

To see how this consumption function fits reality, compare Figure 25.1 to Figure 25.2, which shows the relationship between aggregate real consumption expenditures and real disposable income in the United States for the period 1960 through 1999. Figure 25.2, a scatter plot, shows aggregate real consumption on the vertical axis and aggregate real disposable income on the horizontal axis. Each

consumption function the relationship between consumption spending and its determinants, such as disposable (after-tax) income

marginal propensity to consume (MPC) the amount by which consumption rises when disposable income rises by \$1; we assume that $0 < MPC < 1$

FIGURE 25.1
A Consumption Function.
The consumption function relates households' consumption spending C to disposable income $Y - T$. The vertical intercept of this consumption function is $\bar{C}$, and the slope of the line equals the marginal propensity to consume c.

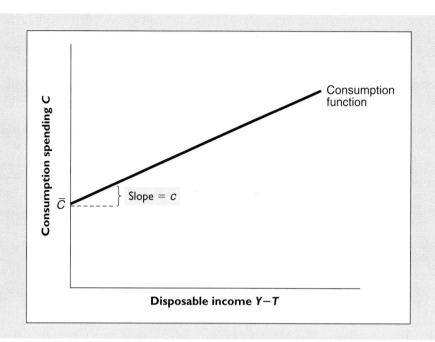

FIGURE 25.2
The U.S. Consumption Function, 1960–1999.
Each point on this figure represents a combination of aggregate real consumption and aggregate real disposable income for a specific year between 1960 and 1999. Note the strong positive relationship between consumption and disposable income.

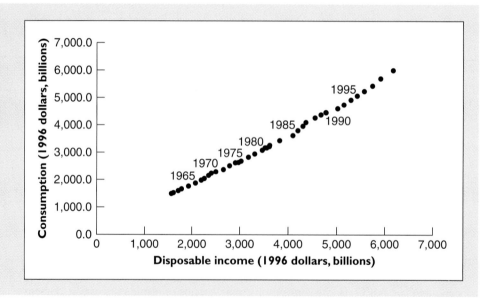

point on the graph corresponds to a year between 1960 and 1999 (selected years are indicated in the figure). The position of each point is determined by the combination of consumption and disposable income associated with that year. As you can see, there is indeed a close relationship between aggregate consumption and disposable income: Higher disposable income implies higher consumption.

AGGREGATE DEMAND AND OUTPUT

Thinking back to Grandma's reminiscences, recall that an important element of her story involved the links among production, income, and spending. As the shoe factories in Grandma's town reduced production, the incomes of both factory workers and factory owners fell. Workers' incomes fell as the number of hours of work per week were reduced (a common practice during the Depression), as some workers were laid off, or as wages were cut. Factory owners' income fell as profits declined. Reduced incomes, in turn, forced both workers and factory owners to curtail their spending, which led to still lower production and further reductions in income.

To capture these links in our model, we need to show how aggregate demand AD is affected by changes in aggregate income Y—which is the same, you may recall, as aggregate output, or GDP. The consumption function, which relates desired consumption to disposable income, helps to establish this relationship. Because consumption spending C is a large part of aggregate demand and because consumption depends on output Y, aggregate demand as a whole depends on output.

To express the connection between aggregate demand and output in an equation, we start with the definition of aggregate demand, Equation 25.1:

$$AD = C + I^p + G + NX.$$

If we substitute the consumption function, Equation 25.2, for consumption C in the definition of aggregate demand just given, the result is

$$AD = [\overline{C} + c(Y - T)] + I^p + G + NX.$$

Although we have discussed the determinants of consumption, we have not yet said anything about the other three components of spending. For now, we will simply assume that planned investment, government purchases, and net exports are given, fixed quantities that are determined outside our model of the economy. Using an overbar to denote a fixed value, we can write this assumption as

$$I^p = \overline{I},$$

$$G = \overline{G},$$

$$NX = \overline{NX}.$$

We will also assume for now that net taxes T are fixed by the government. Because the amount of net taxes collected is assumed to be fixed, we can write $T = \overline{T}$.

Substituting the fixed values for investment, government purchases, net exports, and taxes into the equation defining aggregate demand, we get

$$AD = [\overline{C} + c(Y - \overline{T})] + \overline{I} + \overline{G} + \overline{NX}.$$

Finally, let's rearrange this equation to group together those terms that depend on output Y and those that do not. This rearrangement yields

$$AD = (\overline{C} - c\overline{T} + \overline{I} + \overline{G} + \overline{NX}) + cY. \qquad (25.3)$$

Equation 25.3 shows that if real output Y increases by one unit, then aggregate demand AD increases by c units, where c, the marginal propensity to consume, is between 0 and 1. Thus Equation 25.3 captures the key idea that as real output (Y) changes, aggregate demand (AD) changes with it, in the same direction.

Equation 25.3 also shows that aggregate demand can be divided into two parts, a part that is determined outside the model and a part that is determined within the model. The portion of aggregate demand that is determined *outside* the model is called **autonomous aggregate demand**. In this example, autonomous aggregate demand is given by the first term on the right side of Equation 25.3, $(\overline{C} - c\overline{T} + \overline{I} + \overline{G} + \overline{NX})$. The portion of aggregate demand that is determined *within* the model is called **induced aggregate demand**. Algebraically, induced aggregate demand is given by cY, the second term on the right side of Equation

autonomous aggregate demand the portion of aggregate demand that is determined outside the model

induced aggregate demand the portion of aggregate demand that is determined within the model (because it depends on output Y)

25.3. This portion of aggregate demand is determined within the model because it changes as income Y changes. Autonomous aggregate demand and induced aggregate demand together equal total aggregate demand. Example 25.2 illustrates these ideas numerically.

EXAMPLE 25.2   **Linking aggregate demand to output**

In a particular economy, the following parameter values hold:

$$\overline{C} = 620, c = 0.8, \overline{I} = 220, \overline{G} = 300, \overline{NX} = 20, \overline{T} = 250.$$

a. Write an equation linking aggregate demand to output.

b. Find autonomous aggregate demand and induced aggregate demand.

Substituting the consumption function for consumption C, and treating the other components of aggregate demand as fixed numbers, the algebraic expression for aggregate demand can be written as (see Equation 25.3)

$$AD = [\overline{C} - c\overline{T} + \overline{I} + \overline{G} + \overline{NX}] + cY.$$

Plugging in the numbers in Example 25.2, we have

$$AD = [620 - 0.8(250) + 220 + 300 + 20] + 0.8Y = 960 + 0.8Y.$$

This equation links aggregate demand AD to output Y. As Y increases, aggregate demand increases as well.

Autonomous aggregate demand is the part of aggregate demand that is determined outside the model and hence does not depend on output Y. Induced aggregate demand is the part of aggregate demand that does depend on output. In this example, $AD = 960 + 0.8Y$, so autonomous aggregate demand is 960 and induced aggregate demand is $0.8Y$. Notice that the numerical value of induced aggregate demand depends on the value taken by output.

RECAP   **AGGREGATE DEMAND**

Aggregate demand (AD) is total planned spending on final goods and services. The four components of aggregate demand are consumer expenditure (C), planned investment (I^p), government purchases (G), and net exports (NX). Planned investment differs from actual investment when firms' sales are different from what they expected so that additions to inventory (a component of investment) are different from what firms anticipated.

The largest component of aggregate demand is consumer expenditure, or simply consumption. Consumption depends on disposable, or after-tax, income, according to a relationship known as the *consumption function*. The slope of the consumption function equals the marginal propensity to consume c. The *marginal propensity to consume*, a number between 0 and 1, is the amount by which consumption rises when disposable income rises by $1.

Increases in output, which imply increases in income, cause consumption to rise. As consumption is part of aggregate demand, aggregate demand depends on output as well. The portion of aggregate demand that depends on output, and hence is determined within the model, is called *induced aggregate demand*. The portion of aggregate demand determined outside the model is *autonomous aggregate demand*.

SHORT-RUN EQUILIBRIUM OUTPUT

Now that we have defined aggregate demand and seen how it is related to output, the next task is to determine what output will be. Recall the assumption of the basic Keynesian model: that in the short run, producers leave prices at preset levels and simply meet the demand at those prices. In other words, during the short-run period in which prices are preset, firms produce an amount that is equal to aggregate demand. Accordingly, we define **short-run equilibrium output** as the level of output at which output Y equals aggregate demand AD:

short-run equilibrium output the level of output at which output Y equals aggregate demand AD; the level of output that prevails during the period in which prices are predetermined

$$Y = AD. \quad \text{Definition of short-run equilibrium output} \quad (25.4)$$

Short-run equilibrium output is the level of output that prevails during the period in which prices are predetermined.

We can find the short-run equilibrium output for the economy described in Example 25.2 using Table 25.1. Column 1 in the table gives some possible values for short-run equilibrium output. To find the correct one, we must com-

TABLE 25.1
Numerical Determination of Short-Run Equilibrium Output

(1) Output Y	(2) Aggregate demand AD = 960 + 0.8Y	(3) Y − AD	(4) Y = AD?
4,000	4,160	−160	No
4,200	4,320	−120	No
4,400	4,480	−80	No
4,600	4,640	−40	No
4,800	4,800	0	Yes
5,000	4,960	40	No
5,200	5,120	80	No

pare each to the value of aggregate demand at that output level. Column 2 shows the value of aggregate demand corresponding to the values of output in column 1. Recall that in this example, aggregate demand is determined by the equation

$$AD = 960 + 0.8Y$$

(see Example 25.2). Because consumption rises with output, aggregate demand (which includes consumption) rises also. But if you compare columns 1 and 2, you will see that when output rises by 200, aggregate demand rises by only 160. That is because the marginal propensity to consume in this economy is 0.8, so each dollar in added income raises consumption and aggregate demand by 80 cents.

Again, short-run equilibrium output is the level of output at which $Y = AD$, or equivalently, $Y - AD = 0$. Looking at Table 25.1, we can see there is only one level of output that satisfies that condition, $Y = 4,800$. At that level, output and aggregate demand are precisely equal, so the producers are just meeting the demand.

In this economy, what would happen if output happened to differ from its equilibrium value of 4,800? Suppose, for example, that output were 4,000. Looking at column 2 of Table 25.1, we can see that when output is 4,000, aggregate demand equals 960 + 0.8(4,000), or 4,160. Thus if output is 4.000, firms are not producing enough to meet the demand. They will find that as sales exceed the amounts they are producing, their inventories of finished goods are being depleted by 160 per year, and that actual investment is less than planned investment. Under the assumption that firms are committed to meeting their customers' demand, firms will respond by expanding their production.

Would expanding production to 4,160, the level of aggregate demand firms faced when output was 4,000, be enough? The answer is no, because of induced aggregate demand. That is, as firms expand their output, aggregate income (wages and profits) rises with it, which in turn leads to higher levels of consumption. Indeed, if output expands to 4,160, aggregate demand will increase as well, to $960 + 0.8(4,160)$, or 4,288. So an output level of 4,160 will still be insufficient to meet demand. As Table 25.1 shows, output will not be sufficient to meet aggregate demand until it expands to its short-run equilibrium value of 4,800.

What if output were initially greater than its equilibrium value—say, 5,000? From Table 25.1 we can see that when output equals 5,000, aggregate demand equals only 4,960— less than what firms are producing. So at an output level of 5,000, firms will not sell all they produce and will find that their merchandise is piling up on store shelves and in warehouses (actual investment is greater than planned investment). In response, firms will cut their production runs. As Table 25.1 shows, they will have to reduce production to its equilibrium value of 4,800 before output just matches aggregate demand.

EXERCISE 25.1

Construct a table like Table 25.1 for an economy like the one we have been working with. Use the following values for the parameters:

$$\overline{C} = 820, \ c = 0.7, \ \overline{I} = 600, \ \overline{G} = 600, \ \overline{NX} = 200, \ \overline{T} = 600.$$

What is short-run equilibrium output in this economy? (*Hint:* Try using values for output above 5,000.)

Table 25.1 is useful for understanding why short-run equilibrium output equals 4,800 in the economy described in Example 25.2, but it is a laborious way to find the equilibrium value of output. Example 25.3 illustrates the more direct approach to solving for short-run equilibrium output numerically.

EXAMPLE 25.3   **Finding short-run equilibrium output (numerical approach)**

Solve numerically for short-run equilibrium output for the economy described in Example 25.2.

We can solve numerically for short-run equilibrium output in two steps. First, we know that in this example aggregate demand is related to output by the equation

$$AD = 960 + 0.8Y.$$

Recall that we found this equation by substituting the values given in the problem for each of the four components of aggregate demand into the definition of aggregate demand, Equation 25.1.

Second, we know that short-run equilibrium output must satisfy the equation $Y = AD$. Using the equation $AD = 960 + 0.8Y$ to substitute for AD in the definition of short-run equilibrium output, we get

$$Y = 960 + 0.8Y.$$

The solution to this equation gives us short-run equilibrium output, the level of output at which production equals aggregate demand. Solving for Y we get

$$Y = 4,800,$$

which is the same value obtained from Table 25.1. Box 25.2 summarizes the process of solving the basic Keynesian model numerically.

BOX 25.2: SOLVING THE BASIC KEYNESIAN MODEL NUMERICALLY

Step 1. Find the relationship between aggregate demand AD and output Y.

■ Write the definition of aggregate demand, Equation 25.1:

$$AD = C + I^p + G + NX.$$

■ Substitute for each of the four components of aggregate demand, and simplify. For example, Example 25.2 assumes

$$C = 620 + 0.8(Y - T),$$

$$I^p = \bar{I} = 220,$$

$$G = \bar{G} = 300,$$

$$NX = \overline{NX} = 20,$$

$$T = \bar{T} = 250.$$

Substituting for the components of aggregate demand in Equation 25.1 gives

$$AD = [620 + 0.8(Y - 250)] + 220 + 300 + 20.$$

Simplifying this equation yields the relationship of AD to Y:

$$AD = 960 + 0.8Y.$$

Step 2. Use the definition of short-run equilibrium output, $Y = AD$, to solve for Y.

■ Write the definition of short-run equilibrium output, Equation 25.4:

$$Y = AD.$$

■ Replace AD with the expression found in step 1:

$$Y = 960 + 0.8Y.$$

■ Solve the resulting equation for short-run equilibrium output Y:

$$Y(1 - 0.8) = 960,$$

$$0.2Y = 960,$$

$$Y = 960/0.2,$$

$$Y = 4,800.$$

This answer is the same as the one shown in Table 25.1.

Short-run equilibrium output can also be determined graphically, as Example 25.4 shows.

EXAMPLE 25.4   **Finding short-run equilibrium output (graphical approach)**

Using a graphical approach, find short-run equilibrium output for the economy described in Example 25.2.

Figure 25.3 shows the graphical determination of short-run equilibrium output for the economy described in Example 25.2. Output Y is plotted on the horizontal axis and aggregate demand AD on the vertical axis. The figure contains two lines, one of which is a 45° line extending from the origin. In general, a 45° line from the origin includes the points at which the variable on the vertical axis equals the variable on the horizontal axis. In this case, the 45° line represents the equation $Y = AD$. Recall that short-run equilibrium output must satisfy the condition $Y = AD$. So we know that the value of short-run equilibrium output demand must lie somewhere on the $Y = AD$ line.

The second line in Figure 25.3, less steep than the 45° line, shows the relationship between aggregate demand AD and output Y. Because it summarizes how

FIGURE 25.3
Determination of Short-Run Equilibrium Output (Keynesian Cross).
The 45° line represents the short-run equilibrium condition $Y = AD$. The line $AD = 960 + 0.8Y$, referred to as the expenditure line, shows the relationship of aggregate demand to output. Short-run equilibrium output (4,800) is determined at the intersection of the two lines, point E. This type of diagram is known as a Keynesian cross.

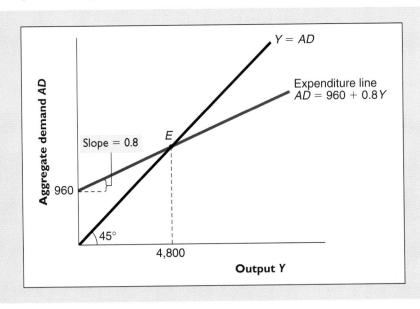

total expenditure depends on output, we will call this line the *expenditure line*. In this example, we know that the relationship between aggregate demand and output (the equation for the expenditure line) is

$$AD = 960 + 0.8Y.$$

According to this equation, when $Y = 0$, the value of AD is 960. Thus 960 is the intercept of the expenditure line, as shown in Figure 25.3. The slope of the line relating aggregate demand to output is 0.8, the value of the coefficient of output in the equation $AD = 960 + 0.8Y$. Where does the number 0.8 come from? (*Hint:* What determines by how much aggregate demand increases when output rises by a dollar?)

Only one point in Figure 25.3 is consistent with both the definition of short-run equilibrium output $Y = AD$ and the given relationship between aggregate demand and output, $AD = 960 + 0.8Y$. That point is the intersection of the two lines, point E. At point E, short-run equilibrium output equals 4,800, which is the same value that we obtained using Table 25.2 and by a direct numerical solution. Notice that at points to the right of E, output exceeds aggregate demand. Hence, to the right of point E, firms will be producing more than they can sell and will tend to reduce their production. Similarly, to the left of point E, aggregate demand exceeds output. In that region, firms will not be producing enough to meet demand and will tend to increase their production. Only at point E, where output equals 4,800, will firms be producing enough to just satisfy aggregate demand.

The diagram in Figure 25.3 is often called the *Keynesian cross*, after its characteristic shape. The Keynesian cross shows graphically how short-run equilibrium output is determined in a world in which producers meet demand at predetermined prices.

EXERCISE 25.2

Find short-run equilibrium output for the economy described in Exercise 25.1 using a Keynesian cross diagram. What are the intercept and the slope of the expenditure line?

AGGREGATE DEMAND AND THE OUTPUT GAP

We are now ready to use the basic Keynesian model to show how insufficient aggregate demand can lead to a recession. To illustrate this idea, we will continue to work with the economy introduced in Example 25.2. We have shown that in this economy, short-run equilibrium output equals 4,800. Let's now make the additional assumption that potential output in this economy also equals 4,800, or $Y^* = 4,800$. In other words, we will assume that at first, actual output equals potential output so that there is no output gap. Starting from this position of full employment, Example 25.5 shows how a fall in aggregate demand can lead to a recession.

A fall in spending leads to a recession

EXAMPLE 25.5

For the economy introduced in Example 25.2, we have found that short-run equilibrium output Y equals 4,800. Assume also that potential output $Y^* = 4,800$ so that the output gap $Y^* - Y$ equals zero.

Suppose, though, that consumers become more pessimistic about the future, so they begin to spend less at every level of current disposable income. We can capture this change by assuming that $\bar{C}$, the vertical intercept of the consumption function, falls from its initial value of 620 to 610. What is the effect of this reduction in aggregate demand on the economy?

The fall in $\bar{C}$ implies a reduction in autonomous aggregate demand, which will affect short-run equilibrium output. To find out precisely what this effect is, let's solve for short-run equilibrium output under the assumption that $\bar{C}$ has fallen from 620 to 610. Once more we can use the steps outlined in Box 25.2. The first step is to find the relationship between aggregate demand AD and output Y after the decline in $\bar{C}$.

Recall the definition of aggregate demand, Equation 25.1:

$$AD = C + I^p + G + NX.$$

To find the relationship of aggregate demand to output, we can substitute for the four components of spending. Planned investment, government purchases, net exports, and net tax collections take the same fixed values as before: $\bar{I} = 220$,

$\overline{G}$ = 300, $\overline{NX}$ = 20, $\overline{T}$ = 250. However, because of the assumed decline in $\overline{C}$ from 620 to 610, consumption is now given by

$$C = \overline{C} + c(Y - T) = 610 + 0.8(Y - 250).$$

If we substitute these values for the four components of spending in the definition of aggregate demand, we get

$$AD = [610 + 0.8(Y - 250)] + 220 + 300 + 20.$$

Simplifying, we find that the relationship of aggregate demand to output is

$$AD = 950 + 0.8Y.$$

Comparing this equation to the result in Example 25.2, we see that the 10-unit decline in $\overline{C}$ has caused autonomous aggregate demand to fall by 10 units, from 960 to 950.

Following the method of Box 25.2, the second step is to solve for short-run equilibrium output Y. We use the relationship $AD = 950 + 0.8Y$ to substitute for AD in the definition of short-run equilibrium output $Y = AD$, which gives us

$$Y = 950 + 0.8Y.$$

Solving this equation for Y, we get

$$Y = 4,750.$$

Thus the decline in consumers' willingness to spend has caused short-run equilibrium output to fall from 4,800 to 4,750. The output gap, which was zero, now equals $Y^* - Y = 4,800 - 4,750 = 50$. We conclude that the fall in consumer spending has led to a recession. From Okun's law, we know that this fall in output also implies an increase in cyclical unemployment.

The same result can be obtained graphically. Figure 25.4 shows the original short-run equilibrium point of the model (E), at the intersection of the $Y = AD$ line and the original expenditure line, representing the equation $AD = 960 + 0.8Y$. As before, the initial value of short-run equilibrium output is 4,800, which corresponds to potential output Y^*. But what happens when $\overline{C}$ declines by 10 from 620 to 610? We have just found that the equation for the expenditure line

FIGURE 25.4
A Decline in Spending Leads to a Recession.
A decline in consumers' willingness to spend at any current level of disposable income reduces autonomous aggregate demand and shifts the expenditure line down. The short-run equilibrium point drops from E to F, reducing output and opening up a recessionary gap.

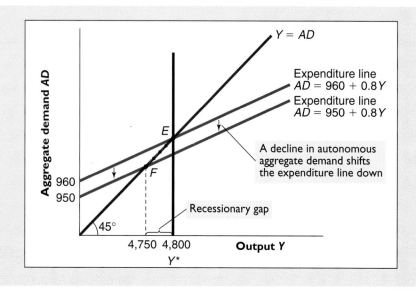

after the drop in consumer spending is $AD = 950 + 0.8Y$. Since the intercept of the expenditure line has decreased, from 960 to 950, but its slope has not changed, the effect of the decline in consumer spending will be to shift the expenditure line down in parallel fashion by 10 units. The blue line in Figure 25.4 indicates this downward shift. The new short-run equilibrium point is F.

As Figure 25.4 shows, the downward shift in aggregate demand reduces short-run equilibrium output from 4,800 to 4,750, opening up a recessionary gap of 50.

EXERCISE 25.3

In Example 25.5, we found a recessionary gap of 50, relative to potential output of 4,800. Suppose that in this economy the natural rate of unemployment u^* is 5 percent. What will the actual unemployment rate be after the recessionary gap appears?

EXERCISE 25.4

For the economy described in Exercise 25.1, suppose planned investment I^P rises from 600 to 630. Assuming the economy had no output gap before the increase in planned investment, show numerically that the change in investment leads to an expansionary output gap.

"These are hard times for retailers, so we should show them our support in every way we can."

What caused the 1990–1991 recession?

As we saw in Chapter 24, the 1990–1991 recession came at the wrong time for President Bush. What caused the output of the U.S. economy to fall below its potential during that period?

Two factors have received a substantial part of the blame for the 1990–1991 recession, one being a *decline in consumer confidence*. Organizations such as the Conference Board and the Survey Research Center of the University of Michigan perform regular consumer surveys, in which people are asked their views about the future of the economy in general, and their own fortunes in particular. Consumer responses are then summarized in measures of "consumer confidence." A high level of confidence implies that people are optimistic about both their own economic futures and the future of the economy in general. Economists have found that when consumers

ECONOMIC NATURALIST 25.1

are optimistic, they are more likely to spend, particularly on "big-ticket" items such as cars and furniture. Hence, when consumer confidence took its sharpest-ever plunge following Iraq's invasion of Kuwait and the associated spike in oil prices in August 1990, economists and policymakers winced. As Americans became increasingly concerned both about U.S. energy security and the possibility of a ground war in the Middle East, aggregate demand and hence output fell, as suggested by Example 25.5.

The second factor, a *credit crunch,* arose from problems in the U.S. banking system. During the 1980s, many U.S. banks had made large real estate loans, taking undeveloped land or commercial real estate as collateral. When land and other real estate prices fell sharply in the late 1980s, banks suffered serious losses. Some regions of the country, such as New England, were hit especially hard. Many financially distressed banks either had no new funds to lend or were not permitted to lend by government regulators. This decline in the supply of credit from banks made credit costlier and more difficult to obtain for many borrowers, especially small- and medium-sized firms. Without access to credit, these firms could not make capital investments, further reducing aggregate demand and output. In terms of the model presented in this chapter, a decline in planned investment spending brought about by a credit crunch can be thought of as a fall in $\bar{I}$. Like the decline in $\bar{C}$ illustrated in Example 25.5, a fall in $\bar{I}$ reduces short-run equilibrium output (see Problem 5 at the end of the chapter).

ECONOMIC NATURALIST 25.2

Why was the deep Japanese recession of the 1990s bad news for the rest of East Asia?

Economic Naturalist 24.1 discussed the severe economic slump in Japan during the 1990s. Japan's economic problems were a major concern not only of the Japanese but of policymakers in other East Asian countries, such as Thailand and Singapore. Why did East Asian policymakers worry about the effects of the Japanese slump on their own economies?

Although the economies of Japan and its East Asian neighbors are intertwined in many ways, one of the most important links is through trade. Much of the economic success of East Asia has been based on the development of export industries, and over the years Japan has been the most important customer for East Asian goods. When the economy slumped in the 1990s, Japanese households and firms reduced their purchases of imported goods sharply. This fall in demand dealt a major blow to the export industries of other East Asian countries. Not just the owners and workers of export industries were affected, though. The decline in exports to Japan reduced net exports, and thus autonomous aggregate demand, in East Asian countries. Falling aggregate demand in turn reduced their short-run equilibrium GDP and contributed to recessionary output gaps. Graphically, the effects were similar to those shown in Figure 25.4.

Japan is not the only country whose economic ups and downs have had a major impact on its trading partners. Because the United States is the most important trading partner of both Canada and Mexico, a recession in the United States would be likely to reduce Canadian and Mexican GDPs as well by reducing U.S. demand for the exports of its neighbors.

THE MULTIPLIER

Note that in Example 25.5, although the initial decline in consumer spending (as measured by the fall in $\bar{C}$) was only 10 units, short-run equilibrium output fell by 50 units. The reason the impact on output and aggregate demand was greater than the initial change in spending is the "vicious circle" effect suggested by Grandma's reminiscences about the Great Depression. Specifically, a fall in consumer spending not only decreases aggregate demand, it also reduces the incomes of workers and owners in the industries that produce consumer goods. As their incomes fall, these workers and capital owners reduce their spending, which reduces the output and incomes of *other* producers in the economy. And these reductions in income lead to still further cuts in spending. Ultimately, these successive rounds of declines in spending and income may lead to a decrease in aggregate demand that is significantly greater than the change in spending that started the process.

The idea that a change in spending may lead to a much larger change in short-run equilibrium output is an important feature of the basic Keynesian model. In Example 25.5 we considered the effects of a decrease in spending, but an increase in spending produces the same effect in reverse. For example, if desired consumption had *increased* rather than decreased by 10, it would have set off successive rounds of increases in income and spending, culminating in a final increase of 50 in short-run equilibrium output. The same type of effect also applies to changes in other components of autonomous aggregate demand. For example, in this hypothetical economy, an increase of 10 in desired investment spending $\bar{I}$, in government purchases $\bar{G}$, or in net exports $\overline{NX}$ would increase short-run equilibrium output by 50.

The effect on short-run equilibrium output of a one-unit increase in autonomous aggregate demand is called the **income-expenditure multiplier**, or the *multiplier* for short. In the economy of Example 25.5 the multiplier is 5. That is, each \$1 increase in autonomous aggregate demand leads to a \$5 increase in short-run equilibrium output, and each \$1 decrease in autonomous aggregate demand implies a \$5 decrease in short-run equilibrium output. Box 25.3 provides more information about the economics of the multiplier and shows how to calculate its numerical value in specific examples.

We stress that, because the basic Keynesian model omits some important features of the real economy, it tends to yield unrealistically high values of the multiplier. Indeed, virtually no one believes that the multiplier in the U.S. economy is as high as 5. Later we will discuss why the basic Keynesian model tends to overstate the value of the multiplier. Nevertheless, the idea that changes in aggregate demand can have important effects on short-run equilibrium output remains a central tenet of Keynesian economics and a major factor in modern policymaking.

income-expenditure multiplier
the effect of a one-unit increase in autonomous aggregate demand on short-run equilibrium output

---

BOX 25.3: THE MULTIPLIER IN THE BASIC KEYNESIAN MODEL

In Example 25.5, a drop in autonomous aggregate demand of 10 units caused a decline in short-run equilibrium output five times as great—an illustration of the *income-expenditure multiplier* in action. To see more precisely why this multiplier effect occurs, note that the initial decrease of 10 in consumer spending in Example 25.5 has two effects. First, because consumption spending is part of aggregate demand, the fall in consumer spending directly reduces aggregate demand by 10. Second, the fall in spending also reduces by 10 the incomes of producers (workers and firm owners) of consumer goods. Under our assumption that the marginal propensity to consume is 0.8, the producers of consumer goods will therefore reduce *their* consumption spending by 8, or 0.8 times their income loss of 10. This reduction in spending cuts the income of *other* producers by 8, leading them to reduce their spending by 6.4, or 0.8 times their income loss of 8. These income reductions of 6.4 lead still other producers to cut their spending by 5.12, or 0.8 times 6.4, and so on. In principle this process continues indefinitely, although after many rounds of spending and income reductions the effects become quite small.

Adding up all these "rounds" of income and spending reductions, the *total* effect on aggregate demand of the initial reduction of 10 in consumer spending is

$$10 + 8 + 6.4 + 5.12 + \cdots .$$

The three dots indicate that the series of reductions continues indefinitely. The total effect of the initial decrease in consumption can also be written as

$$10[1 + 0.8 + (0.8)^2 + (0.8)^3 + \cdots].$$

This expression highlights the fact that the spending that takes place in each round is 0.8 times the spending in the previous round—0.8, because that is the marginal propensity to consume out of the income generated by the previous round of spending.

A useful algebraic relationship, which applies to any number x greater than 0 but less than 1, is

$$1 + x + x^2 + x^3 + \cdots = \frac{1}{1-x}.$$

If we set $x = 0.8$, this formula implies that the total effect of the decline in consumption spending on aggregate demand and output is

$$10\left(\frac{1}{1 - 0.8}\right) = 10\left(\frac{1}{0.2}\right) = 10 \times 5 = 50.$$

This answer is consistent with our earlier calculation, which showed that short-run equilibrium output fell by 50 units, from 4,800 to 4,750.

By a similar analysis we can also find a general algebraic expression for the multiplier in the basic Keynesian model. Recalling that c is the marginal propensity to consume out of disposable income, we know that a one-unit increase in autonomous aggregate demand raises spending and income by one unit in the first round, by $c \times 1 = c$ units in the second round, by $c \times c = c^2$ units in the second round, by $c \times c^2 = c^3$ units in the third round, and so on. Thus the total effect on short-run equilibrium output of a one-unit increase in autonomous aggregate demand is given by

$$1 + c + c^2 + c^3 + \cdots.$$

Applying the algebraic formula given above, and recalling that $0 < c < 1$, we can rewrite this expression as $1/(1 - c)$. Thus, in a basic Keynesian model with a marginal propensity to consume of c, the multiplier equals $1/(1 - c)$. To check this result, we can substitute our assumed numerical value of 0.8 for c and calculate the multiplier in our example as $1/(1 - 0.8) = 1/0.2 = 5$, which is the same value we obtained earlier.

RECAP **SHORT-RUN EQUILIBRIUM OUTPUT**

Short-run equilibrium output is the level of output at which output equals aggregate demand; or in symbols, $Y = AD$. For a specific example economy, short-run equilibrium output can be solved for numerically (see Box 25.2) or graphically. The graphical solution is based on a diagram called the Keynesian cross. The Keynesian cross diagram includes two lines: a 45° line that captures the condition $Y = AD$ and the expenditure line, which shows the relationship of aggregate demand to output. Short-run equilibrium output is determined at the intersection of the two lines. If short-run equilibrium output differs from potential output, an output gap exists.

Increases in autonomous aggregate demand shift the expenditure line upward, increasing short-run equilibrium output, and decreases in autonomous aggregate demand induce declines in short-run equilibrium output. Decreases in autonomous aggregate demand that drive actual output below potential output are a possible source of recessions. Generally, a one-

> unit increase in autonomous aggregate demand leads to a larger increase in short-run equilibrium output, a result of the *income-expenditure multiplier.* The multiplier arises because a given initial increase in spending raises the incomes of producers, which leads them to spend more, raising the incomes and spending of other producers, and so on.

STABILIZING AGGREGATE DEMAND: THE ROLE OF FISCAL POLICY

According to the basic Keynesian model, inadequate spending is an important cause of recessions. To fight recessions—at least, those caused by insufficient demand rather than slow growth of potential output—policymakers must find ways to increase aggregate demand. Policies that are used to affect aggregate demand, with the objective of eliminating output gaps, are called **stabilization policies.**

The two major types of stabilization policy, *monetary policy* and *fiscal policy,* were introduced in Chapter 17. Recall that monetary policy refers to decisions about the size of the money supply, while fiscal policy refers to decisions about the government's budget—how much the government spends and how much tax revenue it collects. In the remainder of this chapter we will focus on fiscal policy (monetary policy will be discussed in Chapters 26 and 27). Specifically, we will consider how fiscal policy works in the basic Keynesian model, looking first at the effects of changes in government purchases of goods and services and then at changes in tax collections. We will conclude the chapter with a discussion of some practical issues that arise in the application of fiscal policy.

stabilization policies
government policies that are used to affect aggregate demand, with the objective of eliminating output gaps

GOVERNMENT PURCHASES AND AGGREGATE DEMAND

Decisions about government spending represent one of the two main components of fiscal policy, the other being decisions about the level and type of taxes. As was mentioned earlier (see Box 25.1), Keynes himself felt that changes in government spending were probably the most effective tool for reducing or eliminating output gaps. His basic argument was straightforward: Government purchases of goods and services are a component of aggregate demand, so aggregate demand is directly affected by changes in government purchases. If output gaps are caused by too much or too little aggregate demand, then the government can help to guide the economy toward full employment by changing its own level of spending. Keynes's views seemed to be vindicated by the events of the 1930s, notably the fact that the Depression did not finally end until governments greatly increased their military spending in the latter part of the decade. Ironically, Adolf Hitler may have been the most successful of all the era's leaders at applying Keynes's prescription (although no evidence suggests that the Nazi dictator was familiar with Keynes's writings). Economic historians credit Hitler's massive rearmament and road-building programs with greatly reducing unemployment in Germany in the 1930s.

Example 25.6 shows how increased government purchases of goods and services can help to eliminate a recessionary gap. (The effects of government spending on transfer programs, such as unemployment benefits, are a bit different. We will return to that case shortly.)

An increase in the government's purchases eliminates a recessionary gap

EXAMPLE 25.6

In Example 25.5, we found that a drop of 10 units in consumer spending creates a recessionary gap of 50. Show that in that economy, a 10-unit increase in government purchases, from $\overline{G} = 300$ to $\overline{G} = 310$, will eliminate the output gap and restore full employment.

Intuitively, the 10-unit increase in government purchases should be just enough to offset the 10-unit decline in autonomous consumption expenditures and restore actual output to the full-employment level of 4,800. Let's confirm this result by solving for the value of short-run equilibrium output after the increase in government purchases.

As before, the first step is to write the relationship between aggregate demand AD and output Y. To do so, we write the definition of aggregate demand, $AD = C + I^p + G + NX$, and substitute for each of the four components. The first component, consumption spending, is given by

$$C = 610 + 0.8(Y - 250),$$

where $\overline{C} = 610$ and taxes $T = \overline{T} = 250$ (see Example 25.5). As before, planned investment I^p equals 220, and net exports NX equals 20. However, government purchases of goods and services, G, has increased from 300 to 310.

Substituting for these four components of aggregate demand yields

$$AD = [610 + 0.8(Y - 250)] + 220 + 310 + 20.$$

Simplifying, we get the relationship between aggregate demand and output:

$$AD = 960 + 0.8Y,$$

which is the same relationship we found for this economy in Examples 25.3 and 25.4.

The second step is to substitute the expression for aggregate demand into the definition of short-run equilibrium output, $Y = AD$. Doing so, we get

$$Y = 960 + 0.8Y.$$

Finally, solving this equation for the value of short-run equilibrium output, we get $Y = 4,800$, which is the same value assumed for potential output Y^*. Thus in this example the increase in government purchases eliminates the recessionary output gap.

The effect of the increase in government purchases is shown graphically in Figure 25.5. After the 10-unit decline in autonomous consumption spending $\overline{C}$,

FIGURE 25.5

An Increase in Government Purchases Eliminates a Recessionary Gap.

After a 10-unit decline in autonomous consumer spending $\overline{C}$, the economy is at point F, with a recessionary gap of 50 (see Figure 25.4). A 10-unit increase in government purchases raises autonomous aggregate demand by 10 units, shifting the expenditure line back to its original position and raising the equilibrium point from F to E. At point E, where output equals potential output ($Y = Y^* = 4,800$), the output gap has been eliminated.

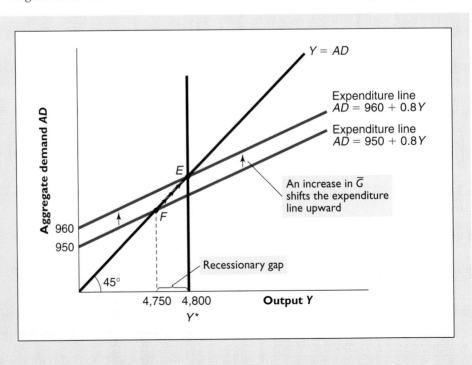

the economy is at point F, with a 50-unit recessionary gap. The 10-unit increase in government purchases raises the intercept of the expenditure line 10 units, causing the expenditure line to shift upward in parallel fashion. The economy returns to point E, where short-run equilibrium output equals potential output ($Y = Y^*$ = 4,800), and the output gap has been eliminated.

EXERCISE 25.5

In Exercise 25.4, you found that for the economy described in Exercise 25.1, an increase in planned investment from 600 to 630 leads to an expansionary output gap. Show how a change in government purchases could be used to eliminate this output gap. Confirm your answer numerically.

To this point we have been considering the effect of fiscal policy on a hypothetical economy. Economic Naturalists 25.3 and 25.4 illustrate the application of fiscal policy in real economies.

Why is Japan building roads nobody wants to use?

Japanese officials recently decided to build a toll road on the northern island of Hokkaido. About 32 miles of the planned 160-mile highway has been completed, at a cost of $1.9 billion, or $60 million per mile. Very few drivers use the road, largely because an existing highway that runs parallel to the new toll road is free. Officials tried to attract drivers by offering prizes and running promotional contests. Though the campaign succeeded in increasing the average number of cars on the road to 862 per day, the route is still the least used highway in Japan (*The New York Times*, Nov. 25, 1999, p. A1). Why is Japan building roads nobody wants to use?

Japan spent most of the 1990s in a deep recession (see Economic Naturalist 24.1), and the government has periodically initiated large spending programs to try to stimulate the economy. Indeed, during the 1990s the Japanese government spent more than $1 trillion on public works projects. More than $10 billion was spent on the Tokyo subway system, an amount so far over budget that subway tokens will have to cost an estimated $9.50 each if the investment is ever to be recouped. (Even more frustrating is that the subway does not run in a complete circle, requiring passengers to make inconvenient transfers to traverse the city.) Other examples of government spending programs include the construction of multimillion-dollar concert halls in small towns, elaborate tunnels where simple roads would have been adequate, and the digging up and relaying of cobblestone sidewalks. Despite all this spending, the Japanese recession has dragged on.

The basic Keynesian model implies that increases in government spending such as those undertaken in Japan should help to increase output and employment. Japanese public works projects do appear to have stimulated the economy, though not enough to pull Japan out of the recession. Why has Japan's fiscal policy proved inadequate to the task? Some critics have argued that the Japanese government was unconscionably slow in initiating the fiscal expansion, and that when spending was finally increased, it was simply not enough, relative to the size of the Japanese economy and the depth of the recession. Another possibility, which lies outside the basic Keynesian model, is that the wasteful nature of much of the government spending demoralized Japanese consumers, who realized that as taxpayers they would at some point be responsible for the costs incurred in building roads nobody wants to use. Reduced consumer confidence implies reduced consumption spending, which may to some extent have offset the stimulus from government spending. Very possibly, more productive investments of Japanese public funds would have had a greater impact on aggregate demand (by avoiding the fall in consumer confidence); certainly, they would have had a greater long-term benefit in terms of increasing the potential output of the economy.

ECONOMIC NATURALIST 25.3

Does military spending stimulate aggregate demand?

An antiwar poster from the 1960s bore the message "War is good business. Invest your son." War itself poses too many economic and human costs to be good for business, but military spending could be a different matter. According to the basic Keynesian model, increases in aggregate demand created by increased government spending may help bring an economy out of a recession or depression. Does military spending stimulate aggregate demand?

Figure 25.6 shows U.S. military spending as a share of GDP from 1940 to 1999. The blue areas in the figure correspond to periods of recession as shown in Table 24.1. Note the spike that occurred during World War II (1941–1945), when military spending reached nearly 38 percent of U.S. GDP, as well as the surge during the Korean War (1950–1953). Smaller increases in military spending relative to GDP occurred at the peak of the Vietnam War in 1967–1969 and during the Reagan military buildup of the 1980s.

FIGURE 25.6
U.S. Military Expenditures as a Share of GDP, 1940–1999.
Military expenditures as a share of GDP rose during World War II, the Korean War, the Vietnam War, and the Reagan military buildup of the early 1980s. Increased military spending is generally associated with an expanding economy and declining unemployment. The blue areas indicate periods of recession.

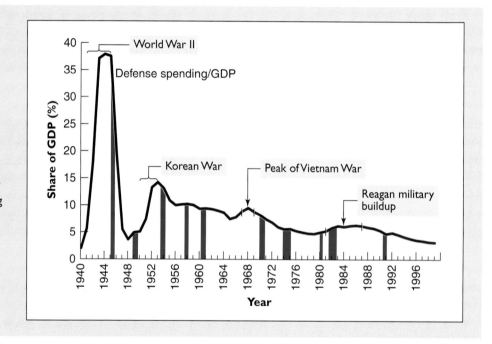

Figure 25.6 provides some support for the idea that expanded military spending tends to promote growth in aggregate demand. The clearest case is the World War II era, during which massive military spending helped the U.S. economy to recover from the Great Depression. The U.S. unemployment rate fell from 17.2 percent of the workforce in 1939 (when defense spending was less than 2 percent of GDP) to 1.2 percent in 1944 (when defense spending was greater than 37 percent of GDP). Two brief recessions, in 1945 and 1948–1949, followed the end of the war and the sharp decline in military spending. At the time, though, many people feared that the war's end would bring a resumption of the Depression, so the relative mildness of the two postwar recessions was something of a relief.

Increases in defense spending during the post-World War II period were also associated with economic expansions. The Korean War of 1950–1953 occurred simultaneously with a strong expansion, during which the unemployment rate dropped from 5.9 percent in 1949 to 2.9 percent in 1953. A recession began the year the war ended, 1954, though military spending had not yet declined much. Finally, economic expansions also occurred during the Vietnam-era military buildup in the 1960s and the Reagan buildup of the 1980s. These episodes support the idea that increases in government spending—in this case, for weapons and military supplies—can help to stimulate the economy.

"Your majesty, my voyage will not only forge a new route to the spices of the East but also create over three thousand new jobs."

TAXES, TRANSFERS, AND AGGREGATE DEMAND

Besides making decisions about government purchases of goods and services, fiscal policymakers also determine the level of tax collections (payments from the private sector to the government) and transfer payments (payments from the government to the private sector, such as welfare payments and Social Security). The basic Keynesian model implies that like changes in government purchases, changes in the level of taxes or transfers can be used to affect aggregate demand and thus to eliminate output gaps.

Unlike changes in government purchases, however, changes in taxes or transfers do not affect aggregate demand directly. Instead they work indirectly by changing disposable income in the private sector. Specifically, either a tax cut or an increase in government transfer payments increases disposable income in the private sector, which according to the consumption function should encourage households to spend more on consumer goods and services. In short, changes in taxes and transfers affect aggregate demand only to the extent that they change the level of spending in the private sector. Example 25.7 shows the effect of a tax cut (or an equal-size increase in transfers) on aggregate demand and short-run equilibrium output.

Using a tax cut to close a recessionary gap

EXAMPLE 25.7

In Example 25.5, we found that in our hypothetical economy, an initial drop in consumer spending of 10 units creates a recessionary gap of 50. Example 25.6 showed that this recessionary gap could be eliminated by a 10-unit increase in government purchases. Suppose that, instead of increasing government purchases, fiscal policymakers decided to stabilize aggregate demand by changing the level of tax collections. By how much should they change taxes to eliminate the output gap?

A common first guess at the answer to this problem is that policymakers should cut taxes by 10, but that guess is not correct. Let's see why.

The source of the recessionary gap in Example 25.5 is the assumption that households have reduced their consumption spending by 10 units at each level of output Y. To eliminate this recessionary gap, the change in taxes must induce households to increase their consumption spending by 10 units at each output level. However, if taxes T are cut by 10 units, raising disposable income $Y - T$ by 10 units, consumption at each level of output Y will increase by only 8 units. The reason is that the marginal propensity to consume out of disposable income is 0.8, so consumption spending increases by only 0.8 times the amount of the tax cut. (The rest of the tax cut is saved.)

To raise consumption spending by 10 units, fiscal policymakers must cut taxes by 12.5 units, from $\overline{T} = 250$ to $\overline{T} = 237.5$. Because $0.8(12.5) = 10$, a tax cut of 12.5 will spur households to increase their consumption by 10 units at each level of output. That increase will just offset the 10-unit decrease in autonomous consumption $\overline{C}$, restoring the economy to full employment.

We can check to see that setting $\overline{T} = 237.5$ will eliminate the recessionary gap. Under the assumptions that $\overline{C}$ takes its lower value of 610 and $\overline{T} = 237.5$, the consumption function is

$$C = 610 + 0.8(Y - 237.5).$$

Using the values for planned investment, government purchases, and net exports given in Example 25.2, we can write aggregate demand as

$$AD = [610 + 0.8(Y - 237.5)] + 220 + 300 + 20.$$

Simplifying in the usual way, we get

$$AD = 960 + 0.8Y,$$

which is the same expression we found in Example 25.2. Using this equation to substitute for AD in the definition of short-run equilibrium output $Y = AD$, we obtain

$$Y = 960 + 0.8Y.$$

Solving for Y, we find $Y = 4,800$, which is also the value of potential output. We conclude that a tax cut of 12.5 will eliminate the recessionary gap and restore full employment in this economy.

Note that since T refers to *net taxes*, or taxes less transfers, the same result could be obtained by increasing transfer payments by 12.5 units. Because households spend 0.8 times any increase in transfer payments they receive, this policy would also raise consumption spending by 10 units at any level of output.

Graphically, the effect of the tax cut is identical to the effect of the increase in government purchases, shown in Figure 25.5. Because it leads to a 10-unit increase in consumption at any level of output, the tax cut shifts the expenditure line up by 10 units. Equilibrium is attained at point E in Figure 25.5, where output again equals potential output.

EXERCISE 25.6

In Exercise 25.5, you eliminated an expansionary output gap from the economy described in Exercise 25.1 by changing government purchases. How could the same effect be achieved by changing tax collections?

RECAP **FISCAL POLICY AND AGGREGATE DEMAND**

Stabilization policies are policies used to affect aggregate demand with the objective of eliminating output gaps. Fiscal policy includes two methods for affecting aggregate demand: changes in government purchases and changes in taxes or transfer payments. An increase in government purchases increases autonomous aggregate demand by an equal amount. A reduction in taxes or an increase in transfer payments increases autonomous aggregate demand by an amount equal to the marginal propensity to consume times the reduction in taxes or increase in transfers. The ultimate effect of

> a fiscal policy change on short-run equilibrium output equals the change in autonomous aggregate demand times the multiplier.
>
> Accordingly, if the economy is in recession, an increase in government purchases, a cut in taxes, or an increase in transfers can be used to stimulate spending and eliminate the recessionary gap.

FISCAL POLICY AS A STABILIZATION TOOL: TWO QUALIFICATIONS

The basic Keynesian model might lead you to think that fiscal policy can be used quite precisely to eliminate output gaps. But as is often the case, the real world is more complicated than economic models. We close the chapter with two qualifications about the use of fiscal policy as a stabilization tool.

First, fiscal policy may affect potential output as well as aggregate demand. In the examples in this chapter we assumed that changes in government purchases, taxes, and transfer payments change aggregate demand without affecting the supply side of the economy, as represented by potential output. But as we saw in Chapter 20, this assumption often is not correct. On the spending side, for example, investments in public capital, such as roads, airports, and schools, can play a major role in the growth of potential output. On the other side of the ledger, tax and transfer programs may well affect the incentives, and thus the economic behavior, of households and firms. For example, a high tax rate on interest income reduces the after-tax return on saving, which may cause people to save less, while a tax break on new investment may encourage firms to increase their rate of capital formation. Such changes in saving or investment will in turn affect potential output. Many other examples could be given of how taxes and transfers affect economic behavior and thus potential output.

Some critics of the Keynesian theory have gone so far as to argue that the *only* effects of fiscal policy that matter are its effects on potential output. This was essentially the view of the so-called *supply-siders,* a group of economists and journalists whose influence reached a high point during the first Reagan administration (1981–1985). Through their arguments that lower taxes would substantially increase potential output, with no significant effect on aggregate demand, the supply-siders provided crucial support for the large tax cuts that took place under the Reagan administration.

A more balanced view is that fiscal policy affects both aggregate demand and potential output. Thus, government policymakers should take into account not only the need to stabilize aggregate demand but also the potential effects of government spending, taxes, and transfers on the economy's productive capacity.

The second qualification about the use of fiscal policy is that *fiscal policy is not always flexible enough to be useful for stabilization.* Our examples have implicitly assumed that the government can change spending or taxes relatively quickly in order to eliminate output gaps. In reality, changes in government spending or taxes must usually go through a lengthy legislative process, which reduces the ability of fiscal policy to respond in a timely way to economic conditions. Budget and tax changes proposed by the President must be submitted to Congress 18 months or more before they actually go into effect. Another factor that limits the flexibility of fiscal policy is that fiscal policymakers have many other objectives besides stabilizing aggregate demand, from assuring an adequate national defense to providing income support to the poor. What happens if, say, the need to strengthen the national defense requires an increase in government spending but the need to stabilize aggregate demand requires a decrease in spending? Such conflicts can be difficult to resolve through the political process.

automatic stabilizers

provisions in the law that imply *automatic* increases in government spending or decreases in taxes when real output declines

This lack of flexibility means that fiscal policy is less useful for stabilizing aggregate demand than the basic Keynesian model suggests. Nevertheless, most economists view fiscal policy as an important stabilizing force for two reasons. The first is the presence of **automatic stabilizers,** provisions in the law that imply *automatic* increases in government spending or decreases in taxes when real output declines. For example, some government spending is earmarked as "recession aid"; it flows to communities automatically when the unemployment rate reaches a certain level. Taxes and transfer payments also respond automatically to output gaps: When GDP declines, income tax collections fall (because households' taxable incomes fall), while unemployment insurance payments and welfare benefits rise—all without any explicit action by Congress. These automatic changes in government spending and tax collections help to increase aggregate demand during recessions and reduce it during expansions, without the delays inherent in the legislative process.

The second reason that fiscal policy is an important stabilizing force is that while fiscal policy may be difficult to change quickly, it may still be useful for dealing with prolonged episodes of recession. The Great Depression of the 1930s and the Japanese slump of the 1990s are two cases in point. However, because of the relative lack of flexibility of fiscal policy, in modern economies aggregate demand is more usually stabilized through monetary policy. The role of monetary policy in stabilizing aggregate demand is the subject of the next chapter.

■ SUMMARY ■

- The basic Keynesian model shows how fluctuations in aggregate spending, or aggregate demand, can cause actual output to differ from potential output. Too little spending leads to a recessionary output gap, while too much spending creates an expansionary output gap. This model relies on two basic assumptions: that aggregate demand fluctuates, and that in the short run, firms will meet the demand for their products at preset prices.

- *Aggregate demand* is total planned spending on final goods and services. The four components of total spending are consumption, investment, government purchases, and net exports. Planned and actual consumption, government purchases, and net exports are assumed to be the same. Actual investment may differ from planned investment, because firms may sell a greater or lesser amount of their production than they expected. If firms sell less than they expected, for example, they are forced to add more goods to inventory than anticipated. And because additions to inventory are counted as part of investment, in this case actual investment (including inventory investment) is greater than planned investment.

- Consumption is related to disposable, or after-tax, income by a relationship called the *consumption function*. The amount by which desired consumption rises when disposable income rises by $1 is called the *marginal propensity to consume* (MPC). The marginal propensity to consume is always greater than 0 but less than 1.

- An increase in real output raises aggregate demand, since higher output (and equivalently, higher income) encourages households to consume more. Aggregate demand can be broken down into two components, autonomous aggregate demand and induced aggregate demand. *Autonomous*

aggregate demand is the portion of aggregate demand that is determined outside the model; *induced aggregate demand* is the portion that is determined within the model. In the model presented in this chapter, induced aggregate demand is the part of aggregate demand that depends on current output.

- At predetermined prices, *short-run equilibrium output* is the level of output that equals aggregate demand. Short-run equilibrium can be determined graphically in a Keynesian cross diagram, drawn with aggregate demand on the vertical axis and output on the horizontal axis. The Keynesian cross contains two lines: an expenditure line, which relates aggregate demand to output, and a 45° line, which represents the condition that short-run equilibrium output equals aggregate demand. Short-run equilibrium output is determined at the point at which these two lines intersect. Algebraically, short-run equilibrium output can be found by setting output equal to aggregate demand and solving for the value of output (see Box 25.2).

- Changes in autonomous aggregate demand will lead to changes in short-run equilibrium output. In particular, if the economy is initially at full employment, a fall in autonomous aggregate demand will create a recessionary gap and a rise in autonomous aggregate demand will create an expansionary gap. The effect of a one-unit increase in autonomous aggregate demand on short-run equilibrium output is called the *multiplier*. An increase in autonomous aggregate demand not only raises spending directly, it also raises the incomes of producers, who in turn increase their spending, and so on. Hence the multiplier is greater than 1; that is, a $1 increase in autonomous aggregate demand raises short-run equilibrium output by more than $1.

- To eliminate output gaps and restore full employment, the government employs *stabilization policies*. The two major types of stabilization policy are monetary policy and fiscal policy. Stabilization policies work by changing aggregate demand, and hence short-run equilibrium output. For example, an increase in government purchases raises aggregate demand, so it can be used to reduce or eliminate a recessionary gap. Similarly, a cut in taxes or an increase in transfer payments increases the public's disposable income, raising consumption and aggregate demand. Higher aggregate demand, in turn, raises short-run equilibrium output.

- Two qualifications must be made to the use of fiscal policy as a stabilization tool. First, fiscal policy may affect potential output as well as aggregate demand. And second, because changes in fiscal policy must go through a lengthy legislative process, fiscal policy is not always flexible enough to be useful for short-run stabilization. However, *automatic stabilizers*—provisions in the law that imply automatic increases in government spending or reductions in taxes when output declines—can overcome the problem of legislative delays to some extent and contribute to economic stability.

▪ KEY TERMS ▪

aggregate demand (*AD*) (659)
automatic stabilizers (682)
autonomous aggregate demand (663)
consumption function (661)

income-expenditure multiplier (673)
induced aggregate demand (663)
marginal propensity to consume
  (*MPC*) (661)

menu costs (658)
short-run equilibrium output (665)
stabilization policies (675)

▪ REVIEW QUESTIONS ▪

1. What are the two key assumptions of the basic Keynesian model? Explain why each of the two assumptions is necessary if one is to accept the view that aggregate spending is a driving force behind short-term economic fluctuations.

2. Give an example of a good or service whose price changes very frequently and one whose price changes relatively infrequently. What accounts for the difference?

3. Define *aggregate demand* and list its components. Why does aggregate demand change when output changes?

4. Explain how planned spending and actual spending can differ. Illustrate with an example.

5. Sketch a graph of the consumption function, labeling the axes of the graph. Discuss the economic meaning of (a) a movement from left to right along the graph of the consumption function and of (b) a parallel upward shift of the consumption function.

6. Sketch the Keynesian cross diagram. Explain in words the economic significance of the two lines graphed in the diagram. Given only this diagram, how could you determine autonomous aggregate demand, induced aggregate demand, the marginal propensity to consume, and short-run equilibrium output?

7. Using the Keynesian cross diagram, illustrate the two causes of the 1990–1991 recession discussed in Economic Naturalist 25.1.

8. Define the *multiplier*. In economic terms, why is the multiplier greater than 1?

9. The government is considering two alternative policies, one involving increased government purchases of 50, the other involving a tax cut of 50. Which policy will stimulate aggregate demand by more? Why?

▪ PROBLEMS ▪

1. Acme Manufacturing is producing $4,000,000 worth of goods this year and is expecting to sell its entire production. It is also planning to purchase $1,500,000 in new equipment during the year. At the beginning of the year the company has $500,000 in inventory in its warehouse. Find actual investment and planned investment if:
   a. Acme actually sells $3,850,000 worth of goods.
   b. Acme actually sells $4,000,000 worth of goods.
   c. Acme actually sells $4,200,000 worth of goods.
   Assuming that Acme's situation is similar to that of other firms, in which of these three cases is output equal to short-run equilibrium output?

2. Data on before-tax income, taxes paid, and consumption spending for the Simpson family in various years are given below.

Before-tax income ($)	Taxes paid ($)	Consumption spending ($)
25,000	3,000	20,000
27,000	3,500	21,350
28,000	3,700	22,070
30,000	4,000	23,600

a. Graph the Simpsons' consumption function, and find their household's marginal propensity to consume.

b. How much would you expect the Simpsons to consume if their income was $32,000 and they paid taxes of $5,000?

c. Homer Simpson wins a lottery prize. As a result, the Simpson family increases its consumption by $1,000 at each level of after-tax income. ("Income" does not include the prize money.) How does this change affect the graph of their consumption function? How does it affect their marginal propensity to consume?

3. An economy is described by the following equations:

$$C = 1{,}800 + 0.6(Y - T),$$

$$I^p = \bar{I} = 900,$$

$$G = \bar{G} = 1{,}500,$$

$$NX = \overline{NX} = 100,$$

$$T = \bar{T} = 1{,}500,$$

$$Y^* = 9{,}000.$$

a. Find an equation linking aggregate demand to output.

b. Find autonomous aggregate demand and induced aggregate demand.

4. For the economy described in Problem 3:

a. Construct a table like Table 25.1 to find short-run equilibrium output. Consider possible values for short-run equilibrium output ranging from 8,200 to 9,000.

b. Solve numerically for short-run equilibrium output.

c. Show the determination of short-run equilibrium output for this economy using the Keynesian cross diagram.

d. What is the output gap for this economy? If the natural rate of unemployment is 4 percent, what is the actual unemployment rate for this economy (use Okun's law)?

5. For the economy described in Problem 3, find the effect on short-run equilibrium output of each of the following changes, taken one at a time:

a. An increase in government purchases from 1,500 to 1,600

b. A decrease in tax collections from 1,500 to 1,400

c. A decrease in planned investment spending from 900 to 800

What is the value of the multiplier for this economy?

6. For the following economy, find autonomous aggregate demand, the multiplier, short-run equilibrium output, and the output gap. By how much would autonomous aggregate demand have to change to eliminate the output gap?

$$C = 3{,}000 + 0.5(Y - T),$$

$$I^p = \bar{I} = 1{,}500,$$

$$G = \bar{G} = 2{,}500,$$

$$NX = \overline{NX} = 200,$$

$$T = \overline{T} = 2,000,$$

$$Y^* = 12,000.$$

7. An economy has zero net exports ($\overline{NX} = 0$). Otherwise, it is identical to the economy described in Problem 6.
   a. Find short-run equilibrium output.
   b. Economic recovery abroad increases the demand for the country's exports; as a result, $\overline{NX}$ rises to 100. What happens to short-run equilibrium output?
   c. Repeat part b, but this time assume that foreign economies are slowing, reducing the demand for the country's exports so that $\overline{NX} = -100$. (A negative value of net exports means that exports are less than imports.)
   d. How do your results help to explain the tendency of recessions and expansions to spread across countries?

8. In a particular economy, planned investment spending is given by the equation

$$I^p = 300 + 0.1Y.$$

   This equation captures the idea that when real GDP rises, firms find it more profitable to make capital investments. Specifically, in this economy, when real GDP rises by a dollar, planned investment spending rises by 10 cents. All the other equations describing this economy are the same as in Problem 6. Find autonomous aggregate demand, the multiplier, short-run equilibrium output, and the output gap. (Be careful: The multiplier is no longer given by the formula $1/(1-c)$. You will need to calculate directly the effect of a change in autonomous aggregate demand on short-run equilibrium output.) By how much would autonomous aggregate demand have to change to eliminate any output gap?

9. An economy is described by the following equations:

$$C = 40 + 0.8(Y - T),$$

$$I^p = \overline{I} = 70,$$

$$G = \overline{G} = 120,$$

$$NX = \overline{NX} = 10,$$

$$T = \overline{T} = 150.$$

   a. Potential output Y^* equals 580. By how much would government purchases have to change to eliminate any output gap? By how much would taxes have to change? Show the effects of these fiscal policy changes in a Keynesian cross diagram.
   b. Repeat part a assuming that $Y^* = 630$.

10. (More difficult) This problem illustrates the workings of automatic stabilizers. Suppose that the components of aggregate demand in an economy take their usual forms: $C = \overline{C} + c(Y - T)$, $I^p = \overline{I}$, $G = \overline{G}$, and $NX = \overline{NX}$. However, suppose that, realistically, taxes are not fixed but depend on income. Specifically, we assume

$$T = tY,$$

where t (a number between 0 and 1) is the fraction of income paid in taxes (the tax rate). As we will see in this problem, a tax system of this sort serves as an automatic stabilizer, because taxes collected automatically fall when incomes fall.
    a. Find an algebraic expression for short-run equilibrium output in this economy.

b. Find an algebraic expression for the multiplier, that is, the amount that output changes when autonomous aggregate demand changes by one unit. Compare the expression you found to the formula for the multiplier when taxes are fixed. Show that making taxes proportional to income reduces the multiplier.

c. Explain how reducing the size of the multiplier helps to stabilize the economy, holding constant fluctuations in the components of autonomous aggregate demand.

d. Suppose $\overline{C} = 500$, $\overline{I} = 1,500$, $\overline{G} = 2,000$, $\overline{NX} = 0$, $c = 0.8$, and $t = 0.25$. Calculate numerical values for short-run equilibrium output and the multiplier.

■ ANSWERS TO IN-CHAPTER EXERCISES ■

25.1 First we need to find an equation that relates aggregate demand to output. We start with the definition of aggregate demand and substitute the numerical values given in the problem:

$$AD = C + I^P + G + NX,$$

$$= [\overline{C} + c(Y - T)] + \overline{I} + \overline{G} + \overline{NX},$$

$$= [820 + 0.7(Y - 600)] + 600 + 600 + 200,$$

$$= 1,800 + 0.7Y.$$

Using this relationship we construct a table analogous to Table 25.1. Some trial and error is necessary to find an appropriate range of guesses for output (column 1).

Determination of Short-Run Equilibrium Output

(1) Output Y	(2) Aggregate demand AD = 1,800 + 0.7Y	(3) Y − AD	(4) Y = AD?
5,000	5,300	−300	No
5,200	5,440	−240	No
5,400	5,580	−180	No
5,600	5,720	−120	No
5,800	5,860	−60	No
6,000	6,000	0	Yes
6,200	6,140	60	No
6,400	6,280	120	No
6,600	6,420	180	No

Short-run equilibrium output equals 6,000, as that is the only level of output that satisfies the condition $Y = AD$.

25.2 The graph shows the determination of short-run equilibrium output, $Y = 6,000$. The intercept of the expenditure line is 1,800, and its slope is 0.7. Notice that the intercept equals autonomous aggregate demand and the slope equals the marginal propensity to consume.

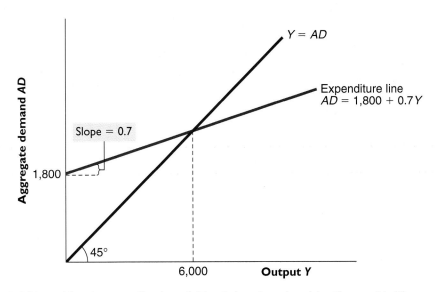

25.3 This problem is an application of Okun's law, introduced in Chapter 24. The recessionary gap in this example is 50/4,800, or about 1.04 percent, of potential output. By Okun's law, cyclical unemployment is one-half the percentage size of the output gap, or 0.52 percent. As the natural rate of unemployment is 5 percent, total unemployment rate after the recessionary gap appears will be approximately 5.52 percent.

25.4 To find short-run equilibrium output after the increase in planned investment spending, we first find the relationship between aggregate demand and output. The steps are the same as in Exercise 25.1 except now we assume $\bar{I} = 630$.

$$AD = C + I^P + G + NX$$

$$= [\bar{C} + c(Y - T)] + \bar{I} + \bar{G} + \overline{NX}$$

$$= [820 + 0.7(Y - 600)] + 630 + 600 + 200$$

$$= 1,830 + 0.7Y.$$

Comparing with Exercise 25.1, we see that the increase of 30 in planned investment spending raises the intercept of the expenditure line by 30.

To solve for short-run equilibrium output, set $Y = AD$, use the expression above to substitute for AD, and solve for Y:

$$Y = AD$$

$$= 1,830 + 0.7Y$$

$$= 6,100.$$

Hence the increase in planned investment causes output to increase from 6,000 (see Exercise 25.1) to 6,100. If the economy had no output gap before the increase in planned investment, the increase leads to an expansionary output gap of $6,100 - 6,000 = 100$.

25.5 The increase in planned investment raised autonomous aggregate demand by 30. A reduction of 30 in government purchases will restore autonomous aggregate demand to its original level and thus eliminate the output gap. It is straightforward to show directly that if $\bar{I} = 630$ and government purchases $\bar{G}$ are lowered from 600 to 570, then

$$AD = 1,800 + 0.7Y.$$

Setting $Y = AD$ and solving for Y, we find that short-run equilibrium output is 6,000, its original value.

25.6   An increase of 30 in planned investment created the output gap, so to eliminate the output gap autonomous aggregate demand must be reduced by 30. The marginal propensity to consume is 0.7 in this economy, so an increase in taxes of $30/0.7 = 42.9$ will achieve a reduction of 30 (or 0.7×42.9) in autonomous consumption spending. To confirm the answer, show that if $\bar{I} = 630$ and $\bar{T} = 600 - 42.9 = 557.1$ then short-run equilibrium output equals 6,000, its original value.

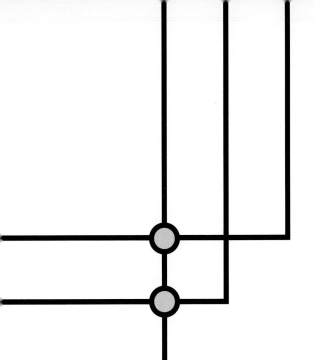

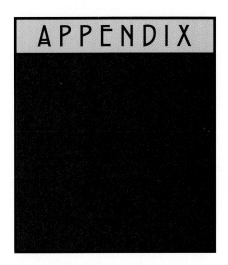

AN ALGEBRAIC SOLUTION OF THE BASIC KEYNESIAN MODEL

■

This chapter showed how to solve the basic Keynesian model in two steps, given specific numerical values for the parameters. In this appendix we will show that the same steps can be used to find a more general algebraic solution for short-run equilibrium output in the basic Keynesian model. This solution has the advantage of showing clearly the links between short-run equilibrium output, the multiplier, and autonomous aggregate demand. The general method can also be applied when we make changes to the basic Keynesian model, as we will see in subsequent chapters.

The model we will work with is the same one presented earlier. It is based on the consumption function, Equation 25.2, and the assumption that the other three components of aggregate demand are fixed. We assume also that tax collections are fixed. These assumptions may be summarized as follows:

$$C = \overline{C} + c(Y - T),$$

$$I^p = \overline{I},$$

$$G = \overline{G},$$

$$NX = \overline{NX},$$

$$T = \overline{T}.$$

The first step in solving the model is to relate aggregate demand to output. The definition of aggregate demand, Equation 25.1, is

$$AD = C + I^p + G + NX.$$

As before, we substitute for the components of aggregate demand to get

$$AD = [\overline{C} - c(Y - \overline{T})] + \overline{I} + \overline{G} + \overline{NX}.$$

Rearranging this equation to separate the terms that do and do not depend on output Y, we obtain

$$AD = (\overline{C} - c\overline{T} + \overline{I} + \overline{G} + \overline{NX}) + cY.$$

This is Equation 25.3. The term in parentheses on the right side of the equation represents autonomous aggregate demand, and the term cY represents induced aggregate demand.

The second step in solving for short-run equilibrium output begins with its definition, $Y = AD$. Using the equation just above to substitute for AD, we have

$$Y = (C - c\overline{T} + \overline{I} + \overline{G} + \overline{NX}) + cY.$$

To solve this equation for Y, it is convenient to group all terms involving Y on the left side of the equation:

$$Y - cY = (\overline{C} - c\overline{T} + \overline{I} + \overline{G} + \overline{NX}),$$

or

$$Y(1 - c) = (\overline{C} - c\overline{T} + \overline{I} + \overline{G} + \overline{NX}).$$

Dividing both sides of the equation by $(1 - c)$ gives the answer:

$$Y = \left(\frac{1}{1 - c}\right)(\overline{C} - c\overline{T} + \overline{I} + \overline{G} + \overline{NX}). \tag{A.1}$$

Equation A.1 gives short-run equilibrium output for our model economy in terms of the values of $\overline{C}$, $\overline{I}$, $\overline{G}$, $\overline{NX}$, and $\overline{T}$ and the marginal propensity to consume c. We can use this formula to solve for short-run equilibrium output in specific numerical examples. For example, suppose we plug in the numerical values assumed in Example 25.2: $\overline{C} = 620$, $\overline{I} = 220$, $\overline{G} = 300$, $\overline{NX} = 20$, $\overline{T} = 250$, and $c = 0.8$. We get

$$Y = \left(\frac{1}{1 - 0.8}\right)[620 - 0.8(250) + 220 + 300 + 20]$$

$$= \frac{1}{0.2}(960) = 5 \times 960 = 4,800,$$

which is the same answer found earlier.

Equation A.1 shows clearly the relationship between autonomous aggregate demand and short-run equilibrium output. Autonomous aggregate demand is the second term on the right side of Equation A.1, equal to $\overline{C} - c\overline{T} + \overline{I} + \overline{G} + \overline{NX}$. The equation shows that a one-unit increase in autonomous aggregate demand increases short-run equilibrium output by $1/(1 - c)$ units. In other words, we can see from Equation A.1 that the *multiplier* for this model equals $1/(1 - c)$, a result that we found more indirectly in Box 25.3.

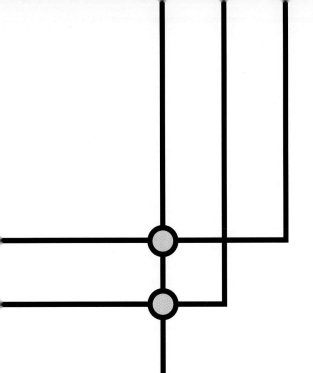

CHAPTER
26

STABILIZING AGGREGATE DEMAND: THE ROLE OF THE FED

■

Financial market participants and commentators go to remarkable lengths to try to predict the actions of the Federal Reserve. For a while, the CNBC financial news program *Squawk Box* reported regularly on what they called the Greenspan Briefcase Indicator. The idea was to spot Fed Chairman Alan Greenspan on his way to meet with the Federal Open Market Committee, the group that determines U.S. monetary policy (see Chapter 23). If Greenspan's briefcase was packed full, presumably with macroeconomic data and analyses, the guess was that the Fed planned to change interest rates. A slim briefcase meant no change in rates was likely.

"It was right 17 out of the first 20 times," the program's anchor Mark Haines told *The New York Times Magazine* (Nov. 28, 1999, p. 35), "but it has a built-in self-destruct mechanism, because Greenspan packs his [own] briefcase. He can make it wrong or right. He has never publicly acknowledged the indicator, but we have reason to believe that he knows about it. We have to consider the fact that he wants us to stop doing it because the last two times the briefcase has been wrong, and that's disturbing."

The Briefcase Indicator is but one example of the close public scrutiny that the Chairman of the Federal Reserve and other monetary policymakers face. Every speech, every congressional testimony, every interview from a member of the Board of Governors is closely analyzed for clues about the future course of monetary policy. In self-defense, Greenspan and other policymakers have become masters of the carefully worded but often ambiguous public statement calculated to leave the "Fed watchers" guessing. The reason for the intense public interest in the Federal Reserve's decisions about monetary policy—and especially the level of interest rates—is that those decisions have important implications for both financial markets and the economy in general.

In this chapter we examine the workings of monetary policy, one of the two major types of *stabilization policy*. (The other type, fiscal policy, was discussed in Chapter 25.) As we saw in Chapter 25, stabilization policies are government policies that are meant to influence aggregate demand, with the goal of eliminating output gaps. Both types of stabilization policy are important and have been useful at various times. However, monetary policy, which can be changed quickly by a decision of the Federal Open Market Committee, is more flexible and responsive than fiscal policy, which can only be changed by legislative action. Under normal circumstances, therefore, monetary policy is used more actively than fiscal policy to help stabilize the economy.

We will begin this chapter by discussing how the Fed uses its ability to control the money supply to influence the level of interest rates, both nominal and real. We then turn to the economic effects of changes in interest rates. Building on our analysis of the basic Keynesian model in Chapter 25, we will see that, in the short run, monetary policy achieves its effects by influencing aggregate demand and thus short-run equilibrium output. We will defer for the moment discussion of the other major effect of monetary policy actions, changes in the rate of inflation. The effects of monetary policy on inflation will be addressed in Chapter 27.

THE FEDERAL RESERVE AND INTEREST RATES

When we introduced the Federal Reserve System in Chapter 23, we focused on the Fed's tools for controlling the money supply: the quantity of currency and checking accounts held by the public. As we first discussed in Chapter 17, the determination of the money supply is the primary task of monetary policymakers. But if you follow the economic news regularly, you may find the idea that the Fed's job is to control the money supply a bit foreign, because the media nearly always focus on the Fed's decisions about *interest rates*. Indeed, the announcement the Fed makes after each meeting of the Federal Open Market Committee nearly always concerns the plan for a particular short-term interest rate, called the *federal funds rate* (more on the federal funds rate later).

Actually, there is no contradiction between the two ways of looking at monetary policy—as control of the money supply or as the setting of interest rates. As we will see in this section, controlling the money supply and controlling the nominal interest rate are two sides of the same coin: Any value of the money supply chosen by the Fed implies a specific setting for the nominal interest rate, and vice versa. The reason for this close connection is that the nominal interest rate is effectively the "price" of money (or, more accurately, its opportunity cost). So, by controlling the quantity of money supplied to the economy, the Fed also controls the "price" of money (the nominal interest rate).

To better understand how the Fed determines interest rates, we will look first at the market for money, beginning with the demand side of that market. We will see that given the demand for money by the public, the Fed can control interest rates by changing the amount of money supplied to the public. Later we will show how the Fed uses control of interest rates to influence aggregate demand and the state of the economy.

THE DEMAND FOR MONEY

Recall from Chapter 23 that *money* refers to the set of assets, such as cash and checking accounts, that are usable in transactions. Money is also a store of value, just as stocks, bonds, or real estate are—in other words, money is a type of financial asset. As a financial asset, money is a way of holding wealth.

Anyone who has some wealth, even a small amount, must determine the *form* in which he or she wishes to hold that wealth. For example, if Louis has wealth of $10,000, he could if he wished hold all $10,000 in cash. Or he could hold $5,000 of his wealth in the form of cash and $5,000 in government bonds. Or he could hold $1,000 in cash, $2,000 in a checking account, $2,000 in government bonds, and $5,000 in rare stamps. Indeed, there are thousands of different real and financial assets to choose from, all of which can be held in different amounts and combinations, so Louis's choices are virtually infinite. The decision about the forms in which to hold one's wealth is called the **portfolio allocation decision.**

What determines the particular mix of assets that Louis or another wealth holder will choose? We discussed some of the factors that affect the portfolio allocation decision in Chapter 23. All else being equal, people generally prefer to hold assets that they expect to pay a high *return* and that do not carry too much *risk.* They may also try to reduce the overall risk they face through *diversification,* that is, by owning a variety of different assets. Many people own some real assets, such as a car or a home, because they provide services (transportation or shelter) and often a financial return (an increase in value, as when the price of a home rises in a strong real estate market).

Here we do not need to analyze the entire portfolio allocation decision, but only one part of it—namely, the decision about how much of one's wealth to hold in the form of *money* (cash and checking accounts). The amount of wealth an individual chooses to hold in the form of money is that individual's **demand for money.** So if Louis decided to hold his entire $10,000 in the form of cash, his demand for money would be $10,000. But if he were to hold $1,000 in cash, $2,000 in a checking account, $2,000 in government bonds, and $5,000 in rare stamps, his demand for money would be only $3,000—that is, $1,000 in cash plus the $2,000 in his checking account.

Consuelo's demand for money

Example 22.1 presented the balance sheet of an individual named Consuelo (see Table 22.1). What is her demand for money? If Consuelo wanted to increase her money holdings by $100, how could she do so? What if she wanted to reduce her money holdings by $100?

Looking back at Table 22.1, we see that Consuelo's balance sheet shows five different asset types: cash, a checking account, shares of stock, a car, and furniture. Of these assets, the first two (the cash and the checking account) are forms of money. As shown in Table 22.1, Consuelo's money holdings consist of $80 in cash and $1,200 in her checking account. Thus Consuelo's demand for money—the amount of wealth she chooses to hold in the form of money—is $1,280.

There are many different ways in which Consuelo could increase her money holdings, or demand for money, by $100. She could sell $100 worth of stock and deposit the proceeds in the bank. That action would leave the total value of her assets and her wealth unchanged (because the decrease in her stockholdings would be offset by the increase in her checking account), but would increase her money holdings by $100. Another possibility would be to take a $100 cash advance on her credit card. That action would increase both her money holdings and her assets by $100, but it would also increase her liabilities—specifically, her credit card balance—by $100. Once again, her total wealth would not change, though her money holdings would increase.

portfolio allocation decision the decision about the forms in which to hold one's wealth

demand for money the amount of wealth an individual chooses to hold in the form of money

EXAMPLE 26.1

To reduce her money holdings, Consuelo need only use some of her cash or checking account balance to acquire a nonmoney asset or pay down a liability. For example, if she were to buy an additional $100 of stock by writing a check against her bank account, her money holdings would decline by $100. Similarly, writing a check to reduce her credit card balance by $100 would reduce her money holdings by $100. You can confirm that though her money holdings decline, in neither case does Consuelo's total wealth change.

How much money should an individual (or household) choose to hold? Application of the *cost-benefit principle* tells us that an individual should increase his or her money holdings only so long as the benefit of doing so exceeds the cost. As we saw in Chapter 23, the principal *benefit* of holding money is its usefulness in carrying out transactions. Consuelo's shares of stock, her car, and her furniture are all valuable assets, but she cannot use them to buy groceries or pay her rent. She can make routine payments using cash or her checking account, however. Because of its usefulness in daily transactions, Consuelo will almost certainly want to hold some of her wealth in the form of money. Furthermore, if Consuelo is a high-income individual, she will probably choose to hold more money than someone with a lower income would, because she is likely to spend more and carry out more transactions than the low-income person.

Consuelo's benefit from holding money is also affected by the technological and financial sophistication of the society she lives in. For example, in the United States, developments such as credit cards, debit cards, and ATMs have generally reduced the amount of money people need to carry out routine transactions, decreasing the public's demand for money at given levels of income. In 1960, for example, *M*1 money holdings (primarily cash and checking account balances) in the United States were about 28 percent of GDP; by 1999 that ratio had fallen to 12 percent.

Although money is an extremely useful asset, there is also a cost to holding money—more precisely, an opportunity cost—which arises from the fact that most forms of money pay little or no interest. Cash pays zero interest, and most checking accounts carry very low interest rates. For the sake of simplicity, we will assume in the rest of this book that *the nominal interest rate on money is zero.* In contrast, most alternative assets, such as bonds or stocks, pay a positive nominal return. Each extra dollar of money that a person holds, therefore, reduces by $1 the value of higher-yielding assets in the person's portfolio. The *opportunity cost* of holding money is thus the interest that could have been earned if the person had chosen to hold interest-bearing assets instead of money. All else being equal, the higher the nominal interest rate, the higher the opportunity cost of holding money, and the less money people will choose to hold.

We have been talking about the demand for money by individuals, but businesses also hold money to carry out transactions with customers and to pay workers and suppliers. The same general factors that determine individuals' money demand also affect the demand for money by businesses. That is, in choosing how much money to hold, a business, like an individual, will compare the benefits of holding money for use in transactions with the opportunity cost of holding a non-interest-bearing asset. While we will not differentiate between the money held by individuals and the money held by businesses in discussing money demand, you should be aware that in the U.S. economy, businesses hold a significant portion—more than half—of the total money stock. Example 26.2 illustrates the determination of money demand by a businessowner.

Innovations such as ATMs have reduced the amount of money that people need to hold for routine transactions.

© Aaron Haupt/Stock Boston

EXAMPLE 26.2   **How much money should Kim's restaurants hold?**

Kim owns several successful restaurants. Her accountant informs her that on the typical day her restaurants are holding a total of $50,000 in cash on the premises. Of this, only $25,000 is essential for carrying out normal business. The accountant points out that if Kim's restaurants reduced their cash holdings, Kim could use the extra cash to purchase interest-bearing government bonds.

The accountant proposes two methods of reducing the amount of cash Kim's restaurants hold. First, she could increase the frequency of cash pickups by her armored car service. The extra service would cost $500 annually but would allow Kim's restaurants to reduce their average cash holding to $40,000. Second, in addition to the extra pickups, Kim could employ a computerized cash management service to help her keep closer tabs on the inflows and outflows of cash at her restaurants. The service costs $700 a year, but the accountant estimates that, together with more frequent pickups, the more efficient cash management provided by the service could help Kim reduce average cash holdings at her restaurants to $30,000.

The interest rate on government bonds is 6 percent. How much money should Kim's restaurants hold? What if the interest rate on government bonds is 8 percent?

Kim's restaurants need cash to carry out their normal business, but holding more cash than absolutely necessary has an opportunity cost, which is the interest those funds could be earning if they were held in the form of government bonds instead of zero-interest cash. As the interest rate on government bonds is 6 percent, each $10,000 by which Kim can reduce her restaurants' money holdings yields an annual benefit of $600 (6 percent of $10,000).

If Kim increases the frequency of pickups by her armored car service, reducing the restaurants' average money holdings from $50,000 to $40,000, the benefit will be the additional $600 in interest income that Kim will earn. The cost is the $500 charged by the armored car company. Since the benefit exceeds the cost, Kim should purchase the extra service and reduce the average cash holdings at her restaurants to $40,000.

Should Kim go a step further and employ the cash management service as well? Doing so would reduce average cash holdings at the restaurants from $40,000 to $30,000, which has a benefit in terms of extra interest income of $600 per year. However, this benefit is less than the cost of the cash management service, which is $700 per year. So Kim should *not* employ the cash management service and instead should maintain average cash holdings in her restaurants of $40,000.

If the interest rate on government bonds rises to 8 percent, then the benefit of each $10,000 reduction in average money holdings is $800 per year (8 percent of $10,000) in extra interest income. In this case the benefit of employing the cash management service, $800, exceeds the cost of doing so, which is $700. So Kim should employ the service, reducing the average cash holdings of her business to $30,000. This example shows that a higher nominal interest rate on alternative assets reduces the quantity of money demanded.

EXERCISE 26.1

The interest rate on government bonds falls from 6 to 4 percent. How much cash should Kim's restaurants hold now?

MACROECONOMIC FACTORS THAT AFFECT THE DEMAND FOR MONEY

In any household or business the demand for money will depend on a variety of individual circumstances. For example, a high-volume retail business that serves thousands of customers each day will probably choose to have more money on hand than a legal firm that bills clients and pays employees monthly. But while individuals and businesses vary considerably in the amount of money they choose to hold, three macroeconomic factors affect the demand for money quite broadly: the nominal interest rate, real output, and the price level. As we see next, the nominal interest rate affects the cost of holding money throughout the economy, while real output and the price level affect the benefits of money.

- *The nominal interest rate* (*i*). We have seen that the interest rate paid on alternatives to money, such as government bonds, determines the opportunity cost of holding money. The higher the prevailing nominal interest rate, the greater the opportunity cost of holding money, and hence the less money individuals and businesses will demand.

What do we mean by *the* nominal interest rate? As we saw in Chapter 23, there are thousands of different assets, each with its own interest rate (rate of return). So can we really talk about *the* nominal interest rate? The answer is, that while there certainly are many different assets, each with its own corresponding interest rate, the rates on those assets tend to rise and fall together. That is to be expected, because if the interest rates on some assets were to rise sharply while the rates on other assets declined, financial investors would flock to the assets paying high rates and refuse to buy the assets paying low rates. So, although there are many different interest rates, speaking of the general level of interest rates usually does make sense. In this book, when we talk about *the* nominal interest rate, what we mean is some average measure of interest rates. This simplification is one more application of the macroeconomic concept of *aggregation,* introduced in Chapter 17.

The nominal interest rate is a macroeconomic factor that affects the cost of holding money. A macroeconomic factor that affects the *benefit* of holding money is:

- *Real income or output* (*Y*). An increase in aggregate real income or output— as measured, for example, by real GDP—raises the quantity of goods and services that people and businesses want to buy and sell. When the economy enters a boom, for example, people do more shopping and stores have more customers. To accommodate the increase in transactions, both individuals and businesses need to hold more money. Thus higher real output raises the demand for money.

A second macroeconomic factor affecting the benefit of holding money is:

- *The price level* (*P*). The higher the prices of goods and services, the more dollars (or yen, or euros) are needed to make a given set of transactions. Thus a higher price level is associated with a higher demand for money.

Today, when a couple of teenagers go out for a movie and snacks on Saturday night, they need probably five times as much cash as their parents did 25 years ago. Because the prices of movie tickets and popcorn have risen steeply over 25 years, more money (that is, more dollars) is needed to pay for a Saturday night date than in the past. By the way, the fact that prices are higher today does *not* imply that people are worse off today than in the past, because nominal wages and salaries have also risen substantially. But in general, higher prices do imply that people need to keep a greater number of dollars available, in cash or in a checking account.

THE MONEY DEMAND CURVE

For the purposes of monetary policymaking, economists are most interested in the aggregate, or economywide, demand for money. The interaction of the aggregate demand for money, determined by the public, and the aggregate supply of money, which is set by the Fed, determines the nominal interest rate that prevails in the economy.

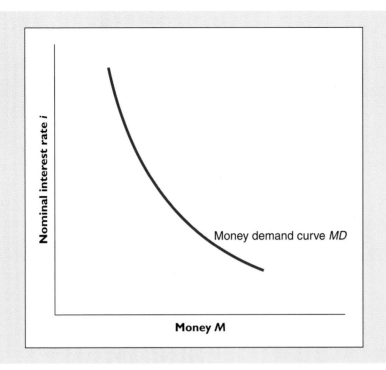

FIGURE 26.1
The Money Demand Curve.
The money demand curve relates the economywide demand for money to the nominal interest rate. Because an increase in the nominal interest rate raises the opportunity cost of holding money, the money demand curve slopes down.

The economywide demand for money can be represented graphically by the *money demand curve* (see Figure 26.1). The **money demand curve** relates the aggregate quantity of money demanded M to the nominal interest rate i. The quantity of money demanded M is a nominal quantity, measured in dollars (or yen, or euros). Because an increase in the nominal interest rate increases the opportunity cost of holding money, which reduces the quantity of money demanded, the money demand curve slopes down.

If we think of the nominal interest rate as the "price" (more precisely, the opportunity cost) of money, and the amount of money people want to hold as the "quantity," the money demand curve is analogous to the demand curve for a good or service (see Chapter 4). As with a standard demand curve, the fact that a higher price of money leads people to demand less of it is captured in the downward slope of the demand curve. Furthermore, as in a standard demand curve, changes in factors other than the price of money (the nominal interest rate) can cause the demand curve for money to shift. Specifically, for a given nominal interest rate, any change that makes people want to hold more money will shift the money demand curve to the right, and any change that makes people want to hold less money will shift the money demand curve to the left. We have already identified two macroeconomic factors other than the nominal interest rate that affect the economywide demand for money: real output and the price level. Because an increase in either of these variables increases the demand for money, it shifts the money demand curve rightward, as shown in Figure 26.2. Similarly, a fall in real output or the general price level reduces money demand, shifting the money demand curve leftward.

The money demand curve may also shift in response to other changes that affect the cost or benefit of holding money, such as the technological and financial advances we mentioned earlier. For example, the introduction of ATMs reduced the amount of money people choose to hold and thus shifted the economywide money demand curve to the left. Economic Naturalist 26.1 describes another potential source of shifts in the demand for money, holdings of U.S. dollars by foreigners.

money demand curve relates the aggregate quantity of money demanded M to the nominal interest rate i; because an increase in the nominal interest rate increases the opportunity cost of holding money, which reduces the quantity of money demanded, the money demand curve slopes down

FIGURE 26.2
A Shift in the Money Demand Curve.
At a given nominal interest rate, any change that makes people want to hold more money—such as an increase in the general price level or in real GDP—will shift the money demand curve to the right.

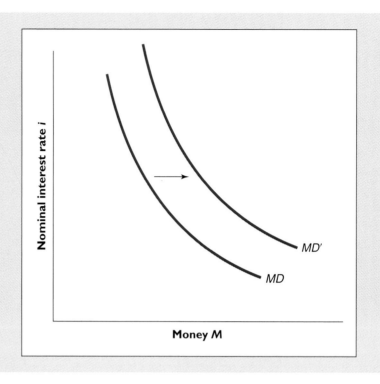

Nominal interest rate i

MD'

MD

Money M

ECONOMIC NATURALIST 26.1

Why does the average Argentine hold more U.S. dollars than the average U.S. citizen?

Estimates are that the value of U.S. dollars circulating in Argentina exceeds $1,000 per person, which is higher than the per capita dollar holdings in the United States. A number of other countries, including those that once made up the former Soviet Union, also hold large quantities of dollars. In all, as much as $250 billion in U.S. currency—more than half the total amount issued—may be circulating outside the borders of the United States. Why do Argentines and other non-U.S. residents hold so many dollars?

U.S. residents and businesses hold dollars primarily for transactions purposes, rather than as a store of value. As a store of value, interest-bearing bonds and dividend-paying stocks are a better choice for Americans than zero-interest money. But such is not necessarily the case for the citizens of other countries, particularly those that are economically or politically unstable. Argentina, for example, endured many years of high and erratic inflation, which sharply eroded the value of financial investments denominated in Argentine pesos. Lacking better alternatives, many Argentines began saving in the form of U.S. currency—dollar bills hidden in the mattress or plastered into the wall—which they correctly believed to be more stable in value than peso-denominated assets. In 1990 Argentina instituted a new monetary system, under which U.S. dollars and Argentine pesos trade freely one for one. Dollars can now be used in any transaction, large or small, in the Argentine economy. To a significant degree, the Argentine economy has become "dollarized," meaning that dollars are used heavily in everyday transactions. (In 2000, Ecuador went one step further and made U.S. dollars the official national currency.)

The countries formed after the breakup of the Soviet Union have endured not only high inflation but political instability and uncertainty as well. In a politically volatile environment, citizens face the risk that their savings, including their bank deposits, will be confiscated or heavily taxed by the government. Often they conclude that a hidden cache of U.S. dollars—an estimated $1 million in $100 bills can be stored in a suitcase—is the safest way to hold wealth.

In practice, changes in the number of U.S. dollars hoarded abroad are an important source of fluctuation in the U.S. money demand curve. For example, large quantities of U.S. dollars flowed abroad during the Gulf War of 1990–1991, reflecting concerns among residents of the Middle East about regional instability. This increase in foreign dollar holdings shifted the U.S. money demand curve substantially to the right, as in Figure 26.2. Because policymakers at the Federal Reserve are primarily concerned with the number of dollars circulating in the U.S. economy, rather than in the world as a whole, they pay close attention to these international flows of greenbacks.

RECAP   **MONEY DEMAND**

For the economy as a whole, the *demand for money* is the amount of wealth that individuals, households, and businesses choose to hold in the form of money. The opportunity cost of holding money is measured by the nominal interest rate i, which is the return that could be earned on alternative assets such as bonds. The benefit of holding money is its usefulness in transactions.

Increases in real GDP (Y) or the price level (P) raise the nominal volume of transactions and thus the economywide demand for money. The demand for money is also affected by technological and financial innovations, such as the introduction of ATMs, that affect the costs or benefits of holding money.

The *money demand curve* relates the economywide demand for money to the nominal interest rate. Because an increase in the nominal interest rate raises the opportunity cost of holding money, the money demand curve slopes downward.

Changes in factors other than the nominal interest rate that affect the demand for money can shift the money demand curve. For example, increases in real GDP or the price level raise the demand for money, shifting the money demand curve to the right, while decreases shift the money demand curve to the left.

THE SUPPLY OF MONEY AND MONEY MARKET EQUILIBRIUM

Where there is demand, can supply be far behind? As we saw in Chapter 23, the *supply* of money is controlled by the central bank—in the United States, the Federal Reserve. The Fed's primary tool for controlling the money supply is *open-market operations*. For example, to increase the money supply, the Fed can use newly created money to buy government bonds from the public (an open-market purchase), which puts the new money into circulation.

Figure 26.3 shows the demand for and the supply of money in a single diagram. The nominal interest rate is on the vertical axis, and the nominal quantity of money (in dollars) on the horizontal axis. As we have seen, because a higher nominal interest rate increases the opportunity cost of holding money, the money demand curve slopes downward. And because the Fed fixes the supply of money, we have drawn the *money supply curve* as a vertical line that intercepts the horizontal axis at the quantity of money chosen by the Fed, denoted M.

As in standard supply and demand analysis, equilibrium in the market for money occurs at the intersection of the supply and demand curves, shown as point E in Figure 26.3. The equilibrium amount of money in circulation M is simply the amount of money the Fed chooses to supply. The equilibrium nominal interest rate i is the interest rate at which the quantity of money demanded by the public, as determined by the money demand curve, equals the fixed supply of money made available by the Fed.

FIGURE 26.3
Equilibrium in the Market for Money.
Equilibrium in the market for money occurs at point E, where the demand for money by the public equals the amount of money supplied by the Federal Reserve. The equilibrium nominal interest rate, which equates the supply of and demand for money, is i.

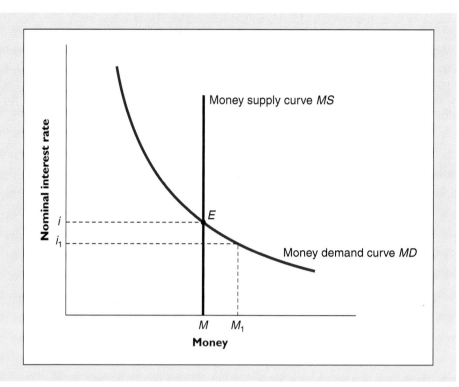

To understand how the market for money reaches equilibrium, it may help to recall the basic relationship between interest rates and the price of bonds that was introduced in Chapter 23 (see Example 23.1). As we saw in Chapter 23, the prices of existing bonds are *inversely related* to the current interest rate. Higher interest rates imply lower bond prices, and lower interest rates imply higher bond prices. With this relationship between interest rates and bond prices in mind, let's ask what happens if, for example, the nominal interest rate is initially below the equilibrium level in the market for money—e.g., at a value such as i_1 in Figure 26.3. At that interest rate the public's demand for money is M_1, which is greater than the actual amount of money in circulation, equal to M. How will the public—households and firms—react if the amount of money they hold is less than they would like? To increase their holdings of money, people will try to sell some of the interest-bearing assets they hold, such as bonds. But if everyone is trying to sell bonds and there are no willing buyers, then all the attempt to reduce bond holdings will achieve is to drive down the price of bonds, in the same way that a glut of apples will drive down the price of apples.

A fall in the price of bonds, however, is equivalent to an increase in interest rates. Thus, the public's collective attempt to increase its money holdings by selling bonds and other interest-bearing assets, which has the effect of lowering bond prices, also implies higher market interest rates. As interest rates rise, the quantity of money demanded by the public will decline (represented by a right-to-left movement along the money demand curve), as will the desire to sell bonds. Only when the interest rate reaches its equilibrium value, i in Figure 26.3, will people be content to hold the quantities of money and other assets that are actually available in the economy.

EXERCISE 26.2

Describe the adjustment process in the market for money if the nominal interest rate is initially above rather than below its equilibrium value. What happens to the price of bonds as the money market adjusts toward equilibrium?

HOW THE FED CONTROLS THE NOMINAL INTEREST RATE

We began this section by noting that the public and the press usually talk about Fed policy in terms of decisions about the nominal interest rate rather than the money supply. Indeed, Fed policymakers themselves usually describe their plans in terms of a target value for the interest rate. We now have the background to understand how the Fed translates the ability to determine the economy's money supply into control of the nominal interest rate.

Figure 26.3 showed that the nominal interest rate is determined by equilibrium in the market for money. Let's suppose that for some reason the Fed decides to lower the interest rate. As we will see, to lower the interest rate the Fed must increase the supply of money, which can be accomplished by using newly created money to purchase government bonds from the public (an open-market purchase).

Figure 26.4 shows the effects of such an increase in the money supply by the Fed. If the initial money supply is M, then equilibrium in the money market occurs at point E in the figure, and the equilibrium nominal interest rate is i. Now suppose the Fed, by means of open-market purchases of bonds, increases the money supply to M'. This increase in the money supply shifts the vertical money supply curve to the right, which shifts the equilibrium in the money market from point E to point F (see Figure 26.4). Note that at point F the equilibrium nominal interest rate has declined, from i to i'. The nominal interest rate must decline if the public is to be persuaded to hold the extra money that has been injected into the economy.

To understand what happens in financial markets when the Fed expands the money supply, recall once again the inverse relationship between interest rates and the price of bonds. To increase the money supply, the Fed must buy government bonds from the public. However, if households and firms are initially satisfied with their asset holdings, they will be willing to sell bonds only at a price that is higher than the initial price. That is, the Fed's bond purchases will drive up the price of bonds in the open market. But we know that higher bond prices imply lower interest rates. Thus the Fed's bond purchases lower the prevailing nominal interest rate.

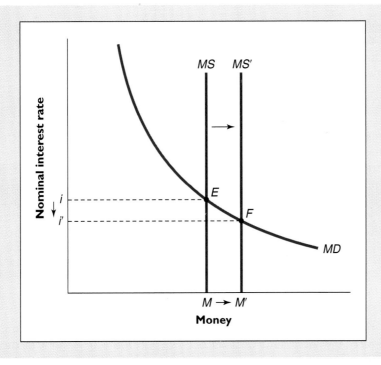

FIGURE 26.4
The Fed Lowers the Nominal Interest Rate. The Fed can lower the equilibrium nominal interest rate by increasing the supply of money. For the given money demand curve, an increase in the money supply from M to M' shifts the equilibrium point in the money market from E to F, lowering the equilibrium nominal interest rate from i to i'.

A similar scenario unfolds if the Fed decides to raise interest rates. To raise interest rates, the Fed must *reduce* the money supply. Reduction of the money supply is accomplished by an open-market sale—the sale of government bonds to the public in exchange for money. (The Fed keeps a large inventory of government bonds, acquired through previous open-market purchases, for use in open-market operations.) But in the attempt to sell bonds on the open market, the Fed will drive down the price of bonds. Given the inverse relationship between the price of bonds and the interest rate, the fall in bond prices is equivalent to a rise in the interest rate. In terms of money demand and money supply, the higher interest rate is necessary to persuade the public to hold less money. Example 26.3 illustrates numerically how the Fed determines interest rates.

EXAMPLE 26.3   **The Fed sets the nominal interest rate**

Suppose the demand for money (in millions of dollars) equals $P(0.5Y - 10,000i)$, where the price level P equals 2.0, real output Y equals 6,000, and the nominal interest rate i is expressed as a decimal (for example, 3 percent = 0.03). The Fed wants to set the nominal interest rate at 5 percent. At what level should Fed policymakers set the money supply? If real output were then to increase to 6,500, could the Fed keep the nominal interest rate unchanged at 5 percent?

Note that the demand for money in this example depends positively on the price level and real output, and negatively on the nominal interest rate, as economic reasoning implies.

Equilibrium in the market for money requires that the money supply equal money demand, or

$$M = P(0.5Y - 10,000i),$$

where M is the money supply set by the Fed. Since and $P = 2.0$ and $Y = 6,000$, we can substitute those values into the equation and rewrite it as

$$M = 2.0(0.5 \times 6,000 - 10,000i)$$

$$= 6,000 - 20,000i.$$

This equation shows the relationship between the money supply set by the Fed and the equilibrium nominal interest rate. To find the money supply that sets the equilibrium interest rate at 0.05, we can substitute 0.05 for i in the equation above and solve for M:

$$M = 6,000 - 20,000(0.05) = 5,000.$$

By setting the money supply at 5,000, the Fed can achieve a 5 percent equilibrium interest rate.

What if real output were to rise from 6,000 to 6,500, increasing the demand for money? As we will show, the Fed can keep the nominal interest rate unchanged at 5 percent, but doing so requires a change in the supply of money. With $Y = 6,500$ and the price level unchanged at 2.0, the condition that money supply equals money demand, $M = P(0.5Y - 10,000i)$, can be written

$$M = 2.0(0.5 \times 6,500 - 10,000i)$$

$$= 6,500 - 20,000i.$$

To find the money supply necessary to maintain a 5 percent equilibrium interest rate after the increase in real output, we substitute 0.05 for i in the equation to get

$$M = 6,500 - 20,000(0.05) = 5,500.$$

Thus the Fed can keep the interest rate constant at 5 percent when output and money demand increase, but to do so it must increase the supply of money from 5,000 to 5,500.

The Fed's stabilization of the interest rate in the face of an increase in output and money demand is illustrated in Figure 26.5. Initially, equilibrium in the money market, point E, occurs at the intersection of the money demand curve marked "Y = 6,000" and the initial money supply of 5,000. At that equilibrium, the nominal interest rate is 0.05, or 5 percent. An increase in output from 6,000 to 6,500 raises money demand, shifting the money demand curve rightward to the curve marked "Y = 6,500." If the Fed took no action, the nominal interest rate would rise (see Exercise 26.3). However, by increasing the money supply to 5,500—an action that shifts the money market equilibrium to point F—the Fed can keep the nominal interest rate at 5 percent.

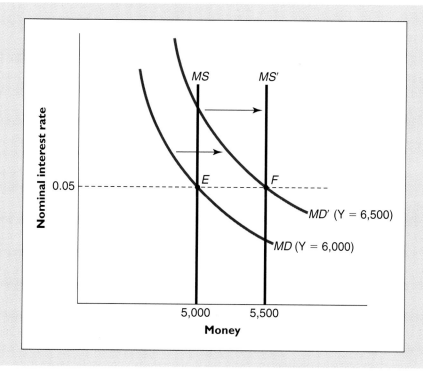

FIGURE 26.5
The Fed Stabilizes the Interest Rate after an Increase in Money Demand.
Initially, money market equilibrium is at point E, with a money supply of 5,000 and a nominal interest rate of 0.05, or 5 percent. An increase in output from 6,000 to 6,500 shifts the money demand curve to the right, as shown. With no action by the Fed, the equilibrium interest rate would rise. But the Fed can keep the nominal interest rate stable at 5 percent by increasing the money supply to 5,500, which reestablishes equilibrium at point F.

EXERCISE 26.3

a. Continuing Example 26.3, suppose that output Y increases from 6,000 to 6,500 but the Fed does not increase the money supply (it remains equal to 5,000). What will happen to the nominal interest rate?

b. Starting from the money market equilibrium in which P = 2.0, Y = 6,000, M = 5,000, and i = 0.05, suppose the price level P increases to 2.5, raising the demand for money. At what level would the Fed have to set the money supply to keep the nominal interest rate equal to 5 percent?

As Example 26.3 illustrates, control of interest rates is not separate from control of the money supply. If Fed officials choose to set the nominal interest rate at a particular level, they can do so only by setting the money supply at a level consistent with the target interest rate. The Fed can *not* set the interest rate and the money supply independently, since for any given money demand curve, a particular interest rate implies a particular size of the money supply, and vice versa.

Since monetary policy actions can be expressed in terms of either the interest rate or the money supply, why does the Fed (and almost every other central bank) choose to communicate policy in terms of a target nominal interest rate rather than a target money supply? One reason, as we will see shortly, is that the main effects of monetary policy on both the economy and financial markets are exerted through interest rates. Consequently, the interest rate is often the best summary of the overall impact of the Fed's actions. Another reason for focusing on interest rates is that they are more familiar to the public than the money supply. Finally, interest rates can be monitored continuously in the financial markets, which makes the effects of Fed policies on interest rates easy to observe. By contrast, measuring the amount of money in the economy requires collecting data on bank deposits, with the consequence that several weeks may pass before policymakers and the public know precisely how Fed actions have affected the money supply.

ECONOMIC NATURALIST 26.2

federal funds rate the interest rate that commercial banks charge each other for very short-term (usually overnight) loans; because the Fed frequently sets its policy in the form of a target for the federal funds rate, this rate is closely watched in financial markets

What's so important about the federal funds rate?

Although thousands of interest rates and other financial data are easily available, the interest rate that is perhaps most closely watched by the public, politicians, the media, and the financial markets is the *federal funds rate*. What is the federal funds rate, and why is it so important?

The **federal funds rate** is the interest rate commercial banks charge each other for very short-term (usually overnight) loans. For example, a bank that has insufficient reserves to meet its legal reserve requirements (see Chapter 23) might borrow reserves for a few days from a bank that has extra reserves. Despite its name, the federal funds rate is not an official government interest rate and is not connected to the federal government.

Because the market for loans among commercial banks is tiny compared to some other financial markets, such as the market for government bonds, one might expect the federal funds rate to be of little interest to anyone other than the managers of commercial banks. But enormous attention is paid to this interest rate, because over most of the past 35 years, the Fed has expressed its policies in terms of a target value for it. Indeed, at the close of every meeting of the Federal Open Market Committee, the Fed announces whether the federal funds rate will be increased, decreased, or left unchanged. Thus, more than any other financial variable, changes in the federal funds rate indicate the Fed's plans for monetary policy.

Why does the Fed choose to focus on this particular nominal interest rate over all others? As we saw in Chapter 23, in practice the Fed affects the money supply through its control of bank reserves. Because open-market operations directly affect the supply of bank reserves, the Fed's control over the federal funds rate is particularly tight. However, if Fed officials chose to do so, they could probably signal their intended policies just as effectively in terms of another short-term nominal interest rate, such as the rate on short-term government debt.

Figure 26.6 shows the behavior of the federal funds rate since 1970. As you can see, the Fed has allowed this interest rate to vary considerably in response to economic conditions. Later in the chapter we will consider a specific episode in which the Fed changed the federal funds rate in response to an economic slowdown.

CAN THE FED CONTROL THE REAL INTEREST RATE?

Through its control of the money supply the Fed can control the economy's *nominal* interest rate. But many important economic decisions, such as the decisions to save and invest, depend on the *real* interest rate (see Chapter 22). To affect those decisions, the Fed must exert some control over the real interest rate.

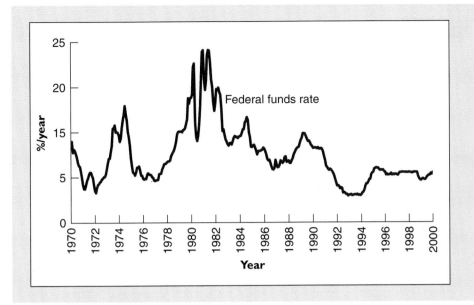

FIGURE 26.6
The Federal Funds Rate,
1970–2000.
The federal funds rate is the
interest rate commercial
banks charge each other for
short-term loans. It is closely
watched because the Fed
expresses its policies in terms
of a target value for the
federal funds rate. The Fed has
allowed the federal funds rate
to vary considerably in
response to economic
conditions. [SOURCE: Federal
Reserve Bank of St. Louis
(www.stls.frb.org/fred/).]

Most economists believe that the Fed can control the real interest rate, at least for some period. To see why, recall the definition of the real interest rate from Chapter 19:

$$r = i - \pi.$$

That is, the real interest rate r equals the nominal interest rate i minus the rate of inflation π. As we have seen, the Fed can control the nominal interest rate quite precisely through its ability to determine the money supply. Furthermore, inflation appears to change relatively slowly in response to changes in policy or economic conditions, for reasons we discuss in Chapter 27. Because inflation tends to adjust slowly, action by the Fed to change the nominal interest rate causes the real interest rate to change by about the same amount.

The idea that the Fed can set the real interest rate appears to contradict the analysis in Chapter 22, which indicated that the real interest rate is determined by the condition that national saving must equal investment in new capital goods. This apparent contradiction is rooted in a difference in the time frame being considered. Because inflation does not adjust quickly, the Fed can control the real interest rate over the short run. In the long run, however—that is, over periods of several years or more—the inflation rate and other economic variables will adjust, and the balance of saving and investment will determine the real interest rate. Later in the chapter we will discuss an implication for monetary policy of the fact that, in the long run, the real interest rate is determined by saving and investment decisions.

In discussing the Fed's control over interest rates, we should also return to a point mentioned earlier in this chapter: that in reality there are many thousands of interest rates in the economy, not just one. Because interest rates tend to move together (allowing us to speak of "the" interest rate), an action by the Fed to change the federal funds rate generally causes other interest rates to change in the same direction. However, the tendency of other interest rates (such as the long-term government bond rate or the rate on bonds issued by corporations) to move in the same direction as the federal funds rate is only a tendency, not an exact relationship. In practice, then, the Fed's control of other interest rates may be somewhat less precise than its control of the federal funds rate—a fact that complicates the Fed's policymaking.

> **RECAP** **THE FEDERAL RESERVE AND THE NOMINAL INTEREST RATE**
>
> In the market for money, the money demand curve slopes downward, reflecting the fact that a higher nominal interest rate increases the opportunity cost of holding money and thus reduces the amount of money people want to hold. The money supply curve is vertical at the quantity of money that the Fed chooses to supply. The equilibrium nominal interest rate i is the interest rate at which the quantity of money demanded by the public equals the fixed supply of money made available by the Fed.
>
> The Federal Reserve controls the nominal interest rate by changing the supply of money. An open-market purchase of government bonds increases the money supply and lowers the equilibrium nominal interest rate. Conversely, an open-market sale of bonds reduces the money supply and increases the nominal interest rate. The Fed can prevent changes in the demand for money from affecting the nominal interest rate by adjusting the quantity of money supplied appropriately. The Fed typically expresses its policy intentions in terms of a target for a specific nominal interest rate, the *federal funds rate*.
>
> Because inflation is slow to adjust, in the short run the Fed can control the real interest rate (equal to the nominal interest rate minus the inflation rate) as well as the nominal interest rate. In the long run the real interest rate is determined by the balance of saving and investment (see Chapter 22).

THE EFFECTS OF FEDERAL RESERVE ACTIONS ON THE ECONOMY

Now that we have seen how the Fed can influence interest rates (both nominal and real), we can turn to the question of how monetary policy can be used to eliminate output gaps and stabilize the economy. The basic idea is relatively straightforward: Aggregate demand (as we will see) depends on the real interest rate. Specifically, a lower real interest rate encourages higher spending by households and firms, while a higher real interest rate reduces spending. By adjusting the real interest rate, the Fed can move aggregate demand in the desired direction. Assuming that firms produce just enough to meet the demand for their output, the stabilization of aggregate demand leads to stabilization of aggregate output and employment as well. In this section we will first explain how aggregate demand is related to the real interest rate. Then we will show how the Fed can use changes in the real interest rate to fight a recession or inflation.

AGGREGATE DEMAND AND THE REAL INTEREST RATE

In Chapter 25 we saw how aggregate demand is affected by changes in real output Y. Changes in output affect the private sector's disposable income, which in turn influences consumption spending, a relationship captured by the consumption function. An increase in output stimulates consumption spending and aggregate demand, while a decline in output reduces aggregate demand.

A second variable that has potentially important effects on aggregate demand is the real interest rate r. In Chapter 22, in our discussion of saving and investment, we saw that the real interest rate influences the behavior of both households and firms.

For households, the effect of a higher real interest rate is to increase the reward for saving, which encourages households to save more.[1] This positive effect of the real interest rate on saving is captured by the upward slope of the supply of savings curve (see Figure 22.7). At a given level of income, households can save more only if they consume less. Thus, the statement that a higher real interest rate increases saving is the same as saying that a higher real interest rate reduces consumption spending. This idea makes sense: Think, for example, about people's willingness to buy consumer durables, such as automobiles or furniture. Consumer durables, which are part of consumption spending, are often financed by borrowing from a bank, credit union, or finance company. When the real interest rate rises, the monthly finance charges associated with the purchase of a car or a piano are higher, and people become less willing or able to make the purchase. Thus a higher real interest rate reduces people's willingness to spend on consumer goods, assuming disposable income and other factors that affect consumption remain constant.

Besides reducing consumption spending, a higher real interest rate also discourages firms from making capital investments. That is the reason the demand for savings curve, introduced in Chapter 22, is downward-sloping. As in the case of a consumer thinking of buying a car or a piano, when the real interest rate rises, increasing financing costs, firms may reconsider their plans to invest. For example, upgrading a computer system may be profitable for a manufacturing firm when the cost of the system can be financed by borrowing at a real interest rate of 3 percent. However, if the real interest rate rises to 6 percent, doubling the cost of funds to the firm, the same upgrade may not be profitable and the firm may choose not to invest.

We conclude that *both consumption spending and planned investment spending decline when the real interest rate increases.* Conversely, a fall in the real interest rate tends to stimulate consumption and investment spending, by reducing financing costs. Example 26.4 shows how to calculate aggregate demand and short-run equilibrium output when aggregate demand depends on the real interest rate set by the Fed. The basic approach is the one used in Chapter 25. After we have seen how to find short-run equilibrium output, we will turn to the question of how the Fed can use control of the real interest rate to eliminate output gaps.

When the real interest rate rises, financing a new car becomes more expensive and fewer cars are purchased.

Short-run equilibrium output when aggregate demand depends on the real interest rate.

EXAMPLE 26.4

In a certain economy, the components of aggregate demand are given by

$$C = 640 + 0.8(Y - T) - 400r,$$

$$I^P = 250 - 600r,$$

$$G = \overline{G} = 300,$$

$$NX = \overline{NX} = 20.$$

The real interest rate r is set by the Fed to equal 0.05 (5 percent), and taxes T are fixed at 250. Find the relationship of aggregate demand to output and then solve for short-run equilibrium output.

This example is similar to several in Chapter 25, except that now the real interest rate r is allowed to affect both consumption and planned investment. For example, the final term in the equation describing consumption, $-400r$, implies

---

[1]Because a higher real interest rate also reduces the amount households must put aside to reach a given savings target, the net effect of a higher real interest rate on saving is theoretically ambiguous. However, empirical evidence suggests that higher real interest rates have a modest positive effect on saving.

that a 1 percent (0.01) increase in the real interest rate reduces consumption spending by $400(0.01) = 4$ units. Similarly, the final term in the equation for planned investment tells us that in this example, a 1 percent increase in the real interest rate lowers planned investment by $600(0.01) = 6$ units.

The procedure for solving for short-run equilibrium output involves the same steps given in Chapter 25. First we must find the relationship of aggregate demand to output. The general definition of aggregate demand is

$$AD = C + I^P + G + NX.$$

Substituting for the four components of aggregate demand, using the numerical values in Example 26.4, we get

$$AD = [640 + 0.8(Y - 250) - 400(0.05)] + [250 - 600(0.05)] + 300 + 20.$$

The first term in brackets on the right side of this equation for aggregate demand is the expression for consumption; the second bracketed term is planned investment. Both are written as they were given in the problem, except that the assumed numerical value of 250 has been substituted for taxes T and the value 0.05 substituted for the real interest rate r. The last two terms on the right side of the equation are the given numerical values for government purchases and net exports. If we simplify this equation and group the terms that do and do not depend on output, we get

$$AD = (640 + 0.8Y - 200 - 20) + (250 - 30) + 300 + 20$$

$$= 960 + 0.8Y.$$

Having obtained an equation relating aggregate demand to output, our next step is to substitute this expression for aggregate demand into the definition of short-run equilibrium output, $Y = AD$:

$$Y = 960 + 0.8Y.$$

Solving this equation for Y, we get

$$Y = 4,800.$$

So short-run equilibrium output in this economy is 4,800.

Short-run equilibrium output can also be found graphically, using the Keynesian cross diagram from Chapter 25. Indeed, since the aggregate demand equation in this example, $AD = 960 + 0.8Y$, happens to be the same as in the example in Chapter 25, Figure 25.3 applies equally well here.

EXERCISE 26.4

For the economy described in Example 26.4, suppose the Fed sets the real interest rate at 3 percent rather than at 5 percent. Find short-run equilibrium output.

THE FED FIGHTS A RECESSION

We have seen that the Fed can control the real interest rate and that the real interest rate in turn affects aggregate demand and short-run equilibrium output. Putting these two results together, we can see how Fed policies help to stabilize aggregate demand and output.

Suppose the economy faces a recessionary gap—a situation in which real output is below potential output and aggregate demand is "too low." To fight a recessionary gap, the Fed should reduce the real interest rate, stimulating consumption and investment spending. According to the theory we have developed, this increase in aggregate demand will increase output, restoring the economy to full employment. Example 26.5 illustrates this point by extending Example 26.4.

The Fed fights a recession

EXAMPLE 26.5

For the economy described in Example 26.4, suppose potential output Y^* equals 5,000. As before, the Fed has set the real interest rate equal to 5 percent. At that real interest rate, what is the output gap? What should the Fed do to eliminate the output gap and restore full employment?

In Example 26.4 we showed that with the real interest rate at 5 percent, short-run equilibrium output for this economy is 4,800. Potential output is 5,000, so the output gap $Y^* - Y$ equals $5,000 - 4,800 = 200$. Because actual output is below potential, this economy faces a recessionary gap.

To fight the recession, the Fed should lower the real interest rate, raising aggregate demand until output reaches 5,000, the full-employment level. By how much should the Fed reduce the real interest rate, given the specific numerical values we have assumed? To find out, let's write out the equation for aggregate demand again. This time, however, we will not substitute a value for the real interest rate r but will leave it as a variable to be solved for. The equation for aggregate demand is

$$AD = C + I^p + G + NX.$$

Substituting for the components of aggregate demand, we get

$$AD = [640 + 0.8(Y - 250) - 400r] + [250 - 600r] + 300 + 20.$$

The first term in brackets on the right side of this equation is consumption, the second term is planned investment, and so on. The only difference from Example 26.4 is that we have not substituted a numerical value for r.

Let's simplify this expression for aggregate demand by grouping together the terms that depend on output and on the real interest rate:

$$AD = (640 - 200 + 250 + 300 + 20) + 0.8Y - (400 + 600)r,$$

$$= 1,010 + 0.8Y - 1,000r.$$

Now that we have an expression for aggregate demand, we can substitute it for AD in the definition of short-run equilibrium output, $Y = AD$. This substitution yields

$$Y = 1,010 + 0.8Y - 1,000r. \tag{26.1}$$

Equation 26.1 relates short-run equilibrium output to the real interest rate set by the Fed. For example, if we set $r = 0.05$, as in Example 26.4, and solve Equation 26.1 for Y, we find the solution $Y = 4,800$.

What real interest rate will set output equal to potential output in this example? Since potential output is 5,000, we can answer this question by setting Y equal to 5,000 in Equation 26.1 and solving for r. Substituting $Y = 5,000$ into Equation 26.1 yields

$$5,000 = 1,010 + 0.8(5,000) - 1,000r.$$

Solving this equation for r, we find

$$r = 0.01 = 1\%.$$

To eliminate the recessionary gap, then, the Fed should lower the real interest rate from 5 to 1 percent. Notice that a decrease in the real interest rate increases short-run equilibrium output, as economic logic suggests.

The Fed's recession-fighting policy is shown graphically in Figure 26.7. The reduction in the real interest rate raises aggregate demand at each level of output, shifting the expenditure line upward. When the real interest rate equals 1 percent, the expenditure line intersects the $Y = AD$ line at $Y = 5,000$, so output and potential output are equal. A reduction in interest rates by the Fed, made with the intention of reducing a recessionary gap in this way, is called an **expansionary monetary policy**, or, less formally, a *monetary easing*.

expansionary monetary policy (or monetary easing) a reduction in interest rates by the Fed, made with the intention of reducing a recessionary gap

EXERCISE 26.5

Continuing Example 26.5, suppose that potential output is 4,850 rather than 5,000. By how much should the Fed cut the real interest rate to restore full employment?

FIGURE 26.7
The Fed Fights a Recession.
When the real interest rate is 5 percent, the expenditure line intersects the $Y = AD$ line at point E. At that point output is 4,800, below the economy's potential output of 5,000 (a recessionary gap of 200). If the Fed reduces the real interest rate to 1 percent, stimulating consumption and investment spending, the expenditure line will shift upward. At the new point of intersection F, output will equal potential output at 5,000.

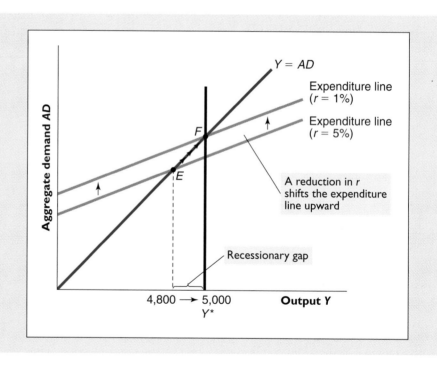

Why did the Fed cut the federal funds rate 23 times between 1989 and 1992?

ECONOMIC NATURALIST 26.3

The federal funds rate fell sharply between 1989 and 1992 (see Figure 26.6). At its peak in March 1989, the funds rate was 9.9 percent; by December 1992 it had fallen to 2.9 percent. During this period the Federal Reserve announced reductions in the target federal funds rate on 23 separate occasions. Why did the Fed cut the federal funds rate so much in this period?

As we saw in Chapter 24, the U.S. economy went into recession in the summer of 1991, about the time Iraq invaded Kuwait. In an attempt to stimulate the economy, the Fed cut the federal funds rate numerous times. By March 1991, the trough of the recession, this key interest rate stood at 6.1 percent—almost 4 percentage points below its value 2 years earlier. Despite the Fed's actions, however, the economy recovered only slowly. Although the recession ended in March 1991, the unemployment rate continued to climb. The media dubbed the weak expansion a "jobless recovery."

The unusually slow recovery from the 1990–1991 recession puzzled economists as well as the media. Alan Greenspan, the Chairman of the Fed, suggested that financial problems such as the credit crunch in the banking sector (see Economic Naturalist 24.2) were creating "financial headwinds" that held back economic growth. The Fed reacted to the sluggish performance of the economy by continuing to cut the federal funds rate, which reached 2.9 percent in December 1992 and remained around 3 percent until the spring of 1994. The Fed's policy appears ultimately to have been successful. Economic growth eventually picked up and the unemployment rate began to fall, reaching record lows by the end of the 1990s. Indeed, as we noted in Chapter 24, the expansion that began in March 1991 ultimately became the longest in U.S. history.

THE FED FIGHTS INFLATION

To this point we have focused on the problem of stabilizing output, without considering inflation. In Chapter 27 we will see how ongoing inflation can be incorporated into our analysis. For now we will simply note that one important cause of inflation is an expansionary output gap—a situation in which aggregate demand, and hence actual output, exceeds potential output. When an expansionary gap exists, firms find that the demand for their output exceeds their normal rate of production. Although firms may be content to meet the excess demand at previously determined prices for some time, if it persists they will ultimately raise their prices, spurring inflation.

Because an expansionary gap tends to lead to inflation, the Fed moves to eliminate expansionary gaps as well as recessionary gaps. The procedure for getting rid of an expansionary gap, a situation in which output is "too high" relative to potential output, is the reverse of that for fighting a recessionary gap, a situation in which output is "too low." As we have seen, the cure for a recessionary gap is to reduce the real interest rate, an action that stimulates aggregate demand and increases output. The cure for an expansionary gap is to *raise* the real interest rate, which reduces consumption and planned investment by raising the cost of borrowing. The resulting fall in aggregate demand leads in turn to a decline in output and to a reduction in inflationary pressures.

The Fed fights inflation

EXAMPLE 26.6

For the economy studied in Examples 26.4 and 26.5, assume that potential output is 4,600 rather than 5,000. At the initial real interest rate of 5 percent, short-run equilibrium output is 4,800, so this economy has an expansionary gap of 200. How should the Fed change the real interest rate to eliminate this gap?

In Example 26.5 we found that in this economy, short-run equilibrium output Y and the real interest rate r are related by

$$Y = 1,010 + 0.8Y - 1,000r$$

(Equation 26.1). This equation was derived by finding an expression for aggregate demand, then using that expression to substitute for AD in the definition of short-run equilibrium output, $Y = AD$. To find the real interest rate that will bring output to the target level of 4,600, we can set Y equal to 4,600 and solve for r. Substituting $Y = 4,600$ into the equation yields

$$4,600 = 1,010 + 0.8(4,600) - 1,000r.$$

Solving for r, we obtain

$$r = 0.09 = 9\%.$$

To eliminate the expansionary gap, then, the Fed must raise the real interest rate from 5 to 9 percent. The higher real interest rate will reduce aggregate demand to a level that is consistent with potential output, eliminating inflationary pressures.

FIGURE 26.8

The Fed Fights Inflation.
When the real interest rate is 5 percent, the expenditure line intersects the $Y = AD$ line at point E, where short-run equilibrium output equals 4,800. If potential output is 4,600, an expansionary output gap of 200 exists. If the Fed raises the real interest rate to 9 percent, reducing aggregate demand, the expenditure line shifts downward. At the new intersection point G, actual output equals potential output at 4,600, and the expansionary gap is eliminated.

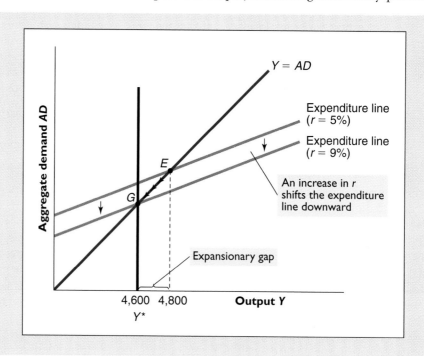

The effects of the Fed's inflation-fighting policy are shown in Figure 26.8. With the real interest rate at 5 percent, the expenditure line intersects the $Y = AD$ line at point E in the figure, where output equals 4,800. To reduce aggregate demand and output, the Fed raises the real interest rate to 9 percent. The higher real interest rate slows consumption and investment spending, moving the expenditure line downward. At the new equilibrium point G, actual output equals potential output at 4,600. The Fed's policy of raising the real interest rate has

*"Personally, I liked this roller coaster a lot better before
the Federal Reserve Board got hold of it."*

eliminated the expansionary output gap, and with it, the threat of inflation. When policymakers at the Fed increase interest rates in this way, with the intention of reducing an expansionary gap, they are said to be pursuing a **contractionary monetary policy,** or a *monetary tightening.*

While the Fed's interest rate policies affect the economy as a whole, they have a particularly important effect on financial markets. The introduction to this chapter noted the tremendous lengths financial market participants will go to in an attempt to anticipate Federal Reserve policy changes. Economic Naturalist 26.4 illustrates the type of information financial investors look for, and why it is so important to them.

contractionary monetary policy (or monetary tightening) an increase in interest rates by the Fed, made with the intention of reducing an expansionary gap

Why does news of inflation hurt the stock market?

Financial market participants watch data on inflation extremely closely. A report that inflation is increasing or is higher than expected often causes stock prices to fall sharply. Why does bad news about inflation hurt the stock market?

Investors in the financial markets worry about inflation because of its likely impact on Federal Reserve policy. As we have seen, faced with signs of an expansionary gap, the Fed is likely to raise interest rates in an attempt to reduce aggregate demand and "cool down" the economy. This type of contractionary monetary policy hurts stock prices in two ways. First, it slows down economic activity, reducing the expected sales and profits of companies whose shares are traded in the stock market. Lower profits, in turn, reduce the dividends those firms are likely to pay their shareholders.

Second, higher real interest rates reduce the value of stocks by increasing the required return for holding stocks. We saw in Chapter 23 that an increase in the return financial investors require to hold stocks lowers current stock prices. Intuitively, if interest rates rise, interest-bearing alternatives to stocks such as newly issued government bonds will become more attractive to investors, reducing the demand for, and hence the price of, stocks.

© 2000 Robert Mankoff from cartoonbank.com. All Rights Reserved.

"Interest rates gyrated wildly today, on rumors that the Federal Reserve Board would be replaced by the cast of 'Saturday Night Live.'"

THE FED'S POLICY REACTION FUNCTION

As we have seen, the Fed attempts to stabilize the economy by manipulating the real interest rate. When the economy faces a recessionary gap, the Fed reduces the real interest rate to stimulate spending; when an expansionary gap exists, so that inflation threatens to increase, the Fed restrains spending by raising the real interest rate. Economists find it convenient to summarize the behavior of the Fed in terms of a *policy reaction function.* In general, a **policy reaction function**

policy reaction function describes how the action a policymaker takes depends on the state of the economy

describes how the action a policymaker takes depends on the state of the economy. Here, the policymaker's action is the Fed's choice of the real interest rate, and the state of the economy is given by factors such as the output gap or the inflation rate. But there are many other examples of policy reaction functions. For example, the funding Congress provides for welfare programs should depend on the fraction of the population that is currently living in poverty. Ideally, policymakers should try to react in such a way as to optimize economic performance.

Economic Naturalist 26.5 describes one attempt to quantify the Fed's policy reaction function.

The Taylor rule

In 1993 the economist John Taylor proposed a "rule," now known as the Taylor rule, to describe the behavior of the Fed.[2] What is the Taylor rule? Does the Fed always follow it?

The rule Taylor proposed is not a rule in any legal sense but is instead an attempt to describe the Fed's behavior in terms of a policy reaction function. Taylor's "rule" can be written as

$$r = 0.01 - 0.5 \left(\frac{Y^* - Y}{Y^*} \right) + 0.5\pi \quad \text{(the Taylor rule)},$$

where r is the real interest rate set by the Fed, $Y^* - Y$ is the current output gap (the difference between potential and actual output), $(Y^* - Y)/Y^*$ is the output gap measured as a percentage of potential output, and π is the inflation rate. According to the Taylor rule, the Fed responds to both output gaps and the rate of inflation. For example, the formula implies that if a recessionary gap equal to 1 percent of potential output develops, the Fed will reduce the real interest rate by 0.5 percentage point, say from 5.0 to 4.5 percent. Similarly, if inflation rises by 1 percentage point, according to the Taylor rule the Fed will increase the real interest rate by 0.5 percentage point. Taylor has shown that his rule does in fact describe the behavior of the Fed under Chairman Alan Greenspan quite accurately. Thus the Taylor rule is a real-world example of a policy reaction function.

Although the Taylor rule has worked well as a description of the Fed's behavior, we reiterate that it is not a rule in a legal sense. The Fed is perfectly free to deviate from it, and does so when circumstances warrant. Still, the Taylor rule provides a useful benchmark for assessing, and predicting, the Fed's actions.

EXERCISE 26.6

This exercise asks you to apply the Taylor rule. Suppose inflation is 3 percent and the output gap is zero. According to the Taylor rule, at what value should the Fed set the real interest rate? The nominal interest rate? Suppose the Fed were to receive new information showing that there is a 1 percent recessionary gap (inflation is still 3 percent). According to the Taylor rule, how should the Fed change the real interest rate, if at all?

Notice that according to the Taylor rule, the Fed responds to two variables: the output gap and inflation. In principle, any number of economic variables, from stock prices to the value of the dollar in terms of the Japanese yen, could affect Fed policy and thus appear in the policy reaction function. For the sake of simplicity, in applying the policy reaction function idea in Chapter 27, we will assume that the Fed's choice of the real interest rate depends on only one variable: the rate of inflation. This simplification will not change our results in any significant way.

---

[2]John Taylor, "Discretion versus Policy Rules in Practice," *Carnegie-Rochester Conference Series on Public Policy,* 1993, pp. 195–214.

Furthermore, as we will see, having the Fed react only to inflation captures the most important aspect of Fed behavior, namely, its tendency to raise the real interest rate when the economy is "overheating" (experiencing an expansionary gap) and to reduce it when the economy is sluggish (experiencing a recessionary gap).

Table 26.1 describes an example of a policy reaction function according to which the Fed reacts only to inflation. According to the policy reaction function given in the table, the higher the rate of inflation, the higher the real interest rate set by the Fed. This relationship is consistent with the idea that the Fed responds to an expansionary gap (which threatens to lead to increased inflation) by raising the real interest rate. Figure 26.9 shows a graph of this policy reaction function. The vertical axis of the graph shows the real interest rate chosen by the Fed; the horizontal axis shows the rate of inflation. The upward slope of the policy reaction function captures the idea that the Fed reacts to increases in inflation by raising the real interest rate.

How does the Fed determine its policy reaction function? In practice the process is a complex one, involving a combination of statistical analysis of the economy and human judgment. However, two useful insights into the process can be drawn even from the simplified policy reaction function shown in Table 26.1 and Figure 26.9. First, as we mentioned earlier in the chapter, though the Fed

TABLE 26.1
A Policy Reaction Function for the Fed

Rate of Inflation π	Real interest rate set by Fed, r
0.00 (= 0%/year)	0.02 (= 2%)
0.01	0.03
0.02	0.04
0.03	0.05
0.04	0.06

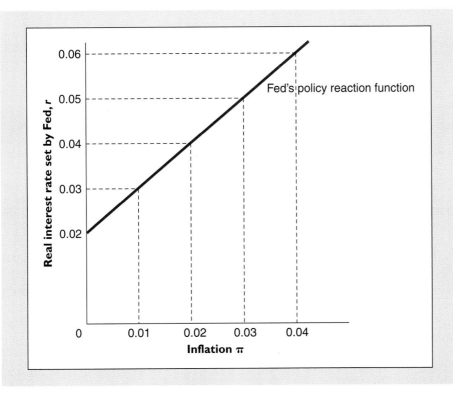

FIGURE 26.9
An Example of a Fed Policy Reaction Function. This example of a policy reaction function for the Fed shows the real interest rate the Fed sets in response to any given value of the inflation rate. The upward slope captures the idea that the Fed raises the real interest rate when inflation rises. The numerical values in the figure are from Table 26.1.

controls the real interest rate in the short run, in the long run the real interest rate is determined by the balance of saving and investment (see Chapter 22). To illustrate the implication of this fact for the Fed's choice of policy reaction function, suppose that the Fed estimates the long-run value of the real interest rate (as determined by the supply and demand for saving) to be 4 percent, or 0.04. By examining Table 26.1, we can see that the Fed's policy reaction function implies a long-run value of the real interest rate of 4 percent only if the inflation rate in the long run is 2 percent. Thus the Fed's choice of this policy reaction function only makes sense if the Fed's long-run target rate of inflation is 2 percent. We conclude that one important determinant of the Fed's policy reaction function is the policymakers' objective for inflation.

Second, the Fed's policy reaction function contains information not only about the central bank's long-run inflation target but also about how aggressively the Fed plans to pursue that target. To illustrate, suppose the Fed's policy reaction function were very flat, implying that the Fed changes the real interest rate rather modestly in response to increases or decreases in inflation. In that case we would conclude that the Fed does not intend to be very aggressive in its attempts to offset movements in inflation away from the target level. In contrast, if the reaction function slopes steeply upward so that a given change in inflation elicits a large adjustment of the real interest rate by the Fed, we would say that the Fed plans to be quite aggressive in responding to changes in inflation.

RECAP   **MONETARY POLICY AND THE ECONOMY**

An increase in the real interest rate reduces both consumption spending and planned investment spending. Through its control of the real interest rate, the Fed is thus able to influence aggregate demand and short-run equilibrium output.

To fight a recession (a recessionary output gap), the Fed should lower the real interest rate, stimulating aggregate demand and output. A reduction in interest rates by the Fed, with the intention of reducing a recessionary gap, is called *expansionary monetary policy.* Conversely, to fight inflation (an expansionary output gap), the Fed should raise the real interest rate. An increase in interest rates by the Fed, made with the intention of reducing an expansionary output gap, is a *contractionary monetary policy.*

The Fed's policy reaction function relates its policy action (specifically, its setting of the real interest rate) to the state of the economy. For the sake of simplicity, we consider a policy reaction function in which the real interest rate set by the Fed depends only on the rate of inflation. Because the Fed raises the real interest rate when inflation rises to contain spending, the Fed's policy reaction is upward-sloping. The Fed's policy reaction function contains information about the central bank's long-run target for inflation and the aggressiveness with which it intends to pursue that target.

MONETARY POLICYMAKING: ART OR SCIENCE?

In this chapter we used a simplified model to explain the basic economics underlying monetary policy. We worked through a number of examples showing the calculation of the real interest rate that is needed to restore output to its full-employment level. While those examples are useful in understanding how monetary policy works, as with our analysis of fiscal policy in Chapter 25, they overstate the precision of monetary policymaking. The real-world economy is highly complex and our knowledge of its workings quite imperfect. For example, though we assumed in our analysis that the Fed knows the exact value of potential output, in reality potential output can be estimated only approximately. As a result, at any given time the Fed has only a rough idea of the size of the output gap. Similarly, Fed policymakers have only an approximate idea of the effect of a given change in the real interest rate on aggregate demand, or the length of time before that effect will occur. Because of these uncertainties, the Fed tends to proceed cautiously. Fed policymakers avoid large changes in interest rates, and rarely raise or lower the federal funds rate more than one-fourth of a percentage point (from 5.25 to 5.00 percent, for example) at any one time.

Is monetary policymaking an art or a science, then? In practice it appears to be both. Scientific analyses, such as the development of detailed statistical models of the economy, have proved useful in making monetary policy. But human judgment based on long experience—what has been called the "art" of monetary policy—plays a crucial role in successful policymaking and is likely to continue to do so.

▪ SUMMARY ▪

- Monetary policy is one of two types of stabilization policy, the other being fiscal policy. Although the Federal Reserve operates by controlling the money supply, the media's attention nearly always focuses on the Fed's decisions about interest rates, not the money supply. There is no contradiction between these two ways of looking at monetary policy, however, as the Fed's ability to control the money supply is the source of its ability to control interest rates.

- The nominal interest rate is determined in the market for money, which has both a demand side and a supply side. For the economy as a whole, the *demand for money* is the amount of wealth households and businesses choose to hold in the form of money (such as cash or checking accounts). The demand for money is determined by a comparison of cost and benefits. The opportunity cost of holding money, which pays either zero interest or very low interest, is the interest that could have been earned by holding interest-bearing assets instead of money. Because the nominal interest rate measures the opportunity cost of holding a dollar in the form of money, an increase in the nominal interest rate reduces the quantity of money demanded. The benefit of money is its usefulness in carrying out transactions. All else being equal, an increase in the volume of transactions increases the demand for money. At the macroeconomic level, an increase in the price level or in real GDP increases the dollar volume of transactions, and thus the demand for money.

- The *money demand curve* relates the aggregate quantity of money demanded to the nominal interest rate. Because an increase in the nominal interest rate increases the opportunity cost of holding money, which reduces the quantity of money demanded, the money demand curve slopes down. Factors other than the nominal interest rate that affect the demand for money will shift the demand curve to the right or left. For example, an increase in the price level or real GDP increases the demand for money, shifting the money demand curve to the right.

- The Federal Reserve determines the supply of money through the use of open-market operations. The supply curve for money is vertical at the value of the money supply set by the Fed. Money market equilibrium occurs at the nominal interest rate at which money demand equals the money supply. The Fed can reduce the nominal interest rate by increasing the money supply (shifting the money supply curve to the right) or increase the nominal interest rate by reducing the money supply (shifting the money supply curve to the left). The nominal interest rate that the Fed targets most closely is the *federal funds rate*, which is the rate commercial banks charge each other for very short-term loans.

- In the short run, the Fed can control the real interest rate as well as the nominal interest rate. Recall that the real interest rate equals the nominal interest rate minus the inflation rate. Because the inflation rate adjusts relatively slowly, the Fed can change the real interest rate by changing the nominal interest rate. In the long run, the real interest rate is determined by the balance of saving and investment (Chapter 22).

- The Federal Reserve's actions affect the economy because changes in the real interest rate affect aggregate demand. Specifically, an increase in the real interest rate raises the cost of borrowing, reducing consumption and planned investment. Thus, by increasing the real interest rate, the Fed can reduce aggregate demand and short-run equilibrium output. Conversely, by reducing the real interest rate, the Fed can stimulate aggregate demand and raise short-run equilibrium output. In both cases, the Fed's ultimate objective is to eliminate output gaps. To eliminate a recessionary output gap, the Fed will lower the real interest rate (an *expansionary monetary policy*). To eliminate an expansionary output gap the Fed will raise the real interest rate (a *contractionary monetary policy*).

- A *policy reaction function* describes how the action a policymaker takes depends on the state of the economy. For example, a policy reaction function for the Fed could specify the real interest rate set by the Fed for each value of inflation.

- In practice, the Fed's information about the level of potential output and the size and speed of the effects of its actions is imprecise. Thus monetary policymaking is as much an art as a science.

■ KEY TERMS ■

contractionary monetary policy (713)
demand for money (693)
expansionary monetary policy (710)

federal funds rate (704)
money demand curve (697)

policy reaction function (713)
portfolio allocation decision (693)

■ REVIEW QUESTIONS ■

1. What is the *demand for money?* How does the demand for money depend on the nominal interest rate? On the price level? On income? Explain in terms of the costs and benefits of holding money.

2. Show graphically how the Fed controls the nominal interest rate. Can the Fed control the real interest rate?

3. What effect does an open-market purchase of bonds by the Fed have on nominal interest rates? Discuss both in terms of (a) the effect of the purchase on bond prices and (b) the effect of the purchase on the supply of money.

4. The Fed significantly increased the money supply prior to January 1, 2000, because of public fears that the so-called Y2K computer bug would disrupt basic services. Why did the Fed take that action? What might have happened to interest rates if Fed policymakers had taken no action?

5. You hear a news report that employment growth is lower than expected. How do you expect that report to affect market interest rates? Explain. (*Hint:* Assume that Fed policymakers have access to the same data that you do.)

6. Why does the real interest rate affect aggregate demand? Give examples.

7. The Fed faces a recessionary gap. How would you expect it to respond? Explain step by step how its policy change is likely to affect the economy.

8. Define *expansionary monetary policy* and *contractionary monetary policy.* For each type of policy, state what happens to the nominal interest rate, the real interest rate, and the money supply. Under what circumstances is each type of policy more likely to be appropriate?

9. Define *policy reaction function.* Sketch a policy reaction function relating the Fed's setting of the real interest rate to the inflation rate.

10. Discuss why the analysis of this chapter overstates the precision with which monetary policy can be used to eliminate output gaps.

■ PROBLEMS ■

1. During the heavy Christmas shopping season, sales of retail stores, online sales firms, and other merchants rise significantly.
   a. What would you expect to happen to the money demand curve during the Christmas season? Show graphically.
   b. If the Fed took no action, what would happen to nominal interest rates around Christmas?
   c. In fact, nominal interest rates do not change significantly in the fourth quarter of the year because of deliberate Fed policy. Explain, and show graphically, how the Fed can ensure that nominal interest rates remain stable around Christmas.

2. The following table shows Uma's estimated annual benefits of holding different amounts of money.

Average money holdings ($)	Total benefit ($)
500	35
600	47
700	57
800	65
900	71
1,000	75
1,100	77
1,200	77

How much money will Uma hold on average if the nominal interest rate is 9 percent? 5 percent? 3 percent? Assume that she wants her money holding to be a multiple of $100. (*Hint:* Make a table comparing the extra benefit of each additional $100 in money holdings with the opportunity cost, in terms of forgone interest, of additional money holdings.)

3. How would you expect each of the following to affect the U.S. demand for money? Explain.
   a. Competition among brokers forces down the commission charge for selling holdings of bonds or stocks.
   b. Grocery stores begin to accept credit cards in payment.
   c. Financial investors become concerned about increasing riskiness of stocks.
   d. Online banking allows customers to check balances and transfer funds between checking and mutual fund investments 24 hours a day.
   e. The economy enters a boom period.
   f. Political instability increases in developing nations.

4. Suppose the economywide demand for money is given by $P(0.2Y - 25,000i)$. The price level P equals 3.0, and real output Y equals 10,000. At what value should the Fed set the nominal money supply if:
   a. It wants to set the nominal interest rate at 4 percent?
   b. It wants to set the nominal interest rate at 6 percent?

5. In a certain economy the demand for money is equal to $2.0(Y) - 10,000i$. The Fed wants to keep the nominal interest rate constant at 5 percent.
   a. How can it accomplish its objective if real output Y equals 2,000? If Y equals 3,000?
   b. Repeat part a under the assumption that the Fed wants to keep the nominal interest rate at 8 percent.

6. An economy is described by the following equations:

$$C = 2,600 + 0.8(Y - T) - 10,000r,$$

$$I^P = 2,000 - 10,000r,$$

$$G = \overline{G} = 1,800.$$

Net exports are zero, taxes T are fixed at 3,000, and the real interest rate r is 10 percent. Find the relationship of aggregate demand to output and then solve for short-run equilibrium output. Show your result graphically using the Keynesian cross diagram.

7. For the economy described in Problem 6:
   a. Potential output Y^* equals 12,000. What real interest rate should the Fed set to bring the economy to full employment?
   b. Repeat part a for $Y^* = 9,000$.
   c. Show that the real interest rate you found in part a sets national saving at potential output, defined as $Y^* - C - G$, equal to planned investment I^P. This result shows that the real interest rate must be consistent with equilibrium in the market for saving when the economy is at full employment.

8. Here is another set of equations describing an economy:

$$C = 14,400 + 0.5(Y - T) - 40,000r,$$

$$I^P = 8,000 - 20,000r,$$

$$G = \overline{G} = 7,000,$$

$$NX = \overline{NX} = -1,800,$$

$$T = \overline{T} = 8,000,$$

$$Y^* = 40,000.$$

    a. At what value should the Fed set the real interest rate to eliminate any output gap?

    b. With the economy at potential output, as ensured by the policy you found in part a, government purchases increase to 7,600. What happens to short-run equilibrium output if the Fed leaves the real interest rate unchanged? What should the Fed do to keep the economy at full employment?

9. Supposing that the Fed follows the Taylor rule (Economic Naturalist 26.5), find the real interest rate and the nominal interest rate that the Fed will set in each of the following situations:

    a. Inflation of 4 percent and an expansionary gap equal to 1 percent of potential output

    b. Inflation of 2 percent and a recessionary gap equal to 2 percent of potential output

    c. Inflation of 6 percent and no output gap

    d. Inflation of 2 percent and a recessionary gap of 5 percent (Can the Fed set a negative real interest rate? If so, how?)

10. By law, the Federal Reserve must report twice each year to Congress about monetary policy and the state of the economy. This report is called the Humphrey-Hawkins Report, after the law that requires it. When the Report is presented, it is customary for the Fed Chairman to testify before Congress to update legislators on the economic situation.

    Obtain a copy of the most recent Humphrey-Hawkins testimony from the Fed's web page, www.bog.frb.fed.us (click "Monetary Policy" and follow the links). In the period covered by the testimony, did monetary policy ease, tighten, or remain neutral? What principal developments in the economy led the Fed to take the actions that it did?

■ ANSWERS TO IN-CHAPTER EXERCISES ■

26.1 At 4 percent interest, the benefit of each $10,000 reduction in cash holdings is $400 per year (4 percent times $10,000). In this case the cost of the extra armored car service, $500 a year, exceeds the benefit of reducing cash holdings by $10,000. Kim's restaurants should therefore continue to hold $50,000 in cash. Comparing this result with Example 26.2, you can see that the demand for money by Kim's restaurants is lower, the higher the nominal interest rate.

26.2 If the nominal interest rate is above its equilibrium value, then people are holding more money than they would like. To bring their money holdings down, they will use some of their money to buy interest-bearing assets such as bonds.

    If everyone is trying to buy bonds, however, the price of bonds will be bid up. An increase in bond prices is equivalent to a fall in market interest rates. As interest rates fall, people will be willing to hold more money. Eventually interest rates will fall enough that people are content to hold the amount of money supplied by the Fed, and the money market will be in equilibrium.

26.3 a. Equilibrium in the money market requires that money supply equal money demand, or $\overline{M} = P(0.5Y - 10,000i)$. With the given values $\overline{M} = 5,000$, $P = 2.0$, and $Y = 6,500$, the equilibrium condition becomes $5,000 = 2.0(3,250 - 10,000i)$, or $5,000 = 6,500 - 20,000i$. Solving for the nominal interest rate we get $i = 0.075 = 7.5$ percent.

    b. If we assume $P = 2.5$ and $Y = 6,000$, the equilibrium condition in the money market becomes $\overline{M} = 2.5(3,000 - 10,000i)$. We want to know the value of the money supply that will keep the nominal interest rate at 5 percent. Setting $i = 0.05$ and solving for $\overline{M}$, we get $\overline{M} = 6,250$. Example 26.3 showed that when $P = 2.0$, a money supply of 5,000 led to an interest rate of 5 percent. So, when the price level rises to 2.5, to keep the nominal interest rate at 5 percent the Fed must increase the money supply from 5,000 to 6,250.

26.4 If $r = 0.03$, then consumption is $C = 640 + 0.8(Y - 250) - 400(0.03) = 428 + 0.8Y$, and planned investment is $I^p = 250 - 600(0.03) = 232$. Aggregate demand is given by

$$AD = C + I^p + G + NX = (428 + 0.8Y) + 232 + 300 + 20 = 980 + 0.8Y.$$

Setting $Y = AD$ and solving for short-run equilibrium output Y, we get

$$Y = 980 + 0.8Y,$$

$$Y(1 - 0.8) = 980,$$

$$Y = 5 \times 980 = 4,900.$$

So lowering the real interest rate from 5 to 3 percent increases short-run equilibrium output from 4,800 (as found in Example 26.4) to 4,900.

26.5 Example 26.5 showed that the relationship between short-run equilibrium output and the real interest rate is given by Equation 26.1:

$$Y = 1,010 + 0.8Y - 1,000r.$$

To find the real interest rate that sets output equal to 4,850, set $Y = 4,850$ in this equation and solve for r:

$$4,850 = 1,010 + 0.8(4,850) - 1,000r.$$

Solving this equation for r, we get $r = 0.04 = 4$ percent.

26.6 If $\pi = 0.03$ and the output gap is zero, we can plug these values into the Taylor rule (see Economic Naturalist 26.5) to obtain

$$r = 0.01 - 0.5(0) + 0.5(0.03) = 0.025 = 2.5\%.$$

So the real interest rate implied by the Taylor rule, when inflation is 3 percent and the output gap is zero, is 2.5 percent. The nominal interest rate equals the real rate plus the inflation rate, or $2.5\% + 3\% = 5.5\%$.

If there is a recessionary gap of 1 percent of potential output, the Taylor rule formula becomes

$$r = 0.01 - 0.5(0.01) + 0.5(0.03) = 0.02 = 2\%.$$

The nominal interest rate implied by the Taylor rule in this case is the 2 percent real rate plus the 3 percent inflation rate, or 5 percent. So the Taylor rule has the Fed lowering the interest rate when the economy goes into recession, which is both sensible and realistic.

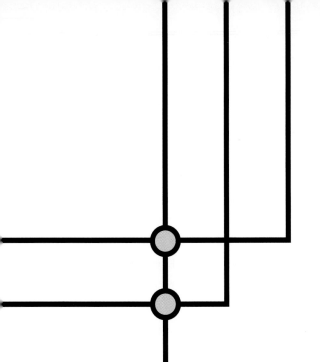

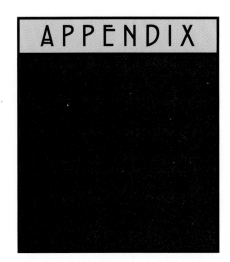

MONETARY POLICY IN THE BASIC KEYNESIAN MODEL

■

T his appendix extends the algebraic analysis of the basic Keynesian model that was presented in the Appendix to Chapter 25 to include the role of monetary policy. The main difference from the Appendix in Chapter 25 is that in this analysis the real interest rate is allowed to affect aggregate demand. We will not describe the supply and demand for money algebraically but will simply assume that the Fed can set the real interest rate r at any level it chooses.

The real interest rate affects consumption and planned investment. To capture these effects, we will modify the equations for those two components of spending as follows:

$$C = \overline{C} + c(Y - \overline{T}) - ar,$$

$$I^p = \overline{I} - br.$$

In these equations, a and b are both fixed numbers greater than zero that measure the strength of the interest rate effect. We will continue to assume that government spending and net exports are fixed numbers.

To solve for short-run equilibrium output, we must first find the relationship of aggregate demand to output. Start as usual with the definition of aggregate demand:

$$AD = C + I^p + G + NX.$$

Substituting the modified equations for consumption and planned investment into this definition, we get

$$AD = [\overline{C} + c(Y - \overline{T}) - ar] + (\overline{I} - br) + \overline{G} + \overline{NX}.$$

Grouping terms that depend on output and those that depend on the real interest rate yields

$$AD = (\overline{C} - c\overline{T} + \overline{I} + \overline{G} + \overline{NX}) - (a + b)r + cY.$$

This equation is similar to Equation 25.3, except that it has an extra term, $-(a + b)r$, on the right side. This extra term captures the idea that an increase in the real interest rate reduces consumption and planned investment, lowering aggregate demand. Notice that the term $-(a + b)r$ is part of the intercept of the expenditure line, so changes in the real interest rate will shift the expenditure line up (if the real interest rate decreases) or down (if the real interest rate increases).

To find short-run equilibrium output, we set $Y = AD$ and solve for Y:

$$Y = AD$$

$$= (\overline{C} - c\overline{T} + \overline{I} + \overline{G} + \overline{NX}) - (a + b)r + cY$$

$$= \left(\frac{1}{1 - c}\right)[\overline{C} - c\overline{T} + \overline{I} + \overline{G} + \overline{NX} - (a + b)r]. \qquad \text{(A.1)}$$

Equation A.1 shows that short-run equilibrium output depends on both autonomous aggregate demand, $\overline{C} - c\overline{T} + \overline{I} + \overline{G} + \overline{NX}$, and the real interest rate r. The equation also shows that the impact of a change in the real interest rate on short-run equilibrium output depends on two factors: (1) the effect of a change in the real interest rate on consumption and planned investment, which depends on the magnitude of $a + b$, and (2) the size of the multiplier, $1/(1 - c)$, which relates changes in spending to changes in short-run equilibrium output. The larger the effect of the real interest rate on consumption and planned investment, and the larger the multiplier, the more powerful will be the effect of a given change in the real interest rate on short-run equilibrium output.

To check Equation A.1, we can use it to re-solve Example 26.4. In that example we are given $\overline{C} = 640$, $\overline{I} = 250$, $\overline{G} = 300$, $\overline{NX} = 20$, $\overline{T} = 250$, $c = 0.8$, $a = 400$, and $b = 600$. The real interest rate set by the Fed is 5 percent, or 0.05. Substituting these values into Equation A.1 and solving, we obtain

$$Y = \left(\frac{1}{1 - 0.8}\right)[640 - 0.8(250) + 250 + 300 + 20 - (400 + 600)0.05]$$

$$= 5 \times 960 = 4,800$$

This result is the same as we found in Example 26.4.

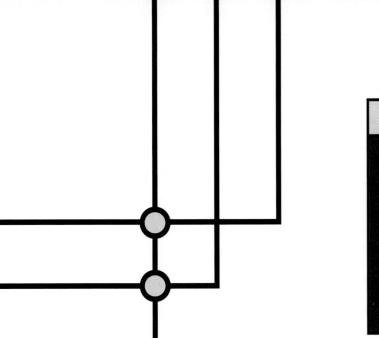

CHAPTER
27

INFLATION, AGGREGATE DEMAND, AND AGGREGATE SUPPLY

◼

On October 6, 1979, the Federal Open Market Committee, the policy-making committee of the Federal Reserve, held a highly unusual, and unusually secretive, Saturday meeting. Fed Chairman Paul Volcker may have called the Saturday meeting because he knew the financial markets would be closed and thus would not be able to respond to any "leaks" to the press about the discussions. Or perhaps he hoped that the visit of Pope John Paul II to Washington on the same day would distract the media from goings-on at the Fed. However unnoticed this meeting may have been at the time, in retrospect it marked a turning point in postwar U.S. economic history.

When Volcker called the October 6 meeting, he had been Chairman of the Fed for only 6 weeks. At 6 feet 8 inches tall with a booming bass voice, and a chain-smoker of cheap cigars, Volcker had a reputation for financial conservatism and personal toughness. Partly for those qualities, President Carter had appointed Volcker to head the Federal Reserve in August 1979. Carter needed a tough Fed Chairman to restore confidence, both in the economy and the government's economic policies. The U.S. economy faced many problems, including a doubling of oil prices following the overthrow of the Shah of Iran and a worrisome slowdown in productivity growth (see Chapter 20). But in the minds of the public, the biggest economic worry was an inflation rate that seemed to be out of control. In the second half of 1979, the annual rate of

Paul Volcker faced a tough assignment.

increase in consumer prices had reached 13 percent; by the spring of 1980 the inflation rate had risen to nearly 16 percent. Volcker's assignment: to bring inflation under control and stabilize the U.S. economy.

Volcker knew that getting rid of inflation would not be easy, and he warned his colleagues that a "shock treatment" might be necessary. His plan was couched in technical details, but in essence he proposed to reduce the rate of growth of the money supply sharply. Everyone in the room knew that slowing the growth of the money supply would cause interest rates to rise and aggregate demand to fall. Inflation might be brought down, but at what cost in terms of recession, lost output, and lost jobs? And how would the financial markets, which were already shaky, react to the new approach?

Officials in the room stirred nervously as Volcker spoke about the necessity of the move. Finally a vote was called. Every hand went up.

What happened next? We'll return to this story before the chapter ends, but first we need to introduce the basic framework for understanding inflation and the policies used to control it. In Chapters 25 and 26 we made the assumption that firms are willing to meet the demand for their products at preset prices. When firms simply produce what is demanded, the level of aggregate demand determines the nation's real GDP. If aggregate demand is lower than potential output, a recessionary output gap develops, and if aggregate demand exceeds potential output, the economy experiences an expansionary gap. As we saw in Chapters 25 and 26, policymakers can attempt to eliminate output gaps by taking actions that affect the level of aggregate demand, such as changing the level of government spending or taxes (fiscal policy) or using government control of the money supply to change the real interest rate (monetary policy).

The basic Keynesian model is useful for understanding the role of aggregate demand in the short-run determination of output, but it is too simplified to provide a fully realistic description of the economy. The main shortcoming of the basic Keynesian model is that it does not explain the behavior of inflation. Although firms may meet demand at preset prices for a time, as assumed in the basic Keynesian model, prices do *not* remain fixed indefinitely. Indeed, sometimes they may rise quite rapidly—the phenomenon of high inflation—imposing significant costs on the economy in the process, as we saw in Chapter 19. In this chapter we will extend the basic Keynesian model to allow for ongoing inflation. As we will show, the extended model can be conveniently represented by a new diagram, called the *aggregate demand–aggregate supply diagram*. Using this extended analysis, we will be able to show how macroeconomic policies affect inflation as well as output, illustrating in the process the difficult trade-offs policymakers sometimes face. We will emphasize numerical and graphical analysis of output and inflation in the body of the chapter. The appendix at the end of the chapter presents a more general algebraic treatment.

AGGREGATE DEMAND AND INFLATION

aggregate demand (AD) curve shows the relationship between aggregate demand and inflation; because short-run equilibrium output equals aggregate demand, the aggregate demand curve also shows the relationship between short-run equilibrium output and inflation; increases in inflation reduce aggregate demand and short-run equilibrium output, so the aggregate demand curve is downward-sloping

Recall from Chapter 25 that *aggregate demand*, denoted *AD*, is total planned spending on final goods and services. We saw in Chapters 25 and 26 that aggregate demand determines output in the short run, according to the relationship $Y = AD$. We also saw that while aggregate demand depends *positively* on the level of output Y, it is related *negatively* to the real interest rate r. These basic points will carry over to the expanded model presented in this chapter.

To incorporate inflation into the model, however, we must introduce a new relationship, between aggregate demand *AD* and the rate of inflation, denoted π. Graphically, this important relationship is captured in what is called the **aggregate demand (AD) curve**, shown in Figure 27.1. Because short-run equilibrium output equals aggregate demand, $Y = AD$, the aggregate demand curve also shows the relationship between short-run equilibrium output and inflation. We will see shortly that, all else being equal, *an increase in the rate of inflation tends to reduce both aggregate demand and short-run equilibrium output.* Therefore, in a diagram showing inflation π on the vertical axis and output Y on the horizontal axis, the aggregate demand curve is downward-sloping.[1] Note that we refer to the *AD* "curve," even though the relationship is drawn as a straight line in Figure 27.1. Although the *AD* curve happens to be a straight line in several of the examples presented in this chapter, in general the *AD* curve can be either straight or curving.

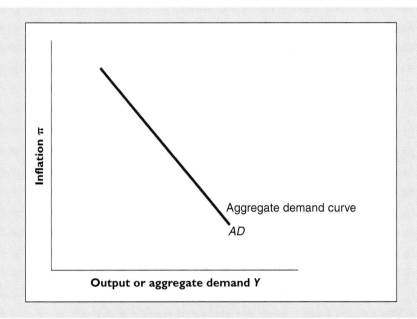

FIGURE 27.1
The Aggregate Demand Curve.
The aggregate demand curve *AD* shows the relationship between aggregate demand and inflation. Because short-run equilibrium output equals aggregate demand, the *AD* curve also shows the relationship between short-run equilibrium output and inflation. The downward slope of the *AD* curve implies that an increase in inflation reduces aggregate demand.

Why does higher inflation lead to a lower level of aggregate demand? As we will see next, one important reason is the Fed's response to increases in inflation.

INFLATION, THE FED, AND AGGREGATE DEMAND

One of the primary responsibilities of the Fed, or any central bank, is to maintain a low and stable rate of inflation. For example, in recent years the Fed has tried to keep inflation in the United States in the range of 2 to 3 percent. By keeping inflation low, the central bank tries to avoid the costs high inflation imposes on the economy (see Chapter 19).

What can the Fed do to keep inflation low and stable? As we have already mentioned, one situation that is likely to lead to increased inflation is an expansionary output gap, in which aggregate demand exceeds potential output. When aggregate demand exceeds potential output, firms must produce at above-normal capacity to meet the demands of their customers. Like Al's ice cream store, described in Chapter 24, firms may be willing to do so for a time, but eventually they will raise their prices, contributing to inflation. To control inflation, then, the Fed needs to dampen aggregate demand when it threatens to exceed potential output.

How can the Fed restrain aggregate demand? As we saw in Chapter 26, the Fed can reduce private spending, and hence aggregate demand, by raising the real interest rate. This behavior by the Fed underlies the link between inflation and

[1]Economists sometimes define the aggregate demand curve as the relationship between aggregate demand and the *price level,* rather than inflation. The definition used here both simplifies the analysis and yields results more consistent with real-world data. For a comparison of the two approaches, see David Romer, "Keynesian Macroeconomics without the LM Curve," *Journal of Economic Perspectives,* Spring 2000, 149–170. The graphical analysis used in this chapter follows closely the approach recommended by Romer.

aggregate demand that is summarized by the aggregate demand curve. When inflation is high, the Fed responds by raising the real interest rate (recall that this behavior is implied by the Fed's *policy reaction function,* introduced in Chapter 26). The increase in the real interest rate reduces consumption and investment spending and hence aggregate demand. Because higher inflation leads, through the Fed's actions, to a reduction in aggregate demand, the aggregate demand (*AD*) curve is downward-sloping, as Figure 27.1 shows. Example 27.1 illustrates this relationship between inflation and aggregate demand numerically.

EXAMPLE 27.1

Inflation, the Fed, and aggregate demand

For the economy described in Examples 26.4 and 26.5, we found the following relationship between aggregate demand, output, and the real interest rate (Equation 26.1):

$$AD = 1,010 + 0.8Y - 1,000r.$$

In this example, as is usually the case, aggregate demand increases when output rises and decreases when the real interest rate rises.

The real interest rate *r* is set by the Fed. Following the policy reaction function introduced in Table 26.1, suppose the real interest rate the Fed sets depends on the current rate of inflation, as follows:

Rate of Inflation π	Real interest rate set by Fed, r
0.00 (= 0%)	0.02 (= 2%)
0.01	0.03
0.02	0.04
0.03	0.05
0.04	0.06

In other words, the higher the rate of inflation, the higher the real interest rate set by the Fed. For each level of inflation from 0 to 4 percent, find the implied level of aggregate demand and short-run equilibrium output.

Suppose, for example, that inflation is 0 percent so the Fed sets the real interest rate at 2 percent, as dictated by its policy reaction function. Substituting $r = 0.02$ into the equation for aggregate demand given in the example, we get

$$AD = 1,010 + 0.8Y - 1,000(0.02)$$

$$= 990 + 0.8Y.$$

To find short-run equilibrium output, as usual we can substitute *Y* for *AD* (because short-run equilibrium output is defined by $Y = AD$) to get

$$Y = 990 + 0.8Y.$$

Solving this equation for output *Y* yields

$$Y = 4,950.$$

So if inflation is 0 percent and the Fed sets the real interest rate at 2 percent, the resulting value of short-run equilibrium output *Y* must be 4,950. Aggregate demand must also equal 4,950, since we know that aggregate demand and short-run equilibrium output are equal.

If instead inflation is 1 percent, the Fed will set the real interest rate at 3 percent, or 0.03. In that case aggregate demand is given by

$$AD = 1{,}010 + 0.8Y - 1{,}000(0.03)$$

$$= 980 + 0.8Y.$$

Substituting Y for AD as before, we find

$$Y = 980 + 0.8Y$$

$$= 4{,}900.$$

So a 1 percent inflation rate implies aggregate demand and short-run equilibrium output of 4,900. If we proceed this way for each value of inflation between 0 and 4 percent, we obtain the results in Table 27.1.

TABLE 27.1
Inflation, the Real Interest Rate, and Output (Example 27.1)

Inflation rate π	Real interest rate r	Output Y
0.00	0.02	4,950
0.01	0.03	4,900
0.02	0.04	4,850
0.03	0.05	4,800
0.04	0.06	4,750

The first two columns of Table 27.1 restate the relationship between inflation and the real interest rate set by the Fed (the policy reaction function), given in the statement of the problem. The third column shows the implied value of short-run equilibrium output (which is the same as aggregate demand) for each value of inflation.

Figure 27.2 graphs the relationship between inflation and output that is shown in Table 27.1. The graph of this relationship is the AD curve for this economy. Because higher inflation leads to higher real interest rates, and hence to lower aggregate demand and output, the AD curve slopes downward.

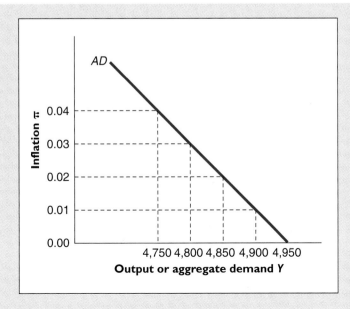

FIGURE 27.2
Numerical Example of an Aggregate Demand Curve.
This figure shows the AD curve that was calculated numerically in Example 27.1. Assuming that an increase in the inflation rate prompts the Fed to raise the real interest rate, we saw that the higher the inflation rate, the lower are aggregate demand and short-run equilibrium output. Hence, the AD curve slopes downward.

OTHER REASONS FOR THE DOWNWARD SLOPE OF THE *AD* CURVE

Although we focus here on the behavior of the Fed as the source of the *AD* curve's downward slope, there are other channels by which higher inflation reduces aggregate demand. One such channel is the effect of inflation on the *real value of money* held by households and businesses. At high levels of inflation, the purchasing power of money held by the public declines rapidly. This reduction in the public's real wealth may cause households to restrain spending, reducing aggregate demand.

A second channel by which inflation may affect aggregate demand is through *distributional effects*. Studies have found that people who are less well off are often hurt more by inflation than wealthier people are. For example, retirees on fixed incomes and workers receiving the minimum wage (which is set in dollar terms) lose buying power when prices are rising rapidly. Less affluent people are also likely to be relatively unsophisticated in making financial investments and hence less able than wealthier citizens to protect their savings against inflation. Moreover, relative to wealthier individuals, people at the lower end of the income distribution tend to spend a greater percentage of their disposable income. Thus if a burst of inflation redistributes resources from less affluent households, who spend most of their income, to more affluent households, who tend to save relatively more, overall spending may decline.

A final link between inflation and aggregate demand operates through the *prices of domestic goods and services sold abroad*. As we will see in Chapter 29, the foreign price of domestic goods depends in part on the rate at which the domestic currency, say dollars, exchanges for foreign currencies, such as the British pound. However, for constant rates of exchange between currencies, a rise in domestic inflation causes the prices of domestic goods in foreign markets to rise more quickly. As domestic goods become relatively more expensive to prospective foreign purchasers, export sales decline. Net exports are part of aggregate demand, and so once more we find that increased inflation is likely to reduce aggregate demand. All these factors contribute to the downward slope of the *AD* curve, together with the behavior of the Fed.

SHIFTS OF THE AGGREGATE DEMAND CURVE

The downward slope of the aggregate demand, or *AD*, curve shown in Figure 27.1 reflects the fact that *all other factors held constant*, a higher level of inflation will lead to lower aggregate demand and lower short-run equilibrium output. Again, the principal reason higher inflation reduces aggregate demand is that the Fed tends to react to increases in inflation by raising the real interest rate, which in turn reduces consumption and planned investment, two important components of aggregate demand.

However, factors other than inflation can affect aggregate demand, as we saw in Chapters 25 and 26. For example, Economic Naturalist 25.1 explained how declines in autonomous consumption and investment spending, $\overline{C}$ and $\overline{I}$, reduced aggregate demand and helped to cause the recession of 1990–1991. For a given level of inflation, any change in the economy that affects aggregate demand and short-run equilibrium output will cause the *AD* curve to shift. If the change increases short-run equilibrium output at each level of inflation, the *AD* curve will shift to the right. If the change reduces short-run equilibrium output at each level of inflation, the *AD* curve will shift to the left. We will focus on two sorts of changes in the economy that shift the aggregate demand curve: changes in *autonomous aggregate demand*, discussed next, and changes in the *Fed's policy reaction function*.

Changes in autonomous aggregate demand In Chapter 25 we defined *autonomous aggregate demand* as the portion of aggregate demand that is determined outside the model.[2] We have seen that, because they shift the expenditure line, changes in autonomous aggregate demand lead to changes in short-run equilibrium output. For example, if at a given level of output households desire to consume more, or firms are willing to invest more, the expenditure line will shift upward and short-run equilibrium output will increase.

Likewise, changes in autonomous aggregate demand can affect the aggregate demand curve. If the rate of inflation and the real interest rate set by the Fed are held constant, an increase in autonomous aggregate demand will raise short-run equilibrium output (Y). Graphically, the AD curve shifts to the right. If for some reason autonomous aggregate demand were to fall, reducing short-run equilibrium output at any given level of inflation, the AD curve would shift to the left. Example 27.2 illustrates the effects of changes in autonomous aggregate demand on the AD curve.

An increase in autonomous aggregate demand shifts the AD curve

EXAMPLE 27.2

In the economy we worked with in Example 27.1, aggregate demand was given by

$$AD = 1,010 + 0.8Y - 1,000r.$$

Suppose firms were to increase the autonomous part of planned investment $\overline{I}$ by 10 at every level of output and real interest rate. Then the equation for aggregate demand would become

$$AD = 1,020 + 0.8Y - 1,000r.$$

Assuming there is no change in the Fed's policy reaction function, given in Example 27.1, graph the AD curve after the increase in autonomous aggregate demand at inflation values ranging from 0 to 4 percent. For comparison, show the AD curve that prevailed before planned investment increased.

As in Example 27.1, we can solve for short-run equilibrium output at each value of inflation. Suppose, for example, that inflation is 0 percent so that (following its policy reaction function) the Fed sets the real interest rate at 2 percent. Substituting $r = 0.02$ into the expression for aggregate demand, we get

$$AD = 1,020 + 0.8Y - 1,000(0.02)$$

$$= 1,000 + 0.8Y.$$

To find short-run equilibrium output, use the fact that $Y = AD$ to substitute for AD:

$$Y = 1,000 + 0.8Y$$

$$= 5,000.$$

Repeating the same exercise for each value of inflation from 1 to 4 percent, we get the results shown in Table 27.2. The first two columns of Table 27.2 give the relationship between the inflation rate and the real interest rate set by the Fed, which is the same as in Example 27.1. The third column shows the value of short-run equilibrium output implied by each real interest rate. The overall relationship

[2]Algebraically, autonomous aggregate demand is given by $\overline{C} - c\overline{T} + \overline{I} + \overline{G} + \overline{NX}$. The portion of aggregate demand that depends on the real interest rate is determined within the model and thus is not part of autonomous aggregate demand.

between inflation (column 1) and short-run equilibrium output (column 3) yields the new *AD* curve for this economy, after the increase in planned investment.

TABLE 27.2
Inflation, the Real Interest Rate, and Output (Example 27.2)

Inflation rate π	Real interest rate r	Output Y
0.00	0.02	5,000
0.01	0.03	4,950
0.02	0.04	4,900
0.03	0.05	4,850
0.04	0.06	4,800

If you compare Table 27.2 to Table 27.1, you will see that the level of output associated with any given inflation rate has increased by 50. Thus the *AD* curve has shifted to the right by 50 units. Figure 27.3 shows the *AD* curves for this economy before and after the increase in autonomous aggregate demand.

FIGURE 27.3
Effect of an Increase in Autonomous Aggregate Demand.
This figure shows the *AD* curve for the economy described in Example 27.2 both *before* (AD) and *after* (AD') an increase in autonomous aggregate demand (an increase in planned investment). If the inflation rate and the real interest rate set by the Fed are held constant, an increase in autonomous aggregate demand will raise short-run equilibrium output. As a result, the *AD* curve will shift to the right, from AD to AD'.

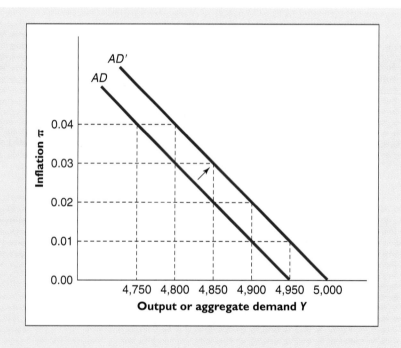

Many other events besides a change in planned investment may affect autonomous aggregate demand and thus the position of the *AD* curve. Here is a list of the components of autonomous aggregate demand (see Equation 25.3), together with an example of a factor that might shift each one:

■ Autonomous consumption $\overline{C}$. *Example:* Autonomous consumption would increase if consumers became more optimistic about the future, and thus more willing to spend at every level of income.

■ Taxes $\overline{T}$. *Example:* Because consumption depends on disposable, or after-tax, income, a cut in taxes stimulates consumer spending and raises autonomous aggregate demand.

■ Autonomous investment spending $\overline{I}$. *Example:* The development of a new cost-saving technology would increase autonomous investment spending as eager firms scrambled to acquire it.

- Government purchases $\overline{G}$. *Example:* An increase in government purchases of military hardware would increase autonomous aggregate demand.

- Net exports $\overline{NX}$. *Example:* Increased demand for U.S. products abroad would increase net exports, which in turn would increase autonomous aggregate demand.

As we see next, a change in the Fed's behavior, as reflected by a shift of its policy reaction function, will also shift the *AD* curve.

Changes in the Fed's policy reaction function Recall that the Fed's policy reaction function describes how the Fed sets the real interest rate at each level of inflation. This relationship is built into the *AD* curve—indeed, it accounts for the curve's downward slope. As long as the Fed sets the real interest rate according to this reaction function, its adjustments in the real rate will not cause the *AD* curve to shift.

However, on occasion the Fed may choose to be "tighter" or "easier" than normal, given the rate of inflation. For example, if inflation is too high and has stubbornly refused to decrease, the Fed might choose a "tighter" monetary policy, setting the real interest rate higher than normal, given the rate of inflation. This change of policy can be interpreted as an upward shift in the Fed's policy reaction function, as shown in Figure 27.4(a). A decision by the Fed to set the real interest rate at a higher level reduces aggregate demand and output at any given rate of inflation. Because an upward shift of the Fed's policy reaction function—a "tightening" of monetary policy—decreases aggregate demand and output at any given rate of inflation, the *AD* curve shifts to the left [Figure 27.4(b)].

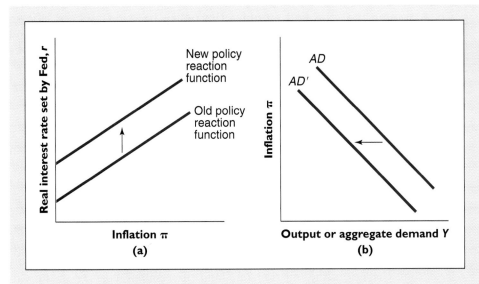

**FIGURE 27.4
A Tightening of Monetary Policy.**
A "tightening" of monetary policy implies that, at any given inflation rate, the Fed sets a higher value of the real interest rate than normal. Graphically, this change corresponds to an upward movement in the Fed's policy reaction function [part (a)]. A tightening of monetary policy shifts the *AD* curve to the left [part (b)]. An "easing" of monetary policy would correspond to a downward movement of the Fed's policy reaction function and a shift to the right of the *AD* curve.

Similarly, if the nation is experiencing an unusually severe recession, the Fed may choose to stimulate the economy by setting the real interest rate lower than normal, given the rate of inflation. This change in policy can be interpreted as a downward shift of the Fed's policy reaction function. Given the rate of inflation, a lower-than-normal setting of the real interest rate will increase aggregate demand and output. Therefore a downward shift of the Fed's policy reaction function—an "easing" of monetary policy—causes the *AD* curve to shift to the right.

EXERCISE 27.1

Explain why a tightening of monetary policy, as shown in Figure 27.4, can be interpreted as a decline in the Fed's long-run target for the inflation rate. (*Hint:* In the long run, the real interest rate set by the Fed must be consistent with the real interest rate determined in the market for saving and investment.)

EXERCISE 27.2

Example 27.1 showed how to find the *AD* curve for an economy with a given policy reaction function. This *AD* curve is graphed in Figure 27.2. Now suppose the Fed changes its policy reaction function as shown below:

Rate of Inflation π	Real interest rate set by Fed, r
0.00 (= 0%)	0.03 (= 3%)
0.01	0.04
0.02	0.05
0.03	0.06
0.04	0.07

a. Graph this policy reaction function and the policy reaction function given in Example 27.1. Explain why the policy reaction function given here represents a "tightening" of monetary policy.

b. Assuming that the Fed employs the policy reaction function shown here, find the new *AD* curve for the economy in Example 27.1, and compare it to the *AD* curve graphed in Figure 27.2. What effect does a tightening of monetary policy have on the *AD* curve?

SHIFTS OF THE *AD* CURVE VERSUS MOVEMENTS ALONG THE *AD* CURVE

Let's end this section by reviewing and summarizing the important distinction between *movements along* the *AD* curve and *shifts* of the *AD* curve.

The downward slope of the *AD* curve captures the inverse relationship between inflation, on the one hand, and aggregate demand and short-run equilibrium output, on the other. As we have seen, a rise in the inflation rate leads the Fed to raise the real interest rate, according to its policy reaction function. The higher real interest rate, in turn, depresses aggregate demand and short-run equilibrium output. Because the downward slope of the *AD* curve embodies this relationship, changes in the inflation rate, and the resulting changes in the real interest rate and short-run equilibrium output, are represented by *movements along* the *AD* curve. In particular, as long as the Fed sets the real interest rate in accordance with a fixed policy reaction function, changes in the real interest rate will *not* shift the *AD* curve.

However, any factor that changes the short-run equilibrium level of output *at a given level of inflation* will shift the *AD* curve—to the right if short-run equilibrium output increases, or to the left if short-run equilibrium output decreases. We have identified two factors that can shift the *AD* curve: changes in autonomous aggregate demand and changes in the Fed's policy reaction function. An increase in autonomous aggregate demand or an easing of monetary policy (a downward shift of the policy reaction function) will increase short-run equilibrium output at every level of inflation, shifting the *AD* curve to the right. A decline in autonomous aggregate demand or a tightening in Fed policy (an upward shift in the policy reaction function) will decrease short-run equilibrium output at every level of inflation, shifting the *AD* curve to the left.

RECAP   **THE AGGREGATE DEMAND (*AD*) CURVE**

- Shows the relationship between aggregate demand (equal to short-run equilibrium output) and inflation. Higher inflation leads the Fed to raise the real interest rate, which reduces aggregate demand and short-run equilibrium output. Therefore the *AD* curve slopes downward.

- Other reasons for the downward slope of the *AD* curve include (1) higher inflation reduces the real value of money held by the public, reducing wealth and spending; (2) inflation redistributes resources from less affluent people, who spend a high percentage of their disposable income, to more affluent people, who spend a smaller percentage of disposable income; and (3) for a constant rate of exchange between the dollar and other currencies, rising prices of domestic goods and services reduce foreign sales and hence net exports (a component of aggregate demand).

- An increase in autonomous aggregate demand raises short-run equilibrium output at each value of inflation and so shifts the *AD* curve to the right. Conversely, a decrease in autonomous aggregate demand shifts the *AD* curve to the left.

- An easing of monetary policy, as reflected by a downward shift in the Fed's policy reaction function, shifts the *AD* curve to the right. A tightening of monetary policy, as reflected by an upward shift in the Fed's policy reaction function, shifts the *AD* curve to the left.

- Changes in inflation correspond to movements *along* the *AD* curve; they do not shift the *AD* curve.

INFLATION AND AGGREGATE SUPPLY

Until this point in the chapter we focused on how changes in inflation affect aggregate demand and short-run equilibrium output, a relationship captured by the *AD* curve. But we have not yet discussed how inflation itself is determined. In the rest of the chapter we will examine the main factors that determine the inflation rate in modern industrial economies, as well as the options that policymakers have to control inflation. In doing so we will introduce a useful diagram for analyzing the behavior of output and inflation, called the *aggregate demand–aggregate supply diagram.*

Physicists have noted that a body will tend to keep moving at a constant speed and direction unless it is acted upon by some outside force, a tendency they refer to as *inertia.* Applying this concept to economics, many observers have noted that inflation seems to be inertial in the sense that it tends to remain roughly constant as long as the economy is at full employment and there are no external shocks to the price level. In the first part of this section we will discuss why inflation behaves in this way.

However, just as a physical object will change speed if it is acted on by outside forces, so various economic forces can change the rate of inflation. Later in this section we will discuss three factors that can cause the inflation rate to change. The first is the presence of an *output gap:* Inflation tends to rise when there is an expansionary output gap and to fall when there is a recessionary output gap. The second factor that can affect the inflation rate is a shock that directly affects prices, which we will refer to as an *inflation shock.* An example would be a large increase in the price of imported oil, which raises the price of gasoline, heating oil, and other fuels, as well as of goods made with oil or services using oil. Finally, the third factor that directly affects the inflation rate is a *shock to potential output,* or a sharp change in the level of potential output—an extreme example would be a natural disaster that destroyed a significant portion of a country's factories and businesses. Together, inflationary shocks and shocks to potential output are known as *aggregate supply shocks.*

INFLATION INERTIA

In low-inflation industrial economies like that of the United States today, inflation tends to change relatively slowly from year to year, a phenomenon that is sometimes referred to as *inflation inertia.* If the rate of inflation in one year is 2 percent, it may be 3 percent or even 4 percent in the next year. But unless the nation experiences a very unusual economic shock, inflation is unlikely to rise to 6 or 8 percent or fall to −2 percent in the following year. This relatively sluggish behavior contrasts sharply with the behavior of economic variables such as stock or commodity prices, which can change rapidly from day to day. For example, oil prices might well rise by 20 percent over the course of a year and then fall 20 percent over the next year. Yet since 1992, the U.S. inflation rate has generally remained in the range of 2 to 3 percent per year.

Why does inflation tend to adjust relatively slowly in modern industrial economies? To answer this question, we must consider two closely related factors that play an important role in determining the inflation rate: the behavior of the public's *inflation expectations* and the existence of *long-term wage and price contracts.*

First, consider the public's expectations about inflation. In negotiating future wages and prices, both buyers and sellers take into account the rate of inflation they expect to prevail in the next few years. As a result, today's *expectations* of future inflation may help to determine the future inflation rate. Suppose, for example, that office worker Fred and his boss Colleen agree that Fred's performance this past year justifies an increase of 2 percent in his real wage for next year. What nominal wage increase should they agree on? If Fred believes that inflation is likely to be 3 percent over the next year, he will ask for a 5 percent increase in his nominal wage to obtain a 2 percent increase in his real wage. If Colleen agrees that inflation is likely to be 3 percent, she should be willing to go along with a 5 percent nominal increase, knowing that it implies only a 2 percent increase in Fred's real wage. Thus the rate at which Fred and Colleen *expect* prices to rise affects the rate at which at least one price—Fred's nominal wage—*actually* rises.

A similar dynamic affects the contracts for production inputs other than labor. For example, if Colleen is negotiating with her office supply company, the prices she will agree to pay for next year's deliveries of copy paper and staples will depend on what she expects the inflation rate to be. If Colleen anticipates that the price of office supplies will not change relative to the prices of other goods and services and that the general inflation rate will be 3 percent, then she should be willing to agree to a 3 percent increase in the price of office supplies. On the other hand, if she expects the general inflation rate to be 6 percent, then she will agree to pay 6 percent more for copy paper and staples next year, knowing that a nominal increase of 6 percent implies no change in the real, or relative, price of office supplies.

Economywide, then, the higher the expected rate of inflation, the more nominal wages and the cost of other inputs will rise. But if wages and other costs of production grow rapidly in response to expected inflation, firms will have to raise their prices rapidly as well to cover their costs. Thus a low rate of expected inflation tends to lead to a low rate of actual inflation, and a high rate of expected inflation tends to contribute to a high rate of actual inflation.

The conclusion that actual inflation is partially determined by expected inflation raises the question of what determines inflation expectations. To a great extent, people's expectations are influenced by their recent experience. If inflation has been low and stable for some time, people are likely to expect it to continue to be low. But if inflation has recently been high, people will expect it to continue to be high. If inflation has been unpredictable, alternating between low and high levels, the public's expectations will likewise tend to be volatile, rising or falling with news or rumors about economic conditions or economic policy.

Figure 27.5 illustrates schematically how low and stable inflation may tend to be self-perpetuating. As the figure shows, if inflation has been low for some time, people will continue to expect low inflation. Increases in nominal wages and other production costs will thus tend to be small. If firms raise prices only by enough to cover costs, then actual inflation will be low, as expected. This low actual rate will in turn promote low expected inflation, perpetuating the "virtuous circle." The same logic applies in an economy with high inflation. A high inflation rate implies high expected inflation, which in turn contributes to a high rate of actual inflation, and so on in a "vicious circle." This role of inflation expectations in the determination of wage and price increases helps to explain why inflation often seems to adjust slowly.

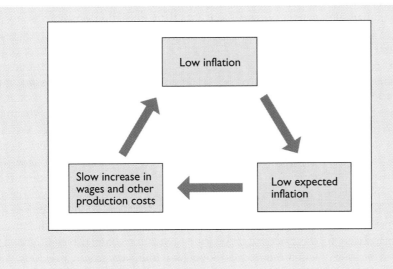

FIGURE 27.5
A Virtuous Circle of Low Inflation and Low Expected Inflation.
Low inflation leads people to expect low inflation in the future. As a result, they agree to accept small increases in wages and the prices of the goods and services they supply, which keeps inflation—and expected inflation—low. In a similar way, high inflation leads people to expect high inflation, which in turn tends to produce high inflation.

The role of inflation expectations in the slow adjustment of inflation is strengthened by a second key element, the existence of *long-term wage and price contracts*. Union wage contracts, for example, often extend for 3 years into the future. Likewise, contracts that set the prices manufacturing firms pay for parts and raw materials often cover several years. Long-term contracts serve to "build in" wage and price increases that depend on inflation expectations at the time the contracts were signed.

To summarize, in the absence of external shocks, inflation tends to remain relatively stable over time, at least in low-inflation industrial economies like that of the United States. In other words, inflation is *inertial* (or as some people put it, "sticky"). Inflation tends to be inertial for two main reasons. The first is the behavior of people's expectations of inflation. All else being equal, a low inflation rate leads people to expect low inflation in the future, which results in reduced pressure for wage and price increases. Similarly, a high inflation rate leads people to expect high inflation in the future, resulting in more rapid increases in wages and prices. The effects of expectations are reinforced by the existence of long-term wage and price contracts, which is the second reason inflation tends to be stable over time. Long-term contracts tend to build in the effects of people's inflation expectations.

Although the rate of inflation is inertial, it does, of course, change over time. We next discuss a key factor causing the inflation rate to change.

THE OUTPUT GAP AND INFLATION

An important factor influencing the rate of inflation is the output gap, or the difference between potential output and actual output ($Y^* - Y$). We have seen that, in the short run, firms will meet the demand for their output at previously determined prices. For example, Al's ice cream shop will serve ice cream to any customer who comes into the shop at the prices posted behind the counter. The level of output that is determined by aggregate demand at preset prices is called short-run equilibrium output.

At a particular time the level of short-run equilibrium output may happen to equal the economy's long-run productive capacity, or potential output. But, as we have seen, that is not necessarily the case. Output may exceed potential output, giving rise to an expansionary gap, or it may fall short of potential output, producing a recessionary gap. Let's consider what happens to inflation in each of these three possible cases: no output gap, an expansionary gap, and a recessionary gap.

If actual output equals potential output, then by definition there is no output gap. When the output gap is zero, firms are satisfied, in the sense that their sales equal their normal production rates. As a result, firms have no incentive either to reduce or increase their prices *relative* to the prices of other goods and services. However, the fact that firms are satisfied with their sales does *not* imply that inflation—the rate of change in the overall price level—is zero.

To see why, let's go back to the idea of inflation inertia. Suppose that inflation has recently been steady at 3 percent per year so that the public has come to expect an inflation rate of 3 percent per year. If the public's inflation expectations are reflected in the wage and price increases agreed to in long-term contracts, then firms will find their labor and materials costs are rising at 3 percent per year. To cover their costs, firms will need to raise their prices by 3 percent per year. Note that if all firms are raising their prices by 3 percent per year, the *relative* prices of various goods and services in the economy—say, the price of ice cream relative to the price of a taxi ride—will not change. Nevertheless, the economywide rate of inflation equals 3 percent, the same as in previous years. We conclude that, *if the output gap is zero, the rate of inflation will tend to remain the same.*

Suppose instead that an expansionary gap exists so that most firms' sales exceed their normal production rates. As we might expect in situations in which the quantity demanded exceeds the quantity firms desire to supply, firms will respond by trying to increase their relative prices. To do so, they will increase their prices by *more* than the increase in their costs. If all firms behave this way, then the general price level will begin to rise more rapidly than before. Thus, *when an expansionary gap exists, the rate of inflation will tend to increase.*

Finally, if a recessionary gap exists, firms will be selling less than their capacity to produce, and they will have an incentive to cut their relative prices so they can sell more. In this case, firms will raise their prices less than needed to cover fully their increases in costs, as determined by the existing inflation rate. As a result, *when a recessionary gap exists, the rate of inflation will tend to decrease.* These important results are summarized in Box 27.1.

BOX 27.1: THE OUTPUT GAP AND INFLATION

Relationship of output to potential output		Behavior of inflation
1. No output gap:	$Y = Y^*$	Inflation remains unchanged
2. Expansionary gap:	$Y > Y^*$	Inflation rises: $\pi \uparrow$
3. Recessionary gap:	$Y < Y^*$	Inflation falls: $\pi \downarrow$

THE AGGREGATE DEMAND–AGGREGATE SUPPLY DIAGRAM

The adjustment of inflation in response to an output gap can be shown conveniently in a diagram. Figure 27.6, drawn with inflation π on the vertical axis and real output Y on the horizontal axis, is an example of an *aggregate demand–aggregate supply diagram,* or *AD-AS diagram* for short. The diagram has three elements, one of which is the downward-sloping *AD* curve, introduced earlier in the chapter. Recall that the *AD* curve shows how aggregate demand, and hence short-run equilibrium output, depend on the inflation rate. The second element is a vertical line marking the economy's potential output Y^*. Because potential output represents the economy's long-run productive capacity, we will refer to this vertical line as the **long-run aggregate supply line,** or *LRAS* line. The third element in Figure 27.6, and a new one, is the *short-run aggregate supply line,* labeled *SRAS* in the diagram. The **short-run aggregate supply line** is a horizontal line that shows the current rate of inflation in the economy, which in the figure is labeled π. We can think of the current rate of inflation as having been determined by past expectations of inflation and past pricing decisions. The short-run aggregate supply line is horizontal because, in the short run, producers supply whatever output is demanded as preset prices.

long-run aggregate supply (LRAS) line a vertical line showing the economy's potential output Y^*

short-run aggregate supply (SRAS) line a horizontal line showing the current rate of inflation, as determined by past expectations and pricing decisions

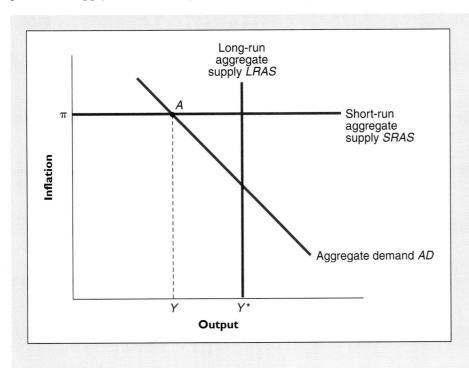

FIGURE 27.6
The Aggregate Demand–Aggregate Supply (AD-AS) diagram.
This diagram has three elements: the *AD* curve, which shows how short-run equilibrium output depends on inflation, the long-run aggregate supply line (*LRAS*), which marks the economy's potential output, and the short-run aggregate supply line (*SRAS*), which shows the current value of inflation (π). Short-run equilibrium output, which is equal to Y here, is determined by the intersection of the *AD* curve and the *SRAS* line (point *A*). Because actual output Y is less than potential output Y^*, this economy has a recessionary gap.

The *AD-AS* diagram can be used to determine the level of output prevailing at any particular time. As we have seen, the inflation rate at any moment is given directly by the position of the *SRAS* line; for example, current inflation equals π in Figure 27.6. To find the current level of output, recall that the *AD* curve shows the level of short-run equilibrium output at any given rate of inflation. Since the inflation rate in this economy is π we can infer from Figure 27.6 that short-run equilibrium output must equal *Y*, which corresponds to the intersection of the *AD* curve and the *SRAS* line (point *A* in the figure). Notice that in Figure 27.6, short-run equilibrium output *Y* is smaller than potential output *Y**, so there is a recessionary gap in this economy.

The intersection of the *AD* curve and the *SRAS* line (point *A* in Figure 27.6) is referred to as the point of *short-run equilibrium* in this economy. When the economy is in **short-run equilibrium**, inflation equals the value determined by past expectations and past pricing decisions, and output equals the level of short-run equilibrium output that is consistent with that inflation rate.

Although the economy may be in short-run equilibrium at point *A* in Figure 27.6, it will not remain there. The reason is that at point *A*, the economy is experiencing a recessionary gap (output is less than potential output, as indicated by the *LRAS* line). As we have just seen, when a recessionary gap exists, firms are not selling as much as they would like to and so they slow down the rate at which they increase their prices. Eventually, the low level of aggregate demand that is associated with a recessionary gap causes the inflation rate to fall.

The adjustment of inflation in response to a recessionary gap is shown graphically in Figure 27.7. As inflation declines, the *SRAS* line moves downward, from *SRAS* to *SRAS'*. Because of inflation inertia (caused by the slow adjustment of the public's inflation expectations and the existence of long-term contracts), inflation adjusts downward only gradually. However, as long as a recessionary gap exists, inflation will continue to fall, and the *SRAS* line will move downward until it intersects the *AD* curve at point *B* in the figure. At that point, actual output equals potential output, and the recessionary gap has been eliminated. Because there is no further pressure on inflation at point *B*, the inflation rate stabilizes at the lower level. A situation like that represented by point *B* in Figure 27.7, in which the inflation rate is stable and actual output equals potential output, is referred to as a **long-run equilibrium** of the

short-run equilibrium a situation in which inflation equals the value determined by past expectations and pricing decisions, and output equals the level of short-run equilibrium output that is consistent with that inflation rate; graphically, short-run equilibrium occurs at the intersection of the *AD* curve and the *SRAS* line

long-run equilibrium a situation in which actual output equals potential output and the inflation rate is stable; graphically, long-run equilibrium occurs when the *AD* curve, the *SRAS* line, and the *LRAS* line all intersect at a single point

FIGURE 27.7
The Adjustment of Inflation When a Recessionary Gap Exists.
At the initial short-run equilibrium point *A*, a recessionary gap exists, putting downward pressure on inflation. As inflation falls gradually, the *SRAS* line moves downward until it reaches *SRAS'* and actual output equals potential output (point *B*). Once the recessionary gap has been eliminated, inflation stabilizes at π*, and the economy settles into long-run equilibrium at the intersection of *AD*, *LRAS*, and *SRAS'* (point *B*).

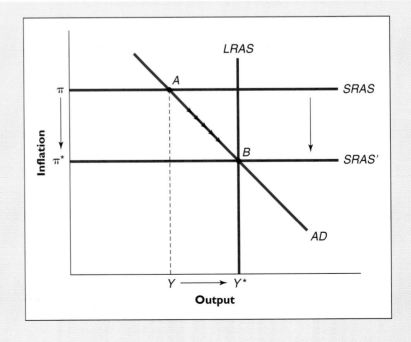

economy. Long-run equilibrium occurs when the *AD* curve, the *SRAS* line, and the *LRAS* line all intersect at a single point. At long-run equilibrium, the *equilibrium principle* applies, so that the economy is performing efficiently.

Figure 27.7 illustrates the important point that when a recessionary gap exists, inflation will tend to fall. It also shows that as inflation declines, short-run equilibrium output rises, increasing gradually from *Y* to *Y** as the short-run equilibrium point moves down the *AD* curve. The source of this increase in output is the behavior of the Federal Reserve, which lowers the real interest rate as inflation falls, stimulating aggregate demand. As output rises, cyclical unemployment, which by Okun's law is proportional to the output gap, also declines. This process of falling inflation, falling real interest rates, rising output, and falling unemployment continues until the economy reaches full employment at point *B* in Figure 27.7, the economy's long-run equilibrium point.

What happens if instead of a recessionary gap the economy has an expansionary gap, with output greater than potential output? An expansionary gap would cause the rate of inflation to *rise*, as firms respond to high demand by raising their prices more rapidly than their costs are rising. In graphical terms, an expansionary gap would cause the *SRAS* line to move upward over time. Inflation and the *SRAS* line would continue to rise until the economy reached long-run equilibrium, with actual output equal to potential output. This process is illustrated in Figure 27.8. Initially, the economy is in short-run equilibrium at point *A*, where *Y* > *Y** (an expansionary gap). The expansionary gap causes inflation to rise over time; graphically, the short-run aggregate supply line moves upward, from *SRAS* to *SRAS'*. As the *SRAS* line rises, short-run equilibrium output falls, the result of the Fed's tendency to increase the real interest rate when inflation rises. Eventually the *SRAS* line intersects the *AD* curve and *LRAS* line at point *B*, where the economy reaches long-run equilibrium, with no output gap and stable inflation.

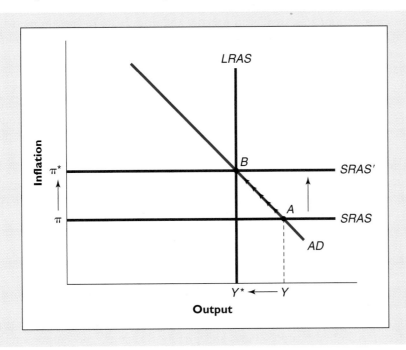

FIGURE 27.8
The Adjustment of Inflation When an Expansionary Gap Exists.
At the initial short-run equilibrium point A, an expansionary gap exists. Inflation rises gradually (the SRAS line moves upward), and output falls. The process continues until the economy reaches long-run equilibrium at point B, where inflation stabilizes and the output gap is eliminated.

THE SELF-CORRECTING ECONOMY

Our analysis of Figures 27.7 and 27.8 makes an important general point, which is that the economy tends to be *self-correcting*. In other words, given enough time, output gaps tend to disappear on their own. Expansionary output gaps are eliminated by rising inflation, while recessionary output gaps are eliminated by falling inflation. This result contrasts sharply with the basic Keynesian model, which does not include a self-correcting mechanism. The difference in results is explained by the fact that the basic Keynesian model concentrates on the short-run period, during which prices do not adjust; it does not take into account the changes in prices and inflation that occur over a longer period.

Does the economy's tendency to self-correct imply that active manipulation of monetary and fiscal policies is not needed to stabilize output? The answer to this question depends crucially on the *speed* with which the self-correction process takes place. If self-correction takes place very slowly so that actual output differs from potential for protracted periods, then active use of monetary and fiscal policy can help to stabilize output. But if self-correction is rapid, then active stabilization policies are probably not justified in most cases, given the lags and uncertainties that are involved in policymaking (see Chapters 25 and 26). Indeed, if the economy returns to full employment quickly, then attempts by policymakers to influence aggregate demand may end up doing more harm than good, for example, by causing actual output to "overshoot" potential output.

The speed with which a particular economy corrects itself depends on a variety of factors, including the prevalence of long-term contracts and the efficiency and flexibility of product and labor markets. (For a case study, see the comparison of U.S. and European labor markets in Chapter 21). However, a reasonable conclusion is that the greater the initial output gap, the longer the economy's process of self-correction will take. This observation suggests that monetary and fiscal policy should not be used actively to eliminate relatively small output gaps, but that they may be quite useful in remedying large gaps—for example, when the unemployment rate is exceptionally high.

The self-correcting tendency of the economy is one reason why the *income-expenditure multiplier* is smaller in practice than the basic Keynesian model suggests (see Chapter 25). Recall that the multiplier results from many rounds of increased spending and production. For example, a $1 increase in government purchases not only raises aggregate demand by $1 immediately, it raises the incomes of producers by $1 as well. This extra dollar of income prompts a second round of increased spending, which raises the incomes of other producers, leading to a third round of increased spending, and so on. If prices never adjusted and firms continued to meet demand, the full impact of this spending would be felt on short-run equilibrium output, as suggested in Chapter 25. In reality, however, inflation is likely to begin to rise before many rounds of spending have occurred. As the Fed increases the real interest rate in response to the resulting rise in inflation, the effects of the increase in aggregate demand will be partially offset. In short, because inflation begins to increase before many rounds of spending and production have taken place, the multiplier is smaller in practice than implied by the basic Keynesian model.

RECAP   *AD-AS* **AND THE SELF-CORRECTING ECONOMY**

The economy is in *short-run equilibrium* when inflation equals the value determined by past expectations and pricing decisions, and output equals the level of short-run equilibrium output that is consistent with that inflation rate. Graphically, short-run equilibrium occurs at the intersection of the *AD* curve and the *SRAS* line.

The economy is in *long-run equilibrium* when actual output equals potential output (there is no output gap) and the inflation rate is stable. Graphically, long-run equilibrium occurs when the *AD* curve, the *SRAS* line, and the *LRAS* line intersect at a common point.

Inflation adjusts gradually to bring the economy into long-run equilibrium (a phenomenon called the economy's *self-correcting tendency*). Inflation rises to eliminate an expansionary gap and falls to eliminate a recessionary gap. Graphically, the *SRAS* line moves up or down as needed to bring the economy into long-run equilibrium.

The more rapid the self-correction process, the less need for active stabilization policies to eliminate output gaps. In practice, policymakers' attempts to eliminate output gaps through changes in aggregate demand are more likely to be helpful when the output gap is large than when it is small.

SOURCES OF INFLATION

We have seen that inflation can rise or fall in response to an output gap. But what creates the output gaps that give rise to changes in inflation? And are there other factors besides output gaps that can affect the inflation rate? In this section we use the *AD-AS* diagram to explore the ultimate sources of inflation. We first discuss how excessive growth in aggregate demand can spur inflation, then turn to factors operating through the supply side of the economy.

EXCESSIVE AGGREGATE DEMAND

One important source of inflation in practice is excessive aggregate demand, or, in more colloquial terms, "too much spending chasing too few goods." Example 27.3 illustrates.

Military buildups and inflation

EXAMPLE 27.3

Wars and military buildups are sometimes associated with increased inflation. Explain why, using the *AD-AS* diagram. Can the Fed do anything to prevent the increase in inflation caused by a military buildup?

Wars and military buildups are potentially inflationary because increased spending on military hardware raises aggregate demand relative to the economy's productive capacity. In the face of rising sales, firms increase their prices more quickly, raising the inflation rate.

The two parts of Figure 27.9 illustrate this process. In Figure 27.9(a), suppose that the economy is initially in long-run equilibrium at point A, where the aggregate demand curve AD intersects both the short-run and long-run aggregate supply lines, $SRAS$ and $LRAS$, respectively. Point A is a long-run equilibrium point, with output equal to potential output and stable inflation. Now suppose that the government decides to spend more on armaments. Increased military spending is an increase in government purchases $\overline{G}$, one of the components of autonomous aggregate demand. We saw earlier that increases in autonomous aggregate demand increase output at each level of inflation, shifting the AD curve to the right. Figure 27.9(a) shows the aggregate demand curve shifting rightward, from AD to AD', as the result of increased military expenditure. The economy moves to a new, short-run equilibrium at point B, where AD' intersects $SRAS$. Note that at point B actual output has risen to $Y > Y^*$, creating an expansionary gap. Because inflation is inertial and does not change in the short run, the immediate effect of the increase in government purchases is to increase aggregate demand and output, just as we saw in Chapter 25.

The process doesn't stop there, however, because inflation will not remain the same indefinitely. At point B an expansionary gap exists, so inflation will gradually begin to increase. Figure 27.9(b) shows this increase in inflation as a shift of the $SRAS$ line from its initial position to a higher level, $SRAS'$. When inflation has risen to π', enough to eliminate the output gap (point C), the economy is

FIGURE 27.9

War and Military Buildup as a Source of Inflation.
(a) An increase in military spending shifts the AD curve to the right, from AD to AD'. At the new short-run equilibrium point B, actual output has risen above potential output Y*, creating an expansionary gap. (b) This gap leads to rising inflation, shown as an upward movement of the SRAS line, from SRAS to SRAS'. At the new long-run equilibrium point C actual output has fallen back to the level of potential output, but at π', inflation is higher than it was originally.

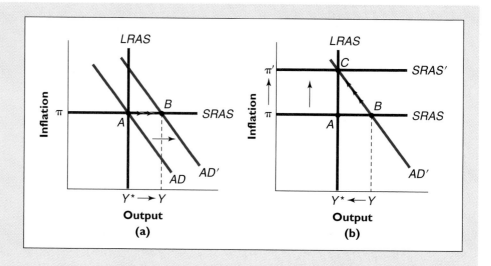

back in long-run equilibrium. We see now that the increase in output created by the military buildup was only temporary. In the long run actual output has returned to the level of potential output, but at a higher rate of inflation.

Does the Fed have the power to prevent the increased inflation that is induced by a rise in military spending? The answer is yes. We saw earlier that a tightening of monetary policy—a decision by the Fed to set a higher real interest rate at any given level of inflation—will shift the AD curve to the left. So if the Fed tightens monetary policy as the military buildup proceeds, it can reverse the rightward shift of the AD curve caused by increased government spending and avoid the development of an expansionary gap with its inflationary consequences. In economic terms, the Fed's policy works because higher real interest rates reduce consumption and investment spending. The reduction in private aggregate demand offsets the increase in demand by the government, eliminating, or at least moderating, the inflationary impact of the military purchases.

We should not conclude, by the way, that avoiding the inflationary consequences of a military buildup makes the buildup cost less to society. As we have just noted, inflation can be avoided only if consumption and investment are reduced by higher real interest rates. Effectively, the private sector must give up some resources so that more resources can be devoted to military purposes. This reduction in resources reduces both current living standards (by reducing consumption) and future living standards (by reducing investment).

How did inflation get started in the United States in the 1960s?

In the United States from 1959 through 1963, inflation hovered around 1 percent per year. Beginning in 1964, however, inflation began to rise, reaching nearly 6 percent in 1970. Why did inflation become a problem in the United States in the 1960s?

Increases in government spending, plus the failure of the Federal Reserve to act to contain inflation, appear to explain most of the increase in inflation during the 1960s. On the fiscal side, military expenditures increased dramatically in the latter part of the decade as the war in Vietnam escalated. Defense spending rose from $50.6 billion, or about 7.4 percent of GDP, in 1965 to $81.9 billion, or 9.4 percent of GDP, in 1968 and remained at a high level for some years. To appreciate the size of this military buildup

ECONOMIC NATURALIST 27.1

relative to the size of the economy, note that the *increase* in military spending alone between 1965 and 1968 was about 2 percent of GDP. In contrast, in 1999 the *total* U.S. defense budget was a little over 3 percent of GDP. Moreover, at about the same time as the wartime military buildup, government spending on social programs—reflecting the impact of President Lyndon Johnson's Great Society and War on Poverty initiatives—also increased dramatically.

These government-induced increases in aggregate demand contributed to an economic boom. Indeed the 1961–1969 economic expansion was the longest in history at the time, being surpassed only recently by the long expansion of the 1990s. However, an expansionary gap developed, and eventually inflation began to rise, as would have been predicted by the analysis in Example 27.3.

An interesting contrast exists between these effects of the 1960s military buildup and those of the 1980s buildup under President Reagan, which did not lead to an increase in inflation. One important difference between the two eras was the behavior of the Federal Reserve. As we saw in Example 27.3, the Fed can offset the inflationary impact of increased government spending by tightening monetary policy and raising the real interest rate. Except for a brief attempt in 1966, the Federal Reserve generally did not try to offset inflationary pressures during the 1960s. That failure may have been simply a miscalculation, or it may have reflected a reluctance to take the politically unpopular step of slowing the economy during a period of great political turmoil and unrest. But in the early 1980s, under Paul Volcker, the Federal Reserve acted vigorously to contain inflation. As a result, inflation actually declined in the 1980s, despite the military buildup.

"I told you the Fed should have tightened."

While output gaps cause gradual changes in inflation, on occasion an economic shock can cause a relatively rapid change. Such jolts to prices, which we call *inflation shocks,* are the subject of the next section.

INFLATION SHOCKS

In late 1973, at the time of the Yom Kippur War between Israel and a coalition of Arab nations, the Organization of Petroleum Exporting Countries (OPEC) sharply cut its supplies of crude oil to the industrialized nations, quadrupling world oil prices. The sharp increase in oil prices was quickly transferred to the prices of gasoline, heating oil, and goods and services that were heavily dependent on oil, such as air travel. The effects of the oil price increase, together with agricultural shortages that increased the price of food, contributed to a significant rise in the overall U.S. inflation rate in 1974.[3]

The increase in inflation in 1974 is an example of what is referred to as an *inflation shock*. An **inflation shock** is a sudden change in the normal behavior of inflation, unrelated to the nation's output gap. An inflation shock that causes an increase in inflation, like the large rise in oil prices in 1973, is called an *adverse* inflation shock. An inflation shock that reduces inflation, such as the sharp decline in oil prices that occurred in 1986, is called a *favorable* inflation shock. Economic Naturalist 27.2 gives more details on the economic effects of inflation shocks.

inflation shock a sudden change in the normal behavior of inflation, unrelated to the nation's output gap

ECONOMIC NATURALIST 27.2

OPEC's 1974 cutback in oil production created long lines, rising prices, and shortages at the gas pump.

© Rick Smolan/Stock Boston

Why did inflation escalate in the United States in the 1970s?

Having risen in the latter half of the 1960s, inflation continued to rise in the 1970s. Already at 6.2 percent in 1973, inflation jumped to 11.0 percent in 1974. After subsiding from 1974 to 1978, it began to rise again in 1979, to 11.4 percent, and reached 13.5 percent in 1980. Why did inflation increase so much in the 1970s?

We have already described the quadrupling of oil prices in late 1973 and the sharp increases in agricultural prices at about the same time, which together constituted an adverse inflation shock. A second inflation shock occurred in 1979, when the turmoil of the Iranian Revolution restricted the flow of oil from the Middle East and doubled oil prices yet again.

Figure 27.10 shows the effects of an adverse inflation shock on a hypothetical economy. Before the inflation shock occurs, the economy is in long-run equilibrium at point A, at the intersection of AD, LRAS, and SRAS. At point A actual output is equal to potential output Y*, and the inflation rate is stable at π. However, an adverse inflation shock directly increases inflation so that the SRAS line shifts rapidly upward to SRAS'. A new short-run equilibrium is established at point B, where SRAS' intersects the aggregate demand curve, AD. In the wake of the inflation shock, inflation rises to π' and output falls from Y* to Y'. Thus an inflation shock creates the worst possible scenario: higher inflation coupled with a recessionary gap. The combination of inflation and recession has been referred to as *stagflation*, or stagnation plus inflation. The United States economy experienced a stagflation in 1973–1975, after the first oil shock, and again in 1980, after the second oil shock.

An adverse inflation shock poses a difficult dilemma for macroeconomic policymakers. To see why, suppose monetary and fiscal policies were left unchanged following an inflationary shock. In that case, inflation would eventually abate and return to its original level. Graphically, the economy would reach its short-run equilibrium at point B in Figure 27.10 soon after the inflation shock. However, because of the recessionary gap that exists at point B, eventually inflation would begin to drift downward, until finally the recessionary gap is eliminated. Graphically, this decline in inflation would be represented by a downward movement of the SRAS line, from SRAS' back to SRAS. Inflation would stop declining only when long-run equilibrium is restored, at point A in the figure, where inflation is at its original level of π and output equals potential output.

However, although a "do-nothing" policy approach would ultimately eliminate both the output gap and the surge in inflation, it would also put the economy through a deep and protracted recession, as actual output remains below potential output until the inflation adjustment process is completed. To avoid such an economically and politically costly outcome, policymakers might opt to eliminate the recessionary gap more quickly. By easing monetary policy, for example, the Fed could shift the AD curve to the right, from AD to AD', taking the economy to a new long-run equilibrium, point C in Figure 27.10. This expansionary policy would help to restore output to the full-

---

[3]In Chapter 19 we distinguished between relative price changes (changes in the prices of individual goods) and inflation (changes in the overall price level). In the 1973–1974 episode changes in the price of individual categories of goods, such as energy and food, were sufficiently large and pervasive that the overall price level was significantly affected. Thus these relative price changes carried an inflationary impact as well.

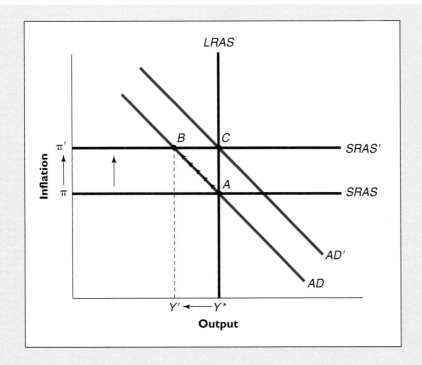

FIGURE 27.10
The Effects of an Adverse Inflation Shock.
Starting from long-run equilibrium at point A, an adverse inflation shock directly raises current inflation, causing the SRAS line to shift upward to SRAS'. At the new short-run equilibrium, point B, inflation has risen to π′ and output has fallen to Y′, creating a recessionary gap. If the Fed does nothing, eventually the economy will return to point A, restoring the original inflation rate but suffering a long recession in the process. The Fed could ease monetary policy, shifting the AD curve to AD′ and restoring full employment more quickly at point C. The cost of this strategy is that inflation remains at its higher level.

employment level more quickly, but as the figure shows, it would also allow inflation to stabilize at the new, higher level.

In sum, inflation shocks pose a true dilemma for policymakers. If they leave their policies unchanged—a "steady-as-she-goes" approach—inflation will eventually subside but the nation may experience a lengthy and severe recession. If instead they act aggressively to expand aggregate demand, the recession will end more quickly but inflation will stabilize at a higher level. In the 1970s, though U.S. policymakers tried to strike a balance between stabilizing output and containing inflation, both recession and increased inflation hobbled the economy.

SHOCKS TO POTENTIAL OUTPUT

In analyzing the effects of increased oil prices on the U.S. economy in the 1970s, we assumed that potential output was unchanged in the wake of the shock. However, the sharp rise in oil prices during that period probably affected the economy's potential output as well. As oil prices rose, for example, many companies retired less energy-efficient equipment or scrapped older "gas-guzzling" vehicles. A smaller capital stock implies lower potential output.

If the increases in oil prices did reduce potential output, their inflationary impact would have been compounded. Figure 27.11 illustrates the effects on the economy of a sudden decline in potential output. For the sake of simplicity, the figure includes only the effects of the reduction in potential output and not the direct effect of the inflation shock. (Problem 8 at the end of the chapter asks you to combine the two effects.)

Suppose once again that the economy is in long-run equilibrium at point A. Then potential output falls unexpectedly from Y* to Y*′, shifting the long-run aggregate supply line leftward from LRAS to LRAS′. After this decline in potential output, is the economy still in long-run equilibrium at point A? The

FIGURE 27.11

The Effects of a Shock to Potential Output.

The economy is in long-run equilibrium at point *A* when a decline in potential output from *Y** to *Y*'* creates an expansionary gap. Inflation rises, and the short-run aggregate supply line shifts upward from *SRAS* to *SRAS'*. A new long-run equilibrium is reached at point *B*, where actual output equals the new, lower level of potential output *Y*'* and inflation has risen to π'. Because it is the result of a fall in potential output, the decline in output is permanent.

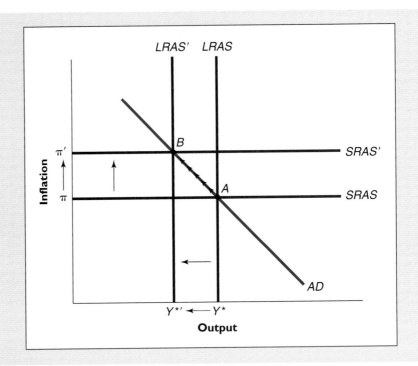

aggregate supply shock either an inflation shock or a shock to potential output; adverse aggregate supply shocks of both types reduce output and increase inflation

answer is no, because output now exceeds potential output at that point. In other words, an expansionary gap has developed. This gap reflects the fact that although aggregate demand has not changed, the capacity of firms to supply goods and services has been reduced.

As we have seen, an expansionary gap leads to rising inflation. In Figure 27.11, increasing inflation is represented by an upward movement of the *SRAS* line. Eventually the short-run aggregate supply line reaches *SRAS'*, and the economy reaches a new long-run equilibrium at point *B*. (Why is point *B* a long-run, and not just a short-run equilibrium?) At that point output has fallen to the new, lower level of potential output *Y*'* and inflation has risen to π'.

Sharp changes in potential output and inflation shocks are both referred to as **aggregate supply shocks**. As we have seen, an adverse aggregate supply shock of either type leads to lower output and higher inflation and therefore poses a difficult challenge for policymakers. A difference between the two types of aggregate supply shock is that the output losses associated with an adverse inflation shock are temporary (because the economy self-corrects and will ultimately return to its initial level of potential output), but those associated with a fall in potential output are permanent (output remains lower even after the economy has reached a new long-run equilibrium).

RECAP   SOURCES OF INFLATION

Inflation may result from excessive aggregate demand, which creates an expansionary output gap and puts upward pressure on prices. Monetary policy or fiscal policy can be used to offset excessive aggregate demand, preventing higher inflation from emerging.

Inflation may also arise from an *aggregate supply shock*, either an inflation shock or a shock to potential output. An *inflation shock* is a sudden change in the normal behavior of inflation, unrelated to the nation's output gap. An example of an inflation shock is a runup in energy and food prices large enough to raise the overall price level. An inflation shock creates stagflation, a combination of recession and higher inflation. Stagflation poses a difficult dilemma for policymakers. If they take no action, eventually inflation will subside and output will recover, but in the interim the economy may suffer a protracted period of recession. If they use monetary or fiscal policy to increase aggregate demand, they will shorten the recession but will also lock in the higher level of inflation.

A *shock to potential output* is a sharp change in potential output. Like an adverse inflation shock, an adverse shock to potential output results in both higher inflation and lower output. Because lower potential output implies that productive capacity has fallen, however, output does not recover following a shock to potential output, as it eventually does following an inflation shock.

CONTROLLING INFLATION

High or even moderate rates of inflation imply significant costs to the economy. Indeed, over the past several decades a consensus has developed among economists and policymakers that low and stable inflation is important and perhaps necessary for sustained economic growth. What, then, should policymakers do if the inflation rate is too high? As Example 27.4 will show, inflation can be slowed by policies that reduce aggregate demand. Unfortunately, such policies are likely to impose significant short-run costs in the form of lost output and increased unemployment.

The effects of anti-inflationary monetary policy

EXAMPLE 27.4

Suppose that, although the economy is at full employment, the inflation rate is 10 percent—too high to be consistent with economic efficiency and long-term economic growth. The Fed decides to tighten monetary policy to reduce the inflation rate to 3 percent. What will happen to output, unemployment, and inflation in the short run? Over the long run?

The economic effects of a monetary tightening are very different in the short run and long run. Figure 27.12(a) shows the short-run effect. Initially, the economy is in long-run equilibrium at point *A*, where actual output equals potential output. But at point *A* the inflation rate, 10 percent, is high, as indicated by the aggregate supply line, *SRAS*.

To bring inflation down to 3 percent, what can policymakers do? To get "tough" on inflation, the Fed must set the real interest rate at a level higher than normal, given the rate of inflation. In other words, the Fed must shift its policy reaction function upward, as in Figure 27.4(a). At a constant rate of inflation, an increase in the real interest rate set by the Fed will reduce consumption and investment spending, lowering aggregate demand at every inflation rate. As we saw earlier in the chapter, this monetary tightening by the Fed causes the *AD* curve to shift leftward, from *AD* to *AD'* in Figure 27.12(a).

After the Fed's action, the *AD'* curve and the *SRAS* line intersect at point *B* in Figure 27.12(a), the new short-run equilibrium point. At point *B* actual output has fallen to *Y*, which is less than potential output *Y**. In other words, the Fed's action has allowed a recessionary gap to develop, one result of which will be that unemployment will exceed the natural rate. At point *B*, however, the inflation rate has not changed, remaining at 10 percent. We conclude that in the short run, a monetary tightening pushes the economy into recession but has little or no effect on the inflation rate, because of inflation inertia.

The short-run effects of the monetary tightening—lower output, higher unemployment, and little or no reduction of inflation—are, to say the least, not very encouraging, and they explain why tight monetary policies are often quite unpopular in their early stages. Fortunately, however, we have not reached the end of the story, because the economy will not remain at point *B* indefinitely. The

FIGURE 27.12

The Short-Run and Long-Run Effects of a Monetary Tightening.

(a) Initially the economy is in long-run equilibrium at point A, with actual output equal to potential and the inflation rate at 10 percent. If a monetary tightening by the Fed shifts the AD curve to the left, from AD to AD', the economy will reach a new short-run equilibrium at point B, at the intersection of AD' and SRAS. As short-run equilibrium output falls to Y, a recessionary gap opens up. The inflation rate does not change in the short run.

(b) After a monetary tightening, a recessionary gap exists at point B, which eventually causes inflation to decline. The short-run aggregate supply line moves downward, from SRAS to SRAS'. Long-run equilibrium is restored at point C. In the long run, real output returns to potential and inflation stabilizes at a lower level (3 percent in this figure).

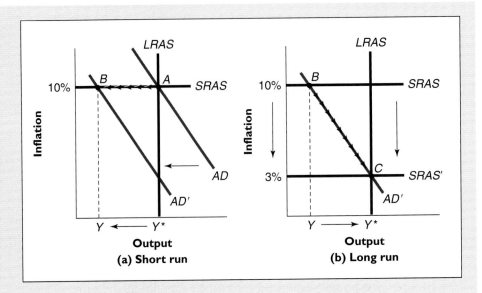

(a) Short run

(b) Long run

reason is that the existence of a recessionary gap at that point eventually causes inflation to decline, as firms become more reluctant to raise their prices in the face of weak demand.

Graphically, the eventual decline in inflation that results from a recessionary gap is represented by the downward movement of the short-run aggregate supply line, from SRAS to SRAS' in Figure 27.12(b). Inflation will continue to fall until the economy returns to long-run equilibrium at point C. At that point, actual output has returned to potential and the inflation rate has stabilized at 3 percent. So we see that a tight monetary policy inflicts short-term pain (a decline in output, high unemployment, and a high real interest rate) to achieve a long-term gain (a permanent reduction in inflation). Similar results arise if fiscal rather than monetary policy is used to reduce aggregate demand. Economic Naturalist 27.3 discusses a real-life episode of Fed tightening.

EXERCISE 27.3

Show the typical time paths of output, inflation, and the real interest rate when the Fed employs an anti-inflationary monetary policy. Draw a separate graph for each variable, showing time on the horizontal axis. Be sure to distinguish the short run from the long run. Specific numerical values are not necessary.

"I don't <u>like</u> six per-cent unemployment, either. But I can live with it."

How was inflation conquered in the 1980s?

After reaching double-digit levels in the late 1970s, inflation in the United States declined sharply in the 1980s. After peaking at 13.5 percent in 1980, the inflation rate fell all the way to 3.2 percent in 1983, and remained in the 2 to 5 percent range for the rest of the decade. In the 1990s inflation fell even lower, holding in the 2 to 3 percent range in most years. How was inflation conquered in the 1980s?

The person who was most directly responsible for the conquest of inflation in the 1980s was Federal Reserve Chairman Paul Volcker. Following the secret Saturday meeting he called on October 6, 1979 (described in the introduction to this chapter), the Federal Open Market Committee agreed to tighten monetary policy significantly in an attempt to rein in inflation. The results of this policy change on the U.S. economy are shown in Table 27.3, which includes selected macroeconomic data for the period 1978–1985.

The data in Table 27.3 fit our analysis of anti-inflationary monetary policy quite well. First, as our model predicts, in the short run the Fed's monetary tightening led to a recession. In fact, two recessions followed the Fed's action in 1979, a short one in 1980 and a deeper one in 1981–1982. Note that growth in real GDP was negative in 1980 and 1982, and the unemployment rate rose significantly, peaking at 9.7 percent in 1982. Nominal and real interest rates also rose, a direct effect of the monetary tightening. Inflation, however, did not respond much during the period 1979–1981. All these results are consistent with the short-run analysis in Figure 27.12.

By 1983, however, the situation had changed markedly. The economy had recovered, with strong growth in real GDP in 1983–1985 (see Table 27.3). In 1984 the unemployment rate, which tends to respond to a recovery relatively late, began to decline. Interest rates remained relatively high, perhaps reflecting other factors besides monetary policy. Most significantly, inflation fell in 1982–1983 and stabilized at a much lower level. Inflation has remained low in the United States ever since.

ECONOMIC NATURALIST 27.3

TABLE 27.3
U.S. Macroeconomic Data, 1978–1985

Year	% Growth in real GDP	Unemployment rate (%)	Inflation rate (%)	Nominal interest rate (%)	Real interest rate (%)
1978	5.4	6.1	7.6	8.3	0.7
1979	2.8	5.8	11.4	9.7	−1.7
1980	−0.3	7.1	13.5	11.6	−1.9
1981	2.3	7.6	10.3	14.4	4.1
1982	−2.1	9.7	6.2	12.9	6.7
1983	4.0	9.6	3.2	10.5	7.3
1984	7.0	7.5	4.3	11.9	7.6
1985	3.6	7.2	3.6	9.6	6.0

SOURCE: *Economic Report of the President,* various tables. Real GDP is measured in 1992 dollars. Inflation is measured by the CPI. The nominal interest rate is the average annual value of the 3-month Treasury bill rate. The real interest rate equals the nominal interest rate minus the inflation rate.

disinflation a substantial reduction in the rate of inflation

A substantial reduction in the rate of inflation, like the one the Fed engineered in the 1980s, is called a **disinflation.** But again, disinflation comes at the cost of a large recessionary gap and high unemployment like that experienced by the United States in the early 1980s. Is this cost worth bearing? This question is not an easy one to answer, because the costs of inflation are difficult to measure. Policymakers around the world appear to agree on the necessity of containing inflation, however, as many countries fought to bring their own inflation rates down to 2 percent or less in the 1980s and 1990s. Canada and Great Britain are among the many industrial countries that have borne the costs of sharp reductions in inflation.

Can the costs of disinflation be reduced? Unfortunately, no one has found a pain-free method of lowering the inflation rate. Accordingly, in recent years central banks around the world have striven to keep inflation at manageable levels so as not to have to face the costs of disinflation. In the United States, under Chairman Alan Greenspan, the Federal Reserve has followed a strategy of *preemptive strikes,* raising interest rates at the first sign that inflation might soon begin to creep upward. This strategy appears to have been quite successful in keeping inflation low and avoiding recession.

■ SUMMARY ■

- This chapter extended the basic Keynesian model to include inflation. First, we showed how aggregate demand and short-run equilibrium output are related to inflation, a relationship that is summarized by the aggregate demand curve. Second, we discussed how inflation itself is determined. In the short run, inflation is determined by past expectations and pricing decisions, but in the long run inflation adjusts as needed to eliminate output gaps.

- The *aggregate demand (AD) curve* shows the relationship between aggregate demand and inflation. Because short-run equilibrium output is equal to aggregate demand, the aggregate demand curve also relates short-run equilibrium output to inflation. Since increases in inflation reduce both aggregate

demand and short-run equilibrium output, the aggregate demand curve is downward-sloping in a diagram with inflation on the vertical axis and output on the horizontal axis.

- The inverse relationship of inflation and aggregate demand is the result, in large part, of the behavior of the Federal Reserve. To keep inflation low and stable, the Fed reacts to rising inflation by increasing the real interest rate. A higher real interest rate reduces consumption and planned investment, lowering aggregate demand. The Fed's objective in restraining aggregate demand is to reduce the risk that an expansionary gap will develop, fueling inflation. Other reasons that the aggregate demand curve slopes downward include the effects of inflation on the real value of money, distributional effects (inflation redistributes wealth from the poor, who save relatively little, to the more affluent), and the impact of inflation on foreign sales of domestic goods.

- For any given value of inflation, an increase in autonomous aggregate demand will raise aggregate demand and short-run equilibrium output, shifting the aggregate demand (*AD*) curve to the right. A decline in autonomous aggregate demand will shift the *AD* curve to the left. The *AD* curve can also be shifted by a change in the Fed's policy reaction function. If the Fed gets "tougher," choosing a higher real interest rate at each level of inflation, the aggregate demand curve will shift to the left. If the Fed gets "easier," setting a lower real interest rate at each level of inflation, the *AD* curve will shift to the right.

- In low-inflation industrial economies like the United States today, inflation tends to be inertial, or slow to adjust to changes in the economy. This inertial behavior reflects the fact that inflation depends in part on people's expectations of future inflation, which in turn depend on their recent experience with inflation. Long-term wage and price contracts tend to "build in" the effects of people's expectations for multiyear periods.

- Although inflation is inertial, it does change over time in response to output gaps. An expansionary gap tends to raise the inflation rate, because firms raise their prices more quickly when they are facing demand that exceeds their normal productive capacity. A recessionary gap tends to reduce the inflation rate, as firms become more reluctant to raise their prices. The *short-run aggregate supply (SRAS) line* is a horizontal line that shows the current rate of inflation, as determined by past expectations and pricing decisions.

- The economy is in *short-run equilibrium* when inflation equals the value determined by past expectations and pricing decisions, and output equals the level of short-run equilibrium output that is consistent with that inflation rate. Graphically, short-run equilibrium occurs at the intersection of the *AD* curve and the *SRAS* line. If an output gap exists, however, the inflation rate will adjust to eliminate the gap. Graphically, the *SRAS* line moves upward or downward as needed to restore output to its full-employment level. When the inflation rate is stable and actual output equals potential output, the economy is in *long-run equilibrium*. Graphically, long-run equilibrium corresponds to the common intersection point of the *AD* curve, the *SRAS* line, and the long-run aggregate supply (*LRAS*) line, a vertical line that marks the economy's potential output.

- Because the economy tends to move toward long-run equilibrium on its own through the adjustment of the inflation rate, it is said to be self-correcting. The more rapid the self-correction process, the smaller the need for active stabilization policies to eliminate output gaps. In practice, the larger the output gap, the more useful such policies are.

- One source of inflation is excessive aggregate demand, which leads to expansionary output gaps. Aggregate supply shocks are another source. *Aggregate supply shocks* include both *inflation shocks*—sudden changes in the normal behavior of inflation, created, for example, by a rise in the price of imported oil—and shocks to potential output. Adverse supply shocks both lower output and increase inflation, creating a difficult dilemma for policymakers.

- To reduce inflation, policymakers must reduce aggregate demand, usually through tight monetary policy. In the short run, the main effects of a reduction in aggregate demand are reduced output and higher unemployment, as the economy experiences a recessionary gap. These short-run costs of *disinflation* must be balanced against the long-run benefits of a lower rate of inflation. Over time, output and employment will return to normal levels and inflation declines. The disinflation engineered by the Fed under Chairman Paul Volcker in the early 1980s followed this pattern.

■ KEY TERMS ■

aggregate demand (*AD*) curve (726)
aggregate supply shock (748)
disinflation (752)
inflation shock (746)

long-run aggregate supply (*LRAS*) line (739)
long-run equilibrium (740)

short-run aggregate supply (*SRAS*) line (739)
short-run equilibrium (740)

■ REVIEW QUESTIONS ■

1. What two variables are related by the aggregate demand (*AD*) curve? Give an economic explanation of the slope of the curve.

2. State how each of the following affects the *AD* curve and explain:
   a. An increase in government purchases
   b. A cut in taxes
   c. A decline in autonomous investment spending by firms

d. A decision by the Fed to lower the real interest rate at each level of inflation

3. Why does the overall rate of inflation tend to adjust more slowly than prices of commodities, such as oil or grain?

4. Discuss the relationship between output gaps and inflation. How is this relationship captured in the aggregate demand–aggregate supply diagram?

5. Sketch an aggregate demand–aggregate supply diagram depicting an economy away from long-run equilibrium. Indicate the economy's short-run equilibrium point. Discuss how the economy reaches long-run equilibrium over a period of time. Illustrate the process in your diagram.

6. True or false, and explain: The economy's self-correcting tendency makes active use of stabilization policy unnecessary.

7. What factors led to increased inflation in the United States in the 1960s and 1970s?

8. Why does an adverse inflation shock pose a particularly difficult dilemma for policymakers?

9. How does a tight monetary policy, like that conducted by the Volcker Fed in the early 1980s, affect output, inflation, and the real interest rate in the short run? In the long run?

■ PROBLEMS ■

---

1. Aggregate demand in Lotusland depends on real GDP and the real interest rate according to the following equation:

$$AD = 3{,}000 + 0.8Y - 2{,}000r.$$

The Bank of Lotusland, the central bank, has announced that it will set the real interest rate according to the following policy reaction function:

Rate of inflation π	Real interest rate r
0.0	0.02
0.01	0.03
0.02	0.04
0.03	0.05
0.04	0.06

For the rates of inflation given, find aggregate demand in Lotusland. Graph the AD curve.

2. An economy is described by the following equations:

$$C = 1{,}600 + 0.6(Y - T) - 2{,}000r,$$

$$I^P = 2{,}500 - 1{,}000r,$$

$$G = \overline{G} = 2{,}000,$$

$$NX = \overline{NX} = 50,$$

$$T = \overline{T} = 2{,}000.$$

Suppose also that the central bank's policy reaction function is the same as in Problem 1.

a. Find an equation relating aggregate demand to output and the real interest rate.

b. Make a table showing the relationship between aggregate demand (short-run equilibrium output) and inflation for inflation rates between 0 and 4 percent. Using this table, graph the AD curve for the economy.

c. Repeat parts a and b, assuming that government purchases have increased to 2,100. How does an increase in government purchases affect the AD curve?

3. For the economy described by the equations in Problem 2, suppose that the central bank's policy reaction function is as follows:

Rate of inflation π	Real interest rate r
0.0	0.04
0.01	0.045
0.02	0.05
0.03	0.055
0.04	0.06

    a. Make a table showing the relationship between aggregate demand and the inflation rate for values of inflation between 0 and 4 percent. Graph the aggregate demand curve of the economy.

    b. Suppose that the central bank decides to lower the real interest rate by half a percentage point at each value of inflation. Repeat part a. How does this change in monetary policy affect the aggregate demand curve?

4. An economy is described by the equations given in Problem 2 and the policy reaction function given in Problem 1. Initially, the inflation rate is 4 percent. Potential output Y^* equals 12,000.
    a. Find inflation and output in short-run equilibrium.
    b. Find inflation and output in long-run equilibrium.
    Show your work.

5. This problem asks you to trace out the adjustment of inflation when the economy starts off with an output gap.
    a. Suppose that the economy's aggregate demand curve is

$$Y = 1{,}000 - 1{,}000\pi,$$

    where Y is short-run equilibrium output and π is the inflation rate, measured as a decimal. Potential output Y^* equals 950, and the initial inflation rate is 10 percent ($\pi = 0.10$). Find output and inflation for this economy in short-run equilibrium and in long-run equilibrium.

    b. Suppose that, each quarter, inflation adjusts according to the following rule:

This quarter's inflation = Last quarter's inflation − 0.0004 × Last quarter's output gap.

    Starting from the initial value of 10 percent for inflation, find the value of inflation for each of the next four quarters. Does inflation come close to its long-run value?

6. For each of the following, use an *AD-AS* diagram to show the short-run and long-run effects on output and inflation. Assume the economy starts in long-run equilibrium.
    a. An increase in autonomous consumption
    b. A reduction in taxes
    c. An easing of monetary policy by the Fed (a downward shift in the policy reaction function)
    d. A sharp drop in oil prices
    e. A war that raises government purchases

7. Suppose that the government cuts taxes in response to a recessionary gap, but that because of legislative delays the tax cut is not put in place for 18 months. Using an *AD-AS* diagram and assuming that the government's objective is to stabilize output and inflation, show how this policy action might actually prove to be counterproductive.

8. Suppose that a permanent increase in oil prices both creates an inflationary shock and reduces potential output. Use an *AD-AS* diagram to show the effects of the oil price increase on output and inflation in the short run and the long run, assuming that there is no policy response. What happens if the Fed responds to the oil price increase by tightening monetary policy?

■ ANSWERS TO IN-CHAPTER EXERCISES ■

27.1 In the long run, the real interest rate set by the Fed must be consistent with the real interest rate determined in the market for saving and investment. To find the Fed's long-run inflation target, take as given the real interest rate determined in the long run by the market for saving and investment and read off the corresponding inflation rate from the Fed's policy reaction function. As the accompanying figure illustrates, a tightening of Fed policy (an upward shift of the policy reaction function) implies that, for any given long-run real interest rate, the Fed's inflation target must be lower.

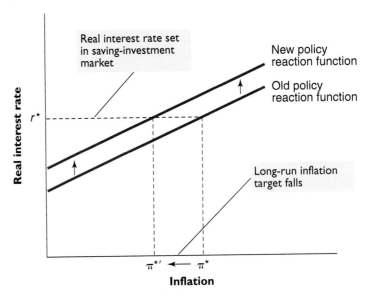

27.2 a. A table like Table 27.1 can be used to show the Fed's original and modified reaction functions. The first column of the table shows alternative values of inflation. The second column shows the real interest rate responses of the Fed given in Example 27.1 (the "old" reaction function). The third column shows the "new" reaction function, in which the real interest rate for each level of inflation is increased by 0.01.

(1) Inflation rate π	(2) Real interest rate r ("old")	(3) Real interest rate r ("new")
0.00	0.02	0.03
0.01	0.03	0.04
0.02	0.04	0.05
0.03	0.05	0.06
0.04	0.06	0.07

A graph of both reaction functions is shown in the next accompanying figure. You can see that "tougher" monetary policy shifts the reaction function upward, reflecting the fact that at each level of inflation, the Fed is setting the real interest rate at a higher level.

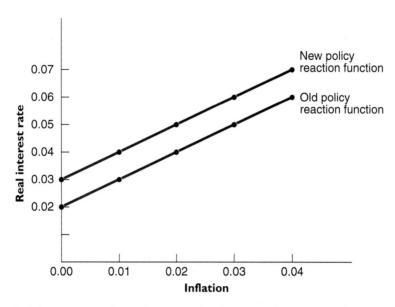

b. To find the aggregate demand curve under the new policy reaction function, for each value of inflation and the Fed's choice of the real interest rate we must find the implied value of short-run equilibrium output. To do this, it is useful to recall that aggregate demand in the economy introduced in Example 27.1 is given by

$$AD = 1{,}010 + 0.08Y - 1{,}000r.$$

Suppose, for example, that inflation is zero. The Fed's choice of real interest rate in that case is $r = 0.03$ (see columns 1 and 3 of the table in the answer to part a above). If $r = 0.03$, then aggregate demand is given by

$$AD = 1{,}010 + 0.8Y - 1{,}000(0.03) = 980 + 0.8Y.$$

To solve for short-run equilibrium output, we use this equation to substitute for AD in the definition of short-run equilibrium output $Y = AD$:

$$Y = 980 + 0.8Y.$$

Solving for output we get $Y = 4{,}900$. Continuing in this way for each value of inflation and the real interest rate, we can construct the following table, similar to Table 27.1:

Inflation rate π	Real interest rate r	Output Y
0.00	0.03	4,900
0.01	0.04	4,850
0.02	0.05	4,800
0.03	0.06	4,750
0.04	0.07	4,700

Comparison of this table with Table 27.1 shows that, for each value of inflation, the implied value of short-run equilibrium output is lower by 50. Thus the toughening of Fed policy causes the AD curve to shift leftward in parallel fashion by 50 units at each value of inflation. This shift is shown in the accompanying diagram.

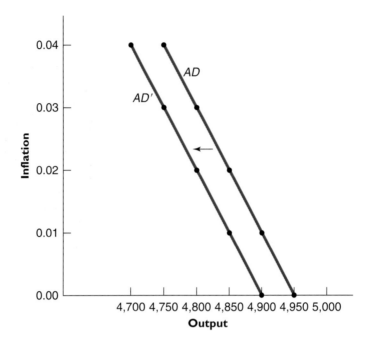

27.3

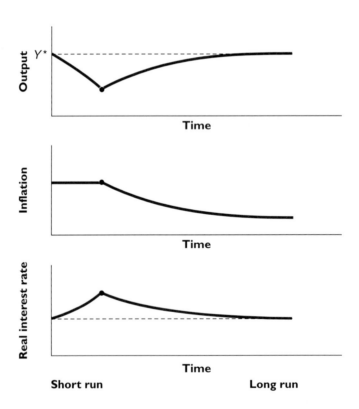

THE ALGEBRA OF AGGREGATE DEMAND AND AGGREGATE SUPPLY

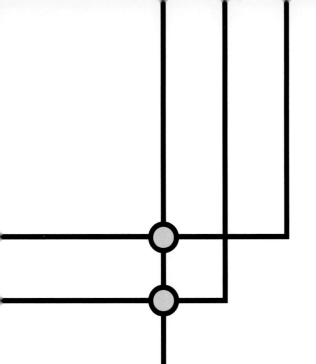

■

I n this appendix we will derive the aggregate demand curve algebraically. Then we will show how together aggregate demand and aggregate supply determine the short-run and long-run equilibrium points of the economy.

THE AGGREGATE DEMAND CURVE

In the Appendix to Chapter 26, Equation A.1 showed that short-run equilibrium output depends on both autonomous aggregate demand and the real interest rate:

$$Y = \left(\frac{1}{1 - c}\right)[\overline{C} - c\overline{T} + \overline{I} + \overline{G} + \overline{NX} - (a + b)r],$$

where $1/(1 - c)$ is the multiplier, $\overline{C} - c\overline{T} + \overline{I} + \overline{G} + \overline{NX}$ is autonomous aggregate demand, and a and b and are positive numbers that measure the effect of changes in the real interest rate on consumption and planned investment, respectively.

The aggregate demand curve incorporates the behavior of the Fed, as described by its policy reaction function. According to its policy reaction function, when inflation rises, the Fed raises the real interest rate. Thus the Fed's policy reaction function can be written as an equation relating the real interest rate r to inflation π:

$$r = \bar{r} + g\pi, \qquad (A.1)$$

where $\bar{r}$ and g are positive constants chosen by Fed officials. This equation states that when inflation π rises by 1 percentage point—say from 2 to 3 percent per year—the Fed responds by raising the real interest rate by g percentage points. So, for example, if $g = 0.5$, an increase in inflation from 2 to 3 percent would lead the Fed to raise the real interest rate by 0.5 percent. The intercept term $\bar{r}$ tells us at what level the Fed would set the real interest rate if inflation happened to be zero (so that the term $g\pi$ dropped out of the equation).

We can combine the equation for short-run equilibrium output with the equation for the policy reaction function by substituting the right-hand side of Equation A.1 for the real interest rate r in the previous equation:

$$Y = \left(\frac{1}{1-c}\right)[\bar{C} - c\bar{T} + \bar{I} + \bar{G} + \overline{NX} - (a + b)(\bar{r} + g\pi)]. \qquad (A.2)$$

This equation, which is the general algebraic expression for the AD curve, summarizes the link between inflation and short-run equilibrium output, as shown graphically in Figure 27.1. Equation A.2 implies that an increase in inflation π reduces short-run equilibrium output Y, so that the AD curve is downward-sloping.

For a numerical illustration of this equation, we can use the parameter values from Example 26.4, which is continued in Example 27.1. For the economy studied in Example 26.4, we assumed that $\bar{C} = 640$, $\bar{T} = 250$, $\bar{I} = 250$, $\bar{G} = 300$, $\overline{NX} = 20$, $c = 0.8$, $a = 400$, and $b = 600$. To derive the AD curve, we also need the parameters for the Fed's policy reaction function. Example 27.1 included a table relating the Fed's choice of the real interest rate to the inflation rate. To express the relationship in the table in the form of an equation, note that when inflation π equals zero, the real interest rate r equals 2 percent. Therefore the constant term in the Fed's policy reaction function, $\bar{r}$, equals 2 percent, or 0.02. Second, the table in Example 27.1 shows that the real interest rate rises one point for each point that inflation rises; therefore the slope of the reaction function, g, equals 1.0. Substituting these numerical values into Equation A.2 and simplifying, we get the following numerical equation for the AD curve in Example 27.1:

$$Y = 5[640 - 0.8(250) + 250 + 300 + 20 - (400 + 600)(0.02 + \pi)]$$

$$= 4{,}950 - 5{,}000\pi. \qquad (A.3)$$

Note that, in this equation, higher values of inflation imply lower values of short-run equilibrium output. To check this equation, recall that in Example 27.1 we found that if inflation is 1 percent, then short-run equilibrium output equals 4,900. Setting $\pi = 0.01$ in Equation A.3 does in fact yield $Y = 4{,}900$. You may want to confirm the other values given in Table 27.1.

SHIFTS OF THE AGGREGATE DEMAND CURVE

Recall that changes in autonomous aggregate demand or in the Fed's policy reaction function will shift the AD curve (see pages 730–734). These results follow directly from Equation A.2. First, the equation shows that, for a given rate of inflation π, an increase in autonomous aggregate demand, $\bar{C} - c\bar{T} + \bar{I} + \bar{G} + \overline{NX}$, will raise short-run equilibrium output Y. Thus an increase in autonomous aggregate demand shifts the AD curve to the right; conversely, a decrease in autonomous aggregate demand shifts the AD curve to the left.

A shift in the Fed's policy reaction can be captured by a change in the intercept term $\bar{r}$ in Equation A.1. For example, suppose the Fed tightens monetary policy by setting the real interest rate 1 percent higher than before at every level of inflation, as in Exercise 27.2a. Such a change is equivalent to raising the intercept term in the policy reaction function $\bar{r}$, by 0.01. If you look at Equation A.2, you will see that with the level of inflation held constant, an increase in $\bar{r}$ reduces short-run equilibrium output. Thus a tightening of monetary policy shifts the AD curve to the left; conversely, an easing of monetary policy (represented by a decline in $\bar{r}$) shifts the AD curve to the right.

EXERCISE A.1

a. **For the economy in Example 27.1, find a numerical equation for the AD curve after autonomous aggregate demand increases by 10. Compare your answer with the results obtained in Example 27.2.**

b. **For the economy in Example 27.1, find a numerical equation for the AD curve after the tightening of monetary policy described in Exercise 27.2a. Compare your answer with the results you obtained in Exercise 27.2b.**

SHORT-RUN EQUILIBRIUM

Recall that in short-run equilibrium, inflation is equal to its previously determined value, and the $SRAS$ line is horizontal at that value. At that level of inflation, the level of output in short-run equilibrium is given by the aggregate demand curve, Equation A.2. For instance, in the economy in Example 27.1, suppose the current value of inflation is 3 percent. The value of short-run equilibrium output is therefore

$$Y = 4{,}950 - 5{,}000\pi = 4{,}950 - 5{,}000(0.03)$$

$$= 4{,}800.$$

LONG-RUN EQUILIBRIUM

Recall that in long-run equilibrium actual output Y equals potential output Y^*. Thus, in long-run equilibrium, the inflation rate can be obtained from the equation for the AD curve by substituting Y^* for Y. To illustrate, let's write the equation for the AD curve in the economy in Example 27.1 once again:

$$Y = 4{,}950 - 5{,}000\pi.$$

Suppose, in addition, that $Y^* = 4{,}900$. Substituting this value for Y in the aggregate demand equation yields

$$4{,}900 = 4{,}950 - 5{,}000\pi.$$

Solving for the inflation rate π, we get

$$\pi = 0.01 = 1\%.$$

When this economy is in long-run equilibrium, then, the inflation rate will be 1 percent. If we start from the value of inflation in short-run equilibrium, 3 percent, we can see that the aggregate supply line must shift downward until inflation reaches 1 percent before long-run equilibrium can be achieved.

A.1 The algebraic solutions for the AD curves in each case, obtained by substituting the numerical values into the formula, are given below. Compare the equation in part a with Table 27.2 and the equation in part b with the table given in the answer to Exercise 27.2b, above. You will find that for any given inflation rate, the equations below predict the same level of short-run equilibrium output as do the tables.

a. $Y = 5,000 - 5,000\pi$

b. $Y = 4,900 - 5,000\pi$

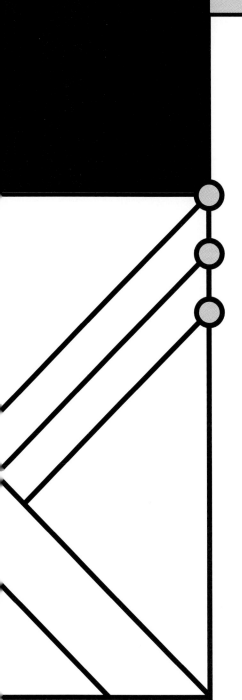

PART

8

THE INTERNATIONAL ECONOMY

■

One of the defining economic trends of recent decades is the "globalization" of national economies. Since the mid-1980s, the value of international trade has increased at nearly twice the rate of world GDP, and the volume of international financial transactions has expanded at many times that rate. From a long-run perspective, the rapidly increasing integration of national economies we see today is not unprecedented: Before World War I, Great Britain was the center of an international economic system that was in many ways nearly as "globalized" as our own, with extensive international trade and lending. But even the most far-seeing nineteenth-century merchant or banker would be astonished by the sense of *immediacy* that recent revolutionary changes in communications and transportation have imparted to international economic relations. For example, teleconferencing and the Internet now permit people on opposite sides of the globe to conduct "face-to-face" business negotiations and transactions.

We introduced international dimensions of the economy at several points in this book already (for example, in our discussion of comparative advantage and trade in Chapter 3 and our analysis of the labor market effects of globalization in Chapter 21). In Part 8 we will look at the international economy in greater detail. Chapter 28 continues our analysis of international trade, considering both the broad benefits of trade and the reasons why we sometimes see attempts to block or reduce trade. Besides trade in goods and services, the chapter also considers the implications of trade in real and financial assets, referred to as *international capital flows*. Chapter 29 focuses on a particularly important variable in international economics, the *exchange rate*. The exchange rate plays a key role in determining patterns of trade. Furthermore, as we will see, the type of exchange rate system a country adopts has important implications for the effectiveness of its macroeconomic policies.

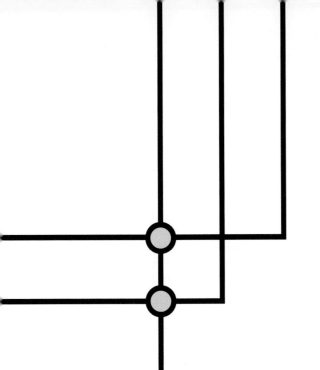

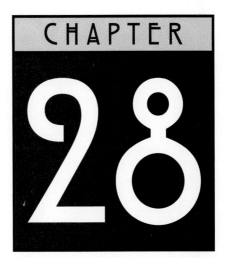

INTERNATIONAL TRADE AND CAPITAL FLOWS

■

On April 13, 1861, Southern troops fired on Fort Sumter in Charleston harbor, initiating the American Civil War. Less than a week later, on April 19, President Lincoln proclaimed a naval blockade of the South. Code-named the Anaconda Plan (after a snake that squeezes its prey to death), the blockade required the Union navy to patrol the Southern coastline, stopping and boarding ships that were attempting to land or depart. The object of the blockade was to prevent the Confederacy from shipping cotton to Europe, where it could be traded for military equipment, clothing, foodstuffs, and other supplies.

Historians are divided on the effectiveness of the Union blockade in choking off Confederate trade. In the early years of the war, the North had too few ships to cover the 3,600-mile Southern coastline, so "running" the blockade was not difficult. But in the latter part of the war the number of Union ships enforcing the blockade increased from about 90 to over 600, and sailing ships were replaced with faster, more lethal ironclad vessels. Still, private blockade-runners—like the fictitious Rhett Butler in Margaret Mitchell's novel, *Gone with the Wind*—attempted to elude the Union navy in small, fast ships. Because the price of raw cotton in Great Britain was between 10 and 20 times what it was in the Confederacy (a differential that indicated disruption in the normal flow of trade), blockade-runners enjoyed huge profits when they were successful. But despite their efforts, by 1864 the Southern war effort was seriously hampered by a lack of military equipment and supplies, at least in part as a result of the blockade.

He appreciated the economic benefits of trade.

Courtesy of the Everett Collection

The use of a naval blockade as a weapon of war highlights a paradox in contemporary attitudes toward trade between nations. Presumably, an attempt by a foreign power to blockade U.S. ports today would be considered a hostile act that would elicit a strong response from the U.S. government. Yet one often hears politicians and others arguing that trade with other nations is harmful to the United States and should be restricted—in effect, that the United States should blockade its own ports! Despite support from President Clinton and virtually all professional economists, for example, many politicians opposed the 1993 signing of the North American Free Trade Agreement (NAFTA), which was intended to increase U.S. trade with Mexico and Canada, on the grounds that it might cost American jobs. In December 1999, opponents of increased trade demonstrated in Seattle, disrupting meetings of the World Trade Organization, an international body set up to promote trade and enforce trade agreements. So is trade a good thing or not? And if it is, why does it sometimes face determined and even violent opposition?

This chapter addresses international trade and its effects on the broader economy. We will begin by reviewing the idea of *comparative advantage,* which we introduced in Chapter 3. We will show that everyone can enjoy more goods and services if nations specialize in those products in which they have a comparative advantage and then trade freely among themselves. Furthermore, if trade is unrestricted, market forces will ensure that countries produce those goods in which they have a comparative advantage.

Having shown the potential benefits of trade, we will turn next to the reasons for opposition to trade. Although opening the economy to trade increases economic welfare overall, some groups—such as workers in industries that face competition from foreign producers—may be made worse off. The fact that open trade may hurt some groups creates political pressure to enact measures restricting trade, such as taxes on imported goods (called *tariffs*) and limits on imports (called *quotas*). We will analyze the effects of trade restrictions, along with other ways of responding to concerns about affected industries and workers. From an economic point of view, providing direct assistance to those who are hurt by increased trade is preferable to blocking or restricting trade, a point that was also emphasized in Chapter 21.

Trade between nations occurs not only in goods and services but in assets, both financial and real. For example, foreign households and firms may acquire domestic stocks and bonds (financial assets) or real estate (real assets); similarly, domestic residents may purchase real and financial assets abroad. Purchases and sales of assets across international borders are called *international capital flows.* As we will see in the latter part of this chapter, international capital flows play a crucial role in modern economies. Capital flows provide a means for countries to finance imbalances in trade so that their exports need not equal their imports in every period. In addition, international capital flows can increase the pool of savings that is available for domestic investment in new capital goods.

COMPARATIVE ADVANTAGE AS A BASIS FOR TRADE

Chapter 3 began with the story of the Nepalese cook Birkhaman, a remarkable jack-of-all-trades who could do everything from butchering a goat to fixing an alarm clock. Yet despite his range of skills, Birkhaman, like most Nepalese, was quite poor. The reason for Birkhaman's poverty, as we saw in Chapter 3, was precisely his versatility. Because he did so many different things, Birkhaman could not hope to become as productive in each separate activity as someone who specializes entirely in that activity.

The alternative to a nation of Birkhamans is a country in which each person specializes in the activity at which he is relatively most efficient, or has a *comparative advantage.* This specialization, combined with trade between producers of different goods and services, allows a society to achieve a higher level of productivity and standard of living than one in which each person is essentially self-sufficient.

This insight, that specialization and trade among individuals can yield impressive gains in productivity, applies equally well to nations. Factors such as climate, natural resources, technology, workers' skills and education, and culture provide countries with comparative advantages in the production of different goods and services. For example, as we saw in Chapter 3, the large number of leading research universities in the United States gives that nation a comparative advantage in the design of technologically sophisticated computer hardware and software. Likewise, the wide international use of the English language endows the United States with a comparative advantage in producing popular films and TV shows. Similarly, France's climate and topography, together with the accumulated knowledge of generations of vintners, provides that country a comparative advantage in producing fine wines, while Australia's huge expanses of arable land give that country a comparative advantage in producing grain.

The *principle of comparative advantage* tells us that we can all enjoy more goods and services when each country produces according to its comparative advantage and then trades with other countries. In the next section we explore this fundamental idea in greater detail.

Climate and long experience give France a comparative advantage in producing fine wines

PRODUCTION AND CONSUMPTION POSSIBILITIES AND THE BENEFITS OF TRADE

In this section we will consider how international trade benefits an individual country. To do so, we will contrast the production and consumption opportunities in a **closed economy**—one that does not trade with the rest of the world—with the opportunities in an **open economy**—one that does trade with other economies. Because we will make use of the *production possibilities curve* (PPC), introduced in Chapter 3, we will begin by briefly reviewing that concept. We will look first at the PPC for a two-person economy and then at the PPC for a many-person economy. After reviewing the PPC, we will see how a country's production possibilities are related to its citizens' ability to consume in a closed economy versus an open economy.

closed economy an economy that does not trade with the rest of the world

open economy an economy that trades with other countries

THE TWO-WORKER PRODUCTION POSSIBILITIES CURVE REVISITED

Recall that (for a two-good economy) the production possibilities curve (PPC) is a graph that shows the maximum amount of each good that can be produced at every possible level of production of the other good.[1] To review how the PPC is constructed, let's consider a hypothetical economy, call it Brazil, which has only two workers, Carlos and Maria. Each of these two workers can produce two goods, coffee and computers.

The PPC for a two-worker economy

Two Brazilian workers, Carlos and Maria, can each produce coffee and computers. Carlos can produce either 100 pounds of coffee or one computer per week. Maria can produce either 100 pounds of coffee or two computers per week. Both Carlos and Maria work 50 weeks per year. Find the production possibilities curve (PPC) for Brazil.

To construct the PPC for this two-person economy, we follow the procedure

EXAMPLE 28.1

---

[1]For a many-good economy, the PPC shows the maximum amount of each good that can be produced at any level of production of all the other goods. Focusing on the two-good case allows us to draw the figures on the two-dimensional page. Our conclusions apply to the many-good case, however.

outlined in Chapter 3. We ask first how much coffee Brazil could produce if both Carlos and Maria worked full-time producing coffee. Between them they can produce 200 pounds of coffee per week, so in 50 weeks they could produce 10,000 pounds of coffee. Thus if we plot coffee production on the vertical axis of the graph of Brazil's PPC, the vertical intercept of the PPC will be 10,000 pounds of coffee per year (point *A* in Figure 28.1). Likewise, if Carlos and Maria produced only computers, between them they could produce three computers per week, or 150 computers per year. So the horizontal intercept of Brazil's PPC is 150 computers per year (point *B* in Figure 28.1).

FIGURE 28.1

Production Possibilities Curve for a Two-Worker Economy.

In the portion of the PPC between points *A* and *C*, only Maria is producing computers, so the slope of the PPC in that range reflects Maria's opportunity cost of computers in terms of coffee production forgone. At point *C*, Maria spends all her time on computers and Carlos spends all his time on coffee. Between points *C* and *B*, any additional computers must be produced by Carlos. Thus between points *C* and *B* the slope of the PPC reflects Carlos's opportunity cost of producing computers, in terms of coffee production forgone.

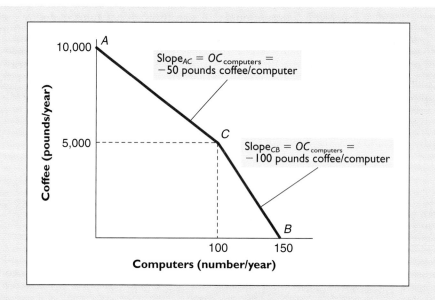

We found where the Brazilian PPC intersects the two axes of the graph. To find the rest of the PPC, imagine that Carlos and Maria are producing only coffee (point *A* in Figure 28.1), when they decide that they would like to have some computers as well.

In this situation, which worker should switch from producing coffee to producing computers?

To determine which worker should switch from coffee to computers, we need to find the one with a *comparative advantage* in producing computers. To do that we must calculate opportunity costs. Carlos can produce either 100 pounds of coffee or one computer per week. Because producing a computer leaves him one fewer week to devote to coffee production, which reduces his coffee output by 100 pounds, Carlos's opportunity cost of producing a computer is 100 pounds of coffee. Maria can produce either 100 pounds of coffee or two computers per week, so her opportunity cost of producing a computer is 100/2, or 50 pounds of coffee. Because Maria's opportunity cost of producing a computer is lower than Carlos's, she has a comparative advantage in producing computers. By the principle of comparative advantage, Maria should be the one to specialize in computer production. For his part, Carlos has a comparative advantage in producing coffee (see Exercise 28.1), so he should specialize in coffee.

Starting from point *A* in Figure 28.1, where only coffee is produced, we can imagine that Maria begins to produce increasing numbers of computers. As we saw in Chapter 3, the slope of the line emanating from point *A* equals Maria's opportunity cost of producing a computer, $OC_{computers}$, where cost is measured as a negative quantity:

$$\text{Slope} = \text{Maria's } OC_{computers} = \frac{\text{Loss in coffee}}{\text{Gain in computers}},$$

$$= \frac{-100 \text{ Pounds coffee/week}}{2 \text{ Computers/week}} = -50 \text{ Pounds coffee/computer.}$$

As Maria increases the share of her time devoted to computer production, we move down along the straight line from point A in Figure 28.1. The slope of the PPC is constant in this region at -50 pounds coffee/computer, Maria's opportunity cost of computers.

Maria's time is limited to 50 weeks/year, however, so if she keeps increasing her computer production, she will eventually reach a point at which she produces only computers and no coffee. At that point annual production by the two workers taken together will be 100 computers (produced by Maria) and 5,000 pounds of coffee (produced by Carlos, who spends all his time producing coffee). This combination of production is shown at point C on the production possibilities curve.

Once Maria's time is fully devoted to making computers, Brazil can increase its computer production only if Carlos begins to build some computers, too. However, Carlos's opportunity cost, measured as pounds of coffee forgone per computer produced, is greater than Maria's. Hence at point C the slope of the PPC changes, creating a "kink" in the graph. The slope of the PPC to the right of point C is given by

$$\text{Slope} = \text{Carlos's } OC_{computers} = \frac{\text{Loss in coffee}}{\text{Gain in computers}},$$

$$= \frac{-100 \text{ Pounds coffee/week}}{1 \text{ Computer/week}} = -100 \text{ Pounds coffee/computer.}$$

Note that the slope of the PPC to the right of point C is more negative than the slope to the left of point C, so the PPC declines more sharply to the right of that point. The fact that the opportunity cost of a computer increases as more computers are produced (the *principle of increasing opportunity cost*) implies the outwardly bowed shape that is characteristic of a production possibilities curve, as shown in Figure 28.1.

EXERCISE 28.1

Example 28.1 showed that Maria has a comparative advantage in producing computers. Show by comparison of opportunity costs that Carlos has a comparative advantage in producing coffee.

THE MANY-WORKER PRODUCTION POSSIBILITIES CURVE

Although the economy considered in Example 28.1 included only two workers, the main ideas apply to economies with more workers. Suppose, for example, that we added a third Brazilian worker, Pedro, whose opportunity cost of producing computers is higher than Maria's but lower than Carlos's. As we saw in Chapter 3, the production possibilities curve for this three-person economy would look something like Figure 28.2. Between points A and C on the PPC shown in Figure 28.2, all computers are produced by Maria, who has the greatest comparative advantage in computer production. Thus the slope of the PPC between points A and C is determined by Maria's opportunity cost, measured as the amount of coffee production forgone for each additional computer produced.

FIGURE 28.2

Production Possibilities Curve for a Three-Worker Economy.

The PPC for a three-person economy has two "kinks," at points C and D. Between points A and C only Maria produces computers, and the slope of the PPC represents her opportunity cost of producing computers. At point C Maria is spending all her time making computers, so any additional computers will be produced by Pedro, whose comparative advantage is the next greatest. Between points C and D the slope of the PPC is determined by Pedro's opportunity cost. At point D Pedro is also fully occupied producing computers, so that Carlos must begin producing them if computer production is to increase further. Between points D and B the slope of the PPC reflects Carlos's opportunity cost.

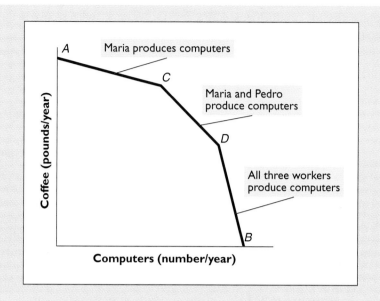

At point C Maria is dedicating all her time to computer production, so someone else must produce any additional computers. Pedro has the next lowest opportunity cost of producing computers, so (following the *principle of increasing opportunity cost*) he begins to produce computers at point C. The slope of the PPC between points C and D is determined by Pedro's opportunity cost, which is greater (more negative) than Maria's opportunity cost. At point D in Figure 28.2, Pedro is producing all the computers he can, so finally Carlos begins to produce computers as well. Thus the slope of the PPC between points D and B reflects Carlos's opportunity cost. Because opportunity cost increases as we move from left to right in the figure, the slope of the PPC becomes more and more negative, leading once again to the outwardly bowed shape.

By similar logic, we can construct a case in which there are many workers, perhaps millions. With many workers, the part of the nation's PPC that is associated with each individual worker becomes very small. As a result, the PPC for an economy with many workers has a smoothly bowed shape, as shown in Figure 28.3. With a smoothly curved PPC, the slope at each point still reflects the opportunity cost of producing an additional computer, as illustrated in Figure 28.3. For example, at point C in Figure 28.3, the opportunity cost of producing an extra computer is given by the slope of the line that just touches the PPC at that point. Because computers will be produced first by workers with the greatest comparative advantage (the lowest opportunity cost), the slope of the PPC becomes more and more sharply negative as we read from left to right in the figure.

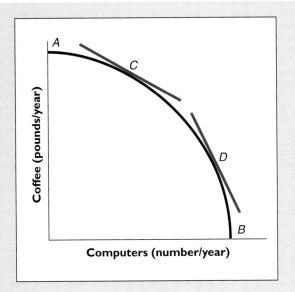

FIGURE 28.3
Production Possibilities Curve for a Many-Worker Economy.
The PPC for a many-worker economy has a smooth, outwardly bowed shape. At each point on the PPC the slope of the curve reflects the opportunity cost, in terms of coffee forgone, of producing an additional computer. For example, the opportunity cost of a computer at point *C* equals the slope of the line that just touches the PPC at that point, and the opportunity cost of a computer at point *D* equals the slope of the line that just touches the PPC there. Because the opportunity cost of producing another computer increases as more computers are produced, the slope of the PPC becomes more and more negative as we read from left to right on the graph.

RECAP   **PRODUCTION POSSIBILITIES CURVES (PPCs)**

■ The *production possibilities curve* (PPC) for a two-good economy is a graph that shows the maximum amount of one good that can be produced at every possible level of production of the other good.

■ The slope of a PPC at any point indicates the opportunity cost, in terms of forgone production of the good on the vertical axis, of increasing production of the good on the horizontal axis by one unit.

■ The more of a good that is already being produced, the greater the opportunity cost of increasing production still further. Thus the slope of the PPC becomes more and more negative as we read from left to right, imparting the characteristic outwardly bowed shape of the curve.

CONSUMPTION POSSIBILITIES WITH AND WITHOUT INTERNATIONAL TRADE

A country's production possibilities curve shows the quantities of different goods that its economy can *produce*. However, economic welfare depends most directly not on what a country can produce but on what its citizens can *consume*. The combinations of goods and services that a country's citizens might feasibly consume are called the country's **consumption possibilities**.

consumption possibilities the combinations of goods and services that a country's citizens might feasibly consume

The relationship between a country's consumption possibilities and its production possibilities depends on whether or not the country is open to international trade. In a closed economy with no trade, people can consume only the goods and services produced within their own country. *In a closed economy, then, society's consumption possibilities are identical to its production possibilities.* A situation in which a country is economically self-sufficient, producing everything its citizens consume, is called **autarky**.

autarky a situation in which a country is economically self-sufficient

The case of an open economy, which trades with the rest of the world, is quite different. In an open economy, people are not restricted to consuming what is produced in their own country, because part of what they produce can be sent abroad in exchange for other goods and services. Indeed, we will see in this section that opening an economy up to trade may allow citizens to consume more of everything. Thus, *in an open economy, a society's consumption possibilities are typically greater than (and will never be less than) its production possibilities.* We will illustrate this critical point with reference to the two-worker economy studied earlier in the chapter, then briefly consider the more general case of a many-worker economy.

EXAMPLE 28.2

Brazil's consumption possibilities with trade

Two Brazilian workers, Carlos and Maria, can produce coffee and computers as described in Example 28.1. Initially the country is closed to trade, and Maria produces only computers, while Carlos produces only coffee. Then the country opens up to trade. World prices are such that 80 pounds of coffee can be traded for one computer on the international market, and vice versa. Assume that these prices are unaffected by Brazil's entry into world markets. How does the opening of Brazil to trade affect Maria's and Carlos's opportunity to consume coffee and computers?

The analysis of this example is similar to the discussion of the small island nation in Chapter 3 (see Figure 3.10). If Maria is producing only computers and Carlos is producing only coffee, then Brazil is at point C on the PPC shown in Figure 28.4 (which is the same as the PPC shown in Figure 28.1). At that point Maria is spending all her time producing 100 computers a year,

FIGURE 28.4
Brazil's Consumption Possibilities with Trade.
Without the opportunity to trade, Brazil's consumption possibilities are the same as the Brazilian PPC, represented by line *ACB*. With the opportunity to trade, however, Brazilians can consume at any point along line *FG*.

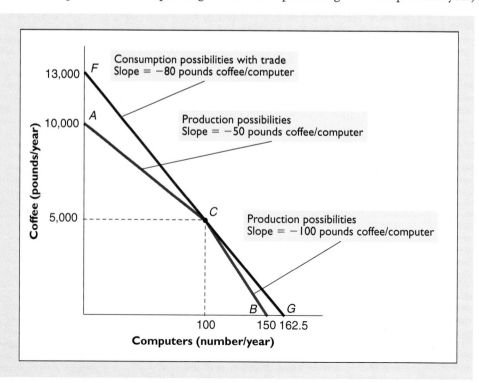

and Carlos is spending all his time producing 5,000 pounds of coffee a year. If Maria and Carlos decided they wanted more coffee, they could obtain it only by settling for fewer computers. Specifically, starting at point C on the PPC, they could obtain 50 additional pounds of coffee by giving up one computer—by having Maria work 1/2 week less on computers and 1/2 week more producing coffee.

If Brazil opens up to trade, however, then Maria and Carlos can get 80 pounds of coffee in exchange for one computer simply by trading computers for coffee on the international market. In other words, they can get an extra 30 pounds of coffee for each computer they give up. To illustrate the degree to which the opportunity to trade benefits Brazil, recall from Example 28.1 that with no trade, Maria's and Carlos's maximum coffee consumption is 10,000 pounds per year (the vertical intercept of the Brazilian PPC). With the opportunity to trade, however, Maria can trade the 100 computers produced at point C for 8,000 pounds of coffee (80 pounds of coffee/computer × 100 computers). Together with the 5,000 pounds of coffee Carlos produces, the coffee obtained through trade raises Brazil's maximum annual coffee consumption from 10,000 to 13,000 pounds per year, as indicated by point F in Figure 28.4. Because trade creates the possibility for Brazil to consume as much as 13,000 pounds of coffee per year, point F is included in Brazil's consumption possibilities, though it would have been unattainable to the Brazilians before the opening up of trade.

Furthermore, with the opportunity to trade, Maria and Carlos can consume any combination of coffee and computers represented on the straight line between points F and C in Figure 28.4. This straight line has a slope of −80 pounds coffee/1 computer, which is the rate at which the two goods can be exchanged on the international market. So, simply by trading computers for coffee, Maria and Carlos can improve their consumption possibilities at any point except C, where their production and consumption possibilities are the same.

Suppose instead that, starting from point C on Brazil's PPC, Maria and Carlos decide they want to consume more computers rather than more coffee. With no ability to trade, the opportunity cost of obtaining one more computer at point C would be 100 pounds of coffee—that is, the amount of coffee that would be lost by having Carlos work one more week at producing an extra computer, and hence one less week at producing coffee. With trade, however, Brazilians can obtain an extra computer at the cost of only 80 pounds of coffee (the price of computers on the international market). In the extreme, if they wanted to consume only computers, the Brazilians could trade the 5,000 pounds of coffee Carlos produces at point C for 5,000/80 = 62.5 computers, for a total consumption (with the 100 computers Maria produces) of 162.5 computers. This maximum consumption amount is indicated by point G in Figure 28.4. Comparing point G with point B, we can see that the opportunity to trade has increased Brazil's maximum consumption of computers from 150 to 162.5. (The half a computer is a laptop.) Furthermore, by trading various amounts of coffee for computers, Brazilians can consume any combination of computers and coffee on the straight line between points C and G in Figure 28.4. Like the segment FC, segment CG has a slope equal to −80 pounds coffee/1 computer, reflecting the rate at which coffee can be traded for computers on the international market. Note that, since segments FC and CG have the same slopes, the line FG is a straight line. The line FG represents Brazil's consumption possibilities—the combinations of coffee and computers that Carlos and Maria might feasibly consume—when the Brazilian economy is open to trade. By comparing Brazil's consumption possibilities without trade (line ACB) and with trade (line FG), we can see that Maria and Carlos have a wider range of consumption opportunities when their economy is open.

EXERCISE 28.2

Prior to the opening of trade, suppose that Brazilian residents consumed 80 computers per year. How much coffee were they able to consume each year? Suppose that the Brazilians open up to trade, but they choose to continue to consume 80 computers per year. Now how much coffee can they consume? In answering, use the PPC and consumption possibilities we found in Example 28.2. Does opening to trade make the Brazilians better off?

The same points just made in Example 28.2, which illustrates a two-worker economy, apply in the case of a many-worker economy. Figure 28.5 shows this more general case. With many workers, the PPC (curve *ACB* in the figure) is smoothly bowed. Point *A*, where the PPC intercepts the vertical axis, indicates the maximum amount of coffee the economy can produce, and point *B*, the horizontal intercept of the PPC, shows the maximum number of computers the economy can produce. The intermediate points on the PPC represent alternative combinations of coffee and computers that can be produced. As in the two-worker economy, the slope at each point on the PPC indicates the opportunity cost of producing one additional computer. The more computers that are already being produced, the greater the opportunity cost of increasing computer production still further. Hence the slope of the PPC becomes more and more negative as we read from left to right.

FIGURE 28.5
Consumption Possibilities in a Many-Worker Economy.
The PPC for a many-worker economy is the smooth, outwardly bowed line *ACB*. If the country is open to trade, its consumption possibilities lie on the line *FG*, which just touches the PPC at point *C*. The slope of this line equals the rate at which coffee can be traded for computers at world prices. The country maximizes its consumption possibilities by producing at point *C* and then trading so as to reach its most desired point on line *FG*.

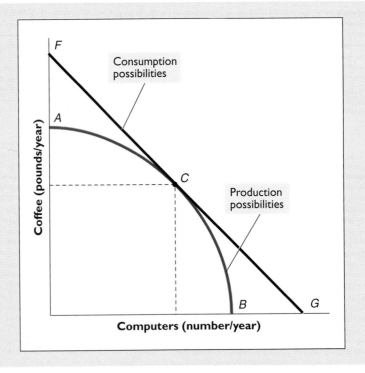

Line *FG* shows the consumption possibilities for this economy if it is open to trade. This line has two key features. First, it is drawn so that it just touches the PPC, at point *C* in Figure 28.5. Second, the slope of line *FG* is determined by the relative prices of coffee and computers on the world market. Specifically, as in the two-worker case (Figure 28.4), the slope of line *FG* tells us how much coffee must be exchanged on world markets to obtain an additional computer.

With access to international trade, Brazil can consume the greatest amount of both coffee and computers by producing at point *C* on the PPC and trading on the international market to obtain the desired combination of coffee and computers on line *FG*. (The exact combination of coffee and computers Brazilians will choose depends on the needs and wants of the population.)

Why should the Brazilians produce at point *C*? At point *C*, and only at that point, the slope of the PPC equals the slope of the consumption possibilities line *FG*. Hence, only at point *C* is the opportunity cost of increasing domestic computer production equal to the opportunity cost of purchasing an extra computer on the world market. If the opportunity cost of producing a computer domestically exceeded the opportunity cost of purchasing a computer on the world market, Brazil would gain by reducing its computer production and importing more computers. Likewise, if the opportunity cost of producing a computer domestically were less than the opportunity cost of purchasing a computer abroad, Brazil would gain by increasing computer production and reducing computer imports. Brazil's best production combination, therefore, is at point *C*, where the domestic and international opportunity costs of acquiring an extra computer, measured in terms of coffee forgone, are equal.

We have already stated the general conclusion that can be drawn from this analysis. Once again, by opening itself up to trade, a country can consume more of *every* good than if it relied solely on its own production (a situation of *autarky*). Graphically, the consumption possibilities line in Figure 28.5 lies above the production possibilities curve, showing that through trade Brazil can consume combinations of computers and coffee that would not be attainable if its economy were closed to trade.[2]

"The repairs will take awhile. We need a part from Mexico, a part from Brazil and one from Taiwan."

RECAP CONSUMPTION POSSIBILITIES AND PRODUCTION POSSIBILITIES

■ A country's *consumption possibilities* are the combinations of goods and services that its citizens might feasibly consume.

■ In an economy that is closed to trade, residents can consume only what is produced domestically (a situation of *autarky*). Hence, in a closed economy, consumption possibilities equal production possibilities.

[2]The single point at which consumption possibilities do *not* lie above production possibilities in Figure 28.5 is at point *C*, where production possibilities and consumption possibilities are the same. If Brazilian residents happen to prefer the combination of computers and coffee at point *C* to any other point on *FG*, then they realize no benefit from trade.

■ The residents of an open economy can trade part of what they produce on international markets. According to the principle of comparative advantage, trade allows everyone to do better than they could otherwise. Thus, in an open economy, consumption possibilities are typically greater than, and will never be less than, production possibilities.

■ Graphically, consumption possibilities in an open economy are described by a downward-sloping line that just touches the production possibilities curve (PPC). The slope of this line equals the amount of the good on the vertical axis that must be traded on the international market to obtain one unit of the good on the horizontal axis. A country maximizes its consumption possibilities by producing at the point where the consumption possibilities line just touches the PPC, and then trading so as to reach its most preferred point on the consumption possibilities line.

ECONOMIC
NATURALIST
28.1

Does cheap foreign labor pose a danger to high-wage economies?

Does "cheap" foreign labor pose a danger to high-wage economies?

Some people argue that high-wage industrialized countries lose by trading with low-wage developing nations. The concern is that the lower average wage that prevails in developing nations will allow those countries to produce most or all goods and services at lower cost. Unable to compete, the industrialized countries will suffer declining wages and rising unemployment. Does "cheap" foreign labor pose a danger to high-wage economies?

The "cheap foreign labor" argument is fallacious because it ignores the principle of comparative advantage and the advantages of specialization. To illustrate the key issues, suppose the United States produces both software and beef. Trade negotiators have proposed to open trade between the United States and a developing nation, Fredonia, which produces the same two products. Real wages are much lower in Fredonia than in the United States. Does this fact imply that Fredonia will undersell the United States in both the software and the beef markets, threatening American workers with the loss of their jobs?

To answer this question, let's first ask *why* wages are lower in Fredonia. As we saw in Chapter 21, real wages are determined by the marginal productivity of labor. Hence, if real wages in Fredonia are radically lower than in the United States, Fredonian workers must be much less productive than U.S. workers. This observation is enough to show why Fredonian producers will not be able to undersell American producers in both industries. Even though Fredonian firms pay lower wages, because of differences in factors such as technology, physical capital, and human capital, a Fredonian worker produces much less output per hour than an American worker. Thus lower Fredonian wages do not necessarily translate into lower production costs.

Indeed, Fredonia's production costs will tend to be lower than U.S. production costs only in those industries in which Fredonia is *relatively* more productive. Recall the principle of comparative advantage. Suppose that Fredonia is half as productive as the United States in producing beef but only one-tenth as productive in producing software. In that case, the United States has an absolute advantage in producing both goods, but Fredonia has a comparative advantage in producing beef and the United States has a comparative advantage in software. As we saw in the examples in this chapter, the United States can gain by producing more software and trading the extra software to Fredonians for beef. Fredonia can gain too by trading its beef for software. Far from being hurt by trading with Fredonia, U.S. consumers can have more of both goods through trade.

While the U.S. economy as a whole gains from trade with Fredonia, the United States will have a larger software sector and a smaller beef-producing sector than it would in the absence of trade. That is, some U.S. software will be exported to Fredonia, but some U.S.-produced beef will be replaced by imported Fredonian beef. Hence, although opportunities for workers in the software sector will increase as a result of trade, employment and wages in the beef sector will fall. We will discuss the sectoral impacts of trade in the next section.

A SUPPLY AND DEMAND PERSPECTIVE ON TRADE

To this point we have shown that a country can improve its overall consumption possibilities by trading with other countries. In this section we will look more carefully at how international trade affects supply and demand in the markets for specific goods. We will see that, when it is costly for workers and firms to change industries, opening up trade with other countries may create groups of winners and losers among producers even as it helps consumers.

Let's see how trade affects the markets for computers and coffee in Brazil. Figure 28.6 shows the supply and demand for computers in that country. As usual, the price is shown on the vertical axis and the quantity on the horizontal axis. For now, think of the price of computers as being measured in terms of coffee rather than in terms of dollars (in other words, we measure the price of computers *relative* to the price of the other good in the economy). As usual, the upward-sloping curve in Figure 28.6 is the supply curve of computers, in this case for computers produced in Brazil, and the downward-sloping curve is the demand curve for computers by Brazilian residents. The supply curve for computers in Brazil reflects the opportunity cost of supplying computers (see Chapter 4). Specifically, at any level of computer production, the relative price at which Brazilian firms are willing to supply an additional computer equals their opportunity cost of doing so. The demand curve, which tells us the number of computers Brazilians will purchase at each relative price, reflects the preferences and buying power of Brazilian consumers.

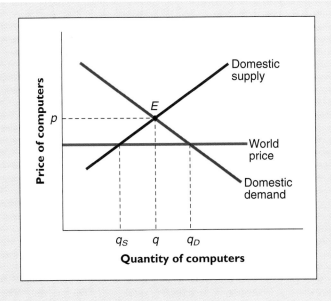

FIGURE 28.6
The Market for Computers in Brazil.
If Brazil is closed to international trade, the equilibrium price and quantity of computers are determined by the intersection of the domestic supply and demand curves at point *E*. But if Brazil is open to trade, the domestic price of computers must equal the world price. At that price, Brazilians will demand q_D computers, but domestic producers will supply only q_S computers. Thus $q_D - q_S$ computers must be imported from abroad.

If the Brazilian economy is closed to international trade, then market equilibrium occurs where the domestic supply and demand curves intersect, at point *E* in Figure 28.6. The equilibrium price will be *p*, and the equilibrium quantity will be *q*.

world price the price at which a good or service is traded on international markets

If Brazil opens its market to trade, however, the relevant price for computers becomes the **world price** of computers, the price at which computers are traded internationally. The world price for computers is determined by the world-wide supply and demand for computers. If we assume that Brazil's computer market is too small to affect the world price for computers very much, the world price can be treated as fixed, and represented by a horizontal line in the figure. Figure 28.6 shows the world price for computers as being lower than Brazil's closed-economy price.

If Brazilians are free to buy and sell computers on the international market, then the price of computers in Brazil must be the same as the world price. (No one in Brazil will buy a computer at a price above the world price, and no one will sell one at a price below the world price.) Figure 28.6 shows that at the world price, Brazilians consumers and firms demand q_D computers, but Brazilian computer producers will supply only q_S computers. The difference between the two quantities, $q_D - q_S$, is the number of computers that Brazil must import from abroad. Figure 28.6 illustrates a general conclusion: *If the price of a good or service in a closed economy is greater than the world price, and that economy opens itself to trade, the economy will tend to become a net importer of that good or service.*

A different outcome occurs in Brazil's coffee market, shown in Figure 28.7. The price of coffee (measured relative to the price of computers) is shown on the vertical axis, and the quantity of coffee on the horizontal axis. The downward-sloping demand curve in the figure shows how much coffee Brazilian consumers want to buy at each relative price, and the upward-sloping supply curve how much coffee Brazilian producers are willing to supply at each relative price. If Brazil's economy is closed to trade with the rest of the world, then equilibrium in the market for coffee will occur at point *E,* where the domestic demand and supply curves intersect. The quantity produced will be q and the price p.

FIGURE 28.7
The Market for Coffee in Brazil.
With no international trade, the equilibrium price and quantity of coffee in Brazil are determined by the intersection of the domestic supply and demand curves (point *E*). But if the country opens to trade, the domestic price of coffee must equal the world price. At the higher world price, Brazilians will demand the quantity of coffee q_D, less than the amount supplied by Brazilian producers, q_S. The excess coffee supplied by Brazilian producers, $q_S - q_D$, is exported.

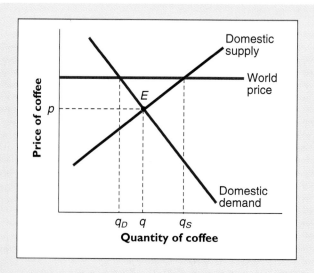

Now imagine that Brazil opens its coffee market to international trade. As in the case of computers, if free trade in coffee is permitted, then the prevailing price for coffee in Brazil must be the same as the world price. Unlike the case of computers, however, the world price of coffee as shown in Figure 28.7 is *higher* than the domestic equilibrium price. How do we know that the world price of coffee will be higher than the domestic price? Recall that the price of coffee is measured relative to the price of computers, and vice versa. If the price of computers relative to the price of coffee is higher in Brazil than in the world market, then the price of coffee relative to the price of computers must be lower, as each price is the reciprocal of the other. More generally, as we saw in Chapter 3, when two people or two countries trade with each other, neither can have a comparative advantage in *every* good and service. Thus, in an example with only two goods, if non-Brazilian producers have a comparative advantage in computers, reflected in the lower cost of computers relative to coffee in the world market, then Brazilian producers must have a comparative advantage in coffee. By definition, this comparative advantage implies that the opportunity cost of coffee in terms of computers must be lower in Brazil than in the rest of the world.

Figure 28.7 shows that at the world price for coffee, Brazilian producers are willing to supply q_S coffee, while Brazilian consumers want to purchase a smaller amount, q_D. The difference between domestic production and domestic consumption, $q_S - q_D$, is exported to the world market. The general conclusion of Figure 28.7 is this: *If the price of a good or service in a closed economy is lower than the world price, and that economy opens itself to trade, the economy will tend to become a net exporter of that good or service.*

These examples illustrate how the market translates comparative advantage into mutually beneficial gains from trade. If trade is unrestricted, then countries with a comparative advantage in a particular good will profit by supplying that good to the world market and using the revenue earned to import goods in which they do not have a comparative advantage. Thus the workings of the free market automatically ensure that goods will be produced where the opportunity cost is lowest, leading to the highest possible consumption possibilities for the world as a whole.

WINNERS AND LOSERS FROM TRADE

If trade is so wonderful, why do politicians so often resist free trade and "globalization"? The reason is that although free trade benefits the economy as a whole, specific groups may not benefit. If groups who are hurt by trade have sufficient political influence, they may be able to persuade politicians to enact policies that restrict the free flow of goods and services across borders.

The supply and demand analyses shown in Figures 28.6 and 28.7 are useful in understanding who gains and who loses when an economy opens up to trade. Look first at Figure 28.6, which shows the market for computers in Brazil. When Brazil opens its computer market to international competition, Brazilian consumers enjoy a larger quantity of computers at a lower price. Clearly, Brazilian computer users benefit from the free trade in computers. In general, *domestic consumers of imported goods benefit from free trade.* However, Brazilian computer producers will not be so happy about opening their market to international competition. The fall in computer prices to the international level implies that less efficient domestic producers will go out of business and that those who remain will earn lower profits. Unemployment in the Brazilian computer industry will rise and may persist over time, particularly if displaced computer workers cannot easily move to a new industry.[3] We see that, in general, *domestic producers of imported goods are hurt by free trade.*

Consumers are helped, and producers hurt, when imports increase. The opposite conclusions apply for an increase in exports (see Figure 28.7). In the example of Brazil, an opening of the coffee market raises the domestic price of coffee to the world price and creates the opportunity for Brazil to export coffee.

---

[3]The wages paid to Brazilian computer workers will also fall, reflecting the lower relative price of computers. We analyzed the effect on workers of increased competition from imports in Chapter 21.

Domestic producers of coffee benefit from the increased market (they can now sell coffee abroad as well as at home) and from the higher price of their product. In short, *domestic producers of exported goods benefit from free trade.* Brazilian coffee drinkers will be less enthusiastic, however, since they must now pay the higher world price of coffee and can therefore consume less. *Thus domestic consumers of exported goods are hurt by free trade.*

TRADE WINNERS AND LOSERS

Winners

- Consumers of imported goods

- Producers of exported goods

Losers

- Consumers of exported goods

- Producers of imported goods

Free trade is *efficient* in the sense that it increases the total "pie" available to the economy. Indeed, the efficiency of free trade is an application of the *equilibrium principle,* that markets in equilibrium leave no unexploited opportunities for individuals. Despite the efficiency of free trade, however, some groups may lose from trade, which generates political pressures to block or restrict trade. In the next section we will discuss the major types of policies used to restrict trade.

PROTECTIONIST POLICIES: TARIFFS AND QUOTAS

protectionism the view that free trade is injurious and should be restricted

tariff a tax imposed on an imported good

quota a legal limit on the quantity of a good that may be imported

The view that free trade is injurious and should be restricted is known as **protectionism.** Supporters of this view believe the government should attempt to "protect" domestic markets by raising legal barriers to imports. (Interestingly, protectionists rarely attempt to restrict exports, even though they hurt consumers of the exported good.) Two of the most common types of such barriers are *tariffs* and *quotas.* A **tariff** is a tax imposed on an imported good. A **quota** is a legal limit on the quantity of a good that may be imported.

Tariffs The effects of tariffs and quotas can be explained using supply and demand diagrams. Suppose that Brazilian computer makers, dismayed by the penetration of "their" market by imported computers, persuade their government to impose a tariff—that is, a tax—on every computer imported into the country. Computers produced in Brazil will be exempt from the tax. Figure 28.8 shows the likely effects of this tariff on the domestic Brazilian computer market. The lower of the two horizontal lines in the figure indicates the world price of computers, not including the tariff. The higher of the two lines indicates the price Brazilian consumers will actually pay for imported computers, including the tariff. We refer to the price of computers including the tariff as p_T. The vertical distance between the two lines equals the amount of the tariff that is imposed on each imported computer.

From the point of view of domestic Brazilian producers and consumers, the imposition of the tariff has the same effects as an equivalent increase in the world price of computers. Because the price (including the tariff) of imported computers has risen, Brazilian computer producers will be able to raise the price they charge for their computers to the world price plus tariff, p_T. Thus the price Brazilian consumers must pay—whether their computers are imported or not—equals p_T, represented by the upper horizontal line in Figure 28.8.

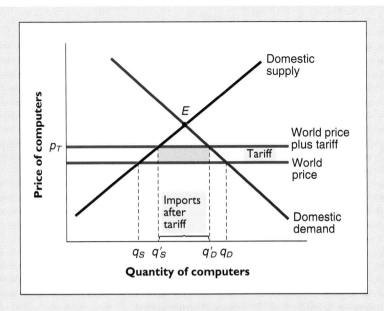

FIGURE 28.8
The Market for Computers after the Imposition of an Import Tariff.
The imposition of a tariff on imported computers raises the price of computers in Brazil to the world price plus tariff, p_T, represented by the upper horizontal line. Domestic production of computers rises from q_S to q'_S, domestic purchases of computers fall from q_D to q'_D, and computer imports fall from $q_D - q_S$ to $q'_D - q'_S$. Brazilian consumers are worse off and Brazilian computer producers are better off. The Brazilian government collects revenue from the tariff equal to the area of the pale blue rectangle.

The rise in the price of computers created by the tariff affects the quantities of computers supplied and the quantities demanded by Brazilians. Domestic computer producers, facing a higher price for computers, increase their production from q_S to q'_S (see Figure 28.8). Brazilian consumers, also reacting to the higher price, reduce their computer purchases from q_D to q'_D. As a result, the number of imported computers—the difference between domestic purchases and domestic production—falls from $q_D - q_S$ to $q'_D - q'_S$.

Who are the winners and the losers from the tariff, then? The winners are the domestic computer producers, who sell more computers and receive a higher price for them. The clearest losers are Brazilian consumers, who must now pay more for their computers. Another winner is the government, which collects revenue from the tariff. The pale blue area in Figure 28.8 shows the amount of revenue the government collects, equal to the quantity of computer imports after the imposition of the tariff, $q'_D - q'_S$, times the amount of the tariff.

A tariff on imported computers

EXAMPLE 28.3

Suppose the demand for computers by Brazilian consumers is given by

$$\text{Demand} = 3,000 - 0.5(\text{Price of computers}).$$

The supply of computers by domestic Brazilian producers is

$$\text{Supply} = 1,000 + 0.5(\text{Price of computers}).$$

a. Assuming that the Brazilian economy is closed to trade, find the equilibrium price and quantity in the Brazilian computer market.

b. Assume the economy opens to trade. If the world price of computers is 1,500, find Brazilian consumption, production, and imports of computers.

c. At the request of domestic producers, the Brazilian government imposes a tariff of 300 per imported computer. Find Brazilian consumption, production, and imports of computers after the imposition of the tariff. How much revenue does the tariff raise for the government?

To find the closed-economy price and quantity, we set supply equal to demand:

$$1,000 + 0.5(\text{Price of computers}) = 3,000 - 0.5(\text{Price of computers}).$$

Solving this equation for the price of a computer gives the equilibrium price, equal to 2,000. Substituting the equilibrium price into either the supply equation or the demand equation, we find the equilibrium quantity of computers in the Brazilian market, equal to 2,000. This equilibrium price and quantity correspond to a point like point E in Figure 28.8.

If the economy opens to trade, the domestic price of computers must equal the world price, which is 1,500. At this price, domestic demand for computers is $3,000 - 0.5(1,500)$, or 2,250; domestic supply is $1,000 + 0.5(1,500)$, or 1,750. These quantities correspond to q_D and q_S, respectively, in Figure 28.8. Imports equal the difference between domestic quantities demanded and supplied, equal to $2,250 - 1,750$, or 500 computers.

The imposition of a tariff of 300 per computer raises the price from 1,500 (the world price without the tariff) to 1,800. To find Brazilian consumption and production at this price, we set the price equal to 1,800 in the demand and supply equations. Thus the domestic demand for computers is $3,000 - 0.5(1,800)$, or 2,100 computers; the domestic supply is $1,000 + 0.5(1,800)$, or 1,900 computers. Imports, the difference between the quantity demanded by Brazilians and the quantity supplied by domestic firms, equal $2,100 - 1,900$, or 200 computers, corresponding to $q'_D - q'_S$ in Figure 28.8. Thus the tariff has raised the price of computers by 300 and reduced imports by 300. The tariff revenues collected by the government equal 300 per imported computer times 200 computers, or 60,000.

EXERCISE 28.3

Repeat parts b and c of Example 28.3 under the assumption that the world price of computers is 1,200. What happens if the world price is 1,800?

Quotas An alternative to a tariff is a quota, or legal limit, on the number or value of foreign goods that can be imported. One means of enforcing a quota is to require importers to obtain a license or permit for each good they bring into the country. The government then distributes exactly the number of permits as the number of goods that may be imported under the quota.

How does the imposition of a quota on, say, computers affect the domestic market for computers? To see the effect of a quota on imported computers, see Figure 28.9, which is similar to Figure 28.8. As before, assume that at first there are no restrictions on trade. Consumers pay the world price for computers, and $q_D - q_S$ computers are imported. Now suppose once more that domestic computer producers complain to the government about competition from foreign computer makers, and the government agrees to act. However, this time, instead of a tariff, the government imposes a quota on the number of computers that can be imported. For comparability with the tariff analyzed in Figure 28.8, let's assume that the quota permits the same level of imports as entered the country under the tariff: specifically, $q'_D - q'_S$ computers. What effect does this ruling have on the domestic market for computers?

After the imposition of the quota, the supply of computers to the Brazilian market is the production of domestic firms plus the $q'_D - q'_S$ imported com-

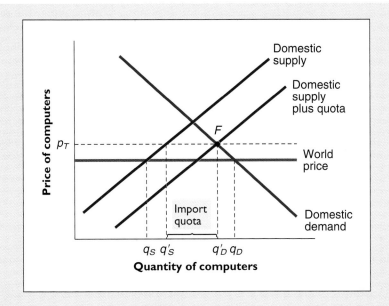

FIGURE 28.9
The Market for Computers after the Imposition of an Import Quota.
The figure shows the effects of the imposition of a quota that permits only $q'_D - q'_S$ computers to be imported. The total supply of computers to the domestic economy equals the domestic supply curve shifted to the right by $q'_D - q'_S$ units (the fixed amount of imports). Market equilibrium occurs at point F. The effects of the quota on the domestic market are identical to those of the tariff analyzed in Figure 28.8. The domestic price rises to p_T, domestic production of computers rises from q_S to q'_S, domestic purchases of computers fall from q_D to q'_D, and computer imports fall from $q_D - q_S$ to $q'_D - q'_S$. The quota differs from the tariff in that under a quota system the government collects no revenue.

puters allowed under the quota. Figure 28.9 shows the supply of computers inclusive of the quota. The total supply curve, labeled "Domestic supply plus quota," is the same as the domestic supply curve except shifted $q'_D - q'_S$ units to the right. The domestic demand curve is the same as in Figure 28.8. Equilibrium in the domestic market for computers occurs at point F in Figure 28.9, at the intersection of the supply curve including the quota and the domestic demand curve. The figure shows that, relative to the initial situation with free trade, the quota (1) raises the domestic price of computers above the world price, to the level marked p_T in Figure 28.9; (2) reduces domestic purchases of computers from q_D to q'_D; (3) increases domestic production of computers from q_S to q'_S; and (4) reduces imports to $q'_D - q'_S$, consistent with the quota. Like a tariff, the quota helps domestic producers by increasing their sales and the price they receive for their output, while hurting domestic consumers by forcing them to pay a higher price.

Interestingly, under our assumption that the quota is set so as to permit the same level of imports as the tariff, the effects on the domestic market of the tariff (Figure 28.8) and the quota (Figure 28.9) are not only similar, they are *equivalent*. Comparing Figures 28.8 and 28.9, you can see that the two policies have identical effects on the domestic price, domestic purchases, domestic production, and imports.

Although the market effects of a tariff and a quota are the same, there is one important difference between the two policies, which is that a tariff generates revenue for the government, while a quota does not.[4] With a quota, the revenue that would have gone to the government goes instead to those firms who hold the import licenses. A holder of an import license can purchase a computer at the world price and resell it in the domestic market at price p_T, pocketing the difference. Thus, with a tariff the government collects the difference between the world price and the domestic market price of the good; with a quota, private firms or individuals collect that difference. Why then would the government ever impose a quota rather than a tariff? One possibility is that the distribution of import licenses is a means of rewarding the government's political supporters. Sometimes, international political concerns may also play a role (see Economic Naturalist 28.2 for a possible example).

EXAMPLE 28.4

Effects of an import quota

Suppose the supply of and demand for computers in Brazil is as given in Example 28.3, and the government imposes an import quota of 200 computers. Find the equilibrium price in the domestic computer market, as well as the quantities produced by domestic firms and purchased by domestic consumers.

The supply of computers by domestic Brazilian producers was stated in Example 28.3 to be 1,000 + 0.5(Price of computers). The quota allows 200 computers to be imported. Thus the total supply of computers, including both domestic production and imports, is 1,000 + 0.5(Price of computers) + 200, or 1,200 + 0.5(Price of computers). Setting the quantity supplied equal to the quantity demanded, we get

$$1,200 + 0.5(\text{Price of computers}) = 3,000 - 0.5(\text{Price of computers})$$

Solving for the unknown, we find that the price of computers in the domestic Brazilian market is 1,800. Domestic production of computers is 1,000 + 0.5(1,800), or 1,900 computers, while domestic demand is 3,000 − 0.5(1,800), or 2,100 computers. The difference between demand and domestic production, 200 computers, is made up by imports.

Note that the domestic price, domestic production, and domestic demand are the same as in Example 28.3 on the effect of a tariff. Thus the tariff and the quota have the same effects on the domestic market for computers. The only difference between the two policies is that with a quota, the government does not get the tariff revenue it got in Example 28.3. That revenue goes instead to the holders of import licenses, who can buy computers on the world market at 1,500 and sell them in the domestic market at 1,800.

Who benefited from, and who was hurt by, voluntary export restraints on Japanese automobiles in the 1980s?

After the oil price increases of the 1970s, American consumers began to buy small, fuel-efficient Japanese automobiles in large numbers. Reeling from the new foreign competition, U.S. automobile producers petitioned the U.S. government for assistance. In response, in May 1981 the U.S. government negotiated a system of so-called *voluntary export restraints*, or VERs, with Japan. Under the VER system, each Japanese auto producer would "voluntarily" restrict exports to the United States to an agreed-upon level. VER quotas were changed several times before the system was formally eliminated in 1994. Who benefited from, and who was hurt by, VERs on Japanese automobiles?

Several groups benefited from the VER system. As should be expected, U.S. auto producers saw increased sales and profits when their Japanese competition was reduced. But Japanese automobile producers also profited from the policy, despite the

ECONOMIC NATURALIST 28.2

---

[4]Unless the government sells rather than gives away import licenses. In that case, a tariff and a quota are also equivalent in terms of government revenue.

reduction in their U.S. sales. The restrictions on the supply of their automobiles to the U.S. market allowed them to raise their prices in the U.S. market significantly—by several thousand dollars per car by the latter part of the 1980s, according to some estimates. From an economic point of view, the VERs functioned like a tariff on Japanese cars, except that the Japanese automobile producers, rather than the U.S. government, got to keep the tariff revenue. A third group that benefited from the VERs was European automobile producers, who saw U.S. demand for their cars rise when Japanese imports declined.

The biggest losers from the VER system were clearly American car buyers, who faced higher prices (particularly for Japanese imports) and reduced selection. During this period dealer discounts on new Japanese cars largely disappeared, and customers often found themselves paying a premium over the list price. Because the economic losses faced by American car buyers exceeded the extra profits received by U.S. automobile producers, the VERs produced a net loss for the U.S. economy that at its greatest exceeded an estimated $3 billion per year.

The U.S. government's choice of a VER system, rather than a tariff or a quota, was somewhat puzzling. If a tariff on Japanese cars had been imposed instead of a VER system, the U.S. government would have collected much of the revenue that went instead to Japanese auto producers. Alternatively, a quota system with import licenses given to U.S. car dealers would have captured some revenue for domestic car dealers rather than Japanese firms. The best explanation for why the U.S. government chose VERs is probably political. U.S. policymakers may have been concerned that the Japanese government would retaliate against U.S. trade restrictions by imposing its own restrictions on U.S. exports. By instituting a system that did minimal financial harm to—or even helped—Japanese auto producers, they may have hoped to avoid retaliation from the Japanese.[5]

Who benefited from "voluntary" export restraints on Japanese cars?

Tariffs and quotas are not the only barriers to trade that governments sometimes erect. Importers may be subject to unnecessarily complex bureaucratic rules (so-called red tape barriers), and regulations of goods that are nominally intended to promote health and safety but sometimes have the side effect, whether intentionally or unintentionally, of restricting trade. One example is European restrictions on imports of genetically modified foods. Although these regulations were motivated in part by concerns about the safety of such foods, they also help to protect Europe's politically powerful farmers from foreign competition.

THE INEFFICIENCY OF PROTECTIONISM

Free trade is efficient because it allows countries to specialize in the production of goods and services in which they have the greatest comparative advantage. Conversely, protectionist policies that limit trade are inefficient—they reduce the total economic pie. (Recall Chapter 4's *efficiency principle:* Efficiency is an important social goal.) Why, then, do governments adopt such policies? The reason is similar to why some city governments impose rent controls (see Chapter 4). Although rent controls reduce economic welfare overall, some people benefit from them, namely, the tenants whose rents are held artificially below market level. Similarly, as we have seen in this section, tariffs and quotas benefit certain groups. Because those who benefit from these restrictions (such as firms facing import competition) are often better organized politically than those who lose from trade barriers (such as consumers in general), lawmakers are sometimes persuaded to enact the restrictions.

The fact that free trade is efficient suggests an alternative to trade restrictions, however. Because eliminating restrictions on trade increases the overall economic pie, in general the winners from free trade will be able to compensate the losers

---

[5]President Reagan's autobiography confirms that policymakers were concerned that an alternative method of limiting Japanese imports would provoke the Japanese into taking measures to limit U.S. exports to Japan. See Ronald Reagan, *An American Life*, New York: Simon and Schuster, 1990, p. 274.

in such a way that everyone becomes better off. Government programs that assist and retrain workers displaced by import competition are an example of such compensation (see Chapter 21). Spreading the benefits of free trade, or at least reducing its adverse effects on certain groups, reduces the incentives of those groups to inhibit free trade.

Although we have focused on the winners and losers from trade, not all opposition to free trade is motivated by economic interest. For example, many of the antitrade protesters in Seattle in 1999 cited environmental concerns. Protecting the environment is an important and laudable goal, but once again the *efficiency principle* suggests that restricting trade is not the most effective means of achieving that goal. Restricting trade lowers world income, reducing the resources available to deal with environmental problems. (Chapter 20 noted that high levels of economic development are associated with lower, not higher, amounts of pollution.) Furthermore, much of the income loss arising from barriers to trade is absorbed by poor nations trying to develop their economies. For this reason, leaders of developing countries are among the strongest advocates of free trade.

RECAP | **A SUPPLY AND DEMAND PERSPECTIVE ON TRADE**

- For a closed economy, the domestic supply of and demand for a good or service determine the equilibrium price and quantity of that good or service.

- In an open economy, the price of a good or service traded on international markets equals the *world price*. If the domestic quantity supplied at the world price exceeds the domestic quantity demanded, the difference will be exported to the world market. If the domestic quantity demanded at the world price exceeds the domestic quantity supplied, the difference will be imported.

- Generally, if the price of a good or service in a closed economy is lower than the world price, and the economy opens to trade, the country will become a net exporter of that good or service. If the closed-economy price is higher than the world price, and the economy opens to trade, the country will tend to become a net importer of the good or service.

- Consumers of imported goods and producers of exported goods benefit from trade, while consumers of exported goods and producers of imported goods are hurt by trade. If those groups that are hurt have sufficient political influence, they may persuade the government to enact barriers to trade. The view that free trade is injurious and should be restricted is called *protectionism*.

- The two most common types of trade barriers are *tariffs,* or taxes on imported goods, and *quotas,* legal limits on the quantity that can be imported. A tariff raises the domestic price to the world price plus the tariff. The result is increased domestic production, reduced domestic consumption, and fewer imports. A quota has effects on the domestic market that are similar to those of a quota. The main difference is that, under a quota, the government does not collect tariff revenue.

- Trade barriers are inefficient; they reduce the overall size of the economic pie. Thus, in general, the winners from free trade should be able to compensate the losers in such a way that everyone becomes better off. Government programs to help workers displaced by import competition are an example of such compensation.

CAPITAL FLOWS AND THE BALANCE OF TRADE

Thus far in our discussion of international trade we have made two important simplifications. First, in our examples we have implicitly assumed that the value of a country's imports equals the value of its exports in every period. In reality, however, trade need not be balanced in every year. That is, the value of a country's exports in any particular year may be greater or less than the value of its imports.

In Chapter 18 we introduced the term *net exports* (*NX*), the value of a country's exports less the value of its imports. Another, equivalent term for the value of a country's exports less the value of its imports is the **trade balance**. Because exports need not equal imports in each quarter or year, the trade balance (or net exports) need not always equal zero. If the trade balance is positive in a particular period so that the value of exports exceeds the value of imports, a country is said to have a **trade surplus** for that period equal to the value of its exports minus the value of its imports. If the trade balance is negative, with imports greater than exports, the country is said to have a **trade deficit** equal to the value of its imports minus the value of its exports.

Figure 28.10 shows the components of the U.S. trade balance since 1960 (see Figure 17.5 for data extending back to 1900). The blue line represents U.S. exports as a percentage of GDP; the red line, U.S. imports as a percentage of GDP. When exports exceed imports, the vertical distance between the two lines gives the U.S. trade surplus as a percentage of GDP. When imports exceed exports, the vertical distance between the two lines represents the U.S. trade deficit. Figure 28.10 shows first that international trade has become an increasingly important part of the U.S. economy in the past several decades. In 1960, only 4.6 percent of U.S. GDP was exported, and the value of imports equaled 4.5 percent of U.S. GDP. In 1999, by comparison, 10.8 percent of U.S. production was sold abroad, and imports amounted to 13.6 percent of U.S. GDP. Second, the figure shows that since the late 1970s the United States has consistently run trade deficits, frequently equal to 2 percent or more of GDP. Why has the U.S. trade balance been in deficit for so long? We will answer that question later in this section.

trade balance (or net exports) the value of a country's exports less the value of its imports in a particular period (quarter or year)

trade surplus when exports exceed imports, the difference between the value of a country's exports and the value of its imports in a given period

trade deficit when imports exceed exports, the difference between the value of a country's imports and the value of its exports in a given period

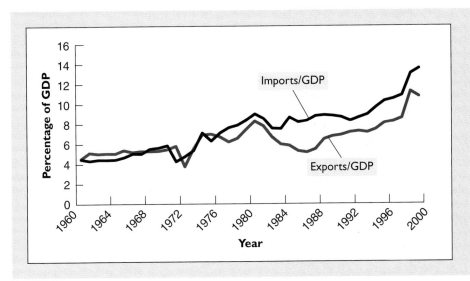

FIGURE 28.10
The U.S. Trade Balance, 1960–1999.
This figure shows U.S. exports and imports as a percentage of GDP. Since the late 1970s the United States has run a trade deficit, with imports exceeding exports. [SOURCE: *Economic Report of the President* (www.access. gpo.gov/eop/index.html).]

The second simplification we have made in our discussions thus far is to ignore the fact that trade among countries occurs in real and financial *assets* as well as in *goods and services*. For example, an American saver may wish to diversify her financial investments by purchasing shares of a Japanese company or a bond issued by the German government. Likewise, a wealthy Argentinean may decide to acquire bonds issued by a U.S. corporation or a time-share in a Miami

international capital flows purchases or sales of real and financial assets across international borders

capital inflows purchases of domestic assets by foreign households and firms

capital outflows purchases of foreign assets by domestic households and firms

condominium. Purchases or sales of real and financial assets across international borders are known as **international capital flows**. From the perspective of a particular country, say the United States, purchases of domestic (U.S.) assets by foreigners are called **capital inflows**; purchases of foreign assets by domestic (U.S.) households and firms are called **capital outflows**. To remember these terms, it may help to keep in mind that capital inflows represent funds "flowing in" to the country (foreign savers buying domestic assets), while capital outflows are funds "flowing out" of the country (domestic savers buying foreign assets). The difference between the two flows is expressed as *net capital inflows*—capital inflows minus capital outflows—or *net capital outflows*—capital outflows minus capital inflows. Note that capital inflows and outflows are *not* counted as exports or imports, because they refer to the purchase of existing real and financial assets rather than currently produced goods and services.

In the remainder of this chapter we will add realism to our discussion of international trade by incorporating both the trade balance and international capital flows. As a first step, we will show that these two apparently very different concepts are in fact closely related.

THE LINK BETWEEN THE TRADE BALANCE AND CAPITAL FLOWS

The trade balance represents the difference between the value of goods and services exported by a country and the value of goods and services imported by the country. Net capital inflows represent the difference between purchases of domestic assets by foreigners and purchases of foreign assets by domestic residents. There is a precise link between these two imbalances, which is that in any given period, *the trade balance and net capital inflows sum to zero*. For future reference, let's write this relationship as an equation:

$$NX + KI = 0. \tag{28.1}$$

where NX is the trade balance (the same as net exports) and we use KI to stand for net capital inflows. The relationship given by Equation 28.1 is an identity, meaning that it is true by definition.

To see why Equation 28.1 holds, consider what happens when (for example) a U.S. resident purchases an imported good, say a Japanese automobile priced at $20,000. Suppose the U.S. buyer pays by check so that the Japanese car manufacturer now holds $20,000 in an account in a U.S. bank. What will the Japanese manufacturer do with this $20,000? Basically, there are two possibilities.

First, the Japanese company may use the $20,000 to buy U.S.-produced goods and services, such as U.S.-manufactured car parts or Hawaiian vacations for its executives. In this case, the United States has $20,000 in exports to balance the $20,000 automobile import. Because exports equal imports, the U.S. trade balance is unaffected by these transactions (for these transactions, $NX = 0$). And because no assets are bought or sold, there are no capital inflows or outflows ($KI = 0$). So under this scenario, the condition that the trade balance plus net capital inflows equals zero, as stated in Equation 28.1, is satisfied.

Alternatively, the Japanese car producer might use the $20,000 to acquire U.S. assets, such as a U.S. Treasury bond or some land adjacent to its plant in Tennessee. In this case, the United States compiles a trade deficit of $20,000, because the $20,000 car import is not offset by an export ($NX = -\$20,000$). But there is a corresponding capital inflow of $20,000, reflecting the purchase of a U.S. asset by the Japanese ($KI = \$20,000$). So once again the trade balance and net capital inflows sum to zero, and Equation 28.1 is satisfied.[6]

---

[6]If the Japanese company simply left the $20,000 in the U.S. bank, it would still count as a capital inflow, since the deposit would still be a U.S. asset acquired by foreigners.

In fact, there is a third possibility, which is that the Japanese car company might swap its dollars to some other party outside the United States. For example, the company might trade its dollars to another Japanese firm or individual in exchange for Japanese yen. However, the acquirer of the dollars would then have the same two options as the car company—to buy U.S. goods and services or acquire U.S. assets—so that the equality of net capital inflows and the trade deficit would continue to hold.

EXERCISE 28.4

A U.S. saver purchases a $20,000 Japanese government bond. Explain why Equation 28.1 is satisfied no matter what the Japanese government does with the $20,000 it receives for its bond.

THE DETERMINANTS OF INTERNATIONAL CAPITAL FLOWS

Capital inflows, recall, are purchases of domestic assets by foreigners, while capital outflows are purchases of foreign assets by domestic residents. For example, capital inflows into the United States include foreign purchases of items such as the stocks and bonds of U.S. companies, U.S. government bonds, and real assets such as land or buildings owned by U.S. residents. Why would foreigners want to acquire U.S. assets, and conversely, why would Americans want to acquire assets abroad?

The basic factors that determine the attractiveness of any asset, either domestic or foreign, are *return* and *risk* (Chapter 23). Financial investors seek high real returns; thus, with other factors (such as the degree of risk and the returns available abroad) held constant, a higher real interest rate in the home country promotes capital inflows by making domestic assets more attractive to foreigners. By the same token, a higher real interest rate in the home country reduces capital outflows by inducing domestic residents to invest their savings at home. Thus, all else being equal, a higher real interest rate at home leads to net capital inflows. Conversely, a low real interest rate at home tends to create net capital outflows, as financial investors look abroad for better opportunities. Figure 28.11 shows the relationship between a country's net capital inflows and the real rate of

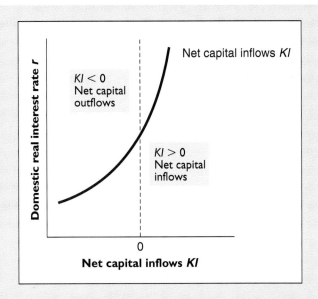

FIGURE 28.11
Net Capital Inflows and the Real Interest Rate.
Holding constant the degree of risk and the real returns available abroad, a high real interest rate in the home country will induce foreigners to buy domestic assets, increasing capital inflows. A high real rate in the home country also reduces the incentive for domestic savers to buy foreign assets, reducing capital outflows. Thus, all else being equal, the higher the domestic real interest rate *r*, the higher will be net capital inflows *KI*.

interest prevailing in that country. When the domestic real interest rate is high, net capital inflows are positive (foreign purchases of domestic assets exceed domestic purchases of foreign assets). But when the real interest rate is low, net capital inflows are negative (that is, the country experiences net capital outflows).

The effect of risk on capital flows is the opposite of the effect of the real interest rate. For a given real interest rate, an increase in the riskiness of domestic assets reduces net capital inflows, as foreigners become less willing to buy the home country's assets, and domestic savers become more inclined to buy foreign assets. For example, political instability, which increases the risk of investing in a country, tends to reduce net capital inflows. Figure 28.12 shows the effect of an increase in risk on capital flows: At each value of the domestic real interest rate, an increase in risk reduces net capital inflows, shifting the capital inflows curve to the left.

FIGURE 28.12

An Increase in Risk Reduces Net Capital Inflows.

An increase in the riskiness of domestic assets, arising, for example, from an increase in political instability, reduces the willingness of foreign and domestic savers to hold domestic assets. The supply of capital inflows declines at each value of the domestic real interest rate, shifting the *KI* curve to the left.

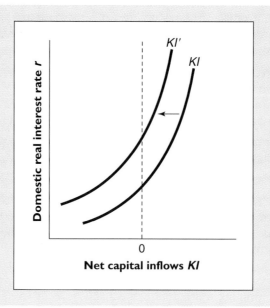

EXERCISE 28.5

For given real interest rate and riskiness in the home country, how would you expect net capital inflows to be affected by an increase in real interest rates abroad? Show your answer graphically.

SAVING, INVESTMENT, AND CAPITAL INFLOWS

International capital flows have a close relationship to domestic saving and investment. As we will see next, capital inflows augment the domestic saving pool, increasing the funds available for investment in physical capital, while capital outflows reduce the amount of saving available for investment. Thus capital inflows can help to promote economic growth within a country, and capital outflows to restrain it.

To derive the relationship among capital inflows, saving, and investment, recall from Chapter 18 that total output or income Y must always equal the sum of the four components of expenditure: consumption (C), investment (I), government purchases (G), and net exports (NX). Writing out this identity, we have

$$Y = C + I + G + NX.$$

Next, we subtract $C + G + NX$ from both sides of the identity to obtain

$$Y - C - G - NX = I.$$

In Chapter 22 we saw that national saving S is equal to $Y - C - G$. Furthermore, Equation 28.1 above states that the trade balance plus capital inflows equals zero, or $NX + KI = 0$, which implies that $KI = -NX$. If we substitute S for $Y - C - G$ and KI for $-NX$ in the above equation, we find that

$$S + KI = I. \tag{28.2}$$

Equation 28.2, a key result, says that the sum of national saving S and capital inflows from abroad KI must equal domestic investment in new capital goods, I. In other words, in an open economy, the pool of saving available for domestic investment includes not only national saving (the saving of the domestic private and public sectors) but funds from savers abroad as well.

Chapter 22 introduced the saving-investment diagram, which shows that in a closed economy, the supply of saving must equal the demand for saving. A similar diagram applies to an open economy, except that the supply of saving in an open economy includes net capital inflows as well as domestic saving. Figure 28.13 shows the open-economy version of the saving-investment diagram. The domestic real interest rate is shown on the vertical axis and saving and investment flows on the horizontal axis. As in a closed economy, the downward-sloping curve I shows the demand for funds by firms that want to make capital investments. The solid upward-sloping curve, marked $S + KI$, shows the total supply of saving, including *both* domestic saving S and net capital inflows from abroad

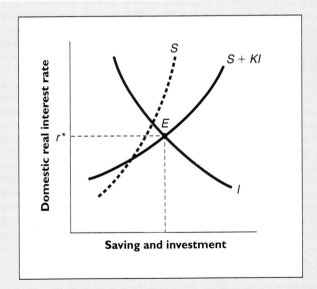

Saving and investment

FIGURE 28.13

The Saving-Investment Diagram for an Open Economy.

The total supply of savings in an open economy is the sum of national saving S and net capital inflows KI. The supply of domestic saving S is shown for comparison. Because a low real interest rate prompts capital outflows ($KI < 0$), at low values of the domestic interest rate the total supply of saving $S + KI$ is smaller than national saving S. The domestic demand for saving for purposes of capital investment is shown by the curve labeled I. The equilibrium real interest rate r^* sets the total supply of saving, including capital inflows, equal to the domestic demand for saving.

KI. Also shown, for comparison, is the supply of domestic saving, marked S. You can see that for higher values of the domestic real interest rate, net capital inflows are positive, so the $S + KI$ curve falls to the right of the curve S showing domestic saving only. But at low enough values of the real interest rate r, the economy sustains net capital outflows, as savers look abroad for higher returns on their financial investments. Thus, at low values of the domestic real interest rate, the net supply of savings is lower than it would be in a closed economy, and the $S + KI$ curve falls to the left of the domestic supply of saving curve S. As Figure 28.13 shows, the equilibrium real interest rate in an open economy, r^*, is the level that sets the total amount of saving supplied (including capital inflows from abroad) equal to the amount of saving demanded for purposes of domestic capital investment.

Figure 28.13 also indicates how net capital inflows can benefit an economy. A country that attracts significant amounts of foreign capital flows will have a larger pool of total saving and hence both a lower real interest rate and a higher rate of investment in new capital than it otherwise would. The United States and Canada both benefited from large inflows of capital in the early stages of their economic development, as do many developing countries today. Because capital inflows tend to react very sensitively to risk (see Figure 28.12), an implication is that countries that are politically stable and safeguard the rights of foreign investors will attract more foreign capital and thus grow more quickly than countries without those characteristics.

Although capital inflows are generally beneficial to the countries that receive them, neither are they costless. Countries that finance domestic capital formation primarily by capital inflows face the prospect of paying interest and dividends to the foreign financial investors from whom they have borrowed. A number of developing countries have experienced *debt crises*, arising because the domestic investments they made with foreign funds turned out poorly, leaving them insufficient income to pay what they owed their foreign creditors. An advantage to financing domestic capital formation primarily with domestic saving is that the returns from the country's capital investments accrue to domestic savers rather than flowing abroad.

THE SAVING RATE AND THE TRADE DEFICIT

We have seen that a country's exports and imports do not necessarily balance in each period. Indeed, the United States has run a trade deficit, with its imports exceeding exports, for many years. What causes trade deficits? Stories in the media sometimes claim that trade deficits occur because a country produces inferior goods that no one wants to buy or because other countries impose unfair trade restrictions on imports. Despite the popularity of these explanations, however, there is little support for them in either economic theory or evidence. For example, the United States has a large trade deficit with China, but no one would claim U.S. goods are generally inferior to Chinese goods. And many developing countries have significant trade deficits even though they, rather than their trading partners, tend to impose the more stringent restrictions on trade.

Economists argue that, rather than the quality of a country's exports or the existence of unfair trade restrictions, *a low rate of national saving is the primary cause of trade deficits.*

To see the link between national saving and the trade deficit, recall the identity $Y = C + I + G + NX$. Subtracting $C + I + G$ from both sides of this equation and rearranging, we get $Y - C - G - I = NX$. Finally, recognizing that national saving S equals $Y - C - G$, we can rewrite the relationship as

$$S - I = NX. \qquad (28.3)$$

Equation 28.3 can also be derived directly from Equations 28.1 and 28.2. According to Equation 28.3, if we hold domestic investment (I) constant, a high rate of national saving S implies a high level of net exports NX, while a low level of national saving implies a low level of net exports. Furthermore, if a country's national saving is less than its investment, or $S < I$, then Equation 28.3 implies that net exports *NX* will be negative. That is, the country will have a trade deficit. The conclusion from Equation 28.3 is that, holding domestic investment constant, low national saving tends to be associated with a trade deficit ($NX < 0$), and high national saving is associated with a trade surplus ($NX > 0$).

Why does a low rate of national saving tend to be associated with a trade deficit? A country with a low national saving rate is one in which households and the government have high spending rates, relative to domestic income and production. Since part of the spending of households and the government is devoted to imported goods, we would expect a low-saving, high-spending economy to have a high volume of imports. Furthermore, a low-saving economy consumes a large proportion of its domestic production, reducing the quantity of goods and services available for export. With high imports and low exports, a low-saving economy will experience a trade deficit.

A country with a trade deficit must also be receiving capital inflows, as we have seen. (Equation 28.1 tells us that if a trade deficit exists so that $NX < 0$, then it must be true that $KI > 0$—net capital inflows are positive.) Is a low national saving rate also consistent with the existence of net capital inflows? The answer is yes. A country with a low national saving rate will not have sufficient savings of its own to finance domestic investment. Thus there likely will be many good investment opportunities in the country available to foreign savers, leading to capital inflows. Equivalently, a shortage of domestic saving will tend to drive up the domestic real interest rate, which attracts capital flows from abroad.

We conclude that a low rate of national saving tends to create a trade deficit, as well as to promote the capital inflows that must accompany a trade deficit. Economic Naturalist 28.3 illustrates this effect for the case of the United States.

Why is the U.S. trade deficit so large?

As shown by Figure 28.9, U.S. trade was more or less in balance until the mid-1970s. Since the late 1970s, however, the United States has run large trade deficits, particularly in the mid-1980s and the latter part of the 1990s. Indeed, in 1999 the trade deficit equaled 2.8 percent of U.S. GDP. Why is the U.S. trade deficit so large?

Figure 28.14 shows national saving, investment, and the trade balance for the United States from 1960 to 1999 (all measured relative to GDP). Note that the trade balance has been negative since the late 1970s, indicating a trade deficit. Note also that trade deficits correspond to periods in which investment exceeds national saving, as required by Equation 28.3.

ECONOMIC NATURALIST 28.3

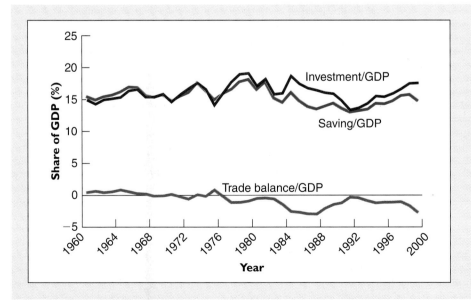

FIGURE 28.14
National Saving, Investment, and the Trade Balance in the United States, 1960–1990. Since the 1970s U.S. national saving has fallen below domestic investment, implying a significant trade deficit. [SOURCE: *Economic Report of the President* (www.access.gpo.gov/eop/index.html) and authors' calculations.]

U.S. national saving and investment were roughly in balance in the 1960s and early 1970s, and hence the U.S. trade balance was close to zero during that period. However, U.S. national saving fell sharply during the late 1970s and 1980s. One factor that contributed to the decline in national saving was the large government deficits of the era (see Chapter 22). Because investment did not decline as much as saving, the U.S. trade deficit ballooned in the 1980s, coming under control only when investment fell during the recession of 1990–1991. Saving and investment both recovered during the 1990s, but in the latter part of the 1990s national saving dropped again. This time the federal government was not at fault, since its budget showed a healthy surplus. Rather, the fall in national saving reflected a decline in private saving, the result of a powerful upsurge in consumption spending. Much of the increase in consumption spending was for imported goods and services, which pushed the trade deficit to record levels.

Is the U.S. trade deficit a problem? The trade deficit implies that the United States is relying heavily on foreign savings to finance its domestic capital formation (net capital inflows). These foreign loans must ultimately be repaid with interest. If the foreign savings are well invested and the U.S. economy continues to grow, repayment will not pose a problem. However, if economic growth in the U.S. slackens, repaying the foreign lenders will impose an economic burden in the future.

"But we're not just talking about buying a car—we're talking about confronting this country's trade deficit with Japan."

■ SUMMARY ■

- According to the principle of comparative advantage, the best economic outcomes occur when each nation specializes in the goods and services at which it is relatively most productive and then trades with other nations to obtain the goods and services its citizens desire.

- The production possibilities curve (PPC) of a country is a graph that describes the maximum amount of one good that can be produced at every possible level of production of the other good. At any point the slope of a PPC indicates the opportunity cost, in terms of forgone production of the good on the vertical axis, of increasing production of the good on the horizontal axis by one unit. The more of a good that is already being produced, the greater the opportunity cost of increasing production still further. Thus the slope of a PPC becomes more and more negative as we read from left to right. When an economy has many workers, the PPC has a smooth, outwardly bowed shape.

- A country's *consumption possibilities* are the combinations of goods and services that might feasibly be consumed by its citizens. In a *closed economy*—one that does not trade with other countries—the citizens' consumption possibilities are identical to their production possibilities. But in an *open economy* that does trade with other countries, consumption possibilities are typically greater than, and never less than, the economy's production possibilities. Graphically, an open economy's consumption possibilities are described by a downward-sloping line that just touches the PPC, whose slope equals the amount of the good on the vertical axis that must be traded to obtain one unit of the good on the horizontal axis. A country achieves its highest consumption possibilities by producing at the point where the consumption possibilities line touches the PPC and then trading to obtain the most preferred point on the consumption possibilities line.

- In a closed economy, the relative price of a good or service is determined at the intersection of the supply curve of domestic producers and the demand curve of domestic consumers. In an open economy, the relative price of a good or service equals the world price—the price determined by supply and demand in the world economy. If the price of a good or service in a closed economy is greater than the world price, and the country opens its market to trade, it will become a net importer of that good or service. But if the closed-economy price is below the world price, and the country opens itself to trade, it will become a net exporter of that good or service.

- Although free trade is beneficial to the economy as a whole, some groups—such as domestic producers of imported goods—are hurt by free trade. Groups that are hurt by trade may be able to induce the government to impose *protectionist* measures, such as tariffs or quotas. A *tariff* is a tax on an imported good that has the effect of raising the domestic price of the good. A higher domestic price increases domestic supply, reduces domestic demand, and reduces imports of the good. A *quota*, which is a legal limit on the amount of a good that may be imported, has the same effects as a tariff, except that the government collects no tax revenue. (The equivalent amount of revenue goes instead to those firms with the legal authority to import goods.) Because free trade is efficient, the winners from free trade should be able to compensate the losers so that everyone becomes better off. Thus policies to assist those who are harmed by trade, such as assistance and retraining for workers idled by imports, are usually preferable to trade restrictions.

- The *trade balance,* or net exports, is the value of a country's exports less the value of its imports in a particular period. Exports need not equal imports in each period. If exports exceed imports, the difference is called a *trade surplus,* and if imports exceed exports, the difference is called a *trade deficit.* Trade takes place in assets as well as goods and services. Purchases of domestic assets (real or financial) by foreigners are called *capital inflows,* and purchases of foreign assets by domestic savers are called *capital outflows.* Because imports that are not financed by sales of exports must be financed by sales of assets, the trade balance and net capital inflows sum to zero.

- The higher the real interest rate in a country, and the lower the risk of investing there, the higher its capital inflows. The availability of capital inflows expands a country's pool of saving, allowing for more domestic investment and increased growth. A drawback to using capital inflows to finance domestic capital formation is that the returns to capital (interest and dividends) accrue to foreign financial investors rather than domestic residents.

- A low rate of national saving is the primary cause of trade deficits. A low-saving, high-spending country is likely to import more than a high-saving country. It also consumes more of its domestic production, leaving less for export. Finally, a low-saving country is likely to have a high real interest rate, which attracts net capital inflows. Because the sum of the trade balance and capital inflows is zero, a high level of net capital inflows is consistent with a large trade deficit.

■ KEY TERMS ■

autarky (772)	international capital flows (788)	trade balance (787)
capital inflows (788)	open economy (767)	trade deficit (787)
capital outflows (788)	protectionism (780)	trade surplus (787)
closed economy (767)	quota (780)	world price (778)
consumption possibilities (771)	tariff (780)	

■ REVIEW QUESTIONS ■

1. Sketch a PPC for a four-worker economy that produces two goods, hot dogs and hamburgers. Give an economic interpretation of the vertical intercept, the horizontal intercept, and the slope of the graph at various points.

2. What is meant by the *consumption possibilities* of a country? How are consumption possibilities related to production possibilities in a closed economy? In an open economy?

3. A small open economy is equally productive in producing coffee and tea. What will this economy produce if the world price of coffee is twice that of tea? Half that of tea? What will the country produce if the world price of coffee happens to equal the world price of tea?

4. True or false, and explain: If a country is more productive in every sector than a neighboring country, then there is no benefit in trading with the neighboring country.

5. Show graphically the effects of a tariff on imported automobiles on the domestic market for automobiles. Who is hurt by the tariff, and why? Who benefits, and why?

6. Show graphically the effects of a quota on imported automobiles on the domestic market for automobiles. Who does the quota hurt, and who benefits? Explain.

7. Explain with examples why, in any period, a country's net capital inflows equal its trade deficit.

8. How would increased political instability in a country likely affect capital inflows, the domestic real interest rate, and investment in new capital goods? Show graphically.

■ PROBLEMS ■

1. An economy has two workers, Anne and Bill. Per day of work, Anne can produce 100 apples or 25 bananas, and Bill can produce 50 apples or 50 bananas. Anne and Bill each work 200 days per year.
   a. Which worker has an absolute advantage in apples? Which has a comparative advantage? Calculate each worker's opportunity cost of producing an additional apple.
   b. Find the maximum number of each type of fruit that can be produced annually in this economy, assuming that none of the other type of fruit is produced. What is the most of each type that can be produced if each worker fully specializes according to his or her comparative advantage?
   c. Draw the PPC for annual production in this economy. Show numerical values for the vertical intercept, the horizontal intercept, and the slopes of each segment of the PPC.

2. A developing economy requires 1,000 hours of work to produce a television set and 10 hours of work to produce a bushel of corn. This economy has available a total of 1,000,000 hours of work per day.
   a. Draw the PPC for daily output of the developing economy. Give numerical values for the PPC's vertical intercept, horizontal intercept, and slope. Relate the slope to the developing country's opportunity cost of producing each good. If this economy does not trade, what are its consumption possibilities?
   b. The developing economy is considering opening trade with a much larger, industrialized economy. The industrialized economy requires 10 hours of work to produce a television set and 1 hour of work to produce a bushel of corn. Show graphically how trading with the industrialized economy affects the developing economy's consumption possibilities. Is opening trade desirable for the developing economy? (*Hint:* When it opens to trade, the developing economy will be fully specialized in one product.)

3. Modifying Example 28.1, suppose that Brazilian worker Carlos can produce either 100 pounds of coffee or one computer per week, and a second worker, Maria, can produce either 150 pounds of coffee or one computer per week. Both Carlos and Maria work 50 weeks per year.
   a. Find the PPC for Brazil. Give numerical values for the graph's intercepts and slopes. How much of each good is produced if each worker fully specializes according to comparative advantage?
   b. World prices are such that one computer trades for 125 pounds of coffee on international markets. If Brazil is open to trade, show Brazil's consumption possibilities graphically. What is the most of each good that Brazilians can consume when the economy is open? Compare to the situation when the economy is closed.
   c. Repeat part b under the assumption that one computer trades for 80 pounds of coffee on world markets.

4. Suppose that Carlos and Maria can produce coffee and computers as described in Problem 3. A third worker, Pedro, joins the Brazilian economy. Pedro can produce either 140 pounds of coffee or one computer per week. Like the other two workers, Pedro works 50 weeks per year.
   a. Find the PPC for Brazil. Give numerical values of the PPC's intercepts and slopes.
   b. Find Brazil's consumption possibilities if the country is open and one computer trades for 125 pounds of coffee on world markets. What is the most of each good that Brazilians can consume when the economy is open? Compare to the situation when the economy is closed.
   c. Repeat part b, assuming that one computer trades for 200 pounds of coffee on world markets.

5. Suppose that a U.S. worker can produce 1,000 pairs of shoes or 10 industrial robots per year. For simplicity, assume there are no costs other than labor costs and firms earn zero profits. Initially, the U.S. economy is closed. The domestic price of shoes is $30 per pair, so a U.S. worker can earn $30,000 annually by working in the shoe industry. The domestic price of a robot is $3,000, so a U.S. worker can also earn $30,000 annually working in the robot industry.

Now suppose that the U.S. opens trade with the rest of the world. Foreign workers can produce 500 pairs of shoes or one robot per year. The world price of shoes after the U.S. opens its markets is $10 per pair, and the world price of robots is $5,000.
a. What do foreign workers earn annually, in dollars?
b. When it opens to trade, which good will the United States import and which will it export?
c. Find the real income of U.S. workers after the opening to trade, measured in (1) the number of pairs of shoes annual worker income will buy and (2) the number of robots annual worker income will buy. Compare to the situation before the opening of trade. Does trading in goods produced by "cheap foreign labor" hurt U.S. workers?
d. How might your conclusion in part c be modified in the short term, if it is costly for workers to change industries? What policy response might help with this problem?

6. The demand for automobiles in a certain country is given by

$$D = 12,000 - 200P,$$

where P is the price of a car. Supply by domestic automobile producers is

$$S = 7,000 + 50P.$$

a. Assuming that the economy is closed, find the equilibrium price and production of automobiles.
b. The economy opens to trade. The world price of automobiles is 18. Find the domestic quantities demanded and supplied and the quantity of imports or exports. Who will favor the opening of the automobile market to trade, and who will oppose it?
c. The government imposes a tariff of 1 unit per car. Find the effects on domestic quantities demanded and supplied and on the quantity of imports or exports. Also find the revenue raised by the tariff. Who will favor the imposition of the tariff, and who will oppose it?
d. Can the government obtain the same results as you found in part c by imposing a quota on automobile imports? Explain.

7. Suppose the domestic demand and supply for automobiles is as given by Problem 6. The world price of automobiles is 16. Foreign car firms have a production cost of 15 per automobile, so they earn a profit of 1 per car.
a. How many cars will be imported, assuming this country trades freely?
b. Now suppose foreign car producers are asked "voluntarily" to limit their exports to the home country to half of free-trade levels. What will be the equilibrium price of cars in the domestic market if foreign producers comply? Find domestic quantities of cars supplied and demanded.
c. How will the "voluntary" export restriction affect the profits of foreign car producers?

8. From the web site of the Bureau of Economic Analysis, www.bea.doc.gov, find data on the components of nominal GDP for the most recent quarter available and for the previous two complete years. Find net exports, national saving (which can be derived from the relationship $S = Y - C - G$), and gross private domestic investment for the period, and verify that they satisfy the relationship $S - I = NX$. How has the U.S. trade balance changed over the past 2 years as a percentage of GDP? Are the changes attributable to changes in the national saving rate, the rate of investment, or both?

9. How do each of the following transactions affect (1) the trade surplus or deficit and (2) capital inflows or outflows for the United States? Show that in each case the identity that the trade balance plus net capital inflows equals zero applies.
a. A U.S. exporter sells software to Israel. She uses the Israeli shekels received to buy stock in an Israeli company.
b. A Mexican firm uses proceeds from its sale of oil to the United States to buy U.S. government debt.

    c. A Mexican firm uses proceeds from its sale of oil to the United States to buy oil drilling equipment from a U.S. firm.

    d. A Mexican firm receives U.S. dollars from selling oil to the United States. A French firm accepts the dollars as payment for drilling equipment. The French firm uses the dollars to buy U.S. government debt.

    e. A British financial investor writes a check on his bank account in New York to purchase shares of General Motors stock (GM is a U.S. company).

10. A country's domestic supply of saving, domestic demand for saving for purposes of capital formation, and supply of net capital inflows are given by the following equations:

$$S = 1,500 + 2,000r,$$

$$I = 2,000 - 4,000r,$$

$$KI = -100 + 6,000r.$$

    a. Assuming that the market for saving and investment is in equilibrium, find national saving, capital inflows, domestic investment, and the real interest rate.

    b. Repeat part a, assuming that desired national saving declines by 120 at each value of the real interest rate. What effect does a reduction in domestic saving have on capital inflows?

    c. Concern about the economy's macroeconomic policies causes capital inflows to fall sharply so that now $KI = -700 + 6,000r$. Repeat part a. What does a reduction in capital inflows do to domestic investment and the real interest rate?

■ ANSWERS TO IN-CHAPTER EXERCISES ■

28.1 The opportunity cost of producing coffee equals the number of computers given up for each extra pound of coffee produced. Carlos can produce either 100 pounds of coffee or 1 computer per week, so his opportunity cost is given by

$$\frac{\text{Loss in computers}}{\text{Gain in coffee}} = \frac{-1 \text{ Computer/week}}{100 \text{ Pounds coffee/week}},$$

$$= \frac{-1/100 \text{ Computer}}{\text{Pound coffee}}.$$

Maria can produce either 100 pounds of coffee or 2 computers per week, so her opportunity cost is

$$\frac{\text{Loss in computers}}{\text{Gain in coffee}} = \frac{-2 \text{ Computer/week}}{100 \text{ Pounds coffee/week}},$$

$$= \frac{-1/50 \text{ Computer}}{\text{Pound coffee}}.$$

Since each pound of coffee Carlos produces requires the sacrifice of 1/100 of a computer, while each pound of coffee produced by Maria sacrifices 1/50 of a computer, Carlos has the smaller opportunity cost of producing coffee. Thus he has a comparative advantage in producing coffee.

28.2 When the economy is closed, the Brazilians can obtain 80 computers by having Maria work 40 weeks making computers. If Maria works the remaining 10 weeks producing coffee and Carlos works 50 weeks producing coffee, the Brazilians will be able to consume $(10 + 50) \times 100 = 6,000$ pounds of coffee per year.

    The world price of computers is 80 pounds of coffee, which is greater than Maria's opportunity cost of producing computers but less than Carlos's opportunity cost. Thus if the economy opens to trade, Maria will specialize in computers and Carlos will specialize in coffee. If Maria produces 100 computers, 80 of which are consumed domestically, 20 computers are available for export. Because a computer is worth 80 pounds of coffee on the world market, the 20 exported computers can be traded for 1,600 pounds of coffee. Carlos still produces 5,000 pounds of coffee. Total coffee consumption in Brazil is thus 1,600 + 5,000 pounds = 6,600 pounds. Opening to trade has allowed the Brazilians to consume 10 percent more coffee at no sacrifice in computers.

28.3 If the world price of computers is 1,200, domestic demand for computers is 3,000 − 0.5(1,200), or 2,400 computers. Domestic supply is 1,000 + 0.5(1,200), or 1,600 computers. The difference between the quantity demanded and the quantity supplied, 800 computers, is imported.

A tariff of 300 raises the domestic price of computers to 1,500. Now domestic demand is 3,000 − 0.5(1,500), or 2,250, and domestic supply is 1,000 + 0.5(1,500), or 1,750. The difference, 500 computers, equals imports. Revenue for the government is 300 per computer times 500 imported computers, or 150,000.

If the world price of computers is 1,800 and there is no tariff, domestic demand is 3,000 − 0.5(1,800), or 2,100; domestic supply is 1,000 + 0.5(1,800), or 1,900; and imports are 200. A tariff of 300 raises the world price to 2,100, which is greater than the domestic price when there is no trade (2,000). No computers are imported in this case, and no tariff revenue is raised.

28.4 The purchase of the Japanese bond is a capital outflow for the United States, or $KI = -\$20,000$. The Japanese government now holds $20,000. What will it do with these funds? There are basically three possibilities. First, it might use the funds to purchase U.S. goods and services (military equipment, for example). In that case the U.S. trade balance equals +$20,000, and the sum of the trade balance and capital inflows is zero. Second, the Japanese government might acquire U.S. assets, for example, deposits in U.S. banks. In that case a capital inflow to the United States of $20,000 offsets the original capital outflow. Both the trade balance and net capital outflows individually are zero, and so their sum is zero.

Finally, the Japanese government might use the $20,000 to purchase non-U.S. goods, services, or assets—oil from Saudi Arabia, for example. But then the non-U.S. recipient of the $20,000 is holding the funds, and it has the same options that the Japanese government did. Eventually, the funds will be used to purchase U.S. goods, services, or assets, satisfying Equation 28.1. Indeed, even if the recipient holds onto the funds (in cash, or as a U.S. bank deposit), they would still count as a capital inflow to the United States, as U.S. dollars or an account in a U.S. bank are U.S. assets acquired by foreigners.

28.5 An increase in the real interest rate abroad increases the relative attractiveness of foreign financial investments to both foreign and domestic savers. Net capital inflows to the home country will fall at each level of the domestic real interest rate. The supply curve of net capital inflows shifts left, as in Figure 28.12.

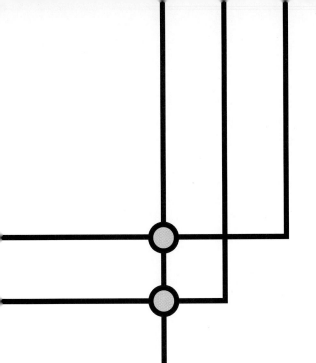

CHAPTER

29

EXCHANGE RATES
AND THE OPEN ECONOMY

■

Two Americans visiting London were commiserating over their problems understanding English currency. "Pounds, shillings, tuppence, thruppence, bob, and quid, it's driving me crazy," said the first American. "This morning it took me twenty minutes to figure out how much to pay the taxi driver."

The second American was more upbeat. "Actually," he said, "since I adopted my new system, I haven't had any problems at all."

The first American looked interested. "What's your new system?"

"Well," replied the second, "now, whenever I take a taxi, I just give the driver all the English money I have. And would you believe it, I have got the fare exactly right every time!"

Dealing with unfamiliar currencies—and translating the value of foreign money into dollars—is a problem every international traveler faces. The traveler's problem is complicated by the fact that *exchange rates*—the rates at which one country's money trades for another—may change unpredictably. Thus the number of British pounds, Russian rubles, Japanese yen, or Australian dollars that a U.S. dollar can buy may vary over time, sometimes quite a lot.

The economic consequences of variable exchange rates are much broader than their impact on travel and tourism, however. For example, the competitiveness of U.S. exports depends in part on the prices of U.S. goods in terms of foreign currencies, which in turn depend on the exchange rate between the U.S. dollar and those currencies. Likewise, the prices Americans pay for imported goods depend in part on the value of the dollar relative to

the currencies of the countries that produce those goods. Exchange rates also affect the value of financial investments made across national borders. For countries that are heavily dependent on trade and international capital flows—the majority of the world's nations—fluctuations in the exchange rate may have a significant economic impact.

This chapter discusses exchange rates and the role they play in open economies. We will start by distinguishing between the *nominal exchange rate*—the rate at which one national currency trades for another—and the *real exchange rate*—the rate at which one country's goods trade for another's. We will show how exchange rates affect the prices of exports and imports, and thus the pattern of trade.

Next we will turn to the question of how exchange rates are determined. Exchange rates may be divided into two broad categories, flexible and fixed. The value of a *flexible* exchange rate is determined freely in the market for national currencies, known as the *foreign exchange market*. Flexible exchange rates vary continually with changes in the supply of and demand for national currencies. In contrast, the value of a *fixed* exchange rate is set by the government at a constant level. Because most large industrial countries, including the United States, have a flexible exchange rate, we will focus on that case first. We will see that a country's monetary policy plays a particularly important role in determining the exchange rate. Furthermore, in an open economy with a flexible exchange rate, the exchange rate becomes a tool of monetary policy, in much the same way as the real interest rate.

Although most large industrial countries have a flexible exchange rate, many small and developing economies fix their exchange rates, so we will consider the case of fixed exchange rates as well. We will explain first how a country's government (usually, its central bank) goes about maintaining a fixed exchange rate at the officially determined level. Though fixing the exchange rate generally reduces day-to-day fluctuations in the value of a nation's currency, we will see that, at times, a fixed exchange rate can become severely unstable, with potentially serious economic consequences. We will close the chapter by discussing the relative merits of fixed and flexible exchange rates.

EXCHANGE RATES

The economic benefits of trade between nations in goods, services, and assets are similar to the benefits of trade within a nation. In both cases, trade in goods and services permits greater specialization and efficiency, whereas trade in assets allows financial investors to earn higher returns while providing funds for worthwhile capital projects. However, there is a difference between the two cases, which is that trade in goods, services, and assets *within* a nation normally involves a single currency—dollars, yen, pesos, or whatever the country's official form of money happens to be—whereas trade *between* nations usually involves dealing in different currencies. So, for example, if an American resident wants to purchase an automobile manufactured in South Korea, she (or more likely, the automobile dealer) must first trade dollars for the Korean currency, called the won. The Korean car manufacturer is then paid in won. Similarly, an Argentine who wants to purchase shares in a U.S. company (a U.S. financial asset) must first trade his Argentine pesos for dollars and then use the dollars to purchase the shares.

NOMINAL EXCHANGE RATES

Because international transactions generally require that one currency be traded for another, the relative values of different currencies are an important factor in international economic relations. The rate at which two currencies can be traded for each other is called the **nominal exchange rate,** or more simply the *exchange rate,* between the two currencies. For example, if one U.S. dollar can be exchanged for 110 Japanese yen, the nominal exchange rate between the U.S. and Japanese currencies is 110 yen/dollar. Since 1991 Argentina has set the value of its currency so that it trades one-for-one with the U.S. dollar. That is, the nominal exchange rate between the Argentine peso and the dollar is 1.00 Argentine peso/dollar. Each country has many nominal exchange rates, one corresponding to each currency against which its own currency is traded. Thus the dollar's value can be quoted in terms of English pounds, Swedish kroner, Israeli shekels, Russian rubles, or dozens of other currencies. Table 29.1 gives exchange rates between the dollar and six other important currencies as of the close of business in New York City on February 8, 2000.

nominal exchange rate the rate at which two currencies can be traded for each other

TABLE 29.1
Nominal Exchange Rates for the U.S. Dollar

Country	Foreign currency/dollar	Dollar/foreign currency
United Kingdom (pound)	0.6208	1.6108
Canada (Canadian dollar)	1.4463	0.6914
Mexico (peso)	9.3970	0.1064
Japan (yen)	109.35	0.00914
Switzerland (Swiss franc)	1.6295	0.6137
South Korea (won)	1,129.20	0.00089

SOURCE: *The New York Times* and *The Wall Street Journal,* Feb. 9, 2000.

As Table 29.1 shows, exchange rates can be expressed either as the amount of foreign currency needed to purchase one dollar (left column) or as the number of dollars needed to purchase one unit of the foreign currency (right column). These two ways of expressing the exchange rate are equivalent: Each is the reciprocal of the other. For example, on February 8, 2000, the U.S.-Canadian exchange rate could have been expressed either as 1.4463 Canadian dollars per U.S. dollar or as 0.6914 U.S. dollars per Canadian dollar, where 0.6914 = 1/1.4463.

Nominal exchange rates

EXAMPLE 29.1

Based on Table 29.1, find the exchange rate between the British and Canadian currencies. Express the exchange rate in both Canadian dollars per pound and pounds per Canadian dollar.

From Table 29.1, we see that 0.6208 British pounds will buy a U.S. dollar, and that 1.4463 Canadian dollars will buy a U.S. dollar. Therefore 0.6208 British pounds and 1.4463 Canadian dollars are equal in value:

0.6208 pounds = 1.4463 Canadian dollars.

Dividing both sides of this equation by 1.4463, we get

0.4292 pounds = 1 Canadian dollar.

In other words, the British-Canadian exchange rate can be expressed as 0.4292 pounds per Canadian dollar. Alternatively, the exchange rate can be expressed as 1/0.4292 = 2.33 Canadian dollars per pound.

EXERCISE 29.1

From the business section of the newspaper or an online source (try the Federal Reserve Bank of St. Louis FRED database, www.stls.frb.org/fred/ data/exchange.html), find recent quotations of the value of the U.S. dollar against the British pound, the Canadian dollar, and the Japanese yen. Based on these data find the exchange rate (a) between the pound and the Canadian dollar and (b) between the Canadian dollar and the yen. Express the exchange rates you derive in two ways (e.g., both as pounds per Canadian dollar and as Canadian dollars per pound).

Figure 29.1 shows the nominal exchange rate for the U.S. dollar for 1973 to 2000. Rather than showing the value of the dollar relative to that of an individual foreign currency, such as the Japanese yen or the British pound, the figure expresses the value of the dollar as an average of its values against other major currencies. This average value of the dollar is measured relative to a base value of 100 in 1973. So, for example, a value of 120 for the dollar in a particular year implies that the dollar was 20 percent more valuable in that year, relative to other major currencies, than it was in 1973.

You can see from Figure 29.1 that the dollar's value has fluctuated over time, sometimes increasing (as in the period 1980–1985) and sometimes decreasing (as in 1985–1987). An increase in the value of a currency relative to other currencies is known as an **appreciation**; a decline in the value of a currency relative to other currencies is called a **depreciation**. So we can say that the dollar appreciated in 1980–1985 and depreciated in 1985–1987. We will discuss the reasons a currency may appreciate or depreciate later in this chapter.

appreciation an increase in the value of a currency relative to other currencies

depreciation a decrease in the value of a currency relative to other currencies

In this chapter we will use the symbol e to stand for a country's nominal exchange rate. Although the exchange rate can be expressed either as foreign currency units per unit of domestic currency, or vice versa, as we saw in Table 29.1, let's agree to define e as *the number of units of the foreign currency that the domestic currency will buy.* For example, if we treat the United States as the "home" or "domestic" country and Japan as the "foreign" country, e will be defined as the number of Japanese yen that one dollar will buy. Defining the nominal exchange rate this way implies that an *increase* in e corresponds to an *appreciation*, or a strengthening, of the home currency, while a *decrease* in e implies a *depreciation*, or weakening, of the home currency.

FIGURE 29.1
The U.S. Nominal Exchange Rate, 1973–2000.

This figure expresses the value of the dollar from 1973 to 2000 as an average of its values against other major currencies, relative to a base value of 100 in 1973. [SOURCE: Federal Reserve Bank of St. Louis, FRED database, (www.stls.frb.org/fred/data/exchange.html).]

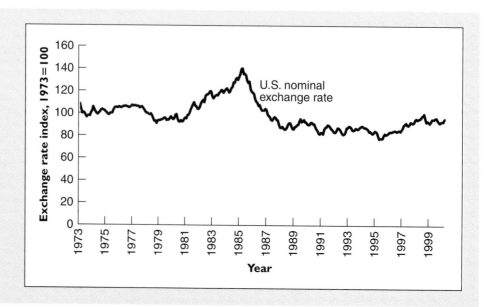

"On the foreign-exchange markets today, the dollar fell against all major currencies and the doughnut."

FLEXIBLE VERSUS FIXED EXCHANGE RATES

As we saw in Figure 29.1, the exchange rate between the U.S. dollar and other currencies isn't constant but varies continually. Indeed, changes in the value of the dollar occur daily, hourly, even minute by minute. Such fluctuations in the value of a currency are normal for countries like the United States, which have a *flexible* or *floating exchange rate*. The value of a **flexible exchange rate** is not officially fixed but varies according to the supply and demand for the currency in the **foreign exchange market**—the market on which currencies of various nations are traded for one another. We will discuss the factors that determine the supply and demand for currencies shortly.

Some countries do not allow their currency values to vary with market conditions but instead maintain a *fixed exchange rate*. The value of a **fixed exchange rate** is set by official government policy. (A government that establishes a fixed exchange rate typically determines the exchange rate's value independently, but sometimes exchange rates are set according to an agreement among a number of governments.) Some countries fix their exchange rates in terms of the U.S. dollar (Argentina, for example), but there are other possibilities. Some French-speaking African countries have traditionally fixed the value of their currencies in terms of the French franc. Under the gold standard, which many countries used until its collapse during the Great Depression, currency values were fixed in terms of ounces of gold. In the next part of the chapter we will focus on flexible exchange rates, but we will return later to the case of fixed rates. We will also discuss the costs and benefits of each type of exchange rate.

flexible exchange rate an exchange rate whose value is not officially fixed but varies according to the supply and demand for the currency in the foreign exchange market

foreign exchange market the market on which currencies of various nations are traded for one another.

fixed exchange rate an exchange rate whose value is set by official government policy

THE REAL EXCHANGE RATE

The nominal exchange rate tells us the price of the domestic currency in terms of a foreign currency. As we will see in this section, the *real exchange rate* tells us the price of the average domestic *good or service* in terms of the average foreign *good or service*. We will also see that a country's real exchange rate has important implications for its ability to sell its exports abroad.

To provide background for discussing the real exchange rate, imagine you are in charge of purchasing for a U.S. corporation that is planning to acquire a large number of new computers. The company's computer specialist has identified two models, one Japanese-made and one U.S.-made, that meet the necessary specifications. Since the two models are essentially equivalent, the company will buy the one with the lower price. However, since the computers are priced in the currencies of the countries of manufacture, the price comparison is not so straightforward. Your mission—should you decide to accept it—is to determine which of the two models is cheaper.

To complete your assignment you will need two pieces of information: the nominal exchange rate between the dollar and the yen and the prices of the two models in terms of the currencies of their countries of manufacture. Example 29.2 shows how you can use this information to determine which model is cheaper.

EXAMPLE 29.2

Comparing prices expressed in different currencies

A U.S.-made computer costs $2,400, and a similar Japanese-made computer costs 242,000 yen. If the nominal exchange rate is 110 yen per dollar, which computer is the better buy?

To make this price comparison, we must measure the prices of both computers in terms of the same currency. To make the comparison in dollars, we first convert the Japanese computer's price into dollars. The price in terms of Japanese yen is ¥242,000 (the symbol ¥ means "yen"), and we are told that ¥110 = $1. To find the dollar price of the computer, then, we observe that for any good or service,

$$\text{Price in yen} = \text{Price in dollars} \times \text{Value of dollar in terms of yen}$$

Note that the value of a dollar in terms of yen is just the yen-dollar exchange rate. Making this substitution and solving, we get

$$\text{Price in dollars} = \frac{\text{Price in yen}}{\text{Yen-dollar exchange rate}},$$

$$= \frac{¥242,000}{¥110/\$1} = \$2,200.$$

Notice that the yen symbol appears in both the numerator and the denominator of the ratio, so it cancels out. Our conclusion is that the Japanese computer is cheaper than the U.S. computer at $2,200, or $200 less than the price of the U.S. computer, $2,400. The Japanese computer is the better deal.

EXERCISE 29.2

Continuing Example 29.2, compare the prices of the Japanese and American computers by expressing both prices in terms of yen.

In Example 29.2, the fact that the Japanese computer was cheaper implied that your firm would choose it over the U.S.-made computer. In general, a country's ability to compete in international markets depends in part on the prices of its goods and services *relative* to the prices of foreign goods and services, when the prices are measured in a common currency. In the hypothetical example of the Japanese and U.S. computers, the price of the domestic (U.S.) good relative to the price of the foreign (Japanese) good is $2,400/$2,200, or 1.09. So the U.S. computer is 9 percent more expensive than the Japanese computer, putting the U.S. product at a competitive disadvantage.

More generally, economists ask whether *on average* the goods and services produced by a particular country are expensive relative to the goods and services produced by other countries. This question can be answered by the country's *real exchange rate*. Specifically, a country's **real exchange rate** is the price of the average domestic good or service *relative* to the price of the average foreign good or service, when prices are expressed in terms of a common currency.

real exchange rate the price of the average domestic good or service *relative* to the price of the average foreign good or service, when prices are expressed in terms of a common currency

To obtain a formula for the real exchange rate, recall that e equals the nominal exchange rate (the number of units of foreign currency per dollar) and that P equals the domestic price level, as measured, for example, by the consumer price index. We will use P as a measure of the price of the "average" domestic good or service. Similarly, let P^f equal the foreign price level. We will use P^f as the measure of the price of the "average" foreign good or service.

The real exchange rate equals the price of the average domestic good or service relative to the price of the average foreign good or service. It would not be correct, however, to define the real exchange rate as the ratio P/P^f, because the two price levels are expressed in different currencies. As we saw in Example 29.2, to convert foreign prices into dollars, we must divide the foreign price by the exchange rate. By this rule, the price in dollars of the average foreign good or service equals P^f/e. Now we can write the real exchange rate as

$$\text{Real exchange rate} = \frac{\text{Price of domestic good}}{\text{Price of foreign good, in dollars}},$$

$$= \frac{P}{P^f/e}.$$

To simplify this expression, multiply the numerator and denominator by e to get

$$\text{Real exchange rate} = \frac{eP}{P^f}, \tag{29.1}$$

which is the formula for the real exchange rate.

To check this formula, let's use it to re-solve the computer example, Example 29.2. (For this exercise, we imagine that computers are the only good produced by the United States and Japan, so the real exchange rate becomes just the price of U.S. computers relative to Japanese computers.) In that example, the nominal exchange rate e was ¥110/\$1, the domestic price P (of a computer) was \$2,400, and the foreign price P^f was ¥242,000. Applying Equation 29.1, we get

$$\text{Real exchange rate (for computers)} = \frac{(¥110/\$1) \times \$2,400}{¥242,000},$$

$$= \frac{¥264,000}{¥242,000},$$

$$= 1.09,$$

which is the same answer we got earlier.

The real exchange rate, an overall measure of the cost of domestic goods relative to foreign goods, is an important economic variable. As Example 29.2 suggests, when the real exchange rate is high, domestic goods are on average more expensive than foreign goods (when priced in the same currency). A high real exchange rate implies that domestic producers will have difficulty exporting to other countries (domestic goods will be "overpriced"), while foreign goods will sell well in the home country (because imported goods are cheap relative to goods produced at home). Since a high real exchange rate tends to reduce exports and increase imports, we conclude that *net exports will tend to be low when the real exchange rate is high*. Conversely, if the real exchange rate is low, then the home country will find it easier to export (because its goods are priced below those of foreign competitors), while domestic residents will buy fewer imports (because imports are expensive relative to domestic goods). *Thus net exports will tend to be high when the real exchange rate is low.*

Equation 29.1 also shows that the real exchange rate tends to move in the same direction as the nominal exchange rate *e* (since *e* appears in the numerator of the formula for the real exchange rate). To the extent that real and nominal exchange rates move in the same direction, we can conclude that net exports will be hurt by a high nominal exchange rate and helped by a low nominal exchange rate.

Does a strong currency imply a strong economy?

Politicians and the public sometimes take pride in the fact that their national currency is "strong," meaning that its value in terms of other currencies is high or rising. Likewise, policymakers sometimes view a depreciating ("weak") currency as a sign of economic failure. Does a strong currency necessarily imply a strong economy?

Contrary to popular impression, there is no simple connection between the strength of a country's currency and the strength of its economy. For example, Figure 29.1 shows that the value of the U.S. dollar relative to other major currencies was greater in the year 1973 than in the year 2000, though U.S. economic performance was considerably better in 2000 than in 1973, a period of deep recession and rising inflation. Indeed, the one period shown in Figure 29.1 during which the dollar rose markedly in value, 1980–1985, was a time of recession and high unemployment in the United States.

One reason a strong currency does not necessarily imply a strong economy is that an appreciating currency (an increase in e) tends to raise the real exchange rate (equal to eP/P^f), which may hurt a country's net exports. For example, if the dollar strengthens against the yen (that is, if a dollar buys more yen than before), Japanese goods will become cheaper in terms of dollars. The result may be that Americans prefer to buy Japanese goods rather than goods produced at home. Likewise, a stronger dollar implies that each yen buys fewer dollars, so exported U.S. goods become more expensive to Japanese consumers. As U.S. goods become more expensive in terms of yen, the willingness of Japanese consumers to buy U.S. exports declines. A strong dollar may therefore imply lower sales and profits for U.S. industries that export, as well as for U.S. industries (like automobile manufacturers) that compete with foreign firms for the domestic U.S. market.

ECONOMIC NATURALIST 29.1

RECAP   EXCHANGE RATES

- The *nominal exchange rate* between two currencies is the rate at which the currencies can be traded for each other. More precisely, the nominal exchange rate *e* for any given country is the number of units of foreign currency that can be bought for one unit of the domestic currency.

- An *appreciation* is an increase in the value of a currency relative to other currencies (a rise in *e*); a *depreciation* is a decline in a currency's value (a fall in *e*).

- An exchange rate can be either *flexible*—meaning that it varies freely according to supply and demand for the currency in the foreign exchange market—or *fixed*, meaning that its value is fixed by official government policy.

- The *real exchange rate* is the price of the average domestic good or service *relative* to the price of the average foreign good or service, when prices are expressed in terms of a common currency. A useful formula for the real exchange rate is eP/P^f, where *e* is the nominal exchange rate, *P* is the domestic price level, and P^f is the foreign price level.

- An increase in the real exchange rate implies that domestic goods are becoming more expensive relative to foreign goods, which tends to reduce exports and stimulate imports. Conversely, a decline in the real exchange rate tends to increase net exports.

THE DETERMINATION OF THE EXCHANGE RATE

Countries that have flexible exchange rates, such as the United States, see the international values of their currencies change continually. What determines the value of the nominal exchange rate at any point in time? In this section we will try to answer this basic economic question. Again, our focus for the moment is on flexible exchange rates, whose values are determined by the foreign exchange market. Later in the chapter we discuss the case of fixed exchange rates.

A SIMPLE THEORY OF EXCHANGE RATES: PURCHASING POWER PARITY (PPP)

The most basic theory of how nominal exchange rates are determined is called *purchasing power parity,* or PPP. To understand this theory, we must first discuss a fundamental economic concept, called *the law of one price.* The **law of one price** states that if transportation costs are relatively small, the price of an internationally traded commodity must be the same in all locations. For example, if transportation costs are not too large, the price of a bushel of wheat ought to be the same in Bombay, India, and Sydney, Australia. Suppose that were not the case—that the price of wheat in Sydney were only half the price in Bombay. In that case grain merchants would have a strong incentive to buy wheat in Sydney and ship it to Bombay, where it could be sold at double the price of purchase. As wheat left Sydney, reducing the local supply, the price of wheat in Sydney would rise, while the inflow of wheat into Bombay would reduce the price in Bombay. According to the *equilibrium principle* (Chapter 4), the international market for wheat would return to equilibrium only when unexploited opportunities to profit had been eliminated—specifically, only when the prices of wheat in Sydney and in Bombay became equal or nearly equal (with the difference being less than the cost of transporting wheat from Australia to India).

> **law of one price** if transportation costs are relatively small, the price of an internationally traded commodity must be the same in all locations

If the law of one price were to hold for all goods and services (which is not a realistic assumption, as we will see shortly), then the value of the nominal exchange rate would be determined, as Example 29.3 illustrates.

EXAMPLE 29.3

How many Indian rupees equal one Australian dollar? (1)

Suppose that a bushel of grain costs 5 Australian dollars in Sydney and 150 rupees in Bombay. If the law of one price holds for grain, what is the nominal exchange rate between Australia and India?

Because the market value of a bushel of grain must be the same in both locations, we know that the Australian price of wheat must equal the Indian price of wheat so that

$$5 \text{ Australian dollars} = 150 \text{ Indian rupees.}$$

Dividing by 5, we get

$$1 \text{ Australian dollar} = 30 \text{ Indian rupees.}$$

So the nominal exchange rate between Australia and India should be 30 rupees per Australian dollar.

> **EXERCISE 29.3**
>
> **The price of gold is \$300/ounce in New York and 2,500 kronor/ounce in Stockholm, Sweden. If the law of one price holds for gold, what is the nominal exchange rate between the U.S. dollar and the Swedish krona?**

purchasing power parity (PPP) the theory that nominal exchange rates are determined as necessary for the law of one price to hold

Example 29.3 and Exercise 29.3 illustrate the application of the purchasing power parity theory. According to the **purchasing power parity (PPP)** theory, nominal exchange rates are determined as necessary for the law of one price to hold.

A particularly useful prediction of the PPP theory is that in the long run, the *currencies of countries that experience significant inflation will tend to depreciate.* To see why, we will extend the analysis in Example 29.3.

EXAMPLE 29.4

How many Indian rupees equal one Australian dollar? (2)

Suppose India experiences significant inflation so that the price of a bushel of grain in Bombay rises from 150 to 300 rupees. Australia has no inflation, so the price of grain in Sydney remains unchanged at 5 Australian dollars. If the law of one price holds for grain, what will happen to the nominal exchange rate between Australia and India?

As in Example 29.3, we know that the market value of a bushel of grain must be the same in both locations. Therefore,

$$5 \text{ Australian dollars} = 300 \text{ rupees.}$$

Equivalently,

$$1 \text{ Australian dollar} = 60 \text{ rupees.}$$

The nominal exchange rate is now 60 rupees/Australian dollar. Before India's inflation, the nominal exchange rate was 30 rupees/Australian dollar (Example 29.3). So in this example, inflation has caused the rupee to depreciate against the Australian dollar. Conversely, Australia, with no inflation, has seen its currency appreciate against the rupee.

This link between inflation and depreciation makes economic sense. Inflation implies that a nation's currency is losing purchasing power in the domestic market. Analogously, exchange rate depreciation implies that the nation's currency is losing purchasing power in international markets.

Figure 29.2 shows annual rates of inflation and nominal exchange rate depreciation for the 10 largest South American countries from 1992 to 1999. (Data for Brazil begin in 1994 because Brazil adopted a new currency in that year. Prior

FIGURE 29.2
Inflation and Currency Depreciation in South America, 1992–1999.
The annual rates of inflation and nominal exchange-rate depreciation (relative to the U.S. dollar) in 10 South American countries varied considerably during 1992–1999. (Data for Brazil are for 1994–1999.) High inflation was associated with rapid depreciation of the nominal exchange rate. (SOURCE: International Monetary Fund, *International Financial Statistics,* and authors' calculations.)

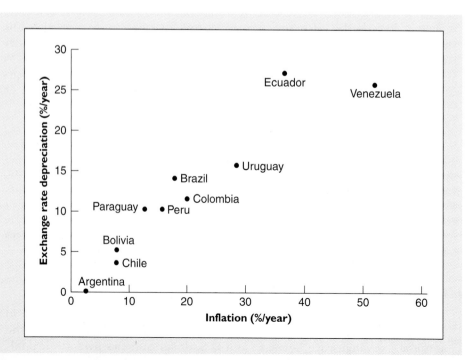

to 1994 Brazil experienced both very high inflation and rapid depreciation.) Inflation is measured as the annual rate of change in the country's consumer price index; depreciation is measured relative to the U.S. dollar. As you can see, inflation varied greatly among South American countries during the period. For example, Argentina's inflation rate was essentially the same as that of the United States, while Venezuela's was over 50 percent per year.

Figure 29.2 shows that, as the PPP theory implies, countries with higher inflation during the 1992–1999 period tended to experience the most rapid depreciation of their currencies.

SHORTCOMINGS OF THE PPP THEORY

Empirical studies have found that the PPP theory is useful for predicting changes in nominal exchange rates over the relatively long run. In particular, this theory helps to explain the tendency of countries with high inflation to experience depreciation of their exchange rates, as shown in Figure 29.2. However, the theory is less successful in predicting short-run movements in exchange rates.

A particularly dramatic failure of the PPP theory occurred in the United States in the early 1980s. As Figure 29.1 indicates, between 1980 and 1985 the value of the U.S. dollar rose nearly 50 percent relative to the currencies of U.S. trading partners. This strong appreciation was followed by an even more rapid depreciation during 1986 and 1987. PPP theory could explain this roller-coaster behavior only if inflation were far lower in the United States than in U.S. trading partners from 1980 to 1985, and far higher from 1986 to 1987. In fact, inflation was similar in the United States and its trading partners throughout both periods.

Why does the PPP theory work less well in the short run than the long run? Recall that this theory relies on the law of one price, which says that the price of an internationally traded commodity must be the same in all locations. The law of one price works well for goods such as grain or gold, which are standardized commodities that are traded widely. However, *not all goods and services are traded internationally,* and *not all goods are standardized commodities.*

Many goods and services are not traded internationally, because the assumption underlying the law of one price—that transportation costs are relatively small—does not hold for them. For example, for Indians to export haircuts to Australia, they would need to transport an Indian barber to Australia every time a Sydney resident desired a trim. Because transportation costs prevent haircuts from being traded internationally, the law of one price does not apply to them. Thus, even if the price of haircuts in Australia were double the price of haircuts in India, market forces would not necessarily force prices toward equality in the short run. (Over the long run, some Indian barbers might emigrate to Australia.) Other examples of nontraded goods and services are agricultural land, buildings, heavy construction materials (whose value is low relative to their transportation costs), and highly perishable foods. In addition, some products use nontraded goods and services as inputs: A McDonald's hamburger served in Moscow has both a tradable component (frozen hamburger patties) and a nontradable component (the labor of counter workers). In general, the greater the share of nontraded goods and services in a nation's output, the less precisely the PPP theory will apply to the country's exchange rate.[1]

The second reason the law of one price and the PPP theory sometimes fail to apply is that not all internationally traded goods and services are perfectly standardized commodities, like grain or gold. For example, U.S.-made automobiles and Japanese-made automobiles are not identical; they differ in styling,

---

[1]Trade barriers, such as tariffs and quotas, also increase the costs associated with shipping goods from one country to another. Thus trade barriers reduce the applicability of the law of one price in much the same way that physical transportation costs do.

horsepower, reliability, and other features. As a result, some people strongly prefer one nation's cars to the other's. Thus if Japanese cars cost 10 percent more than American cars, U.S. automobile exports will not necessarily flood the Japanese market, since many Japanese will still prefer Japanese-made cars even at a 10 percent premium. Of course, there are limits to how far prices can diverge before people will switch to the cheaper product. But the law of one price, and hence the PPP theory, will not apply exactly to nonstandardized goods.

To summarize, the PPP theory works reasonably well as an explanation of exchange rate behavior over the long run, but not in the short run. Because transportation costs limit international trade in many goods and services, and because not all goods that are traded are standardized commodities, the law of one price (on which the PPP theory is based) works only imperfectly in the short run. To understand the short-run movements of exchange rates we need to incorporate some additional factors. In the next section we will study a supply and demand framework for the determination of exchange rates.

THE DETERMINATION OF THE EXCHANGE RATE: A SUPPLY AND DEMAND ANALYSIS

Although the PPP theory helps to explain the long-run behavior of the exchange rate, supply and demand analysis is more useful for studying its short-run behavior. As we will see, dollars are demanded in the foreign exchange market by foreigners who seek to purchase U.S. goods and assets and are supplied by U.S. residents who need foreign currencies to buy foreign goods and assets. The equilibrium exchange rate is the value of the dollar that equates the number of dollars supplied and demanded in the foreign exchange market. In this section we will discuss the factors that affect the supply and demand for dollars, and thus the U.S. exchange rate.

One note before we proceed: In Chapter 26 we described how the supply of money by the Fed and the demand for money by the public help to determine the nominal interest rate. However, the supply and demand for money in the domestic economy, as presented in Chapter 26, are *not* equivalent to the supply and demand for dollars in the foreign exchange market. As mentioned, the foreign exchange market is the market in which the currencies of various nations are traded for one another. The supply of dollars to the foreign exchange market is *not* the same as the money supply set by the Fed; rather, it is the number of dollars U.S. households and firms offer to trade for other currencies. Likewise, the demand for dollars in the foreign exchange market is *not* the same as the domestic demand for money, but the number of dollars holders of foreign currencies seek to buy. To understand the distinction, it may help to keep in mind that while the Fed determines the total supply of dollars in the U.S. economy, a dollar does not "count" as having been supplied to the foreign exchange market until some holder of dollars, such as a household or firm, tries to trade it for a foreign currency.

The supply of dollars Anyone who holds dollars, from an international bank to a Russian citizen whose dollars are buried in the backyard, is a potential supplier of dollars to the foreign exchange market. In practice, however, the principal suppliers of dollars to the foreign exchange market are U.S. households and firms. Why would a U.S. household or firm want to supply dollars in exchange for foreign currency? There are two major reasons. First, a U.S. household or firm may need foreign currency *to purchase foreign goods or services*. For example, a U.S. automobile importer may need yen to purchase Japanese cars, or an American tourist may need yen to make purchases in Tokyo. Second, a U.S. household or firm may need foreign currency *to purchase foreign assets*. For example, an American mutual fund may wish to acquire stocks issued by Japanese companies, or an individual U.S. saver may want to purchase Japanese government bonds.

Because Japanese assets are priced in yen, the U.S. household or firm will need to trade dollars for yen to acquire these assets.

The supply of dollars to the foreign exchange market is illustrated in Figure 29.3. We will focus on the market in which dollars are traded for Japanese yen, but bear in mind that similar markets exist for every other pair of traded currencies. The vertical axis of the figure shows the U.S.-Japanese exchange rate as measured by the number of yen that can be purchased with each dollar. The horizontal axis shows the number of dollars being traded in the yen-dollar market.

Note that the supply curve for dollars is upward-sloping. In other words, the more yen each dollar can buy, the more dollars people are willing to supply to the foreign exchange market. Why? At given prices for Japanese goods, services, and assets, the more yen a dollar can buy, the cheaper those goods, services, and assets will be in dollar terms. For example, if a video game costs 5,000 yen in Japan, and a dollar can buy 100 yen, the dollar price of the video game will be $50. However, if a dollar can buy 200 yen, then the dollar price of the same video game will be $25. Assuming that lower dollar prices will induce Americans to increase their expenditures on Japanese goods, services, and assets, a higher yen-dollar exchange rate will increase the supply of dollars to the foreign exchange market. Thus the supply curve for dollars is upward-sloping.

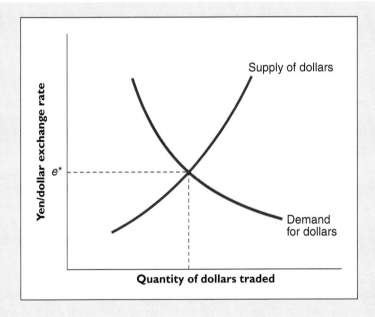

FIGURE 29.3
The Supply and Demand for Dollars in the Yen-Dollar Market.
The supply of dollars to the foreign exchange market is upward-sloping, because an increase in the number of yen offered for each dollar makes Japanese goods, services, and assets more attractive to U.S. buyers. Similarly, the demand for dollars is downward-sloping, because holders of yen will be less willing to buy dollars the more expensive they are in terms of yen. The equilibrium exchange rate e^*, also called the *fundamental value of the exchange rate,* equates the quantities of dollars supplied and demanded.

The demand for dollars In the yen-dollar foreign exchange market, demanders of dollars are those who wish to acquire dollars in exchange for yen. Most demanders of dollars in the yen-dollar market are Japanese households and firms, although anyone who happens to hold yen is free to trade them for dollars. Why demand dollars? The reasons for acquiring dollars are analogous to those for acquiring yen. First, households and firms that hold yen will demand dollars *so that they can purchase U.S. goods and services.* For example, a Japanese firm that wants to license U.S.-produced software needs dollars to pay the required fees, and a Japanese student studying in an American university must pay tuition in dollars. The firm or the student can acquire the necessary dollars only by offering yen in exchange. Second, households and firms demand dollars *in order to purchase U.S.*

assets. The purchase of Hawaiian real estate by a Japanese company or the acquisition of Microsoft stock by a Japanese pension fund are two examples.

The demand for dollars is represented by the downward-sloping curve in Figure 29.3. The curve slopes downward because the more yen a Japanese citizen must pay to acquire a dollar, the less attractive U.S. goods, services, and assets will be. Hence, the demand for dollars will be low when dollars are expensive in terms of yen and high when dollars are cheap in terms of yen.

The equilibrium value of the dollar   As mentioned earlier, the United States maintains a flexible, or floating, exchange rate, which means that the value of the dollar is determined by the forces of supply and demand in the foreign exchange market. In Figure 29.3 the equilibrium value of the dollar is e^*, the yen-dollar exchange rate at which the quantity of dollars supplied equals the quantity of dollars demanded. The equilibrium value of the exchange rate is also called the **fundamental value of the exchange rate.** In general, the equilibrium value of the dollar is not constant but changes with shifts in the supply of and demand for dollars in the foreign exchange market.

fundamental value of the exchange rate (or equilibrium exchange rate) the exchange rate that equates the quantities of the currency supplied and demanded in the foreign exchange market

CHANGES IN THE SUPPLY OF DOLLARS

Recall that people supply dollars to the yen-dollar foreign exchange market in order to purchase Japanese goods, services, and assets. Factors that affect the desire of U.S. households and firms to acquire Japanese goods, services, and assets will therefore affect the supply of dollars to the foreign exchange market. Some factors that will *increase* the supply of dollars, shifting the supply curve for dollars to the right, include:

- An increased preference for Japanese goods. For example, suppose that Japanese firms produce some popular new consumer electronics. To acquire the yen needed to buy these goods, American importers will increase their supply of dollars to the foreign exchange market.

- An increase in U.S. real GDP. An increase in U.S. real GDP will raise the incomes of Americans, allowing them to consume more goods and services (recall the consumption function, introduced in Chapter 25). Some part of this increase in consumption will take the form of goods imported from Japan. To buy more Japanese goods, Americans will supply more dollars to acquire the necessary yen.

- An increase in the real interest rate on Japanese assets. Recall that U.S. households and firms acquire yen in order to purchase Japanese assets as well as goods and services. Other factors such as risk held constant, the higher the real interest rate paid by Japanese assets, the more Japanese assets Americans will choose to hold. To purchase additional Japanese assets, U.S. households and firms will supply more dollars to the foreign exchange market.

Conversely, reduced demand for Japanese goods, a lower U.S. GDP, or a lower real interest rate on Japanese assets will *reduce* the number of yen Americans need, in turn reducing their supply of dollars to the foreign exchange market and shifting the supply curve for dollars to the left. Of course, any shift in the supply curve for dollars will affect the equilibrium exchange rate, as Example 29.5 shows.

Supplying dollars, demanding yen.

EXAMPLE 29.5

Video games, the yen, and the dollar

Suppose Japanese firms come to dominate the video game market, with games that are more exciting and realistic than those produced in the United States. All else being equal, how will this change affect the relative value of the yen and the dollar?

The increased quality of Japanese video games will increase the demand for the games in the United States. To acquire the yen necessary to buy more

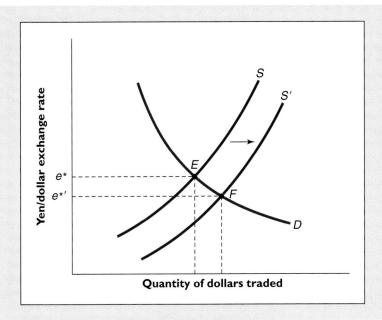

FIGURE 29.4
An Increase in the Supply of Dollars Lowers the Value of the Dollar.
Increased U.S. demand for Japanese video games forces Americans to supply more dollars to the foreign exchange market to acquire the yen they need to buy the games. The supply curve for dollars shifts from S to S', lowering the value of the dollar in terms of yen. The fundamental value of the exchange rate falls from e^* to $e^{*\prime}$.

Japanese video games, U.S. importers will supply more dollars to the foreign exchange market. As Figure 29.4 shows, the increased supply of dollars will reduce the value of the dollar. In other words, a dollar will buy fewer yen than it did before. At the same time, the yen will increase in value: A given number of yen will buy more dollars than it did before.

EXERCISE 29.4

The U.S. goes into a recession, and real GDP falls. All else equal, how is this economic weakness likely to affect the value of the dollar?

CHANGES IN THE DEMAND FOR DOLLARS

The factors that can cause a change in the demand for dollars in the foreign exchange market, and thus a shift of the dollar demand curve, are analogous to the factors that affect the supply of dollars. Factors that will *increase* the demand for dollars include:

■ An increased preference for U.S. goods. For example, Japanese airlines might find that U.S.-built aircraft are superior to others, and decide to expand the number of American-made planes in their fleets. To buy the American planes, Japanese airlines would demand more dollars on the foreign exchange market.

■ An increase in real GDP abroad, which implies higher incomes abroad, and thus more demand for imports from the United States.

■ An increase in the real interest rate on U.S. assets, which would make those assets more attractive to foreign savers. To acquire U.S. assets, Japanese savers would demand more dollars.

MONETARY POLICY AND THE EXCHANGE RATE

Of the many factors that could influence a country's exchange rate, among the most important is the monetary policy of the country's central bank. As we will see, monetary policy affects the exchange rate primarily through its effect on the real interest rate.

FIGURE 29.5
A Tightening of Monetary Policy Strengthens the Dollar.
Tighter monetary policy in the United States raises the domestic real interest rate, increasing the demand for U.S. assets by foreign savers. An increased demand for U.S. assets in turn increases the demand for dollars. The demand curve shifts from D to D', leading the exchange rate to appreciate from e^* to $e^{*'}$.

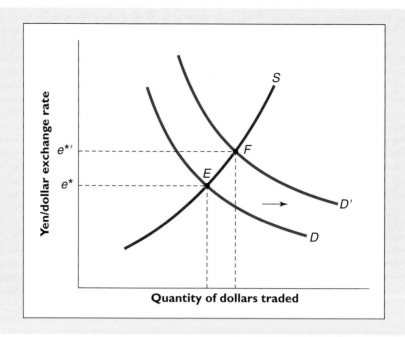

Suppose the Fed is concerned about inflation and tightens U.S. monetary policy in response. The effects of this policy change on the value of the dollar are shown in Figure 29.5. Before the policy change, the equilibrium value of the exchange rate is e^*, at the intersection of supply curve S and the demand curve D (point E in the figure). The tightening of monetary policy raises the domestic U.S. real interest rate r, making U.S. assets more attractive to foreign financial investors. The increased willingness of foreign investors to buy U.S. assets increases the demand for dollars, shifting the demand curve rightward from D to D' and the equilibrium point from E to F. As a result of this increase in demand, the equilibrium value of the dollar rises from e^* to $e^{*'}$.

In short, a tightening of monetary policy by the Fed raises the demand for dollars, causing the dollar to appreciate. By similar logic, an easing of monetary policy, which reduces the real interest rate, would weaken the demand for the dollar, causing it to depreciate.

ECONOMIC NATURALIST 29.2

Why did the dollar appreciate nearly 50 percent in the first half of the 1980s?

Figure 29.1 showed the strong appreciation of the U. S. dollar in 1980–1985, followed by a sharp depreciation in 1986–1987. We saw earlier that the PPP theory cannot explain this roller-coaster behavior. What *can* explain it?

Tight monetary policy, and the associated high real interest rate, were important causes of the dollar's remarkable appreciation during 1980–1985. As we saw in Economic Naturalist 27.3, U.S. inflation peaked at 13.5 percent in 1980. Under the leadership of Chairman Paul Volcker, the Fed responded to the surge in inflation by raising the real interest rate sharply in hopes of reducing aggregate demand and inflationary pressures. As a result, the real interest rate in the United States rose from negative values in 1979 and 1980 to more than 7 percent in 1983 and 1984 (see Table 27.3). Attracted by these high real returns, foreign savers rushed to buy U.S. assets, driving the value of the dollar up significantly.

The Fed's attempt to bring down inflation was successful. By the middle of the 1980s the Fed was able to ease U.S. monetary policy. The resulting decline in the real interest rate reduced the demand for U.S. assets, and thus for dollars, at which point the dollar fell back almost to its 1980 level.

THE EXCHANGE RATE AS A TOOL OF MONETARY POLICY

In a closed economy, monetary policy affects aggregate demand solely through the real interest rate. For example, by raising the real interest rate, a tight monetary policy reduces consumption and investment spending. We will see next that in an open economy with a flexible exchange rate, the exchange rate serves as another channel for monetary policy, one that reinforces the effects of the real interest rate.

To illustrate, suppose that policymakers are concerned about inflation and decide to restrain aggregate demand. To do so, they increase the real interest rate, reducing consumption and investment spending. But, as Figure 29.5 shows, the higher real interest rate also increases the demand for dollars, causing the dollar to appreciate. The stronger dollar, in turn, further reduces aggregate demand. Why? As we saw in discussing the real exchange rate, a stronger dollar reduces the cost of imported goods, increasing imports. It also makes U.S. exports more costly to foreign buyers, which tends to reduce exports. Recall that net exports—or exports minus imports—is one of the four components of aggregate demand. Thus, by reducing exports and increasing imports, a stronger dollar (more precisely, a higher real exchange rate) reduces aggregate demand.

In sum, when the exchange rate is flexible, a tighter monetary policy reduces net exports (through a stronger dollar) as well as consumption and investment spending (through a higher real interest rate). Conversely, an easier monetary policy weakens the dollar and stimulates net exports, reinforcing the effect of the lower real interest rate on consumption and investment spending. Thus, relative to the case of a closed economy we studied earlier, *monetary policy is more effective in an open economy with a flexible exchange rate.*

The tightening of monetary policy under Fed Chairman Volcker in the early 1980s illustrates the effect of monetary policy on net exports (the trade balance). As we saw in Economic Naturalist 29.2, Volcker's tight-money policies were a major reason for the 50 percent appreciation of the dollar during 1980–1985. In 1980 and 1981, the United States enjoyed a trade surplus, with exports that modestly exceeded imports. Largely in response to a stronger dollar, the U.S. trade balance fell into deficit after 1981. By the end of 1985 the U.S. trade deficit was about 3 percent of GDP, a substantial shift in less than half a decade.

RECAP   DETERMINING THE EXCHANGE RATE

- The most basic theory of nominal exchange rate determination, *purchasing power parity (PPP),* is based on the law of one price. The *law of one price* states that if transportation costs are relatively small, the price of an internationally traded commodity must be the same in all locations. According to the PPP theory, the nominal exchange rate between two currencies can be found by setting the price of a traded commodity in one currency equal to the price of the same commodity expressed in the second currency.

- A useful prediction of the PPP theory is that the currencies of countries that experience significant inflation will tend to depreciate over the long run. However, the PPP theory does not work well in the short run. The fact that many goods and services are nontraded, and that not all traded goods are standardized, reduces the applicability of the law of one price, and hence of the PPP theory.

- Supply and demand analysis is a useful tool for studying the short-run determination of the exchange rate. U.S. households and firms supply dollars to the foreign exchange market to acquire foreign currencies, which they need to purchase foreign goods, services, and assets. Foreigners demand dollars in the foreign exchange market to purchase U.S. goods, services, and assets. The equilibrium exchange rate, also called the *fundamental value of the exchange rate*, equates the quantities of dollars supplied and demanded in the foreign exchange market.

■ An increased preference for foreign goods, an increase in U.S. real GDP, or an increase in the real interest rate on foreign assets will increase the supply of dollars on the foreign exchange market, lowering the value of the dollar. An increased preference for U.S. goods by foreigners, an increase in real GDP abroad, or an increase in the real interest rate on U.S. assets will increase the demand for dollars, raising the value of the dollar.

■ A tight monetary policy raises the real interest rate, increasing the demand for dollars and strengthening the dollar. A stronger dollar reinforces the effects of tight monetary policy on aggregate spending by reducing net exports, a component of aggregate demand. Conversely, an easy monetary policy lowers the real interest rate, weakening the dollar.

FIXED EXCHANGE RATES

So far we have focused on the case of flexible exchange rates, the relevant case for most large industrial countries like the United States. However, the alternative approach, fixing the exchange rate, has been quite important historically and is still used in many countries, especially small or developing nations. In this section we will see how our conclusions change when the nominal exchange rate is fixed rather than flexible. One important difference is that when a country maintains a fixed exchange rate, its ability to use monetary policy as a stabilization tool is greatly reduced.

HOW TO FIX AN EXCHANGE RATE

In contrast to a flexible exchange rate, whose value is determined solely by supply and demand in the foreign exchange market, the value of a fixed exchange rate is determined by the government (in practice, usually the finance ministry or treasury department, with the cooperation of the central bank). Today, the value of a fixed exchange rate is usually set in terms of a major currency (for instance, Argentina pegs its currency one-for-one to the dollar), or relative to a "basket" of currencies, typically those of the country's trading partners. Historically, currency values were often fixed in terms of gold or other precious metals, but in recent years precious metals have rarely if ever been used for that purpose.

Once an exchange rate has been fixed, the government usually attempts to keep it unchanged for some time.[2] However, sometimes economic circumstances force the government to change the value of the exchange rate. A reduction in the official value of a currency is called a **devaluation;** an increase in the official value is called a **revaluation.** The devaluation of a fixed exchange rate is analogous to the depreciation of a flexible exchange rate; both involve a reduction in the currency's value. Conversely, a revaluation is analogous to an appreciation.

devaluation a reduction in the official value of a currency (in a fixed-exchange-rate system)

revaluation an increase in the official value of a currency (in a fixed-exchange-rate system)

[2]There are exceptions to this statement. Some countries employ a *crawling peg* system, under which the exchange rate is fixed at a value that changes in a preannounced way over time. For example, the government may announce that the value of the fixed exchange rate will fall 2 percent each year. Other countries use a *target zone* system, in which the exchange rate is allowed to deviate by a small amount from its fixed value. To focus on the key issues, we will assume that the exchange rate is fixed at a single value for a protracted period.

The supply and demand diagram we used to study flexible exchange rates can be adapted to analyze fixed exchange rates. Let's consider the case of a country called Latinia, whose currency is called the peso. Figure 29.6 shows the supply and demand for the Latinian peso in the foreign exchange market. Pesos are *supplied* to the foreign exchange market by Latinian households and firms who want to acquire foreign currencies to purchase foreign goods and assets. Pesos are *demanded* by holders of foreign currencies who need pesos to purchase Latinian goods and assets. Figure 29.6 shows that the quantities of pesos supplied and demanded in the foreign exchange market are equal when a peso equals 0.1 dollars (10 pesos to the dollar). Hence 0.1 dollars per peso is the *fundamental value* of the peso. If Latinia had a flexible-exchange-rate system, the peso would trade at 10 pesos to the dollar in the foreign exchange market.

But let's suppose that Latinia has a fixed exchange rate and that the government has decreed the value of the Latinian peso to be 8 pesos to the dollar, or 0.125 dollars per peso. This official value of the peso, 0.125 dollars, is indicated by the solid horizontal line in Figure 29.6. Notice that it is greater than the fundamental value, corresponding to the intersection of the supply and demand curves. When the officially fixed value of an exchange rate is greater than its fundamental value, the exchange rate is said to be **overvalued.** The official value of an exchange rate can also be lower than its fundamental value, in which case the exchange rate is said to be **undervalued.**

In this example, Latinia's commitment to hold the peso at 8 to the dollar is inconsistent with the fundamental value of 10 to the dollar, as determined by supply and demand in the foreign exchange market (the Latinian peso is overvalued). How could the Latinian government deal with this inconsistency? There are several possibilities. First, Latinia could simply devalue its currency, from 0.125 dollars per peso to 0.10 dollars per peso, which would bring the peso's official value into line with its fundamental value. As we will see, devaluation is often the ultimate result of an overvaluation of a currency. However, a country with a fixed exchange rate will be reluctant to change the official value of its exchange rate every time the fundamental value changes. If a country must continuously adjust its exchange rate to market conditions, it might as well switch to a flexible exchange rate.

As a second alternative, Latinia could try to maintain its overvalued exchange rate by restricting international transactions. Imposing quotas on imports and prohibiting domestic households and firms from acquiring foreign assets would effec-

overvalued exchange rate an exchange rate that has an officially fixed value greater than its fundamental value.

undervalued exchange rate an exchange rate that has an officially fixed value less than its fundamental value

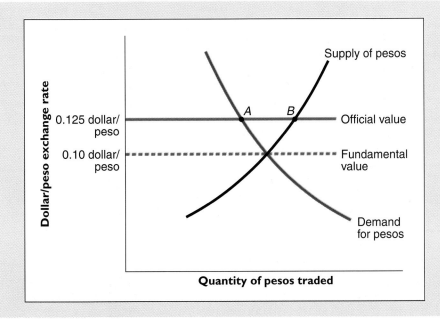

FIGURE 29.6
An Overvalued Exchange Rate.
The peso's official value (0.125 dollars) is shown as greater than its fundamental value (0.10 dollars), as determined by supply and demand in the foreign exchange market. Thus the peso is overvalued. To maintain the fixed value, the government must purchase pesos in the quantity *AB* each period.

tively reduce the supply of pesos to the foreign exchange market, raising the fundamental value of the currency. An even more extreme action would be to prohibit Latinians from exchanging the peso for other currencies without government approval, a policy that would effectively allow the government to determine directly the supply of pesos to the foreign exchange market. Such measures might help to maintain the official value of the peso. However, restrictions on trade and capital flows are extremely costly to the economy, because they reduce the gains from specialization and trade and deny domestic households and firms access to foreign capital markets. Thus, a policy of restricting international transactions to maintain a fixed exchange rate is likely to do more harm than good.

The third and most widely used approach to maintaining an overvalued exchange rate is for the government to become a demander of its own currency in the foreign exchange market. Figure 29.6 shows that at the official exchange rate of 0.125 dollars per peso, the private sector supply of pesos (point *B*) exceeds the private sector demand for pesos (point *A*). To keep the peso from falling below its official value, in each period the Latinian government could purchase a quantity of pesos in the foreign exchange market equal to the length of the line segment *AB* in Figure 29.6. If the government followed this strategy, then at the official exchange rate of 0.125 dollars per peso, the total demand for pesos (private demand at point *A* plus government demand *AB*) would equal the private supply of pesos (point *B*). This situation is analogous to government attempts to keep the price of a commodity, like grain or milk, above its market level. To maintain an official price of grain that is above the market-clearing price, the government must stand ready to purchase the excess supply of grain forthcoming at the official price. In the same way, to keep the "price" of its currency above the market-clearing level, the government must buy the excess pesos supplied at the official price.

To be able to purchase its own currency and maintain an overvalued exchange rate, the government (usually the central bank) must hold foreign currency assets, called **international reserves,** or simply *reserves*. For example, the Latinian central bank may hold dollar deposits in U.S. banks or U.S. government debt, which it can trade for pesos in the foreign exchange market as needed. In the situation shown in Figure 29.6, to keep the peso at its official value, in each period the Latinian central bank will have to spend an amount of international reserves equal to the length of the line segment *AB*.

Because a country with an overvalued exchange rate must use part of its reserves to support the value of its currency in each period, over time its available reserves will decline. The net decline in a country's stock of international reserves over a year is called its **balance-of-payments deficit.** Conversely, if a country experiences a net increase in its international reserves over the year, the increase is called its **balance-of-payments surplus.**

international reserves foreign currency assets held by a government for the purpose of purchasing the domestic currency in the foreign exchange market

balance-of-payments deficit the net decline in a country's stock of international reserves over a year

balance-of-payments surplus the net increase in a country's stock of international reserves over a year

EXAMPLE 29.6

Latinia's balance-of-payments deficit

The demand for and supply of Latinian pesos in the foreign exchange market are

$$\text{Demand} = 25,000 - 50,000e,$$

$$\text{Supply} = 17,600 + 24,000e,$$

where the Latinian exchange rate *e* is measured in dollars per peso. Officially, the value of the peso is 0.125 dollars. Find the fundamental value of the peso and the Latinian balance-of-payments deficit, measured in both pesos and dollars.

To find the fundamental value of the peso, equate the demand and supply for pesos:

$$25,000 - 50,000e = 17,600 + 24,000e.$$

Solving for *e,* we get

$$7,400 = 74,000e,$$

$$e = 0.10.$$

So the fundamental value of the exchange rate is 0.10 dollars per peso, as in Figure 29.6.

At the official exchange rate, 0.125 dollars/peso, the demand for pesos is 25,000 − 50,000(0.125) = 18,750, and the supply of pesos is 17,600 + 24,000(0.125) = 20,600. Thus the quantity of pesos supplied to the foreign exchange market exceeds the quantity of pesos demanded by 20,600 − 18,750 = 1,850 pesos. To maintain the fixed rate, the Latinian government must purchase 1,850 pesos per period, which is the Latinian balance-of-payments deficit. Since pesos are purchased at the official rate of 8 pesos to the dollar, the balance-of-payments deficit in dollars is (1,850 pesos) × (0.125 dollars/peso) = $(1,850/8) = $231.25.

EXERCISE 29.5

Repeat Example 29.6 under the assumption that the fixed value of the peso is 0.15 dollars/peso. What do you conclude about the relationship between the degree of currency overvaluation and the resulting balance-of-payments deficit?

Although a government can maintain an overvalued exchange rate for a time by offering to buy back its own currency at the official price, there is a limit to this strategy, since no government's stock of international reserves is infinite. Eventually the government will run out of reserves, and the fixed exchange rate will collapse. As we will see next, the collapse of a fixed exchange rate can be quite sudden and dramatic.

EXERCISE 29.6

Diagram a case in which a fixed exchange rate is *undervalued* rather than overvalued. Show that, to maintain the fixed exchange rate, the central bank must use domestic currency to purchase foreign currency in the foreign exchange market. With an undervalued exchange rate, is the country's central bank in danger of running out of international reserves? (*Hint:* Keep in mind that a central bank is always free to print more of its own currency.)

SPECULATIVE ATTACKS

A government's attempt to maintain an overvalued exchange rate can be ended quickly and unexpectedly by the onset of a *speculative attack*. A speculative attack involves massive selling of domestic currency assets by both domestic and foreign financial investors. For example, in a speculative attack on the Latinian peso, financial investors would attempt to get rid of any financial assets—stocks, bonds, deposits in banks—denominated in pesos. A speculative attack is most likely to occur when financial investors fear that an overvalued currency will soon be devalued, since in a devaluation, financial assets denominated in the domestic currency suddenly become worth much less in terms of other currencies. Ironically, speculative attacks, which are usually prompted by *fear* of devaluation, may turn out to be the *cause* of devaluation. Thus a speculative attack may actually be a self-fulfilling prophecy.

speculative attack a massive selling of domestic currency assets by financial investors

The effects of a speculative attack on the market for pesos are shown in Figure 29.7. At first, the situation is the same as in Figure 29.6: The supply and demand for Latinian pesos are indicated by the curves marked S and D, implying a fundamental value of the peso of 0.10 dollars per peso. As before, the official value of the peso is 0.125 dollars per peso—greater than the fundamental value—so the peso is overvalued. To maintain the fixed value of the peso, each period the Latinian central bank must use its international reserves to buy back pesos, in the amount corresponding to the line segment AB in the figure.

Suppose, though, that financial investors fear that Latinia may soon devalue its currency, perhaps because the central bank's reserves are getting low. If the peso were to be devalued from its official value of 8 pesos to the dollar to its fundamental value of 10 pesos per dollar, then a 1 million peso investment, worth $125,000 at the fixed exchange rate, would suddenly be worth only $100,000. To try to avoid these losses, financial investors will sell their peso-denominated assets and offer pesos on the foreign exchange market. The resulting flood of pesos into the market will shift the supply curve of pesos to the right, from S to S' in Figure 29.7.

This speculative attack creates a serious problem for the Latinian central bank. Prior to the attack, maintaining the value of the peso required the central bank to spend each period an amount of international reserves corresponding to the line segment AB. Now suddenly the central bank must spend a larger quantity of reserves, equal to the distance AC in Figure 29.7, to maintain the fixed exchange rate. These extra reserves are needed to purchase the pesos being sold by panicky financial investors. In practice, such speculative attacks often force a devaluation by reducing the central bank's reserves to the point where further

FIGURE 29.7

A Speculative Attack on the Peso.

Initially, the peso is overvalued at 0.125 dollars per peso. To maintain the official rate, the central bank must buy pesos in the amount AB each period. Fearful of possible devaluation, financial investors launch a speculative attack, selling peso-denominated assets and supplying pesos to the foreign exchange market. As a result, the supply of pesos shifts from S to S', lowering the fundamental value of the currency still further and forcing the central bank to buy pesos in the amount AC to maintain the official exchange rate. This more rapid loss of reserves may lead the central bank to devalue the peso, confirming financial investors' fears.

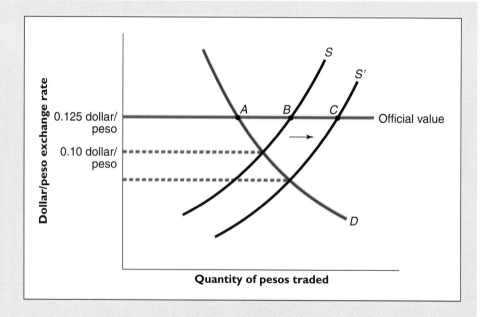

defense of the fixed exchange rate is considered hopeless. Thus a speculative attack ignited by fears of devaluation may actually end up producing the very devaluation that was feared.

MONETARY POLICY AND THE FIXED EXCHANGE RATE

We have seen that there is no really satisfactory way of maintaining a fixed exchange rate above its fundamental value for an extended period. A central bank can maintain an overvalued exchange rate for a time by using international reserves to buy up the excess supply of its currency in the foreign exchange market. But a country's international reserves are limited and may eventually be exhausted by the attempt to keep the exchange rate artificially high. Moreover, speculative attacks often hasten the collapse of an overvalued exchange rate.

An alternative to trying to maintain an overvalued exchange rate is to take actions that increase the fundamental value of the exchange rate. If the exchange rate's fundamental value can be raised enough to equal its official value, then the overvaluation problem will be eliminated. The most effective way to change the exchange rate's fundamental value is through monetary policy. As we saw earlier in the chapter, a tight monetary policy that raises the real interest rate will increase the demand for the domestic currency, as domestic assets become more attractive to foreign financial investors. Increased demand for the currency will in turn raise its fundamental value.

The use of monetary policy to support a fixed exchange rate is shown in Figure 29.8. At first, the demand and supply of the Latinian peso in the foreign exchange market are given by the curves D and S, so the fundamental value of the peso equals 0.10 dollars per peso—less than the official value of 0.125 dollars per peso. Just as before, the peso is overvalued. This time, however, the

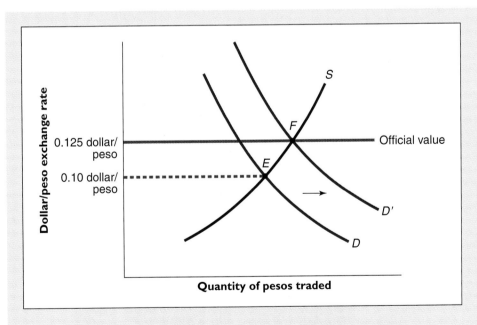

FIGURE 29.8
A Tightening of Monetary Policy Eliminates an Overvaluation.
With the demand for the peso given by D and the supply given by S, equilibrium occurs at point E and the fundamental value of the peso equals 0.10 dollars per peso—below the official value of 0.125 dollars per peso. The overvaluation of the peso can be eliminated by tighter monetary policy, which raises the domestic real interest rate, making domestic assets more attractive to foreign financial investors. The resulting increase in demand for the peso, from D to D', raises the peso's fundamental value to 0.125 dollars per peso, the official value. The peso is no longer overvalued.

Latinian central bank uses monetary policy to eliminate the overvaluation problem. To do so, the central bank increases the domestic real interest rate, making Latinian assets more attractive to foreign financial investors and raising the demand for pesos from D to D'. After this increase in the demand for pesos, the fundamental value of the peso equals the officially fixed value, as can be seen in Figure 29.8. Because the peso is no longer overvalued, it can be maintained at its fixed value without loss of international reserves or fear of speculative attack. Conversely, an easing of monetary policy (a lower real interest rate) could be used to remedy an undervaluation, in which the official exchange rate is below the fundamental value.

Although monetary policy can be used to keep the fundamental value of the exchange rate equal to the official value, using monetary policy in this way has some drawbacks. In particular, *if monetary policy is used to set the fundamental value of the exchange rate equal to the official value, it is no longer available for stabilizing the domestic economy.* Suppose, for example, that the Latinian economy were suffering a recession due to insufficient aggregate demand at the same time that its exchange rate is overvalued. The Latinian central bank could lower the real interest rate to increase spending and output, or it could raise the real interest rate to eliminate overvaluation of the exchange rate, *but it cannot do both.* Hence, if Latinian officials decide to maintain the fixed exchange rate, they must give up any hope of fighting the recession using monetary policy. The fact that a fixed exchange rate limits or eliminates the use of monetary policy for the purpose of stabilizing aggregate demand is one of the most important features of a fixed-exchange-rate system.

The conflict monetary policymakers face, between stabilizing the exchange rate and stabilizing the domestic economy, is most severe when the exchange rate is under a speculative attack. A speculative attack lowers the fundamental value of the exchange rate still further, by increasing the supply of the currency in the foreign exchange market (see Figure 29.7). To stop a speculative attack, the cen-

"It's just a flesh wound. I got it defending the dollar."

tral bank must raise the fundamental value of the currency a great deal, which requires a large increase in the real interest rate. (In a famous episode in 1992, the Swedish central bank responded to an attack on its currency by raising the short-term interest rate to 500 percent!) However, because the increase in the real interest rate that is necessary to stop a speculative attack reduces aggregate demand, it can cause a severe economic slowdown. Economic Naturalist 29.3 describes a real-world example of this phenomenon.

What were the causes and consequences of the East Asian crisis of 1997–1998?

During the past three decades the countries of East Asia have enjoyed impressive economic growth and stability. But the "East Asian miracle" seemed to end in 1997, when a wave of speculative attacks hit the region's currencies. Thailand, which had kept a constant value for its currency in terms of the U.S. dollar for more than a decade, was the first to come under attack, but the crisis spread to other countries, including South Korea, Indonesia, and Malaysia. Each of these countries was ultimately forced to devalue its currency. What caused this crisis, and what were its consequences?

Because of the impressive economic record of the East Asian countries, the speculative attacks on their currencies were unexpected by most policymakers, economists, and financial investors. With the benefit of hindsight, however, we can identify some problems in the East Asian economies that contributed to the crisis. Perhaps the most serious problems concerned their banking systems. In the decade prior to the crisis, East Asian banks received large inflows of capital from foreign financial investors hoping to profit from the East Asian miracle. Those inflows would have been a boon if they had been well invested, but unfortunately, many bankers used the funds to make loans to family members, friends, or the politically well-connected—a phenomenon that became known as *crony capitalism*. The results were poor returns on investment and defaults by many borrowers. Ultimately, foreign investors realized that the returns to investing in East Asia would be much lower than expected. When they began to sell off their assets, the process snowballed into a full-fledged speculative attack on the East Asian currencies.

Despite assistance by international lenders such as the International Monetary Fund (see Box 29.1), the effects of the speculative attacks on the East Asian economies were severe. The prices of assets such as stocks and land plummeted, and there were bank runs in several nations. (See Chapter 23 for a discussion of bank runs.) In an attempt to raise the fundamental values of their exchange rates and stave off additional devaluation, several of the countries increased their real interest rates sharply. However, the rise in real interest rates depressed aggregate demand, contributing to sharp declines in output and rising unemployment.

Fortunately, by 1999 most East Asian economies had begun to recover. Still, the crisis impressed the potential dangers of fixed exchange rates quite sharply in the minds of policymakers in developing countries. Another lesson from the crisis is that banking regulations need to be structured so as to promote economically sound lending rather than crony capitalism.

ECONOMIC NATURALIST 29.3

BOX 29.1: THE INTERNATIONAL MONETARY FUND

The International Monetary Fund (IMF) was established after World War II. An international agency, the IMF is controlled by a 24-member Executive Board. Eight Executive Board members represent individual countries (China, France, Germany, Japan, Russia, Saudi Arabia, the United Kingdom, and the United States); the other 16 members each represent a group of countries. A Managing Director oversees the IMF's operations and its approximately 2,600 employees.

The original purpose of the IMF was to help manage the system of fixed exchange rates, called the Bretton Woods system, put in place after the war. Under Bretton Woods, the IMF's principal role was to lend international reserves to member countries who needed them so that those countries could maintain their exchange rates at the official values. However, by 1973 the United States, the United Kingdom, Germany, and most other industrial nations had abandoned fixed exchange rates for flexible rates, leaving the IMF to find a new mission. Since 1973 the IMF has been involved primarily in lending to developing countries. It lent heavily to Mexico when that country experienced speculative attacks in 1994, and it made loans to East Asian countries during the 1997–1998 crisis. Other countries that received large IMF loans in recent years include Russia and Brazil.

The IMF's performance in recent crises has been controversial. Many observers credit the IMF with helping Mexico, the East Asian nations, and others to recover quickly from the effects of speculative attacks and contend that the IMF plays a vital role in maintaining international economic stability. However, some critics have charged that the IMF has required recipients of its loans to follow economic policies—such as tight monetary policies and fiscal cutbacks—that have turned out to be ill-advised. Others have claimed that the IMF's loans help foreign financial investors and the richest people in the countries receiving loans, rather than the average person. (The IMF has been severely embarrassed by reports that much of the nearly $5 billion it lent to Russia in 1998 has disappeared into the bank accounts of unscrupulous citizens, including gangsters.)

The IMF has also come into conflict with the World Bank, a separate international institution that was set up at about the same time as the IMF. The World Bank, whose mission is to provide long-term loans to help poor nations develop their economies, has complained that IMF interventions in poor countries interfered with World Bank programs and objectives. In 2000, a report commissioned by the U.S. Congress recommended reducing the IMF's powers (as well as, incidentally, those of the World Bank). The debate over the IMF's proper role will no doubt continue.

How did policy mistakes contribute to the Great Depression?

Chapter 17 introduced the study of macroeconomics with the claim that policy mistakes played a major role in causing the Great Depression. Now that we are close to completing our study of macroeconomics, we can be more specific about that claim. How did policy mistakes contribute to the Great Depression?

Many policy mistakes (as well as a great deal of bad luck) contributed to the severity of the Depression. For example, U.S. policymakers, in an attempt to protect domestic industries, imposed the infamous Hawley-Smoot tariff in 1930. Other countries quickly retaliated with their own tariffs, leading to the virtual collapse of international trade.

However, the most serious mistakes by far were in the realm of monetary policy.[3] As we saw in Chapter 23, the U.S. money supply contracted by one-third between 1929 and 1933 (Table 23.7). Associated with this unprecedented decline in the money supply were sharply falling output and prices and surging unemployment.

At least three separate policy errors were responsible for the collapse of the U.S. money supply between 1929 and 1933. First, the Federal Reserve tightened monetary

---

[3]A classic 1963 book by Milton Friedman and Anna Schwartz, *A Monetary History of the United States: 1867–1960* (Princeton University Press), was the first to provide detailed support for the view that poor monetary policy helped to cause the Depression.

ECONOMIC NATURALIST 29.4

policy significantly in 1928 and 1929, despite the absence of inflation. Fed officials took this action primarily in an attempt to "rein in" the booming stock market, which they feared was rising too quickly. Their "success" in dampening stock market speculation was more than they bargained for, however, as rising interest rates and a slowing economy contributed to a crash in stock prices that began in October 1929.

The second critical policy error was allowing thousands of U.S. banks to fail during the banking panics of 1930 to 1933. Apparently officials believed that the failures would eliminate only the weakest banks, strengthening the banking system overall. However, the banking panics sharply reduced bank deposits and the overall money supply, for reasons discussed in Economic Naturalist 23.4.

The third policy error, related to the subject of this chapter, arose from the U.S. government's exchange rate policies. When the Depression began, the United States, like most other major countries, was on the gold standard, with the value of the dollar officially set in terms of gold.[4] By establishing a fixed value for the dollar, the United States effectively created a fixed exchange rate between the dollar and other currencies whose values were set in terms of gold. As the Depression worsened, Fed officials were urged by Congress to ease monetary policy to stop the fall in output and prices. However, as we saw earlier, under a fixed exchange rate monetary policy cannot be used to stabilize the domestic economy. Specifically, policymakers of the early 1930s feared that if they eased monetary policy, foreign financial investors might perceive the dollar to be overvalued and launch a speculative attack, forcing a devaluation of the dollar or even the abandonment of the gold standard altogether. The Fed therefore made no serious attempt to arrest the collapse of the money supply.

With hindsight, we can see that the Fed's decision to put a higher priority on remaining on the gold standard than on stimulating the economy was a major error. Indeed, countries that abandoned the gold standard in favor of a floating exchange rate, such as Great Britain and Sweden, or which had never been on the gold standard (Spain and China), were able to increase their money supplies and to recover much more quickly from the Depression than the United States did. The Fed evidently believed, erroneously as it turned out, that stability of the exchange rate would somehow translate into overall economic stability.

Upon taking office in March 1933, Franklin D. Roosevelt reversed several of these policy errors. He took active measures to restore the health of the banking system, and he suspended the gold standard. The money supply stopped falling and began to grow rapidly. Output, prices, and stock prices recovered rapidly during 1933 to 1937, although unemployment remained high. However, ultimate recovery from the Depression was interrupted by another recession in 1937–1938.

RECAP   **FIXED EXCHANGE RATES**

- The value of a fixed exchange rate is set by the government. The official value of a fixed exchange rate may differ from its fundamental value, as determined by supply and demand in the foreign exchange market. An exchange rate whose officially fixed value exceeds its fundamental value is *overvalued;* an exchange rate whose officially fixed value is below its fundamental value is *undervalued.*

- For an overvalued exchange rate, the quantity of the currency supplied to the foreign exchange market at the official exchange rate exceeds the quantity demanded. The government can maintain an overvalued exchange rate for a time by using its *international reserves* (foreign currency assets) to purchase the excess supply of its currency. The net decline in a country's stock of international reserves during the year is its *balance-of-payments deficit.*

---

[4]The value of the dollar in 1929 was such that the price of 1 ounce of gold was fixed at $20.67.

■ Because a country's international reserves are limited, it cannot maintain an overvalued exchange rate indefinitely. Moreover, if financial investors fear an impending devaluation of the exchange rate, they may launch a *speculative attack,* selling domestic currency assets and supplying large amounts of the country's currency to the foreign exchange market—an action that exhausts the country's reserves even more quickly. Because rapid loss of reserves may force a devaluation, financial investors' fear of devaluation may prove a self-fulfilling prophecy.

■ A tight monetary policy, which increases the real interest rate, raises the demand for the currency and hence its fundamental value. By raising a currency's fundamental value to its official value, tight monetary policies can eliminate the problem of overvaluation and stabilize the exchange rate. However, if monetary policy is used to set the fundamental value of the exchange rate, it is no longer available for stabilizing the domestic economy.

SHOULD EXCHANGE RATES BE FIXED OR FLEXIBLE?

Should countries adopt fixed or flexible exchange rates? In briefly comparing the two systems, we will focus on two major issues: (1) the effects of the exchange rate system on monetary policy and (2) the effects of the exchange rate system on trade and economic integration.

On the issue of monetary policy, we have seen that the type of exchange rate a country has strongly affects the central bank's ability to use monetary policy to stabilize the economy. A flexible exchange rate actually strengthens the impact of monetary policy on aggregate demand. But a fixed exchange rate prevents policymakers from using monetary policy to stabilize the economy, because they must instead use it to keep the exchange rate's fundamental value at its official value (or else risk speculative attack).

In large economies like that of the United States, giving up the power to stabilize the domestic economy via monetary policy makes little sense. Thus large economies should nearly always employ a flexible exchange rate. However, in small economies, giving up this power may have some benefits. We have mentioned the case of Argentina, which maintains a one-to-one exchange rate between its peso and the U.S. dollar. Although in the past Argentina has suffered periods of hyperinflation, since the peso was pegged to the dollar early in the 1990s, Argentina's inflation rate has essentially equaled that of the United States. By tying its currency to the dollar and giving up the freedom to set its monetary policy, Argentina may have effectively committed itself to avoiding the inflationary policies of the past, and instead placed itself under the "umbrella" of the Federal Reserve.

The second important issue is the effect of the exchange rate on trade and economic integration. Proponents of fixed exchange rates argue that fixed rates promote international trade and cross-border economic cooperation by reducing uncertainty about future exchange rates. For example, a firm that is considering building up its export business knows that its potential profits will depend on the future value of its own country's currency relative to the currencies of the countries to which it exports. Under a flexible-exchange-rate regime, the value of the home currency fluctuates with changes in supply and demand and is therefore difficult to predict far in advance. Such uncertainty may make the firm reluctant to expand its export business. Supporters of fixed exchange rates argue that if the exchange rate is officially fixed, uncertainty about the future exchange rate is reduced or eliminated.

One problem with this argument, which has been underscored by episodes like the East Asian crisis, is that fixed exchange rates are not guaranteed to remain fixed forever. Although they do not fluctuate from day to day as flexible rates do, a speculative attack on a fixed exchange rate may lead suddenly and unpredictably to a large devaluation. Thus a firm that is trying to forecast the exchange rate 10 years into the future may face as much uncertainty if the exchange rate is fixed as if it is flexible.

The potential instability of fixed exchange rates caused by speculative attacks has led some countries to try a more radical solution to the problem of uncertainty about exchange rates: the adoption of a common currency. Economic Naturalist 29.5 describes an important instance of this strategy.

Why have 11 European countries adopted a common currency?

Effective January 1, 1999, eleven western European nations, including France, Germany, and Italy, adopted a common currency, called the euro. In several stages the euro will replace the French franc, the German mark, the Italian lira, and other national currencies. Why have these nations adopted a common currency?

For some decades the nations of Western Europe have worked to increase economic cooperation and trade among themselves. European leaders recognized that a unified and integrated European economy would be more productive and perhaps more competitive with the U. S. economy than a fragmented one. As part of this effort, these countries established fixed exchange rates under the auspices of a system called the European Monetary System (EMS). Unfortunately, the EMS did not prove stable. Numerous devaluations of the various currencies occurred, and in 1992 severe speculative attacks forced several nations, including Great Britain, to abandon the fixed-exchange-rate system.

In December 1991, in Maastricht in the Netherlands, the member countries of the European Community (EC) adopted a treaty popularly known as the Maastricht Treaty. One of the major provisions of the Treaty, which took effect in November 1993, was that member countries would strive to adopt a common currency. This common currency, known as the euro, was formally adopted on January 1, 1999. The advent of the euro means that Europeans will no longer have to change currencies when trading with other European countries, much as Americans from different states can trade with each other without worrying that a "New York dollar" will change in value relative to a "California dollar." The euro should help to promote European trade and cooperation while eliminating the problem of speculative attacks on the currencies of individual countries.

Because Western Europe now has a single currency, it also must have a common monetary policy. The EC members agreed that European monetary policy would be put under the control of a new European Central Bank (ECB), a multinational institution located in Frankfurt, Germany. The ECB has in effect become "Europe's Fed." One potential problem with having a single monetary policy for 11 different countries is that different countries may face different economic conditions, so a single monetary policy cannot respond to all of them. What will the ECB do, for example, if Italy is suffering from a recession (which requires an easing of monetary policy) while Germany is worried about inflation (which requires a tightening)? Whether the requirement of a single monetary policy will create conflicts of interest among the member nations of the European Community remains to be seen.

ECONOMIC NATURALIST 29.5

▪ SUMMARY ▪

- The *nominal exchange rate* between two currencies is the rate at which the currencies can be traded for each other. A rise in the value of a currency relative to other currencies is called an *appreciation;* a decline in the value of a currency is called a *depreciation.*

- Exchange rates can be flexible or fixed. The value of a *flexible exchange rate* is determined by the supply and demand for the currency in the *foreign exchange market,* the market on which currencies of various nations are traded for one another. The government sets the value of a *fixed exchange rate.*

- The *real exchange rate* is the price of the average domestic good or service *relative* to the price of the average foreign good or service, when prices are expressed in terms of a common currency. An increase in the real exchange rate implies that domestic goods and services are becoming more expensive relative to foreign goods and services, which tends to reduce exports and increase imports. Conversely, a decline in the real exchange rate tends to increase net exports.

- A basic theory of nominal exchange rate determination, the *purchasing power parity* (PPP) theory, is based on the law of one price. The *law of one price* states that if transportation costs are relatively small, the price of an internationally traded commodity must be the same in all locations. According to the PPP theory, we can find the nominal exchange rate between two currencies by setting the price of a commodity in one of the currencies equal to the price of the commodity in the second currency. The PPP theory correctly predicts that the currencies of countries that experience significant inflation will tend to depreciate in the long run. However, the fact that many goods and services are not traded internationally, and that not all traded goods are standardized, makes the PPP theory less useful for explaining short-run changes in exchange rates.

- Supply and demand analysis is a useful tool for studying the determination of exchange rates in the short run. The equilibrium exchange rate, also called the *fundamental value of the exchange rate,* equates the quantities of the currency supplied and demanded in the foreign exchange market. A currency is supplied by domestic residents who wish to acquire foreign currencies to purchase foreign goods, services, and assets. An increased preference for foreign goods, an increase in the domestic GDP, or an increase in the real interest rate on foreign assets will all increase the supply of a currency on the foreign exchange market and thus lower its value. A currency is demanded by foreigners who wish to purchase domestic goods, services, and assets. An increased preference for domestic goods by foreigners, an increase in real GDP abroad, or an increase in the domestic real interest rate will all increase the demand for the currency on the foreign exchange market and thus increase its value.

- If the exchange rate is flexible, a tight monetary policy (by raising the real interest rate) increases the demand for the currency and causes it to appreciate. The stronger currency reinforces the effects of the tight monetary policy on aggregate demand by reducing net exports. Conversely, easy monetary policy lowers the real interest rate and weakens the currency, which in turn stimulates net exports.

- The value of a fixed exchange rate is officially established by the government. A fixed exchange rate whose official value exceeds its fundamental value in the foreign exchange market is said to be *overvalued.* An exchange rate whose official value is below its fundamental value is *undervalued.* A reduction in the official value of a fixed exchange rate is called a *devaluation;* an increase in its official value is called a *revaluation.*

- For an overvalued exchange rate, the quantity of the currency supplied at the official exchange rate exceeds the quantity demanded. To maintain the official rate, the country's central bank must use its *international reserves* (foreign currency assets) to purchase the excess supply of its currency in the foreign exchange market. Because a country's international reserves are limited, it cannot maintain an overvalued exchange rate indefinitely. Moreover, if financial investors fear an impending devaluation of the exchange rate, they may launch a *speculative attack,* selling their domestic currency assets and supplying large quantities of the currency to the foreign exchange market. Because speculative attacks cause a country's central bank to spend its international reserves even more quickly, they often force a devaluation.

- A tight monetary policy, by raising the fundamental value of the exchange rate, can eliminate the problem of overvaluation. However, if monetary policy is used to set the fundamental value of the exchange rate equal to the official value, it is no longer available for stabilizing the domestic economy. Thus under fixed exchange rates, monetary policy has little or no power to affect domestic output and employment.

- Because a fixed exchange rate implies that monetary policy can no longer be used for domestic stabilization, most large countries employ a flexible exchange rate. A fixed exchange rate may benefit a small country by forcing its central bank to follow the monetary policies of the country to which it has tied its rate. Advocates of fixed exchange rates argue that they increase trade and economic integration by making the exchange rate more predictable. However, the threat of speculative attacks greatly reduces the long-term predictability of a fixed exchange rate.

■ KEY TERMS ■

---

appreciation (804)
balance-of-payments deficit (820)
balance-of-payment surplus (820)
depreciation (804)
devaluation (818)
fixed exchange rate (805)
flexible exchange rate (805)

foreign exchange market (805)
fundamental value of the exchange
rate (814)
international reserves (820)
law of one price (809)
nominal exchange rate (803)

overvalued exchange rate (819)
purchasing power parity (PPP) (810)
real exchange rate (806)
revaluation (818)
speculative attack (821)
undervalued exchange rate (819)

■ REVIEW QUESTIONS ■

---

1. Japanese yen trade at 110 yen/dollar and Mexico pesos trade at 10 pesos/dollar. What is the nominal exchange rate between the yen and the peso? Express in two ways.

2. Define *nominal exchange rate* and *real exchange rate*. How are the two concepts related? Which type of exchange rate most directly affects a country's ability to export its goods and services?

3. Would you expect the law of one price to apply to crude oil? To fresh milk? To taxi rides? To compact discs produced in different countries by local recording artists? Explain your answer in each case.

4. Why do U.S. households and firms supply dollars to the foreign exchange market? Why do foreigners demand dollars in the foreign exchange market?

5. Under a flexible exchange rate, how does an easing of monetary policy (a lower real interest rate) affect the value of the exchange rate? Does this change in the exchange rate tend to weaken or strengthen the effect of the monetary ease on output and employment? Explain.

6. Define *overvalued exchange rate*. Discuss four ways in which government policymakers can respond to an overvaluation. What are the drawbacks of each approach?

7. Use a supply and demand diagram to illustrate the effects of a speculative attack on an overvalued exchange rate. Why do speculative attacks often result in a devaluation?

8. Contrast fixed and flexible exchange rates in terms of how they affect (a) the ability of monetary policy to stabilize domestic output and (b) the predictability of future exchange rates.

■ PROBLEMS ■

---

1. Using the data in Table 29.1, find the nominal exchange rate between the Mexican peso and the Japanese yen. Express in two ways. How do your answers change if the peso appreciates by 10 percent against the dollar while the value of the yen against the dollar remains unchanged?

2. A British-made automobile is priced at £20,000 (20,000 British pounds). A comparable U.S.-made car costs $26,000. One pound trades for $1.50 in the foreign exchange market. Find the real exchange rate for automobiles from the perspective of the United States and from the perspective of Great Britain. Which country's cars are more competitively priced?

3. Between last year and this year, the CPI in Blueland rose from 100 to 110 and the CPI in Redland rose from 100 to 105. Blueland's currency unit, the blue, was worth $1 (U.S.) last year and is worth 90 cents (U.S.) this year. Redland's currency unit, the red, was worth 50 cents (U.S.) last year and is worth 45 cents (U.S.) this year.

   Find the percentage change from last year to this year in Blueland's *nominal* exchange rate with Redland and in Blueland's *real* exchange rate with Redland. (Treat Blueland as the home country.) Relative to Redland, do you expect Blueland's exports to be helped or hurt by these changes in exchange rates?

4. The demand for U.S.-made cars in Japan is given by

   Japanese demand = 10,000 − 0.001(Price of U.S. cars in yen).

Similarly, the demand for Japanese-made cars in the United States is

U.S. demand = 30,000 − 0.2(Price of Japanese cars in dollars).

The domestic price of a U.S.-made car is $20,000, and the domestic price of a Japanese-made car is ¥2,500,000. From the perspective of the United States, find the real exchange rate in terms of cars and net exports of cars to Japan, if:

a. The nominal exchange rate is 100 yen/dollar.

b. The nominal exchange rate is 125 yen/dollar.

How does an appreciation of the dollar affect U.S. net exports of automobiles (considering only the Japanese market)?

5. a. Gold is $350/ounce in the United States and 2,800 pesos/ounce in Mexico. What nominal exchange rate between U.S. dollars and Mexican pesos is implied by the PPP theory?

b. Mexico experiences inflation so that the price of gold rises to 4,200 pesos/ounce. Gold remains $350/ounce in the United States. According to the PPP theory, what happens to the exchange rate? What general principle does this example illustrate?

c. Gold is $350/ounce in the United States and 4,200 pesos/ounce in Mexico. Crude oil (excluding taxes and transportation costs) is $30/barrel in the U.S. According to the PPP theory, what should a barrel of crude oil cost in Mexico?

d. Gold is $350/ounce in the United States. The exchange rate between the United States and Canada is 0.70 U.S. dollars/Canadian dollar. How much does an ounce of gold cost in Canada?

6. How would each of the following be likely to affect the value of the dollar, all else being equal? Explain.

a. U.S. stocks are perceived as having become much riskier financial investments.

b. European computer firms switch from U.S.-produced software to software produced in India, Israel, and other nations.

c. As East Asian economies recover, international financial investors become aware of many new, high-return investment opportunities in the region.

d. The U.S. government imposes a large tariff on imported automobiles.

e. The Federal Reserve reports that it is less concerned about inflation and more concerned about an impending recession in the United States.

f. U.S. consumers increase their spending on imported goods.

7. The demand for and supply of shekels in the foreign exchange market is

$$Demand = 30,000 − 8,000e,$$
$$Supply = 25,000 + 12,000e,$$

where the nominal exchange rate is expressed as U.S. dollars per shekel.

a. What is the fundamental value of the shekel?

b. The shekel is fixed at 0.30 U.S. dollars. Is the shekel overvalued, undervalued, or neither? Find the balance-of-payments deficit or surplus in both shekels and dollars. What happens to the country's international reserves over time?

c. Repeat part b for the case in which the shekel is fixed at 0.20 U.S. dollars.

8. The annual demand for and supply of shekels in the foreign exchange market is as given in Problem 7. The shekel is fixed at 0.30 dollars per shekel. The country's international reserves are $600. Foreign financial investors hold checking accounts in the country in the amount of 5,000 shekels.

a. Suppose that foreign financial investors do not fear a devaluation of the shekel, and thus do not convert their shekel checking accounts into dollars. Can the shekel be maintained at its fixed value of 0.30 U.S. dollars for the next year?

b. Now suppose that foreign financial investors come to expect a possible devaluation of the shekel to 0.25 U.S. dollars. Why should this possibility worry them?

c. In response to their concern about devaluation, foreign financial investors withdraw all funds from their checking accounts and attempt to convert those shekels into dollars. What happens?

d. Discuss why the foreign investors' forecast of devaluation can be considered a "self-fulfilling prophecy."

9. Eastland's currency is called the eastmark, and Westland's currency is called the westmark. In the market in which eastmarks and westmarks are traded for each other, the supply of and demand for eastmarks is given by

$$\text{Demand} = 25,000 - 5,000e + 50,000(r_E - r_W).$$
$$\text{Supply} = 18,500 + 8,000e - 50,000(r_E - r_W).$$

The nominal exchange rate e is measured as westmarks per eastmark, and r_E and r_W are the real interest rates prevailing in Eastland and Westland, respectively.

a. Explain why it makes economic sense for the two real interest rates to appear in the demand and supply equations in the way they do.

b. Initially, $r_E = r_W = 0.10$, or 10 percent. Find the fundamental value of the eastmark.

c. The Westlandian central bank grows concerned about inflation and raises Westland's real interest rate to 12 percent. What happens to the fundamental value of the eastmark?

d. Assume that the exchange rate is flexible and that Eastland does not change its real interest rate following the increase in Westland's real interest rate. Is the action of the Westlandian central bank likely to increase or reduce aggregate demand in Eastland? Discuss.

e. Now suppose that the exchange rate is fixed at the value you found in part b. After the action by the Westlandian central bank, what will the Eastlandian central bank have to do to keep its exchange rate from being overvalued? What effect will this action have on the Eastlandian economy?

f. In the context of this example, discuss the effect of fixed exchange rates on the ability of a country to run an independent monetary policy.

■ ANSWERS TO IN-CHAPTER EXERCISES ■

29.1 No answer given.

29.2 The dollar price of the U.S. computer is $2,400, and each dollar is equal to 110 yen. Therefore the yen price of the U.S. computer is (110 yen/dollar) × ($2,400), or 264,000 yen. The price of the Japanese computer is 242,000 yen. Thus the conclusion that the Japanese model is cheaper does not depend on the currency in which the comparison is made.

29.3 Since the law of one price holds for gold, its price per ounce must be the same in New York and Stockholm:

$$\$300 = 2,500 \text{ kronor.}$$

Dividing both sides by 300, we get

$$\$1 = 8.33 \text{ kronor.}$$

So the exchange rate is 8.33 kronor/dollar.

29.4 A decline in U.S. GDP reduces consumer incomes and hence imports. As Americans are purchasing fewer imports, they supply fewer dollars to the foreign exchange market, so the supply curve for dollars shifts to the left. Reduced supply raises the equilibrium value of the dollar.

29.5 At a fixed value for the peso of 0.15 dollars, the demand for the peso equals 25,000 − 50,000(0.15) = 17,500. The supply of the peso equals 17,600 + 24,000(0.15) = 21,200. The quantity supplied at the official rate exceeds the quantity demanded by 3,700. Latinia will have to purchase 3,700 pesos each period, so its balance-of-payments deficit will equal 3,700 pesos, or 3,700 × 0.15 = 555 dollars. This balance-of-payments deficit is larger than we found in Example 29.6. We conclude that the greater the degree of overvaluation, the larger the country's balance-of-payments deficit is likely to be.

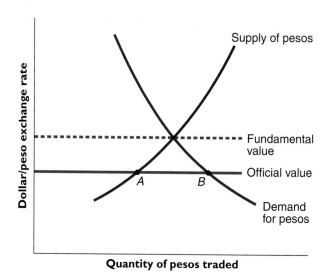

29.6   The figure shows a situation in which the official value of the currency is *below* the fundamental value, as determined by the supply of and demand for the currency in the foreign exchange market, so the currency is undervalued. At the official value of the exchange rate, the quantity demanded of the domestic currency (point *B*) exceeds the quantity supplied (point *A*). To maintain the official value, the central bank must supply domestic currency to the foreign exchange market each period in the amount *AB*. In contrast to the case of an overvalued exchange rate, here the central bank is providing its own currency to the foreign exchange market and receiving foreign currencies in return.

   The central bank can print as much of its own currency as it likes, and so with an undervalued currency there is no danger of running out of international reserves. Indeed, the central bank's stock of international reserves increases in the amount *AB* each period, as it receives foreign currencies in exchange for the domestic currency it supplies.

A

Absolute advantage. One person has an absolute advantage over another if he or she takes fewer hours to perform a task than the other person.

Accounting profit. The difference between a firm's total revenue and its explicit costs.

Adverse selection. The pattern in which insurance tends to be purchased disproportionately by those who are most costly for companies to insure.

Aggregate demand (*AD*). Total planned spending on final goods and services.

Aggregate demand (*AD*) curve. Shows the relationship between aggregate demand and inflation; because short-run equilibrium output equals aggregate demand, the aggregate demand curve also shows the relationship between short-run equilibrium output and inflation; increases in inflation reduce aggregate demand and short-run equilibrium output, so the aggregate demand curve is downward-sloping.

Aggregate supply shock. Either an inflation shock or a shock to potential output; adverse aggregate supply shocks of both types reduce output and increase inflation.

Aggregation. The adding up of individual economic variables to obtain economywide totals.

Allocative function of price. Changes in prices direct resources away from overcrowded markets and toward markets that are underserved.

Appreciation. An increase in the value of a currency relative to other currencies.

Assets. Anything of value that one owns.

Asymmetric information. Situations in which buyers and sellers are not equally well informed about the characteristics of goods and services for sale in the marketplace.

Attainable point. Any combination of goods that can be produced using currently available resources.

Autarky. A situation in which a country is economically self-sufficient.

Automatic stabilizers. Provisions in the law that imply *automatic* increases in government spending or decreases in taxes when real output declines.

Autonomous aggregate demand. The portion of aggregate demand that is determined outside the model.

Average benefit. Total benefit of undertaking *n* units of an activity divided by *n*.

Average cost. Total cost of undertaking *n* units of an activity divided by *n*.

Average labor productivity. Output per employed worker.

B

Balance-of-payments deficit. The net decline in a country's stock of international reserves over a year.

Balance-of-payments surplus. The net increase in a country's stock of international reserves over a year.

Bank reserves. Cash or similar assets held by commercial banks for the purpose of meeting depositor withdrawals and payments.

Banking panic. An episode in which depositors, spurred by news or rumors of the imminent bankruptcy of one or more banks, rush to withdraw their deposits from the banking system.

Barrier to entry. Any force that prevents firms from entering a new market.

Barter. The direct trade of goods or services for other goods or services.

Basic elements of a game. The players, the strategies available to each player, and the payoffs each player receives for each possible combination of strategies.

Bequest saving. Saving done for the purpose of leaving an inheritance.

Better-than-fair gamble. A gamble whose expected value is positive.

Board of Governors. The leadership of the Fed, consisting of seven governors appointed by the President to staggered 14-year terms.

Bond. A legal promise to repay a debt, usually including both the principal amount and regular interest payments.

Boom. A particularly strong and protracted expansion.

Breakeven income level. Under a negative income tax, the level of before-tax income at which a family's tax liability exactly offsets its initial tax credit.

C

Capital gains. Increases in the value of existing assets.

Capital good. A long-lived good, which is itself produced and used to produce other goods and services.

Capital inflows. Purchases of domestic assets by foreign households and firms.

Capital losses. Decreases in the value of existing assets.

Capital outflows. Purchases of foreign assets by domestic households and firms.

Cartel. A coalition of firms that agrees to restrict output for the purpose of earning an economic profit.

Change in demand. A shift of the entire demand curve.

Change in supply. A shift of the entire supply curve.

Change in the quantity demanded. A movement along the demand curve that occurs in response to a change in price.

Change in the quantity supplied. A movement along the supply curve that occurs in response to a change in price.

Closed economy. An economy that does not trade with the rest of the world.

Coase theorem. If at no cost people can negotiate the purchase and sale of the right to perform activities that cause externalities, they can always arrive at efficient solutions to the problems caused by externalities.

Collective good. A good or service that, to at least some degree, is nonrival but excludable.

Commitment device. A way of changing incentives so as to make otherwise empty threats or promises credible.

Commitment problem. A situation in which people cannot achieve their goals because of an inability to make credible threats or promises.

Comparable worth legislation. Legislation that would set wages for a job not by market forces but by collective judgments about the social value of the job.

Comparative advantage. One person has a comparative advantage over another if his or her opportunity cost of performing a task is lower than the other person's opportunity cost.

Compensating wage differential. A difference in the wage rate—negative or positive—that reflects the attractiveness of a job's working conditions.

Complements. Two goods are complements in consumption if an increase in the price of one causes a leftward shift in the demand curve for the other.

Compound interest. The payment of interest not only on the original deposit but on all previously accumulated interest.

Constant. A quantity that is fixed in value.

Constant returns to scale. A production process is said to have constant returns to scale if, when all inputs are changed by a given proportion, output changes by the same proportion.

Consumer price index (CPI). For any period, measures the cost in that period of a standard basket of goods and services relative to the cost of the same basket of goods and services in a fixed year, called the *base year*.

Consumer surplus. The economic surplus gained by the buyers of a product as measured by the cumulative difference between their respective reservation prices and the price they actually paid.

Consumption. Spending by households on goods and services, such as food, clothing, and entertainment.

Consumption function. The relationship between consumption spending and its determinants, such as disposable (after-tax) income.

Consumption possibilities. The combinations of goods and services that a country's citizens might feasibly consume.

Contractionary monetary policy. An increase in interest rates by the Fed, made with the intention of reducing an expansionary gap; also known as *monetary tightening*.

Costly-to-fake principle. To communicate information credibly to a potential rival, a signal must be costly or difficult to fake.

Cost-plus regulation. A method of regulation under which the regulated firm is permitted to charge a price equal to its explicit costs of production plus a markup to cover the opportunity cost of resources provided by the firm's owners.

Coupon payments. Regular interest payments made to the bondholder.

Coupon rate. The interest rate promised when a bond is issued.

Credible promise. A promise to take an action that is in the promiser's interest to keep.

Credible threat. A threat to take an action that is in the threatener's interest to carry out.

Cross-price elasticity of demand for two goods. The percentage by which the quantity demanded of the first good changes in response to a 1 percent change in the price of the second.

Crowding out. Occurs when private firms cancel planned investment projects because of higher interest rates caused by government borrowing.

Customer discrimination. The willingness of consumers to pay more for a product produced by members of a favored group, even if the quality of the product is unaffected.

Cyclical unemployment. The extra unemployment that occurs during periods of recession.

D

Deadweight loss. The deadweight loss caused by a policy is the reduction in economic surplus that results from adoption of that policy.

Decision tree (or game tree). A diagram that describes the possible moves in a game in sequence and lists the payoffs that correspond to each possible combination of moves.

Deflating (a nominal quantity). The process of dividing a nominal quantity by a price index (such as the CPI) to express the quantity in real terms.

Deflation. A situation in which the prices of most goods and services are falling over time so that inflation is negative.

Demand curve. A curve or schedule showing the total quantity of a good that buyers wish to buy at each price.

Demand for money. The amount of wealth an individual or firm chooses to hold in the form of money.

Dependent variable. A variable in an equation whose value is determined by the value taken by another variable in the equation.

Deposit insurance. A system under which the government guarantees that depositors will not lose any money even if their bank goes bankrupt.

Depreciation. A decrease in the value of a currency relative to other currencies.

Depression. A particularly severe or protracted recession.

Devaluation. A reduction in the official value of a currency (in a fixed-exchange-rate system).

Diminishing returns to capital. If the amount of labor and other inputs employed is held constant, then the greater the amount of capital already in use, the less an additional unit of capital adds to production.

Diminishing returns to labor. If the amount of capital and other inputs in use is held constant, then the greater the quantity of labor already employed, the less each additional worker adds to production.

Disappearing political discourse. The theory that people who support a position may remain silent, because speaking out would create a risk of being misunderstood.

Discount rate. The interest rate that the Fed charges commercial banks to borrow reserves.

Discount window lending. The lending of reserves by the Federal Reserve to commercial banks.

Discouraged workers. People who say they would like to have a job but have not made an effort to find one in the past 4 weeks.

Disinflation. A substantial reduction in the rate of inflation.

Diversification. The practice of spreading one's wealth over a variety of different financial investments to reduce overall risk.

Dividend. A regular payment received by stockholders for each share that they own.

Dominant strategy. One that yields a higher payoff no matter what the other players in a game choose.

Dominated strategy. Any other strategy available to a player who has a dominant strategy.

Duration. The length of an unemployment spell.

E

Earned-income tax credit (EITC). A policy under which low-income workers receive credits on their federal income tax.

Economic efficiency. *See* **Efficiency.**

Economic loss. An economic profit that is less than zero.

Economic profit. The difference between a firm's total revenue and the sum of its explicit and implicit costs; also called *excess profit.*

Economic rent. That part of the payment for a factor of production that exceeds the owner's reservation price, the price below which the owner would not supply the factor.

Economic surplus. The economic surplus from taking any action is the benefit of taking the action minus its cost.

Economics. The study of how people make choices under conditions of scarcity and of the results of those choices for society.

Efficiency (or economic efficiency). Condition that occurs when all goods and services are produced and consumed at levels that produce the maximum economic surplus for society.

Efficient (or Pareto-efficient). A situation is efficient if no change is possible that will help some people without harming others.

Efficient markets hypothesis. The theory that the current price of stock in a corporation reflects all relevant information about its current and future earnings prospects.

Efficient point. Any combination of goods for which currently available resources do not allow an increase in the production of one good without a reduction in the production of the other.

Efficient quantity. The efficient quantity of any good is the quantity that maximizes the economic surplus that results from producing and consuming the good.

Elastic. The demand for a good is elastic with respect to price if its price elasticity of demand is greater than 1. The supply of a good is elastic with respect to price if its price elasticity of supply is greater than 1.

Employer discrimination. An arbitrary preference by the employer for one group of workers over another.

Entrepreneurs. People who create new economic enterprises.

Equation. A mathematical expression that describes the relationship between two or more variables.

Equilibrium. A stable, balanced, or unchanging situation in which all forces at work within a system are canceled by others.

Equilibrium exchange rate. *See* **Fundamental value of the exchange rate.**

Equilibrium price and equilibrium quantity. The price and quantity of a good at the intersection of the supply and demand curves for the good.

Excess demand (or shortage). The difference between the quantity supplied and the quantity demanded when the price of a good lies below the equilibrium price; buyers are dissatisfied when there is excess demand.

Excess supply (or surplus). The difference between the quantity supplied and the quantity demanded when the price of a good exceeds the equilibrium price; sellers are dissatisfied when there is excess supply.

Expansion. A period in which the economy is growing at a rate significantly above normal.

Expansionary gap. A negative output gap, which occurs when actual output is higher than potential output.

Expansionary monetary policy. A reduction in interest rates by the Fed, made with the intention of reducing a recessionary gap; also known as *monetary easing.*

Expected value of a gamble. The sum of the possible outcomes of the gamble multiplied by their respective probabilities.

Explicit costs. The actual payments a firm makes to its factors of production and other suppliers.

External benefit (or positive externality). A benefit of an activity received by people other than those who pursue the activity.

External cost (or negative externality). A cost of an activity that falls on people other than those who pursue the activity.

Externality. An external cost or benefit of an activity.

F

Factor of production. An input used in the production of a good or service.

Fair gamble. A gamble whose expected value is zero.

Federal funds rate. The interest rate that commercial banks charge each other for very short-term (usually overnight) loans; because the Fed frequently sets its policy in the form of a target for the federal funds rate, this rate is closely watched in financial markets.

Federal Open Market Committee (FOMC). The committee that makes decisions concerning monetary policy.

Federal Reserve System. The central bank of the United States; also called the *Fed.*

Final goods or services. Goods or services consumed by the ultimate user; because they are the end products of the production process, they are counted as part of GDP.

Financial intermediaries. Firms that extend credit to borrowers using funds raised from savers.

First-dollar insurance coverage. Insurance that pays all expenses generated by the insured activity.

Fiscal policy. Decisions that determine the government's budget, including the amount and composition of government expenditures and government revenues.

Fisher effect. The tendency for nominal interest rates to be high when inflation is high and low when inflation is low.

Fixed cost. A cost that does not vary with the level of an activity.

Fixed exchange rate. An exchange rate whose value is set by official government policy.

Fixed factor of production. An input whose quantity cannot be altered in the short run.

Flexible exchange rate. An exchange rate whose value is not officially fixed but varies according to the supply and demand for the currency in the foreign exchange market.

Flow. A measure that is defined *per unit of time.*

Foreign exchange market. The market on which currencies of various nations are traded for one another.

Fractional-reserve banking system. A banking system in which bank reserves are less than deposits so that the reserve-deposit ratio is less than 100 percent.

Free-rider problem. An incentive problem in which too little of a good or service is produced because nonpayers cannot be excluded from using it.

Frictional unemployment. The short-term unemployment associated with the process of matching workers with jobs.

Fundamental value of the exchange rate (or equilibrium exchange rate). The exchange rate that equates the quantities of the currency supplied and demanded in the foreign exchange market.

G

Game tree. *See* **Decision tree.**

Government budget deficit. The excess of government spending over tax collections $(G - T)$.

Government budget surplus. The excess of government tax collections over government spending $(T - G)$; the government budget surplus equals public saving.

Government purchases. Purchases by federal, state, and local governments of final goods and services; government purchases do not include *transfer payments,* which are payments made by the government in return for which no current goods or services are received, nor do they include interest paid on the government debt.

Gross domestic product (GDP). The market value of the final goods and services produced in a country during a given period.

H

Head tax. A tax that collects the same amount from every taxpayer.

Health maintenance organization (HMO). A group of physicians that provides health services to individuals and families for a fixed annual fee.

Human capital. An amalgam of factors such as education, training, experience, intelligence, energy, work habits, trustworthiness, initiative, and others that affect the value of a worker's marginal product.

Human capital theory. A theory of pay determination that says a worker's wage will be proportional to his or her stock of human capital.

Hurdle method of price discrimination. The practice by which a seller offers a discount to all buyers who overcome some obstacle.

Hyperinflation. A situation in which the inflation rate is extremely high.

I

Imperfectly competitive firm. A firm that has at least some control over the market price of its product.

Implicit costs. All the firm's opportunity costs of the resources supplied by the firm's owners.

Income elasticity of demand. The percentage by which a good's quantity demanded changes in response to a 1 percent change in income.

Income-expenditure multiplier. The effect of a one-unit increase in autonomous aggregate demand on short-run equilibrium output; also known as the *multiplier.*

Increasing returns to scale. A production process is said to have increasing returns to scale if, when all inputs are changed by a given proportion, output changes by more than that proportion; also called *economies of scale.*

Independent variable. A variable in an equation whose value determines the value taken by another variable in the equation.

Indexing. The practice of increasing a nominal quantity each period by an amount equal to the percentage increase in a specified price index. Indexing prevents the purchasing power of the nominal quantity from being eroded by inflation.

Induced aggregate demand. The portion of aggregate demand that is determined within the model.

Inefficient point. Any combination of goods for which currently available resources enable an increase in the production of one good without a reduction in the production of the other.

Inelastic. The demand for a good is inelastic with respect to price if its price elasticity of demand is less than 1.

Inferior good. A good whose demand curve shifts leftward when the incomes of buyers increase.

Inflation shock. A sudden change in the normal behavior of inflation, unrelated to the nation's output gap.

In-kind transfer. A payment made not in the form of cash but in the form of a good or service.

Intermediate goods or services. Goods or services used up in the production of final goods and services and therefore not counted as part of GDP.

International capital flows. Purchases or sales of real and financial assets across international borders.

International reserves. Foreign currency assets held by a government for the purpose of purchasing the domestic currency in the foreign exchange market.

Investment. Spending by firms on final goods and services, primarily capital goods and housing.

Invisible hand theory. A theory stating that the actions of independent, self-interested buyers and sellers will often result in the most efficient allocation of resources.

L

Labor force. The total number of employed and unemployed people in the economy.

Labor union. A group of workers who bargain collectively with employers for better wages and working conditions.

Law of diminishing returns. A property of the relationship between the amount of a good or service produced and the amount of a variable factor required to produce it; the law says that when some factors of production are fixed, increased production of the good eventually requires ever larger increases in the variable factor.

Law of one price. If transportation costs are relatively small, the price of an internationally traded commodity must be the same in all locations.

Lemons model. George Akerlof's explanation of how asymmetric information tends to reduce the average quality of goods offered for sale.

Liabilities. The debts one owes.

Life-cycle saving. Saving to meet long-term objectives, such as retirement, college attendance, or the purchase of a home.

Logrolling. The practice whereby legislators support one another's legislative proposals.

Long run. A period of time of sufficient length that all the firm's factors of production are variable.

Long-run aggregate supply (LRAS) line. A vertical line showing the economy's potential output Y^*.

Long-run equilibrium. A situation in which actual output equals potential output and the inflation rate is stable; graphically, long-run equilibrium occurs when the AD curve, the SRAS line, and the LRAS line all intersect at a single point.

M

M1. Sum of currency outstanding and balances held in checking accounts.

M2. All the assets in M1 plus some additional assets that are usable in making payments but at greater cost or inconvenience than currency or checks.

Macroeconomic policies. Government actions designed to affect the performance of the economy as a whole.

Macroeconomics. The study of the performance of national economies and the policies that governments use to try to improve that performance.

Marginal benefit. The marginal benefit of an activity is the increase in total benefit that results from carrying out one additional unit of the activity.

Marginal cost. The marginal cost of an activity is the increase in total cost that results from carrying out one additional unit of the activity.

Marginal labor cost. The amount by which a monopsonist's total wage bill goes up if it hires an extra worker.

Marginal product of labor. The additional output a firm gets by employing one additional unit of labor.

Marginal propensity to consume (MPC). The amount by which consumption rises when disposable income rises by \$1; we assume that $0 < MPC < 1$.

Marginal revenue. The change in a firm's total revenue that results from a one-unit change in output.

Marginal utility. The additional utility gained from consuming an additional unit of a good.

Market. The market for any good consists of all buyers or sellers of that good.

Market equilibrium. Occurs when all buyers and sellers are satisfied with their respective quantities at the market price.

Market power. A firm's ability to raise the price of a good without losing all its sales .

Means-tested. A benefit program is means-tested if its benefit level declines as the recipient earns additional income.

Medium of exchange. An asset used in purchasing goods and services.

Menu costs. The costs of changing prices.

Microeconomics. The study of individual choice under scarcity and its implications for the behavior of prices and quantities in individual markets.

Monetary policy. Determination of the nation's money supply.

Money. Any asset that can be used in making purchases.

Money demand curve. Relates the aggregate quantity of money demanded M to the nominal interest rate i; because an increase in the nominal interest rate increases the opportunity cost of holding money, which reduces the quantity of money demanded, the money demand curve slopes down.

Monopolistically competitive firm. One of a large number of firms that produce slightly differentiated products that are reasonably close substitutes for one another.

Monopsony. A market with only a single buyer.

Mutual fund. A financial intermediary that sells shares in itself to the public, then uses the funds raised to buy a wide variety of financial assets.

N

Nash equilibrium. Any combination of strategies in which each player's strategy is his or her best choice, given the other players' strategies.

National saving. The saving of the entire economy, equal to GDP less consumption expenditures and government purchases of goods and services, or $Y - C - G$.

Natural monopoly. A monopoly that results from economies of scale.

Natural rate of unemployment (u^*). The part of the total unemployment rate that is attributable to frictional and structural unemployment; equivalently, the unemployment rate that prevails when cyclical unemployment is zero, so the economy has neither a recessionary nor an expansionary output gap.

Negative externality. *See* External cost.

Negative income tax. A system under which the government would grant every citizen a cash payment each year, financed by an additional tax on earned income.

Net exports. Exports minus imports.

Nominal exchange rate. The rate at which two currencies can be traded for each other.

Nominal GDP. A measure of GDP in which the quantities produced are valued at current-year prices; nominal GDP measures the *current dollar value* of production.

Nominal interest rate. The annual percentage increase in the nominal value of a financial asset; also called the *market interest rate.*

Nominal price. Absolute price of a good in dollar terms.

Nominal quantity. A quantity that is measured in terms of its current dollar value.

Nonexcludable good. A good that is difficult, or costly, to exclude nonpayers from consuming.

Nonrival good. A good whose consumption by one person does not diminish its availability for others.

Normal good. A good whose demand curve shifts rightward when the incomes of buyers increase.

Normal profit. The opportunity cost of the resources supplied by the firm's owners; Normal profit = Accounting profit − Economic profit.

Normative analysis. Addresses the question of whether a policy *should* be used; normative analysis inevitably involves the values of the person doing the analysis.

O

Okun's law. States that each extra percentage point of cyclical unemployment is associated with about a 2 percentage point increase in the output gap, measured in relation to potential output.

Oligopolist. A firm that produces a product for which only a few rival firms produce close substitutes.

100 percent reserve banking. A situation in which banks' reserves equal 100 percent of their deposits.

Open economy. An economy that trades with other countries.

Open-market operations. Open-market purchases and open-market sales.

Open-market purchase. The purchase of government bonds from the public by the Fed for the purpose of increasing the supply of bank reserves and the money supply.

Open-market sale. The sale by the Fed of government bonds to the public for the purpose of reducing bank reserves and the money supply.

Opportunity cost. The opportunity cost of an activity is the value of the next-best alternative that must be forgone to undertake the activity.

Optimal combination of goods. The affordable combination that yields the highest total utility.

Output gap $(Y^* - Y)$. The difference between the economy's potential output and its actual output at a point in time.

Overvalued exchange rate. An exchange rate that has an officially fixed value greater than its fundamental value.

P

Pareto-efficient. *See* Efficient.

Participation rate. The percentage of the working-age population in the labor force (that is, the percentage that is either employed or looking for work).

Payoff matrix. A table that describes the payoffs in a game for each possible combination of strategies.

Peak. The beginning of a recession, the high point of economic activity prior to a downturn.

Perfect hurdle. One that completely segregates buyers whose reservation prices lie above some threshold from others whose reservation prices lie below it, imposing no cost on those who jump the hurdle.

Perfectly competitive market. A market in which no individual supplier has significant influence on the market price of the product.

Perfectly discriminating monopolist. A firm that charges each buyer exactly his or her reservation price.

Perfectly elastic demand. The demand for a good is perfectly elastic with respect to price if its price elasticity of demand is infinite.

Perfectly elastic supply curve. A supply curve whose elasticity with respect to price is infinite.

Perfectly inelastic demand. The demand for a good is perfectly inelastic with respect to price if its price elasticity of demand is zero.

Perfectly inelastic supply curve. A supply curve whose elasticity with respect to price is zero.

Personal Responsibility Act. The 1996 federal law that transferred responsibility for welfare programs from the federal level to the state level and placed a 5-year lifetime limit on payment of AFDC benefits to any given recipient.

Policy reaction function. Describes how the action a policymaker takes depends on the state of the economy.

Pork barrel spending. A public expenditure that is larger than the total benefit it creates but that is favored by a legislator because his or her constituents benefit from the expenditure by more than their share of the resulting extra taxes.

Portfolio allocation decision. The decision about the forms in which to hold one's wealth.

Positional arms control agreement. An agreement in which contestants attempt to limit mutually offsetting investments in performance enhancement.

Positional arms race. A series of mutually offsetting investments in performance enhancement that is stimulated by a positional externality.

Positional externality. Occurs when an increase in one person's performance reduces the expected reward of another's in situations in which reward depends on relative performance.

Positive analysis. Addresses the economic consequences of a particular event or policy, not whether those consequences are desirable.

Positive externality. *See* External benefit.

Potential output. The amount of output (real GDP) that an economy can produce when using its resources, such as capital and labor, at normal rates; also called *potential GDP* or *full-employment output.*

Poverty threshold. The level of income below which the federal government classifies a family as poor.

Precautionary saving. Saving for protection against unexpected setbacks, such as the loss of a job or a medical emergency.

Present value. When the annual interest rate is r, the present value (PV) of a payment M to be received T years from now is the amount that would have to be deposited today at an annual interest rate r to generate a balance of M after T years: $PV = M/(1 + r)^T$.

Price ceiling. A maximum allowable price, specified by law.

Price discrimination. The practice of charging different buyers different prices for essentially the same good or service.

Price elasticity of demand. The percentage change in the quantity demanded of a good or service that results from a 1 percent change in its price.

Price elasticity of supply. The percentage change in the quantity supplied that will occur in response to a 1 percent change in the price of a good or service.

Price floor. A law or regulation that guarantees that suppliers will receive at least a specified amount for their product.

Price index. A measure of the average price of a given class of goods or services relative to the price of the same goods and services in a base year.

Price level. A measure of the overall level of prices at a particular point in time as measured by a price index such as the CPI.

Price setter. A firm with at least some latitude to set its own price.

Price taker. A firm that has no influence over the price at which it sells its product.

Principal amount. The amount originally lent.

Prisoner's dilemma. A game in which each player has a dominant strategy, and when each plays it, the resulting payoffs are smaller than if each had played a dominated strategy.

Private saving. The saving of the private sector of the economy is equal to the after-tax income of the private sector minus consumption expenditures $(Y - T - C)$; private saving can be further broken down into household saving and business saving.

Producer surplus. The economic surplus gained by the sellers of a product as measured by the cumulative difference between the price received and their respective reservation prices.

Production possibilities curve. A graph that describes the maximum amount of one good that can be produced for every possible level of production of the other good.

Profit. The total revenue a firm receives from the sale of its product minus all costs—explicit and implicit—incurred in producing it.

Profit-maximizing firm. A firm whose primary goal is to maximize the difference between its total revenues and total costs.

Progressive tax. One in which the proportion of income paid in taxes rises as income rises.

Proportional income tax. One under which all taxpayers pay the same proportion of their incomes in taxes.

Protectionism. The view that free trade is injurious and should be restricted.

Public good. A good or service that, to at least some degree, is both nonrival and nonexcludable.

Public saving. The saving of the government sector is equal to net tax payments minus government purchases $(T - G)$.

Purchasing power parity (PPP). The theory that nominal exchange rates are determined as necessary for the law of one price to hold.

Pure commons good. One for which nonpayers cannot easily be excluded and for which each unit consumed by one person means one less unit available for others.

Pure monopoly. The only supplier of a unique product with no close substitutes.

Pure private good. One for which nonpayers can easily be excluded and for which each unit consumed by one person means one less unit available for others.

Pure public good. A good or service that, to a high degree, is both nonrival and nonexcludable.

Q

Quota. A legal limit on the quantity of a good that may be imported.

R

Rate of inflation. The annual percentage rate of change in the price level, as measured, for example, by the CPI.

Rational person. Someone with well-defined goals who tries to fulfill those goals as best he or she can.

Rationing function of price. Changes in prices that distribute scarce goods to those consumers who value them most highly.

Real exchange rate. The price of the average domestic good or service *relative* to the price of the average foreign good or service, when prices are expressed in terms of a common currency.

Real GDP. A measure of GDP in which the quantities produced are valued at the prices in a base year rather than at current prices; real GDP measures the actual *physical volume* of production.

Real interest rate. The annual percentage increase in the purchasing power of a financial asset; the real interest rate on any asset equals the nominal interest rate on that asset minus the inflation rate.

Real price. Dollar price of a good relative to the average dollar price of all other goods and services.

Real quantity. A quantity that is measured in physical terms—for example, in terms of quantities of goods and services.

Real wage. The wage paid to workers measured in terms of real purchasing power; the real wage for any given period is calculated by dividing the nominal (dollar) wage by the CPI for that period.

Recession. A period in which the economy is growing at a rate significantly below normal; also called a *contraction*.

Recessionary gap. A positive output gap, which occurs when potential output exceeds actual output.

Regressive tax. A tax under which the proportion of income paid in taxes declines as income rises.

Relative price. The price of a specific good or service *in comparison to* the prices of other goods and services.

Rent-seeking. The socially unproductive efforts of people or firms to win a prize.

Reservation price. The highest price someone is willing to pay to obtain any good or service, or the lowest payment someone would accept for giving up a good or performing a service.

Reserve requirements. Set by the Fed, the minimum values of the ratio of bank reserves to bank deposits that commercial banks are allowed to maintain.

Reserve-deposit ratio. Bank reserves divided by deposits.

Revaluation. An increase in the official value of a currency (in a fixed-exchange-rate system).

Risk premium. The rate of return that financial investors require to hold risky assets minus the rate of return on safe assets.

Risk-averse person. Someone who would refuse any fair gamble.

Risk-neutral person. Someone who would accept any gamble that is fair or better.

S

Saving. Current income minus spending on current needs.

Saving rate. Saving divided by income.

Shortage. *See* **Excess demand.**

Short run. A period of time sufficiently short that at least some of the firm's factors of production are fixed.

Short-run aggregate supply (*SRAS*) line. A horizontal line showing the current rate of inflation, as determined by past expectations and pricing decisions.

Short-run equilibrium. A situation in which inflation equals the value determined by past expectations and pricing decisions, and output equals the level of short-run equilibrium output that is consistent with that inflation rate; graphically, short-run equilibrium occurs at the intersection of the *AD* curve and the *SRAS* line.

Short-run equilibrium output. The level of output at which output *Y* equals aggregate demand *AD*; the level of output that prevails during the period in which prices are predetermined.

Skill-biased technological change. Technological change that affects the marginal products of higher-skilled workers differently from those of lower-skilled workers.

Slope. In a straight line, the ratio of the vertical distance the straight line travels between any two points (*rise*) to the corresponding horizontal distance (*run*).

Speculative attack. A massive selling of domestic currency assets by financial investors.

Stabilization policies. Government policies that are used to affect aggregate demand, with the objective of eliminating output gaps.

Statistical discrimination. The practice of making judgments about the quality of people, goods, or services based on the characteristics of the groups to which they belong.

Stock. A claim to partial ownership of a firm; also called *equity*.

Stock. A measure that is defined *at a point in time*.

Store of value. An asset that serves as a means of holding wealth.

Structural policy. Government policies aimed at changing the underlying structure, or institutions, of the nation's economy.

Structural unemployment. The long-term and chronic unemployment that exists even when the economy is producing at a normal rate.

Substitutes. Two goods are substitutes in consumption if an increase in the price of one causes a rightward shift in the demand curve for the other.

Sunk cost. A cost that is beyond recovery at the moment a decision must be made.

Supply curve. A curve or schedule showing the total quantity of a good that sellers wish to sell at each price.

Surplus. *See* **Excess supply.**

T

Tariff. A tax imposed on an imported good.

Time value of money. The fact that a given dollar amount today is equivalent to a larger dollar amount in the future, because the money can be invested in an interest-bearing account in the meantime.

Total economic surplus. The total economic surplus in a market is the sum of all the individual economic surpluses gained by buyers and sellers who participate in the market.

Total expenditure = Total revenue. The dollar amount consumers spend on a product is equal to the dollar amount sellers receive.

Trade balance (or net exports). The value of a country's exports less the value of its imports in a particular period (quarter or year).

Trade deficit. When imports exceed exports, the difference between the value of a country's imports and the value of its exports in a given period.

Trade surplus. When exports exceed imports, the difference between the value of a country's exports and the value of its imports in a given period.

Tragedy of the commons. The tendency for a resource that has no price to be used until its marginal benefit falls to zero.

Transfer payments. Payments the government makes to the public for which it receives no current goods or services in return.

Trough. The end of a recession, the low point of economic activity prior to a recovery.

U

Ultimatum bargaining game. One in which the first player has the power to confront the second player with a take-it-or-leave-it offer.

Unattainable point. Any combination of goods that cannot be produced using currently available resources.

Undervalued exchange rate. An exchange rate that has an officially fixed value less than its fundamental value.

Unemployment rate. The number of unemployed people divided by the labor force.

Unemployment spell. A period during which an individual is continuously unemployed.

Unit elastic demand. The demand for a good is unit elastic with respect to price if its price elasticity of demand is equal to 1.

Unit of account. A basic measure of economic value.

Utilitarianism. A moral theory in which the right course of action is the one that results in the highest total utility.

V

Value added. For any firm, the market value of its product or service minus the cost of inputs purchased from other firms.

Value of marginal product of labor (*VMP*). The dollar value of the additional output a firm gets by employing one additional unit of labor.

Variable. A quantity that is free to take a range of different values.

Variable cost. A cost that varies with the level of an activity.

Variable factor of production. An input whose quantity can be altered in the short run.

Vertical intercept. The value taken by the dependent variable when the independent variable equals zero.

W

Wealth. The value of assets minus liabilities.

Winner-take-all labor market. One in which small differences in human capital translate into large differences in pay.

Worker mobility. The movement of workers between jobs, firms, and industries.

Workers' compensation. A government insurance system that provides benefits to workers who are injured on the job.

World price. The price at which a good or service is traded on international markets.

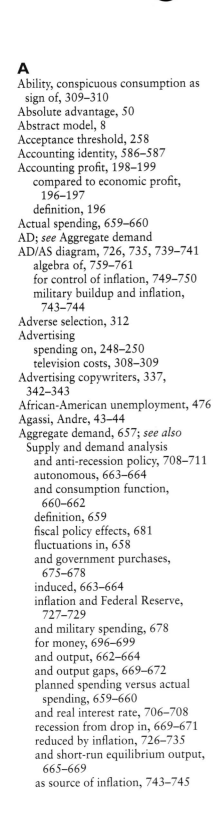

A

Ability, conspicuous consumption as sign of, 309–310
Absolute advantage, 50
Abstract model, 8
Acceptance threshold, 258
Accounting identity, 586–587
Accounting profit, 198–199
   compared to economic profit, 196–197
   definition, 196
Actual spending, 659–660
AD; *see* Aggregate demand
AD/AS diagram, 726, 735, 739–741
   algebra of, 759–761
   for control of inflation, 749–750
   military buildup and inflation, 743–744
Adverse selection, 312
Advertising
   spending on, 248–250
   television costs, 308–309
Advertising copywriters, 337, 342–343
African-American unemployment, 476
Agassi, Andre, 43–44
Aggregate demand, 657; *see also*
Supply and demand analysis
   and anti-recession policy, 708–711
   autonomous, 663–664
   and consumption function, 660–662
   definition, 659
   fiscal policy effects, 681
   fluctuations in, 658
   and government purchases, 675–678
   induced, 663–664
   inflation and Federal Reserve, 727–729
   and military spending, 678
   for money, 696–699
   and output, 662–664
   and output gaps, 669–672
   planned spending versus actual spending, 659–660
   and real interest rate, 706–708
   recession from drop in, 669–671
   reduced by inflation, 726–735
   and short-run equilibrium output, 665–669
   as source of inflation, 743–745

stabilization policies, 675–681
   and taxes, 679–680
   and transfer payments, 679–680
Aggregate demand curve, 726–735
   algebra of, 759–760
   downward slope of, 730
   movement along, 734–735
   numerical example, 729
   shifts of, 730–734, 760–761
Aggregate demand equation, 660
Aggregate income, 403, 663
Aggregate spending, 638
   components of, 659
Aggregate supply; *see also* AD/AS
diagram; Supply and demand
analysis
   and inflation, 735–743
   and inflation expectations, 736–737
   inflation inertia, 736–738
   output gap and inflation, 738–739
   and self-correcting economy, 741–743
Aggregate supply shocks, 748
Aggregation
   national, 447
   US exports, 448
AIDS epidemic, 514
Aid to Families with Dependent
Children, 413, 417, 588
Airline industry, 43
   advertising spending, 248–250
   barriers to entry, 204
   and hurdle method, 242
   net cost of compensation policy, 181
   overbooking, 179–182
   regulated, 208–209
Akerlof, George A., 306
Allen, Paul, 113
Allocative function of price, 203–204
   with free market entry/exit, 204–205
Alternatives, next-best, 32–33
Aluminum prices, 149
Amazon.com, 301
Ambrose, Stephen E., 514n
American Cancer Society, 337, 338
American Civil War, 765
Anabolic steroids, 287
Anaconda Plan, 765
Analyze This, 247, 259

Antipoverty programs, 209; *see also*
Income-support programs
Antitrust laws, 234
   history of, 352–353
Apple Computer, 335
Appreciation, 804
   raising real exchange rate, 808
   of US dollar in 1980s, 811, 816
Arab-Israeli War of 1973, 531
Arbitration agreements, 290
Arcnet, Inc., 338–339
Argentina
   currency board, 501
   dollars in circulation, 698–699
   monetary policy, 828
Aristotle, 76
Arms races, 288–289
AS; *see* Aggregate supply
Asian crisis, 672
   causes of, 825
   International Monetary Fund response, 826
Asprey and Garrard, 401
Assets, 577
   of banking system, 619–620
   bonds and stocks, 609–613
   money, 606
   real and financial, 787–788
   risk and return, 789
   varying interest rates, 696
Asymmetric information, 305–312
   adverse selection, 310
   conspicuous consumption, 309–310
   costly-to-fake principle, 308–309
   credibility problem, 307–308
   lemons model, 306–307
   statistical discrimination, 310–312
AT&T, 222
Attainable point, 57
Auction price-setting, 650
Auctions of pollution permits, 364–365
Australian dollar, 809–810
Autarky, 772, 775
Automatic stabilizers, 682
Automatic teller machines, 17, 694
Automation, 522–523
Automobile industry, 17
   and gas prices, 114
   increasing sophistication of, 559
   production data, 456